# *Research Design and Statistical Analysis*

**Second Edition**

# Research Design and Statistical Analysis

## Second Edition

**Jerome L. Myers**
**Arnold D. Well**
University of Massachusetts

**LEA**
**LAWRENCE ERLBAUM ASSOCIATES, PUBLISHERS**
2003    Mahwah, New Jersey                                    London

| | |
|---|---|
| Senior Editor: | Debra Riegert |
| Textbook Marketing Manager: | Marisol Kozlovski |
| Editorial Assistant: | Jason Planer |
| Cover Design: | Kathryn Houghtaling Lacey |
| Textbook Production Manager: | Paul Smolenski |
| Full-Service Compositor: | TechBooks |
| Text and Cover Printer: | Hamilton Printing Company |

This book was typeset in 10/12 pt. Times, Italic, Bold, and Bold Italic.
The heads were typeset in Futura, Italic, Bold, and Bold Italic.

Lawrence Erlbaum Associates, Inc., Publishers
10 Industrial Avenue
Mahwah, New Jersey 07430


**Library of Congress Cataloging-in-Publication Data**

Myers, Jerome L.
    Research design and statistical analysis / Jerome L. Myers, Arnold D. Well.– 2nd ed.
        p.   cm.
    Includes bibliographical references and index.
    ISBN 0-8058-4037-0 (case only : alk. paper)
    1. Experimental design.   2. Mathematical statistics.   I. Well, A. (Arnold)   II. Title.
QA279 .M933   2002
519.5–dc21

                                                                                                2002015266


Books published by Lawrence Erlbaum Associates are printed on
acid-free paper, and their bindings are chosen for strength and durability.

Printed in the United States of America
10  9  8  7  6  5  4  3  2

*To Nancy and Susan*

# Contents

# Preface

In writing this book, we had two overriding goals. The first was to provide a textbook from which graduate and advanced undergraduate students could really learn about data analysis. Over the years we have experimented with various organizations of the content and have concluded that bottom-up is better than top-down learning. In view of this, most chapters begin with an informal intuitive discussion of key concepts to be covered, followed by the introduction of a real data set along with some informal discussion about how we propose to analyze the data. At that point, having given the student a foundation on which to build, we provide a more formal justification of the computations that are involved both in exploring and in drawing conclusions about the data, as well as an extensive discussion of the relevant assumptions. The strategy of bottom-up presentation extends to the organization of the chapters. Although it is tempting to begin with an elegant development of the general linear model and then treat topics such as the analysis of variance as special cases, we have found that students learn better when we start with the simpler, less abstract, special cases, and then work up to more general formulations. Therefore, after we develop the basics of statistical inference, we treat the special case of analysis of variance in some detail before developing the general regression approach. Then, the now-familiar analyses of variance, covariance, and trend are reconsidered as special cases. We feel that learning statistics involves many passes; that idea is embodied in our text, with each successive pass at a topic becoming more general.

Our second goal was to provide a source book that would be useful to researchers. One implication of this is an emphasis on concepts and assumptions that are necessary to describe and make inferences about real data. Formulas and statistical packages are not enough. Almost anybody can run statistical analyses with a user-friendly statistical package. However, it is critically important to understand what the analyses really tell us, as well as their limitations and their underlying assumptions. No text can present every design and analysis that researchers will encounter in their own research or in their readings of the research literature. In view of this, we build a conceptual foundation that should permit the reader to generalize to new situations, to comprehend the advice of statistical consultants, and to understand the content of articles on statistical methods. We do this by emphasizing such basic concepts as sampling distributions, expected mean squares, design efficiency, and statistical models. We pay close attention to assumptions that are made about the data, the consequences of their violation, the detection of those violations, and alternative methods that might be used in the face of severe violations. Our concern for alternatives to standard analyses has led us to integrate nonparametric procedures into relevant design chapters rather than to collect them together in a single last chapter, as is often the case. Our approach permits us to explicitly compare the pros and cons of alternative data analysis procedures within the research context to which they apply.

Our concern that this book serve the researcher has also influenced its coverage. In our roles as consultants to colleagues and students, we are frequently reminded that research is not just experimental. Many standard textbooks on research design have not adequately served the needs of researchers who observe the values of independent variables rather than manipulate them. Such needs are clearly present in social and clinical psychology, where sampled social and personality measures are taken as predictors of behavior. Even in traditionally experimental areas, such as cognitive psychology, variables are often sampled. For example, the effects of word frequency and length on measures of reading are often of interest. The analysis of data from observational studies requires knowledge of correlation and regression analysis. Too often, ignorant of anything other than analysis of variance, researchers take quantitative variables and arbitrarily turn them into categorical variables, thereby losing both information and power. Our book provides extensive coverage of these research situations and the proper analyses.

## MAJOR CHANGES IN THE SECOND EDITION

This second edition of *Research Design and Statistical Analysis* is a major revision of the earlier work. Although it covers many of the same research designs and data analyses as the earlier book, there have been changes in content and organization. Some new chapters have been added; some concepts not mentioned in the first edition have been introduced, and the coverage of some concepts that were previously discussed has been expanded. We have been motivated in part by our sense that data analysis too often consists of merely tabling means or correlation coefficients, and doing time-honored analyses on them without really looking at the data. Our sense that we can learn more from our data than we often do has been reinforced by the recent publication of the American Psychological Association's guidelines for statistical methods (Wilkinson, 1999). Among other things, these guidelines urge researchers to plot and examine their data, to find confidence intervals, to use power analyses to determine sample size, and to calculate effect sizes. We illustrate these, and other, procedures throughout this book. It may be helpful to consider the changes from the first to the second edition in greater detail.

***Statistics and Graphics.***    One change from the first edition is the expansion of the section, Sample Distributions: Displaying the Data, into two chapters in the present edition. Because it would take an entire volume to do justice to the array of statistics and graphic devices available in many statistical computer packages, Chapters 2 and 3 provide only some of the more basic ways of displaying univariate and bivariate data. However, these should provide more insight into data than is usually the case. Furthermore, we believe that an important contribution of the present text is that we then present such displays in many subsequent chapters, using them to inform subsequent decisions about, and interpretation of, the data analyses.

**Confidence Intervals.**    Although we presented confidence intervals and discussed their interpretation in the first edition, we now emphasize them in two ways. First, in our chapters on inferences based on normal and $t$ distributions, we present confidence intervals before we present hypothesis tests. This is in accord with our belief that they deserve priority because—as we point out—they provide the information available from hypothesis tests, and more. Furthermore, they focus on the right question: What is the size of the effect? rather than Is there an effect? Second, we make the calculation of confidence intervals a part of the data analysis process in many of the subsequent chapters, illustrating their application in various designs and with various statistics.

**Standardized Effect Size.**    The calculation of standardized effect sizes has been urged by several statisticians, most notably Cohen (1977). The standardized effect, in contrast to the raw effect, permits comparisons across experiments and dependent variables, and it is a necessary input to power analyses. This new edition introduces the standardized effect size early in the book (Chapter 6), and then it routinely illustrates its calculation in subsequent chapters featuring different research designs and analyses.

**Power Analyses.**    Power analyses, both to determine the required sample size and to assess the power of an experiment already run, were discussed in the earlier edition. There, we relied on charts that provided approximate power values. Currently, however, several statistical software packages either provide direct calculations of power or provide probabilities under noncentral distributions, which in turn allow the calculation of power. Individuals lacking access to such programs can instead access software available on the Internet that is easy to use and is free. We use two such programs in illustrations of power analyses. In view of the ready accessibility of exact power analyses in both commercial packages such as SAS, SPSS, and SYSTAT and in free programs such as GPOWER and UCLA's statistical calculators, we have dropped the power charts, which are cumbersome to use and at best provide approximate results. As with graphic displays, confidence intervals, and effect size calculations, we present several examples of power calculations in the present edition.

**Tests of Contrasts.**    We believe that much research is, or should be, directed at focused questions. Although we present all the usual omnibus tests of main effects and interactions, we deal extensively with contrasts. We discuss measures of effect size and power analyses for contrasts, and how to control Type 1 errors when many contrasts are considered. We illustrate the calculation of tests of contrasts earlier (Chapter 6), presenting such tests as merely a special case of $t$ tests. We believe this simplifies things, paving the way for presenting calculations for more complex designs in later chapters.

**Elementary Probability.**    We have added a chapter on probability to review basic probability concepts and to use the binomial distribution to introduce hypothesis testing. For some students, reviewing the material in Chapter 4 may be unnecessary, but we have found that many students enter the course lacking a good understanding of basic concepts such as independence, or of the distinction between $p(A|B)$ and $p(B|A)$. The latter distinction is particularly important because $\alpha$, $\beta$, statistical power, and the $p$ values associated with hypothesis tests are all examples of conditional probabilities. The chapter also serves the purpose of introducing hypothesis testing in a relatively transparent context in which the student can calculate probabilities, rather than take them as given from some table.

***Correlation and Regression.***    The section on correlation and regression has been reorganized and expanded. The basic concepts are introduced earlier, in Chapter 3, and are followed up in Chapters 18–21. A major emphasis is placed on the kinds of misinterpretations that are frequently made when these analyses are used. The treatment of power for correlation and regression, and of interaction effects in multiple regression, is considerably expanded. Significance tests for dependent correlations have been addressed both by calculations and by software available on the Internet. Trend analysis and analysis of covariance are presented in Chapters 10 and 15 in ways that require only a limited knowledge of regression, and then they are revisited as instances of multiple regression analyses in Chapters 20 and 21. Nonorthogonal analysis of variance is first addressed in Chapter 12, and then it is considered within the multiple regression framework in Chapter 21. We believe that the coverage of multiple regression can be more accessible, without sacrificing the understanding of basic concepts, if we develop the topic without using matrix notation. However, there is a development that uses matrix notation on the accompanying CD.

***Data Sets.***    The CD-ROM accompanying the book contains several real data sets in the *Data Sets* folder. These are provided in SPSS (.sav), SYSTAT (.syd), and ASCII (.txt) formats, along with readme files (in Word and ASCII formats) containing information about the variables in the data sets. The *Seasons* folder contains a file with many variables, as well as some smaller files derived from the original one. The file includes both categorical variables (e.g., sex, occupation, and employment status) and continuous variables (e.g., age, scores in each season on various personality scales, and physical measures such as cholesterol level). The *Royer* folder contains files with accuracy and response time scores on several arithmetic skills for boys and girls in first to eighth grades. The *Wiley_Voss* folder contains a number of measures from an experiment that compares learning from text with learning from Web sites. The *Probability Learning* folder contains a file from an experiment that compares various methods of teaching elementary probability. In addition, there is an *Exercises* folder containing artificial data sets designed for use with many of the exercises in the book.

The "real-data" files have provided examples and exercises in several chapters. They should make clear that real data often are very different from idealized textbook examples. Scores are often missing, particularly in observational studies, variables are often not normally distributed, variances are often heterogeneous, and outliers exist. The use of real data forces us to consider both the consequences of violations of assumptions and the responses to such violations in a way that abstract discussions of assumptions do not. Because there are several dependent variables in these files, instructors may also find them useful in constructing additional exercises for students.

***Supplementary Material.***    We have also included three files in the *Supplementary Materials* folder of the accompanying CD to supplement the presentation in the text. As we note in Chapter 6, confidence intervals can be obtained for standardized effect sizes. We provided references to recently published articles that describe how to find these confidence intervals in the text, and we illustrate the process in the "Confidence Intervals for Effect Sizes" file in the Supplementary Materials folder. In addition, as we note in Chapter 20, although not necessary for understanding the basic concepts, matrix algebra can greatly simplify the presentation of equations and calculations for multiple regression. To keep the length of the book within bounds, we have not included this material in the text; however, we have added a file, "Chapter 20A, Developing Multiple Regression Using Matrix Notation," to the folder. Finally, when we discussed testing for the interaction between two quantitative variables in multiple regression in the text, we mentioned that if we do not properly specify the model, we might wind up thinking that we have an interaction when, in fact, we have curvilinearity. We discuss this issue in the "Do We Have an Interaction or Do We Have Curvilinearity or Do We Have Both?" file.

**Chapter Appendices.**    Although we believe that it is useful to present some derivations of formulas to make them less "magical" and to show where assumptions are required, we realize that many students find even the most basic kinds of mathematical derivations intimidating and distracting. In this edition, we still include derivations. However, most have been placed in chapter appendices, where they are available for those who desire a more formal development, leaving the main text more readable for those who do not.

**Instructors' Solutions Manual.**    In the "Answers to Selected Exercises" contained in the text, we usually have provided only short answers, and we have done that only for the odd-numbered exercises. The Solutions Manual contains the intermediate steps, and in many cases further discussion of the answers, and does so for all exercises.

## ACKNOWLEDGMENTS

Many individuals have influenced our thinking of, and teaching of, statistics. Discussions with our colleague Alexander Pollatsek have been invaluable, as has been the feedback of our teaching assistants over the years. Most recently these have included Kristin Asplin, Mary Bryden-Miller, Joseph DiCecco, Patricia Collins, Katie Franklin, Jill Greenwald, Randall Hansen, Pam Hardiman, Celia Klin, Susan Lima, Jill Lohmeier, Laurel Long, Robert Lorch, Edward O'Brien, David Palmer, Jill Shimabukuro, Scott Van Manen, and Sarah Zemore. We would also like to thank the students in our statistics courses who encouraged us in this effort and made useful suggestions about earlier drafts of the book. Special thanks go to those individuals who reviewed early chapters of the book and made many useful suggestions that improved the final product: Celia M. Klin, SUNY Binghamton; Robert F. Lorch, University of Kentucky; Jay Maddock, University of Hawaii at Manoa; Steven J. Osterlind, University of Missouri at Columbia; and Thomas V. Petros, University of North Dakota.

We wish to thank Mike Royer for making the *Royer* data available, Jenny Wiley and Jim Voss for the *Wiley_Voss* data, and Ira Ockene for permission to use the *Seasons* data. The Seasons research was supported by National Institutes of Health, National Heart, Lung, and Blood Institute Grant HL52745 awarded to University of Massachusetts Medical School, Worcester, Massachusetts.

We would like to express our gratitude to Debra Riegert, a senior editor at Erlbaum, who encouraged us in this work and provided important editorial assistance. We also wish to thank the American Statistical Association, the Biometric Society, and the *Biometrika* Trustees for their permission to reproduce statistical tables.

As in all our endeavors, our wives, Nancy and Susan, have been very supportive and patient throughout the writing of this book. We gratefully acknowledge that contribution to our work.

# Research Design and Statistical Analysis

## Second Edition

# Chapter 1
## Introduction

## 1.1 VARIABILITY AND THE NEED FOR STATISTICS

Empirical research is undertaken to answer questions that often take the form of whether, and to what extent, several variables of interest are related. For example, an educator may be interested in whether the whole language method of teaching reading is more effective than another method based mostly on phonics; that is, whether reading performance is related to teaching method. A political scientist may investigate whether preference for a political party is related to gender. A social psychologist may want to determine the relation between income and attitude toward minorities. In each case, the researcher tries to answer the question by first collecting relevant measures and then analyzing the data. For example, the educator may decide to measure the effectiveness of reading training by first obtaining scores on a standard test of reading comprehension and then determining whether the scores are better for one of the teaching methods than for the other.

A major problem in answering the research question is that there is variability in the scores. Even for a single teaching method, the reading comprehension scores will differ from one another for all sorts of reasons, including individual differences and measurement errors. Some children learn to read faster than others, perhaps because they are brighter, are more motivated, or receive more parental support. Some simply perform better than others on standardized tests. All this **within-treatment variability** presents a number of major challenges. Because the scores differ from one another, even within a single treatment group, the researcher has to consider how to describe and characterize sets of scores before they can be compared. Considerable attention will be given in this book to discussing how best to display, summarize, and compare distributions of scores. Usually, there are certain summary measures that are of primary interest. For example, the educational researcher may be primarily interested in the *average* reading test score for each method of teaching reading. The political scientist may want to know the *proportion* of males and females who vote for each political party. The social psychologist may want a numerical index, perhaps a *correlation or regression coefficient*, that reflects the relation between income and some attitude score. Although each of these summary statistics may provide useful information, it is important to bear in mind that each tells only part of the story. In Chapters 2 and 3, we return to this point, considering statistics and data plots that provide a fuller picture of treatment effects.

A major consequence of all the within-treatment variability is that it causes us to refine the research question in a way that distinguishes between samples and populations. If there was no within-treatment variability, research would be simple. If we wanted to compare two teaching methods, we would only have to find the single reading comprehension score associated with each teaching method and then compare the two scores. However, in a world awash with variability, there is no single score that completely characterizes the teaching method. If we took two samples of students who had been taught by one of the methods, and then found the average reading comprehension score for each sample, these averages would differ from one another. The average of a sample of comprehension scores is an imperfect indicator of teaching effectiveness because it depends not only on the teaching method but also on all the sources of variability that cause the scores to differ from one another. If we were to find that a sample of scores from students taught by one teaching method had a higher average than a sample from students taught by the other, how could we tell whether the difference was due to teaching method or just to uncontrolled variability? What score could be used to characterize reading performance for each teaching method to answer the question?

We generally try to answer the research question by considering the **populations** of scores associated with each of the teaching methods; that is, *all* the scores that are relevant to the question. To answer the question about teaching methods, we would ideally like to know the comprehension scores for all the students who might be taught by these methods, now and in the future. If we knew the **population parameters,** that is, the summary measures of the populations of scores, such as the average, we could use these to answer questions about the effectiveness of the teaching methods.

Obviously, we usually do not have access to the entire population of scores. In the current example, the populations of comprehension scores are indefinitely large, so there is no way that we can measure the population means directly. However, we can draw inferences about the population parameters on the basis of **samples** of scores selected from the relevant populations. If the samples are appropriately chosen, summary measures of the sample—the **sample statistics**—can be used to estimate the corresponding population parameters. Even though the sample statistics are imperfect estimators of the population parameters, they do provide evidence about them. The quality of this evidence depends on a host of factors, such as the sizes of the samples and the amount and type of variability. The whole field of **inferential statistics** is concerned with what can be said about population parameters on the basis of samples selected from the population. Most of this book is about inferential statistics.

It should be emphasized that, for population parameters to be estimated, the samples must be chosen appropriately. The statistical procedures we discuss in this book assume the use of what are called **simple random samples**; these samples are obtained by methods that give all possible samples of a given size an equal opportunity to be selected. If we can assume that all samples of a given size are equally likely, we can use the one sample we actually select to calculate the likelihood of errors in the inferences we make.

Even when randomly selected, the sample is not a miniature replica of the population. As another example, consider a study of the change in arithmetic skills of third graders who are taught arithmetic by use of computer-assisted instruction (CAI). In such a study, we are likely to want to estimate the size of the change. We might address this by administering two tests to several third-grade classes. One test would be given at the beginning of third grade, and one would follow a term of instruction with CAI. The sample statistic of interest, the average change in the sample, is unlikely to be exactly the same as the population parameter, the average change that would have been observed if measurements were available for the entire population of third graders. This is because there will be many sources of variability that will cause the change scores to vary from student to student. Some students are brighter than others and would learn arithmetic skills faster no matter how they were taught. Some may have had experience with computers at home, or may have a more positive attitude toward using a computer. If the variability of scores is large, even if we choose a random sample, then the sample may look very different from the population because we just may happen, by chance, to select a disproportionate number of high (or low) scores. We can partly compensate for variability by increasing sample size, because larger samples of data are more likely to look like the population. If there were no, or very little, variability in the population, samples could be small, and we would not need inferential statistical procedures to enable us to draw inferences about the population.

Because of variability, the researcher has a task similar to that of someone trying to understand a spoken message embedded in noise. Statistical procedures may be thought of as filters, as methods for extracting the message in a noisy background. No one procedure is best for every, or even for most, research questions. How well we understand the message in our data will depend on choosing the research design and method of data analysis most appropriate in each study. Much of this book is about that choice.

## 1.2 SYSTEMATIC VERSUS RANDOM VARIABILITY

In the example of the study of CAI, the researcher might want to contrast CAI with a more traditional instructional method. We can contrast two different types of approaches to the research: experimental and observational. In an **experiment**, the researcher *assigns* subjects to the treatment groups in such a way that there are no *systematic* differences between the groups except for the treatment. One way to do this is to randomly assign students to each of the two instructional methods. In contrast, in an **observational** or **correlational study**, the researcher does not assign subjects to treatment conditions, but instead obtains scores from subjects who just happen to be exposed to the different treatments. For example, in an observational approach to the study of CAI, we might examine how arithmetic is taught in some sample of schools, finding some in which CAI is used, others where it is not, and comparing performances across the two sets of schools. In either the experimental or the observational study, the instructional method is the **independent variable**. However, in an experiment, we say that the independent variable is *manipulated*, whereas in an observational study, we say the independent variable is *observed*. The **dependent variable** in both approaches would be the score on a test of arithmetic skills. A problem with the observational approach is that the treatment groups may differ *systematically* from one another because of factors other than the treatment. These systematic differences often make it very difficult or impossible to assess the effect of the treatment.

As we previously indicated, variables other than the independent variable could influence the arithmetic test scores. In both the experimental and the observational approaches, the groups might differ by chance in ability level, exposure to computers outside of the classroom, or parental encouragement. We will refer to these as **nuisance variables**. Although they influence performance, and may be of interest in other studies, they are not the variables of current interest and will produce unwanted, nuisance, variability. In an experiment, we might account for the influence of nuisance variables by assigning students to the teaching methods by using randomization; that is, by employing a procedure that gave each student an equal chance of being assigned to each teaching method. **Random assignment** does not perfectly match the experimental groups on nuisance variables; the two groups may still differ on such dimensions as previous experience with computers, or ability level. However, random assignment does guard against systematic differences between the groups. When assignment to experimental conditions is random, differences between groups on nuisance variables are limited to "chance" factors. If the experiment is repeated many times, in the long run neither of the instructional methods will have an advantage caused by these factors. The statistical analyses that we apply to the data have been developed to take chance variability into account; they allow us to ask whether differences in performance between the experimental groups are more than would be expected if they were due only to the chance operation of nuisance variables. Thus, if we find very large differences on the arithmetic skills test, we can reasonably conclude that the variation in instructional methods between experimental groups was the cause.

In an observational study we observe the independent variable rather than manipulate it. This would involve seeking students already being taught by the two teaching methods and measuring their arithmetic performance. If we did this, not only would the instructional groups differ because of chance differences in the nuisance variables, it is possible that some of them might vary systematically across instructional conditions, yielding systematic differences between groups that are not readily accounted for by our statistical procedures. For example, school districts that have the funds to implement CAI may also have smaller class sizes, attract better teachers with higher salaries, and have students from more affluent families, with parents who have more time and funds to help children with their studies. If so, it would be difficult to decide whether superior performance in the schools using CAI was due to the instructional method, smaller class size, more competent teachers, or greater parental support. We describe this situation by saying that CAI is *confounded* with income level. Because there is often greater difficulty in disentangling the effects of nuisance and independent variables in observational studies, the causal effects of the independent variable are more readily assessed in experiments.

Although we can infer causality more directly in experiments, observational studies have an important place in the research process. There are many situations in which it is difficult or impossible to manipulate the independent variable of interest. This is often the case when the independent variable is a physical, mental, or emotional characteristic of individuals. An example of this is provided in a study conducted by Räkkönen, Matthews, Flory, Owens, and Gump (1999). Noting that ambulatory blood pressure (BP) had been found to be correlated with severity of heart disease, they investigated whether it in turn might be influenced by certain personality characteristics, specifically, the individual's level of optimism or pessimism and general level of anxiety. These two predictor variables were assessed by tests developed in earlier studies of personality. The dependent variable, BP, was monitored at 30-minute intervals over 3 days while the 50 male and 50 female participants went about their usual activities. An important aspect of the study was that participants kept diaries that enabled the investigators to separate out the effects of several nuisance variables, including mood, physical activity, posture (sitting and standing versus reclining), and intake of caffeinated beverages such as coffee. By doing so, and by applying sophisticated statistical procedures to analyze their data, the investigators were able to demonstrate that stable personality characteristics (optimism, pessimism, and general anxiety level) influenced BP beyond the transient effects of such variables as mood. Thus, it is possible to collect data on all the important variables and to test causal models. However, such analyses are more complicated and inferences are less direct than those that follow from performing an experiment.

## 1.3 ERROR VARIANCE AGAIN

Let's review some of the concepts introduced in Section 1.1, using some of the terms we introduced in Section 1.2. Even if subjects have been randomly assigned to experimental conditions, the presence of nuisance variables will result in **error variance**, variability among scores that cannot be attributed to the effects of the independent variable. Scores can be thought of as consisting of two components: a **treatment component** determined by the independent variable and an **error component** determined by nuisance variables. Error components will always exhibit some variability, even when scores have been obtained under the same experimental treatment. This error variance may be the result of individual differences in such variables as age, intelligence, and motivation. Error variance may also be the result of within-individual variability when measures are obtained from the same individuals at different times, and it is influenced by variables such as attentiveness, practice, and fatigue.

Error variance tends to obscure the effects of the independent variable. For example, in the CAI experiment, if two groups of third graders differ in their arithmetic scores, the difference could be due, at least in part, to error variance. Similarly, if BP readings are higher in more pessimistic individuals, as Räkkönen et al. (1999) found, we must ask whether factors other than pessimism could be responsible. The goal of data analysis is to divide the observed variation in performance into variability attributable to variation in the independent variable, and variability attributable to nuisance variables. As we stated at the beginning of this chapter, we have to extract the message (the effects of the independent variable) from the noise in which it is embedded (error variance). Much of the remainder of this book deals with principles and techniques of inferential statistics that have been developed to help us decide whether variation in a dependent variable has been caused by the independent variable or is merely a consequence of error variability.

## 1.4 REDUCING ERROR VARIANCE

If we can reduce error variance through the design of the research, it becomes easier for us to assess the influence of the independent variable. One basic step is to attempt to hold nuisance variables constant. For example, Räkkönen et al. (1999) took BP measurements from all subjects on the same 3 days of the week; 2 were workdays and 1 was not. In this way, they minimized any possible effects of the time at which measurements were taken.

In a study such as the CAI experiment, it is important that teachers have similar levels of competence and experience, and, if possible, classes should be similar in the distribution of ability levels. If only one level of a nuisance variable is present, it cannot give any advantage to any one level of the independent variable, nor can it contribute to the variability among the scores. Each research study will have its own potential sources of error variance, but, by careful analysis of each situation, we can eliminate or minimize many of them.

We can also minimize the effects of error variance by choosing an efficient research design; that is, we can choose a design that permits us to assess the contribution of one or more nuisance variables and therefore to remove that contribution from the error variance. One procedure that is often used in experiments is **blocking**, sometimes also referred to as **stratification**. Typically, we divide the pool of subjects into blocks on the basis of some variable whose effects are not of primary interest to us, such as gender or ability level. Then we randomly assign subjects within each block to the different levels of the independent variable. In the CAI experiment, we could divide the pool of third graders into three levels of arithmetic skill (low, medium, and high) based on a test administered at the start of the school year. We might then randomly assign students at each skill level to the two instructional methods, yielding six combinations of instruction and initial skill level. The advantage of this design is that it permits us to remove some of the contribution of initial skill level from the total variability of scores, thus reducing error variance. The blocking design is said to be more **efficient** than the design that randomly assigns subjects to instructional methods without regard to ability level. Chapter 12 presents the analysis of data when a blocking design has been used. For some independent variables (instructional method is not one of them), even greater efficiency can be achieved if we test the same subject at each level of the independent variable. This **repeated-measures design** is discussed in Chapter 13. Other designs that enable us to remove some sources of error variance from the total variability are the Latin Squares of Chapter 17.

Often, blocking is not practical. Morrow and Young (1997) studied the effects of exposure to literature on reading scores of third graders. Although reading scores were obtained before the start of the school year (pretest scores), the composition of the third-grade classes was established by school administrators prior to the study. Therefore, the blocking design we just described was not a possibility. However, the pretest score could still be used to reduce error variance. Morrow and Young adjusted the posttest scores, the dependent variable, essentially removing that portion of the score that was predictable from the pretest score. In this way, much, though not all, of the variability caused by the initial level of ability was removed from the final data set. This statistical adjustment, called **analysis of covariance**, is presented in Chapter 15. Both blocking designs and analysis of covariance use measures that are not affected by the independent variable but are related to the dependent variable to reduce the error variance, thus making it easier to assess the variability caused by the independent variable.

Usually the greater efficiency that comes with more complicated designs and analyses has a cost. For example, additional information is required for both blocking and the analysis of covariance. Furthermore, the appropriate statistical analysis associated with more efficient approaches is usually based on more stringent assumptions about the nature of the data. In view of this, a major theme of this book is that there are many possible designs and analyses, and many considerations in choosing among them. We would like to select our design and method of data analysis with the goal of reducing error variance as much as possible. However, our decisions in these matters may be constrained by the resources and subjects that are available and by the assumptions that must be made about the data. Ideally, the researcher should be aware of the pros and cons of the different designs and analyses, and the trade-offs that must be considered in making the best choice.

## 1.5 OVERVIEW OF THE BOOK

Although most researchers tend to compute a few summary statistics and then carry out statistical tests, data analyses should begin by exploring the data more thoroughly than is usually done. This means not only calculating alternative statistics that tell us something about the location, variability, and shape of the distribution of data, but also graphing the data in various ways. Chapter 2 presents useful statistics and methods of graphing for univariate data, that is, for cases involving a single variable. Chapter 3 does the same for bivariate data, cases in which the relation between two variables is of interest.

Theoretical distributions play a central role in procedures for drawing inferences about population parameters. These can be divided into two types: discrete and continuous. A variable is **discrete** if it assumes a finite, countable, number of values; the number of individuals who solve a problem is an example. In contrast, a **continuous variable** can take on any value in an interval. Chapter 4 presents an important discrete distribution, the binomial distribution, and uses it to review some basic concepts involved in testing hypotheses about population parameters. Chapter 5 provides a similar treatment of an important continuous distribution, the normal distribution, extending the treatment of inference to concepts involved in estimating population parameters, and intervals in which they may lie. Chapter 6 continues the treatment of continuous distributions and their applications to inferences about population parameters in the context of the $t$ distribution, and it also introduces the concept of **standardized effect size**, a measure that permits comparisons of treatment effects obtained in different experiments or with different measures. Chapter 7 concludes our review of continuous distributions with a discussion of the chi-square ($\chi^2$) and $F$ distributions.

As we noted in the preceding section, there are many different experimental designs. We may assign subjects to blocks on the basis of a pretest score, or age, or gender, or some other variable. We may test the same subject under several levels of an independent variable. We may sequence the presentation of such levels randomly or in an arbitrary order designed to balance practice or fatigue effects across treatments. These various experimental designs, and the analyses appropriate for each, are discussed in Chapters 8–17.

Most of the analyses presented in the experimental design chapters are usually referred to as analyses of variance. An analysis of variance, or ANOVA, is a special case of *multiple regression analysis*, or *MRA*, a general method of analyzing changes in the dependent variable that are associated with changes in the independent variable. Chapters 18–21 develop this regression framework, including estimation and statistical tests, and its relation to ANOVA.

## 1.6 CONCLUDING REMARKS

In the initial draft of a report of a special task force of the American Psychological Association (Task Force on Statistical Inference, 1996, posted at the APA Web site; see also Wilkinson, 1999), the committee noted that "the wide array of quantitative techniques and the vast number of designs available to address research questions leave the researcher with the non-trivial task of matching analysis and design to the research question." The goal of this book is to aid in that task by providing the reader with the background necessary to make these decisions. No text can present every design and analysis that researchers will encounter in their own work or in the research literature. We do, however, consider many common designs, and we attempt to build a conceptual framework that permits the reader to generalize to new situations and to comprehend both the advice of statistical consultants and articles on statistical methods. We do this by emphasizing basic concepts; by paying close attention to the assumptions on which the statistical methods rest and to the consequences of violations of these assumptions; and by considering alternative methods that may have to be used in the face of severe violations.

The special task force gave their greatest attention to "approaches to enhance the quality of data usage and to protect against potential misrepresentation of quantitative results." One result of their concern about this topic was a recommendation "that more extensive descriptions of the data be provided...." We believe this is important not only as a way to avoid misrepresentation to reviewers and readers of research reports, but also as the researcher's first step in understanding the data, a step that should precede the application of any inferential procedure. In the next two chapters, we illustrate some of the descriptive methods that are referred to in the report.

## KEY CONCEPTS

Boldfaced terms in the text are important to understand. In this chapter, many concepts were only briefly introduced. Nevertheless, it will be useful to have some sense of them even at a basic level. They are listed here for review.

| | |
|---|---|
| within-treatment variability | population |
| sample | population parameter |
| sample statistic | inferential statistics |
| random sample | experiment |
| observational study | independent variable |
| dependent variable | nuisance variables |
| random assignment | treatment component |
| error component | error variance |
| blocking | design efficiency |
| repeated-measures design | analysis of covariance |
| discrete variable | continuous variable |

## EXERCISES

**1.1** A researcher requested volunteers for a study comparing several methods to reduce weight. Participants were told that if they were willing to be in the study, they would be assigned randomly to one of three methods. Thirty individuals agreed to this condition and participated in the study.
(a) Is this an experiment or an observational study?

(b) Is the sample random? If so, characterize the likely population.

(c) Describe and discuss an alternative research design.

**1.2**  A study of computer-assisted learning of arithmetic in third-grade students was carried out in a private school in a wealthy suburb of a major city.

(a) Characterize the population that this sample represents. In particular, consider whether the results permit generalizations about CAI for the broad population of third-grade students. Present your reasoning.

(b) This study was done by assigning one class to CAI and one to a traditional method. Discuss some potential sources of error variance in this design.

**1.3**  Investigators who conducted an observational study reported that children who spent considerable time in day care were more likely than other children to exhibit aggressive behavior in kindergarten (Stolberg, 2001). Although this suggests that placement in day care may cause aggressive behavior—either because of the day-care environment or because of the time away from parents—other factors may be involved.

(a) What factors other than time spent in day care might affect aggressive behavior in the study cited by Stolberg?

(b) If you were carrying out such an observational study, what could you do to try to understand the effects on aggression of factors other than day care?

(c) An alternative approach to establishing the effects of day care on aggressive behavior would be to conduct an experiment. How would you conduct such an experiment and what are the pros and cons of this approach?

**1.4**  It is well known that the incidence of lung cancer in individuals who smoke cigarettes is higher than in the general population.

(a) Is this evidence that smoking causes lung cancer?

(b) If you were a researcher investigating this question, what further lines of evidence would you seek?

**1.5**  In the Seasons study (the data are in the Seasons file in the *Seasons* folder on the CD accompanying this book), we found that the average depression score was higher for men with only a high school education than for those with at least some college education. Discuss the implications of this finding. In particular, consider whether the data demonstrate that providing a college education will reduce depression.

**1.6**  In a 20-year study of cigarette smoking and lung cancer, researchers recorded the incidence of lung cancer in a random sample of smokers and nonsmokers, none of whom had cancer at the start of the study.

(a) What are the independent and dependent variables?

(b) For each, state whether the variable is discrete or continuous.

(c) What variables other than these might be recorded in such a study? Which of these are discrete or continuous?

# Chapter 2
## Looking at Data:
## Univariate Distributions

## 2.1 INTRODUCTION

This chapter and the next are primarily concerned with how to look at and describe data. Here, we consider how to characterize the **distribution** of a single variable; that is, what values the variable takes on and how often these values occur. We consider graphic displays and descriptive statistics that tell us about the location, or central tendency, of the distribution, about the variability of the scores that make up the distribution, and about the shape of the distribution. Although we present examples of real-life data sets that contain many different variables, and sometimes compare several of them, in this chapter our focus is on the description of single variables. In Chapter 3 we consider relations among variables and present plots and statistics that characterize relations among two or more variables.

Data analyses should begin with graphs and the calculation of descriptive statistics. In some instances, description is an end in itself. A school district superintendent may wish to evaluate the scores on a standardized reading test to address various questions, such as What was the average score? How do the scores in this district compare with those in the state as a whole? Are most students performing near the average? Are there stragglers who require added help in learning? If so, which schools do they come from? Do boys and girls differ in their average scores or in the variability of their scores? We must decide which statistics to compute to answer these and other questions, and how to graph the data to find the most salient characteristics of the distribution and to reveal any unusual aspects.

In other instances, we may want to draw inferences about a population of scores on the basis of a sample selected from it. Summarizing and graphing the data at hand is important for that purpose as well. The exploration of the data may suggest hypotheses that we might not otherwise have considered. For example, we may have begun the study with an interest in comparing treatment averages but find that one treatment causes greater variability than the others. A close look at our data may also suggest potential problems for the statistical tests we planned. For example, the validity of many standard statistical tests depends on certain assumptions about the distributions of scores. Many tests assume that the distributions of scores associated with each treatment are bell shaped; that is, they have a so-called normal distribution.[1] Some tests make the assumption that the variability of scores is the same for each treatment. If these assumptions are not supported by the data, we may wish to consider alternative procedures.

## 2.2 EXPLORING A SINGLE SAMPLE

Suppose we have carried out a study of arithmetic performance by elementary school students. Given the data set, there are many questions we could ask, but the first might be, How well are the students doing? One way to answer this is to calculate some average value that typifies the distribution of scores. "Typifies" is a vague concept, but usually we take as a typical value the mean or median. These measures provide a sense of the **location**, or the **central tendency**, of the distribution. We calculate the **arithmetic mean** for our sample by adding together the students' scores and dividing by the number of students. To obtain the **median** value, we rank order the scores and find the middle one if the number of scores is odd, or we average the two middle scores if the number of scores is even. No matter which average we decide to calculate, it provides us with limited information. For example, in a study of the arithmetic skills of elementary school children conducted by Royer, Tronsky, and Chan (1999; see the Royer data file in the *Royer* folder on the CD), the mean percentage correct addition score for 28 second-grade students was 84.607 and the median was 89.[2] This tells us that, on the average, the students did quite well. What it does not tell us is whether everyone scored close to the mean or whether there was considerable variability. Nor does the average tell us anything about the shape of the distribution. If most students have scored near the median but a few students have much lower scores, than we should know this because it alerts us to the fact that there are children having problems with simple addition.

Table 2.1 presents the scores for the 28 students in the Royer study under the label "Royer" together with a second set of 28 scores ($Y$) that we created that has the same mean and median. A quick glance at the numbers suggests that, despite the fact that the two data sets have the same means and medians, there are differences between the distributions. Specifying the differences on the basis of an examination of the numbers is difficult, and would be even more so if we had not placed them in order, or if the data sets were larger. We need a way of getting a quick impression of the distributions of the scores—their location,

**TABLE 2.1**  THE ROYER GRADE 2 ADDITION SCORES AND AN ARTIFICIAL SET ($Y$) WITH THE SAME MEAN AND MEDIAN

| | | | | | | | | | | |
|---|---|---|---|---|---|---|---|---|---|---|
| | 47 | 50 | 50 | 69 | 72 | 74 | 76 | 82 | 82 | 83 |
| Royer | 84 | 85 | 88 | 89 | 89 | 90 | 93 | 94 | 94 | 94 |
| | 94 | 95 | 95 | 100 | 100 | 100 | 100 | 100 | | |
| | | | | | | | | | | |
| | 31 | 32 | 79 | 83 | 83 | 85 | 85 | 85 | 87 | 87 |
| $Y$ | 87 | 89 | 89 | 89 | 89 | 89 | 89 | 90 | 90 | 91 |
| | 91 | 91 | 91 | 92 | 92 | 93 | 95 | 95 | | |

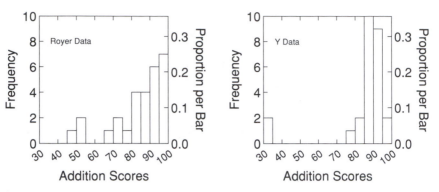

**Fig. 2.1** Histograms of the data in Table 2.1.

variability, and shape. Histograms, graphs of the frequency of groups of scores, provide one way to view the data quickly. They can be generated by any one of several statistical (e.g., SPSS, SAS, or SYSTAT) or graphic (e.g., Sigma Plot, StatGraphics, or PsiPlot) programs or spread sheets (e.g., Excel or Quattro Pro). Figure 2.1 presents such histograms for the two data sets of Table 2.1.

### 2.2.1 Histograms of the Data

In these histograms, the $X$ axis (the abscissa) has been divided into intervals of 5 points each. The label on the left-hand $Y$ axis (the ordinate) is the frequency, the number of scores represented by each bar; the label on the right side is the proportion of the 28 scores represented by each bar. Important characteristics of each distribution, as well as similarities and differences among the distributions, should now be more evident than they would be from a listing of the scores. For example, whereas the modal (most frequent) category in the Royer data is the interval 96–100, the modal category in the $Y$ data is the interval 86–90, and the bar corresponding to the $Y$ mode is noticeably higher than that of the Royer mode. Another difference is that, despite being equal in both means and medians, the $Y$ distribution contains two scores much lower than any in the Royer data.

The gap we observe in both the $Y$ and Royer distributions is typical of many real data sets, as is the obvious asymmetry in both distributions. Micceri (1989) examined 440 distributions of achievement scores and other psychometric data and noted the prevalence of such departures from the classic bell shape as asymmetry (or skew), and "lumpiness," or more than one mode (the most frequently observed value). Similarly, after analyzing many data distributions based on standard chemical analyses of blood samples, Hill and Dixon (1982) concluded that their real-life data distributions were "asymmetric, lumpy, and have relatively few unique values" (p. 393). We raise this point because the inferential procedures most commonly encountered in journal reports rest on strong assumptions about the shape of the distribution of data in the population. It is worth keeping in mind that these assumptions are often not met, and it is therefore important to understand the consequences of the mismatch between assumptions and the distribution of data. We consider those consequences when we take up each inferential procedure.

Most statistical packages enable the user to determine the number of histogram intervals and their width. There is no one perfect choice for all data sets. We chose to display

```
Stem and Leaf Plot of variable:      ROYER, N = 28
    Minimum:      47.000
    Lower hinge:     79.000
    Median:       89.000
    Upper hinge:     94.500
    Maximum:    100.000

        4  7
        5  00
* * * Outside Values * * *
        6  9
        7  24
        7 H 6
        8  2234
        8 M 5899
        9 H 034444
        9  55
       10  00000
```

**Fig. 2.2** Stem-and-leaf plot of the Royer data in Table 2.1.

14 intervals between 30 and 100, each 5 points wide. We had previously constructed the histograms with 7 intervals, each 10 points wide. However, this construction lost certain interesting differences among the distributions. For example, because scores from 91 to 100 were represented by a single bar, the distributions looked more similar than they actually were at the upper end. It is often helpful to try several different options. This is easily done because details such as the interval width and number of intervals, or the upper and lower limits on the axes, can be quickly changed by most computer graphics programs.

Histograms provide only one way to look at our data. For a more detailed look at the numerical values in the Royer Grade 2 data, while still preserving information about the distribution's shape, we next consider a different kind of display.

### 2.2.2 Stem-and-Leaf Displays

Figure 2.2 presents a stem-and-leaf display of the Royer data. The display consists of two parts. The first part contains five values, beginning with the **minimum** and ending with the **maximum**. This first part is sometimes referred to as the **5-point summary**. The minimum and maximum are the smallest and largest values in the data set. Before we consider the second part of the display, the actual stem-and-leaf plot, let's look at the remaining 3 points in the 5-point summary.

**The Median.**    If the number of scores, $N$, is an odd number, the median is the middle value in a set of scores ordered by their values. If $N$ is an even number, the median is the value halfway between the middle two scores. Another way of thinking about this is to define the position of the median in an *ordered* set of scores; this is its *depth*, $d_M$, where

$$d_M = (N + 1)/2 \tag{2.1}$$

For example, if

$$Y = 1, 3, 4, 9, 12, 13, 18$$

then $N = 7$, $d_M = 4$, and the median is the fourth score, 9. If the preceding set contained an additional score, say 19, we would have $N = 8$ and $d_M = 4.5$. This indicates that the median would be the mean of the fourth and fifth scores, 9 and 12, or 10.5. In the Royer data, there are 28 scores; therefore $d_M = 14.5$, and, because the 14th and 15th scores are both 89, the median is 89.

**The Hinges.**    There are many possible measures of the spread of scores that are based on calculating the difference between scores at two positions in an ordered set of scores. The **range**, the difference between the largest and the smallest scores, has intuitive appeal, but its usefulness is limited because it depends only on two scores and is therefore highly variable from sample to sample. Other measures of spread are based on differences between other positions in the ordered data set. The **interquartile range**, or **IQR**, is one such measure. The first quartile is that value which equals or exceeds one fourth of the scores (it is also referred to as the 25th **percentile**). The second quartile is the median (the 50th percentile), and the third quartile is the value that equals or exceeds three fourths of the scores (the 75th percentile). The IQR is the difference between the first and third quartile. Calculating the first or third quartile value is often awkward, requiring linear interpolation. For example, if there are seven scores, the first quartile is the value at the 1.75 position, or three fourths of the distance between the first and second score. Somewhat simpler to calculate, but close to the first and third quartile, are the **hinges**. As an example of their calculation, and of the **interhinge distance**, or **H spread**, consider the Royer data of Table 2.1. Then take the following steps:

1.  Find the location, or depth, of the median $d_M = (N + 1)/2$. With 28 scores, $d_M = 14.5$.
2.  When $d_M$ has a fractional value—that is, when $N$ is an even number—drop the fraction. We use brackets to represent the integer; that is, $[d_M] = 14$. The lower and upper hinges are simply the medians of the lower and of the upper 14 scores.
3.  Find the depth of the lower hinge, $d_{LH}$. This is given by

$$d_{LH} = \frac{[d_M] + 1}{2} \tag{2.2}$$

In our example, $d_{LH} = 7.5$; this means that the lower hinge will be the score midway between the seventh score (76) and the eighth score (82), or 79. The upper hinge will lie midway between the seventh and eighth scores from the top; this is 94.5 in the Royer data. The $H$ spread is therefore $94.5 - 79$, or 15.5.

The 5-point summary provides a rough sense of the data. The median tells us that at least half of the Grade 2 students have a good grasp of addition. When we consider the minimum and maximum together with the median, it is clear that there are some stragglers; the distance from the minimum to the median is almost four times greater than that of the maximum to the median. However, that distance could be due to just one student with a low score. More telling is the comparison of the top and bottom fourths; 25% of the students have scores between 95 and 100, whereas another 25% fall between 47 and 79.

Most of our readers are probably more familiar with the arithmetic mean than with the median, and with the variance (or its square root, the standard deviation) than with the $H$ spread. It is worth noting that the mean and variance are more sensitive to individual scores than the median and $H$ spread. If we replaced the 47 in the data set with a score of 67, the median and $H$ spread would be unchanged but the mean would be increased and the variance would be decreased. Because they change less when the values of individual scores are changed, we say that the median and $H$ spread are **resistant statistics**. This does not necessarily mean that they are better measures of location and variability than the mean and variance. The choice of measures should depend on our purpose. The median and $H$ spread are useful when describing location and variability. However, the mean and variance play a central role in statistical inference.

**The Stem-and-Leaf Plot.**    The plot in Fig. 2.2 is essentially a histogram laid on its side. The length of each row gives a sense of the frequency of a particular range of scores, just as in the histogram. However, this plot provides somewhat more information because it allows us to reconstruct the actual numerical values of Table 2.1. The left-hand column of values, beginning with 4 and ending with 10, is called the stem. For the Royer data, to obtain a score, we multiply the stem by 10 and add the leaf, the value to the right of the stem. Thus the first row of the plot represents the score of 47. The next row informs us that there are two scores of 50. The next two rows contain the scores 69, 72, and 74. The row following this indicates the score of 76 and has an $H$ between the stem (7) and the sole leaf (6). The $H$ indicates that the (lower) hinge lies in the range of scores from 75 to 79. Note that it does not mean that the lower hinge is 76; the hinges and the median do not necessarily correspond to observed scores; in this case, the actual hinge is 79, midway between the observed scores of 76 and 82.

The stem-and-leaf plot provides a sense of the shape of the distribution, although the gap between 50 and 71 is not as immediately evident as it was in the histogram. The trade-off between the histogram and the stem-and-leaf plot is that the former usually provides a more immediate sense of the overall shape whereas the latter provides more detail about the numerical values. In addition, it provides summary statistics in the hinges and median, and, as we discuss shortly, it also clearly marks outliers, scores that are very far from most of the data.

The values by which the stem and leaf should be multiplied depend on the numerical scale. Consider a set of 30 Standardized Achievement Test (SAT) scores, the first 10 of which are 394, 416, 416, 454, 482, 507, 516, 524, 530, and 542. Figure 2.3 presents SYSTAT's stem-and-leaf display for the entire data set. To obtain an approximation to the actual scores, multiply the stem by 100 and the leaf by 10. Thus the first row tells us that there is a score between 390 and 399, actually 394. The next row tells us that there are two scores between 410 and 419; both are actually 416. Although we cannot tell the exact score from this plot, we clearly have more information than the histogram would have provided, and we still have a sense of the shape of the distribution.

**Outliers.** In both Figs. 2.2 and 2.3, $H$ marks the intervals within which the hinges fall and $M$ marks the interval that contains the median. The values above the "Outside Values" line in the Royer plot, and outside the two such lines in Fig 2.3, are called outliers. In the Royer data, the outliers call our attention to students whose performances are far below those of the rest of the class; these students may require remedial help. Of course, there are other possible reasons for outliers in data sets. The students who produced the scores of 47 and 50 may have been ill on the day the test was administered, or have performed below their capabilities for other reasons. In some cases, outliers may reflect clerical errors. In situations in which interest resides primarily in the individuals tested, it is important to identify outliers and try to ascertain whether the score truly represents the ability or

```
Stem and Leaf Plot of variable:        Y, N = 30
Minimum:     394.000
Lower hinge:      524.000
Median:     581.000
Upper hinge:      602.000
Maximum:      753.000

          3  9
    * * * Outside Values * * *
          4   11
          4
          4  5
          4
          4  8
          5  01
          5 H 23
          5  445
          5  667
          5 M 888889
          6 H 00001
          6  23
          6  5
    * * * Outside Values * * *
          7  5
```

**Fig. 2.3**  Stem-and-leaf plot of 30 SAT scores.

characteristic being assessed. In studies in which we are primarily interested in drawing inferences about a population—for example, in deciding which of two treatments of a medical condition is superior—outliers should also be considered. If they are due to clerical errors in transcribing data, they can distort our understanding of the results, and therefore should be corrected. In some cases, there is no obvious reason for an outlier. It may reflect a subject's lack of understanding of instructions, a momentary failure to attend, or any number of other factors that distort the behavioral process under investigation. Unfortunately, there is no clear consensus about how to deal with such data. Some researchers do nothing about such nonclerical outliers. Most either replace the outlier by the nearest nonoutlying score, or just drop the outlier from the data set.

Our present concern is to understand how outliers are defined. The criterion for the outside values in Fig. 2.3 was calculated in the following steps:

1. Calculate the $H$ spread. In Fig. 2.3, this is $602 - 524$, or 78.
2. Multiply the $H$ spread by 1.5. The result is 117.
3. Subtract 117 from the lower hinge and add 117 to the upper hinge. The resulting values, 407 and 719, are called **inner fences**. Scores below 407 and above 719 are outliers.

Equation 2.3 represents these steps: a score, $Y$, is an outlier if

$$Y < H_L - 1.5\,(H_U - H_L) \text{ or } Y > H_U + 1.5\,(H_U - H_L) \tag{2.3}$$

where $H_L$ and $H_U$ are the lower and upper hinges, respectively. **Outer fences** may be calculated by multiplying the $H$ spread by 3, rather than 1.5. The lower outer fence would be $524 - 234$, or 290, and the upper outer fence would be $602 + 234$, or 836. Values beyond these two points would be labeled **extreme outliers**.

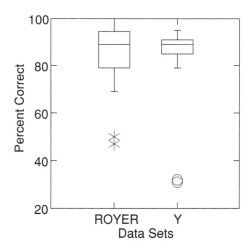

**Fig. 2.4**  Box plots of the data in Table 2.1.

Histograms and stem-and-leaf displays provide considerable information about the shape of the distribution. A less detailed view, but one that provides a quick snapshot of the main characteristics of the data, may be obtained by still another type of plot, which we consider next.

### 2.2.3 Box Plots

Figure 2.4 presents box plots of the Royer Grade 2 addition accuracy data and of the $Y$ data of Table 2.1. The top and bottom sides of the "boxes" are at the hinges. The lines somewhat above the middle of the boxes are at the medians. The lines extending vertically from the boxes are sometimes referred to as "whiskers." Their endpoints are the most extreme scores that are not outliers.

For the Royer data, the 5-point summary of Fig. 2.2 informs us that the hinges are at 79 and 94.5. Therefore, the $H$ spread is 15.5, and the lower fence is $79 - 1.5 \times 15.5$, or 55.75. The asterisks represent outliers, scores below 55; in this example, these are the 47 and the two 50s in Table 2.1. There are no extreme outliers in the Royer data but there are two in the $Y$ data (scores of 31 and 32; see Table 2.1); these are represented by small circles rather than asterisks. The bottom whisker in the Royer data extends to 69, the lowest value in Table 2.1 that was not an outlier. Note that the whisker does not extend to the fence; the fence is not represented in the plot.

The box plot quickly provides information about the main characteristics of the distribution. The crossbar within the box locates the median, and the length of the box gives us an approximate value for the $H$ spread. The box plot for the Royer data tells us that the distribution is skewed to the left because the bottom whisker is longer than the top, and there are three low outliers. Thus, at a glance, we have information about location, spread, skewness, tail length, and outliers. Furthermore, we can see at a glance that the $H$ spread is much smaller for the $Y$ data, that the two medians are similar, and, with the exception of the two extreme outliers, the $Y$ data are less variable than the Royer data. To sum up, the stem-and-leaf and box plots provide similar information. However, the stem-and-leaf plot gives us numerical values of hinges, medians, and outliers, and it provides a more precise view of the distribution. In contrast, the box plot makes the important characteristics of the distribution immediately clear and provides an easy way of comparing two or more distributions with respect to those characteristics.

## 2.3 COMPARING TWO DATA SETS

Suppose we have measures of anxiety for male and female samples. We might wish to know whether men and women differ with respect to this measure. Typically, researchers translate this into a question of whether the mean scores differ, but there may be more to be learned by also comparing other characteristics of the distributions. For example, researchers at the University of Massachusetts Medical School collected anxiety measures, as well as several other personality measures, during each season of the year, from male and female patients of various ages.[3] We calculated the average of the four seasonal anxiety scores for each participant in the study for whom all four scores were available. The means for the two groups are quite similar: 4.609 for female participants and 4.650 for male participants. Nor is there a marked difference in the medians: 4.750 for female participants and 4.875 for male participants. However, plotting the distributions suggested that there is a difference. Figure 2.5 contains box plots and histograms created with the data from 183 female and 171 male participants. If we look first at the box plots, it appears that the *H* spread (the length of the box) is slightly greater for women, suggesting greater variability in their anxiety scores. We further note that there are more outlying high scores for the women. Turning to the histograms, we confirm this impression. Why this difference in variability

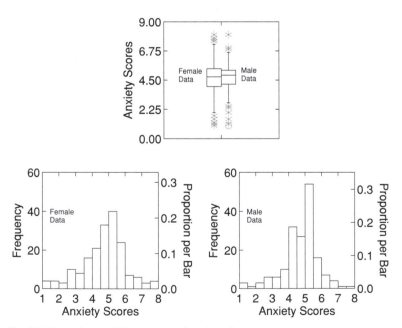

**Fig. 2.5** Box plots and histograms of anxiety data.

occurs and what the implications are for the treatment of anxiety, if any, is something best left to the medical investigators. We only note that plotting the data reveals a difference in the distributions that may be of interest, a difference not apparent in statistics reflecting location.

This is not to suggest that we disregard measures of location, but that we supplement them with other statistics and with plots of the data. With respect to measures of location, it is a good idea to bear in mind that there are many situations in which the mean and median will differ. In any salary dispute between labor and management, management may argue that salaries are already high, pointing to the mean as evidence. Workers, recognizing that a few highly paid individuals have pushed the mean upward, may prefer to negotiate on the basis of a lower value, the median, arguing that 50% of employees have salaries below that figure. Similar discrepancies between mean and median also arise with many behavioral measures. The data in the Seasons file (*Seasons* folder in the CD) present one illustration. In examining Beck depression scores for the winter season for men of various ages, we found a difference between the mean (over seasons) of the youngest group (<40 years, mean = 6.599) and that of a group between 50 and 59 years old (mean = 5.502). However, the medians were identical at 4.500.

Plotting the Beck depression data for the two groups is a first step in clarifying why the means are further apart than the medians. The upper panel of Fig. 2.6 presents box plots for the two groups. As in all plots of Beck depression scores, most of the scores are at the low (normal) end of the scale in the histograms for both age groups. We say that the distributions are skewed to the right because of the straggling right-hand (upper) tails. The explanation for the difference in means is readily apparent. The younger group has

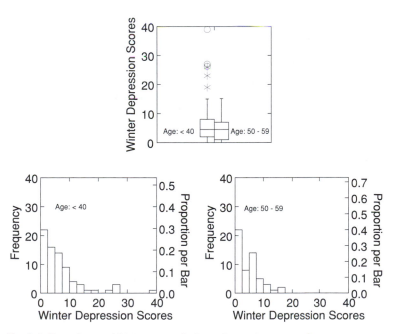

**Fig. 2.6** Box plots and histograms of winter depression scores for two age groups of men.

several individuals with scores above 18; these are depicted as outliers in the box plot for that group. Some of the outliers, depicted by open circles, are extreme outliers according to the definition of Subsection 2.2.2. No score is an outlier in the older group. Although the medians are identical, the greater number of extreme high scores in the younger group has moved that mean higher than the mean of the older group. The histograms in the lower panel of Fig. 2.6 provide a complementary view of the data. Again, the more pronounced right-hand tail in the younger group is evident. Just why there are more extremely depressed men in the under-40 group is not clear. It may be due to chance, in which case other samples from the same population may not exhibit the pattern of medians and means we have noted. It may be that, for some reason, more depressed older men are not in the pool of patients included in the study. For now, we withhold judgment about the cause of the pattern we have observed, while noting that calculating both the mean and the median, and plotting the data, may be more informative than calculating only one of the two measures of location.

## 2.4 OTHER MEASURES OF LOCATION AND SPREAD: THE MEAN AND STANDARD DEVIATION

Thus far, using stem-and-leaf and box plots has focused our attention on the median and the $H$ spread. However, there are many other statistics that can aid us in understanding our data, and these are readily obtained from most statistical packages. For example, a sequence of clicks ("Analyze," "Descriptive Statistics," and "Explore") in SPSS provides the statistics in Table 2.2, summarizing the data of Table 2.1. We have already considered several of these statistics—the median, minimum, maximum, range, and IQR. Others, such as the confidence interval, are explained in Chapter 5. In this section, we focus on the mean, standard deviation, and variance; although we suspect that they are familiar from an introductory course, it may be useful to review their definitions and properties. We also discuss the standard errors (labeled Std. Error in Table 2.2) of Table 2.1. Later in this chapter, we consider skewness and kurtosis, statistics that summarize aspects of the shape of the data distribution. In presenting some statistical formulas, we occasionally use a summation sign, a capital Greek sigma, $\Sigma$. The use of notation provides a shorthand; if a picture is worth a thousand words, a Greek symbol, or an equation, is often worth at least a dozen. Although our use of notation is intended to be easily understood, readers may find it helpful to refer to Appendix A, which reviews the algebra of summation and derives several properties of statistics that we state in this chapter.

### 2.4.1 The Arithmetic Mean

The familiar arithmetic mean, symbolized by $\overline{Y}$ ($Y$ bar), is just the sum of all scores divided by the number of scores. Expressing this as an equation, we have

$$\overline{Y} = \frac{1}{N} \sum_{i=1}^{N} Y_i \tag{2.4}$$

where $N$ represents the number of scores in a sample. For example, the mean of $Y = 1, 2, 3, 5, 9, 10, 12$ is $\overline{Y} = 42/7 = 6$. The widespread use of the mean reflects two advantages it

**TABLE 2.2**  SUMMARY STATISTICS FOR THE DATA OF TABLE 2.1

| Score Set | Descriptives | | Statistic | Std. Error |
|---|---|---|---|---|
| Royer | Mean | | 84.61 | 2.89 |
| | 95% confidence | Lower Bound | 78.68 | |
| | Interval for Mean | Upper Bound | 90.54 | |
| | 5% Trimmed Mean | | 85.79 | |
| | Median | | 89.00 | |
| | Variance | | 234.025 | |
| | Std. Deviation | | 15.30 | |
| | Minimum | | 47 | |
| | Maximum | | 100 | |
| | Range | | 53 | |
| | Interquartile Range | | 17.25 | |
| | Skewness | | −1.326 | .441 |
| | Kurtosis | | 1.124 | .858 |
| Y | Mean | | 84.61 | 2.92 |
| | 95% confidence | Lower Bound | 78.62 | |
| | Interval for Mean | Upper Bound | 90.59 | |
| | 5% Trimmed Mean | | 86.99 | |
| | Median | | 89.00 | |
| | Variance | | 238.099 | |
| | Std. Deviation | | 15.43 | |
| | Minimum | | 31 | |
| | Maximum | | 95 | |
| | Range | | 64 | |
| | Interquartile Range | | 6.00 | |
| | Skewness | | −3.195 | .441 |
| | Kurtosis | | 9.664 | .858 |

*Note.* Table is output from SPSS's Explore module.

**TABLE 2.3**  EXAMPLE OF MEANS BASED ON DIFFERENT SAMPLE SIZES

| | Clinics | | | |
|---|---|---|---|---|
| Parameter | A | B | C | D |
| Mean | 17.5 | 18.3 | 19.2 | 22.6 |
| Sample size ($n$) | 26 | 17 | 31 | 24 |

has over other measures of location. First, we can manipulate it algebraically, and, second, it has certain properties that are desirable when we estimate the mean of the population from which the sample was drawn. The role of the sample mean as an estimator of the population mean is discussed in Chapter 5. In this chapter, we summarize several useful algebraic properties. These properties can be proven by using the rules of summation in

Appendix A. They can be demonstrated by using the preceding set of numbers, or any other numbers you choose.

1. Adding a constant, $k$, to every score in the sample results in the mean being increased by the amount $k$; that is, $\Sigma(Y + k)/N = \overline{Y} + k$. For example, if we add 10 to each of the values in the preceding set of 7 numbers, the mean increases from 6 to 16.
2. Multiplying every score in the sample by a constant, $k$, results in the mean being multiplied by $k$; that is, $\Sigma(kY)/N = k\overline{Y}$. For example, multiplying each of the scores in the example by 2 increases the mean from 6 to 12.
3. Perhaps most importantly, means can be combined. For example, given the means of depression scores and the sample sizes from several clinics, we are able to calculate the mean based on the combined data sets.

The means and sample sizes ($n$) for each of four clinics are presented in Table 2.3. It is tempting to add the four means and divide by 4 to get the mean of the combined data sets. However, because the four $n$s vary, this will not do. The mean for Clinic C should carry more weight and that for Clinic B less weight in combining the means because of their relative sample sizes. The correct approach requires us to obtain the sum of all the scores in all four data sets and then divide by $N$, the sum of the $n$s. We obtain the sum of scores for each clinic by multiplying the clinic mean by the number of scores for that clinic. Summing these four sums, and dividing the grand total by $N$, the total number of scores, we have the grand mean of all the scores:

$$\overline{Y} = [(26 \times 17.5) + (17 \times 18.3) + (31 \times 19.2) + (24 \times 22.6)]/98 = 19.426$$

We might have rewritten this slightly:

$$\overline{Y} = \left(\frac{26}{98}\right)(17.5) + \left(\frac{17}{98}\right)(18.3) + \left(\frac{31}{98}\right)(19.2)\left(\frac{24}{98}\right)(22.6) \tag{2.5}$$

Equation 2.5 suggests that the mean can be represented as a sum of weighted values where the weights are proportions or probabilities. The weight for Clinic A is 26/98 because 26 of the 98 depression scores come from Clinic A. To take a somewhat different example, consider a student who has spent two semesters in College A and compiles a 3.2 grade point average (GPA). She then transfers to College B, where she earns a 3.8 GPA for the next three semesters. The student's overall GPA for the five semesters is calculated as in the preceding example of the clinic means. The overall GPA is a weighted mean in which the weights are 2/5 and 3/5:

$$\overline{Y} = (2/5)(3.2) + (3/5)(3.8) = 3.56$$

In general, the preceding calculations may be represented by

$$\overline{Y} = \sum p(y) \cdot y \tag{2.6}$$

Equation 2.6 is the formula for a **weighted mean**. It indicates that each distinct value of $Y$ is to be multiplied by its weight, $p(y)$, the proportion of all scores with that value. All of these products are then added together. Note that the usual expression for the arithmetic mean $\overline{Y} = \sum Y/N$ is a special case of the preceding formula for the weighted mean; here each of the $N$ scores in the sample is given a weight of $1/N$.

Two other properties of the mean, proven in Appendix A at the end of the book, may help convey the sense in which it reflects the central tendency of a data set:

4. The mean is the balance point of the data in the sense that the sum of the deviations about the mean is zero; that is, $\sum(Y - \overline{Y}) = 0$.
5. The sum of squared deviations of scores from the mean is smaller than the sum of squared differences taken from any point other than the mean; that is, $\sum[Y - (\overline{Y} + k)]^2$ has its smallest value when $k = 0$.

Every value in a set of scores is incorporated into the calculation of the mean. One benefit of this is that, as in our example of the four clinics, means can be combined without access to the individual values on which they are based. This strength is, however, also a potential weakness. A few extreme scores can bias the value of the mean, and they may result in the mean's taking on a value that does not typify the distribution of scores. As we discussed earlier in this chapter, the median provides an alternative measure of location that is resistant to the influence of extreme scores.

## 2.4.2 The Standard Deviation and the Variance

We group these statistics together because the variance is the square of the standard deviation. The sample variance, $S^2$, is the average squared deviation of scores about their mean; that is, $S^2 = \sum(Y - \overline{Y})^2/N$. However, as most statistical packages do, we will divide by $N - 1$, rather than $N$. The divisor $N - 1$ is used, rather than $N$, because it results in a better estimate of the population variance. We delay further consideration of this point to the discussion of estimation in Chapter 5. We denote this revised definition by $s^2$, rather than $S^2$, to indicate that we are dividing by $N - 1$. Thus, our formula for $s^2$ is

$$s^2 = \frac{\sum(Y - \overline{Y})^2}{N - 1} \tag{2.7}$$

The calculation of $s^2$ is illustrated with the following set of seven scores:

$$Y = 1, 2, 3, 5, 9, 10, 12$$

The sum of the scores is 42, and, therefore, $\overline{Y} = 42/7 = 6$. Finding the deviations from the mean, we have

$$Y - \overline{Y} = -5, -4, -3, -1, 3, 4, 6$$

squaring these deviations, we have

$$(Y - \overline{Y})^2 = 25, 16, 9, 1, 9, 16, 36$$

and summing the squared deviations, we have $\sum(Y - \overline{Y})^2 = 112$. Then, $s^2 = 112/6 = 18.667$. Because the variance is based on the squared deviations of the scores about the mean, the standard deviation, the square root of the variance, is usually preferred as a measure of spread. In the preceding example, $s = \sqrt{18.667} = 4.320$.

Two properties of the standard deviation should be noted:

1. When a constant is added to all scores in a distribution, the standard deviation is unchanged. That is, if $Y' = Y + k$, where $k$ is a constant, then $s_{Y'} = s_Y$. Intuitively, each score is increased (or decreased) by the same amount so the spread of scores is unchanged. The range and the $H$ spread also are unchanged when a constant is added, and it is a desirable property of any measure of variability.

2. When each score is multiplied by a positive constant, $k$, the standard deviation of the new scores is $k$ times the old standard deviation. If $k$ is negative, multiplying each score by $k$ is equivalent to multiplying the standard deviation by $-k$; the reason for this is that the standard deviation must always be a positive number. You can verify these multiplication properties by multiplying the preceding values of $Y$ by 10, and then by $-10$, and recalculating both $s$ and $s^2$ in each case. The new standard deviation is 43.2, 10 times the original value, and the new variance is 1866.7, 100 times the value on the original scale.

We can summarize the properties of the standard deviation as follows:

1. If $Y' = Y + k$, then $s_{Y'} = s_Y$.
2. If $Y' = kY$, then $s_{Y'} = ks_Y$ when $k > 0$ and $s_{Y'} = -ks_Y$ when $k < 0$.

These properties are proven in Appendix A at the back of the book.

Although the standard deviation is less intuitive than other measures of variability, it has two important advantages. First, the standard deviation is important in drawing inferences about populations from samples. It is a component of formulas for many significance tests, for procedures for estimating population parameters, and for measures of relations among variables. Second, it (and its square, the variance) can be manipulated arithmetically in ways that other measures cannot. For example, knowing the standard deviations, means, and sample sizes of two sets of scores, we can calculate the standard deviation of the combined data set without access to the individual scores. This relation between the variability within groups of scores and the variability of the total set plays an important role in data analysis. Both of the properties just noted will prove important throughout this book.

The main drawback of the standard deviation is that, like the mean, it can be greatly influenced by a single outlying score. Recall that for $Y = 1, 2, 3, 5, 9, 10$, and 12, $\overline{Y} = 6$ and $s = 4.320$. Suppose we add one more score. If that score is 8, a value within the range of the scores, then the new mean and standard deviation are 6.25 and 4.062, a fairly small change. However, if the added score is 20, then we now have $\overline{Y} = 7.75$ and $s = 6.364$. The standard deviation has increased by almost 50% with the addition of one extreme score. The $H$ spread (or its fraternal twin, the IQR) is resistant to extreme scores and is often a more useful measure for describing the variability in a data set. We again emphasize that there is no one best measure of variability (or for that matter, of location or shape), but that there is a choice, and that different measures may prove useful for different purposes, or may sometimes supplement each other.

## 2.4.3 The Standard Error of the Mean

Among the many statistics commonly available from statistical packages is one labeled the standard error ("Std. Error" in the SPSS output of Table 2.2), or *standard error of the mean*

(*SEM*). The *SEM* is a simple function of the standard deviation:

$$SEM = s/\sqrt{N} \qquad (2.8)$$

To understand the *SEM*, assume that many random samples of size $N$ are drawn from the same population, and that the mean is calculated each time. The distribution of these means is the **sampling distribution** of the mean for samples of size $N$. The *SEM* that is calculated from a single sample is an estimate of the standard deviation of the sampling distribution of the mean. In other words, it is an estimate of how much the mean would vary over samples. If the *SEM* is small, the one sample mean we have is likely to be a good estimate of the population mean because the small *SEM* suggests that the mean will not vary greatly across samples, and therefore any one sample mean will be close to the population mean. We have considerably more to say about the *SEM* and its role in drawing inferences in later chapters. At this point, we introduced it because of its close relation to the standard deviation, and because it provides an index of the variability of the sample mean.

### 2.4.4 The 5% Trimmed Mean

The SPSS output of Table 2.2 includes the value of the 5% trimmed mean. This is calculated by rank ordering the scores, dropping the highest and lowest 5%, and recalculating the mean. The potential advantage of trimming is that the *SEM* will be smaller than for the untrimmed mean in distributions that have long straggling tails, or have so-called "heavy" tails that contain more scores than in the normal distribution. In view of the preceding discussion of the *SEM*, this suggests that in some circumstances the trimmed mean will be a better estimator of the population mean. However, decisions about when to trim and how much to trim are not simple. Rosenberger and Gasko (1983) and Wilcox (1997) have written good discussions on this topic.

### 2.4.5 Displaying Means and Standard Errors

A graph of the means for various conditions often provides a quick comparison of those conditions. When accompanied by a visual representation of variability, such as $s$, or the *SEM*, the graph is still more useful. How best to graph the data should depend on the nature of the independent variable. Although graphics programs will provide a choice, the American Psychological Association's Publication Manual (2001) recommends that "**Bar graphs** are used when the independent variable is categorical" and "**Line graphs** are used to show the relation between two quantitative variables" (p. 178). We believe this is good advice. When the independent variable consists of categories that differ in type, rather than in amount, we should make it clear that the shape of a function relating the independent and dependent variables is not a meaningful concept. Figure 2.7 presents mean depression scores[4] from the Seasons data set as a function of marital status and sex; the numbers on the $x$ axis are the researchers' codes: 1 = single; 2 = married; 3 = living with partner; 4 = separated; 5 = divorced; 6 = widowed. At least in this sample, depression means are highest for single men and women, and for divorced women, and the means are low for those living with a partner. Without a more careful statistical analysis, and without considering the size of these samples, we hesitate to recommend living with a partner without marriage, but we merely note that the bar graph presents a starting point for comparing the groups. The vertical lines at the top of each bar represent the *SEM*s. Note that the *SEM* bars

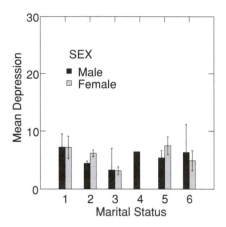

**Fig. 2.7** Bar graph of mean depression scores as a function of marital status and sex.

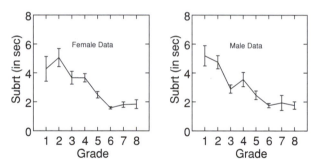

**Fig. 2.8** Line graph of subtraction response times as a function of grade and gender.

indicate that the male data are more variable than the female data, particularly in categories 3 and 6.

Figure 2.8 presents mean times in seconds to do subtraction problems (labeled "Subrt") from the Royer data set as a function of grade and gender. Because grade level is quantitative, it is useful to plot the data as line curves, providing a sense of the shape of the functional relation. It appears that response times for both genders decrease as a function of grade and seem to level off near the sixth grade. It also appears that variability decreases with grade, as indicated by the general decrease in the length of the *SEM* bars. Comparing across panels, we see that the main difference between boys' and girls' times appears to be in the early grades. We plotted these data in two panels because the two curves are close together and the error bars are difficult to disentangle if presented within a single panel.

Software capable of bar and line plots usually offer several options such as the choice of placing different plots in one panel (as in Fig. 2.7) or in separate panels (as in Fig. 2.8), or choosing the error bars to represent standard deviations, standard errors, or confidence intervals. The best advice is to become thoroughly familiar with the software being used, and then to think carefully about which options will enable you to best communicate the points you believe are important.

## 2.5 STANDARDIZED (z) SCORES

An individual's score, by itself, is not very informative. If a student earns a score of 70 on a math test, is that good or bad? On one hand, if told that a score of 70 was at the 90th percentile—that it had been exceeded by only 10% of all scores—we would probably feel that the performance was quite good. On the other hand, we would be considerably less impressed if the same raw score fell at the 40th percentile. Although information about percentile values tells us where a score ranks relative to other scores, it provides no information about distances among scores. For example, a score at the 90th percentile could be many points higher than the average or only a little higher; it depends on how variable the scores are. Standardized, or $z$, scores tell us more about where the score is located within the distribution—specifically, how many standard deviation units the score is above or below the mean. Given a distribution of scores with mean, $\overline{Y}$, and standard deviation, $s$, the $z$ score corresponding to a score $Y$ is calculated as

$$z_Y = (Y - \overline{Y})/s \qquad (2.9)$$

For example, if the mean is 75 and the standard deviation is 15, for a score of 90, we would have $z_{90} = (90 - 75)/15 = 1$; thus, this score is one standard deviation above the mean. Statistical packages generally include an option such as SPSS's Descriptive Statistics (in the "Analyze" menu) for calculating $z$ scores.

Standardizing a group of scores changes the scale to one of standard deviation units, thus permitting comparisons with scores that were originally on a different scale. Nevertheless, there are aspects of the original distribution that remain unchanged. The following are two things that remain constant:

1. An individual's $z$ score has the same percentile rank as did that individual's original score. This is because subtracting a constant, $\overline{Y}$, from every score does not change the rank order of the scores; nor is the order changed by dividing all scores by a constant, $s$.

2. The shape of the distribution of $z$ scores is the same as that of the original data. Subtraction of $\overline{Y}$ shifts the original distribution and division by $s$ squeezes the points closer together, but shape information is preserved. If the original distribution was symmetric, the distribution of $z$ scores will be also. However, if the original distribution was skewed, this will also be true of the distribution of $z$ scores.

As we see in Chapter 5, $z$ scores are used in drawing inferences when scores can reasonably be assumed to be normally distributed. However, the preceding point should make clear that *z scores are not necessarily (or even usually) normally distributed.* Their distribution depends on the distribution of the scores prior to the $z$ transformation.

Two other characteristics of $z$ scores should be noted:

3. The mean (and therefore also the sum) of a set of $z$ scores is zero. We stated earlier that when a constant is subtracted from every score, the mean is also changed

by that constant. In the case of $z$ scores, $\overline{Y}$ is subtracted from each of the $Y$ values. Therefore the mean of the $z$ scores is $\overline{Y} - \overline{Y}$, or 0.

4. The variance of a group of $z$ scores is 1.0, and, therefore, so is the standard deviation. Because the average $z$ score is zero, we need only square each member of the group of $z$ scores, sum the squared values, and divide by $N-1$ to obtain the variance. Doing so yields

$$
\begin{aligned}
s_z^2 &= \frac{\sum (Y - \overline{Y})^2 / s^2}{N - 1} \\
&= \frac{\sum (Y - \overline{Y})^2 / (N - 1)}{s^2} \\
&= \frac{s^2}{s^2} = 1
\end{aligned}
$$

Standardized scores can be useful in our understanding of a data set because they provide a way of comparing performances on different scales. For example, the mean and standard deviation of the subtraction accuracy scores in the Royer data set were 88.840 and 11.457, respectively; the corresponding values for multiplication accuracy scores were 87.437 and 13.996. Even though a subtraction score of 70 is higher than a multiplication score of 65, it is actually worse, relative to the other scores in the distribution. You may verify that, for subtraction, $z_{70}$ is $-1.64$ (that is, the score of 70 is 1.64 standard deviations below the mean of the subtraction scores), whereas for multiplication, $z_{65}$ is $-1.60$.

Standardized scores play other roles as well. In Chapter 5, we discuss how $z$ scores provide percentile information when the population distribution has an approximate bell shape. More immediately, in Chapter 3, we consider the correlation coefficient as an average product of $z$ scores. The underlying reason that $z$ scores play a role in deriving a statistic reflecting the relation between two variables is that such a statistic should not be influenced by differences in the scales of the two variables. This criterion can be met by converting the original values to $z$ scores. We show in Appendix 2.1 that the magnitudes of $z$ scores are unchanged if we change scales by adding a constant to each score and/or by multiplying each score by a constant. For example, if we measure the weights of each student in a class, the $z$ score of an individual student will be the same whether we measure weights in pounds or kilograms.

## 2.6 MEASURES OF THE SHAPE OF A DISTRIBUTION

Early in this chapter, we displayed addition accuracy scores for second graders in a study by Royer, together with an artificial data set that had the same mean and median as the Royer data (Table 2.1 and Fig. 2.1). Table 2.2 presented those statistics, as well as several others, for the Royer data and for the artificial set, $Y$. Note that not only are the means and medians of the $Y$ and Royer data identical, but the standard deviations are very similar. Nevertheless, a look back at Fig. 2.1 suggests that there are differences in the shapes of the two distributions. These differences are reflected in the skewness and kurtosis values in Table 2.2. We will consider those values shortly, but first we consider why measures of shape should interest us.

As Fig. 2.1 and the statistics of Table 2.2 indicate, measures of location and spread may fail to fully characterize a distribution, or differences between distributions. It is useful to have summary numbers that reflect aspects of the shape of the distribution. Although, as with measures of location and spread, there are several measures of shape and none are perfect, they do extend our ability to describe the distribution of data.

Improved description is not the only reason for being interested in numerical indices of aspects of shape. Many of the most widely used inferential procedures rest on the assumption that the sampled population of scores can be described by a particular equation that describes a family of bell-shaped, or normal, curves. If the population distribution from which a researcher samples can be adequately described by this equation, there are many useful inferential procedures that require only information about sample means and standard deviations. This assumption of a normally distributed population accounts for the emphasis on the mean and standard deviation, and on the procedures that use them, in statistical texts and research reports. In recent years, however, it has become clear that real data are rarely normally distributed; as we noted, the Royer data and the Beck depression data are not unusual in their departures from normality. In cases in which there are marked departures from normality, the reliance on the mean and standard deviation may be inappropriate. For example, although the mean and median of a symmetric population distribution are identical, the sample mean is usually considered the better estimate of the location of the population distribution. However, if the population distribution has long straggling tails, the sample median, or a trimmed mean, is more likely to have a value close to that of the center of the population distribution (Rosenberger & Gasko, 1983), and therefore it would be a better estimate of the location of the population.

The preceding discussion points to two reasons for calculating measures of shape: we may wish to describe the data we have collected more precisely, or to assess the validity of the assumption of normality underlying inferential procedures under consideration. There is a third reason for our interest in measures of shape. An important stage in understanding the processes that underlie behavior is the construction of mathematical or computer models, models precise enough to predict the behavior in question. Comparing predicted and observed measures of the shape of the data distribution provides additional tests of such models.

Two aspects of shape have received the most attention from statisticians: the degree of **skewness**, or departure from symmetry; and **tail weight**, or the proportion of data in the extreme tails of the distribution. Indices of these two attributes of shape can be obtained from various computer packages; those in Table 2.2 were generated by SPSS 10, but most packages will provide the same results. We next consider the skewness and kurtosis values in Table 2.2.

## 2.6.1 Skewness

Skewness statistics are designed to reflect departures from symmetry. The standard definition of skewness, generally denoted by $\sqrt{b_1}$, is the average cubed deviation of scores from the mean divided by the cubed standard deviation: For a sample, the formula is

$$\sqrt{b_1} = \frac{\sum (Y - \overline{Y})^3 / N}{\left[ \sum (Y - \overline{Y})^2 / N \right]^{3/2}} \tag{2.10}$$

Table 2.2 reports G1, a modified version of this formula that provides a better estimate of the population skewness parameter. There are several points to consider. First, both the $Y$ and Royer skewness values are negative, indicating that the distributions are skewed to the left. This reflects the fact that the left tails in Fig. 2.1 are considerably longer than the right tails of their respective distributions. If the distributions had been perfectly symmetric, the skewness values would have been zero. Second, the artificial $Y$ data have a more negative value than the actual Royer data. Recall that the $Y$ data contained two scores that were much lower than any in the Royer data; these increased the absolute value of the skewness statistic. Third, note how much larger the absolute skewness values are than their standard errors, the *SE skewness* values. The standard error of skewness, like the *SE* of the mean encountered earlier, is based on the idea of drawing many random samples of size $N$ from the same population, and then calculating G1 for each sample. The *SE* is an estimate of the standard deviation of those G1 values. A ratio of skewness (ignoring the sign) to its *SE* greater than 2 suggests that asymmetry is present in the population that we sampled from, and did not occur just by chance in the sample.

## 2.6.2 Midsummary Scores Based on Different Tail Cutoffs

A problem with Equation 2.10 (or the closely related G1) is that, like the mean and standard deviation, its value may be distorted by a single outlying point. Several more intuitively appealing alternatives have been suggested (Hill & Dixon, 1982; Elashoff & Elashoff, 1978; Hogg, 1974). These typically involve ratios of distances among points in the left and right tails.

Our own preference involves somewhat more (but simple) calculations and does not provide a single number, but it does yield a comprehensive picture of the distribution that can be easily understood (see Hoaglin, 1983, for a more extensive presentation). The basic idea is to find **midsummary scores**; these are scores midway between values that cut off different fractions of the data in the upper and lower tails of the distribution. For example, one midsummary score might be midway between values cutting off the upper and lower eighths of the distribution; another might be midway between values cutting off the upper and lower fourths. If all of these midsummary scores equal the median, it indicates that the distribution is symmetrical. If they are not all the same, the way they vary provides us with information about how the distribution departs from symmetry.

We begin by recalling the definition of the median, presented earlier. For the Royer and $Y$ data, the depth of the median is

$$d_M = (N + 1)/2 = 29/2 = 14.5$$

Thus, the median is the mean of the 14th and 15th scores when the scores are rank ordered. Also, recall that the depth of the hinges was

$$d_H = \{[d_M] + 1\}/2$$

where the brackets imply dropping any fraction. Therefore, when $N = 28$,

$$d_H = (14 + 1)/2 = 7.5$$

The hinge is sometimes referred to as the "**fourth**," because roughly one fourth of the data will always lie below the lower fourth and one fourth will lie above the upper fourth. For example, if $d_{\text{fourth}}$ is 7.5, the lower fourth value for the Royer data is the mean of the 7th and

**TABLE 2.4**  LETTER VALUES AND MIDSUMMARIES FOR TABLE 2.1 ROYER DATA

| Letter | Letter Depth | Lower Value | Midsummary | Upper Value |
|---|---|---|---|---|
| Median | 14.5 | | 89 | |
| F (4th) | 7.5 | 79 | 86.75 | 94.5 |
| E (8th) | 4 | 69 | 84.5 | 100 |
| D (16th) | 2.5 | 50 | 75 | 100 |

8th scores from the bottom, or 79, and the upper fourth value is the mean of the 21st and 22nd scores (i.e., the 7th and 8th scores from the top), or 94.5. The **midsummary score** is the mean of these upper and lower values; here it is 86.75.

We can define other, more extreme fractions of the distribution in the same way. We can talk about upper and lower eighths or sixteenths, where, for example,

$$d_{eighth} = \frac{[d_{fourth}] + 1}{2} \quad \text{and} \quad d_{sixteenth} = \frac{[d_{eighth}] + 1}{2}$$

The general formula for the depth of the next fraction is

$$\frac{[d_{previous}] + 1}{2}$$

For example,

$$d_{eighth} = (7 + 1)/2 = 4$$

Table 2.4 presents the depths for fourths ($F$), eighths ($E$), and sixteenths ($D$), the upper and lower values, and the midsummaries for the Royer data. Note the use of **letter values** to stand for the various positions in the distribution.

If a distribution is perfectly symmetric, all of its midsummaries should equal the median of the distribution. The midsummaries for the Royer data decline in an orderly fashion as we move further from the median, indicating that the distribution is not symmetric, but is skewed to the left.

### 2.6.3 Kurtosis

Kurtosis values reflect departures from the normal distribution, and they are generally sensitive to the height of the peak and to the tail weight of a distribution. The standard kurtosis statistic, $b_2$, is defined as

$$b_2 = \frac{\sum (Y - \overline{Y})^4/N}{\left[\sqrt{\sum (Y - \overline{Y})^2/N}\right]^4} \tag{2.11}$$

The values reported in Table 2.2 are designated G2 and are modifications of $b_2$ derived to improve the estimate of the population kurtosis value. Turning back once again to Fig. 2.1, note that the $Y$ data have a very pronounced peak in the interval 86–90, as well as several scores in the extreme left tail. These two characteristics contribute to the G2 value for $Y$ that is much higher than that for the Royer data, and much larger than its own *SE*. G2 has a value of zero for the normal distribution ($b_2$ is 3 in that case, and the reported value is often $b_2 - 3$ to provide a simpler comparison with the normal distribution). Distributions with high peaks and heavy tails (relative to the normal distribution) will have positive G2 values, whereas the G2 values will be negative for flatter, shorter-tailed distributions. Heavy-tailed distributions are of particular interest because inferences based on the assumption of normality have often been shown to be affected by this departure from normality. With such data, increasing the sample size or removing extreme scores (trimming) may improve the quality of our inferences. We elaborate on this point in future chapters. For now, we note that high kurtosis values may signal the need for remedial action. However, kurtosis is sensitive to more than just the tails of the distribution, and therefore interpretation is often difficult. Good discussions of kurtosis, together with figures illustrating various shapes and the accompanying effect on $b_2$, are provided in several sources (e.g., Balanda & MacGillivray, 1988; DeCarlo, 1997). These and other articles and chapters (e.g., Hogg, 1974; Rosenberger & Gasko, 1983) also suggest alternative measures of tail weight that are often more resistant to outlying points and that are more readily interpreted.

### 2.6.4 A Graphic Check on Normality

Because so many commonly used statistical procedures are based on the assumption that the data were sampled from a normally distributed population, it is helpful to have several ways of looking at possible violations of this assumption. Skewness and heavy tails in stem-and-leaf and box plots indicate nonnormality. However, a more direct indication is available in various computing packages. Basically, those programs rank order the scores and then plot their expected $z$ scores (assuming normality) against the actual scores. Figure 2.9 presents two such plots. The left panel presents the plot for multiplication response times for students in the fifth through eighth grades; the right panel presents the plot for response speeds that are obtained by taking the reciprocals of the response times. If the data are sampled from a normally distributed population, the data points fall reasonably close to a straight line. This is clearly not the case in the left panel. The points in the right panel, except for the lowest speeds, do fall quite close to the line, indicating that if the population of response speeds is not normal, it is more nearly so than the population of response times. In Chapter 8, we present other evidence that data analyses might better be based on the speed than on the time measure.

Investigators who have precise enough theoretical models to predict distribution functions other than the normal, or who seek to fit the distribution as part of an effort to better

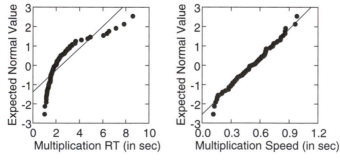

**Fig. 2.9** Normal probability (Q-Q) plots of multiplication response times (MULTRT) and speeds (SPEEDMRT).

understand their data, will find the Q-Q plot options helpful. There are many options other than the normal distribution. For each, the expected value, assuming that distribution, is plotted against the observed values.

## 2.7 CONCLUDING REMARKS

The first step in any data analysis should be an examination of the data. The point seems obvious, but our experience suggests that many, perhaps most, researchers note only means and (sometimes) standard deviations, and, when a measure of relation between two variables is of interest, correlation coefficients. Our view of this first step is that it should provide more information. Researchers should plot their data, perhaps using a variety of graphic devices. Such plots should not only involve means but also provide a sense of the distribution of data. Alternative indices of location, spread, and shape should be obtained. This wealth of information is available at the click of a mouse, and the payoff can be large. Multiple modes in a histogram may suggest subpopulations differing in the effect of the independent variable. Outliers in a box plot may suggest individuals whose performance should be examined further, and perhaps excluded from further analyses. Differences in shape statistics for two different experimental conditions may suggest different processes underlying behavior in these conditions. Marked departures from the theoretical normal distribution may indicate either that more data should be collected or that the researcher should consider alternatives to the planned analysis that are less dependent on the assumption of normality. Knowledge of the shape of the distribution can inform the development of theoretical models. All these, and more, are possible consequences of exploring data sets. The present chapter introduced some basic ways in which such exploration can be carried out. More extensive discussions and other types of graphs may be found in many sources. In particular, we recommend the three volumes edited by Hoaglin, Mosteller, and Tukey (1983, 1985, 1991). They provide a clear presentation of many topics beyond the scope of this book, as well as further discussion and examples of topics we have introduced. Other suggestions of possible ways of plotting data, and references to useful sources, may be found in the report of the American Psychological Association's Task Force on Statistical Inference (Wilkinson, 1999).

## KEY CONCEPTS

| | |
|---|---|
| distribution | central tendency (location) |
| arithmetic mean | median |
| histogram | stem-and-leaf display |
| minimum | maximum |
| 5-point summary | median |
| $d_M$ | hinges |
| range | interquartile range (IQR) |
| percentile | $H$ spread |
| resistant statistics | outliers |
| inner fences | outer fences |
| extreme outliers | box plot |
| weighted mean | standard deviation |

sampling distribution     standard error of the
trimmed means             mean (*SEM*)
line graphs                 bar graphs
skewness                  standardized scores (*z* scores)
midsummary scores        tail weight
kurtosis                  letter values

## EXERCISES

**2.1** We have scores for 16 individuals on a measure of problem-solving ability: $Y = 21$, 40, 34, 34, 16, 37, 21, 38, 32, 11, 34, 38, 26, 27, 33, 47. Without using statistical software, find (a) the mean; (b) the median; (c) $(\sum_i Y_i)^2$; (d) $\sum_i Y_i^2$; (e) the standard deviation; and (f) the upper and lower hinges for these data. Then check your results, using any software of your choice.

**2.2** (a) Transform the scores in Exercise 2.1 to a new scale so that they have a mean of 100 and a standard deviation of 15.

    (b) What will the new values of the median and hinges be?

**2.3** Following are several sets of scores in ranked order. For each data set, is there any indication that it does not come from a normal distribution? Explain, presenting descriptive statistics and graphs to support your conclusion.

    (a) $X = $ 10 16 50 50 50 55 55 55 57 61 61 62 63 72 73 75 83 85 107 114

    (b) $X = $ 15 25 26 37 37 39 45 45 48 49 49 52 53 61 61 63 68 70 72 76

    (c) $X = $ 9 9 10 12 14 14 15 16 16 16 17 18 24 28 31 32 32 35 47 59

**2.4** For Exercise 2.3 (c), find the median, fourths, and eighths (*E* and *F* letter values), and midsummary values. Are these consistent with the conclusion you drew about normality? Explain.

**2.5** Given the five scores 37, 53, 77, 30, and 28,

    (a) what sixth score must be added so that all six scores together have a mean of 47?

    (b) What sixth score should be added so that the set of six scores has the smallest possible variance?

In order to do the following two problems, you may wish to review Appendix A at the back of the book.

**2.6** Given: $Y_1 = 7$, $Y_2 = 11$, $Y_3 = 14$, $Y_4 = 21$, $Y_5 = 9$, $X_1 = 6$, $X_2 = 5$, $X_3 = 7$, $X_4 = 1$, $X_5 = 11$, $a = 3$, and $b = 9$, find (a) $\sum_{i=1}^{4} (X_i + Y_i)$; (b) $\sum_{i=1}^{5} X_i^2$; (c) $(\sum_{i=1}^{5} X_i)^2$; (d) $\sum_{i=1}^{5} X_i Y_i$; and (e) $\sum_{i=1}^{5} (X_i + aY_i^2 + ab)$.

**2.7** We have the following three groups of scores:

| Cond 1 | Cond 2 | Cond 3 |
|--------|--------|--------|
| 7 | 11 | 3 |
| 31 | 15 | 12 |
| 16 | 40 | 15 |
| 21 | 42 | 19 |
| 35 | 45 | 4 |

Given that $Y_{ij}$ is the $i$th score in the $j$th column, find (a) $\overline{Y}_{.1}$; (b) $\overline{Y}_{2.}$; (c) $\overline{Y}_{..}$; (d) $\sum_{i=1}^{5} \sum_{j=1}^{3} Y_{ij}^2$; and (e) $\sum_{j=1}^{3} \overline{Y}_{.j}^2$.

**2.8**    This problem uses the Ex2_8 data set on the CD accompanying this book. Using any statistical package that you like, explore the distributions and their relationships by displaying (a) histograms, (b) box plots, (c) stem-and-leaf plots, (d) descriptive statistics (include the median, as well as measures of skewness and kurtosis), and (e) probability plots. Summarize what you have learned about the distributions of $X$, $Y$, and $Z$. Be sure to refer to such concepts as the location, spread, and shapes of the distributions, in particular whether or not they seem to be normally distributed.

**2.9**    Suppose we standardized $X$, $Y$, and $Z$ (i.e., converted to standard or $z$ scores) in the Ex2_8 data set. How would this affect the characteristics of the distributions?

**2.10**    Find the Royer multiplication accuracy and response time data (Royer Mult Data in the *Royer* folder) on your CD. Using whichever descriptive statistics and graphs you find useful, describe any differences in location, variability, and shape of male and female distributions in the third and fourth grades. In particular, comment on whether gender differences change from third to fourth grade. Also comment on whether the patterns you note are the same or different for accuracy and for reaction time (RT). Finally, consider whether outlying scores may have an influence on any of these comparisons.

**2.11**    The Seasons study was carried out to see if there was variation in the physical or psychological characteristics of the sampled population over seasons.
(a) Using the data in the Seasons file (*Seasons* folder in the CD), plot Beck_A (anxiety) means as a function of seasons for each age group (Agegrp). Use either a bar or line graph. Which do you think is preferable? Why?
(b) Discuss the graph in part (a), noting any effects of age, seasons, or both.
(c) Box or stem-and-leaf plots reveal a skewed distribution with many outliers. Do you think the pattern of outliers contributed to your conclusions in part (b)?

**2.12**    On the CD, in the *Seasons* folder, find the Sayhlth data set. This includes self-ratings from 1 (excellent health) to 4 (fair); only three participants rated themselves in poor health and they were excluded from this file. The file also includes Beck_D (depression) scores for each season. It is reasonable to suspect that individuals who feel less healthy will be more depressed.
(a) Selecting any statistics and graphs you believe may help, evaluate this hypothesis.
(b) Discuss any trends over seasons. Are there differences in trends as a function of self-ratings of health?

**2.13**    Scores for 30 students on two tests may be found in the Ex2_13 file.
One student received a score of 41 on Test 1 and a score of 51 on Test 2. She was delighted with the improvement.
(a) Should she have been? Explain.
(b) What score on Test 2 would be an improvement for this student, given your answer to (a)?
(c) Graph the data for each test and describe the distributions.

## APPENDIX 2.1

### Additional Properties of z Scores

Suppose we have a set of scores $Y_1, Y_2, Y_3, \ldots, Y_N$. The mean of these scores is $\overline{Y} = \sum_i Y_i/N$ and the variance is $s_Y^2 = \sum_i (Y_i - \overline{Y})^2/(N - 1)$. The $z$ score corresponding to the score $Y_i$ is $z_{Y_i} = (Y_i - \overline{Y})/s_Y$, where $s_Y = \sqrt{s_Y^2}$ is the standard deviation of the $Y$ scores.

If we multiply each $Y$ score by the constant $b$ and add the constant $a$ to each of the resulting products, then the transformed scores can be expressed as $Y_i' = a + bY_i$. From the properties of the mean stated in Subsection 2.4.1, we know that adding a constant to each score increases the mean by that constant, and multiplying each score by a constant results in multiplication of the mean by that constant. Therefore, $\overline{Y'} = \overline{a + bY} = a + b\overline{Y}$. From the properties of the standard deviation stated in Subsection 2.4.2, we know that the addition of a constant to each score does not change the standard deviation. Subsection 2.4.2 also demonstrated that if $Y' = kY$, then $s_{Y'} = ks_Y$ when $k > 0$ and $s_{Y'} = -ks_Y$ when $k < 0$. Therefore, $s_{a+bY} = +b\,s_Y$ when $b$ is positive and $s_{a+bY} = -b\,s_Y$ when $b$ is negative.

Putting this all together, we find that the $z$ score of a transformed score $a + bY_i$ is given by

$$
\begin{aligned}
z_{a+bY_i} &= \frac{a + bY_i - \overline{a + bY}}{s_{a+bY}} \\
&= \frac{a + bY_i - (a + b\overline{Y})}{\pm b\,s_Y} \\
&= \pm\frac{b(Y_i - \overline{Y})}{b\,s_Y} \\
&= \pm z_{Y_i}
\end{aligned}
$$

Thus the $z$ score of the transformed score is identical to that of the untransformed score if $b$ is positive, and it is identical in magnitude, but opposite in sign, if $b$ is negative.

# Chapter 3

## Looking at Data: Relations Between Quantitative Variables

### 3.1 INTRODUCTION

In Chapter 2 we considered how to graph and summarize distributions of single variables. However, we rarely study individual variables in isolation; rather, we usually are interested in how variables are related to one another. For example, we may wish to know if depression varies with the season of the year, how cholesterol level changes with age, or whether math skills are related to verbal skills in children. Because variability is always present, it is important to emphasize that, when variables are related, they are usually not perfectly related. Tall fathers tend to have tall sons, but because of a host of factors, the tallest fathers do not always have the tallest sons. There is a relation between educational level and income, but some uneducated people are wealthy and many educated people are not. Variables may be related in ways that vary in type and degree. Therefore, the major goals of this chapter are to discuss how to graph the data in ways that help us see how, and how strongly, the variables are related, and to present statistics that summarize important aspects of the relation.

Also, if two variables are related, it should be possible to use information about one variable to predict the other. For example, knowing a father's height will be useful in predicting the height of his son. If we make lots of predictions, even though any single prediction may not be very accurate, on the average we can predict a son's height more accurately if we use information about the father's height than if we do not. Clearly, the stronger the relation, the better our ability to predict. But no matter how strongly the variables are related, we wish to make the best predictions that are possible with the information that we have available. Equations that use information about one variable to make predictions about a second variable are referred to as **bivariate regression equations**.

### 3.2 SOME EXAMPLES

Let's first consider two variables from the Royer data set that is on the accompanying CD—subtraction and multiplication accuracy scores (percentage of correct answers) for third

**TABLE 3.1**   DESCRIPTIVE STATISTICS FOR THIRD-GRADE
SUBTRACTION AND MULTIPLICATION ACCURACY

|                 | Subtraction | Multiplication |
|-----------------|-------------|----------------|
| No. of cases    | 32          | 28             |
| Median          | 89.182      | 79.447         |
| Mean            | 87.014      | 78.469         |
| *SE*            | 2.081       | 3.426          |
| Std. dev.       | 11.770      | 18.127         |
| Skewness (G1)   | −1.430      | −0.835         |
| *SE* skewness   | 0.414       | 0.441          |
| Kurtosis (G2)   | 3.078       | 0.813          |
| *SE* kurtosis   | 0.809       | 0.858          |

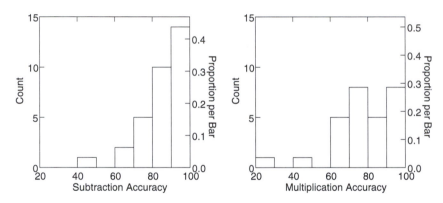

**Fig. 3.1**  Histograms for subtraction and multiplication accuracy for third graders.

graders. The basic statistics for each variable are given in Table 3.1, and their histograms
are presented in Fig. 3.1. For subtraction accuracy, the median and mean are both high,
89.182 and 87.014, respectively. The distribution of scores is negatively skewed, G1 =
−1.430; most scores are high, but there is a "tail" of lower scores. For multiplication,
performance is less good, with both the median and mean approximately 10 points lower
than in the subtraction data. The distribution is again negatively skewed, but less so than for
subtraction (G1 = −0.835). The distribution is flatter; G2 = 0.813 as compared with 3.078
for subtraction. There is less of a pileup of scores toward the high end for multiplication,
and, because the scores are more spread out, measures of variability have larger values. The
standard deviation is 18.127 for multiplication, compared with 11.770 for subtraction. The
multiplication scores not only tend to be smaller than subtraction scores, but also exhibit
greater variability.

### 3.2.1 Scatterplots

But how are subtraction and multiplication accuracy *related* in this sample of third graders?
We might expect that children with larger subtraction scores will also have larger multiplication scores, because we know that some children are better at arithmetic than others. The
most common way of displaying the relation between two variables is to use a **scatterplot**,

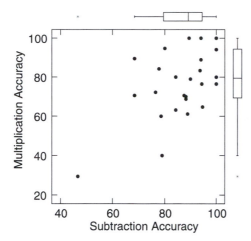

**Fig. 3.2** Scatterplot for subtraction and multiplication accuracy for the 28 third-grade children having both scores; box plots for each variable appear on the borders.

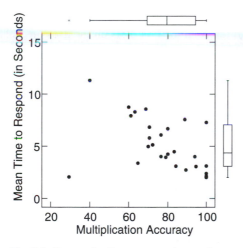

**Fig. 3.3** Scatterplot for response time and multiplication accuracy for third grade.

which is simply a plot in which each point has coordinates corresponding to paired values on each of the variables. The scatterplot for the 28 third graders for whom we have both multiplication accuracy and subtraction accuracy scores is presented in Fig. 3.2. Note that some statistical packages, in this case SYSTAT, allow us to present the univariate distributions such as histograms or box plots along the borders of the scatterplot, so we can see information about both the univariate and joint distributions in the same display.

What we see in the scatterplot is a tendency for larger multiplication scores to go together with larger subtraction scores; when this happens we say there is a **positive relation** or association between the two variables. If larger scores on one variable tend to go together with *smaller* scores on the other, we have a **negative relation**. The scatterplot in Fig. 3.3,

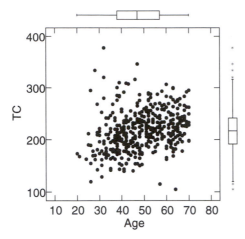

**Fig. 3.4** Scatterplot for TC score and age.

in which mean time to answer multiplication problems is plotted against multiplication accuracy, shows a strong negative relation, reflecting the tendency for children who are more accurate to take less time to answer. A notable exception is the child represented by the data point in the lower left of the display, who took the least time to answer but also had the lowest accuracy. We can also see from the box plots on the axes that this data point is labeled as an outlier with respect to the multiplication accuracy distribution.

We conclude this section with two additional examples of scatterplots to which we refer later in the chapter. To obtain the first, presented in Fig. 3.4, we found the mean of the four seasonal total cholesterol (TC) scores for each of the 431 individuals who had scores in all four seasons in the Seasons study conducted by researchers at the University of Massachusetts Medical School; we then plotted TC against age. Although there is a great deal of variability in the cholesterol scores, there seems to be a positive relation between cholesterol level and age; that is, there is a tendency for older people to have higher cholesterol scores.

The second example uses data obtained from an elementary statistics class. Table 3.2 contains two scores for each of 18 students—the score on a math-skills pretest taken during the first week of class and the score on the final exam. The scatterplot for the 18 data points is presented in Fig. 3.5. Not surprisingly, the pretest and final scores covary. We would like to be able to develop ways to summarize how the two variables are related and to use the pretest scores to predict final exam performance. If we could find the equation that did the best job in predicting the 18 final exam scores from the pretest scores, it could be useful in predicting final exam performance for students who take the pretest in other classes.

## 3.2.2 Extracting the Systematic Relation Between Two Variables

Scatterplots can be very useful in helping us understand how, and to what extent, the variables are related. For example, it is quite clear in Fig. 3.3 that there is a strong tendency for the time taken to perform multiplication to decrease as accuracy improves. However, real data are often extremely messy. Any systematic relation that exists between the variables may be

**TABLE 3.2**   STATISTICS CLASS EXAMPLE DATA

| Pretest Score (X) | Final Exam Score (Y) |
|---|---|
| 29 | 47 |
| 34 | 93 |
| 27 | 49 |
| 34 | 98 |
| 33 | 83 |
| 31 | 59 |
| 32 | 70 |
| 33 | 93 |
| 32 | 79 |
| 35 | 79 |
| 36 | 93 |
| 34 | 90 |
| 35 | 77 |
| 29 | 81 |
| 32 | 79 |
| 34 | 85 |
| 36 | 90 |
| 25 | 66 |

obscured by variability caused by factors such as individual differences and measurement error. In such cases we try to see through the "noise" in order to extract the "signal," that is, the underlying systematic relation, if one exists. This can be difficult to do by eye, especially when there are many data points and a great deal of variability, as in the plot of cholesterol level against age in Fig. 3.4.

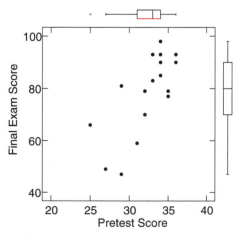

**Fig. 3.5**  Scatterplot for pretest and final exam scores in a statistics class.

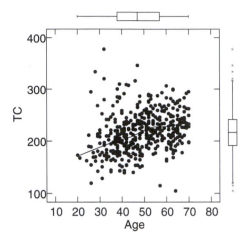

**Fig. 3.6** Scatterplot for TC and age with
LOWESS curve.

One way of trying to get at the underlying relation is to use some type of averaging to reduce the complexity of the display. In Chapter 2 we used the average to represent a univariate distribution of scores. Here we can find the average cholesterol score for each age and plot it against age. Some statistical packages assist us in understanding the relation by fitting curves called **smoothers** to the data points in the scatterplot. We can use these curves to smooth out some of the random variability by plotting a "moving average" of cholesterol scores against age, such that the height of the curve for a particular age represents the mean or the median of the cholesterol scores corresponding to a range of neighboring ages. There are different types of smoothing functions available in both SAS and SYSTAT, some of which have the desirable property of being **resistant** in the sense that they give less weight to outlying data points than to those near the average. We can choose not to put any preconditions on the curve, or we can plot the best-fitting curve of a particular type, such as the best-fitting straight line or logarithmic function.

An example of one kind of smoothing is provided by Fig. 3.6, which displays the scatterplot for cholesterol and age with local weighted scatterplot smoothing (LOWESS; Cleveland, 1979) by using SYSTAT 10. For each value of $X$, LOWESS smoothing plots the $Y$ score predicted by a procedure that gives more weight to data points near the value of $X$ than to data points that are further away (for details, see Cook & Weisberg, 1999). The resulting curve indicates a positive relation between cholesterol and age that approximates a straight line.

In practice, we usually first look to see whether there is a systematic tendency for the variables to have a straight line relation, because this is the simplest and most common way that two variables can be related. We then look further to see whether there are also systematic departures from linearity. The most common numerical measures that are used to summarize the relation between two quantitative variables are those that (a) indicate how well a straight line captures the scatterplot, and (b) describe the straight line that gives the best fit. In Section 3.4 we introduce the first type of measure, the **Pearson correlation coefficient**, which is a measure of the extent to which two variables are linearly related. In Section 3.5 we introduce the idea of **linear regression**, which provides a way to find the straight line equation that fits the data points best, in the sense that it allows the best prediction of one of the variables from the other. We first take a closer look at what it means for two variables to be linearly related.

## 3.3 LINEAR RELATIONS

Each of the scatterplots in Fig. 3.7 contains a number of $(X,Y)$ data points. If all of the data points fall exactly on a straight line, we say there is a perfect **linear relation** between $X$

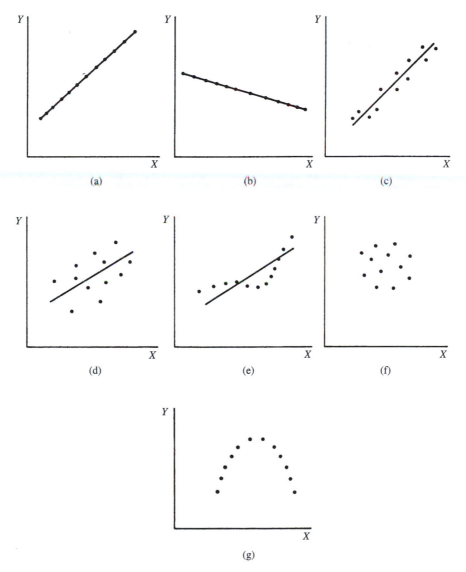

**Fig. 3.7** Examples of scatterplots.

and $Y$. This linear relation is said to be positive if the slope of the line is positive; that is, if $Y$ increases as $X$ increases as in panel (a). The linear relation is negative if $Y$ decreases as $X$ increases as in panel (b). In panel (c), there is a systematic increase in $Y$ as $X$ increases. However, not all the data points fall on the straight line that seems to best capture this systematic increase, although they cluster closely around it. In this case, we say that there is a strong positive linear relation between $X$ and $Y$ but not a perfect one. In panel (d) there is less clustering around the line, indicating a weaker linear relation. In panel (e) there is a linear component to the relation between $X$ and $Y$; that is, the best-fitting straight line seems to capture part of how $Y$ and $X$ are related. However, not only do the points fail to cluster closely around the line, but also there seems to be a systematic nonlinear component to the relation. In panels (f) and (g), there is no overall linear relation between $X$ and $Y$; no straight line passing through the center of either "cloud" of data points is better at characterizing the overall relation between $X$ and $Y$ than a line parallel to the $X$ axis. In (g), however, $X$ and $Y$ are positively related for small values of $X$ but negatively related for large values, whereas in (f) there does not seem to be any indication of a linear relation for any part of the $X$ distribution.

A straight line can be represented by an equation of the form

$$Y = b_0 + b_1 X \tag{3.1}$$

where $b_0$ and $b_1$ are constants, because all points $(X, Y)$ that satisfy this **linear equation** fall on a straight line. The constant $b_1$ is called the **slope** of the line and indicates the rate of change of $Y$ with $X$. We can see in Equation 3.1 that, for every one-unit change in $X$, $Y$ changes by $b_1$ units. The constant $b_0$ is the **$Y$ intercept**, the value of $Y$ when $X$ is equal to zero. We show later that the regression line for Fig. 3.4 that best predicts cholesterol level from age is

$$\text{cholesterol level} = 171.702 + 0.945 \times \text{age}$$

For this line, the slope is 0.945; that is, the predicted cholesterol level increases by 0.945 units for each additional year of age.

## 3.4 THE PEARSON PRODUCT-MOMENT CORRELATION COEFFICIENT

### 3.4.1 Obtaining the Correlation Coefficient

The Pearson correlation is a measure of the extent to which two quantitative variables are linearly related. We indicated in the previous section that the more tightly the data points are clustered about the best-fitting straight line, the stronger the degree of linear relation. The notion of clustering around a straight line leads directly to a useful measure of linear relation. However, in developing this idea further, we consider standardized or $z$ scores instead of raw scores. When raw scores are used, the appearance of the scatterplot and the apparent degree of clustering around the best-fitting straight line depends on the units in which $X$ and $Y$ are measured. This is not true for $z$ scores.

In Section 2.5 we indicated that each member of a set of scores $X_1, X_2, X_3, \ldots, X_N$ can be converted to a $z$ score by using

$$z_{X_i} = \frac{X_i - \overline{X}}{s_X} \tag{3.2}$$

where $\overline{X}$ is the mean of the set of scores and $s_X$ is the standard deviation. The $z$ score that corresponds to a raw score just tells us the number of standard deviations the raw score is above or below the mean of the distribution. In Section 2.5 we showed that the mean of a complete set of $z$ scores is zero, and that the standard deviation and variance both have a value of 1. An equation that will be useful in understanding the correlation coefficient is

$$\frac{1}{N-1} \sum_{i=1}^{N} z_{X_i}^2 = 1 \tag{3.3}$$

This equation follows from the fact that the variance of a set of $z$ scores is 1 and the expression for this variance is

$$\frac{1}{N-1} \sum_{i=1}^{N} (z_{X_i} - \overline{z}_X)^2 = \frac{1}{N-1} \sum_{i=1}^{N} z_{X_i}^2$$

because $\overline{z}_X$, the mean of a set of $z$ scores, is equal to 0.

If $X$ and $Y$ are positively related, larger scores in the $Y$ distribution will tend to be paired with larger scores in the $X$ distribution and smaller scores in the $Y$ distribution will tend to be paired with the smaller $X$s. This means that large positive values of $z_Y$ will tend to be paired with large positive values of $z_X$, small values of $z_Y$ will tend to be paired with small values of $z_X$, and large negative values of $z_Y$ will tend to be paired with large negative values of $z_X$. It can be shown (see Appendix 3.1) that, if there is a perfect positive linear relation between $X$ and $Y$, $z_Y$ is exactly equal to $z_X$, and if there is a perfect negative linear relation, $z_Y$ is exactly equal to $-z_X$. If there is no linear relation between $X$ and $Y$, there is no overall tendency for larger $z_Y$ scores to be paired with either larger or smaller $z_X$ scores, or for positive $z_Y$ scores to be paired with either positive or negative $z_X$ scores.

The Pearson product-moment correlation coefficient for two variables, $X$ and $Y$, is defined as

$$r_{XY} = \frac{1}{N-1} \sum_{i=1}^{N} z_{X_i} z_{Y_i} \tag{3.4}$$

The letter $r$ is used to denote the Pearson correlation coefficient in a sample, and $\rho$ (the Greek letter rho) denotes the correlation in a population. The correlation coefficient is basically the average of the cross products of the corresponding $z$ scores (it would be exactly the average if we divided by $N$ instead of $N-1$ when we obtained the standard deviations of $X$ and $Y$). We can think of $r_{XY}$ as a measure of how similar, on the average, $z_{Y_i}$ is to $z_{X_i}$. If there is a perfect positive relation between $X$ and $Y$, then for each data point $(X,Y)$, $z_Y = z_X$, so that the correlation is

$$r_{XY} = \frac{1}{N-1} \sum_{i=1}^{N} z_{X_i} z_{Y_i} = \frac{1}{N-1} \sum_{i=1}^{N} z_{X_i}^2 = 1$$

from Equation 3.3. If there is a perfect negative relation, $z_Y = -z_X$, so that $r_{XY} = -1$. If there is no linear relation between $Y$ and $X$, there will be no tendency for $z_{Y_i}$ and $z_{X_i}$ to have the same or different signs. Their cross products $z_{X_i} z_{Y_i}$ should be equally likely to be positive (when $z_{X_i}$ and $z_{Y_i}$ have the same sign) or negative (when $z_{X_i}$ and $z_{Y_i}$ have opposite signs). Therefore we would expect the cross products to sum to 0, so that $r_{XY} = 0$.

In summary, $r_{XY}$ provides a numerical measure of the degree to which $X$ and $Y$ are linearly related. It takes on a value of $+1$ when there is a perfect positive linear relation, a value of $-1$ when there is a perfect negative linear relation, and a value of 0 when there is no overall linear relation between $X$ and $Y$. Intermediate values provide measures of the "strength" of the linear relation. Going back to the examples we introduced earlier in the chapter, for multiplication and subtraction accuracy for third graders (Fig. 3.2), $r = .594$; for multiplication accuracy and the time taken to answer (Fig. 3.3), $r = -.487$; for cholesterol level and age (Fig. 3.4), $r = .286$; and for final exam and pretest score (Fig. 3.5), $r = .725$.

### 3.4.2 Interpreting the Correlation Coefficient

Although it is easy to calculate a correlation coefficient, we must be cautious in how we interpret it. Rodgers and Nicewander (1988) discussed 13 different ways to look at the correlation coefficient, and others (e.g., Falk & Well, 1996, 1998; Rovine & Von Eye, 1997) have considered additional interpretations. Although we have a good deal more to say about the correlation coefficient in Chapter 18, here we list some basic things to keep in mind when interpreting a correlation coefficient.

First, how large must a correlation coefficient be in order to indicate that there is a "meaningful" linear relation? Cohen (1977, 1988) discussed guidelines according to which $r$s of .10, .30, and .50 correspond to small, medium, and large effects. Cohen arrived at these values by noting the sizes of correlations encountered in the behavioral sciences and by considering how strong a correlation would have to be before the relation could be perceived by an observer. These values should be considered only as loose guidelines and not as criteria for importance. As we discuss later, in some contexts, even small correlations might be of great practical significance. We should also emphasize that unless the sample is large, the correlation may be quite different in the sample than in the population from which the sample was selected. Later we discuss what the sample allows us to say about the population.

Second, we must always keep in mind the fact that the Pearson correlation coefficient is a measure of strength of the *linear* relation between $X$ and $Y$. The correlation coefficient is not a measure of relation in general, because it provides no information about whether or not there is a systematic nonlinear relation between the two variables. As can be seen in panels (e) and (g) of Fig. 3.7, two variables can have a systematic curvilinear component to their relation in addition to, or instead of, a linear one. Therefore, finding a correlation of 0 does not necessarily mean that the variables are independent. The data points in all four panels of Fig. 3.8 (see Table 3.3) have identical correlations and best-fitting straight lines. However, whereas panel (a) displays a moderate linear relation with no curvilinear component, panel (b) displays a strong curvilinear relation that has a linear component. It cannot be emphasized strongly enough that, to understand how variables are related, one must plot them and not simply rely on statistics such as the correlation coefficient or the slope of the best-fitting straight line.

**TABLE 3.3**   FOUR HYPOTHETICAL DATA SETS

| | Data Set | | | | | |
|---|---|---|---|---|---|---|
| | *a–c* | *a* | *b* | *c* | *d* | *d* |
| | | | Variable | | | |
| Case No. | X | Y | Y | Y | X | Y |
| 1 | 10.0 | 8.04 | 9.14 | 7.46 | 8.0 | 6.58 |
| 2 | 8.0 | 6.95 | 8.14 | 6.77 | 8.0 | 5.76 |
| 3 | 13.0 | 7.58 | 8.74 | 12.74 | 8.0 | 7.71 |
| 4 | 9.0 | 8.81 | 8.77 | 7.11 | 8.0 | 8.84 |
| 5 | 11.0 | 8.33 | 9.26 | 7.81 | 8.0 | 8.47 |
| 6 | 14.0 | 9.96 | 8.10 | 8.84 | 8.0 | 7.04 |
| 7 | 6.0 | 7.24 | 6.13 | 6.08 | 8.0 | 5.25 |
| 8 | 4.0 | 4.26 | 3.10 | 5.39 | 19.0 | 12.50 |
| 9 | 12.0 | 10.84 | 9.13 | 8.15 | 8.0 | 5.56 |
| 10 | 7.0 | 4.82 | 7.26 | 6.42 | 8.0 | 7.91 |
| 11 | 5.0 | 5.68 | 4.74 | 5.73 | 8.0 | 6.89 |

*Note.* From "Graphs in Statistical Analysis," by F. J. Anscambe, 1973, *American Statistician, 27*, pp. 17–21. Copyright 1973 by The American Statistical Association.

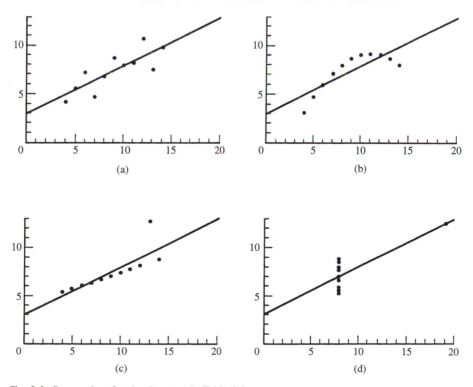

**Fig. 3.8** Scatterplots for the data sets in Table 3.3.

Third, expressions for the correlation coefficient are *symmetric* in $X$ and $Y$. The correlation of $X$ with $Y$ is the same as the correlation of $Y$ with $X$. The correlation between cholesterol level and age is the same as the correlation between age and cholesterol level.

Fourth, although a nonzero correlation coefficient indicates that there is a linear component to the relation between two variables, it generally doesn't *describe* the best-fitting straight line. Figure 3.9 displays several scatterplots that all have the same correlation even though the slopes of the best-fitting straight lines vary considerably. We show later on that the correlation between $X$ and $Y$ depends not only on the slope but also on the standard deviations of $X$ and $Y$.

Fifth, the Pearson correlation coefficient is not a resistant statistic. It can often be changed considerably by the presence of just a few extreme data points. In Fig. 3.10 we used SYSTAT to display the **influence plot** for multiplication and subtraction accuracy for the sample of third graders. The influence plot is just a scatterplot in which each case is plotted as an open or filled circle that can vary in size. The size of the circle indicates how much the correlation would change if that point was omitted, and whether the circle is filled or open indicates whether omitting the data point would make the correlation larger or smaller. The very large open circle in the left of the plot indicates that the corresponding data point has a large effect on the correlation. If we omit this one data point, the correlation drops from .594 to .388. It is important to identify these influential data points because we would have less confidence in the value of a correlation coefficient if it was strongly influenced by a few extreme data points. There are measures of correlation that are more resistant than the Pearson coefficient because they diminish the importance of extreme scores. An example is the **Spearman rho coefficient**, for which the $X$ and $Y$ scores are first ranked, and then the ranks are correlated. We have more to say about such measures in Chapter 18.

Sixth, because the correlation coefficient is defined in terms of $z$ scores, the size of the correlation coefficient does not change if we change the units in which we measure either of the variables by a linear transformation (i.e., if we multiply each score by a constant or add a constant to each score, as when we change units from ounces to kilograms, or from degrees Fahrenheit to degrees Celsius – see Appendix 2.1, in which we showed that such transformations do not change the sizes of the $z$ scores). It follows from this that knowing the correlation between two variables tells us nothing about the mean or variance of either variable.

Seventh, because correlation is a measure of strength of relation, it is tempting to consider the correlation coefficient as a measure of the extent to which changes in $X$ *cause* changes in $Y$. However, correlation does not imply causation—in fact, no statistic implies causation. Just because two variables are correlated does not necessarily mean that they are causally related. For example, the fact that in elementary school there is a positive correlation between shoe size and verbal ability does not mean that foot growth causes enhanced verbal ability or vice versa. Rather, the correlation follows from the fact that both physical and mental growth occur as children get older.

### 3.4.3 Some Other Ways of Expressing the Pearson Correlation Coefficient

The value of the Pearson correlation coefficient can always be obtained from Equation 3.4. However, other expressions are often encountered. If we substitute the expressions for

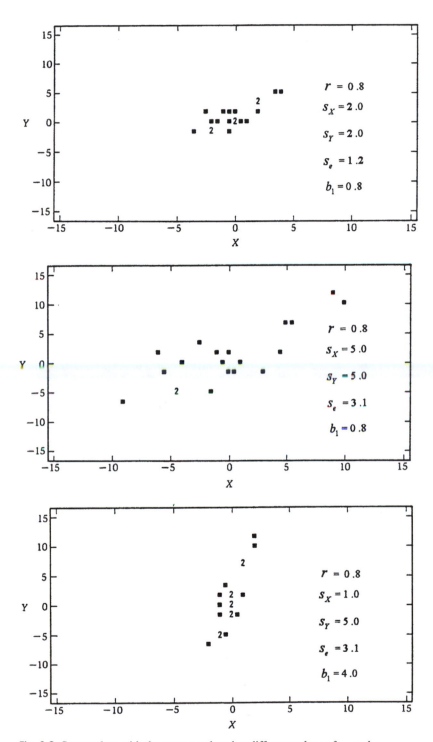

**Fig. 3.9** Scatterplots with the same $r$ values but different values of $s_X$ and $s_Y$.

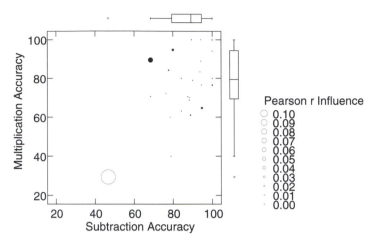

**Fig. 3.10** Influence plot for third-grade multiplication and subtraction accuracy.

$z$ scores (Equation 3.2) into Equation 3.4, we get

$$r_{XY} = \frac{1}{N-1} \sum_{i=1}^{N} \left( \frac{X_i - \overline{X}}{s_X} \right) \left( \frac{Y_i - \overline{Y}}{s_Y} \right)$$

$$= \frac{s_{XY}}{s_X s_Y}$$

where

$$s_{XY} = \frac{1}{N-1} \sum_{i=1}^{N} (X_i - \overline{X})(Y_i - \overline{Y}) = r_{XY} s_X s_Y \tag{3.5}$$

is the sample **covariance** of $X$ and $Y$.

Although the covariance, $s_{XY}$ (i.e., the *amount* of variance shared by $X$ and $Y$), plays an important role in statistics, it is not usually employed as a measure of relation because it changes value when we change the units of measurement. For example, if we measured the heights and weights of a number of people and then found the covariance of height and weight, the covariance would be 12 times larger if we measured height in inches than if we measured it in feet. The correlation coefficient would be the same in either case. The correlation can be thought of as the standardized covariance; that is, the covariance of the $z$ scores.

Another expression that is commonly encountered in elementary textbooks is the so-called **computational formula** for the Pearson correlation coefficient:

$$r_{XY} = \frac{\sum X_i Y_i - \left[ \left( \sum X_i \right) \left( \sum Y_i \right)/N \right]}{\sqrt{\sum X_i^2 - \left[ \left( \sum X_i \right)^2/N \right]} \sqrt{\sum Y_i^2 - \left[ \left( \sum Y_i \right)^2/N \right]}}$$

The computational formula gives the same result as Equation 3.4, within rounding error, but it is less "transparent" than Equation 3.4; that is, the interpretation of the expression is less readily apparent. However, it has the advantage of allowing simpler calculations and less rounding error if it is used to calculate the correlation by hand or with a simple calculator. Although computational ease may have been an important factor in the past when researchers used simple calculators, it is not today, when almost all serious computation is performed by computer, and even inexpensive hand calculators can calculate the correlation at the press of a button. Therefore, we generally do not deal with computational formulas in this book, but instead concentrate on **conceptual (or definitional) formulas** that are expressed in ways that make their meanings most apparent.

## 3.5 LINEAR REGRESSION

### 3.5.1 Predicting Y From X With the Least-Squares Criterion

How do we find the best-fitting straight line for a set of data points $(X, Y)$ represented in a scatterplot? What we usually mean by the "best-fitting straight line" is the line that best predicts the value of $Y$ corresponding to each value of $X$, the **linear regression equation**. The linear regression equation that predicts $Y$ from $X$ has the form

$$\hat{Y}_i = b_0 + b_1 X_i \tag{3.6}$$

where $\hat{Y}_i$ is the predicted value of $Y$ when $X = X_i$, and $b_0$ and $b_1$ are constants chosen in a way that results in the smallest amount of prediction error. Before we can find $b_0$ and $b_1$ we must decide what to use as the measure of error. If, on a given trial, we predict that $Y$ has a value of $\hat{Y}_i$ and it actually has a value of $Y_i$, then the error in prediction is $e_i = Y_i - \hat{Y}_i$. The mean of these errors for a set of $N$ predictions is not a good index of error because positive and negative errors cancel, so the mean error could be small even if there were large positive and negative errors. An index of error that is often used is the mean of the *squared* prediction error. This measure is equal to zero only if prediction is perfect for the entire set of data points and it is also easy to work with mathematically.[1] Regression equations that minimize the mean of the squared errors are said to be optimal or best according to the **least-squares criterion**.

Thus, to find the best linear regression equation according to the least-squares criterion, we must find values of $b_0$ and $b_1$ that minimize the mean of the squared errors, $MSE$, where

$$MSE = \frac{1}{N} \sum (Y_i - \hat{Y}_i)^2 = \frac{1}{N} \sum (Y_i - b_0 - b_1 X_i)^2 \tag{3.7}$$

It can be shown (see Appendix 3.2) that these values are given by

$$b_1 = r \frac{s_Y}{s_X} \tag{3.8}$$

$$b_0 = \overline{Y} - b_1 \overline{X} \tag{3.9}$$

Applying Equations 3.8 and 3.9 to the statistics class data in Table 3.2 allows us to find the linear equation that best predicts final exam performance from pretest score. Substituting into the expressions for $b_1$ and $b_0$, or obtaining the output from a computer package, when we regress $Y$ on $X$ (i.e., when we predict $Y$ from $X$), we find that the regression equation is

$$\hat{Y} = -36.08 + 3.55X$$

A difference of 1 point on the pretest translates into a predicted difference of about 3.6 points on the final exam. Our prediction for the final exam score of a student who scored 30 on the pretest would be $-36.08 + (3.55)(30) = 70.42$, or 70, rounding to the nearest integer.

Note that in the general case for which $s_X \neq s_Y$, the regression equation and the correlation coefficient tell us different things about the linear relation. In Equation 3.6, $X$ and $Y$ play different roles: $X$ is the **predictor variable** and $Y$ is the **criterion variable**, the variable that is predicted. In contrast, the correlation coefficient is symmetric in $X$ and $Y$; both variables are treated in the same way. The regression equation describes the straight line that is best for predicting $Y$ from $X$, whereas the correlation coefficient serves as a measure of the extent to which $Y$ and $X$ are linearly related. If we solve for $r$ in Equation 3.8, we get

$$r = b_1 \frac{s_X}{s_Y} \tag{3.10}$$

From this equation we can see that the same correlation may arise from different combinations of the slope and the standard deviations of $X$ and $Y$. For example, both of the combinations $b_1 = 1$, $s_X = 3$, $s_Y = 5$ and $b_1 = .5$, $s_X = 6$, $s_Y = 5$ will correspond to $r$s of .6. Because of this, we have to be extremely cautious if we wish to compare the relation between $X$ and $Y$ in different groups. Two groups that have the same slope may have different correlations, and two groups that have the same correlation may have different slopes. If we are primarily concerned with the rate of change of $Y$ with $X$, we should compare the slopes, not the correlation coefficients.

We conclude this section by pointing out that there are several additional ways of writing the regression equation that can be useful. Substituting the expression for $b_0$ in Equation 3.9 into Equation 3.6 yields

$$\hat{Y} = \overline{Y} + b_1(X_i - \overline{X}) = \overline{Y} + r\frac{s_Y}{s_X}(X_i - \overline{X}) \tag{3.11}$$

Note that, in Equation 3.11, if $X_i = \overline{X}$, then $\hat{Y} = \overline{Y}$. This tells us that the least-squares regression line always must pass through $(\overline{X}, \overline{Y})$. In addition, if we subtract $\overline{Y}$ from both sides of Equation 3.11 and divide both sides by $s_Y$, we get

$$\frac{\hat{Y}_i - \overline{Y}}{s_Y} = r\frac{X_i - \overline{X}}{s_X}$$

or

$$\hat{z}_Y = rz_X \tag{3.12}$$

the $z$ score form of the regression equation. Note that the regression line that predicts $z_Y$ has slope $r$ and passes through the origin.

### 3.5.2 Predicting X From Y

So far, we have discussed the regression equation for predicting $Y$ from $X$ that is optimal in the sense that it minimizes $\sum(Y - \hat{Y})^2/N$; see panel (a) of Fig. 3.11. Exactly the same reasoning can be used to find the regression equation for predicting $X$ from $Y$. In this case, the index of error that is minimized is $\sum(X_i - \hat{X}_i)^2/N$, the mean of the squared prediction errors when $Y$ is used to predict $X$. These prediction errors are indicated in panel (b) of Fig. 3.11.

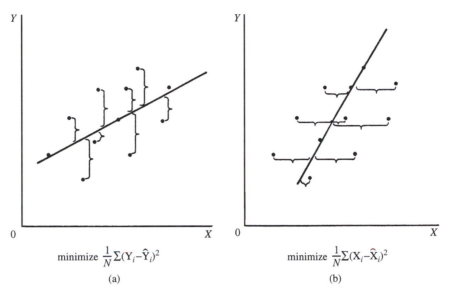

$$\text{minimize } \frac{1}{N}\Sigma(Y_i - \hat{Y}_i)^2 \qquad\qquad \text{minimize } \frac{1}{N}\Sigma(X_i - \hat{X}_i)^2$$

(a) (b)

**Fig. 3.11** Graphical representation of (a) the regression of $Y$ on $X$ and (b) the regression of $X$ on $Y$.

The expressions that have been developed for predicting $Y$ from $X$ can be transformed into expressions for predicting $X$ from $Y$ by simply interchanging $X$ and $Y$. For example,

$$\hat{X}_i = r\frac{s_X}{s_Y}(Y_i - \overline{Y}) + \overline{X}$$

or

$$\hat{z}_{X_i} = r z_{Y_i} \tag{3.13}$$

Of course, whether it makes any sense to predict $X$ from $Y$ depends on the nature of the variables. It is unlikely that we would want to predict pretest scores from final exam scores because pretest scores are available first.

Figure 3.12 indicates how the regression lines that best predict $z_Y$ from $z_X$ and $z_X$ from $z_Y$ differ from one another. Imagine that the elliptical "envelope" that has been drawn in the figure to represent an imperfect linear relation contains a large number of data points. Imagine further that the ellipse is divided into a number of narrow vertical strips. Notice that even though the envelope is symmetrical about a straight line with a slope of 1 drawn through the origin (i.e., $z_Y = z_X$), the mean value of $z_Y$ associated with any given value of $z_X$ is closer to 0 than $z_X$ is. The line that best fits the points representing the mean values of $z_Y$ in the vertical strips will approximate $\hat{z}_Y = r z_X$, the regression equation[2] for predicting $z_Y$ from $z_X$.

In contrast, if we divide the ellipse into a large number of narrow horizontal strips, the line that best fits the mean values of $z_X$ in the strips will approximate the regression equation for predicting $z_X$ from $z_Y$, $\hat{z}_X = r z_Y$. It should be apparent from Fig. 3.12 that these two regression lines are not the same.

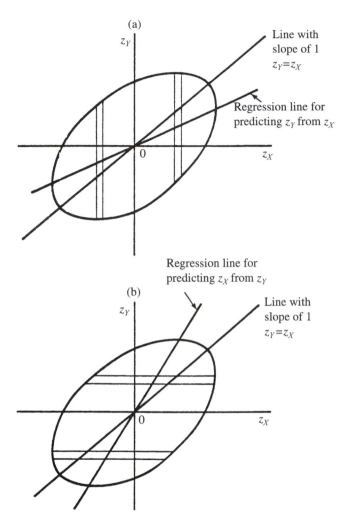

**Fig. 3.12** Regression lines for predicting (a) $z_Y$ from $z_X$ and (b) $z_X$ from $z_Y$ when there is an imperfect relation between $X$ and $Y$.

## 3.6 THE COEFFICIENT OF DETERMINATION, $r^2$

The square of the correlation coefficient, $r^2$, called the **coefficient of determination**, is another commonly encountered measure of strength of linear relation. The $r^2$ measure is usually defined as "the proportion of the variance in $Y$ accounted for by $X$."[3] What this actually means is that $r^2$ is the proportion by which prediction error is reduced if the regression equation is used to predict the $Y$ scores instead of using $\overline{Y}$ to predict each of the $Y$s. The specific interpretation is as follows:

1. If we do not use any information about $X$ in predicting the corresponding value of $Y$, the best prediction for each $Y$ can be shown to be $\overline{Y}$, the mean of the $Y$ scores.

In this case, the sum of the squared prediction errors for the set of $N$ $Y$ scores is the total variability in the $Y$ scores, the **sum of squares of $Y$**, $SS_Y = \sum_i (Y_i - \overline{Y})^2$.

2. If we use the regression equation to predict the $Y$s, the sum of the squared prediction errors is $SS_{error} = \sum (Y_i - \hat{Y}_i)^2$, where the $\hat{Y}_i$s are obtained by using the regression equation. Substituting the expression for $\hat{Y}_i$ from Equation 3.11 and simplifying, we can show the sum of the squared prediction errors to be $SS_{error} = (1 - r^2)SS_Y$.

3. The *amount* by which prediction error is reduced when the regression equation is used is, therefore, $SS_{regression} = SS_Y - SS_{error} = SS_Y - (1 - r^2)\, SS_Y = r^2\, SS_Y$. Therefore, the *proportion* by which prediction error is reduced (or the proportion of the variability in $Y$ accounted for by the regression on $X$) is

$$\frac{SS_{regression}}{SS_Y} = \frac{r^2 SS_Y}{SS_Y} = r^2$$

Therefore, $r^2$ is simply a measure of how well the linear regression equation fits the data. According to the Cohen (1977, 1988) guidelines introduced in Subsection 3.4.2, $r^2$ values of .01, .09, and .25 correspond to small, medium, and large linear relations, respectively.

For the statistics class data, the correlation between the pretest and the final exam score is .725, so the coefficient of determination is $(.725)^2 = .53$. This tells us that the variability of the $Y$ scores about the regression line is $(1 - .53) = .47$ of their variability about their mean. Therefore, if we use the regression equation to predict $Y$ instead of using $\overline{Y}$, we will reduce the squared prediction error by approximately one half. However, measures of the actual variability about the regression line such as the **variance of estimate** (basically, the mean of the squared prediction errors) or its square root, the **standard error of estimate**, provide more useful information than either $r$ or $r^2$ about the accuracy of the predictions of $Y$ based on $X$. Such measures are available in most statistical software and are discussed further in Chapter 19.

We conclude this section by noting that $r^2$ has frequently been misinterpreted, and that some of these misinterpretations have resulted in inappropriate claims being made. For example, the statement has been made in a number of psychology textbooks that children achieve about 50% of their adult intelligence by the age of 4 years. The origin of this statement can be traced to a misinterpretation of the data from a longitudinal study that found IQ scores at age 17 to have a correlation of about .7 with IQ at age 4. The resulting $r^2$ of about .5 (or 50%) provides an indication of how predictable adult IQ is from IQ at age 4, using a linear equation. However, it says nothing about the relative levels of intelligence at age 4 and age 17, and therefore provides no evidence for the statement.

## 3.7 INFLUENTIAL DATA POINTS AND RESISTANT MEASURES OF REGRESSION

Although the least-squares procedures described here are easy to work with, they produce best-fitting straight lines that are sensitive to the effects of extreme scores. All of the major statistics packages provide diagnostics that allow us to identify unduly influential data points and assess how much the regression statistics would change if the extreme data points were not present. We describe these diagnostics in Chapter 19. There are also "robust" regression procedures that provide better fits to the majority of data points than ordinary least-squares procedures because they are resistant to the effects of extreme data points. They are resistant because they somehow reduce the influence of extreme scores by trimming them or giving them less weight, by using ranks, or by using more resistant measures of prediction error such as the median of the squared errors or the mean of the absolute errors. Some of these procedures are discussed by Hoaglin et al. (1985), Neter, Kutner, Nachtscheim, and Wasserman (1996), and Rousseeuw and Leroy (1987).

## 3.8 DESCRIBING NONLINEAR RELATIONS

In the past few sections, we focused on describing the linear component of the relation between two variables, and on measures of its strength. Indeed, correlation coefficients and regression slopes are by far the mostly commonly reported measures of relation for quantitative variables. This is reasonable, given that an approximately linear relation is the simplest and most common way that two variables can be related. However, there will certainly be situations in which it is apparent from the scatterplot and the smoothers that the relation has a nonlinear component. How are we to describe and measure the strength of this component or to describe the overall function that best seems to fit the data? We address this question when we discuss trend analysis in Chapter 10, and again after we extend our knowledge of regression in Chapter 20.

## 3.9 CONCLUDING REMARKS

When we explore how two quantitative variables are related in a sample of data, the first step is to plot the data and look at both the scatterplot and the univariate distributions. Inspecting the scatterplot by eye and using smoothers, we can try to extract, and describe, any underlying systematic relation. We can use the Pearson correlation as a measure of the strength of linear relation and the regression equation as a description of the straight line that allows the best prediction of one variable from the other. We can then try to determine if there are any systematic departures from linearity, and, if so, we can describe them. Later we discuss how to assess the fit of various kinds of functions to the scatterplot.

We must also consider the variability in the distribution of data points. The processes that determine how the variables are related may not be the same for all cases. Separate clusters of points may suggest the presence of subpopulations for which the variables are related differently or have different means (more about this later). Outliers or "extreme" data should be examined closely because they may have a very large influence on statistics such as the correlation or regression slope. Extreme data points may come from subjects who perform in ways that are qualitatively different from the majority of subjects. Extreme data points may also arise because of errors in data collection or copying. If there are a few extreme outliers, we should examine our data records for errors, and we may wish to describe the data both when the extreme scores are included and when they are not. Statistical packages make it easy to identify outliers and to perform these analyses.

As Wilkinson (1999) states in his guidelines for statistical methods in psychology journals:

As soon as you have collected your data, before you compute *any* statistics, *look at your data*. Data screening is not data snooping. It is not an opportunity to discard data or change values to favor your hypotheses. However, if you assess hypotheses without examining your data, you run the risk of publishing nonsense.... Computer malfunctions tend to be catastrophic: A system crashes; a file fails to import; data are lost. Less well-known are the more subtle bugs that can be more catastrophic in the long run. For example, a single value in a file may be corrupted in reading or writing (often the first or last record). This circumstance usually produces a major value error, the kind of singleton that can make large correlations change sign and small correlations become large. (p. 597)

Finally, it should be noted that, in Chapters 2 and 3, we have been concerned with describing *samples* of data. We have yet to address the issue of what we can infer about the populations from which these samples were selected. In Chapter 4, we begin to develop a framework for **statistical inference** that will allow us to do this.

## KEY CONCEPTS

| | |
|---|---|
| scatterplot | positive relation |
| negative relation | smoothers |
| resistant measures | Pearson correlation coefficient |
| linear relation | linear equation |
| slope | $Y$ intercept |
| influence plot | covariance of $X$ and $Y$ |
| conceptual formula | computational formula |
| linear regression equation | least-squares criterion |
| predictor variable | criterion variable |
| coefficient of determination | the sum of squares of $Y$, $SS_Y$ |
| variance of estimate | standard error of estimate |

## EXERCISES

**3.1**  Given the following data,

| X | Y |
|---|---|
| 1 | 11 |
| 2 | 3 |
| 3 | 7 |
| 4 | 9 |
| 5 | 9 |
| 6 | 21 |

(a) Draw a scatterplot.
(b) What is the correlation between $Y$ and $X$?
(c) What is the least-squares equation for the regression of $Y$ on $X$?
(d) What is the proportion of variance in $Y$ accounted for by $X$?
(e) Find the equation for the regression of $X$ on $Y$.
(f) What is the proportion of the variance in $X$ accounted for by $Y$?

**3.2** Given the following data for three variables $X$, $Y$, and $W$,

| W | X | Y |
|----|----|----|
| 12 | 4  | 7  |
| 8  | 6  | 9  |
| 4  | 11 | 3  |
| 17 | 12 | 14 |
| 18 | 13 | 16 |

and, using a statistical package, find the correlations among $W$, $X$, and $Y$. Standardize the variables and recompute the correlations. They should be identical. Why?

**3.3** (a) Using the Royer data set on the CD, find the correlation between multiplication accuracy (MULTACC) and the time taken to solve multiplication problems (MULTRT) for third graders.

(b) Generate the influence plot for these variables.

(c) What is the correlation coefficient if the single most influential point is removed?

**3.4** (a) A psychologist is interested in predicting $Y$ from $X$ in two distinct situations and finds the following results:

| Sit. 1 | Sit. 2 |
|--------|--------|
| $b_1 = 38.41$ | $b_1 = 0.25$ |
| $s_Y = 512.31$ | $s_Y = 8.44$ |
| $s_X = 2.00$ | $s_X = 23.17$ |

In which situation is the correlation between $X$ and $Y$ higher?

(b) You are given a large number of data points $(X,Y)$ and find that the correlation between $X$ and $Y$ is $r_{XY} = 0.70$. You now add 10 to each of the $X$ scores. What happens to the correlation coefficient (i.e., what is the new correlation between $Y$ and the transformed $X$)?

(c) You have the same situation as in (b)—except instead of adding 10 to each of the $X$ scores, you multiply each of the $Y$ scores by 3. Now what is the value of the correlation coefficient?

(d) Now perform both operations: multiply each $Y$ score by 3 and add 10 to the product. What happens to the correlation coefficient?

**3.5** For parts (a)–(c), indicate whether the use of the correlation coefficient is reasonable. If it is not, indicate why not.

(a) A social critic has long held the view that providing enriched programs for disadvantaged students is a waste of money. As evidence to support this position, the critic describes the following study:

Two thousand 8-year-old children were selected from economically deprived homes, given a battery of mental tests, and then randomly assigned to either Group 1 or Group 2. The 1,000 children in Group 1 entered special enriched programs, whereas the 1,000 children in Group 2 continued in their regular classes. After 3 years, another battery of mental tests was given to all the children. It was found that the correlations between children's IQ scores at age 8 and their IQ scores at age 11 was just about the same in Group 1 as it was in Group 2.

Our critic claims that finding very similar correlations in the enriched and regular groups proves that the enriched classes are ineffective in improving IQ.

(b) The research division of the Old Southern Casket and Tobacco Corporation has just released the results of a study that they argue is inconsistent with the negative health claims made against cigarette smoking. For a large sample of heavy smokers, a substantial positive correlation was found between the total number of cigarettes smoked during a lifetime and length of life, a result they claim leads to the conclusion that cigarette smoking is beneficial to health.

(c) It is found that, for eighth-grade children, there is a fairly strong negative correlation between the amount of television watched and school performance as measured by grades. It is claimed that this finding constitutes proof that watching television interferes with intellectual ability and has a negative effect on the ability to focus attention. Does this argument seem valid?

**3.6** In a large study of income $(Y)$ as a function of years on job $(X)$, the data for 2,000 men and 2,000 women in a certain profession are

|  | Men | | Women | |
| --- | --- | --- | --- | --- |
|  | Income $(Y)$ | Years $(X)$ | Income | Years |
| Mean | 80 | 15 | 76 | 10 |
| $s^2$ | 324 | 100 | 289 | 25 |
| $r_{XY}$ | | .333 | | .235 |

Note that income is recorded in thousands of dollars.

(a) Find $b_{YX}$ (i.e., $b_{\text{Income, Years}}$, the regression coefficient for the regression of Income on Years of Service) for men and for women. What is your best estimate of the amount by which salary increases per year for males and females? Is this result consistent with differences in the correlations? Explain.

(b) Using separate regression equations for men and women, what salary would you predict for men and women with 10 years of experience? With 20 years of experience?

**3.7** Using the Seasons data file on the CD, correlate height with weight, and then correlate height with weight separately for men and women. How might you account for the discrepencies among the three correlations?

**3.8** $SS_{\text{error}} = \sum (Y_i - \hat{Y}_i)^2$ is the sum of the squared errors in prediction for a set of $N$ data points. Starting with Equations 3.10 and 3.11, show that $SS_{\text{error}} = (1 - r^2)SS_Y = SS_Y - b_1^2 SS_X$, where $r$ is the correlation of $X$ and $Y$, $b_1$ is the slope of the regression of $Y$ on $X$, $SS_Y = \sum (Y_i - \overline{Y})^2$, and $SS_X = \sum (X_i - \overline{X})^2$.

**3.9** Given that $r_{XY} = .60$, and starting with Equations 3.10 and 3.11, find the correlations between (a) $Y$ and $\hat{Y}$, (b) $Y$ and $Y - \hat{Y}$, and (c) $\hat{Y}$ and $Y - \hat{Y}$.

---

## APPENDIX 3.1

---

### Proof that $z_Y = \pm z_X$ when $Y = b_0 + b_1 X$

We want to show that if $X$ and $Y$ have a perfect linear relation, $z_Y = z_X$ when the relation is positive and $z_Y = -z_X$ when the relation is negative.

For any data point $(X, Y)$ that falls on a straight line, we have $Y = b_0 + b_1 X$. Substituting into the usual expressions for the mean and standard deviation and simplifying, we have $\overline{Y} = b_0 + b_1\overline{X}$ and $s_Y = \pm b_1 s_X$, with $s_Y = +b_1 s_X$ when $b_1$ is positive and $s_Y = -b_1 s_X$ when $b_1$ is negative (see Appendix 2.1). Therefore, if there is a perfect linear relation between $X$ and $Y$,

$$
\begin{aligned}
z_Y &= \frac{Y - \overline{Y}}{s_Y} \\
&= \frac{b_0 + b_1 X - (b_0 + b_1\overline{X})}{\pm b_1 s_X} \\
&= \frac{X - \overline{X}}{\pm s_X} \\
&= \pm z_X
\end{aligned}
$$

---

## APPENDIX 3.2

---

### Where Do the Expressions for $b_0$ and $b_1$ Come From?

Here we sketch out the procedures that produce Equations 3.8 and 3.9, although knowing the details is not necessary for understanding any of the rest of the chapter. Finding expressions for $b_0$ and $b_1$, the $Y$ intercept and slope of the regression line, is just a minimization problem in calculus—we want to find the equation of the straight line that minimizes prediction error. We first take partial derivatives of the error measure (the mean of the squared prediction errors, $MSE$) with respect to both $b_0$ and $b_1$; that is, we find

$$
\frac{\partial MSE}{\partial b_0} \quad \text{and} \quad \frac{\partial MSE}{\partial b_1}
$$

Setting these partial derivatives equal to zero and simplifying, we obtain a set of what are called **normal equations**:

$$
b_0 N + b_1 \sum X_i - \sum Y_i = 0
$$
$$
b_0 \sum X_i + b_1 \sum X_i^2 - \sum X_i Y_i = 0
$$

Solving the normal equations for $b_1$ and $b_0$ yields Equations 3.8 and 3.9. Note that $b_1$ can be expressed in any of a number of equivalent ways, including

$$
\frac{s_{XY}}{s_X^2}, \quad \frac{\sum X_i Y_i - (\sum X_i)(\sum Y_i)/N}{\sum X_i^2 - (\sum X_i)^2/N}, \quad r\frac{\sqrt{SS_Y}}{\sqrt{SS_X}}, \quad r\frac{s_Y}{s_X},
$$

where $s_{XY}$ is the covariance of $X$ and $Y$, $SS_Y = \sum_{i=1}^{N}(Y_i - \overline{Y})^2$, $SS_X = \sum_{i=1}^{N}(X_i - \overline{X})^2$, and $s_Y$ and $s_X$ are the standard deviations of $Y$ and $X$, respectively.

# Chapter 4

## Probability and the Binomial Distribution

## 4.1 INTRODUCTION

In a study of long-term memory for childhood events, N. A. Myers and Chen (1996) tested 20 teenagers who had previously participated in an experiment at the University of Massachusetts as 3- to 5-year-old children 12 years earlier. In the earlier experiment, the children had been exposed to a number of objects. The teenagers were presented with four objects, only one of which they had seen as children. They were asked to decide which of the four objects they had seen 12 years earlier.[1] At one level, the question is whether the teenagers remember the earlier event. But just what does this mean? We need to frame this question more precisely if we are to use the data to answer it. A more precise statement of the question requires us to place the experiment in a clear conceptual framework, one which we introduced in Chapter 1.

We begin by noting that the 20 teenagers may be viewed as a sample from a population of participants of similar age and experience. Accordingly, the responses in the experiment are viewed as a sample of responses in the population. The researchers are interested in whether the responses of the 20 participants provide evidence of memory in the population. We restate this question as, Is the proportion of correct responses in the population greater than we would expect by chance? We are closer to the goal of stating the question precisely enough that we may use the data to answer it, but now we need a definition of "chance."

We can think of chance performance as that which would occur if none of the teenagers retained any memory of the objects they were exposed to 12 years earlier. When they were required to choose one of the objects, we assume they would simply "guess" in such a way that each of the four objects would be equally likely to be chosen. Therefore, assuming chance performance, the probability of a correct choice is 1/4, or .25. If the experiment was performed many times, each time employing a new random sample of 20 teenagers from a population that had experienced the correct object in childhood, we would expect that, "on the average," 5 of the 20 would choose correctly. Note that this assumption of chance responding does not mean that in any one replication of the experiment there will be exactly five correct responses, but that the average number of correct responses will be five if the experiment were carried out many times.

However, the experiment is performed only once. Given that the probability of a correct choice is .25, finding exactly 5 correct responses would be consistent with the assumption of chance responding. But suppose 6 of the 20 teenagers responded correctly. Would this demonstrate that the probability of a correct response in the population was greater than .25? Not necessarily. It is at best weak evidence in favor of memory because 6 correct responses out of 20 could easily occur if the probability of a correct choice was .25. Suppose, however, that 18 of the 20 choices were correct. This would seem to be strong evidence that more than chance is involved, because it seems very unlikely that this result could occur if the probability of a correct choice was .25. How much evidence does it take to convince us that the probability of a correct response is greater than .25—8 correct? 10 correct? In order to make a reasonable decision about whether or not there is evidence of long-term memory for the childhood experience, we need two things:

1.  We need to know the **probability distribution**, assuming only chance responding. If the members of the population had no memory for the childhood event, and if the experiment was performed many times, each time employing a new random sample of teenagers from a population that had experienced the correct object in childhood, what proportion of such experiments would yield 11 correct? Or 12 correct? Or any other number of correct responses from 0 to 20?

2.  We need a **decision rule** for deciding whether the observed number of correct responses is so much greater than 5, the number expected by chance, that we are willing to reject the hypothesis that only chance factors (and not memory) are involved.

In summary, our inferences are fallible because performances vary as a function of many factors beyond the researcher's control. Statistics such as the proportion of correct responses in a sample, or the sample mean and variance, will rarely, if ever, exactly match the population parameters they estimate. However, despite this uncertainty, inferences about population parameters can be made. The data from the sample, together with certain assumptions about the population of scores, provide a basis for such inferences. Understanding the process by which inferences are drawn requires understanding random variables, their distributions, and probability. In the next part of this chapter, we present these topics. Given that conceptual foundation, we can then return to the question of whether the participants in the Chen and Myers experiment exhibited better than chance memory. To develop a statistical test to address this question, we will make use of a particular probability distribution, the binomial. Although the applicability of the statistical test we present is somewhat limited, it should be easy to understand. Furthermore, the issues raised, and the concepts defined, are basic to inferential processes in general.

## 4.2 DISCRETE RANDOM VARIABLES

Continuing with our example of the memory experiment, we state that the number of participants (out of 20) who correctly choose the object seen in the earlier experiment might be symbolized by $Y$. $Y$ is referred to as a **random variable**; in this example, the variable $Y$ can take on any of the 21 integer values in the range from 0 to 20. $Y$ is a **discrete** random variable because there are values within the range of $Y$ that cannot occur. Although only whole numbers can be observed in the preceding example, the potential values of a variable need not be integer or even equally spaced for the variable to be discrete. We might discuss the results of the experiment in terms of the proportion of participants who were correct, in which case the random variable would take on the fractional values 0, 1/20, 2/20, . . . , 20/20.

Variables that can take on *any* value within their range are called **continuous** random variables. Consider the time it takes a participant to make a response in some experimental task. Typically, in this era of high-speed microcomputers, response time can be measured to the nearest millisecond. Although we may not be able to observe response times more accurately, response time is a continuous random variable. The clock may not be capable of recording it, but any time can occur; the limitation is in the measuring instrument and not in the variable itself. Considerably more will be said about continuous random variables in Chapter 5 and, in fact, throughout this book. In this chapter, the focus is on discrete random variables simply because the ideas we wish to develop about inference are more easily understood in this context.

## 4.3 PROBABILITY DISTRIBUTIONS

As we indicated in Section 4.1, we are frequently interested in whether scores that are actually observed, or statistics based on these scores, differ very much from what would be expected by chance. In this section, we begin to clarify what we mean by the expression "expected by chance." Consider the participants in a memory experiment similar to the one just described, but, to simplify things at this stage, assume that each participant is presented with only two objects, one of which is the correct (i.e., previously presented) one. In this simplified memory experiment, if a participant were to make a response by guessing, the probability of being correct on any problem would be .5. For now we also restrict our discussion to only 4 participants in this memory experiment. An appropriate random variable reflecting the performance of this group of participants would be $Y$, the number of participants responding correctly. Given that each response must either be correct ($C$) or in error ($E$), and assuming 4 participants, there are only $2^4$ (or 16) possible patterns of correct and error responses; each of these is associated with a value of $Y$. These patterns are presented in Table 4.1, together with the corresponding values of $Y$.

If the participants are guessing, any of the possible values of $Y$ may occur, although some values are more likely to occur than others. The set of probabilities corresponding to each possible value of $Y$ is called the **probability distribution** of $Y$. The column labeled $p(y)$ in Table 4.1 contains the probabilities associated with guessing, assuming that there are only two choices. These probabilities are also plotted in Fig. 4.1.

Where do these probabilities come from? How can they be used in answering questions that may be of interest to us? We will consider each of these issues in turn.

The probability distribution is derived by beginning with a **statistical model**, a set of assumptions about how responses are generated that is explicit enough for probabilities to be calculated. Different sets of assumptions will lead to different values of $p(y)$. In the current situation, a desirable model would be one that allows the calculation of probabilities

**TABLE 4.1**    POSSIBLE PATTERNS OF $C$ AND $E$ RESPONSES
FOR 4 PARTICIPANTS

| Pattern | No. Correct $(y)$ | $p(y)$ |
|---|---|---|
| $\langle E_1 E_2 E_3 E_4 \rangle$ | 0 | $1/16 = .0625$ |
| $\langle E_1 E_2 E_3 C_4 \rangle$ | 1 | |
| $\langle E_1 E_2 C_3 E_4 \rangle$ | 1 | |
| $\langle E_1 C_2 E_3 E_4 \rangle$ | 1 | $4/16 = .25$ |
| $\langle C_1 E_2 E_3 E_4 \rangle$ | 1 | |
| $\langle E_1 E_2 C_3 C_4 \rangle$ | 2 | |
| $\langle E_1 C_2 E_3 C_4 \rangle$ | 2 | |
| $\langle E_1 C_2 C_3 E_4 \rangle$ | 2 | |
| $\langle C_1 E_2 E_3 C_4 \rangle$ | 2 | $6/16 = .375$ |
| $\langle C_1 E_2 C_3 E_4 \rangle$ | 2 | |
| $\langle C_1 C_2 E_3 E_4 \rangle$ | 2 | |
| $\langle C_1 C_2 C_3 E_4 \rangle$ | 3 | |
| $\langle C_1 C_2 E_3 C_4 \rangle$ | 3 | |
| $\langle C_1 E_2 C_3 C_4 \rangle$ | 3 | $4/16 = .25$ |
| $\langle E_1 C_2 C_3 C_4 \rangle$ | 3 | |
| $\langle C_1 C_2 C_3 C_4 \rangle$ | 4 | $1/16 = .0625$ |
| | | $\sum p(y) = 1$ |

*Note.* The subscripts denote the 4 different individuals.

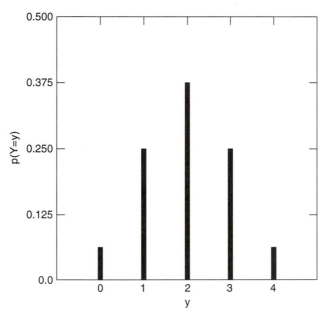

**Fig. 4.1**  Theoretical distribution of the number of correct
responses when $p(C) = .5$.

to be relatively simple, yet captures the essential features of what we mean by guessing. We employ the following model:

1. On each trial (in the example, for each participant) the probability of a correct response is .5.
2. The responses are **independent** of one another; that is, the probability of a correct response on any trial does not depend on the outcomes of any other trials. In our example, the probability that any one participant makes a particular choice does not depend on the choice of any other participant.

The first assumption seems reasonable given that each participant has only two possible responses. It is equivalent to assuming that participants perform as though they are randomly selecting responses from a box containing two slips of paper, one marked with the word "correct" and the other with "error." Each participant shakes the box vigorously and one of the slips of paper is selected. The second assumption requires that after selecting a slip of paper, the participant replaces it so that the next participant is not influenced by the preceding participant's response.

Given these assumptions, it makes sense that all 16 patterns in Table 4.1 are equally likely to occur. Therefore, the probability of 0 correct responses is 1/16 or .0625; we usually write $p(Y = 0) = .0625$. Similarly, because we know there are four equally likely sequences with one correct response, we know that $p(Y = 1) = 4/16$ or .25. We have just assigned numbers called probabilities to the events $Y = 0$ and $Y = 1$. In general, we calculate $p(Y = y)$, where $Y$ is the random variable and $y$ is a specific value that $Y$ can take. As we noted earlier, these values, which we collectively refer to as $p(y)$, are presented in Table 4.1 and are also graphed in Fig. 4.1, in which the height of each bar indicates the probability of the corresponding value of $Y$.

It should be emphasized that different assumptions lead to different probability distributions. If, as in the Chen and Myers memory experiment, there were four alternatives rather than two, assumption 1 would have to be modified to state that the probability of a correct response on each problem was .25 (as though there were now four slips of paper in the box, one marked "correct" and three marked "error"). All the response patterns and the corresponding values of $Y$ listed in Table 4.1 would still be possible, although the probabilities associated with them would change. As you might guess, the probability of getting three or four problems correct would now be much less than indicated in Table 4.1. If the participants were not guessing and we could assume that the probability of a correct response was, for example, .8, still another probability distribution would be indicated. Later in the chapter, we develop a general formula for calculating values of $p(Y = y)$.

Keep in mind why we generated the probability distribution of Table 4.1: to answer questions about whether or not the participants were guessing, we had to get some idea of what kind of data to expect if they were, in fact, guessing. The probability distribution we generated is called a **theoretical probability distribution** because it was generated on the basis of a statistical model. In this case, our statistical model was a theory we had about how people would respond if they were guessing. If the assumptions we made were valid, and if we performed many random replications of the memory experiment (assuming four participants and two choices), in 1/16 of the experiments no one would be correct; in 1/4 of the experiments one participant would be correct; and so on. In short, the proportions of experiments yielding various values of $Y$ would match the theoretical values in Table 4.1. We can see this, and get a better sense of what we mean by "many random replications

**TABLE 4.2** PROPORTION OF SIMULATED EXPERIMENTS IN WHICH THERE WERE Y CORRECT RESPONSES

| No. Correct (y) | No. of Experiments | | | | Theoretical Prob. |
|---|---|---|---|---|---|
| | 10 | 100 | 1,000 | 10,000 | |
| 0 | .1 | .09 | .058 | .0603 | .0625 |
| 1 | .2 | .25 | .256 | .2493 | .2500 |
| 2 | .4 | .34 | .389 | .3772 | .3750 |
| 3 | .3 | .28 | .237 | .2552 | .2500 |
| 4 | 0 | .04 | .060 | .0580 | .0625 |

*Note.* $p(c) = .5$ and $n = 4$.

of the experiment," by considering the results of computer simulations of the experiments. We simulated participants performing according to our model in either 10, 100, or 10,000 "experiments," each of which had four participants for whom the probability of a correct response was .5. We then recorded a value of $Y$ for each simulated experiment; recall that $Y$ is the number of correct responders out of four participants. The observed probability distributions of $Y$ are presented in Table 4.2, together with the theoretical values of $p(y)$. The numbers in each column are the proportions of experiments in which there were $y$ correct responses; note that each column sums to 1.0. When there are only 10 simulated experiments, the probabilities clearly differ from those for the theoretical distribution, though the distribution shapes have some similarity. The observed proportions more closely approach the theoretical probabilities as the sample size increases. Thus, the theoretical probabilities may be viewed as the proportions of an infinitely large set of experiments having a particular value of $Y$, assuming the statistical model is correct.

The idea of repeating an experiment many times and obtaining the value of some statistic (here $Y$, the number of correct responses in the example) from each experiment is basic to the inferential procedures described throughout this book and used by most researchers. The idea is important enough for us to summarize the general steps:

1. A statistical model is formulated.
2. On the basis of this model, a theoretical distribution of a statistic of the experiment is derived; this distribution is called a **sampling distribution**. This is the distribution we would obtain if our model is correct and we were to repeat the experiment many times, plotting the distribution of the statistic ($Y$ in the example) over the many replications of the experiment.
3. The sampling distribution is then employed, together with the data from our experiment, to draw inferences about the population.

We have our statistical model and a theoretical sampling distribution (Table 4.1) for four trials (participants) and $p = .5$. Now we can use this theory together with observed data to investigate whether people in the memory experiment are simply guessing. To accomplish this, we have to be clearer about the question. We can formulate it this way: Is the probability of a correct response in the sampled population .5 or does our experimental evidence indicate it is higher than .5? One possible decision rule is to conclude that performance is better than chance if 3 or 4 responders—more than 50% of the sample of responders—are correct.

However, the values in Table 4.1 suggest that 3 or 4 correct is not strong evidence that performance is better than we would expect by chance. As we can see from that table, assuming our model of chance guessing, the chance a sample would have 3 or 4 correct responses is .3125 (that is, .25 + .0625). In other words, even if participants were guessing, there is almost one chance in three of getting at least 3 correct responses. Stronger evidence of memory would be provided if we require all 4 participants to be correct. According to our model, if people are guessing, only 1/16 of similar experiments (.0625) would yield 4 correct responses. Therefore, if all 4 participants are correct, either they are guessing and a relatively unlikely event has occurred, or performance in the population is better than chance.

We can now outline the rationale underlying statistical testing. If in the context of a particular experiment we wish to examine the hypothesis that only chance is involved, a model of chance performance is used to generate a probability distribution. There are certain outcomes, consistent with an alternative hypothesis (e.g., that the probability of a correct response is above the chance level), that will be very unlikely if the model is valid. If one of this set of outcomes is obtained in the experiment, we will conclude that the model is not valid and that something other than chance is involved. Although these basic ideas are involved in a variety of statistical tests, the advantage of first developing ideas about inference by using a discrete random variable is that the relevant probabilities are easier to understand and calculate. Although we will not have to deal with very complicated aspects of probability, a thorough understanding of a few basic concepts will be required. The next section provides an introduction to some of these concepts. Following that, we present a class of probability distributions of which the one in Fig. 4.1 is a member. These are then used to demonstrate further how inferences can be drawn from data.

## 4.4 SOME ELEMENTARY PROBABILITY

Suppose we have a class of 100 students, of whom 60 are men and 40 are women. The instructor, a kindly statistician, gives no grades lower than C. The number of male and female students receiving each grade is presented in Table 4.3. Suppose further that the sex of each student, along with his or her grade, is written on a separate slip of paper. The 100 slips are placed in a box. If a slip of paper is randomly selected from the box, we can determine the probability that the slip drawn belongs to a particular sex and has a particular grade written on it. We can use this very simple "probability experiment" to introduce some basic ideas about probability.

**TABLE 4.3**  DISTRIBUTION OF GRADES FOR MEN AND WOMEN

| Sex | Grade | | | Total |
| --- | --- | --- | --- | --- |
|  | A | B | C |  |
| Female | 12 | 24 | 4 | 40 |
| Male | 15 | 36 | 9 | 60 |
| Total | 27 | 60 | 13 | 100 |

First, by **random selection**, we mean selecting a slip of paper in such a way that each slip is equally likely to be chosen. We might achieve this by vigorously shaking the box before selecting the slip. There are 100 slips of paper and one of them will be selected. There are only 100 possible outcomes, each corresponding to a value of sex and grade. The possible outcomes of a probability experiment are called **elementary events**, and the complete set of elementary events is called the **sample space** for the experiment. Here, if we assume random selection, each of the 100 elementary events has an equal probability of occurring.

We are frequently not so much interested in the probability of a particular elementary event as we are in the probability of meaningful collections of elementary events, which are usually called **event classes** or simply **events**. We might be interested in the probability of the event "getting a grade of A," which we can denote by $p(A)$. When the probabilities of elementary events are equal, the probability of an event is easily computed. In this case,

$$p(A) = \frac{n(A)}{n(S)} \tag{4.1}$$

where $n(A)$ is the number of elementary events in $A$ and $n(S)$ is the number of elementary events in the entire sample space. For our probability experiment,

$$p(A) = \frac{27}{100}$$

because there are only 100 elementary events and 27 of them belong to the event $A$. It should be clear that $p(A)$ cannot take on any values greater than one or less than zero. Similarly, if the event of interest is $M$, "being male," $p(M) = 60/100 = .60$. Because events like $A$ and $M$ contain all the elementary events in a row or a column of the table, their probabilities are often referred to as **marginal probabilities**.

## 4.4.1 Joint Probabilities

The probability of obtaining a particular *combination* of events is referred to as a **joint probability**. For example, $p(A$ and $M)$, which is read as "the probability of A and M," is the probability of the joint event $\langle A, M \rangle$; that is, it is the probability of selecting a slip of paper with both "A" and "male" written on it. If the probabilities of the elementary events are equal, $p(A$ and $M)$ can be obtained by using

$$p(A \text{ and } M) = \frac{n(A \text{ and } M)}{n(S)} \tag{4.2}$$

where $n(A$ and $M)$ is the number of elementary events that belong to both events $A$ and $M$. For the data of Table 4.3, $p(A$ and $M) = .15$, because 15 of the 100 slips of paper correspond to grades of A obtained by male students. Similarly, if the events $B$ and $F$ correspond to "getting a grade of B" and "being female," respectively, $p(B$ and $F) = 24/100 = .24$. Note that $p(A)$ must always be at least as large as $p(A$ and $M)$ because event $A$ will always contain at least as many elementary events as joint event $\langle A, M \rangle$. These ideas may be clarified by reconsidering Table 4.3. Each column represents the event of a letter grade and has two nonoverlapping parts. For example, the column representing event $A$ consists of joint events $\langle A, M \rangle$ and $\langle A, F \rangle$. Note that $n(A) = n(A$ and $M) + n(A$ and $F)$, and it follows from Equations 4.1 and 4.2 that $p(A) = p(A$ and $M) + p(A$ and $F)$. An additional fact to note is that, because of the way in which it is defined, $p(A$ and $M) = p(M$ and $A)$.

## 4.4.2 Probabilities of Unions of Events

The **union** of two elementary events consists of all the elementary events belonging to either of them. The elementary events forming the union of events $A$ and $M$ are the following cells of Table 4.3: $\langle A, F \rangle$, $\langle A, M \rangle$, $\langle B, M \rangle$, and $\langle C, M \rangle$. The expression $p(A \cup M)$, or $p(A$ or $M)$ refers to the probability of obtaining an elementary event belonging to either $A$ or $M$, that is, falling into any of the four cells just noted. Therefore,

$$p(A \text{ or } M) = \frac{n(A \text{ or } M)}{n(S)} \tag{4.3}$$

$$= \frac{12 + 15 + 36 + 9}{100} = .72$$

because 72 of the 100 elementary events belong either to $A$ or to $M$. Note that $n(A$ or $M)$ does not equal the sum of $n(A)$ and $n(M)$. As should be clear from Table 4.3, this sum counts twice the 15 elementary events that belong to both $A$ and $M$. Verify for yourself that $p(A$ or $M) = p(A) + p(M) - p(A$ and $M)$. Also verify that $p(A$ or $F) = 55/100 = .55$. In general, if $E_1$ and $E_2$ are two events of interest,

$$p(E_1 \text{ or } E_2) = p(E_1) + p(E_2) - p(E_1 \text{ and } E_2) \tag{4.4}$$

## 4.4.3 Conditional Probabilities

We may be interested in the probability of obtaining a grade of A when only the male students in the class are considered. This probability is called a **conditional probability** because it is the probability of $A$ given the condition that $M$ occurs. It is denoted by $p(A|M)$, and it is read as "the probability of $A$ given $M$." There are 60 slips of paper labeled "male" and 15 of them correspond to grades of A. Therefore, $p(A|M) = 15/60 = .25$. More generally, $p(A|M)$ is the proportion of all elementary events in $M$ that also belong to $A$, or

$$p(A|M) = \frac{n(A \text{ and } M)}{n(M)} = \frac{p(A \text{ and } M)}{p(M)} \tag{4.5}$$

Verify that, for the current example, $p(B|M) = 36/60 = .60$; $p(M|A) = 15/27 = .56$; and $p(A|B) = 0/60 = 0$.

Two important ideas about conditional probabilities should be noted. First, people have a tendency to confuse conditional probabilities with joint probabilities. Look carefully at Equations 4.2 and 4.5. The conditional probability $p(A|M)$ is the probability of selecting a slip of paper that is labeled "A" if a selection is made from only the 60 slips labeled "male." The joint probability $p(A$ and $M)$ is the probability of selecting a slip labeled both "A" and "male" if selection is randomly made from *all* 100 slips of paper. A conditional probability has to be at least as large as, and generally is larger than, the corresponding joint probability because the set from which we sample is a subset of the entire sample. For example, when we calculate $p(A|M)$, we are dividing by only the number of male students, a number less than the total sample. Bear in mind, however, that although joint and conditional probabilities are not the same, they are related, as Equation 4.5 demonstrates.

The second idea is that for any two events $A$ and $M$, there are two conditional probabilities, $p(A|M)$ and $p(M|A)$. These two conditional probabilities will generally not have the same values; in our current example, $p(A|M) = 15/60 = .25$ and $p(M|A) = 15/27 = .56$. As this example illustrates, the denominators are based on different subsets of the entire sample, and these often will have different numbers of elementary events.

An important extension of the ideas about joint and conditional probability is incorporated into Bayes' Rule, a mathematical formulation that has implications for understanding the relations among conditional and joint probabilities, and that has also provided the foundation for an entirely different approach to statistics, Bayesian analysis. An introduction to Bayes' Rule and an example of its application may be found in Appendix 4.3 at the end of this chapter.

### 4.4.4 Mutually Exclusive, Exhaustive, and Independent Events

Two events $E_1$ and $E_2$ are **mutually exclusive** if they are incompatible; that is, if an elementary event belongs to $E_1$, it cannot belong to $E_2$. It follows that if $E_1$ and $E_2$ are mutually exclusive, $p(E_1 \text{ and } E_2) = 0$, $p(E_1|E_2) = 0$, and $p(E_2|E_1) = 0$. In our current example (Table 4.3), $p(A \text{ and } B) = 0$, because if a student received a grade of A in the course, he or she did not receive a B; $p(A \text{ and } M)$ is not equal to 0 because some of the men in the course did receive As.

A set of events is **exhaustive** if it accounts for all of the elementary events in the sample space. In our example, the events $A$, $B$, and $C$ collectively account for all the students in the class and are also mutually exclusive. Therefore, $p(A \text{ or } B \text{ or } C) = 1.00$ and we can say that $A$, $B$, and $C$ constitute an exhaustive and mutually exclusive set of events.

Two events $E_1$ and $E_2$ are **independent** if $p(E_1|E_2) = p(E_1)$; that is, if the probability of event $E_1$ is the same whether or not event $E_2$ occurs. We may wish to ask questions such as, Is getting a grade of A independent of sex? This is another way of asking whether the probability of getting an A is the same for male and female students. If there is independence, $p(A|M) = p(A|F) = p(A)$. Returning to Table 4.3, we see that $p(A|M) = 15/60 = .25$; $p(A|F) = 12/40 = .30$; and $p(A) = .27$. Clearly, for these data, getting an A is not independent of being a male or female student, so $\langle A, M \rangle$ and $\langle A, F \rangle$ are pairs of events that are not independent. In contrast, $p(B|M) = p(B|F) = p(B)$, so getting a grade of B is independent of the student's sex. For both male and female students, the probability of getting a B is .60.

We may also wish to ask more general questions, such as Are the variables grade and sex independent of each other? For the answer to be yes, each of the six pairs of events formed by combining levels of sex and grade, specifically, $\langle A, M \rangle$, $\langle A, F \rangle$, $\langle B, M \rangle$, $\langle B, F \rangle$, $\langle C, M \rangle$, and $\langle C, F \rangle$, would have to be independent. The variables, sex and grade, are not independent of each other in this example.

Several important concepts concerning independence should be noted. First, if $E_1$ and $E_2$ are two independent events, $p(E_1 \text{ and } E_2) = p(E_1) \times p(E_2)$. To see why this is so, consider the definition of conditional probability, given by Equation 4.5:

$$p(E_1|E_2) = p(E_1 \text{ and } E_2)/p(E_2)$$

Multiplying both sides of this equation by $p(E_2)$ yields

$$p(E_1|E_2) \times p(E_2) = p(E_1 \text{ and } E_2)$$

However, we know that if $E_1$ and $E_2$ are independent, $p(E_1|E_2) = p(E_1)$. Replacing $p(E_1|E_2)$ by $p(E_1)$ in the last equation, we have, if $E_1$ and $E_2$ are independent events,

$$p(E_1 \text{ and } E_2) = p(E_1) \times p(E_2)$$

It is important to understand that if events $E_1$ and $E_2$ are mutually exclusive, they cannot be independent. If $E_1$ and $E_2$ are mutually exclusive, $E_1$ cannot occur if $E_2$ does. Therefore, *if $E_1$ and $E_2$ are mutually exclusive*, then their joint probability and both conditional probabilities must be zero; that is,

$$p(E_1 \text{ and } E_2) = 0, \; p(E_1|E_2) = 0, \text{ and } p(E_2|E_1) = 0$$

However, $p(E_1)$ and $p(E_2)$ may be greater than zero, so the basic condition for independence—that $p(E_1|E_2) = p(E_1)$ or $p(E_2|E_1) = p(E_2)$—is not met.

### 4.4.5 Rules of Probability

We can now summarize the basic rules of elementary probability.

**The Multiplication Rule.** If $E_1$ and $E_2$ are two independent events,

$$p(E_1 \text{ and } E_2) = p(E_1) \times p(E_2) \tag{4.6}$$

In Table 4.3, the events $B$ and $M$ are independent, so $p(B \text{ and } M) = p(B)p(M) = (.60)(.60) = .36$. Note that Equation 4.6 does *not* hold if the events are not independent; for example, $A$ and $M$ are not independent and $p(A \text{ and } M) = .15$, but $p(A)p(M) = (.27)(.60) = .162$. As indicated in the last section, Equation 4.6 follows directly from the definitions of independence and conditional probability. The rule can be extended to any number of independent events; for example, if three events $E_1$, $E_2$, and $E_3$ are independent of one another,

$$p(E_1 \text{ and } E_2 \text{ and } E_3) = p(E_1) \times p(E_2) \times p(E_3) \tag{4.7}$$

Although in this chapter we are concerned with independent events, the multiplication rule can be extended to events that are not independent. In this case,

$$p(E_1 \text{ and } E_2) = p(E_1) \times p(E_2|E_1) = p(E_2) \times p(E_1|E_2) \tag{4.8}$$

Equation 4.8 follows directly from the definition of conditional probability (Equation 4.5):

$$p(E_1|E_2) = p(E_1 \text{ and } E_2)/p(E_2)$$

Multiplying both sides of this last equation by $p(E_2)$ yields

$$p(E_2) \times p(E_1|E_2) = p(E_1 \text{ and } E_2).$$

For example, applying Equation 4.8 to the data of Table 4.3, we can see that $p(A \text{ and } M) = p(M) \, p(A|M) = (.60)(15/60) = .15$.

**The Addition Rule.** If $E_1$ and $E_2$ are two mutually exclusive events,

$$p(E_1 \text{ or } E_2) = p(E_1) + p(E_2) \tag{4.9}$$

**TABLE 4.4**  SOME PROBABILITY DEFINITIONS AND RULES

| Definition or Rule | Formula |
| --- | --- |
| Some probability definitions | |
| Probability of event $A$ | $p(A) = n(A)/n(S)$ |
| Probability of joint event $A$ and $B$ | $p(A \text{ and } B) = n(A \text{ and } B)/n(S)$ |
| Probability of the union of events $A$ and $B$ | $p(A \text{ or } B) = n(A \text{ or } B)/n(S)$ |
| Conditional probability of $A$ given $B$ | $p(A\|B) = p(A \text{ and } B)/p(B)$ |
| | $= n(A \text{ and } B)/n(B)$ |
| Some probability rules | |
| The addition rule for unions of events | $p(A \text{ or } B) = p(A) + p(B) - p(A \text{ and } B)$ |
| Special case of the addition rule if the events are mutually exclusive | $p(A \text{ or } B) = p(A) + p(B)$ |
| The multiplication rule for joint events | $p(A \text{ and } B \text{ and } C)$ |
| | $= p(A)p(B\|A)\,p(C\|A \text{ and } B)$ |
| Special case of the multiplication rule for independent events | $p(A \text{ and } B \text{ and } C) = p(A)p(B)p(C)$ |

This can be extended to any number of mutually exclusive events; for example, if $E_1$, $E_2$, and $E_3$ are mutually exclusive events,

$$p(E_1 \text{ or } E_2 \text{ or } E_3) = p(E_1) + p(E_2) + p(E_3)$$

As we explained in Subsection 4.4.2 (and see Table 4.3), if events $E_1$ and $E_2$ are not mutually exclusive,

$$p(E_1 \text{ or } E_2) = p(E_1) + p(E_2) - p(E_1 \text{ and } E_2) \tag{4.10}$$

For example, in Table 4.3, $p(A \text{ or } M) = p(A) + p(M) - p(A \text{ and } M) = .27 + .60 - .15 = .72$.

Table 4.4 summarizes much of what has been presented in Section 4.4 to this point. It includes important definitions and the rules embodied in Equations 4.6–4.10.

Although the multiplication and addition rules are very simple, people often mix them up. It should be emphasized that the multiplication rule tells us how to calculate $p(E_1$ and $E_2)$, the probability of the joint occurrence of $E_1$ and $E_2$. The addition rule tells us how to calculate $p(E_1$ or $E_2)$, the probability that $E_1$ or $E_2$ occurs. This union of $E_1$ and $E_2$ ($E_1$ or $E_2$) will include the joint event $\langle E_1$ and $E_2 \rangle$, but it also includes occurrences of $E_1$ without $E_2$ and of $E_2$ without $E_1$.

## 4.4.6 The Sample Space for an Experiment

In the previous few sections, we discussed a sample space in which the elementary events were the 100 combinations of sex and grade that could be sampled from a class. We now apply some of the ideas that we have developed about probability to the memory experiment that was introduced earlier. In the terminology we have developed, each of the possible patterns of 4 correct and error responses presented earlier in Table 4.1 may be viewed as an elementary event. These elementary events are mutually exclusive and exhaust the sample space for an experiment with four participants, each making either a correct or incorrect response. Figure 4.2 represents the events of Table 4.1 in a **tree diagram**.

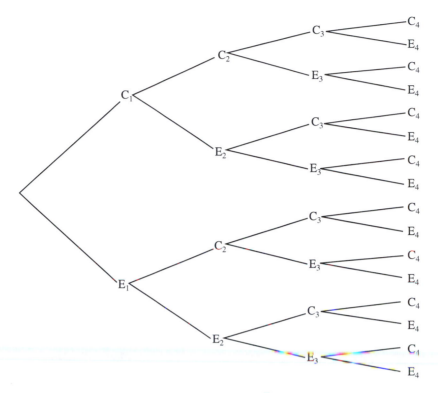

**Fig. 4.2** Tree diagram for four trials ($C$ = correct, $E$ = error).

In Fig. 4.2, the top branch corresponds to the pattern $\langle C_1, C_2, C_3, C_4 \rangle$, the next is $\langle C_1, C_2, C_3, E_4 \rangle$, and so on. The subscripts indicate the 4 individuals in the experiment. The 16 patterns are mutually exclusive and exhaust the possibilities that can occur. If we assume independent outcomes for the 4 participants, we can find the probability of each pattern by using the multiplication rule. If $p(C_j) = 1/2$ for $j = 1, 2, 3$, and 4, then

$$p(C_1 \text{ and } C_2 \text{ and } C_3 \text{ and } C_4) = p(C_1)p(C_2)p(C_3)p(C_4)$$
$$= (1/2)(1/2)(1/2)(1/2) = 1/16$$

and the probabilities for each of the other 15 sequences are also $1/16$.

We can now obtain the probability distribution of $Y$, the number of correct responses, using the addition rule as necessary; for example,

$$p(Y = 0) = p(E_1 \text{ and } E_2 \text{ and } E_3 \text{ and } E_4) = 1/16$$
$$p(Y = 1) = p(C_1 \text{ and } E_2 \text{ and } E_3 \text{ and } E_4) + \cdots + p(E_1 \text{ and } E_2 \text{ and } E_3 \text{ and } C_4)$$
$$= 4/16$$

and similarly for the rest of the possible values of $Y$. The rules of probability allow us to generate the theoretical probability distribution that was presented in Table 4.1 and Fig. 4.1.

The outcome probabilities can easily be calculated, no matter what the probability of a correct answer is for either problem. In the Chen and Myers experiment, each participant had to select one of four objects. Assuming guessing, $p(C)$, the probability of a correct response is $1/4$ and $p(E) = 3/4$. Then, for example, the probability of exactly 1 correct response is now

$$p(Y = 1) = p(C_1 \text{ and } E_2 \text{ and } E_3 \text{ and } E_4) + \cdots + p(E_1 \text{ and } E_2 \text{ and } E_3 \text{ and } C_4)$$
$$= (1/4)(3/4)(3/4)(3/4) + \cdots + (3/4)(3/4)(3/4)(1/4)$$
$$= 4 \times 27/256 = 108/256 = .422$$

Before ending this introduction to probability, we should emphasize several points. The sample space, $S$, consists of all of the elementary events, and the probabilities of the elementary events must sum to 1. This must be the case because the elementary events are by definition mutually exclusive and exhaustive. In the memory experiment example, the events 0, 1, 2, 3, and 4 correct responses are also mutually exclusive and exhaustive and so their probabilities must also sum to 1. In general,

$$p(S) = 1 \tag{4.11}$$

The sample space can always be partitioned into two mutually exclusive and exhaustive sets of elementary events; call these $A$ and $\tilde{A}$ ("not $A$" and called the **complement** of $A$). For example, let $A$ be "zero correct responses" in the 4-participant memory experiment. Then $\tilde{A}$ is "1 or more correct." We could calculate $p(1 \text{ or more correct})$ by using the addition rule; that is, we could add $p(1 \text{ correct}) + p(2 \text{ correct}) + p(3 \text{ correct}) + p(4 \text{ correct})$. It is simpler to note that, because $p(S) = 1$, $p(1 \text{ or more correct})$ must equal $1 - p(0 \text{ correct})$. In general,

$$p(\tilde{A}) = 1 - p(A) \tag{4.12}$$

It should be evident from the definition of probability in Equation 4.1 that a probability must have a value within the range from zero to one. More precisely,

$$0 \leq p(A) \leq 1 \tag{4.13}$$

### 4.4.7 Sampling With and Without Replacement

Suppose we select two individuals from the sample summarized by Table 4.3. What is the probability that both will be men? When sampling is done **with replacement**, if a man is selected on the first draw, he is put back into the sample (i.e., replaced) and is therefore eligible to be selected again on the second draw. This means that if sampling is performed with replacement, selecting a man on the first draw $(M_1)$ and selecting a man on the second draw $(M_2)$ are independent events, so $p(M_1 \text{ and } M_2) = p(M_1)\, p(M_2) = (60/100)(60/100) = .360$. However, when sampling is performed **without replacement**, if a man is selected on the first draw, he is not replaced, so there is one less man eligible for selection on the second draw. Consequently, the events $M_1$ and $M_2$ are not independent. Now, $p(M_1 \text{ and } M_2) = p(M_1)\, p(M_2|M_1) = (60/100)(59/99) = .358$. Note that here, even though the events are not independent, the probability is similar to that calculated by assuming independence, because the sample is fairly large (see Appendix 4.2).

This concludes our introduction to probability. It is brief and far from complete. Nevertheless, it provides the basis for discussing a particular type of probability distribution known as the binomial. In turn, the binomial distribution provides a context within which we can introduce aspects of inference involved in the use of many other statistical distributions. So, without further ado, let's consider the binomial distribution.

## 4.5 THE BINOMIAL DISTRIBUTION

Figure 4.1 and the $p(y)$ column of Table 4.1 present the distribution of one random variable, the number of correct responses, for the special case in which there are four trials and the probability of a correct response on each trial is .5. It would be useful to have a general formula for the probability distribution for any number of trials and for any probability of a correct response. For example, in the Chen and Myers experiment, 20 teenage participants were presented with four objects, one of which they had been exposed to in a laboratory task when they were preschoolers. In order to decide whether memory for the previously seen object was at a better than chance level, the chance probability distribution had to be determined. The question becomes, If the participants are guessing, what is the probability distribution? In this example, $p(C) = .25$, and $n$, the number of trials (participants), is 20. Once we have the chance distribution, we can formulate a decision rule. For example, using an equation that we develop in the next two sections, we can calculate that if $p(C) = .25$ and $n = 20$, the probability of 9 or more correct responses is less than .05 (.041). Therefore, if 9 or more participants are correct, either they are guessing and are very lucky, or $p$ is actually greater than .25. Given that guessing is very unlikely to produce 9 or more correct responses, we might form the following decision rule: If 9 or more responses are correct, reject the hypothesis that the true probability of a correct response is .25 in favor of the hypothesis that it is greater than .25. To form such decision rules for any experiment of this type, we need to be able to calculate the theoretical probability distribution assuming chance performance. We now develop a formula to enable us to do just that.

### 4.5.1 Basic Assumptions

Look again at Figs. 4.1 and 4.2. They represent specific instances of a general experimental situation that has the following three characteristics:

1. **Bernoulli Trials**. On a Bernoulli trial, there are exactly two possible outcomes; examples would be "correct" or "error," "head" or "tail," and "success" or "failure." The two outcomes possible on each trial will be referred to as $A$ and $\tilde{A}$ ("not $A$") and their respective probabilities will be denoted by $p$ and $q$. Because $A$ and $\tilde{A}$ exhaust the possible outcomes on a trial, $p + q = 1$.
2. **Stationarity**. This is the assumption that $p$ and $q$ stay constant ("stationary") over trials. Thus, if the probability of a correct response is $1/4$ on trial 1, it is $1/4$ on all trials.
3. **Independence**. In the example of the memory experiment, we assumed that the probability that a participant responded correctly was the same regardless of how other participants responded. In general, the assumption of independence is that the probability of an outcome of any trial does not depend on the outcome of any other trial.

The preceding assumptions justify the probability calculations that yield the **binomial distribution**. If that distribution is used to draw inferences about some population, and the underlying assumptions are not correct, the inferences may not be valid. We will have more to say about the consequences of violating assumptions after illustrating the use of the binomial distribution in testing hypotheses about the population.

### 4.5.2 The Binomial Function

Consider an experiment with $n$ Bernoulli trials, each with possible outcomes $A$ and $\tilde{A}$. The outcome probabilities, $p$ and $q$, are stationary over trials and do not depend on the outcomes of other trials. We want a formula for $p(Y = y)$, where $Y$ is a discrete random variable and the values it can take on are the possible number of $A$ responses that can occur in $n$ trials. In an $n$-trial experiment, $Y$ can take on the values 0, 1, 2, ..., $n$. Suppose that $n$ and $p$ are specified and we calculate $p(Y = y)$ for each possible value of $Y$ in turn. The result is a probability distribution; the distribution in Fig. 4.1 is a specific example obtained by setting $n$ at 4 and $p$ at .5. An infinite number of distributions that belong to this general family can be generated by using different combinations of $p$ and $n$. Any distribution in this family is referred to as a binomial distribution. In this section, we develop a formula for calculating the probability of $y$ responses as a function of $n$ and $p$. This binomial probability function will be denoted by $p(y; n, p)$ to indicate that it is the probability of $y$ responses of type $A$ when there are $n$ trials with $p(A) = p$ on each trial.

Table 4.1 and Fig. 4.2 present the 16 possible sequences for a four-trial experiment. Note that the trial outcomes, $A$ and $\tilde{A}$, need not come from different individuals as they did in the example of the memory experiment. For example, $A$ and $\tilde{A}$ could represent correct and error responses by an individual on four multiple-choice questions. Then each pattern would represent a sequence of such responses for the four questions and $p$ would be the proportion of correct responses in a population of such items. From now on, we will use the more general term **combination** to refer to a sequence or pattern of $A$ and $\tilde{A}$ responses.

Suppose we wish to find the probability of obtaining exactly three $A$ responses in four trials. Assuming that the responses $A$ and $\tilde{A}$ are independently distributed over trials, we can use the multiplication rule developed earlier to calculate the probability for each combination of $A$ and $\tilde{A}$ responses. For example, the probability of the combination $\langle A, A, A, \tilde{A} \rangle$ would be $(p)(p)(p)(q)$ or $p^3 q$. What we want, however, is $p(3, 4, p)$, the probability of exactly 3 $A$ responses in four trials. That is, $p(\langle \tilde{A}, A, A, A \rangle$ or $\langle A, \tilde{A}, A, A \rangle$ or $\langle A, A, \tilde{A}, A \rangle$ or $\langle A, A, A, \tilde{A} \rangle)$. These four combinations are mutually exclusive (i.e., exactly one will occur in a four-trial experiment in which there are three $A$ responses and one $\tilde{A}$ response). Therefore, the probability of three $A$ and one $\tilde{A}$ response in any order is the sum of the probabilities of the combinations, or $4p^3 q$. In general, we calculate the probability of a combination having $y$ $A$ responses; we then multiply by the number of such combinations.

The approach can be generalized to any value of $n$. The probability of any one specific combination of $y$ $A$ responses and $n - y$ $\tilde{A}$ responses is $p^y q^{n-y}$. The probability of exactly $y$ $A$ responses and $n - y$ $\tilde{A}$ responses is

$$p(y; n, p) = kp^y q^{n-y} \tag{4.14}$$

where $k$ is the number of combinations consisting of $y$ $A$ and $n - y$ $\tilde{A}$ responses. We just about have our binomial function; all we still need is a formula for $k$, the number of ways in which $y$ $A$ and $(n - y)$ $\tilde{A}$ responses can be combined. This number of combinations is

$$k = \binom{n}{y}$$

This is referred to as the binomial coefficient. The derivation of this coefficient is presented in Appendix 4.1 at the end of this chapter. Its formula is

$$\binom{n}{y} = \frac{n!}{y!(n-y)!} \tag{4.15}$$

where $n! = (n)(n-1)(n-2)\ldots(3)(2)(1)$ and $0! = 1$. Also, note that

$$\binom{n}{y} \text{ and } \binom{n}{n-y}$$

have the same value. Substituting $y = 0, 1, 2, 3$, and 4 in turn into Equation 4.15, verify that the formula yields the values 1, 4, 6, 4, and 1, respectively; these are the numbers of combinations that appear in Table 4.1. Of course, writing out and counting all the combinations becomes rather tedious when there are many trials. For large $n$s, Equation 4.14 becomes quite useful.

Replacing $k$ in Equation 4.14 with the formula for $k$ in Equation 4.15 yields the binomial probability function:

$$p(y; n, p) = \binom{n}{y} p^y q^{n-y} = \frac{n!}{y!(n-y)!} p^y q^{n-y} \tag{4.16}$$

Numerical values of this probability for various values of $n$, $p$, and $y$ are contained in Appendix C at the back of the book (Table C.1). You may use the values contained there to verify our statement that the probability of 9 or more correct in 20 trials is .041 if $p = .25$.

Figure 4.3 presents several binomial distributions for various values of $n$ and $p$. For easier comparison across different values of $n$, the outcome probability is plotted as a function of the proportion of $A$ responses, $Y/n$. For example, when $n = 10$ and $p = .5$, we expect to observe 40% correct responding (4 $A$ responses in 10 trials) with probability .2051. In the long run (i.e., if the experiment were repeated many times), the proportion of experiments with 4 $A$ and 6 $\tilde{A}$ responses should equal .2051, if the binomial model is correct. Several points should be noted about these distributions. First, when $p = .5$, the distributions are symmetric. Second, when $p = .25$ and skewness (asymmetry) is present, as $n$ increases the distribution becomes more symmetric about the value of $Y/n$ that corresponds to $p$. Third, the distributions appear more continuous in form as $n$ increases. The importance of these observations lies in the fact that if $n$ is sufficiently large, particularly when $p$ is close to .5, the binomial distribution looks much like the normal distribution, which then can be used to get binomial probabilities with considerably easier calculations. This point is developed in Chapter 5.

A fourth detail to note about Fig. 4.3 is that the probability of getting a value of $Y/n$ close to $p$ increases with $n$. Consider the probability if $p = .5$ that $Y/n$ lies in the range from .4 to .6; that is, $p(.4 \leq Y/n \leq .6)$. When $n$ is 10, $p(.4 \leq Y/n \leq .6)$ is the probability that $Y = 4, 5$, or 6, which is $.2051 + .2461 + .2051$, or .6563. When $n$ is 20, $p(.4 \leq Y/n \leq .6)$ is the probability that $Y = 8, 9, 10, 11$, or 12, which is $.1201 + .1602 + .1762 + .1602 + .1201$, or .7368. When $n$ is 40, the probability is .8461. This point is very important; it means that as $n$ grows larger, the proportion of $A$ responses observed in a single experiment is more likely to be close to the population parameter. We do not prefer larger data sets to smaller

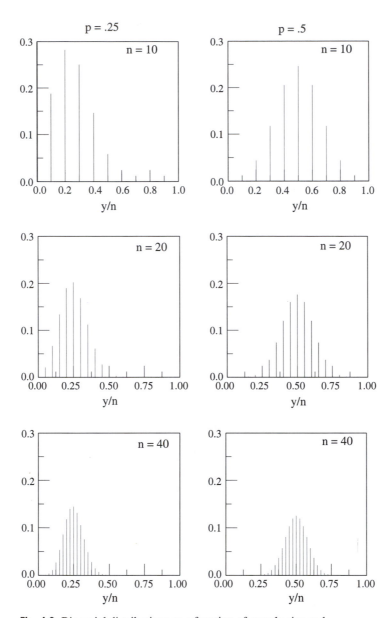

**Fig. 4.3**  Binomial distributions as a function of sample size and probability.

ones because of some deeply ingrained work ethic; we do so because it is more likely to result in a sample statistic that is closer to the population parameter of interest. Statistics that have a higher probability of being within any fixed range of the population parameter as $n$ increases are called **consistent** estimators of the parameter. We have more to say about this desirable property of sample statistics, and about other properties important to estimating population parameters, in Chapter 5.

## 4.6 MEANS AND VARIANCES OF DISCRETE DISTRIBUTIONS

In drawing statistical inferences, we are concerned with the parameters of a theoretical population of scores; quite often the population mean and variance will be the parameters of interest. Equations 2.4 and 2.7 for the sample mean and variance are not directly applicable to the calculation of the population mean and variance, because the individual scores in the population usually are not available for summing and the number of such scores is often infinite. However, when the random variable is discretely distributed, we usually know its possible values, and, assuming some theoretical distribution such as the binomial, we also know the probability of each value. This provides us with a way of defining the mean and variance for discrete distributions. We present the necessary equations in the following section, using the binomial distribution to illustrate. In Chapter 5, we present analogs to these equations, suitable for dealing with the mean and variance of continuously distributed random variables.

### 4.6.1 The Population Mean

Now that we have developed the probability distribution of a discrete random variable, we can take the opportunity to demonstrate how to find the mean of the distribution. The concept of a weighted average provides a good way to think about population means. For example, reconsider Table 4.1, which presents the probability distribution of the number of correct responses ($Y$) when there are four independent trials and $p$ is .5 on each trial. We can conceive of doing this four-trial experiment many times, each time recording the number of successes. Thus, we have a hypothetical population of numbers from 0 to 4 and we wish to know what the mean of that population is: Over an infinite number of replications of the experiment, what will the average number of successes be? This population mean will be referred to as the **expected value** of $Y$ and denoted as $E(Y)$, and often by the Greek letter, $\mu$ (mu). In our example, $Y$ can take on the values 0, 1, 2, 3, and 4, and we can calculate the proportion of each of these values in the population by using the binomial formula.

The equation for $E(Y)$ is the same as Equation 2.5 for the weighted mean of an observed set of numbers; the proportions are replaced by $p(y)$, the theoretical probabilities of each value of $Y$. Then we define the expected value as

$$E(Y) = \sum_y yp(y) \tag{4.17}$$

Appendix B at the back of the book presents some useful information about expectations.

If $n = 4$ and $p = .5$, Equation 4.17 yields the following result for the mean of a binomial distribution:

$$E(Y) = (0)(\tfrac{1}{2})^4 + (1)[(4)(\tfrac{1}{2})^4] + (2)[(6)(\tfrac{1}{2})^4] + (3)[(4)(\tfrac{1}{2})^4] + (4)(\tfrac{1}{2})^4$$
$$= (0)(.0625) + (1)(.25) + (2)(.375) + (3)(.25) + (4)(.0625)$$
$$= 2.$$

In words, take each possible value of $Y$ (zero through four in the example of the four-trial experiment), multiply it by its probability of occurrence, and sum the products. The probabilities in this example are given by the binomial equation, 4.16, and appear in Table 4.2. It is as if we had a very large number of people, each tossing four fair coins. We note the number of heads obtained by each person. The average number should be two. In Appendix

B, which presents the algebra of expectations, we demonstrate that the mean number of successes in $n$ independent Bernoulli trials is $pn$, where $p$ is the probability of a success on a single trial. In the preceding example, $p = .5$ and $n = 4$ and $(.5)(4) = 2$.

### 4.6.2 The Population Variance

Analogous to the sample variance, the population variance is the average squared deviation of scores about their mean, or $E(Y - \mu)^2$. We denote this quantity by $\sigma^2$ (the Greek letter, sigma). We can calculate this population variance by

$$\sigma^2 = \sum_y (y - \mu)^2 p(y) \tag{4.18}$$

Applying this equation to our example of the binomial distribution with $n = 4$ and $p = .5$, and recalling that $\mu = 2$ in this case, we have

$$\sigma^2 = (0 - 2)^2(.0625) + (1 - 2)^2(.25) + (2 - 2)^2(.375) + (3 - 2)^2(.25) + (4 - 2)^2(.0625)$$
$$= 1$$

In the case of the binomial distribution, this result can be obtained more simply; $\sigma^2 = p(1 - p)n$, as we demonstrate in Appendix B.

## 4.7 HYPOTHESIS TESTING

### 4.7.1 A Significance Test

Now that we have a probability distribution, the binomial, we can apply it to the example presented at the beginning of this chapter. Recall that there were 20 participants, each of whom had been exposed to a set of objects in the University of Massachusetts laboratory 12 years earlier, and who were now required to choose the one object from a set of four that they had seen in the earlier experiment. The sample statistic of interest will be the number of participants who make a correct response. In the language developed earlier, we have 20 independent Bernoulli trials; $n = 20$ and $Y$ is the number of correct responses.

Before proceeding with the actual significance test, a review of the conceptual framework is helpful. Imagine a population of 15- to 17-year-olds who had been in the experiment 12 years previously. Further imagine that a lottery has been held such that each individual in the population had an equal chance to appear in our study. In this sense, the 20 students who participated in our study can be viewed as a random sample from a hypothetical population of 15- to 17-year-olds. The 20 responses actually obtained in the study can be regarded as having been sampled from the hypothetical population of responses that could be obtained from this population. Our estimate of the probability of a correct response in the population will be $p$, the proportion of correct responders in the sample. We denote the population probability by the Greek letter $\pi$ (pi). From now on we will use Greek letters to stand for population parameters and the more common Latin letters to stand for sample statistics in order to lessen confusion between the two.

We now must decide between two hypotheses about $\pi$: the **null hypothesis**, $H_0$, and the **alternative hypothesis**, $H_1$. Here, the null hypothesis states that the members of the population are guessing; that is, the probability of a correct response is .25:

$$H_0: \pi = .25$$

The alternative hypothesis states that the probability of a correct response is higher than the chance level; that is, $p$ is greater than .25:

$$H_1: \pi > .25$$

If we assume that the null hypothesis is true, we can specify the probability distribution of the random variable, $Y$, the number of correct responses out of 20 responses. We use the theoretical distribution that $Y$ should have if the null hypothesis is true to assess whether we have enough evidence to reject the null hypothesis. Letting $n$ be 20 and replacing $p$ by $\pi$ (.25 if $H_0$ is true) in Equation 4.16, we can generate the values of $p(y)$ found in the $\pi = .25$ column of Table 4.5.

The next step is to determine those values of $Y$ that, if obtained in the study, would lead to rejection of $H_0$ in favor of $H_1$. Such values constitute a **rejection region**. This is a set of possible values of $Y$ that are consistent with $H_1$ and very improbable if $H_0$ is assumed to be true. Indeed, these values are so unlikely if $H_0$ is assumed that their occurrence leads us to reject $H_0$. An arbitrarily chosen value, $\alpha$ (alpha), defines exactly how unlikely "so unlikely" is. Traditionally, researchers have set $\alpha$ at .05. We want very strong evidence against $H_0$ before we reject it.

**TABLE 4.5** THE BINOMIAL DISTRIBUTION

| No. Correct | $p(y)$ | | |
|---|---|---|---|
| $y$ | $\pi = .25$ | $\pi = .35$ | $\pi = .50$ |
| 0 | .0032 | .0002 | .0000 |
| 1 | .0211 | .0020 | .0000 |
| 2 | .0669 | .0100 | .0002 |
| 3 | .1339 | .0323 | .0011 |
| 4 | .1897 | .0738 | .0046 |
| 5 | .2023 | .1272 | .0148 |
| 6 | .1686 | .1712 | .0370 |
| 7 | .1124 | .1844 | .0739 |
| 8 | .0609 | .1614 | .1201 |
| 9 | .0271 | .1158 | .1602 |
| 10 | .0099 | .0686 | .1762 |
| 11 | .0030 | .0336 | .1602 |
| 12 | .0008 | .0136 | .1201 |
| 13 | .0002 | .0045 | .0739 |
| 14 | .0000 | .0012 | .0370 |
| 15 | .0000 | .0003 | .0148 |
| 16 | .0000 | .0000 | .0046 |
| 17 | .0000 | .0000 | .0011 |
| 18 | .0000 | .0000 | .0002 |
| 19 | .0000 | .0000 | .0000 |
| 20 | .0000 | .0000 | .0000 |

*Note.* The binomial distribution is shown for $n = 20$ and $\pi = .25, .35,$ and .50.

We will now establish a rejection region for the Chen and Myers experiment. Turn to the $\pi = .25$ column of Table 4.5 and sum the probabilities, beginning at the bottom of the column. We begin at the bottom (larger values of $Y$) because these are the values of $Y$ consistent with $H_1$; values of $Y$ at the top of the table are consistent with $H_0$ being true. If $H_0$ is true, the probability that $Y$ has a value between 9 and 20 is

$$p(9 \leq Y \leq 20) = .0271 + .0099 + .0030 + .0008 + .0002 + 0 = .0410$$

Note that if we included $Y = 8$ in the rejection region, the probability of obtaining a value of $Y$ in that region (assuming $H_0$ to be true) would be .1019, which is greater than the value of $\alpha$ we had set. Therefore, our decision rule for this experiment is to reject $H_0$ if 9 or more subjects in the experiment make the correct response.

The logic of our approach underlies the application of many other statistical tests. Therefore, it is worth reviewing the basic steps in hypothesis testing:

1. State a null and alternative hypothesis.
2. Obtain the distribution of the **test statistic** assuming $H_0$ to be true. In our example, $H_0$ implies $\pi = .25$. The test statistic is $Y$, the number of correct responses. In general, the test statistic (a) is a quantity calculated from the data that is sensitive to the truth or falsity of the null hypothesis; and (b) has a known probability distribution when $H_0$ is assumed to be true.
3. Decide on a value of $\alpha$ and establish a rejection region. If $H_0$ is true, the probability that the experiment yields a value of the test statistic within the rejection region should be less than or equal to $\alpha$. Typically, this **significance level** is .05. Because we are dealing with a discrete distribution, that value of $\alpha$ was not available to us, so in our example $\alpha$ was .041.
4. Run the experiment and calculate the value of the test statistic. If it lies within the rejection region, $H_0$ is rejected in favor of $H_1$. Otherwise, fail to reject $H_1$.

A **statistically significant** result means that a value of the test statistic has occurred that is unlikely if $H_0$ is true. Of course, "unlikely" is not the same as "impossible." We may be rejecting a true null hypothesis. Such incorrect rejections of the null hypothesis are called **Type 1 errors**. Alpha ($\alpha$) is the probability of such errors; that is, $\alpha = p(\text{reject } H_0 | H_0 \text{ true})$. Note that $\alpha$ is a conditional probability, the probability of rejecting $H_0$ given that $H_0$ is true. A useful way to conceptualize this is that if the individuals in the population are actually guessing ($H_0$ is true), and if we were to replicate the experiment many times, we can expect to obtain a value of $y$ in the rejection region in .041 of these experiments. By setting $\alpha$ at this level, we express a level of risk of a Type 1 error that we are willing to tolerate.

Statistical packages usually report an exact **$p$ value**, that is, the probability that a result at least as "extreme" as that obtained in the experiment would occur, if the null hypothesis was true. A result is statistically significant if $p$ is less than the value of $\alpha$ that has been chosen. For example, if $Y$ was 12, $p = p(Y \geq 12 | \pi = .25)$; that is,

$$p = p(Y = 12) + p(Y = 13) + p(Y = 14) + \cdots + p(Y = 19) + p(Y = 20) = .001$$

The result is statistically significant because $p$ is less than the alpha value of .05. Researchers have tended to misinterpret these $p$ values in at least two ways. First, they often view the reported $p$ value as the probability that the null hypothesis is true. This amounts to viewing $p$ as $p(H_0 \text{ true} | \text{data})$. But, in fact, $p$ is the probability of the observed data given that the null hypothesis is true, or $p(\text{data} | H_0 \text{ true})$. It would be nice if we could calculate the probability of the status of $H_0$ from our analysis of the data, but we cannot. What we can do is calculate the probability of the data under the assumption that the null hypothesis is true, and that is a very different thing. Second, there is a tendency to compare $p$ values across experiments or experimental conditions, concluding that if one $p$ value is smaller than another, it must represent a larger, or more important, effect. However, $p$ values depend on sample size and variability as well as effect size, and direct comparisons are rarely valid. This is one reason why we present ways to estimate effect sizes in the following chapters, and emphasize the importance of such methods.

### 4.7.2 One- and Two-Tailed Tests

The test we just described for the Chen and Myers study is referred to as a **one-tailed** test, or directional test. Because we were interested in whether the sampled population performs better than chance, the rejection region consisted of only the largest values of $Y$. On one hand, in the context of this research example, that makes sense. On the other hand, one can conceive of many situations in which a departure from the null hypothesis in either direction would be of interest. For example, in the case of Royer's data on arithmetic skills (see Chapter 2), we might wish to know if there is a significant difference in performance on arithmetic and subtraction; if there was, it might influence the way in which these skills were taught. We might assign a plus to each student who had a higher addition than subtraction score, and we might assign a minus if the subtraction score was higher. Then we ask if the probability of a plus (or, equivalently, a minus) was significantly different from .5. As another example, as described in Chapter 2, University of Massachusetts medical school researchers collected data on seasonal variation in clinical states such as depression and anxiety. Comparing depression scores in winter and summer, we might assign a plus if the winter score was higher, or a minus if it was lower. In both of these examples, $H_0$ would be

$$H_0: \pi = .5$$

The alternative hypothesis would be

$$H_1: \pi \neq .5$$

Suppose $n$ is again 20. Turning to the column labeled $\pi = .50$ in Table 4.5, and assuming that equal weight is given to both directions and $\alpha$ is close to .05, we would reject $H_0$ if $Y \leq 5$ or $Y \geq 15$. This is usually referred to as a **two-tailed** or nondirectional test. Note that, if we use these rejection regions, the actual probability of a Type 1 error is $.021 + .021 = .042$. A larger, but still symmetric, rejection region would include the next value of $Y$ in each tail; then $\alpha$ would be $.042 + .037 + .037$, or $.116$.

### 4.7.3 The Power of a Statistical Test

In deciding whether or not to reject a null hypothesis, a researcher can make two types of errors. If the null hypothesis is true, rejecting it is called a Type 1 error. The probability of such an error is alpha and it is determined by the experimenter in the way we have illustrated. Suppose the null hypothesis is false. Failure to reject a false null hypothesis is called a **Type 2 error**, and its probability is referred to as $\beta$ (the Greek letter beta). The probability of rejecting a false null hypothesis, that is, $p(\text{reject } H_0 | H_0 \text{ is false})$, is called the **power** of the test. The sum of power and $\beta$ is one.

The following table may help to clarify the meanings of $\alpha$, $\beta$, and power:

| $H_0$ | Decision | |
| --- | --- | --- |
| | Reject | Fail to Reject |
| True | $\alpha$ | $1 - \alpha$ |
| False | power $= 1 - \beta$ | $\beta$ |

The rows represent two mutually exclusive events: $H_0$ is either true or false. Given either of these two events, the researcher may make one of two mutually exclusive decisions: reject or do not reject $H_0$. The cell probabilities are conditional probabilities representing the probability of the decision given the event. Because one of the two decisions must be made, the probabilities in each row sum to one.

The Chen and Myers experiment on memory for a childhood event will serve to illustrate the general principles involved in computing power and should clarify the relation between power and other quantities such as $\alpha$ and $n$. We begin by noting that the power of a statistical test depends on how false $H_0$ is. If the probability of a correct response in the sampled population is .9, it is very likely that the sample of 20 subjects will yield a value of $Y$ in the rejection region; therefore, the statistical test has high power. In contrast, if the true value of $\pi$ is only .6, the probability of a large value of $Y$ is much less and so, therefore, is power.

Of course, the true value of the population parameter is never known. However, if some value of the parameter is assumed, the power of the test against that alternative can be calculated. For example, suppose we wish to test $H_0: \pi = .25$ against the alternative hypothesis, $H_1: \pi > .25$. We can calculate the power of the test for different assumed values of $\pi$. If we assume a **specific alternative hypothesis**, say,

$$H_A: \pi = .35$$

we can determine the power of the statistical test of $H_0$ against $H_A$. In other words, we can calculate the probability of rejecting $H_0$ if the probability of a correct response is .35 in the sampled population.

Table 4.5 can be used to obtain the value of power for this example. On the basis of $H_0$, $H_1$, and $\alpha$, the rejection region was determined to be $Y \geq 9$. Power is the probability of obtaining a value in this region when $H_A$ is true. The actual steps in this calculation are as follows:

1.  Calculate the probability distribution of $Y$, assuming $H_0$ to be true. In this example, the distribution is presented in the $\pi = .25$ column of Table 4.5.
2.  Determine the rejection region. In this example ($n = 20$, $\alpha = .05$, $H_1: \pi > .25$), the rejection region is $Y \geq 9$.
3.  Calculate the probability distribution of $Y$, assuming $H_A$ is true. In this example, $p$ in Equation 4.16 is replaced by .35. The results are presented in the $\pi = .35$ column of Table 4.5.
4.  Sum the probabilities for $Y \geq 9$ (the rejection region) in the .35 column. This sum is $p(Y \geq 9 | H_A = .35)$, the power of the test of $H_0$ against $H_A$. In this case, power $= .1158 + .0686 + .0336 + .0136 + .0045 + .0012 + .0003 = .2376$.

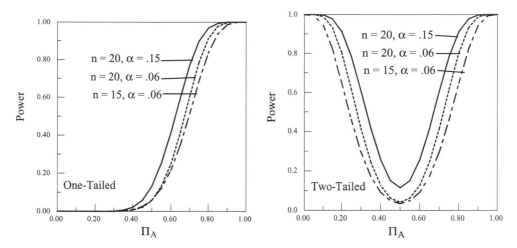

**Fig. 4.4** Power functions based on the binomial distribution.

The Type 2 error probability, $\beta$, is $1 - .238$, or $.762$. These calculations mean that a test of $H_0$: $\pi = .25$ has $.238$ probability of yielding a significant result if $\pi$ is actually $.35$. If the true value of $\pi$ is even greater than $.35$, the power of the test will be greater than $.238$. Using the $\pi = .5$ column, verify that power against this alternative to the null hypothesis is $.748$.

The approach just illustrated underlies power calculations for all statistical tests. The possible values of the test statistic are divided into rejection and nonrejection regions; this division is determined by the value of the parameter under $H_0$ and the nature of $H_1$ (one or two tailed). Then the probability of obtaining a value of the test statistic that falls in the rejection region is obtained, with the assumption that a specific alternative distribution is the true one.

It is important to be clear about the distinction between $H_1$ and $H_A$. $H_1$ is the class of alternative hypotheses that determines where the rejection region is placed (right or left tail, or in both tails). $H_A$ is a *specific alternative*; power is calculated for the test of $H_0$ by assuming $H_A$ to be true.

Figure 4.4 presents the power of the binomial test of $H_0$: $\pi = .50$ against several alternatives. The power functions have been plotted for three conditions: (1) $n = 20, \alpha = .15$; (2) $n = 20, \alpha = .06$; and (3) $n = 15, \alpha = .06$; $\Pi_A$ represents specific alternative values of $\pi$. The left panel presents power for a one-tailed alternative and the right panel presents power for a two-tailed alternative. Three points should be noted that are typical for power functions for all statistical tests. First, power increases as $\alpha$ increases. This is because the increase in $\alpha$ requires an increase in the rejection region. For example, when $n = 20$ and the alternative is one tailed, the rejection region increases from $Y \geq 14$ to $Y \geq 13$ as $\alpha$ increases from $.06$ to $.15$. Because power is also calculated for this larger set of $Y$ values, it too is increased. Second, power is affected by the nature of $H_0$ and $H_1$. In the left panel of Fig. 4.4, the alternative hypothesis is $H_1$: $\pi > .5$. This one-tailed test has more power than the two-tailed test in the right panel whenever $\pi$ is greater than $.5$. This is because the rejection region is concentrated in that tail of the distribution in the case of the one-tailed test, whereas it is divided in half and distributed over the two tails in the case of the two-tailed test. In contrast, the one-tailed test has virtually no power against specific alternatives of the form $\pi < .5$, whereas the two-tailed test does have power to reject $H_0$ against these alternatives.

The third aspect of power illustrated in Fig. 4.4 is that increased sample size, $n$, results in increased power. This follows from the discussion of Fig. 4.3 in which it was noted that $Y/n$ is a consistent estimator of $\pi$. This means that as $n$ increases, $Y/n$ is more likely to be close to the true value of the parameter. Therefore, if $H_0$ is false, a larger $n$ increases the probability of getting values of $Y$ consistent with the alternative hypothesis; therefore, power is increased.

The study of power functions has other implications for researchers. First, power functions for different statistical tests of the same $H_0$ can be compared. Assuming that the choice among tests is not dictated by some other factor (such as validity of assumptions, ease of calculations, or availability of tables), the test with the higher power function should be chosen. Second, the effects of violations of assumptions on power functions can be assessed. For example, when the population of scores is normally distributed, the $t$ test is more powerful than other tests that can be used to compare two experimental conditions. However, when the population of scores is not normally distributed, other tests may achieve markedly more power (Blair & Higgins, 1980, 1985). Finally, and most important, the relation between power and sample size can be used to decide how much data should be collected. Suppose we want power of at least .90 to reject $H_0$ if $\pi$ is at least .75. We can derive power functions for various values of $n$ similar to those depicted in Fig. 4.4. The $n$ we want for our study is the one that gives rise to a power function such that there is an ordinate value (power) of at least .90 when the abscissa value ($\pi$) is .75.

The last point deserves further comment. The null hypothesis is almost always false. If we collect enough data, we are likely to obtain statistically significant results. Whether the results will be of practical importance or theoretical significance is another matter. The effect may be trivially small, or in a direction that makes no sense in terms of any theory, or practical concern. Therefore, it makes good sense before we collect data to ask these questions: What is the smallest size effect that would be of interest? and What power do we want to detect such an effect? The answer to these two questions will be major factors in determining the sample size for our research. Sometimes the required $n$ will be impractically large and we will have to compromise, have less power, or target a larger effect; or we may be able to redesign the research so that a smaller sample will achieve the desired power against the specific alternative hypothesis we had in mind. We return to these issues in discussions of power in subsequent chapters.

## 4.8 INDEPENDENCE AND THE SIGN TEST

Throughout the preceding sections on hypothesis testing and power, we have assumed that $Y$ has a binomial distribution. All the computed probabilities have been based on Equation 4.16. The derivation of that equation rests on the assumption that $p$ is constant across trials (stationarity) and that the probability of an outcome on any one trial is independent of the outcome on any other trial. The assumption of independence is of particular importance for several reasons. First, it is frequently violated in psychological research. Several measures taken from the same participant will usually be correlated. In addition, whenever responses are obtained from members of the same discussion group, school class, or litter of animals, the responses obtained are likely to be correlated. Social, environmental, and biological factors will tend to affect the members of such units in a similar way. Second, violation of the independence assumption frequently will result in a Type 1 error rate very different from the alpha assumed by the experimenter. Some assumptions can be violated with minor consequences, but the independence assumption is often quite critical. Third, the independence assumption plays some role in all statistical test procedures. The binomial test is used to illustrate the consequences of its violation, but the implications are much more general.

Consider a study in which 10 pairs of participants discuss a topic. After the discussion, each of the 20 participants casts a "yes" or "no" vote on the issue under consideration. Previous research has established that votes are evenly divided between the two positions when there is no discussion. However, theoretical principles lead the researcher to believe that "yes" votes will be more frequent than "no" votes following discussion. Thus, the null hypothesis is $H_0$: $p(\text{yes}) = .5$ and the alternative hypothesis is $H_1$: $p(\text{yes}) > .5$. If alpha is set equal to .06, the binomial table indicates that $H_0$ should be rejected if the observed number of "yes" responses is 14 or more.

There is a problem with this procedure: the two individuals in each discussion pair may have influenced each other and their responses may not be independent. Let's see what this means and then attempt to understand the implications for our testing procedure. We begin with a case in which the independence assumption is valid. Suppose we had a population of such discussion pairs. Randomly label one member of each pair $M_1$ and the other $M_2$. Over all pairs in the population, the joint probabilities of "yes" and "no" responses might look like this:

|          |     | $M_1$ |     |     |
|----------|-----|-------|-----|-----|
|          |     | yes   | no  |     |
| $M_2$    | yes | .49   | .21 | .70 |
|          | no  | .21   | .09 | .30 |
|          |     | .70   | .30 |     |

In .49 of the pairs, both members voted "yes," in .21 of the pairs, $M_1$ voted "yes" and $M_2$ voted "no," and so on. Comparing the products of the marginal probabilities with the joint probabilities (e.g., $.7 \times .7 = .49$), we should find it apparent that the response of each member in a pair is independent of that made by the other member. We can verify this by calculating conditional probabilities; the probability of one member's response is .7 regardless of whether the other member responded "yes" or "no."

Unfortunately, this independence result is not the usual outcome in studies of social interaction. The joint probabilities in the population are more likely to look something like this:

|  |  | $M_1$ | | |
|---|---|---|---|---|
|  |  | yes | no | |
|  | yes | .30 | .20 | .50 |
| $M_2$ | | | | |
|  | no | .20 | .30 | .50 |
|  |  | .50 | .50 | |

A check of the products of the marginal probabilities against the joint probabilities reveals that the independence assumption no longer holds. Calculate conditional probabilities and verify that the probability that a pair member votes "yes" is higher when the partner also votes "yes" than when the partner votes "no."

In order to make clear what the consequences of this dependency within pairs is for the binomial test, we consider an extreme example. Suppose the joint probabilities of votes were

|  |  | $M_1$ | | |
|---|---|---|---|---|
|  |  | yes | no | |
|  | yes | .50 | 0 | .50 |
| $M_2$ | | | | |
|  | no | 0 | .50 | .50 |
|  |  | .50 | .50 | |

In this case, the dependence within pairs is complete: The conditional probability of a "yes" vote is 1 when the partner votes "yes" and 0 when the partner votes "no." Note, however, that the null hypothesis [$p(\text{yes}) = .5$] is true.

Recall that the researcher had sampled 10 pairs from this population and, on the basis of the binomial distribution table, had decided to reject $H_0$ if there were 14 or more "yes" votes from the 20 individuals; the researcher assumed a .06 significance level. Unknown to the researcher, the two members of each pair vote the same way. Therefore, the probability of 14 or more "yes" votes is really the probability that 7, 8, 9, or 10 pairs vote "yes." There are only 10 independent events; they are the pair (not the individual) votes. If this violation of the independence assumption occurs, the probability of a Type 1 error is not the .058 assumed by the researcher; rather it is the probability that $Y = 7, 8, 9,$ or 10 when $n = 10$ and $p(\text{yes}) = .5$. Using Equation 4.15, we can show that probability to be .172. The Type 1 error rate is much higher than the researcher believed. Most researchers would feel that it is an unacceptably high Type 1 error rate.

Although complete dependence between the members of the pair is improbable in a real experiment, some dependence is often likely. Consequently, the distortion in Type 1 error rate will be smaller than in our example, but there will be distortion. Frequently, the true error rate will be intolerably high. The opposite result occurs when responses are negatively related. For example, suppose that the null hypothesis is false, but in a high proportion of pairs, the partners agree to split their votes. In cases such as this, power will be greatly reduced. Thus, depending on the nature of the dependency, either Type 1 or Type 2 error rates will be increased. Positive dependencies are far more likely, and, therefore, the greatest danger is an increased rate of rejection of true null hypotheses.

## 4.9 MORE ABOUT ASSUMPTIONS AND STATISTICAL TESTS

Independence is only one assumption that plays a role in many statistical tests. In general, the consequences of failures of assumptions are not simple and have to be thought through in each research situation. Many factors affect error rates. The example in the preceding section illustrates two of these—the magnitude and direction of the failure of the assumption. A third factor is which assumption is violated. Some assumptions, despite being used in the derivation of the test statistic, are less critical; their violation has little effect on error rates. A fourth factor is sample size; certain assumptions (but not all) are less critical when there are many observations. Appendix 4.2 provides an example of the interaction of assumptions and sample size.

In summary, every inferential procedure involves some statistical distribution, and the derivation of that distribution rests on certain assumptions. The consequences of violating these assumptions will vary depending on the factors noted herein. Throughout this book, we emphasize the statistical model underlying each inferential procedure, detailing the conditions that cause assumptions to be violated, the results of such violations, and alternative analyses that remedy the situation when the violations are severe enough to make the proposed analysis untrustworthy.

## 4.10 CONCLUDING REMARKS

The only thing certain about the inferences we draw from samples of data is that there is no certainty. As a consequence, one cornerstone of inferential statistics is probability. Accordingly, this chapter provided a brief review of elementary probability. Inferences from a sample to a population require a statistical model, a set of assumptions that underlie the probabilities associated with our conclusions. Chapter 4 has illustrated this, developing the relation between assumptions of independence and stationarity and an important theoretical distribution, the binomial. Finally, we used the binomial distribution to illustrate how a theoretical distribution can be used in one kind of inferential process, significance testing. In doing so, we introduced many of the concepts and much of the machinery of hypothesis testing in general. Throughout this chapter, we focused on discrete random variables because the relationship between the assumptions and the resulting theoretical probability distribution is quite transparent. In subsequent chapters, continuous random variables are introduced, and the role of their probability distributions in making inferences is discussed.

A limitation of this chapter has been its focus on hypothesis testing. In the example of the memory experiment, we asked whether the true probability of a correct response was greater than .25. We might have asked a related but different question: What is the actual value of $\pi$, the population probability of a correct response? Our best estimate of that parameter is the sample proportion of correct responses, $p$. However, such a **point estimate** of a population parameter is of limited value. It is a best guess about the population parameter, but we do not know how good a guess it is. If we ran the experiment several times, we would have as many estimates as experimental replications. If the estimates were close to each other, we might feel confident that any one estimate was close to the population parameter. Unfortunately, like most researchers, we will run our study only once. From that one data set, we would like an idea of how good our estimate is, how close it is likely to be to the parameter being estimated. The statistic we calculate to accomplish this is called a **confidence interval**. In future chapters, we develop formulas for confidence intervals for various population parameters, illustrate their interpretation and use, and discuss their relation to significance tests.

## KEY CONCEPTS

| | |
|---|---|
| probability distribution | continuous random variable |
| discrete random variable | statistical model |
| theoretical probability distribution | sampling distribution |
| random selection | elementary event |
| sample space | event classes (events) |
| marginal probability | joint probability |
| union of events | conditional probability |
| mutually exclusive events | exhaustive set of events |
| independent events | tree diagram |
| complement of an event | sampling with replacement |
| sampling without replacement | Bernoulli trial |
| stationarity | independence |
| binomial distribution | combination of events |
| binomial probability function | significance test |
| null hypothesis | alternative hypothesis |
| rejection region | test statistic |
| significance level | statistically significant result |
| Type 1 error | $p$ value |
| one- and two-tailed tests | Type 2 error |
| power of a test | specific alternative hypothesis |
| sign test | point estimate |
| decision rule | |

## EXERCISES

**4.1**  Suppose an experiment is designed to test for the existence of ESP (extrasensory perception—the supposed ability to be aware of events in the environment through means that do not use the normal sensory channels). An experimenter is seated in a room with a deck of five different cards, which we can refer to as 1, 2, 3, 4, and 5. On each trial of the experiment, the experimenter shuffles the cards well and then randomly selects one of them. A participant, $P$, who is seated in a room in a different building, knows when each trial of the experiment is to occur and tries to "perceive" and then record each card that was chosen by the experimenter. Evidence that $P$ does better than would be expected by chance will be taken as support for ESP. Therefore, it is important to be able to calculate what we could expect as a result of pure chance. Suppose $P$ has no ESP and simply picks one of the five cards on each trial. Assuming independence, what is the probability that $P$ is (a) correct on the first trial? (b) correct on each of the first three trials? (c) correct on the second trial but wrong on the first and third? (d) correct on exactly one of the first three trials? (e) correct on at least one of the first three trials? (f) correct on exactly two of the first three trials? (g) correct for the first time on the fifth trial?

**4.2** Suppose a certain trait is associated with eye color. Three hundred randomly selected individuals are studied with the following results:

| | Eye Color | | |
|---|---|---|---|
| Trait | Blue | Brown | Other |
| Yes | 70 | 30 | 20 |
| No | 20 | 110 | 50 |

Suppose a person is chosen at random from the 300 in the study.

(a) For each of the following pairs of events, indicate whether or not they are exhaustive, whether or not they are mutually exclusive, and whether or not they are independent: (i) "yes" and "no," (ii) "blue" and "brown," and (iii) "yes" and "brown."

(b) Find: (i) $p(\text{blue}|\text{yes})$; (ii) $p(\text{yes}|\text{blue})$; (iii) $p(\text{yes or blue})$; and (iv) $p(\text{yes and blue})$.

Suppose two people are chosen at random from the 300.

(c) What is the probability that the first person has the trait and has brown eyes?

(d) What is the probability that both people have the trait and have brown eyes if they are selected *with replacement*?

(e) What is the probability that both people have the trait and have brown eyes if they are selected *without replacement*?

**4.3** The following demonstrates why it is hard to screen populations for the presence of low-incidence diseases: enzyme-linked immunosorbent assay (ELISA) tests are used to screen donated blood for the presence of the HIV virus. The test actually detects antibodies, substances that the body produces when the virus is present. However, the test is not completely accurate. It can be wrong in two ways: first, by giving a positive result when there are no antibodies (false positive), and second, by giving a negative result when there actually are antibodies (false negative).

When antibodies are present, ELISA gives a positive result with a probability of about .997 and a negative result (false negative) with a probability of about .003. When antibodies are not present, ELISA gives a positive result (false positive) with a probability of about .015 and a negative result with a probability of .985. That is,

$$p(\text{correct positive}) = p(\text{positive}|\text{HIV}) = .997$$
$$p(\text{false negative}) = p(\text{negative}|\text{HIV}) = .003$$
$$p(\text{false positive}) = p(\text{positive}|\text{no HIV}) = .015$$
$$p(\text{correct negative}) = p(\text{negative}|\text{no HIV}) = .985$$

Suppose 100,000 blood samples are obtained from a population for which the incidence of HIV infection is 1.0%; that is, $p(\text{HIV}) = .01$.

(a) Using the information given here, fill in the cells in the following 2 × 2 table:

| Test Results | HIV | No HIV | Total |
| --- | --- | --- | --- |
| Positive | | | |
| Negative | | | |
| Total | | | |

(b) Given that a randomly chosen sample tests positive, what is the probability that the donor is infected?

(c) Given that a randomly chosen sample tests negative, what is the probability that the donor is not infected?

**4.4** We are often able to use key words such as "and," "or," and "given" to decide among probability rules. In the following problem, we use more everyday language, so read carefully and for each part think about whether the wording dictates marginal, joint, or conditional probability.

Suppose that a survey of 200 people in a college town has yielded the following data on attitudes toward liberalizing rules on the sale of liquor:

| | Male | | Female | | |
| --- | --- | --- | --- | --- | --- |
| Attitude | Student | Nonstudent | Student | Nonstudent | Row Total |
| For | 70 | 10 | 40 | 0 | 120 |
| Against | 5 | 30 | 10 | 20 | 65 |
| No opin. | 5 | 0 | 10 | 0 | 15 |
| Col. total | 80 | 40 | 60 | 20 | 200 |

(a) What is the probability that someone is *for* if that person is male?

(b) What is the probability that a randomly selected individual is a female who has no opinion?

(c) What is the probability that a female student would have no opinion?

(d) What is the probability that a student would have no opinion?

(e) What is the probability that someone with no opinion is male?

**4.5** Assume that, in a particular research area, .30 of the null hypotheses tested are true. Suppose a very large number of experiments are conducted, each with $\alpha = .05$ and power $= .80$.

(a) What proportion of true null hypotheses will be rejected?

(b) What proportion of false null hypotheses will not be rejected?

(c) What proportion of nonrejected null hypotheses will actually be true?

(d) What proportion of all null hypotheses will be rejected?

**4.6** A study reported in the local newspapers indicated that a psychological test has been developed with the goal of predicting whether elderly people are at high risk for developing dementia in the near future. For healthy people at age 79, the probability of developing dementia within the next 4 years is approximately .20. In the study, a group of healthy 79-year-olds was given the test. For those who went on to develop dementia within the next 4 years, the probability of a positive test at age 79 was found to be .17; that is, $p(\text{positive}|\text{dementia}) = .17$. For those who did not develop dementia within the next 4 years, the probability of a positive test was .008; that is, $p(\text{positive}|\text{no dementia}) = .008$.

(a) What is $p(\text{negative}|\text{dementia})$?

(b) What is $p(\text{negative}|\text{no dementia})$?

From the data given here, find the predictive accuracy of the test. That is, find the probability that a 79-year-old who takes the test will develop dementia within the next 4 years **(c)** if the test result is positive and **(d)** if the test result is negative. Bayes' rule (Appendix 4.3) can be used to answer parts (c) and (d); alternatively, see our answer to Exercise 4.5.

**4.7** For each of the following, state the null and alternative hypotheses.

(a) The recovery rate for a disease is known to be .25. A new drug is tried with a sample of people who have the disease in order to determine if the probability of recovering is increased.

(b) An experiment such as that described in Exercise 4.1 is conducted to provide evidence for the existence of ESP.

(c) In the ESP experiment of Exercise 4.1, a proponent of ESP (Claire Voyant?) claims that she will be successful on more than 60% of the trials.

**4.8** Use the binomial table (Appendix Table C.1) to find the rejection region in each of the following cases ($\pi$ is the population probability):

| Case | $H_0$ | $H_1$ | $n$ | $\alpha$ |
|------|-------|-------|-----|----------|
| (a) | $\pi = .25$ | $\pi > .25$ | 20 | .01 |
| (b) | $\pi = .25$ | $\pi > .25$ | 5 | .01 |
| (c) | $\pi = .25$ | $\pi < .25$ | 20 | .05 |
| (d) | $\pi = .5$ | $\pi \neq .5$ | 20 | .01 |

**4.9** In an experiment, data are collected such that, when a hypothesis test is conducted, the null hypothesis is rejected with $p = .003$.

(a) Can you conclude that $H_0$ is true with probability .003? Why or why not?

(b) Can you conclude that $H_1$ is true with probability .997? Why or why not?

**4.10** In each of the following, (i) State the null and alternative hypotheses; (ii) state $n$; and (iii) state the appropriate rejection region assuming $\alpha = .05$.

(a) An important quality in clinical psychologists is empathy, the ability to perceive others as they perceive themselves. In a simplified version of one investigation of empathy, 5 first-year graduate students were asked to rate a target individual on a particular trait as they believed the individual would rate himself or herself.

A 4-point scale was used. The question of interest was whether the raters would do better than chance.

(b) In a study of group problem solving, the investigator uses the solution rate for individuals in a previous study to predict that 40% of 3-person groups will reach the correct solution. Fifteen groups are run in the study. The question of interest is whether the theory is correct.

**4.11** Suppose a sign test is to be done with $H_0: \pi = .50$, $H_1: \pi < .50$, $n = 20$, and $\alpha = .060$.

(a) What is the rejection region?

(b) What is the power of the test if $\pi$ is actually .35?

(c) What would the rejection region be if the alternative hypothesis was nondirectional, that is, if $H_1: \pi \neq .50$ ?

(d) What is the power with an assumption of a two-tailed rejection region and an alternative of $\pi = .35$?

**4.12** Ten students took a course to improve reasoning skills. Before the course they took a pretest designed to measure reasoning ability, and after the course they took a posttest of equal difficulty. The results for the 10 students are as follows:

| Student | 1 | 2 | 3 | 4 | 5 | 6 | 7 | 8 | 9 | 10 |
|---|---|---|---|---|---|---|---|---|---|---|
| Pretest score | 25 | 27 | 28 | 31 | 29 | 30 | 32 | 21 | 25 | 20 |
| Posttest score | 28 | 29 | 33 | 36 | 32 | 34 | 31 | 18 | 32 | 25 |

The instructors of the course try to decide whether performance on the posttest is significantly different from performance on the pretest by looking at the signs of the difference scores, on the reasoning that if the course had no effect whatsoever, each student would be equally likely to get a plus or minus.

(a) State $H_0$ and $H_1$.

(b) Perform a sign test on these data ($\alpha = .06$) and report your conclusion.

(c) The researchers believe that if at least 75% of the population sampled improves on the posttest, the reasoning course is worth using more widely. They redo the analysis, testing the null hypothesis that $\pi = .75$ against the alternative that it is less than .75. Do you see a problem with this approach? Explain.

**4.13** A researcher studying memory performs an experiment that compares two strategies for remembering pairs of words. Twelve students are each given a number of sets of word pairs to learn. They learn half the sets by using rote memorization and the other half by using imagery. The order of conditions is counterbalanced appropriately. It is found that 9 students do better with the imagery strategy and 3 do better with rote memorization.

(a) Using the binomial distribution, test the null hypothesis that both strategies are equally effective using $\alpha = .05$. Write down the appropriate null and alternative hypothesis and describe the steps you take in testing the null hypothesis. What is the result of the significance test?

(b) What is the power of this test if the probability of doing better using the imagery strategy is actually .9 in the population (so that the probability of doing better using the rote strategy would be .1)?

**4.14**  Reconsider the study of empathy described in Exercise 4.10, part (a).
  **(a)** If the true probability of an empathetic response is .5, what is the power of the significance test in your answer to the earlier question?
  **(b)** What is meant by "true probability"?

**4.15**  Consider the hypothetical population that corresponds to a random variable $Y$ where $Y$ takes on each of the values 2, 4, 6, and 8 with probability .25.
  **(a)** What are the values of $E(Y)$ and var$(Y)$?
  **(b)** Samples consisting of two scores are drawn with replacement from this population, and the mean of each sample, $\overline{Y}$, is obtained. Complete the following table, generating the sampling distribution of $\overline{Y}$:

$$\overline{Y} = 2 \quad 3 \quad 4 \quad 5 \quad 6 \quad 7 \quad 8$$
$$p(\overline{Y}) = ?$$

  **(c)** Find $E(\overline{Y})$ and var$(\overline{Y})$ for the distribution in (b). How do these values relate to your answer to part (a)?

**4.16**  Given a parent population that consists of just five scores, 2, 4, 6, 8, and 10:
  **(a)** What is the mean, $\mu$, and the variance, $\sigma^2$, of the population?
  **(b)** Consider all the samples of two scores that can be selected with replacement from the population. Generate the sampling distribution. That is, state each possible value of the sample mean and its probability of occurrence.
  **(c)** Find the mean and variance of this sampling distribution.

**4.17**  It is known that, in a school with several thousand students, the mean IQ is 100. You select a random sample of 5 students. The first student you select has an IQ of 150. Given the above information, answer the following questions and justify your answers.
  **(a)** What is your best estimate of the mean IQ of the next 4 students you select?
  **(b)** What is your best estimate of the mean IQ of all 5 students in the sample?
  **(c)** Do either of your answers to (a) and (b) change if the sample size is increased to 10? If so, what is the nature of the change?

**4.18**  Suppose we draw all samples of size 2 *without replacement* from the population of five scores in Exercise 4.16.
  **(a)** Generate the sampling distribution of the mean.
  **(b)** What is the mean and variance of this sampling distribution?

# APPENDIX 4.1

## Understanding the Combinatorial Formula (Equation 4.15)

Consider five individuals who are running for positions on the city council; the two top vote getters will be elected. First consider all the possible assignments of individuals to ranks where the ranks are the position in the final vote. There are five possibilities for the first position in the vote count, and four possibilities for the second position (e.g., A could be followed by B, C, D, or E). The total number of sequences is (5)(4)(3)(2)(1) or 5! In general, there are $n!$ sequences of $n$ objects.

Suppose the question is, How many outcomes can this election have? Here, by "out-come" we mean patterns of election and nonelection. For example, A and B might be elected and C, D, and E fail to be elected. Notice that the order of finish within each of the two classes (elected and nonelected) is irrelevant. The following sequences are all equivalent in that they constitute the same outcome: A and B elected, and C, D, and E not elected:

| | |
|---|---|
| A,B/C,D,E | B,A/C,D,E |
| A,B/C,E,D | B,A/C,E,D |
| A,B/D,C,E | B,A/D,C,E |
| A,B/D,E,C | B,A/D,E,C |
| A,B/E,C,D | B,A/E,C,D |
| A,B/E,D,C | B,A/E,D,C |

Note that the two (2!) possible sequences of A and B, paired with the six (3!) possible combinations of C, D, and E, correspond to one **combination** (A and B elected; C, D, and E not elected). In general, $r!(n-r)!$ sequences will correspond to a single combination when $n$ items are split into one class with $r$ items and one with $n-r$ items. Therefore, the number of combinations is $n!/r!(n-r)!$ In our example, the number of ways the election can turn out is

$$\binom{5}{3} = \binom{5}{2} = \frac{5!}{2!3!} = \frac{120}{(2)(6)} = 10$$

In general, the number of different ways of selecting $r$ items from $n$ items is

$$\binom{n}{r} = \frac{n!}{r!(n-r)!}$$

## APPENDIX 4.2

## Sample Size and Violations of the Independence Assumption

Although violations of assumptions can often lead to erroneous inferences, the consequences can sometimes (though not always) be minimized by using large samples. The violation of the independence assumption in calculating probabilities provides a nice illustration of this point. Consider an urn containing five red and five black balls. We draw a marble three times from the urn. If we assume that the marble is replaced and the urn is thoroughly shaken after each draw, so that we have independence, according to the multiplication rule, the probability of drawing three red marbles is $p(R_1$ and $R_2$ and $R_3) = p(R)p(R)p(R) = (5/10)^3 = .125$. However, suppose that the drawn marble has not been replaced each time. This violates our assumption of independence. We can see this by the following analysis: If a red ball is drawn on trial 1, the probability of drawing a second red ball is now 4/9, whereas if a black ball is drawn on the first draw, the probability of a red on the second draw is 5/9. In fact, the probability of drawing a red (or black) ball on any trial depends on the sequence of preceding draws. So, although our assumption of independence leads us to conclude that $p(R_1 \text{ and } R_2 \text{ and } R_3) = .125$, the true probability is $p(R_1 \text{ and } R_2 \text{ and } R_3) = p(R_1)p(R_2|R_1)p(R_3|R_1 \text{ and } R_2) = (5/10)(4/9)(3/8) = .063$, roughly half the inferred probability.

Suppose the urn consists of 50 red and 50 black balls. Our assumption of independence leads us to the same probability, .125. This time, however, the true probability if we select without replacement is $p(R_1 \text{ and } R_2 \text{ and } R_3) = (50/100)(49/99)(48/98) = .121$, and the true and inferred probabilities are quite close; that is, the violation of the independence assumption did not lead to a very large error.

There are two implications of our examples that extend beyond simple probability calculations and violations of the independence assumption. First, violations may lead to very wrong conclusions, as the urn with 10 marbles attests. Second, the consequences of violations of assumptions may be less damaging when sample size is large. Neither of these statements will be true for every inferential procedure, but they are often true and therefore worth bearing in mind.

## APPENDIX 4.3

### Bayes' Rule

We defined conditional probability in Subsection 4.4.3. For any two events, $X$ and $Y$, there are two conditional probabilities: the probability of event $X$ given event $Y$,

$$p(X|Y) = \frac{p(X \text{ and } Y)}{p(Y)} \tag{4.19}$$

and the probability of $Y$ given $X$,

$$p(Y|X) = \frac{p(Y \text{ and } X)}{p(X)} \tag{4.20}$$

We also mentioned that people tend to confuse the opposite conditional probabilities, $p(X|Y)$ and $p(Y|X)$, and to confuse both of them with the joint probability $p(X \text{ and } Y)$. Bayes' rule provides a way of expressing one conditional probability in terms of the other. Because $p(Y \text{ and } X) = p(X \text{ and } Y)$, from Equations 4.19 and 4.20 we have

$$p(Y|X) = \frac{p(X|Y)p(Y)}{p(X)} \tag{4.21}$$

Also, because when $X$ occurs, $Y$ either occurs or does not occur, we can write

$$\begin{aligned} p(X) &= p(X \text{ and } Y) + p(X \text{ and } \tilde{Y}) \\ &= p(X|Y)p(Y) + p(X|\tilde{Y})p(\tilde{Y}) \end{aligned} \tag{4.22}$$

where $\tilde{Y}$ represents "not $Y$." Combining Equations 4.21 and 4.22, we can write Bayes' rule as

$$p(Y|X) = \frac{p(X|Y)p(Y)}{p(X|Y)p(Y) + p(X|\tilde{Y})p(\tilde{Y})}$$

$$= \left[ \frac{p(X|Y)}{p(X|Y)p(Y) + p(X|\tilde{Y})p(\tilde{Y})} \right] p(Y) \tag{4.23}$$

These equations tell us a number of useful things. From Equation 4.21, we see that $p(X|Y) = p(Y|X)$ only if $p(X) = p(Y)$. Equation 4.23 provides a way to find $p(Y|X)$, given that we know the opposite conditional probability, $p(X|Y)$, and have some appropriate additional information. Equation 4.23 can also be thought of as providing a way of updating probabilities in the light of additional information. Suppose you know $p(Y)$ and are now given information about $X$. Equation 4.23 gives you a way of updating your estimate of the probability of $Y$ given the information $X$, resulting in $p(Y|X)$. When the equation is used in this way, $p(Y)$ is called the **prior** probability and $p(Y|X)$ is called the **posterior** probability.

The importance of distinguishing between opposite conditional probabilities is illustrated by the following example. For diagnostic tests, one can distinguish between the predictive accuracy, $p(\text{disease}|\text{positive result})$, and the retrospective accuracy, $p(\text{positive result}|\text{disease})$, of the test. Consider the ELISA test that is used to detect the presence of HIV antibodies in samples of donated blood. The test is not completely accurate, and it can be wrong in two ways: it can give a positive result when there are no antibodies (false positive), and it can give a negative result when there actually are antibodies (false negative).

Although accuracy varies somewhat from laboratory to laboratory, when antibodies are present, the ELISA test gives a positive result with a probability of about .997 and a negative result (false negative) with a probability of about .003 (these two numbers have to add to 1). When antibodies are not present, ELISA gives a positive result (false positive) with a probability of about .015 and a negative result with a probability of .985. That is,

$$p(\text{correct positive}) = p(\text{positive}|\text{HIV}) = .997$$
$$p(\text{false negative}) = p(\text{negative}|\text{HIV}) = .003$$
$$p(\text{false positive}) = p(\text{positive}|\text{no HIV}) = .015$$
$$p(\text{correct negative}) = p(\text{negative}|\text{no HIV}) = .985$$

Suppose a blood sample is randomly selected from a population known to have an HIV infection rate of 2%. Before the blood sample is tested, $p(\text{HIV}) = .02$. Now suppose the ELISA test is performed on a sample and gives a positive result. What is the probability that the sample contains HIV antibodies given that we know the test was positive, $p(\text{HIV}|\text{positive})$?

According to Bayes' rule,

$$p(\text{HIV}|\text{positive}) = \left[ \frac{p(\text{positive}|\text{HIV})}{p(\text{positive}|\text{HIV})p(\text{HIV}) + p(\text{positive}|\text{no HIV})p(\text{no HIV})} \right] p(\text{HIV})$$

$$= \left[ \frac{(.997)}{(.997)(.02) + (.015)(.98)} \right] (.02) = 0.576$$

Note that whereas $p(\text{positive}|\text{HIV}) = .997$, $p(\text{HIV}|\text{positive})$ is only .576 given the information presented here. The two conditional probabilities would be equal only if the rate of HIV infection was 50%; that is, $p(\text{HIV}) = p(\text{no HIV})$.

Even though the probability of a positive test is much higher when antibodies are present than when they are not, with only a 2% infection rate, almost half the positive tests will come from samples that do not contain antibodies because there are so many more of them. To see this more clearly, suppose we tested 100,000 blood samples. Of the expected 2,000 samples with antibodies, we would expect $(.997)(2,000) = 1994$ positive tests. Of the expected 98,000 samples without antibodies, we would expect $(.015)(98,000) = 1,470$ positive tests. Therefore, of the $1,994 + 1,470 = 3,464$ positive tests, 1,994 would come from samples with HIV antibodies, so that $p(\text{HIV}|\text{positive}) = 1,994/3,464 = .576$. Bayes' rule is just a way of formalizing this type of reasoning.

# Chapter 5

## Estimation and Hypothesis Tests: The Normal Distribution

## 5.1 INTRODUCTION

In this chapter, we review many of the concepts introduced in Chapter 4, but with new procedures. For example, we again consider hypothesis tests and the errors associated with them. However, whereas we previously employed the binomial distribution as a basis for our inferences, we now use the normal distribution for that purpose.

The general outline of this chapter is as follows. Because the normal distribution is continuous, we begin by expanding on the brief statement in Chapter 4 about continuous distributions. Next, we consider the normal distribution and some reasons for its central role in much of statistical inference. Following that, we discuss sampling distributions (also introduced in Chapter 4), and we provide several illustrations. This enables us to address questions such as, What do the statistics of our data set tell us about the parameters of the population? What are the characteristics of a "good" estimate of a population parameter? How do we set limits on our estimate so that we have an interval within which we are reasonably confident the parameter falls? We then analyze several measures from the Seasons data set (*Seasons* folder on the CD) collected at the University of Massachusetts Medical School to illustrate interval estimation and hypothesis testing, basing probabilities on the normal distribution. In Chapter 6, we consider smaller samples and introduce additional concepts; our inferences there are based on the *t* distribution.

## 5.2 CONTINUOUS RANDOM VARIABLES

### 5.2.1 The Density Function

A **continuous random variable** is one that can take any value within a given interval. A common example in psychological research is response time, which theoretically takes on any value from zero to infinity. Of course, observed response times usually fall between some

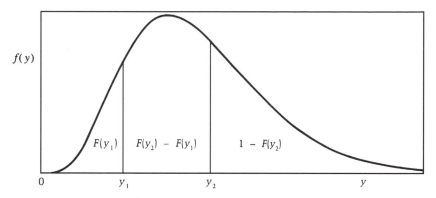

**Fig. 5.1** Example of a continuous distribution.

bounds such as 200 ms and 10 s. Even within such bounds, continuity is more theoretical than real because the best laboratory timing devices rarely record in units smaller than thousandths of a second. Not all the possible values of a continuous random variable can be recorded. Nevertheless, the concept is important because many inferential procedures assume continuously distributed random variables.

A logical problem arises when we try to deal with the probabilities of values of a continuous random variable. We can see this by considering a relatively crude clock, one capable of registering response times within a tenth of a second. Times longer than .95 but shorter than 1.05 s will be registered as 1 s. Suppose we now substitute a more accurate clock capable of measuring to the nearest hundredth of a second. Only response times in the interval from .995 to 1.005 s now will be registered as 1 s. Of course, there will be fewer times between .995 and 1.005 s than between .95 and 1.05 s; the probability of registering 1 s is lower with the more accurate clock. Extending the argument, we should find it apparent that the probability of a response time with a duration of *exactly* 1 s is essentially zero.

We may understand the issue better by considering Fig. 5.1. The distribution in the figure is continuous. The area segment between $y_1$ and $y_2$ represents the proportion of observations that falls between these two values. If $y_1$ and $y_2$ are placed closer together, the probability of a score between these two values becomes smaller. Theoretically, we could make that probability as close to zero as we desired by just reducing the separation between $y_1$ and $y_2$.

This line of reasoning suggests that it is not sensible to speak of the probability of some exact value of $Y$ when $Y$ is a continuous random variable. To distinguish among continuous random variables having different distributions, we need to represent the distribution by some function of $Y$ other than its probability. One function we can define is $F(y)$, the **cumulative probability function.** For example, $F(y_1)$ is the probability of getting a value less than $y_1$; in terms of Fig. 5.1, it is the area to the left of $y_1$. The area in the segment between $y_1$ and $y_2$ is $F(y_2) - F(y_1)$. This is the probability that $y$ takes on a value between $y_1$ and $y_2$. This probability forms the basis for another function often used to characterize a distribution: let

$$f(y) = [F(y_2) - F(y_1)]/[y_2 - y_1] \tag{5.1}$$

when $y_2 - y_1$ is very small. This ratio is the **probability density function** for continuous distributions. We can view $f(y)$ as the height of the curve at the value $y$. To see why this is so, realize that we are dividing an area (between $y_1$ and $y_2$) by its width ($y_2 - y_1$);

area/width = height. Even though the area gets increasingly close to zero as the width gets smaller, the ratio approaches a constant value that ordinarily is greater than zero. The value of $f(y)$ will depend on just what the value of $y$ is, but the formula for $f(y)$ will allow us to calculate the probability density for any $y$. In other words, if we had a formula for $f(y)$ for the distribution of Fig. 5.1, we could plug values of $y$ into it and plot the distribution in that figure.

In contrast to $f(y)$, $F(y)$ *is* a probability, a proportion of the curve up to the point $y$. It will be of primary interest in most inferential procedures; recall, for example, that the hypothesis test in Chapter 4 involved evaluating the area in the tails of the binomial distribution. Nevertheless, $f(y)$ is important because continuous probability distributions are characterized not by $p(y)$, the probability that the variable, $Y$, has the value $y$, but by $f(y)$, the probability density function. This function represents the limiting ratio obtained when the probability of a very small interval is divided by the width of that interval. The density function is different for different distributions and provides a way of characterizing a continuous distribution, just as Equation 4.16 characterizes the binomial distribution.

## 5.2.2 Expected Values

The expected value of a discrete random variable was defined in Chapter 4 as $E(Y) = \sum yp(y)$. Because $p(y)$ is essentially zero when $Y$ is continuously distributed, the definition for the continuous case involves the calculus. We present that definition, together with rules for defining expected values, in Appendix B at the back of the book. For now, it is only important to understand that the expected value of a population distribution is its average. We use the notation $E(Y)$, or the Greek letter mu ($\mu$), to indicate the mean of the population of $Y$ scores. The variance of the distribution is, as in discrete distributions, the average squared deviation of scores from the mean:

$$\sigma^2 = E(Y - \mu)^2 \tag{5.2}$$

This can also be written as (see Appendix B for the derivation)

$$\sigma^2 = E(Y - \mu)^2 = E(Y^2) - \mu^2 \tag{5.3}$$

## 5.3 THE NORMAL DISTRIBUTION

The assumption that scores are normally distributed plays a central role in many inferential procedures. In large part, this is because the derivations of other distributions such as the chi-square, $t$, and $F$ rest on that assumption. There is some justification for the assumption of normality; many random variables do have at least an approximately normal distribution. Consideration of an individual's score on a test such as the SAT may clarify why this is so. The score might be represented as

$$Y = \mu + \varepsilon \tag{5.4}$$

where $Y$ is the obtained score, $\mu$ is the mean of the population of test takers, and $\varepsilon$ (Greek letter epsilon) is a sum of "errors," positive and negative deviations from the population mean that are due to many random factors that affect the obtained performance. Such factors would include test-taking skills, amount of knowledge relevant to the test, amount and type of preparation, motivation, and the current state of alertness. There is an important theorem, the **central limit theorem**, which says that the sum of many such effects will be normally distributed. Therefore, if $\varepsilon$ can be viewed as a sum of many independent random effects, such as the ones we have indicated, it (and therefore $Y$) will tend to be normally distributed. Another consequence of the central limit theorem is that even if $Y$ is not normally distributed, the distribution of the sample mean will tend toward the normal as the sample size increases. Because of this, tests on means may be valid even when the data are not normally distributed.

Although the normal distribution is a reasonable approximation to the distribution of many variables, many others are not normally distributed. We cited published reviews of data sets in Chapter 2 and presented examples from the Royer and Seasons data sets that make this point. With this in mind, in several chapters, we consider the consequences of nonnormality and the alternatives to those classical statistical procedures that rest on the assumption of normality. Nevertheless, because of its central role in statistical inference, we devote much of this chapter to considering the normal distribution. The normal distribution also merits our consideration because it provides a relatively simple context within which to continue our presentation of inferential procedures such as interval estimation and hypothesis testing.

The normal distribution is characterized by its density function:

$$f(y) = \frac{1}{\sigma\sqrt{2\pi}} e^{-(y-\mu)^2/2\sigma^2} \tag{5.5}$$

where $\mu$ and $\sigma$ are the mean and standard deviation of the population and $\pi$ and $e$ are mathematical constants. The random variable $Y$ can take on any value between $-\infty$ and $+\infty$, and the curve is symmetric about its mean, $\mu$.

Infinitely many normal distributions are possible, one for each combination of mean and variance. However, inferences based on these normal distributions are aided by the fact that all of the possible normal distributions are related to a single distribution. This **standardized normal distribution** is obtained by subtracting the distribution mean from each score and dividing the difference by the distribution standard deviation; specifically, it is the distribution of the $z$ **score**:

$$z = \frac{Y - \mu}{\sigma} \tag{5.6}$$

As we showed in Chapter 2, the mean of the distribution of $z$ scores is zero and its standard deviation is one. This is true of any complete set of $z$ scores. In addition, if the variable $Y$ is normally distributed, the corresponding distribution of $z$ scores also will be normal. In this case, the variable $z$ is often referred to as a **standardized normal deviate**.

Standardization provides information about the relative position of an individual score, and it is very helpful. For example, assume a normally distributed population of scores with $\mu = 500$ and $\sigma = 15$. A value $Y$ of 525 would correspond to a $z$ score of 1.67; $z = (525 - 500)/15 = 1.67$. Turning to Appendix Table C.2, we find that $F(z) = .9525$ when $z$ is 1.67. $F(z)$ is the proportion of standardized scores less than $z$ in a normally distributed population of such scores. In this example, we may conclude that the score of 525 exceeds .9525 of the population. Of course, this conclusion may not be valid if our values of $\mu$ and $\sigma$ are incorrect or if $Y$ is not normally distributed.

Equation 5.6 defined a $z$ score as $(Y - \mu)/\sigma$. In fact, this is just a special case of a general formula for a $z$ score. Instead of $Y$, we could have any observed quantity; examples would be the sample mean, the difference between two sample means, or some other statistic. Call this $V$ for *observed variable*. To transform $V$ into a $z$ score, subtract its expected value from it. Then divide the difference by $\sigma_V$. To conceptualize $\sigma_V$, assume that many samples have been drawn from a population and a value of the statistic $V$ is calculated for each sample. The standard deviation of these values is $\sigma_V$, which we refer to as the **standard error of the sampling distribution** of $V$. Thus, a general formula for $z$ is

$$z_V = \frac{V - E(V)}{\sigma_V} \tag{5.7}$$

The variable $z_V$ will be normally distributed if (*and only if*) $V$ is normally distributed. In that case, we can assess the probability that $V$ exceeds some specified value by referring to Appendix Table C.2, which tables probabilities under the normal distribution. We illustrate the application of the table and Equation 5.7 for drawing inferences about means in Sections 5.5–5.8, but first we consider the general issue of estimating population parameters.

## 5.4 POINT ESTIMATES OF POPULATION PARAMETERS

The basic problem in using the statistics of a single study to draw inferences about population parameters is that the values of the statistics are not identical to those of the parameters they estimate. The sample mean will vary over independent replications of a study, as will all other statistics we can compute from a sample. This raises many questions, among which are the following: What does the sampling distribution of a given statistic look like? Can more than one statistic be used to estimate a particular population parameter? If so, how do we decide between these possible estimates? These are some of the issues we deal with in the following subsections.

### 5.4.1 What Is a Sampling Distribution?

The concept of a sampling distribution, introduced in Chapter 4, is implicit in statistical inference. For example, consider the following marketing study. Fifty individuals are sampled from some well-defined population and asked to rate a new brand of breakfast cereal. The ratings range from 1 ("strongly dislike") to 11 ("strongly like") with 6 as the neutral point. We might wish to test whether the mean of the sampled population is different from the midpoint of the scale, 6. The mean of the sampled ratings is 8.6. On one hand, if the sample mean changed little from one sample to another, this value would provide strong evidence against the hypothesis that $\mu = 6$. On the other hand, if the sample mean was quite variable over samples, then a sample value of 8.6 could well have occurred even when the population mean was 6. The critical point is that it is useful to picture many random replications of the 50-subject sampling experiment with each replication giving rise to a value of $\overline{Y}$. This hypothetical probability distribution of $\overline{Y}$ is called the sampling distribution of the mean for samples of size 50. As we can see from our example, knowing the properties of this sampling distribution may help us evaluate inferences made on the basis of a single sampled value of $\overline{Y}$. If we know that the sampling distribution has little variability, we have considerable confidence that our one estimate is close to the population parameter; conversely, we are less satisfied with an estimate when the variability of the sampling distribution is high. Furthermore, as we shall see, if we have knowledge of the shape of the sampling distribution—for example, that it can be described by the normal density function—we can draw various inferences about the parameter. Every statistic has a sampling distribution, because, each time a new sample is drawn from a population, the sample statistic is based on a new set of values. For now, we focus on the mean and variance of the sampling distribution of $\overline{Y}$. These two properties of the sampling distribution of the mean will prove useful to know when we study subsequent developments.

## 5.4.2 The Sampling Distribution of the Mean

We can never observe the sampling distribution of a statistic, because we never take a large number of samples from the same population. Fortunately, we can derive properties of the sampling distribution without actually drawing even one sample. This point may be clearer if we consider some examples.

***Sampling from a Population with Equiprobable Values.***   Assume that we toss a single die. As usual, the die has six sides, each with a different one of the values from 1 to 6. If this experiment is carried out many times, and the resulting number is recorded each time, we have the distribution displayed in Fig. 5.2(a); in the long run, each possible

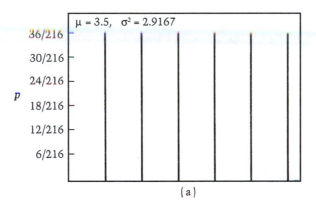

(a)

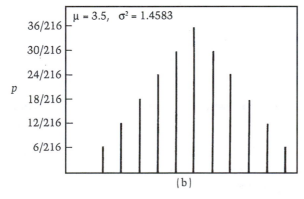

(b)

**Fig. 5.2**  (a) A discrete population distribution and (b) the sampling distribution of the mean for $n = 2$.

integer from 1 to 6 will occur on 1/6 of the trials, if we assume that the trial outcomes are independent and that each value has probability 1/6 of occurring.

Now let's change the experiment slightly so that a trial consists of tossing two dice. If we record the mean of the two numbers that come up on each of many trials, then—still assuming independence and equal probability of the six values for each die—the sampling distribution of the trial mean will be that depicted in Fig. 5.2(b). The distribution now has a definite peak. For example, the sample mean is more likely to equal 3.5 than 1 or 6. The reason for this follows from the multiplication rule for independent events. The mean will equal 1 only if both dice on a trial result in a 1, an event that occurs with probability $p = 1/6 \times 1/6$. In contrast, the mean will equal 3.5 if one die shows a 1 and the other shows a 6, or if either die has a 2 while the other shows a 5, or if the result is a 3 and a 4. Therefore, there are six outcomes that can yield a sum of 7, or a mean of 3.5. Each outcome has a probability of 1/36, so the probability of a mean of 3.5 is $6 \times 1/36$. If we were to further increase the number of dice tossed in each replication of the experiment, consistent with the central limit theorem, the resulting sampling distribution of the mean would be more closely approximated by the normal density function of Equation 5.5.

Figure 5.2(a) includes values of the population mean and variance, and Fig. 5.2(b) includes the mean and variance of the sampling distribution when two dice are thrown; that is, when $n = 2$. Note that the mean of the sampling distribution of the mean, $\mu_{\overline{Y}}$, is identical to the mean of the population, $\mu_Y$; that is,

$$\mu_{\overline{Y}} = E(\overline{Y}) = \mu_Y \tag{5.8}$$

In words, the expected, or average, value of the sample means equals the population mean. In Appendix 5.1, we show that Equation 5.8 must be true for all sampling distributions regardless of the shape of the population distribution. Also note that, when there are two scores (e.g., two dice are thrown) in the sample, the variance of the sample means, $\sigma_{\overline{Y}}^2$, is $1/2$ the population variance. In general, if the scores are independently distributed, $\sigma_{\overline{Y}}^2 = \sigma_Y^2/N$, where $N$ is the sample size (see Appendix 5.1 for examples). For example, in panel (a), the population variance is 2.917, and in panel (b), which depicts the sampling distribution of means of samples of size 2, the variance is 2.917/2, or 1.458. If we construct the sampling distribution of means for samples of size 10, the variance would be .2917.

In summary, (a) the average of many sample means will be the same as the population mean, and (b) the sample-to-sample variability of the sample mean will be less when $N$ is large. Therefore, a single sample mean is more likely to be close to the population mean it estimates when the sample is large than when it is small. This makes sense; the larger the sample, the more likely it is to resemble other samples from the same population and the closer its mean will be to those of other samples.

***Sampling from a More Representative Population Distribution.*** As Micceri (1989) and others have noted, distributions of many, perhaps most, variables measured by psychologists and educators are not normally distributed; they tend to be skewed, or have pronounced peaks, or marked gaps among values, or some combination of these. To consider a distribution with some of these characteristics, we created a distribution with mean, standard deviation, skewness, and kurtosis similar to that of the sample of Beck depression seasonal change (winter − spring) scores in the Seasons data set. This population distribution is displayed in Fig. 5.3(a). There is a slight asymmetry and a marked peak

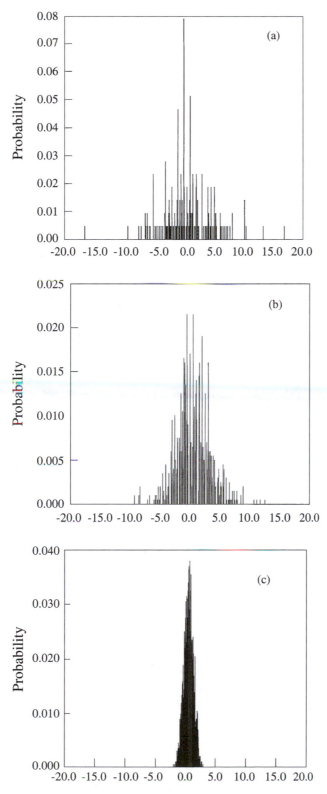

**Fig. 5.3** (a) A population distribution, and sampling distributions of the mean for (b) $n = 2$ and (c) $n = 25$.

near the mean, as well as several outliers, all characteristics present in the Seasons data. Another salient characteristic is the presence of several large gaps among the values. We drew 2,000 samples of size 2 from this population; the sampling distribution of the 2,000 means is displayed in panel (b). The sampling distribution is still slightly skewed to the right but there are now fewer gaps, and the peak and outliers are less prominent. Averaging the infrequent high scores with the more frequently occurring zero values has produced these effects. Panel (c) displays the sampling distribution of 2,000 means, each based on samples of 25 scores. Now we can see the central limit theorem at work; the gaps have been filled in and the distribution is beginning to look more like that described by the normal density function. Skewness and kurtosis values are quite close to the theoretical value of zero for the normal density function. This does not mean that a sample of size 25 will always suffice to yield a sampling distribution approximated by the normal density function. With a very skewed population distribution, a still larger $n$ would be required.

In summary, the following points should be kept in mind:

1. The sampling distribution of the mean approaches the normal distribution as sample size increases. This approach will be slower when the population distribution is not symmetric.
2. The mean of the sampling distribution of the mean equals the mean of the population. Because of this, we say that the sample mean is an **unbiased estimate** of the population mean. This and other properties of estimators are discussed in Subsection 5.4.3.
3. The variance of the sampling distribution of the mean of a sample of size $N$ equals the population variance divided by $N$. The square root of this variance is known as the **standard error of the mean** (*SEM*) and plays an important role in many inferential procedures.
4. Not all sampling distributions are described by the normal density function when $n$ is large. The central limit theorem applies only to linear combinations[1] of variables, and even then an $N$ so large as to be impractical may be required before the normal distribution is a good fit to the sampling distribution.

The mean of the sampling distribution and its standard deviation (the *SEM*) provide the key to understanding the estimation of population parameters. Having developed some basic ideas about sampling distributions, we can now consider the properties of estimators.

## 5.4.3 Some Properties of Estimators

An infinite number of possible estimators of any single population parameter exist. The population mean might, for example, be estimated by the sample mean, the sample median, or even the first score drawn from the sample. The choice of an estimator may seem intuitively obvious. Why not just estimate the population mean by the sample mean, the population variance by the sample variance, and so on? The answer is that the "obvious" estimator may not be a very good estimator. For example, suppose we wanted to estimate the height of the tallest man in a country; call this parameter $G$. Intuitively, we might use $g$, the tallest height in a sample of men, to estimate $G$. However, it is unlikely that the tallest man in the country will be included in a random sample of men; $g$ usually will be less than $G$. Why use an estimator that, on the average, will give a value that is systematically too small?

Sometimes intuition suggests competing choices for estimators. Suppose a sample is taken from a symmetrically distributed population of scores. Then, the population mean and median are identical. In that case, intuition leaves two choices for an estimator. Do we take the sample mean as the estimate? The sample median? Does it matter? Clearly, we need something more than intuition to guide us in estimating (and testing hypotheses about) population parameters. The decision about which quantity best estimates a particular population parameter can be made by establishing criteria for good estimators, and then examining how closely various estimators meet these criteria. The criteria that are generally agreed on are based on knowledge of the sampling distribution of the estimator. We consider three important criteria for selecting estimates in turn.

**Unbiasedness.**   Suppose we wish to estimate some population parameter, $\theta$ (theta); $\theta$ might be a mean, a variance, or any other quantity of interest. A statistic, $\hat{\theta}$, is calculated from a sampled set of $N$ scores. One desirable quantity for a good estimator is that the mean of its sampling distribution should equal the parameter being estimated; that is,

$$E(\hat{\theta}) = \theta \tag{5.9}$$

If Equation 5.9 holds for an estimator, the average of many independent estimates will equal the population parameter. Estimators conforming to Equation 5.9 are called **unbiased estimators**. One example of biased estimation is the use of the largest score in a sample ($g$) to estimate the largest score in a population ($G$). We noted earlier that $E(g) < G$. A second example is $S^2$ as an estimator of $\sigma^2$, where $S^2 = \sum(Y_l - \overline{Y})^2/N$. In Appendix B, we show that

$$E(s^2) = \sigma^2 \tag{5.10}$$

where $s^2 = \sum(Y - \overline{Y})^2/(N - 1)$. Therefore, because $S^2 = [(N - 1)/N)]s^2$,

$$E(S^2) = \left(\frac{N - 1}{N}\right)\sigma^2 \tag{5.11}$$

and $E(S^2) < \sigma^2$. In other words, $s^2$ is an unbiased estimator of the population variance but $S^2$ is a biased estimate. Equations 5.10 and 5.11 together convey this message: If we were to take many samples, and compute $S^2$ and $s^2$ each time, the average value of $S^2$ would be smaller than the population variance, $\sigma^2$, whereas the average value of $s^2$ would equal $\sigma^2$. Because $S^2$ tends to underestimate $\sigma^2$, we follow the usual practice of calculating $s^2$ rather than $S^2$ for the sample variance.

Bias, or the lack of it, cannot be the sole, or even the most important, property of an estimator. Suppose we took the first score, $Y_1$, in a sample as an estimate of $\mu$. If we drew many samples, discarded all but the first score each time, and then calculated the mean of the sampling distribution of $Y_1$, that mean would equal $\mu$. Thus, the first score (or, for that matter, any single score) drawn from a sample is an unbiased estimate of $\mu$. Nevertheless, this estimator does not feel right. For one thing, it violates our work ethic; collecting more data in the sample does not improve our estimate because we are discarding all but one score. This line of reasoning suggests the next criterion for an estimator.

**Consistency.**   Again, let $\hat{\theta}$ be some estimator of $\theta$. It is a **consistent estimator** of $\theta$ if its value is more likely to be close to $\theta$ as $N$ increases.[2] A familiar example of a consistent estimator is the sample mean; because $\sigma_{\overline{Y}}^2 = \sigma_Y^2/N$, it is evident that the sampling variability of $\overline{Y}$ about $\mu$ decreases as $N$ increases. Because inferences based on consistent estimators are more likely to be correct as sample size increases, consistency is an important property of an estimator. Nevertheless, even consistency combined with unbiasedness is not a sufficient basis for selecting between possible estimators of a parameter. A very important consideration in selecting an estimator of a parameter is its variance about the parameter being estimated. The less variable the sampling distribution is, the more likely it is that any single estimate will have a value close to that of the population parameter. We consider this criterion next.

**Relative Efficiency.**    Assume that a sample of size $n$ has been drawn from a symmetric population. In that case, the sample mean and median are both unbiased estimators of the population mean because the population mean and median have the same value in any symmetric distribution. Furthermore, both the sample mean and median are consistent estimates of $\mu$. They do differ in one respect, however. For any sample of size $n$, the sampling distributions of the median and mean will differ in their variances. Assume that many samples are drawn from a normally distributed population and the average squared deviations of the sample means and medians about $\mu$ are then calculated. For large samples, the variance of the sample means will be approximately 64% of the variance of the sample medians *when the population is normally distributed*. This smaller variance of the mean relative to that of the median is expressed by saying that the **relative efficiency** (RE) of the median to the mean as estimators of the mean of a normally distributed population is .64. Conversely, the relative efficiency of the mean to the median is 1/.64 or 157%. Because of its greater efficiency, the mean is preferred to the median as an estimator of the mean of a normally distributed population.

In general, assume a population parameter, $\theta$, which can be estimated by either of two statistics, $\hat{\theta}_1$ or $\hat{\theta}_2$. The RE of $\hat{\theta}_1$ to $\hat{\theta}_2$ is

$$\text{RE}_{1 \text{ to } 2} = \frac{E(\hat{\theta}_2 - \theta)^2}{E(\hat{\theta}_1 - \theta)^2} \tag{5.12}$$

Thus, RE is the ratio of two averages of squared deviations of estimates about the same population parameter. Note that this is a measure of the efficiency of the estimator in the denominator relative to that in the numerator.

## 5.4.4 Which Estimator?

Most of the estimation and hypothesis testing procedures presented in this and similar books, and in published journal articles, make use of the sample mean, $\overline{Y}$, and the unbiased variance estimate, $s^2$. If the population from which the data are drawn has a normal distribution, these statistics will be efficient relative to their competitors. Consequently, estimates based on them are more likely to be close to the true value of the parameter being estimated, and hypothesis tests are more likely to lead to correct inferences. But what if the population distribution is not normal? We address this question by considering the relative efficiencies of several estimators of $\mu$ for different population distributions.

To examine the efficiencies of various estimators, we used a computer to draw 2,000 random samples of size 20 from a normally distributed population that had $\mu = 0$ and $\sigma = 1$. Three statistics were calculated for each sample. These were the mean $(\overline{Y})$, the median

**TABLE 5.1**  VARIANCES AND REs OF THREE ESTIMATES OF A POPULATION MEAN

| Statistic | Normal Distribution | | Mixed-Normal Distribution | |
|---|---|---|---|---|
| | Variance | RE | Variance | RE |
| $\overline{Y}$ | .051 | 1.000 | .260 | 1.000 |
| $\tilde{Y}$ | .073 | 0.700 | .079 | 3.293 |
| $\overline{Y}_{.10}$ | .054 | 0.952 | .061 | 4.238 |

*Note.* RE for each statistic is its sampling variance relative to that of the sample mean.

$(\tilde{Y})$, and the 10% trimmed mean $(\overline{Y}_{.10})$; this last statistic is obtained by rank ordering the scores in the sample, discarding the highest and lowest 10% (the top and bottom two scores for $n = 20$), and then calculating the arithmetic mean. The variances of the 2,000 values of these three statistics are presented in the first column of Table 5.1. The column also contains the efficiencies of $\tilde{Y}$ and $\overline{Y}_{.10}$ relative to $\overline{Y}$; these are obtained by taking ratios of the variances, as in Equation 5.12. It appears that, when the population of scores is normal, the mean is the more efficient statistic and therefore the better estimator of the population mean. The situation is quite different if we make one change. Suppose 19 of the 20 scores in each sample were drawn from the population with $\mu = 0$ and $\sigma = 1$; however, one score is drawn from a population with $\mu - 0$ and $\sigma - 3$. This second population looks much like the first except that extreme scores are more likely. Think of the extreme scores as coming from those rare individuals who come to the experiment hung over from the previous night's party. Such scores might contribute to the variance, increasing the proportion of very small and very large scores. Variances of the three statistics and efficiencies relative to the mean are presented in the second column of Table 5.1. The interesting result here is that the variances of the sampling distributions of both the trimmed mean and the median are markedly less than that of the mean, and their relative efficiencies, accordingly, are greater.

Contrary to popular mythology and intuition, the sample mean is not always the best estimator of the population mean. Other estimators may be more efficient when the population is skewed, or is symmetric but with long tails, or when there are a few outlying scores, as in the example of Table 5.1. This happens because the sampling variance of the mean is increased much more than that of the trimmed mean or median by the inclusion of even a few extreme scores. The sampling procedure we used to generate the results in the second column of Table 5.1 is probably representative of what happens in many studies. The result of the occasional inclusion of a deviant score is that we have less confidence in our inferences about population parameters. In many cases, it might be best to use inferential procedures that do not rest on the sample mean. Several nonparametric, or distribution free, procedures are presented in this book; these procedures will be particularly useful in fairly simple designs, but less so in more complex designs involving several independent variables. Another possible approach implicit in the results presented in Table 5.1 is to trim data from the tails of sample distributions. This involves adjusting estimates of population variances. Hogg, Fisher, and Randles (1975) describe a *t* test based on trimming, and they compare it with several nonparametric tests (as well as with the standard *t* test) for distributions exhibiting various degrees of tail weight and skew. They also suggest ways of estimating tail weight and skew and of using these estimates to select the best hypothesis-testing procedure.

To sum up the developments of this section, we state that unbiasedness, consistency, and efficiency are desirable properties in the statistics we use in drawing inferences. The prevalent use of inferential procedures based on $\overline{Y}$ and $\sigma_{\overline{Y}}$ reflect the fact that these statistics are known to have these properties under many conditions. However, there will be situations in which we encounter distributions for which other statistics will be more efficient. The researcher should be aware of this and, when such situations arise, consider alternative approaches to inference.

## 5.5 INFERENCES ABOUT POPULATION MEANS: THE ONE-SAMPLE CASE

One of the measures available to us in the Seasons data set is the seasonal total cholesterol score (TC1, . . . , TC4). We calculated the average over the four seasons (the variable labeled TC) for those participants who had been measured in all four seasons (some participants missed at least one of the four sessions); the data are in the TC file in the *Seasons* folder on the CD; We decided to use our sample data to estimate the mean TC of a subpopulation—namely, male participants who were 50 years of age or older (Agegrps 3 and 4 in the file). Keeping in mind that doctors frequently recommend that TC levels should be at 200 or less, we also wanted to know if the subpopulation mean differed from this recommended maximum level. In what follows, we analyze the TC data of 117 male participants in Agegrps 3 and 4 to estimate the mean of a population of such individuals, and to test the null hypothesis that the population mean equals 200.

### 5.5.1 A First Look at the Data

Figure 5.4 presents a plot of the data obtained from SYSTAT's *t*-test module. Several aspects of the plot are of interest. First consider the box plot of the TC scores. Because the median approximately bisects the box, and the whiskers are of about equal length, it appears that the distribution is symmetric. Note that the median is clearly above the recommended maximum TC level of 200. Furthermore, the lower hinge is to the right of the dashed line that represents this level; therefore, at least 75% of the participants have TC scores above the recommended

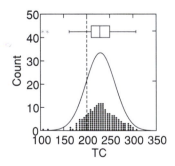

**Fig. 5.4** SYSTAT graphs of the TC data for 117 male subjects in Agegrps 3 and 4 (50 years of age or older in the Seasons study).

maximum. There is some good news, however. None of the participants have a TC level as high as 300, a value that would clearly signal a high-risk patient. Nevertheless, the box plot warns us that cholesterol level may be a problem for many of these patients. One other point should be noted in the box plot. There are two extreme outliers, TC scores close to 100. Such scores are very unusual, and it might be wise to consider rechecking these patients' cholesterol levels. One possibility that should be considered is that the scores represents clerical errors.

The **_dot plot_** at the bottom of the figure shows the distribution of scores in a very detailed manner. Our impression of symmetry is confirmed and we again see the low outliers. The curve above the dot plot is a normal distribution having the same mean and standard deviation as the sample of 117 TC scores. Because the normal distribution is symmetric, the peak is at its mean, and again we can see that the mean is clearly above the recommended maximum level indicated by the dashed line. Comparing the dot plot and the theoretical normal distribution, we find it evident that the distribution in the sample is flatter and "shorter tailed" than the normal distribution. In the following sections, in which we draw inferences from our data, we comment on the consequences of this apparent departure from normality.

To draw inferences about the population mean, based on the normal distribution, we need three pieces of information: the sample size ($N$), the sample mean ($\overline{Y}$), and the sample standard deviation ($s$). The mean and standard deviation are readily obtained from any statistical package; in this example, we have

$$N = 117, \overline{Y} = 224.684, s = 31.302$$

We are now ready to estimate an interval containing the population mean and to test whether that mean differs significantly from the theoretical value of 200. The calculations that follow are based on the normal probability distribution. Strictly speaking, because we do not *know* $\sigma$, but instead have estimated it, the $t$ distribution provides more valid inferences. However, because $N$ is large, there will be little difference between the results based on the normal and on the $t$ distributions. We have used the normal probability distribution in this chapter to postpone certain complexities in our discussion of inferences about means.

## 5.5.2 A Confidence Interval for $\mu$

The sample mean, $\overline{Y} = 224.684$, provides a **point estimate** of $\mu$, the population mean TC score for male participants older than 50 years. However, the sample mean might be close to the parameter, or it might be considerably in error. To have a sense of the reliability of such estimates, we calculate a **confidence interval** (CI), a pair of numbers that provide bounds for the parameter being estimated. How is this confidence interval calculated? What assumptions underlie the calculations? How should we interpret the results? We consider these questions next, first noting that although our example involves the confidence interval for the population mean, the interpretation of confidence intervals for other parameters is similar to that for the mean.

Assume that many samples of 117 TC scores are drawn from a population of such scores. Further assume that the mean of each sample is converted into a standardized ($z$) score by subtracting the mean of the sampling distribution and then dividing the remainder by the standard error of the mean. If the scores are independently sampled from a normal population, Appendix Table C.2 tells us that .95 of the sampled $z$ values will lie between $-1.96$ and $1.96$. That is,

$$p\left(-1.96 \leq \frac{\overline{Y} - \mu}{\sigma_{\overline{Y}}} \leq 1.96\right) = .95 \tag{5.13}$$

To obtain the bounds on $\mu$, consider each inequality separately. First, consider

$$-1.96 \leq (\overline{Y} - \mu)/\sigma_{\overline{Y}}$$

Solving for $\mu$, we have the upper bound:

$$\mu \leq \overline{Y} + 1.96\,\sigma_{\overline{Y}}$$

Similarly, we can solve for the lower bound. From the inequality

$$(\overline{Y} - \mu)/\sigma_{\overline{Y}} \leq 1.96$$

we arrive at

$$\overline{Y} - 1.96\,\sigma_{\overline{Y}} \leq \mu$$

Putting it all together, we have

$$p(\overline{Y} - 1.96\,\sigma_{\overline{Y}} \leq \mu \leq \overline{Y} + 1.96\,\sigma_{\overline{Y}}) = .95 \tag{5.14}$$

Recall that $\overline{Y} = 224.684$ and $s = 31.302$. Dividing $s$ by the square root of $N$, $\sqrt{117}$, we have 2.894, an estimate of $\sigma_{\overline{Y}}$. Because $N$ is large and the statistic $s$ is a consistent estimate of $\sigma$, we expect $s$ to be very close in value to $\sigma$, and we feel justified in using it in our calculations.[3] Substituting into Equation 5.14, we find that the upper and lower bounds of the .95 confidence interval for $\mu$ are

$$\text{CI} = \overline{Y} \pm 1.96\sigma_{\overline{Y}}$$
$$= 224.68 \pm 5.67$$
$$= 219.01, 230.36$$

Consistent with our earlier look at plots of the data, we see that the lower limit of the CI is above the recommended maximum TC of 200, but we are reasonably confident that the population mean is not dangerously high for the population of over-50 males from which we have sampled.

What exactly do these numerical limits mean? In what sense do we have .95 confidence that the population mean is contained within them? We cannot say that "the probability is .95 that $\mu$ lies between 219 and 230"; $\mu$ is either in this interval or it is not. Equation 5.14 tells us that, if we were to select many samples and find the .95 CI for each sample, in the long run, .95 of these intervals will contain $\mu$. Therefore, our confidence is .95 that the one interval calculated for this data set contains $\mu$.

Ideally, the narrower the interval, the better our estimate of $\mu$. Returning to Equation 5.14, we can see that the interval width depends on the *SE*; the smaller the variability of the sample mean, the smaller the distance between the two limits. If we recall that $\sigma_{\overline{Y}} = \sigma/\sqrt{N}$, it follows that the interval decreases with increased sample size and with decreased variability. In short, we can increase the precision of our estimate by doing whatever we can to reduce error variance, and by collecting as many observations as is practical. A third factor, not immediately obvious in Equation 5.14, also affects the width of the CI. We refer to the level of confidence. Turning to Appendix Table C.2, note that if the level of confidence is set at .90, rather than .95, the critical $z$ score is 1.645. Replacing 1.96 by 1.645, we see that the new limits are 219.92 and 229.44; we have less confidence but a slightly narrower interval. There is a trade-off between confidence and interval width.

### 5.5.3 A Test of the Null Hypothesis

We originally asked whether the mean of the sampled population of TC scores differed from a value of 200. The CI limits we just calculated suggest that the answer is that there is a significant difference. We reason as follows: First, we have .95 confidence that the computed interval, which has the limits 219 and 230, contains the population mean. Second, that interval does not contain 200. Thus, we conclude with .95 confidence that the population mean TC score differs from 200.

Most researchers tend not to calculate the CI and instead directly test whether the population mean equals the theoretical value. We believe this is a mistake because it addresses the question, Is the mean 200? rather than the question, What is the mean? Nevertheless, the practice of hypothesis testing is widespread. Furthermore, a presentation of the test permits us to again address related concepts such as Type 1 and Type 2 errors. For these reasons, we use the standardized normal distribution to test whether $\mu$ differs from 200. In Section 5.8, we present a more detailed discussion of the relation between the CI and the significance test.

As in our discussion of the binomial test in Chapter 4, we establish a null and alternative hypothesis; these are again designated $H_0$ and $H_1$, respectively. Letting $\mu_{TC}$ represent the mean of the population of TC scores, we can restate our two hypotheses. The null hypothesis is that $\mu = 200$ and is stated as

$$H_0: \mu_{TC} = 200$$

The alternative hypothesis is

$$H_1: \mu_{TC} \neq 200$$

Once these two hypotheses have been formulated, we need a test statistic whose value will enable us to decide between them. Recall the general form of the $z$ statistic (Equation 5.7):

$$z = \frac{V - E(V)}{\sigma_V}$$

To test whether the mean TC score is significantly different from 200, we replace $V$ by $\overline{Y}_{TC}$, $E(V)$ by the population mean specified by $H_0$ ($\mu_{hyp}$), and $\sigma_V$ by the *SEM*. Consequently, we have

$$z = \frac{\overline{Y}_{TC} - \mu_{hyp}}{\sigma/\sqrt{N}} \tag{5.15}$$

Substituting the values presented in Subsection 5.5.2, we have

$$z = \frac{224.684 - 200}{2.894} = 8.53$$

This $z$ score informs us that the observed mean is more than 8 standard deviation units above the hypothesized mean of 200.

Now that we have a numerical value for our test statistic, we must use it to decide between $H_0$ and $H_1$. We do this by determining those values of $z$ that would lead to rejection of $H_0$ in favor of $H_1$. Such values constitute the rejection region, the set of possible values of $z$ that are consistent with $H_1$ and very improbable if $H_0$ is assumed to be true. Indeed, those values are so improbable if $H_0$ is assumed that their occurrence leads us to reject $H_0$. An arbitrarily chosen value, $\alpha$ (alpha), defines exactly how unlikely "so unlikely" is. Traditionally, researchers have set $\alpha$ at .05. Again, we want very strong evidence against $H_0$ before we reject it.

Once we have decided on a value of $\alpha$, we can establish a rejection region for our study. Turning to Appendix Table C.2, we find that 1.96 is exceeded by .025 of the standardized normal curve; because the curve is symmetric, .025 of the area also lies below $-1.96$. Thus, if the null hypothesis is true, there is only a 5% probability of obtaining a value greater than 1.96 or less than $-1.96$. Equivalently, we reject $H_0$ if the absolute value of $z$, $|z|$, is greater than 1.96. Obviously, the $z$ we calculated is much larger than 1.96 and therefore we reject $H_0$.

To summarize the steps in testing the null hypothesis (also see Chapter 4):

1. State the null and alternative hypotheses.
2. Decide on a test statistic; in the present example, this is the $z$ defined by Equation 5.15.
3. Decide on a value of alpha and establish a rejection region. If $\alpha = .05$, and the test is two tailed, reject $H_0$ when $z > 1.96$ or $z < -1.96$.

The obtained value of the test statistic falls well into the rejection region, so we can reject the null hypothesis.

Alternatively, in step 3 we can find the $p$ value, the probability that the value of the test statistic would be at least as extreme as we actually obtained, if the null hypothesis was true. We reject the null hypothesis if $p \leq \alpha$. Here, the $p$ is $p(z > 8.53) + p(z < -8.53)$; to three decimal places, $p = .000$.

The two-tailed rejection region was selected because we tested whether cholesterol scores were significantly different from (lower or higher than) 200. However, we might have decided that low cholesterol scores are good and our interest lies only in detecting high values. In that case the rejection region would have been one tailed and the null and alternative hypotheses would have been

$$H_0: \mu_{TC} \leq 200 \text{ and } H_1: \mu_{TC} > 200$$

In this situation, if the population of scores is normally and independently distributed, and we know the population variance, we again can use the $z$ test. Accordingly, we turn to Appendix Table C.2. Again, the rejection region consists of those extreme values of $z$ that are consistent with the alternative hypothesis. In this case, because our test is one tailed, the region consists only of the largest 5% of the $z$ distribution. Therefore, again assuming that $\alpha = .05$, we will reject $H_0$ if the $z$ calculated from our data is greater than 1.645. Also, in the one-tailed case, the $p$ value is determined only by the part of the distribution beyond the value of the test statistic in the direction consistent with the alternative hypothesis.

The choice between one- and two-tailed tests should be made before the data are collected. To understand why, consider the following scenario. Suppose we originally hypothesized that the average TC score should be above 200; we have a one-tailed hypothesis.

However, upon examining the data, we find that the sample mean is less than 200, and we now restate our hypotheses, testing at the .05 level for a significant difference in the direction opposite to that originally hypothesized. Because we have already considered one tail (mean TC scores above 200) and are now considering the other tail (the mean is below 200), the true alpha level is greater than .05. In essence, we failed to find evidence for one alternative hypothesis at the .05 level and are now seeking evidence for a different alternative, again at the .05 level. But $2 \times .05 = .10$, the true alpha level in this approach to the data.

Why not always carry out the two-tailed test? Doing so would allow us to test for departures from the null hypothesis in both directions. The answer lies in a consideration of power. Note that the two-tailed test requires a cutoff of 1.96 in the right-hand tail of the normal distribution, whereas the one-tailed test requires a cutoff of 1.645. In other words, if the alternative hypothesis is that the population mean is greater than 200, the one-tailed test has a more lenient criterion for rejection. Therefore, as we illustrated with the binomial distribution of Chapter 4 (see Fig. 4.4), when the null hypothesis is true the one-tailed test has more power against that alternative. We illustrate the calculation of the power of the normal probability ($z$) test and discuss the factors affecting it in Section 5.7. Before doing this, and also before considering the assumptions underlying the inferences we have drawn, we first consider a second example.

## 5.6 INFERENCES ABOUT POPULATION MEANS: THE CORRELATED-SAMPLES CASE

A major purpose of the study carried out by researchers at the University of Massachusetts Medical School was to determine whether changes in the seasons affect various personality and physical attributes. One measure that might reflect seasonal change is the Beck depression score. We subtracted the depression score obtained in the spring from that obtained in the winter for each participant in the Seasons study who had scores in both seasons. Note that once we have carried out this subtraction and obtained the sample of change (or difference) scores, our data set resembles the set of TC scores. That is, although we began with two samples (winter and spring depression scores), we now have a single sample of change scores. We refer to this as the **correlated-scores case** because each participant contributes a winter and spring score to the change score, and the seasonal scores are therefore likely to be correlated. Correlated scores also are a product of research designs in which individuals are matched on some measure other than the dependent variable (such as IQ or a pretest score), or are paired because they are siblings (or, often, twins), and each member of the pair is randomly assigned to one of two treatments. In these cases, difference scores are obtained for each pair, and CI and significance test calculations reduce to those previously illustrated in Section 5.5. In summary, the correlated-scores case is really a one-sample case in which the sample consists of difference scores. Because one-sample data sets are most common in studies in which two measures are taken from one individual, or individuals are matched on the basis of some variable, we focus on the example of seasonal change scores for the rest of this chapter.

Summary statistics based on the seasonal Beck depression change scores are presented separately for male and female participants in Table 5.2. These statistics are based on the

**TABLE 5.2**  DEPRESSION SEASONAL CHANGE (WINTER – SPRING) SCORES BY GENDER

|                  | Males    | Females  |
|------------------|----------|----------|
| No. of cases     | 211      | 215      |
| Minimum          | −13.054  | −16.205  |
| Maximum          | 22.054   | 16.500   |
| Median           | 0.000    | 0.026    |
| Mean             | 0.028    | 0.557    |
| 95% CI upper      | 0.588    | 1.080    |
| 95% CI lower      | −0.532   | 0.033    |
| Std. error       | 0.284    | 0.266    |
| Standard dev.    | 4.126    | 3.897    |
| Variance         | 17.028   | 15.185   |
| Skewness(G1)     | 1.096    | 0.235    |
| *SE* skewness    | 0.167    | 0.166    |
| Kurtosis(G2)     | 6.527    | 2.548    |
| *SE* kurtosis    | 0.333    | 0.330    |

*Note.* Output is from SYSTAT.

difference between winter and spring (Beck_D1 − Beck_D2) scores in the Beck_D file in the *Seasons* folder of the CD. We first use these statistics to draw inferences about the mean difference in depression scores in the female population. In Section 5.10, we investigate the difference between the mean change scores of the male and female populations.

Substituting the values of the sample statistics for female participants into Equation 5.14 yields the following CI on the mean change score:

$$CI = .557 \pm (1.96)(.266)$$
$$= .036, 1.078$$

These values differ slightly from those in Table 5.2 (.033, 1.080). Because the population standard deviation is not known, but is estimated, our statistical package used critical values of the $t$ distribution rather than the normal. For large $N$, the normal and $t$ distributions are very similar. If we had substituted the critical value of $t$, 1.971, rather than 1.96 into Equation 5.14, we would have obtained the confidence limits shown in Table 5.2.

The CI limits we just calculated suggest that there is a significant change in depression scores between the winter and spring seasons because the computed interval, which has the limits .04 and 1.08, does not contain zero. Thus, we conclude with .95 confidence that there is an average difference in the population; the mean depression score is higher in the sampled population in the winter than in the spring. As in our analysis of cholesterol scores in Section 5.5, we can carry out a direct test. Letting $\mu_{change}$ represent the mean of the population of change scores, we can state two hypotheses. Assuming that we wish to determine whether there is a difference in either direction, the hypothesis that the mean change is zero is the null hypothesis,

$$H_0: \mu_{change} = 0$$

and the alternative hypothesis is

$$H_1: \mu_{\text{change}} \neq 0$$

Once these two hypotheses have been formulated, we need a test statistic whose value will enable us to decide between them. As in Section 5.5,

$$z = \frac{\overline{Y}_{\text{change}} - \mu_{\text{hyp}}}{\sigma_{\text{change}}/\sqrt{N}}$$

Substituting the mean and *SE* values from Table 5.2 yields

$$z = \frac{.557 - 0}{.266} = 2.09$$

Setting $\alpha = .05$, we see that the rejection region is $z \geq 1.96$ or $z \leq -1.96$, and we reject $H_0$ because $2.09 > 1.96$. Alternatively, we can find the *p* value, which is .036. Because .036 is less than our $\alpha$, .05, we again conclude that the null hypothesis is false. Note that $\mu_{\text{hyp}}$ need not be zero. The value of the mean under the null hypothesis might be some other value, perhaps based on a mathematical model or on norms gathered from a different population, or in previous studies.

## 5.7 THE POWER OF THE *Z* TEST

Following a data analysis in which the null hypothesis was not rejected, the researcher might wish to know what power the test had, given the effect size that was observed, the variability of the data, and the number of observations. Another investigator might wish to know what the power would be if a different sample size were used. In these cases, *N*, $\sigma$ (or an estimate), and a specific effect size (such as the mean change score) are known and power is to be determined. Ideally, researchers should take power into consideration when planning the experiment. We should ask what sample size we need to have a specified level of power to reject $H_0$, assuming a specific effect size. In this case, power, $\sigma$, and the effect size are known and *N* is to be determined. To reinforce our understanding of what power means, we provide an example of how power is calculated when *N*, $\sigma$, and a specific effect size are given. Further examples of the determination of power, and also of *N*, using software available on the Internet, are presented in Chapter 6.

### 5.7.1 Determining the Power of the Normal Probability (z) Test

Suppose that a research group in another part of the country wants to know if the effects of seasonal change on female depression scores can be replicated in their area, an area in which seasonal climates differ from those in Massachusetts. Further suppose that their sample of female participants is limited to an *N* of 100. This is a smaller sample than the 215 tested by the University of Massachusetts researchers. Would this second group of researchers have reasonable power to reject the null hypothesis if it is false? To answer this question, we have to follow the steps outlined in Chapter 4, in which power was discussed in the context of the binomial test. We first have to establish a specific alternative hypothesis. A reasonable approach is to test $H_0$ against an alternative suggested by the results of the Seasons study;

therefore, we will base the specific hypothesis, $H_A$, on the observed mean change, .557. Furthermore, we decide on a one-tailed test. Then, the null hypothesis is $H_0$: $\mu_{change} = 0$, the alternative hypothesis is $H_1$: $\mu_{change} > 0$, and the specific alternative is $H_A$: $\mu_{change} = .557$. Having specified a one-tailed test, and setting $\alpha = .05$, we see that the decision rule is to reject if $z \geq 1.645$.

The basic principles in computing power are the same that dictated the power calculations of Subsection 4.7.3. Simply put, we have to calculate the area in the rejection region assuming $H_A$ is true. We do this by finding the distance in *SE* units between the mean assuming the alternative hypothesis and the mean assuming the null hypothesis; the alternative value, $\mu_A$, is .557 and the value assuming the null hypothesis, $\mu_{hyp}$, is zero. If $\overline{Y}$ represents the mean change score, its *SE* is $\sigma_{\overline{Y}} = \sigma_{change}/\sqrt{N}$. In words, the *SEM* is the standard deviation of the change scores divided by the square root of the sample size. To find the numerical value of the *SE*, we assume that $\sigma_{change} = 3.897$, the value of $s_{change}$ obtained in the Seasons study. Therefore, $SE = 3.897/10$, or .390. Now we can calculate the distance in standardized error units between $\mu_A$ and $\mu_{hyp}$. This is a $z$ score; specifically,

$$z = (\mu_A - \mu_{hyp})/\sigma_{\overline{Y}}$$
$$= (.557 - 0)/.390$$
$$= 1.43$$

Figure 5.5 presents two standardized normal distributions. The left one is the distribution assuming the null hypothesis to be true; its mean is at zero, and the rejection region is the shaded area to the right of 1.645, the cutoff established when we selected our alpha level. The right distribution has its mean at $\mu_A$, which we have just shown is 1.429 standard errors to the right of $\mu_{hyp}$. The power of the hypothesis test is the proportion of this distribution to the right of $z = 1.645$ in this alternative distribution. To find the size of this area, do the following:

1. Find the $z$ score of the cutoff with respect to the alternative distribution. This value is .216, because if we look at the null distribution, the critical $z$ score is $1.645 - 1.429 = .216$ units greater than the $z$ of $\mu_A$.
2. Turn to Appendix Table C.2 and find the area to the right of a $z$ of .216.

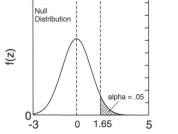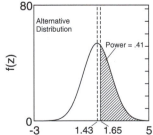

**Fig. 5.5** Null and alternative distributions (shaded areas are rejection regions).

In our example, this area, the power of our test, is approximately .41. In words, if the mean change score in the population is .557, the probability is .41 of rejecting the null hypothesis that the mean change is zero. The rather low value of power serves to remind us of the critical effect variability has on our inferences. Despite what many laboratory scientists would consider to be a large sample, power is low against what appears to be a reasonable alternative hypothesis (on the basis of an actual study), and, accordingly, the Type 2 error rate is very high. The situation is considerably better—though hardly great—in the actual study in which the $N$ was larger; power against the specific alternative ($\mu = .557$) with an $N$ of 215 instead of 100 is approximately .67. Clearly, the variability in Beck depression scores makes it difficult to achieve precise parameter estimates or high power to test hypotheses, even with relatively large samples.

## 5.7.2 Factors Affecting Power

In general, the power of a test depends on several factors, all of which have effects qualitatively similar to those noted in the discussion of power in Chapter 4. First, power increases as $\alpha$ increases because the increase in $\alpha$ requires an increase in the range of values included in the rejection region. If alpha is .10, the critical value in Fig. 5.5 shifts from 1.645 to 1.28, increasing the rejection region, and consequently the area above it. Second, power is affected by the nature of $H_0$ and $H_1$. If the statement of $H_1$ is two tailed, with alpha still at .05, the decision is to reject $H_0$ if $z < -1.96$ or $z > 1.96$. Then there would be two critical values in Fig. 5.5: $-1.96$ and $1.96$. Power would correspond to the areas to the right of 1.96 and to the left of $-1.96$ under the $H_A$ distribution. As we can see in Fig. 5.5, the probability of $z < -1.96$ if $H_A$ is true is essentially zero and the probability that $z > 1.96$ is less than the probability that $z > 1.645$. Therefore, the one-tailed test is more powerful against the specific alternative, $\mu_A = .557$. In contrast, this one-tailed test has virtually no power against specific alternatives of the form $\mu < \mu_{hyp}$, whereas the two-tailed test has the same probability of rejecting $H_0$ against these alternatives as against those of the form $\mu > \mu_{hyp}$.

Two other factors affecting power are the population variance and the sample size; reduced variance and larger $N$ yield smaller $SEM$s. As the $SEM$ decreases, the sample mean is more likely to be close to the true parameter value. As we have noted previously, a smaller $SEM$ increases the probability of getting values of $\overline{Y}$ close to the true population mean. Thus a decreased $SEM$ will result in increased power to reject false null hypotheses. Of course, as we pointed out in Chapter 4, most null hypotheses are false at least to some extent. We should always consider whether we have had so large an $N$ that an effect of little practical or theoretical importance was detected. This is one reason why CIs are an important part of our analyses. Very large sample sizes may sometimes result in rejection of a null hypothesis even if the effect is trivial, but the CI, by providing a bounded estimate of the effect, enables us to assess its importance.

We can influence variability by our choice of measures and experimental design, as well as by controlling extraneous factors that might contribute to chance variability. How large an $N$ we need will depend on the other factors noted herein and the power we want, as well as the smallest size effect we want to be able to reject with that power. A sample size of as little as 40 would have provided more than the .41 power we calculated if the variance of the depression scores had been smaller, or if $\mu_A$ had been larger than .557. Many sources, including books (e.g., Cohen, 1988; Kraemer & Thiemann, 1987), software, and

Web sites, enable researchers to calculate the sample size needed to have a certain level of power against a specified alternative. We illustrate this important application of power analyses in later chapters.

Examining power as a function of the variables that affect it has proven useful in deciding between alternative methods of analyses (e.g., Blair & Higgins, 1980, 1985; Levine & Dunlap, 1982; Ratcliff, 1993; Zimmerman & Zumbo, 1993). For example, power functions for different statistical tests can be compared. Assuming that the choice among tests is not dictated by some other factor (such as validity of assumptions, ease of calculations, or availability of tables), we should choose the test with the higher power function. We can also consider the effects of violations of assumptions on the power of various statistical tests. For example, the *t* test is more powerful than other tests that can be used to compare two experimental conditions when the population is normally distributed. However, when the population of scores is not normally distributed, other tests may achieve markedly more power, particularly when a one-tailed hypothesis is tested (Sawilosky & Blair, 1992). One way to increase power is to increase sample size when practical. Other approaches to the problem are discussed at various points in this book.

## 5.8 HYPOTHESIS TESTS AND CIs

The relation between CIs and significance tests may be understood by considering the usual decision rule for a two-tailed test: Assuming $\alpha = .05$, reject $H_0$ if

$$\frac{\overline{Y} - \mu_{\text{hyp}}}{\sigma_{\overline{Y}}} > 1.96 \quad \text{or} \quad \frac{\overline{Y} - \mu_{\text{hyp}}}{\sigma_{\overline{Y}}} < -1.96$$

Some algebra will show that this is equivalent to the following rule: Reject if

$$\mu_{\text{hyp}} < \overline{Y} - 1.96\,\sigma_{\overline{Y}} \quad \text{or} \quad \mu_{\text{hyp}} > \overline{Y} + 1.96\,\sigma_{\overline{Y}}$$

However, $\overline{Y} \pm 1.96\,\sigma_{\overline{Y}}$ are the lower and upper limits of a 95% CI on $\mu$. Therefore, the null hypothesis will be rejected at the .05 level (two tailed) whenever the hypothesized value of the population mean is less than the lower bound, or more than the upper bound of a .95 CI. In the example of the seasonal change in depression scores, the value zero was below the lower limit of the .95 CI, allowing us to reject at the .05 level of significance the hypothesis of no mean change in the sampled population. Note that the CI permits evaluation of any null hypothesis; any hypothesized parameter value that falls outside the limits will lead to rejection by a significance test (assuming $\alpha$ is set at one minus the confidence level), whereas null hypotheses that assert values of the parameter within the CI will not be rejected.

We can also use the confidence interval to carry out one-tailed tests of significance. We might wish to test the null hypothesis of no seasonal change in depression scores against the one-tailed alternative that the winter–spring difference is positive; that is, that the mean depression score for women is higher in winter than in spring. Then we test $H_0$: $\mu = 0$ against the directional alternative, $H_1$: $\mu > 0$. Because the lower bound of our .95 CI is .03, we have .975 confidence that the true population mean is greater than .03. Therefore, $H_0$: $\mu = 0$ is very unlikely to be true. In fact, we can reject this null hypothesis at the .025 level of significance. The .90 CI would provide a one-tailed test of the null hypothesis at the .05 level.

A CI provides several advantages over a hypothesis test. First, it provides a bounded estimate of the population parameter, thus focusing attention on the parameter value rather than on whether that parameter has one specific value. Second, the CI permits tests of all possible null hypotheses simultaneously, thus providing considerably more information than does the hypothesis test. Finally, the interval width provides information about the precision of the research. A significant result, coupled with a very narrow interval, may suggest that power was so great as to enable us to reject even a trivial effect. In contrast, a nonsignificant result, together with a wide interval, suggests that our experiment lacked precision, pointing to the need for either a less variable measure, more careful application of experimental procedures, or a larger sample. Note that the width of the interval is influenced by the same variables that influence power. The narrower the interval, the more powerful a test of any particular null hypothesis will be. The interval narrows, and power increases, as $N$ increases and as $s$ decreases. Furthermore, increasing $\alpha$ and decreasing confidence have parallel effects. An increase in $\alpha$ increases power at the cost of increasing the Type 1 error rate. There is a similar trade-off between confidence and the interval width; decreasing confidence yields a narrower interval providing a more precise estimate but with less confidence in that estimate.

## 5.9 VALIDITY OF ASSUMPTIONS

The validity of the inferences we made based on the calculations of CIs and hypothesis tests in the preceding sections rests on three assumptions. Scores are assumed to be independently and normally distributed, and they have a known standard deviation, $\sigma$. Let's consider each of these assumptions in turn.

### 5.9.1 The Independence Assumption

Two scores, $Y_i$ and $Y_j$, are independent of each other if the probability of any value of one is independent of the value of the other. In the notation of Chapter 4, we have two independent scores if $p(Y_j | Y_i) = p(Y_j)$. In simple English, two scores are independent if knowing one score provides no information about the value of any other score. If scores are not independently distributed, the CI for $\mu$ may be invalid and Type 1 error rates and power associated with tests of hypotheses about $\mu$ may be seriously affected. In the Seasons data, spring and winter scores are likely to be correlated, and therefore not independent; individuals who are more depressed than others in the winter will also tend to be so in the spring. For this reason we cannot treat the winter and spring samples as independent of each other. To draw inferences about the difference in the winter and spring mean depression scores, we created a single change score for each participant in the study. The statistics of Table 5.2 are based on these change scores. We have one such score for each participant in the study, and the assumption of independence is that these change scores are independently distributed. Assuming that our participants were randomly sampled, we can analyze the change scores to provide inferences about $\mu_{change}$, the mean of the population of change scores.

If we treat the spring and winter scores as though they were independent of each other, using calculations we present later in Section 5.10, we find that the CI will be overly wide and power will be low relative to that in the correct analysis. The reason for this is that the standard error of the difference between two independent means is larger than that for two dependent means.[4] By treating the means as independent when they are not, we use too large an estimate of the variability in this research design. In other research designs, the result of a failure to take nonindependence into account in the data analysis may result in an inflation of Type 1 error rate. Chapter 16 presents an example of this.

## 5.9.2 The Normality Assumption

The skewness and kurtosis values in Table 5.2 indicate that the change scores are not normally distributed. As we noted in Chapter 2, G1 is zero if the distribution is perfectly symmetric and G2 is zero for the normal distribution. In Table 5.2, both of these statistics have values more than twice as large as their *SE*s, providing evidence against the assumption that the population of change scores is normally distributed. However, the issue for any assumption is not whether it is correct but rather whether it is sufficiently close to being correct that our inferences are valid. In the example of the depression change scores, the departure from normality is not likely to be a problem. Our inferences are based on the assumption that the sampling distribution of the mean change score is normal. Even if the population of scores is not normal, because we have a large number (215) of change scores, the central limit theorem leads us to believe that the sampling distribution of the mean is approximately normal. This approach to normality with increasing sample size was illustrated in Fig. 4.3.

## 5.9.3 The Assumption of a Known Value of the Standard Deviation

Although we can be certain that the population standard deviation is not exactly 3.90, the value of $s$ in Table 5.2 is an unbiased estimate of $\sigma$, and a consistent one. Consistency implies that, as the sample grows larger, the probability increases that $s$ lies close to $\sigma$. Because our sample size is large, using the sample value of the standard deviation in our calculations in place of the true (unknown) population value should not present a problem. We have one indication that this is the case when we compare the CI calculated by using values from the table of normal probabilities with those in Table 5.2, which were based on the $t$ distribution. Although the $t$ distribution assumes an estimate of $\sigma$ rather than a known value, the two sets of results are very similar.

Further evidence that violations of the normality and known-$\sigma$ assumptions are not critical when $N$ is large derives from a computer study we conducted. We drew 2,000 samples of 215 scores each from the population distribution in Fig. 5.3(a) and we calculated a CI for each sample. This population was constructed to have characteristics—mean, standard deviation, skewness, and kurtosis—similar to those of the sample of 215 scores.[5] The proportion of samples yielding limits containing the mean of the simulated population was .945, quite close to the theoretical value of .95.[6] In terms of a two-tailed test of the null hypothesis, this implies a rejection rate of .055. The close approximation of confidence and significance values to the theoretical values indicates that even if the population is not normally distributed, the normal probability function and an estimate of the population standard deviation can provide adequate inferences when the sample is large. This raises the question of how large is large. There is no simple answer to this. Using the population of Fig. 5.3 and drawing samples of size 30 instead of 215, we found that .940 of the

2,000 CIs contained the true value of the population mean, a reasonable approximation to the theoretical value of .95. However, the results may not be quite as satisfactory with small samples if the population distribution deviates more markedly from normality.

## 5.10 COMPARING MEANS OF TWO INDEPENDENT POPULATIONS

In the developments thus far, we had winter and spring depression scores for 215 women who participated in the Seasons study. Because each participant's depression score was obtained twice, once in each season, the scores are correlated; $r = .819$. Consequently, although we estimated and tested the difference between two means, we did this by first obtaining a single distribution of scores. A change score was obtained for each participant and the mean of the population of change scores was estimated and submitted to a hypothesis test. In this section, we consider a comparison of two means that are based on two independently (and therefore uncorrelated) distributed sets of scores. Specifically, we consider the difference between the effect of the seasons on changes in male and female depression scores.

The change scores for the women and men are displayed in histograms in Fig. 5.6. The data are from the Beck_D file. Both distributions are roughly symmetric, although the right tail is more pronounced than the left, particularly in the sample of male scores. The other notable difference is that there are more scores in the male than in the female histogram in the two most frequent categories. These differences are reflected in Table 5.2, presented earlier in this chapter. The fact that the right tail extends further for the male histograms is consistent with the higher skewness value for men, and the difference in the peaks of the distributions is also reflected in the higher kurtosis value. The difference in the right tails is also reflected in the difference in the maximum values in the table. In summary, there are proportionately more men than women in the categories close to zero change, and also slightly more in the most extreme right tail. Turning to measures of location in Table 5.2, we find the medians either at zero (men) or very close to zero (women). The means present a somewhat different picture. The mean change score is higher for women, suggesting that, on the average, they exhibit a greater increase in depression scores from spring to winter. Also note that the male CI contains zero, whereas the lower limit of the female CI is greater than zero. Nevertheless, the difference in the mean change scores (.028 vs. .557) seems small relative to the range of scores. Before we draw any conclusions, it would be wise to consider this difference further.

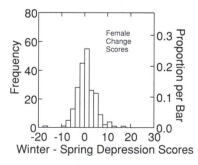 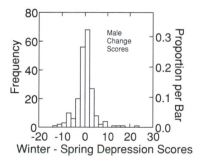

**Fig. 5.6**  Histograms of winter–spring Beck depression scores by gender.

### 5.10.1 Assumptions

We continue to use the normal distribution, tabled in Appendix Table C.2, as the basis for our inferences. More specifically, we assume two populations of independently and normally distributed depression change (winter–spring ) scores, one for men and one for women. We assume that many pairs of samples of size 211 (male) and 215 (female) are drawn at random from the two populations. Following each draw, the difference in the sample means, $\overline{Y}_F - \overline{Y}_M$, is computed. Consequently, we generate a sampling distribution of these differences. The mean and $SE$ of that sampling distribution are $\mu_F - \mu_M$. and $\sigma_{\overline{Y}_F - \overline{Y}_M}$, respectively.

### 5.10.2 Interval Estimation

Let $\mu_M$ and $\mu_F$ be the means for the male and female populations of change scores, respectively. We want a .95 CI that bounds $\mu_F - \mu_M$. It is helpful in deriving that interval to consider a general form for the CI:

$$p[V - 1.96\sigma_V \leq E(V) \leq V + 1.96\sigma_V] = .95 \tag{5.16}$$

To obtain the .95 CI for $\mu_F - \mu_M$, $V = \overline{Y}_F - \overline{Y}_M = .557 - .028 = .529$ and $E(V) = \mu_F - \mu_M$. All that remains is to calculate $\sigma_V$. We begin by noting that $\sigma_V$ is $\sigma_{\overline{Y}_F - \overline{Y}_M}$, and $\overline{Y}_F - \overline{Y}_M$ is a linear combination of the two means; that is,

$$\overline{Y}_F - \overline{Y}_M = (1)(\overline{Y}_F) + (-1)(\overline{Y}_M)$$

In Appendix 5.1 we prove that the variance of the difference between two independently distributed quantities is the sum of their variances. Therefore,

$$\sigma^2_{\overline{Y}_F - \overline{Y}_M} = \sigma^2_{\overline{Y}_F} + \sigma^2_{\overline{Y}_M} \tag{5.17}$$

Because the variance of the sampling distribution of the mean is the population variance divided by the sample size, the $SE$ of the sampling distribution of the difference between the means is

$$\sigma_{\overline{Y}_F - \overline{Y}_M} = \sqrt{\frac{\sigma^2_F}{n_F} + \frac{\sigma^2_M}{n_M}} \tag{5.18}$$

and, substituting the values in Table 5.2, we have

$$\sigma_{\overline{Y}_F - \overline{Y}_M} = \sqrt{\frac{17.028}{211} + \frac{15.185}{215}} = .389$$

We may now rewrite Equation 5.16 for the special case in which $V = \overline{Y}_F - \overline{Y}_M$:

$$p\left[(\overline{Y}_F - \overline{Y}_M) - 1.96\sqrt{\frac{\sigma^2_F}{n_F} + \frac{\sigma^2_M}{n_M}} \leq \mu_F - \mu_M \leq (\overline{Y}_F - \overline{Y}_M) + 1.96\sqrt{\frac{\sigma^2_F}{n_F} + \frac{\sigma^2_M}{n_M}}\right] = .95$$

$$\tag{5.19}$$

Substituting numerical values, the lower and upper limits for $\mu_F - \mu_M$ are

$$CI = (.557 - .028) \pm (1.96)(.389)$$
$$= .529 \pm .762$$
$$= -.23, 1.29.$$

We have .95 confidence that the difference between male and female seasonal change scores lies between $-.23$ and $1.29$. It appears that the difference between the male and female populations is quite small. In fact, the confidence interval is consistent with the hypothesis that there is no gender difference; $\mu_F - \mu_M = 0$ lies within the interval. As usual, that hypothesis can be tested directly and we consider such a test before further discussing the relation of seasonal depression score changes to gender.

## 5.10.3 The Hypothesis Test

Testing the null hypothesis that the difference between two population means has some specified value (usually, but not always, zero) follows directly from the developments of the preceding section. Equation 5.7 stated that

$$z = [V - E(V)]/\sigma_V$$

From our work with the CI for $\mu_F - \mu_M$, we know that $V = \overline{Y}_F - \overline{Y}_M = .557 - .028 = .529$, $E(V) = \mu_F - \mu_M$, and $\sigma_V = \sqrt{(\sigma_M^2/n_M) + (\sigma_F^2/n_F)} = .389$. To test $H_0$: $\mu_F - \mu_M = 0$ against the alternative $\mu_F - \mu_M \neq 0$, assuming the sampling distribution of the difference in means is normal, we form the decision rule: Reject $H_0$ if $|z| > 1.96$. Substituting numbers into Equation 5.7, we find that $z = (.529 - 0)/.389 = 1.36$. As the confidence limits indicated, $H_0$ cannot be rejected.

There is an apparent inconsistency if we consider results obtained when CIs (or significance tests) are calculated for the mean change scores for men and for women separately. This can be seen by reviewing the results obtained in each case. Table 5.3 presents the mean and $SE$ of the sampling distribution, and the upper and lower .95 confidence limits, for each of three variables: the mean change score for women, the mean change score for men, and the difference in gender means. Considering the confidence limits, we conclude that there is a significant seasonal change in mean depression scores for women, but not for men. This implies that there is a difference between the genders in their mean change scores. However, the confidence limits for the difference between genders fail to support the inference that the male and female populations differ in their mean change scores.

This pattern of results raises two issues. The first is why separate tests on the male and female samples indicate that the null hypothesis of no seasonal change can be rejected for women but not for men, whereas a test of the mean female change score minus the mean male change score does not support the hypothesis that the change is greater in the female population. The explanation lies in consideration of the $SE$s and the interval widths. Note that the $SE$ and the interval is larger for the sampling distribution of $\overline{Y}_F - \overline{Y}_M$ than for either $\overline{Y}_F$ or $\overline{Y}_M$. We have less precision in estimating the difference in population means than in estimating either population mean alone. Consistent with the wider interval for

**TABLE 5.3**   SUMMARY STATISTICS FOR SEASONAL CHANGE SCORES

| Sex | Mean | SE | CI Limit Lower | CI Limit Upper |
|-----|------|-----|-------|-------|
| Men | .028 | .284 | $-.532$ | 0.588 |
| Women | .557 | .266 | .033 | 1.080 |
| Gender diff. | .529 | .389 | $-.233$ | 1.291 |

$\mu_F - \mu_M$, hypothesis tests about the difference between population means have less power than hypothesis tests about either population mean alone.

The second issue raised by the results in Table 5.3 is, What can we conclude? Is the mean greater in the population of female seasonal change scores than in the male population, or isn't it? Problems similar to this frequently arise when the results of data analyses are reviewed, but there is no simple answer. In the current example, we calculated the power to reject a specific alternative based on the observed difference in change scores; despite the large sample sizes, power was low, approximately .27. Consequently, it is difficult to reach a conclusion about the difference in the mean change scores of the two populations. We have sufficient evidence to reject the null hypothesis of no seasonal change in the female population but lack sufficient evidence to reject the hypothesis of no difference between the mean changes of the male and female populations. However, given the lack of power in the test of the difference, there is no support for concluding that the population means are the same.

The medians of the change scores provide a complementary picture of the relation between the two distributions. Note that the male and female medians in Table 5.2, unlike the means, are quite similar and are both very close to zero. This suggests that there is no median change in either population. The significant mean change for women may reflect a few extreme positive change scores, a suggestion that is supported if we delete all eight (positive and negative) outliers from the data set; in that analysis, the mean change for women is no longer significant and both medians and means suggest no difference in location between the male and female populations. In this particular instance, the medians seem more representative of the data and we would be inclined to conclude that (a) the population midpoints (i.e., the medians) are close to zero and differ very little, if at all, and (b) the female mean change score, although significantly different from zero, probably reflects a few scores that are considerably more depressed in winter than in spring.

Although the statistics at hand, and the further calculations based on them, are important in influencing our conclusions, other factors may also play a role. Consider a situation in which behavioral changes are recorded with two drugs in order to select one to be marketed. Assume the change is significant with one drug and not with the other but, as in the direct comparison of men and women, there is no significant difference between the drugs. We might be inclined to market the drug that produced the significant change. However, the situation becomes more complicated if we stipulate that the other drug is considerably less expensive to manufacture. Should we go ahead with the more expensive drug if the direct comparison does not provide clear evidence of its superiority? This example suggests that there will be situations in which results will be inconclusive and further research, perhaps with larger samples or with less variable measures, may be desirable.

## 5.11 THE NORMAL APPROXIMATION TO THE BINOMIAL DISTRIBUTION

When we worked with the binomial distribution in Chapter 4, probabilities were obtained either by calculation or by using tables of the binomial distribution. However, for large samples this is unnecessary, because we can estimate binomial probabilities by using tables of the normal distribution. In Chapter 4, we showed that as the number of trials increased, the binomial distribution began to look more symmetric, and more like the normal distribution (see Fig. 4.3), particularly when the probability of a success on a trial, $p$, was .5. In fact,

**TABLE 5.4**  TAIL PROBABILITIES, $P(Y > y)$, FOR THE BINOMIAL
AND NORMAL DISTRIBUTIONS ($N = 20$)

| | $p = .5$ | | $p = .75$ | |
|---|---|---|---|---|
| $y$ | Binomial | Normal | Binomial | Normal |
| 11 | .4119 | .4115 | .9861 | .9899 |
| 12 | .2517 | .2512 | .9591 | .9646 |
| 13 | .1316 | .1318 | .8982 | .9016 |
| 14 | .0577 | .0588 | .7858 | .7807 |
| 15 | .0207 | .0221 | .6172 | .6019 |
| 16 | .0059 | .0070 | .4148 | .3981 |
| 17 | .0013 | .0018 | .2252 | .2193 |
| 18 | .0002 | .0004 | .0913 | .0984 |
| 19 | .0000 | .0001 | .0243 | .0354 |
| 20 | .0000 | .0000 | .0032 | .0101 |

with $N$ as small as 20, the normal distribution provides an excellent approximation to the tail probabilities of the binomial. To use the normal probability table of Appendix Table C.2 to get the probability of $y$ or more successes when $y$ is greater than $pN$, calculate

$$z = \frac{y - pN - .5}{\sqrt{p(1 - p)N}} \tag{5.20}$$

where $pN$ is the mean value of $Y$, $p(1-p)N$ is the variance of $Y$, and the .5 is a **correction for continuity.** The correction reflects the fact that the binomial is a discrete distribution. Suppose we want the probability of 15 or more successes in 20 trials. Because 15 may be viewed as representing a point from 14.5 to 15.5 along a continuum, we "correct" 15 by subtracting .5; in other words, we find the area above 14.5 under the normal distribution. If $y < pN$, we add the .5 instead of subtracting it.

Table 5.4 presents tail probabilities [$p(Y \geq y)$] when $N = 20$, $p = .5$ or .75, for values of $y$ from 11 to 20. The normal approximation to the binomial is almost perfect when $p = .5$ and it is fair when $p = .75$. The approximation when $p = .75$ can be improved by increasing $N$. A rough rule of thumb is that in order to use the normal approximation to the binomial, the smaller of $Np$ and $N(1 - p)$ should be greater than 5.

## 5.12 CONCLUDING REMARKS

We have focused on two inferential procedures—CIs and hypothesis tests. Once again, we emphasize that CIs have inherent advantages. They provide a bounded estimate of the size of the effect and, at the same time, a sense of the precision of the research through the width of the interval. Furthermore, the very act of defining a null and alternative hypothesis invites the researcher to make a dichotomous decision between the existence and nonexistence of an effect, whereas the establishment of a .95 interval should serve to remind us that the true effect may lie outside the calculated confidence limits. When hypothesis tests are carried out, they should be accompanied by power calculations. The result of such calculations can influence our view of hypothesis test (or CI) results. If power is low (or the interval is wide), we should be skeptical of nonsignificant results. If we have very high power (or a very narrow interval) to detect a very small effect, we should consider whether the effect is large enough to be of interest, or whether statistical significance merely reflects the collection of a very large amount of data. The minimum effect size of interest can be determined on the basis of practical considerations in applied research or, in more theoretical work, on the basis of theory and previous research. Determining this targeted effect size, and therefore the specific alternative hypothesis, has the healthy consequence of forcing us to think about how large an effect should be before it is important to detect. We have much more to say about effect sizes, and we provide some guidelines for what is small, medium, or large, in the next chapter.

The development of CIs and hypothesis tests has been carried out within the context of the normal distribution because it allowed us to focus on basic concepts and procedures, postponing certain complexities to subsequent chapters. In addition, although the normal density function rarely plays a direct role in data analyses, the assumption that the population is normally distributed underlies procedures based on the $t$, chi-square, and $F$ distributions. This assumption is rarely true; data distributions in psychological and educational research tend to be skewed, or have longer tails than the normal, or have gaps, or lumps. Several of these characteristics were present in the Seasons data analyzed in this chapter, and those data are quite typical of other psychometric measures in those respects. Despite this, distributions of means and of differences among means will tend to be symmetric, and with large samples will be adequately approximated by the normal density function. With smaller samples, the consequences of violating assumptions are not readily summarized because they depend on many factors—for example, the actual shape of the population distribution, the sample size, and whether the hypothesis test is one or two tailed. We consider these factors further in subsequent chapters.

A critically important concept that underlies all the developments in this chapter is that of the sampling distribution. We usually have a single data set from which to draw inferences about the population of scores that has been sampled. The concept of the sampling distribution provides a bridge between the sample and the population. Our interpretation of the confidence level is based on the proposition that if we were to take many random samples, computing a CI for each, the proportion of intervals containing the parameter of interest would match the nominal confidence level. Similarly, when we say that the probability of a Type 1 error is .05, we say in effect that *if the null hypothesis is true*, .05 of independent replications of the experiment will result in rejecting that hypothesis. Furthermore, our criteria for estimates of parameters—unbiasedness, consistency, and relative efficiency— are based on properties of the sampling distribution.

Another important concept introduced in this chapter was that of linear combinations, that is, weighted sums or averages. Linear combinations will play an important role in future developments. Appendix 5.1 notes several important linear combinations such as the mean, sum, and weighted average. Still another application is provided when the mean of one set of conditions is pitted against the mean of another set of conditions, as, for example, in a test of whether depression scores are higher in the fall and winter than they are in the spring and summer. These more general linear combinations, or contrasts, together with their CIs and significance tests, are introduced in Chapter 6, and they are discussed further in Chapters 9 and 10.

Although this chapter focused on the inferential process, exemplified by CIs and hypothesis tests based on the normal density function, it is important to be aware that we begin to have an understanding of the data by looking at the data. This means a consideration not just of arithmetic means but of the diverse statistics that summarize location, spread, and shape of the distribution. It means viewing graphs that provide an insight into the spread among scores, the shape of the distribution, and the presence or absence of outliers that may influence summary statistics. A close examination of the data will often influence the interpretation of the results, sometimes suggesting the presence of effects we did not anticipate, or influencing the interpretation of the results of inferential procedures. In some circumstances, it may indicate that critical assumptions have been violated, providing a spur to consider other forms of analysis, or to at least qualify conclusions. Researchers typically invest considerable thought, time, and effort into data collection. Too often, the data analysis involves considerably less thought, consisting of significance tests or correlation coefficients commonly calculated with similar data. The data analysis process should be more extensive, and we should begin it by tabulating and graphing more than means.

## KEY CONCEPTS

| | |
|---|---|
| continuous random variable | cumulative probability function |
| probability density function | central limit theorem |
| standardized normal distribution | $z$ score |
| standardized normal deviate | standard error |
| unbiased estimator | consistent estimator |
| relative efficiency | dot plot |
| point estimate | confidence interval |
| correlated scores | correction for continuity |

In some of the following problems, it may be helpful to consult Appendix 5.1, which contains equations for the variances of linear combinations.

## EXERCISES

5.1   A standard IQ test yields scores that are normally distributed with $\mu = 100$ and $\sigma = 15$. $Y$ is a randomly selected score on the test.

(a) (i) What is $p(Y > 130)$? (ii) $p(85 < Y < 145)$? (iii) $p(Y > 70)$? (iv) $p(70 < Y < 80)$?

(b) What scores define the middle 80% of the distribution?

(c) What is the 75th percentile (score such that it exceeds 75% of the scores)?

(d) What is the probability that a randomly selected student will have a score greater than 115?

(e) What is the probability that the mean IQ of a group of 10 randomly selected students will be greater than 115?

5.2   On a new test of logical reasoning, the mean and standard deviations for a population of men are $\mu = 170$ and $\sigma = 50$; for women, $\mu = 200$ and $\sigma = 60$.

(a) What is the probability that a randomly selected woman will have a score greater than 170?

**(b)** What is the probability that the mean of a group of 9 randomly sampled women will be greater than 170?

**(c)** Assume that many pairs of female ($F$) and male ($M$) scores are drawn from their respective populations and a difference score, $d = F - M$, is calculated for each pair. What is the mean and standard deviation of the population of such difference scores?

**(d)** What is the probability that a randomly selected woman will have a higher score than a randomly selected man? Note: $p(F > M) = p(F - M > 0)$.

**5.3** Assume that $X$ and $Y$ are independently and normally distributed variables. For $X$, $\mu = 30$ and $\sigma = 20$; for $Y$, $\mu = 20$ and $\sigma = 16$.

**(a)** What is the probability of sampling an $X$ score (i) <25? (ii) >60? (iii) between 15 and 40?

**(b)** What is $p(X > \mu_Y)$?

**(c)** Let $W = X + Y$. What is $p(W > 35)$?

**(d)** An individual's $X$ score is at the 85th percentile (i.e., it exceeds .85 of the population of $X$ scores); this person's $Y$ score is at the 30th percentile of the $Y$ distribution. What percentage of the population of $W$ scores does the individual's $W$ score exceed?

**5.4** Assume that a population of scores is uniformly distributed between 0 and 1. This means that $f(y)$ is a line bounded by 0 and 1 with a slope of zero and that $F(y)$, the probability of sampling a score less than $y$, equals $y$. For example, $p(Y < .8) = .8$. The mean and standard deviation of this uniformly distributed population are .5 and $1/\sqrt{12}$.

**(a)** (i) What is $p(Y < .6)$? (ii) What is the probability that a sample of two scores are both less than .6? Express your answer as a probability raised to a power. (iii) What is the probability that a sample of 20 scores are all less than .6?

**(b)** Assume we draw many samples of 20 scores and calculate the mean of each sample. Describe the shape of the sampling distribution. What is its mean and variance?

**(c)** On the basis of your answer to part (b), what is the probability that the mean of a sample of 20 scores is less than .6?

**(d)** Briefly state your justification for your approach to part (c). Would the same approach be appropriate in answering part (a), (iii)? Explain.

**5.5** In this problem, we use the normal probability distribution to test a hypothesis about a proportion.

A population of individuals has a disease, is treated, and symptoms are no longer present. However, .4 of this population suffers a reoccurrence of the symptoms within 1 year. A new drug developed to prevent recurrence of the disease is tried on a sample of 48 patients. We wish to determine whether the probability of failure (i.e., recurrence of symptoms) is less than .4.

**(a)** Let $\pi$ equal the probability of failure in the population sampled. State $H_0$ and $H_1$.

**(b)** Let $p$ equal the probability of failure in the sample. If $H_0$ is true, the mean of the sampling distribution of $p$ is $\pi = .4$ and its variance is $\pi(1 - \pi)/N$. In the study, only 12 of the 48 participants suffered a recurrence of symptoms after 1 year. Use the normal probability distribution to test the null hypothesis. State your conclusions.

(c) In part (b), we used the normal probability ($z$) table to test a hypothesis about a population probability. (i) What assumption about the sampling probability of $p$ is implied by this procedure? (ii) What justifies this assumption? (iii) Would the assumption of normality be as justifiable if the sample had only 10 people in it? Explain.

**5.6** A national survey of a large number of college students in 1983 yielded a mean "authoritarianism" score of 52.8 and a standard deviation of 10.5. For all practical purposes, we may view these as population parameters.

(a) Suppose we wish to examine whether authoritarian attitudes have increased in the years since the survey by examining a random sample of 50 students. State $H_0$, $H_1$, and the rejection region, assuming $\alpha = .05$.

(b) Assume that the mean of the sample of 50 scores is 56.0. Carry out the significance test and state your conclusion.

(c) Suppose the true population mean is now 57.00. What is the power of your significance test?

(d) On the basis of your sample (and assuming the population variance has stayed the same), what is the 95% CI for the current population mean of authoritarianism scores?

(e) In part (d) you found the 95% CI. What exactly *is* a 95% CI? What exactly is supposed to happen 95% of the time?

**5.7** We have a population in which $p(X = 0) = .8$ and $p(X = 1) = .2$. Let $\pi = p(X = 1)$ and $1 - \pi = p(X = 0)$.

(a) (i) Calculate the population mean, $\mu_X$, and variance, $\sigma_X$ [$E(X)$ and var($X$)]. Note that var($X$) = $E(X^2) - [E(X)]^2$ and $E(X) = (\pi)(1) + (1 - \pi)(0)$. (ii) Assume we draw samples of size 3 from this population. What would be the variance of the sampling distribution of the mean [var($\overline{X}$)]?

(b) Assume we draw samples of size 3. If we define the outcome of the experiment as a value of $Y$ where $Y = \sum X$, there are four possible outcomes. Complete the following table ($S^2$ is the sum of squares divided by $N$, whereas $s^2$ is the sum of squares divided by $N - 1$):

| $Y$ | $p(Y)$ | | $\overline{X}$ | $S^2_X$ | $S^2_{\overline{X}}$ | $s^2_{\overline{X}}$ |
|---|---|---|---|---|---|---|
| 0 | $.8^3$ | $= .512$ | | | | |
| 1 | $(3)(.8^2)(.2)$ | $= .384$ | | | | |
| 2 | $(3)(.8)(.2^2)$ | $= .096$ | | | | |
| 3 | $.2^3$ | $.008$ | | | | |

(c) Using the entries in this table, find (i) $E(Y)$, (ii) $E(\overline{X})$, (iii) $E(S^2_{\overline{X}})$, and (iv) $E(s^2_{\overline{X}})$.

(d) How do $E(Y)$ and $E(\overline{X})$ compare with the value of $E(X)$ obtained in part (a)?

(e) How do $E(S^2_{\overline{X}})$ and $E(s^2_{\overline{X}})$ compare with the value of var($\overline{X}$) obtained in part (a)?

(f) What do your answers to parts (d) and (e) say about which sample statistics are biased or unbiased estimators?

**5.8** Two random samples are available from a population with unknown mean. Sample 1 has $n_1$ scores and has a mean of $\overline{Y}_1$; sample 2 has $n_2$ scores and a mean of $\overline{Y}_2$.

Consider two possible estimates of the population mean, $\mu_Y$, that are based on both samples: One estimate is the unweighted mean of the sample means, UM, where

$$\text{UM} = \frac{\overline{Y}_1 + \overline{Y}_2}{2}$$

and the other is the weighted mean of the sample means, WM, where

$$\text{WM} = \frac{n_1 \overline{Y}_1 + n_2 \overline{Y}_2}{n_1 + n_2}$$

(a) Is UM an unbiased estimator of the population mean? Show why or why not.

(b) Is WM an unbiased estimator of the population mean? Show why or why not.

(c) Calculate the variance of UM if $n_1 = 20$ and $n_2 = 80$, and the population variance, $\sigma^2$, equals 4.

(d) Calculate the variance of WM if $n_1 = 20$ and $n_2 = 80$, and the population variance, $\sigma^2$, equals 4.

(e) Is UM or WM a better estimate of the population mean? Why?

(f) Are either UM or WM better estimators of the population mean than $\overline{Y}_1$ or $\overline{Y}_2$? Why?

**5.9** Assume that we have a treatment ($T$) and a control ($C$) population for which $\mu_T$ is larger than $\mu_C$. Assume that both populations are normally distributed and have the same variance, $\sigma^2$.

(a) Let $T$ and $C$ be randomly sampled scores from their respective populations. If $\mu_T$ is $.5\sigma$ larger than $\mu_C$, express the mean and variance of the sampling distribution of $T - C$ in terms of $\mu_T$, $\mu_C$, and $\sigma$.

(b) What is the probability that a randomly chosen score from the treatment population will be larger than a randomly chosen score from the control population? It is not necessary to have numerical values for $\mu_T$, $\mu_C$, and $\sigma$.

(c) Cohen (1988) has suggested that, for two independent groups, we should consider a medium-sized effect to correspond to a difference of $.5\sigma$ between the population means. He also suggested that small and large effects be considered to correspond to differences between the population means of $.2\sigma$ and $.8\sigma$, respectively. We have assumed a medium effect in parts (a) and (b). Given this assumption, (i) what is the probability that the mean of 9 randomly chosen scores from the treatment population will be larger than the mean of 9 randomly chosen scores from the control population? (ii) What is the probability if the effect is small?

**5.10** A population of voters consists of equal numbers of conservatives and liberals. Furthermore, .9 of the liberals prefer the Democratic candidate in the upcoming election, whereas only .3 of the conservatives prefer the Democratic candidate.

(a) What is $P_D$, the probability of sampling an individual from the entire population who prefers the Democratic candidate?

(b) The variance of a proportion $p$ is $p(1 - p)/N$ (see Appendix B for the proof). With this in mind, what is the variance of the sampling distribution of $p_D$, the proportion of Democratic voters in a sample of 50 individuals who are randomly selected from the population of voters?

(c) Suppose you are a pollster who knows that the population is equally divided between liberals and conservatives, but you do not know what the proportion of Democratic voters is. You sample 50 individuals with the constraint that 25 are liberals and 25 are conservatives; this is referred to as stratified sampling.

   (i) From the information presented at the start of this problem, what is the variance of the sampling distribution of $p_{D|L}$, the proportion of Democratic voters in a sample of 25 liberals?

   (ii) What is the variance of the sampling distribution of $p_{D|C}$, the proportion of Democratic voters in a sample of 25 conservatives?

   (iii) The proportion of Democrats in the stratified sample is $p_D = (1/2)(p_{D|L} + p_{D|C})$. What is the variance of the sampling distribution of $P$ when stratification is employed?

   (iv) In view of your answers to (b) and (c), (iii) discuss the effect of stratification.

**5.11** Following are summary statistics for the total cholesterol scores for the winter (TC1) and spring (TC2) seasons for men; the data are in the TC file of the *Seasons* folder on the CD.

$$\overline{Y}_1 = 224.059 \qquad \overline{Y}_2 = 218.818$$
$$s_1 = 40.793 \qquad s_2 = 40.113$$
$$r = .855 \qquad N = 220$$

  **(a)** Find the *SE* of the difference in the means. Reference to Appendix 5.1 may be helpful.

  **(b)** Using the result in part (a), find the .95 CI for the difference in the two seasonal means.

  **(c)** Carry out the $z$ test of the null hypothesis of no seasonal effect; $\alpha = .05$.

  **(d)** Using any statistical package you have, check your results for parts (b) and (c), using the data set in the TC file in the *Seasons* folder on your CD. Note: there will be a slight difference because most packages conduct a $t$ test, but with large $N$, as in this case, the results should be very close.

**5.12** **(a)** Assuming on the basis of the analysis of the winter–spring TC data (Exercise 5.11) that $\sigma_d = 20$, how large should $N$ be to have a .95 CI of 4 points?

  **(b)** Cohen (1988) has defined a standardized effect as $\overline{d}/s_d$, and he suggested that effects of .2, .5, and .8 be viewed as small, medium, and large, respectively. For the data in Exercise 5.11, the standardized effect $= 5.241/21.779 = .24$, a fairly small effect although quite significant. Assume that we wish to replicate our study of cholesterol differences in a new sample of men. If we have only 100 participants available, what is the power to detect a standardized effect of .24? Assume a one-tailed test with $\alpha = .05$.

**5.13** In the TC file, we created an educational level (EL) variable. If Schoolyr $= 1$, 2, or 3, EL $= 1$; if Schoolyr $= 4$, 5, or 6, EL $= 2$; and if Schoolyr $= 7$ or 8, EL $= 3$. El $= 1$ corresponds to individuals with a high school education or less, EL $= 2$ corresponds to those with education beyond high school but not including a bachelor's degree, and EL $= 3$ corresponds to those with a college or graduate school education.

  **(a)** Calculate a .95 CI for the difference in the TC population means between the EL $= 1$ and the EL $= 2$ groups. What can you conclude about this difference based on the CI?

  **(b)** Another researcher elsewhere in the country wishes to replicate the study of effects of education on cholesterol levels (TC). The researcher has two EL groups, each with 100 participants. Assuming that the each population has $\sigma = 40$, that

$\alpha = .05$, that the test is one-tailed, and that the investigator wants to detect a difference of at least 15 points, what power will the test have?

**5.14** We decide to run a study of cholesterol levels in a population of patients. On the basis of the TC data in the present Seasons study, we assume that the population standard deviation is 30. We would like power $= .80$ to detect effects of small size ($.2\sigma$ or 6 points) above a level of 200.

(a) What are the null and alternative hypotheses for the proposed study?

(b) What is the specific alternative hypothesis?

(c) How many participants should we recruit for our study? Assume $\alpha = .05$.

**5.15** In this exercise, we use the Mean_D variable in the Beck_D file of the *Seasons* folder. This is an average of the four seasonal depression scores for those individuals who were tested in all four seasons. Note that there are missing values of the Mean_D measure because not all individuals were tested in all four seasons.

(a) Tabulate descriptive statistics separately for male and female participants, and compare these. Then graph the two data sets any way you choose, relating characteristics of the plots to the statistics. Comment on location, spread, and shape.

(b) Using the statistics you obtained, construct a .95 CI for $\mu_F - \mu_M$ (female – male Beck_D population means) and decide whether the male and female means differ significantly at the .05 level. Do you think the assumption of normality is valid?

(c) Outlying scores frequently influence our conclusions. Considering the male and female data separately, what values would be outliers?

(d) Redo parts (a) and (b) with the outliers excluded. How does this affect the results in parts (a) and (b)? Note: If the file is sorted by sex and then by Mean_D, outliers can more easily be extracted.

---

## APPENDIX 5.1

---

### Linear Combinations

So far, we have considered the means and variances of individual distributions of scores. However, we are often interested in combinations of scores. For example, suppose each of the $N$ students in a class takes three tests. We refer to the score of the $i$th student on test 1 as $Y_{i1}$, where the first subscript indicates the student and the second indicates the test. Similarly, $Y_{i2}$ indicates the score of the $i$th student on test 2, and so on. From Chapter 2, we know that the mean of all the scores on test 1 is

$$\overline{Y}_{.1} = \frac{\sum\limits_{i=1}^{N} Y_{i1}}{N}$$

where the subscript ".1" indicates that we are averaging over all $N$ of the scores on test 1. The variance of the scores on test 1 is given by

$$s_1^2 = \frac{\sum\limits_{i=1}^{N} (Y_{i1} - \overline{Y}_{.1})^2}{N - 1}$$

Now suppose we want the total score on the three tests for each student. We can express this as $T_i = (+1)Y_{i1} + (+1)Y_{i2} + (+1)Y_{i3}$; or we might want the average score of the three tests, $\overline{Y}_{i.} = (+1/3)Y_{i1} + (+1/3)Y_{i2} + (+1/3)Y_{i3}$; here the subscript "$i.$" means that we are averaging over all the scores for the $i$th student. Perhaps we want the difference between test 1 and test 2. We can express this difference as $D_i = (+1)Y_{i1} + (-1)Y_{i2}$. Or the final grade, $G$, might give test 3 twice the weight of test 1 and test 2; $G_i = (+1)Y_{i1} + (+1)Y_{i2} + (+2)Y_{i3}$. All of the above are examples of **linear combinations** of the $Y$ variables. They are all of the form

$$L_i = w_1 Y_{i1} + w_2 Y_{i2} + \cdots + w_a Y_{ia} = \sum_{j=1}^{a} w_j Y_{ij} \tag{5.21}$$

or simply $L = \sum_j w_j Y_j$, where, for example, in the equation for $G$, the weights are $w_1 = 1$, $w_2 = 1$, and $w_3 = 2$. $L$ is referred to as a *linear* combination of the $Y$s because the $Y$s are not raised to a power other than 1 or multiplied by one another. The weights can be any numbers. As the preceding examples illustrate, they need not be equal to one another, or be integers, or even be positive numbers.

Many statistics of interest to researchers are linear combinations. For example, the mean of the three test scores for a student is a linear combination for which the weights each have the value 1/3. To draw inferences about the population parameters estimated by these statistics, we need to know something about means and standard deviations of linear combinations. Therefore, we consider these next.

## MEANS OF LINEAR COMBINATIONS

Suppose we want the mean of the $L_i$ scores in Equation 5.21. This is

$$\overline{L} = \frac{1}{N} \sum_{i=1}^{N} L_i$$

$$= \frac{1}{N} \sum_{i=1}^{N} \sum_{j=1}^{a} w_j Y_{ij}$$

$$= \sum_{j=1}^{a} w_j \left[ \frac{1}{N} \sum_{i=1}^{N} Y_{ij} \right] \tag{5.22}$$

$$= \sum_{j=1}^{a} w_j \overline{Y}_{.j}$$

The quantity $\overline{Y}_{.j}$ is the mean score on the $j$th variable. Equation 5.22 indicates that the mean of a set of linear combinations is a linear combination of the variable means.

The same general rule holds for a population of values of $L$. The mean of the population can be represented as the linear combination of the population means. That is,

$$\mu_L = E(L) = \sum_{j} w_j \mu_j \tag{5.23}$$

We can now show why Equation 5.11, $\mu_{\overline{Y}} = E(\overline{Y}) = \mu_Y$, must be true. We know that

$$\overline{Y} = \sum_i \frac{Y_i}{N} = \frac{1}{N} \sum_i (Y_1 + Y_2 + \cdots + Y_i + \cdots + Y_n)$$

so that

$$E(\overline{Y}) = \frac{1}{N} [E(Y_1) + E(Y_2) + \cdots + E(Y_n)]$$

$$= \frac{1}{N} [\mu_Y + \mu_Y + \cdots + \mu_Y]$$

because the expected value of each score drawn in a sample is the population mean. Therefore, $E(\overline{Y}) = (1/N)(N\mu_Y) = \mu_Y$.

# VARIANCES OF LINEAR COMBINATIONS

## The Variance of the Sums and Differences of Two Variables

The variance of a linear combination depends both on the variances of the variables and on the covariance of each pair of variables. To keep things as simple as possible, first consider two linear combinations of the variables $X$ and $Y - T = X + Y$ and $D = X - Y$. The variance of any linear combination, $L$, is $\sum_i (L_i - \overline{L})^2/(N - 1)$. Therefore, for the variance of $X + Y$,

$$s_{X+Y}^2 = \frac{1}{N-1} \sum_i (X_i + Y_i - \overline{X+Y})^2$$

But

$$\overline{X+Y} = \frac{1}{N} \sum_i (X_i + Y_i) = \overline{X} + \overline{Y}$$

Therefore,

$$s_{X+Y}^2 = \frac{1}{N-1} \sum_i (X_i + Y_i - \overline{X} - \overline{Y})^2$$

$$= \frac{1}{N-1} \sum_i \left[ (X_i - \overline{X}) + (Y_i - \overline{Y}) \right]^2$$

$$= \frac{1}{N-1} \sum_i \left[ (X_i - \overline{X})^2 + (Y_i - \overline{Y})^2 + 2(X_i - \overline{X})(Y_i - \overline{Y}) \right]$$

$$= s_X^2 + s_Y^2 + 2s_{XY}$$

where $s_{XY} = r_{XY}s_X s_Y$, the covariance of $X$ and $Y$ (see Equation 3.5). Therefore,

$$s_{X+Y}^2 = s_X^2 + s_Y^2 + 2r_{XY}s_X s_Y \tag{5.24}$$

The variance of the difference scores has a similar form:

$$s_{X-Y}^2 = s_X^2 + s_Y^2 - 2r_{XY}s_X s_Y \tag{5.25}$$

The only difference in the two expressions is in the sign of the covariance term. Note that if the two variables are uncorrelated, both the variance of $X + Y$ and $X - Y$ is $s_X^2 + s_Y^2$, the sum of the variances of $X$ and $Y$.

Analogous expressions hold when we consider population parameters. The population variances for $X + Y$ and $X - Y$ are

$$\sigma_{X+Y}^2 = \sigma_X^2 + \sigma_Y^2 + 2\rho_{XY}\sigma_X\sigma_Y \tag{5.26}$$

$$\sigma_{X-Y}^2 = \sigma_X^2 + \sigma_Y^2 - 2\rho_{XY}\sigma_X\sigma_Y \tag{5.27}$$

If $X$ and $Y$ are uncorrelated, the variances of both $X + Y$ and $X - Y$ are $\sigma_X^2 + \sigma_Y^2$. These expressions are important in the development of many inferential procedures.

## The General Case

So far we have considered the variances of only very simple linear combinations: only two variables have been considered, and they have either been added or subtracted. We now generalize to linear combinations that deal with any number of variables and weights other than $+1$ and $-1$. Consider $N$ individuals with $a$ scores each, $Y_1, Y_2, \ldots, Y_a$. The general linear combination was defined by Equation 5.21 and its mean by Equation 5.22. The variance of a linear combination, $L$, can be proven to be

$$s_L^2 = \sum_j w_j^2 s_j^2 + \sum_{i \neq i'} \sum_{j'} w_j w_{j'} r_{jj'} s_j s_{j'} \tag{5.28}$$

If the variables are independently distributed, all the covariance terms are all 0, and

$$s_L^2 = \sum_j w_j^2 s_j^2 \tag{5.29}$$

The corresponding expression for population parameters is

$$\sigma_L^2 = \sum_j w_j^2 \sigma_j^2 \tag{5.30}$$

Of particular interest is the variance of the sampling distribution of the mean. Assuming that the individual scores are independently distributed, and letting $w_i = 1/N$ for all $i$, we find that substitution into Equation 5.30 yields

$$\sigma_{\bar{Y}}^2 = \sum_{i=1}^{N} \left(\frac{1}{N}\right)^2 \sigma_i^2$$

Because the variance of the $i$th score over many samples is $\sigma^2$, the preceding equation becomes

$$\sigma_{\bar{Y}}^2 = \left(\frac{1}{N}\right)^2 \sum_{i=1}^{N} \sigma^2 = \frac{\sigma^2}{N} \tag{5.31}$$

# Chapter 6

## Estimation, Hypothesis Tests, and Effect Size: The *t* Distribution

## 6.1 INTRODUCTION

When we analyze large data sets, such as those used in Chapter 5, it makes little difference whether inferences are based on the normal or the *t* distribution. However, in many studies, either we have a more limited pool of participants available, or we are interested in a smaller subset of the entire sample. In those cases, the *t* distribution of Appendix Table C.3 is better suited to the data analysis. The primary purposes of this chapter are to review the applications of the *t* distribution and to discuss the standardized effect size, a measure of the importance of the difference between means that we observe in our sample.

To illustrate applications of the *t* distribution, we again consider only the winter and spring Beck depression scores in the Seasons data set. More precisely, we subtracted the score obtained in the spring from that obtained in the winter to get a single change score for each participant. Whereas in Chapter 5 we drew inferences from a large sample of such change scores, in this chapter we limit our attention to change scores of participants under 36 years of age. Seasonal Beck depression scores for both men (sex = 0) and women (sex = 1) in this age bracket can be found in the Under 36 file in the *Seasons* folder on the CD. Table 6.1 presents the depression change score (the Diff1_2 variable in the file) statistics for the male and female subgroups that meet this age criterion. A comparison with the values in Table 5.2 will reveal several differences, but our initial concern is with the differences in sample size. With over 200 participants, we felt justified in using the normal probability distribution as the basis for calculations of confidence intervals (CI) and for testing hypotheses. However, with the smaller number of participants, the standard error *(SE)* is likely to be considerably more in error as an estimate of the standard deviation of the sampling distribution of the mean, and, consequently, the denominator of the *z* statistic will be in error. The *t* statistic provides a remedy for this problem.

**TABLE 6.1**  STATISTICS FOR MALE AND FEMALE WINTER – SPRING
DEPRESSION CHANGE SCORES

| Gender = | Male | Female |
|---|---|---|
| N of cases | 30 | 32 |
| Minimum | −8.825 | −6.197 |
| Maximum | 15.838 | 8.009 |
| Median | −0.178 | 0.000 |
| Mean | −0.745 | 0.747 |
| 95% CI Upper | 0.901 | 2.093 |
| 95% CI Lower | −2.391 | −0.599 |
| Std. Error | 0.805 | 0.660 |
| Standard Dev | 4.407 | 3.733 |
| Variance | 19.425 | 13.934 |
| Skewness(G1) | 1.490 | 0.121 |
| *SE* Skewness | 0.427 | 0.414 |
| Kurtosis(G2) | 6.260 | −0.582 |
| *SE* Kurtosis | 0.833 | 0.809 |

*Note.* From SYSTAT for subjects under 36 years of age.

## 6.2 INFERENCES ABOUT A POPULATION MEAN

### 6.2.1 The *t* Statistic

In Chapter 5, we considered statistics that had the general form of $[V - E(V)]/\sigma_V$. In this expression, $V$ represents a statistic such as the sample mean, or the difference between two means, and $\sigma_V$ is the standard error (*SE*) of the sampling distribution of that statistic. If we assume that $\sigma_V$ is a constant, only the numerator of the ratio will vary over samples. If that numerator has a normally distributed sampling distribution, the ratio will be normally distributed. If $N$ is large, say more than 40, an estimate of $\sigma_V$ based on the data will vary only slightly across samples. In that case, we can replace $\sigma_V$ by the estimate and the normal distribution of Table C.2 will adequately approximate the sampling distribution of the test statistic. In many experiments, $N$ is not large; consequently, the estimate of the **standard error of the mean** (*SEM*) will vary considerably over samples. In that case, the distribution of the ratio is the *t* distribution tabled in Appendix C.3. The *t* distribution has a more prominent peak than the standardized normal, and more of the *t* distribution's area is in its tails. This means that if $\sigma$ is estimated from a relatively small sample, inferences based on the normal distribution may be in error.

The *t* statistic has the general definition

$$t = \frac{V - E(V)}{s_V} \tag{6.1}$$

where, as before, $V$ refers to an observed variable that estimates a population parameter, $E(V)$, and $s_V$ is the sample statistic that estimates the *SE* of the sampling distribution of $V$.

Note that the *t* statistic is identical to the *z* statistic, except that the denominator of Equation 6.1 is an estimate of the *SE* of *V* rather than its actual value. As in the case of *z*, it is assumed that scores are independently and normally distributed.

With respect to the example of Table 6.1, $E(V)$ is the mean of the population of change scores, $\mu_{change}$ (i.e., $\mu_{winter} - \mu_{spring}$), *V* is $\overline{Y}_{change}$, and $s_V$ is the sample standard deviation, $s_{change}$, divided by $\sqrt{N}$. There is no single *t* distribution; rather, there is a family of *t* distributions whose members look more like the normal distribution as sample size increases. This increasing approximation to the normal distribution with increasing *N* reflects the fact that $s_V$ is a consistent estimator of $\sigma_v$; as *N* increases, the statistic $s_V$ becomes less variable over samples and approaches the parameter, $\sigma_v$. For large *N*, values of *t* closely approximate the values of the standardized normal deviate, *z*.

It is a slight oversimplification to tie the shape of the *t* distribution to *N*. It really depends on something called **degrees of freedom**, frequently referred to as *df*. The concept of degrees of freedom is closely related to sample size but is not quite the same thing. Because degrees of freedom are a parameter of other distributions that play a role in data analysis, they deserve further discussion.

## 6.2.2 Degrees of Freedom (*df*) and the *t* Distribution

The degrees of freedom associated with any quantity are the number of *independent* observations on which that quantity is based. The meaning of "independent observations" is best illustrated by using an example. Suppose that we are asked to choose 10 numbers that sum to 50. We can freely choose any 9 values, but the 10th must be 50 minus the sum of the first 9. In this case, there are 10 scores, but because only 9 can be chosen independently, there are only 9 *df*. There is a restriction, because the numbers must sum to 50 and that costs us a "degree of freedom." The same situation occurs when we calculate a sample standard deviation. This requires us to subtract each score from the mean. However, as we noted in Chapter 2, the sum of deviations of all scores about their mean must be zero; that is, $\sum (Y - \overline{Y}) = 0$. Rewriting this last result, we have $\sum Y = N\overline{Y}$. If the sample mean is 5 and *N* is 10, we have the original example in which the sum of 10 scores must equal 50. Therefore, the sample standard deviation is based on $10 - 1$, or 9, *df*.

At this point, it looks as if the degrees of freedom are always just $N - 1$. That is true if the statistic of interest involves only one restriction. But suppose we draw two samples from some population; one sample is of size $n_1$ and the other of size $n_2$. We want to estimate the population variance but we have two estimates. As we will see shortly, these can be averaged; however, the point now is that there are two restrictions if two sample variances are computed: the sum of the $n_1$ scores in the first sample must equal $n_1\overline{Y}_1$ and the sum of the $n_2$ scores in the second sample must equal $n_2\overline{Y}_2$. There are $n_1 - 1$ *df* associated with the variance for the first sample and $n_2 - 1$ *df* associated with that for the second sample. The degrees of freedom associated with a statistic involving some combination of these two variances will be $df = (n_1 - 1) + (n_2 - 1) = n_1 + n_2 - 2$. The message is that the degrees, of freedom are not necessarily the number of scores minus 1. Rather

$df$ = number of independent observations

= total number of observations minus number of restrictions on those

observations

In the two-sample example, there are $n_1 + n_2$ observations and two restrictions caused by taking deviations about each of the sample means.

Turn again to Table C.3. Each row of the table corresponds to a different value of degrees of freedom. The columns are proportions of the sampling distribution of $t$ exceeding some cutoff; note that each column is headed by one-tailed and two-tailed proportions. Find the column corresponding to a one-tailed proportion of .025 (and a two-tailed proportion of .05) and the row for $df = 9$. The critical value in the cell is 2.262. This value is exceeded by .025 of the sampling distribution of $t$ when there are 9 $df$; .05 of the distribution is greater than 2.262 or less than $-2.262$. Now look down the same column to the row labeled "infinity." The critical value in that cell is 1.96. This means that the probability is .025 of exceeding 1.96, and the probability of $t > 1.96$ or $t < -1.96$ is .05. This is exactly the critical value in Table C.2, the normal probability table. In general, the critical value of $t$ decreases as the degrees of freedom increase, rapidly approaching the critical value in Table C.2 for the normal distribution. The reason for this is that our estimate of $\sigma$ exhibits less sampling variability as $N$ increases. In short, as $N$ increases, $s$ more closely approximates $\sigma$, and therefore the distribution of $t$ more closely approximates that of a normally distributed $z$ score. In general, Table C.3 will provide more accurate inferences than Table C.2, although there is little difference when sample sizes are large. For example, on the basis of the normal distribution of Table C.2, we calculated the .95 confidence limits for the mean change score for the 215 female participants to be .035 and .078. If we use the $t$ distribution on 214 $df$ instead of the normal distribution, the critical value is 1.971 instead of 1.96, the value in Table C.2—and the confidence limits are .033 and .080.

## 6.2.3 Confidence Intervals and $t$ Tests: The One-Sample Case

We first consider a single sample of scores. Specifically, we draw inferences based on the sample of seasonal depression change scores for women under the age of 36 years in the Seasons study. Before considering the confidence interval (CI) for the mean change score, and the test of the null hypothesis of no change, look at the plots of the data in Fig. 6.1. Both the box and dot plots suggest that the data distribution is not symmetric; in addition, the dot plot appears flat, in contrast to the theoretical normal distribution having the same mean and standard deviation. Looking back at Table 6.1, neither the skewness (G1) nor the kurtosis (G2) values are very different from the value of zero that would be appropriate for normally distributed data; neither statistic exceeds its $SE$ by a ratio of 2 or more. This suggests that the departure from normality may not be a problem. We discuss the possible consequences of nonnormality later in this chapter.

Let's turn now to the statistics presented in Fig. 6.1. In this one-sample case, confidence intervals (CIs) and significance tests follow the procedures developed in Chapter 5. The only difference is that critical values are obtained from the $t$, rather than the $z$, distribution. The general form of the CI in the one-sample case is

$$p\left(\overline{Y} - t_{N-1,\,\alpha/2}\frac{s}{\sqrt{N}} \leq \mu \leq \overline{Y} + t_{N-1,\,\alpha/2}\frac{s}{\sqrt{N}}\right) = 1 - \alpha \qquad (6.2)$$

where $t_{N-1,\alpha/2}$ is the value of $t$ such that $\alpha/2$ of the distribution on $N - 1$ $df$ lies to the right of it. In the example of seasonal changes in Beck depression scores, with 32 female participants under the age of 36, $\mu$ represents the mean of the population of change scores,

Data for the following results were selected according to:

(AGE < 36) AND (*SEX* = "FEMALE")

One-sample *t* test of DIFF with 32 cases;   Ho: Mean =    0.000

Mean =    0.747         95.00% CI =    −0.599 to    2.093

SD =    3.733                          *t* =    1.132

*df* =   31   Prob =    0.266

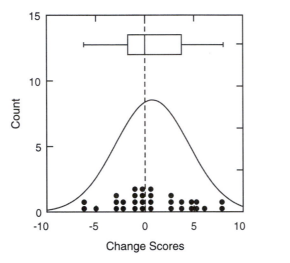

Fig. 6.1  Data plots, CI, and *t*-test results based
on the female data of Table 6.1 (from SYSTAT).

*df* = 31, and the critical *t* value for a .95 CI is approximately 2.04 (by linear interpolation between 2.042 and 2.021). Substituting the sample mean and *SE* of the change scores into Equation 6.2, we have

$$p[.747 - (2.04)(.660) \leq \mu_{\text{change}} \leq .747 + (2.04)(.660)] = .95$$

Completing the calculations, we obtain the values reported in Table 6.1 and Fig. 6.1: −.599 and 2.093.

Note that the CI for the sample of women under 36 years of age is much wider than that obtained for the entire sample of 215 women (those limits were .033 and 1.080). One contributing factor to the reduced precision of the estimate is the slightly larger value of *s* in the analysis of the smaller data set. A more important factor is the difference in sample sizes, which affects the CIs in two ways. First, with the smaller sample, the critical *t* value is 2.04, rather than 1.97. Second, and more important, *s* is divided by 14.663 (the square root of 215) in the earlier analysis, but by only 5.657 (the square root of 32) in the analysis of the under-36 group. Therefore, even if *s* were the same in both analyses, the *SE* would be roughly 2.6 times larger for the smaller sample and the CI would be that much larger. To improve our estimates of population parameters, we need to do all we can to reduce variability and we should collect as much data as is practical.

Because the CI contains zero, it should be evident that a two-tailed test of $H_0$: $\mu_{change} = 0$ at the .05 level will not yield a significant result. The direct test parallels that developed in Chapter 5; the only difference is that we replace $\sigma$ by an estimate, $s$. We calculate

$$t_{N-1} = \frac{\overline{Y} - \mu_{hyp}}{s/\sqrt{N}} \tag{6.3}$$

and, if the test is two tailed, reject $H_0$ if $|t| > t_{N-1,\alpha/2}$. In the present example, $\mu_{hyp} = 0$, and the denominator is .660, the $SE$ in Table 6.1. Therefore, $t = .747/.660 = 1.132$, which is much smaller than the critical value of 2.040. As reported in Fig. 6.1, the actual probability of obtaining a value of $t$ greater than 1.132 or less than $-1.132$, *assuming $H_0$ to be true*, is .266 . If we were to reject $H_0$ based on these results, there would be more than a one in four chance of making a Type 1 error. Generally, researchers consider these rather poor odds.

## 6.3 THE STANDARDIZED EFFECT SIZE

The mean difference between the winter and spring depression scores for women under the age of 36 years (.747) is the **raw effect size**. The advantage of the raw effect size is that the units are on the original scale and therefore differences on that scale should be meaningful to the researcher. The disadvantage of the raw effect size is that it *is* on the original scale, and therefore it is difficult to make comparisons with results of research conducted with other measures of depression. When comparing effects across groups, even if the same measurement scale is used, we often find it useful to consider differences between group means relative to their standard deviations. Because differences in variability and in the measurement scale make direct comparisons of raw effect sizes difficult to interpret, the **standardized effect size**,[1] $E_S$, is an important tool for understanding our data. It provides a scale-free index of the importance of the effect, something that neither CIs on the raw effect nor the $p$ values associated with $t$ tests can do. Furthermore, $E_S$ provides information required for estimates of the power of hypotheses tests, and it is used in meta-analyses, analyses that combine results from several studies. The CI for the raw effect, although informative, is dependent on the original measurement scale. The $p$ value is often misleading; very small effects, perhaps unimportant in any practical sense, may be very significant because the sample sizes are large and, conversely, large effects may not be significant because the sample was too small, or variability too great, to have much power. It is not unusual to find in a comparison of two variables that the one associated with the lower $p$ value actually has the smaller effect size.

There is increasing agreement that measures of effect size are important and should be reported along with the results of statistical tests. A growing number of journals now explicitly require that measures of effect size be reported, and the fifth edition of the *Publication Manual of the American Psychological Association* (2001) states, "For the reader to fully understand the importance of your findings, it is almost always necessary to include some index of effect size or strength of relationship in your Results section" (p. 25).

### 6.3.1 Estimating $E_S$

In the example of the seasonal change scores, we conceived of a population of such scores. The mean of that population is $\mu_{change}$ (i.e., $\mu_{winter} - \mu_{spring}$), and its standard deviation is

$\sigma_{\text{change}}$. In general in the one-sample case, we define the standardized effect score as

$$E_S = (\mu_A - \mu_{\text{hyp}})/\sigma \tag{6.4}$$

where $\mu_{\text{hyp}}$ is the mean assuming the null hypothesis to be true and $\mu_A$ is the mean under an alternative hypothesis. In the example of the change scores, $\mu_{\text{hyp}} = 0$, and $\mu_A$ is the true mean of the population of change scores, $\mu_{\text{change}}$. In the example summarized by Table 6.1 and Fig. 6.1, $E_S = (\mu_{\text{change}} - 0)/\sigma_{\text{change}}$ and is estimated as

$$\hat{E}_S = (\overline{Y}_{\text{change}} - 0)/s_{\text{change}} \tag{6.5}$$

In the example of the seasonal change scores for the sample of 32 women under the age of 36, we substitute the mean and standard deviation of the seasonal change scores (from Table 6.1 or Fig. 6.1) into Equation 6.5; then,

$$\hat{E}_S = (.747 - 0)/3.733 = .200$$

In the one-sample case, there is a simple relation between $\hat{E}_S$ and $t$:

$$\hat{E}_S = t/\sqrt{N}$$
$$= 1.132/\sqrt{32} = .200 \tag{6.6}$$

A rough rule of thumb suggested by Cohen (1988), and widely adopted, is that effect sizes of .2, .5, and .8 should be considered small, medium, and large, respectively. According to that guideline, the seasonal change in the mean Beck scores is small relative to the variability in the change scores. Note that "small" does not necessarily mean "unimportant." If we were testing a new cancer treatment, even a small improvement in remission rate, or increase in life expectancy, might be worthwhile. In theoretical work, small effects—particularly when unexpected, or not predicted by a competing theory—might prove important. Cohen's guidelines are just that—guides, not mandates, and each effect size should be evaluated in terms of the researcher's goals and knowledge of the relevant research and theory.

Confidence limits for $E_S$ may aid our evaluation of the effect size. For example, if $E_S$ is .75, Cohen's guidelines would suggest it is large. However, it is just an estimate; we would feel surer that the population effect size was large if confidence limits were close to this value than if they were widely separated. Steiger and Fouladi (1997; also see Cumming & Finch, 2001) describe one method for calculating limits on $E_S$. We have included a brief illustration of this method in the *Supplementary Materials* folder of the accompanying CD. Hedges and Olkin (1985) describe a second, approximate method, and the entire August, 2001 issue of *Educational and Psychological Measurement* is devoted to the topic of CIs for measures of effect size. Interested readers may consult these sources.

### 6.3.2 *p* Values and Effect Sizes

As we suggested earlier, the significance level, or *p* value, obtained in a study can be misleading about the importance of an effect, or about the relative size of effects in two studies. Table 6.2 presents the results of two experiments that differed only in the number of participants and in the dependent variable; in both cases, two scores were obtained from each participant, allowing a comparison of two treatments. The higher *t* and lower *p* values in Experiment 2 might lead us to believe that the measure in Experiment 2 was more sensitive; the larger raw effect in Experiment 2 would seem to support that inference. However, the standardized effect size is almost twice as large in Experiment 1, indicating

**TABLE 6.2**  COMPARISON OF (TWO-TAILED) $P$ VALUES AND EFFECT SIZES

|  | Experiment 1 | Experiment 2 |
|---|---|---|
| $N$ | 16 | 64 |
| $\overline{Y}_1 - \overline{Y}_2$ | 15 | 40 |
| $s$ | 33 | 152 |
| $t$ | 1.818 | 2.105 |
| $p$ | .089 | .039 |
| $\hat{E}_S$ | .455 | .263 |

that Experiment 1 may have lacked power to reject the null hypothesis because of the relatively small sample. Note that, according to Cohen's (1988) guidelines, the effect in Experiment 1 is medium whereas that in Experiment 2 is small.

## 6.4 POWER OF THE ONE-SAMPLE *t* TEST

Here we consider two uses of power functions: The **post hoc calculation of power** refers to the calculation of the power of the hypothesis test to detect an effect estimated from previously collected data; the **a priori calculation of power** refers to the estimation of the sample sizes needed to achieve a specified level of power to detect a specific value of $E_S$. In terms of the example of the seasonal depression change scores of the 32 women under age 36, we might wish to know what power our experiment had to reject $H_0$ if the population effect size was .2, the value of $E_S$ we estimated from our data. Once we find that value of power, assuming it is lower than we wish, we might determine what sample size would be needed in subsequent research to achieve a specific value of power that was higher than that in the study already run. Of course, a priori calculations do not require that we have previously collected data. Any basis for specifying an effect size can be used. If effect sizes in an area of the literature are all small, we might specify the effect size for a new study as .2, and calculate the sample size needed to achieve some desired level of power.

Power can be calculated by several standard software programs, including SAS's CDF module, SYSTAT's Design of Experiments (under "Statistics") module, and SPSS's NCDF.F program (under "Compute"). Those lacking access to these packages will find programs for calculating power freely available from several Internet sources.[2] We describe the use of two such sources—a Web site developed by the UCLA statistics department, and a downloadable program, GPOWER. However, before illustrating the calculations, we consider the concept of the power of the *t* test.

### 6.4.1 The Noncentral *t* Distribution

As with the binomial (Chapter 4) and normal probability (Chapter 5) tests, we can conceive of two distributions: one when the null hypothesis is true and one when it is false by a specifiable amount. For example, we have one distribution corresponding to $H_0$: $E_S = 0$ and an alternative distribution corresponding to $H_A$: $E_S = .2$. When the null hypothesis is true, the *t* distribution has a mean of zero. The area exceeding any particular value of *t* depends on the degree of freedom, and this "tail probability" may be found in Appendix

Table C.3. We refer to the distribution of *t* under the null hypothesis as the **central *t* distribution.** To calculate the power to reject a specific alternative hypothesis, we also must consider the alternative distribution; for example, we must consider the distribution of *t* when $E_S = .2$. In this case, the mean of the *t* distribution is no longer at zero, and the distribution of *t* is referred to as a **noncentral *t* distribution.** As with other statistical tests, we first determine the critical region—the values of *t* that lead to rejection of the null hypothesis. The critical value can be obtained from Table C.3, or from most statistical software packages. Once we know the rejection region, we can calculate power by finding the probabilities of the values in that region, assuming the alternative distribution. This second step is more difficult than it was with the normal probability test because the noncentral *t* distribution is not merely displaced from the null distribution; it has a different variance and shape.

The location, variance, and shape of the noncentral *t* distribution is determined by the degree of freedom and a **noncentrality parameter, δ** (the Greek letter delta). This parameter incorporates information about variability ($\sigma$), sample size ($N$), and the effect size under the alternative hypothesis. Assuming a sample of $N$ difference scores, as in the example of the change between winter and spring depression scores, we see that the formula for δ is

$$\delta = \frac{\mu_{change}}{\sigma_{change}/\sqrt{N}}$$
$$= \frac{\mu_{change}\sqrt{N}}{\sigma_{change}} \tag{6.7}$$

where $\mu_{change}$ is the mean of the sampled population of difference, or change, scores and $\sigma_{change}$ is the standard deviation of that population. The noncentrality parameter is closely related to the standardized effect size; when considering a population of change scores, we see that $E_S = \mu_{change}/\sigma$; therefore, we can rewrite Equation 6.7 as

$$\delta = E_S\sqrt{N} \tag{6.8}$$

Some software programs require a value of δ in order to calculate power, whereas others require $E_S$ (or, equivalently, Cohen's *d*) and the value of $N$ (or the degree of freedom). In either case, we need to estimate the effect size. We can estimate δ by first estimating $E_S$ and then using Equation 6.8. However, from Equations 6.6 and 6.8, we can see that δ is also estimated by the value of the test statistic, *t*.

### 6.4.2 Post Hoc Power Calculations

Previously, we found that the standardized effect of the change in seasons (from winter to spring) on the depression scores of 32 women under 36 years of age was .2. We determine the power of the experiment to detect this effect size by using two different methods based on software freely available on the Internet.

***The UCLA Calculator.*** One useful Internet site provided by the UCLA department of statistics at this time is http://www.stat.ucla.edu/calculators/cdf/. When you enter this site, a table appears. The rows provide a choice of distributions, including the normal and the central *t* (labeled "Student"), and the columns allow calculations or plots based on either the cumulative or probability density functions. Assuming that we have already obtained the critical value from Appendix Table C.3 (if not, we can obtain it by clicking on the cell in the "Student" row and "CDF" column), click on the CDF (cumulative distribution function) calculator in the "Noncentral Student" (noncentral *t* distribution) row of the table. Then, follow these steps:

1. For the "X value," provide the critical *t* required for significance. For 31 *df*, $\alpha = .05$, and a one-tailed test of $H_0$: $\mu = 0$ versus $H_1$: $\mu > 0$, the critical *t* is 1.696.
2. Type the degrees of freedom (31) in the "Degrees of Freedom" row.
3. Type the estimate of $\delta$ in the "Noncentrality Parameter" row. In the current example, $E_S = .20$ and $N = 32$; then from Equation 6.8 our estimate of $\delta$ is 1.1314. Power is the probability of exceeding the "X value" in a noncentral *t* distribution whose location is determined by the value of $\delta$.
4. Type ? in the "Probability" row and click on "Complete Me!"

The probability returned is always the probability of a value *less than* the critical *t*. If we were to look at a plot of the alternative (noncentral) *t* distribution we specified, the probability returned would correspond to the area to the left of the critical value of *t*. If the critical *t* is positive, this probability is $\beta$, the probability of accepting a false null hypothesis. Therefore, power is obtained by subtracting that value from 1. If the critical *t* is negative, the values to the left of the critical *t* form the rejection region and, in this case, the probability returned will correspond directly to power. In the current example, completing the table returns the value .705 in the Probability row, so the power is $1 - .705 = .295$. Verify that if we estimate the power for $E_S = .2$ with a new *N* of 120, we obtain a value of .703 (remember that the critical *t* should be based on the new degrees of freedom, and $\delta$ will also change because of the change in *N*).

**GPOWER.**  An alternative that is versatile, simple to use, and can be downloaded to your own computer is the free software, GPOWER, available at the Web site http://www.psychologie.uni-trier.de:8000/projects/gpower.html. Documentation (Erdfelder, Faul, & Buchner, 1996) is available at this site but the software is quite simple to use. It can be downloaded from the World Wide Web, and it requires less than half of the space of a standard diskette. Both Macintosh and PC versions are available. We illustrate GPOWER's use, continuing with the example of the hypothesis test based on seasonal change scores. Figure 6.2 presents a reproduction of the screen for a post hoc calculation in the one-sample (or correlated-scores) case.

Moving to the main screen, we click on "Tests," which brings up a menu that includes the *t* for two means, the *t* test of the correlation coefficient, "Other *t* Tests," chi-square tests, and *F* tests. In the present instance, although we have two seasonal means, they are not independent because they are based on the same set of participants. We really have a single sample of change scores. Therefore, click on "Other *t* Tests." Then:

1. Click on "Post hoc" under "Analysis" to determine what power the *t* test had to reject $H_0$: $\mu_{change} = 0$ against the specific alternative $E_S = .2$ (the effect size we estimated from our data).
2. Select "One tailed" from the choice of one and two tails.
3. In the choice between "Speed" and "Accuracy," choose "Accuracy" unless you have a very slow computer.

| _ Tests  Colors | | 159kB free | 16:39:35 |
|---|---|---|---|
| | | | Analysis |
| Calculate _    Calc Effect size _ | Graph  _ | | ( ) A priori |
| _____   _____ | | | (x) Post hoc |
| Effect size f    0.2    Delta   ? | | | ( ) Compromise |
| Alpha        0.05    Critical *t* = ? | | | I prefer... |
| | | | ( ) Speed |
| N        32    Power   ? | | | (x) Accuracy |
| *df*        31 | | | Test is.. |
| | | | (x) One tailed |
| | | | ( ) Two tailed |

**Fig. 6.2**  GPOWER screen for a post hoc analysis.

4. Double click on "Effect size"[3] and type ".2."
5. Enter the values of alpha (.05), *N* (32), and *df* (31).
6. Click on "Calculate" and the question marks on the screen are replaced by

$$\text{Delta} = 1.1314$$
$$\text{Critical } t(31) = 1.6955$$
$$\text{Power} = .2952$$

The delta value is the noncentrality parameter that we obtained by using Equation 6.8 and entered into the UCLA calculator. The power is the same low value obtained with the UCLA software. To increase power, we must either use a less variable measure of depression than the Beck scale or increase the sample size.

### 6.4.3 *A Priori* Power Calculations

At this point, we have an estimated standardized effect size that was not large enough to allow rejection of $H_0$. We might wish to ask the following question: If the actual effect was .2, what sample size should we use in future research in this area to achieve a power of, say, .8? With $N = 32$, power was about .3; it is evident that to increase power to .8, we will need many more participants. Let's see just how many "many more" is.

GPOWER has an a priori option under "Analysis" but this is not available for "Other *t* Tests." However, by trying various values of *N* and degrees of freedom ($= N - 1$) in the "Post hoc" analysis, we quickly find that $N = 155$ provides .80 (actually .7979) power. Although the UCLA calculator does not calculate the *N* needed directly, as with GPOWER we can try various values to obtain the desired power. Note that for each value of $N$ we try with the UCLA calculator, we would have to insert values of the critical $t$, degrees of freedom, and estimated $\delta$ based on that value.

Our calculations indicate that if we are serious about studying seasonal depression score changes, either we are going to have to collect a large data sample, or we are going to have to improve our measuring instrument so as to reduce variability. Another possibility is to attempt to standardize data collection to reduce variability. For example, some of the winter scores were collected early in the winter; others were collected later. The same is true, of course, for depression scores placed in the spring category.

### 6.4.4 Consequences of Violations of Assumptions

The inferences we have drawn thus far in this chapter rest on two assumptions: first, the scores are independently distributed, and second, the population distribution is normal. We discussed these assumptions in Chapter 5 with respect to the use of the normal probability tables. As we noted there, it is reasonable to view the seasonal change (winter – spring) scores as independently distributed. We also noted in Chapter 5 that, although the population was unlikely to be normally distributed, the sampling distribution of the mean would tend to be normal because each mean was based on 215 scores. However, the sampling distribution of the mean will be less well approximated by the normal distribution in the current example, in which we have only 32 scores. In general, with samples of approximately this size, problems may arise if the population distribution is very skewed. We have drawn 10,000 samples of sizes 10 and 40 from the right-skewed exponential distribution depicted in Fig. 6.3. This distribution has a high peak at its minimum point and then the density quickly decreases as the scores increase. The population from which we sampled had a mean of one and we tested $H_0\colon \mu = 1$ at the .05 level. The results of these computer experiments can be seen in Table 6.3. In each case, the theoretical error rate is .05. We can see that when the alternative was $H_1\colon \mu > 1$, there were far too few rejections. When the alternative hypothesis was $H_1\colon$

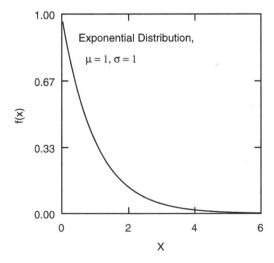

**Fig. 6.3** An exponential distribution.

**TABLE 6.3** TYPE 1 ERROR RATES FOR THE DISTRIBUTION OF FIG. 6.3 ($\alpha = .05$)

| Sample Size ($N$) | Alternative Hypothesis | Type 1 Error Rate |
|:---:|:---:|:---:|
| 10 | $\mu > 1$ | .014 |
| 10 | $\mu < 1$ | .131 |
| 10 | $\mu \neq 1$ | .097 |
| 40 | $\mu > 1$ | .025 |
| 40 | $\mu < 1$ | .096 |
| 40 | $\mu \neq 1$ | .072 |

$\mu < 0$, there were many more than .05 rejections. Two-tailed tests also resulted in inflated Type 1 error rates.

Although our data are frequently skewed, they are rarely as skewed as in the exponential distribution plotted in Fig. 6.3. The resulting Type 1 error rates of Table 6.3 represent a worst-case scenario. Furthermore, the situation is clearly better when $N = 40$ than when $N = 10$. If we used still larger samples, the empirical error rates would eventually stabilize at .05 even in the exponential condition; this is a consequence of the central limit theorem. Larger data sets not only yield increased power and narrower CIs, but also tend to offset clear violations of the normality assumption.

If there is evidence of extreme skew, efforts should be made to collect larger samples. If small samples are drawn from very skewed populations, there are few remedies. One possibility is to transform the data by performing some operation on all the scores and then applying the *t* test. For example, the logarithm of exponentially distributed scores will tend to be more nearly normally distributed than will the original scores. We have more to say about transformations in Chapter 8.

Departures from normality may also affect the power of the *t* test and the precision of interval estimates. For example, if the distribution of scores is symmetric but has a longer tail than the normal distribution, the *SEM* may be large and, consequently, power may be low and CIs may be wide. Precision of estimation and the power of hypothesis tests are often improved by "trimming" the data, which consists of deleting the most extreme scores prior to calculating a modified *t* statistic (Wilcox, 1997). An alternative to the *t* test based on the ranks of the scores, the Wilcoxon Signed Rank Test, may also improve power. This alternative to the standard one-sample *t* test is discussed in Chapter 13.

## 6.5 THE *t* DISTRIBUTION: TWO INDEPENDENT GROUPS

Looking back at Table 6.1, we see that the average change scores for men and women seem quite different. The mean winter–spring change in the Beck depression score is −.745 for men but .747 for women. In other words, the means of the seasonal change scores suggest that men in this age group are more depressed in spring than in winter, but women are more depressed in winter than in spring. The medians, however, suggest a different picture; the male median is negative (−.18) but close to zero and the female median is zero. Figure 6.4 presents box plots of the seasonal change scores for the two groups that should help clarify the reasons for the discrepancy between comparisons of medians and means. Recall that the horizontal line dividing the box into two segments represents the median and that the ends of

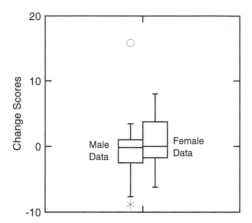

**Fig. 6.4** Box plots of male and female seasonal change scores.

the box are the hinges, approximately the 25th and 75th percentiles. In the female data, the 25% of the scores between the median and the lower hinge are mainly negative but close to zero, whereas the 25% of the scores between the median and the upper hinge include values further from the median, thus moving the mean in the positive direction. The situation is reversed in the male data, where the scores between the median and the upper hinge tend to be closer to zero (with the exception of one extreme outlier represented by a small circle) than the mostly negative values between the median and the lower hinge. The other aspect of the box plot that merits our attention is that there is a considerable range of scores, and there are outliers in both directions in the male data. In view of the apparent variability, and the somewhat conflicting picture presented by means and medians, we will further analyze the data.

Before we can calculate confidence limits or conduct significance tests, we need to consider the relevant sampling distribution, its *SE*, and how that *SE* should be estimated. We turn next to these matters.

## 6.5.1 The *SE* of the Difference Between Two Independent Means

Suppose we drew many independent random samples of size $n_1$ and $n_2$ from two independently and normally distributed populations of scores. If we carried out this sampling procedure, we could compute a difference between the means for each pair of samples drawn. The standard deviation of the sampling distribution of this difference, the *SE*, is the quantity to be estimated by the denominator of the *t* in the two-group study. The issue is how to calculate that estimate.

In Chapter 5, we noted that if the $n_1 + n_2$ scores are independently distributed, the *SE* of the sampling distribution of the difference between the two group means is (Equation 5.18)

$$\sigma_{\overline{Y}_1 - \overline{Y}_2} = \sqrt{\frac{\sigma_1^2}{n_1} + \frac{\sigma_2^2}{n_2}}$$

The *t* distributions of Appendix Table C.3 require one additional assumption, that the two population variances are equal; that is,

$$\sigma_1^2 = \sigma_2^2 = \sigma^2$$

This is usually referred to as the assumption of **homogeneity of variance**, or **homoscedasticity**. Given this assumption, we can rewrite the *SE* of the sampling distribution of the difference between the means as

$$\sigma_{\overline{Y}_1 - \overline{Y}_2} = \sqrt{\frac{\sigma^2}{n_1} + \frac{\sigma^2}{n_2}}$$

$$= \sigma\sqrt{\frac{1}{n_1} + \frac{1}{n_2}}$$

We have a single population variance ($\sigma^2$) and two possible estimates of it—the variances of the two groups sampled in an experiment. To obtain the best single estimate of $\sigma$, we need to average the two group variances and take the square root of the result. Because variance estimates are consistent statistics, the estimate based on the larger group is more likely to be close to the true variance. Therefore, the best estimate of $\sigma^2$ is a weighted average of the two group variances. This is often referred to as the **pooled-variance estimate**, or $s_{pooled}^2$, and it is calculated as

$$s_{pooled}^2 = \left[\frac{n_1 - 1}{n_1 + n_2 - 2}\right] s_1^2 + \left[\frac{n_2 - 1}{n_1 + n_2 - 2}\right] s_2^2 \tag{6.9}$$

Note that the weight on each group variance in Equation 6.9 is obtained by dividing the degrees of freedom for that group by the sum of the degrees of freedom for the two groups $[(n_1 - 1) + (n_2 - 1)]$. The degrees of freedom rather than the *n*s are used in these weights because this yields an unbiased estimate of $\sigma_{\overline{Y}_1 - \overline{Y}_2}$. The pooled-variance estimate can also be written as

$$s_{pooled}^2 = \frac{SS_1 + SS_2}{n_1 + n_2 - 2} \tag{6.10}$$

where the *SS* for the *j*th group is a sum of squared deviations of the scores about the mean of the group; that is,

$$SS_j = \sum_i (Y_{ij} - \overline{Y}_{.j})^2 \tag{6.11}$$

This quantity is usually referred to as the **sum of squares**, and it plays an important role in the remaining chapters.

We can now state the expression for the estimate of the *SE* of the sampling distribution of the difference of two independent means:

$$s_{diff} = s_{pooled}\sqrt{\frac{1}{n_1} + \frac{1}{n_2}} \tag{6.12}$$

When $n_1 = n_2 = n$, as is frequently the case in experimental research, Equations 6.10 and 6.12 simplify:

$$s_{pooled}^2 = \frac{SS_1 + SS_2}{2(n - 1)} \tag{6.10'}$$

$$s_{diff} = s_{pooled}\sqrt{2/n} \tag{6.12'}$$

To illustrate the calculation of $s_{\text{diff}}$, let's substitute values from Table 6.1. In other words, let's get a numerical estimate of the $SE$ of the sampling distribution of the difference between the means of the male and female change scores. From Equation 6.12,

$$s_{\text{diff}} = s_{\text{pooled}}\sqrt{\frac{1}{n_M} + \frac{1}{n_F}}$$

$$= \sqrt{\frac{(n_M - 1)s_M^2 + (n_F - 1)s_F^2}{n_M + n_F - 2}}\sqrt{\frac{1}{n_M} + \frac{1}{n_F}}$$

$$= \sqrt{\frac{(29)(19.425) + (31)(13.934)}{60}}\sqrt{\frac{1}{30} + \frac{1}{32}}$$

$$= (4.073)(.254)$$

$$= 1.035$$

## 6.5.2 CIs and $t$ Tests

With a formula for the $SE$ of the difference between the means, we can estimate confidence limits on the difference in mean change scores for the under-36 groups of men and women. We begin by stating the general form of the CI; if the confidence level is $1 - \alpha$, then

$$p(V - t_{df,\,\alpha/2}s_V \leq E(V) \leq V + t_{df,\,\alpha/2}s_V) = 1 - \alpha \tag{6.13}$$

and the confidence limits are

$$\text{CI} = V \pm t_{df,\,\alpha/2}s_V \tag{6.14}$$

where, as usual, $V$ is the statistic that estimates the relevant population parameter, $s_V$ is the estimate of the $SE$ of the sampling distribution of $V$, and $t_{df,\,\alpha/2}$ is the value of $t$ exceeded by $\alpha/2$ of the $t$ distribution on $n_1 + n_2 - 2$ $df$. Replacing the $V$ in Equation 6.14 by the difference between the male and female change means, we have

$$\text{CI} = (\overline{Y}_1 - \overline{Y}_2) \pm t_{df,\,\alpha/2}s_{\text{diff}} \tag{6.15}$$

We can now substitute values from Table 6.1 to obtain the .95 limits on $\mu_F - \mu_M$, the difference between the means of the two populations of change scores. The difference in the group means is $\overline{Y}_F - \overline{Y}_M = .747 - (-.745) = 1.492$, and the estimate of the $SE$ of this difference, $s_{\text{diff}}$, was computed previously as 1.035.

Turning to Appendix Table C.3, we see that the two-tailed $t$ required for significance at the .05 level when $df = 60$ is 2.000. Substituting these values into Equation 6.15, we find that the confidence limits are

$$\text{CI} = 1.492 \pm (1.035)(2.000)$$

$$= 1.492 \pm 2.070$$

$$= -.58, 3.56$$

The interval bounds give a sense of the likely range of differences between the male and female change scores. The interval is wide, more than 4 points, indicating that our estimate of the difference in mean change scores is not very reliable. We also note that the interval contains zero. Therefore, despite the fact that the mean seasonal change score was positive for women and negative for men, we cannot reject the null hypothesis of no difference. However, the wide interval suggests that power may be less than desirable. We consider the power of the significance test in Section 6.7.

A direct test of $H_0: \mu_1 - \mu_2 = 0$ against the alternative $H_1: \mu_1 - \mu_2 \neq 0$ follows from the preceding developments. The test statistic is

$$t = \frac{(\overline{Y}_1 - \overline{Y}_2) - (\mu_1 - \mu_2)_{\text{hyp}}}{s_{\text{pooled}}\sqrt{\dfrac{1}{n_1} + \dfrac{1}{n_2}}} \tag{6.16}$$

Substituting numerical values, we have

$$t = \frac{[(.747) - (-.745)] - 0}{(4.073)(.254)}$$

$$= 1.44$$

Because this value is less than 2.00, the result is clearly not significant. However, the CI is quite wide, wider than any encountered previously in either Chapter 5 or 6, indicating that the point estimate of the difference between the sexes may be in considerable error. The wide CI also suggests that power to reject $H_0$ will be low, if we assume the current group sizes and the estimated values of the population parameters. In the following sections, we proceed as we did in Sections 6.3 and 6.4, calculating first the standardized effect size for the two sample case and then the power of the significance test.

## 6.6 STANDARDIZED EFFECT SIZE FOR TWO INDEPENDENT MEANS

Following the developments of Section 6.3, we define the standardized effect size $E_S$ as

$$E_S = [(\mu_1 - \mu_2) - \Delta]/\sigma \tag{6.17}$$

where $\mu_1$ and $\mu_2$ are the actual population means, and $\Delta$ (Greek uppercase delta) is the population difference assuming $H_0$ is true; $\Delta$ is usually, but not always, zero. In the two-sample case, $E_S$ is estimated as

$$\hat{E}_S = [(\overline{Y}_1 - \overline{Y}_2) - \Delta]/s_{\text{pooled}} \tag{6.18}$$

In the example of the contrast of male and female seasonal change scores, we previously determined that $\overline{Y}_F - \overline{Y}_M = 1.492$ and $s_{\text{pooled}} = 4.073$. Therefore,

$$\hat{E}_S = 1.492/4.073 = .37$$

Following Cohen's (1988) guidelines, we find that the standardized effect size of gender on the seasonal change in Beck depression scores for individuals less than 36 years of age falls somewhere between small and medium.

Although the measure of effect size we have presented is the most common one, others are possible and, particularly when homogeneity of variance is suspect, such alternatives should be considered. Grissom and Kim (2001) provide an excellent review of the assumptions involved in calculating effect size, and they discuss the pros and cons of several alternatives to $E_S$.

## 6.7 POWER OF THE TEST OF TWO INDEPENDENT MEANS

If the actual effect size in the population equals the estimate, .37, what is the probability of rejecting the null hypothesis? In other words, if the experiment was replicated many times and the true $E_S$ was .37, in what proportion of those replications would the null hypothesis be rejected? The underlying process of obtaining a numerical value of power involves the same two stages involved in finding power for the normal probability and one-sample $t$ tests. Assuming $H_0$ to be true, and given the nature of the alternative (one or two tailed) and the value of $\alpha$, we use Appendix Table C.3 to decide on the critical region, those values of $t$ that will lead to rejection of $H_0$. Then, we find the probability of obtaining a value of $t$ that falls within that region under a specified alternative distribution.

Power calculations can be performed by several standard statistical software packages, as well as by programs at the UCLA Web site or by using GPOWER. With GPOWER, use the default "$t$ test for means." As in the one-sample case, we again need to specify an effect size. One possibility is to use the value of $E_S$ determined from the data (.37 in our example). This is the practice followed by many researchers. Alternatively, because .37 falls about midway between Cohen's (1988) guidelines for small and medium effects, we might compute power by assuming $E_S = .2$ or .5. Whatever value is used, the process of calculating power is straightforward with GPOWER. Indicate that the calculation is post hoc and enter the effect size value. The default value of alpha is .05, but this can be changed if we want to test at a different significance level. Complete the input by inserting the values of $n_1$ and $n_2$, and by indicating whether a one- or two-tailed test is desired. Then click on "*Calculate*." For a two-tailed test against the specific alternative, $H_A$: $E_S = .37$, power $= .29$. It appears that even if the null hypothesis was false, we had little power to reject it. This is consistent with the wide interval we noted when the CI was calculated.

Using the noncentral Student CDF calculator at the UCLA Web site to calculate power yields the same result. For the two-tailed test with 60 $df$, the critical values of the $t$ distribution are $\pm 2.00$. Entering 2.00 for "X Value," ? for "Probability," 60 for "Degrees of Freedom," and the observed $t$, 1.44, for "Noncentrality Parameter" returns a probability value of .71. Because this is $\beta$, the area below the cutoff, the power associated with the upper region of rejection is $1 - .71 = .29$, the same value obtained by using GPOWER. No additional power is obtained by using the lower region of rejection. If we insert $-2.00$ instead of $+2.00$ for "X Value," the probability returned is .000. In this instance, because a negative value of $t$ was inserted, the probability returned corresponds directly to power. No power is gained by considering the area below the lower critical value.

Ideally, we should determine the $n$ required to obtain a specific level of power prior to collecting our data. From previous work with the Beck depression scores, we might be aware that small effects were generally obtained. In that case, using GPOWER, we set the effect size parameter at .2, select "A priori" under "Analysis," indicate the desired level of power, and click on "Calculate." For a two-tailed test with $\alpha = .05$, if $E_S = .2$, GPOWER estimates that we will need $n = 394$ in order for the power to equal .80. No a priori power calculations are directly available with UCLA's noncentral Student calculator, although we could use it to find the power for different sample sizes. If we wish to use the UCLA noncentral $t$ calculator (or the noncentral $t$ functions in statistical packages such as SPSS) to calculate a priori power for two-group $t$ tests, we should note that the noncentrality parameter can be estimated from

$$\delta = E_S \sqrt{\frac{n_1 n_2}{n_1 + n_2}}$$

## 6.8 ASSUMPTIONS UNDERLYING THE TWO-GROUP *t* TEST

When using the *t* distribution as a basis for inferences about two independent population means, we assume that the two populations of scores are independently and normally distributed and have the same variance. As we discussed earlier, violation of the independence assumption will often result in distorted Type 1 error rates. Nonnormality is less of a problem, at least in large samples. The impact of heterogeneity of variance also depends on the absolute sample sizes, as well as on the relative sizes of the two samples. Let's consider these issues more closely.

### 6.8.1 The Assumption of Normality

From our discussion of the central limit theorem, we know that the sampling distribution of the difference of means approaches normality as the combined sample size $(n_1 + n_2)$ increases. As a consequence, the actual Type 1 error rates associated with the test statistic will closely approximate the values for the *t* distribution in Table C.3 if the combined sample size is moderately large. "Moderately large" may be as small as 20 if $n_1 = n_2$ and if the two populations have symmetric distributions, or even if they are skewed but have the same direction and degree of skewness. Our rather liberal attitude with respect to skewness may seem surprising in view of the fact that the one-sample *t* required quite large *n*s to achieve honest Type 1 error rates when the parent population was skewed. However, here we are concerned with the sampling distribution of the difference between independent means. If two populations are skewed in the same direction, and if the samples are equal in size, then the differences in sample means are as likely to be positive as negative, and the sampling distribution of those differences will tend to be symmetric. For most situations the researcher will encounter, combined sample sizes of 40 should be sufficient to guarantee an honest Type 1 error rate.

When populations are skewed or have outliers, the sampling distribution of $\overline{Y}_1 - \overline{Y}_2$ will tend to be long tailed. In such cases, estimates of the difference between population means will be less precise, and the *t* test will be less powerful than when the normality assumption holds. As in the one-sample case, trimming extreme scores (Wilcoxon, 1997) and tests based on ranks often will be more powerful than the *t* test. We consider the latter approach in Chapter 13.

### 6.8.2 The Assumption of Homogeneity of Variance

The denominator of the equation for the two-sample *t* test is based on the pool of two variance estimates (Equation 6.9); the underlying assumption is that the two group variances estimate the same population variance. If this is not true—if the population variances are heterogeneous—then the sampling distribution of the *t* statistic of Equation 6.16 may not

**TABLE 6.4**  TYPE 1 ERROR RATES FOR THE $t$ TEST AS A FUNCTION
OF POPULATION VARIANCES AND SAMPLE SIZES

| $n_1$ | $n_2$ | $\sigma_1^2/\sigma_2^2$ | $\alpha = .05$ | $\alpha = .01$ |
|---|---|---|---|---|
| 5 | 5 | 4 | .060 | .014 |
| 5 | 5 | 16 | .061 | .019 |
| 5 | 5 | 100 | .066 | .024 |
| 15 | 15 | 4 | .056 | .010 |
| 15 | 15 | 16 | .054 | .015 |
| 15 | 15 | 100 | .059 | .017 |
| 5 | 10 | 4 | .095 | .031 |
| 5 | 10 | .25 | .021 | .003 |
| 10 | 15 | 4 | .073 | .023 |
| 10 | 15 | .25 | .040 | .006 |
| 10 | 20 | 4 | .091 | .031 |
| 10 | 20 | .25 | .021 | .003 |
| 20 | 30 | 4 | .067 | .027 |
| 20 | 30 | .25 | .037 | .004 |

have a true $t$ distribution. Table 6.4 gives some sense of what may happen in this case. We drew 2,000 pairs of samples of various sizes from two normal populations with identical means but different variances. Proportions of rejections for $\alpha = .01$ and $\alpha = .05$ are presented.

Several points about the results should be noted. First, if the two sample sizes are equal, the difference between the empirical and theoretical Type 1 alpha rates tends to be at most 1%, except when $n$ is very small (i.e., $n = 5$) and the variance ratio is very large (i.e., $\sigma_1^2/\sigma_2^2 = 100$). Second, when $n$s are unequal, whether the Type 1 error rate is inflated or deflated depends on the direction of the relation between sample size and population variance. The reason for this can be understood by considering the fact that the denominator of the $t$ is based on a weighted average of two variance estimates; the weights are proportions of degrees of freedom. Therefore, when the larger group is drawn from the population with the larger variance, the larger variance estimate receives more weight than the smaller estimate. The denominator of the $t$ test tends to be large and the $t$ small; the rejection rate is less than it should be. Conversely, when sample size and population variance are negatively correlated, the smaller variance estimate gets the larger weight; the denominator of the $t$ statistic tends to be small and the $t$ large; the rejection rate is inflated.

Unequal sample sizes should be avoided when possible. However, we recognize that there will be many cases in which sample sizes will differ, often markedly. For example, the response rate to questionnaires may be quite different for two populations such as male and female, or college and noncollege educated. We do not advocate discarding data from the larger sample; this would increase sampling variability for statistics computed from that sample. Instead, we recommend an alternative to the standard $t$ test. One such alternative is a $t$ that does not use the pooled estimate of the population variance. The denominator of this statistic would be that of the $z$ test for two independent groups with variance estimates instead of known population variances. We define

$$t' = \frac{(\overline{Y}_1 - \overline{Y}_2) - (\mu_1 - \mu_2)}{\sqrt{s_1^2/n_1 + s_2^2/n_2}} \tag{6.19}$$

This statistic is sometimes referred to as **Welch's** *t* (Welch, 1938). If the scores have been drawn from normally distributed populations, $t'$ is distributed approximately as *t* but not with the usual degrees of freedom. The degrees of freedom are

$$df' = \frac{(s_1^2/n_1 + s_2^2/n_2)^2}{\dfrac{s_1^4}{n_1^2(n_1 - 1)} + \dfrac{s_2^4}{n_2^2(n_2 - 1)}} \tag{6.20}$$

where $s^4$ is the square of the variance, $s^2$. The degrees of freedom are rounded to the nearest integer when the value of $t'$ is evaluated or when CIs are obtained.

Most statistical packages compute values of both $t'$ and *t* when an independent-groups *t* test is performed. For example, SYSTAT outputs both a **separate-variance** *t* and a **pooled-variance** *t*, and SPSS outputs a result for "Equal variances not assumed" and "Equal variances assumed." The former is the $t'$ of Equation 6.19 and the pooled-variance *t* is the standard *t* statistic of Equation 6.16. Tables 6.5a and 6.5b present SPSS's output of the *t* statistics and CIs for the comparison of mean seasonal depression change scores of men and

**TABLE 6.5a**   THE *t* TEST COMPARING MEAN SEASONAL CHANGE SCORES FOR MEN AND WOMEN: GROUP STATISTICS

| SEX | N | Mean | Std. Deviation | Std. Error Mean |
|---|---|---|---|---|
| DIFF   MALE | 30 | −.7450 | 4.4074 | .8047 |
|         FEMALE | 32 | .7469 | 3.7328 | .6599 |

*Note.* Output is from SPSS.

**TABLE 6.5b**   *THE t TEST COMPARING MEAN SEASONAL CHANGE SCORES FOR MEN AND WOMEN: INDEPENDENT SAMPLES TEST*

| | | Levene's Test for Equality of Variances | | t-test for Equality of Means | | | | | | 95% Confidence Interval of the Difference | |
|---|---|---|---|---|---|---|---|---|---|---|---|
| | | F | Sig. | t | df | Sig. (2-tailed) | Mean Difference | Std. Error Difference | | Lower | Upper |
| DIFF | Equal variances assumed | .038 | .847 | −1.441 | 60 | .155 | −1.4919 | 1.0350 | | −3.5623 | .5785 |
| | Equal variances not assumed | | | −1.434 | 57.003 | .157 | −1.4919 | 1.0406 | | −3.5758 | .5920 |

*Note.* Output is from SPSS.

women under 36 years of age. The values of the $t$ based on the pooled-variance estimate ("Equal variances assumed") and that of $t'$ ("Equal variances not assumed") are almost identical. This is because the group sizes are very similar, as are the standard deviations. Further evidence of homogeneity of variance is provided by Levene's (1960) test, which has a clearly nonsignificant result. This test evaluates the difference between groups with respect to the average absolute deviation of scores about their respective means. We have more to say about this test in subsequent chapters, in which we also discuss the Brown–Forsythe test of homogeneity of variance (Brown & Forsythe, 1974a). That test is similar to Levene's but is based on the average absolute deviation of scores about the median instead of the mean.

## 6.9 CONTRASTS INVOLVING MORE THAN TWO MEANS

Contrasts are linear combinations in which the weights sum to zero; for example, the contrast between the winter and spring mean depression scores may be represented by $(1)(\mu_{winter}) + (-1)(\mu_{spring})$. Occasionally, we are interested in contrasts involving more than two means. We designate contrasts by $\psi$ (the Greek letter, psi); all contrasts have the general form

$$\psi = \sum_{j=1}^{J} w_j \mu_j \tag{6.21}$$

with the added condition that the weights sum to zero; that is,

$$\sum_{j=1}^{J} w_j = 0$$

where $J$ is the number of conditions in the contrast (two in our example), and the $w_j$ are the weights on the means (1 and −1 in our example). Note that when the total number of groups is more than two, some weights may be zero.

Suppose we wanted to estimate the contrast between the average winter score and the average score in the other three seasons. This would be a repeated-measures contrast because several seasonal measures are obtained from each participant in the study. An example of a contrast involving several independent group means might be the difference between the mean depression score for college graduates and the combined mean for high school and vocational school graduates. Because the repeated-measures and independent-group contrasts involve slightly different calculations, we consider them separately.

### 6.9.1 Repeated-Measures Contrasts

The contrast between the population mean of Beck depression scores obtained in the winter season and the mean for the other three seasons is

$$\psi = \mu_{winter} - (\mu_{spring} + \mu_{summer} + \mu_{fall})/3$$

which, following the form of Equation 6.21, we can rewrite as a linear combination of the population means:

$$\psi = (1)(\mu_{winter}) + (-1/3)(\mu_{spring}) + (-1/3)(\mu_{summer}) + (-1/3)(\mu_{fall})$$

To obtain a CI for $\psi$, we first must estimate the contrast:

$$\hat{\psi} = (1)(\overline{Y}_{\text{winter}}) + (-1/3)(\overline{Y}_{\text{spring}}) + (-1/3)(\overline{Y}_{\text{summer}}) + (-1/3)(\overline{Y}_{\text{fall}})$$

To carry out the calculations for the CI, we obtain a contrast score for each participant, subtracting the average of the depression means for spring, summer, and fall from the individual's winter score. These scores can be found in the column labeled PSI_D in the Under 36 file. Most statistical packages perform transformations such as this (and more complicated ones) quite easily. Once we have the set of contrast scores, the mean and standard deviation are obtained. Then CIs are constructed, and a hypothesis test is conducted, using Equations 6.2 and 6.3 for a single sample. We calculated contrast scores from the depression data for 24 female participants under 36 years of age; 8 under-36 participants did not have a score for all four seasons and their data were therefore omitted from the analysis. The mean contrast score, $\hat{\psi}$, was 1.289 and its $SE$ was $3.030/\sqrt{24}$, or .619. The critical $t$ value, $t_{23,.025}$, is 2.069, and, after substitution into Equation 6.2, the .95 confidence limits on $\psi$ are

$$\text{CI} = 1.289 \pm (2.069)(.619) = .01, 2.57$$

The CI provides limits for our estimate of the contrast, indicating that the mean depression score for the under-36 population of women is higher in winter than in the remainder of the year because zero is not contained in the interval.

If only the null hypothesis $H_0$: $\psi = 0$ is of interest, we can calculate the $t$ statistic directly. The $t$ for these data is $\hat{\psi}$ divided by its $SE$. Therefore,

$$t = 1.289/.619 = 2.082$$

Because this exceeds the critical $t$ value on 23 *df* (2.07), we again have evidence that the mean winter depression score is higher than the mean of scores in the other three seasons.

Converting $\hat{\psi}$ to an estimate of the **standardized contrast**, $\psi_s$, requires only that we divide $\hat{\psi}$ by its standard deviation. In our example, $\hat{\psi}_s = 1.289/3.030 = .425$. The effect is slightly less than half the standard deviation greater than zero, a medium sized effect.

We may wish to assess the power of the test of $H_0$: $\psi = 0$ against the alternative, $H_A$: $\psi = .425$, with $\alpha = .05$. Many software programs for calculating power require a value of the noncentrality parameter, $\delta$. In the repeated-measures design, this was defined in Equation 6.8 as

$$\delta = \psi_s \sqrt{N}$$

Substituting our estimate of $\psi_s$ (.425), and the $N$ (24), we find that $\delta = 2.082$, the value we calculated for $t$. Using the UCLA calculator (or any other available software that has the noncentral $t$ function such as SAS's CDF module), we can find the power of the test. Assuming a one-tailed test of $H_0$, enter 1.714, the critical value that cuts off the upper .05 of the $t$ distribution with 23 *df* in the "X value" row. Also enter 23 in the "Degrees of Freedom" row and 2.082 in the "Noncentrality Parameter" row. The value of "Probability" returned is .354. This is $\beta$, the probability of a Type 2 error; therefore, the power of the $t$ test is $1 - .354 = .646$. GPOWER returns the same result. The only procedural difference is that the values of $E_S$ and $\alpha$, rather than $\delta$ and the critical $t$, are input to the program. Using either of these programs, or any other software, verify that if we obtained the same effect size with 60 participants, the noncentrality parameter would be $(.425)\sqrt{60} = 3.292$, and the test of the null hypothesis would have a power of about .95.

We sometimes lose track of just what we are doing when we use these programs. With any statistical test, power is the probability of exceeding some critical value (e.g., 1.714) when we have a specific alternative to the distribution hypothesized under $H_0$. $E_S$ or $\delta$, specifies the alternative distribution. No matter how we obtain a value of power, we basically go through the same steps: first, decide on a critical region based on the null hypothesis, the direction of the alternative (that is, is it one or two tailed?), the value of $\alpha$, and degrees of freedom (or sample size in the case of some tests); second, find the probability that the test statistic will fall within that critical region when the true distribution is a specific alternative to the null distribution.

### 6.9.2 Independent-Groups Contrasts

Myers, Hansen, Robson, and McCann (1983) investigated the relative effectiveness of three methods of teaching elementary probability. They wrote three texts, which they referred to as the Standard (S), the Low Explanatory (LE), and the High Explanatory (HE) texts. Each text was studied by a different group of 16 undergraduates, none of whom had any previous formal exposure to probability . The participants were then tested on two series of problems—formula problems and story problems. The data are in the PL_data file in the *PL* folder. The means and variances of the proportion of story problems correct are presented in Table 6.6.

The mean proportion of correct responses is higher in the HE group than in the other two groups, which differ only slightly from one another. Myers et al. carried out a test of the HE mean against the average of the other two means. In terms of the three population means, the implied contrast is

$$\psi = (1/2)(\mu_S + \mu_{LE}) - \mu_{HE}$$
$$= (1/2)\mu_S + (1/2)\mu_{LE} + (-1)\mu_{HE}$$

Replacing population means by sample means, we estimate the contrast:

$$\hat{\psi} = (1/2)\overline{Y}_S + (1/2)\overline{Y}_{LE} + (-1)\overline{Y}_{HE} \tag{6.22}$$

The CI for $\psi$ follows the general form of CIs developed in this chapter; specifically,

$$p(\hat{\psi} - t_{df,\alpha/2}s_{\hat{\psi}} \leq \psi \leq \hat{\psi} + t_{df,\alpha/2}s_{\hat{\psi}}) = 1 - \alpha \tag{6.23}$$

**TABLE 6.6** MEANS AND VARIANCES FROM THE MYERS ET AL. STUDY

|          | Condition | | |
|----------|-------|-------|-------|
|          | S     | LE    | HE    |
| Mean     | .396  | .406  | .531  |
| Variance | .031  | .038  | .023  |

Equation 6.22 provides a basis for calculating $\hat{\psi}$, and a formula for the *SE* of $\hat{\psi}$ was derived in Appendix 6.1 (Equation 6.32):

$$s_{\hat{\psi}} = s_{\text{pooled}} \sqrt{\sum_{j=1}^{J} \frac{w_j^2}{n_j}}$$

where

$$s_{\text{pooled}} = \sqrt{\frac{(n_1 - 1)s_1^2 + (n_2 - 1)s_2^2 + \cdots + (n_J - 1)s_J^2}{\sum_{j=1}^{J} n_j - J}}$$

Using these equations, we can calculate the .95 confidence limits on $\psi$. The calculations are presented in Table 6.7. The CI does not contain zero and therefore a two-tailed test of $H_0$ can reject the null hypothesis. The *t* statistic has also been calculated in Table 6.7 and leads to the same conclusion.

A sense of the magnitude of the effect can be obtained by estimating the standardized contrast, $\psi_S$. This also provides a basis for comparison with the effects of other methods, or with the effects of these methods on other types of problems. The standardized contrast

---

**TABLE 6.7**  CALCULATIONS OF CONFIDENCE LIMITS, *t* TEST, AND STANDARDIZED CONTRAST

---

**1.** First calculate an estimate of the population contrast:

$$\hat{\psi} = [.531 - (1/2)(.396 + .406)] = .130$$

**2.** Because the *n*s are equal, the formula for the pooled standard deviation simplifies to $s_{\text{pooled}} = \sqrt{\sum s_j^2/J}$, where *J* is the number of groups. Therefore

$$s_{\text{pooled}} = \sqrt{(.031 + .038 + .023)/3} = \sqrt{.092/3} = .175$$

**3.** Then,

$$s_{\hat{\psi}} = s_{\text{pooled}} \sqrt{\sum_{j=1}^{3} \frac{w_j^2}{n_j}} = .175\sqrt{\frac{1.5}{16}} = .054$$

**4.** The critical values of *t* on 45 *df* for $\alpha = .05$, two tailed, can be obtained by linear interpolation in Table C.3. The critical value that cuts off the upper .025 of the distribution is 2.015. Substituting this and the results of the previous steps into Equation 6.23, we find that the .95 confidence limits are CI $= .130 \pm (2.015)(.054) = .02, .24$.

**5.** To conduct the *t* test,

$$t = \hat{\psi}/s_{\hat{\psi}} = .130/.054 = 2.41$$

The result is clearly larger than the critical value of 2.015, and so we reject the null hypothesis of no difference between performance with the HE text and the average performance with the other two texts.

**6.** Finally, we calculate the standardized contrast: $\hat{\psi}_S = \hat{\psi}/s_{\text{pool}} = .130/.175 = .74$.

---

*Note.* Calculations are based on the statistics of Table 6.6.

is defined as

$$\psi_S = \frac{\psi}{\sigma} \tag{6.24}$$

Assuming homogeneity of variance, we estimate $\psi_S$ by

$$\hat{\psi}_S = \frac{\hat{\psi}}{\hat{\sigma}} = \sum_{j=1}^{J} \frac{w_j \overline{Y}_j}{s_{\text{pooled}}} \tag{6.25}$$

Numerical values have been substituted into Equation 6.25 as indicated in Table 6.7. According to Cohen's (1977, 1988) guidelines, the standardized contrast, .767, would be considered large.

We can use a program such as SAS's CDF function or the UCLA calculator to find the power of the test of the null hypothesis. Suppose we wish to assess the power of a two-tailed t test of $H_0$: $\psi_S = 0$ against the specific alternative $H_A$: $\psi_S = .743$. Using the UCLA program, we provide the "X value," the "Degrees of Freedom," and the "Noncentrality Parameter." Because the test is two tailed, we reject $H_0$ when $t > 2.015$ or $t < -2.015$. For the "X value," enter 2.015, and also the $df$, 45. The noncentrality parameter is, as before, a function of the standardized effect, and it is defined as

$$\delta = \psi / \sigma \sqrt{\sum_{j=1}^{J} \frac{w_j^2}{n_j}} \tag{6.26}$$

$$= \psi_s / \sqrt{\sum_{j=1}^{J} \frac{w_j^2}{n_j}}$$

Substituting values from Table 6.7, we find $\delta = 2.407$. When the three numbers (2.015, 45, and 2.407) are entered, a "Probability" of .347 is returned. This is the area below 2.015 in the noncentral $t$ distribution determined by $\delta = 2.307$. The area above 2.015 plus the area below $-2.015$ is power, the probability of rejecting $H_0$ when the test is two tailed. The area above 2.015 is $1 - .347$, or .653. The area below $-2.015$ may be found by replacing the "X value" with $-2.015$. That area is essentially zero, so the power is approximately .65.

## 6.10 CORRELATED SCORES OR INDEPENDENT GROUPS?

In Chapters 5 and 6, we encountered analyses of data sets in which each participant contributed more than one score, such as a score for each of two or more seasons. The scores for the different seasons will be correlated. Such designs are often referred to as **repeated-measures** or **within-subjects designs**. Correlated scores will also result from **matched-pair** designs. For example, we might wish to compare the effects of two instructional methods on a participant pool of 40 students. The scores of the students might be ordered on the basis of a pretest of ability. The students would then be divided into 20 pairs, with the members of each pair having approximately equal scores on the pretest. In an **independent-groups** or **between-subjects** design, scores in the different conditions are independent of each other. This was the case in our analyses of gender and educational effects. The study of instructional methods could also be carried out in an independent-groups design. In that situation, assignment to instructional methods would be completely random except for the restriction that there would be 20 children in each condition. What are the advantages and disadvantages of the two designs?

When both types of design are feasible, the independent-groups design has two advantages. First, it involves more degrees of freedom in the *t* test. Because each group provides an independent estimate of the population variance, each based on *n* scores, the *t* is distributed on $2(n-1)$ *df*. The matched-pairs design involves only $n-1$ *df* because there is a single set of *n* difference scores. Looking at Appendix Table C.3, we find it evident that the critical value of *t* becomes smaller as degrees of freedom increase. In fact, the power of the *t* test increases and the CI is narrower for larger degrees of freedom. A second advantage of the independent-groups design is that it does not require an additional measure for matching participants. Sometimes, such a measure can be difficult to obtain.

Why, then, should we use a repeated-measures or matched-pairs design? The answer lies in a comparison of the denominators of the *t* statistics (the *SE* of the difference between the means) for the two designs. In the independent-groups design, the *SE* is based on the pooled variability of the individual scores, whereas in the repeated-measures design, the *SE* is based on the variability of the *n* difference scores. The latter *SE* will generally be smaller. To understand why, consider a data set in which the scores are perfectly correlated. For example, the scores for 10 subjects tested under both an experimental (E) and control (C) condition might be

|       |     |     |     |     | Subject |     |     |     |     |     |
| ----- | --- | --- | --- | --- | ------- | --- | --- | --- | --- | --- |
| Group | 1   | 2   | 3   | 4   | 5       | 6   | 7   | 8   | 9   | 10  |
| E     | 5   | 10  | 3   | 7   | 12      | 13  | 9   | 4   | 8   | 15  |
| C     | 7   | 12  | 5   | 9   | 14      | 15  | 11  | 6   | 10  | 17  |

Note that when two sets of scores are perfectly correlated, the difference is constant across subjects. In the repeated-measures design, the variance of the difference is the denominator of the *t*. In the preceding example, this variance would be zero, and *any* difference between the E and C means would be significant. This would be true no matter how variable the scores within a condition are. Although we never have correlations this high, the correlations usually achieved by testing each subject under both conditions, or by matching subjects, will usually reduce the *SE* of the mean difference considerably compared with the variability of the individual scores.

A more formal argument is as follows. From Appendix 5.1, we may write the variance of the sampling distribution of the difference of two means as

$$\sigma_D^2 = \sigma_{\bar{Y}_1}^2 + \sigma_{\bar{Y}_2}^2 - 2\rho_{\bar{Y}_1\bar{Y}_2}\sigma_{\bar{Y}_1}\sigma_{\bar{Y}_2}$$

where $\rho$ is the correlation between the means. Because $\sigma_{\bar{Y}}^2 = \sigma^2/n$, and assuming homogeneous variances, we can rewrite the equation as

$$\sigma_D^2 = (1/n)(2\sigma^2 - 2\rho\sigma^2) = (1/n)(2\sigma^2)(1-\rho)$$

That correlation should be zero for the independent-groups design but greater than zero in both matched-pairs and repeated-measures designs. As a result, $\sigma_D^2$ will be smaller in correlated-scores designs ($\sigma^2_{cor}$) than in independent-groups designs ($\sigma^2_{ind}$). In fact, $\sigma^2_{cor}/\sigma^2_{ind}$ will equal $1 - \rho$. Therefore, correlated-scores designs will have smaller denominators and consequently larger $t$ ratios than independent-group designs. There will be some trade-off because the $t$ statistic for the correlated-scores design is distributed on fewer degrees of freedom than that for the independent-groups design. Nevertheless, if the same participants are tested under both conditions, or if participants are matched on the basis of a measure that is related to the dependent variable in the experiment, $\rho$ usually will be large enough to more than offset the loss in degrees of freedom. Ordinarily, the $t$ test will be more powerful and the CI narrower when scores are correlated than when scores are independent. The repeated-measures design is used extensively in behavioral research, largely for the reasons just presented. However, not all variables can be manipulated in this way. It would make no sense to use both methods of arithmetic instruction on the same participants. Nor is gender readily manipulated within participants. Furthermore, the researcher should be aware of the possibility of "contrast effects." Some experimental treatments (e.g., one amount of reward) have a very different effect when the same participant has been exposed to other treatments (e.g., other amounts of reward) than when the participant has experienced only that treatment.

## 6.11 CONCLUDING REMARKS

This chapter focused on various applications of the $t$ distribution and on concepts related to the $t$ statistic. We discussed CIs and $t$ tests for differences between means, together with formulas for effect size, with examples for both repeated-measures and independent-groups designs. Examples of the use of computer software to perform post hoc and a priori power calculations were also presented. Attention to all of these tools should help researchers to understand their data. To focus only on significance tests is to risk ignoring considerable additional information that is readily available. CIs focus on estimates of population effect sizes and provide a sense of the precision of those estimates. Standardized effect sizes, $E_S$, permit comparisons of results obtained under different conditions, or from different measurement scales, or from different experiments or laboratories. As a result of Cohen's (1988) work, we also have guidelines to judge whether the effect is small, large, or somewhere in between. Finally, $E_S$ provides an input needed for calculating power, and the $n$ required to achieve a specified level of power. Such power calculations can now be easily carried out with one of several statistical packages or with programs freely available on the Internet. In this chapter, we illustrated the use of two of these, GPOWER (which can be downloaded to your computer) and the UCLA calculator. We have occasion to refer to these again in future chapters.

## KEY CONCEPTS

| | |
|---|---|
| $t$ statistic | degrees of freedom |
| raw effect size | standardized effect size |
| post hoc calculation of power | *a priori* calculation of power |
| central $t$ distribution | noncentral $t$ distribution |
| noncentrality parameter, $\delta$ | homogeneity of variance (homoscedasticity) |

| pooled-variance estimate | sum of squares |
|---|---|
| separate-variance *t* | pooled-variance *t* |
| Welch's *t* statistic | contrast |
| standardized contrast | repeated-measures (within-subjects) designs |
| matched-pairs design | independent-groups (between-subjects) design |

## EXERCISES

**6.1**  An investigator wants to determine whether the difficulty of material to be learned influences the anxiety of college students. A random sample of 10 students is given both hard and easy material to learn (order of presentation is counterbalanced). After part of each task is completed, anxiety level is measured by using a questionnaire. The anxiety scores are as follows:

|      |    |    |    |    |    | Student |    |    |    |    |    |    |
|------|----|----|----|----|----|---------|----|----|----|----|----|----|
| Task | 1  | 2  | 3  | 4  | 5  | 6 | 7 | 8  | 9  | 10 | 11 | 12 |
| Hard | 48 | 71 | 65 | 47 | 53 | 55 | 68 | 71 | 59 | 31 | 80 | 77 |
| Easy | 40 | 59 | 58 | 51 | 49 | 55 | 70 | 61 | 57 | 32 | 70 | 69 |

(a) Find the 95% CI for the difference in the population means corresponding to the two conditions.

(b) Test whether anxiety is significantly different in the two difficulty conditions by using a matched-group *t* test. State $H_0$ and $H_1$ and indicate the rejection region for $\alpha = .05$.

(c) Redo parts (a) and (b), assuming that the experiment had been done with two independent groups of 12 participants each. What are the strengths and weaknesses of each design? Note any differences in results of the analyses and the reasons for them in your answer, as well as any other considerations that you believe are important.

**6.2**  A sample of nine 30-day-old protein-deficient infants are given a motor skills test. The mean for a normal population is 60. The data are

40 69 75 42 38 47 37 52 31

(a) Find a .90 CI for the mean of the protein-deficient population.

(b) Is the mean score of the protein-deficient children significantly below that of a normal population?

(c) Our estimate of the mean of the protein-deficient population is very imprecise. Using the value of *s* calculated in part (a), estimate the sample size needed to have a CI width of only 12 points.

(d) After 3 months on a normal diet, the nine children have scores of

48 68 77 46 47 46 41 51 34

Estimate the mean of the population after 3 months of a normal diet. Calculate the .90 CI and test whether this population mean is below the normal value of 60. Assume $\alpha = .05$.

(e) Calculate difference scores and test whether there has been an improvement from the first test to the second. Assume $\alpha = .05$.

(f) Calculate the standardized effect of the normal diet.

**6.3** For a matched-group design, we wish to test $H_0$: $\mu_D = 0$ against $H_1$: $\mu_D > 0$ at $\alpha = .05$. Using a sample of 16 participants, we find $\overline{D} = 2.0$ and $s_D = 5.6$.

(a) Carry out the $t$ test.

(b) Calculate the standardized effect size.

(c) What power did the $t$ test have to reject the null hypothesis, given the value of $E_S$ calculated in part (b)?

(d) What power would the $t$ test have to reject the null hypothesis, given the value of $E_S$ calculated in part (b) and $N = 36$ instead of 16?

(e) What $N$ would be required to have power equal to or greater than .80?

(f) In parts (c) and (d), you should have found the power of the $t$ test. Redo the power calculations in part (c), using the standardized normal distribution (see Chapter 5 for a review of the method) for $N = 16$ and for the $N$ in your answer to part (e). How good an approximation are these results to the results you obtained with the $t$ distribution? Is the approximation better or worse as $n$ increases? Why might this be?

**6.4** In an independent-groups design, we find

| Group 1 | Group 2 |
|---|---|
| $n_1 = 18$ | $n_2 = 14$ |
| $s_1^2 = 16$ | $s_2^2 = 20$ |
| $\overline{Y}_1 = 30.1$ | $\overline{Y}_2 = 27.7$ |

(a) Find the 95% CI for $\mu_1 - \mu_2$. Assuming we wish to test $H_0$: $\mu_1 = \mu_2$ against a two-tailed alternative, what can we conclude?

(b) Calculate the standardized effect size. With this effect size, what power did the experiment have to reject the null hypothesis?

(c) Suppose we wished to redo the study with equal $n$ and want .8 power to reject $H_0$, assuming the effect size calculated in part (b). What size $n$ would we need?

(d) Using the $n$ from part (c), and assuming the variances given in part (a), what would the width of the new CI be?

**6.5** In an independent-groups design we have

| Group 1 | Group 2 |
|---|---|
| $n_1 = 21$ | $n_2 = 11$ |
| $s_1^2 = 8$ | $s_2^2 = 30$ |
| $\overline{Y}_1 = 30.2$ | $\overline{Y}_2 = 27.0$ |

(a) Test the null hypothesis at $\alpha = .05$ against a two-tailed alternative by using the pooled-variance $t$ test.

(b) Test the null hypothesis at $\alpha = .05$ against a two-tailed alternative by using the separate-variance (Welch) $t$ test.

(c) Explain any differences in your conclusions in parts (a) and (b).

**6.6** An arithmetic skills test is given to 8- and 10-year-old boys and girls. There are 10 children in each of the four cells of this research design. The means and standard deviations are given as follows:

| Children | 8 Years | 10 Years |
|----------|---------|----------|
| Boys     |         |          |
| $\overline{Y}$ | 58 | 72 |
| $s$      | 2.7     | 2.1      |
| Girls    |         |          |
| $\overline{Y}$ | 53 | 60 |
| $s$      | 2.9     | 2.2      |

(a) (i) Calculate a .90 CI for the difference in population means for 8- and 10-year-old girls ($\mu_{10,G} - \mu_{8,G}$). (ii) Assume you wish to test the null hypothesis against $H_1: \mu_{10,G} > \mu_{8,G}$. What can you conclude on the basis of the CI?

(b) There is considerable data showing that boys do better than girls on tests such as this arithmetic test. An interesting question is whether this advantage increases with age. In other words, is the difference between boys and girls greater at age 10 than at age 8? (i) State $H_0$ and $H_1$ in terms of a linear combination of the four population means. (ii) Carry out a $t$ test of your null hypothesis, briefly reporting the conclusion.

**6.7** Three groups of participants are required to solve problems under varying levels of environmental stress (noise: low, medium, and high). The experimenter has hypothesized an inverted U-shaped function, with the belief that performance should be best under medium stress and about equal for the high- and low-stress conditions. The necessary information for the three groups is presented as follows:

|        | Low     | Medium  | High    |
|--------|---------|---------|---------|
| $n$    | 15      | 18      | 21      |
| $\overline{Y}$ | 67.333 | 70.611 | 66.048 |
| $s$    | 6.102   | 6.137   | 6.128   |

To test his or her theory, the experimenter carries out two statistical tests. In each case, state $H_0$, $H_1$, and the rejection region, and carry out the test, reporting your conclusion.

(a) According to the theory, the average performance of low and high populations should not differ from each other.

(b) According to the theory, the average of a medium population should be higher than the average of the combined low and high populations.

(c) Calculate the standardized effect associated with each of the two contrasts.

**6.8** Several researchers have compared laboratory reading (participants knew they would be tested for recall) with natural reading (participants read material without knowing they would be tested). In one such study, two groups of 9 participants each (lab, natural groups) were tested twice on the same materials, once on each of two different days. Free-recall percentages (correct responses) were as follows:

| Group | Percentage |
|---|---|
| Lab | |
| Day 1 | 45  60  42  57  63  38  36  51 |
| Day 2 | 43  38  28  40  47  23  16  32 |
| Natural | |
| Day 1 | 64  51  44  48  49  55  32  31 |
| Day 2 | 21  38  19  16  24  27  22  35 |

(a) For each group, find the .95 CI for the population mean of the change in recall over the 2 days.

(b) We wish to compare the two groups on Day 2. Assuming a two-tailed test, can we reject $H_0$ at the .05 level?

(c) From part (a), we have a change score for each subject. We wish to test whether the amount of change is the same for the two populations of readers. State the null and alternative hypotheses. Do the test at the .05 level.

**6.9** The data for this problem are in the TC file in the *Seasons* folder of the CD.

(a) Calculate the standardized effect size ($E_S$) for the winter – spring difference in TC scores (TC1 − TC2) for the sayhlth = 2 (very good) and for the sayhlth = 4 (fair) group. How would you characterize the effects in terms of Cohen's guidelines? (See Chapter 6 to review the guidelines.)

(b) Calculate the winter – spring CIs for the two sayhlth groups of part (a). In which is the CI narrower? Also calculate the $t$ statistic for each. Which has the larger $t$? The lower $p$ value?

(c) Considering the various statistics, discuss the effects of seasons (winter versus spring) on TC level.

The next problems are open ended but represent the task faced by the investigator with a large data set.

**6.10** The Royer_acc file on the CD contains subtraction, addition, multiplication, and mean percentage correct for male and female third to eighth graders who had accuracy scores for all three arithmetic operations. Considerable attention has been given to the relative quantitative skills of male and female students. What differences, if any, are there between the sexes in performance? Support your conclusions with graphs, and any statistics—including significance test results, CIs, and effect sizes—that you find relevant.

⬤   **6.11**   Using the Royer_rt file, which provides response times paralleling the accuracy scores in this exercise, discuss differences, if any, between the sexes, again supporting your answer with graphs and statistics.

---

## APPENDIX 6.1

### The *SE* of a Contrast

To obtain a CI, or to test the null hypothesis about $\psi$, we require an estimate of the *SE* of the sampling distribution of $\hat{\psi}$. To derive an expression for that estimate, we note that $\hat{\psi}$ is a linear combination of the sample means. In Appendix 5.1, we proved that a linear combination $(L)$ of independently distributed variables $(V)$ of the form

$$L = w_1 V_1 + w_2 V_2 + \cdots + w_J V_J \tag{6.27}$$

has variance

$$\sigma_L^2 = w_1^2 \sigma_1^2 + w_2^2 \sigma_2^2 + \cdots + w_J^2 \sigma_J^2 \tag{6.28}$$

where the $w_k$ are weights and $\sigma_k^2$ is the variance of $V_k$. Replacing $L$ by $\psi$ and substituting parameter estimators into Equation 6.27, we have

$$
\begin{aligned}
s_{\hat{\psi}}^2 &= w_1^2 s_{\bar{Y}_1}^2 + w_2^2 s_{\bar{Y}_2}^2 + \cdots + w_J^2 s_{\bar{Y}_J}^2 \\
&= w_1^2 \frac{s_1^2}{n_1} + w_2^2 \frac{s_2^2}{n_2} + \cdots + w_J^2 \frac{s_J^2}{n_J}
\end{aligned} \tag{6.29}
$$

Assuming homogeneity of variance, we may rewrite Equation 6.29 as

$$
\begin{aligned}
s_{\hat{\psi}}^2 &= \left( \frac{w_1^2}{n_1} + \frac{w_2^2}{n_2} + \cdots + \frac{w_J^2}{n_J} \right) s_{\text{pooled}}^2 \\
&= s_{\text{pooled}}^2 \sum_{j=1}^{J} \frac{w_j^2}{n_j}
\end{aligned} \tag{6.30}
$$

where $s_{\text{pooled}}^2$ is the weighted (by degrees of freedom) average of the group variances; that is,

$$s_{\text{pooled}}^2 = \frac{(n_1 - 1)s_1^2 + (n_2 - 1)s_2^2 + \cdots + (n_J - 1)s_J^2}{\displaystyle\sum_{j=1}^{J} n_j - J} \tag{6.31}$$

and $J$ is the number of groups. Substituting the pooled-variance estimate into Equation 6.30 and taking the square root yields an expression for the estimate of the *SE* of $\hat{\psi}$:

$$s_{\hat{\psi}} = s_{\text{pooled}} \sqrt{\sum_{j=1}^{J} \frac{w_j^2}{n_j}} \tag{6.32}$$

# Chapter 7

## The Chi-Square and
## *F* Distributions

## 7.1 INTRODUCTION

The chi-square ($\chi^2$) distribution is of interest both because of its role in data analyses and its relation to the normal, $t$, and $F$ distributions. With respect to data analyses, the most common application is to frequency data. In such applications, the $\chi^2$ distribution is used to determine how well a theoretical distribution fits an observed distribution, and in testing whether two or more categorical variables are independent. An example of the **goodness-of-fit** application would be in testing whether the distribution of letter grades in a class conformed to some theoretical distribution such as 15% As and Fs, 20% Bs and Ds, and 30% Cs. An example of the **test of independence** would be one in which we ask whether the distribution of letter grades is the same in the populations of male and female students. That is, is the distribution of grades independent of gender? An introduction to these applications of the chi-square statistic may be found in almost every introductory statistics textbook, and entire textbooks have presented detailed treatments, particularly of tests of independence in multifactor designs (e.g., Bishop, Fienberg, & Holland, 1975; Fienberg, 1977; Fliess, 1973).

In this chapter, we limit our presentation of $\chi^2$ to defining the distribution and illustrating how it can be used to draw inferences about population variances. If the scores in the population are distributed independently and normally, confidence intervals (CI) may be calculated for the variance, and hypothesis tests about the variance may also be carried out. We also consider the consequences of violating the assumptions upon which the chi-square test rests. After this discussion of the application of the chi-square statistic to inferences about variances, we develop the relation of $\chi^2$ to the $F$ distribution. Whereas the $\chi^2$ distribution allows us to draw inferences about a single population variance, the $F$ distribution provides a basis for inferences about the ratio of two population variances.

Perhaps the most common application of the $F$ distribution is in **analysis of variance** (**ANOVA**), a focus of much of this book. In an ANOVA, the numerator of the $F$ ratio is a variance of a set of sample means, and the denominator is a measure of chance, or error, variance. The $F$ test in an ANOVA addresses the question of whether the variability of the group means is greater than what could reasonably be attributed to chance. If the $F$ ratio is large enough, the null hypothesis that the population means are all equal can be rejected. In the present chapter, we define the $F$ statistic, and we apply it to situations in which we compare the variances of two independent samples in order to test the null hypothesis that the two sampled population variances are equal. We also develop relations that exist among the chi-square, $t$, and $F$ statistics.

## 7.2 THE $\chi^2$ DISTRIBUTION

Assume that $N$ scores are randomly sampled from a population of scores that are independently and normally distributed with mean $\mu$ and standard deviation $\sigma$. Each of the sampled scores is transformed into a $z$ score by first subtracting $\mu$ and then dividing the result by $\sigma$. These $z$ scores are then squared and summed. Translating our verbal description into an equation for the chi-square statistic, we have

$$\chi_N^2 = \sum_{i=1}^{N} \frac{(Y_i - \mu)^2}{\sigma^2} \tag{7.1}$$

If many such random samples of size $N$ are drawn from a normal population, and $\chi^2$ is calculated for each sample, the sampling distribution will have a characteristic density that will depend on degrees of freedom. The quantity in Equation 7.1 has $N$ $df$ (as indicated by the subscript on $\chi^2$) because $N$ independent values of $Y$ have entered into the statistic. Because the values of $\mu$ and $\sigma$ are values of population parameters, there are no constraints on the $N$ values of $Y$ and therefore no degrees of freedom are lost.

As Figure 7.1 illustrates, the $\chi^2$ distribution is skewed; the skew is less pronounced as the degrees of freedom increase. Several other properties of the distribution should be noted. First, the mean of the distribution is equal to its degrees of freedom and its variance is twice the degrees of freedom:

$$E(\chi^2) = df \quad \text{and} \quad var(\chi^2) = (2)(df)$$

Second, the sum of independently distributed $\chi^2$ variables also has a $\chi^2$ distribution. The degrees of freedom associated with the sum is the sum of the degrees of freedom for the component values of $\chi^2$. For example, a quantity obtained by summing a chi-square statistic with 2 $df$ and one with 3 $df$ will have 5 $df$. This is the **additive property** for independent chi-square statistics.

Appendix Table C.4 presents critical values of $\chi^2$ for various numbers of degrees of freedom. Because a $\chi^2$ with 1 $df$ is just a squared $z$ score, the values in the first row of Table C.4 are related to those in Table C.2 for the normal distribution. For example, .95 of a normally distributed population of scores lies between $z = -1.96$ and $z = 1.96$. Therefore, .95 of $\chi^2$ values on 1 $df$ should lie between 0 and $1.96^2$, that is, between 0 and 3.8416. This in turn implies that .05 of scores should exceed 3.8416. This is, in fact, the .05 critical value of $\chi^2$ when $df = 1$ in Table C.4. Note that the mean of any $\chi^2$ distribution is equal to its

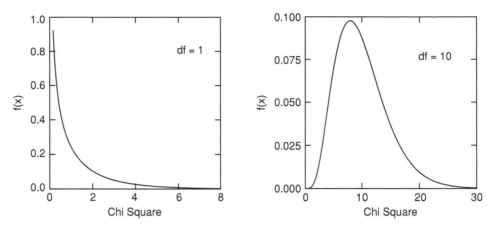

**Fig. 7.1** Two $\chi^2$ distributions. For $\alpha = .05$, the critical values are 3.84 ($df = 1$) and 25.00 ($df = 10$).

degrees of freedom. Therefore, as the degrees of freedom increase, the distribution shifts to the right and the critical values of $\chi^2$ for any $\alpha$ level become larger.

In Equation 7.1, we subtracted the *population* mean from each of the $N$ scores in the sample. Suppose we repeated our sampling experiment but, this time, we subtract the *sample* mean from each score instead of the population mean. In other words, we draw a sample of $N$ scores from a normally distributed population. For each score, we subtract the sample mean, square the result, and then divide by the population variance. Then we sum these transformed scores. Equation 7.2 summarizes these operations:

$$\chi^2_{N-1} = \sum_{i=1}^{N} \frac{(Y_i - \overline{Y})^2}{\sigma^2} \tag{7.2}$$

Because

$$\sum \frac{(Y - \overline{Y})^2}{N-1} = s^2$$

we often find Equation 7.2 written as

$$\chi^2_{N-1} = \frac{(N-1)s^2}{\sigma^2} \tag{7.3}$$

This statistic is also distributed as $\chi^2$, but on $N-1$ $df$ in contrast to the quantity in Equation 7.1, which is distributed on $N$ $df$. The loss of a degree of freedom is caused by taking deviations of $N$ scores about their mean; because the sum of these deviations must equal zero, 1 $df$ is lost. By capitalizing on the additive property of $\chi^2$, Appendix 7.1 demonstrates more formally why the statistic in Equation 7.2, or 7.3, is distributed on $N-1$ $df$.

## 7.3 INFERENCES ABOUT THE POPULATION VARIANCE

Equation 7.3 provides the basis for drawing inferences about variances. We consider that application of the chi-square statistic next. In the example we present, we have a hypothesis that predicts both the mean and variance of a set of scores. The $t$ test of Chapter 6 provides a test of the prediction about the mean. Here we illustrate the application of the chi-square statistic to a test of the prediction about the variance.

## 7.3.1 An Example

Consider a population of chronically ill patients whose symptoms fluctuate unpredictably over time, even when the patients are maintained on standard drug therapy. When given monthly tests, the patients are equally likely to have "good" and "bad" months; that is, they are equally likely to exhibit symptom levels that are better or worse than their baseline levels. Thirty of these patients are selected for a study in which they are given a new drug and tested monthly for 1 year. If the new drug is no more effective than the old one, and if month-to-month fluctuations can be considered to be independent of one another, the number of "good" months for each patient tested should follow a binomial distribution with $\pi = .5$. From Chapter 4, we know that the mean number of good months for patients should be $\pi m$, where $m$ is the number of monthly tests. In this example, that would be $(.5)(12)$, or 6. We know something else as well about the binomial distribution; the variance is $\pi(1 - \pi)m$. Therefore, the theoretical variance of the number of good months out of the 12 months tested is $(.5)(.5)(12)$, or 3. In summary, the hypothesis that the new drug produces the same chance variation over months that the old one did implies two null hypotheses: $H_{01}$: $\mu = 6$, and $H_{02}$: $\sigma^2 = 3$, where $\mu$ is the mean number of "good" months in the population of patients, and $\sigma^2$ is the variance of the number of "good" months.

The observed mean number of good months $(\overline{Y})$, averaging over the 30 patients, is 6.4, and the observed variance $(s^2)$ is 5.1. A $t$ statistic on 29 $df$ provides a test of $H_{01}$: $\mu = 6$;

$$t = \frac{6.4 - 6}{\sqrt{5.1/30}} = 0.97$$

Thus, the observed number of good months is not large enough to cause us to reject the hypothesis that the new and old drugs are equally effective.

We can also use the sample variance to further investigate the effectiveness of the new drug. We first construct a CI for $\sigma^2$. Assume that the population of scores (in our example, a score is the number of "good" months in the 12 months tested) is normally distributed. Then it follows from Equation 7.3 that $(N - 1)s^2/\sigma^2$ is a chi-square statistic and therefore

$$p\left[\chi^2_{N-1,1-\alpha/2} < (N - 1)s^2/\sigma^2 < \chi^2_{N-1,\alpha/2}\right] = 1 - \alpha \qquad (7.4)$$

where $\chi^2_{N-1,\alpha/2}$ is exceeded by $\alpha/2$ of the $\chi^2$ distribution on $N - 1$ $df$. For example, if we want a .95 CI, $\alpha = .05$, and $\chi^2_{N-1,\alpha/2}$ is the value of $\chi^2$ exceeded by .025 of the distribution for 29 (because we have 30 patients) $df$. The value of $\chi^2_{N-1,1-\alpha/2}$ is that value exceeded by .975 of the $\chi^2$ distribution. Finding the .975 and .025 critical $\chi^2$ values from Appendix Table C.4, and replacing $N$ by 30 and $s^2$ by the observed value, 5.1, we can rewrite Equation 7.4 as

$$p(16.047 < (20)(5.1)/\sigma^2 < 45.722) = .95$$

What we want, however, are bounds on $\sigma^2$. Algebraic manipulation of Equation 7.4 yields the general form of the CI:

$$p\left[\frac{(N-1)s^2}{\chi^2_{N-1,\alpha/2}} < \sigma^2 < \frac{(N-1)s^2}{\chi^2_{N-1,1-\alpha/2}}\right] = 1 - \alpha \tag{7.5}$$

Substituting numerical values into this equation, we have

$$p\left[\frac{(29)(5.1)}{45.722} < \sigma^2 < \frac{(29)(5.1)}{16.047}\right] = .95$$

and, doing the arithmetic,

$$p(3.235 < \sigma^2 < 9.217) = .95$$

Two points are worth noting about the preceding result. First, in Chapters 5 and 6, CIs based on the normal and $t$ distributions were symmetric about the statistic estimating the population parameter; for example, in the estimation of $\mu$, the bounds were equidistant from $\overline{Y}$. However, because the $\chi^2$ distribution is not symmetric, the CI just calculated is not symmetric about $s^2$, our estimate of $\sigma^2$. The second point is that because the theoretical variance, 3, does not fall within the .95 CI, we may reject at the .05 level the null hypothesis, $H_{02}: \sigma^2 = 3$, in favor of the two-tailed alternative, $H_1: \sigma^2 \neq 3$. We can also test $H_{02}$ directly. Table 7.1 presents the test statistic and summarizes the test procedure against three possible forms of the alternative hypothesis.

The test of the null hypothesis against a two-tailed alternative indicates that the variance is larger than we would expect it to be if the test and standard drugs were equally effective and the use of the binomial distribution was appropriate. Because the sample mean is consistent with the hypothesis that the drugs are equally effective, one possibility is that the new drug is more effective than the standard drug for some patients, but less effective for other patients—leading to a situation in which, on the average, the drugs are equally effective, but with too much variance for the drugs to be equally effective for each patient. If this was the case, a next step in the research would be to look for differences in two subsets of patients—those who improved with the new drug therapy and those who did not. Another possibility is that the assumption of random short-term fluctuations of symptoms over time is not valid, but rather that during the course of the disease, the patients have periods during which either good months or bad months occur more frequently. If this is the case, the use of the binomial distribution to calculate the theoretical variance is not appropriate, because the assumption of independence does not hold. To obtain a more definitive answer about drug effectiveness, we would really need to also have a control group of patients treated with the standard drug, and we would have to look at the variances and the sequences of good and bad months in both groups. Although our example is an artificial one, medical treatments may have positive effects for some individuals and negative effects for others. In such cases, the mean may be little affected but the treatment may increase variability.

The model testing procedure we have just illustrated has certain risks. Failing to reject the null hypothesis that the population variance (or any other parameter whose value is predicted by the model) has the predicted value provides support for the model. Sloppy researchers who have small $N$s may find support for their position because of a lack of power. Confidence intervals are helpful in assessing the validity of a conclusion based on a statistical test. If the interval containing the population variance is wide, we should

**TABLE 7.1**   USING THE CHI-SQUARE STATISTIC TO TEST HYPOTHESES ABOUT VARIANCES

**1.**

| If $H_1$ is | Reject $H_0$ if |
|---|---|
| $\sigma^2 > \sigma_{hyp}^2$ | $\chi^2 > \chi_\alpha^2$ |
| $\sigma^2 < \sigma_{hyp}^2$ | $\chi^2 < \chi_{1-\alpha}^2$ |
| $\sigma^2 \neq \sigma_{hyp}^2$ | $\chi^2 < \chi_{1-\alpha/2}^2$ or $\chi^2 > \chi_{\alpha/2}^2$ |

where

$$\chi^2 = \frac{(N-1)(s^2)}{\sigma_{hyp}^2}$$

If $\alpha = .05$, and $df = 29$ (as in our example),

| If $H_1$ is | Reject $H_0$ if |
|---|---|
| $\sigma^2 > \sigma_{hyp}^2$ | $\chi^2 > 42.557$ |
| $\sigma^2 < \sigma_{hyp}^2$ | $\chi^2 < 17.708$ |
| $\sigma^2 \neq \sigma_{hyp}^2$ | $\chi^2 < 16.047$ or $\chi^2 > 45.722$ |

**2.** Now calculate the value of $\chi^2$ based on the data. In the example presented in the text,

$$\chi^2 = [(29)(5.1)]/3$$
$$= 49.30$$

Note that the value of $\sigma^2$ is the value assumed under $H_0$.

**3.** Compare the result with the appropriate critical value. If the alternative hypothesis is $\sigma^2 > \sigma_{hyp}^2$, or if the test is two tailed, the null hypothesis can be rejected. If the null hypothesis is true, the probability of exceeding 49.3, the observed value of $\chi^2$ in our example, is .011. This exact probability can be obtained from many sources, including the transformation menus in SYSTAT or SPSS, or from the UCLA Web site described in Chapter 6.

---

view a failure to reject the null hypothesis with some skepticism; a wide range of predicted parameter values would also have been consistent with the data. If the interval is very narrow, and the observed variance is close to the theoretical value, rejection of $H_0$ may imply high statistical power; we may be rejecting a model that—although not perfect—does a very good job of accounting for the data.

## 7.3.2 Violation of the Normality Assumption

We calculated the CI and conducted the hypothesis test of Table 7.1 under the assumption that the population distribution was normal. However, in the example of this section, we were dealing with a binomial distribution. Does this invalidate the inferences drawn?

The answer is that in this application we have no problem. The reason lies in the central limit theorem, which states that sums, and more generally linear combinations, tend to be normally distributed as $N$ increases. Each of the scores in our study is actually a sum of ones (correct responses) and zeros (errors); because there are 12 responses contributing to each score, they will tend to be normally distributed. Consequently, the true Type 1 error rate will tend to be approximately .05 when the significance test is carried out at the .05 level.

What about the validity of the test in other situations? There are many mathematical models that yield numerical predictions for means and variances of various statistics, and a test of whether the observed variance is consistent with that predicted by the model would contribute to an assessment of the model. Unfortunately, in many of these cases, the distribution whose variance is of interest may well be very skewed. Frequently, the theoretical distribution of interest looks much like the exponential distribution of Fig. 6.3 (see, e.g., Bower, 1961). In such cases, the true Type 1 error rate may be much greater than the nominal significance level. This returns us to one of our favorite themes: always plot the data or, when testing a theoretical model, plot the theoretical distribution of the variable of interest. If either the theory, or the data, indicate a clearly nonnormal population distribution, inferences about variances based on the chi-square statistic are likely to be invalid. Alternative procedures exist that do not depend on the normality assumption. The jackknife and bootstrap methods are two possible alternatives that are described in several sources (Efron, 1982; Efron & Gong, 1983; Miller, 1974; Mosteller & Tukey, 1977).

## 7.4 THE F DISTRIBUTION

To understand the $F$ distribution, we begin with a sampling experiment. Assume the existence of two independently and normally distributed populations with variances $\sigma_1^2$ and $\sigma_2^2$, respectively. Suppose we draw a random sample of size $n_1$ from the first population and a sample of size $n_2$ from the second population. The $F$ statistic is the ratio

$$F = \frac{s_1^2/\sigma_1^2}{s_2^2/\sigma_2^2} \tag{7.6}$$

If the two population variances are the same, we may write the preceding ratio as

$$F = s_1^2/s_2^2 \tag{7.7}$$

This provides the basis for tests of whether the population variances estimated by the sample variances are the same. If the ratio in Equation 7.7 is much smaller or much larger than one, it suggests that the sampled populations have different variances. We will shortly consider how we can determine whether the ratio is very large or small. The distribution of the $F$ ratio is determined by both the degrees of freedom of the numerator, $df_1$, and of the denominator, $df_2$.

Equation 7.6 provides a way of relating $F$ to $\chi^2$. Recall that

$$\chi^2 = \frac{\sum (Y - \overline{Y})^2}{\sigma^2}$$

Dividing the left and right side by the degrees of freedom, $n - 1$, we have

$$\frac{\chi^2}{(n-1)} = \frac{\sum (Y - \overline{Y})^2/(n-1)}{\sigma^2}$$
$$= s^2/\sigma^2$$

Comparing this with the components that form the $F$ ratio of Equation 7.6, we find that it follows that the $F$ statistic is essentially a ratio of two independent chi-square statistics, each divided by its degrees of freedom. Therefore, we can also write the $F$ ratio as

$$F = \frac{\chi_1^2/(n_1 - 1)}{\chi_2^2/(n_2 - 1)} \tag{7.8}$$

where the subscripts refer to the populations being sampled.

If we repeatedly draw random samples of sizes $n_1$ and $n_2$ from their respective populations, the sampling distribution of the ratio of sample variances will be distributed as $F$. Turning to Appendix Table C.5, we find critical values of the $F$ distribution for various values of $\alpha$, $df_1$, and $df_2$. The tabled values are those exceeded by $\alpha$ of the samples, assuming that the sampled populations are independently and normally distributed and have equal variances. The $df_1$ are the degrees of freedom associated with the numerator of the $F$ distribution, and $df_2$ are those associated with the denominator. When we form a ratio of sample variances from two populations, as in Equation 7.6, the numerator and denominator degrees of freedom are $n_1 - 1$ and $n_2 - 1$, respectively. In future chapters in which we consider other applications of the $F$ ratio, the degrees of freedom take on other values.

From the fact that the critical values of $F$ depend on the degrees of freedom, it should be evident that the $F$, like the $t$ and $\chi^2$ distributions, is not one distribution but a family of distributions, one for each possible combination of numerator and denominator degrees of freedom. If we were to repeatedly draw samples, computing the $F$ ratio each time, the average of the $F$s would be a function of the denominator degrees of freedom; more precisely,

$$E(F) = \frac{df_2}{df_2 - 2}$$

As the denominator degrees of freedom increase, the expected value of $F$ approaches one. Therefore, ratios of sample variances much less than, or much greater than, one indicate that the two sample variances are not estimating the same population variance. How different they must be in order to draw this conclusion depends on the degrees of freedom. For example, if $df_1 = 8$ and $df_2 = 10$, from Table C.5 we find that an $F$ of 3.07 will be exceeded with probability .05 when the two sample variances estimate the same population variance. In terms of the hypothesis testing logic applied in previous chapters, an $F$ larger than 3.07 suggests that either the population variances are equal and by chance a large value of $F$ has been obtained, or the null hypothesis of equal variances is false.

Although Table C.5 provides critical values, at best it provides only a rough sense of the $F$ distribution. We can improve our sense of the distribution by viewing the two examples in Fig. 7.2. Several points should be noted. First, as is typical for the $F$ distribution, the distributions are skewed to the right. Second, the values of $F$ are positive because $F$ is a ratio of variances, and variances are sums of squared quantities. Third, the value of $F$ exceeded by .05 of the distribution is smaller when there are 20 denominator degrees of freedom than when there are 5. In general, a smaller critical value is required as either numerator or denominator degrees of freedom increase. If we think about this for a moment, it makes good sense. If our samples were very large, the ratio of sample variances would closely approximate the ratio of population variances, and therefore even an $F$ only slightly different from one would suggest that the population variances differed.

One other point, not evident from the figure, should be noted. Because we are usually interested in whether the $F$ is significantly large, tables such as Table C.5 present only critical values in the right tail. We may occasionally be interested in probabilities associated

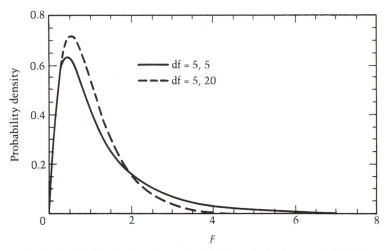

**Fig. 7.2** Two *F* distributions. For $\alpha = .05$, the critical values are 6.39 ($df_1$, $df_2 = 5$) and 2.90 ($df_1 = 5$, $df_2 = 20$).

with very small *F* ratios. For example, in subsequent chapters on the ANOVA, the logic is such that very small *F*s would suggest a failure of certain assumptions. More immediately, a CI on the ratio of two population variances requires a lower bound and depends on finding a critical value in the left (lower) tail. One way to find critical values from the lower tail of the distribution is to note that such critical values are related to those in the upper tail. Let the critical value that is exceeded with probability $\alpha$ be designated as $F_{\alpha, df_1, df_2}$ and the value that is exceeded with probability $1 - \alpha$ be designated as $F_{1-\alpha, df_1, df_2}$. The relation between these is

$$F_{1-\alpha, df_1, df_2} = 1/F_{\alpha, df_2, df_1} \qquad (7.9)$$

Suppose that $\alpha = .05$, $df_1 = 8$, and $df_2 = 12$. Then the critical value in the right tail is $F_{.05, 8, 12} = 2.85$. From Equation 7.9 we have

$$F_{.95, 8, 12} = 1/F_{.05, 12, 8} = 1/3.28 = .305$$

With access to various software packages such as SYSTAT, SPSS, and SAS, or to the Internet, we find that the solution to the "lower-tail problem" is simpler. If you do not have software capable of providing exact *p* values, access to the Internet can solve the problem. One solution is to use the *F* CDF calculator at the UCLA Web site referenced in Chapter 6. Supply a question mark for "X Value," and .05, 8, and 12 for the probability, and numerator and denominator degrees of freedom slots, and the answer, .3045, is quickly provided. The UCLA calculator is also useful for data sets for which one or both degrees of freedom values are not in Table C.5. GPOWER, the downloadable program we described in Chapter 6, provides a second solution. Select "Other *F* Tests" from the "Tests" menu, and then (ignoring other inputs) input the $\alpha$, and the numerator and denominator degrees of freedom. For the .05 lower-tail value to be obtained, the $\alpha$ should be .95. Note that the UCLA calculator requires that *p* be the area *below* the *F* you want, whereas GPOWER requires that you enter the area *above* the required *F*.

## 7.5 INFERENCES ABOUT POPULATION VARIANCE RATIOS

We are usually interested in comparing measures of the location of distributions, in particular, means. Nevertheless, there are times when a comparison of measures of variability may be of interest. The reason usually given for such comparisons is to determine whether the population variances meet the assumption of homogeneity of variance underlying the $t$ test (and the ANOVA). However, that rationale is not very compelling. As we saw in Chapter 6, the variances must be very unequal, or the $n$s must differ, before the error rate of the $t$ test is distorted. In those cases, the separate-variance $t$ test is available. Of greater interest is the possibility that two treatments differ in their effects on variability. For example, we may find little difference in the mean of a behavioral measure for two groups given different medication for depression, but greater variability in the scores of one of the groups. This would raise the possibility that the more variable data set represents some individuals who improved and others who became more depressed, something certainly worth investigating further. In some areas of research, we may be able to formulate precise enough theories to predict the effects of certain factors on variability as well as on averages, thus providing a more sensitive test of the theory. In such situations, comparisons of measures of variability in different conditions should be made. In what follows, we will use a subset of the Seasons data to illustrate some approaches to drawing inferences about population variances.

### 7.5.1 A Confidence Interval

Table 7.2 presents summary statistics based on the anxiety scores of men and women over 60 years of age. These data were extracted from the Seasons data file. Figure 7.3 presents histograms of the means over seasons. From Table 7.2, we see that the variance of the female mean scores is more than twice as great as that of the male mean scores. The histogram in Fig. 7.3 reinforces our sense that variability is greater in the sample of female anxiety scores. Confidence limits on the ratio of variances will provide a better sense of the possible range of values of this ratio.

**TABLE 7.2**    ANXIETY STATISTICS FOR MEN AND
WOMEN OVER 60 YEARS OF AGE

| Sex = | Male | Female |
|---|---|---|
| N of cases | 55 | 41 |
| Minimum | 2.000 | 1.250 |
| Maximum | 6.500 | 7.750 |
| Median | 4.875 | 4.625 |
| Mean | 4.618 | 4.451 |
| Standard Dev | 0.927 | 1.356 |
| Variance | 0.860 | 1.840 |
| Skewness(G1) | −0.836 | −0.280 |
| SE Skewness | 0.322 | 0.369 |
| Kurtosis(G2) | 0.903 | 0.985 |
| SE Kurtosis | 0.634 | 0.724 |

*Note.* Output is from SYSTAT.

**TABLE 7.3**   CI FOR THE RATIO OF THE VARIANCES IN TABLE 7.2

In our example, let $\sigma_F^2$ be the variance of the female population and $\sigma_M^2$ be the variance of the male population. The $F$ ratio, $s_F^2/s_M^2$, $= 2.14$ and is distributed on 40 numerator $df$ and 54 $df$. From the UCLA Web site (see Chapter 6), we find the $F$ values required by Equation 7.11:

$$F_{.925,54,40} = .564 \quad \text{and} \quad F_{.025,54,40} = 1.819$$

Substituting these values and the values of the variances from Table 7.2 into Equation 7.10, we have

$$p\left[(.564)\left(\frac{1.84}{.86}\right) \le \frac{\sigma_1^2}{\sigma_2^2} \le (1.819)\left(\frac{1.84}{.86}\right)\right] = .95$$

Completing the arithmetic, we find that the upper and lower confidence limits are 1.207 and 3.892, respectively. Because the lower bound is greater than one, we can reject the null hypothesis of homogeneous variances at the .05 level.

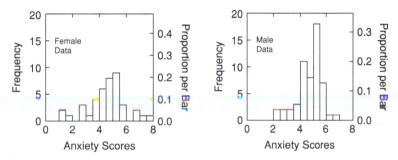

**Fig. 7.3**  Histograms of anxiety data for men and women over 60 years of age.

We begin by establishing limits on the variance ratio of Equation 7.6. From that definition of the $F$ statistic, we have

$$p\left(F_{1-\alpha/2,df_1,df_2} \le \frac{s_1^2/\sigma_1^2}{s_2^2/\sigma_2^2} \le F_{\alpha/2,df_1,df_2}\right) = 1 - \alpha$$

Algebraic manipulation and application of Equation 7.9 yields the general form of the CI:

$$p\left[\left(\frac{s_1^2}{s_2^2}\right)F_{1-\alpha/2,df_2,df_1} \le \frac{\sigma_1^2}{\sigma_2^2} \le \left(\frac{s_1^2}{s_2^2}\right)F_{\alpha/2,df_2,df_1}\right] = 1 - \alpha \tag{7.10}$$

Table 7.3 illustrates the application of Equation 7.10 by using the variances and sample sizes in Table 7.2. The confidence bounds indicate that the variance of the population of female anxiety scores is at least somewhat larger than that for the males.

Note that for the degrees of freedom in this data set, critical $F$ values are not available in Appendix Table C.5. In the past, researchers had to resort to linear interpolation in tables, or to obtaining an approximate $p$ value. With the availability of various statistical packages, such approximations are no longer necessary. As we pointed out in Section 7.4, The UCLA CDF calculator or GPOWER, as well as many other programs, can provide the necessary $F$ values. Commonly used packages such as SYSTAT, SPSS, and SAS will also provide the exact probability associated with many statistics such as $F$, $t$, $z$, and $\chi^2$.

**TABLE 7.4**  APPLYING THE F RATIO TO TEST HOMOGENEITY OF VARIANCE

**1.** Let $F = s_1^2/s_2^2$. Then

| If $H_1$ is | Reject $H_0$ if |
|---|---|
| $\sigma_1^2 > \sigma_2^2$ | $F > F_\alpha$ |
| $\sigma_1^2 < \sigma_2^2$ | $F < F_{1-\alpha}$ |
| $\sigma_1^2 \neq \sigma_2^2$ | $F > F_{\alpha/2}$ or $F < F_{1-\alpha/2}$ |

In our example, let $\sigma_F^2$ be the variance of the female population and $\sigma_M^2$ be the variance of the male population. The $F$ ratio, $s_F^2/s_M^2$, is distributed on 40 numerator $df$ and 54 denominator $df$. From the UCLA Web site, we find that

$$F_{.05,40,54} = 1.617, \ F_{.95,40,54} = 0.606, \ F_{.025,40,54} = 1.773, \ \text{and} \ F_{.975,40,54} = 0.550.$$

Therefore, the decision rule for this example is

| If $H_1$ is | Reject $H_0$ if |
|---|---|
| $\sigma_1^2 > \sigma_2^2$ | $F > 1.617$ |
| $\sigma_1^2 < \sigma_2^2$ | $F < .606$ |
| $\sigma_1^2 \neq \sigma_2^2$ | $F > 1.773$ or $F < .550$ |

**2.** From the statistics in Table 7.2, the $F$ ratio in our example is

$$F = 1.840/.86 = 2.14$$

Because we have no prior reason to expect greater variability in the scores of either gender, the test in our example is two tailed. Because $2.14 > 1.773$, the null hypothesis of equal population variances is rejected. With $df_1 = 40$ and $df_2 = 54$, the two-tailed $p = .01$.

## 7.5.2 The F Test

We can directly test the null hypothesis of equal variances. To illustrate the application of the $F$ test of variances, we again apply it to the Seasons anxiety scores of men and women over 60 years of age. Table 7.4 presents decision rules for the test, and calculations based on the statistics of Table 7.2. We again conclude that the population variances are not equal. It may not be immediately obvious, but, as is the case with other statistical tests, the test of the null hypothesis derived from the confidence limits in Table 7.3 and the direct test in Table 7.4 are equivalent. We illustrate the relation between the two procedures in Appendix 7.2.

## 7.5.3 The Normality Assumption

The validity of the $F$ test of the variance ratio illustrated in Table 7.4 rests on the assumption that the two populations are normally distributed. When the population distributions are skewed or have longer tails than the normal distribution, Type 1 error rates associated with this test are often inflated. This distortion *increases* as sample sizes increase because the shapes of the sample distributions more closely approximate those of the populations. Deciding whether a sample may reasonably be viewed as drawn from a normally distributed population is difficult. A useful graphic device is the normal probability plot that we described and illustrated in Chapter 2. As previously noted, such plots are available in many statistical packages. The expected values under the normality assumption are plotted as a function of the observed scores, and marked departures from linearity indicate nonnormality. In addition, it can be helpful to plot box plots and histograms, looking for obvious discrepancies between sample means and medians, and seeing if kurtosis and skewness values are large relative to their standard errors ($SE$). For confirmation, researchers can test for nonnormality by using the Shapiro–Wilk $W$ test, available in SPSS and SAS (Shapiro & Wilk, 1965). This test has good power for samples of 50 smaller. For larger samples, D'Agostino, Belanger, and D'Agostino (1990) describe alternative tests that take kurtosis and skewness statistics as inputs.

When the investigator is interested in assessing differences between conditions in variability and when the validity of the normality assumption is in doubt, the Levene (1960) or Brown–Forsythe (1974a) tests described in Chapter 6 provide an alternative to the $F$ test of variances. Although neither directly tests whether the population variances are equal, they do permit a comparison of the average spread of scores. As described in Chapter 6, the Levene test is based on the average absolute deviation of scores about the group mean, and the Brown–Forsythe test is based on the average absolute deviation of scores about the median. If the normality assumption is valid, these tests will be less powerful than the $F$ test of the variances. However, the Levene and Brown–Forsythe tests are less affected by violations of the normality assumption than the $F$ test based on the sample variances. The Brown–Forsythe test has been found to be more powerful than the Levene test under some conditions and therefore provides a reasonable alternative when normality is suspect, though users should be aware that when the population distributions differ in shape from one another, the actual Type 1 error rate may differ from the nominal error rate.

## 7.6 RELATIONS AMONG DISTRIBUTIONS

In this chapter, we have noted the relation of $\chi^2$ and $F$ to each other, and to the normal distribution. Both are also related to the $t$ distribution. We consider these relations next. We may write the one-sample $t$ statistic of Chapter 6 as

$$t = \frac{(\bar{Y} - \mu)}{\sqrt{\sum(Y - \bar{Y})^2/[(N)(N - 1)]}} \tag{7.11}$$

In order to show the relation of $t$ to $\chi^2$, we rearrange the quantities in Equation 7.11, divide numerator and denominator by $\sigma^2$, and then square the result:

$$t^2 = \frac{(\bar{Y} - \mu)^2/(\sigma^2/N)}{[\sum(Y - \bar{Y})^2/\sigma^2]/(N - 1)} \tag{7.12}$$

If $Y$ is normally distributed, the numerator on the right-hand side of Equation 7.12 is distributed as $\chi^2$ on 1 $df$; the denominator is distributed as $\chi^2$ on $N - 1$ $df$, divided by

$N - 1$. Therefore,

$$t = \frac{\sqrt{\chi_1^2}}{\sqrt{\chi_{N-1}^2/(N-1)}} \qquad (7.13)$$

The $t$ statistic for the two-sample case has a similar form. Beginning with the square of the usual formula for $t$, we have

$$t_{n_1+n_2-2}^2 = \frac{[(\overline{Y}_1 - \overline{Y}_2) - (\mu_1 - \mu_2)]^2}{s_{pooled}^2 (1/n_1 + 1/n_2)} \qquad (7.14)$$

Dividing the numerator and denominator of Equation 7.14 by $\sigma^2(1/n_1 + 1/n_2)$, we have

$$t_{n_1+n_2-2}^2 = \frac{[(\overline{Y}_1 - \overline{Y}_2) - (\mu_1 - \mu_2)]^2/\sigma^2 (1/n_1 + 1/n_2)}{s_{pooled}^2/\sigma^2} \qquad (7.15)$$

If the two population variances are the same, then $\sigma^2(1/n_1 + 1/n_2)$ is the variance of the sampling distribution of $\overline{Y}_1 - \overline{Y}_2$. If, in addition, $Y$ is normally distributed, the numerator of Equation 7.15 is distributed as $\chi^2$ on 1 $df$.

Under the assumptions of normality and homogeneity of variance, the denominator of Equation 7.15 is also related to $\chi^2$. We can rewrite the denominator as

$$\frac{(SS_1 + SS_2)/\sigma^2}{n_1 + n_2 - 2}$$

If the sums of squares (the $SS$ quantities) are numerators of estimates of the same population variance, this quantity is distributed as $\chi^2$ divided by its degrees of freedom. In that case, the two-sample $t$ statistic is of the same form as Equation 7.13.

If we square the right-hand side of Equation 7.13 and slightly rewrite the numerator, we have

$$t_{n_1+n_2-2}^2 = \frac{\chi_1^2/1}{\chi_{n_1+n_2-2}^2/(n_1 + n_2 - 2)} \qquad (7.16)$$

In other words, $t^2$ is the ratio of two chi-squared variables, each divided by its degrees of freedom. But this is exactly the definition of $F$ given by Equation 7.8. Therefore, a squared $t$ statistic is an $F$ with one numerator degree of freedom.

## 7.7 CONCLUDING REMARKS

This chapter had two major goals: first, to introduce the $\chi^2$ and $F$ distributions, two prominent players in statistical inference; second, to consider applications of these distributions to inferences about variances. With respect to the latter goal, it is worth repeating that when evaluating the effects of an independent variable, researchers focus on means or, less often, other measures of location, almost exclusively. However, knowledge of how other aspects of the data distributions are affected can contribute to both practical applications and the development of theory. This chapter provided one set of tools for investigating one aspect of a distribution's shape—its variance.

Inferential procedures based on the distributions considered thus far in the book play a major role in data analysis. The $t$ and $F$ distributions, in particular, have starring roles throughout the remainder of this book. This reflects the prominence of these distributions in data analyses reported in the research literature, a prominence resulting from ease of calculation, applicability to data from many research designs, and a reliance on statistics that are good estimators of population parameters under many conditions. Perhaps most importantly, *when their underlying assumptions are met*, the tests based on these distributions are **uniformly most powerful tests**; no alternative test will have greater power to reject the null hypothesis. Bear in mind, however, that when assumptions are violated, other procedures may provide more valid inferences. These may be tests based on other distributions, such as alternatives to the $t$ test based on ranked data, or modifications of the usual test statistic, such as $t'$ when variances are heterogeneous. With this in mind, we emphasize that there are several considerations prior to choosing a method of analysis: First, do the data indicate departures from assumptions? Second, if so, are these departures severe enough to distort CIs, increase Type 1 error rate, or decrease power? Third, if so, are there alternative procedures that are likely to yield more valid inferences? Answering these questions requires that we begin our data analysis by looking at the data. Summary statistics and data plots available in most statistical packages will aid this process.

## KEY CONCEPTS

| | |
|---|---|
| goodness-of-fit | test of independence |
| analysis of variance (ANOVA) | chi-square statistic |
| additive property of $\chi^2$ | $F$ statistic |
| uniformly most powerful tests | |

## EXERCISES

**7.1** Equation 7.5 states that $(N - 1)s^2/\sigma^2$ is distributed as a chi-square variable if each score in the sample is randomly drawn from an independently and normally distributed population of scores. Let's see what this implies.

**(a)** Suppose we draw many samples of size $N$ from a normally distributed population. We calculate the ratio, $(N - 1)s^2/\sigma^2$, for each sample. If $N = 6$, (i) what is the probability that this ratio is less than 9.236? (ii) What is the probability that the ratio lies between 1.145 and 6.626?

**(b)** The population sampled in part a has a variance of 10. If we still assume $N = 6$, in what proportion of samples will $s^2$ be less than 8.703?

**7.2** We are interested in a new method of teaching arithmetic. We use the new method with a sample of 31 students, and at the end of a trial period we give them a standardized test. In the past, the population of scores on the test has been approximately normally distributed with a mean of 64 and a variance of 10. Following the training period, the mean test score is 66 and the variance is 14.

**(a)** Has the new method of teaching led to a significant improvement in test scores? Let $\alpha = .05$.

**(b)** One interpretation of the increased variability on the test is that the new method helps some students but hurts the learning of other students. Is the increase in variability significant? Let $\alpha = .05$.

(c) We might better consider the variability under the new method by obtaining a CI. Find the .90 CI for $\sigma^2$.

**7.3** On the basis of a review of large amounts of data, it is well established that the variance of a population of ratings of the quality of a particular wine is 12.64. A new method for training raters is established in hopes of reducing the variance. In a sample of 10 judges trained under the new method, $s^2$ is 3.51.

(a) Would you conclude that the new method has effectively reduced the variance of ratings? Explain your reasoning.

(b) Suppose the population of scores was not normally distributed. Why is this a problem for the approach you took in part (a)? Would it be less of a problem if your sample size were larger? Explain.

**7.4** A sample of 7 scores is selected randomly from a normally distributed population. The scores are 22, 2, 0, 30, 28, 26, and 32.

(a) Find the 90% CI for the population variance.

(b) Assuming $\alpha = .05$, test the null hypothesis that the population standard deviation is 10 against the alternative hypothesis that it is greater than 10. Relate your conclusion to the confidence limits you calculated in part (a).

**7.5** We have samples of reading scores from 5 boys and 11 girls. We form a ratio of the variances of the two samples, $s_B^2/s_G^2$; call this $F$ in accord with Equation 7.7.

(a) If many samples of sizes 5 and 11 are drawn, (i) what is the proportion of $F$ values greater than 2.61 that we should expect? (ii) What is the proportion less than 4.47?

(b) What assumptions are implied in your approach to answering part (a)?

**7.6** Samples of scores are obtained from 9 male and 13 female subjects. Assuming $\alpha = .05$, answer the follwing.

(a) What is the rejection region if the researcher wishes to detect a difference in the variances?

(b) How large must $s_M^2/s_F^2$ be for you to conclude that the variance is greater in the population of boys' scores?

**7.7** In Exercise 6.5, we carried out a test of the means against a two-tailed alternative, using the pooled- and separate-variance $t$ test. It is of interest to decide whether the separate-variance test is justified. Assuming that the scores were sampled from a normal population, test whether the variances are equal against the alternative hypothesis that they are not. The $n$s were 21 and 11, and the variances were 8 and 30, respectively.

**7.8** An experimenter drew four independent random samples each of size 5 from one normally distributed population. The variance of the four sample means about their grand mean is 84.

(a) (i) Estimate the variance of the population from which the samples were drawn. (ii) How many degrees of freedom are associated with your estimate?

The experimenter also has a sample of 15 independent observations that are believed to be from the same population from which the original four samples were taken. The variance of the 15 scores is 384.

(b) Perform a statistical test to determine whether the 15 scores do come from the same population as the four samples of 5.

**7.9** In viewing summary statistics for multiplication accuracy in the Royer data (Royer_acc file in the *Royer* folder), we noted that in the fourth grade the male multacc scores seemed to be considerably more variable than the female scores.

(a) Find the .95 CI for the ratio of population variances $(s_M^2/s_F^2)$ for fourth-grade multiplication accuracy.

(b) Is there a significant difference in the variances? State the null and alternative hypotheses.

(c) Plot the two density distributions in any way you find helpful. This can include box plots, density plots, histograms, or stem-and-leaf plots. Does the plot provide any insight into the reason for the difference in variances? If so, can you suggest a further analysis of the data?

(d) Do you see any problem in the calculation of confidence limits and significance tests for this data set?

**7.10** Further analyzing the Royer_acc data of Exercise 7.10, calculate the Brown–Forsythe $t$ statistic to test whether there is a significant effect of gender on the variability of the fourth-grade multiplication accuracy scores.

**7.11** The Royer_rt file contains response times for addition, subtraction, and multiplication, a well as a variable labeled $rt$; this is the mean of the three measures.

(a) Plot the mean and standard deviations of the $rt$ variable as a function of grade, from Grade 3 to Grade 8. Describe the two functions.

(b) Test whether the variances of the sixth- and eighth-grade response times (RTs) differ at the .05 level. State $H_0$ and $H_1$.

# APPENDIX 7.1

## Chi-Square and Degrees of Freedom

We begin with the identity

$$Y_i - \mu = (Y_i - \overline{Y}) + (\overline{Y} - \mu)$$

Squaring both sides of the equation, summing the $N$ quantities, and applying the summation rules of Appendix A, we have

$$\sum_{i=1}^{N}(Y_i - \mu)^2 = \sum_{i=1}^{N}(Y_i - \overline{Y})^2 + N(\overline{Y} - \mu)^2 + 2(\overline{Y} - \mu)\sum_{i=1}^{N}(Y_i - \overline{Y})$$

Because $\sum(Y - \overline{Y}) = 0$, the preceding equation reduces to

$$\sum_{i=1}^{N}(Y_i - \mu)^2 = \sum_{i=1}^{N}(Y_i - \overline{Y})^2 + N(\overline{Y} - \mu)^2$$

Rearranging terms, and dividing both sides by the population variance, $\sigma^2$, yields

$$\frac{\sum(Y - \mu)^2}{\sigma^2} - \frac{N(\overline{Y} - \mu)^2}{\sigma^2} = \frac{\sum(Y - \overline{Y})^2}{\sigma^2}$$

or

$$\frac{\sum(Y - \mu)^2}{\sigma^2} - \frac{(\overline{Y} - \mu)^2}{\sigma^2/N} = \frac{\sum(Y - \overline{Y})^2}{\sigma^2}$$

However, the leftmost quantity is a chi-square statistic distributed on $N$ $df$. The quantity subtracted from it is a chi-square statistic on 1 $df$ because a single value $(\overline{Y})$ is subtracted from its expected value ($\mu$), and divided by the variance of its sampling distribution. From the additive property of chi square, it follows that the rightmost term is distributed on $N - 1$ *df*. That is, $\chi_N^2 - \chi_1^2 = \chi_{N-1}^2$.

---

## APPENDIX 7.2

---

## Relation Between the *F* test and the Confidence Interval for $\sigma_1^2/\sigma_2^2$

Equation 7.10 established confidence limits on the ratio of population variances:

$$p\left[\left(\frac{s_1^2}{s_2^2}\right) F_{1-\alpha/2,\, df_2,\, df_1} \leq \frac{\sigma_1^2}{\sigma_2^2} \leq \left(\frac{s_1^2}{s_2^2}\right) F_{\alpha/2,\, df_2,\, df_1}\right] = 1 - \alpha$$

Let $F_{\text{obs}}$ stand for the observed $F$ ratio, $s_1^2/s_2^2$. Let $F_L$ and $F_U$ stand for the lower and upper critical $F$ values. Then we can rewrite the preceding equation:

$$p\left(F_{\text{obs}} F_L \leq \frac{\sigma_1^2}{\sigma_2^2} \leq F_{\text{obs}} F_U\right) = 1 - \alpha$$

With respect to the CI, we reject $H_0$ if the value 1.00 does not fall within the interval. That is, we reject the null hypothesis if $1 < F_L F_{\text{obs}}$ or $1 > F_U F_{\text{obs}}$. Note that we can rewrite $1 < F_L F_{\text{obs}}$ as $1/F_L < F_{\text{obs}}$. However, $1/F_L = F_U$ is the upper critical value of the $F$ distribution; therefore, asking if one is less than the lower limit of the CI is the same as asking if the upper critical value of the $F$ distribution is less than the observed $F$ computed from the data. Similarly, asking whether the upper bound of the CI is less than one is equivalent to asking whether the observed $F$ is less than the lower critical value of the $F$ distribution. In summary, we can reject $H_0$ (that the population variances are equal) if the observed $F$ is greater than the upper critical value of the $F$ distribution or less than the lower critical value.

# Chapter 8

## Between-Subjects Designs: One Factor

## 8.1 INTRODUCTION

This chapter deals with the analysis of data from a research design that serves as a building block for the more complex designs we consider in subsequent chapters. In the one-factor, between-subjects design, the scores of several groups of participants are analyzed in order to decide whether the means of the **treatment populations,** the populations represented by the groups, are equal. In such studies, participants may either be selected from existing populations or be randomly assigned to one of several experimental conditions, or treatment levels. An example of the former is the Seasons study in which individuals were sampled from populations differing with respect to several factors, including gender, educational level, and occupation. Strictly speaking, that study would be classified as an observational study. True experiments involve random assignment of participants to levels of an independent variable; the independent variable is said to be manipulated and the design is often referred to as **completely randomized**. An example we mentioned in Chapter 6 was the experiment by Myers et al. (1983). In that experiment, participants were randomly assigned to study one of three texts presenting elementary rules of probability.

Whether the levels of the independent variable are observed or manipulated, the data analysis has much the same form and the underlying assumptions are the same. What characterizes the designs of this and the following chapter is that each participant yields a single score. These designs are **between-subjects designs**; all the variability in the data is due to differences between participants. In **within-subjects designs** the same participants are tested under several conditions, and there is variability within each participant's set of scores. Within-subject designs are also called **repeated-measures designs**. In later chapters we also consider **mixed designs**, in which there are both between- and within-subjects factors.

Between-subjects designs have the advantage of simplicity. Inferences require fewer assumptions than are required by designs in which each participant responds on several trials or under several conditions. Each additional assumption underlying the derivation of the test statistic is one more assumption that may be violated, possibly undermining the validity of the statistical inference. The between-subjects design also has the advantage of computational simplicity relative to other designs. This is less important in the present era of electronic calculators and fast computers than it was in the past. Nevertheless, it is useful to be able to obtain and check results quickly. The chief disadvantage of the between-subjects design is its relative inefficiency. Because individuals differ on so many dimensions, chance variability will often tend to be great, sometimes obscuring real effects and reducing the power of the statistical test. As we discussed in Chapter 6, matching participants on the basis of some measure other than the dependent variable, or testing each participant in several conditions, will often lead to a reduction in chance variability. We consider matching, or blocking, designs in Chapter 12 and repeated-measures designs in Chapter 13.

In this chapter, we begin by looking at part of the data on which the article by Myers et al. was based. As usual, this means generating and looking at descriptive statistics and plotting the data in several ways. We then use the data to illustrate a conceptual framework in which each score is viewed as a sum of components, and the total variability of the scores is viewed as a sum of the variabilities of those components. This leads us into the **analysis of variance**, or **ANOVA**, a partitioning of the total variability into parts that provide the basis for an $F$ test of the hypothesis that the treatment population means are the same. Having illustrated the ANOVA with our data set, we consider the underlying theory. We present a **structural model**, a model of the relation between each score and the population parameters, and we state other assumptions necessary to justify the $F$ test. Following this, we present several measures of effect size, and we consider the power of the $F$ test. Finally, we consider the consequences of violations of assumptions, and we examine possible remedies when those violations are thought to be severe enough to threaten the validity of our inferences.

This is a rather extensive menu of theory and calculations. To avoid presenting too many new ideas at once, we have placed the following restrictions on the presentation of material in this chapter:

1. We consider only the subset of between-subjects designs that involve a single independent variable; these are one-factor designs. We extend the development to multifactor between-subjects designs in Chapter 11.

2. We consider only **fixed-effect** variables. This means that we view the population of levels of the independent variable as consisting only of those that have been selected for the experiment. We have more to say about this in Chapter 13. At that point, we also introduce the concept of **random-effect** variables. The levels of these variables are assumed to be randomly sampled from a population of levels.

3. We consider only tests of the **omnibus null hypothesis**: $\mu_1 = \mu_2 = \cdots \mu_j = \cdots \mu_a$, where $\mu_j$ is the mean of a population of scores of individuals tested under $A_j$, the $j$th level of the independent variable, $A$, and there are $a$ levels of $A$ in the study. In Chapters 9 and 10, we extend the analysis of data from between-subjects designs to contrasts among means of subsets of conditions, and to the analysis of mathematical functions of quantitative independent variables, such as number of trials, time in therapy, or hours of sleep deprivation.

## 8.2 EXPLORING THE DATA

In the probability-learning experiment conducted by Myers et al. (1983), each of 48 participants studied one of three texts that presented elementary probability concepts such as the addition and multiplication rules, and conditional and joint probability. The participants were tested on 6 story and 6 formula problems immediately following study, and they were tested on a second set of 12 problems 2 days later. Half of each group of participants received the story problems first, and the other half received the formula problems first. The researchers were primarily interested in whether the relative performances of the groups differed on the two types of problems.[1] However, we will analyze the proportion correct of the 12 story problems, ignoring other aspects of the design and proceeding as if we had a one-factor design with three levels, and 16 participants at each level. The story problem scores are presented in Table 8.1, together with various summary statistics for each group. The standard text is abbreviated by S, the Low Explanatory text by LE, and the High Explanatory text by HE. The texts differed with respect to the kinds of examples used and the presence or absence of illustrations such as tree diagrams.

Figure 8.1 presents box plots of the three groups of data. Several aspects of the plot stand out. First, there is little difference between the S and LE data sets, whereas the HE set is noticeably different in several respects. It appears that the HE distribution is somewhat skewed because the median lies above the midpoint of the box. Also, with the exception of one outlying score, the HE data seem less variable. We note the apparent skew of the HE group and its smaller interhinge distance because, as with the $t$ test of Chapter 6, normality and homogeneity of variance are assumptions underlying the $F$ test of means. However, the skew is not so pronounced nor, as the variances in Table 8.1 indicate, are the spreads

**TABLE 8.1**   PROPORTION OF CORRECT SCORES IN THE MYERS ET AL. (1983) STUDY

| | S | LE | HE | |
|---|---|---|---|---|
| | .083 | .083 | .333 | |
| | .167 | .167 | .333 | |
| | .250 | .250 | .333 | |
| | .250 | .250 | .417 | |
| | .250 | .250 | .417 | |
| | .333 | .333 | .500 | |
| | .333 | .333 | .500 | |
| | .333 | .417 | .500 | |
| | .417 | .417 | .583 | |
| | .500 | .417 | .583 | |
| | .500 | .417 | .583 | |
| | .500 | .500 | .583 | |
| | .500 | .583 | .583 | |
| | .583 | .583 | .667 | |
| | .583 | .667 | .667 | |
| | .750 | .833 | .917 | |
| $\overline{Y}_{\cdot j} =$ | .396 | .406 | .531 | $\overline{Y}_{\cdot\cdot} = .444$ |
| $s^2 =$ | .031 | .038 | .023 | |

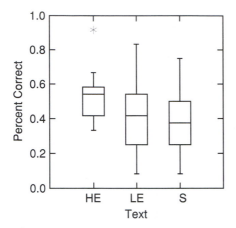

**Fig. 8.1** Box plots of the data in Table 8.1.

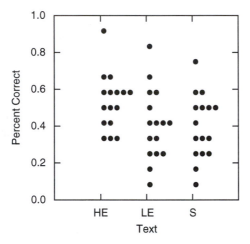

**Fig. 8.2** Dot-density plot of the data in
Table 8.1.

different enough to cause concern about the *F* test we present shortly. We can also see that
there is an outlier in the HE plot. This suggests the possibility that the higher HE mean in
Table 8.1 is merely a reflection of this one score. However, other aspects of the plot suggest
this is not the case; the median, which is not influenced by the outlier, is also higher in the
HE condition and the entire distribution is displaced upward relative to the other two. This
displacement is also apparent in the **dot-density** plot of Fig. 8.2. Such plots provide an
alternative to histograms, with each small circle or "dot" representing a score. In Fig. 8.2,
the advantage of the HE condition is reflected in the fact that almost one third (5 of 16)
of the scores in the S and LE conditions lie below the lowest score in the HE condition.
Whether this advantage of the HE group is large enough relative to the variability in the
data to enable us to conclude that it holds for the populations represented by these three
groups of scores is a question we consider shortly.

## 8.3 THE ANALYSIS OF VARIANCE

Before participants were assigned to the text conditions, they could be viewed as a sample from a single, infinitely large population. Assume that each individual in this parent population is randomly assigned to one of the three treatments (texts) applied in the experiment. There are then three treatment populations, very large populations of scores that potentially differ systematically from each other. Within this framework, we may view each of the sets of 16 scores in Table 8.1 as a random sample from the corresponding treatment population. Usually, the first question of interest is whether there are any differences among the means of the three populations of scores. More precisely, we wish to test the omnibus null hypothesis:

$$H_0 : \mu_S = \mu_{\text{LE}} = \mu_{\text{HE}}$$

In general, we assume that there are $a$ levels of the treatment, $A$, and the omnibus null hypothesis is

$$H_0 : \mu_1 = \mu_2 = \cdots = \mu_j = \cdots = \mu_a$$

The alternative hypothesis is that there is at least one inequality among the means of the $a$ treatment populations.

Suppose the null hypothesis in the probability-learning experiment is true; the three texts do not differ in their effects on the proportion correct on the story-problem test. Even if this were so, the three group means would differ from each other. By chance, the 16 individuals in one group may be more motivated, more alert, or more knowledgeable about probability than those in another group. In addition, there may be chance variations caused by other factors that affect test performance, such as the times at which the participants are tested. The test of the null hypothesis is really a test of whether the group means differ more than would be expected on the basis of these chance factors. If they do, then something more than chance variation is involved. That "something more" is presumably the effect of the independent variable (the text studied), and the null hypothesis should be rejected.

In the ANOVA, we attempt to determine whether more than chance variability is involved by comparing two independent estimates of the population error variance, estimates that do not differ significantly if the null hypothesis is true. One of these, the **between-groups mean square**, is based on the variance of the group means and is influenced by both chance variability and—if $H_0$ is false—the effects of the independent variable. We label this mean square $MS_A$. The second estimate of variance, the **error mean square**, is the average of the variances of scores in each group; it reflects only chance variability. We refer to this as $MS_{S/A}$ (the mean square for subjects within levels of A). If $MS_A$ is much larger than $MS_{S/A}$, we may decide that the spread among the group means is too large to have resulted only from chance variability. If so, we will conclude that the treatment population means are not all equal; that is, $H_0$ is false.

In the following sections, we develop formulas for the mean squares. We begin by partitioning the total variability in the data set into two components that provide the numerators of the mean squares. We discuss why the two mean squares are estimates of the same chance, or error, variability when $H_0$ is true and why, therefore, their ratio is distributed as $F$. Following this, we present a more formal discussion, including a model of the structure of the scores in terms of population parameters, and an explicit statement of assumptions.

### 8.3.1 Partitioning the Total Variability

Mean squares are ratios of sums of squared deviations to degrees of freedom. As we noted in Chapter 6, these sums of squared deviations are referred to as **sums of squares (SS)**. In this section we show that $SS_A$ and $SS_{S/A}$ together account for the total variability in the data of the one-factor design. We begin by partitioning the deviation of the $i$th score in the $j$th group $(Y_{ij})$ from the grand mean $(\overline{Y}..)$, the mean of all $an$ scores, into two components: first, the deviation of the score from the mean of its own treatment group $(\overline{Y}._j)$, and second, the deviation of the group mean from the grand mean:

$$Y_{ij} - \overline{Y}.. = (\overline{Y}._j - \overline{Y}..) + (Y_{ij} - \overline{Y}._j) \tag{8.1}$$

Table 8.2 illustrates this partitioning, using the data of Table 8.1. The table is divided into three sets of three columns. The first three columns contain the values of $Y_{ij} - \overline{Y}..$ for each of the three texts. The next three columns contain the effects of the three texts, $\overline{Y}._j - \overline{Y}...$ These **treatment effects** actually reflect both the effect of the treatment and chance variability. If there is a treatment effect in the population—that is, if the treatment population means differ—that population effect should be reflected in differences among the group means, and therefore in a deviation of any group mean from the grand mean. But even if $H_0$ is true, the group means will still differ, because there are different individuals in each group and they will perform differently because of many factors. The **residual** terms, $Y_{ij} - \overline{Y}._j$, are contained in the last three columns, and they reflect the variation in the performance of individuals who have received the same treatment. By squaring both sides of Equation 8.1, summing, and applying the rules of summation of Appendix A, we

**TABLE 8.2**  BREAKDOWN OF THE SCORES FROM THE MYERS ET AL. (1995) EXPERIMENT

| Scores − Grand Mean $(Y_{ij} - \overline{Y}..)$ | | | = | Text Effect $(\overline{Y}._j - \overline{Y}..)$ | | | + | Residual $(Y_{ij} - \overline{Y}._j)$ | | |
|---|---|---|---|---|---|---|---|---|---|---|
| −.361 | −.361 | −.111 | | −.049 | −.038 | .087 | | −.313 | −.323 | −.198 |
| −.277 | −.277 | −.111 | | −.049 | −.038 | .087 | | −.229 | −.239 | −.198 |
| −.194 | −.194 | −.111 | | −.049 | −.038 | .087 | | −.146 | −.156 | −.198 |
| −.194 | −.194 | −.027 | | −.049 | −.038 | .087 | | −.146 | −.156 | −.114 |
| −.194 | −.194 | −.027 | | −.049 | −.038 | .087 | | −.146 | −.156 | −.114 |
| −.111 | −.111 | .056 | | −.049 | −.038 | .087 | | −.063 | −.073 | −.031 |
| −.111 | −.111 | .056 | | −.049 | −.038 | .087 | | −.063 | −.073 | −.031 |
| −.111 | −.027 | .056 | | −.049 | −.038 | .087 | | −.063 | .011 | −.031 |
| −.027 | −.027 | .139 | | −.049 | −.038 | .087 | | .021 | .011 | .052 |
| .056 | −.027 | .139 | | −.049 | −.038 | .087 | | .104 | .011 | .052 |
| .056 | −.027 | .139 | | −.049 | −.038 | .087 | | .104 | .011 | .052 |
| .056 | .056 | .139 | | −.049 | −.038 | .087 | | .104 | .094 | .052 |
| .056 | .139 | .139 | | −.049 | −.038 | .087 | | .104 | .177 | .052 |
| .139 | .139 | .223 | | −.049 | −.038 | .087 | | .187 | .177 | .136 |
| .139 | .223 | .223 | | −.049 | −.038 | .087 | | .187 | .261 | .136 |
| .306 | .389 | .473 | | −.049 | −.038 | .087 | | .354 | .427 | .386 |

$SS_{tot} = \sum_j \sum_i (Y_{ij} - \overline{Y}..)^2 = (-.361)^2 + (-.277)^2 + \cdots + (.473)^2 = 1.561$

$SS_{Text} = n \sum_j (\overline{Y}._j - \overline{Y}..)^2 = (16)[(-.049)^2 + (-.038)^2 + (.087)^2] = .182$

$SS_{Res} = \sum_j \sum_i (Y_{ij} - \overline{Y}._j)^2 = (-.313)^2 + (-.229)^2 + \cdots + (.386)^2 = 1.379$

find that the **total sum of squares** ($SS_{tot}$) is partitioned into two component sources of variability, the **between-groups sum of squares** ($SS_A$, the sum of squares for $A$), and the **within-groups sum of squares** ($SS_{S/A}$, the sum of squares for subjects within levels of $A$). We have carried out this squaring and summing operation with the numbers in Table 8.2, and, as indicated at the bottom of the table, the $SS_A$ and $SS_{S/A}$ do indeed sum to the $SS_{tot}$. A general proof that $SS_{tot} = SS_A + SS_{S/A}$ is presented in Appendix 8.1. The end result is

$$\sum_{j}^{a} \sum_{i}^{n} (Y_{ij} - \overline{Y}..)^2 = \sum_{j}^{a} \sum_{i}^{n} (Y_{ij} - \overline{Y}._j)^2 + n \sum_{j}^{a} (\overline{Y}._j - \overline{Y}..)^2 \qquad (8.2)$$

$$SS_{tot} \quad = \quad SS_{S/A} \quad + \quad SS_A$$

The $SS_{tot}$ of Equation 8.2 is the numerator of the variance of all $an$ scores about the grand mean. Accordingly, it is distributed on $an - 1$ df. The within-groups sum of squares, $SS_{S/A}$, is the sum, or "pool" of the numerators of each of the group variances. Because each group variance is distributed on $n - 1$ df, $SS_{S/A}$ is distributed on the sum of the group degrees of freedom, or $a(n - 1)$ df. The between-groups sum of squares, $SS_A$, is $n$ times the numerator of the variance of the $a$ group means about the grand mean and is therefore distributed on $a - 1$ df. Note that

$$an - 1 = a(n - 1) + (a - 1)$$
$$df_{tot} = df_{S/A} + df_A \qquad (8.3)$$

Equation 8.3 demonstrates that the degrees of freedom are partitioned into two nonoverlapping parts corresponding to the sums of squares. This partitioning of the degrees of freedom provides a partial check on the partitioning of the total variability in more complex designs in which some term in the analysis may be overlooked, or the total variability may be misanalyzed in some other way. When designs have many factors, and therefore many components of the total variability, it is wise to find the degrees of freedom associated with each term and to check to see if these add up to the total number of scores minus one.

Equation 8.2 defines the sums of squares for the one-factor between-subjects design, and, accordingly, we refer to the component terms as **definitional formulas**. Using such formulas with a calculator can result in rounding errors, and therefore textbooks have generally provided so-called computational or **raw-score formulas**. Such formulas are of less practical use today because most analyses are carried out by computer packages, or by calculators that have a high degree of accuracy. Therefore, we ordinarily will not include raw-score formulas. However, Appendix 8.2 presents the raw-score equivalent of the terms in Equation 8.2, and it provides some rules that will generally enable the calculation of sums of squares in more complex designs provided the user knows the correct degrees of freedom for the terms. The use of the raw-score formulas is illustrated in Appendix 8.2 with the data of Table 8.1.

Dividing the sums of squares by degrees of freedom results in the mean squares. These quantities provide the components of the $F$ statistic that tests the omnibus null hypothesis. We consider these mean squares next.

## 8.3.2 Mean Squares, F, and the ANOVA Table

Suppose we draw $a$ samples of $n$ scores from the same population; we represent the variance of the population (the **error variance**) by $\sigma_e^2$. The variance of the $a$ sample means is an estimate of the variance of the sampling distribution of the mean; that is,

$$\frac{\sum_j^a (\overline{Y}_{.j} - \overline{Y}..)^2}{a - 1} = \hat{\sigma}_{\overline{Y}}^2$$

The caret above the $\sigma$ stands for "estimated." Recall that the variance of the sampling distribution of the mean is the population variance divided by $n$. Therefore, we can rewrite the preceding equation as

$$\frac{\sum_j^a (\overline{Y}_{.j} - \overline{Y}..)^2}{a - 1} = \frac{\hat{\sigma}_e^2}{n}$$

and, multiplying both sides by $n$,

$$\frac{n \sum_j^a (\overline{Y}_{.j} - \overline{Y}..)^2}{a - 1} = \hat{\sigma}_e^2 \qquad (8.4)$$

The left side of Equation 8.4 is the $SS_A$ divided by $df_A$; or $MS_A$. The entire equation states that $MS_A$, the between-groups mean square, is an estimate of chance, or error, variance when the $a$ groups of scores are sampled from the same population.

Now assume that each group of scores is sampled from one of $a$ treatment populations, and that the population parameters are identical; that is,

$$\mu_1 = \mu_2 = \cdots = \mu_j = \cdots \mu_a \quad \text{and} \quad \sigma_1^2 = \sigma_2^2 = \cdots = \sigma_j^2 = \cdots \sigma_a^2$$

Under this assumption, the situation is the same as if we sampled the $a$ groups of scores from one population. Therefore, *if the null hypothesis is true and there is homogeneity of variance,* the **between-groups mean square** is an estimate of the error variance common to the $a$ treatment populations.

The **within-groups mean square**, $MS_{S/A}$, provides a second estimate of error variance. We have

$$MS_{S/A} = \frac{SS_{S/A}}{a(n - 1)}$$
$$= \frac{\sum_j \sum_i (Y_{ij} - \overline{Y}_{.j})^2}{a(n - 1)} \qquad (8.5)$$

We may rewrite Equation 8.5 as

$$MS_{S/A} = \frac{1}{a} \sum_j \left[ \frac{1}{n - 1} \sum_i (Y_{ij} - \overline{Y}_{.j})^2 \right]$$

The expression in the square brackets on the right side is the variance of the $j$th group of scores, and the entire right side is an average of the $a$ group variances. Therefore, $MS_{S/A}$ is an average of $a$ estimates of the population variance, $\sigma_e^2$.

The point of the preceding development is that, if the null hypothesis is true, $MS_A$ and $MS_{S/A}$ both estimate the same population error variance. Therefore, their ratio should be about one. Usually the ratio will be a little more or a little less than one; it would be surprising if two independent estimates of the same population variance were identical. *If*

$H_0$ *is true,* the ratio, $MS_A/MS_{S/A}$, is distributed as $F$ on $a-1$ and $a(n-1)$ *df*. As we noted in Chapter 7, critical values are tabled in Appendix C.5 and can also be obtained from various software packages and Web sites.

Suppose the null hypothesis is false. For example, suppose that the text studied does affect performance on story problems in the Myers et al. experiment. Then the means of the groups of scores in Table 8.1 will differ not only because the scores in the different groups differ by chance but also because the participants studied different texts. In other words, if $H_0$ is false, $MS_A$, which is $n$ times the variance of the group means, reflects not only chance variability but also variability that is due to the independent variable. However, the within-group variance should not be affected by the independent variable because all participants in a group receive the same treatment. Therefore, when $H_0$ is false, the ratio $MS_A/MS_{S/A}$ should be greater than one.

In summary, under the assumptions of the null hypothesis, homogeneity of variance, and independently distributed scores, $MS_A$ and $MS_{S/A}$ are two independent estimates of the population error variance, $\sigma_e^2$. From Chapter 7, we know that if we add the assumption that the population of scores is normally distributed, the ratio of two independent estimates of the same population variance has an $F$ distribution. Therefore, under these assumptions, the ratio $MS_A/MS_{S/A}$ is distributed as $F$. Because the numerator is an estimate of the variance of $a$ population means, it has $a-1$ *df*. The denominator has $a(n-1)$ *df* because the variance estimate for each group is based on $n-1$ *df* and the $a$ group variances are averaged.

Table 8.3 summarizes the developments so far, presenting the formulas for sums of squares, degrees of freedom, mean squares, and the $F$ ratio for the one-factor between-subjects design; Table 8.4 presents SYSTAT ANOVA output for the probability-learning data of Table 8.1. Despite the apparent advantage of the HE text in Figs. 8.1 and 8.2, the $p$ value, .062, is slightly larger than the usual standard for statistical significance, $p = .05$. We cannot reject $H_0: \mu_S = \mu_{LE} = \mu_{HE}$. However, neither can we accept the null hypothesis. The usual criterion for $p$, .05, is not a magic number, and it is good to keep in mind that the $p$ value reflects not only the variance of the treatment population means but also error variance and sample size. As we have noted in previous chapters, effects large enough to be of practical or theoretical importance may not be statistically significant, and trivial effects may be if enough data are collected. With this in mind, we should look at one or more indices of importance. We discuss several in Section 8.5, but we now briefly note one index that accompanies the ANOVA output in Table 8.4, and that is also provided by other statistical packages, such as SPSS.

**TABLE 8.3**  ANOVA FOR THE ONE-FACTOR BETWEEN-SUBJECTS DESIGN

| SV | df | SS | MS | F |
|---|---|---|---|---|
| Total | $an-1$ | $\sum\limits_{j=1}^{a}\sum\limits_{i=1}^{n}(Y_{ij}-\overline{Y}..)^2$ | | |
| A | $a-1$ | $n\sum\limits_{j=1}^{a}(\overline{Y}._j-\overline{Y}..)^2$ | $SS_A/df_A$ | $MS_A/MS_{S/A}$ |
| S/A | $a(n-1)$ | $\sum\limits_{j=1}^{a}\sum\limits_{i=1}^{n}(Y_{ij}-\overline{Y}._j)^2$ | $SS_{S/A}/df_{S/A}$ | |

*Note.* SV = source of variance.

**TABLE 8.4**   ANOVA OF THE DATA IN TABLE 8.1

Categorical values encountered during processing are:
TEXT (3 levels)
  HE, LE, S

Dep Var: Y   N: 48   Multiple R: .341   Squared multiple R: .116

Analysis of Variance

| Source | Sum-of-Squares | df | Mean-Square | F-ratio | P |
|--------|---------------|----|-------------|---------|-----|
| TEXT   | .182          | 2  | .091        | 2.965   | .062 |
| Error  | 1.379         | 45 | .031        |         |      |

*Note.* ANOVA output is from SYSTAT.

### 8.3.3 The Coefficient of Multiple Determination

The sums of squares provide one possible index of the importance of the independent variable. The ratio, $SS_A/SS_{tot}$, is the proportion of the total variability attributable to the independent variable. This ratio is often called $\eta^2$ (**eta squared**) and is similar to $r^2$, the coefficient of determination introduced in Chapter 3. Recall that we defined $r^2$ as $SS_{regression}/SS_Y$, where $SS_{regression}$ (the sum of squares for regression) was the sum of the squared deviations of the predicted scores about the grand mean and $SS_Y$ was the sum of squared deviations of the actual scores about the grand mean. The best prediction we have for each score is the mean of the group to which it belongs. Replacing $SS_{regression}$ by $SS_A$ and $SS_Y$ by $SS_{tot}$, we have the **coefficient of multiple determination**:

$$R^2 = \frac{SS_A}{SS_{tot}} \tag{8.6}$$

This ratio of the between-groups to the total sum of squares may be viewed as a measure of how well the group means predict the individual scores. The better this prediction—that is, the larger the portion of the total variability accounted for by the independent variable—the higher the value of $R^2$.

The $R^2$ for the probability-learning data is reported in Table 8.4 as a **squared multiple R** of .116 (SPSS reports it as eta squared). Following Equation 8.6, the $SS_A$ was divided by $SS_{tot}$ ($SS_A + SS_{S/A}$):

$$R^2 = \frac{.182}{.182 + 1.379} = .116$$

The multiple $R$ of .341 is the square root of .116.

$R^2$ overestimates the actual proportion of variability in the population that is due to the independent variable. To understand why, assume that the treatment population means are identical. In that case, none of the variability in the population would be due to the independent variable; therefore, $R^2$ should be zero. However, $R^2$ will be greater than zero because—in contrast to the population means—the sample means will vary because of chance. To correct for this, Wherry (1931) proposed a formula for **shrunken $R^2$** (also called the adjusted, corrected, or attenuated $R^2$, depending on the source):

$$R^2_{adj} = 1 - \left(\frac{N-1}{N-a}\right)(1 - R^2) \tag{8.7}$$

where $N = na$. For the current example, the adjusted $R^2$ is

$$R^2_{adj} = 1 - \left(\frac{47}{45}\right)(1 - .116) = .077$$

and the corresponding $R_{adj}$ is .277.

Given that the participants in the study probably varied with respect to motivation, mathematical background, and aptitude, as well as other factors that can affect learning, it is not surprising that the independent variable appears to account for only a small portion of the total variability, roughly 8%. Of course, this does not mean that the effects of the text are unimportant. Nor are they as small as it might appear. According to guidelines suggested by Cohen (1988), an adjusted $R^2$ of .077 corresponds to a medium-sized effect. In any event, judgment of the importance of the independent variable should be guided by knowledge of the research situation and the potential application. If the difference of approximately 13% correct between the mean in the HE condition and the other two conditions held for the population, most instructors would consider it an important gain in performance.

$R^2$ is only one possible index of the importance of the independent variable. It has the advantage of being easy to compute and understand, but other measures deserve consideration and are discussed in Section 8.5. These measures are best interpreted in terms of the parameters of the ANOVA model. Therefore, we first consider the model in a more formal way than we have so far.

## 8.4 THE MODEL FOR THE ONE-FACTOR DESIGN

In Subsection 8.3.2, we presented a somewhat informal statement of assumptions and justification of the ratio of mean squares as an $F$ ratio. In this section, we take a closer look at these assumptions and see how they lead to an important concept, that of expected mean squares.

### 8.4.1 The Structural Model

We can view an observed score as consisting of two components—the treatment population mean and an **error component**. We represent this as

$$Y_{ij} = \mu_j + \varepsilon_{ij} \tag{8.8}$$

where $\mu_j$ is the mean of the $j$th treatment population and is a component of all the scores in that population, and $\varepsilon_{ij}$ (the Greek letter epsilon) is the unique contribution to the score of the $i$th individual in the $j$th treatment population. Any differences among the treatment population means reflect differences in the effects of the treatments, whereas variation in the error components reflects differences caused by differences in characteristics of the individuals (such as ability or motivation) and differences in conditions of measurement (such as the time of testing).

Equation 8.8 is unchanged if on the right side we both add and subtract the constant $\mu$, resulting in

$$Y_{ij} = \mu + (\mu_j - \mu) + \varepsilon_{ij}$$

where $\mu = \sum \mu_j / a$, the average of the $a$ treatment population means. We may rewrite the preceding equation as

$$Y_{ij} = \mu + \alpha_j + \varepsilon_{ij} \tag{8.9}$$

where $\alpha_j = \mu_j - \mu$ is the **effect of treatment $A_j$**. Equation 8.9 provides a structure within which we view a score as a sum of the following three components:

1. *The parent population mean, $\mu$.* This quantity may be viewed as the average of the treatment population means and is a constant component of all scores in the data set.
2. *The effect of treatment $A_j$, $\alpha_j$.* This is a constant component of all scores obtained under $A_j$ but may vary over treatments (levels of $j$). The null hypothesis asserts that the $a$ values of $\alpha_j$ are all zero.
3. *The error, $\varepsilon_{ij}$.* This is the deviation of the $i$th score in group $j$ from $\mu_j$ and reflects uncontrolled, or chance, variability. It is the only source of variation within the $j$th group, and if the null hypothesis is true, the only source of variation within the data set.

Two other points about treatment effects should be noted. First, researchers often refer to the effects of an independent variable as in "$A$ had a significant effect upon performance." A somewhat wordy, but precise, translation of such a statement is that one or more of the levels of $A$ had an effect. In terms of the structural model, at least one of the $\alpha_j$ was not zero. Second, a distinction that will be important is that between **fixed-effects variables,** independent variables whose levels have been arbitrarily selected, and **random-effects variables**, variables whose levels have been randomly sampled. When levels have been arbitrarily selected—as when we select three texts for study—it is as if we have exhausted the population of levels. There is no statistical basis for generalizing from the results of this experiment to draw conclusions about the effects of texts not included in the experiment. In this situation, $\sum_j (\mu_j - \mu) = 0$ (or, equivalently, $\sum_j \alpha_j = 0$) because the sum of deviations of all values about their mean is zero. We deal exclusively with fixed-effect treatment variables in this chapter.

Equation 8.9 is not sufficient for deriving parameter estimates and significance tests. In addition, the following assumptions about the distribution of $\varepsilon_{ij}$ are required:

1. The $\varepsilon_{ij}$ are independently distributed. This means that the probability of sampling some value of $\varepsilon_{ij}$ does not depend on other values of $\varepsilon_{ij}$ in the sample. An important consequence of this is that the $\varepsilon_{ij}$ are uncorrelated.
2. The $\varepsilon_{ij}$ are normally distributed with mean zero in each of the $a$ treatment populations.
3. The distribution of the $\varepsilon_{ij}$ has variance $\sigma_e^2$ in each of the $a$ treatment populations; that is, $\sigma_1^2 = \sigma_2^2 = \cdots = \sigma_j^2 = \cdots = \sigma_a^2 = \sigma_e^2$. This is usually referred to as the assumption of **homogeneity of variance**.

Although we never have access to the populations of scores, plots of the data will provide information about the validity of our assumptions. Chapter 2 described some procedures that will prove helpful, and we illustrated one other (the dot-density plot) in this chapter. In later sections of this chapter, we discuss the problems that may arise when our assumptions are violated, and how alternative data analyses may provide a solution to these problems. For now, we assume that Equation 8.9 is valid and that the populations of error components are independently and normally distributed with equal variances. This provides the basis for a more formal justification of the $F$ test presented in this chapter.

## 8.4.2 Expected Mean Squares

In Section 8.3 we argued that the ratio of mean squares, $MS_A/MS_{S/A}$, was a reasonable test statistic for the null hypothesis of equality of the treatment population means. The idea is that if $H_0$ is true, $MS_A$ and $MS_{S/A}$ are both estimates of $\sigma_e^2$, the treatment population error variance. Because they both estimate the same quantity, their average values over many random replications of the experiment should be about the same size. If $H_0$ is false, however, $MS_A$ reflects the differences among the treatment population means in addition to chance variability. In that case, on the average, $MS_A$ will tend to be larger than $MS_{S/A}$. In this section, we provide a somewhat different version of this argument, one based on the average values of $MS_A$ and $MS_{S/A}$ over many replications of the experiment.

Suppose we draw $a$ samples of $n$ scores from their respective treatment populations, and calculate the two mean squares. Now suppose that we draw another $a$ samples of $n$ scores, and again calculate $MS_A$ and $MS_{S/A}$. We could repeat this sampling experiment many times, and arrive at two sampling distributions, one for $MS_A$ and another for $MS_{S/A}$. Given the arguments of Section 8.3, the average value of $MS_A$ will reflect both error variance and treatment effects, whereas the average value of $MS_{S/A}$ will reflect only error variance. These averages of the sampling distributions of the two mean squares are the expected values of the mean squares, or the **expected mean squares (EMS)**. They play an important role both in understanding the analysis of variance (ANOVA) and in deciding a number of practical issues. To cite just one application, in more complex designs there will be many possible sources of variance; the EMS dictates the appropriate error term for any particular source. Given the structural model of Equation 8.9, and assuming that the $\varepsilon_{ij}$ are independently distributed with variance $\sigma_e^2$, we can derive the EMS of Table 8.5 (Kirk, 1995; Myers & Well, 1995).

Look again at Table 8.5. Note that if the null hypothesis is true (i.e., if the $\mu_j$ are all equal), both expectations equal $\sigma_e^2$; in any one experiment, the two mean squares we have calculated will not be identical, but they rarely should be very different if $H_0$ is true. In contrast, if the $\mu_j$ differ, $MS_A$ has a larger expected value than $MS_{S/A}$ and therefore their ratio should be greater than one. When we look at Table 8.5, it appears that this ratio increases

**TABLE 8.5**  EMS FOR THE ONE-FACTOR BETWEEN-SUBJECTS DESIGN

| SV | EMS |
|----|-----|
| A | $\sigma_e^2 + n\theta_A^2$ |
| S/A | $\sigma_e^2$ |

*Note.* $\theta_A^2 = \left[\sum_j (\mu_j - \mu)^2\right]/(a-1)$. We use the $\theta^2$ notation rather than $\sigma^2$ to remind us that the treatment component of the EMS involves division by degrees of freedom rather than by the number of levels, as it would in the formula for a population variance.

with increases in $n$, with increases in the spread among the $\mu_j$, and with decreases in the error variance. Therefore, we can expect greater power when we run more subjects, when the effects of the independent variable are larger, and when error variance is reduced. The error variance will depend on the subject population sampled, the measure selected, and the experimental design. An example of the last factor—the experimental design—was the comparison of the correlated-scores and independent-groups designs in Chapters 5 and 6.

In the one-factor design, there are only two mean squares and therefore it requires no great insight to decide that $MS_{S/A}$ is the **error term**—the denominator of the $F$ test, against which $MS_A$ is to be tested. The choice of an error term is more complicated in designs in which there are several possible error terms. However, that choice is guided by a simple rule:

Choose an error term such that its EMS and the EMS of the term to be tested are identical when the null hypothesis is true.

In summary, if the $\varepsilon_{ij}$ are independently distributed with variance $\sigma_e^2$, the mean squares have the expectations presented in Table 8.5. If, in addition, the null hypothesis is true, $\theta_A^2 = 0$, and the two expectations are the same. Finally, if the $\varepsilon_{ij}$ are normally distributed, the ratio of mean squares, $MS_A/MS_{S/A}$, is distributed as $F$ and the probabilities of exceeding various values are those tabled in Appendix C.5.

### 8.4.3 ANOVA With Unequal Group Sizes

The $n$s in conditions in a study may vary for one of several reasons. The populations may be equal in size but data may be lost from some conditions, perhaps because of a malfunction of equipment, or a participant's failure to complete the data-collection session. Usually, individuals can be replaced, but sometimes this is impossible. In other instances, the treatments may affect the availability of scores; for example, animals in one drug condition may be less likely to survive the experiment than animals in another condition. In still other instances, usually when we collect data from existing populations, some conditions may naturally have more individuals available for participation than others will. For example, in the Seasons data, we find different numbers of participants at various levels of educational experience, and in different occupations. In educational and clinical settings, there may naturally be different numbers of individuals in different conditions, such as grade levels, or diagnostic categories. Discarding participants to equalize the group $n$s will reduce error degrees of freedom and, consequently, power, and this may also misrepresent the relative size of the populations sampled. In the latter case, the effects of some conditions may be weighted too heavily or too lightly in the data analysis. In all of these circumstances involving unequal $n$, the ANOVA is a straightforward modification of the equal-$n$ case, at least in the one-factor between-subjects design. (Complications arise when more than one factor is involved; these are treated in Chapters 11 and 21.) Table 8.6 presents the ANOVA formulas and EMS for the unequal-$n$ case. Note that if the $n_j$ are equal, these formulas reduce to the definitional formulas in Table 8.3 and the EMS formulas of Table 8.5.

Table 8.7 presents statistics based on the average (over seasons) Beck depression scores (Beck_D) for four groups of male subjects who participated in the University of Massachusetts Medical School research on seasonal effects (the Seasons data). For the purposes of this example, we excluded some participants (those having only no or some high

**TABLE 8.6** ANOVA FOR THE ONE-FACTOR BETWEEN-SUBJECTS DESIGN WITH UNEQUAL GROUP SIZES

| SV | df | SS | MS | F | EMS |
|---|---|---|---|---|---|
| Total | $N - 1$ | $\sum\limits_{j=1}^{a} \sum\limits_{i=1}^{n_j} (Y_{ij} - \overline{Y}..)^2$ | | | |
| A | $a - 1$ | $\sum\limits_{j=1}^{a} n_j (\overline{Y}._j - \overline{Y}..)^2$ | $SS_A/df_A$ | $MS_A/MS_{S/A}$ | $\sigma_e^2 + \frac{1}{a-1} \sum\limits_{j} n_j \alpha_j^2$ |
| S/A | $N - a$ | $\sum\limits_{j=1}^{a} \sum\limits_{i=1}^{n_j} (Y_{ij} - \overline{Y}._j)^2$ | $SS_{S/A}/df_{S/A}$ | | $\sigma_e^2$ |

*Note.* $n_j$ is the number of scores in the $j$th group and $N = \sum_{j=1}^{a} n_j$.

school education, and those with vocational training or an associate's degree). The remaining groups are HS (high school diploma only), C (some college), B (bachelor's degree), and GS (graduate school). The data may be found in the Male_educ file in the *Seasons* folder.

The group of males participants with high school diplomas have higher average depression scores, both means and medians, than those of the other three groups; whereas the three groups with more education have means ranging from 3.331 to 4.847, the HS group has a mean depression score of almost 7 (6.903). The groups with the highest depression scores (HS and GS) also have the highest variances, a finding that suggests that heterogeneity of variance may affect the validity of conclusions based on the ANOVA of these data. Skew and kurtosis are most pronounced in the B group. This is of interest because nonnormality is most problematic when distributions vary in shape (Lindquist, 1953, pp. 78–90). Box plots obtained from SPSS are presented in Fig. 8.3. They provide a more direct view of the distributions, and the differences in location, spread, and skew are quite evident, as is the presence of outliers in the B and GS groups. These characteristics of the plot suggest that the assumptions of the ANOVA are violated. In Section 8.7 we discuss those assumptions, together with alternative analyses developed to respond to violations of them.

**TABLE 8.7** SUMMARY STATISTICS FOR BECK DEPRESSION SCORES IN FOUR EDUCATIONAL LEVELS

| | Education | | | |
|---|---|---|---|---|
| | HS | C | B | GS |
| N of cases | 19 | 33 | 37 | 39 |
| Median | 6.272 | 2.875 | 2.265 | 3.031 |
| Mean | 6.903 | 3.674 | 3.331 | 4.847 |
| Variance | 34.541 | 5.970 | 9.861 | 26.218 |
| Skewness(G1) | .824 | 0.368 | 2.047 | 1.270 |
| Kurtosis(G2) | .168 | −0.919 | 5.837 | .745 |

*Note.* HS = high school diploma only; C = some college; B = bachelor's degree; GS = graduate school. Data may be found in the Male_educ file in the *Seasons* folder.

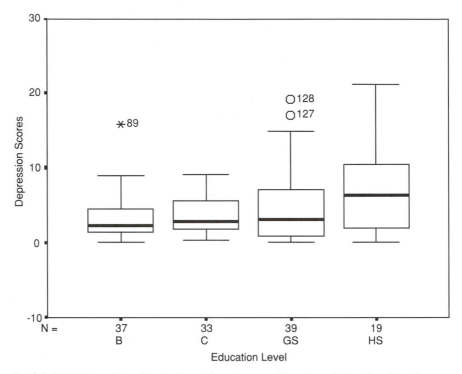

**Fig. 8.3** SPSS Box plots of Beck depression scores as a function of educational level. Note that the numbers next to the outliers are case numbers and the asterisk represents an extreme outlier.

The output is based on an analysis of Beck depression means for those participants for whom scores in all four seasons were available. It contains considerable information in addition to the ANOVA table. First note the squared multiple $R$ of .079. Under Cohen's (1988) guidelines, this would be a medium-sized association between the dependent and independent variable. The ANOVA table follows and it is clear that the omnibus null hypothesis can be rejected. The last thing to note is the warning that two scores are outliers, using the studentized residual as a criterion.[2] Upon examining these two cases, we found that one belonged to the HS group and the other to the GS group. We redid the ANOVA with these cases excluded, and the result was no longer significant; the new $p$ value was .065. Deleting just 2 of 128 scores changed the $p$ value from .016 to .065, and a finding of statistical significance to nonsignificance. Despite the fact that statistical significance depended on the presence of the two outliers, there are reasons to suspect that the population distributions of depression scores do differ. First, even after the two outliers were excluded, the medians of the three groups with some education beyond high school were about 3 or less, whereas that for the HS group was more than twice as high. Second, examination of the four distributions revealed that 26% of the HS scores were above 10, the cutoff for dysphoria, roughly defined as a state of dissatisfaction (16 is the cutoff for depression) and 20% of the GS group exceeded that cutoff; in contrast, only one individual in the other two groups had an average Beck depression score exceeding 10. The point we wish to make is that we need to look beyond the significance test and examine the sample distributions to better understand

**TABLE 8.8**  ANOVA OF THE DATA SUMMARIZED IN TABLE 8.7

```
Dep Var: D_SCORE      N: 128      Multiple R: .282      Squared multiple R: .079

                         Analysis of Variance

Source        Sum-of-Squares      df      Mean-Square      F-ratio      P

EDUC$             186.501          3         62.167         3.562      .016

Error            2164.061         124        17.452
```

```
*** WARNING ***
Case          14 is an outlier           (Studentized Residual =    3.665)
Case         114 is an outlier           (Studentized Residual =    3.622)

Durbin-Watson D Statistic       1.995
First Order Autocorrelation     -.006
```

*Note.* ANOVA output is from SYSTAT.

our data. In addition, we should supplement the omnibus $F$ test results with measures of importance, such as those we consider in Section 8.5. Finally, CIs and significance tests on specific contrasts (for example, the HS group against the combined mean of the other three groups) will be informative. We introduced such contrasts in Chapter 6 and have more to say about them in Chapter 9. For example, there we pursue the question of whether the HS mean differs significantly from the mean of the other three groups combined, as the means and medians suggest.

Significance tests and confidence intervals (CIs), examination of contrasts, measures of importance, examination of group distributions—these combine to provide a sense of whether the sampled populations differ and in what ways. The cause of the differences can be elusive. For example, it is not clear why high school graduates (and possibly also those with graduate school education) are more likely to be depressed than individuals in the other two categories, if this difference proves to be reliable. Two possible causes of such differences are occupational and age differences among the groups. Individuals with only a high school education may be more dissatisfied with their jobs, and individuals with graduate school education may feel overqualified for theirs. If the four groups differ in age, there may be differences in health and, therefore, in depression scores. In summary, even if we conclude that the populations differ in some respects, we must ask why they differ.

## 8.5 ASSESSING THE IMPORTANCE OF THE INDEPENDENT VARIABLE

Too often, researchers view .05 as a boundary dividing real effects from null effects. However, there is nothing magical about $p = .05$; it is merely one possible index of the effect of the independent variable. Usually, when $p$ is less than or equal to .05, researchers reject the null hypothesis. But should we really have so much less confidence that there is an effect if $p = .06$? And if $p = .01$, does this statistically significant result reflect an effect of practical or theoretical importance, or does it reflect a researcher with access to a large pool of subjects? There is no statistic that carries a magic dividing line; however, there are several measures that complement $p$, and that are more directly related to the variance of the treatment means, and therefore are more easily interpreted. Using the example of the probability-learning experiment, we considered one such measure, $R^2$, the proportion of variability accounted for by the independent variable. $R^2$ may also be viewed as a measure of the strength of association between the dependent and independent variable. In what follows, we consider another measure of the strength of association, as well as a standardized effect statistic that parallels the $E_S$ presented in Chapter 6. The development of both statistics follows from our knowledge of the expected mean squares.

## 8.5.1 Measuring Strength of Association: $\omega^2$ (Omega Squared)

When we perform an ANOVA, $R^2$ is the ratio of the between-groups sum of squares to the total sum of squares. An alternative measure of the strength of association between the dependent and independent variable is the ratio of the population variance of the means to the total population variance. Following Hays' (1994) notation, we label this ratio as $\omega^2$. The numerator of the ratio is the variance of the treatment population means (the $\mu_j$) or, equivalently, the variance of the treatment effects (the $\alpha_j$):

$$\sigma_A^2 = \frac{\sum_j^a (\mu_j - \mu)^2}{a}$$
$$= \frac{\sum_j^a \alpha_j^2}{a} \tag{8.10}$$

The denominator of $\omega^2$ is the total population variance; that is, it is the treatment population error variance, $\sigma_e^2$, plus the variance of the treatment population means, $\sigma_A^2$. Therefore,

$$\omega^2 = \frac{\sigma_A^2}{\sigma_e^2 + \sigma_A^2} \tag{8.11}$$

We cannot know this ratio but we can use Equations 8.10 and 8.11 to derive an estimate of it. More precisely, we derive estimates of $\sigma_A^2$ and $\sigma_e^2$. We begin by restating the EMS equations of Table 8.5:

$$E(MS_A) = \sigma_e^2 + n\theta_A^2 \tag{8.12}$$
$$E(MS_{S/A}) = \sigma_e^2 \tag{8.13}$$

To obtain an estimate of $\sigma_A^2$ we first subtract Equation 8.13 from Equation 8.12, and divide by $n$; then we have

$$\frac{MS_A - MS_{S/A}}{n} \doteq \theta_A^2$$

where the symbol $\hat{=}$ means "is an estimate of." However, the numerator of $\omega^2$ as defined by Equation 8.11 involves $\sigma_A^2$, not $\theta_A^2$. Because $\sigma_A^2 = [(a-1)/a]\theta_A^2$, our estimate is

$$\hat{\sigma}_A^2 = \left(\frac{a-1}{a}\right)\left(\frac{MS_A - MS_{S/A}}{n}\right) \tag{8.14}$$

where the "caret" above the $\sigma$ indicates "the estimate of." We now have estimates of the numerator and denominator of $\omega^2$, and, therefore, substituting into Equation 8.11, we have an estimate of $\omega^2$: for the one-factor between-subjects design, we have

$$\hat{\omega}^2 = \frac{[(a-1)/a](1/n)(MS_A - MS_{S/A})}{[(a-1)/a](1/n)(MS_A - MS_{S/A}) + MS_{S/A}} \tag{8.15}$$

We may write Equation 8.15 in a different form, one that allows us to calculate $\hat{\omega}^2$ from knowledge of the $F$ ratio, $a$, and $n$. The advantages are that the expression is somewhat simpler, and, perhaps more important, because most research reports contain this information we can estimate the strength of association for data collected by other investigators. We begin by defining $F_A = MS_A/MS_{S/A}$. Then, multiplying the numerator and denominator of Equation 8.15 by $an$, and dividing by $MS_{S/A}$, we have

$$\hat{\omega}^2 = \frac{(a-1)(F_A - 1)}{(a-1)(F_A - 1) + na} \tag{8.16}$$

Let's review what Equation 8.15 (or 8.16) represents. If we replicate the experiment many times, the average value of the right-hand term will approximately equal $\omega^2$, the proportion of the total variance in the $a$ treatment populations that is attributable to the variance of their means. We say "approximately equal" because the expected value of a ratio is not the same as the ratio of expected values. The approximation is reasonably accurate and the expression is much simpler than that for the correct expression.

One other aspect of Equation 8.16 should be noted. If the null hypothesis is true, it is quite possible that the $F$ will have a value less than one, because in that case we have two independent estimates of the error variance and either one could be the larger of the two. Then, $\hat{\omega}^2$ would be less than zero and we should conclude that $\omega^2 = 0$; that is, none of the total population variance is attributable to the independent variable.

We can apply Equation 8.16 to the probability-learning experiment. In that experiment, $a = 3$, $n = 16$, and (from Table 8.3) $F = 2.965$. Then, inserting these values into Equation 8.16, we have

$$\hat{\omega}^2 = \frac{(2)(1.965)}{(2)(1.965) + 48} = .076$$

This is very close to the value we calculated earlier for $R_{adj}^2$. That the values of $R_{adj}^2$ and $\omega^2$ are so close is not unusual; Maxwell, Camp, and Arvey (1981) found that the two rarely differ by more than .02. With respect to assessing the importance of either measure, Cohen (1988) suggested that values of .01, .06, and .14 may be viewed as small, medium, and large, respectively. According to those guidelines, the proportion of variability accounted for may be judged to be medium. Again, however, we caution that the importance attached to any value must be assessed in the context of the research problem and the investigator's knowledge of the research literature.

## 8.5.2 Measuring Effect Size

$R^2$ and $\hat{\omega}^2$ have intuitive appeal because their values are on a scale of zero to one and they can be directly interpreted in terms of the variability accounted for by the independent variable. However, standardized effect sizes such as those presented in Chapter 6 have other advantages. They play an important role in meta-analysis, a procedure for combining the results of several experiments (Hedges & Olkin, 1985), and, as we saw in Chapters 5 and 6, standardized effect sizes, together with $\alpha$ and $n$, determine power. In Chapter 6, we defined the standardized effect size as

$$E_S = \frac{\mu_1 - \mu_2}{\sigma}$$

Cohen (1988) suggested another standardized effect-size measure, $f$, which is a useful adjunct to ANOVA:

$$f = \sqrt{\sigma_A^2 / \sigma_e^2}$$

$$= \sqrt{\frac{\sum_{j=1}^{a} (\mu_j - \mu)^2 \big/ a}{\sigma_e^2}} \tag{8.17}$$

$$= \sqrt{\frac{\sum_{j=1}^{a} \alpha_j^2 \big/ a}{\sigma_e^2}}$$

The quantity under the square root sign in Equation 8.17 is the ratio of $\sigma_A^2$, the variance of the treatment population means, to $\sigma_e^2$, the population error variance. An estimate of $\sigma_A^2$ is provided by Equation 8.14 and the error variance is estimated by $MS_{S/A}$. Therefore, our estimate of $f$ is

$$\hat{f} = \sqrt{\frac{(a-1)(MS_A - MS_{S/A})}{anMS_{S/A}}} \tag{8.18}$$

$$= \sqrt{(a-1)(F_A - 1)/an}$$

Substituting values from the output in Table 8.4 into the last equation, we have

$$\hat{f} = \sqrt{\frac{(2)(2.965 - 1)}{48}} = .286$$

Cohen (1988) has suggested that $f = .10, .25,$ and $.40$ corresponds to small, medium, and large effect sizes, respectively. Using these guidelines, we judge the effect to be of medium size. This corresponds to the conclusion reached when we estimated $\omega^2$. This is not surprising because the two measures are directly related:

$$\omega^2 = f^2/(1 + f^2) \quad \text{and} \quad f^2 = \omega^2/(1 - \omega^2).$$

Estimates of either of two other parameters are often used in obtaining the power of the $F$ test. When the null hypothesis is false, the ratio of mean squares has a **noncentral F distribution,** with **noncentrality parameter, $\lambda$ (lambda).** This parameter serves as one of the inputs to software programs for finding power, such as SAS's CDF module

**TABLE 8.9**   SOME PARAMETERS AND STATISTICS FOR THE ONE-FACTOR
BETWEEN-SUBJECTS DESIGN

| Parameters | Estimators |
|---|---|
| $\sigma_A^2 = \sum \alpha_j^2/a$ | $\hat{\sigma}_A^2 = [(a-1)/a][(MS_A - MS_{S/A})/n]$ |
| $\sigma_e^2 = E\left(\varepsilon_{ij}^2\right)$ | $\hat{\sigma}_e^2 = MS_{S/A}$ |
| $f = \sigma_A/\sigma_e$ | $\hat{f} = \sqrt{\hat{\sigma}_A^2/\hat{\sigma}_e^2}$ |
| $\omega^2 = \sigma_A^2/(\sigma_A^2 + \sigma_e^2)$ | $\hat{\omega}^2 = \hat{\sigma}_A^2/\left(\hat{\sigma}_A^2 + \hat{\sigma}_e^2\right)$ |
| $\quad = f^2/(1+f^2)$ | $\quad = [SS_A - (a-1)MS_{S/A}]/(SS_{\text{tot}} + MS_{S/A})$ |
| | $\quad = [(a-1)(F-1)]/[(a-1)(F-1) + na]$ |
| $\lambda = n\sum\alpha_j^2/\sigma_e^2$ | $\hat{\lambda} = na\hat{\sigma}_A^2/\hat{\sigma}_e^2$ |
| $\quad = naf^2 = a\phi^2$ | $\quad = [(a-1)(MS_A - MS_{S/A})]/MS_{S/A}$ |
| | $\quad = (a-1)(F-1)$ |
| $\phi = f\sqrt{n} = \sqrt{\lambda/a}$ | $\hat{\phi} = \sqrt{n\hat{\sigma}_A^2/\hat{\sigma}_e^2}$ |
| | $\quad = \hat{f}\sqrt{n} = \sqrt{\hat{\lambda}/a}$ |

and the UCLA calculator. Another parameter, used in conjunction with power charts that are found in many textbooks, is $\phi$ (phi). These two parameters, as well as $f$ and $\omega^2$, together with formulas for estimating them, and relations among them, are presented in Table 8.9.

## 8.5.3 Measures of Importance With Unequal Group Sizes

When there are different numbers of scores in each condition, we need a different way of estimating $\sigma_A^2$ than that presented in Table 8.9; we cannot just divide by $n$ because there is no single value of $n$. However, if the $n$s vary by chance and are not too different, the average $n$ might replace the $n$ in the denominator of the estimator of Table 8.6. That is, we might define

$$\hat{\sigma}_A^2 = \left(\frac{a-1}{a}\right)\left(\frac{MS_A - MS_{S/A}}{\bar{n}}\right)$$
$$= \frac{(a-1)(MS_A - MS_{S/A})}{a(N/a)} \tag{8.19}$$
$$= \frac{(a-1)(MS_A - MS_{S/A})}{N}$$

The first line in Equation 8.19 is identical to that for the equal-$n$ case (Equation 8.14), except that $n$ has been replaced by the average of the $n$s.

We can arrive at Equation 8.19 in a somewhat different way. Suppose the populations do differ in size. Then the definition of $\sigma_A^2$ is

$$\sigma_A^2 = \sum_j p_j \alpha_j^2 \qquad (8.20)$$

where the $p_j$ sum to one and are weights reflecting the relative population sizes. From the EMS in Table 8.6,

$$(a - 1)\left(\frac{MS_A - MS_{S/A}}{N}\right) \doteq \sum_j \frac{n_j}{N}\alpha_j^2$$

which is a reasonable estimate of the parameter defined by Equation 8.20 if $n_j/N$ is an adequate estimate of $p_j$. Although the rationales differ, the left-hand side of this equation is identical to the last line of Equation 8.19.

To obtain estimates of the other parameters in Table 8.9 in the unequal-$n$ case, we need only substitute the expression for $\hat{\sigma}_A^2$ in Equation 8.19 into the other expressions in the table.

### 8.5.4 Measures of Importance: Limitations

In an introductory chapter to an edited collection aptly titled *What if There Were No Significance Tests?*, Harlow (1997, pp. 5–6) reported that 11 of the book's other 13 chapters "were very much in favor" of reporting measures such as $R^2$, $\omega^2$, and $E_S$, and the remaining two contributors "at least mildly endorsed such use." Similar support for measures such as these can be found in The American Psychological Associations's guidelines for statistical usage (Wilkinson, 1999), which urge researchers to report effect size statistics. Nevertheless, there are potential pitfalls. Values of these statistics may depend on the experimental design (for example, between or within subjects), the choice and number of levels of the independent variable, the dependent variable, and the population sampled. Another concern is that squared coefficients tend to be small and it is sometimes easy to dismiss an effect as trivial because of a small value of $\omega^2$. These arguments suggest that we must be careful in generalizing the results of any one study, or of making comparisons across studies that differ with respect to the factors just cited. In addition, we should treat guidelines such as those set forth by Cohen (1988) as suggestions, not as definitive boundaries between important and unimportant effects. Even a very small advantage of one therapy over another may be important. In theoretical work, a small effect predicted by a theory may be important support for that theory. In summary, if care is taken in interpreting measures of strength, statistics such as $\hat{f}$ and $\hat{\omega}^2$ are useful additions to the test statistics usually computed.

## 8.6 POWER OF THE *F* TEST

Power calculations can play an important role in planning the experiment. Ideally, researchers would have an estimate of $f$ or $\omega^2$ from previous studies; these could then be used to determine the sample size needed to achieve a specific level of power. However, such estimates may be unavailable or very wrong, or the required $n$ may be too large to be practical. In such cases, it is still helpful to estimate the power of the $F$ test after the data have been collected. We describe this post hoc use of power functions first. Then we consider a priori applications in which the researcher uses the power function of the *F* to decide on a sample size before running the experiment.

## 8.6.1 Post Hoc Power Calculations

There are several situations in which it is important to have a sense of the power of the data analysis. In one case, the researcher predicts effects of the independent variable and there is a clear trend among the observed means that supports the researcher's prior hypothesis. However, the result is not statistically significant. Therefore, either there really are no effects of importance in the sampled population and the pattern of observed means is due to chance, or the treatment population means do differ but the research had too little power to detect this treatment variance. In this situation we may ask what power the *F* test had to reject $H_0$ assuming the population effect size estimated from the data. If this power is low, the research may be replicated with a larger *n* or with procedures or measures designed to reduce error variance.

In a second case, the researcher predicts no effect and does not obtain a significant result. In this situation, before claiming a successful prediction, the researcher should demonstrate that power to detect the effects estimated from the data was high and therefore the failure to achieve significance was because the independent variable had no, or trivially small, effects. Finally, in a third situation, the experimenter predicts no effect but the *F* test produces a significant result. Here, if power is very high to detect even very small effects, the effects estimated from the data, although possibly real, may not be large enough to be of theoretical or practical interest.

In all of these situations, estimates of $f$ and $\omega^2$ will be important in discussing the results because they help provide a sense of the absolute and relative contributions of the independent variable to the total variability. Calculations of power supplement these statistics and place the results of our statistical text in a useful context.

The power of the *F* test (and of other tests; see the discussions in Chapters 4–6) depends on several factors:

1. *The significance level,* $\alpha$. As we reduce the rejection region, say from .05 to .01, we lower the probability of rejecting false, as well as true, null hypotheses. In other words, a reduced Type 1 error rate is accompanied by reduced power.
2. *The values of a and n.* Increases in either numerator or denominator degrees of freedom yield increased power. Ordinarily, the value of *a* is determined by the goals of the experiment; *n* is usually more arbitrarily selected, although constrained by practical concerns such as time, effort, and cost. In Subsection 8.6.2, we consider how power calculations can, and should, influence decisions about sample size.
3. *The error variance,* $\sigma_e^2$. The less noise in our data, the easier it will be to detect treatment effects. Therefore, power increases with decreases in error variance. This variance will be a function of the dependent variable, the subject population, and the experimental design.
4. *The variance of the treatment effects,* $\sigma_A^2$. In the case of the *F* test, we will have more power to reject the null hypothesis of equal treatment population means when the differences among them are larger.

To determine the power of the $F$ test, we need the numerical values of the four factors just cited, and we then need to find some way of relating power to them. Assuming we have run the experiment, we know $df_1$ and $df_2$, and have decided on $\alpha$, we see that $MS_{S/A}$ provides an estimate of $\sigma_e^2$. An estimate of the variance of the treatment effects is provided by $\hat{\sigma}_A^2$, which was defined in Equation 8.14. To obtain a value of power, we calculate one of several closely related indices that are based on the ratio $\hat{\sigma}_A/\hat{\sigma}_e$. Some sources (including the previous edition of this book) contain "nomographs," charts in which power is plotted as a function of $\phi = f \times \sqrt{n}$, with different curves for different values of $df_1$, $df_2$, and $\alpha$. These charts are awkward to use, and provide at best approximate results.[3] A somewhat better approximation may be obtained by using an estimate of $f$ (defined by Equation 8.18) together with tables provided by Cohen (1988). Of course, no chart or table can provide power values for every possible combination of degrees of freedom or for every possible value of $\alpha$. The best solution to the problem of calculating power is to use a software application that calculates power when the necessary information is input. Several statistical packages such as SYSTAT, SAS, and SPSS[4] will do this, at least for some tests. Furthermore, a number of easy-to-use programs are freely available on the Internet. We used two of these, GPOWER and the UCLA calculator, to obtain the power of the $t$ test in Chapter 6. Table 8.10 illustrates the application of both these programs to find the power of the $F$ test, using the data from the probability-learning experiment.

It is easy to become so focused on the process that we forget what the result means. What the estimated power of .39 in Table 8.10 means is the following: Given the sample size we ran, and assuming the $MS_{S/A}$ is a reasonable estimate of $\sigma_e^2$, there is a probability of about .39 that we will reject the null hypothesis, if the effects in the population are of the order of magnitude estimated from our data. Put somewhat differently, if the treatment population means are about as different as our sample means suggest, we still have a .61 $(1 - .39)$ probability of making a Type 2 error. Noting the low power, the $p$ value that fell only a little short of .05, and the medium-sized estimate of $f$ (or $\omega^2$), we find evidence that the independent variable may have an effect. Although we cannot reject the null hypothesis, there is some basis for believing that a more powerful replication of the experiment might produce a statistically significant effect. If we replicate the experiment, we might attempt to improve its sensitivity. One way to do this is to increase the number of participants. Another way would be to increase the number of items on the test given to the participants. This would decrease the variance of the test score, and thus decrease the error variance. Decreasing the variance of the dependent variable is often possible, and often less expensive in time and resources than running more subjects.

## 8.6.2 A Priori Power Calculations

Ideally, we should have some idea of the size of the effect we want to detect *before* running an experiment. Pilot data, or a review of related experiments, might suggest that effects will be of a certain magnitude. It is not necessary to have a precise estimate of $f$; usually, some sense of whether the effect is small, medium, or large (using Cohen's 1988 guidelines) will do. Certainly, a decision about sample size based on any estimate of $f$ will be an improvement over an arbitrary selection of $n$. In some cases, the $n$ required to achieve a certain level of power against a specified effect size will be impractically large. We can then calculate what power we have with the largest $n$ available for our study. If that power is very

**TABLE 8.10**   CALCULATING THE POWER OF THE *F* TEST

---

Using GPOWER
1. Under "Tests," select "*F* Tests (ANOVA)."
2. Fill in these values from the probability-learning experiment:
$$f = .286$$
$$\text{Alpha} = .05$$
$$\text{Total sample size} = 48$$
$$\text{Groups} = 3$$
3. Click on "Calculate.",  The results are:
$$\text{Lambda} = 3.9262$$
$$\text{Critical } F = 3.2043$$
$$\text{Power} = .3852.$$
   Note that $f$ was estimated previously (Subsection 8.5.2) by using Equation 8.2;
   also, $\lambda = anf^2 = 48 \times .286^2$.

Using the UCLA calculator
1. Go to the UCLA calculator (see Table 8.4 or Chapter 6 for the URL).
2. Click on "Noncentral F CDF Calculator."
3. Fill in these values:
$$\text{X value} = 3.2043 \text{ (the critical value of } F \text{ for } \alpha = .05)$$
$$\text{Probability} = ?$$
$$\text{Numerator } df = 2$$
$$\text{Denominator } df = 45$$
$$\text{Noncentrality parameter} = 3.9262 \ (\lambda)$$
4. Click on "Complete Me!"
5. The question mark is replaced by .6148; this is beta, the probability of a Type 2
   error. Subtracting from 1, we have power = .3852.

---

*Note.* The X value can be obtained from Table D.5, which contains critical values of the central *F* distribution for various combinations of α and degrees of freedom. If the degrees of freedom for your data set are not in Table D.5, interpolation will usually provide a reasonable approximation to the required X value. Better still, the central *F* calculator at the above Web site will provide the necessary result.

low, consideration should be given to ways of decreasing variability—perhaps a different research design, or a different dependent variable.

Finding the required *n* is simple with GPOWER. Select "*F* Tests" and "A priori." Indicate the value of $f$, the α level, the desired power, and the number of groups. If power $= .8$, $f = .25$ (medium), $\alpha = .05$, and there are three groups, the total $N$ is 159, or $n = 53$ participants in each group. If the UCLA calculator is used, the process involves trial and error. Having selected a trial $N$ (the total number of participants, $na$), you must calculate the denominator degrees of freedom, find the $F$ needed for significance at the desired α level (the "X Value"), and calculate the noncentrality parameter, $\lambda$. Enter these together with the numerator degrees of freedom and a question mark in the probability space. If the probability that is returned is greater than one minus the desired power (remember, the calculator returns β), increase the *n*; this means recalculating the denominator degrees of freedom, the critical $F$ value, and $\lambda$. If β is very small, you can decrease the *n* and make the necessary adjustments in the variables needed for the calculator. The same parameters are entered into the SPSS "Compute" module.

## 8.7 ASSUMPTIONS UNDERLYING THE *F* TEST

Although the critical values of $F$ in Appendix Table C.5 are derived from the assumptions presented previously, it does not follow that violations of the assumptions necessarily invalidate the $F$ test. For example, in view of our discussion of the central limit theorem and the $t$ test (in Chapter 6), we might guess that the ratio of mean squares will be distributed approximately as $F$ even when the populations are not normal. In this section, we look at the role of assumptions more closely. We ask what the consequences of violations of assumptions are and, in those cases in which there are undesirable consequences, what alternatives to the standard analysis exist.

### 8.7.1 Validity of the Structural Model

It is important to bear in mind that the ANOVA for the one-factor design begins with the assumption of Equation 8.9. That equation implies that only one factor systematically influences the data and that the residual variability ($MS_{S/A}$) represents random error. However, researchers sometimes ignore factors that have been manipulated but are not of interest in themselves. If those factors contribute significant variability, the one-factor model is not valid for the research design. Common examples arise when half of the subjects are male and half are female, or when subject running is divided equally between two experimenters, or when the position of an object is counterbalanced in an experiment involving a choice. Although the researcher may consider these variables irrelevant to the purpose of the research, they may affect the outcome. If so, the $MS_{S/A}$ represents both error variance and variance caused by gender, experimenter, or position, but the variance caused by these "irrelevant" variables will not contribute to $MS_A$ because—for example—there will be an equal number of male and female subjects at each level of $A$. The analysis based on the one-factor model then violates the principle that the numerator and denominator of the $F$ ratio should have the same expectation when $H_0$ is true. In such situations, the denominator has a larger expectation because the irrelevant variable makes a contribution. The result is a loss of power that can be considerable if the irrelevant variable has a large effect. We say that the $F$ test is **negatively biased** in this case. As a general rule, the researcher should formulate a complete structural model, one which incorporates all systematically varied factors, even those thought to be irrelevant or uninteresting. In the examples cited, this would mean viewing the study as one involving two factors, $A$ and gender (or experimenter, or position), and carrying out the analysis presented in Chapter 11.

### 8.7.2 The Independence Assumption

When only one observation is obtained from each participant, and participants are randomly assigned to treatments or randomly sampled from distinct populations, the assumption that the scores are independently distributed should be met. There are exceptions, however, that are often unrecognized by researchers. For example, suppose we wished to compare attitudes on some topic for male and female participants. Further suppose that before being tested, the participants are involved in three-person discussions of the relevant topic. The scores of individuals who were part of the same discussion group will tend to be positively correlated. If this failure of the independence assumption is ignored (and it often is; see Anderson & Ager, 1978, for a review), there will be a **positive bias**—an inflation of Type 1 error rate—in an *F* test of the gender effect. Why this is so, and the nature of the proper analysis, is explained in Chapter 16. Another potential source of failure of the independence assumption is the "bottom-of-the-barrel" problem. Researchers at universities often feel that as the semester progresses, the performance of volunteer participants in experiments tends to become poorer because less motivated participants usually volunteer for research credit late in the semester. Then scores obtained close in time will tend to be correlated.

**Autocorrelation plots**, such as those in Fig. 8.4, provide one diagnostic tool. The bars represent the average correlations of residuals ( $Y_{ij} - \bar{Y}._j$ ) that are various temporal distances ("lags") apart. If any of the bars exceed the confidence limits indicated by the two horizontal lines, the independence assumption may be invalid. In the upper panel of Fig. 8.4, the correlation tends to be larger for scores nearer together in time, suggesting some failure of the independence assumption. However, all the bars are within the CI and the correlations are generally small. The bottom panel represents an artificial data set into which we built a tendency for scores to become worse over time. As a result, scores near each other had very high positive correlations and scores far apart tended to have a negative correlation. Scatter diagrams of scores versus time of test may also be useful in checking for trends over time (e.g., that performances were deteriorating or becoming more variable as the semester progressed). Departures from a best-fitting line with slope of zero, or changes in the spread of scores as a function of time, would suggest that scores were dependent on when they were obtained.

### 8.7.3 The Normality Assumption

Mathematical proofs (Scheffé, 1959) and computer-sampling studies (e.g., Donaldson, 1968; Lindquist, 1953, pp. 78–90) have shown that the Type 1 error probability associated with the *F* test is little affected by sampling from nonnormal populations unless the samples are quite small and the departure from normality extremely marked. This reflects the role played by the central limit theorem; the distribution of means and their differences will tend to be normal as *n* increases even when the distribution of the parent populations is not. The *F* test's **robustness** with respect to Type 1 error rate appears to hold even when the independent variable is discretely distributed, as it is whenever rating data or response frequencies are analyzed. Computer-sampling studies indicate that Type 1 error rates are relatively unaffected when such measures are submitted to an ANOVA. With as few as two rating points (Lunney, 1970) and two groups of 3 participants each (Bevan, Denton, & Myers, 1974; Hsu & Feldt, 1969), in all but the most skewed distributions the proportion of rejections of the null hypothesis fell within two standard deviations of the theoretical alpha. Furthermore, the distance between the empirical and theoretical alpha decreased with more rating points, larger samples, and more symmetric distributions.

Although the Type 1 error rate is relatively unaffected by nonnormality in most instances, power may be a concern. When treatment distributions are not normal, there are alternatives to the ANOVA that will be more powerful. Such **nonparametric tests** do not require the assumption that the population distribution is normal. We consider two such tests next.

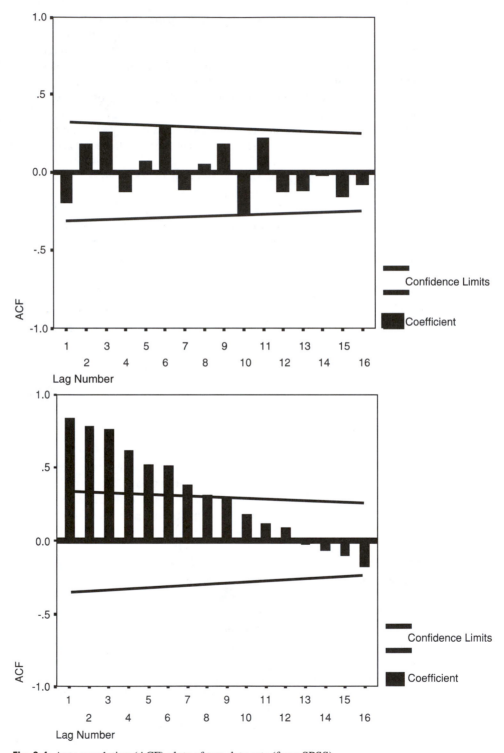

**Fig. 8.4** Autocorrelation (ACF) plots of two data sets (from SPSS).

## 8.7.4 Tests Based on Ranks: The Kruskal–Wallis *H* and the Rank-Transform *F* Tests

These tests are based on an analysis of ranks and are closely related. Both tests require that all scores are ordered with a rank of 1 assigned to the lowest score in the data set and a rank of $N$ assigned to the largest, where $N$ is the total number of scores in the data set. In case of ties, the median rank is assigned. For example, if the 5 lowest scores are 1, 4, 7, 9, and 9, they would receive ranks of 1, 2, 3, 4.5, and 4.5 respectively. The Kruskal–Wallis $H$ test (Kruskal & Wallis, 1952) is available from the nonparametric menu of statistical packages such as SPSS, SYSTAT, and SAS. Basically, it is the treatment sum of squares based on the ranks, divided by the variance of $N$ consecutive integers. Recall from Chapter 7 that the ratio of a sum of squared deviations of normally distributed variables divided by the population variance is distributed as $\chi^2$ if the variables are normally distributed. If the $n_j$ are not very small—5 or more is the usually recommended cutoff—the means of the group ranks will be approximately normally distributed and, under the null hypothesis, $H$ will be distributed as $\chi^2$ on $a - 1$ $df$. A computing formula is

$$H = \left[ \frac{12}{N(N+1)} \right] \left[ \sum_j \frac{T_{\cdot j}^2}{n_j} \right] - 3(N+1) \tag{8.21}$$

where $n_j$ is the number of scores in the $j$th group, $N$ is the total number of scores, and $T_{\cdot j}$ is the sum of ranks in the $j$th group.

The rank-transform $F$ test (Conover & Iman, 1981) is conceptually even simpler. After the scores are transformed, the usual one-way ANOVA is performed on the ranks and the test statistic, $F_R$, is evaluated on $a-1$ and $N - a$ $df$. $H$ and $F_R$ will generally result in similar $p$ values. This is not surprising given that they are related by the following equation:

$$F_R = \frac{(N-a)H}{(a-1)(N-1-H)}$$

Neither test requires the assumption that the treatment populations are normally distributed. However, the test of equal population means rests on the assumption that the population distributions have identical shapes; that is, that they have the same values of variance, skewness, and kurtosis. Under this constraint, the alternative to the null hypothesis is referred to as the **shift hypothesis,** so called because it implies that the alternative is that the treatment has shifted the distributions but not influenced them in any other way. If the populations are not normally distributed but have the same shapes, then these tests will often have more power than the $F$ test. Furthermore, they are only slightly less powerful than the $F$ test when the distributions are normal. These points are illustrated in Table 8.11, which presents the proportion of rejections for $F$ and $H$ in 1,000 computer-sampling experiments with three different population distributions. The mixed-normal distribution is symmetric but has heavier tails than the normal and the exponential is extremely skewed. When $H_0$ is true (distance $= 0$), the empirical rejection rate is usually within two standard deviations (or .014) of .05, the theoretical value of $\alpha$. When the null hypothesis is false (distance $= .4$ or .8), the $F$ has a slight power advantage over the Kruskal–Wallis and rank-transform $F$ tests if the populations are normally distributed. However, for the two nonnormal distributions, the nonparametric tests generally have more power.

There has been considerable confusion in journal articles and statistics texts about the null hypothesis tested by $H$ and $F_R$. It has frequently been claimed that the Kruskal–Wallis

**TABLE 8.11**    EMPIRICAL REJECTION RATES FOR THE $F$ AND KRUSKAL-WALLIS $H$ TESTS

| | | Distance Between Adjacent Population Means | | | | | |
| | | 0 | | .4 | | .8 | |
| $n$ | Test | $F$ | $H$ | $F$ | $H$ | $F$ | $H$ |
|---|---|---|---|---|---|---|---|
| 5 | Normal | .054 | .049 | .167 | .144 | .504 | .441 |
| 5 | Mixed-normal | .055 | .055 | .119 | .122 | .363 | .357 |
| 5 | Exponential | .048 | .047 | .197 | .243 | .578 | .616 |
| 10 | Normal | .048 | .036 | .308 | .285 | .876 | .852 |
| 10 | Mixed-normal | .038 | .040 | .205 | .234 | .644 | .720 |
| 10 | Exponential | .035 | .047 | .365 | .528 | .859 | .936 |

$H$ test should be used instead of the usual $F$ test when there is heterogeneity of variance. However, if the treatment populations do not have identical distributions, then $H$ and $F_R$ tests may reject the null hypothesis because of differences in the shapes of the distributions, not their locations. On the basis of a computer-sampling study, Oshima and Algina (1992) warn against using the Kruskal–Wallis test when the homogeneity of variance assumption is suspect. A detailed discussion of what is tested by the Kruskal–Wallis and rank-transform tests under various conditions is provided by Vargha and Delaney (1998). Our view is that these tests can be useful when two conditions are met: first, there is clear evidence that the data are not normally distributed; second, the treatment distributions are similar in shape. Researchers entertaining the possibility of using either nonparametric alternative should first view a normal probability plot of their data. As shown in Chapter 2, clear departures from a straight line indicate a departure from normality. In addition, as discussed in Chapter 7, tests of normality are available in SPSS and SAS.

If there is evidence of nonnormality, the next step would be to compare plots of the data from the different treatment groups, using box plots, histograms, or dot-density plots. Obvious differences in shape, or marked differences among variance, skewness, or kurtosis measures, would suggest that the $H$ or $F_R$ statistic is not appropriate for testing equality of population means.[5]

When there are only two groups, the Kruskal–Wallis test is equivalent to the Wilcoxon rank sum (or the equivalent Mann–Whitney $U$) test, and the rank-transform $F$ test produces the same result as a $t$ test applied to the ranks. One drawback in using these rank-based procedures is that although CIs on the median difference can be established, the process is somewhat tedious and requires tables of the Mann–Whitney $U$ test. Steps for calculating the CI are outlined by Marascuilo and Serlin (1988, p. 242), and the necessary tables are in the appendix to their book.

## 8.7.5 The Homogeneity of Variance Assumption

Variances may differ across conditions for one of several reasons. One possible cause of heterogeneity of variance is an interaction of an experimental treatment with individual characteristics. For example, a drug tested for its effects on depression may result in a higher variance, but the same mean score, as a placebo. This would suggest that some individuals had improved but others had been adversely affected by that drug. A second possible reason for unequal variances is that some populations are more variable than others on a particular task. For example, although boys may have higher average scores on some measure of mathematical ability, they may also have a higher variance. Still another factor in findings of heterogeneity of variance are floor, or ceiling, effects. Variability may be reduced in one condition relative to another because of a lower, or upper, limit on performance that is due to the measuring instrument. Finally, variances tend to be correlated, usually positively, with means; the normal distribution is the sole exception in which the means and variances are independently distributed. For all of these reasons, homogeneity of variance is rarely present in the populations sampled in our research. In this section, we summarize some consequences of the failure of this assumption; in the sections following we consider alternatives to the standard *F* test.

When there are the same number of scores in all conditions, heterogeneous variances usually will cause Type 1 error rates to be inflated. The inflation is usually less than .02 at the .05 level, and less than .005 at the .01 level, provided the ratio of the largest to smallest variance is no more than 4:1, and *n* is at least 5. Even larger ratios may not be a problem, but this will depend on sample size, the number of groups, and the shape of the population distributions. The results of computer simulations employing these factors are discussed in articles by Clinch and Keselman (1982) and Tomarken and Serlin (1986).

When there are different numbers of scores in each condition, simulation studies clearly demonstrate that heterogeneous variances are a problem. Sampling from sets of either 3 or 4 normally distributed populations, Tomarken and Serlin found that at a nominal .05 level, the actual Type 1 error rate was as low as .022 when the group size was positively correlated with the variance and as high as .167 when the correlation was negative. Sampling from heavy-tailed and skewed distributions, and using variance ratios of largest to smallest as high as 16:1, Lix and Keselman (1998) found that error rates were as high as .50 in some conditions. The expected mean squares may clarify why heterogeneous variances are more troublesome when *n*s are unequal. For simplicity, assume the null hypothesis is true. Then, it can be shown that

$$E(MS_A) = \frac{1}{a-1} \sum_{j=1}^{a} \left( \frac{N-n_j}{N} \right) \sigma_j^2 \tag{8.22}$$

$$E(MS_{S/A}) = \frac{1}{N-a} \sum_{j=1}^{a} (n_j - 1) \sigma_j^2 \tag{8.23}$$

where $N = \sum_j n_j$ and $\sigma_j^2$ is the variance of the *j*th treatment population. If the $n_j$ all equal *n*, then $N = an$, and both expressions reduce to the same quantity; under the null hypothesis, $E(MS_A) = E(MS_{S/A}) = \sum_j \sigma_j^2/a$, the average population variance. This equality of expectations does not mean that the ratio of mean squares will be distributed as *F* when variances are heterogeneous; we have already noted that there may be inflation of Type 1 error rate even when *n*s are equal. Nevertheless, the equality does constrain the degree to which the distribution of mean squares will vary from the theoretical *F* distribution.

The larger the $n_j$, the smaller the contribution of the *j*th population variance to $E(MS_A)$ in Equation 8.22, because $N - n_j$ decreases as $n_j$ increases. The opposite is true for $E(MS_{S/A})$; the larger the $n_j$, the greater the contribution of the *j*th population variance to the denominator because $n_j - 1$ increases as $n_j$ does. Therefore, when large variances are paired with large group sizes, they will increase the denominator relatively more than the numerator; as a result, the true Type 1 error rate will be below the theoretical value and power against false null hypotheses is likely to be reduced; there is negative bias. In contrast, when large variances are paired with small group sizes, they tend to contribute relatively more to the numerator of the $F$ test than to its denominator. In this case, the bias is positive; the Type 1 error rate is inflated.

There is evidence that extreme variance ratios do occur in the research literature (Wilcox, 1987), and a host of simulation studies make clear that heterogeneity of variance can inflate Type 1 error rates and deflate power, depending on various factors such as sample sizes and the type of distribution sampled. That leaves us with two questions. First, for a given data set, how do we decide whether to abandon the standard ANOVA for some remedial procedure? Second, if we do decide that unequal variances are a threat to the validity of the standard $F$ test, what alternative should we use? We consider these questions next.

### 8.7.6 Detecting Heterogeneity of Variance

As always, we urge that researchers begin the data analysis by examining summary statistics and plots of the data. SPSS's Explore module (click on "Analyze" followed by "Descriptive Statistics") is very helpful in this respect. It provides descriptive statistics, tests of homogeneity of variance, and box plots. The box plot for the Beck depression data as a function of educational level was presented in Fig. 8.3 and, as we noted there, differences among the groups in shape and spread are quite evident. The range of variances in Table 8.7 strongly suggests that the alpha level reported in Table 8.8 may not be the actual probability of a Type 1 error. For confirmation of this, we may wish to test whether the variances are homogeneous. Several tests of homogeneity of variance have been proposed. Some of these (Bartlett, 1937; Cochran, 1941; Hartley, 1950) have been shown not to be robust in the face of data that are not normally distributed and therefore are not considered further. The Box–Scheffé (1953, 1959) test provides Type 1 error rates that are close to the nominal alpha but lacks power relative to other procedures (Games, Keselman, & Clinch, 1979). A test proposed by Levene (1960) is available in several statistical packages such as SYSTAT, SPSS, BMDP, and SAS. In this test, the absolute residual of each score from its group mean, $\left|Y_{ij} - \overline{Y}_{.j}\right|$, is computed and these residuals are then submitted to the ordinary ANOVA. Although these residuals do not directly represent the variance, they are an index of the spread of scores. For the data summarized in Table 8.7, SPSS's Explore module reports the value of this statistic as 7.722, which, on 3 and 124 $df$, is very significant ($p = .000$) and indicates that the mean absolute residual varies significantly as a function of education level. The SPSS output also reports three other "Levene statistics." The first of these, actually developed by Brown and Forsythe (1974a), is similar to the Levene test except that the data are absolute deviations from the group medians, rather than the means. This test should be less sensitive to outliers. The second alternative to the Levene test is a further modification of the Brown–Forsythe test, in which degrees of freedom are adjusted as a function of the group variances. The third alternative is one in which an ANOVA is performed on residuals from the trimmed group means. The **trimmed means** are obtained by removing the highest and lowest 5% of the scores in each group, and then calculating the means. This provides another way of reducing the impact of outliers. With respect to the depression scores, all four methods produced $p$ values of .005 or less, confirming our sense that the spread of scores was indeed a function of the educational level.

How robust are these tests of the null hypothesis of equal variances? The Levene test appears to have an unacceptably high Type 1 error rate when the population distributions are skewed or bimodal. Empirical rejection probabilities reach as high as .25 with very skewed distributions when the nominal Type 1 error rate is .05 (Church & Wike, 1976). We recommend the Brown–Forsythe test based on deviations from the median. Sampling studies indicate it has only a slightly inflated Type 1 error rate and good power relative to various competitors even when *ns* are not equal and distributions depart markedly from the normal (Games et al., 1979).

Once we conclude that the population variances are not equal, the next question is, What shall we do about it? One possible response is to seek a transformation of the data that yields homogeneity of variance on the scale resulting from the transformation. A second possibility is to compute an alternative to the usual *F* test. We consider each of these approaches next.

### 8.7.7 Transformations of the Data

Statisticians have frequently recommended transforming data, for example by raising all scores to some power, or by taking the logarithm of all scores. Transformations have been used to transform skewed distributions into more nearly normal distributions, to reduce heterogeneity of variance, and to remedy a condition known as "nonadditivity" in designs in which each participant is tested on several trials or under several treatment levels. We delay discussion of this third purpose until Chapter 13. For now, we note that a transformation that best achieves one purpose may not be equally suitable for other purposes, although it is true that transformations that equate variances do tend to yield more normally distributed scores. Our focus here is on transformations designed to achieve homogeneous variances.

Typically, a variance-stabilizing transformation can be found when there is a functional relation between cell variances and cell means. Smith (1976) has presented the rationale underlying the derivation of transformation based on the relation between variances and means, as well as several transformations representing different functional relations. Emerson and Stoto (1983) have described a general approach that will frequently produce more nearly equal variances. The technique involves plotting the log of the *H* spread (or interquartile range; see Chapter 2) as a function of the log of the median and then finding the slope of the best-fitting straight line. Then, if *Z* is the transformed score, the **power transformation** is

$$Z = Y^{1-\text{slope}} \tag{8.24}$$

If the slope equals one, the power equals zero, and the appropriate transformation is $Z = \log(Y)$. SPSS provides a **spread versus level** plot of $\log(H$ spread) as a function of $\log(\text{median})$, and outputs the slope and power. Select "Analyze," Descriptive Statistics," and "Explore," and then choose the "Plots" option and, within that, "Power Transformations." We followed this procedure with data from Royer's (1999) study of arithmetic skills in elementary school children. Submitting response times (RTs) on multiplication problems to SPSS's Explore module, we found that the slope of the spread-versus-level plot was 2.227 and the recommended power was therefore $-1.227$. We rounded this, letting $Z = Y^{-1} = 1/Y$, thus reexpressing RT as response speed, a measure that is easily understood. Table 8.12 presents the group means and variances on the original and new data scales. On the original RT scale, the ratio of largest to smallest variance is almost 15:1; on the speed scale, that ratio is only 1.4:1. To provide a further check on the adequacy of the transformation, we had SPSS plot the spread-versus-level function for the speed data. The slope of this function was $-.144$ and therefore the power to which each score should be raised is $1-$ slope $=$

**TABLE 8.12** MEANS AND VARIANCES OF MULTIPLICATION RTs FROM THE ROYER DATA

| Mean or Variance | Grade | | | |
| --- | --- | --- | --- | --- |
| | 5 | 6 | 7 | 8 |
| RT Mean | 3.837 | 1.998 | 1.857 | 1.935 |
| RT Variance | 4.864 | .612 | .328 | .519 |
| Speed Mean | .350 | .560 | .586 | .583 |
| Speed Variance | .033 | .028 | .031 | .038 |

1.144. But this is close to one, indicating that no improvement is likely to be obtained by a further transformation.

The choice of a dependent variable is often arbitrary and some transformation of the original scale may be preferable if the distribution on the new scale has desirable properties, such as normality or homogeneity of variance, that are lacking in the original data. One potential problem is that values on the new scale may be less easily interpreted than on the original scale. For example, the percentage of correct answers on a test ($y$) is easily understood and communicated, but this is less true, for example, of the arc sine transformation ($\sin^{-1} \sqrt{y}$, the angle whose sine is the square root of $y$), often recommended to stabilize the variances of percentage scores. Another potential problem is that, although variance-stabilizing transformations will usually maintain the ordering of the group means, the relative distances among means may change, creating problems when the effects of the manipulated factors are interpreted. Suppose a researcher has predicted that response time (RT) will vary as a linear function of the levels of the independent variable. There is an excellent chance that a test of linearity on a transformed scale will fail to support the prediction because the means on the new scale are likely to fall on a curve. Transformations only make sense when predictions are not dependent on the measurement scale. When the measuring scale is arbitrary, the researcher may find it helpful to seek a transformation, assessing the success of the transformation by plotting a spread-versus-level function as we described in our example of the multiplication RTs and speeds. Keep in mind that although it is perfectly reasonable to try several transformations, assessing each by plotting spread against level, it is not appropriate to conduct a significance test after each transformation, settling for the data scale that yields the largest $F$ value. Such a procedure is bound to increase the probability of a Type 1 error if the population means do not differ.

Often the researcher will not wish to transform the data, either because of the difficulty of interpreting effects (or lack of effects) on the new scale, or because a strong theory dictates the dependent variable. In other instances, it may be impossible to find a variance-stabilizing transformation. Fortunately, there are other solutions that, although they also are not always satisfactory, can often solve the heterogeneity problem. We turn now to consider modifications of the standard $F$ test.

## 8.7.8 Alternative Tests When Variances Are not Equal

Several alternatives to the standard $F$ test of the equality of the $a$ population means have been proposed (Alexander & Govern, 1994; Brown & Forsythe, 1974b; James, 1951, 1954;

Welch, 1951), but no one test is best under all conditions. Each has strengths and weaknesses, depending on the shapes of the treatment distributions, the relative sample sizes, and the ratio of variances. Detailed information about the influences of these factors on alternative tests of the null hypothesis is provided in articles by Coombs, Algina, and Oltman (1996), Grissom (2000), and Lix, Keselman, and Keselman (1996). These, particularly the Grissom article, will in turn provide many additional references.

When the data are normally distributed and *n*s are equal, most of the procedures are reasonably robust with respect to Type 1 error rate; however, the standard *F* is slightly more powerful if the population variances are equal. When the variances are not equal, which test is best depends on the degree of skew and kurtosis, whether outliers are present, the degree of heterogeneity of variance, the relation between group sizes and group variances, and the total *N* (Clinch & Keselman, 1982; Coombs et al., 1996; Lix et al., 1996; Tomarken & Serlin, 1986). Although there is rarely a clear-cut choice for any given data set, we illustrate the application of the **Welch test, $F_w$**, to the data summarized in Table 8.7. $F_w$ performs well relative to various competitors except when the data are highly skewed (skew > 2.0) or group sizes are less than 10 (Tomarken & Serlin, 1986; Lix et al., 1996). Furthermore, the test is available in BMDP and SAS/IML. Table 8.13 presents the necessary formulas and illustrates their application to the statistics of Table 8.7. The resulting *p* value is considerably higher than the .016 we obtained by using the standard *F* calculations. The discrepancy can

**TABLE 8.13**  FORMULAS FOR THE WELCH ($F_W$) TEST AND APPLICATION TO THE STATISTICS OF TABLE 8.7

The Welch test

$$F_W = \frac{A}{B}$$

where

$$A = \frac{1}{a-1} \sum w_j (\overline{Y}_{\cdot j} - \overline{Y}_{\cdot\cdot})^2$$

$$B = 1 + \left[ \frac{2(a-2)}{a^2-1} \right] \sum \frac{[1-(w_j/u)]^2}{n_j-1}$$

$$w_j = n_j/s_j^2; \quad u = \sum w_j; \quad \overline{Y}_{\cdot\cdot} = \frac{\sum w_j \overline{Y}_{\cdot j}}{u}$$

$$df_1 = a - 1$$

$$\frac{1}{df_2} = \left( \frac{3}{a^2-1} \right) \sum \frac{[1-(w_j/u)]^2}{n_j-1}$$

Substituting Table 8.7 values in the preceding equations

|  | HS | C | B | GS |
|---|---|---|---|---|
| $w_j$ | .550 | 5.528 | 3.752 | 1.488 |
| $\overline{Y}_{\cdot j}$ | 6.903 | 3.674 | 3.331 | 4.847 |

Then, $u = 11.318$, $\overline{Y}_{\cdot\cdot} = 3.871$, $A = 2.594$, $B = 1.024$, and $F = 2.533$; also, $df_1 = 3$, $df_2 = 1.018 = 55$, and $p = .066$.

be accounted for by noting that the correlation between $n_j$ and $s_j^2$ is negative $-.59$. There are only 19 participants in the group having only a high school education (HS), whereas the other groups all have at least 33 participants. That smaller group size is paired with the largest group variance. As we noted earlier in the chapter, when larger groups have smaller variances, they have too much weight in the denominator of the $F$ test, with a resulting inflated probability of Type 1 errors. The Welch test has compensated for this by taking the inequalities in group sizes and variances into account.

In summary, we recommend the following with respect to alternative tests:

1. Look at summary statistics, including skew and kurtosis measures, and plot the data. Box plots are widely available and will often provide a sufficient basis for deciding whether heterogeneity of variance is a problem. Visual inspection will often be sufficient, but tests of homogeneity such as the Brown–Forsythe test can provide confirmation (Brown & Forsythe, 1974a).

2. If the $n$s are equal and the ratio of largest to smallest variance is no more than 4:1, the ordinary $F$ test will have a Type 1 error rate close to its nominal value and will have slightly more power than alternative tests against false null hypotheses. However, when in doubt, it is probably best to consider an alternative. Even when all the assumptions of the $F$ test are met, the evidence suggests that the power of the $F$ will exceed that of competitors such as $F_w$ by less than .04.

3. Although there is no one test that combines honest Type 1 error rates with higher power than its competitors, we recommend the Welch test. It is available in statistical packages and performs reasonably well except when the distributions are very skewed and the $n$s are less than 10. For $n < 6$, the Brown–Forsythe test of the means (Brown & Forsythe, 1974b) appears to have Type 1 error rates closer to the nominal value and power roughly equal to that of $F_w$. Another possibility is to apply a test such as the Welch or Brown–Forsythe test to means based on data from which the highest and lowest 20% have been trimmed. Computer-sampling results for this procedure are promising (Lix & Keselman, 1998; also see Wilcox, 1997, p. 134, for a description of the procedure). The main drawback is the computational complexity, but Wilcox has made a program available at a Web site linked to the Academic Press Web site: (http://www.apnet.com).

No one test will be best in every situation. The relative merits of various procedures will depend on a complex combination of factors. Researchers with heterogeneous variances should turn to articles that have reported the effects of various combinations of factors on error rates and power (e.g., Coombs et al., 1996; Lix et al., 1996; Lix & Keselman, 1998; Tomarken & Serlin, 1986). A test may then be selected on the basis of consideration of the relative Type 1 error rates and power under conditions similar to the researcher's own study. In some cases, there will be no test that clearly meets the researcher's needs. In such instances, information about the distributions in the various conditions, including plots of the data, should be presented in research reports. Indeed, such information should be routinely presented regardless of whether significance test results are presented. Whatever approach is taken, decisions about the appropriate null hypothesis test should never be made by running several tests and selecting the one that yields the lowest $p$ value; this procedure is likely to inflate the Type 1 error rate.

## 8.8 CONCLUDING REMARKS

Most studies involve more than a single factor. There may be several treatment variables or, as in the Seasons data, participants may be categorized in several ways. Furthermore, in many studies, participants are tested under several conditions or on several trials. Nevertheless, important concepts and issues have been raised in this context, and these will require consideration regardless of the design of the research. We should always consider the appropriate structural model for our data, and we should always be concerned about whether assumptions have been met and, if not, what the consequences are likely to be and what remedies are available. In understanding our data and in assessing the validity of assumptions, we should be guided by summary statistics and data plots readily available from many computer packages. Normal probability plots, box plots, dot-density plots, stem-and-leaf plots, and spread-versus-level plots can all be helpful.

We have focused on tests of the omnibus null hypothesis in this chapter because they are routinely conducted and routinely presented in research reports, and they provide an overview of the effects of the independent variable. However, we believe that the omnibus null hypothesis is rarely, if ever, of primary interest to researchers. Usually, either because of reasons based on theory or prior knowledge, or because of the observed pattern of cell means, we are most interested in estimating and testing contrasts of means. As we demonstrated in Chapter 6, the $t$ distribution provides the basis for CIs and tests of contrasts, and these calculations are straightforward. Nevertheless, inferences about contrasts raise certain issues, some of which are as much philosophical as statistical. We turn to these in the next chapter.

## KEY CONCEPTS

| | |
|---|---|
| treatment populations | completely randomized design |
| between-subjects designs | within-subjects (repeated-measures) designs |
| structural model | fixed-effect variables |
| random-effect variables | omnibus null hypothesis |
| dot-density plot | between-groups mean square |
| treatment effect | error component |
| total sum of squares ($SS_{tot}$) | between-groups sum of squares ($SS_A$) |
| within-groups sum of squares ($SS_{S/A}$) | definitional formulas |
| raw-score formulas | $\eta^2$ |
| shrunken $R^2$ | expected mean squares (EMS) |
| error term | $\omega^2$ |
| noncentral $F$ distribution | noncentrality parameter, $\lambda$ |
| negative bias of the $F$ test | positive bias |
| autocorrelation plots | robustness |
| nonparametric tests | Kruskal–Wallis $H$ test |
| rank-transform $F$ test | shift hypothesis |
| trimmed means | power transformation |
| spread-versus-level plot | Welch test, $F_w$ |

## EXERCISES

**8.1**   A data set has three groups of 5 scores each. Because the scores involve decimal values, each score is multiplied by 100.

(a) How will the mean squares change (relative to an analysis on the original data set)?

(b) Should the $F$ ratio change?

(c) In general, what happens to a variance when every score is multiplied by a constant?

(d) Suppose we just added a constant, say 10, to all 15 scores. How would that effect the mean squares and $F$ ratio?

(e) Suppose we added 5 to all scores in the first group, 10 to all scores in the second group, and 15 to all scores in the third group. Should $MS_A$ change? Should $MS_{S/A}$? Explain.

**8.2**   Following are summary statistics from a three-group experiment. Present the ANOVA table when (a) $n_1 = n_2 = n_3 = 10$ and (b) $n_1 = 6$, $n_2 = 8$, and $n_3 = 10$ (T.$_j$ is the total, or sum of scores, for group $j$).

$$
\begin{array}{cccc}
 & A_1 & A_2 & A_3 \\
T._j = & 30 & 48 & 70 \\
s_j^2 = & 3.2 & 4.1 & 5.7
\end{array}
$$

**8.3**   The data are:

$$
\begin{array}{ll}
A_1 & 27\ 18\ 16\ 33\ 24 \\
A_2 & 23\ 33\ 26\ 19\ 38
\end{array}
$$

(a) Perform the ANOVA.

(b) Next, do a $t$ test. How are the results of parts (a) and (b) related?

**8.4**   The file Ex8_4 (*Exercise* folder) on the CD contains three groups of 15 scores.

(a) Explore the data; examine statistics and graphs relevant to assessing the normality and homogeneity of variance assumptions.

(b) Calculate the $F$ and Kruskal–Wallis $H$ tests for these data and comment on the outcome, relating your discussion to your answer to part (a).

**8.5**   (a) Calculate treatment and residual effects for the scores in Ex8_4. What should the average treatment effect be? The average residual? Are the results as expected?

(b) Multiply the sum of the squared treatment effects by $n$ and compare the result with the between-groups sum of squares from Ex8_4, part (b). Also sum the squared residuals and compare the result with the within-groups sum of squares from Ex8_4, part (b).

**8.6**   The following are the results of two experiments, each with three levels of the independent variable.

| | Table 1 | | | Table 2 | |
|---|---|---|---|---|---|
| SV | df | MS | SV | df | MS |
| $A$ | 2 | 80 | $A$ | 2 | 42.5 |
| $S/A$ | 27 | 5 | $S/A$ | 12 | 5 |

(a) (i) For each of the two tables, calculate $F$ and estimates of $\omega_A^2$.

    (ii) What does a comparison of the two sets of results suggest about the effect of the change in n upon these three quantities?

(b) Calculate $\eta_A^2$ for each table. How does $n$ effect the value of $\eta_A^2$ ?

(c) Suppose $F = 1$. (i) What must the value of $\omega_A^2$ be? (ii) What must the value of $\eta_A^2$ be (as a function of $a$ and $n$)?

(d) Comment on the relative merits of the various statistics calculated as indices of the importance of $A$.

**8.7** The results of an ANOVA of a data set based on three groups of 10 scores each is as follows:

| SV | df | SS | MS | F |
|----|----|----|----|---|
| A | 2 | 192 | 96 | 3.2 |
| S/A | 27 | 810 | 30 | |

(a) Is there a significant $A$ effect if $\alpha = .05$?

(b) Estimate Cohen's $f$ for these results.

(c) Assuming this is a good estimate of the true effect of $A$, what power did the experiment have?

(d) How many participants would be required to have power $= .8$ to detect a medium-sized effect? Use Cohen's guidelines (Subsection 8.5.1 for $\omega^2$ and Subsection 8.5.2 for $f$) for effect size.

**8.8** According to a mathematical model for the experiment in Exercise 8.7, the predicted scores are 10 in Condition 1, 14 in Condition 2, and 18 in Condition 3. If the theory is correct, what sample size would be needed to achieve .8 power to reject the null hypothesis of no difference among the means? Assume that the error mean square is a good estimate of the population variance, and $\alpha = .05$.

**8.9** In this chapter, we examined descriptive statistics for the probability-learning data of Myers et al. (1983; see Table 8.1). Although we decided that heterogeneity of variance was not a problem, we should test this assumption.

(a) Perform the Brown–Forsythe test of equality of spread.

(b) We also concluded that nonnormality was not a problem. However, we did not examine normal probability plots for each condition. Do so.

(c) Perform the Kruskal–Wallis $H$ test of the probability-learning data. Does it lead to a different conclusion than the $F$ test result reported in this chapter?

**8.10** Open the Sayhlth file in the *Seasons* folder of your CD. This file contains Sayhlth scores (self-ratings of health) of 1–4 (excellent to fair; 3 participants with poor ratings in the Seasons file are not included). The four categories will be the independent variable in this exercise and the Beck_D score will be the dependent variable in the following analyses. The Beck_D score is an average of the four seasonal Beck depression scores and is available only for those subjects whose scores were recorded in all four seasons. The distribution of Beck_D scores tends to be skewed, and, as in most nonnormal distributions, heterogeneity of variance is often a problem.

(a) Explore the data, using any statistics and plots you think are relevant, and comment on the relative locations, shapes, and variabilities of the scores in the four categories.

(b) Using the four Sayhlth categories, plot the spread versus level; as stated in Chapter 8, this is the log of the $H$ spread plotted against the log of the median. Several statistical software packages make this plot available. Find the best-fit regression line for this plot and transform the Beck_D scores by raising them to the power, $1 -$ slope.

(c) Explore the distribution of the transformed scores at each Sayhlth category. Has the transformation had any effect on the shape of the distributions or on their variances? Test for homogeneity of variance.

(d) Next let's try a different transformation. Calculate log(Beck_D +1) and discuss the effects of this transformation.

(e) What might be the advantges of transforming data to a scale on which they are normally distributed with homogeneous variances?

8.11 Continuing with the Sayhlth file, perform the following steps.

(a) Using the four Sayhlth categories as your independent variable, do separate ANOVAs of the Beck_D data for men and for women.

(b) Calculate Cohen's $f$ for each sex and compare the effect sizes (see Equation 8.19).

8.12 The Sayhlth file also categorizes individuals by employment category: $1 =$ employed full time; $2 =$ employed part time; and $3 =$ not employed.

(a) Explore the Beck_D data in each Employ category, looking at relevant graphs and statistics. Comment on the validity of the ANOVA assumptions.

(b) In Exercise 8.10, we considered transformations of the Beck_D data, one of which appeared to provide results more in accord with the ANOVA model. Use that transformation and again explore the data. Are the results more in accord with the ANOVA model?

(c) Perform ANOVAs on the Beck_D scores and the transformed scores as a function of employment status. Discuss the results.

(d) Calculate Cohen's $f$ for both the original and the transformed data. How would you characterize the effect sizes?

# APPENDIX 8.1

## Partitioning the Total Variability in the One-Factor Design

The following developments involve two indices of summation: $i$ indexes a value from 1 to $n$ within each group, where $n$ is the number of individuals in a group; $j$ indexes a value from 1 to $a$, where $a$ is the number of groups. Appendix A at the back of the book provides an explanation of the use of this notation, using several examples.

Squaring both sides of Equation 8.1 yields

$$(Y_{ij} - \overline{Y}..)^2 = (Y_{ij} - \overline{Y}._j)^2 + (\overline{Y}._j - \overline{Y}..)^2 + 2(Y_{ij} - \overline{Y}._j)(\overline{Y}._j - \overline{Y}..)$$

Summing over $i$ and $j$, and applying the rules of Appendix A on summation, we have

$$\sum_{j}^{a}\sum_{i}^{n}(Y_{ij}-\overline{Y}..)^2 = \sum_{j}^{a}\sum_{i}^{n}(Y_{ij}-\overline{Y}.j)^2 + n\sum_{j}^{a}(\overline{Y}.j-\overline{Y}..)^2$$

$$+ 2\sum_{j}^{a}\sum_{i}^{n}(Y_{ij}-\overline{Y}.j)(\overline{Y}.j-\overline{Y}..)$$

Rearranging terms, we can show that the rightmost (cross-product) term equals zero:

$$2\sum_{j}^{a}\sum_{i}^{n}(Y_{ij}-\overline{Y}.j)(\overline{Y}.j-\overline{Y}..) = 2\sum_{j}^{a}(\overline{Y}.j-\overline{Y}..)\sum_{i}^{n}(Y_{ij}-\overline{Y}.j)$$

$$= 2\sum_{j}^{a}(\overline{Y}.j-\overline{Y}..)(0) = 0$$

The last result follows because the sum of deviations of scores about their mean is zero.

## APPENDIX 8.2

## Raw-Score Formulas for Sums of Squares

The raw-score formula for $SS_{tot}$ is obtained by squaring each score, summing, and subtracting a "**correction term**," $C$, where $C = an\overline{Y}..^2 = \left(\sum_{j=1}^{a}\sum_{i=1}^{n}Y_{ij}\right)^2/an$, and

$$SS_{tot} = \sum_{j=1}^{a}\sum_{i=1}^{n}Y_{ij}^2 - C$$

$C$ corrects for the fact that we are subtracting deviations about the grand mean.

Raw-score formulas for most designs can be readily obtained from the relation between degrees of freedom and $SS$. Let $T.j$ stand for the sum of the $n$ scores in the $j$th group, and let $T..$ stand for the sum of all $an$ scores. Now consider the $SS_{S/A}$.

1. Expand the corresponding degrees of freedom: $a(n-1) = an - a$. If the group sizes are not equal, $df_{S/A} = N - a$, where $N = \sum_{j} n_{j}$.
2. Each degree of freedom in the expanded term corresponds to a squared quantity. Therefore, we now have

$$\sum_{j=1}^{a}\sum_{i=1}^{n_j}Y_{ij}^2 - \sum_{j=1}^{a}T.j^2$$

Note that each squared quantity must have subscripts that correspond exactly to the indices of summation to its left. Any indices that are not subscripted according to this rule are replaced by dots, indicating that summation has taken place for that index prior to squaring. The designation $T_{.j}^2$ indicates that we have summed the $n_j$ scores in group $j$ and then squared the total.

3. Divide each squared quantity by the number of values on which it is based. Because $Y_{ij}$ is a single score, it is divided by one. However, $T_{..j}$ is a sum of $n_j$ scores, so

$$SS_{S/A} = \sum_j \sum_i Y_{ij}^2 - \sum_j \frac{T_{.j}^2}{n_j}$$

Following these rules, because $df_A = a-1$,

$$SS_A = \sum_j \frac{T_{.j}^2}{n_j} - C$$

where $C = T_{..}^2/N$.

**EXAMPLE 1**  Applying these formulas to the data of Table 8.1, we have

$$C = (21.33^2)/48 = 9.48$$
$$SS_{\text{tot}} = 11.04 - 9.48$$
$$= 1.56$$
$$SS_A = (6.33^2 + 6.50^2 + 8.50^2)/16 - 9.48$$
$$= .18$$
$$SS_{S/A} = 1.56 - .18$$
$$= 1.38$$

# Chapter 9
## Contrasts Among Means

## 9.1 INTRODUCTION

In Chapter 8, we tested the effects of educational level on male depression scores in the Seasons data set. That is, we tested the null hypothesis that the population means of male depression scores at each educational level are identical. Such tests of the **omnibus null hypothesis** are conducted in part because tradition demands it, and in part because there is a belief that such a preliminary screening is required before we can address the questions that really interest us. A significant $F$ indicates that not all of the population means are equal. However, it does not reveal which population means differ. Presumably, we are interested in testing, and constructing confidence intervals (CIs) for, such differences as those between the HS (high school education only) and C (some college) means, or between the HS and the combined C, B (bachelor's degree), and GS (graduate school) means. The calculations for such tests and CIs are straightforward; we have already illustrated them as examples of applications of the $t$ statistic in Chapter 6. However, evaluating several contrasts raises a number of issues.

The first issue we confront is that the risk of a Type 1 error increases as we conduct more significance tests. To understand why this is so, assume that three contrasts among population means are tested. Further assume that the null hypothesis is true in all three cases so that any rejection is a Type 1 error. Finally, assume that the three significance tests are independent; the result of any one test does not change the probability of the result of any of the other tests. There are eight possible patterns of test results. For example, there might be a significant result on the first test followed by nonsignificant results on the second and third test. Assuming $H_0$ to be true and that the test results are independent, we find that the probability of this is $.05 \times .95 \times .95$. Of the eight possible patterns of results, seven have at least one rejection; that is, at least one Type 1 error. In fact, the probability of *at least one* Type 1 error is one minus the probability that *no* test results in a rejection; this is $1 - .95^3$, or .143. This is notably higher than the .05 we associate with an individual test. Furthermore, the more tests that are performed, the higher this error probability becomes. Although the conditions we set in this example—all null hypotheses true and all tests independent of each other—will not usually hold in our studies, the general principle does. As the number of tests increases, there is also an increase in the probability of at least one Type 1 error; this probability is referred to as the **familywise error rate**, or **FWE**. There have been many proposals for controlling the error rate associated with a family of tests, and a major purpose of this chapter is to sort through these and make recommendations.

The second issue is, What is a family? In a one-factor design such as those considered in Chapter 8, the answer seems obvious; it is the set of all tests conducted. However, suppose we conducted two different sets of three tests each. For example, the contrasts among educational levels might be performed on the depression data and on one other measure, perhaps anxiety scores. Is there a single family consisting of six tests, or two families of three tests each? The answer will influence the inferences that are drawn because a larger value of $t$ will be needed for significance when the FWE is based on six, as opposed to three, tests. We discuss this issue in Section 9.4.

A third issue centers on the distinction between **planned contrasts**, those determined before the data were collected, and **post hoc contrasts**, those based on "data snooping," testing differences that look interesting after the data have been collected. Should this distinction influence the process by which we arrive at our inferences, and, if so, how? We will argue that the distinction is important, and, in separate sections for planned and post hoc contrasts, we discuss procedures for controlling the FWE.

The results of tests conducted on the Myers et al. (1983) probability-learning experiment data in Chapters 6 and 8 raise yet a fourth issue. In Chapter 6, a $t$ test on these data revealed that the mean of the HE (high explanatory) condition was significantly higher than the mean of the combined S (standard) and LE (low explanatory) conditions. However, the $F$ test in Chapter 8 failed to reject the omnibus null hypothesis that all three population means are equal; the $p$ was .062. Because the omnibus $F$ was not significant, some investigators would argue that no further tests should have been carried out. These individuals view the omnibus $F$ test as a gatekeeper and therefore would not proceed to tests of contrasts in the absence of a significant result in the test of the omnibus null hypothesis. However, *if the FWE is maintained at or below its nominal level*, not only is there no need for a prior test of the omnibus null hypothesis before testing contrasts, but requiring such a test before proceeding further will lead to a reduction of power.

The plan for this chapter is as follows. We first define some basic terms and present examples of contrasts. Following this, we review calculations of $t$ statistics for testing hypotheses about contrasts, noting possible modifications under conditions of unequal $n$s or unequal variances. We then address the issues raised previously in this introduction. We illustrate methods for maintaining the FWE in several different situations—when a subset of all possible contrasts has been planned, when all possible contrasts based on pairs of means are made, when each of several treatment means is contrasted with the mean of a control group, and when contrasts are selected for testing after an inspection of the data.

## 9.2 DEFINITIONS AND EXAMPLES OF CONTRASTS

We define a **contrast**, or **comparison**, of population means as a linear combination of the means. We denote contrasts by the Greek letter, psi ($\psi$):

$$\psi = \sum_j w_j \mu_j \tag{9.1}$$

where at least one $w_j$ is not zero and $\sum_j w_j = 0$. Some examples are

$$\psi_1 = \mu_4 - \mu_3$$
$$\psi_2 = (1/2)(\mu_3 + \mu_4) - \mu_2$$
$$\psi_3 = (1/3)(\mu_2 + \mu_3 + \mu_4) - \mu_1 \tag{9.2}$$
$$\psi_4 = (1/2)(\mu_1 + \mu_2) - (1/2)(\mu_3 + \mu_4)$$

For example, $\psi_3$ contrasts the average of the last three treatment population means with the first population mean. The point estimate of $\psi$ is

$$\hat{\psi} = \sum_j w_j \overline{Y}_{.j} \tag{9.3}$$

For the contrasts in Equation 9.2, the point estimates are

$$\hat{\psi}_1 = (0)(\overline{Y}_{.1}) + (0)(\overline{Y}_{.2}) + (-1)(\overline{Y}_{.3}) + (1)(\overline{Y}_{.4})$$
$$\hat{\psi}_2 = (0)(\overline{Y}_{.1}) + (-1)(\overline{Y}_{.2}) + (1/2)(\overline{Y}_{.3}) + (1/2)(\overline{Y}_{.4})$$
$$\hat{\psi}_3 = (-1)(\overline{Y}_{.1}) + (1/3)(\overline{Y}_{.2}) + (1/3)(\overline{Y}_{.3}) + (1/3)(\overline{Y}_{.4}) \tag{9.4}$$
$$\hat{\psi}_4 = (1/2)(\overline{Y}_{.1}) + (1/2)(\overline{Y}_{.2}) + (-1/2)(\overline{Y}_{.3}) + (-1/2)(\overline{Y}_{.4})$$

Each of these estimates a different contrast of the four population means and therefore provides the basis for testing a different null hypothesis.

Because any set of weights that sum to zero is allowed under the definition of a contrast, there are an infinite number of possible contrasts. In practice, researchers are usually interested in contrasts between the means of two treatment populations; $\psi_1$ is an example. Such contrasts are often referred to as **pairwise comparisons**. Less often, we are interested in more complex contrasts in which at least one of the two means is itself an average of several means; the remaining three contrasts in Equation 9.4 are all examples of this. If we have four treatments, there will be six pairwise comparisons and 19 additional contrasts involving subsets of means, such as $\psi_2$, $\psi_3$, and $\psi_4$. Such an abundance of testable hypotheses may tempt us to test them all or, what is essentially the same thing, to look at the various differences between sets of means, selecting the largest one and testing it. As we indicated earlier, this may cause a greatly inflated Type 1 error rate. We present methods for controlling error rates even for large families of tests, but we must be aware that these methods involve a cost. As we increase the number of contrasts we test while holding the FWE at some reasonable level (ordinarily .05 or .10), power is lost. In view of this, we should think hard about which hypotheses are of interest before we collect the data. We need to focus both the research design and the power of our significance tests on those questions that are of most interest to us.

## 9.3 CALCULATIONS OF THE $t$ STATISTIC FOR TESTING HYPOTHESES ABOUT CONTRASTS

In Chapter 6, we presented calculations for the $t$ statistic for contrasts.[1] In this section we review those calculations with another example, and we discuss the selection of weights when $n$s are unequal, and alternative calculations when variances are unequal. Consider the response speeds on a multiplication test for the fifth- to eighth-grade students in Royer's study (Royer et al., 1999). Suppose we had initially hypothesized that between fifth and sixth grade, there was a clear change in speed, but little, if any, further improvement in subsequent grades. This suggests that the fifth-grade mean will differ from the mean of the combined sixth through eighth graders, and that there will be no pairwise differences among the higher three grades.[2] This in turn suggests the following set of four null hypotheses:

$$H_{01}: \psi_1 = (1/3)(\mu_6 + \mu_7 + \mu_8) - \mu_5 = 0$$
$$H_{02}: \psi_2 = \mu_7 - \mu_6 = 0$$
$$H_{03}: \psi_3 = \mu_8 - \mu_6 = 0$$
$$H_{04}: \psi_4 = \mu_7 - \mu_8 = 0$$

Table 9.1 presents the means and variances of the four groups, and the group sizes, and it illustrates the calculation of the $t$ statistic for the first contrast. Note that the weights for $\psi_1$ ($w_j$) have been multiplied by 3 so that all weights are now integers. This does not change the value of the $t$ statistic because both the numerator and the denominator are increased by a

**TABLE 9.1**    THE $t$ TEST OF $H_{01}: \psi_1 = (1/3)(\mu_6 + \mu_7 + \mu_8) - \mu_5 = 0$

| | Grade | | | | |
|---|---|---|---|---|---|
| | 5 | 6 | 7 | 8 | |
| Mean | 0.350 | 0.560 | 0.586 | 0.583 | |
| Variance | 0.033 | 0.028 | 0.031 | 0.038 | |
| $n$ | 23 | 26 | 21 | 20 | $N = 90$ |

$MS_{S/A} = (22/86)(.033) + (25/86)(.028) + (20/86)(.031) + (19/86)(.038) = .032$
and $df_{S/A} = 90 - 4 = 86$. To test $H_{01}$, we calculate

$$t = \hat{\psi}/S_{\hat{\psi}}$$
$$= \frac{\sum_j w_j \overline{Y}_j}{s_{pooled}\sqrt{\sum_j \frac{w_j^2}{n_j}}}$$

In this example,

$$\hat{\psi}_1 = (\overline{Y}_6 + \overline{Y}_7 + \overline{Y}_8) - (3)(\overline{Y}_5) = .679,$$

$$s_{pooled} = \sqrt{MS_{S/A}} = .179,$$

$$\sqrt{\sum_j (w_j^2/n_j)} = \sqrt{9/23 + 1/26 + 1/21 + 1/20} = .726$$

Therefore,

$$S_{\hat{\psi}} = (.179)(.726) = .130$$
$$t = \hat{\psi}/S_{\hat{\psi}}$$
$$= .679/.130$$
$$= 5.212$$

**TABLE 9.2a** CONTRAST COEFFICIENTS AND TESTS FOR MEAN MULTIPLICATION SPEEDS

**Contrast Coefficients**

| Contrast | GRADE | | | |
|:---:|:---:|:---:|:---:|:---:|
| | **5** | **6** | **7** | **8** |
| 1 | −3 | 1 | 1 | 1 |
| 2 | 0 | 1 | −1 | 0 |
| 3 | 0 | 1 | 0 | −1 |
| 4 | 0 | 0 | 1 | −1 |

**TABLE 9.2b**

**CONTRAST TESTS**

| | | Contrast | Value of Contrast | Std. Error | *t* | df | Sig. (2-tailed) |
|---|---|:---:|:---:|:---:|:---:|:---:|:---:|
| SPEEDMRT | Assume equal variances | 1 | .680140 | .129976 | 5.233 | 86 | .000 |
| | | 2 | 2.62E-02 | 5.25E-02 | −.500 | 86 | .619 |
| | | 3 | 2.36E-02 | 5.32E-02 | −.443 | 86 | .659 |
| | | 4 | 2.64E-03 | 5.59E-02 | .047 | 86 | .962 |
| | Does not assume equal variances | 1 | .680140 | .131143 | 5.186 | 38.3 | .000 |
| | | 2 | 2.62E-02 | 5.05E-02 | −.519 | 41.7 | .606 |
| | | 3 | 2.36E-02 | 5.44E-02 | −.434 | 37.3 | .667 |
| | | 4 | 2.64E-03 | 5.83E-02 | .045 | 38.2 | .964 |

*Note:* Table 9.2 output is from SPSS.

factor of 3. It does simplify the calculations and makes rounding errors less likely. However, one caution is in order: Confidence limits based on these weights will also be increased by a factor of 3. To get back on the original speed scale, the limits are divided by 3. Note that when we compare CIs, we must be sure they are all on the same scale. This can be achieved by always transforming back to the original scale, or by adopting the convention that the negative contrast weights should add to −1 and the positive weights to +1.

Tables 9.2a and 9.2b present the SPSS output for all four contrasts. There are two sets of results depending on whether homogeneity of variance is assumed. We discuss calculations when the assumption of equal variances is violated in Subsection 9.3.2. The "Value of Contrast" column in Table 9.2b contains the values of the $\hat{\psi}$s, and the "Std. Error" column is for $s_{\hat{\psi}}$. (The value of the *t* for $\psi_1$ is slightly different from ours because we rounded the group means.)

## 9.3.1 Weighting Means When *ns* Are Unequal

In the multiplication speed data, the four grades had different numbers of students. However, there is no reason to view the four sampled populations as unequal in size. If the sixth- through eighth-grade populations are equal in size, then they should receive equal weight when their mean is contrasted against the mean of the fifth-grade population. Therefore, the weights used in testing $H_{01}$ $(-3,1,1,1)$ are appropriate. Equal weighting of means that are averaged on one side of a contrast usually will also be appropriate in the analysis of data from any true experiment in which the independent variable is manipulated. In contrast, in many observational studies, differences in group $n$s reflect differences in population size. A case in point is the Seasons study, which we cited previously. In Chapter 8, we tested the omnibus null hypothesis that mean depression scores were equal for four populations defined by their education level. The four groups were male participants with only a high school education (HS), some college experience (C), a bachelor's degree (B), or graduate school experience (GS). Table 9.3a presents group sizes, means, and variances.

Assume that one question of interest was whether the mean depression scores differed between men with a graduate school education and all other men. We might weight the

**TABLE 9.3a** SUMMARY STATISTICS FOR DEPRESSION SCORES AS A FUNCTION OF EDUCATIONAL LEVEL

| Educational Level | $n$ | Mean | Variance |
|---|---|---|---|
| HS | 19 | 6.903 | 34.541 |
| C | 33 | 3.674 | 5.970 |
| B | 37 | 3.331 | 9.861 |
| GS | 39 | 4.847 | 26.218 |

**TABLE 9.3b** SPSS OUTPUT FOR DEPRESSION SCORES AS A FUNCTION OF EDUCATIONAL LEVEL

**CONTRAST COEFFICIENTS**

| Contrast | Educational Level | | | |
|---|---|---|---|---|
| | HS | C | B | GS |
| 1 | 1 | 1 | 1 | −3 |
| 2 | 19 | 33 | 37 | −89 |

**Contrast Tests**

| | Contrast | | Value of Contrast | Std. Error | $t$ | df | Sig. (2-tailed) |
|---|---|---|---|---|---|---|---|
| D_SCORE | Assume equal variances | 1 | −.6329 | 2.4385 | −.260 | 124 | .796 |
| | | 2 | −55.7348 | 71.3989 | −.781 | 124 | .437 |
| | Does not assume equal variances | 1 | −.6329 | 2.8837 | −.219 | 60.134 | .827 |
| | | 2 | −55.7348 | 80.8897 | −.689 | 55.239 | .494 |

*Note.* Table 9.3b is output from SPSS.

means (from HS to GS) 1, 1, 1, and $-3$; in this way we can test

$$H_0: \mu_{HS} + \mu_C + \mu_B - (3)(\mu_{GS}) = 0$$

This weights the HS mean the same as the C and B means, despite the fact that the relative frequencies suggest that the HS population is considerably smaller than the others. Alternatively, we can assume that the four populations vary in size such that weights proportional to their size would be $w_{HS}, w_C, w_B$, and $w_{GS}$. Then the mean of the first three populations—call it $\mu_{<GS}$ ("less than graduate school")—would be a weighted average; that is,

$$\mu_{<GS} = \frac{w_{HS}\,\mu_{HS} + w_C\,\mu_C + w_B\,\mu_B}{w_{HS} + w_C + w_B}$$

and the contrast of interest is

$$\psi = \frac{w_{HS}\,\mu_{HS} + w_C\,\mu_C + w_B\,\mu_B}{w_{HS} + w_C + w_B} - \mu_{GS}$$

Because the $t$ test of a contrast is not affected by multiplying all weights by a constant, we can simplify things by multiplying the expression by $w_{HS} + w_C + w_B$, giving us

$$\psi = w_{HS}\,\mu_{HS} + w_C\,\mu_C + w_B\,\mu_B - (w_{HS} + w_C + w_B)\mu_{GS}$$

and we test

$$H_0: w_{HS}\,\mu_{HS} + w_C\,\mu_C + w_B\,\mu_B - (w_{HS} + w_C + w_B)\mu_{GS} = 0$$

Unless we know the actual sizes of the populations, we now need estimates of the $w$s. In many situations, the most reasonable and simplest estimate will be the group sizes. Table 9.3b presents output from SPSS when the weights are 1, 1, 1, and $-3$ and when they are based on the group sizes provided in Table 9.3a. Results are reported when equal variances are assumed and when they are not; we consider the latter case shortly. For now, note that, in the second contrast, the $w$s have been replaced by their corresponding $n$s. Although neither contrast is statistically significant, there are clear differences between the two $t$ values, and between their $p$ values.

Equal weighting and weighting by frequency will not always yield very different results; the distribution of group sizes is the critical factor. We originally intended to contrast the HS mean with the mean of the three groups having at least some college education but soon found that the two sets of weights ($-3, 1, 1, 1$ versus $-109, 33, 37, 39$) yielded very similar results. The reason for this becomes evident if we divide the latter set of weights by 36; we get $-3.028, .917, 1.028$, and $1.083$—not very different from $-3, 1, 1$, and $1$.

Bear in mind that the issue of weights arises only with contrasts in which one or both subsets are based on at least two means. When pairwise comparisons are tested (by far the most common situation), the weights will always be 1 and $-1$ for the two means involved in the comparison, and 0 for all other means.

## 9.3.2 Testing Contrasts When Variances Are not Equal

Suppose we wish to contrast the depression mean for the HS group with the mean of individuals with more than a high school education. We use the weights 3, $-1, -1$, and $-1$. Before continuing our calculations, we note in Tables 9.3 that the variances of depression scores are very different at the four educational levels. As we noted in both Chapters 6

**TABLE 9.4a**   WELCH'S $t'$ TEST OF $H_{01}$: $\mu_{HS} = (1/3)(\mu_C + \mu_B + \mu_{GS}) = 0$.

From Table 9.3, $\hat{\psi} = (3)(\overline{Y}_{HS}) - (\overline{Y}_C + \overline{Y}_B + \overline{Y}_{GS}) = 8.857$
The denominator of $t'$ is

$$s_{\hat{\psi}} = \sqrt{\sum_{j=1}^{a} \frac{w_j^2 s_j^2}{n_j}}$$

$$= \sqrt{\frac{(3^2)(34.541)}{19} + \frac{5.970}{33} + \frac{9.861}{37} + \frac{26.218}{39}}$$

$$= 4.181$$

Then $t' = 8.857/4.181 = 2.118$. From Equation 9.6, the degrees of freedom are

$$df' = \frac{s_{\hat{\psi}}^4}{\dfrac{(3^4)(34.541^2)}{(19^2)(18)} + \dfrac{5.970^2}{(33^2)(32)} + \dfrac{9.861^2}{(37^2)(36)} + \dfrac{26.218^2}{(39^2)(38)}}$$

$$= \frac{305.577}{14.887}$$

$$\approx 21$$

**TABLE 9.4b**   CONTRAST COEFFICIENTS AND TESTS FOR
DEPRESSION SCORES

**Contrast Coefficients**

| Contrast | Education Level | | | |
|:---:|:---:|:---:|:---:|:---:|
| | HS | C | B | GS |
| 1 | 3 | −1 | −1 | −1 |

**Contrast Tests**

| Contrast | | | Value of Contrast | Std. Error | $t$ | df | Sig. (2-tailed) |
|---|---|:---:|:---:|:---:|:---:|:---:|:---:|
| D_SCORE | Assume equal variances | 1 | 8.8572 | 3.1169 | 2.842 | 124 | .005 |
| | Does not assume equal | 1 | 8.8572 | 4.1810 | 2.118 | 20.5 | .047 |

*Note.* Output is printed from SPSS.

and 8, when the homogeneity of variance assumption is violated, the error rates associated with the standard $t$ and $F$ tests may be badly distorted. The $t'$ solution proposed by Welch (1947) was presented as an alternative to the usual $t$ and $F$ tests. A general form of the $t'$ statistic can be applied even when more than two groups are involved in the contrast. The test statistic is

$$t' = \hat{\psi} \Big/ \sqrt{\sum_{j=1}^{a} \frac{w_j^2 s_j^2}{n_j}} \tag{9.5}$$

and the degrees of freedom are

$$df' = \frac{\left(\sum_{j=1}^{a} \frac{w_j^2 s_j^2}{n_j}\right)^2}{\sum_{j=1}^{a} \frac{w_j^4 s_j^4}{n_j^2(n_j - 1)}} \tag{9.6}$$

Table 9.4a illustrates the calculations for the contrast of the HS mean with the mean of the combined other three educational groups. The calculations are somewhat tedious, but fortunately, as Table 9.4b illustrates, the same result can be obtained from most statistical software packages. These provide results under both the assumption of equal population variances (in which case the standard error of the mean, $SEM$, is based on the $MS_{S/A}$) and under the more general assumption that the variances are not equal.

There are two situations in which the $MS_{S/A}$ is not an appropriate error term. In one case, the contrast to be tested involves conditions for which the assumption of equal variances is suspect. Here, $t'$ should be calculated. In other instances, the variances corresponding to the conditions involved in the contrast are very similar but different from the variances of those conditions not included in the contrast (that is, having zero weight). The standard $t$ is appropriate here but the denominator should be based only on the pool of the variances corresponding to the included conditions. For example, if there are three groups with variances 10, 11, and 5, and the means of the first two groups are to be compared, the variance of 5 should not be included in the denominator because the estimate of the standard error ($SE$) of the contrast will be too small, and the Type 1 error rate will be inflated. In summary, when there is reason to doubt that all population variances are equal, only those corresponding to means involved in the contrast should be included. If the equal-variance assumption is at all suspect even for those variances, calculate $t'$. Finally, as usual, we warn that such decisions should be made a priori; basing decisions about which result to report on the output of both analyses invalidates the inference process.

## 9.4 THE PROPER UNIT FOR THE CONTROL OF TYPE 1 ERROR

As we argued in the introduction to this chapter, the probability of a Type 1 error increases with the number of significance tests. Therefore, if the probability of each significance test is set without regard to how many tests might be conducted, the error rate for the entire collection of tests may rise to an unacceptable level. Statisticians and researchers are generally agreed that the proper unit for control of the Type 1 error rate is not the individual test but a set of contrasts called a **family**. Before we address the question of how to limit the Type 1 error rate for the family, we more closely consider possible definitions of a family of contrasts.

We begin by distinguishing between the **error rate per contrast** (EC)—the probability that a single contrast results in a Type 1 error—and the FWE—the probability that a set, or family, of contrasts will contain at least one Type 1 error. For a family of $K$ independent tests,

$$FWE = p(\text{at least one Type 1 error in the family})$$
$$= 1 - p(\text{no Type 1 errors in the family})$$
$$= 1 - p(\text{no Type 1 error on a single test})^K$$

The probability of a Type 1 error on a single test is the EC. Therefore,

$$FWE = 1 - (1 - EC)^K \tag{9.7}$$

If a family consists of six independent tests, each conducted at EC = .05, substitution in Equation 9.7 results in FWE $= 1 - (1 -.05)^6 = .265$, considerably greater than .05. If the six tests are not independent, the FWE is less than .265 but more than .05, although the exact value is difficult to calculate. In any event, the larger the family, the more the FWE exceeds the EC.

One extreme view we might take with respect to the discrepancy between the EC and the FWE is simply to ignore the FWE. We could choose a value for the EC without considering the total number of contrasts tested, and we could test each contrast by using that $p$ value, perhaps .05, as the criterion for significance. The problem with this approach is that even if there are no differences among the treatment population means, we would have a good chance of finding "significant" results if we performed a large enough number of tests, because the FWE would then be large. Publishing such findings could result in wasted effort spent investigating and attempting to replicate effects that did not exist. In view of this, we want the EC to be such that the FWE for a family of contrasts will be kept within acceptable bounds. The exact criterion for significance for the test of any one contrast will depend on how large the family is. If we want to keep the FWE constant as family size increases, the EC will have to decrease. This line of reasoning requires that we decide exactly what we mean by a family of contrasts.

An investigator working in a research area over a period of years might perform hundreds of experiments and test thousands of hypotheses. If we considered these thousands of tests to form a single family and set the FWE equal to .05, the EC would be infinitesimally small. Although this ultraconservative approach would result in a very low Type 1 error rate, the Type 2 error rate would soar to unacceptable levels. The experimenter could be confident that significant results revealed real effects but would miss finding many real effects. Because lowering the EC results in a reduction of power, the definition of family must be based on a compromise between concerns about Type 1 and Type 2 errors.

When we conduct an experiment with one independent variable and one dependent variable, the definition of the family seems straightforward. If we have four levels of the independent variable, and plan three specific contrasts, the family is of size 3. If we test every possible pairwise contrast, the family is of size 6. If we scan the data, and select the largest possible contrast, the family size is infinite because there are an infinite number of sets of weights possible. The situation is different if we have several independent or dependent variables in a single study. For example, consider the study of seasonal variation in psychological and physical measures that we have referenced several times previously. We might conduct pairwise comparisons among four educational levels on depression means and on anxiety means. We might do this separately for male and for female participants. We have six pairwise comparisons for one measure for one sex. Because there are two measures and two sexes, there are a total of 24 comparisons. Do we control the FWE for a family of 24 comparisons, or for each of four families of 6 comparisons? We recommend the second option—viewing each combination of factor level and dependent variable as the basis for defining the family. This seems a reasonable compromise between Type 1 and Type 2 errors. Furthermore, it provides a natural basis for comparison with other studies. Suppose another investigator carries out a study of the effects of educational level on depression scores in female participants and also tests all six possible pairwise comparisons. Any comparison of the FWEs of the two studies should be based on the same definition of family. Because the second study used only female participants, and only the depression measure, such a comparison is possible only if we have also defined the family in this way, rather than in terms of all 24 comparisons we made.

## 9.5 PLANNED VERSUS POST HOC CONTRASTS

In Chapter 8, we analyzed depression scores as a function of educational level; the educational groups were HS, C, B, and GS. We tested the omnibus null hypothesis that the four population means were equal. With respect to contrasts, consider two scenarios:

1.  After inspecting the data, we find that the mean depression score for the HS group is higher than that for the other three groups. Accordingly, we test the contrast of the HS group mean against the combined mean of the other three groups; that is, we test $H_0$: $\mu_{HS} = (1/3)(\mu_C + \mu_B + \mu_{HS})$.
2.  Before conducting the experiment, we predict on the basis of theory or previous research that the HS mean will differ from that of individuals having at least some college experience. On this basis, we test the same null hypothesis as in Scenario 1.

Assuming the result of the $t$ test is significant at the .05 level, we should have more confidence that the difference exists in the population in the second scenario than in the first. If the null hypothesis is true and, without looking at the data, we select a single contrast to be tested at $\alpha = .05$, the probability of a Type 1 error is .05. However, if we first examine the data by looking for a difference, and then we test the largest effect we observe, it is as if we have carried out many significance tests. The EC is .05 but the FWE, the probability of at least one Type 1 error, is considerably higher. The first scenario represents a situation in which tests of contrasts are post hoc (or a posteriori), whereas the second scenario represents a situation in which the contrasts are planned (or a priori).

A simple analogy may make the distinction clearer. Assume that I bet you at even odds that the fourth toss of a coin will be a head. Assuming the coin is a fair one, so is the bet; the probability of a head on the fourth toss is exactly .5. This is similar to a planned (predicted) contrast. Now assume instead that I bet you at even odds that there will be a head somewhere in the sequence of four tosses. Either refuse the bet or ask for (much) better odds because the probability of at least one head in four tosses is considerably more than .5. This situation is similar to a post hoc test of a contrast.

Before considering ways of controlling the FWE in each of these situations, we wish to raise several points. First, plan ahead. If there is only one planned contrast, the EC and FWE will be the same because the family is of size 1. Although we usually plan more than one contrast, typically the family of planned contrasts will be fairly small. Consequently, the EC will not be greatly reduced relative to the FWE. As we noted earlier, the larger the family, the lower the EC, and the lower the power of each individual test. For example, although there are methods for controlling the FWE for the family of all pairwise comparisons, if we test only a few that were decided on before we looked at the data, we will have greater power and narrower CIs for each test.

The second point is that, although contrasts should be planned, often the pattern of means is unexpected but suggests something interesting, although unanticipated. It is not only legitimate to inspect one's data and carry out tests of contrasts that look interesting, it should be obligatory. However, the criterion for significance of such post hoc tests should be such that the FWE is held to a reasonable level.

A third consideration is the nature of that reasonable level. What should the FWE be? Traditionally, the FWE has been set at the .05 level. That seems reasonable for small families of planned contrasts. However, Scheffé (1959), in a classic text on ANOVA, suggested that for post hoc tests, the FWE could be set at .10. The effective size of a family of post hoc contrasts is determined not by the number of contrasts actually tested but by those that might conceivably have been tested had the data suggested it was worth doing so. This family is large and the power to test contrasts will often be extremely low if the FWE is set at .05 in this situation. Bear in mind that the EC and FWE are different concepts, and there is no reason that traditional EC levels of significance need be applied to the FWE. Even with the FWE at .10, the EC will generally be quite low.

## 9.6 CONTROLLING THE FWE FOR FAMILIES OF *K* PLANNED CONTRASTS

Here, we discuss some very general methods for dealing with planned contrasts. All use the $t$ statistic presented in Table 9.1, or Welch's $t'$ (Subsection 9.3.2) if variances are unequal. However, they differ in their criteria for significance, and in whether they allow the construction of CIs. These methods are very versatile. Although we illustrate their use with multiple $t$ tests, it should be emphasized that they can be used with any statistical tests, parametric or nonparametric. Furthermore, if the summary statistics and plots of the data indicate that the population variances are not equal, then these methods can be used with Welch's $t'$ test. Most important, it is not necessary that the omnibus $F$ be significant prior to testing planned contrasts, provided the FWE is controlled. In fact, power is lost by requiring a significant $F$ before carrying out planned tests with a procedure that controls the FWE. What is critical is that the contrasts are decided on before the data are collected and a method for evaluating significance of the tests is used that maintains the FWE at or below a reasonable level, presumably .05 or .10.

### 9.6.1 Methods Based on the Bonferroni Inequality

Equation 9.7 describes the relation between the FWE and EC when the $K$ tests are independent. Because this condition rarely holds, a more general statement of the relation is

$$\text{FWE} \leq 1 - (1 - \text{EC})^K \tag{9.8}$$

In other words, the FWE is equal to *or less than* the term on the right, with the inequality holding when the tests are not independent. Furthermore, if $K$ tests are conducted with error rates $EC_1, EC_2, \ldots, EC_K$, then

$$FWE \leq \sum_k EC_k \tag{9.9}$$

where $EC_k$ is the probability of a Type 1 error for the $k$th contrast. The relationship expressed in Equation 9.9 is known as the **Bonferroni inequality**, and it is the basis for several procedures for testing planned contrasts. From the inequality, it follows that if each of the $K$ contrasts that make up the family is tested at $EC = FWE/K$, the probability of a Type 1 error for the family cannot exceed the FWE. If, for example, the family contains five planned contrasts, the FWE will not be larger than .05 if each contrast in the family is tested at the .01 level.

To illustrate methods based on the Bonferroni inequality, we reconsider the SPSS output in Table 9.2. The significance values reported by SPSS are the ECs. In this instance, it appears that we reach the same conclusion whether our criterion is the EC or the FWE. The first contrast has such a small $p$ value that it should be significant by any criterion, whereas the last three contrasts are clearly not significant by any reasonable standard. Nevertheless, we consider how each of two methods controls the FWE for this set of tests.

**The Dunn–Bonferroni method** follows from Equation 9.9. (Dunn, 1961). If there are $K$ contrasts, the FWE will not exceed a nominal value if the EC is set at that value divided by $K$. For example, assuming a FWE of .05, we test the four contrasts in Table 9.2 at the .0125 (.05/4) alpha level. To conduct the test, calculate

$$t = \frac{\sum_j w_j \overline{Y}_j}{\sqrt{MS_e \sum_j \frac{w_j^2}{n_j}}} \tag{9.10}$$

where the $MS_e$ (error mean square) will be $MS_{S/A}$ in the one-factor design and the error degrees of freedom ($df_e$) will be $N - a$, where $N = \sum_j n_j$. If the exact $p$ value is available, as for example in the SPSS output of Table 9.2, to control the FWE we compare it with $FWE/K$, and reject $H_0$ only for those contrasts such that $p < FWE/K$. Alternatively, Appendix Table C.7 provides critical values of $t$ as a function of the FWE, $df_e$, and $K$. Note that these values assume that the alternative hypothesis is two tailed. To illustrate the use of the table, suppose we have five tests and FWE = .05. Further assume that $df_e = 20$. According to Table C.7, we require $t = 2.845$ for significance. If our tests were one tailed, 2.845 would correspond to FWE = .025. To maintain the FWE at .05 for a set of one-tailed tests, the critical value of $t$ is 2.528.

For $df_e$ not listed in the table, the critical value of $t$ can be readily obtained from statistical packages such as SAS, SYSTAT, or SPSS. For example, with a data file containing a $p$ value and the degrees of freedom, SPSS's IDF.T function will yield the corresponding value of $t$ (to use this function, first click on "Transform," and then on "Compute"). The CDF calculator for the Student distribution at the UCLA Statistics Department Web site (see Chapter 6 or 8 for the URL) allows us to input any two of these three: $X$ (the value of $t$), the degrees of freedom, or the $p$ value, with a question mark for the third variable. We enter 86 for the degrees of freedom and, assuming the test is two tailed, .00625 ($1/2 \times$ .0125) for the probability; the result is 2.551. If programs such as these are not available, an approximation based on the normal probability table can be calculated:

$$t_\alpha = z_\alpha + \frac{z_\alpha^3 + z_\alpha}{4(df_e - 2)} \tag{9.11}$$

We see that $z_\alpha$, the $z$ exceeded by .00625, is slightly less than 2.50, approximately 2.4975. Substituting this value for $z_\alpha$, we again have $t_\alpha = 2.551$.

With this value of $t_\alpha$ and the $SE$s of the four contrasts, we can compute CIs. The equation for the CI is exactly the same as in Chapter 6; the difference is that the critical $t$ is based on the FWE of .0125 (two tailed), not the EC of .05. For $\psi_1$, the limits are

$$\text{CI} = \hat{\psi}_1 \pm t_\alpha s_{\hat{\psi}_1} \tag{9.12}$$

Substituting the critical $t$ and values from Table 9.2, we find that the limits are

$$.680 \pm (2.551)(.130) = .348, 1.012$$

Because we used weights of $-3$, 1, 1, and 1, we divide the limits by 3 to return to the original data scale. The limits on the difference between the mean speeds of the fifth-grade students and the mean of the other three grades are .116 and .337.

When CIs are based on the FWE, as in this example, they are interpreted somewhat differently than when they are based on the EC. It may help to understand the distinction if we assume many random replications of an experiment. In each replication, a set of four CIs, one for each of the planned contrasts, is calculated and the critical value of $t$ is 2.551. We expect that, in .95 of the replications, each of the four intervals will contain the estimated population contrast. In other words, the probability is .95 that the CIs for *all* members of the family of contrasts will contain their corresponding $\psi$ values. Because of this property, intervals based on the FWE are referred to as **simultaneous CIs**.

Division of the FWE by $K$ provides an approximate value of the EC. However, an exact solution to Equation 9.7 is possible. This solution, originally proposed by Šidák (1967), is obtained by solving for EC in Equation 9.7:

$$\text{EC} = 1 - (1 - \text{FWE})^{1/K} \tag{9.13}$$

In the **Dunn–Šidák method**, $H_{0k}$: $\psi_k = 0$ is rejected if $p_k \le 1 - (1 - \text{FWE})^{1/K}$. Because $1 - (1 - \text{FWE})^{1/K} > \text{FWE}/K$, this method has more power and a narrower CI than the original Dunn–Bonferroni procedure. However, the difference is very small, as can be seen in Table 9.5; this table presents values of the EC for the original Dunn–Bonferroni test ($EC_1$) and for the Dunn–Šidák revision ($EC_2$).

A feature of the Bonferroni-based methods is that they allow the possibility of weighting contrasts unequally (Myers, 1979; Rosenthal & Rubin, 1983). From Equation 9.9, it follows that the FWE does not have to be divided into $K$ equal parts. Suppose tests of three contrasts are planned but one is of greater interest than the other two. Instead of a division of the FWE by 3 in the Dunn–Bonferroni procedure, the most important contrast might be tested at the .025 level, and the other two each at .0125. The FWE is still less than or equal to .05, but power is increased in the test of the most interesting contrast at the expense of the other two. An important qualification is that the determination of the division of the FWE should be made before the data are collected.

**TABLE 9.5**   DUNN–BONFERRONI AND ŠIDÁK VALUES OF EC
WHEN FWE = .05 OR .10

| $K$ | FWE = .05 | | FWE = .10 | |
|---|---|---|---|---|
| | $EC_1$ | $EC_2$ | $EC_1$ | $EC_2$ |
| 2 | .025000 | .025321 | .050000 | .051317 |
| 3 | .016667 | .016952 | .033333 | .034511 |
| 4 | .012500 | .012741 | .025000 | .025996 |
| 5 | .010000 | .010206 | .020000 | .020852 |
| 6 | .008333 | .008512 | .016667 | .017407 |
| 7 | .007143 | .007301 | .014286 | .014939 |
| 8 | .006250 | .006391 | .012500 | .013084 |
| 9 | .005556 | .005683 | .011111 | .011638 |
| 10 | .005000 | .005116 | .010000 | .010481 |

*Note.* $EC_1 = FWE/K$ and $EC_2 = 1 - (1 - FWE)^{1/K}$.

### 9.6.2 Hochberg's Sequential Method

The Dunn–Bonferroni and Dunn–Šidák procedures are **simultaneous methods**. A further increment in power is provided by **sequential methods** (also referred to as stepwise, or multistage), in which tests of contrasts involve several stages. The simplest of these are Holm's sequentially rejective method (Holm, 1979), and Hochberg's step-up method (Hochberg, 1988). We describe only the latter method here because it is the more powerful of the two. The $K$ contrasts are rank ordered according to their $p$ values, with $p_1$ being the smallest and $p_K$ being the largest. In the example of Table 9.2, the contrasts would be ordered as $\psi_1, \psi_2, \psi_3,$ and $\psi_4$. If $p_K \leq FWE$, all $K$ null hypotheses are rejected. If not, consider the next largest $p$ value, $p_{K-1}$. If $p_{K-1} \leq FWE/2$, then reject the null hypothesis corresponding to the $K - 1$ contrast and all remaining contrasts. If this test is not significant, then test whether $p_{K-2} \leq FWE/3$, $p_{K-3} \leq FWE/4$, and so on. Using the example of Table 9.2, and assuming FWE = .05, we first compare .962 with .05. This fails and we compare the next largest $p$ value, .659, against .025. This fails and .619 is compared with .0167. The only significant comparison is that of .000 with .0125, and we can reject only $H_0: \psi_1 = 0$. The power of this procedure can be increased at the cost of greater complexity (Hommel, 1988; Rom, 1990).

   The choice between the Bonferroni-based methods and the Hochberg procedure should depend on whether the researcher wants CIs. If only tests of hypotheses are required, use the Hochberg method because it provides a more powerful test while still maintaining the FWE at the targeted level. When CIs are to be calculated, the Dunn–Bonferroni or Dunn–Šidák methods should be used because readily interpretable CIs are not available for sequential methods.

## 9.7   TESTING ALL PAIRWISE CONTRASTS

It is quite common for researchers to decide to contrast all possible pairs of means. The methods used in the preceding section are applicable, but there are other procedures that provide slightly greater power. Of these, the ones we present are based on $q$, **the studentized range statistic**. This statistic is the range of a set of observations from a normally distributed population, divided by the estimated standard deviation of the population. If the observations are group means,

$$q = \frac{\overline{Y}_{max} - \overline{Y}_{min}}{s_{\overline{Y}}} \tag{9.14}$$

where $\overline{Y}_{max}$ and $\overline{Y}_{min}$ are the largest and smallest means in a set of $a$ ordered means and $s_{\overline{Y}}$, the *SEM*, is

$$s_{\overline{Y}} = \sqrt{MS_e/n} \tag{9.15}$$

assuming homogeneity of variance and equal $n$s. Critical values of $q$ can be found in Appendix Table C.9 as a function of the FWE, $a$ (the number of means), and the degrees of freedom associated with the error mean square.

If we were to carry out a $t$ test of the difference between the same two means, assuming equal variances and group sizes in a one-factor design, the statistic would be

$$t = \frac{\overline{Y}_{max} - \overline{Y}_{min}}{\sqrt{MS_{S/A}(2/n)}}$$
$$= q/\sqrt{2}$$

This relation can be useful in comparing the results of procedures based on $t$ (such as the Dunn–Bonferroni method) with those based on $q$; it has also been the basis for dealing with unequal $n$s and unequal variances.

In the following sections, we consider several procedures for testing all $\binom{a}{2}$ pairwise contrasts. It is not necessary to conduct a preliminary test of the omnibus null hypothesis prior to using any of these methods, because each method maintains the FWE at or below its nominal value. In fact, requiring rejection of the omnibus null hypothesis before applying a procedure that controls the FWE for the set of $\binom{a}{2}$ comparisons is likely to increase the probability of failing to detect true differences between means.

### 9.7.1 Tukey's HSD Test

Tukey's HSD (honestly significant difference; Tukey; 1953) test controls the FWE for the set of all possible pairwise comparisons. We illustrate the test by using the means and standard deviations for the fifth- through eighth-grade multiplication speed scores in the Royer study. These were presented in Table 9.1. However, because Equation 9.14 requires that the $n$s be equal, assume that there are 16 students in each of the four grades. (We will shortly redo the calculations with the true $n$s, using a version of the Tukey test modified to deal with unequal $n$s.) Table 9.6 presents the necessary steps in testing all pairwise contrasts and in constructing simultaneous CIs, assuming equal $n$s and equal variances. The results are also readily obtained from many statistical software packages.

In many studies, only a few of the possible pairwise comparisons will be of interest. In such cases, the Dunn–Bonferroni procedure may provide more power and narrower CIs. The ratio of interval widths of the Tukey to the Dunn–Bonferroni method is simply the ratio

**TABLE 9.6**  TUKEY'S HSD TEST AND CIs

1. Order the means in Table 9.1 from smallest to largest:

   | Grade: | 5 | 6 | 8 | 7 |
   |--------|------|------|------|------|
   | Mean: | .350 | .560 | .583 | .586 |

   We assume the means are based on 16 scores each.

2. Find the value of $q$ required for significance when FWE = .05, $a = 4$, and $df = a(n - 1) = 60$. That value is 3.74.

3. Calculate the *SEM* by using the values of the variance in Table 9.1, but assuming $n = 16$. Averaging the variances (assuming equal $n$), $MS_{S/A} = .0325$, and

$$s_{\bar{Y}} = \sqrt{MS_{S/A}/n} = .045$$

4. A value of $q$ can now be calculated for each of the six possible pairwise contrasts by dividing each of the six differences between means by .045, and comparing the result with the critical value, 3.74. For example, the difference between the fifth- and seventh-grade means is .236 and therefore $q = .236/.045 = 5.24$. Because this is larger than 3.74, we conclude that these two means differ significantly. We can therefore proceed to test the next largest difference. If we proceed in this way, successively testing each smaller difference, we stop testing when we encounter a nonsignificant difference.

   Alternatively, we can find a critical difference between the means against which the observed differences can be compared. In this example,

$$d_{\text{crit}} = q_{.05,4,76}s_{\bar{Y}} = (3.74)(.045) = .169$$

   Compare the largest difference with $d_{\text{crit}}$, rejecting the null hypothesis if the observed difference exceeds .169. Continue testing in the order of decreasing differences until a difference does not exceed $d_{\text{crit}}$. This procedure is only applicable when the $n$s are equal.

5. The equivalent test can be carried out by using the $t$ distribution. Calculate the usual $t$ statistic and compare with $q_{.05,4,60}/\sqrt{2}$, or 2.645. To carry out the test by using the differences, calculate

$$s_{\hat{\psi}} = \sqrt{MS_{S/A}\,(2/n)} = .064$$
$$d_{\text{crit}} = (2.645)(.064) = .169$$

6. Simultaneous CIs can also be constructed by using Tukey's method. If the FWE is .05, then the probability is .95 that all possible pairwise contrasts are contained within intervals of the form $\hat{\psi} \pm q_{.05,a,df}s_{\bar{Y}}$ or, equivalently, $\hat{\psi} \pm (q_{.05,a,df}/\sqrt{2})s_{\hat{\psi}}$. For example, The .95 confidence limits on the difference in mean speeds of the fifth- and sixth-grade populations are

$$.21 \pm (2.645)(.064) = .041, .379$$

of the critical values of their respective test statistics,

$$\frac{q_{\text{FWE}}/\sqrt{2}}{t_{\text{FWE}/K}}$$

where $K$ is the number of comparisons and is equal to $\binom{a}{2}$; for example, if $a$ (the number of groups) $= 4$, then $K = 6$. Dunn (1961) has evaluated this ratio for various combinations of $K, a, df_e$ (the degrees of freedom associated with the error term for the omnibus $F$ test), and the FWE. When all possible pairwise comparisons are tested, the Tukey procedure will have the narrower interval (and the more powerful test); that is, the ratio of intervals will be less

**TABLE 9.7**   CRITICAL VALUES OF $t$ FOR THE D–B METHOD AS $K$ VARIES

| $K$ | EC | $t$ | | Ratio (D–B/HSD) | |
|---|---|---|---|---|---|
| | | $df_e = 20$ | $df_e = 60$ | $df_e = 20$ | $df_e = 60$ |
| 6 | .0083 | 2.927 | 2.728 | 1.045 | 1.032 |
| 5 | .01 | 2.845 | 2.660 | 1.016 | 1.006 |
| 4 | .0125 | 2.744 | 2.575 | 0.980 | 0.974 |
| 3 | .0167 | 2.613 | 2.463 | 0.933 | 0.931 |
| 2 | .025 | 2.423 | 2.299 | 0.865 | 0.869 |

*Note.* Critical values are made with the assumption that $a = 4$, $df = 20$, $df = 60$, and FWE = .05. D–B = Dunn–Bonferroni. The ratio (D–B/HSD) divides the critical $t$ for the D–B method by that for the Tukey HSD method. A ratio less than 1 indicates that the D–B method requires a smaller $t$ for significance and therefore is more powerful and has a narrower CI.

than 1. For fixed $a$, the advantage of the Tukey procedure declines as the FWE decreases, the degrees of freedom increases, or $K$ decreases. Table 9.7 illustrates that if only a subset of all possible pairwise comparisons is planned and tested, a point is reached at which the Dunn–Bonferroni procedure is more powerful. More precisely, if only four comparisons are tested, the Dunn–Bonferroni method requires a smaller value of $t$ for significance than does Tukey's method. Therefore, it has the narrower CI (when $K \leq 4$) and greater power; the advantage of the Dunn–Bonferroni method increases if even fewer comparisons are made. Although the crossover point at which the Dunn–Bonferroni method has the advantage is a function of $K$, it usually does not require $K$ to be very small. For example, if $a = 5$, the crossover point occurs when 7 of the possible 10 contrasts are planned if $df_e = 60$, and when 6 are planned if $df_e = 20$.

### 9.7.2 When *ns* Are Unequal: The Tukey–Kramer Test

In the Royer study, the number of students in the fifth through eighth grades varied, as indicated in Table 9.1. A modification of Tukey's HSD test suggested by Kramer (1956) may be applied in such situations. The standard $t$ statistic is calculated and compared with $q_{\text{FWE},a,df}/\sqrt{2}$. SPSS provides an alternative approach. The $s_{\hat{\psi}}$ and $p$ values, as well as the .95 confidence limits, can be obtained from SPSS; the output for all pairwise comparisons is presented in Table 9.8. The Tukey–Kramer $t$ equals the mean difference ($\hat{\psi}$) value divided by the Std. (standard) Error ($s_{\hat{\psi}}$).

If the necessary software is lacking, the studentized range table (Appendix Table C.9) can be used. In the example of the speed data, $a = 4$ and $df_e = 86$. However, there is no entry in Table C.9 for these degrees of freedom; the closest are for $df = 60$ and 120. To obtain the critical $q$ value for $df = 86$, we can use a nonlinear interpolation method proposed by Harter, Clemm, and Guthrie (1959). We first find $q_{.05,4,.60} = 3.74$ and $q_{.05,4.,120} = 3.69$ from the table, and the reciprocals of 86 (.0116), 60 (.0167), and 120 (.0083). The critical value for $df_e = 86$ is then given by

$$q_{.05,4,86} = 3.74 - \left( \frac{.0167 - .0116}{.0167 - .0083} \right)(3.74 - 3.69) = 3.710$$

**TABLE 9.8**   SPSS OUTPUT FOR TUKEY–KRAMER TESTS OF THE DATA OF TABLE 9.1: MULTIPLE COMPARISONS

*Multiple Comparisons*

*Dependent Variable: SPEEDMRT*
*Tukey HSD*

| (I) GRADE | (J) GRADE | Mean Difference (I-J) | Std. Error | Sig. | 95% Confidence Interval | |
|---|---|---|---|---|---|---|
| | | | | | Lower Bound | Upper Bound |
| 5 | 6 | −.210099* | 5.12E-02 | .001 | −.344329 | −7.5869E-02 |
| | 7 | −.236340* | 5.40E-02 | .000 | −.377872 | −9.4808E-02 |
| | 8 | −.233701* | 5.47E-02 | .000 | −.377071 | −9.0332E-02 |
| 6 | 5 | .210099* | 5.12E-02 | .001 | 7.58695E-02 | .344329 |
| | 7 | −2.624E-02 | 5.25E-02 | .959 | −.163820 | .111340 |
| | 8 | −2.360E-02 | 5.32E-02 | .971 | −.163071 | .115868 |
| 7 | 5 | .236340* | 5.40E-02 | .000 | 9.48076E-02 | .377872 |
| | 6 | 2.624E-02 | 5.25E-02 | .959 | −.111340 | .163820 |
| | 8 | 2.638E-03 | 5.59E-02 | 1.000 | −.143872 | .149149 |
| 8 | 5 | .233701* | 5.47E-02 | .000 | 9.03316E-02 | .377071 |
| | 6 | 2.360E-02 | 5.32E-02 | .971 | −.115868 | .163071 |
| | 7 | 2.638E-03 | 5.59E-02 | 1.000 | −.149149 | .143872 |

*Note.* The dependent variable is SPEEDMRT.
*The mean difference is significant at the .05 level.

Then, assuming FWE = .05, we find $q_{\text{FWE},a,df}/\sqrt{2} = 3.710/1.414 = 2.623$. To test the difference between the fifth- and sixth-grade means, we calculate the $t$ statistic of Equation 6.17 (with $s_{\text{pooled}}$ replaced by $MS_{S/A}$):

$$t = \frac{.560 - .350}{\sqrt{(.032)(1/26 + 1/23)}}$$

$$= .21/.051 = 4.101$$

This clearly exceeds 2.623 and is therefore significant. Note that this is the ratio based on the Table 9.8 output.

### 9.7.3   When Variances Are Unequal

In Chapter 8, in our analysis of the effects of education level on mean depression scores of male subjects in the Seasons study, we found that the variances were quite heterogeneous. Several methods have been proposed to deal with this problem. Most use Welch's $t'$ (Equation 9.5) and $df'$ (Equation 9.6) but differ in the criterion against which $t'$ is evaluated. In the **Games–Howell test**, $t'$ is compared with $q_{\text{FWE},a,df'_e}/\sqrt{2}$ (Games & Howell, 1976). The procedure is illustrated in Table 9.9, using the depression data.

Investigations of the error rates associated with the Games–Howell test indicate that if the variances are fairly homogeneous and the group sizes are less than 50, the FWE may

**TABLE 9.9**    GAMES–HOWELL PROCEDURE FOR TESTING ALL PAIRWISE COMPARISONS WHEN VARIANCES ARE NOT EQUAL

Applying Equations 9.5 and 9.6 to the fifth- and sixth-grade speed statistics of Table 9.1, we have

$$t' = \frac{.560 - .350}{\sqrt{166^2/26 + .180^2/23}} = 4.227$$

$$df' = \frac{(.166^2/26 + .180^2/23)^2}{.166^4/[(26^2)(25)] + .180^4/[(23^2)(22)]} \approx 45$$

To obtain the critical value of $t$ corresponding to 45 $df$, interpolate in Appendix Table C.3 between $df = 40$ and $df = 60$, with $a = 4$, FWE $= .05$. The critical $q$ value is 3.773. Then

$$t_{.05,4,45} = 3.773/\sqrt{2} = 2.668$$

Because $4.227 > 2.668$, we reject $H_0$: $\mu_5 = \mu_6$. In similar fashion, values of $t'$ and $df'$ can be calculated for each of the remaining five pairwise comparisons and evaluated against 2.668.

---

sometimes be as high as .07 when the nominal probability is .05 (Dunnett, 1980; Games, Keselman, & Rogan, 1981). Even when the variances are not homogeneous, with $ns$ less than 6, the FWE may be inflated. However, these same studies indicate that under most other conditions the FWE is quite close to the nominal level. Furthermore, the test is more powerful than any of the several competitors that have been proposed and, as might therefore be expected, has narrower CIs for each comparison. If the researcher is concerned about the possible inflation of the FWE, Dunnett's T3 test (Dunnett, 1980) appears to be the most powerful of several alternatives that maintain the FWE at less than or equal to the nominal value. The test requires tables of the studentized maximum modulus distribution. Miller has described the procedure and has provided tables of the distribution (Miller, 1981, pp. 70–75). Statistical packages provide a welcome shortcut to the analytic labor involved in these tests. Table 9.10 presents SPSS output for the Games–Howell and Dunnett T3 methods applied to the depression data. Note that the $p$ values (in the "Sig." Column) are consistently lower for the Games–Howell procedure.

## 9.7.4 The Fisher–Hayter Test

Although the tests considered so far do not require a preliminary test of the omnibus null hypothesis, there are procedures for controlling the FWE that include such a test as a first stage. In Fisher's LSD (least significant difference) procedure (Fisher, 1935), the first stage is the omnibus $F$ test. Pairwise comparisons are tested by the usual $t$ test at the .05 level in a second stage, but only if the first stage yields a significant result. The LSD test has been shown to have an inflated FWE for $a > 3$. However, Hayter's modification of the LSD test maintains the FWE at or below its nominal level (Hayter 1986). In the Fisher–Hayter test, the first stage consists of the omnibus $F$ test. If this test yields a significant result, then all pairwise comparisons may be tested. Standard $t$ statistics are formed and tested against the criterion $q_{\text{FWE},\ a-1,df_e}/\sqrt{2}$. Note that in Appendix Table C.9, the column corresponding to $a - 1$ means provides the critical value. Table 9.11 provides an example, again using the Royer multiplication speed data.

As with other sequential testing methods, power is gained relative to simultaneous tests but at the loss of the ability to construct simultaneous CIs. Therefore, the choice between

**TABLE 9.10** RESULTS OF THE DUNNETT T3 AND GAMES–HOWELL TESTS OF ALL PAIRWISE COMPARISONS

**Multiple Comparisons**

**Dependent Variable: D_MEAN**

| | (I) | (J) | Mean Difference (I − J) | Std. Error | Sig. | 95% Confidence Interval Lower Bound | 95% Confidence Interval Upper Bound |
|---|---|---|---|---|---|---|---|
| **Dunnett T3** | HS | C | 3.2288 | 1.2031 | .170 | −.8314 | 7.2890 |
| | | B | 3.5724 | 1.1791 | .115 | −.5579 | 7.7028 |
| | | GS | 2.0562 | 1.1688 | .723 | −2.3523 | 6.4646 |
| | C | HS | −3.2288 | 1.2031 | .170 | −7.2890 | .8314 |
| | | B | .3436 | 1.0003 | .996 | −1.4671 | 2.1543 |
| | | GS | −1.1727 | .9881 | .745 | −3.6871 | 1.3418 |
| | B | HS | −3.5724 | 1.1791 | .115 | −7.7028 | .5579 |
| | | C | −.3436 | 1.0003 | .996 | −2.1543 | 1.4671 |
| | | GS | −1.5163 | .9587 | .534 | −4.1427 | 1.1101 |
| | GS | HS | −2.0562 | 1.1688 | .723 | −6.4646 | 2.3523 |
| | | C | 1.1727 | .9881 | .745 | −1.3418 | 3.6871 |
| | | B | 1.5163 | .9587 | .534 | −1.1101 | 4.1427 |
| **Games–Howell** | HS | C | 3.2288 | 1.2031 | .133 | −.7023 | 7.1600 |
| | | B | 3.5724 | 1.1791 | .091 | −.4176 | 7.5625 |
| | | GS | 2.0562 | 1.1688 | .568 | −2.2214 | 6.3337 |
| | C | HS | −3.2288 | 1.2031 | .133 | −7.1600 | .7023 |
| | | B | .3436 | 1.0003 | .956 | −1.4188 | 2.1061 |
| | | GS | −1.1727 | .9881 | .586 | −3.6180 | 1.2727 |
| | B | HS | −3.5724 | 1.1791 | .091 | −7.5625 | .4176 |
| | | C | −.3436 | 1.0003 | .956 | −2.1061 | 1.4188 |
| | | GS | −1.5163 | .9587 | .406 | −4.0726 | 1.0400 |
| | HS | HS | −2.0562 | 1.1688 | .568 | −6.3337 | 2.2214 |
| | | C | 1.1727 | .9881 | .586 | −1.2727 | 3.6180 |
| | | B | 1.5163 | .9587 | .406 | −1.0400 | 4.0726 |

*Note:* Output is from SPSS.

the Fisher–Hayter test and the Tukey (or Tukey–Kramer) test depends on whether such CIs are desired. Another consideration is whether variances are assumed to be homogenous. The Fisher–Hayter test was derived under that assumption, and therefore a test such as the Games–Howell or the Dunnett T3 test should be used if homogeneity of variance is in doubt.[3] Another issue is the choice of the omnibus test used in the first stage of testing. Although the $F$ test is usually referenced with respect to the Fisher–Hayter method, the $q$ (or $q/\sqrt{2}$) statistic applied to the largest difference between means provides an alternative test of the omnibus null hypothesis. Seaman, Levin, and Serlin (1991) found that there was little difference in the power of the Fisher–Hayter method as a function of whether $F$ or $q$ was used in the first stage. Which procedure had the advantage depended on the pattern

**TABLE 9.11** EXAMPLE OF THE FISHER–HAYTER TEST APPLIED TO THE STATISTICS OF TABLE 9.1

1. In the first stage, the ANOVA is performed. Because the result (see the SPSS output below) is significant, we can proceed to the second stage, testing all pairwise contrasts.

**ANOVA**

**SPEEDMRT**

|  | Sum of Squares | df | Mean Square | F | Sig. |
|---|---|---|---|---|---|
| Between Groups | 0.880 | 3 | .293 | 9.153 | .000 |
| Within Groups | 2.755 | 86 | 3.203E-02 | | |
| Total | 3.634 | 89 | | | |

2. Assuming homogeneous variances, we now perform the pairwise tests. To obtain the critical value of $q$ in Appendix Table C.9, we interpolate between the reciprocals of 60 and 120 in the column corresponding to three means (one less than the total number of groups). The value of $q_{.05,3,86}$ is 3.376 and, dividing by $\sqrt{2}$, we find that the critical value of $t$ is 2.387. The $t$ statistic may now be calculated for each contrast, and the null hypothesis corresponding to any given contrast will be rejected if the corresponding $t$ exceeds 2.387.

*Note.* The ANOVA output is from SPSS.

of the means. However, it should be noted that the $q$ test of the largest difference between means is appropriate for the first stage only if the $n$s are equal; otherwise, the largest raw difference may not correspond to the largest standardized effect.

### 9.7.5 Pairwise Comparisons: Summing Up

Seaman et al. (1991) simulated tests of all pairwise comparisons under conditions of equal $n$s and equal variances. With respect to the methods we have presented, averaging over $n$s of 5, 10, and 19, the Tukey HSD test generally had a power advantage of 2–3% over the Dunn–Bonferroni method. The Fisher–Hayter method had a power advantage over the Tukey method that varied from about 2% to as much as 9%, with the most typical difference being about 6%. The advantage of the Fisher–Hayter method decreased as $a$ increased from 3 to 5, and as $n$ decreased from 19 to 10. In summary, if (a) all pairwise contrasts are to be tested, (b) the power to detect differences is the primary consideration, and (c) homogeneity of variance can reasonably be assumed, then the Fisher–Hayter procedure is the method of choice. If only some subset of pairwise comparisons are of interest, the Dunn–Bonferroni procedure may prove more powerful than the alternatives. If CIs are desired, use the Tukey procedure, or the Dunn–Bonferroni one if only a few of the possible comparisons are of interest. If there is any evidence of unequal variances, use the Games–Howell test, or the Dunnett T3 test if $n < 6$.

Seaman et al. compared 23 different methods (including variations such as whether $F$ or $q$ was used in the first stage of the Fisher–Hayter method), and even this set of methods is not exhaustive. We have excluded from the current discussion some methods that yield FWEs that often are considerably in excess of the nominal value. Among these are Fisher's LSD test, the Student–Newman–Keuls test (Keuls, 1952; Newman, 1939), and Duncan's multiple range test (Duncan, 1955). We have also excluded several procedures that maintain the FWE at or below its nominal level and have slightly more power than the Fisher–Hayter method under some combinations of number of groups and group size. On the basis of various sampling studies, the very slight power advantage of these methods (usually 1–2%) does not warrant the added complexity they usually entail. The omitted methods include proposals by Peritz (1970), Ramsay (1978, 1981), Shaffer (1979, 1986), and Welsch (1977). Descriptions of these methods, together with results of sampling experiments, may be found in the article by Seaman et al. (1991). Other discussions of several tests of pairwise comparisons may be found in review articles by Zwick (1993) and Shaffer (1995), and in Toothaker's (1993) monograph on multiple comparison procedures.

## 9.8 COMPARING $a - 1$ TREATMENT MEANS WITH A CONTROL: DUNNETT'S TEST

Dunnett (1955, 1964) proposed a test for studies in which the researcher plans to contrast each of several treatments with a control. If these are the only comparisons of interest, methods that control the FWE for a family consisting of *all* pairwise comparisons will be overly conservative, power will be lost and simultaneous CIs will be wider than necessary. The Dunn–Bonferroni procedure with $K = a - 1$ will be an improvement but will still offer less power and wider intervals than the Dunnett test.

Assuming that the group sizes are equal and that variances are homogeneous, we see that the test is quite simple. To test the difference between the mean of the $j$th group and the control group mean, compute the usual $t$ statistic for each of the $a - 1$ contrasts:

$$t = \frac{\overline{Y}_j - \overline{Y}_C}{\sqrt{MS_{S/A}(2/n)}} \tag{9.16}$$

where $\overline{Y}_C$ is the mean of the control group and the error mean square ($MS_{S/A}$) is the average of all $a$ within-group variances. This $t$ statistic is evaluated against the critical values of $d_{FWE,a,df_e}$ in Appendix Table C.8 where $a$ is the number of means including the control and $df_e$ is the number of degrees of freedom associated with the ANOVA error term. Dunnett (1964) has provided tables that allow comparisons when the standard error of $\overline{Y}_C$ differs from that of the treatment group means. If the treatment group $n$s are not equal, replace $2/n$ in Equation 9.16 by $1/n_j + 1/n_C$, and use the Dunn–Bonferroni procedure with $K = a - 1$. If the treatment group variances are heterogeneous, use Welch's $t'$ and again use the Dunn–Bonferroni criterion.

Of course, the Dunn–Bonferroni method can be used even when the assumptions underlying the Dunnett test are met. However, the Dunnett test has a power advantage in those circumstances. For example, suppose we want to compare the sixth-, seventh-, and eighth-grade mean speeds with the mean speed of the fifth graders. Further assume the means and standard deviations in Table 9.1 but assume that the $n$s are all 16, as in Table 9.6. If the FWE is .05, for a contrast to be significant by use of the Dunnett criterion, the $t$ statistic must exceed 2.43. Using the Bonferroni criterion, we see that the EC is .05/3, or .0167, and the

$t$ statistic must exceed 2.46. The difference is small but nonetheless the power advantage lies with the Dunnett procedure. The CIs exhibit a similar relation. Let $s_{\hat{\psi}} = .064$, the value calculated in Table 9.6. Then the Dunnett confidence limits for any contrast with the fifth-grade mean are

$$\overline{Y}_c - \overline{Y}_j \pm (2.43)(.064)$$

and the Dunn–Bonferroni limits are

$$\overline{Y}_c - \overline{Y}_j \pm (2.46)(.064)$$

The interval widths for the Dunnett and the Dunn–Bonferroni methods are .311 and .315, respectively. Again, the difference is not large but the Dunnett method does have a slight advantage.

## 9.9 CONTROLLING THE FAMILYWISE ERROR RATE FOR POST HOC CONTRASTS

Sometimes observed patterns in the data suggest one or more effects that were not anticipated. When the corresponding null hypotheses are tested to determine whether these effects are significant, we should be quite conservative in evaluating the result. In testing contrasts "after the fact" we are, in effect, investigating the family of all possible outcomes. There are an infinite number of possible contrasts and therefore the methods we present are quite conservative because they control for the probability of at least one Type 1 error in a very large set of possible contrasts.

### 9.9.1 Scheffé's Method

Assuming that the populations are normally distributed and have equal variances, Scheffé's method maintains the FWE at its nominal level when the family consists of all possible contrasts associated with a source of variance (Scheffé, 1959). The test statistic is the $t$ of Equation 9.10 and it is evaluated against

$$S = \pm\sqrt{df_1 \cdot F_{FWE, df_1, df_2}} \tag{9.17}$$

where $df_1$ and $df_2$ are the numerator and denominator degrees of freedom associated with the omnibus $F$ test.

Using the fifth- to eighth-grade multiplication speeds as an example, assume that we did not anticipate the pattern of means in Table 9.1 but, after viewing the data, realized that the sixth through eighth grades had very similar means, each higher than the fifth-grade mean. We might wish to test whether the mean of the fifth-grade times differed significantly from that of the three combined sixth- through eighth-grade times; that is, we might test

$$H_0: \mu_5 - (1/3)(\mu_6 + \mu_7 + \mu_8) = 0$$

We calculated the $t$ statistic in Table 9.1 as 5.212. Because the test was not planned, we use the Scheffé method to test the preceding null hypothesis. With FWE $= .05$, $f = 3$, and $df_e = 86$, the critical value of $F$ is 2.71 (by interpolation in Appendix Table C.5, or by using the UCLA calculator or software such as SYSTAT, SPSS, or SAS). Therefore,

$$S = \sqrt{(3)(2.71)} = 2.851$$

We reject $H_0$ if $t > S$ or $t < -S$; because $5.264 > 2.851$, the contrast is significant.

CIs can also be calculated. The probability is $1-$ FWE that the values of all possible contrasts in a family are simultaneously contained within intervals bounded by

$$\hat{\psi} \pm s_{\hat{\psi}} \sqrt{f \cdot F_{FWE, f, df_e}} \tag{9.18}$$

From Table 9.1, we find that for the contrast in our example, $\hat{\psi} = .679$ and $s_{\hat{\psi}} = .130$. The original weights were all multiplied by 3 to yield integer weights. Therefore, the confidence limits on $3\mu_5 - (\mu_6 + \mu_7 + \mu_8)$ are

$$.679 \pm (.130)(2.851) = .308, 1.050$$

However, we want limits on the original scale and we therefore divide these values by 3, yielding .103 and .350. In Subsection 9.6.1, we treated this contrast as planned and found the Dunn–Bonferroni limits, .116 and .337. The Scheffé interval is wider than the Dunn–Bonferroni interval, revealing the price we pay in precision of estimation and power when contrasts are not planned. A good strategy is to plan all those contrasts that might conceivably be of interest, and then use the Dunn–Bonferroni or Fisher–Hayter method. Although the power of these methods decreases as $K$, the number of planned contrasts, increases, a rather large number of comparisons must be planned before the Scheffé criterion requires a smaller value of $t$ for significance. For a more detailed comparison of the Dunn–Bonferroni and the Scheffé methods, consult the article by Perlmutter and Myers (1973).

Experimenters who have used both the standard ANOVA (analysis of variance) tests and the Scheffé procedure have sometimes been surprised to find the omnibus null hypothesis rejected by the ANOVA test but no contrasts significant by the Scheffé criterion. The source of this apparent contradiction is that the overall $F$ test has exactly the same power as the *maximum possible contrast* tested by the Scheffé procedure. That contrast may be of little interest and may not therefore have been tested. It could be something like $(11/37)\mu_1 + (26/37)\mu_2 - (17/45)\mu_3 - (28/45)\mu_4$. In summary, although rejection of the omnibus null hypothesis indicates that at least one contrast is significant by the Scheffé criterion, there is no guarantee that any obvious or interesting contrast will be significant.

As with all the tests we have considered so far (except the Fisher–Hayter test), there is no logical necessity that the Scheffé tests of contrasts be preceded by a significant omnibus $F$. In contrast, even the largest possible contrast will not be significant if the overall $F$ test is not. There seems little point in expending energy on a series of post hoc Scheffé tests unless first determining, by the $F$ test of the omnibus null hypothesis, whether there is any possibility that a contrast of interest might be significant.

### 9.9.2 The Brown–Forsythe Method

Brown and Forsythe (1974b) proposed that Welch's $t'$ and $df'$ (Equations 9.5 and 9.6) be used with a criterion similar to Scheffé's $S$ when the assumption of homogeneity of variance is in question. The only difference is that the critical value of $S$ against which $t'$ is evaluated is based on $df'$. As an example, reconsider the Seasons data. Let us contrast the mean depression scores of individuals with only a high school education (HS) with the mean of individuals with more than a high school education (some college, C; bachelor's degree, B; and graduate school, GS). We test

$$H_0: \mu_{HS} - (1/3)(\mu_C + \mu_B + \mu_{GS}) = 0$$

Turning back to Table 9.4, we find $df_e$ $(df') = 20.527$, or approximately 21. With $df_1 = a - 1$, or 3, and FWE $= .05$, the critical value of $F$ is 3.07. Therefore,

$$S = \sqrt{(3)(3.07)} = 3.035$$

and, because $t' = 2.118$ (see Table 9.4), the result is not significant. The .95 limits on the simultaneous CI of the contrast were calculated after all coefficients were multiplied by 3; those limits are

$$8.8574 \pm (4.1811)(3.035) = -3.832, 21.547$$

Dividing by 3 to return to the original scale, we have $-1.277, 7.182$. The interval provides an alternative test of the null hypothesis; the fact that it contains zero informs us that the null hypothesis cannot be rejected.

## 9.10 THE SUM OF SQUARES ASSOCIATED WITH A CONTRAST

The $t$ statistic used throughout this chapter provides one approach to testing hypotheses about contrasts. An alternative, but equivalent, test is based on components of $SS_A$, the sums of squares for the $A$ source of variance. We develop this approach now in order to emphasize the continuity between the ANOVA and test of contrasts, and to enhance our understanding of contrasts. Furthermore, the relation between contrasts and sums of squares will prove useful in the developments of the next chapter on trend analysis. A central idea is that any contrast of the group means corresponds to a component of the $SS_A$, the sum of squares for the variable, $A$. That component sum of squares, $SS_{\hat{\psi}}$, will be distributed on 1 $df$ and the contrast can be tested by dividing it by $MS_{S/A}$. Because, as we showed in Chapter 7, $F_{1,df_e} = t^2_{df_e}$, the $F$ statistic formed in this way will equal $t^2$. This relation leads us directly to a formula for $SS_{\hat{\psi}}$:

$$F = t^2 = \frac{\hat{\psi}^2}{s^2_{\hat{\psi}}} = \frac{\left(\sum w_j \overline{Y}_{\cdot j}\right)^2}{MS_{S/A} \sum w_j^2/n_j}$$

$$= \frac{\left(\sum w_j \overline{Y}_{\cdot j}\right)^2 / \left(\sum w_j^2/n_j\right)}{MS_{S/A}}$$

$$= \frac{SS_{\hat{\psi}}}{MS_{S/A}}$$

so that

$$SS_{\hat{\psi}} = \frac{\hat{\psi}^2}{\sum w_j^2/n_j} = \frac{\left(\sum w_j \overline{Y}_{\cdot j}\right)^2}{\sum w_j^2/n_j} \tag{9.19}$$

**TABLE 9.12**   CONTRASTS OF THE MEANS IN TABLE 9.1, ASSUMING $n = 16$

The contrasts are

$$\hat{\psi}_1 = (1)\bar{Y}_5 + (1)\bar{Y}_6 + (1)\bar{Y}_7 + (-3)\bar{Y}_8$$
$$\hat{\psi}_2 = (1)\bar{Y}_5 + (1)\bar{Y}_6 + (-2)\bar{Y}_7 + (0)\bar{Y}_8$$
$$\hat{\psi}_3 = (1)\bar{Y}_5 + (-1)\bar{Y}_6 + (0)\bar{Y}_7 + (0)\bar{Y}_8$$

The ANOVA table is

| SV | df | SS | MS | F |
|----|----|----|----|----|
| A | 3 | 0.621 | .207 | 6.37 |
| $\psi_1$ | 1 | 0.085 | .085 | 2.62 |
| $\psi_2$ | 1 | 0.183 | .183 | 5.63 |
| $\psi_3$ | 1 | 0.353 | .353 | 10.86 |
| S/A | 60 | 1.95 | .033 | |

To illustrate and to further develop the relation between contrasts and the ANOVA, reconsider the multiplication speed scores in the Royer study. The means (from Table 9.1) are .350, .560, .586, and .583 for the fifth through eighth grades, and to simplify calculations we again assume $n = 16$ in all grades. Table 9.12 presents three contrasts and the ANOVA table containing all relevant sums of squares, degrees of freedom, mean squares, and $F$ tests. The contrasts represent (a) the difference between the mean for the eighth grade and the mean for the other three grades, (b) the difference between the seventh-grade mean and the mean of the combined fifth and sixth grades, and (c) the difference between the fifth- and sixth-grade means. An important point is that the $SS_{\hat{\psi}}$s in Table 9.12 sum to .621, the $SS_A$; that is,

$$.085 + .183 + .353 = .621$$
$$SS_{\hat{\psi}_1} + SS_{\hat{\psi}_2} + SS_{\hat{\psi}_3} = SS_A$$

We can think of the treatment sum of squares as a pie and each contrast as a piece of the pie. In the example of Table 9.1, the pieces are nonoverlapping, and together they account for the whole pie. Here, the contrast of the fifth- and sixth-grade means ($\psi_3$) is the biggest piece, accounting for about 57% (.353/.621) of the variability among the treatment means. As with any pie, the $SS_A$ can be divided into pieces in many ways. For example, let

$$\hat{\psi}_1 = (-3)\bar{Y}_5 + (-1)\bar{Y}_6 + (1)\bar{Y}_7 + (3)\bar{Y}_8$$
$$\hat{\psi}_2 = (-1)\bar{Y}_5 + (1)\bar{Y}_6 + (1)\bar{Y}_7 + (-1)\bar{Y}_8 \quad (9.20)$$
$$\hat{\psi}_3 = (-1)\bar{Y}_5 + (3)\bar{Y}_6 + (-3)\bar{Y}_7 + (1)\bar{Y}_8$$

Applying Equation 9.19, we find the corresponding sums of squares for these contrasts to be .421, .181, and .019; these values again sum to .621.

Will every set of contrasts result in sums of squares that add to $SS_A$? Not at all; in each of the preceding examples, the contrasts making up the set had a particular property that resulted in their accounting for different portions of the variability, for nonoverlapping pieces of the pie. When this is the case, the contrasts are said to be **orthogonal**. In addition, the number of orthogonal contrasts in each set, $a - 1$, was equal to the degrees of freedom of the treatment sum of squares. The sums of squares of $df_A$ orthogonal contrasts will always add to $SS_A$.

Before defining orthogonality more precisely, let's consider an example in which it does not occur. Let's test

$$H_{01}: \mu_5 - \mu_6 = 0 \quad \text{and} \quad H_{02}: \mu_5 - (1/3)(\mu_6 + \mu_7 + \mu_8) = 0$$

If the mean of the fifth-grade population ($\mu_5$) differs from that of the sixth-grade population ($\mu_6$), there is a good chance that it will also differ from the combined mean of $\mu_6$, $\mu_7$, and $\mu_8$, because that mean contains $\mu_6$. In other words, there is a positive relation between the two contrasts. This lack of independence between the two contrasts is called **nonorthogonality**. It becomes evident in our example when we calculate the sums of squares corresponding to the two contrasts. The sums of squares for the tests of $H_{01}$ and $H_{02}$ are .353 and .615, respectively. The sum is clearly greater than $SS_A$, .621. The two pieces of the pie overlap.

We do not have to add the sums of squares to determine whether two contrasts are, or are not, orthogonal. Consider two contrasts, $\psi_p$ and $\psi_q$, such that

$$\psi_p = \sum_j w_{jp}\mu_j \quad \text{and} \quad \psi_q = \sum_j w_{jq}\mu_j$$

If there are $n$ scores at all levels of $A$, the criterion for orthogonality is

$$\sum_j w_{jp}w_{jq} = 0 \tag{9.21}$$

For example, we know that the first two contrasts in Equation 9.20 are orthogonal because

$$(-3)(-1) + (-1)(1) + (1)(1) + (3)(-1) = 0$$

If the $n$s vary across treatment conditions, the criterion for orthogonality becomes

$$\sum_j \frac{w_{jp}w_{jq}}{n_j} = 0 \tag{9.22}$$

Several points about orthogonality deserve emphasis. First, a set of $a - 1$ orthogonal contrasts can be thought of as asking $a - 1$ logically independent questions that collectively "use up" all the degrees of freedom and variability associated with the independent variable. Note that the variability can be partitioned in different ways, so that it is possible to find different sets of orthogonal contrasts. Also, whether or not two contrasts are orthogonal depends on the contrast weights, not on the values of the means being contrasted. One way of thinking about this is that orthogonality depends on what questions are addressed by the contrasts, not on what the answers turn out to be. The second point is that we choose to test contrasts because they are of substantive interest, whether or not they are orthogonal to one another. For example, researchers commonly test pairwise comparisons; these are not orthogonal, but they are often of interest and should be tested when they are.

## 9.11 CONCLUDING REMARKS

Table 9.13 summarizes the conditions under which each of the methods described in the preceding sections is appropriate. The methods that are listed do not exhaust all the possibilities. We have excluded some methods because they allow the FWE to exceed its nominal

**TABLE 9.13**  SUMMARY OF METHODS FOR CONTROLLING FWEs

| Contrast | CI | Group Size (n) | Pop. Variances[a] | Test Stat. | Method |
|---|---|---|---|---|---|
| Planned | Yes | NR | Equal | $t$ | D–B or D–S |
| | Yes | NR | Not equal | $t'$ | D–B or D–S |
| | No | NR | Equal | $t$ | Hochberg |
| | No | NR | Not equal | $t'$ | Hochberg |
| vs. Control | Yes | Equal | Equal | $t$ | Dunnett |
| | Yes | Not equal | Equal | $t$ | D–B or D–S |
| | Yes | NR | Not equal | $t'$ | D–B or D–S |
| All pairwise | Yes | Equal | Equal | $q$ or $t$ | Tukey |
| | Yes | Not equal | Equal | $q$ or $t$ | T–K |
| | Yes | NR | Not equal | $t'$ | G–H or T3 |
| | No | NR | Equal | $F$ or $q$, then $q$ or $t$ | F–H |
| General post hoc | Yes | NR | Equal | $t$ | Scheffé |
| | Yes | NR | Not equal | $t'$ | Scheffé |

*Note.* NR = not relevant; D–B = Dunn–Bonferroni; D–S = Dunn–Šidák; T–K = Tukey–Kramer; G–H = Games–Howell; T3 = Dunnett's T3; F–H = Fisher–Hayter; $t$ = $t$ statistic with $SE$ based on $MS_{S/A}$; $t'$ = Welch's $t$ using $df'$; see Equations 9.5 and 9.6.
[a] For population variances: Equal = the population variances are assumed to be homogeneous; Not equal = homogeneity of variance assumption is suspect.

level, and others because they provide a very small gain in power at the cost of added complexity. The methods listed in Table 9.13 are easy to use and are available in several software packages such as SPSS and SAS. Further discussions of these procedures and descriptions of other methods may be found in the previously cited review article by Shaffer (1995). Seaman et al. (1991) also describe many methods for controlling FWEs for the family of all pairwise comparisons and present the results of a large-scale computer-sampling study of error rates and power.

In closing, we emphasize two points. First, among the tests we have presented, only the Fisher–Hayter procedure requires that the omnibus null hypothesis be rejected before contrasts are tested. Such a requirement causes a loss of power in using the Bonferroni-based, or the Tukey, or the Dunnett methods. In the case of Scheffé's test, the preliminary $F$ is useful in possibly saving unnecessary labor because if it is not significant, no test of a contrast will have a significant outcome; however, the omnibus test is not logically necessary. In other instances, for example, when several contrasts have been planned, a significant outcome of the omnibus test suggests that something is going on and if the planned contrasts are not significant, the investigator may wish to do some data snooping, using the Scheffé method. However, if the omnibus null hypothesis is not rejected, planned contrasts can still be tested provided the FWE is maintained at or below the nominal value. The second point, which cannot be emphasized too strongly, is the importance of planning contrasts. A procedure such as the Dunn–Bonferroni may be considerably more powerful than the Tukey procedure if only a few of the pairwise comparisons are of any possible interest. In addition, close consideration to the questions that are of primary, or perhaps sole, interest may lead to research designs that are more closely focused on those questions.

## KEY CONCEPTS

| | |
|---|---|
| omnibus null hypothesis | planned contrasts |
| post hoc contrasts | family |
| familywise error rate (FWE) | error rate per contrast (EC) |
| Bonferroni inequality | Dunn–Bonferroni method |
| simultaneous CIs | Dunn–Šidák method |
| simultaneous methods | sequential methods |
| Hochberg's sequential method | the studentized range statistic ($q$) |
| Tukey's HSD test | Tukey–Kramer test |
| Games–Howell test | Fisher–Hayter test |
| Dunnett's test | Scheffé's method |
| Brown–Forsythe method | orthogonal contrasts |
| nonorthogonality | |

## EXERCISES

**9.1** There are five treatment conditions in a problem-solving study, each with $n = 20$. Two groups, $F1$ and $F2$, are given instructions designed to facilitate problem solving. The third group is a control group given neutral instructions. The fourth and fifth groups, $I1$ and $I2$, are given instructions designed to interfere with problem solving. The data are as follows:

| | $F1$ | $F2$ | $C$ | $I1$ | $I2$ |
|---|---|---|---|---|---|
| $\overline{Y}._j$ | 14.6 | 14.9 | 13.8 | 11.8 | 11.7 |
| $s_j^2$ | 3 | 4 | 5 | 4 | 4 |

Test each of the following hypotheses with $\alpha = .05$. State $H_0$ and $H_1$.
(a) The average of the facilitation group population means is greater than the mean of the control population.
(b) The average of the interference population means is different from the mean of the control population.
(c) The average of the facilitation means is not the same as the average of the interference means.

**9.2** (a) Assume that all three tests in Exercise 9.1 were planned prior to data collection. Using the Dunn–Bonferroni method, construct .90 simultaneous CIs for the three contrasts. Reevaluate whether the null hypotheses in parts (b) and (c) should be rejected, using the Dunn–Bonferroni criterion with FWE = .10.
(b) Assume the contrasts were chosen after the means were viewed. Use the Scheffé method to construct simultaneous CIs. Reevaluate whether the null hypotheses in parts (b) and (c) of Exercise 9.1 should be rejected with FWE = .10.

**9.3** The following group means are each based on 10 scores:

| $A_1$ | $A_2$ | $A_3$ |
|-------|-------|-------|
| 24    | 16    | 14    |

(a) Calculate $SS_A$.

(b) Calculate the sum of squares for each of the following contrasts: (i) $\hat{\psi}_1 = \overline{Y}_{.1} - \overline{Y}_{.2}$; (ii) $\hat{\psi}_{21} = \overline{Y}_{.1} - (1/2)(\overline{Y}_{.2} + \overline{Y}_{.3})$; (iii) $\hat{\psi}_3 = \overline{Y}_{.1} - \overline{Y}_{.3}$. What should be true of the relation between $SS_A$ and the sums of squares for $\hat{\psi}_1$ and $\hat{\psi}_2$? Why?

(c) We can remove the effect associated with $\hat{\psi}_1$ from the data by setting the means at $A_1$ and $A_2$ equal to their average. The adjusted means are as follows:

| $A_1$ | $A_2$ | $A_3$ |
|-------|-------|-------|
| 20    | 20    | 14    |

Redo part (b), (ii) and (iii). Are either of the sums of squares different from those calculated for the original (unadjusted) means? Explain, emphasizing the relation of the results to the concept of orthogonality.

**9.4** (a) Suppose the group sizes in Exercise 9.3 were not equal; the $n_j$s are 8, 10, and 12, respectively. Returning to the original means, calculate $SS_A$. Then calculate the sums of squares for $\hat{\psi}_1$ and $\hat{\psi}_2$. Now, what is the relation between the sums of squares for $\hat{\psi}_1$ and $\hat{\psi}_2$ and $SS_A$?

(b) Redefine the $\psi_2$ contrast so that it is orthogonal to that for $\psi_1$ for the samples sizes stated in this exercise. Calculate $SS_{\hat{\psi}_2}$. Does $SS_{\hat{\psi}_1} + SS_{\hat{\psi}_2} = SS_A$?

**9.5** Consider the means in Exercise 9.3. Assume that $MS_{S/A} = 900$.

(a) Assuming $n = 10$ in all three groups, calculate the standardized contrast, $\hat{\psi}_S$, for part (b), (ii) of Exercise 9.3. (See Chapter 6 to review definitions and calculations.)

(b) Repeat part (a), but assume the unequal $n$s of Exercise 9.4 and define the contrast as in part (b).

**9.6** The following is suggested by a study conducted by Fenz and Epstein (1967). In a study of conflict in parachutists, galvanic skin response (GSR) measures were obtained for five different groups of 5 participants who differed with respect to when the measures were taken: 2 weeks before the jump (BJ − 2), one week before (BJ − 1), on the day of the jump prior to jumping (DJ − P), and on the day of the jump after jumping (DJ − A). There was also a control group of normal (nonjumping) cowards (C). The $MS_{error}$ for the ANOVA $= 4.0$, and it is reasonable to assume homogeneity of variance. The means were as follows:

| BJ − 2 | BJ − 1 | DJ − A | DJ − P | C |
|--------|--------|--------|--------|---|
| 5      | 5      | 7      | 9      | 2 |

(a) Suppose the investigator had planned to compare each of the four experimental groups with the control (C). With $\alpha = .05$ (two tailed), test the difference between the DJ − P and C means, using (i) the Dunn–Bonferroni procedure, and (ii) the Dunnett procedure.

(b) Suppose that the experimenter tested all possible pairwise comparisons. Redo the test in part (a), using the appropriate procedure for controlling the FWE at .05.

(c) Comment on the relative power of these three procedures, justifying your conclusion by citing relevant information in your preceding answers. Explain why these situations give rise to the differences in power that you indicate.

(d) Calculate the CIs obtained with each of the three procedures and relate the results to your answer to part (c).

**9.7** A sample of humanities majors are divided into three groups of 10 each in a study of statistics learning. One group receives training on relevant concepts *before* reading the text, a second receives the training *after* reading the text, and a third is a no-training *control*. Summary statistics on a test are as follows:

|         | Before | After | Control |
|---------|--------|-------|---------|
| $\overline{Y}_{.j}$ | 20 | 14 | 13 |
| $s_j^2$ | 72 | 62 | 76 |

(a) We want to test whether the mean of the Before population is higher than the average of the other two populations combined. In answering the following parts, assume FWE = .05.

(i) State the null and alternative hypotheses. (ii) What is the estimate of the variance of the sampling distribution of $\hat{\psi}$ (assume homogeneity of variance)? (iii) Calculate the $t$ statistic appropriate for testing $H_0$.

(b) Evaluate the test statistic you just calculated, assuming (i) the test was the sole contrast tested and had been planned before viewing the data; (ii) the test was a result of viewing the data.

**9.8** We have five group means, each based on 10 scores, with $MS_{S/A} = 4.0$. The means are as follows:

| $A_1$ | $A_2$ | $A_3$ | $A_4$ | $A_5$ |
|-------|-------|-------|-------|-------|
| 8.6 | 9.5 | 9.2 | 8.0 | 10.4 |

(a) We plan five contrasts with FWE = .05. Test the contrast of $A_5$ against the average of the other four groups. State the criterion required for significance, and whether $H_0$ can be rejected.

(b) Suppose we had decided on the contrast in part (a) after inspecting the data. Now what is the result of the significance test? Be sure to show your criterion statistic.

(c) Find the CIs corresponding to the tests in parts (a) and (b). Explain the difference in widths.

(d) Suppose we did all possible pairwise tests. Actually calculate the test for $A_1$ against $A_2$. What is the criterion statistic? What conclusion do you reach about $H_0$?

(e) Suppose the only contrast we planned pitted the average of $A_1$ and $A_2$ against the average of the remaining three groups. Do the calculations and report the results, showing the criterion statistic.

**9.9**  In an attitude change study, four groups of participants are presented with persuasive messages about a topic. Two groups read the messages; there is a positive message for one group and a negative message for the other. Two other groups receive the messages by viewing a videotape. A fifth, control, group receives no message. Each group has its attitude assessed by a questionnaire for which larger scores mean a more positive attitude. There are 7 participants in each group and $MS_{S/A} = 20$. The group means are as follows:

| $A_1$ Video/Pos. | $A_2$ Video/Neg. | $A_3$ Read/Pos. | $A_4$ Read/Neg. | $A_5$ Control |
|---|---|---|---|---|
| 71 | 42 | 63 | 47 | 52 |

(a) Determine which experimental conditions differ significantly from the control using the Dunnett test with FWE = .05.

(b) Test the hypothesis that the difference between the positive and negative messages is the same whether they are read, or are presented by videotape. Assume this is the only planned comparison.

(c) By how much would two groups have to differ before they would be considered significantly different by the Tukey test with FWE = .05?

**9.10**  The Male_educ file in the *Seasons* folder contains means (over seasons) for four of the Schoolyr categories (3 = only high school, 5 = some after high school, 7 = bachelor's degree, 8 = graduate school). In what follows, assume that all pairwise differences are tested.

(a) Test the difference between the Schoolyr = 3 and Schoolyr = 5 Beck_D means using (i) the Tukey–Kramer method, and (ii) the Dunn–Bonferroni method, assuming all pairwise comparisons. Assume homogeneous variances. (iii) Compare the CIs.

(b) Perform the Games–Howell test of the difference in part (a). Compare the results with those in part (a). In particular, which of these procedures should be used with these data?

**9.11**  The Sayhlth file in the *Seasons* folder contains Beck depression scores as a function of several factors.

(a) Test whether employment status significantly affects mean_d, the mean (over seasons) depression score.

(b) Calculate all simultaneous CIs (FWE = .05) by using the Tukey–Kramer method. Assume homogeneous variances.

(c) Redo part (b), using the Dunn–Bonferroni method. Assume homogeneous variances.

**9.12**  **(a)** Is the assumption of homogeneity of variance reasonable for the data in Exercise 9.11? Support your conclusion with statistical evidence.

**(b)** Assume we wish to know if the mean depression score for fully employed individuals (Category 1) differs from that of those who are not fully employed (Categories 2 and 3 in the Sayhlth file). Test whether the difference is significant, assuming this is the sole comparison tested and was planned prior to the collection of data.

# Chapter 10
## Trend Analysis

## 10.1 INTRODUCTION

In Chapter 9 we discussed methods for comparing the mean scores of two groups, or of two subsets of groups. Our primary concern was to address questions that are most appropriate when the independent variable is qualitative. Qualitative variables are variables whose "levels" differ in type, such as type of therapy, method of instruction, and diagnostic category. In contrast, quantitative variables are variables whose levels differ in amount, such as hours of therapy or instruction, drug dosage, and stimulus intensity. Even with variables such as these, contrasts of two means can be tested. We did just that in contrasting multiplication speed scores for different grades. However, when the independent variable is quantitative, it often is more informative to consider the overall trend in the treatment group means, rather than to make specific comparisons between two means. We might want to determine whether there is a trend for means to increase as the level of the independent variable increases, or whether the function relating the means and the level of the independent variable is significantly curved. For example, Fig. 10.1 presents the mean multiplication speeds (filled circles) for fifth- through eighth-grade students in the Royer study, together with a straight line that minimizes the average squared distance of the points to the line, a curve that indicates predicted speed as a function of grade and grade$^2$, which also represents a least-squares fit, and equations for these two functions. In the equations, $Y$ represents mean speed and $X$ represents the grade. Because the slope of the best-fitting straight line (.074) is positive, we know that there is a trend for the speeds to increase with grade level. The fit of the straight line is at best fair; the average absolute deviation of grade means from the predicted values based on the line is .053. The grade means are clearly closer to the curve; the average absolute deviation is less than .02. If our goal is to fit the observed means, we can do even better by adding an $X^3$ term to the equation for the curve and replotting accordingly. The means would then fall right on the resulting curve. Usually, however, we want to draw inferences about the function that describes the relation between the population means and

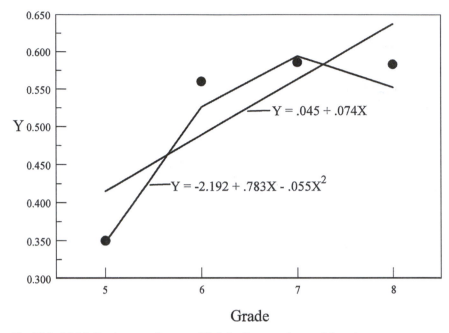

**Fig. 10.1** Multiplication speed means ($Y$) fit by linear and curved functions.

the independent variable. We recognize that the pattern of observed means may be due to chance, and therefore we usually want to test hypotheses about the slope and curvature of the *population* function. We usually want to address the following questions: Is the slope of the straight line that best fits the population means different from zero? Do the population means fall on that line or is the best-fitting function curved? In the sections that follow, we state null hypotheses corresponding to these questions and present the calculations necessary to test those hypotheses. In Chapter 11, we consider analyses of trends in multifactor designs, comparing the slopes and curves of several functions.

## 10.2 LINEAR TREND

Here we review equations for linear regression and the associated sums of squares, and then we proceed to develop significance tests of hypotheses about the shape of functions based on our data. We begin our discussion of trend analysis by considering linear regression because it provides a relatively simple context within which to develop the basic ideas. To simplify things still further, we assume that $n$s are equal throughout the chapter. A more general treatment of trend analysis can be found in Chapter 20.

### 10.2.1 The Equation for a Straight Line

Suppose we have $a$ levels of a quantitative independent variable. For example, we have four levels of school grade in the Royer study; we represent the values as $X = 5, 6, 7$, and 8. We can draw a straight line relating the group means to the $X$ values. The line is described by the equation

$$\overline{Y}_{\text{pre},j} = b_0 + b_1 X_j \tag{10.1}$$

where $\overline{Y}_{\text{pre},j}$ is the mean predicted for group $j$ and $b_0$ and $b_1$ are the **intercept** and slope (or **linear regression coefficient**), respectively. As we noted in Chapter 3, the intercept is the value predicted for $Y$ when $X = 0$, and the slope is the amount $Y$ changes for each unit change in $X$. Paralleling the developments in Chapter 3, and assuming equal $n$, we have the following least-squares formulas for $b_0$ and $b_1$:

$$b_1 = \frac{\sum (\overline{Y}_{.j} - \overline{Y}_{..})(X_j - \overline{X}_{.})}{\sum (X_j - \overline{X}_{.})^2} \tag{10.2}$$

$$b_0 = \overline{Y}_{..} - b_1 \overline{X}_{.} \tag{10.3}$$

Equation 10.1 enables us to predict a mean for any group, provided we have numerical values of the intercept and slope. That prediction is not necessarily accurate; the best-fitting straight line may not be a good fit. The observed group means may not lie on the best-fitting straight line, or even be reasonably close to it. However, the predicted points do provide the basis for testing whether the best-fitting straight line has a slope significantly different from zero. That is, they underlie the test of whether there is a linear trend in the population, a tendency for the population means to increase (or decrease) as $X$ increases.

The linear regression coefficient, $b_1$, is an estimate of the population parameter $\beta_1$. We can represent the best-fitting straight line relating the treatment population means to the levels of the independent variable by

$$\hat{\mu}_j = \beta_0 + \beta_1 X_j \tag{10.4}$$

When we test for linear trend, we test the null hypothesis

$$H_0: \beta = 0$$

In words, the null hypothesis is that the straight line that best fits the treatment population means has a slope of zero.

Several points about this last statement must be understood. First, the $\mu_j$ may vary even if the preceding hypothesis is true; that is, they may vary even if there is no linear trend. To see this, suppose that the $\mu_j$ fall on a perfectly symmetric inverted U-shaped function. These means would exhibit no linear trend; a best-fitting straight line would have a slope ($\beta_1$) of zero. Nevertheless, there would be variability among the means.

The second point to keep in mind is that the straight lines described by Equations 10.1 and 10.4 are lines of best fit. Many straight lines can be drawn to describe a set of means. We choose our values of $b_0$ and $b_1$ to minimize $\sum (\overline{Y}_{\text{pre},j} - \overline{Y}_{.j})^2$, the sum of squared distances between $\overline{Y}_{\text{pre},j}$ and $\overline{Y}_{.j}$, the predicted and observed values of the group means. This is usually referred to as the **least-squares criterion** and it is what we mean by "best fit."

The third point to note is that rejection of the null hypothesis of no linear trend does not allow us to conclude that the population means are well fit by a straight line but only that the best-fitting straight line has a slope other than zero. Again, we emphasize that the best-fitting straight line is not necessarily a good fit. Still, inferences about linear trend are important. For example, in a study of the effects of hours of practice on learning, a significant linear trend would support the hypothesis that the probability of a correct response tends to increase with practice.

Equations 10.1–10.3 provide the basis for testing the null hypothesis that $\beta_1 = 0$, and for obtaining confidence intervals (CI) for $\beta_1$. In the next section, we present a numerical example and use it to develop one approach to an $F$ test of the null hypothesis. CIs are presented in Chapter 20 within a more general regression framework.

## 10.2.2 Testing $H_0$: $\beta_1 = 0$

Consider an experimental study of stimulus generalization. A mild shock is presented in the presence of a rectangle of light 11 in. high and 1 in. wide. Participants are then randomly divided into five groups of 10, each of which is tested in the presence of a rectangle of light, but with no shock. The independent variable is the height of the rectangle of light on these test trials; the five groups see a rectangle whose height is either 7, 9, 11, 13, or 15 in. high. An average galvanic skin response (GSR) measure is obtained for each participant. The experimenters' hypothesis is that two processes are at work in this experiment. First, they believe that the magnitude of conditioned responses should vary directly with the magnitude of the test stimulus; this implies that GSR scores should increase as a function of the height of the rectangle of light. Second, the experimenters expect a generalization effect. There should be a trend for GSR scores to be higher the closer the test stimulus is to the training stimulus. The result of this generalization process would be a symmetric inverted U-shaped curve. If only this process were operating, GSR would be highest in response to the 11-in. test stimulus and lowest for the 7- and 15-in. test stimuli.

The five group means, each of which is based on 10 scores, are presented in Table 10.1 ("Obs. mean GSR") and are plotted in Fig. 10.2. If the experimenters' theory is correct, the observed curve in Fig. 10.2 is the sum of two component functions. One of the two

**TABLE 10.1**   OBSERVED AND PREDICTED GROUP MEANS, AND CALCULATIONS FOR A TEST OF LINEARITY

| Statistics | | | | | | Mean |
|---|---|---|---|---|---|---|
| Stimulus Height $(X)$ | 7 | 9 | 11 | 13 | 15 | 11 |
| Obs. mean GSR $(\overline{Y}_{.j})$ | 1.910 | 3.560 | 4.440 | 3.580 | 3.830 | 3.464 |
| Pred. mean GSR $(\overline{Y}_{pre,j})$ | 2.692 | 3.078 | 3.464 | 3.850 | 4.236 | 3.464 |
| $\overline{Y}_{pre,j} - \overline{Y}_{..}$ | −0.772 | −0.386 | 0 | .386 | .772 | 0 |
| Variance $(s_j^2)$ | 2.218 | 2.563 | 1.964 | 2.881 | 1.659 | 2.257 |

*Note.*

$$b_1 = \frac{\sum (X_j - \overline{X}_.)(\overline{Y}_{.j} - \overline{Y}_{..})}{\sum (X_j - \overline{X}_.)^2}$$

$$= \frac{(7 - 11)(1.910 - 3.464) + \cdots + (15 - 11)(3.830 - 3.464)}{(7 - 11)^2 + \cdots + (15 - 11)^2}$$

$$= \frac{7.720}{40} = .193$$

Furthermore, the predicted means follow from Equation 10.5. For example,

$$\overline{Y}_{pre,1} = \overline{Y}_{..} + b_1(X_1 - \overline{X}_.)$$

$$= 3.464 + (.193)(7 - 11) = 2.692$$

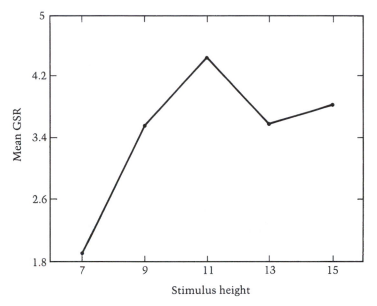

**Fig. 10.2** Mean GSR plotted as a function of stimulus height.

hypothesized functions increases with stimulus height and the other increases and then decreases as height increases, with a peak when the height is 11 in. Therefore, in this particular example, we want to test each of the two kinds of effects independently. **Trend analysis** permits us to answer the following questions. First, if we fit a straight line to the five means, will its slope be significantly different from zero? This addresses the hypothesis that there is an increase in the population means with increasing test stimulus height. Second, if we fit a symmetric inverted U-shaped curve to the five group means, will the points on this function vary significantly? This addresses the hypothesis that there is a generalization effect in the sampled population of GSR scores.

There are other questions we could ask about these data. For example, note the slight upturn in the rightmost data point. If this upturn is due to more than chance variability, it is not accounted for by the straight line representing stimulus height effects and the inverted U-shaped curve representing generalization effects. There is the possibility that some process that produces an S-shaped function is also at work. We present tests of possible curvilinear components such as the inverted U and the S in later sections of this chapter. In this section, let's focus our attention on the test of linearity; that is, we test whether the best-fitting straight line has a slope significantly different from zero.

One way of testing linear trend follows directly from the preceding discussion of the equation for a line of best fit. This approach involves finding the group means predicted by the best-fitting straight line and then calculating the sums of squared deviations of these predicted means about their average, $\overline{Y}...$. This sum of squares can then be tested against the usual within-groups error term, $MS_{S/A}$, which has a value of 2.257 in the generalization example.

We will shortly illustrate a computationally simpler way to calculate the sum of squares, one that avoids the necessity of calculating the predicted group means. However, our first approach is useful in reminding us that the test of the null hypothesis of zero slope is a test of the variability of the means predicted by Equation 10.1.

Replacing $b_0$ in Equation 10.1 by the right side of Equation 10.3, we have

$$
\begin{aligned}
\overline{Y}_{\text{pre},j} &= b_0 + b_1 X_j \\
&= (\overline{Y}.. - b_1 \overline{X}.) + b_1 X_j \\
&= \overline{Y}.. + b_1 (X_j - \overline{X}.)
\end{aligned}
\tag{10.5}
$$

Using the $X$ and $\overline{Y}._j$ values in Table 10.1, we have calculated the value of $b_1$ and used it to obtain the predicted values of the group means ("Predicted mean GSR"). If the null hypothesis of no linear trend is true then $\beta_1 = 0$, and, therefore, we would expect $b_1$ to be small. In turn, this implies that the **predicted group means**, the $\overline{Y}_{\text{pre},j}$, do not vary greatly and are close to their average, the grand mean, $\overline{Y}..$ . In contrast, considerable variability of the predicted means would suggest that the null hypothesis of no linear trend is false and should be rejected. This variability of the predicted means, the sum of squares for linearity, is defined as

$$
SS_{\text{lin}} = n \sum_j (\overline{Y}_{\text{pre},j} - \overline{Y}..)^2
\tag{10.6}
$$

Like $SS_A$ as defined in Chapter 8, $SS_{\text{lin}}$ is $n$ times the sum of squared deviations of group means about their average. The difference is that these are *predicted*, not observed, group means. Unlike $SS_A$, $SS_{\text{lin}}$ is distributed on only 1 *df*. This is because it reflects the deviation of one quantity, $b_1$, from zero.

Applying Equations 10.5 and 10.6 to the data of Table 10.1, we have

$$
SS_{\text{lin}} = (10)\,[(2.692 - 3.464)^2 + \cdots + (4.236 - 3.464)^2] = 14.9
$$

We can now test $H_0$: $\beta_1 = 0$:

$$
F_{1,a(n-1)} = \frac{SS_{\text{lin}}}{MS_{S/A}}
\tag{10.7}
$$

Because $MS_{S/A}$ is the average within-group variance, 2.257,

$$
F = 14.9/2.257 = 6.602
$$

This $F$ ratio, which is on 1 and 45 *df*, is quite significant. We therefore reject the null hypothesis of no linear trend. It appears that the $\mu_j$ tend to increase in magnitude as $X$, the height of the rectangle of light, increases. However, this test tells us nothing about the shape of the function that describes the population means. To draw inferences about whether the function is curved, we must consider functions somewhat more complicated than straight lines. In Section 10.3, we do just that. However, we first present a much simpler way to calculate $SS_{\text{lin}}$.

## 10.2.3 $SS_{\text{lin}}$ as a Single-degrees-of-freedom Contrast

From Equation 10.5, we know that

$$
\overline{Y}_{\text{pre},j} - \overline{Y}.. = b_1(X_j - \overline{X})
$$

Substituting the right-hand side of the preceding equation into Equation 10.6, we obtain

$$SS_{\text{lin}} = n \sum_j (\overline{Y}_{\text{pre},j} - \overline{Y}..)^2$$

$$= n \sum_j [b_1(X_j - \overline{X}.)]^2$$

Substituting for $b_1$ from Equation 10.2 and simplifying, we can rewrite Equation 10.6 as

$$SS_{\text{lin}} = \frac{\left[\sum (X_j - \overline{X}.)\overline{Y}_{.j}\right]^2}{\sum (X_j - \overline{X}.)^2/n} \tag{10.8}$$

$$= \frac{\left[\sum w_j \overline{Y}_{.j}\right]^2}{\sum w_j^2/n}$$

where $w_j = X_j - \overline{X}..$

The important point to recognize is that if we divide the last line of Equation 10.8 by $MS_{S/A}$, the result is the $F$ test of a single-degree-of-freedom contrast as defined in Chapter 9. The advantage of recognizing that the numerator of that $F$ test, $SS_{\text{lin}}$, can be written as a sum of squares for a single-degree-of-freedom contrast is that we do not have to calculate $b_1$ and use it to calculate the predicted group means. Furthermore, we soon will show that tests of other trends can also be viewed as tests of single-degree-of-freedom contrasts. The only difference is that when nonlinear trends are tested, the weights (the $w_j$) in Equation 10.8 are quantities other than $X_j - \overline{X}..$

The linear weights for the generalization example were the deviations of the stimulus lengths about their average: $-4, -2, 0, 2,$ and $4$. $SS_{\text{lin}}$ is unchanged if we multiply or divide all the weights by a constant; this is because the squared constant appears in both numerator and denominator of Equation 10.8. Therefore, we can get the same value of $SS_{\text{lin}}$ if we divide $X_j - \overline{X}.$ by two; the new weights are

$$\xi_{\text{lin}} = -2, -1, 0, 1, 2$$

The $\xi_{\text{lin}}$ (Greek xi; the subscript refers to linearity) are weights that can be used in Equation 10.8 in place of $X_j - \overline{X}.$ to test the linearity hypothesis whenever (a) the values of the independent variable are equally spaced, and (b) each mean is based on the same number of scores. If the $X_j$ are equally spaced, $X_j - \overline{X}.$ will differ from $\xi_{\text{lin},j}$ by a constant multiplier and, as already noted, $SS_{\text{lin}}$ will not be affected. For the general case in which spacing or $n$s are not equal, refer to Chapter 20 on multiple regression.

Turn now to Appendix Table C.6, labeled "Coefficients of Orthogonal Polynomials." Find the block of coefficients for $a = 5$ (five levels of the independent variable) and look at the first row, the linear coefficients. These are the $\xi_{\text{lin}}$ listed previously. The table also lists linear coefficients for other values of $a$, that is, for experiments in which there are more or fewer levels of the independent variable. For each row of linear coefficients, (a) $\sum \xi_{\text{lin},j} = 0$ and (b) provided the values of $X$ (the independent variable) are equally spaced, the linear coefficients are a straight line function of $X$. From now on, if the values of $X$ are equally spaced and the $n_j$ are all equal, Equation 10.8 can be used to calculate $SS_{\text{lin}}$, but with the linear coefficients of Table 6 replacing $w_j$.

As you may have guessed, the coefficients in the rows labeled "Quadratic," "Cubic," and so on enable us to test other hypotheses about the shape of the function that best describes the treatment population means. We now discuss these hypotheses and the related significance tests.

## 10.3 TESTING NONLINEAR TRENDS

### 10.3.1 A General Test

One question we might wish to ask is whether the group means in Table 10.1 depart significantly from the best-fitting straight line. The null hypothesis is that the population means fall on a straight line; there is no curvature. The experimenters expect generalization, which implies that this null hypothesis should be false; the population means should deviate from a straight line. A general test of the null hypothesis of no curvature follows from recognizing that $SS_A$, the variability among the group means, can be partitioned into two components. The first of these is the $SS_{lin}$ that we discussed in the preceding section. Recall that this reflects the difference between the best-fitting straight line and a line with slope of zero. The second component of $SS_A$ is $SS_{nonlin}$ ("sum of squares for nonlinearity"), which reflects the departure of the observed group means from the best-fitting straight line. This partitioning of $SS_A$ follows from the identity

$$(\overline{Y}_{.j} - \overline{Y}_{..}) = (\overline{Y}_{.j} - \overline{Y}_{pre,j}) + (\overline{Y}_{pre,j} - \overline{Y}_{..})$$

Squaring both sides of the preceding equation, and summing over subjects and groups, we have

$$\underbrace{n \sum (\overline{Y}_{.j} - \overline{Y}_{..})^2}_{SS_A} = \underbrace{n \sum (\overline{Y}_{.j} - \overline{Y}_{pre,j})^2}_{SS_{nonlin}} + \underbrace{n \sum (\overline{Y}_{pre,j} - \overline{Y}_{..})^2}_{SS_{lin}} \tag{10.9}$$

To the extent that the observed group means differ from the means predicted by a straight line, the function is curved. The sum of those squared differences (between the observed means and the means predicted by a straight line) is exactly what $SS_{nonlin}$ reflects. Because $SS_{lin}$ is distributed on 1 $df$, $SS_{nonlin}$ must be distributed on $a - 2$ $df$. Another way of thinking about these degrees of freedom is that $SS_{nonlin}$ represents the variability of $a$ data points about a line; 2 $df$ are lost because the line is determined by estimates of two parameters, $\beta_0$ and $\beta_1$, leaving $a - 2$ $df$.

It follows from Equation 10.9 that $SS_{nonlin}$ is calculated as the difference between $SS_A$ and $SS_{lin}$. Therefore, to test the hypothesis that the population means fall on a straight line, calculate

$$F = \frac{(SS_A - SS_{lin})/(a - 2)}{MS_{S/A}} \tag{10.10}$$

Applying Equation 10.10 to the data of Table 10.1, we have

$$SS_{nonlin} = SS_A - SS_{lin} = 35.241 - 14.9 = 20.341$$

and

$$F = \frac{20.341/3}{2.257} = 3.004$$

This result is significant at the .05 level, leading us to conclude that the function relating $\mu_j$ and $X_j$ is not a straight line.

Let's summarize what we have learned so far from the analysis of trend in the generalization example. First, the test of linearity reveals that there is a trend for the treatment population means to increase as $X$ increases; the linear regression coefficient is significantly greater than zero. Second, the test of nonlinearity reveals that the straight line by itself is not sufficient to account for the variation in the population means. Consistent with the idea of stimulus generalization, the best-fitting function appears to be curved.

$SS_{nonlin}$ can be further partitioned into $a - 2$ components, each distributed on 1 $df$. We next consider how these components are calculated and what they represent.

### 10.3.2 Orthogonal Polynomials

In the example of the generalization experiment (Table 10.1), we have so far established that there are both linear and nonlinear components of the population function. In many analyses, tests of these two components will be enough. However, more precise theories motivate more precise statistical tests. For example, in the generalization experiment, the theory specifies two independent processes that combine to generate the treatment means. The absolute magnitude of the stimulus is thought to produce a linear effect; for each increment of one unit in $X$, the $\mu_j$ should increase by some constant amount. Distance of the test stimulus from the training stimulus results in a quadratic effect; if only this generalization effect were present, the $\mu_j$ would be a symmetric inverted U-shaped function of $X$. Note that this statement of the theory is more specific than one that only states that there will be deviations from the best-fitting straight line. The theory requires a very specific kind of nonlinearity. It says that the population means are adequately described by a **second-order polynomial function** of the form

$$\mu_j = \beta_0 + \beta_1 X_j + \beta_2 X_j^2 \tag{10.11}$$

This function is also called a **quadratic function**, and $\beta_2$ is often referred to as the **quadratic coefficient**.

Equation 10.11 is a special case of the general **polynomial function of order $a - 1$**:

$$\mu_j = \beta_0 + \beta_1 X_j + \beta_2 X_j^2 + \cdots + \beta_p X_j^p + \cdots + \beta_{a-1} X_j^{a-1} \tag{10.12}$$

Note the restriction that if there are $a$ points, the order of the polynomial is at most $a - 1$. For example, if we have only two values of $X$, we can draw a line between the two data points, thus establishing a linear function of the form of equation 10.1. However, we do not have enough data to estimate more than the two coefficients, $\beta_0$ and $\beta_1$; therefore, two data points restrict us to a linear, or first-order, polynomial function. Similarly, three data points permit us to estimate $\beta_0$, $\beta_1$, and $\beta_2$, and therefore allow us to fit a quadratic, or second-order polynomial, function. The order of the polynomial function can be less than $a - 1$ because some of the higher order coefficients such as $\beta_{a-1}$ or $\beta_{a-2}$ can be zero.

Because there are five group means in the generalization example of Table 10.1, the data could conceivably be fit by a function having **cubic** ($X^3$) and **quartic** ($X^4$) terms. Our theory, however, holds that only the linear and quadratic components are necessary to account for the variation among the treatment population means. Because $SS_{lin}$ was significant, we have already demonstrated the presence of a linear component. Now we would like to determine whether, in accord with the theory, the only significant nonlinear component is the quadratic one. In order to construct independent tests of the quadratic, cubic, and quartic components of the function for our five group means, we make use of the orthogonal polynomial coefficients of Appendix Table C.6. Turning to the table, again focus on the block for which $a = 5$. Several points hold for the four rows of coefficients:

1. The plot of the coefficients in a given row is closely related to the component we wish to test. In Fig. 10.3, we have plotted each row as a function of $X$. Note that the linear coefficients, the $\xi_{lin}$, lie on a straight line. The quadratic coefficients, the $\xi_{quad}$, lie on a symmetric U-shaped function; multiplication by $-1$ would give us the inverted U hypothesized for the generalization experiment. Sums of squares and values of test statistics are not affected by reversing the sign of the coefficients, or indeed by multiplying all coefficients by any constant.

2. As with the linear coefficients, and all the sets of contrast weights encountered in Chapter 5, the coefficients sum to zero. That is, $\sum_j \xi_{p,j} = 0$, where $\xi_{p,j}$ is the $j$th value in the $p$th row.

3. All pairs of rows are orthogonal by the definition provided in Chapter 9. Recall that a necessary condition for two sets of weights, $w_{jp}$ and $w_{jq}$, to be orthogonal

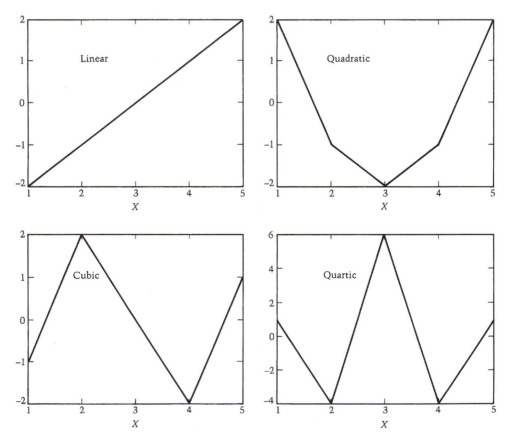

**Fig. 10.3** Examples of polynomial functions.

is that $\sum_j w_{jp} w_{jq}$ must be zero. This requirement is met for the six pairs of rows here. For example,

$$\sum_j \xi_{\text{lin},j} \xi_{\text{quad},j} = (-2)(2) + (-1)(-1) + (0)(-2) + (1)(-1) + (2)(-2) = 0$$

Using $\xi_{p,j}$, we can rewrite Equation 10.12 as a sum of orthogonal polynomial components. The advantage of this form of the polynomial function over Equation 10.12 is that it enables us to independently test the null hypothesis for each orthogonal component. The general form of this relation between the population means and the $\xi_{p,j}$ is

$$\mu_j = \beta_0' + \beta_1' \xi_{\text{lin},j} + \beta_2' \xi_{\text{quad},j} + \cdots + \beta_p' \xi_{p,j} + \cdots + \beta_{a-1}' \xi_{a-1,j} \tag{10.13}$$

Tests of null hypotheses about the population parameters follow from the developments in Chapter 9. The sums of squares for a single-degree-of-freedom contrast is the numerator of the $F$ ratio in Equation 9.19:

$$SS_{\hat{\psi}} = \frac{\left(\sum w_j \overline{Y}_{.j}\right)^2}{\sum w_j^2 / n_j}$$

Replacing the $w_j$ by values of $\xi$, we can compute the sums of squares needed to test whether various terms in Equation 10.13 contribute to the variability among the group means. To test $H_0$: $\beta_p' = 0$, calculate

$$SS_{p(A)} = \frac{\sum_j (\xi_{p,j} \overline{Y}_{.j})^2}{\sum_j \xi_{p,j}^2 / n} \tag{10.14}$$

For example, to test whether there is a quadratic component contributing to the population GSR function, calculate

$$SS_{\text{quad}(A)} = \frac{[(2)(1.91) + (-1)(3.56) + \cdots + (2)(3.83)]^2}{[2^2 + (-1)^2 + \cdots + 2^2]/10} = 14.723$$

Table 10.2 presents the ANOVA, including tests of all four possible components of $SS_A$. Several points should be noted. First, note that the polynomial sums of squares are all tested against the $MS_{S/A}$. That is,

$$F = SS_{p(A)} / MS_{S/A} \tag{10.15}$$

**TABLE 10.2**   TREND ANALYSIS OF THE MEANS OF TABLE 10.1

| SV | | df | SS | MS | F |
|---|---|---|---|---|---|
| A | | 4 | 35.241 | 8.811 | 3.90* |
| | lin(A) | 1 | 14.900 | 14.900 | 6.60** |
| | quad(A) | 1 | 14.722 | 14.722 | 6.52** |
| | cubic(A) | 1 | 3.534 | 3.534 | 1.57 |
| | quart(A) | 1 | 2.085 | 2.085 | 0.92 |
| S/A | | 45 | 101.565 | 2.257 | |

*p < .05; **p < .01.

Second, considering the *SS* column, note that the four sums of squares corresponding to the polynomial components sum to $SS_A$. This is because, as discussed earlier in this section, the $\xi_p$ are orthogonal coefficients. Consequently, the corresponding sums of squares are nonoverlapping sources of variability and together account for the total variability among the means. Keep in mind, however, that this holds only if the $n_j$ are equal and the values of $X$ are equally spaced. As we see in Chapter 20, orthogonal partitioning of the $SS_A$ is possible when these conditions are not met but the values in Appendix Table C.6 are no longer appropriate.

The third point to note about Table 10.2 is that only the linear and quadratic components of $SS_A$ are significant. We reject the null hypotheses

$$H_0: \beta_1' = 0 \quad \text{and} \quad H_0: \beta_2' = 0$$

and we fail to reject the null hypotheses

$$H_0: \beta_3' = 0 \quad \text{and} \quad H_0: \beta_4' = 0$$

This is consistent with our theory about the shape of the generalization function; the best-fitting straight line has a slope greater than zero, indicating that response magnitude increases with the magnitude of the test stimulus, and there is a quadratic component reflecting stimulus generalization. The results of the significance test lead us to conclude that these are the only two processes at work; linear and quadratic components appear adequate to describe the variation among the group means. We conclude that, for this population and these stimulus values, the mean GSR is best described by

$$\mu_j = \beta_0' + \beta_1' \xi_{\text{lin},j} + \beta_2' \xi_{\text{quad},j}$$

In many studies, it is informative to plot the estimated population function. To do this, we must first calculate the values of the $b_p'$. The $\beta_p'$ are estimated by

$$b_0' = \overline{Y}.. \tag{10.16}$$

and, for $p > 0$,

$$b_p' = \frac{\sum\limits_{j} \xi_{p,j} \overline{Y}_{.j}}{\sum\limits_{j} \xi_{p,j}^2} \tag{10.17}$$

For example, the quadratic coefficient, $b_2'$, would be calculated as follows. First, we find the values of $\xi_{2,j}$ from Appendix Table C.6; when there are five groups, these are 2, −1, −2, −1, 2. Then, substituting these values and the group means into Equation 10.17, we have

$$b_2' = \frac{(2)(1.91) + (-1)(3.56) + \cdots + (2)(3.83)}{2^2 + (-1)^2 + \cdots + 2^2}$$

$$= \frac{-4.54}{14} = -.324$$

Because our data provide evidence only for the contributions of linear and quadratic components, we calculate only $b_0'$, $b_1'$, and $b_2'$. Table 10.3 presents their values, the values of $b_1' \xi_{\text{lin},j}$ and $b_2' \xi_{\text{quad},j}$ (the estimates of the components of the population function), and the predicted values for each group. The predicted value for group $j$ is obtained by adding $b_0'$,

**TABLE 10.3** REGRESSION COEFFICIENTS AND SIGNIFICANT COMPONENTS OF FIG. 10.2

| Component | $b'_p$ | $b'_p \xi_{p,1}$ | $b'_p \xi_{p,2}$ | $b'_p \xi_{p,3}$ | $b'_p \xi_{p,4}$ | $b'_p \xi_{p,5}$ |
|---|---|---|---|---|---|---|
| | | | $b'_0 (\overline{Y}..) = 3.464$ | | | |
| Linear | 0.386 | −0.772 | −0.386 | 0 | 0.386 | 0.772 |
| Quadratic | −0.324 | −0.649 | 0.324 | 0.649 | 0.324 | −0.649 |
| Pred. value | | 2.043 | 3.462 | 4.113 | 4.174 | 3.587 |

*Note.* The predicted value is the sum of the grand mean and the linear and quadratic components of the observed function. The value of $b'_p$ is computed by using Equation 10.6, and the values of the $\xi'_{p,j}$ are obtained from Appendix Table C.6. For example, $b'_{\text{lin}}\xi_{\text{lin},1}$ is $(.386)(-2)$; $-2$ is the linear coefficient for the first group.

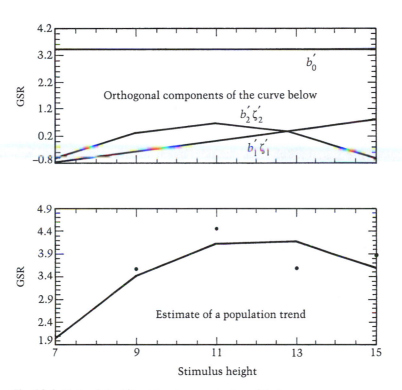

**Fig. 10.4** Plots of significant trend components and their sum.

$b'_1\xi_{\text{lin},j}$, and $b'_2\xi_{\text{quad},j}$. For example, the value predicted for the group tested with the 7-in. stimulus (Group 1) would be $3.464 + (-.772) + (-.649) = 2.043$.

The grand mean ($b'_0$) of the 50 scores, and the linear and quadratic components of Table 10.3, are plotted in the upper panel of Fig. 10.4; they have been summed in the bottom panel to provide our best estimate of the shape of the population function. If we included the cubic and quartic components as well, the points representing the observed group means would fall on the resulting curve. However, our significance tests indicate that these two components do not reflect real trends in the population. Therefore, the deviations of the five group means about the function plotted in the bottom panel are attributed to chance variability, and the plotted function is our best estimate of the true population function.

### 10.3.3 Strategies in Testing Trend

We generally prefer to carry out the minimum number of significance tests required to evaluate our theory. When more polynomial components are tested, the probability of a Type 1 error increases unless a procedure such as the Dunn–Bonferroni (described in Chapter 9) procedure is used to control it. However, in that case, the fewer tests performed, the greater the power each has to detect true contributions to the population function. Therefore, although we have presented $F$ tests for each of the four possible polynomial components in our example, in practice we would perform only three tests. Because our theory predicted linear and quadratic effects, and no polynomial contribution beyond these, we would test the linear and quadratic components, as indicated earlier. In addition, to determine whether the hypothesized components are sufficient to account for the pattern of the $a$ means, we would also test the residual between-groups ($A$) variability; the numerator sum of squares for this test is calculated simply as

$$SS_{A\,res} = SS_A - (SS_{lin} + SS_{quad})$$

and $MS_{A\,res} = SS_{A\,res}/df_{A\,res}$, where $df = (a - 1) - 2$ in our example. If $MS_{A\,res}$ is significant when tested against $MS_{S/A}$, we have evidence that one or more of the polynomial components included in $SS_{A\,res}$ (the cubic and quartic components in our example) is contributing to the $A$ effects. This significant result may be followed by tests of the components of the residual term if the outcome of such tests will help us reformulate our theory. In practice, however, cubic and higher-order terms usually are difficult to interpret.

## 10.4 CONCLUDING REMARKS

Trend analysis is a powerful tool for analyzing functional relations among variables. However, it is important to keep in mind that, when variables have fixed effects, trend analysis provides statistical support only for conclusions about levels of the manipulated variable that were included in the experiment. For example, conclusions about the shape of the generalization function in our example hold only for the values of stimulus height in the experiment. Would the function in Fig. 10.1 decline further or level off if heights greater than 15 had been included? We might infer the answer to questions such as this by using our knowledge of the variables, theoretical considerations, and results of other studies. However, such extrapolation beyond the stimulus levels in the current experiment has a different status than the statistical inferences based on the stimulus levels in the study. The best advice is to include in the study the range of variables that are of possible interest, and to include a sufficient number of levels within that range to provide a good sense of the shape of the function.

Another concern is the routine application of trend analysis whenever one or more independent variables are quantitative. Any set of $a$ data points can be fitted by a polynomial of order $a - 1$, but if the population function is not a polynomial (e.g., a sine curve, or an exponential function), the polynomial analysis can be misleading. It is also dangerous to freely identify significant components with psychological processes. It is one thing to hypothesize a cubic component of a variable, to then test for its contribution, and to find it significant, thus substantiating the theory. It is another matter to assign psychological meaning to a significant component that has not been hypothesized prior to the collection of data. An unexpected significant component should be of interest and should alert the researcher to the possible need to reexamine the hypotheses that led to the study. However, such a result should be viewed with even more than the usual skepticism until validated by further research. If these caveats are kept in mind, trend analysis can be a powerful tool for establishing the true shapes of data functions. As such, this method of analysis should accompany the development of precise quantitative behavioral hypotheses.

## KEY CONCEPTS

| | |
|---|---|
| linear trend | intercept |
| linear regression coefficient | trend analysis |
| predicted group means | orthogonal polynomials |
| polynomial function of order $a - 1$ | quadratic coefficient |
| cubic coefficient | quartic coefficient |

## EXERCISES

**10.1**  Four groups of 8 participants each are tested on a problem; time to solve is the dependent variable. The independent variable is the number of previous practice problems. The group means are

| Previous problems: | 1 | 2 | 3 | 4 |
|---|---|---|---|---|
| Mean time: | 6.49 | 4.82 | 4.25 | 3.80 |

The average within-group variance is 1.42.
  (a) Calculate the value of $b_1$, the least-squares linear regression coefficient defined by Equation 10.2.
  (b) Using the result in part (a), calculate the predicted mean for each of the four groups.
  (c) (i) Use Equation 10.6 to calculate $SS_{lin}$. (ii) Redo the calculations by using Equation 10.8, the single degree of freedom formula for a contrast. Carry out the significance test. (iii) What would a significant $F$ ratio tell us about the results of this experiment?

**10.2**  (a) Are the means in Exercise 10.1 adequately described by a straight line? Present evidence to justify your response.
  (b) A somewhat different test of $SS_{lin}$ than that we present here has been proposed on several occasions. The procedure is to test $SS_{lin}$ against $MS_{residual}$; $SS_{residual} = SS_{tot} - SS_{lin}$, $df_{residual} = (an - 1) - 1$, and $MS_{residual} = SS_{residual}/df_{residual}$. What is the underlying assumption of this test procedure? What are its potential advantages and disadvantages?

**10.3**  In a study of the effects of group problem solving, group size $= 2, 3, 4$, or $5$. Professor Smith believes that "the more the merrier" and predicts that scores will increase as size increases. Professor Brown believes that "there can be too much of a good thing"

and predicts that scores will improve and then drop as size increases. There are five groups in each size condition, and each group attempts 10 problems. The dependent variable is the number each group gets correct. The means and standard deviations for each size condition are

$$
\begin{array}{lcccc}
\text{Size} = 2 & 3 & 4 & 5 \\
\text{Mean} = 2.8 & 4.6 & 7.4 & 6.0 \\
s = 3.578 & 1.788 & 1.720 & 1.414
\end{array}
$$

Do a trend analysis. Which prediction do the results support?

**10.4**  (a) Equation 10.15, defining the $F$ ratio for testing polynomial terms, may be rewritten so that its square root is the ratio of the polynomial coefficient to its standard error $(SE)$. The square root of that $F$ ratio is a $t$ statistic. That is,

$$
t = \frac{b'_p}{\sqrt{MS_{S/A}/n \sum_j \xi_{j,p}^2}}
$$

Use this equation to test linear trend and confirm that the resulting $t$ is the square root of the $F$ ratio computed in Exercise 10.3.

(b) Find the .95 CI for $b'_1$.

(c) Convert this into a CI for $b_1$, the slope of the line that best fits $Y$ as a function of $X$.

**10.5**  A method used in some memory studies involves requiring participants to respond yes or no within a predetermined interval to a probe of memory. For example, Corbett and Wicklegren (1978) presented the name of a category (e.g., *bird*) for 2 seconds, and then a second word (e.g., *robin*); participants then had $s$ seconds to respond as to whether the second word was a member of the category. One mathematical model predicts that, as $s$ increases, accuracy should at first be flat, then increase, and finally flatten out again. Although experiments using this deadline procedure are usually run as within-subject designs, we will assume that there are seven groups of six subjects, each of which are tested with a different response interval, ranging from 0.2 seconds to 1.4 in intervals of 0.2.

(a) Which trend component(s) should be significant?

(b) The file Ex10_5 contains the scores. The independent variable is Time and the dependent variable is d_prime $(d')$, a measure of accuracy. Test for the trend component(s) you listed in answer to part (a). Also test whether any other component(s) are significant.

**10.6**  For the data in the Ex10_5 file, construct a plot based only on the significant components (see Fig. 10.4). What does this plot represent?

**10.7**  The file Ex10_7 contains a data set from a hypothetical drug experiment. The four levels of the factor $A$ represent drug dosages in milligrams. The dependent variable $Y$ is a performance measure.

(a) Plot the means of the $Y$ data against the levels of $A$; include standard error bars.

(b) Perform an ANOVA (analysis of variance) on the data, including tests of each of the three polynomial components of $A$.

(c) Discuss the results of part (b) with respect to the plot of the means.

**10.8**  The concept of orthogonal components may be clarified by further analysis of the data in the Ex10_7 file.

(a) Using Equations 10.16 and 10.17, calculate $b'_3$. Then, calculate the cubic component for each group, $b'_3 \xi_{cubic}$. Call this *cubic*. The $\xi_{cubic}$ values can be obtained from Appendix Table C.6.

(b) Subtract each cubic value calculated in part (a) from the $Y$ scores in the corresponding group. Call the result $V$. Find $SS_A$ for the dependent variable, $V$. How is this quantity related to the results of the ANOVA in Exercise 10.8?

(c) Calculate the linear and quadratic sums of squares for the $V$ variable. Compare the results with those in part (c) of Exercise 10.7.

# Chapter 11

## Multifactor Between-Subjects Designs: Significance Tests in the Two-Way Case

## 11.1 INTRODUCTION

In this chapter, we extend the between-subjects design of Chapter 8 to include a second factor. In an example of this design, Wiley and Voss (1999) had 64 students read about the Irish potato famine of the first half of the 19th century. One factor was the format: whether the material was presented in a single textbooklike chapter (text format) or divided among eight sources in a computer weblike (web format) environment. A second factor was the instructions participants received; they were told to either write a narrative ($N$), a summary ($S$), an explanation ($E$), or an argument ($A$) about what produced changes in Ireland's population between 1800 and 1850. In summary, the experiment was a $2 \times 4$ ("two by four") design involving two types of format (text or web) and four types of instructions (narrative, summary, explanation, or argument). The 64 participants were assigned randomly to the eight cells with the restriction that there were 8 participants in each cell.

Including several factors within the same experiment allows us to use one data set to investigate several issues. In the Wiley–Voss study, the researchers wanted to test whether the argument instruction promoted "more conceptual understanding" as evidenced by the effects of instructions on writing, inference, and analogy tasks. They also were interested in whether the more difficult web format, which forced readers to integrate material obtained from several sources, would lead to a deeper understanding. Another focus of the experiment was the **interaction** of format and instructions; the researchers were interested in whether any difference between the effects of the argument instruction and the other instructions would vary depending on the format.

In the next section, we view tables and graphs summarizing one of the measures from the Wiley–Voss study. Those data will then be used to illustrate the ANOVA (analysis of variance) and several possible follow-up tests for a two-factor design. This is followed by a more formal development of the model underlying the analysis. Chapter 12 continues the development of multifactor designs. Topics in that chapter include analyses of effect size and power, problems raised when cell frequencies are unequal, alternative structural models, and matching participants on a concomitant variable. Chapter 12 also extends previous developments to designs involving more than two factors.

## 11.2 A FIRST LOOK AT THE DATA

### 11.2.1 Summary Statistics

Wiley and Voss tested readers' understanding of the material in several ways, one of which was a 10-item inference verification test (IVT). Table 11.1 presents the percent correct IVT scores, together with cell and marginal means, and cell variances. Looking at the marginal format means in the rightmost column, we observe that performance for the web format ($\overline{Y}_{web}$) was better than that for the text format ($\overline{Y}_{text}$). We will soon consider whether this difference reflects a difference in the means of populations tested under these conditions, or whether it is caused by chance. Looking at the cell means, we see that the difference in the marginal means seems largely due to the argument ($A$) instructional condition; although

**TABLE 11.1**   IVT SCORES, WITH SUMMARY STATISTICS

| Format | Instructions[a] | | | | |
|---|---|---|---|---|---|
| | $N$ | $S$ | $E$ | $A$ | |
| Text | 70 | 50 | 70 | 70 | |
| | 80 | 90 | 80 | 70 | |
| | 80 | 60 | 70 | 60 | |
| | 70 | 80 | 60 | 60 | |
| | 60 | 70 | 60 | 70 | |
| | 50 | 80 | 80 | 90 | |
| | 80 | 80 | 70 | 90 | |
| | 80 | 70 | 60 | 80 | |
| $\overline{Y}_{text,k} =$ | 71.25 | 72.5 | 68.75 | 73.75 | $\overline{Y}_{text} = 71.56$ |
| $s^2_{text,k} =$ | 126.79 | 164.29 | 69.64 | 141.07 | |
| Web | 100 | 70 | 60 | 100 | |
| | 80 | 70 | 60 | 90 | |
| | 60 | 80 | 80 | 100 | |
| | 60 | 50 | 80 | 80 | |
| | 60 | 90 | 80 | 90 | |
| | 70 | 60 | 60 | 100 | |
| | 90 | 100 | 80 | 70 | |
| | 90 | 70 | 80 | 90 | |
| $\overline{Y}_{web,k} =$ | 76.25 | 73.75 | 72.5 | 90 | $\overline{Y}_{web} = 78.1$ |
| $s^2_{web,k} =$ | 255.36 | 255.36 | 107.14 | 114.29 | |
| | $\overline{Y}_N = 73.75$ | $\overline{Y}_S = 73.13$ | $\overline{Y}_E = 70.63$ | $\overline{Y}_A = 81.88$ | |
| | | $\overline{Y}_{...} = 74.84$ | | | |

*Note.* $N$ = narrative, $S$ = summary, $E$ = explanation, and $A$ = argument.

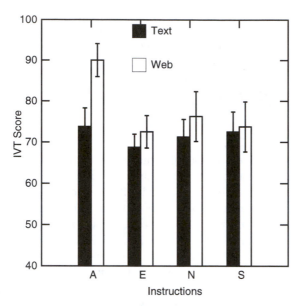

**Fig. 11.1** Bar graph of the Wiley–Voss (1999) IVT data.

the web format has a higher mean than the text format in all instructional conditions, the differences between web and text cell means are small except in the *A* column. Turning next to the marginal instructional means ($\overline{Y}_N$, $\overline{Y}_S$, $\overline{Y}_E$, and $\overline{Y}_A$), we find the IVT mean to be higher in the argument condition than in any of the others. Again, however, we must qualify this; looking at the cell means in the two format conditions, we see that the advantage of the argument condition is apparently quite pronounced for the web format, but rather small in the text format. Whether we view the data as showing that the difference between format means depends on instructions, or as showing that the differences among instruction means depend on format, we are concerned with an interaction of format and instructions. This is clearer in the bar graph of Fig. 11.1. Although web learning has an advantage in all four instructional conditions, that advantage is clearly more pronounced in the *A* condition than in any of the other three.

Table 11.1 also reports the cell variances. In three of the four instructional conditions, the variance is larger in the web than in the text condition. However, the cell frequencies are equal and the ratio of smallest to largest variance is less than 4, suggesting that the inequality of variances may not seriously violate the ANOVA's homogeneity of variance assumption. Another index of variability is provided by the lines projecting from the top of each bar in Fig. 11.1; these indicate the standard errors (*SE*) of the cell means. Consistent with our conclusion based on Table 11.1, the variation in the heights of the *SE* lines appears slight. We next consider this further, armed with graphic displays and the results of a test of the null hypothesis of equality of spread.

### 11.2.2 Evaluating the Validity of Assumptions

Ultimately, we wish to conduct tests of null hypotheses about the population means. As stated in the preceding chapters, the distributions of the *F* and *t* statistics are derived under

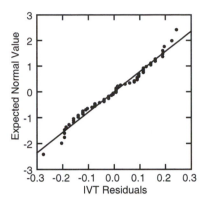

**Fig. 11.2** Normal probability plot of the Wiley–Voss IVT residuals.

assumptions of independence, normality, and homogeneity of variance. We examine those assumptions for the IVT data, and we also check for the presence of any outliers that might be responsible for the apparent superiority of the $A$/web condition. Given that participants in the study were randomly assigned to conditions, there is no reason to suspect a violation of the independence assumption. The normality assumption may not hold because the scores tend to be high and the upper tail will tend to be truncated by the ceiling of 100. However, as we discussed in Chapters 6 and 8, computer-sampling studies indicate that Type 1 error rates are not usually greatly affected by departures from normality. To be sure that the departure from normality is not severe, we used the SPSS software to plot the $z$ scores expected under the normality assumption against residuals (the residual is the difference between a score and its cell mean). This normal probability plot is presented in Fig. 11.2. The advantage of using residuals, which are available in most statistical packages, is that the effects of experimental treatments are removed from the data. As we discussed in Chapter 2, if the data are perfectly fit by a normal distribution, the points fall on a straight line. In fact, the points, although not all on the line, fall quite close. We also used SPSS's Explore module to apply the Kolmogorov–Smirnov test of normality to the residual distribution of 64 scores; the result was a nonsignificant $p$ value of .20.

What about the possibility of heterogeneous variances? In viewing Table 11.1, we saw indications that the population variances might not be equal. However, none of the set of four test results provided by SPSS's Explore module resulted in a $p$ value less than .39. The Brown–Forsythe test (Brown & Forsythe, 1974a), recommended in Chapter 7, yielded an $F$ on 7 and 56 $df$ of .692. Apparently, the differences in the variances of the eight groups are no more than we would expect by chance, assuming the population variances are equal.

We also checked the data for outliers. Figure 11.3 presents box plots of the data in the eight cells. There are no outliers using the criterion defined in Chapter 2. Therefore, we doubt that the apparent advantage of the $A$/web condition is due to a deviant score either increasing that mean, or lowering other means. This conclusion is supported by finding that the pattern of the medians is similar to that for the means: as with the means, it is the $A$/web condition that seems most deviant.[1]

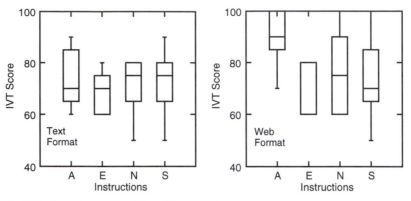

**Fig. 11.3** Box plots of the Wiley–Voss IVT data.

## 11.3 TWO-FACTOR DESIGNS: THE ANOVA

In this section, we discuss the nature of main and interaction effects in data from a two-factor completely randomized design, and we develop the ANOVA (analysis of variance) to test those effects. In these designs, there are two independent variables, $A$ and $B$, with $a$ levels of $A$, $b$ levels of $B$, and $n$ scores in each of the $ab$ cells. We represent a score as $Y_{ijk}$, the $i$th score at the $j$th level of $A$ and the $k$th level of $B$. We begin by considering the decomposition of $Y_{ijk}$ into several components, and then we build on this to develop the partitioning of sums of squares. Throughout the section, we use the Wiley–Voss IVT scores to illustrate developments. In this example, we index the levels of format by $j(j = 1$ or 2, corresponding to text or web), and the levels of instruction by $k(k = 1, 2, 3,$ or 4, corresponding to $N$, $S$, $E$, or $A$). The cell frequency, $n$, is 8 and the total number of scores, $abn$ or $N$, is 64.

### 11.3.1 Components of the Scores

In the one-factor design of Chapter 8, we viewed a score as consisting of three components: the grand mean, the treatment main effect, and a residual, or error, component. We represented this by

$$Y_{ij} = \overline{Y}_{..} + (\overline{Y}_{.j} - \overline{Y}_{..}) + (Y_{ij} - \overline{Y}_{.j})$$
$$\text{score} = \text{grand mean} + \text{treatment effect} + \text{residual} \tag{11.1}$$

Subtracting the grand mean from both sides, we have

$$(Y_{ij} - \overline{Y}_{..}) = (\overline{Y}_{.j} - \overline{Y}_{..}) + (Y_{ij} - \overline{Y}_{.j})$$
$$\text{score} - \text{grand mean} = \text{treatment effect} + \text{residual} \tag{11.2}$$

Equation 11.2 provides the basis for the partitioning of the total sum of squares ($SS_{\text{tot}}$), and therefore for the ANOVA. By squaring and summing each component, we saw that the total sum of squares equaled the between-groups sum of squares plus the within-groups sum of squares. That is,

$$\sum_j \sum_i (Y_{ij} - \overline{Y}_{..})^2 = n \sum_j (\overline{Y}_{.j} - \overline{Y}_{..})^2 + \sum_j \sum_i (Y_{ij} - \overline{Y}_{.j})^2$$

$$\quad SS_{\text{tot}} \quad = \quad SS_A \quad + \quad SS_{S/A} \tag{11.3}$$

In the two-factor design, we can also view a score as consisting of the three components of Equation 11.2. In a manner similar to that of Equation 11.2, we could write

$$(Y_{ijk} - \overline{Y}_{...}) \quad = (\overline{Y}_{.jk} - \overline{Y}_{...}) + (Y_{ijk} - \overline{Y}_{.jk})$$

$$\text{score} - \text{grand mean} = \quad \text{cell effect} \quad + \quad \text{residual} \tag{11.4}$$

where a cell is the combination of a level of $A$ and a level of $B$; for example, the combination of narrative instructions and text format ($N$/text) is one of eight cells in the Wiley–Voss design.

The **residual**, the deviation of a score from its cell mean, reflects chance, or error, variability; a subject's score differs from those of other people in the same cell, and therefore from the average for that cell, because of individual differences or random variation within the experimental conditions. The variance of these residuals is the error term in the ANOVA, our best estimate of chance, or error, variance in the $ab$ treatment populations. The **cell effect**, the deviation of the cell mean from the grand mean, may be decomposed further into components that reflect the questions of interest to the researcher. In the Wiley–Voss example, the cell deviation can be partitioned into a format component, an instruction component, and a third component reflecting the interaction of format and instruction. The format and instruction components of this effect are **main effects**, and the interaction component is the **interaction effect**. On occasion, we refer to some variable such as format as having a significant effect (or a significant main effect). More precisely, we mean that the population effects at the levels of the variable are not all zero or, equivalently, that the population means at these levels are not all the same. The relation of the cell effect to the main and interaction effects is

$$(\overline{Y}_{.jk} - \overline{Y}_{...}) = (\overline{Y}_{.j.} - \overline{Y}_{...}) + (\overline{Y}_{..k} - \overline{Y}_{...}) + (\overline{Y}_{.jk} - \overline{Y}_{.j.} - \overline{Y}_{..k} + \overline{Y}_{...})$$

$$\text{cell effect} = \text{main effect} + \text{main effect of} + \quad \text{interaction effect} \tag{11.5}$$

$$\text{of } A \text{ (format)} \quad B \text{ (instructions)}$$

Equation 11.5 provides one way of thinking about the interaction effect; if we subtract the two main effect terms from both sides, we find that the interaction is what remains of the cell effect after the main effects have been subtracted.

Substituting the right side of Equation 11.5 for the cell effect in Equation 11.4, we have the basis for the ANOVA:

$$(Y_{ijk} - \overline{Y}_{...}) = (\overline{Y}_{.j.} - \overline{Y}_{...}) + (\overline{Y}_{..k} - \overline{Y}_{...}) + (\overline{Y}_{.jk} - \overline{Y}_{.j.} - \overline{Y}_{..k} + \overline{Y}_{...}) + (Y_{ijk} - \overline{Y}_{.jk})$$

$$\tag{11.6}$$

In words,

$$\text{score} - \text{grand mean} = \text{main effect of } A \text{ (format)} + \text{main effect of } B \text{ (text)}$$

$$+ \text{interaction effect (format} \times \text{text)} + \text{residual}$$

Table 11.2 displays a breakdown of the IVT scores into the components of Equation 11.6. For example, the value $-4.844$ in the $N$ column of the top row of the scores$-$grand mean panel is the sum of the corresponding values in each of the panels on the right; that is,

$$70 - 74.844 = (-3.281) + (-1.094) + (.781) + (-1.25)$$

**TABLE 11.2**  A BREAKDOWN OF THE IVT SCORES FROM THE WILEY–VOSS EXPERIMENT

| Format | $N$ | $S$ | $E$ | $A$ |
|--------|-----|-----|-----|-----|
| | Scores $-$ Grand Mean $(Y_{ijk} - \overline{Y}_{...})$ | | | |
| Text | $-4.844$ | $-24.844$ | $-4.844$ | $-4.844$ |
| | $5.156$ | $15.156$ | $5.156$ | $-4.844$ |
| | $\dots$ | $\dots$ | $\dots$ | $\dots$ |
| | $5.156$ | $-4.844$ | $-14.844$ | $5.156$ |
| Web | $25.156$ | $-14.844$ | $-4.844$ | $25.156$ |
| | $5.156$ | $-4.844$ | $-14.844$ | $15.156$ |
| | $\dots$ | $\dots$ | $\dots$ | $\dots$ |
| | $15.156$ | $-4.844$ | $5.156$ | $15.156$ |
| | $=$ Format Effect $(\overline{Y}_{.j.} - \overline{Y}_{...})$ | | | |
| Text | $-3.281$ | $-3.281$ | $-3.281$ | $-3.281$ |
| | $-3.281$ | $-3.281$ | $-3.281$ | $-3.281$ |
| | $\dots$ | $\dots$ | $\dots$ | $\dots$ |
| | $-3.281$ | $-3.281$ | $-3.281$ | $-3.281$ |
| Web | $3.281$ | $3.281$ | $3.281$ | $3.281$ |
| | $3.281$ | $3.281$ | $3.281$ | $3.281$ |
| | $\dots$ | $\dots$ | $\dots$ | $\dots$ |
| | $3.281$ | $3.281$ | $3.281$ | $3.281$ |
| | $+$ Instruction Effect $(\overline{Y}_{..k} - \overline{Y}_{...})$ | | | |
| Text | $-1.094$ | $-1.719$ | $-4.219$ | $7.031$ |
| | $-1.094$ | $-1.719$ | $-4.219$ | $7.031$ |
| | $\dots$ | $\dots$ | $\dots$ | $\dots$ |
| | $-1.094$ | $-1.719$ | $-4.219$ | $7.031$ |
| Web | $-1.094$ | $-1.719$ | $-4.219$ | $7.031$ |
| | $-1.094$ | $-1.719$ | $-4.219$ | $7.031$ |
| | $\dots$ | $\dots$ | $\dots$ | $\dots$ |
| | $-1.094$ | $-1.719$ | $-4.219$ | $7.031$ |
| | $+$ Interaction $(\overline{Y}_{.jk} - \overline{Y}_{.j.} - \overline{Y}_{..k} + \overline{Y}_{...})$ | | | |
| Text | $0.781$ | $2.656$ | $1.406$ | $-4.844$ |
| | $0.781$ | $2.656$ | $1.406$ | $-4.844$ |
| | $\dots$ | $\dots$ | $\dots$ | $\dots$ |
| | $0.781$ | $2.656$ | $1.406$ | $-4.844$ |
| Web | $-0.781$ | $-2.656$ | $-1.406$ | $4.844$ |
| | $-0.781$ | $-2.656$ | $-1.406$ | $4.844$ |
| | $\dots$ | $\dots$ | $\dots$ | $\dots$ |
| | $-0.781$ | $-2.656$ | $-1.406$ | $4.844$ |

**TABLE 11.2**  (continued)

| Format | N | S | E | A |
|---|---|---|---|---|
| | | $+$ Residuals $\left(Y_{ijk} - \overline{Y}_{.jk}\right)$ | | |
| Text | −1.25 | −22.50 | 1.25 | −3.75 |
| | 8.75 | 17.50 | 11.25 | −3.75 |
| | . . . | . . . | . . . | . . . |
| | 8.75 | −2.50 | −8.75 | 6.25 |
| Web | 23.75 | −3.75 | −12.50 | 10.00 |
| | 3.75 | −3.75 | −12.50 | 0.00 |
| | . . . | . . . | . . . | . . . |
| | 13.75 | −3.75 | 7.50 | 0.00 |

*Note.*

$$\sum_j \sum_k \sum_i (Y_{ijk} - \overline{Y}_{...})^2 = 32 \sum_j (\overline{Y}_{.j.} - \overline{Y}_{...})^2 + 16 \sum_j (\overline{Y}_{..k} - \overline{Y}_{...})^2 + 8 \sum_j \sum_k (\overline{Y}_{.jk} - \overline{Y}_{.j.} - \overline{Y}_{..k} + \overline{Y}_{...})^2$$

$$+ \sum_j \sum_k \sum_i (Y_{ijk} - \overline{Y}_{.jk})^2$$

$$SS_{tot} = SS_{format} + SS_{instructions} + SS_{format \times instructions} + SS_{S/format \times instructions}$$
$$10,998.44 = 689.06 + 1142.19 + \quad 529.69 \quad + \quad 8637.50$$

Notice that the same value, −4.844, in the *A* column in that same top row has some different components:

$$70 − 74.844 = (−3.281) + (7.031) + (−4.844) + (−3.75)$$

Each panel corresponds to a term in Equation 11.6. The grand mean (74.844) is subtracted from every score, giving rise to the values to the left of the equals sign. The format effect is −3.281 for those scores in the text condition (the top half of each panel) and 3.281 for those scores in the web condition (the bottom half of each panel). The text and web effects sum to zero because they are deviations of the text and web means from their average, the grand mean; as we pointed out in Chapter 2, the sum of deviations of scores about their average is zero. For the same reason, the four instruction effects also sum to zero, as do the interaction effects when summed over either rows or columns.

Turning to the panel representing the Instruction Effects, note that the average *N* and *S* scores are −1.094 and −1.719 below the grand mean. The *E* mean is further below the grand mean (−4.219), and the argument mean is 7.031 points above it. Although the same information could have been obtained from the means in Table 11.1, the display of effect sizes should immediately make clear that the argument instructions had a strong positive effect on the inference scores.

If Instructions and Format were the only factors (other than chance) influencing the results, the Interaction panel would have all zeros in it. However, the combinations of Instructions and Format make additional contributions to the data. As in Table 11.1 and Fig. 11.1, we see in this panel that the spread between text and web effects is greater under argument (*A*) instructions than in any of the other instructional conditions.

Finally, look at the residuals. Although, to conserve space, we have omitted many of the rows in these panels, the residuals that are displayed indicate that there is considerable error variability in the data. We see absolute values as large as 23.50 and as small as zero. Such variability of the residual terms is informative. On one hand, if there is considerable variability, effects that appear large may be due to chance. On the other hand, if the effects are not due to chance, the power of the hypothesis test may be low because of the large error variability. In general, when there is considerable error variability, we can be less confident about how to interpret nonsignificant effects.

## 11.3.2 The ANOVA Table

If we square each of the 64 values of $Y_{ijk} - \overline{Y}_{...}$ in Table 11.2, and then sum those squared quantities, we have $SS_{tot}$, a measure of the total variability in the data set. Similarly, squaring each of the 64 terms in each panel to the right of the equals sign and summing results in a component of the total sum of squares. For example, consider the Instructions Effects. Squaring the values of each of the four effects ($-1.094$, $-1.719$, $-4.29$, and $7.031$) and then multiplying by 16 yields $SS_{instructions}$. The equations at the bottom of Table 11.2 demonstrate the partitioning of sums of squares, and the parallel to the decomposition of scores.

Table 11.3 presents the ANOVA of the data of Table 11.1. Formulas for degrees of freedom and $SS$ have been presented, assuming $a$ texts and $b$ instructions; numerical values based on the IVT data are presented with these formulas. The **sources of variance (SV)**

**TABLE 11.3**   ANOVA OF THE WILEY–VOSS DATA

| SV | df | SS | MS | F |
|---|---|---|---|---|
| Total | $abn - 1 = 63$ | $\sum_{j}^{a}\sum_{k}^{b}\sum_{i}^{n}(Y_{ijk} - \overline{Y}_{...})^2$ $= 10{,}998.44$ | | |
| Between cells | $ab - 1 = 7$ | $n\sum_{j}^{a}\sum_{k}^{b}(\overline{Y}_{.jk} - \overline{Y}_{...})^2$ $= 2{,}360.94$ | | |
| Format ($F$) | $a - 1 = 1$ | $nb\sum_{j}^{a}(\overline{Y}_{.j.} - \overline{Y}_{...})^2$ $= 689.06$ | $\dfrac{SS_F}{df_F} = 689.06$ | $\dfrac{MS_F}{MS_{S/FI}} = 4.47^a$ |
| Instructions ($I$) | $b - 1 = 3$ | $na\sum_{k}^{b}(\overline{Y}_{..k.} - \overline{Y}_{...})^2$ $= 1{,}142.19$ | $\dfrac{SS_I}{df_I} = 380.73$ | $\dfrac{MS_I}{MS_{S/FI}} = 2.47^b$ |
| FI | $(a-1)(b-1) = 3$ | $SS_{cells} - SS_F - SS_I$ $= 529.69$ | $\dfrac{SS_{FI}}{df_{FI}} = 176.56$ | $\dfrac{MS_{FI}}{MS_{S/FI}} = 1.14^c$ |
| S/FI | $ab(n-1) = 56$ | $SS_{tot} - SS_{cells}$ $= 8{,}637.50$ | $\dfrac{SS_{S/FI}}{df_{S/FI}} = 154.24$ | |

$^a p = .039;\ ^b p = .071;\ ^c p = .337.$

reflect, first, the partitioning of the total variability into a between-cell ($SS_{cells}$) and a within-cell ($SS_{S/FI}$) component, and, second, the further partitioning of the between-cell component into the Main and Interaction Effects of Table 11.2. These SV then dictate the values of the degrees of freedom. The variability among cell means is based on 7 $df$ because deviations are calculated for eight cell means about the grand mean of the 64 scores. The between-cell variability usually is not of interest in itself because it has several possible sources. The eight cell means may differ because they represent different formats, different instructions, or different combinations of formats and instructions. There is 1 $df$ for the Format SV because the mean of the 32 scores from the text condition is compared with the mean of the 32 scores for the web condition. Similarly, there are 3 $df$ for the Instruction SV because it represents the variance of the four instruction means about the grand mean. Calculating the $SS_{FI}$ involves taking deviations of cell means about the grand mean, and removing the variability caused by Format and Instruction; therefore, the 7 $df$ for the cells SV are reduced by 1 (Format) and 3 (Instruction), leaving 3 $df$ for the Format × Instruction interaction. In general, if there are $a$ levels of a variable, $A$, and $b$ levels of $B$, the interaction degrees of freedom are

$$df_{AB} = (ab - 1) - (a - 1) - (b - 1) = (a - 1)(b - 1)$$

reflecting the adjustment of cell variability for the variability caused by $A$ and $B$. In practice, we can generate the degrees of freedom for an interaction just by multiplying the degrees of freedom for the interacting variables.

The $df_{S/AB}$ may be thought of as the difference between $df_{tot}$ and $df_{cells}$; in our example, this is $63 - 7$, or 56. We can also view these degrees of freedom as the result of summing the degrees of freedom for variability within each cell; there are $ab$ cells, each with $n - 1$ $df$, yielding $ab(n - 1)$ $df$, which is $8 \times 7$ in our example. The two ways of thinking about degrees of freedom, as a difference between the total degrees of freedom and the cell degrees of freedom, or as a sum over cells, are equivalent; that is,

$$df_{AB} = (abn - 1) - (ab - 1) = ab(n - 1)$$

The $SS$ formulas in Table 11.3 are essentially instructions to operate on the effects in Table 11.2. These formulas were first presented in that table and were used to calculate the numerical values in Table 11.3. Note that, just as the various deviation scores in Table 11.2 summed to $Y_{ijk} - \overline{Y}_{...}$, the corresponding sums of squares sum to the $SS_{tot}$. The formulas presented in Table 11.3 define the sums of squares and therefore should provide a sense of the variability represented by each term. We calculated the results in Table 11.3 by using SPSS; other statistical packages such as SAS, SYSTAT, or BMDP would have done as well. In the absence of suitable software, a calculator that has a variance key can quickly provide the desired results. For example, the $SS_{tot}$ is $abn - 1$ times the variance of all the scores, the $SS_A$ is $bn(a - 1)$ times the variance of the $A$ marginal means, and the $SS_{cells}$ is $n(ab - 1)$ times the variance of the $ab$ cell means.

As in the one-factor design, the $MS$ of Table 11.3 are ratios of $SS$ to degrees of freedom. Conceptually, however, the mean squares for the main effects are simple functions of variances. For example, $MS_I$ is the variance of the four marginal means in the instructional conditions, multiplied by 16, the number of scores on which each mean is based. The error mean square, $MS_{S/FI}$, is an average of the within-cell variances; we can calculate it as

$$MS_{S/FI} = \left(\frac{1}{ab}\right) \sum_j \sum_k s_{jk}^2$$

where $s_{jk}^2$ is the variance of the $n$ scores in the cell defined by $A_j$ and $B_k$. All three $F$ ratios are formed by using the $MS_{S/FI}$ in the denominator. For example, the $F$ ratio for the Format SV is $689.06/154.24$, which equals $4.47$. The reason for this choice of denominator follows from the discussion of expected mean squares (EMS) in Chapter 8. Under the assumptions presented there, if the means of the text and web populations do not differ, both $MS_F$ and $MS_{S/FI}$ estimate the population error variance, $\sigma_e^2$. Therefore, forming a ratio of these two mean squares follows the rule that the numerator and denominator $MS$ of an $F$ ratio must have the same expectation when the null hypothesis represented by the numerator is true. The same rationale also justifies testing the Instruction and Format $\times$ Instruction mean squares against $MS_{S/FI}$. We take a closer look at the expected mean squares and the model underlying their derivation in the next section.

As the experimenters hypothesized, a significantly higher proportion of inferences were correctly verified by participants in the web than in the text format condition. To understand what this means, consider eight populations differing with respect to the type of format and instructions. The $F$ test of the Format source of variance addresses the null hypothesis that the average of the four populations of IVT scores obtained under the web format does not differ from the average of the four populations of IVT scores obtained under the text format. In terms of Table 11.1, it is the **marginal means**, $\overline{Y}_{\text{web}}$ (78.13) and $\overline{Y}_{\text{text}}$ (71.56), that differ significantly. It is important to understand that this test informs us only about the marginal means; by itself, it does not provide information about the difference between format effects at any particular level of instructions.

The experimenters also were interested in whether instructions would affect performance. They reported that the effect was "marginally significant" because the $p$ value was .07, short of the .05 level usually required for statistical significance. We pursue the question of the effect of instructions in Chapter 12, where we calculate measures of effect size, using the Wiley–Voss IVT data to illustrate such calculations for two-factor designs. We also calculate the power of the test of instructions in Chapter 12.

The $F$ test of the Format $\times$ Instructions interaction tests the null hypothesis that the effects of instructions are the same under text as under web learning. One statement of the null hypothesis of no interaction is that the difference between the text and web population means is the same under all types of instructions. This may be represented as

$$H_0: (\mu_{\text{text}, N} - \mu_{\text{web}, N}) = (\mu_{\text{text}, S} - \mu_{\text{web}, S}) = (\mu_{\text{text}, E} - \mu_{\text{web}, E}) = (\mu_{\text{text}, A} - \mu_{\text{web}, A})$$

where, for example, $\mu_{\text{text}, N}$ is the mean of the population of scores obtained under the narrative instructions and the text format. The difference between the observed text and web means under argument ($A$) instructions appears considerably larger than the other differences, as evidenced in the means of Table 11.1 and the bar graph of Fig. 11.1, as well as by the panel displaying interaction effects in Table 11.2. Nevertheless, the $F$ test of the interaction fell well short of significance. This raises several questions. Given that the Instructions and the Format $\times$ Instructions sources of variance were not significant, is it proper to proceed with tests of contrasts related to those sources? If so, how should the families of tests be defined? How should the familywise error rate (FWE) be controlled?

What is the appropriate error term? We consider those questions later in this chapter. First, however, we take a closer look at the model underlying the ANOVA of Table 11.3.

## 11.4 THE STRUCTURAL MODEL AND EXPECTED MEAN SQUARES

The formal justification of the ANOVA of data from multifactor designs lies in a set of assumptions, including a model of the relation between the observed scores and various population parameters. To understand this **structural model**, we need to define certain population parameters. Table 11.4 defines the population means, effects based on these means, the quantities that estimate these parameters, and the EMS.

The EMS show how the population parameters may contribute to the variability in the data. Note that $\sigma_e^2$ contributes to each of the EMS. In the $A$, $B$, and $AB$ rows, there is an

**TABLE 11.4**  POPULATION PARAMETERS AND ESTIMATES, AND EMS FOR A TWO-FACTOR DESIGN

### The Model

$$Y_{ijk} = \mu + \alpha_j + \beta_k + (\alpha\beta)_{jk} + \varepsilon_{ijk}$$

where $Y_{ijk} = i$th score at the $j$th level of $A$ and the $k$th level of $B$.

| Population Means | Estimates |
|---|---|
| $\mu_{jk} =$ mean of the pop. of scores at $A_j$ and $B_k$ | $\overline{Y}_{.jk} = \sum_i \dfrac{Y_{ijk}}{n}$ |
| $\mu_{j.} = \sum_k \dfrac{\mu_{jk}}{b}$ | $\overline{Y}_{.j.} = \sum_i \sum_k \dfrac{Y_{ijk}}{nb}$ |
| $\mu_{.k} = \sum_j \dfrac{\mu_{jk}}{a}$ | $\overline{Y}_{..k} = \sum_i \sum_j \dfrac{Y_{ijk}}{na}$ |
| $\mu = \sum_j \sum_k \dfrac{\mu_{jk}}{ab}$ | $\overline{Y}_{...} = \sum_i \sum_j \sum_k \dfrac{Y_{ijk}}{nab}$ |

| SV | EMS |
|---|---|
| $A$ | $\sigma_e^2 + nb\sum_j (\mu_{j.} - \mu)^2/(a-1) = \sigma_e^2 + nb\sum_j \alpha_j^2/(a-1)$ |
| $B$ | $\sigma_e^2 + na\sum_k (\mu_{.k} - \mu)^2/(b-1) = \sigma_e^2 + na\sum_k \beta_k^2/(b-1)$ |
| $AB$ | $\sigma_e^2 + n\sum_j \sum_k (\mu_{jk} - \mu_j - \mu_k + \mu)^2/(a-1)(b-1)$ |
|  | $\quad = \sigma_e^2 + n\sum_j \sum_k (\alpha\beta)_{jk}^2/(a-1)(b-1)$ |
| $S/AB$ | $\sigma_e^2$ |

*Note.*

$\alpha_j = \mu_{j.} - \mu,\ \beta_k = \mu_{.k} - \mu$ and $(\alpha\beta)_{jk} = (\mu_{jk} - \mu) - \alpha_j - \beta_k = (\mu_{jk} - \mu_{j.} - \mu_{.k} + \mu)$

additional term involving the sum of squared population effects, multiplied by a coefficient. The coefficient is the number of scores on which each of the relevant means are based. For example, the $A$ SV reflects the variability among $a$ means that are each based on $bn$ scores, whereas the $AB$ SV involves the variability of $ab$ means that are each based on $n$ scores. $MS_{S/AB}$ is the appropriate error term for all $F$ tests because, if $H_0$ is true, the numerator and denominator $MS$ will have the same expectation, $\sigma_e^2$.

Scores obtained under the same combination of $A$ and $B$ may differ simply because they were obtained from different individuals or because of other chance factors such as variation in the time of day. These individual differences and errors of measurement contribute to $\sigma_e^2$, the error component defined in Table 11.4.

Deciding whether the variability in the scores is caused by anything more than chance variability is what the analysis is about. For example, consider the factor $A$; if it does not matter what level of $A$ is administered to subjects, the $\mu_{j.}$ would be identical and, therefore, the $\alpha_j$ would all equal zero. The $F$ test of the $A$ source of variance will evaluate the variance of the $\overline{Y}_{.j.}$; the issue is whether the variance of those means is about what one would expect on the basis of chance variability alone, or whether it is so large as to suggest that the population means, the $\mu_{j.}$, vary. An important point to keep in mind is that this test will not tell us about whether the factor $A$ has an effect at any particular level of $B$. The means being compared are each based on all $bn$ scores at a level of $A$.

In summary, variability in the data has four possible sources. These are as follows:

1. *The error component,* $\varepsilon_{ijk}$. We assume that the errors are independently and normally distributed with mean zero and variance $\sigma_e^2$, within each treatment population defined by a combination of levels of $A$ and $B$.

2. *The main effect of treatment A,* $\alpha_j$. The factor $A$ is assumed to have fixed effects; that is, the $a$ levels have been arbitrarily selected and are viewed as representing the population of levels. Then $\sum_j \alpha_j = 0$. The $F$ test of the $A$ main effect tests the null hypothesis that

$$H_0: \mu_{1.} = \mu_{2.} = \cdots = \mu_{j.} = \cdots = \mu_{a.}$$

or, equivalently,

$$H_0: \alpha_1 = \alpha_2 = \cdots = \alpha_j = \cdots = \alpha_a = 0$$

3. *The main effect of treatment B,* $\beta_k$. This is also a fixed-effect variable and so $\sum_k \beta_k = 0$. The $F$ test of the $B$ main effect tests the null hypothesis that

$$H_0: \mu_{.1} = \mu_{.2} = \cdots = \mu_{.k} = \cdots = \mu_{.b}$$

or, equivalently,

$$H_0: \beta_1 = \beta_2 = \cdots = \beta_k = \cdots = \beta_b = 0$$

4. The interaction effect of $A_j$ and $B_k$, $(\alpha\beta)_{jk}$. Because both $A$ and $B$ have fixed effects, $\sum_j (\alpha\beta)_{jk} = \sum_k (\alpha\beta)_{jk} = 0$. The relevant null hypothesis is

$$H_0: (\alpha\beta)_{11} = (\alpha\beta)_{12} = \cdots = (\alpha\beta)_{jk} = \cdots = (\alpha\beta)_{ab} = 0$$

The relations among these population parameters and the data are summarized by the structural model stated in Table 11.4.

## 11.5 MAIN EFFECT CONTRASTS

Suppose we wish to test, or construct confidence intervals (CIs) for, contrasts of the marginal instructional means in Table 11.1. Such tests follow the guidelines recommended in Chapter 9. If a set of $K$ contrasts is planned before the data are viewed, the researcher can apply any of the methods described in Chapter 9 to deal with this case (e.g., the Dunn–Bonferroni or the Dunn–Šidák methods). For example, in using the Dunn–Bonferroni method, and assuming that the FWE is .05, we see that each contrast would be tested at the .05/$K$ significance level. Such tests can be conducted whether or not the $F$ test of the main effect was significant. In contrast, if the researcher has decided to test all pairwise comparisons, then the Tukey HSD procedure would apply. Finally, if a contrast that was not planned is tested, the Scheffé criterion should be applied. In all of these cases, the appropriate test statistic for contrasts among means at various levels of the factor $B$ is

$$t = \frac{\hat{\psi}}{s_{\hat{\psi}}} = \frac{\sum_{k=1}^{b} w_k \overline{Y}_{..k}}{\sqrt{MS_{\text{error}} \left( \sum_{k=1}^{b} w_{.k}^2 / an \right)}} \tag{11.7}$$

where $\overline{Y}_{..k}$ is the average of the $an$ scores at $B_k$ and $w_{.k}$ is the weight on that mean. Alternatively, we can calculate the contrast sum of squares ($SS_{\hat{\psi}}$) and divide it by the $MS_{\text{error}}$. The resulting $F$ ratio is the square of the $t$ statistic of Equation 11.7. The numerator for this $F$ test is calculated as

$$SS\hat{\psi} = \frac{\hat{\psi}^2}{\sum_{k=1}^{b} w_{.k}^2 / an} = \frac{\left( \sum_{k=1}^{b} w_{.k} \overline{Y}_{..k} \right)^2}{\sum_{k=1}^{b} w_{.k}^2 / an} \tag{11.8}$$

In testing a contrast of the instruction means in the Wiley–Voss data set, we find that $an = 2 \times 8$, the number of scores in each instructional condition. The error mean square, $MS_{\text{error}}$, is the average within-cell variance, $MS_{S/FI}$ (154.24), if the assumption of homogeneous variances is tenable. Summary statistics and data plots will help to decide whether or not the $ab$ population variances are homogeneous. Preliminary tests, such as the Levene test or the Brown–Forsythe test, provide additional information. If there is any indication that the population variances differ—either through eyeballing the variances or because $p < .25$ in a preliminary test—we recommend calculating $MS_{\text{error}}$ as the average of only the within-cell variances corresponding to the cells involved in the contrast. Otherwise, the error term may be too small or too large, and consequently there will be too many either Type 1 or Type 2 errors.

Tests of contrasts can usually be performed by statistical software packages. However, to make clear just what is involved, we illustrate the calculations for each of the tests performed in this section. As an example of the application of Equation 11.7, assume that Wiley and Voss tested the contrast of the argument marginal mean with the average of the other three means. Then the null hypothesis is

$$H_0 : \mu_A - (1/3)(\mu_N + \mu_S + \mu_E) = 0$$

The value of the $t$ statistic is unchanged if we multiply all weights by 3, yielding integers. Using the revised weights, and the means from Table 11.1, we find that the numerator of the $t$ is

$$\hat{\psi} = (3)(81.88) - (73.75 + 73.13 + 70.63) = 28.13$$

Assuming that the eight population variances are equal, we replace $MS_{\text{error}}$ by $MS_{S/FI}$ in the denominator of Equation 11.7. The final result is

$$t = \frac{28.13}{\sqrt{(154.24\,(12/16)}} = 2.62$$

Assume that the FWE is .05 and this test was one of four planned tests. Then, with the use of the Dunn–Bonferroni method, the test is conducted with $\alpha = .05/4$, or .0125; the $t$ required for significance at this (two-tailed) alpha level, with 56 $df$, is 2.58. Because the calculated $t$ exceeds this critical value, the null hypothesis would be rejected.

If the test of the null hypothesis was selected after the data were viewed, the Scheffé criterion is applied:

$$S = \pm\sqrt{df_1 \cdot F_{FWE,df_1,df_e}}$$

where the numerator degrees of freedom, $df_1, = b - 1$ or 3 in our example, and the error degrees of freedom, $df_e, = 56$, assuming the error term is $MS_{S/FI}$. In that case, with the FWE set at .05, the critical value of $S = 3.27$, clearly larger than the $t$ statistic we calculated. Therefore, the post hoc contrast is not significant.

There was actually no need to perform the significance test because no contrast will be significant when the Scheffé criterion is used unless the omnibus $F$ test was significant. Nevertheless, the CI will provide some added information. To calculate either the Dunn–Bonferroni or the Scheffé limits, we need the $SE$ of the contrast. Because we multiplied the original weights by 3, we return to the original scale by multiplying by 1/3. Therefore, $\hat{\psi} = (1/3)(28.13) = 9.38$ and its $SE$ is $s_{\hat{\psi}} = (1/3)\sqrt{(154.24)(12/16)} = 3.59$. On the original scale, the Dunn–Bonferroni limits are

$$CI = \hat{\psi} \pm s_{\hat{\psi}}\,t_{\text{FWE}/K} = (1/3)(28.13) \pm (3.59)(2.58) = 0.11,\ 18.64$$

Replacing 2.58 by the critical value of $S$, 3.27, we find that the confidence limits for the Scheffé method are $-2.36$ and 21.11. Note that not only does the Scheffé interval include zero, indicating that the contrast is not significant but also that it is a wider interval than that obtained when the contrast had been planned. Once again, we see the price in precision of the estimate of the contrast and, by implication, power of the significance test when contrasts are not planned.

## 11.6 MORE ABOUT INTERACTION

### 11.6.1 When Effects Are Additive

Look again at Table 11.3. Consistent with the partitioning of the deviation of the cell mean from the grand mean (Table 11.2), $SS_{FI}$ can be obtained by subtracting $SS_F$ and $SS_I$ from $SS_{\text{cells}}$. In other words, the interaction sum of squares represents the variability among cell means that still remains when variability caused by the main effects of the two factors has been removed. Although this definition of interaction is correct, it is not satisfying. Ordinarily, we would like to make a statement about an interaction in terms of the plot of the original cell means. One way to develop this sort of interpretation is to consider what the data would look like if there were no interaction. When there is no interaction, the effects of the factors in the design are **additive**; each cell mean is obtained by adding the main effects to the grand mean. If the interaction components in Table 11.2 were zero, the cell means would be the sum of the grand mean and the format and instructions components. For example, in the absence of interaction effects, the mean for the scores in the text format, narrative instruction condition would be the sum of the grand mean, the text format effect, and the narrative instruction effect; that is, $74.844 + (-3.281) + (-1.094) = 70.469$. Summing the Grand Mean, the Format effects, and the Instruction effects while ignoring the Interaction panel of Table 11.2, we have the eight cell means in Table 11.5. For comparison, we have also included the observed cell means in parentheses in the Cell Means panel.

The interesting point about the "interactionless" cell means is that the difference between the web and text format is exactly 6.562 under all four sets of instructions. We may also compare the instruction means in the two formats. For example, the difference between the Summary ($S$) and Narrative ($N$) means is .625 in both the Web and the Format row. The difference between the $A$ and $E$ columns is 11.25 in both rows. The point is that *when there is no interaction*, the difference between any two row means will be the same in all columns and, equivalently, the difference between any two column means will be the same in all rows. The point should be clear in Fig. 11.4, which contains a plot of two functions, one for the web and one for the text format.[2] These lines, based on the cell means with no interaction effects, are parallel. Of course, no sets of means based on real data will ever be exactly parallel; however, *interaction is a significant departure from parallelism.*

**TABLE 11.5**   WILEY–VOSS CELL MEANS WHEN INTERACTION EFFECTS ARE REMOVED FROM THE DATA

| Format | N | S | E | A |
|---|---|---|---|---|
| | | Grand Mean | | |
| Text | 74.844 | 74.844 | 74.844 | 74.844 |
| Web | 74.844 | 74.844 | 74.844 | 74.844 |
| | | + Format Effects | | |
| Text | −3.281 | −3.281 | −3.281 | −3.281 |
| Web | 3.281 | 3.281 | 3.281 | 3.281 |
| | | + Instruction Effects | | |
| Text | −1.094 | −1.719 | −4.219 | 7.031 |
| Web | −1.094 | −1.719 | −4.219 | 7.031 |
| | | = Cell Means | | |
| Text | 70.469 (71.25) | 69.844 (72.50) | 67.344 (68.75) | 78.594 (73.75) |
| Web | 77.031 (76.25) | 76.406 (73.75) | 73.906 (72.50) | 85.156 (90.00) |
| Difference | 6.562 (5.00) | 6.562 (1.25) | 6.562 (5.75) | 6.562 (16.25) |

*Note.* Observed cell means are in parentheses.

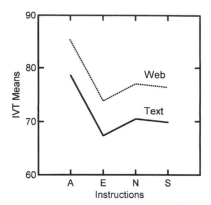

**Fig. 11.4** The Wiley–Voss IVT data with no interaction.

## 11.6.2 Testing Interaction Contrasts

When the interaction of two variables is significant, main effects are insufficient for an understanding of our data. For example, if the Format × Instruction interaction had been significant in the Wiley–Voss study, it would indicate that the size of the population format effects depended on instructions. In this case, we might wish to test what Tukey (1991) has termed "**cross comparisons**." These comparisons would include various 2 × 2 subsets of means. An example of such a comparison would be the comparison of the difference between the $A$ and $N$ instructions in the web and format conditions. This is essentially a contrast of contrasts.[3] Tests of possible 2 × 2 interactions, embedded within a larger design (such as the 2 × 4 of Wiley and Voss), are straightforward. For illustrative purposes, we test a more complex cross comparison, one relevant to the pattern of means in the IVT data.

Assume that we wish to know if the contrast of the $A$ mean against the average of the other three is significantly different in the web and format conditions; this is the difference between $\psi_{I/\text{web}}$ (instructional contrast within the web condition) and $\psi_{I/\text{text}}$. The relevant null hypothesis is

$$H_0: \quad [\mu_{\text{web}, A} - (1/3)(\mu_{\text{web}, N} + \mu_{\text{web}, S} + \mu_{\text{web}, E})]$$
$$-[\mu_{\text{text}, A} - (1/3)(\mu_{\text{text}, N} + \mu_{\text{text}, S} + \mu_{\text{text}, E})] = 0$$

Rewriting to make the weights ($w_{jk}$) more obvious, we have $H_0: \psi = 0$, where

$$\psi = (1)\mu_{\text{web}, A} + (-1/3)\mu_{\text{web}, N} + (-1/3)\mu_{\text{web}, S}(-1/3)\mu_{\text{web}, E}$$
$$+(-1)\mu_{\text{text}, A} + (1/3)\mu_{\text{text}, N} + (1/3)\mu_{\text{text}, S} + (1/3)\mu_{\text{text}, E} = 0$$

The $t$ statistic for each of these contrasts is similar to the statistic in Equation 11.7:

$$t = \frac{\hat{\psi}}{s_{\hat{\psi}}} = \frac{\sum\limits_{j=1}^{a} \sum\limits_{k=1}^{b} w_{jk}\overline{Y}_{.jk}}{\sqrt{MS_{\text{error}}\left(\sum\limits_{j=1}^{a} \sum\limits_{k=1}^{b} w_{jk}^2/n\right)}} \tag{11.9}$$

Alternatively, the $F$ statistic can be obtained by calculating the sum of squares for the contrast and dividing by $MS_{\text{error}}$. The equation for the contrast sum of squares is similar to Equation 11.8:

$$SS_{\hat{\psi}} = \frac{\hat{\psi}^2}{\sum_j \sum_k w_{jk}^2/n} = \frac{\left(\sum_j \sum_k w_{jk}\overline{Y}_{.jk}\right)^2}{\sum_j \sum_k w_{jk}^2/n} \tag{11.10}$$

The $t$ and $F$ statistics are calculated in Table 11.6.

How shall we evaluate the result of our calculations? If this is one of $K$ planned interaction contrasts, we would use a method such as the Dunn–Bonferroni method to control the FWE. Such a test can be performed whether or not the omnibus test of the interaction was significant. If the test was post hoc, perhaps based on noticing the apparent difference between the web and text contrasts, the Scheffé method should be applied. The critical value of $S$ is calculated as

$$S = \pm\sqrt{(a-1)(b-1) \cdot F_{\text{FWE},(a-1)(b-1),df_{\text{error}}}}$$
$$= \pm\sqrt{3 \cdot F_{.05,3,56}} = \pm\sqrt{(3)(2.77)} = \pm 2.88$$

The $t$ calculated in Table 11.6 is clearly smaller than $S$ and, therefore, we would not reject $H_0$. In fact, whichever method we use, even setting $\alpha = .05$ (as if there were exactly one planned

---

**TABLE 11.6**   CALCULATIONS FOR TESTS OF A CROSS COMPARISON

Because we want a difference between two contrasts, we begin by calculating $\hat{\psi}_{I/\text{web}}$ and $\hat{\psi}_{I/\text{text}}$, the instructional contrast of interest within the web and text conditions. We have

$$\hat{\psi}_{I/\text{text}} = \overline{Y}_{.\text{text},A} - (1/3)(\overline{Y}_{.\text{text},N} + \overline{Y}_{.\text{text},S} + \overline{Y}_{.\text{text},E})$$
$$= 73.75 - (1/3)(71.25 + 72.5 + 68.75) = 2.917$$

and, similarly, we find that $\hat{\psi}_{I/\text{web}} = 15.833$. Then the contrast we wish to test is

$$\hat{\psi} = \hat{\psi}_{I/\text{web}} - \hat{\psi}_{I/\text{text}} = 15.833 - 2.917 = 12.916$$

The $SE$ of this contrast is

$$s_{\hat{\psi}} = \sqrt{MS_{\text{error}}\left(\sum_{j=1}^{a} \sum_{k=1}^{b} w_{jk}^2/n\right)}$$

The $MS_{\text{error}}$ (assuming homogeneity of variance) is 154.24 and the sum of the eight squared weights is 24/9, or 2.67. Therefore $s_{\hat{\psi}} \sqrt{(154.24)(2.67/8)}$, or 7.17, and $t = 12.92/7.17$, or 1.80.

To calculate the $F$ statistic, we find

$$SS_{\hat{\psi}} = \frac{\left(\sum_j \sum_k w_{jk}\overline{Y}_{.jk}\right)^2}{\sum_j \sum_k w_{jk}^2/n} = \frac{12.92^2}{2.67/8} = 499.844$$

Dividing by $MS_{S/FI}$, we find $F = 3.24$, which equals the square of the $t$, 1.80.

---

*Note.* The sum of the squared weights is $1^2 + (3)(-1/3)^2 + (-1)^2 + (3)(1/3)^2 = 24/9$.

contrast), we find that the result is not significant. In the case of the Scheffé method, the fact that the test of the interaction was not significant meant that tests of interaction contrasts could not be significant. Nevertheless, it may be of interest to calculate $S$ in order to find the CI. Nonsignificance is a failure to reject, not an acceptance of, the null hypothesis. Therefore, it still makes sense to estimate the effect and to have an index of the precision of the estimate. As calculated in Table 11.6, the estimate of $\psi$ is 12.92 and the confidence limits for the Scheffé method are

$$\hat{\psi} \pm S \cdot s_{\hat{\psi}} = 12.92 \pm (2.88)(7.17) = -7.73, 33.57$$

This rather wide interval reflects the variability of the IVT scores and attests to the impreci-sion of the estimate and implies that our test had little power. As we have preached at other points in the text, it is usually better to anticipate the contrasts of interest before collecting the data. This permits a narrower definition of the family, and consequently a more precise estimate and higher power of the significance test.

The effects of one variable at a specific level of another variable—for example, the ef-fects of format under the argument instructions—are called **simple effects**. An interaction is significant when the simple effects of one variable depend on the level of the second variable. We now take a closer look at the nature of such effects and at related significance tests.

## 11.7 SIMPLE EFFECTS

Tables 11.7a and 11.7b display estimates of the Simple Effects of Format and Instructions on the IVT scores. To calculate the values in the panel labeled Simple Effects of Format, we subtracted each column (instructional) mean from the cell means in that column. For example, the average of the text scores in the narrative ($N$) condition is 2.5 points below the mean of that condition. This value, $-2.5$, is the simple effect of the text format in the narrative condition. The other values in the simple effects panel have been obtained in the same way. Two points should be noted about these simple effects of format. First, just as the main effects of format sum to zero, so do its simple effects. Second, the means of the two rows in the simple effects panel are $-3.281$ and $3.281$; these are the main effects originally computed for the text and web formats in Table 11.2. In general, *the main effects of a variable are an average of its simple effects*. If all interaction effects are zero, all the simple effects in a row equal the row main effect. In this data set, the simple effects vary somewhat; the Simple Effects of Format are greater in the $A$ condition than in any other instructional condition. Although this is evident from the original cell means in Table 11.1, by carrying out the subtraction illustrated in Table 11.7a, we immediately see both the direction and size of the effects of format at each instructional level.

Table 11.7b presents the Simple Effects of Instruction in each format condition. To calculate these effects, we subtracted the row means from each cell mean. The sum of the instruction simple effects (i.e., the sum of the four values in each row) is again zero and the average of the simple effects of any instruction equals the instructional main effect; for example, the average of $-.313$ and $-1.875$ is the $N$ main effect of $-1.094$ found in Table 11.2, or Table 11.5. We again see that the combination of the argument instructions and the web format has a distinct effect; the distance between the $A$ simple effect and those for $N$, $S$, and $E$ is greater in the web than in the text condition.

**TABLE 11.7**   SIMPLE EFFECTS OF FORMAT AND INSTRUCTIONS IN THE WILEY–VOSS DATA

| Format | N | S | E | A |
|---|---|---|---|---|
| *(a)* Format Simple Effects | | | | |
| | | Cell Means | | |
| Text | 71.250 | 72.500 | 68.750 | 73.750 |
| Web | 76.250 | 73.750 | 72.500 | 90.000 |
| | | − Column Means | | |
| Text | 73.750 | 73.125 | 70.625 | 81.875 |
| Web | 73.750 | 73.125 | 70.625 | 81.875 |
| | | = Simple Effects of Format | | |
| Text | −2.500 | −0.625 | −1.875 | −8.125 |
| Web | 2.500 | 0.625 | 1.875 | 8.125 |
| | | | | |
| *(b)* Instruction Simple Effects | | | | |
| | | Cell Means | | |
| Text | 71.250 | 72.500 | 68.750 | 73.750 |
| Web | 76.250 | 73.750 | 72.500 | 90.000 |
| | | − Row Means | | |
| Text | 71.563 | 71.563 | 71.563 | 71.563 |
| Web | 78.125 | 78.125 | 78.125 | 78.125 |
| | | = Simple Effects of Instructions | | |
| Text | −0.313 | 0.937 | −2.813 | 2.187 |
| Web | −1.875 | −4.375 | −5.625 | 11.875 |

## 11.7.1 Testing Simple Effects

There are differences of opinion about when simple effects should be tested. Some individuals recommend that such tests should be performed only if the interaction is significant.[4] We believe that this should not be a necessary condition provided the tests were planned and the FWE is controlled. As an example of the test for significance of simple effects, we test the effect of instructions in the web condition. At issue is whether the means of the four instructional populations of IVT scores in the web format condition differ from each other; the null hypothesis is

$$H_0: \mu_{\text{web, } N} = \mu_{\text{web, } S} = \mu_{\text{web, } E} = \mu_{\text{web, } A}$$

The numerator for the $F$ test is the sum of squares for instructions within the web condition. We denote this by $SS_{I/\text{web}}$ (sum of squares for instructions within the web condition). This sum of squares is calculated as if the design were a one-factor design with four levels of instructions, and 8 subjects in each instructional condition; the data for the text conditions are ignored. Then $SS_{I/\text{web}}$ is obtained by squaring each of the four entries in the Web row of the Simple Effects of the Instructions panel of Table 11.7, and multiplying by $n$ (8):

$$SS_{I/\text{web}} = n \sum_{k=1}^{4} (\overline{Y}_{.2k} - \overline{Y}_{.2.})^2$$
$$= (8)[(-1.875)^2 + (-4.375)^2 + (-5.625)^2 + (11.875)^2]$$
$$= 1562.50$$

There are two possible error terms in this analysis: one based on all eight cells and one based only on the cells involved in the significance test. Use of the error term from the omnibus $F$ tests, $MS_{S/FI}$, is supported by finding that neither the Levene nor the Brown–Forsythe test of the homogeneity of the eight cell variances provided any evidence that the population variances differed. However, the real issue in testing the effects of instructions in the web condition is whether the average variance in the web cells differs from that of the format cells. If so, we should use only the four web cell variances. Following this reasoning, we subtracted each score from its cell median, took the absolute value of this difference, and then performed a two-factor ANOVA on these absolute deviations from the median. The $p$ value for the format main effect was .47, providing no evidence of a difference between the average population variances in the web and text format conditions. In view of these results, we tested the simple effects of instructions within the web condition by dividing $MS_{I/\text{web}}$ by $MS_{S/FI}$. The $MS_{I/\text{web}}$ is the $SS_{I/\text{web}}$ divided by the degrees of freedom for instructions, or 1562/3. Therefore, $F = (1562.5/3)/154.24 = 3.38$, with 3 and 56 $df$.

Before we decide whether this result is significant, we have to decide on the criterion for significance. Because there are two possible tests of simple effects, one at each format level, we recommend that each test be carried out at the .025 level. Then the result is significant in the web condition, $p = .024$, but not in the text condition. In summary, we recommend that tests of simple effects of variable $A$ at each level of $B$ should be evaluated with $\alpha = \text{FWE}/b$; similarly, $\alpha = \text{FWE}/a$ for tests of equality for each of the $B$ simple effects.

Tests of contrasts of simple effects may also be carried out. For example, all pairwise comparisons of instructional means within each format level could be tested. In that case, we would apply the Tukey HSD method with $\alpha = .025$.

## 11.7.2 Interactions and Simple Effects

In the IVT data, the Format × Instructions interaction was not significant. Nevertheless, when tests were planned, the simple effects of instructions were significant in the web format conditions, but not in the text conditions, a result that implies an interaction. Given the lack of a significant interaction in the analysis of the IVT scores, many researchers would argue against testing simple effects. However, we recommend proceeding as we have indicated. If the tests were planned, the Dunn–Bonferroni or a similar procedure is appropriate. When the results of the tests of simple effects are not consistent with the test of interaction, we have to be careful about our conclusions. The lack of a significant interaction means that we cannot conclude that there is an interaction in the population, but it also does not permit us to *accept* the null hypothesis of no interaction. We can conclude, as Wiley and Voss did, that instructions had a significant effect within the web condition. That is all we can conclude on the basis of our tests.

Why do we frequently see results of tests of simple effects that suggest the presence of interaction in the population when the test of interaction does not have a significant outcome? Consideration of a $2 \times 2$ design suggests an answer. We can represent the cell means as follows:

|        | $B_1$             | $B_2$             |
|--------|-------------------|-------------------|
| $A_1$  | $\overline{Y}_{.11}$ | $\overline{Y}_{.12}$ |
| $A_2$  | $\overline{Y}_{.21}$ | $\overline{Y}_{.22}$ |

The simple effect of $B$ at $A_1$ is a contrast: $\hat{\psi}_{B/A_1} = \overline{Y}_{.11} - \overline{Y}_{.12}$. The interaction is also a contrast equivalent to the difference between the simple effects, $\hat{\psi}_{B/A_1}$ and $\hat{\psi}_{B/A_2}$; we denote this as $\hat{\psi}_{AB} = (\overline{Y}_{.11} - \overline{Y}_{.12}) - (\overline{Y}_{.21} - \overline{Y}_{.22})$. Note that $\hat{\psi}_{AB}$ may also be viewed as the difference between the $A$ simple effects at the levels of $B$, $(\overline{Y}_{.11} - \overline{Y}_{.21}) - (\overline{Y}_{.21} - \overline{Y}_{.22})$, or, with a little further manipulation, as the difference between diagonal elements, $(\overline{Y}_{.11} + \overline{Y}_{.22}) - (\overline{Y}_{.12} + \overline{Y}_{.21})$. The $t$ statistic to test the $AB$ interaction is

$$ t_{AB} = \frac{\hat{\psi}_{AB}}{\sqrt{MS_{\text{error}}(4/n)}} \qquad (11.11) $$

The 4 in the denominator represents the sum of the squared weights. To test the simple effect of $B$ at $A_1$, we calculate

$$ t_{B/A_1} = \frac{\hat{\psi}_{B/A_1}}{\sqrt{MS_{\text{error}}(2/n)}} \qquad (11.12) $$

Some algebra shows that $t_{AB} \geq t_{B/A_1}$ only if $\hat{\psi}_{AB} \geq (\sqrt{2})(\hat{\psi}_{B/A_1})$. The point is that the $SE$ of the interaction involves the variance of differences among four means, whereas that for the simple effect involves the variance of only two means. Because the variance of a linear combination of independent entities is the sum of their variances, the interaction contrast has to be roughly 1.4 (i.e., $\sqrt{2}$) times larger than the simple contrast to achieve the same size $t$.

## 11.8 TWO-FACTOR DESIGNS: TREND ANALYSIS

In this section, as in Chapter 10, we consider only experiments in which at least one independent variable is quantitative, the levels are equally spaced, and there are equal numbers of observations in each cell. Most of the concepts and notation were originally developed in Chapter 10, and a review of that material should be helpful. The calculations are those for sums of squares of contrasts and follow closely from earlier developments in this chapter; in particular, Equations 11.8 and 11.10 will be especially relevant although the weights will be dictated by questions concerning the slope and shape of functions.

In Chapter 10, we described an experiment in which a GSR (galvanic skin response) response was conditioned to a stimulus 11 in. high. Different groups of participants were tested with either a 7-, 9-, 11-, 13-, or 15-in. stimulus, and the resulting GSR generalization gradient was analyzed into orthogonal polynomial components. In this section, we introduce

**TABLE 11.7** GROUP GSR MEANS FOR A TWO-FACTOR EXPERIMENT

| Personality Type (A) | Test Stim. Height (in.) (B) | | | | | Mean ($\overline{Y}_{.j.}$) |
| --- | --- | --- | --- | --- | --- | --- |
| | 7 | 9 | 11 | 13 | 15 | |
| Control group | 1.24 | 3.96 | 4.44 | 4.48 | 3.08 | 3.440 |
| Schizophrenic group | 3.66 | 4.16 | 4.22 | 4.30 | 4.08 | 4.084 |
| Mean ($\overline{Y}_{..k}$) | 2.45 | 4.06 | 4.33 | 4.39 | 3.58 | 3.762 |

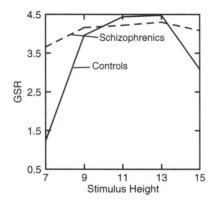

**Fig. 11.5** Plot of GSR means for control groups and schizophrenic groups (Table 11.8).

a second factor. Assume that we sample participants from two populations: 30 patients diagnosed as schizophrenic ($S$) and 30 normal controls ($C$). The 30 participants from each population are randomly assigned to each of the five test stimulus conditions described in Chapter 10. In general, we have $a$ levels of $A$, $b$ levels of $B$, and $n$ subjects in each of the $ab$ cells. In this example, $A$ denotes personality type ($a = 2$), $B$ denotes stimulus height ($b = 5$), and $n = 6$. The cell means for this design are presented in Table 11.8 and plotted in Fig. 11.5.

Given a design of this sort, there are a number of questions we can ask. We can analyze the source of variance for stimulus height into its trend components just as we did in the one-factor design. That allows us to answer questions such as, Averaging over the two personality types, are there linear trends? That is, is the slope of the straight line that best fits the five marginal means significantly different from zero? Does the function describing those marginal means have a quadratic component? Is there *any* significant component of curvature? We can also partition the interaction sum of squares, allowing us to address issues raised by personality theorists who have hypothesized that individuals with schizophrenia tend to discriminate less among stimuli than do individuals without it. This hypothesis has two possible consequences: First, the group with schizophrenia ($S$) should show a less pronounced increase in GSR than a control group ($C$) with increases in stimulus magnitude. If so, the linear coefficient of the generalization function should be lower in the group with schizophrenia than in the control group. That is, the slope of the straight line that best fits the five means should be lower for the $S$ than for the $C$ subjects. Second, the generalization gradient should be flatter in the schizophrenic population than in the control population. This implies that there will be significant differences in the curvature of the two functions of stimulus height. Because the generalization gradient in Chapter 10 contained only a linear and quadratic component, we would expect that the difference in curvature would show up in the quadratic coefficient, which would be predicted to be less in the $S$ groups than in the $C$ groups. As we can see in Fig. 11.5, it appears that the data support our two hypotheses. Although the figure is compelling, in what follows we develop the statistical tests needed to ensure that the apparent differences in position and curvature of the two functions of stimulus height are not merely because of error variance.

## 11.8.1 The Analysis of Main Effects

The questions here are about the slope and shape of the average curve for the two personality types. The relevant data are the marginal means for each of the test stimuli based on the 12 participants tested with that stimulus. More generally, we are interested in the $q$th polynomial component of $B$, and each of the $b$ means is based on $an$ scores. Most statistical packages have a polynomial option in the ANOVA (or GLM, general linear model) module and will perform the necessary calculations. Regression analyses (see Chapter 20), which are not limited to equal spacing and equal $n$, can also be performed by such packages. However, the sums of squares can also readily be obtained with a calculator, once cell means are calculated. To carry out such calculations, we need to weight each mean as in any contrast. Assume we want to calculate the sum of squares for the $q$th component of the sum of squares, for example, for the linear component. Let $\xi_{k,q}$ represent the weight that multiplies $\overline{Y}_{.k}$, the mean of the scores at $B_k$; for example, $\xi_{k,\text{lin}}$ would represent the linear weight for $\overline{Y}_{.k}$. The formula for the sums of squares for the $q$th component of $B$ (e.g., the linear component of the stimulus height function) is

$$SS_{q(B)} = \frac{an\left(\sum_k \xi_{k,q}\overline{Y}_{.k}\right)^2}{\sum_k \xi_{k,q}^2} \tag{11.13}$$

Substituting the marginal stimulus height ($B$) means from Table 11.8 and the linear coefficients from Appendix Table C.6 into Equation 11.13, we find that the sum of squares for the linear component of $B$ is

$$SS_{\text{lin}(B)} = \frac{(2)(6)[(-2)(2.45) + (-1)(4.06) + (0)(4.33) + (1)(4.39) + (2)(3.58)]}{(-2)^2 + (-1)^2 + 0^2 + 1^2 + 2^2}$$
$$= 80.50/10 = 8.05$$

This quantity represents the degree to which the line that best fits the relation between GSR and stimulus height (averaging over the two personality types) departs from a straight line. Whether the slope of that line differs significantly from zero—that is, whether there is a tendency for GSR to increase with stimulus height—is tested shortly. First, however, we consider the components of the interaction.

## 11.8.2 The Analysis of Interaction Effects

As we have noted, in normal populations, GSR tends to increase as the magnitude of the test stimulus increases, but this is combined with a generalization gradient, an inverted U-shaped curve. We hypothesized that such linear and quadratic trends should be less pronounced in schizophrenic populations, who generally are less able to discriminate among stimuli. This implies that the *AB* (Personality type × Stimulus height) interaction should be significant. However, although this is necessary to support our predictions, it is not sufficient. We predicted something more specific than a lack of parallelism; we predicted that the nonparallelism of curves for the two populations would be due to variation in the linear and quadratic components.

Table 11.9a presents point estimates of the population regression coefficients for the two personality types [$A \times q(B)$] and the coefficients based on the combined group data. These values were obtained by using Equation 10.15. They are consistent with our predictions for the two types of participants. The absolute values of the linear and quadratic regression coefficients are larger for the control subjects than for the schizophrenic subjects, suggesting that the control subjects discriminate better among the test stimuli. The cubic and quartic coefficients appear to be small for both groups. Of course, we still have to view the results of significance tests. The differences we have noted may be due to chance variability, and the apparently small cubic and quartic coefficients might differ significantly from zero when tested against a measure of error variance.

The results of a complete ANOVA are presented in Table 11.9b. We have already discussed the calculations for the sums of squares of the trend components of stimulus height [$q(B)$]. The calculations of the interaction components follows directly from earlier developments in the analysis of qualitative contrasts. Specifically, Equation 11.10 stated that the sum of squares for the difference between contrasts is

$$
SS_{\hat{\psi}} = \frac{\left( \sum_j \sum_k w_{jk} \overline{Y}_{.jk} \right)^2}{\sum_j \sum_k w_{jk}^2 / n}
$$

Table 11.6 provided an example of the calculations using this equation. In trend analysis the $w$s are replaced by the polynomial coefficients, the $\xi$s. For example, suppose we wanted to calculate $SS_{A \times \text{lin}(B)}$. This is based on the difference between the linear coefficients for the control and schizophrenic groups. For the control groups, the weights are $-2, -1, 0, 1$, and $2$; for the schizophrenic groups, the weights are $2, 1, 0 -1, -2$. Because we are contrasting two quadratic coefficients, the sum of squares is distributed on 1 *df*.

The results of the ANOVA seem clear. The difference in the mean GSR scores for the two personality types is significant; the schizophrenic subjects are more responsive. The significant stimulus SV indicates significant variation in mean GSR as a function of stimulus height, and the significant linear and quadratic components indicate that the average GSR tends to increase with stimulus height but there is also quadratic curvature. An equation describing the population function would be of the form GSR $= \beta_0 + \beta_1 H + \beta_2 H^2$, where $H$ is the stimulus height. The significant difference in the trends for the control and schizophrenic groups [$A \times \text{lin}(B)$ and $A \times \text{quad}(B)$] indicates that the function

**TABLE 11.9a**   REGRESSION COEFFICIENTS FOR THE GSR MEANS OF TABLE 11.8

| Personality Type (A) | Regression Coefficients | | | |
| --- | --- | --- | --- | --- |
| | Linear | Quadratic | Cubic | Quartic |
| Control group | .42 | −.62 | .08 | −.04 |
| Schizophrenic group | .10 | −.10 | .01 | −.01 |
| Mean [$q(B)$] | .260 | −.360 | .045 | −.025 |

**TABLE 11.9b**   ANOVA OF THE MEANS IN TABLE 11.8

| SV | df | SS | MS | F | P |
| --- | --- | --- | --- | --- | --- |
| Personality (A) | 1 | 6.221 | 6.221 | 9.327 | .004 |
| Stimulus (B) | 4 | 30.723 | 7.681 | 11.516 | .000 |
|   lin(B) | 1 | 8.050 | 8.050 | 12.069 | .001 |
|   quad(B) | 1 | 21.859 | 21.859 | 32.773 | .000 |
|   cubic(B) | 1 | 0.265 | 0.265 | 0.397 | .531 |
|   quart(B) | 1 | 0.549 | 0.549 | 0.823 | .369 |
| AB | 4 | 14.711 | 3.678 | 5.514 | .001 |
|   A × lin(B) | 1 | 3.111 | 3.111 | 4.663 | .036 |
|   A × quad(B) | 1 | 11.294 | 11.294 | 16.933 | .000 |
|   A × cubic(B) | 1 | 0.131 | 0.131 | 0.196 | .660 |
|   A × quart(B) | 1 | 0.175 | 0.175 | 0.262 | .611 |
| S/AB | 50 | 33.333 | 0.667 | | |

is less steep and less curved for the clinical population; the schizophrenic group appears to discriminate less well among the stimuli.

## 11.9 CONCLUDING REMARKS

In this chapter, we considered experiments in which each participant contributed one score to a cell in a design in which all possible combinations of two factors were represented. We defined, illustrated, and distinguished among main, interaction, and simple effects. We provided examples of tests of contrasts of levels of a factor, both when the factor was qualitative (e.g., instructions) and when it was quantitative (e.g., stimulus intensity). Although we illustrated calculations involved in many of the significance tests and CIs discussed, we emphasize that most statistical software packages will provide the same results and also allow the researcher to control the FWE appropriate to the situation.

Although we have covered considerable ground with respect to between-subjects designs, we have not exhausted the topic. In the next chapter, we pursue additional analyses that we believe to be equal in importance to those already considered—for example, calculations of effect size and power. We also extend our coverage to between-subjects designs involving more than two factors.

## KEY CONCEPTS

| | |
|---|---|
| main effects | interaction effects |
| residual | cell effect |
| sources of variance (SV) | marginal means |
| structural model | additivity of effects |
| cross comparisons | simple effects |

## EXERCISES

**11.1**  **(a)** Plot the marginal and cell means for the data set that follows. Discuss the pattern of means.

| | $B_1$ | | | | $B_2$ | | | |
|---|---|---|---|---|---|---|---|---|
| | $A_1$ | $A_2$ | $A_3$ | $A_4$ | $A_1$ | $A_2$ | $A_3$ | $A_4$ |
| | 14 | 22 | 31 | 18 | 42 | 46 | 20 | 41 |
| | 12 | 34 | 33 | 21 | 15 | 18 | 25 | 30 |
| | 26 | 24 | 43 | 19 | 27 | 17 | 15 | 44 |

   **(b)** Estimate the population main and interaction effects.
   **(c)** Using the results in (b), calculate the main and interaction sums of squares.

**11.2**  We have the following cell means and variances; $n = 10$.

| | Means | | | Variances | | |
|---|---|---|---|---|---|---|
| | $B_1$ | $B_2$ | $B_3$ | $B_1$ | $B_2$ | $B_3$ |
| $A_1$ | 2.6 | 4.3 | 6.5 | 2.75 | 5.00 | 5.50 |
| $A_2$ | 4.3 | 3.6 | 3.4 | 1.75 | 2.25 | 3.75 |

   **(a)** Carry out the ANOVA and present the tabled results.
   **(b)** Test the simple effects of $A$ at $B_3$.
   **(c)** Test the simple effects of $B$ at $A_2$.
   **(d)** Briefly justify your choice of error terms for parts (b) and (c).

**11.3**  To conserve space, most psychology journals do not publish ANOVA tables except when the analysis is complicated and there are many significant sources of variance. Thus, usually all we can expect to find is a table of means, a report of the obtained values of $F$, and sometimes the error $MS$s. At times, however, we wish that the researcher had published other analyses of the data. Often we can perform these analyses for ourselves, even though the researcher has not provided us with the raw data from the study. Suppose we have been given the following table of cell means from a between-subjects design with two factors:

|       | $B_1$ | $B_2$ | $B_3$ |
|-------|-------|-------|-------|
| $A_1$ | 12    | 16    | 14    |
| $A_2$ | 18    | 14    | 12    |

We have been told that only the $AB$ interaction is significant, $F = 8.0$, and $p = .002$.

(a) Assuming $n = 6$, reconstruct the entire ANOVA summary table.

(b) Test the simple effect of $B$ at $A_2$. What assumption is needed to justify this test?

**11.4** Consider each of the following sets of hypotheses. Which SV should be significant? Plot a data set consistent with the theory.

(a) In a bar press experiment, we hypothesize that $Y = KDP$, where $Y$ is the bar pressing rate (the dependent variable), $K$ is a constant, $D$ is the hours of deprivation, and $P$ is the number of practice trials.

(b) In impression formation studies, we give subjects some information on the attractiveness ($A$) and intelligence ($I$) of an individual and then ask them to rate the individual. We believe that the rating, $R, = (A + I)/2$.

(c) Patients in a mental hospital are divided into experimental groups on the basis of their socioeconomic level ($SE$, three levels) and the kind of treatment they receive ($T$, two levels, psychotherapy and behavior therapy). The investigator predicts that first, psychotherapy will be less effective than behavior therapy, and second, psychotherapy will be more effective the higher the socioeconomic level of the patient, but that this will not be true for behavior therapy. In fact, no main effect of socioeconomic level is predicted.

**11.5** Assume 40 subjects are divided into good and poor readers on the basis of a pretest. They then read either intact or scrambled text, and they are tested for their recall. The means are as follows:

|              | Text      |        |
|--------------|-----------|--------|
| Read. Ability | Scrambled | Intact |
| Good         | 62.944    | 53.889 |
| Poor         | 48.222    | 43.333 |

Assign weights to the cells and calculate $SS_{\hat{\psi}}$ for reading ability, for text, and for their interaction.

**11.6** Each cell in the following table contains a mean based on 10 scores:

|       | $A_1$ | $A_2$ | $A_3$ |
|-------|-------|-------|-------|
| $B_1$ | 20    | 10    | 6     |
| $B_2$ | 6     | 10    | 8     |

(a) Find the sums of squares accounted for by each of the following contrasts of the $A$ marginal means: $\psi_1 = \mu_{1.} - (1/2)(\mu_{2.} + \mu_{3.}); \psi_2 = \mu_{2.} - \mu_{3.}$.

(b) Are the two contrasts orthogonal?

(c) Find $SS_A$ and compare it with the sum of the two sums of squares found in part (a).

(d) We wish to determine whether either of the above contrasts varies as a function of $B$. Find the $SS$ terms associated with each of the relevant significance tests. Add these terms and compare them with $SS_{AB}$.

**11.7** Ninety children, varying in age ($A_1 = 5$, $A_2 = 7$, and $A_3 = 9$) are taught by one of three mnemonic methods (methods for memorizing; $B_1$, $B_2$, and $B_3$). All subjects are then shown a series of objects and their recall is scored. Thus we have nine groups of 10 children each. The cell means and variances are as follows:

|       | Means | | | Variances | | |
|-------|-------|-------|-------|-------|-------|-------|
|       | $A_1$ | $A_2$ | $A_3$ | $A_1$ | $A_2$ | $A_3$ |
| $B_1$ | 44    | 58    | 78    | 75    | 79    | 84    |
| $B_2$ | 56    | 66    | 83    | 61    | 82    | 85    |
| $B_3$ | 52    | 70    | 79    | 90    | 71    | 77    |

(a) Perform an ANOVA by using these statistics.

(b) $B_2$ and $B_3$ both involve the use of imagery, whereas $B_1$ involves repeating the object names. Therefore a contrast of the $B_1$ mean against the average of the $B_2$ and $B_3$ means is of interest. Calculate a CI for this contrast. Does the contrast differ significantly from zero?

(c) Test whether the contrast in part (b) is different at $A_1$ than at $A_3$.

**11.8** In an experiment on memory, a passage was presented to subjects one word at a time at a rate of either 300, 450, or 600 words per minute. The texts were either intact or the order of sentences was scrambled. The dependent variable was the percentage of idea units recalled. The summary statistics were as follows:

|           | Word Rate/Minute | | | | | |
|-----------|-------|-------|-------|-------|-------|-------|
|           | Means | | | Variances | | |
| Text      | 300   | 450   | 600   | 300   | 450   | 600   |
| Intact    | 66.250 | 59.875 | 43.375 | 68.492 | 79.549 | 81.415 |
| Scrambled | 54.375 | 49.750 | 45.875 | 33.977 | 54.214 | 55.267 |

There are 8 subjects in each cell.

(a) There is some reason to believe that recall decreases as rate increases from 300 to 450 words per minute, but then levels off. What does the hypothesis predict about the polynomial components? Perform an analysis of trend to test the hypothesis.

(b) Test whether the contrasts indicated in part (a) are significantly different for the intact and the scrambled text conditions.

(c) Calculate the $SS_{\text{Rate} \times \text{Text}}$. How should the results in part (b) relate to this value?

(d) Discuss the results of these analyses.

**11.9** Errors in a memory task are recorded for male and female participants of ages 5, 6, 7, and 8 years. There are 5 subjects in each of the eight cells, the average within-cell variance is 8.75, and the cell means are as follows:

|  | Age | | | |
|---|---|---|---|---|
|  | 5 | 6 | 7 | 8 |
| Male | 16.3 | 7.2 | 6.5 | 7.4 |
| Female | 12.1 | 7.3 | 6.7 | 6.2 |

(a) Plot the means and carry out the ANOVA, including trend components of the age variable. Is the decrease in errors with age significant? Is the apparent curvature significant?

(b) There is some indication that the slope of the function relating errors and age is less negative for female subjects. Test whether this difference in slopes is significant.

**11.10** The meaning of polynomial components of interaction such as the lin(Age) × Sex term in Exercise 11.9 [part (b)] may be clearer if we redo part (b) in the following way. Find the equation (see Equation 10.13) for the best-fitting straight line for the male subjects, and calculate the predicted mean errors at each of the four ages. Do the same for the female participants. At this point you have a table of means much like the one in Exercise 11.9 except that those means were observed and these are predicted. Calculate the Sex × Age interaction sum of squares by using the predicted means (remember that $n = 5$) and compare it to $SS_{\text{lin(Age)} \times \text{Sex}}$.

**11.11** In an attempt to develop better approaches to postgraduate clinical training, a study comparing three training methods ($M$) was conducted. To determine if there was some optimal point in time at which no further training was beneficial (within practical limits), a second variable, time ($T$; 3, 6, 9, or 12 months) was included. At the end of the training period, a committee of clinical faculty rated the individuals on a 10-point scale. There were 5 trainees in each cell and the error sum of squares was 87.84. The mean ratings are as follows:

| Method | Time (in months) | | | |
|---|---|---|---|---|
|  | 3 | 6 | 9 | 12 |
| $M_1$ | 5.4 | 5.2 | 5.6 | 7.8 |
| $M_2$ | 5.4 | 5.6 | 6.2 | 8.4 |
| $M_3$ | 5.2 | 5.8 | 5.4 | 5.6 |

(a) Plot the means and describe any trends in the data. Then present the ANOVA table. Include tests of the polynomial components of $T$.

**(b)** We wish to know if the linear trend for $M_3$ differs significantly from the average linear trend for $M_1$ and $M_2$. (i) State the null hypothesis in terms of the regression coefficients for the three training populations. Use the notation $\beta_{11}, \beta_{12},$ and $\beta_{13},$ where the first subscript indicates linearity and the second subscript indicates the level of $M$. (ii) Carry out the significance test.

**11.12** **(a)** The file Ex11_12 in the *Exercises* folder of the CD contains a $3 \times 3$ data set. Table and plot the marginal and cell means. Describe the pattern of means.

**(b)** Carry out an ANOVA on the data and present the results in a table.

**(c)** Assume that we planned to test the all pairwise comparisons among the marginal $A$ means. Perform the tests with FWE $= .05$ and report which comparisons are significant.

**11.13** In this chapter, we analyzed the IVT scores from the Wiley–Voss study (Wiley & Voss, 1999). These investigators also analyzed several other measures of memory and comprehension. These measures may be found in the Wiley file in the *Wiley_Voss* folder of the CD. The variable CAUSAL represents the number of causal connections subjects introduced into essays based on the information obtained, and it reflects their understanding of relations among events in the source (web or text format) material. [Note: format $= 1$ and $2$ corresponds to text and web, respectively; instructions 1 through 4 correspond to narrative ($N$), summary ($S$), explanation ($E$), and argument ($A$), respectively.]

**(a)** Using whatever plots and statistics you wish, describe location, variability, and shape of the distributions.

**(b)** Carry out an ANOVA with format and instructions as the independent variables.

**(c)** Transform the data by log(CAUSAL $+ 1$). How has this affected the results in parts (a) and (b)?

# Chapter 12

## Multifactor Between-Subjects Designs: Further Developments

## 12.1 INTRODUCTION

Chapter 11 presented the model and calculations for the analysis of variance for the two-factor between-subjects design. That chapter also included follow-up tests and confidence intervals. In this chapter, we continue consideration of two-factor designs. Again, using the Wiley–Voss data to illustrate calculations, we compute measures of importance and the power of the $F$ test. The tests based on the Wiley–Voss inference verification task (IVT) data revealed a significant effect of the format ($F$) by which information was presented to participants, but the instructional ($I$) variable was not quite significant ($p = .07$) and the $F \times I$ interaction did not approach significance. Nevertheless, descriptive statistics and graphs revealed considerable error variability, and plots of the data suggested that the $I$ and $F \times I$ sources of variance might be more important than the significance test results indicated. This is not unusual in research, and it is a major motivation for considering something other than $p$ values in assessing a variable's importance. It is also a reason to question whether there was sufficient power to detect effects that might be of interest. We consider these topics in this chapter.

Chapter 12 covers several other topics as well and extends the discussion to the general case in which there are more than two factors. Throughout, we assume that each participant contributes one score to the data analysis and that the levels of each independent variable are fixed; that is, we assume that the levels have been arbitrarily selected, not randomly sampled from a universe of levels.

## 12.2 MEASURES OF EFFECT SIZE

As we noted in Chapter 8, several different measures of effect size have been proposed and are encountered in the literature. Among those we considered was $R^2$, the ratio $SS_A/SS_{\text{tot}}$ in the one-factor design. In multifactor designs, $R^2$ is $SS_{\text{cells}}/SS_{\text{tot}}$. In other words, it is the

**TABLE 12.1**   MEASURES OF IMPORTANCE FOR TWO-FACTOR DESIGNS WITH FIXED-EFFECT VARIABLES

| (a) | Variance | Estimator |
|---|---|---|
| | $\sigma_A^2 = \sum_j \alpha_j^2/a$ | $\hat{\sigma}_A^2 = \left(\dfrac{a-1}{a}\right)\left(\dfrac{MS_A - MS_{S/AB}}{bn}\right)$ |
| | $\sigma_B^2 = \sum_k \beta_k^2/b$ | $\hat{\sigma}_B^2 = \left(\dfrac{b-1}{b}\right)\left(\dfrac{MS_B - MS_{S/AB}}{an}\right)$ |
| | $\sigma_{AB}^2 = \sum_j \sum_k (\alpha\beta)_{jk}^2/ab$ | $\hat{\sigma}_{AB}^2 = \left(\dfrac{(a-1)(b-1)}{ab}\right)\left(\dfrac{MS_{AB} - MS_{S/AB}}{n}\right)$ |
| | $\sigma_e^2$ | $\hat{\sigma}_e^2 = MS_{S/AB}$ |

| (b) | Measure | Estimator |
|---|---|---|
| | $\eta_{\text{Effect}}^2$ | $\eta_{\text{Effect}}^2 = SS_{\text{Effect}}/(SS_{\text{Effect}} + SS_{S/AB})$ |
| | $\omega_{\text{Effect}}^2 = \sigma_{\text{Effect}}^2/(\sigma_e^2 + \sigma_{\text{Effect}}^2)$ | $\hat{\omega}_{\text{Effect}}^2 = \hat{\sigma}_{\text{Effect}}^2/(\hat{\sigma}_e^2 + \hat{\sigma}_{\text{Effect}}^2)$ |
| | | $= df_{\text{Effect}}(F_{\text{Effect}} - 1)/[df_{\text{Effect}}(F_{\text{Effect}} - 1) + N]$ |
| | $f_{\text{Effect}} = \sigma_{\text{Effect}}/\sigma_e$ | $\hat{f}_{\text{Effect}} = \sqrt{\hat{\sigma}_{\text{Effect}}^2/\hat{\sigma}_e^2}$ |
| | | $= \sqrt{(df_{\text{Effect}}/N)(F_{\text{Effect}} - 1)}$ |
| | $\lambda_{\text{Effect}} = N\sigma_{\text{Effect}}^2/\sigma_e^2$ | $\hat{\lambda}_{\text{Effect}} = N\hat{\sigma}_{\text{Effect}}^2/\hat{\sigma}_e^2 = df_{\text{Effect}}(F_{\text{Effect}} - 1)$ |

*Note. $N = abn$; the subscript Effect refers to $A$, $B$, or $AB$.*

proportion of the total variability accounted for by the factors in the design. $R^2$ is sometimes referred to as $\eta^2$ (**eta squared**). If there are more than two factors and the analysis of variance (ANOVA) is carried out using SPSS's General Linear Model module (univariate) and the option "Effect Size" is checked, a value of $\eta^2$ is reported for each effect. It is defined as in Table 12.1 a and b, in which the subscript "Effect" represents $A$, $B$, or $AB$. For example,

$$\eta_A^2 = SS_A/(SS_A + SS_e)$$

Although $\eta^2$ can be a useful indicator of the importance of a source of variance, it is a descriptive statistic. One limitation is that $\sigma_e^2$ contributes to the variability among condition means and therefore to the numerator of $\eta^2$. This is remedied by Hays' (1988) $\omega^2$ (omega squared), in which he defined as the variance of the treatment population means divided by the sum of the population variances. Rather than dividing by the sum of the four variances as Hays proposed, we define an adjusted $\omega^2$ in Table 12.1. For example, in assessing the contribution of the $A$ source of variance, $\omega^2$ would be defined as

$$\omega_A^2 = \sigma_A^2/(\sigma_A^2 + \sigma_e^2)$$

This is sometimes referred to as a **partial $\omega^2$**. This adjustment allows us to estimate the contribution of one source of variance independent of the size of the contribution of other variables. An advantage is that we can compare the contributions of a factor in experiments having different numbers of factors.

**Cohen's** $f$ (1988) provides still another measure of effect size. It can be used both in conjunction with Cohen's (1988) power tables and with the free software package GPOWER, whose URL was provided in Chapter 6. Cohen defined $f$ as the ratio of the standard deviation of the treatment population means to the population error standard deviation; for example,

$$f_A = \sigma_A/\sigma_e$$

$$= \frac{\sqrt{\sum_j (\mu_{j.} - \mu)^2/a}}{\sigma_e}$$

We have included one other indicator of effect size in Table 12.1, $\lambda$ **(lambda)**. This was introduced in Chapter 8 as the parameter of the noncentral $F$ distribution. As we noted there, some programs for calculating power take $\lambda$ as their input. As we showed in Table 8.9, $\omega^2$, $f$, and $\lambda$ are all closely related; for example, $\lambda = Nf^2$.

The upper panel of Table 12.1a presents formulas for defining and estimating the variances referenced in the formulas in Table 12.1b. The variance estimators are derived from the expected mean squares as was previously discussed in Chapter 8. For example,

$$E(MS_A) = \sigma_e^2 + bn \sum_j (\mu_{j.} - \mu)^2/(a - 1)$$

$$E(MS_{S/AB}) = \sigma_e^2$$

Then

$$E(MS_A - MS_{S/AB})/bn = \sum_j (\mu_{j.} - \mu)^2/(a - 1)$$

Multiplying both sides by $(a - 1)/a$, we have

$$\frac{(a - 1)}{a} \cdot \frac{E(MS_A - MS_{S/AB})}{bn} = \frac{\sum_j (\mu_{j.} - \mu)^2}{a} = \sigma_A^2$$

The formula in Table 12.1 follows directly. Estimators of variances for $B$ and $AB$ have a similar form and are also in the table.

Substituting the formulas for the variance estimators into the formulas in the lower panel, we can obtain numerical estimates of $\omega^2$, $f$, and $\lambda$. Alternatively, the statistics can be written in terms of the total $N$, degrees of freedom, and $F$ ratio for the effect of interest. This is useful because it allows us to calculate measures of importance for published reports that usually include the $F$ ratios even when measures of association or effect size have not been included. A comparison with Table 8.9 for the one-factor design reveals that the formulas are the same, as they will be for designs having more than two fixed factors (and no random factors).

Using the Wiley–Voss IVT data, Table 12.2 presents calculations based on the definitions and formulas in Table 12.1. Following Cohen's (1988) suggestion that $f$ of .1 reflects a small-sized effect and $f$ of .25 a medium-sized effect, it appears that both the format $(F)$ and instruction $(I)$ variables are of medium size, whereas the interaction contributes relatively little variability. Because $\omega^2$, $f$, and $\lambda$ are closely related, they present a consistent picture. The $\eta^2$ value for the $F \times I$ interaction is larger than we would expect on the basis of the other measures, presumably reflecting the contribution of error variance to the $SS_{F \times I}$. It is interesting to note that the $F$ value is larger and the $p$ value smaller for the format than for

**TABLE 12.2**  VARIANCE ESTIMATES AND MEASURES OF IMPORTANCE FOR THE WILEY–VOSS DATA (TABLE 11.1)

| Variance | Calculation | Estimate |
|---|---|---|
| $\sigma_F^2$ | $\left(\dfrac{1}{2}\right)\left(\dfrac{689.06 - 154.24}{32}\right)$ | 8.357 |
| $\sigma_I^2$ | $\left(\dfrac{3}{4}\right)\left(\dfrac{380.73 - 154.24}{16}\right)$ | 10.617 |
| $\sigma_{F \times I}^2$ | $\left(\dfrac{3}{8}\right)\left(\dfrac{176.56 - 154.24}{8}\right)$ | 1.046 |
| $\sigma_e^2$ | | 154.24 |

| SV | df | SS | MS | F | $\eta^2$ | $\hat{\omega}^2$ | $\hat{f}$ | $\hat{\lambda}$ |
|---|---|---|---|---|---|---|---|---|
| F | 1 | 689.06 | 689.06 | 4.467* | .074 | .051 | .233 | 3.468 |
| I | 3 | 1,142.19 | 380.73 | 2.468** | .117 | .064 | .262 | 4.393 |
| $F \times I$ | 3 | 529.69 | 176.56 | 1.145 | .058 | .007 | .082 | .430 |
| S/FI | 56 | 8,637.50 | 154.24 | | | | | |
| Total | 63 | 10,998.44 | | | | | | |

*$p = .039$; **$p = .071$.

the instructional source of variance, whereas the relation is slightly reversed when we look at other statistics in the bottom panel. This should serve to remind us of several points: (1) $F$ ratios or $p$ values are indices of statistical significance; (2) this is not the same as practical or theoretical significance; and (3) therefore, $F$ ratios should be supplemented with other measures. In addition to calculating measures of importance, contrasts should be targeted before the data are collected; these should be tested and confidence intervals constructed, with proper attention to the control of familywise error rates. Measures of importance, such as $E_S$ (Cohen's $d$; see Chapter 6) can also be calculated for such contrasts.

## 12.3 POWER OF THE *F* TEST

The appropriate use of tables (e.g., Cohen, 1988), charts (e.g., Kirk, 1995; Myers & Well, 1995), and computer programs for power calculations is to determine the sample size required *prior* to collecting data. Nevertheless, it can be enlightening to obtain a post hoc estimate of power. Investigators are often surprised to find how little power they had to detect even medium-sized effects. Consider, for example, the instructional source of variance in the Wiley–Voss study. Recall that the effect was not significant at the standard .05 level, but our measures of importance suggested that the effect was medium in size. How much power does a $2 \times 4$ design with 8 subjects in each cell have to detect a medium-sized effect ($f = .25$) based on 3 and 56 $df$? The answer is .336 or, put differently, there is a .66 probability of a Type 2 error in a design of this dimensionality and $N$, if we wish to detect an effect of medium size.

Several computer programs and statistical packages will produce this result. They are far more versatile and accurate than tables or graphs. Two of these, GPOWER and the UCLA calculator, are freely available from the Internet. We illustrated their use in determining the power of the $F$ test in one-factor designs in Chapter 8 (see Table 8.10). When using GPOWER with multifactor designs, select "other $F$ tests" from the test menu because the standard $F$ test choice does not handle interaction. The resulting menu asks for $f^2$ (.0625 for a medium effect), $\alpha$, $N$, and the numerator and denominator $df$. It returns not only a value of power, but also $\lambda$ and the critical $F$. The application of the UCLA calculator is exactly the same as in Chapter 8. The drawback to both is that neither GPOWER's "other $F$ tests" nor the UCLA noncentral $F$ program calculate the $N$ needed to achieve a specified level of power. However, by trying different $N$s, this can be determined fairly quickly and accurately. Among commercial statistical packages, we have found SYSTAT 10 easiest to use. By clicking on "Statistics," followed by "Design of Experiments, and then "Power," the user has a choice of statistical tests, a choice between post hoc and a priori power, and a choice among three measures of effect size. Of these, the "standardized average squared effect" is $f^{2\cdot}$. Whichever program is used, assuming Wiley and Voss' $2 \times 4$ design, $\alpha = .05$, and a medium-sized instructions effect, the required cell frequency ($n$) needed to achieve .80 power is 23. You would need $8 \times 23$, or $N = 184$ subjects to have this level of power. In many studies, this will be impractical and therefore consideration of additional or alternative measures or alternative designs is advisable. When some measure related to the dependent variable is available (a **concomitant variable**), the analysis of covariance (ANCOVA) may greatly reduce error variance and thus increase power. That procedure is discussed in Chapter 15.

## 12.4 UNEQUAL CELL FREQUENCIES

### 12.4.1 The Problem

In Chapter 11, and in the developments thus far in this chapter, we have considered only cases in which the number of observations is the same in each of the $ab$ cells. Problems arise when this is not the case. As we noted in Chapter 6, unequal $n$s exaggerate the consequences of heterogeneity of variance. Furthermore, when the $n_{jk}$ (the cell frequencies) are not equal, the sums of squares for $A$, $B$, and $AB$ will usually not add to the $SS_{cells}$ when each is calculated ignoring the other effects. This is because such sums of squares are not independently distributed. As in our discussion of contrasts (Chapter 8), we say that these three sources are not orthogonal and that we have a **nonorthogonal design**. Table 12.3 illustrates the problem. The difference between the column ($B$) means is 5 in both the $A_1$ and $A_2$ rows, indicating that there is no $AB$ interaction. According to our discussion of simple and interaction effects in Chapter 11, the difference in the $B$ main effects should also equal 5 because in designs with equal $n$s when the interaction effects are zero, the simple effects equal the main effects. However, in the example in Table 12.3, the difference between the two column means is $22 - 8$ or 14.

The results are even stranger if we calculate the $A$, $B$, and $AB$ sums of squares in the usual way:

$$SS_A = (10)[(24 - 15)^2 + (6 - 15)^2] = 1620$$
$$SS_B = (10)[(8 - 15)^2 + (22 - 15)^2] = 980$$
$$SS_{cells} = (2)(20 - 15)^2 + (8)(25 - 15)^2 + (8)(5 - 15)^2 + (2)(10 - 15)^2$$
$$= 1700$$

**TABLE 12.3**    EXAMPLE WITH DISPROPORTIONATE CELL FREQUENCIES

|        |                      | $B_1$ | $B_2$ | $n_{j.}$ | $\overline{Y}_{.j.}$ |
|--------|----------------------|-------|-------|----------|----------------------|
| $A_1$  | $n_{1k}$             | 2     | 8     | 10       |                      |
|        | $\overline{Y}_{.1k}$ | 20    | 25    |          | 24                   |
| $A_2$  | $n_{2k}$             | 8     | 2     | 10       |                      |
|        | $\overline{Y}_{.2k}$ | 5     | 10    |          | 6                    |
|        | $n_{.k}$             | 10    | 10    | $n_{..} = 20$ |                 |
|        | $\overline{Y}_{..k}$ | 8     | 22    |          | $\overline{Y}_{...} = 15$ |

*Note.* $\overline{Y}_{.j.} = \sum_k n_{jk}\overline{Y}_{.jk}/n_{j.}$; for example, $24 = [(2)(20) + (8)(25)]/10$. The column means are computed in a similar way. The grand mean (15) is the sum of all scores divided by the total $n$.

To obtain the interaction sum of squares, we calculate

$$SS_{\text{cells}} - (SS_A + SS_B) = -900$$

Of course, a negative sum of squared deviations makes no sense. Apparently, this approach to calculating sums of squares does not work with nonorthogonal designs.

The reason for the strange results of the calculations carried out on the means of Table 12.3 may become clearer if we consider an extreme case of nonorthogonality. Suppose the $n$s were

|        | $B_1$ | $B_2$ |
|--------|-------|-------|
| $A_1$  | 0     | 8     |
| $A_2$  | 8     | 0     |

Now $SS_A$ and $SS_B$ are identical; both are based solely on the difference between the $A_1B_2$ and $A_2B_1$ cell means, and therefore the $A$ and $B$ main effects are perfectly correlated. In Table 12.3, the correlation is no longer perfect, but it is still high. The magnitude of both $SS_A$ and $SS_B$ will still depend primarily (although not entirely) on the difference between the $A_1B_2$ and $A_2B_1$ means.

Figure 12.1 contains a graphic representation of the situation when cell frequencies are unequal. The square represents the $SS_{\text{tot}}$. The circles represent $SS_A$, $SS_B$, and $SS_{AB}$. When cell frequencies are equal, these three circles do not overlap; the overlap represents the covariance of effects that is a result of nonorthogonal designs. Such covariances can be positive or negative so that somehow subtracting the covariance from a sum of squares might result in a smaller quantity (if the covariance is positive) or a larger one (if the covariance is negative). The presence of correlations among effects poses a difficult problem in data analysis and interpretation. For example, we could calculate $SS_A$ in the usual way. We say that we obtain the sum of squares for $A$ *ignoring* $B$ and $AB$. Such a calculation corresponds to the areas $t$, $u$, $v$, and $w$ in Fig. 12.1. Or, we could *adjust* $SS_A$ for the contribution of the other main effect $B$. This $SS_{A|B}$ corresponds to the areas $t$ and $w$. Or we could adjust $SS_A$ for the contributions of $B$ and $AB$, in which case the adjusted $SS_A$, $SS_{A|B,AB}$

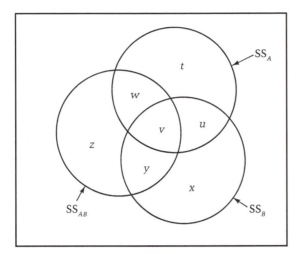

**Fig. 12.1** The partitioning of variability in a two-factor design.

would consist only of $t$. Similar options are available with respect to the other sources of variance.

All three of the alternatives just considered are available in various computer packages. In SPSS, clicking on the model menu in the GLM module provides access to several types of sums of squares. **Type I** $SS_A$ yields the sum of squares for $A$ *ignoring B* effects; **Type II** $SS_A$ is the sum of squares *adjusted for B* effects, $SS_{A|B}$; and **Type III** $SS_A$ is the sum of squares *adjusted for both B* and *AB* effects, $SS_{A|B,AB}$. Let us consider the results of each type of analysis, using data from the Seasons data set.

## 12.4.2 Three Types of Sums of Squares: An Example

The upper panel of Table 12.4 presents means and $n$s for male and female participants in four educational categories, based on average (over seasons) Beck depression scores collected at the University of Massachusetts Medical School as part of the Seasons study. The $n$s are clearly not equal; in particular, many more women than men had only a high school education in this study. The lower panel presents four different partitions of the sums of squares. Note that the error term is the same in all four analyses, as is the interaction sum of squares. The latter may be viewed as represented by area $z$ in Fig. 12.1, and is the variability due to the $AB$ interaction after adjusting for, or removing, the variability attributable to $A$ and $B$. In what follows, we consider each type of sum of squares in turn.

***Type III Sums of Squares.*** The default in most current statistical packages (e.g., SAS, SPSS, SYSTAT) is the **Type III sums of squares.** In this analysis, the sum of squares for each main effect is adjusted for the variability due to all other main and interaction effects. Because of this, we will refer to the Type III sum of squares for $A$ as $SS_{A|B,AB}$ (sum of squares for $A$ adjusted for $B$ and $AB$). In terms of Fig. 12.1, the sum of squares for Education (the $A$ circle) corresponds to the area labeled $t$, the area that does not overlap

**TABLE 12.4**  THREE PARTITIONS OF SUMS OF SQUARES USING THE SEASONS DEPRESSION DATA

| | Means and Cell Frequencies (in Parentheses) | | | |
|---|---|---|---|---|
| | HS | C | B | GS |
| Male | 6.903 (19) | 3.674 (33) | 3.331 (37) | 4.847 (39) |
| Female | 5.703 (48) | 7.081 (26) | 6.774 (29) | 4.735 (35) |

*Note.* $HS$ = high school education; $C$ = some college; $B$ = bachelor's degree; $GS$ = graduate school.

| | | Three Types of Sums of Squares | | | |
|---|---|---|---|---|---|
| SV | df | Type III SS | Type II SS | Type Ia SS | Type Ib SS |
| Education ($A$) | 3 | 78.13 ($t$) | 33.44 ($t + w$) | 68.28 ($t + w + v + u$) | 33.44 ($t + w$) |
| Gender ($B$) | 1 | 118.91 ($x$) | 120.77 ($x + y$) | 120.77 ($x + y$) | 156.61 ($x + y + v + u$) |
| $A \times B$ | 3 | 260.12 ($z$) | 260.12 ($z$) | 260.12 ($z$) | 260.12 ($z$) |
| S/AB | 258 | 6,516.05 | 6,516.05 | 6,516.05 | 6,516.05 |

*Note.* For the Type Ia $SS$, the $A$ sum of squares was calculated ignoring all other sources, and the $B$ sum of squares was calculated after adjusting for (removing variability due to) $A$ effects. For the Type Ib $SS$, the $B$ sum of squares was calculated ignoring all other sources, and the $A$ sum of squares was calculated after adjusting for (removing variability due to) $B$ effects. The letters in parentheses refer to the corresponding areas in Fig. 12.1. See the text for further explanation.

with the $B$ or $AB$ circles. Thus, Type III sums of squares are sums of squares for a source of variance after removing other effects from the analysis.

Although the Type III sum of squares is usually calculated by means of a regression analysis, as described in Chapter 21, the same result can be obtained by using formulas similar to those in the standard ANOVA (analysis of variance) calculations. This is usually referred to as an **unweighted means analysis** because the marginal means are not based on the weighted average of the cell means. For example, the unweighted mean for the high school scores ($\overline{Y}_{..1(U)}$) in Table 12.4 would be $(1/2)(6.903 + 5.703)$. Note that the two cell means are not weighted by the number of scores on which each is based, but instead are given equal weights. Accordingly, the Type III sums of squares for Education in Table 12.4 tests the null hypothesis

$$H_0: (\tfrac{1}{2})(\mu_{11} + \mu_{21}) = (\tfrac{1}{2})(\mu_{12} + \mu_{22}) = (\tfrac{1}{2})(\mu_{13} + \mu_{23}) = (\tfrac{1}{2})(\mu_{14} + \mu_{24})$$

where the first subscript refers to gender and the second to educational level. Appendix 12.1 provides an example of the calculation of the sums of squares for educational level, using standard sums of squares formulas with equal weights on the cell means. The result is identical to the regression analysis result provided by most statistical packages.

In summary, because the results are the same as those produced in an ANOVA in which the means are equally weighted (as illustrated in Appendix 12.1), this method of analysis is appropriate whenever it is reasonable to assume that the sampled populations are of equal size and the unequal $n$s reflect chance variation. For example, Type III sums of squares should be calculated when the data come from true experiments in which the independent variables have been manipulated, and the loss of data is caused by factors such as the random failure of individuals in various conditions to appear for the experiment. This approach would not be appropriate if the loss of data were systematic. Such systematic loss would occur, for example, if certain conditions were more aversive than others, thus leading to a greater loss of participants and their data in those conditions.

**Type II Sums of Squares.**   A second option available in the analysis of data from nonorthogonal designs is the calculation of Type II sums of squares. In this analysis, the variability due to a main effect is adjusted only for the variability caused by effects of the same or lower order. In the two-factor design, this requires adjusting the sum of squares for each main effect for variability from the other main effect, but not for the interaction. Therefore, we refer to the $A$ sum of squares as $SS_{A|B}$ (sum of squares for $A$ adjusted for $B$). The underlying assumption is that interaction effects are absent in the sampled populations. Appelbaum and Cramer (1974; Cramer & Appelbaum, 1980) have been the primary proponents of the Type II analysis, arguing that main effects should not be adjusted for interaction effects when the usual test of interaction has a nonsignificant result. The potential advantage is that such tests of main effects will have more power when small or no interaction variances are ignored in the analysis. The trouble with this approach is that weak tests of the interaction may cause us to fail to adjust for substantial interaction variance, thus increasing the Type 1 error rate in tests of the main effect. More conservative criteria for nonsignificance of the interaction could be used, such as requiring that the interaction not be significant at the .25 level, but there is insufficient understanding of the consequences of even this approach. As a general rule, Type II sums of squares should not be calculated unless there is strong a priori reason to assume no interaction effects, and a clearly nonsignificant interaction sum of squares.

In comparing the Type III and Type II results in Table 12.4, note that the $A$ (Education) sum of squares is smaller in the Type II analysis than in the Type III analysis even though the Type II analysis involves an additional area of Fig. 12.1 (i.e., $t + w$ versus $t$). The reason for this is that the areas of overlap in Fig. 12.1 represent covariances, numerators of correlation coefficients, and as such can be positive or negative. The area labeled $w$ is the covariance of the $A$ and $AB$ effects, adjusted for the contribution of $B$ effects. The fact that the Type II sums of squares are smaller than the Type I indicates that this covariance is negative.

The Type II sums of squares can also be obtained by carrying out an analysis in which the cell means are weighted. However, because the weights are not very meaningful, we will not develop this approach here. Interested readers may consult Carlson and Timm (1974).

**Type I Sums of Squares.**   In calculating Type I sums of squares, a hierarchical analysis is carried out. For example, in the Type 1a analysis reported in Table 12.4, the sum of squares for education was calculated ignoring gender and the interaction. This sum of squares is represented by the full circle $(t + w + v + u)$ in Fig. 12.1. The gender sum of squares was then calculated after adjusting for education; this corresponds to the $x + y$ area. Finally, the Gender × Education $(A \times B)$ sum of squares was calculated after adjusting for both main effects. Note that the gender sum of squares in the Type I and II analyses are identical because, in both cases, gender has been adjusted for the effects of education. In the Type Ib analysis, the effects of gender were removed first, and then the education sum of squares, adjusted for gender effects, was computed. Which approach should be taken, a or b, depends on the question. For example, if our primary interest is in whether educational level affects depression scores, we might first remove the variability due to gender, and then test the adjusted education source to determine if there was any further contribution due to that variable. The topic of the order of adjustments, and of the interpretation of results when variables are correlated and adjustments are made, is a complex one. We will have more to say about this issue in Chapters 15, 20, and 21 on analysis of covariance and multiple regression.

Once again, a cell means analysis provides an equivalent computational approach. For example, assuming weights based on the observed cell frequencies, the weighted marginal population mean for individuals with a high school (HS) education is

$$\mu_{HS} = \left(\frac{19}{19 + 48}\right)\mu_{11} + \left(\frac{48}{19 + 48}\right)\mu_{21}.$$

More generally, the marginal mean for any column, $k$, may be represented by

$$\mu_{.k} = \left(\frac{n_{1k}}{n_{1k} + n_{2k}}\right)\mu_{1k} + \left(\frac{n_{2k}}{n_{1k} + n_{2k}}\right)\mu_{2k}$$

and the null hypothesis of equality of effects of educational level is the hypothesis that the four marginal means are equal. Appendix 12.1 contains an example of sums of squares based on the weighted means.

### 12.4.3 Other Analyses

Several other approaches to unequal $n$s have been used by researchers. The "method of unweighted means" (Horst & Edwards, 1982) is computationally simple, but gives results equivalent to adjusting each sum of squares for its overlap with all others only when there are exactly two levels of all variables. Another approach used to equally weight cell means has been to randomly drop scores from cells to equate cell frequencies. Dropping scores results in a loss of degrees of freedom and consequently of power. It is also inappropriate if the original cell $n$s reflect the proportions in the populations, which will often be the case with categorical values. Investigators have also estimated missing scores to achieve equal $n$s. The reliability of missing score estimates will depend on the number of scores available in the cell. And again, we may be imposing an equality of cell frequencies that is unrepresentative of the relative sizes of the population. The availability of many computer packages designed to do unequal-$n$ analyses makes such short cuts and approximations superfluous. (It should also be noted that any program for regression analysis can accomplish any series of adjustments; Chapter 21 will discuss this further.) It is important, however, to recognize that statistical packages provide options for calculating sums of squares. The choice among such options has consequences for the data analysis and deserves careful thought before doing the ANOVA.

## 12.5 THREE-FACTOR DESIGNS

### 12.5.1 A 2 × 2 × 2 ($2^3$) Example

Let's add a hypothetical third factor to the design of the Wiley–Voss experiment. For example, suppose there were just two levels of instruction ($I$), summary and argument; two

**TABLE 12.5**   MEANS FOR A HYPOTHETICAL EXTENSION OF THE WILEY–VOSS EXPERIMENT

|  |  | Summary | Argument | Mean |
|---|---|---|---|---|
| Novice | Text | 71.25 | 73.75 | 72.50 |
|  | Web | 76.50 | 90.00 | 83.25 |
|  | Mean | 73.875 | 81.875 | 77.875 |
| Expert | Text | 70.50 | 74.00 | 72.25 |
|  | Web | 88.25 | 89.75 | 89.00 |
|  | Mean | 79.375 | 81.875 | 80.625 |
|  |  | Averaging Over Novices and Experts | | |
|  | Text | 70.875 | 73.875 | 72.375 |
|  | Web | 82.375 | 89.875 | 86.125 |
|  | Mean | 76.625 | 81.875 | 79.25 |

formats ($F$), text and web; and we divided participants with respect to experience ($E$)—those who either had prior experience searching the Internet (Experts) and those who were Novices. Assume that there are 10 scores in each cell; that is, $n = 10$ and $N = 80$. The means for this hypothetical experiment are presented in Table 12.5.

**Main Effects.**   In the ANOVA, there will be three sources of main effects—$I$, $F$, and $E$. We can view these main effects by calculating the marginal means. For example, the test of the $F$ source of variance involves a comparison of the text and web marginal means. These means are obtained by averaging over the four combinations of instructions and experience. As can be seen in the lower panel of Table 12.5, the text and web means are 72.375 and 86.125, respectively. The significance test is a test of the null hypothesis that, *averaging over the four populations corresponding to the combinations of experience and instructions*, there is no difference between the population text and web means. Because the difference between the web and text means is distributed on 1 $df$, $SS_F$ can be calculated as a contrast. The numerator is the squared difference between the means, and the denominator is the sum of the squared weights (1 and $-1$) divided by the number of scores upon which each mean is based ($4 \times 10$). Therefore,

$$SS_F = \frac{(\overline{Y}_{\text{Text}} - \overline{Y}_{\text{web}})^2}{1^2/4n + (-1)^2/4n}$$
$$= (2n)(72.375 - 86.125)^2 = 3781.25$$

The $SS_I$ and $SS_E$ are calculated in a similar manner.

**First-Order (Two-Factor) Interactions.**   There are three possible two-factor interactions: $F \times I$, $F \times E$, and $I \times E$. The $F \times E$ interaction is of particular interest because there is no reason to predict that computer experience would have an effect in the text condition, but it well might in the web condition. The interpretation of this interaction is essentially the same as if $F$ and $E$ were the only factors in the experiment, except that, in this case, the relevant means are obtained by averaging over the levels of the third variable, instructions. These means are in the rightmost column in the upper panel of Table 12.5. The interaction contrast is the difference between the format simple effects at the two levels of experience (or, equivalently, the difference between the experience simple effects computed for each format). This contrast is estimated as

$$\hat{\psi}_{F \times E} = (83.25 - 72.50) - (89.00 - 72.25) = -6$$

In words, the advantage of the web format over the text format is six points greater for experts than for novices. The sum of squares for this contrast is calculated as

$$SS_{F \times E} = \hat{\psi}_{F \times E}^2 \Big/ \left( \sum w^2 / 2n \right)$$

In this case, the weights ($w$) are 1, $-1$, $-1$, and 1, and the sum of their squared values is divided by 20, the number of scores on which each of the four means is based. Therefore,

$$SS_{F \times E} = (-6)^2 / (4/20) = 180$$

In the actual Wiley–Voss experiment, the error mean square was 154. Assuming a similar value for our hypothetical study, we lack sufficient evidence to reject the hypothesis of no interaction. In other words, we cannot conclude that the advantage of the web format over the text format is significantly greater for experts than for novices.

***The Second-Order (Three-Factor) Interaction.*** The eight cell means in Table 12.5 are plotted in Fig. 12.2. We assigned instructions to the $X$ axis, and had the experts' means in one panel and the novices in the other, with different lines for the two formats. However, this assignment of variables in the plot is arbitrary. We could have had the two formats, or the two types of instructions, in different panels. We will soon discuss some factors that may influence the decision when plotting means from a three-factor experiment. For now, let's focus on the interpretation of the second-order interaction. In the $2^3$ design, it is helpful to think of the interaction as a contrast of simple two-factor interactions. For example, in the right, expert, panel of the figure, the advantage of the web format over the text format is greater under summary than under argument instructions. However, the opposite is true in the left, novice, panel; there, the difference between web and text formats is smaller in the argument than in the summary condition. Looking at the actual means, the $F \times I$ contrast in the novice condition is

$$\hat{\psi}_{F \times I \mid \text{Novice}} = (71.25 - 73.75) - (76.50 - 90) = 11$$

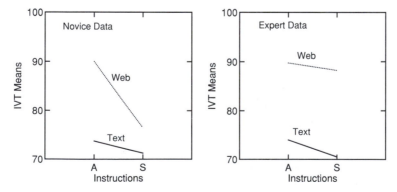

**Fig. 12.2** A plot of the means in Table 12.5.

The simple $F \times I$ interaction in the expert condition is

$$\hat{\psi}_{F \times I | \text{Expert}} = (70.50 - 74) - (88.25 - 89.75) = -2$$

The $F \times I \times E$ interaction contrast is the difference between the two simple interactions; that is,

$$\hat{\psi}_{F \times I \times E} = \hat{\psi}_{F \times I | \text{Novice}} - \hat{\psi}_{F \times I | \text{Expert}} = 11 - (-2) = 13$$

This interaction term is also distributed on 1 $df$. We can see this by a process of subtraction. Because there are eight cell means, $df_{\text{cells}} = 7$. Subtracting 3 $df$s for the three main effects and three more for the 3 two-factor interactions leaves 1 $df$ for the three-factor interaction. Because the $F \times I \times E$ term is distributed on 1 $df$, we can again calculate the sum of squares as a contrast:

$$SS_{F \times I \times E} = \hat{\psi}^2_{F \times I \times E} \Big/ \left( \sum \frac{w^2}{n} \right)$$

In this instance, the sum of the squared weights is 8 because each cell mean in the contrast is multiplied by either 1 or $-1$. This sum is divided by $n$ because each of the eight means is based on $n$ scores. Accordingly,

$$SS_{F \times I \times E} = (13^2)/(8/10) = 211.25$$

Again assuming that $MS_{\text{error}} = 154$, we conclude that the three-factor interaction is not significant. We cannot conclude that the $F \times I$ population interaction differs as a function of the level of experience with computers. Nor does the $F \times E$ interaction differ as a function of instructions, nor the $I \times E$ as a function of the format. No matter which simple two-factor interactions are contrasted, the result of the $F \times I \times E$ contrast will always be 13.

## 12.5.2 More on Three-Factor Interactions

It is important to realize that a three-factor interaction means that the simple interaction effects of any two variables vary as a function of the level of the third variable. Researchers often understand this to mean that, whenever the plot of the $AB$ combinations looks different at different levels of $C$, the three-factor interaction is likely to be significant. However, this is not true. Saying that the simple interaction effects of $AB$ are the same at all levels of $C$ is not the same as saying that the pattern of means is the same at all levels of $C$. The following set of means should help us understand this point.

| | $C_1$ | | $C_2$ | |
|---|---|---|---|---|
| | $B_1$ | $B_2$ | $B_1$ | $B_2$ |
| $A_1$ | 22 | 11 | 34 | 23 |
| $A_2$ | 20 | 14 | 23 | 17 |

Figure 12.3 presents a plot of the eight cell means under consideration. If these were population means, would you think that there is a second-order interaction? The pattern of means looks different at $C_1$ than at $C_2$; the lines cross in the $C_1$ panel, but not in the $C_2$ panel. As a result, students usually believe that an $ABC$ interaction is present. In fact, if we

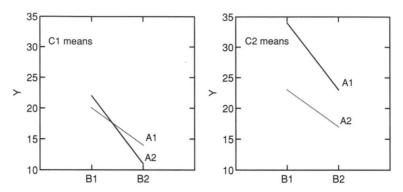

**Fig. 12.3** A $2^3$ plot with no $ABC$ interaction.

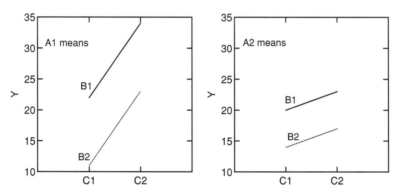

**Fig. 12.4** An alternative plot of the means in Fig. 12.3.

calculate the interaction contrast, we find it is exactly zero, so there cannot be an $A \times B \times C$ interaction. For example, calculating the simple $AB$ interaction contrast at each level of $C$, and subtracting,

$$\hat{\psi}_{ABC} = \hat{\psi}_{AB|C_1} - \hat{\psi}_{AB|C_2} = [(22 - 11) - (20 - 14)] - [(34 - 23) - (23 - 14)] = 0.$$

The reader should verify that the outcome is the same if we contrast the $AC$ simple interaction effects at the levels of $B$, or the $BC$ simple interaction effects at the levels of $A$.

One implication of this example is that the pattern of means can be deceptive. However, some patterns will clearly signal the possibility of a three-factor interaction. If the lines in an $AB$ plot are approximately parallel (i.e., there is no $AB$ interaction) at one or more levels of $C$, but there is a simple interaction at least at one other level of $C$, then this indicates an $ABC$ interaction. Also, if the lines in one panel converge, whereas those in other panels diverge, an $ABC$ interaction is indicated. If the two $AB$ plots are the same (or displaced by a constant amount), except for one point, there is reason to expect a three-factor interaction. Sometimes plotting the data in different ways is helpful. In Fig. 12.4, we have replotted the data from Fig. 12.3. Several points are now clearer than in the original plot. In particular, it should be evident that there is no $BC$ interaction, which was not at all clear in Fig. 12.3. It also appears that there is an $AB$ interaction because the spread among the $B$ lines is greater in the $A_1$ panel than in the $A_2$ panel. Finally, it appears that there is no second-order interaction because the $BC$ interaction contrast is zero in both panels. Of course, these are idealized data points, lacking the variability present in real data. However, the point still stands; it is often helpful to plot data in several ways. Different patterns may become evident, making clearer why certain effects in the ANOVA were significant, whereas others were not.

## 12.5.3 Three-Factor Between-Subjects Designs: The General Case

To understand formulas for sums of squares, and for components of the expected means measure (EMS), we require some notation. In general, we have three independent variables: $A$, $B$, and $C$, with $n$ subjects in each of the $abc$ cells. The relevant indices are

$$i = 1, 2, \ldots, n; \quad j = 1, 2, \ldots, a; \quad k = 1, 2, \ldots, b; \quad and \quad m = 1, 2, \ldots, c.$$

To define the sums of squares, we begin by partitioning the deviation of a score from the grand mean into two components, one corresponding to the deviation of the score from its cell mean and the other corresponding to the deviation of the cell mean from the grand mean:

$$Y_{ijkm} - \overline{Y}_{....} = (Y_{ijkm} - \overline{Y}_{.jkm}) + (\overline{Y}_{.jkm} - \overline{Y}_{....}) \tag{12.1}$$

Deviation of the score from its cell mean provides the basis for the error term in the ANOVA. Considering a single cell, if we square the $n$ deviations and divide by $n - 1$, we have $s^2_{jkm}$, an estimate of error variance. If we do this for every cell, then add the cell variances and divide by the number of cells, we have the error mean square; that is,

$$MS_{S/ABC} = \sum_{j=1}^{a} \sum_{k=1}^{b} \sum_{m=1}^{c} s^2_{jkm} \bigg/ abc \tag{12.2}$$

Deviation of the cell mean from the grand mean can be further partitioned into components that provide the basis for the sums of squares for main and interaction sources of variance. Each of the component deviations estimates a population parameter. For example, $\overline{Y}_{.j..} - \overline{Y}_{....}$ estimates $\alpha_j$, the effect of $A_j$ in the sampled population. Table 12.6 presents the components of the cell deviation and pairs it with the parameter it estimates. Summing the entries in the Effects column yields $\overline{Y}_{.jkm} - \overline{Y}_{....}$, the deviation of the cell mean from the grand mean. In the same way, the sum of squares based on the $abc$ cell means can be partitioned into the sums of squares for main and interaction sources of variance. The $df_{\text{cells}}$ can be partitioned into components representing the various sources of variance:

$$abc - 1 = (a - 1) + (b - 1) + (c - 1) + (a - 1)(b - 1) + (a - 1)(c - 1)$$
$$+ (b - 1)(c - 1) + (a - 1)(b - 1)(c - 1)$$

The only new term in the preceding equation is $(a - 1)(b - 1)(c - 1)$, the $df_{ABC}$. The partitioning of the $SS_{\text{tot}}$ and the $df_{\text{tot}}$, together with definitional formulas of the sums of squares, is presented in Table 12.7.

The $S/ABC$ source of variance is the error term against which all main and interaction terms, as well as any contrasts that are of interest, are tested. The rationale for this choice of error term lies, as usual, in the expected mean squares, which are presented in Table 12.8.

**TABLE 12.6** EFFECTS AND THE PARAMETERS THEY ESTIMATE IN A THREE-FACTOR DESIGN

| Source | Effect | Parameter |
|---|---|---|
| A | $\overline{Y}_{.j..} - \overline{Y}_{....}$ | $\alpha_j = \mu_{j..} - \mu_{...}$ |
| B | $\overline{Y}_{..k.} - \overline{Y}_{....}$ | $\beta_k = \mu_{.k.} - \mu_{...}$ |
| C | $\overline{Y}_{...m} - \overline{Y}_{....}$ | $\gamma_m = \mu_{..m} - \mu_{...}$ |
| AB | $\overline{Y}_{.jk.} - \overline{Y}_{.j..} - \overline{Y}_{..k.} + \overline{Y}_{....}$ | $(\alpha\beta)_{jk} = (\mu_{jk.} - \mu_{...}) - \alpha_j - \beta_k$ |
| AC | $\overline{Y}_{.j.m} - \overline{Y}_{.j..} - \overline{Y}_{...m} + \overline{Y}_{....}$ | $(\alpha\gamma)_{jm} = (\mu_{j.m} - \mu_{...}) - \alpha_j - \gamma_m$ |
| BC | $\overline{Y}_{..km} - \overline{Y}_{..k.} - \overline{Y}_{...m} + \overline{Y}_{....}$ | $(\beta\gamma)_{km} = (\mu_{.km} - \mu_{...}) - \beta_k - \gamma_m$ |
| ABC | $\overline{Y}_{.jkm} + \overline{Y}_{.j..} + \overline{Y}_{..k.} + \overline{Y}_{...m}$ | $(\alpha\beta\gamma)_{jkm} = (\mu_{jkm} - \mu_{...}) - \alpha_j - \beta_k$ |
|  | $\quad - \overline{Y}_{.jk.} - \overline{Y}_{.j.m} - \overline{Y}_{..km} - \overline{Y}_{....}$ | $\quad - \gamma_m - (\alpha\beta)_{jk} - (\alpha\gamma)_{jm} - (\beta\gamma)_{km}$ |

**TABLE 12.7** PARTITIONING THE TOTAL DEGREES OF FREEDOM AND SUMS OF SQUARES IN A THREE-FACTOR DESIGN

| SV | df | SS |
|---|---|---|
| Total | $abcn - 1$ | $\sum_i \sum_j \sum_k \sum_m (Y_{ijkm} - \overline{Y}_{....})^2$ |
| Between cells | $abc - 1$ | $n \sum_j \sum_k \sum_m (\overline{Y}_{.jkm} - \overline{Y}_{....})^2$ |
| A | $a - 1$ | $nbc \sum_j (\overline{Y}_{.j..} - \overline{Y}_{....})^2$ |
| B | $b - 1$ | $nac \sum_k (\overline{Y}_{..k.} - \overline{Y}_{....})^2$ |
| C | $c - 1$ | $nab \sum_m (\overline{Y}_{...m} - \overline{Y}_{....})^2$ |
| AB | $(a - 1)(b - 1)$ | $nc \sum_j \sum_k (\overline{Y}_{.jk.} - \overline{Y}_{.j..} - \overline{Y}_{..k.} + \overline{Y}_{....})^2$ |
| AC | $(a - 1)(c - 1)$ | $nb \sum_j \sum_m (\overline{Y}_{.j.m} - \overline{Y}_{.j..} - \overline{Y}_{...m} + \overline{Y}_{....})^2$ |
| BC | $(b - 1)(c - 1)$ | $na \sum_k \sum_m (\overline{Y}_{..km} - \overline{Y}_{..k.} - \overline{Y}_{...m} + \overline{Y}_{....})^2$ |
| ABC | $(a - 1)(b - 1)(c - 1)$ | $n \sum_j \sum_k \sum_m (\overline{Y}_{.jkm} + \overline{Y}_{.j..} + \overline{Y}_{..k.} + \overline{Y}_{...m}$ |
|  |  | $\quad - \overline{Y}_{.jk.} - \overline{Y}_{.j.m} - \overline{Y}_{..km} - \overline{Y}_{....})^2$ |
| S/ABC (within cells) | $abc(n - 1)$ | $SS_{\text{tot}} - SS_{B.\text{cells}}$ |

These have been derived from the structural model in the upper part of the table under the usual assumptions that the scores in the *abc* treatment populations are independently distributed and that the population variances all equal $\sigma_e^2$. In addition, all three factors are assumed to have fixed effects; that is, the levels have been arbitrarily selected and not randomly sampled from a universe of treatment levels.

As in the two-factor design, the *EMS* play an important role in estimating the variances of effects, and these in turn enable us to estimate measures of effect size such as Cohen's *f*

**TABLE 12.8**   STRUCTURAL MODEL AND EXPECTED MEAN SQUARES (EMS) FOR THE THREE-FACTOR DESIGN

The Structural Model

$$Y_{ijkm} = \mu + \alpha_j + \beta_k + \gamma_m + (\alpha\beta)_{jk} + (\alpha\gamma)_{jm} + (\beta\gamma)_{km} + (\alpha\beta\gamma)_{jkm} + \varepsilon_{ijkm}$$

| SV | EMS |
|---|---|
| A | $\sigma_e^2 + nbc \sum_j \alpha_j^2/(a-1)$ |
| B | $\sigma_e^2 + nac \sum_k \beta_k^2/(b-1)$ |
| C | $\sigma_e^2 + nab \sum_m \gamma_m^2/(c-1)$ |
| AB | $\sigma_e^2 + nc \sum_j \sum_k (\alpha\beta)_{jk}^2/[(a-1)(b-1)]$ |
| AC | $\sigma_e^2 + nb \sum_j \sum_m (\alpha\gamma)_{jm}^2/[(a-1)(c-1)]$ |
| BC | $\sigma_e^2 + na \sum_k \sum_m (\beta\gamma)_{km}^2/[(b-1)(c-1)]$ |
| ABC | $\sigma_e^2 + n \sum_j \sum_k \sum_m (\alpha\beta\gamma)_{jkm}^2/[(a-1)(b-1)(c-1)]$ |
| S/ABC | $\sigma_e^2$ |

*Note.* The parameters of the structural model are defined in Table 12.6.

(1988), $\omega^2$, and $\lambda$. These, as in the one- and two-factor designs, are of interest in themselves and also are used in calculations of power. Calculations of estimates of variances of main and interaction effects are similar to those in Table 12.1. For example, assume a design in which $n = 6$, $a = 2$, $b = 3$, and $c = 3$. A portion of the ANOVA table might contain the following values:

| SV | df | MS | F | p |
|---|---|---|---|---|
| AB | 2 | 34 | 3.40 | .038 |
| ABC | 4 | 24 | 2.40 | .048 |
| S/ABC | 90 | 10 | | |

Given these values, we can estimate the population variances. The estimate of $\sigma_e^2$ is

$$\hat{\sigma}_e^2 = MS_{S/ABC} = 10$$

and from the equations in Table 12.8, we have

$$E(MS_{AB}) = \sigma_e^2 + nc \sum_j \sum_k (\alpha\beta)_{jk}^2/[(a-1)(b-1)]$$

Therefore,

$$(MS_{AB} - MS_{S/ABC})/nc \doteq \sum_j \sum_k (\alpha\beta)_{jk}^2/[(a-1)(b-1)]$$

($\hateq$ means "is an estimate of") and multiplying both sides of the preceding equation by $(a - 1)(b - 1)/ab$, the estimator of $\sigma^2_{AB}$ is

$$\hat{\sigma}^2_{AB} = [(a - 1)(b - 1)/ab] \times [(MS_{AB} - MS_{S/ABC})/nc]$$
$$= (2/6)[(34 - 10)/18] = .444$$

Various measures of effect size can now be estimated. For example Cohen's $f$ is estimated as

$$\hat{f}_{AB} = \hat{\sigma}_{AB}/\hat{\sigma}_e = \sqrt{.444/10} = .21$$

In a similar way, we can show that $\hat{\sigma}^2_{ABC} = .519$ and $\hat{f}_{ABC} = .228$. Note that $\hat{f}$ (and other measures of effect size) is larger for $ABC$, although the $F$ ratio is larger and the $p$ value smaller for $AB$.

## 12.6 MORE THAN THREE INDEPENDENT VARIABLES

The analyses of data from between-subject designs involving more than three factors are, in all respects, straightforward generalizations of the material presented for two- and three-factor designs. Each variable and each possible combination of variables are potential contributors to the total variability, and so is the variability among scores within each cell of the design. As might be guessed, the degrees of freedom for any higher-order interaction are a product of the degrees of freedom for the variables entering into the interaction. For example, an $ABCD$ interaction would have $(a - 1)(b - 1)(c - 1)(d - 1)$ $df$. The interpretation of such higher-order interactions is often difficult. We can say that a significant four-way interaction indicates that the interaction of any three variables is a function of the level of the fourth variable, but that is not very enlightening. Unless we have prior grounds for expecting such interactions to be significant, or can attribute the interaction to some subset of cell means, care should be taken before making too much of the result.

## 12.7 POOLING IN FACTORIAL DESIGNS

### 12.7.1 What Is Pooling?

When two or more sources of variance are pooled, the sums of squares are added together and divided by the sum of the degrees of freedom. For example, in a two-factor design, the pool of the $AB$ term and the $S/AB$ term is

$$MS_{\text{pool}} = \frac{SS_{AB} + SS_{S/AB}}{df_{AB} + df_{S/AB}} \tag{12.3}$$

Equation 12.3 can be rewritten as the weighted average of the two mean squares:

$$MS_{\text{pool}} = \left(\frac{df_{AB}}{df_{AB} + df_{S/AB}}\right) MS_{AB} + \left(\frac{df_{S/AB}}{df_{AB} + df_{S/AB}}\right) MS_{S/AB} \tag{12.4}$$

This form of the equation raises the question: When is it proper to average two mean squares? The answer is that, if the two mean squares estimate the same population variance, or variances, pooling is proper. In the example of Equation 12.4, the assumption is that $\sigma_{AB}^2 = 0$; therefore, we have assumed a structural model that omits the $(\alpha\beta)_{jk}$ term and, consequently, both $MS_{AB}$ and $MS_{S/AB}$ are assumed to estimate $\sigma_e^2$. The advantage of pooling two or more estimates of the population error variance is that $MS_{\text{pool}}$ is distributed on more $df$s than $MS_{S/AB}$; therefore, $F$ tests based on the pooled error term may be more powerful than tests based on $MS_{S/AB}$. Of course, we never *know* that $\sigma_{AB}^2 = 0$. If it is not, we may lose power in using the pooled error term to test a false null hypothesis about a main effect. To see why, look again at Equation 12.4. If, contrary to the assumption on which pooling is based, $E(MS_{AB}) = \sigma_e^2 + \sigma_{AB}^2$, then the weighted average of this expectation and of $\sigma_e^2$ will be larger than $\sigma_e^2$. As a result, the $F$ test of a main effect will be **negatively biased**; the expectation of the error term involves more than just $\sigma_e^2$, and there will be too many Type II errors. Somewhat surprisingly, when the null hypothesis about the main effect is true, there may actually be an increase in Type I errors. The reason for this is that if $MS_{AB}$ and $MS_{S/AB}$ do not both estimate $\sigma_e^2$, the ratio of $MS_A$ (or $MS_B$) to $MS_{\text{pool}}$ will not be distributed as $F$, and the tail area may be larger than the nominal $\alpha$. In view of these considerations, it is not clear when, if ever, to pool. We consider this issue next.

### 12.7.2 When (If Ever) to Pool

Although the subject of pooling is a contentious one, the most common recommendation is a **"sometimes-pool" rule** recommended by Bozivich, Bancroft, and Hartley (1956). In this procedure, pooling is carried out if a preliminary test (e.g., $AB$ against $S/AB$) is not significant at the .25 level. Using this rule, in a two-factor design, the $AB$ and $S/AB$ terms would be pooled to provide an error term against which to test $A$ and $B$ if the $MS_{AB}/MS_{S/AB}$ ratio was not significant at the .25 level. However, the Bozivich et al. recommendation was based on results for a nested design (see Chapter 16). More relevant to the designs of the current chapter are the results obtained by Mead, Bancroft, and Han (1975). They investigated pooling of the $AB$ and $S/AB$ terms in the context of a design with two fixed-effect factors. For designs in which cell frequencies were equal, they found that the sometimes-pool rule, even with the criterion $\alpha$ set at .50, often resulted in a loss of power when the null hypothesis about the main effect was false, and an increase in Type I error rate when it was true. Although there were conditions under which the sometimes-pool rule was beneficial, these involved cases in which the $n$s were proportional and distributed in such a way that the interaction $df$ equaled those for the within-cell error term, or were greater. Such distributions of cell frequencies are very unlikely. Therefore, in designs in which all factors have fixed effects, we recommend never pooling. We consider whether the sometimes-pool rule is advisable in other designs when we discuss those designs.

### 12.7.3 Unintended Pooling

Researchers often pool terms without realizing they have done so. Typically, in such cases, there are one or more treatment variables and then one "nuisance" variable that the researcher regards as irrelevant. For example, the position of a reward may appear equally often in all experimental conditions of a discrimination study, or each of several experimenters may run an equal number of subjects in each condition. Table 12.9 presents an example of two analyses of data from a design in which $A$ is the treatment of interest and $B$ is a nuisance

**TABLE 12.9** AN EXAMPLE OF ANOVAS IN WHICH ONE FACTOR IS A NUISANCE VARIABLE

The Full Structural Model: $Y_{ijk} = \mu + \alpha_j + \beta_k + (\alpha\beta)_{jk} + \varepsilon_{ijk}$

| SV | df | SS | MS | F | p | EMS |
|----|----|----|----|----|----|----|
| A | 2 | 240 | 120 | 3.24 | .049 | $\sigma_e^2 + 16\sum_j \alpha_j^2/2$ |
| B | 1 | 75 | 75 | 2.03 | .162 | $\sigma_e^2 + 24\sum_k \beta_k^2$ |
| AB | 2 | 160 | 80 | 2.16 | .128 | $\sigma_e^2 + 8\sum_j \sum_k (\alpha\beta)_{jk}^2/2$ |
| S/AB | 42 | 1554 | 37 | | | $\sigma_e^2$ |

The Reduced Structural Model: $Y_{ijk} = \mu + \alpha_j + \varepsilon_{ijk}$

| SV | df | SS | MS | F | p | EMS |
|----|----|----|----|----|----|----|
| A | 2 | 240 | 120 | 3.02 | .059 | $\sigma_e^2 + 16\sum_j \alpha_j^2/2$ |
| Pooled Error | 45 | 1789 | 39.76 | | | $\sigma_e^2$ |

variable, such as position of the reward, or experimenter, or gender. In an analysis based on the full model, the treatment ($A$) has a significant effect. When the $B$ variable is ignored in the ANOVA, we implicitly assume the structural model in the lower panel of Table 12.9. In this particular case, the treatment effect is no longer significant. Note that the pooled error sum of squares is the sum of $SS_B$, $SS_{AB}$, and $SS_{S/AB}$, and the pooled error $df$ are summed in the same way.

We cannot know which model is correct; nor can we know whether the null hypothesis is false, as the full ANOVA indicates. However, we do know that if the reduced model in the lower panel is not correct, and if there are $B$ and/or $AB$ effects in the population; then, the pooled error mean square estimates more than just error variance. Specifically, assuming that the full model of the upper panel is correct, pooling results in an inflated error term and a ratio of mean squares that is not distributed as $F$. The expectation of that error term is

$$E(MS_{\text{pool}}) = (42/45)\sigma_e^2 + (1/45)\left(\sigma_e^2 + 24\sum_k \beta_k^2\right)$$

$$+ (2/45)\left(\sigma_e^2 + 8\sum_j \sum_k (\alpha\beta)_{jk}^2/2\right)$$

$$= \sigma_e^2 + (24/45)\sum_k \beta_k^2 + (16/45)\sum_j \sum_k (\alpha\beta)_{jk}^2/2$$

As we noted in discussing Mead et al.'s (1975) results, we run the risk of a loss of power if the null hypothesis is false, or an increased Type I error rate if it is true. The message is simple: Consider all the factors that go into your design and test the full model.

## 12.8 BLOCKING TO REDUCE ERROR VARIANCE

Between-subject designs usually involve considerable variance because individuals differ on many dimensions that will influence the data. There are several ways in which we can attempt to reduce error variance and thus increase the precision of our estimates and the power of hypothesis tests. One approach is to use designs in which participants are tested under all levels of the independent variable. We consider variations of such repeated-measures designs in several of the following chapters. However, in many cases, such designs make no sense. In a test of drug treatments for some disorder, we are unlikely to test the same individuals under all the drugs in the study. Nor are we likely to compare several methods of instruction with the same group of students. In short, there are many situations in which the nature of the treatment variable requires that different individuals be assigned to different levels. In such studies, we can often make use of a concomitant variable, $X$, a measure that we have reason to believe is correlated with the dependent variable $Y$. There are two ways in which $X$ can be used. One way is to perform a regression analysis, **ANCOVA**, in which data are adjusted for variability attributable to $X$. Chapter 15 describes this method and compares it with the method we consider in this section. In this section, we use $X$ to create blocks of subjects and remove its main and interaction effects from the total variability.

This approach uses $X$ in the design of an experiment. Suppose we had four instructional conditions ($a = 4$) whose effects on reading skill we wished to compare. $X$ might be a measure of reading readiness obtained before the start of the school year. Assume that we have 80 children available for this study. We might rank these 80 children in terms of their reading readiness score. We could then divide them into five blocks of 16 children; block 1 ($B_1$) would consist of the 16 children with the highest reading readiness score, $B_2$ would consist of the 16 with the next highest $X$ values, and so on. Then we would randomly assign each of the 16 children in $B_1$ to one of the four instructional conditions with the constraint that there would be exactly four children in each instructional condition. We would do the same thing for each of the other reading readiness blocks. The result is that we would have a two-factor design in which $a = 4$, $b = 5$, and $n = 4$. This two-factor **Treatments** $\times$ **Blocks design** usually will have less error variance than the one-factor design based on the same total number of subjects because the four subjects within each $A \times B$ cell will be less variable in reading readiness than the 20 subjects within each level of $A$ would have been if we had used a one-factor design in which 20 subjects were randomly assigned to each level of $A$ without regard to reading readiness.

How many blocks should be used? If the total $N$ is held constant, increasing the number of blocks will decrease the error variance because with more blocks individuals within a block will be more similar with respect to reading readiness. However, increasing the number of blocks also decreases the error $df$, potentially decreasing power and precision of estimates. In our example, in the one-factor design, the error $df$ are $df_{S/A} = df_{tot} - df_A = 79 - 3 = 76$. In the treatment $\times$ blocks design, the error $df$ are $df_{S/AB} = df_{tot} - (df_A + df_B + df_{AB}) = 79 - (3 + 4 + 12) = 60$. But supposing we used 10, rather than 5 blocks. Still holding $N$ at 80, $a = 4$, $b = 10$, and $n = 2$. The error $df$ are now 40, a loss of 20 $df$. The point is that there is an optimal number of blocks that depends on $N$, $a$, and the correlation between the concomitant and dependent measures. Feldt (1958) has discussed these issues and provided recommendations for selecting the value of $b$. That article should be consulted before using the design.

## 12.9 CONCLUDING REMARKS

The between-subjects factorial designs of this and the preceding chapters have several advantages. Assuming equal cell frequencies, the analysis of the data is much simpler than for most other designs. For any given number of scores, the error degrees of freedom will be larger than for any comparable design. The requirements of the underlying model are more easily met by these between-subjects designs than by other designs, and violations of assumptions are less likely to affect the distribution of the $F$ ratio. The between-subjects designs share one major deficit. Because the within-cell variance—which is the basis for the error term for all $F$ tests—is a function of individual differences, the efficiency of the design is low compared with that of other designs. That is, other designs, which allow the removal of individual difference variability from the error variance, generally will yield smaller error terms and therefore more precise estimates of population effects and more powerful tests of hypotheses. The between-subjects designs are most useful whenever participants are relatively homogeneous for the variable being measured; whenever a large $N$ is available, compensating somewhat for the variability of measurements; or whenever it is feasible to block participants, or adjust variability, on the basis of a concomitant measure related to the dependent variable. Also, there are many experiments in which it is impossible to do anything but assign different participants to different levels of the variable. This is self-evident when the independent variable is personality type or training technique. It may also be true when much time is needed to obtain a measure from the participant, and it is therefore preferable to obtain only one measure from each person. Nevertheless, particularly when several factors are manipulated, participants are usually tested under several levels of the independent variable. In Chapter 13, we consider such repeated-measures, or within-subject, designs.

## KEY CONCEPTS

partial $\omega^2$

$\eta^2$ (eta squared)                          $\lambda$ (lambda)

concomitant variable                            nonorthogonal design

$SS_{A|B}$                                       $SS_{A|B,AB}$

Type I sums of squares                          Type II sums of squares

Type III sums of squares                        pooling sums of squares

negatively biased $F$ test                      "sometimes-pool" rule

analysis of covariance (ANCOVA)                 Treatments $\times$ Blocks design

harmonic mean                                   unweighted means analysis

weighted means analysis

## EXERCISES

**12.1**  Consider the following means from a $2 \times 2 \times 2$ ($2^3$) design.
  **(a)** State the contrasts ($\psi$) corresponding to $A$, $BC$, and $ABC$ sources of variance.
  **(b)** Use the contrast formula to calculate the sums of squares for each contrast in part (a). Assume $n = 10$.

|       | $C_1$ |       |       | $C_2$ |       |
|-------|-------|-------|-------|-------|-------|
|       | $B_1$ | $B_2$ |       | $B_1$ | $B_2$ |
| $A_1$ | 12    | 14    | $A_1$ | 8     | 13    |
| $A_2$ | 17    | 16    | $A_2$ | 10    | 18    |

**12.2** Assume that in a multifactor experiment, $a = 4$, $b = 3$, and $c = 2$ and $N = 96$. Given that $MS_A = 56.8$ and the $F = 2.84$,

(a) What is $n$? $MS_{S/ABC}$?

(b) Estimate $\sigma^2$ and $f^2$ for the $A$ effect.

(c) Assuming the effect size and error variance calculated in part (a), what power do we have to test the $A$ effect (at $\alpha = .01$) if the study is redone with $n = 8$?

**12.3** In a study designed to examine changes in attention with age, 180 children are required to sort decks of cards into two piles according to the value of a relevant dimension contained on the card. For example, if the relevant dimension is shape, the child may be asked to sort all the cards in a deck that contain a circle into one pile and all the cards that contain a square into another pile. To investigate how well a child is able to focus on a single dimension, the amount of irrelevant information present on the card is varied across different experimental conditions: there is either no irrelevant information ($I_1$); one irrelevant dimension, such as color ($I_2$); or two irrelevant dimensions ($I_3$). To summarize the design, there are three *age* levels (3, 5, and 7 years), three levels of *irrelevant information*, and both male and female participants; there are 10 participants in each of these 18 cells. The dependent variable is the average (mean) time required to sort a deck of cards.

(a) Write down the ANOVA table for this design (SV, *df*, and EMS).

(b) The following hypotheses are made: (i) older children are generally faster at doing the task; (ii) irrelevant information interferes with performance, and there is more interference for younger children than for older children; (iii) the tendency for younger children to be more influenced by the irrelevant information than older children is more pronounced for boys than for girls.

If the hypotheses are correct, what terms would you expect to be significant?

**12.4** A large scale study of programmed instruction is carried out with three variables: method (linear program, branching program, material is just read); ability level of students (low, average, high); and instruction time per day (30, 45, or 60 min). Several hypotheses are:

$H_1$: High-ability (*HiA*) students perform better than low-ability (*LoA*) students.

$H_2$: Programmed instruction (*LP, BP*) is superior to nonprogrammed instruction (*NP*).

$H_3$: *HiA* students readers improve less with increased instructional time than *LoA* students.

$H_4$: Performance improves as instruction time increases, but the improvement is smaller between 45 and 60 min than between 30 and 45 min.

$H_5$: The improvement in performance with increased time is greater for the *NP* (no program) conditions.

(a) Plot a set of means consistent with these hypotheses.

(b) What significance tests would you carry out to test this set of hypotheses?

**12.5** Following is a data set with unequal $n$s. The cell totals ($T_{.jk}$) and the $ns$ ($n_{jk}$) are given ($T_{.jk}/n_{jk}$):

|       | $B_1$  | $B_2$  |
|-------|--------|--------|
| $A_1$ | 20/2   | 40/4   |
| $A_2$ | 16/2   | 4/2    |

(a) Calculate $SS_{cells}$. The equation is $SS_{cells} = \sum_j \sum_k n_{jk}(\overline{Y}._{jk} - \overline{Y}...)^2$.

(b) In the same way you did part (a), calculate $SS_A$ and $SS_B$. Then subtract these from $SS_{cells}$ to get $SS_{AB}$. Do you see any problem with this procedure? Explain.

(c) Calculate $\hat{\alpha}_1$ and $\hat{\alpha}_2$. This requires finding the marginal (row) means for $A_1$ and $A_2$ and subtracting the grand mean. If you have done this correctly, $\sum_j n_{j.}\hat{\alpha}_j = 0$ ($n_{j.}$ is the total $n$ for row $j$).

(d) Subtract $\hat{\alpha}_j$ from each cell mean in row $j$. Look at the table of means that results. Using these adjusted means, what are $SS_B$ and $SS_{AB}$? How does this result compare with your answer in part (b)?

**12.6** Consider the following table of cell means. We will adjust these means for the effects of $A$ under different assumptions about cell frequencies and, by observing what happens to the column means, infer the consequences of equal, proportional, and disproportional cell frequencies for ANOVA. The cell means are:

|       | $B_1$ | $B_2$ | $B_3$ |
|-------|-------|-------|-------|
| $A_1$ | 12    | 8     | 22    |
| $A_2$ | 8     | 6     | 13    |
| $A_3$ | 1     | 3     | 16    |

(a) Assume that the cell frequencies are all the same. (i) Calculate the row and column means. (ii) Calculate estimates of the row effects ($\hat{\alpha}_j$). (iii) Subtract each value of $\hat{\alpha}_j$ from the three cell means in the corresponding row. How do the column means of this adjusted (for $A$ effects) matrix compare with those in part (i)?

(b) Assume the original cell means presented here. This time, however, assume the following cell frequencies ($n_{jk}$):

|       | $B_1$ | $B_2$ | $B_3$ |
|-------|-------|-------|-------|
| $A_1$ | 4     | 8     | 12    |
| $A_2$ | 3     | 6     | 9     |
| $A_3$ | 1     | 2     | 3     |

Redo (i)–(iii) of part (a). Be careful in calculating the row, column, and grand means; the values being averaged must be weighted by their corresponding frequency. For example, the mean of the first row is $[(4)(12) + (8)(8) + (12)(22)]/24$. Similarly, the grand mean is the weighted average of the 12 cell means (or of the three row or column means).

(c) Again assume the original set of means. This time, the $n_{jk}$ are:

|       | $B_1$ | $B_2$ | $B_3$ |
|-------|-------|-------|-------|
| $A_1$ | 5     | 10    | 4     |
| $A_2$ | 5     | 5     | 10    |
| $A_3$ | 10    | 3     | 5     |

Again, do (i)–(iii).

(d) Review your answers to this problem and draw a conclusion about the effects of equal, proportional, and disproportional cell frequencies about the partitioning of variability in ANOVA.

**12.7** (a) In Exercise 11.12, based on the file Ex11_12, we found that the $B$ source of variance had an associated $p$ value slightly greater than .05. This does not provide a good sense of the effect size. Calculate both Cohen's $f$ and partial $\omega^2$ for the $B$ effect.

(b) Calculate the power to detect a medium $B$ effect ($f = .25$), given the design of Ex11_12. Do you think the $N$ in the study was sufficient?

**12.8** The file Ex12_8 contains an artificial data set modeled on results reported by Roediger, Meade, and Bergman (2001). They varied three factors in a study of social influence on memory: (1) a confederate included false recalls in the presence of the participant [Context = exptal (i.e., experimental)] or did not include such reports (Context = control); (2) false items were highly related to items actually present in the to-be-remembered list or were low related (Related = high or low), and the time to view the items during the study period was either 15, 30, or 45 seconds. (In the actual study, the context and relatedness variables were within-subject factors, and there were only two viewing times.) The dependent variable in our file is the percentage of false recognitions by the participants.

(a) Plot the means and describe the trends in the data.

(b) Perform an analysis of variance, including trend tests you believe to be appropriate. Discuss the results.

**12.9** The Wiley_Voss file (*Wiley* folder on the CD) contains several dependent variables. Here, we analyze the SVT (sentence verification task) measure.

(a) Plot the cell means, including standard error bars.

(b) Perform the ANOVA.

(c) Calculate the standardized effects (Cohen's $f$) for the main and interaction effects.

(d) Compare the relative sizes of the $f$ values with the $p$ values for the ANOVA. If there is a difference in ordering, discuss why this has happened.

(e) What $N$ would you need to have .8 power to reject $H_0$ if the Format $f$ value was .25 (medium, by Cohen's guidelines)? What $N$ would you need for the Instruction effect? Is there a difference? If so, why?

**12.10**   The file Ex12_10 on the CD contains data modeled after that collected in a study by Bless, Bohner, Schwarz, and Strack (1990). These investigators manipulated the mood (1 = happy, 2 = sad) of their participants, and presented them with a message (1 = strong, 2 = weak) designed to influence their attitude about student service fees. Subjects' focus (1 = content, 2 = language) was also varied. The dependent measure in our data set is the recommended fee (in dollars) after reading the message.

(a) Plot a bar graph of the eight cell means. Describe the pattern. What main and interaction effects are suggested by the plot?

(b) Perform an ANOVA on the data in the file. Discuss the results with reference to the plot of the means in part (a).

(c) Calculate $\omega^2$ for each of the sources of variance. How do the values relate to the results of the ANOVA?

**12.11**   Bless et al. (see Exercise 12.10) also collected data from a control group ($n = 10$) that received no message but were asked to assess a fee. Assume that the mean for the control group is 48 and the standard deviation is 4.5. Test the difference between the control group and each of the eight experimental groups. Which of the experimental groups differed significantly ($\alpha = .10$) from the control group? Be explicit about the method for controlling the FWE and the selection of the error term(s).

---

## APPENDIX 12.1

---

## Calculating Type III and Type I Sums of Squares in Cell Means Analyses

### The Harmonic Mean

Calculating the Type III sum of squares involves the harmonic means of cell frequencies. Assume we have $a$ rows and $b$ columns, with $n_{jk}$ scores in each cell. Then, the harmonic mean of the number of scores in column $k$ is

$$\tilde{n}_{.k} = \frac{a}{\sum_{j=1}^{a}(1/n_{jk})} \tag{12.5}$$

### Type III Sums of Squares for B (Unweighted Means Analysis)

The unweighted marginal mean of column $k$ is obtained by adding the cell means in the column and dividing by the number of rows; that is,

$$\overline{Y}_{..k(U)} = \sum_{j=1}^{a} \overline{Y}_{.jk}\Big/a \tag{12.6}$$

As in the usual formula for the $B$ sum of squares, we need the squared deviation of the column mean from the grand mean. In this case, the "grand mean" is calculated differently, depending on whether we want the $A$ or $B$ sum of squares. For the Type III $B$ sum of squares, the grand mean is obtained by multiplying each unweighted column mean by the harmonic mean of the $n_{jk}$ in that column, summing these products and dividing by the sum of the column harmonic means. In equation form, we have

$$\overline{Y}_{G(B)} = \sum_{k=1}^{b} \tilde{n}_{.k} \overline{Y}_{.k(U)} \bigg/ \sum_{k=1}^{b} \tilde{n}_{.k} \tag{12.7}$$

Substituting numerical values from Table 12.4 in Equations 12.5, 12.6, and 12.7, we have the values needed to calculate the $SS_{B|A,AB}$ (the Type III sum of squares for $B$) in this cell means analysis:

$$\tilde{n}_{.k} = 27.224, 29.085, 32.515, \text{ and } 36.892$$

$$\overline{Y}_{..k(U)} = 6.303, 5.378, 5.052, \text{ and } 4.791$$

$\sum_{k=1}^{b} \tilde{n}_{.k} = 125.716$ and $\overline{Y}_{G(B)} = 5.322$. The $SS_{B|A,AB}$ formula looks much like the standard definitional formula for $SS_B$ in an orthogonal design, except that $n$ is replaced by $\tilde{n}_{.k}$ and the grand mean is calculated as in Equation 12.7:

$$SS_{B|A,AB} = a \sum_{k=1}^{b} \tilde{n}_{.k} (\overline{Y}_{..k(U)} - \overline{Y}_{G(B)})^2 \tag{12.8}$$

After substituting the previously calculated values in Equation 12.8, the result is $SS_{B|A,AB} = 78.13$, as in Table 12.4.

## Type I Sums of Squares for $B$ (Weighted Means Analysis)

In this analysis, the column (educational level) means are obtained by weighting each cell mean by its relative frequency; that is,

$$\overline{Y}_{..k(W)} = \sum_{j=1}^{a} n_{jk} \overline{Y}_{.jk} \bigg/ n_{.k} \tag{12.9}$$

where $n_{.k}$ is the total number of scores in column $k$. The "grand mean" is

$$\overline{Y}_{...W} = \sum_{k=1}^{b} n_{.k} \overline{Y}_{..k(W)} \bigg/ N \tag{12.10}$$

where $N$ is the total number of scores. Substituting numbers from Table 12.4 in Equation 12.10, the weighted column means are 6.044, 5.176, 4.844, and 4.794, and $\overline{Y}_{...(W)} = 5.206$. The $SS_B$ is

$$SS_B = \sum_{k=1}^{b} n_{.k} (\overline{Y}_{..k(W)} - \overline{Y}_{...(W)})^2 \tag{12.11}$$

and, after further substitution in Equation 12.11, $SS_B = 68.28$.

# Chapter 13
## Repeated-Measures Designs

## 13.1 INTRODUCTION

The preceding chapters have focused on research designs in which $N$ participants are distributed among the conditions, and each participant contributes exactly one score to the data set. In many studies, however, participants contribute scores in several conditions. Such studies include experiments in which the conditions are levels of a manipulated independent variable, with the order of presentation randomized independently for each participant, as well as studies in which measures are obtained from the same individuals at different points in time. An example of the latter use of a repeated-measures design is the Seasons study carried out by researchers at the University of Massachusetts Medical School. The upper panel of Table 13.1 presents Beck depression scores for each season for each of 14 men under the age of 35 who served in the Seasons study, and for whom scores were available in all four seasons. Each row of the data set represents a different participant, and each column represents a season. The column means indicate that depression scores are lower in the summer than in any other season, and the analysis of variance (ANOVA) results in Table 13.2 indicate that we can reject the hypothesis that the population means for the four seasons are equal. We have more to say about these results later in this chapter, and we also consider the analysis of the trend over seasons.

In general, we have $n$ subjects, each tested in each of $a$ conditions. A single score is denoted by $Y_{ij}$, the score for the $i$th subject in the $j$th condition of the variable $A$. The design is a departure from the between-subjects designs considered so far because each individual contributes more than one score. However, in one sense there is nothing new about this design. Its layout is essentially that of a two-factor ($S \times A$) design with one score in each of the $an$ cells of the design. Therefore, the calculations of sums of squares and mean squares in Table 13.2 are nearly the same as in the two-factor between-subject design of Chapters 11 and 12. Of course, there is one difference: Because only one score is present in each cell, there is no within-cell error term. Instead, we use $MS_{SA}$ as the denominator for the $F$ test of $A$. The structural model and other assumptions underlying the data analysis will

**TABLE 13.1**   SEASONAL DEPRESSION SCORES AND ANOVA FOR MALES UNDER 35 YEARS OF AGE

| Subject | Winter | Spring | Summer | Fall | Mean |
|---------|--------|--------|--------|------|------|
| 1 | 7.500 | 11.554 | 1.000 | 1.208 | 5.316 |
| 2 | 7.000 | 9.000 | 5.000 | 15.000 | 9.000 |
| 3 | 1.000 | 1.000 | 0.000 | 0.000 | 0.500 |
| 4 | 0.000 | 0.000 | 0.000 | 0.000 | 0.000 |
| 5 | 1.059 | 0.000 | 1.097 | 4.000 | 1.539 |
| 6 | 1.000 | 2.500 | 0.000 | 2.000 | 1.375 |
| 7 | 2.500 | 0.000 | 0.000 | 2.000 | 1.125 |
| 8 | 4.500 | 1.060 | 2.000 | 2.000 | 2.390 |
| 9 | 5.000 | 2.000 | 3.000 | 5.000 | 3.750 |
| 10 | 2.000 | 3.000 | 4.208 | 3.000 | 3.052 |
| 11 | 7.000 | 7.354 | 5.877 | 9.000 | 7.308 |
| 12 | 2.500 | 2.000 | 0.009 | 2.000 | 1.627 |
| 13 | 11.000 | 16.000 | 13.000 | 13.000 | 13.250 |
| 14 | 8.000 | 10.500 | 1.000 | 11.000 | 7.625 |
| Mean | 4.290 | 4.712 | 2.585 | 4.943 | 4.133 |

**TABLE 13.2**   ANOVA OF THE DATA IN TABLE 13.1

| SV | df | SS | MS | F | p |
|----|-----|-----|-----|-----|-----|
| Subjects ($S$) | $n - 1$ $= 13$ | $a \sum_i (\overline{Y}_{i.} - \overline{Y}_{..})^2$ $= 779.01$ | $SS_S / df_S$ $= 59.931$ | $MS_S / MS_{SA}$ $= 11.295$ | .000 |
| Seasons ($A$) | $a - 1$ $= 3$ | $n \sum_j (\overline{Y}_{.j} - \overline{Y}_{..})^2$ $= 47.781$ | $SS_A / df_A$ $= 15.927$ | $MS_A / MS_{SA}$ $= 3.001$ | .042 |
| $S \times A$ | $(n-1)(a-1)$ $= 39$ | $\sum_i \sum_j (\overline{Y}_{ij} - \overline{Y}_{i.} - \overline{Y}_{.j} + \overline{Y}_{..})^2$ $= 206.973$ | $SS_{SA} / df_{SA}$ $= 5.306$ | | |
| Total | $an - 1 = 55$ | $\sum_i \sum_j (Y_{ij} - \overline{Y}_{..})^2$ $= 1033.838$ | | | |

be presented shortly and will be used to generate expected mean squares, thus justifying the $S \times A$ error term. Before then, however, we consider some ways in which the design differs from the between-subjects designs considered so far.

One advantage of the repeated-measures design is that it requires fewer subjects than the between-subjects design does. This is important when subjects are members of a population that is limited in size, as are many clinical populations; or when subjects are difficult to recruit, as when the task is very boring or dangerous; or when subjects are expensive animals such as monkeys. Even without these constraints on subject availability, the repeated-measures design may prove more practical than a between-subjects design. For example, if it takes very little time to obtain a score from a subject, it may be more efficient to run one subject under several conditions than to run several subjects, each under a different condition.

Practicality is an important factor in the choice of a design, but efficiency—the size of the error variance—is even more important. Therefore, to understand the potential advantages of repeated-measures designs, we should consider the nature of the error variance. Recall that the structural model for the one-factor between-subjects design is

$$Y_{ij} = \mu + \alpha_j + \varepsilon_{ij}$$

We might think of $\varepsilon_{ij}$ in a between-subjects design as the sum of two components: (1) an **individual differences component** that occurs because participants who differ from one another in ability, training, and other personal characteristics would respond differently even if tested at exactly the same moment under exactly the same conditions and (2) a **measurement error component** that occurs because even the same individuals respond differently when tested on different occasions because of fluctuations in attention, changes in the physical environment, chance variability in the stimulus, and a host of other factors. Because there is usually considerable variability in the way different individuals perform, $\sigma_e^2$ (and $MS_{S/A}$, our best estimate of it) tends to be large in between-subjects designs. Other designs with no more observations may yield more power, and less variable estimates of parameters, than between-subjects designs by removing some or all of the individual differences component from $\sigma_e^2$.

In the Treatment × Blocks design discussed in Chapter 12, error variance was reduced by introducing a blocking factor that allowed some of the individual differences variability to be removed from the total variability. In repeated-measures designs, the idea of blocking is taken a step further; a blocking factor, subjects, is introduced. This factor has $n$ levels, one for each subject. As can be seen in the ANOVA of Table 13.2, we now are able to remove variability due to individual differences by subtracting a sum of squares for subjects from the total sum of squares. The error term, $MS_{SA}$, still includes variability due to measurement error. However, because of the elimination of variability from individual differences, the error variance in the repeated-measures design will be much smaller than that in a between-subjects design with the same number of data points. As a result, when $H_0$ is false, $F$ ratios will be larger and treatment effects will be more easily detected. In addition, confidence intervals for differences based on pairs of treatments will be narrower in the repeated-measures design; we can more precisely estimate effects.

Repeated-measures designs make efficient use of subjects, both in the sense of requiring fewer subjects than between-subjects designs, and in the sense of having less error variance. However, not all independent variables lend themselves to such designs. For example, subject variables—such as gender, intelligence, and clinical category—must be treated as between-subjects factors. Except under rather unusual circumstances, a given subject cannot be expected to contribute one score as a male and a second score as a female. Also, for some independent variables, once participants are tested at one level, it does not make sense to test them at a second level. For example, in an experiment designed to compare the effectiveness of different methods of teaching mathematics, knowledge achieved by being exposed to one of the methods cannot be miraculously expunged so that it can be relearned using a second method.

Although the between-subjects designs we considered in previous chapters may be inefficient, they are relatively simple. Scores in different groups can be considered to be independent, and the within-cell variance can be used as the error term for testing any effect. The repeated-measures designs we introduce in the present chapter are potentially more efficient, but we pay for the increased efficiency with some additional complexity.

We must be aware of the possibility of **carry-over effects**, the possibility that a score at one point in time is influenced by the treatment at a preceding point in time. A second consideration is that, because each individual contributes several scores, these scores are likely to be correlated; this will have implications for the validity of the $F$ test calculated in Table 13.2. Another difference from the between-subjects design is that the within-cell variance cannot be used as the error term to test all effects. In most repeated-measures designs, there is no within-cell variance; because subjects are a factor in the design, each cell contains a single score. When there are several independent variables, there will usually be an appropriate error term to test each source of interest, but what is used as the error term will depend on which source of variance is tested. These inferential issues—implications of correlated scores and the choice of error term—will be developed in subsequent sections.

## 13.2 THE ADDITIVE MODEL AND EXPECTED MEAN SQUARES FOR THE $S \times A$ DESIGN

We first develop and discuss a very simple structural model for the design of Table 13.1. In this **additive model**, subject ($S$) and treatment ($A$) effects are assumed to add (together with an error component) to account for the deviation of a single score, $Y_{ij}$, from the grand mean, $\overline{Y}_{..}$. We then consider the **nonadditive model** in which an $S \times A$ interaction effect is added to the main effects to account for the structure of the data. Although the nonadditive model provides a more realistic account of many data sets, it raises certain inferential problems. Therefore, we begin our discussion of repeated-measures designs with the simpler additive model.

### 13.2.1 The Structural Equation and Expected Mean Squares (EMS)

Consider a group of $n$ subjects, each of whom is tested once under each of $a$ levels of the treatment variable $A$. The order in which the participant is tested in the different treatment conditions is randomly determined, and randomization is conducted independently for each participant. We assume that the $n$ subjects are a random sample from an infinitely large population of individuals. We view $Y_{ij}$, the score of the $i$th subject under treatment $A_j$ as being composed of a **true score**, $\mu_{ij}$, and measurement error, $\varepsilon_{ij}$; that is,

$$Y_{ij} = \mu_{ij} + \varepsilon_{ij} \tag{13.1}$$

To establish the basis for the ANOVA, we need to express the true score, $\mu_{ij}$, in terms of the population grand mean and the contributions of subjects and treatments. To do this, we have to define some averages of the true scores. In turn, this requires us to distinguish between **fixed-effect** and **random-effect** variables. A treatment variable, $A$, is said to have fixed effects when we assume that its levels have been arbitrarily selected. Therefore, the average true score for subject $i$, $\mu_{i.}$, is the average over the $a$ levels of $A$ selected for our experiment. This is reflected in its definition in Table 13.3. The subject variable, $S$, is assumed to have random effects because the $n$ subjects in the experiment are assumed to be a random sample from the population of subjects. Therefore, the average of the population of true scores at any level of $A$ is an expected value of an infinite set of true scores. Accordingly, Table 13.3

**TABLE 13.3**    DEFINITIONS AND ASSUMPTIONS FOR PARAMETERS OF THE ADDITIVE MODEL

| Parameter | Definition |
|-----------|------------|
| $\mu_{i.}$ | $\sum_j \mu_{ij}/a$ |
| $\mu_{.j}$ | $E(\mu_{ij})$ |
| $\mu$ | $\sum_j \mu_{.j}/a = E(\mu_{i.})$ |
| $\eta_i$ | $\mu_{i.} - \mu$ |
| $\alpha_j$ | $\mu_{.j} - \mu$ |

The following conditions hold for $\alpha_j$, $\eta_i$, and $\varepsilon_{ij}$:

1. The $\alpha_j$, $\eta_i$, and $\varepsilon_{ij}$ are distributed independently of each other.

2. If $A$ is a fixed-effect variable (so that the entire population of levels of $A$ is considered to be represented in the design), then

$$\sum_j \alpha_j = \sum_j (\mu_{.j} - \mu) = 0$$

because the sum of all deviations of treatment means about their mean must be 0. The variance of the treatment effects is

$$\sigma_A^2 = \sum_j \alpha_j^2 / a$$

The null hypothesis about the effects of treatments is

$$H_0 : \alpha_1 = \alpha_2 = \ldots = \alpha_j = \ldots = \alpha_a = 0$$

or, equivalently, that $\sigma_A^2 = 0$.

3. Because we have assumed that the subjects in the experiment are a random sample from an infinite population, the sum of the $n$ values of $\eta_i$ sampled in the experiment are unlikely to sum to zero; that is,

$$\sum_{i=1}^{n} \eta_i \neq 0$$

However, the average value of all such effects for the population of subjects will be zero; that is, $E(\eta_i) = 0$. We assume that the population of $\eta_i$ values is distributed independently and normally with variance $\sigma_S^2 = E(\eta_i^2)$. We can summarize these distributional assumptions by stating that the $\eta_i$ are distributed $IN(0, \sigma_S^2)$; that is, independently and normally with mean zero and variance, $\sigma_S^2$.

4. The error component, $\varepsilon_{ij}$, is assumed to be distributed independently and normally with mean $E(\varepsilon_{ij}) = 0$ and variance $\sigma_e^2 = E(\varepsilon^2)$. That is, the $\varepsilon_{ij}$ are distributed $IN(0, \sigma_e^2)$.

presents the definition of $\mu_{.j}$, the mean of the population of scores at the $j$th level of $A$, as an expected value. The mean of all $a$ populations, $\mu$, is defined as an average of the $\mu_{.j}$ or, equivalently, as an expected value of the $\mu_{i.}$.

The definitions presented in Table 13.3 provide the basis for defining the subject ($\eta_i$) and treatment ($\alpha_j$) effects. Their definitions are also presented in Table 13.3. We assume that the deviation of the true score, $\mu_{ij}$, from the grand mean, $\mu$, is due to the subject and treatment. Therefore, Equation 13.1 can be rewritten as

$$Y_{ij} = \mu + \alpha_j + \eta_i + \varepsilon_{ij} \tag{13.2}$$

Equation 13.2 is the structural model under the assumption of additivity; the term "additivity" reflects the adding of $\alpha_j$ and $\eta_i$ in the model, and the assumption that there are no interaction effects. In the nonadditive model, considered later in this chapter, a term will be added to Equation 13.2 to reflect an $S \times A$ interaction, and the consequences of that additional assumption will be developed. To complete our presentation of the additive model, we state certain conditions on $\alpha_j$, $\eta_i$, and $\varepsilon_{ij}$. These are presented in the lower panel of Table 13.3.

Equation 13.2 and the preceding assumptions about its component parameters provide the basis for deriving EMS. We have

| SV | EMS |
|---|---|
| Subjects ($S$) | $\sigma_e^2 + a\sigma_S^2$ |
| Treatment ($A$) | $\sigma_e^2 + n\theta_A^2$ |
| $S \times A$ | $\sigma_e^2$ |

where $\theta_A^2 = \frac{1}{a-1} \sum \alpha_j^2$. The preceding table indicates that, under the additive model, $MS_{SA}$ is the appropriate error term for testing null hypotheses about both $S$ and $A$. In either test, if the null hypothesis is true, the numerator and denominator of the $F$ ratio have the same expected value.

The additive model and the EMS derived from it have implications for more than the $F$ tests. In the next few sections, we consider several of these aspects of the design.

## 13.2.2 The Efficiency of the Repeated-Measures Design

As we noted in the introduction to this chapter, the error variance in the between-subjects design of Chapter 8 has contributions from both individual differences and measurement error. We might rewrite the expectation of the error mean square in the between-subjects design as

$$E(MS_{S/A}) = \sigma_m^2 + \sigma_S^2 \tag{13.3}$$

where the subscript $m$ indicates that the variance is due to measurement error, and the subscript $S$ indicates variance caused by individual differences in the population of subjects. In contrast, in the repeated-measures design, the subject variability has been removed from the error term because subjects are a factor in the design. Therefore, under the assumption of additivity, the error mean square in this design is an estimate only of error of measurement error. That is,

$$E(MS_{SA}) = \sigma_m^2 \tag{13.4}$$

From Equations 13.3 and 13.4, it follows that $E(MS_{SA}) < E(MS_{S/A})$. Therefore, assuming that both designs have the same number of observations ($an$), $F$ ratios based on the $S \times A$ error term will generally be larger than those based on the $S$-within-levels-of-$A$ error term. Although $df_{SA} < df_{S/A}$ [i.e., $(a-1)(n-1) < a(n-1)$] and power generally depends on $df$, the $S/A$ error variance is usually so much larger due to its individual difference component that the repeated-measures design will almost always result in more power. Another way to think about this is that the repeated-measures design will require fewer subjects, and therefore fewer data points, to achieve the same power. It is more efficient than the between-subjects design. In Appendix 13.1, we have derived an expression for the efficiency of the repeated-measures design relative to that of the completely randomized (i.e., between-subjects) design. The relevant formula, which takes into account differences in error $df$, is

$$RE = \frac{(df_{CR} + 1)(df_{RM} + 3)}{(df_{CR} + 3)(df_{RM} + 1)} \times \frac{n(a - 1)MS_{SA} + (n - 1)MS_S}{(an - 1)MS_{SA}} \qquad (13.5)$$

This is the efficiency of the repeated-measures (RM) design relative to that of the completely randomized (CR) design. As an example of Equation 13.5, consider the efficiency of the design represented by the data set in Table 13.1. There are four depression scores, one for each season, for each of 14 subjects. In the alternative completely randomized design with the same number of observations, there would be 56 subjects, 14 tested in each season. Substituting values of error degrees of freedom and mean squares into Equation 13.5 from the ANOVA of Table 13.2, we have

$$RE = \frac{(53)(42)}{(55)(40)} \times \frac{(14)(3)(5.306) + (13)(59.931)}{(55)(5.306)} = 3.47$$

In practical terms, if this study were run with different subjects in each season, the design would require 3.47 times as many observations for each season to obtain the same power. The completely randomized design would have required about 49 subjects in each season, or 196 observations, instead of the 56 observations in the repeated-measures study.

### 13.2.3 Measures of Effect Size

On the basis of the expected mean squares, we can again measure the effect of the independent variable, $A$, by calculating Cohen's $f$ or partial $\omega^2$. As in Chapters 8 and 12 (e.g., see Table 12.1), estimates of population variances are obtained from the expected mean squares and inserted into the formulas for the measure of effect. Cohen's $f$ is defined as

$$f_A = \sqrt{\sigma_A^2 / \sigma_e^2}$$

Therefore,

$$\hat{f}_A = \sqrt{\frac{(a - 1)(MS_A - MS_{SA})}{anMS_{SA}}} = \sqrt{[(a - 1)/an](F_A - 1)} \qquad (13.6)$$

where $F_A = MS_A / MS_{SA}$. Partial $\omega^2$ is defined as

$$\omega_A^2 = \sigma_A^2 / (\sigma_e^2 + \sigma_A^2)$$

and is estimated by

$$\hat{\omega}_A^2 = \frac{(a - 1)(MS_A - MS_{SA})}{anMS_{SA} + (a - 1)(MS_A - MS_{SA})} = \frac{(a - 1)(F_A - 1)}{an + (a - 1)(F_A - 1)} \qquad (13.7)$$

As in previous chapters, there is a simple relation between the partial $\omega^2$ and $f$:

$$\hat{\omega}_A^2 = \hat{f}_A^2 / (1 + f_A^2)$$

Inserting $F$ ratios from the ANOVA table in Table 13.2 into Equation 13.6, the estimate of $f$ is

$$\hat{f}_A = \sqrt{[(a-1)/an](F_A - 1)} \tag{13.8}$$

$$= \sqrt{(3/56)(2.001)} = .33$$

According to Cohen's (1988) guidelines, seasons have an effect between medium and large ($f = .25$ for a medium effect and .4 for a large effect) on depression scores. In a similar manner, substituting into Equation 13.7, we find that the value of $\hat{\omega}_A^2$ is .10.

### 13.2.4 Estimating Missing Scores

Suppose that a subject does not show up to be tested in Condition $A_j$ or that the data in Condition $A_j$ were not recorded properly for one subject. The Seasons data file on the CD accompanying this book has many such missing scores. Still assuming additivity of subjects and treatments, it is possible to estimate the missing score using the $a - 1$ scores that the subject provided in the other treatment conditions and the $n - 1$ scores provided by the other subjects in Condition $A_j$. Call the missing score $X_{ij}$. Because $E(\varepsilon_{ij}) = 0$, assuming an additive model we can estimate $X_{ij}$:

$$E(X_{ij}) = \mu + \eta_i + \alpha_j \tag{13.9}$$

$$= \mu + (\mu_{i.} - \mu) + (\mu_{.j} - \mu)$$

$$= \mu_{i.} + \mu_{.j} - \mu$$

We now need estimates of the population means in Equation 13.9. Some notation will help. Let $T_{..}$ be the sum of the $an - 1$ scores that were actually obtained, $T_{i.}$ be the sum of the $a - 1$ scores from Subject $i$, and $T_{.j}$ be the sum of the $n - 1$ scores from the other subjects in treatment Condition $A_j$. Our best estimate of $\mu$ is the grand total of all the scores divided by the number of scores, $an$. In this case, the grand total is the observed total plus the missing score: $T_{..} + X_{ij}$. Similarly, we can estimate $\mu_{i.}$ and $\mu_{.j}$. Replacing the parameters of Equation 13.9 by their estimates, we have

$$\hat{X}_{ij} = \frac{T_{i.} + \hat{X}_{ij}}{a} + \frac{T_{.j} + \hat{X}_{ij}}{n} - \frac{T_{..} + \hat{X}_{ij}}{an}$$

and solving for $\hat{X}_{ij}$,

$$\hat{X}_{ij} = \frac{nT_{i.} + aT_{.j} - T_{..}}{(a-1)(n-1)} \tag{13.10}$$

Because the missing score is estimated from the remaining scores, it does not contribute a degree of freedom, so that the error degrees of freedom are reduced by one; that is, $df_{SA} = (n-1)(a-1) - 1$.

To illustrate the procedure, assume that the score for the 11th subject in the winter season is missing from Table 13.1. The sum of the three remaining scores in the row is 22.231, the sum of the remaining scores in the winter season is 53.059, and the total of all scores other than the missing one is 224.426. Substituting into Equation 13.10, the missing score is estimated as

$$\hat{X}_{ij} = \frac{(14)(22.231) + (4)(53.059) - 224.426}{(3)(13)} = 7.668$$

The result is reasonably close to the "true" missing score of 7.

The procedure can be extended to situations in which we have more than one missing value—say both $Y_{1,4}$ and $Y_{5,3}$ are missing. Begin by "guessing" the value of one of the scores (e.g., assigning $Y_{5,3}$ an arbitrary value such as its column mean). Treating this guess as though it were a real score, $\hat{Y}_{1,4}^{(1)}$, a first approximation to $Y_{1,4}$, may be obtained by using Equation 13.10. Then, treating $\hat{Y}_{1,4}^{(1)}$ as though it were a real score, Equation 13.10 can be used to obtain $\hat{Y}_{5,3}^{(1)}$, an approximation to $Y_{5,3}$. The procedure is then repeated, using $\hat{Y}_{5,3}^{(1)}$ in Equation 13.10 to produce $\hat{Y}_{1,4}^{(2)}$, a second approximation to $Y_{1,4}$, then using $\hat{Y}_{1,4}^{(2)}$ to produce $\hat{Y}_{5,3}^{(2)}$, and so on. This can be continued until two successive cycles show as small a change in the estimates as desired. Note that when the data are analyzed, the degrees of freedom for the error term are reduced by 1 for each score that is estimated. This method is called an **iterative procedure** (because of the iteration, or repetition, of steps). The procedure can be extended to situations with more than two missing scores. However, unless a computer program is written to implement it, calculations will quickly get out of hand.

This procedure for estimating missing data rests on the assumption of the additive model, Equation 13.2. If subjects and treatments interact, alternative methods exist but they also require rather strong assumptions. The procedure described here is fairly simple and provides a reasonable approximation for many data sets.

## 13.2.5 Tukey's Test of Nonadditivity and Transformations

In many experiments, the effects of treatments may vary over subjects. To take just one of many possible examples, the effects of many different variables on reading comprehension are likely to depend on such individual factors as reading ability, familiarity with the topic, current state of alertness, and motivation to perform well in the experiment. In such cases, the additive model of Equation 13.2 may not provide a valid description of the structure of data. One consequence of nonadditivity, noted earlier, is that Equation 13.10 provides only a rough estimate of missing scores when interaction terms are present in the model. A second consequence is that the Type 1 error rate associated with the $F$ test of $A$ against $S \times A$ will be inflated. Although this is an important problem, we shall see when we discuss the nonadditive model that there are a number of ways to handle it. Our view is that additivity is desirable because the Subject $\times$ Treatment interaction contributes noise, reducing the power of the test of treatments. When the additivity assumption holds, it provides more precise estimates of population effects and a more powerful $F$ test of those effects.

Assuming that additivity of subject and treatment effects is desirable, we have to decide whether the assumption is reasonable for a given data set and, if it is not, whether a transformation exists that will improve things. We might plot $n$ curves, one for each subject, and attempt to decide if they depart sufficiently from parallelism to justify concluding that subjects and treatments interact in the population. However, distinguishing between variability due to chance and variability due to interaction effects is usually difficult, particularly if

**TABLE 13.4**   TUKEY'S TEST OF NONADDITIVITY AND A RELATED TRANSFORMATION

1. Calculate the product of each score multiplied by the deviations of its row and column means from the grand mean, and sum these products:
$$P_1 = \sum_i \sum_j Y_{ij}(\overline{Y}_{i.} - \overline{Y}_{..})(\overline{Y}_{.j} - \overline{Y}_{..})$$
For example, using the data of Table 13.1, the winter score for Subject 1 (7.5) would be multiplied by its row deviation (5.316 − 4.133) and its column deviation (4.290 − 4.133). If we consider all 56 scores in Table 13.1, $P_1 = 108.544$.

2. Calculate the sum of the squared deviations of the row means from the grand mean and the sum of the squared deviations of the column means from the grand mean, and multiply these two sums:
$$P_2 = \sum_i (\overline{Y}_{i.} - \overline{Y}_{..})^2 \sum_j (\overline{Y}_{.j} - \overline{Y}_{..})^2 = 664.716$$

3. The numerator of the $F$ test of nonadditivity is distributed on 1 $df$ and is calculated as $SS_{\text{nonadd}} = P_1^2/P_2$. For the data of Table 13.1, $SS_{\text{nonadd}} = 17.725$.

4. The denominator $SS$ (the "balance") is distributed on $(n − 1)(a − 1) − 1$ $df$ and is calculated as $SS_{\text{bal}} = SS_{SA} - SS_{\text{nonadd}}$; $SS_{\text{bal}} = 189.228$. Dividing by $df_{\text{bal}}$, 39 − 1, $MS_{\text{bal}} = 4.980$, and $F = SS_{\text{nonadd}}/MS_{\text{bal}} = 3.559$, $p = .067$.

5. The Anscombe–Tukey power transformation is $Y' = Y^{\text{power}}$, where power $= 1 − (P_1/P_2)\overline{Y}_{...}$. In the current example, power $= 1 − (108.544/664.716)(4.133) = .325$. The Tukey test for nonadditivity is available in the Scale/Reliability Analysis module of SPSS; click on "Analyze," "Scale", "Reliability", and "Statistics."

there are more than a very few subjects, as in the example of the 14 subjects in this chapter. Although it will not detect all forms of nonadditivity, Tukey's (1949) test is helpful, not just because it provides a significance test, but also because a transformation to additivity can sometimes be found using some of the results of the calculations. The test is based on partitioning $SS_{SA}$ into two components: one that represents a specific type of nonadditivity and the other that serves as the basis for an error term.

Table 13.4 presents the formulas for Tukey's test of nonadditivity, and the results of applying them to the data of Table 13.1. Although the $F$ test of nonadditivity was not significant at the .05 level, the $p$ value of .067 suggests that subjects and treatments may interact. This suggestion is supported when Anscombe and Tukey's (1963) proposed data transformation is calculated. Such **power transformations** are easily carried out in most statistical packages. When each score was raised to the .325 level, in accord with the result in Table 13.4, the $F$ test of nonadditivity yields a $p$ value of .488, indicating that the transformation was successful. Furthermore, an ANOVA on the transformed data resulted in an $F$ of 4.077, $p = .013$. That $p$ value is considerably smaller than the .042 on the original untransformed depression scores.

Because raising scores to a power of .325 seemed unnatural, we also tried a square root transformation of the scores in Table 13.1; that is, we raised each score to the .5 power, reasoning that this was not too far from the Anscombe–Tukey result. The outcome was similar to that obtained with the .325 transform. Now the test of nonadditivity resulted in a $p$ value of .891. The $F$ test of the Seasons source of variance was again significant at the .013 level. The averages of the square roots of the scores in Table 13.1 were

| Winter | Spring | Summer | Fall |
|--------|--------|--------|------|
| 1.867  | 1.752  | 1.186  | 1.894 |

This pattern is similar to that for the original means in that the one mean that is clearly different from the others is that for the summer. For these 14 men, both the original and the transformed data indicate that depression scores are considerably lower in the summer.

These results with a real data set indicate that data transformations may increase power and the precision of estimates of population parameters. However, it is important to realize that the tests of null hypotheses and parameter estimates are based on a different scale than the original. If the original scale is more meaningful, or the transformation badly distorts the pattern of means, the gain in efficiency may not be worthwhile. On the other hand, the original scale is often quite arbitrary, and taking the square root, or log, or reciprocal of scores may be equally meaningful. Researchers may increase their comfort levels by retransforming the means; for example, by squaring the means based on the transformed data.

## 13.3 THE NONADDITIVE MODEL FOR THE $S \times A$ DESIGN

In many studies, the effects of treatments may vary over subjects with the result that the additive model of Equation 13.2 fails to provide a valid description of the structure of the data. For example, the effects of rate of presentation of text material on comprehension may depend on such individual factors as reading ability, familiarity with the topic, current state of alertness, and motivation to perform well in the experiment. In such cases, it may be impossible to find a transformation to additivity, or it may be important to retain the original scale. Therefore, in this section, we consider a more general, nonadditive model that includes a term to represent $S \times A$ interaction effects.

### 13.3.1 The Structural Equation

For the nonadditive model, we add an interaction component to the additive model of Equation 13.2. Therefore, the equation for the nonadditive case is

$$Y_{ij} = \mu + \alpha_j + \eta_i + (\alpha\eta)_{ij} + \varepsilon_{ij} \tag{13.11}$$

Assumptions about the distribution of the terms that were in Equation 13.2 are unchanged. The interaction effect associated with the $ij$th cell is defined as

$$\begin{aligned}
(\eta\alpha)_{ij} &= (\mu_{ij} - \mu) - \eta_i - \alpha_j \\
&= (\mu_{ij} - \mu) - (\mu_{i.} - \mu) - (\mu_{.j} - \mu) \\
&= \mu_{ij} - \mu_{i.} - \mu_{.j} + \mu
\end{aligned} \tag{13.12}$$

Assuming that the levels of $A$ have been arbitrarily selected, the mean of the interaction effects for a subject is zero; that is, $\sum_j (\eta\alpha)_{ij}/a = 0$. When the effects of $A$ are fixed, the average of the interaction components for any subject is zero, because all the levels of $A$ that have been selected are involved in the average.

At each level of $A$, $(\eta\alpha)_{ij}$ is assumed to be normally and independently distributed. The mean of each of these $a$ distributions of interaction effects, $E(\eta\alpha)_{ij}$, is zero, and the variance is $E(\eta\alpha)_{ij}^2$, which we will refer to as $\sigma_{SA}^2$. The mean of the population of interaction effects at $A_j$ is an expected value because we assume an infinite population of subjects, and therefore of interaction effects, at $A_j$. However, only a *sample* of $n$ of the population of interaction effects at $A_j$ are included in the data. Because this sample will be different at each level of $A$, the $S \times A$ interaction will contribute to differences among the observed means at the various levels of $A$. In contrast, because $A$ is a fixed-effects variable, the mean for each subject involves an average of *all* interaction effects for the subject. That mean will be zero and so interaction effects do not contribute to the variability among the observed subject means. Consistent with this analysis, we shall see that the expected mean square for $A$ contains a component due to the interaction of $S$ and $A$, whereas the expected mean square term for $S$ does not.

Table 13.5 may clarify the preceding discussion. The table presents the true scores for a rather small population of four subjects. Note that the treatment population (column) means are identical; the null hypothesis is true. Also, note that the average interaction effect in each column and in each row is zero; this is an algebraic result of the definition of an interaction effect. Now assume an "experiment" in which two of the four subjects—say $S_1$ and $S_2$—are selected by random sampling. Ordinarily, there would be more subjects in an experiment, but this should be enough to make our point. We also have set all $\varepsilon_{ij}$ equal to zero; that is, we have made the observed scores $(Y_{ij})$ in our experiment equal to the true scores so that $\sigma_e^2$ will not be a factor in our discussion. Taking the "data" from the two subjects in the experiment ($S_1$ and $S_2$), we find that the means at the levels of $A$, the $\overline{Y}_{.j}$, are 9, 9.5, and 5.5. Note that, although the $\mu_{.j}$ are identical, the $\overline{Y}_{.j}$ are not. This is not because of error

**TABLE 13.5**   DATA FOR A POPULATION OF FOUR SUBJECTS

| | \multicolumn{6}{c}{With Interaction Effects Present} | | |
| | $A_1$ | | $A_2$ | | $A_3$ | | | |
| | $Y_{i1}$ | $(\eta\alpha)_{i1}$ | $Y_{i2}$ | $(\eta\alpha)_{i2}$ | $Y_{i3}$ | $(\eta\alpha)_{i3}$ | $\mu_i$ | $\eta_i$ |
|---|---|---|---|---|---|---|---|---|
| $S_1$ | 8 | −1 | 10 | 1 | 9 | 0 | 9 | −.5 |
| $S_2$ | 10 | 3 | 9 | 2 | 2 | −5 | 7 | −2.5 |
| $S_3$ | 11 | −1 | 12 | 0 | 13 | 1 | 12 | 2.5 |
| $S_4$ | 9 | −1 | 7 | −3 | 14 | 4 | 10 | .5 |
| $\mu_j$ | 9.5 | | 9.5 | | 9.5 | | $\mu = 9.5$ | |

| | \multicolumn{3}{c}{Without Interaction Effects Present} | | |
| | $Y_{i1}$ | $Y_{i2}$ | $Y_{i3}$ | $\mu_i$ | $\eta_i$ |
|---|---|---|---|---|---|
| $S_1$ | $8 - (-1) = 9$ | $10 - 1 = 9$ | $9 - 0 = 9$ | 9 | −.5 |
| $S_2$ | $10 - 3 = 7$ | $9 - 2 = 7$ | $2 - (-5) = 7$ | 7 | −2.5 |
| $S_3$ | $11 - (-1) = 12$ | $12 - 0 = 12$ | $13 - 1 = 12$ | 12 | 2.5 |
| $S_4$ | $9 - (-1) = 10$ | $7 - (-3) = 10$ | $14 - 4 = 10$ | 10 | 0.5 |
| $\mu_j$ | 9.5 | 9.5 | 9.5 | | |

of measurement because there is none in this artificial data set. It is entirely due to the fact that the two average *sampled* interaction effects are different at the three levels of $A$. To demonstrate this, each value of $(\eta\alpha)_{ij}$ has been subtracted from the corresponding value of $Y_{ij}$. For example, $Y_{11}$ is $8 - (-1) = 9$ and $Y_{21} = 10 - 3 = 7$; this population of scores, obtained by removing the interaction effects, is presented in the lower panel of Table 13.5. Because there are no interaction effects (and no error components), the treatment means for the first two (or any set of) subjects, like the population treatment means, are identical. The point of all this is that interaction among subjects and treatments will contribute to the variability among the $\overline{Y}_{.j}$, and therefore to $MS_A$. Which treatment means will be most raised or lowered relative to their population values will depend on the pattern of interaction effects that have been sampled from each treatment population.

One other point follows from our two-subject experiment. Note that the subject means, $\overline{Y}_{.j}$, are unchanged if the interaction effects are subtracted from the scores in Table 13.5; $MS_S$ is not affected by the pattern of sampled interactions. This is because $A$ is a fixed-effect variable. When we get the mean for a subject, we average over *all* the $(\eta\alpha)_{ij}$ for that subject; that average will always be zero.

This artificial example was intended to provide some intuition about the nature of the expected mean squares. We next present a more precise statement of these expectations and consider certain implications.

## 13.3.2 EMS

Table 13.6 presents the sources of variance (SV), degrees of freedom ($df$), and *EMS* under the additive and nonadditive models. Although we have not repeated the calculations of

**TABLE 13.6** PARAMETER DEFINITIONS AND EXPECTED MEAN SQUARES FOR THE S × A DESIGN

| Model Definition |
|---|

The additive model: $Y_{ij} = \mu + \eta_i + \alpha_j + \varepsilon_{ij}$

The nonadditive model: $Y_{ij} = \mu + \eta_i + \alpha_j + (\eta\alpha)_{ij} + \varepsilon_{ij}$

where $\eta = \mu_i - \mu$, $\quad \alpha_j = \mu_j - \mu$, $\quad (\eta\alpha)_{ij} = \mu_{ij} - \mu_i - \mu_j + \mu$

$\mu_{ij} = E(Y_{ij})$, $\quad \mu_j = E(\mu_{ij})$, $\quad \mu_i = \sum_j \mu_{ij}/a$, $\quad \mu = E(\mu_i) = \sum_j \mu_j/a$

$\sum_j \alpha_j = \sum_j (\eta\alpha)_{ij} = 0$ $\quad$ and $\quad E[(\eta\alpha)_{ij}] = E(\varepsilon_{ij}) = 0$

$E(\varepsilon_{ij}^2) = \sigma_e^2$, $E(\eta_i^2) = \sigma_S^2$, $E[(\eta\alpha)_{ij}^2] = \sigma_{SA}^2$, $\quad$ and $\quad \sum_j \dfrac{\alpha_j^2}{a-1} = \theta_A^2$

| SV | df | Additive EMS | Nonadditive EMS | F |
|---|---|---|---|---|
| S | $n-1$ | $\sigma_e^2 + a\sigma_S^2$ | $\sigma_e^2 + a\sigma_S^2$ | $\dfrac{MS_S}{MS_{SA}}$ |
| A | $a-1$ | $\sigma_e^2 + n\theta_A^2$ | $\sigma_e^2 + \sigma_{SA}^2 + n\theta_A^2$ | $\dfrac{MS_A}{MS_{SA}}$ |
| SA | $(n-1)(a-1)$ | $\sigma_e^2$ | $\sigma_e^2 + \sigma_{SA}^2$ | |

Table 13.2, it should be noted that the numerical values of the sums of squares and the mean squares are the same for the two models. Furthermore, in both cases, the $A$ source of variance would be tested against $MS_{SA}$. However, in the presence of nonadditivity, the repeated-measures design is less efficient because the interaction effects contribute added "noise" to the data set. This can be seen by considering the ratio of $EMS$ under the two models. If additivity holds, that ratio is

$$\frac{E(MS_A)}{E(MS_{SA})} = 1 + \frac{n \sum_j (\mu_j - \mu)^2/(a-1)}{\sigma_e^2}$$

However, if the nonadditive model is valid, the ratio is smaller:

$$\frac{E(MS_A)}{E(MS_{S \times A})} = 1 + \frac{n \sum_j (\mu_j - \mu)^2/(a-1)}{\sigma_e^2 + \sigma_{SA}^2}$$

$S \times A$ interaction effects will reduce the precision of parameter estimates and the power of the significance test. It is important to understand, however, that such interaction variance will almost always be less than the individual difference variance associated with completely randomized designs. Therefore, even when the data do not conform to the additive model, the repeated-measures design will yield more powerful tests of the null hypothesis than will the completely randomized design with the same number of observations.

An increase in error variance is not the only price that nonadditivity exacts. Although the expected mean squares in Table 13.6 do not suggest bias in the test of the independent variable, $A$, there is a potential problem, which we consider next.

## 13.4 HYPOTHESIS TESTS ASSUMING NONADDITIVITY

As previously stated, a necessary condition for a mean square to be a proper error term to test some null hypothesis is the following: If $H_0$ is true, then the expectations of the numerator and denominator mean squares should be identical. As can be seen in Table 13.6, this requirement is met by the expected mean squares in both the additive and nonadditive cases. However, meeting this requirement is not sufficient for $MS_A/MS_{SA}$ to have an $F$ distribution. Rouanet and Lepine (1970) and Huynh and Feldt (1976) have shown that an assumption called **sphericity** (or circularity) must also be met; when that assumption is violated, Type 1 error rates will be inflated, sometimes severely. The following sections describe the sphericity assumption, its consequences, and the procedures to use when the assumption is violated.

### 13.4.1 Sphericity (Homogeneity of Variances of Difference Scores)

The concept of sphericity is illustrated in the upper panel (Data Set A) of Table 13.7. Data are presented for five subjects at three levels of $A$. We have also calculated all possible difference scores for each subject: $d_{i,12} = Y_{i1} - Y_{i2}$, $d_{i,13} = Y_{i1} - Y_{i3}$, and $d_{i,23} = Y_{i2} - Y_{i3}$. The assumption of sphericity states that the three populations of difference scores have identical variances. In general, if we have $a$ treatment levels, there will be $(1/2)(a)(a-1)$ possible populations of difference scores, and it is assumed that all have the same variance, $\sigma_d^2$. Note that the three sample values of $\sigma_d^2$ are identical in the example in the upper panel;

**TABLE 13.7**   DATA EXHIBITING SPHERICITY (SET A) AND NONSPHERICITY (SET B)

| | Data Set A (Exhibits Sphericity) | | | | | |
| | $A_1$ | $A_2$ | $A_3$ | $Y_{i3} - Y_{i2}$ | $Y_{i2} - Y_{i1}$ | $Y_{i3} - Y_{i1}$ |
|---|---|---|---|---|---|---|
| $S_1$ | 21.050 | 7.214 | 26.812 | 19.598 | −13.836 | 5.760 |
| $S_2$ | 6.915 | 29.599 | 16.366 | −13.233 | 22.684 | 9.451 |
| $S_3$ | 3.890 | 21.000 | 41.053 | 20.053 | 17.110 | 37.163 |
| $S_4$ | 11.975 | 12.401 | 18.896 | 6.495 | .426 | 6.921 |
| $S_5$ | 31.169 | 34.786 | 31.872 | −2.914 | 3.617 | .703 |
| Mean | 15.000 | 21.000 | 27.000 | 6.000 | 6.000 | 12.000 |
| $\hat{\sigma}^2$ | 124.000 | 132.000 | 100.000 | 208.000 | 208.000 | 208.000 |

*Note.* $MS_{SA} = 104 = (1/2)\sigma_d^2$.

| | Data Set B (Exhibits Nonsphericity) | | | | | |
| | $A_1$ | $A_2$ | $A_3$ | $Y_{i3} - Y_{i2}$ | $Y_{i2} - Y_{i1}$ | $Y_{i3} - Y_{i1}$ |
|---|---|---|---|---|---|---|
| $S_1$ | 1.7 | 3.9 | 6.0 | 2.1 | 2.2 | 4.3 |
| $S_2$ | 4.4 | 6.5 | 14.5 | 8.0 | 2.1 | 10.1 |
| $S_3$ | 7.8 | 13.3 | 18.6 | 5.3 | 5.5 | 10.8 |
| $S_4$ | 6.6 | 9.4 | 14.5 | 5.1 | 2.8 | 7.9 |
| $S_5$ | 9.1 | 15.2 | 23.5 | 8.3 | 6.1 | 14.4 |
| Mean | 5.92 | 9.66 | 15.42 | 5.76 | 3.74 | 9.50 |
| $\hat{\sigma}^2$ | 8.557 | 21.793 | 41.457 | 6.378 | 3.653 | 13.914 |

*Note.* $MS_{SA} = 3.991 = (1/2)(6.378 + 3.653 + 13.914)/3$.

the sphericity assumption is met by these data.[1] The data in the lower panel (Data Set $B$) exhibit considerably more heterogeneity of variance of difference scores (nonsphericity); if such heterogeneity exists in the population, Type 1 error rates will be higher than the nominal $\alpha$ level. We will shortly consider what to do about this, but first we note some conditions under which the sphericity assumption will hold.

Additivity is a sufficient, but not necessary condition, for the sphericity assumption to hold. Additivity is sufficient because if there are no $S \times A$ interaction effects, the difference between the scores under any two treatments, $A_j$ and $A_{j'}$, will not vary over subjects. But this means that the variance of the difference scores based on $A_j$ and $A_{j'}$ is zero, and this is true for all $j$ and $j'$. Thus, additivity implies constant (zero) variance of difference scores. However, Data Set $A$ of Table 13.7 indicates that additivity is not necessary for sphericity to hold. Although there is an interaction between $A$ and $S$, the variances of difference scores are identical.

Another condition under which sphericity occurs is **compound symmetry**, which is defined by homogeneity of the population treatment variances and homogeneity of the population covariances; that is, there is compound symmetry if $\sigma_1^2 = \ldots = \sigma_j^2 = \ldots \sigma_a^2$ and

$\rho_{12}\sigma_1\sigma_2 = \dots \rho_{jj'}\sigma_j\sigma_{j'} = \dots = $ a constant; $\rho_{jj'}$ is the population correlation between the scores at $A_j$ and $A_{j'}$, and $\rho_{jj'}\sigma_j\sigma_{j'}$ is the covariance. In Chapter 5 (see Appendix 5.2), we showed that, if $d_{jj'} = Y_{.j} - Y_{.j'}$, then the variance of the population of difference scores is

$$\sigma_d^2 = \sigma_j^2 + \sigma_{j'}^2 - 2\rho_{jj'}\sigma_j\sigma_{j'} \tag{13.13}$$

If compound symmetry holds in the population, all variances of difference scores will involve the same variances and covariances of scores and therefore they must be identical. However, although compound symmetry is sufficient, it too is not necessary for sphericity. In Data Set $A$, the variances of the individual scores are not the same; they are 124, 132, and 100. Nor are the covariances identical. They are 24 for conditions 1 and 2, 8 for conditions 1 and 3, and 12 for conditions 2 and 3.

Nonsphericity, or heterogeneity of variance of difference scores, is analogous in both form and consequences to heterogeneity of variance in the between-subjects designs of Chapters 8, 11, and 12. In Chapter 8, the error term, $MS_{S/A}$, was the average of the group variances. We showed that if the null hypothesis is true, and if there are $n$ scores at each treatment level, then $E(MS_A) = E(MS_{S/A})$ even if the group variances are very different from each other. However, even though this heterogeneity of variance does not effect the ratio of expected mean squares, it does effect the sampling distribution of the ratio of mean squares. More precisely, when the null hypothesis is true, heterogeneity of variance inflates the probability of sampling large $F$ values.

We have a similar situation in the repeated-measures design. As can be seen in Data Sets $A$ and $B$ of Table 13.7, the error term, $MS_{SA}$, is one half the average of the three values of $s_d^2$; this relation between the variances of the difference scores and $MS_{SA}$ will hold for any number of levels of $A$. If these variances are very different, the Type 1 error rate will be inflated, as is the case when group variances differ in the between-subjects design. Mauchly (1940) derived a test of the null hypothesis that the variances of difference scores are homogeneous. The test result is available in some computer packages (e.g., in SPSS's GLM module). However, if the population distributions are not normal, the Mauchly test tends to yield significant results even when sphericity holds. Therefore, we recommend against using this test to determine whether there is a problem in the data set. Rogan, Keselman, and Mendoza (1979) present some simulation results relevant to this point, together with a good discussion of the general topic of the analysis of repeated measurements.

There are three data-analysis strategies that protect the researcher against inflation of Type 1 error rates due to nonsphericity. These are: (1) **the univariate $F$ test with $\varepsilon$-adjusted degrees of freedom**; (2) **the multivariate analysis of variance**, or **MANOVA**; and (3) **tests of planned contrasts**. The first two involve calculating the covariances of scores. The reason for this lies in the relation, expressed in Equation 13.13, between the variances and covariances of scores and the variance of the difference scores. We next consider each of these three approaches.

## 13.4.2 The $\varepsilon$-Adjusted $F$ Test

Box (1954) showed that the statistic $MS_A/MS_{SA}$ is distributed approximately as $F$ when the assumption of sphericity is violated; however, with violations of sphericity, the degrees of freedom are adjusted by a factor, $\varepsilon$; $df_A = (a - 1)\varepsilon$ and $df_{SA} = (a - 1)(n - 1)\varepsilon$. The

**TABLE 13.8**  ANOVA OF THE DATA OF TABLE 13.1

Within Subjects

| Source | SS | df | MS | F | P | G-G | H-F |
|--------|------|------|--------|-------|------|------|------|
| Beck_D | 47.781 | 3 | 15.927 | 3.001 | .042 | .053 | .042 |
| Error | 206.953 | 39 | 5.306 | | | | |

Greenhouse--Geisser Epsilon: 0.8316
Huynh-Feldt Epsilon      : 1.0000

Multivariate Repeated Measures Analysis

Test of: Beck_D

| Statistic | Value | Hypoth. df | Error df | F | P |
|-----------|-------|-------|-------|-------|------|
| Wilks' Lambda | .608 | 3 | 11 | 2.366 | .127 |
| Pillai Trace | .392 | 3 | 11 | 2.366 | .127 |
| H-L Trace | .645 | 3 | 11 | 2.366 | .127 |

*Note.* Output printed from SYSTAT.

adjustment, $\varepsilon$, is a function of the degree of nonsphericity. If the variances of difference scores are homogeneous—that is, if there is sphericity—$\varepsilon$ will be 1 and the usual degrees of freedom apply. Under conditions in which the assumption is severely violated, $\varepsilon$ approaches a lower bound of $1/(a - 1)$. In this case, $F$ would be distributed on 1 and $n - 1\,df$. In summary, as nonsphericity increases, the degrees of freedom decrease, with the result that a larger value of $F$ is required for significance. In this way, the $\varepsilon$ adjustment compensates for the inflation of Type 1 error rate caused by the failure of the sphericity assumption.

Estimating $\varepsilon$ requires calculating covariances for all pairs of levels of $A$, as well as variances for each level of $A$. Fortunately, common statistical computer programs—such as SPSS, SAS, and SYSTAT—do these calculations. The upper panel of Table 13.8 presents the ANOVA output from SYSTAT. The $p$ value for the conventional degrees of freedom is presented in the "P" column. The next column, labeled G-G, presents the $p$ value for the degrees of freedom adjusted by $\hat{\varepsilon}$, the $\varepsilon$ estimate first derived by Box (1954) and subsequently extended to the designs of Chapter 14 by Greenhouse and Geisser (1959). The $p$ value in the far right column, labeled H-F, is based on degrees of freedom adjusted by $\tilde{\varepsilon}$, a second estimator of $\varepsilon$ derived by Huynh and Feldt (1976).

Both $\hat{\varepsilon}$ and $\tilde{\varepsilon}$ are biased estimates of $\varepsilon$, and there is no consensus as to which should be used. The H-F estimate, $\tilde{\varepsilon}$, is always at least as large as that of $\hat{\varepsilon}$ and therefore provides greater power. However, it also appears that $\tilde{\varepsilon}$ has a higher Type 1 error rate under many conditions (Gary, 1981). One reason for this is that $\tilde{\varepsilon}$ can exceed 1.0, in which case it is set to 1. Usually, the two adjustments lead to the same conclusion. When they do not, as in the results presented in Table 13.8, the conservative course is to rely on the G-G adjustment, $\hat{\varepsilon}$.

In this case, we fail to reject the null hypothesis of an effect of seasons on Beck depression scores.

In the rare case in which the researcher lacks access to statistical software that calculates $\hat{\epsilon}$ and $\tilde{\epsilon}$, the calculations can be tedious and time-consuming. Although formulas are available in many sources (e.g., Myers & Well, 1995), Greenhouse and Geisser have suggested a three-step approach to significance testing that frequently will avoid the necessity of carrying out such calculations:

1. First test the $F$ ratio in question with the conventional degrees of freedom (i.e., $a - 1$ and $(n - 1)(a - 1)$). If the $F$ test is not significant using these $df$, it certainly will not be if the $df$ are reduced by the $\epsilon$ adjustment. The null hypothesis cannot be rejected.
2. If the $F$ test using conventional degrees of freedom is significant, perform the conservative $F$ test using 1 and $n - 1$ $df$ [i.e., the test that assumes $\epsilon$ takes on its lowest possible value of $1/(a - 1)$]. If this conservative test is significant, the null hypothesis can be rejected without further testing.
3. If the conventional $F$ test is significant, but the conservative $F$ test is not, the correction factor $\epsilon$ must be estimated.

Given the availability of computers and the fact that estimates of $\epsilon$ are available in most, if not all, statistical software, the degree-of-freedom correction should be used. Because the inflation in Type 1 error rate can be very great if the $df$ are not adjusted, the univariate $F$ should never be evaluated without an adjustment. Note, however, that an adjustment does not apply if $A$ has only two levels. In that case, there is only one set of $n$ difference scores and, therefore, only one variance of difference scores. Therefore, homogeneity of variance of difference scores is not an issue.

### 13.4.3 MANOVA

If the data have a multivariate-normal distribution, the MANOVA provides an alternative to the univariate test that does not require the assumption of sphericity. Although a detailed discussion of MANOVA is beyond the scope of this book, we do provide a brief introduction to the topic.

If there are $a$ within-subject conditions, the null hypothesis of equality of population means is equivalent to assuming that a series of $a - 1$ pairwise differences are all equal to zero. One such null hypothesis would be

$$H_0 : \mu_1 - \mu_2 = 0, \mu_2 - \mu_3 = 0, \ldots, \quad \text{and} \quad \mu_{a-1} - \mu_a = 0$$

and still another would be

$$H_0 : \mu_1 - \mu_2 = 0, \mu_1 - \mu_3 = 0, \ldots, \quad \text{and} \quad \mu_1 - \mu_a = 0$$

This suggests transforming the $a$ scores for each subject into a set of $a - 1$ difference scores. For example, the successive differences for the depression scores of subject 1 (see Table 13.1) are $d_{12} = 7.5 - 11.554 = -4.054$, $d_{23} = 11.554 - 1 = 10.554$, and $d_{34} = 1 - 1.208 = -.208$. Similarly, difference scores can be obtained for all 14 subjects. The difference scores for each subject are then weighted and summed to create a single score;

call this score $U$. For example, the $U$ score for subject 1 based on the successive differences is

$$U_1 = (w_1)(-4.054) + (w_2)(10.554) + (w_3)(-.208)$$

The derivation of the weights requires some knowledge of matrix algebra, but the important point is that they have the property of maximizing a $t$ ratio. That $t$ looks very much like the standard one-sample $t$, that is, it is the mean of the $n$ values of $U_i$ divided by the standard error of the mean:

$$t = \overline{U}/s_{\overline{U}} \tag{13.14}$$

The squared value of this $t$ is ordinarily calculated using matrix algebra and is usually referred to as Hotelling's $T^2$ (1931). The $F$ ratio reported in the MANOVA part of Table 13.8 is $T^2$ multiplied by $(n - a + 1)/[(n - 1)(a - 1)]$. This statistic has the $F$ distribution on $a - 1$ and $n - a + 1$ $df$. Because $n - a + 1$ must be greater than zero, the multivariate test, unlike the univariate, requires that $n$ be greater than $a - 1$. Also, if $a = 2$, $(n - a + 1)/[(n - 1)(a - 1)] = 1$, and $F = t^2$. Stated differently, when there are only two conditions, the multivariate $F$ reduces to the univariate because both are equivalent to calculating a squared $t$ statistic for matched pairs.

In Table 13.8, we see three different statistics listed, all of which result in the same value of $F$. When there is no between-subjects variable, or when there are only two levels of the within-subject variable, these statistics will always result in the same $F$. In other instances, they will usually yield similar results. Several books discuss the various statistics and provide a far more detailed discussion of MANOVA as it applies to the designs of this and the next chapter. Harris (1985) and Morrison (1990) are two excellent sources.

By now, the reader may have noted that, whereas the univariate $F$ test resulted in either a significant (at the .05 level) or near-significant result, the $p$ value for the multivariate analysis is considerably higher. This forces us to confront a fundamental question: Which set of results should we accept? More generally, we must consider the Type 1 and Type 2 error rates under various conditions. We turn next to this topic.

### 13.4.4 ANOVA or MANOVA?

There is no simple answer to this question. The relative powers of the two procedures depend on the value of $\varepsilon$, and on $a$ and $n$. If the population value of $\varepsilon$ is 1, then the univariate test will be more powerful because its denominator $df$, $(a - 1)(n - 1)$, will be greater than the multivariate $df$, $n - a + 1$. For example, as can be seen in Table 13.8, the univariate error $df$ are 39, whereas those for the multivariate test are 11. As $n$ increases, the error $df$ increase for both tests and the power advantage of the univariate test decreases.

When sphericity does not hold, MANOVA may provide the more powerful test. Based on simulations, Algina and Keselman (1997) recommended the multivariate test if: (a) $a \leq 4$, $n \geq a + 15$, and $\tilde{\varepsilon} \leq .90$, or (b) $5 \leq a \leq 8$, $n \geq a + 30$, and $\tilde{\varepsilon} \leq .85$. In the example of the seasonal depression data, these recommendations would indicate that the univariate test is more powerful. Two points should be kept in mind, however. First, the simulations are not exhaustive; different results might be obtained with combinations of $n$, $a$, and $\varepsilon$ other than those investigated. Second, as Algina and Keselman state, even in their simulations, "selection of the multivariate test according to these rules is not a guarantee of increased power; our results indicate that some percentage of the time this rule will result in choosing the wrong test" (1997, p. 215). Nevertheless, it is apparent that as estimates of $\varepsilon$ decrease, and as $n$ increases relative to $a$, the advantage of the univariate test will decrease, and at some point the multivariate test will tend to be more powerful.

Transformation of the data to produce additivity, and therefore sphericity, can be helpful. As we noted earlier in this chapter, a square root transformation of the data in Table 13.1 resulted in a significant $F$ test of the effects of seasons with $p = .01$. Even with the Greenhouse–Geisser $\hat{\varepsilon}$ adjustment, $p = .02$. Even the multivariate test produced a significant result with these transformed data: $p = .04$. Again, we caution that transformations that yield additivity (and therefore more powerful tests and narrower confidence intervals) cannot always be found, and even if available, may not be meaningful. However, the option is often worth consideration.

## 13.4.5 Testing Single *df* Contrasts

In many, perhaps most, studies, pairwise comparisons or more complex contrasts are of primary interest. As we pointed out in Chapter 6, such contrasts—pairwise or complex—are distributed on 1 *df*. Sphericity is not an issue because there is only a single contrast score for each subject. In the example of seasonal effects on depression, we might wish to test all pairwise comparisons. The calculations are straightforward and, in any event, paired $F$ or $t$ tests can be carried out by most statistical software. There are two issues, however. The first is whether to test each of the six possible pairwise comparisons against $MS_{SA}$ or against the variance of the comparison under consideration. $MS_{SA}$ is distributed on more error degrees of freedom, $(a-1)(n-1)$, and therefore the $F$ test with this denominator is potentially more powerful. Nevertheless, the default error term in statistical packages is the variance of the contrast being tested. For example, to test the difference between winter and summer mean depression scores, the mean $(\bar{d})$ and standard deviation $(s_d)$ of the 14 differences would be calculated. Then

$$t = \bar{d}/(s_d/\sqrt{n})$$
$$= 1.705/(2.622/\sqrt{14}) = 2.433$$

The $F$ reported by some software is the squared $t$. The reason for using the standard deviation of the contrast, rather than $MS_{SA}$, in the denominator is that if there is nonsphericity in the data set, the variances of difference scores may vary greatly across comparisons. Because $MS_{SA}$ is one half of the average of the six variances, it will be too small when testing some of the comparisons and too large when testing others. Boik (1981) showed that even small departures from sphericity can create serious distortions in Type 1 and Type 2 error rates, and in the widths of confidence intervals when the denominator of the $t$ (or $F$) is based on $MS_{SA}$.

The second issue in testing the six possible pairwise comparisons is the control of familywise error rate. Tukey's HSD procedure, described in Chapter 9, would seem to be the natural approach. However, the test performs badly if there is nonsphericity. Maxwell (1980) compared the Type 1 error rates and powers of various methods of controlling the familywise error (FWE) rate and concluded that the Bonferroni approach, with the error term based on the contrast being tested, provided the best solution. In the current example, we would calculate a different $s_d$ for each of the six comparisons and compare each $p$ value against $.05/6$.

**TABLE 13.9**   SPSS POLYNOMIAL ANALYSIS OF THE DATA OF TABLE 13.1

**Tests of Within-Subjects Contrasts**

**Measure: MEASURE_1**

| Source | DEPRESS | Type III Sum of Squares | df | Mean Square | F | Sig. |
|--------|---------|------------------------|-----|-------------|------|------|
| DEPRESS | Linear | 1.936E-02 | 1 | 1.936E-02 | .003 | .954 |
|  | Quadratic | 13.124 | 1 | 13.124 | 3.424 | .087 |
|  | Cubic | 34.638 | 1 | 34.638 | 5.438 | .036 |
| Error (DEPRESS) | Linear | 74.310 | 13 | 5.716 |  |  |
|  | Quadratic | 49.831 | 13 | 3.833 |  |  |
|  | Cubic | 82.811 | 13 | 6.370 |  |  |

*Note.* Output is from SPSS.

More complex contrasts are sometimes of interest. In the example of seasonal effects on depression scores, we might be interested in the shape of the function relating the Beck depression scores to the four seasons, starting with winter. As part of the repeated-measures output (in the GLM module), SPSS provides the polynomial analysis shown in Table 13.9. The only significant component is the cubic, indicating that the population means may be described by an *S*-shaped function with a slope of zero. The *F* ratio for the cubic term may be calculated as follows. The equation for the sum of squares for the contrast is

$$SS_{\hat{\psi}} = \frac{\left(\sum_j w_j \overline{Y}_{.j}\right)^2}{\sum_j w_j^2/n} \tag{13.15}$$

For the cubic term, $w_j = -1, 3, -3,$ and $1$. Substituting these values and the means from Table 13.1 into Equation 13.15, we have

$$SS_{\hat{\psi}} = 7.034^2/(20/14)$$

which (within rounding error) equals 34.638, the result in the SPSS output. The error mean square may be calculated directly as

$$MS_{S \times \hat{\psi}} = s_{\hat{\psi}}^2 \Big/ \sum_j w_j^2 \tag{13.16}$$

where $s_{\hat{\psi}}^2$ is the variance of *n* contrast scores. These contrast scores are obtained by multiplying each subject's scores by the corresponding weights and adding the products; the contrast score for the *i*th subject is $\hat{\psi}_i = \sum_j w_j Y_{ij}$. Substituting into Equation 13.16, we have

$$MS_{S \times \hat{\psi}} = 127.401/20 = 6.370$$

and *F* is the ratio: 34.638/6.370. Note that each polynomial component in Table 13.9 is tested against a different error term.

## 13.5 POWER OF THE *F* TEST

Assuming sphericity, power calculations are conducted as for other designs (Koele, 1982). For example, in Section 13.2.3, Cohen's $f$ was calculated as .33 for the depression data of Table 13.1. Using GPOWER, we select "Other $F$ Tests" and then enter the values of $f^2$, numerator and denominator $df$, and $\alpha$. The result is .48, the power of the test of the Seasons source of variance. The noncentrality parameter, $\lambda$, equals $Nf^2$, or 6.10. Using the UCLA calculator, we enter the $F$ needed for significance at the .05 level with 3 and 39 $df$, the numerator and denominator $df$, and $\lambda$. The critical $F$ is 2.845 and $\lambda = 6.10$. The calculator returns $\beta$, the Type 2 error probability. This value is .52 and, subtracting from 1, we again have the power, .48.

Unfortunately, the sphericity assumption is often violated; in that case, the ratio of mean squares is not distributed as $F$ on $a - 1$ and $(a - 1)(n - 1)$ $df$. As we discussed earlier in this chapter, $MS_A/MS_{SA}$ is approximately distributed as $F$ on $\varepsilon(a - 1)$ and $\varepsilon(a - 1)(n - 1)$ $df$. Because, under nonsphericity, $\varepsilon$ is a fraction greater than or equal to $1/(a - 1)$, the degrees of freedom that we should use to calculate power are actually less than $a - 1$ and $(a - 1)(n - 1)$ and, therefore, power is less than in the standard method described previously. Therefore, we can consider the power of .48 in our example as an upper limit on the true power. If we decide on the $n$ before running a study, we also run into the sphericity problem. To decide on the $n$ needed to achieve a certain power against a specified $f^2$ (or $\lambda$), we can try out different values and change the $df_{SA}$ accordingly. However, the $n$ we arrive at will be an underestimate of the $n$ we actually need, if there is nonsphericity.

Muller and Barton (1989, 1991) have presented an approximate solution to the non-sphericity problem. Expected values of $\hat{\varepsilon}$ and $\tilde{\varepsilon}$ can be calculated, and the $df$ that are entered into power calculations can be adjusted by these expected values. The formulas for these expected values are complex, but SAS programs are available (Algina & Keselman, 1997; Muller, LaVange, Ramey, & Ramey, 1992).

Although there are problems in determining power, or the sample size needed to attain a specific level of power, when the numerator has more than 1 $df$, there is no difficulty in determining power or $n$ when pairwise comparisons or contrasts are of interest. The appropriate procedures were described in Chapter 6.

## 13.6 MULTIFACTOR REPEATED-MEASURES DESIGNS

So far, we have considered only the $S \times A$ repeated-measures design; however, there is no reason why additional within-subject factors cannot be included in the design. For example, in a study designed to shed light on the processes underlying facial recognition, Murray, Yong, and Rhodes (2000) presented each of 24 subjects with photos of several faces. There were three versions of each photo—an unaltered version, a distortion in which eyes and mouth were inverted, and a distortion in which the pupils of the eye were whitened and the teeth blackened. Each subject viewed each face for 3 seconds in 1 of 7 positions, from upright to upside down. Subjects were asked to rate each face for bizarreness, with normal being 1 and very bizarre being 7. Both types of distortion (3 levels) and orientation (7 levels) were within-subject variables.[2]

The Murray et al. study is an example of a multifactor repeated-measures design. In such designs, $n$ randomly sampled subjects are each tested at every combination of levels of the other factors. Therefore, if there are two within-subjects factors, $A$ and $B$, with $a$ and $b$ levels, respectively, each subject is tested $ab$ times. If $A$ and $B$ both have fixed effects, the EMS and $F$ tests in the $S \times A \times B$ design are similar to those in the $S \times A$ design. If $A$ or $B$ is assumed to have random effects (i.e., the levels selected to be included in the experiment have been randomly selected), significance tests and estimation of variance components are somewhat more complicated. Let us consider each case in turn.

## 13.6.1 The $S \times A \times B$ Design, with $A$ and $B$ Fixed

Consider an experiment similar to that reported by Murray et al. (2000). Factor $A$ is *orientation* of the faces; there are three levels instead of the seven in the actual experiment. $B$ is the type of *distortion* of the photo: $B_1$ photos are unaltered, $B_2$ photos have the eyes and mouth upside down, and $B_3$ photos have the eyes whitened and teeth blackened. Data in Table 13.10 are made-up averages of ratings of several photos in each condition, but the pattern of the means plotted in Fig. 13.1 is similar to the pattern in the Murray et al. article.

Table 13.11 presents formulas and numerical results for the $S \times A \times B$ ANOVA. The formulas for degrees of freedom and sums of squares parallel those developed earlier in this chapter and in previous chapters. The $F$ tests are based on the nonadditive model, assuming $A$ and $B$ both have fixed effects and subjects are a random sample from an infinite-sized population of subjects. Note that $A$ is tested against $S \times A$, $B$ is tested against $S \times B$, and $A \times B$ is tested against $S \times A \times B$. The expected mean squares that justify these error terms will be presented in Section 13.6.3. With respect to the results, orientation ($A$), distortion ($B$), and their interaction are all very significant, particularly distortion. The huge $F$ for

**TABLE 13.10**   DATA FOR A TWO-FACTOR REPEATED-MEASURES EXPERIMENT

| Subjects | $B_1$ | | | $B_2$ | | | $B_3$ | | |
| --- | --- | --- | --- | --- | --- | --- | --- | --- | --- |
| | $A_1$ | $A_2$ | $A_3$ | $A_1$ | $A_2$ | $A_3$ | $A_1$ | $A_2$ | $A_3$ |
| 1 | 1.18 | 2.40 | 2.48 | 4.76 | 4.93 | 3.13 | 5.56 | 4.93 | 5.21 |
| 2 | 1.14 | 1.55 | 1.25 | 4.81 | 4.73 | 3.89 | 4.85 | 5.43 | 4.89 |
| 3 | 1.02 | 1.25 | 1.30 | 4.98 | 3.85 | 3.05 | 4.28 | 5.64 | 6.49 |
| 4 | 1.05 | 1.63 | 1.84 | 4.91 | 5.21 | 2.95 | 5.13 | 5.52 | 5.69 |
| 5 | 1.81 | 1.65 | 1.01 | 5.01 | 4.18 | 3.51 | 4.90 | 5.18 | 5.52 |
| 6 | 1.69 | 1.67 | 1.04 | 5.65 | 4.56 | 3.94 | 4.12 | 5.76 | 4.99 |

| | Cell and Marginal Means | | | |
| --- | --- | --- | --- | --- |
| | $A_1$ | $A_2$ | $A_3$ | $\overline{Y}_{..k}$ |
| $B_1$ | 1.32 | 1.69 | 1.49 | 1.50 |
| $B_2$ | 5.02 | 4.58 | 3.41 | 4.34 |
| $B_3$ | 4.81 | 5.41 | 5.47 | 5.23 |
| $\overline{Y}_{.j.}$ | 3.72 | 3.89 | 3.46 | |
| | | | $\overline{Y}_{...} = 3.69$ | |

*Note.* $A$ is orientation and $B$ is distortion.

**TABLE 13.11**   ANOVA OF THE DATA OF TABLE 13.10

| SV | df | SS | MS | F |
|----|----|----|----|----|
| Total | $abn - 1 = 54$ | $\sum_i \sum_j \sum_k (Y_{ijk} - \overline{Y}_{...})^2 = 156.133$ | | |
| S | $n - 1 = 5$ | $ab \sum_i (\overline{Y}_{i..} - \overline{Y}_{...})^2 = .544$ | .109 | |
| A | $a - 1 = 2$ | $nb \sum_j (\overline{Y}_{.j.} - \overline{Y}_{...})^2 = 1.749$ | .874 | $\dfrac{MS_A}{MS_{SA}} = 9.23$ |
| SA | $(n - 1)(a - 1) = 10$ | $b \sum_j \sum_i (\overline{Y}_{ij.} - \overline{Y}_{i..} - \overline{Y}_{.j.} + \overline{Y}_{...})^2$ $= .947$ | .095 | |
| B | $b - 1 = 2$ | $na \sum_k (\overline{Y}_{..k} - \overline{Y}_{...})^2 = 136.554$ | 68.277 | $\dfrac{MS_B}{MS_{SB}} = 302.56$ |
| SB | $(n - 1)(b - 1) = 10$ | $a \sum_k \sum_i (\overline{Y}_{i.k} - \overline{Y}_{i..} - \overline{Y}_{..k} + \overline{Y}_{...})^2$ $= 2.257$ | .226 | |
| AB | $(a - 1)(b - 1) = 4$ | $n \sum_j \sum_k (\overline{Y}_{.jk} - \overline{Y}_{.j.} - \overline{Y}_{..k} + \overline{Y}_{...})^2$ $= 8.560$ | 2.140 | $\dfrac{MS_{AB}}{MS_{SAB}} = 7.75$ |
| SAB | $(n - 1)(a - 1)(b - 1)$ $= 20$ | $SS_{tot} - SS_S - SS_A - SS_{SA}$ $-SS_B - SS_{SB} - SS_{AB} = 5.522$ | .276 | |

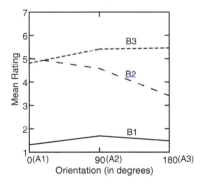

**Fig. 13.1** Plot of the means in Table 13.10

Distortion is largely due to the difference between the average bizarreness rating of the unaltered photo and the means for the two altered photos. Adjusting the degrees of freedom by the conservative Greenhouse–Geisser estimate of $\varepsilon$ (using SPSS's repeated-measures program) did not change the $p$ values markedly ($p < .012$ for all three tests).

Our hypothetical experiment provides an opportunity to consider contrasts among means within the two-factor repeated-measures design. We continue with our example in the following section to illustrate the calculations and interpretation of the results. Following the discussion of contrasts, we return to a discussion of the choice of error terms in Table 13.11, and also consider changes in expected mean squares and error terms when one of the two factors has random effects.

## 13.6.2 Testing Contrasts in the $S \times A \times B$ Design

Several contrasts are of possible interest in the Orientation $\times$ Distortion experiment. We might test whether the average rating in the two distorted conditions ($B_2$ and $B_3$) differs from the mean in the unaltered condition ($B_1$). Or, we might be interested in whether the slope and curvature of the curves in Fig. 13.1 differ as a function of the distortion condition. Most statistical software packages have options for performing such contrasts. They can also be tested by creating a contrast score for each subject and performing the appropriate tests on these. The contrast scores can be obtained by using a calculator or by using the transformation option in statistical software. Because the analysis of contrast scores is simple and may make the nature of the tests clearer, we illustrate this method in tests of two null hypotheses. The first is that the average slope of the three curves in Fig. 13.1 does not differ significantly from zero; that is, $H_{01} : \beta_{lin} = 0$, where $\beta_{lin}$ is the mean of the three population linear regression coefficients. The second null hypothesis is that the three slopes are equal; that is, $H_{02} : \beta_{1,lin} = \beta_{2,lin} = \beta_{3,lin}$. Table 13.12 presents the linear score

**TABLE 13.12**   TREND ANALYSIS FOR THE DATA OF TABLE 13.10

A contrast score for subject $i$ at $B_k$ is $\hat{\psi}_{ik} = \sum_j w_j Y_{ijk}$. For example, the linear contrast score for subject 1 at $B_1$ in Table 13.9 is $\hat{\psi}_{1,lin} = (-1)(1.18) + (0)(2.40) + (1)(2.48) = 1.30$. The other linear contrast scores derived from the ratings in Table 13.10 are:

| | Linear Contrast Scores | | | |
|---|---|---|---|---|
| Subject | $B_1$ | $B_2$ | $B_3$ | Row Means |
| 1 | 1.30 | −1.63 | −0.35 | −0.227 |
| 2 | 0.11 | −0.92 | 0.04 | −0.257 |
| 3 | 0.28 | −1.93 | 2.21 | 0.187 |
| 4 | 0.79 | −1.96 | 0.56 | −0.203 |
| 5 | −0.80 | −1.50 | 0.62 | −0.560 |
| 6 | −0.65 | −1.70 | 0.87 | −0.493 |
| Column Means | 0.172 | −1.608 | .658 | −0.259 |

The test of whether the average linear regression coefficient (the slope) differs significantly from zero is essentially a one-sample $t$ test, as in Chapter 6. Divide the mean of all the linear contrasts by its standard error, $SE(\hat{\psi})$, where $SE(\hat{\psi})$ is the standard deviation of the $n$ row means divided by the square root of $n$. In the present example, to test $H_{01}: \beta_{lin} = 0$,

$$t_5 = -.259/(.264/\sqrt{6}) = -2.403$$

To check our result, we used SPSS's GLM (repeated-measures) ANOVA program that includes an $F$ test of the polynomial components of the orientation SV. The reported $F$ of 5.772 is the square of the $t$ calculated above (within rounding error), as it should be. The $p$ value is .061; assuming $\alpha = .05$, we cannot reject the null hypothesis that the population slope is zero.

To test $H_{02}: \beta_{1,lin} = \beta_{2,lin} = \beta_{3,lin}$, we perform a repeated-measures $S \times B$ ANOVA in which the scores are the linear contrast scores at each level of $B$. From the SPSS output, we have

| SV | df | SS | MS | F | p |
|---|---|---|---|---|---|
| Linear $(B)$ | 2 | 8.543 | 4.272 | 12.528 | .002 |
| $S \times$ Linear $(B)$ | 10 | 3.414 | .341 | | |

for each subject at each level of $B$ followed by tests of the two null hypotheses. With three levels of $A$, the linear coefficients are 1, 0, and $-1$ (or any multiple of these numbers).

As the results in Table 13.12 show, the average of the three slopes does not differ significantly from zero. However, the three slopes do differ significantly from each other. This is because the $B_2$ slope in Fig. 13.1 is negative, whereas the other two slopes are slightly positive. The $B_2$ condition is the one in which the distortion involved turning the eyes and mouth upside down. The slope may be negative because the $B_2$ faces seem less bizarre when seen upside down (at $A_3$, 180 degrees rotation) than when not rotated ($A_1$); in the upside-down condition, the eyes and mouth are in their normal orientation.

The methods illustrated in Table 13.12 are quite general. We can use them to test contrasts involving quadratic curvature using the coefficients $-1, 2$, and $-1$ (or any multiple of these), or to test qualitative contrasts among either the $A$ or $B$ means.

## 13.6.3 The S $\times$ A $\times$ B Design, A Fixed and B Random

In the Murray et al. (2000) experiment, photos of eight different faces were presented to subjects in each combination of distortion and orientation. Faces are a variable, one we view as having random effects. Presumably, the sampling of the photos is carried out in a way that ensures that they can be reasonably viewed as a random sample from a large population of photos. Otherwise, there are no statistical grounds for generalizing conclusions about the effects of the independent variable to photos that were not included in the experiment.

There are many types of experiments in which we would like to generalize the results to stimuli other than those actually used. We may, for example, be concerned with ratings of pictures that vary along some dimension, the number of trials taken to solve problems that differ in difficulty, time to comprehend sentences with different syntactic structures, or responses to words in different experimental conditions. What can reasonably be viewed as a random set of $b$ stimuli is not a simple issue and will be discussed in more detail later in this chapter. Until then, we assume that $B$ is a random-effects factor and consider the implications of this assumption for data analysis.

Table 13.13 presents $EMS$ assuming $B$ has either fixed or random effects. Comparing the two sets of $EMS$, it should be apparent that, if $B$ is random, additional components of variance are present. This is because the data represent samples of the populations of $S \times A$, $A \times B$, and $S \times A \times B$ interaction effects at each level of $A$. The means of these samples of interaction effects will not be zero and will tend to have different values at each level of $A$, depending on the particular interaction effects sampled. Therefore, the interaction variances will influence the value of $MS_A$.

Because of the additional variance components found in the expected mean squares when $B$ is random, there is no obvious error term against which to test $A$, the variable of primary interest. The error term should be a mean square that has an expectation of $\sigma_e^2 + b\sigma_{SA}^2 + n\sigma_{SB}^2 + \sigma_{SAB}^2$. As can be seen in Table 13.13, there is no source of variance that has this expectation. The problem disappears if $\sigma_{SA}^2$ or $\sigma_{AB}^2$ is zero; in either of those cases, an error term is readily found, $MS_{AB}$ if $\sigma_{SA}^2 = 0$ or $MS_{SA}$ if $\sigma_{AB}^2 = 0$. This observation raises the possibility of a preliminary test of the $S \times A$ or the $A \times B$ term against $MS_{SAB}$. If, for example, we had prior grounds for assuming that $\sigma_{AB}^2 = 0$ and the $A \times B$ term was not significant at the .25 level, we might delete $(\alpha\beta)_{jk}$ from the model, in which case $MS_{SA}$ would be an appropriate error term for testing the $A$ source of variance. As we noted in discussing pooling in Chapter 12, there is considerable debate about whether such preliminary tests should be used. If a Type 2 error is made in the preliminary test, then the Type 1 error

**TABLE 13.13**   *EMS* FOR THE $S \times A \times B$ DESIGN

| SV | df | EMS | |
|---|---|---|---|
| | | A,B fixed | A fixed, B random |
| S | $n - 1$ | $\sigma_e^2 + ab\sigma_S^2$ | $\sigma_e^2 + a\sigma_{SB}^2 + ab\sigma_S^2$ |
| A | $n - 1$ | $\sigma_e^2 + b\sigma_{SA}^2 + nb\theta_A^2$ | $\sigma_e^2 + b\sigma_{SA}^2 + n\sigma_{AB}^2 + \sigma_{SAB}^2 + nb\theta_A^2$ |
| SA | $(n - 1)(a - 1)$ | $\sigma_e^2 + b\sigma_{SA}^2$ | $\sigma_e^2 + \sigma_{SAB}^2 + b\sigma_{SA}^2$ |
| B | $b - 1$ | $\sigma_e^2 + a\sigma_{SB}^2 + na\theta_B^2$ | $\sigma_e^2 + a\sigma_{SB}^2 + na\sigma_B^2$ |
| SB | $(n - 1)(b - 1)$ | $\sigma_e^2 + a\sigma_{SB}^2$ | $\sigma_e^2 + a\sigma_{SB}^2$ |
| AB | $(a - 1)(b - 1)$ | $\sigma_e^2 + \sigma_{SAB}^2 + n\theta_{AB}^2$ | $\sigma_e^2 + \sigma_{SAB}^2 + n\sigma_{AB}^2$ |
| SAB | $(n - 1)(a - 1)(b - 1)$ | $\sigma_e^2 + \sigma_{SAB}^2$ | $\sigma_e^2 + \sigma_{SAB}^2$ |

Forming $F$ Ratios

Assuming $H_0$ is true, the ratio of EMS for the numerator and denominator must be 1.

*Rules for EMS*

1. $\sigma_e^2$ contributes to all lines.

2. The component corresponding to the $SV$ under consideration (the null hypothesis component)

   should be present. For example, $E(MS_A)$ includes a $\theta_A^2$ component.

3. Any other variance component will be included if: (1) its subscripts include the letter(s) in the present $SV$, and (2) if *all* of its other subscripts represent random factors. For example, under the model in which $A$ and $B$ are both fixed, $\sigma_{SA}^2$ contributes to $E(MS_A)$, because $SA$ includes $A$ and the remaining subscripts ($S$) is a random factor. When $S$ and $B$ are both random factors, $E(MS_A)$ includes $SA$, $AB$, and $SAB$ components because when $A$ is ignored, the remaining letter (s) represent random factors.

4. The coefficient multiplying each variance component reflects the number of scores involved in the subscribed combinations. For example, there are $n$ scores in each $AB$ combination, so $\theta_{AB}^2$ is multiplied by $n$; however, there are $nb$ scores at each level of $A$, so $\theta_A^2$ is multiplied by $nb$.

associated with the test of $A$ against $MS_{AB}$ will be inflated. In studies of the "sometimes-pool" rule, Type 1 error rates have ranged from .07 to .11 with the nominal $\alpha$ level at .05 (Janky, 2000). Presumably, a similar inflation of Type 1 error rate is possible when a preliminary test is used to justify testing $A$ against $A \times B$ or $S \times A$. Furthermore, there will rarely be prior grounds for deleting a term from the complete nonadditive model. Therefore, an alternative approach, the **quasi-$F$ test**, is recommended. We consider this next.

## 13.6.4 Quasi-$F$ ($F'$) Tests

Assuming that the effects of the independent variable will vary across subjects ($S$) and items ($B$), and that $B$ is a random-effects variable, we are faced with the issue of testing the hypothesis of no treatment effects. One solution is to calculate a quasi-$F$ ratio ($F'$)—a ratio of combinations of mean squares whose expectations are equal under the null hypothesis. One possibility is

$$F_1' = \frac{MS_A}{MS_{AB} + MS_{SA} - MS_{SAB}} \tag{13.17}$$

The rationale for this ratio is that the ratio of *EMS* is

$$\frac{\sigma_e^2 + \sigma_{SAB}^2 + b\sigma_{SA}^2 + n\sigma_{AB}^2 + bn\theta_A^2}{\sigma_e^2 + \sigma_{SAB}^2 + b\sigma_{SA}^2 + n\sigma_{AB}^2}$$

which equals 1 if the null hypothesis ( $\theta_A^2 = 0$) is true.

That the ratio of *EMS* terms equals one is a necessary, but not a sufficient, condition for the ratio of mean squares to be distributed as $F$. As we saw in Chapter 7, an important condition is that both the numerator and denominator must be distributed as chi-square variables divided by their degrees of freedom. Satterthwaite (1946) has shown that, under the usual assumptions of analysis of variance, a linear combination of mean squares has approximately this sampling distribution. The appropriate *df* for the denominator are

$$df = \frac{(MS_{AB} + MS_{SA} - MS_{SAB})^2}{MS_{AB}^2/df_{AB} + MS_{SA}^2/df_{SA} + MS_{SAB}^2/df_{SAB}} \tag{13.18}$$

Other quasi-$F$ ratios can be calculated. One that has been widely recommended is

$$F_2' = \frac{MS_A + MS_{SAB}}{MS_{AB} + MS_{SA}} \tag{13.19}$$

As with $F_1'$, the ratio of EMS is again 1 under the null hypothesis. The numerator *df* are

$$df_{\text{num}} = \frac{(MS_A + MS_{SAB})^2}{MS_A^2/df_A + MS_{SAB}^2/df_{SAB}} \tag{13.20}$$

and the denominator *df* are

$$df_{\text{den}} = \frac{(MS_{AB} + MS_{SA})^2}{MS_{AB}^2/df_{AB} + MS_{SA}^2/df_{SA}} \tag{13.21}$$

Should $F_1$ or $F_2'$ be calculated? $F_2'$ was consistently more powerful under conditions examined in simulation studies by Hudson and Krutchkoff (1968) and Davenport and Webster (1973); however, the advantage appears to be slight, except when *df* are small ( $n = a = b = 3$) or the *SA, AB*, and *SAB* population variances are all very small. Another advantage of $F_2'$ is that it takes on only positive values, whereas $F_1'$ can be negative when $MS_{SAB}$ is large. However, the variance of $F_1'$ "is considerably smaller" than that of $F_2'$ (Davenport & Webster, 1973). Presumably, this is because a ratio based on a chi-square variable and an approximately distributed chi-square variable is a better approximation to the $F$ ratio than one based on two approximately distributed chi-square variables. Neither procedure is clearly preferable under all circumstances, but we lean toward $F_2'$ because its power is somewhat greater under conditions in which power will tend to be low.

Equations 13.18, 13.20, and 13.21 for degrees of freedom are special cases of a general formula. If we have a **linear combination of mean squares** (CMS) such that $CMS = MS_1 \pm MS_2 \pm \cdots \pm MS_K$, it is distributed on *df* calculated as

$$df_{CMS} = \frac{(MS_1 \pm MS_2 \pm \cdots \pm MS_K)^2}{MS_1^2/df_1 + MS_2^2/df_2 + \ldots + MS_K^2/df_K}. \tag{13.22}$$

The ratios formed in Equations 13.17 and 13.19 involve linear combinations of mean squares in which the weights by which the mean squares are multiplied are 1 and $-1$. In some circumstances, we will use other weights to combine mean squares or variances. A case in point is the Brown–Forsythe statistic, $F^*$, which was presented in Chapter 8 as a way of testing treatment effects when variances are heterogeneous. To obtain a denominator mean square for $F^*$, we combined group variances instead of mean squares, and the weights were a function of the group sizes. Nevertheless, $F^*$ is a quasi-$F$ statistic because its denominator is a linear combination of the general form

$$CMS = w_1 V_1 + w_2 V_2 + \cdots + w_k V_k + \cdots + w_K V_K \tag{13.23}$$

where $w_k$ is any real number and $V_k$ is either a mean square or a variance. The degrees of freedom associated with this is

$$df_{CMS} = \frac{(CMS)^2}{\sum_k \left( w_k^2 V_k^2 / df_k \right)} \tag{13.24}$$

The $df_k$ are the degrees of freedom associated with the $k$th mean square or variance.

In many studies, observations are missing and therefore not all $S \times A \times B$ combinations are available. If so, it will be impossible to calculate $MS_{SAB}$ and, therefore, neither $F_1'$ nor $F_2'$ can be calculated. A conservative remedy in this situation is to calculate $F_1'$ or $F_2'$ without $MS_{SAB}$. We can see from Equations 13.17 and 13.19 that $MS_A / (MS_{AB} + MS_{SA})$ must be less than $F_1'$ or $F_2'$, which is why we call this approach conservative. In actual practice, this minimum quasi-F (**min $F'$**; Clark, 1973; Forster & Dickinson, 1976) is computed as follows:

1.  Find the average of the scores in each $S \times A$ combination; presumably there will be a few scores in each combination, even if some values are missing. Compute $F_1 = MS_A / MS_{SA}$.
2.  Find the average of the scores in each $A \times B$ combination. Compute $F_2 = MS_A / MS_{AB}$.
3.  Compute

$$\min F' = \frac{F_1 F_2}{F_1 + F_2} \tag{13.25}$$

and

$$df_{error} = \frac{(F_1 + F_2)^2}{F_1^2 / df_{AB} + F_2^2 / df_{SA}}. \tag{13.26}$$

The numerator $df$ are just $a - 1$. Appendix 13.2 presents the derivation of the two preceding equations.

What about the effects of violations of the sphericity assumption on the distribution of $F'$? Somewhat surprisingly, Maxwell and Bray (1986) have found evidence that non-sphericity does not inflate the Type 1 error rate for $F'$. Their article presents an interesting discussion of the reasons for this.

One last comment is in order. If $B$ is a random-effects variable, $b$ should be as large as possible. Interactions of $A$ with both $S$ and $B$ contribute to the error variance against which treatment effects are to be evaluated. It is important to have sufficient degrees of freedom associated with both variables to ensure powerful tests of $A$. Furthermore, the limited evidence we have suggests that the distribution of $F'$ more closely approximates that of $F$ as $a$, $b$, and $n$ increase.

## 13.7 FIXED OR RANDOM EFFECTS?

It should be clear from our discussion so far that designating effects as fixed or random has important implications for both significance testing and parameter estimation, as well as for the degree to which we can generalize our results. Therefore, we need to consider further the decision about classifying effects.

The decision to classify a variable as having fixed or random effects is not always a simple one. At one extreme, we have variables that clearly should be viewed as having fixed effects. The levels of the variable have been arbitrarily selected for inclusion in the experiment, and because of the way in which they have been selected, there is no basis for viewing them as a random sample of levels from a population of levels. This class includes most manipulated variables such as the type of distortion or the orientation of the photo in the Murray et al. (2000) experiment, or observed characteristics of individuals such as gender or clinical category. It also would include a variable such as seasons because the four seasons included as an independent variable in the study exhaust the population of possible seasons.

At the other extreme, we have random sampling from some well-defined population. This is rarely realized in practice, and it is therefore difficult to determine to which population our results can be generalized. Can we reasonably view our subjects as a random sample of adults? College students? College students interested in psychology? College students who attend the particular university in which the study was run? The answer depends not only on the sampling process, but also on the particular study. In studies of sensory processes, like visual acuity, we might generalize to the population of adults having normal vision. In studies of human learning, we might define the population more narrowly, reserving judgment as to whether our conclusions will hold for populations having a markedly different average level of ability from that characterizing the institution in which our study was run. When in doubt, generalizations should be restricted to the more narrowly defined population.

Even though the population is rarely as well defined as we would like, it should be clear from the preceding comments that we do view subjects as a random-effects variable. Our justification is that subjects are not arbitrarily selected. Other individuals are provided an equal opportunity to participate and might well serve if replications of the experiment were run.

Classifying stimuli, such as words and pictures, presents greater difficulty. For many experiments, we can argue, on much the same grounds that we presented in discussing subjects, that such stimuli are a random sample from a (possibly ill-defined) population of potential items; that is, the stimuli are not arbitrarily selected, and there are many other items that had an equal opportunity of being included in the study under the sampling procedure used. In many other experiments, however, the choice of stimuli is so constrained that it is difficult to imagine a population from which this set of items is one relatively small sample. In studies involving responses to words, for example, restrictions are often placed on the grammatical class, length in both syllables and letters, familiarity, and number of associates of each word. The experimenter may find it difficult to meet those restrictions. Under such conditions, it is not clear that stimuli should be treated as having random effects. Two rough guidelines may be helpful. First, under the existing constraints, could independent investigators produce other samples of items? Second, if the answer to the first question is positive—there is a reasonably large population of items—was there an equal likelihood that all members of the population could be included in the study? If this answer is also positive, it is reasonable to treat the stimuli as having random effects with all that this implies for our data analyses and the scope of our conclusions.

## 13.8 NONPARAMETRIC PROCEDURES FOR REPEATED-MEASURES DESIGNS

In Chapter 8, two tests based on ranks were presented, the Kruskal–Wallis $H$ test and the rank-transformation test (Conover & Iman, 1981). These tests are often more powerful than the $F$ test when the treatment population distributions have heavy tails or are skewed. Similar analyses of ranked scores can be applied to data from repeated-measures designs. We consider these as well as a test for situations in which all scores are either zeros or ones.

### 13.8.1 Friedman's $\chi^2$ Test

Consider a data set with $n$ rows (subjects) and $a$ columns (treatment levels). Assume that the scores for each subject have been assigned ranks from 1 (for the lowest) to $a$ (for the highest). If appropriate statistical software is available, we need not rank the data ourselves. For example, SPSS's nonparametric module ("$K$ Related Samples") takes the original data of Table 13.1 as its input and yields a chi-square statistic and its associated $p$ value. In the absence of such software, ranking can be done by hand and calculations can be carried out. *If there are no ties*, Friedman's (1937) test statistic may be written as

$$\chi_F^2 = \frac{SS_A}{a(a+1)/12} \tag{13.27}$$

where

$$SS_A = n \sum_{j=1}^{a} (\overline{R}_{.j} - \overline{R}_{..})^2 \tag{13.28}$$

and $\overline{R}_{.j}$ is the mean of the $n$ ranks (the $R_{ij}$) at $A_j$, $\overline{R}_{..}$ is the mean of the $an$ ranks, and $\chi_F^2$ is distributed on $a - 1$ $df$. The denominator of Equation 13.27 is the variance of a set of $a$ consecutive integers or untied ranks. Recall that the ratio of a sum of squares to the variance of its population is distributed as chi-square (see Chapter 7) if the scores are independently and normally distributed; for correlated observations, sphericity is required. Therefore, the ratio in Equation 13.27 has an exact chi-square distribution on $a - 1$ $df$ if sphericity holds for the population of ranks and the sampling distribution of the mean of the ranks is normal. The central limit theorem assures us that, for reasonably large $n$, the normality requirement will be met and, therefore, the use of the chi-square table (Appendix Table C.4) to evaluate $\chi_F^2$ will be appropriate. A conservative strategy for using the chi-square table is to require $an > 30$. Odeh (1977) has tabled exact $p$ values for $\chi_F^2$ for values of $a$ and $n$ as large as 6; these may be used to evaluate significance in small samples.

Ties require a modification of Equation 13.27. Because the calculations are somewhat complicated, and several software packages take ties into consideration,[3] we will not illustrate the process here. Interested readers may consult a textbook on nonparametric procedures; Lehmann (1975) provides details of the calculations and a numerical example.

## 13.8.2 The Rank-Transformation $F$ Test ($F_R$)

A rather simple alternative to ANOVA has been applied to data from several experimental designs, including the repeated-measures design (Iman, Hora, & Conover, 1984; Hora & Iman, 1988). There are two steps: first, assign ranks to all $an$ scores from smallest to largest, assigning midranks in case of ties—note that, unlike Friedman's procedure, each subject's scores are not ranked separately; and second, do the standard $S \times A$ ANOVA on the rank values. This means that once the $Y_{ij}$ have been converted to $R_{ij}$, the transformed values can be submitted to any program that analyzes data from a repeated measures design. Table 13.14 presents the $R_{ij}$ transforms of the data of Table 13.1, together with the results of an ANOVA performed by SYSTAT. The $p$ value for this test is .03.

## 13.8.3 Which Test?

When the distributions of scores in the treatment populations are the same, the usual $F$ test, $\chi_F^2$, and $F_R$ all test the null hypothesis of equal treatment population means. If, in addition, those populations can be assumed to be normal or to have short tails (as when the

**TABLE 13.14** RANKS AND ANOVA FOR THE RANK-TRANSFORMATION ($F_r$) TEST

| Winter | Spring | Summer | Fall |
|---|---|---|---|
| 45.0 | 52.0 | 14.0 | 20.0 |
| 42.5 | 47.5 | 39.0 | 55.0 |
| 14.0 | 14.0 | 5.5 | 5.5 |
| 5.5 | 5.5 | 5.5 | 5.5 |
| 17.5 | 5.5 | 19.0 | 35.0 |
| 14.0 | 30.0 | 5.5 | 24.5 |
| 30.0 | 5.5 | 5.5 | 24.5 |
| 37.0 | 17.5 | 24.5 | 24.5 |
| 39.0 | 24.5 | 33.0 | 39.0 |
| 24.5 | 33.0 | 36.0 | 33.0 |
| 42.5 | 44.0 | 41.0 | 47.5 |
| 30.0 | 24.5 | 11.0 | 24.5 |
| 50.5 | 56.0 | 53.5 | 53.5 |
| 46.0 | 49.0 | 14.0 | 50.5 |

| $\overline{R}_{.j}$ | 31.286 | 29.179 | 21.929 | 31.607 |
|---|---|---|---|---|

| SV | df | SS | MS | F | p | G–G | H–F |
|---|---|---|---|---|---|---|---|
| Seasons | 3 | 854.821 | 284.940 | 3.437 | .026 | .035 | .026 |
| S/seasons | 39 | 3233.304 | 82.905 | | | | |

Greenhouse–Geisser epsilon:  0.8302
Huynh–Feldt epsilon :  1.0000

*Note.* Ranks are based on the data of Table 13.1.

data are ratings from a scale with only a few points), the $F$ test will be most powerful. As the discussion in Chapter 8 suggests, the relative power of the $F$ and the rank-based tests changes when treatment populations are skewed or heavy tailed. Several studies (Hora & Iman, 1988; Iman et al., 1984; Kepner & Robinson, 1988) indicate that, in these conditions, both $F_R$ and $\chi_F^2$ usually have Type 1 error rates close to the nominal .05 level, and both are more powerful, often considerably so, than the $F$ test.[4] As for the relative power of the two rank-based tests, Iman et al. (1984) found that $F_R$ was more powerful than $\chi_F^2$ except when the number of levels of the independent variable was 10, or the distribution was very heavy-tailed. In those cases, power was about equal. However, Hora and Iman (1988) and Kepner and Robinson (1988) found that the relative powers of $F_R$ and $\chi_F^2$ depend not only on $a$ and the shape of the treatment population distribution, but also on a number of other factors, including the within-subject correlation, and the variability of subject means. The power advantage moves to the Friedman test as the correlation or subject effects increase. Because of the influence of so many factors, there is no simple rule of thumb, but we recommend $F_R$ unless $a$ is more than 5 and the data are very skewed.

## 13.8.4 The Wilcoxon Signed-Rank (WSR) Test

Neither $F_R$ nor $\chi_F^2$ has good power when $a = 2$. The WSR test (1949) provides a powerful alternative when the population of difference scores is symmetrically and independently distributed. The test is only slightly less powerful than the $t$ when the data are normally distributed and can be considerably more powerful when the difference scores are symmetrically (but not necessarily normally) distributed with heavy tails (Blair & Higgins, 1985). However, power is lost for the WSR test, but not for the $t$ test, when difference scores are zero because such differences are discarded in the WSR test.

Table 13.15 presents fall-summer difference scores and signed ranks for the Beck depression scores for 12 of the 14 subjects in Table 13.1. Two of these difference scores were zero, and therefore were discarded before the analysis. The first step in the analysis of the remaining $n$ pairs is to rank the difference scores, from smallest to largest, ignoring the sign of the difference. This has been done in Table 13.15. When several absolute values of differences are tied, each receives the median rank. After ranks are assigned, a + or − sign is attached, depending on the sign of the original difference score. Then the sum of the positive ranks ($T_+$) and the absolute value of the sum of the negative ranks ($|T_-|$) are obtained. Rules for rejecting the null hypothesis are presented in Table 13.15. Note that they depend on the alternative hypothesis. The $z$ score calculated in the table can also be obtained from several statistical software packages. However, bear in mind that the $p$ value reported assumes a normal distribution of the signed ranks; therefore, for $n$ less than 50, it will be more accurate to compare the $T$ statistic with the critical $T$ value in Appendix Table C.10.

One reminder is in order with respect to the WSR test. Researchers often take the descriptive phrase "distribution free" too literally. Although the test does not depend on the assumption that the population of difference scores is normally distributed, that distribution should be symmetric, or at least not markedly skewed. To see why this is so, consider the following set of scores and their assigned ranks:

| Scores: | −4 | −3 | −2 | +2 | +3 | +4 |
|---|---|---|---|---|---|---|
| Ranks: | −5.5 | −3.5 | −1.5 | +1.5 | +3.5 | +5.5 |

**TABLE 13.15** THE *WSR* TEST APPLIED TO DIFFERENCE SCORES BASED ON THE FALL AND SUMMER DEPRESSION SCORES OF TABLE 13.1

### REJECTION RULES

The null hypothesis is rejected if the test statistic is less than the critical value of $T$ ($T_C$). The test statistic depends on the null hypothesis in the following way:

| $H_1$ | Test Statistic |
|---|---|
| $\mu_{\text{diff}} > 0$ | $|T_-|$ |
| $\mu_{\text{diff}} < 0$ | $T_+$ |
| $\mu_{\text{diff}} \neq 0$ | Smaller of $|T_-|$ and $T_+$ |

### FALL–SUMMER DIFFERENCE SCORES AND RANKS

| Subject | 1 | 2 | 3 | 5 | 6 | 8 | 9 | 10 | 11 | 12 | 13 | 14 |
|---|---|---|---|---|---|---|---|---|---|---|---|---|
| Differences | 10.554 | 4 | 1 | −1.097 | 2.5 | −.94 | −1 | −1.208 | 1.477 | 1.991 | 3 | 9.5 |
| Signed Ranks | 12 | 10 | 2.5 | −4 | 8 | −1 | −2.5 | −5 | 6 | 7 | 9 | 11 |

Assuming a two-tailed alternative, the test statistic for these data is the smaller total, $|T_-| = |(-1) + (-2.5) + (-4) + (-5)| = 12.5$. From Appendix Table C.10, we find that the critical value, $T_C$, for $n = 12$, $\alpha = .05$, is 13. Because $|T_-| < T_C$, reject $H_0$. If $n > 50$, the test statistic can be converted to a $z$ score, and the associated $p$ value can be obtained from the normal probability table, Appendix Table C.2. The conversion formula is

$$z = \frac{\min(T_+, T_-) - n(n+1)/4}{\sqrt{n(n+1)(2n+1)/24 - \sum_{j=1}^{J}\left(t_j^3 - t_j\right)/48}}$$

where $n$ is the number of nonzero differences, $J$ is the number of ties, and $t_j$ is the number of differences in the $j$th tie. In the example, $n = 12$ and there are no ties; therefore,

$$z = (12.5 - 39)/\sqrt{(12)(13)(25)/24} = -2.08$$

and $p = .038$.

The median is zero, and $T_+ = |T_-| = (n)(n+1)/4$. Suppose we now skew the distribution of scores as follows:

| Scores: | −6 | −5 | −2 | +2 | +3 | +4 |
|---|---|---|---|---|---|---|
| Ranks: | −6 | −5 | −1.5 | +1.5 | +3 | +4 |

The median is still zero, but $T_+$ no longer equals $|T_-|$. Thus, a true null hypothesis about a population median may be rejected if the distribution is skewed.

Although we have discussed the WSR test in terms of difference scores, it can be applied to any contrast among means. For example, given four levels of a variable $A$, we might wish to test whether the combined average of the $A_1$ and $A_2$ populations of scores differs from that for $A_3$ and $A_4$. In that case, we calculate $(1/2)(Y_{i1} + Y_{i2}) - (1/2)(Y_{i3} + Y_{i4})$, and then rank and sign these contrast scores.

### 13.8.5 Cochran's Q Test

A common research situation is one in which each subject responds on several trials, or under several different conditions, and each response is classified in one of two ways. For example, suppose we record a success or failure for each subject on each of four mathematical problems that varied in their conceptual distance from a practice problem. The question is whether the probability of success depended on the problem type. In general, $Y_{ij} = 1$ or $0$, indicating a success or failure by subject $i$ in condition $j$. If $\pi_j$ is the probability of a success in the population of responses under $A_j$, then the null hypothesis is

$$H_0 : \pi_1 = \pi_2 = \ldots = \pi_j \ldots = \pi_a$$

The $Q$ statistic is defined as

$$Q = SS_A / MS_{A/S} \tag{13.29}$$

$MS_{A/S}$ is the average of $n$ variances, in which each variance is based on the $a$ scores for a subject. If we denote the sum of scores for subject $i$ as $T_i$, then

$$MS_{A/S} = \frac{a \sum_i T_{i.} - \sum_i T_{i.}^2}{an(a-1)} \tag{13.30}$$

We can also calculate $MS_{A/S}$ by performing an ANOVA on the scores:

$$MS_{A/S} = \frac{SS_A + SS_{SA}}{n(a-1)} \tag{13.31}$$

Cochran (1950) proved that the ratio in Equation 13.29 is distributed as chi-square when $n$ is large and the population correlation for any pair of conditions is the same as for any other pair. Therefore, the null hypothesis is rejected when $Q$ exceeds the critical value of chi-square on $a - 1$ $df$.

As we stated in Chapter 7, the chi-square distribution rests on the assumption that the variable of interest is normally distributed. Under the central limit theorem, this assumption is essentially true when $n$ is large. This raises the question of how large an $n$ is large. The answer depends on the values of the $\pi_j$; when $\pi_j$ is closer to .5, $n$ can be smaller because the distribution is more symmetric. Another factor is the number of subjects who exhibit no variability (i.e., all zeros or ones); such subjects contribute nothing to the value of $Q$ and therefore do not contribute to the effective $n$. Based on a review of several simulation studies, Myers, DiCecco, White, and Borden (1982) recommended that the effective $n$ (for $a = 3$) be at least 16. When $n$ is small, empirical rejection rates of true null hypotheses are less than the nominal $\alpha$, and power is quite low.

Table 13.16 presents data for 16 subjects on four math problems of different types. Although the analysis can be done easily by hand, statistical packages can also be used. For example, SPSS provides a $Q$ test program (under "Nonparametrics," "$K$ Related Samples"), which yields the exact $p$ value of .037. The 0/1 data can also be submitted to a repeated-measures ANOVA. In fact, Myers et al. (1982) report that the $F$ and $Q$ tests have very similar Type 1 error rates for $n \geq 16$; for smaller $n$, the $F$ test's Type 1 error rate may be

**TABLE 13.16**  AN EXAMPLE OF COCHRAN'S Q TEST

| Subject | $P_1$ | $P_2$ | $P_3$ | $P_4$ | $T_{i.}$ | $T_{i.}^2$ |
|---|---|---|---|---|---|---|
| | | | Problems | | | |
| 1 | 1 | 0 | 1 | 0 | 2 | 4 |
| 2 | 1 | 0 | 1 | 0 | 2 | 4 |
| 3 | 1 | 0 | 0 | 0 | 1 | 1 |
| 4 | 0 | 0 | 0 | 1 | 1 | 1 |
| 5 | 1 | 0 | 0 | 0 | 1 | 1 |
| 6 | 1 | 0 | 1 | 0 | 2 | 4 |
| 7 | 1 | 1 | 0 | 1 | 3 | 9 |
| 8 | 1 | 0 | 1 | 0 | 2 | 4 |
| 9 | 0 | 0 | 1 | 1 | 2 | 4 |
| 10 | 1 | 1 | 1 | 0 | 3 | 9 |
| 11 | 1 | 0 | 1 | 0 | 2 | 4 |
| 12 | 0 | 1 | 0 | 1 | 2 | 4 |
| 13 | 0 | 1 | 1 | 0 | 2 | 4 |
| 14 | 1 | 0 | 1 | 0 | 2 | 4 |
| 15 | 1 | 1 | 0 | 0 | 2 | 4 |
| 16 | 1 | 0 | 0 | 0 | 1 | 1 |
| $T_{.j}$ | 12 | 5 | 9 | 4 | 30 | 62 |

*Note.* Substituting into Equation 13.30,

$$MS_{P/S} = \frac{(4)(30) - 62}{(4)(16)(3)} = .302$$

and $SS_P = n \sum_j [(T_{j.}/n) - (T_{..}/an)]^2 = 2.563$. Therefore, $Q = 2.563/.302 = 8.48$. Evaluated as a chi-square statistic on 3 *df*, the result is significant at the .05 level.

inflated. Some indication of this is present in the example; the *p* value reported for the *F* was .031, slightly less than that obtained in the chi-square test.

## 13.9 CONCLUDING REMARKS

The research literature abounds with examples of designs involving repeated measurements. Repeated-measures designs potentially have greater precision than designs that use only between-subjects factors and are particularly useful when the supply of subjects is limited relative to the number of treatment combinations to be studied, or when the experimenter's goal is to collect data on some performance measure as a function of time. However, experimenters should understand the potential problems associated with repeated-measures designs, the assumptions that are made, and the consequences of violating these assumptions. We have, for example, (a) indicated that tests on within-subjects factors having more than two levels will be positively biased when the sphericity assumption is violated and have recommended that a degree-of-freedom correction, or MANOVA, be used to counteract this bias; (b) shown that there will not always be obvious error terms in designs that contain several random-effect factors, but that hypotheses may often be tested using quasi-$F$ tests; and (c) indicated that there are a number of negative consequences of nonadditivity and that sometimes it may be desirable to transform the data to an additive scale. These techniques provide a good starting point for coping with some of the problems that may result from using the repeated-measures design. Even more important, awareness of potential problems is necessary to decide whether to use the repeated-measures design and to evaluate the results of significance tests intelligently.

It should also be emphasized that, when the independent variable is something other than time or trial, the order of presentation of treatments should be randomized independently for each subject. Proper randomization will guard against confounding the effects of time and treatments (what inference can be drawn in the extreme case in which treatment 1 is always presented first, treatment 2 always second, and so on?). Randomization will also reduce the possibility of severe heterogeneity of covariance and violations of the sphericity assumption. Scores for treatments close together in time should be more highly correlated than scores for treatments further apart. By randomizing the order of treatments for each subject, each pair of treatments is given an equal opportunity to appear any given length of time apart.

Sufficient time between presentations of treatments may help minimize carry-over effects. If participating in a particular experimental condition results in the subject becoming fatigued, the effects should be allowed to wear off before the next condition is presented. Even if the different orders of presentation balance so that treatments and trials are not confounded, carry-over effects, if present, will result in increased variability among orders of presentation, and thus reduce the efficiency of the design.

The "pure" repeated-measures designs represent only a subset of designs that use within-subjects factors. In the next chapter, we discuss designs that combine between-subjects and within-subjects factors, and following that we consider designs in which the orders of treatments are systematically counterbalanced. A solid understanding of the contents of the present chapter should provide the necessary preparation for these extensions of the repeated-measures design.

## KEY CONCEPTS

repeated-measures designs
measurement error component
additive model
true score
random-effects variables
power
sphericity
univariate $F$ test with $\varepsilon$-adjusted
   degrees of freedom
quasi-$F$ test
min $F'$
rank-transformation $F$ test ($F_R$)
Cochran's $Q$ test

individual differences component
carry-over effects
nonadditive model
fixed-effects variables
Tukey's test of nonadditivity
transformations
compound symmetry
multivariate analysis of variance
   (MANOVA)
linear combination of mean
   squares (CMS)
Friedman's $\chi^2$ test
Wilcoxon signed-rank (WSR) test

## EXERCISES

**13.1**  The following data set consists of 3 scores for each of four subjects:

|       | $A_1$ | $A_2$ | $A_3$ |
|-------|-------|-------|-------|
| $S_1$ | 12    | 14    | 15    |
| $S_2$ | 9     | 8     | 10    |
| $S_3$ | 10    | 9     | 12    |
| $S_4$ | 8     | 6     | 7     |

(a) Carry out the ANOVA.

(b) Assuming additivity, present the EMS.

(c) Use your answer to part (b) to estimate partial $\omega_A^2$.

(d) If there were four different subjects at each level of $A$, the error variance would have been larger. Estimate what $MS_{S/A}$ would have been from the ANOVA of part (a). The appropriate formula is given by Equation 13.5. (Note that this estimate is a weighted average of the $S$ and $S \times A$ mean squares.)

(e) Estimate the power each design would have had to reject $H_0$ at the .05 level, assuming the effects in the data represent the true population effects.

**13.2**  Consider the following data set:

| Subject | $A_1$ | $A_2$ | $A_3$ |
|---------|-------|-------|-------|
| 1       | 1.7   | 2.4   | 2.7   |
| 2       | 4.6   | 6.3   | 7.0   |
| 3       | 6.9   | 6.8   | 10.2  |
| 4       | 3.6   | 6.1   | 7.5   |
| 5       | 4.3   | 4.4   | 8.2   |
| 6       | 5.1   | 5.2   | 5.8   |

(a) For each subject, calculate the three difference scores $d_{12}$, $d_{13}$, and $d_{23}$, where $d_{jj'}$ represents the difference, $Y_{ij'} - Y_{ij}$. Find the variances of each set of difference scores.

(b) Calculate the variance-covariance matrix. Using those results, calculate the three variances of difference scores. The result should be the same as in part (a).

(c) Perform an ANOVA on the data and show that $MS_{SA} = (1/2) \times$ (average of the three variances calculated in the preceding two parts).

(d) Perform the $t$ test of the difference between the $A_1$ and $A_2$ means (i) using $MS_{SA}$ and (ii) using the variance of $d_{12}$. Find the $p$ value for each procedure. Which analysis do you think should be preferred? Why?

(e) Calculate the $t$ to test the null hypothesis that $(1/2)(\mu_2 + \mu_3) - \mu_1 = 0$.

**13.3**   Huynh and Feldt (1970) present the following variance–covariance matrix. Does it satisfy compound symmetry? Does it satisfy sphericity?

$$
\begin{array}{cccc}
 & A_1 & A_2 & A_3 \\
A_1 & 1.0 & .5 & 1.5 \\
A_2 & & 3.0 & 2.5 \\
A_3 & & & 5.0
\end{array}
$$

**13.4**   Consider the following data set:

|        | $A_1$ | $A_2$ | $A_3$ | $A_4$ |
|--------|-------|-------|-------|-------|
| $S_1$  | 1.8   | 2.2   | 3.2   | 2.4   |
| $S_2$  | 2.4   | 1.5   | 1.9   | 2.7   |
| $S_3$  | 1.9   | 1.7   | 2.5   | 3.5   |
| $S_4$  | 2.7   | 2.6   | 2.4   | 3.1   |
| $S_5$  | 4.7   | 4.8   | 4.4   | 4.8   |
| $S_6$  | 3.6   | 3.1   | 4.2   | 5.4   |
| $S_7$  | 4.4   | 4.2   | 4.1   | 4.9   |
| $S_8$  | 5.8   | 6.1   | 6.4   | 6.6   |

(a) Carry out the ANOVA on these data and find the lower and upper bounds on the $p$ value, assuming sphericity and nonsphericity, respectively. Assuming $\alpha = .05$, can you reach a conclusion with respect to the $A$ source of variance?

(b) Assume that we planned all pairwise comparisons for the preceding data set. Find the .95 confidence interval for $\overline{Y}._4 - \overline{Y}._2$, controlling for the *FWE*.

**13.5**   Assume that the levels of $A$ in Exercise 13.4 are equally spaced. Perform a trend analysis, testing each of the three polynomial components.

**13.6**   An educational psychologist wishes to develop a measure of articulation that can then be used in examining the relation between reading comprehension and the ability to articulate words. She has 40 third graders read aloud each of 20 words and measures the time required for the response. A Subjects × Words ANOVA yields the following results:

| SV            | df  | MS          | F       |
|---------------|-----|-------------|---------|
| Subjects (S)  | 39  | 208,305.017 | 244.158 |
| Words (W)     | 19  | 739.141     | .866    |
| S × W         | 741 | 853.157     |         |

One measure of the reliability of a measuring instrument is $r_{11}$, the proportion of the total variance attributable to differences among the subjects.

(a) Because the variability due to words is clearly negligible, obtain an error mean square by pooling the $W$ and $S \times W$ mean squares.

(b) Estimate $\sigma_S^2$ and $\sigma_e^2$.

(c) Using the results from parts (a) and (b), calculate $r_{11}$.

**13.7** Four subjects each were tested on three successive days. Unfortunately, the record for subject 1 on Day 2 was accidentally deleted from the computer disk. The remaining scores are presented below.

|        | $D_1$ | $D_2$ | $D_3$ |
|--------|-------|-------|-------|
| $S_1$  | 19    | —     | 42    |
| $S_2$  | 24    | 27    | 45    |
| $S_3$  | 21    | 30    | 47    |
| $S_4$  | 16    | 21    | 39    |

(a) Estimate the missing score.
(b) Suppose both $Y_{12}$ and $Y_{43}$ were missing. Use the iterative estimation procedure described in this chapter to estimate the missing scores.

**13.8** Ten randomly sampled clerical workers ($W$) are observed on each of five randomly sampled occasions ($O$) with each of four word processing programs ($P$). The programs have been selected for comparison purposes to decide which ones to buy for the entire work force. A score is obtained for each worker with each processor on each occasion. An ANOVA is then carried out. The results are:

| SV                     | df  | MS   | EMS |
|------------------------|-----|------|-----|
| $W$                    | 9   | 2580 |     |
| $P$                    | 3   | 2610 |     |
| $O$                    | 4   | 690  |     |
| $W \times P$           | 27  | 330  |     |
| $W \times O$           | 36  | 370  |     |
| $P \times O$           | 12  | 640  |     |
| $W \times P \times O$  | 108 | 320  |     |

(a) Write out the *EMS* for the above table, first specifying which factors have random effects and which have fixed effects.
(b) Calculate a quasi-$F$ test of the $P$ source. Let $\alpha = .05$.
(c) Perform an alternative to the quasi-$F$ test of $P$. What assumption is implied in doing this test?

**13.9** In research on personality, there has been much discussion of the relative importance of traits and situations. The basic research design involves $n$ subjects, and $t$ tasks representing a random sample of situations. Measures are obtained for each subject ($\eta_i$) on each task ($\alpha_j$) on each of $b$ randomly sampled occasions ($\beta_k$).
(a) Assuming the completely additive model, $Y_{ijk} = \mu + \eta_i + \alpha_j + \beta_k + \varepsilon_{ijk}$, present expressions for the *SV*, *df*, and *EMS*.
(b) Present expressions for estimates of the variance components for subjects, tasks, and occasions.
(c) Assume we have evidence from previous studies that subjects and tasks interact. State the revised model, the revised ANOVA table (*SV*, *df*, and *EMS*), and revised estimates of the variance components.

**13.10** Each of five subjects is tested at four equally spaced points in time on a visual detection task. The numbers of errors for each test are:

|          | Time |   |   |   |
|----------|------|---|---|---|
| Subject  | 1    | 2 | 3 | 4 |
| 1        | 9    | 6 | 7 | 5 |
| 2        | 11   | 8 | 6 | 6 |
| 3        | 6    | 8 | 7 | 5 |
| 4        | 13   | 10| 10| 9 |
| 5        | 12   | 8 | 9 | 6 |

(a) Time 1 provides a baseline. The experimenter wishes to test whether the mean at Time 1 differs significantly from the combined mean for the other three times. (i) State the null hypothesis and carry out the test with $\alpha = .05$. Calculate a confidence interval for the contrast.

(b) Test whether there is a significant linear trend.

(c) Test whether the means depart significantly from a straight line.

**13.11** In the following data set, $B$ represents 3 statements that are rated before ($A_1$) and after ($A_2$) reading a persuasive communication.

|       | $A_1$ |       |       | $A_2$ |       |       |
|-------|-------|-------|-------|-------|-------|-------|
|       | $B_1$ | $B_2$ | $B_3$ | $B_1$ | $B_2$ | $B_3$ |
| $S_1$ | 2     | 3     | 4     | 8     | 9     | 8     |
| $S_2$ | 3     | 3     | 4     | 6     | 7     | 9     |
| $S_3$ | 7     | 4     | 6     | 4     | 9     | 9     |
| $S_4$ | 2     | 2     | 4     | 7     | 9     | 8     |
| $S_5$ | 1     | 2     | 2     | 5     | 4     | 5     |

(a) Assume $B$ is fixed and do an $S \times A \times B$ ANOVA.

(b) Find the mean at $A_1$ and at $A_2$ for each subject. Now do an ANOVA for this $S \times A$ design.

(c) Now assume $B$ is a random-effects variable (as seems more reasonable). Present the EMS.

(d) Test the $A$ source of variance under the model of part (c).

(e) What is the problem with the (commonly performed) ANOVA of part (b) when $B$ has random effects?

**13.12** Following are response times (in milliseconds) obtained under four different conditions for eight subjects:

| Subject | $A_1$ | $A_2$ | $A_3$ | $A_4$ |
|---|---|---|---|---|
| 1 | 2036 | 2220 | 2211 | 2316 |
| 2 | 2034 | 2042 | 2094 | 2077 |
| 3 | 2198 | 2612 | 2272 | 2348 |
| 4 | 2593 | 2629 | 2652 | 2647 |
| 5 | 2347 | 2408 | 2416 | 2479 |
| 6 | 2308 | 2352 | 2463 | 2358 |
| 7 | 2454 | 2501 | 2475 | 2461 |
| 8 | 2462 | 2394 | 2491 | 2659 |

Carry out (a) the ANOVA, (b) Friedman's $\chi^2$ test, and (c) the rank transform test on these scores.

**13.13** (a) For the data of the preceding exercise, use the WSR procedure to test whether the $A_1$ and $A_2$ conditions are significantly different. Assume a two-tailed alternative hypothesis and $\alpha = .05$.

(b) Continuing with the data set of Exercise 13.13, use the WSR procedure to test whether there is a significant linear trend.

**13.14** Twenty people underwent a 1-week program aimed to help them quit cigarette smoking. The researchers running the program checked on the progress of the participants after 3, 6, and 9 months. The results follow, with a 1 signifying that the individual has smoked at least once during the preceding 3-month period and a 0 indicating that the individual has not smoked during that period.

|  | Subjects | | | | | | | | | | | | | | | | | | | |
|---|---|---|---|---|---|---|---|---|---|---|---|---|---|---|---|---|---|---|---|---|
| Period | 1 | 2 | 3 | 4 | 5 | 6 | 7 | 8 | 9 | 10 | 11 | 12 | 13 | 14 | 15 | 16 | 17 | 18 | 19 | 20 |
| 1 | 1 | 0 | 0 | 0 | 1 | 0 | 0 | 0 | 0 | 0 | 0 | 0 | 0 | 1 | 1 | 0 | 0 | 1 | 1 | 1 | 0 |
| 2 | 1 | 1 | 1 | 1 | 1 | 0 | 1 | 0 | 0 | 1 | 1 | 0 | 1 | 0 | 0 | 1 | 0 | 0 | 1 | 1 |
| 3 | 1 | 1 | 1 | 1 | 1 | 0 | 0 | 1 | 1 | 1 | 1 | 1 | 0 | 1 | 0 | 1 | 1 | 1 | 1 | 0 |

The investigators want to know if there has been a significant change in the percentage of smokers over the three periods in the follow-up study. Perform an analysis to answer this question and state your conclusion.

**13.15** The file Daylight in the *Seasons* folder of the *CD* contains hours/weekday of exposure to daylight for the oldest group of subjects in the Seasons study. This was of interest to the researchers because it is believed that exposure to daylight affects mood.

(a) Perform an ANOVA on the female (i.e., sex = 1) DIRWDC (Direct exposure to daylight during weekdays) scores; 1 = winter, 2 = spring, 3 = summer, and 4 = fall.

(b) Calculate the partial $\omega^2$ for the effects of Seasons.

(c) Perform a trend analysis.

**13.16** Transform the data in Exercise 13.15 by Log(DIRWDC + 1) and redo parts (a)–(c). Comment on any differences in results.

(a) Using any graphs or descriptive statistics you find useful, comment on any changes in the distributions of scores due to the transformation.

---

## APPENDIX 13.1
---

## Relative Efficiency of a Repeated-Measures Design

We assume that over many replications of the experiment, the average total sum of squares will be the same for the completely randomized (CR) and repeated-measures (RM) designs. That is,

$$E(SS_{tot,CR}) = E(SS_{tot,RM})$$

Replacing the total sums of squares by their component sums of squares, we have

$$(a-1)E(MS_{A,CR}) + a(n-1)E(MS_{S/A}) = (a-1)\,E(MS_{A,RM}) + (n-1)E(MS_S)$$
$$+(a-1)(n-1)E(MS_{SA})$$

We next substitute variance components, ignoring the treatment variance because it should be the same in both designs. Therefore,

$$(a-1)E(MS_{A,CR}) + a(n-1)E(MS_{S/A}) = (an-1)\sigma^2_{e,CR}.$$

Similarly, combining the $A$ and $S \times A$ terms on the right, we have

$$(an-1)\sigma^2_{e,CR} = n(a-1)\sigma^2_{e,RM} + (n-1)E(MS_S)$$

Then, our estimate of the error variance for the completely randomized population can be derived from the mean squares calculated from the repeated-measures design by substitution:

$$estMS_{S/A} = [n(a-1)MS_{SA} + (n-1)MS_S]/(an-1)$$

Dividing this estimate by the $MS_{SA}$ calculated from our data yields Equation 13.5, the efficiency of the repeated-measures design relative to the completely randomized design.

---

## Appendix 13.2
---

## Deriving the min $F'$ Statistic

When $MS_{SAB}$ cannot be calculated, we can conceive of the quasi-$F$ as

$$\min F' = \frac{MS_A}{MS_{SA} + MS_{AB}}$$

Multiplying numerator and denominator by $MS_A/(MS_{SA} \cdot MS_{AB})$, we find that the numerator of min $F'$ becomes

$$\left(\frac{MS_A}{MS_{SA}}\right) \times \left(\frac{MS_A}{MS_{AB}}\right) = F_1 \times F_2$$

The denominator is

$$MS_{SA}\left(\frac{MS_A}{MS_{SA} \cdot MS_{AB}}\right) + MS_{AB}\left(\frac{MS_A}{MS_{SA} \cdot MS_{AB}}\right) = F_2 + F_1$$

Therefore, min $F' = F_1 F_2/(F_2 + F_1)$. The error degrees of freedom for min $F'$ are

$$df_{\text{error}} = \frac{(MS_{SA} + MS_{AB})^2}{MS_{AB}^2/df_{AB} + MS_{SA}^2/df_{SA}}$$

Multiplying the numerator by $MS_A^2/(MS_{SA} \cdot MS_{AB})^2$, we have

$$\left[MS_{SA}\left(\frac{MS_A}{MS_{SA} \cdot MS_{AB}}\right) + MS_{AB}\left(\frac{MS_A}{MS_{SA} \cdot MS_{AB}}\right)\right]^2 = (F_2 + F_1)^2$$

and also multiplying the denominator by the same quantity, we have

$$\left(\frac{MS_{AB}^2}{df_{AB}}\right)\left(\frac{MS_A^2}{MS_{SA}^2 \cdot MS_{AB}^2}\right) + \left(\frac{MS_{SA}^2}{df_{SA}}\right)\left(\frac{MS_A^2}{MS_{SA}^2 \cdot MS_{AB}^2}\right) = F_1^2/df_{AB} + F_2^2/df_{SA}$$

Therefore,

$$df_{\text{error}} = (F_1 + F_2)^2/\left(F_1^2/df_{AB} + F_2^2/df_{SA}\right).$$

# Chapter 14

## Mixed Designs: Between-Subjects and Within-Subjects Factors

### 14.1 INTRODUCTION

In Chapter 13, we analyzed the effects of seasons on Beck depression scores for a group of male patients. We might have included a group of female patients as well. This would have allowed us to test whether there was a significant difference between the average (over seasons) depression scores as a function of gender. We could also have tested the interaction of gender and seasons; in particular, we might have tested whether there were differences in the slopes and shapes of the two functions of seasons. Gender is a between-subjects factor, and seasons is a within-subjects factor in this example. Designs like this that involve both between-subjects and within-subjects factors will be referred to as **mixed designs** (sometimes called **split-plot designs**). Such designs are very common. They are a compromise between a desire to use within-subjects factors to reduce error variance (and thus increase power and the precision of estimation) and the reality that certain variables simply cannot be treated as within-subjects factors. Examples of variables that are inherently between-subjects factors are those whose levels are selected rather than manipulated (e.g., individual differences variables, such as gender, age, or clinical diagnostic category) and manipulated variables that entail carry-over effects (e.g., training method). In this chapter, we consider the structural models and analyses for various mixed designs.

### 14.2 ONE BETWEEN-SUBJECTS AND ONE WITHIN-SUBJECTS FACTOR

Table 14.1 presents a data set for a hypothetical experiment in which one group was taught probability by a standard instructional method ($A_1$), a second group was given additional problems ($A_2$), and a third group received additional problems from a computer that provided immediate feedback ($A_3$). All three groups were tested at the end of the instructional period, and then once every 2 weeks until four different tests had been given. Assume that the tests

**TABLE 14.1**  DATA FOR A DESIGN WITH ONE BETWEEN-SUBJECTS (A) AND ONE
WITHIN-SUBJECTS (B) VARIABLE

| Method of Instruction | | $B_1$ | $B_2$ | $B_3$ | $B_4$ | $\overline{Y}_{ij.}$ |
|---|---|---|---|---|---|---|
| | | \multicolumn{4}{c}{Time of Test} | |
| $A_1$ | $S_{11}$ | 82 | 48 | 41 | 53 | 56 |
| | $S_{21}$ | 72 | 70 | 51 | 45 | 62 |
| | $S_{31}$ | 43 | 35 | 30 | 12 | 30 |
| | $S_{41}$ | 77 | 41 | 61 | 31 | 50 |
| | $S_{51}$ | 43 | 43 | 21 | 29 | 34 |
| | $S_{61}$ | 67 | 39 | 30 | 40 | 44 |
| | $\overline{Y}_{.1k}$ | 64 | 46 | 39 | 35 | $\overline{Y}_{.1.} = 46$ |
| $A_2$ | $S_{12}$ | 71 | 53 | 50 | 62 | 59 |
| | $S_{22}$ | 89 | 67 | 76 | 68 | 75 |
| | $S_{32}$ | 82 | 84 | 83 | 71 | 80 |
| | $S_{42}$ | 56 | 56 | 55 | 45 | 53 |
| | $S_{52}$ | 64 | 44 | 44 | 52 | 51 |
| | $S_{62}$ | 76 | 74 | 64 | 74 | 72 |
| | $\overline{Y}_{.2k}$ | 73 | 63 | 62 | 62 | $\overline{Y}_{.2.} = 65$ |
| $A_3$ | $S_{13}$ | 84 | 80 | 75 | 77 | 79 |
| | $S_{23}$ | 84 | 72 | 63 | 81 | 75 |
| | $S_{33}$ | 76 | 54 | 57 | 61 | 62 |
| | $S_{43}$ | 84 | 66 | 61 | 77 | 72 |
| | $S_{53}$ | 67 | 69 | 55 | 69 | 65 |
| | $S_{63}$ | 61 | 67 | 55 | 61 | 61 |
| | $\overline{Y}_{.3k}$ | 76 | 68 | 61 | 71 | $\overline{Y}_{.3.} = 69$ |
| | $\overline{Y}_{..k}$ | 71 | 59 | 54 | 56 | $\overline{Y}_{...} = 60$ |

were equated for difficulty so that any differences could be attributed to the passage of time. This design permits us to compare the instructional methods ($A$) and also to see the time course ($B$) of performance following the end of instruction for each method. Notice that the design is a mixture of the between-subjects design of Chapter 8 and the within-subject design of Chapter 13. If we average the four test scores for each subject, we have a between-subjects design and can conduct the ANOVA exactly as in Chapter 8. If, on the other hand, we retain the four test scores but ignore the instructional factor, we have an $S \times B$ design in which 18 subjects have scores at the four levels of $B$. In designs such as the one in Table 14.1, $n$ subjects are tested at $A_1$, $n$ other subjects are tested at $A_2$, and so on. All $an$ subjects are tested at each of the $b$ levels of the independent variable $B$. Therefore, $abn - 1$ df must be accounted for in the analysis of variance (ANOVA). With respect to notation, we refer to $Y_{ijk}$, where $i$ indexes the subject ($i = 1, 2, \ldots, n$), $j$ indexes the level of the between-subjects variable ($j = 1, 2, \ldots, a$), and $k$ indexes the level of the within-subjects variable ($k = 1, 2, \ldots b$). In the current example, $n = 6$, $a = 3$, and $b = 4$.

We begin our discussion of mixed designs by analyzing the data of Table 14.1. First, we examine how the total sum of squares is partitioned into sources of variance that provide the components of $F$ tests. We do this by analogy to the analyses of the between-subjects design of Chapter 8 and the within-subjects designs of Chapter 13. Following this, we present a more formal structural model to justify the partitioning and expected mean squares to justify the error terms used in the $F$ tests.

## 14.2.1 Partitioning the Sums of Squares and Degrees of Freedom

Mixed designs might at first glance seem more complicated than pure between-subjects or repeated-measures designs. However, we can obtain the appropriate model for any mixed design—and hence the entire ANOVA table for the design—using what we already know about the pure designs. A simple way to find the appropriate sources of variance for any mixed design involves two steps: (1) first ignore the between-subjects factors and obtain the $SV$ terms for the resulting repeated-measures design, then (2) partition the $SV$ terms that contain the "subjects" variable, $S$, to reflect the effects of the between-subjects factors. If we ignore the between-subjects variable, $A$, in Table 14.1, we have an $S \times B$ repeated-measures design with $an$ ($3 \times 6$) subjects and $b$ (4) levels of the within-subjects factor, $B$. For this simplified design, we know from Chapter 13 that the appropriate sources of variance and degrees of freedom are those presented in panel (a) of Table 14.2. Note that the total

**TABLE 14.2**   SOURCES OF VARIANCE, DEGREES OF FREEDOM, AND SUMS OF SQUARES FOR THE MIXED DESIGN OF TABLE 14.1

| (a) Appropriate $SV$ and $df$ If Factor $A$ Is Ignored | | |
|---|---|---|
| $SV$ | $df$ | $SS$ |
| Total | $abn - 1 = 71$ | $\sum_k \sum_j \sum_i (Y_{ijk} - \overline{Y}...)^2 = 20{,}956$ |
| Between-Subjects ($S$) | $an - 1 = 17$ | $b \sum_j \sum_i (\overline{Y}_{ij}. - \overline{Y}...)^2 = 14{,}448$ |
| Within-Subjects ($W\,Ss$) | $an(b - 1) = 54$ | $\sum_k \sum_j \sum_i (Y_{ijk} - \overline{Y}_{ij}.)^2 = 6{,}508$ |
| $B$ | $b - 1 = 3$ | $an \sum_k (\overline{Y}..k - \overline{Y}...)^2 = 3{,}132$ |
| $SB$ | $(an - 1)(b - 1) = 51$ | $SS_{tot} - SS_S - SS_B = 3{,}376$ |

| (b) Complete Partitioning of the $SS$ and $df$ | | |
|---|---|---|
| $SV$ | $df$ | $SS$ |
| Total | $abn - 1 = 71$ | $\sum_k \sum_j \sum_i (Y_{ijk} - \overline{Y}...)^2 = 20{,}956$ |
| Between-Subjects ($S$) | $an - 1 = 17$ | $b \sum_j \sum_i (\overline{Y}_{ij}. - \overline{Y}...)^2 = 14{,}448$ |
| $A$ | $a - 1 = 2$ | $bn \sum_j (\overline{Y}_{.j}. - \overline{Y}...)^2 = 7{,}248$ |
| $S/A$ | $a(n - 1) = 15$ | $SS_S - SS_A = 7{,}200$ |
| Within-Subjects ($W\,Ss$) | $an(b - 1) = 54$ | $SS_{tot} - SS_S = 6{,}508$ |
| $B$ | $b - 1 = 3$ | $an \sum_k (\overline{Y}..k - \overline{Y}...)^2 = 3{,}132$ |
| $SB$ | $(an - 1)(b - 1) = 51$ | $SS_{W\,Ss} - SS_B = 3{,}376$ |
| $AB$ | $(a - 1)(b - 1) = 6$ | $n \sum_j \sum_k (\overline{Y}_{.jk} - \overline{Y}...)^2 - SS_A - SS_B$ $= 1{,}056$ |
| $SB/A$ | $a(n - 1)(b - 1) = 45$ | $SS_{W\,Ss} - SS_B - SS_{AB} = 2{,}320$ |

sum of squares is completely accounted for by variability between subjects ($SS_S$) and within subjects ($SS_{WSs}$); that is,

$$SS_{tot} = SS_S + SS_{WSs}$$

In a similar manner, the total degrees of freedom can be divided into between-subject and within-subject components:

$$df_{tot} = df_S + df_{WSs}$$
$$abn - 1 = (an - 1) + an(b - 1)$$

The within-subjects degrees of freedom reflect the fact that the variance of each subject's $b$ scores is distributed on $b - 1$ $df$, and this variability is then summed over the $an$ subjects. The within-subject variability ($SS_{WSs}$) can be further partitioned into a term due to $B$ and one due to the interaction of $S$ and $B$:

$$SS_{WSs} = SS_B + SS_{SB}$$

The $df_{WSs}$ is similarly partitioned:

$$df_{WSs} = df_B + df_{SB}$$
$$an(b - 1) = (b - 1) + (an - 1)(b - 1)$$

The model and analysis suggested by this partitioning are incomplete because panel (a) of Table 14.2 does not include an $A$ source of variance. The $SS_A$ and $df_A$ are components of the between-subjects sum of squares ($SS_S$) and degrees of freedom ($df_S$). $SS_S$ represents the variability of the $an$ subject means, the $\overline{Y}_{ij.}$. Some of this variability may be due to effects of $A$, and some is due to individual differences among subjects within each level of $A$. If we analyze the $an$ subject means, we have a one-factor between-subjects design with $n$ scores at each level of $A$. Just as we partitioned the total variability in the one-factor design of Chapter 8, we can partition the between-subject variability here:

$$SS_S = SS_A + SS_{S/A}$$

The corresponding degrees of freedom are

$$df_S = df_A + df_{S/A}$$
$$an - 1 = (a - 1) + a(n - 1)$$

The $S \times B$ variability can also be further partitioned by crossing $A$ and $S/A$ with $B$; this yields

$$SS_{SB} = SS_{AB} + SS_{SB/A}$$

The degrees of freedom can be partitioned in a similar way:

$$df_{SB} = df_{AB} + df_{SB/A}$$
$$(an - 1)(b - 1) = (a - 1)(b - 1) + a(n - 1)(b - 1)$$

These partitionings of the $S$ and $SB$ terms complete the breakdown of $SS_{tot}$ into its components. The final result is presented in panel (b) of Table 14.2.

Scanning the sources of variance in panel (b) you may wonder why there is no $S \times A$ term present. The answer lies in the distinction between **crossing** and **nesting**. When data are obtained for all combinations of levels of one factor with all levels of another, we say that the two factors cross. For example, in the current design, $A$ and $B$ cross, as do $S$ and $B$; however, $A$ and $S$ do not cross. Here, $A$ is a between-subjects factor; that is, each subject provides data at a single level of $A$. We describe this situation by saying that subjects are "nested within levels of $A$," and we indicate nesting by using a "/" in our $SV$ terms, as in $S/A$. It is not possible for two factors to interact with one another unless they cross. There is no possibility of an interaction between $S$ and $A$ because the question of whether the difference between any two subjects is greater at $A_1$ than at $A_2$ is meaningless unless the subjects provide data both at $A_1$ and at $A_2$.

How do we interpret the nested terms? It is as though the sums of squares were obtained separately at each level of $A$ and then pooled. Thus, $SS_{S/A}$ could be obtained by computing, for each level of $A$, the variability of the $n$ subject means about the mean for that level of $A$, and then adding up the terms for the $a$ levels of $A$. The $n - 1$ $df$ obtained from each of the $a$ levels of $A$ are added to make up the $a(n - 1)$ $df$ associated with $S/A$. Similarly, we could obtain $SS_{SB/A}$ by computing $SS_{SB}$ separately at each level of $A$ [accounting for $(n-1)(b-1)$ $df$ at each level of $A$] and then summing the resulting $a$ terms [thus accounting for the $a(n-1)(b-1)$ $df$ associated with $SB/A$].

The sums of squares formulas and numerical results are presented in Table 14.2. Although these are not too laborious to obtain with a calculator, with more data, and particularly with more variables, we advise the use of a computer program. In addition to saving labor, packages such as SAS, SPSS, BMDP, and SYSTAT are capable of providing much additional information, such as summary statistics, plots of scores and residuals, tests of contrasts, and adjustments for nonsphericity.

The mean squares in Table 14.3 are, as always, ratios of sums of squares to degrees of freedom. The basis for the choice of error terms also follows our standard rule: The error term has the same expectation as the numerator mean square, assuming $H_0$ is true. The validity of the entries in the expected mean squares (EMS) column rests on the validity of certain underlying assumptions that we will present next.

### 14.2.2 The Structural Model

As usual, the $F$ tests (Table 14.3) are based on expected mean squares whose derivation requires a structural model. Table 14.4 defines the parameters that are components

**TABLE 14.3**   ANOVA OF THE DATA IN TABLE 14.1

| SV | df | SS | MS | Error term | F | EMS |
|----|----|----|----|------------|---|-----|
| Total | 71 | 20,956 | | | | |
| Between-Subjects | 17 | 14,448 | | | | |
| $A$ | 2 | 7,248 | 3,624.000 | $S/A$ | 7.55[a] | $\sigma_e^2 + b\sigma_{S/A}^2 + bn\theta_A^2$ |
| $S/A$ | 15 | 7,200 | 480.000 | | | $\sigma_e^2 + b\sigma_{S/A}^2$ |
| Within-Subjects | 54 | 6,508 | | | | |
| $B$ | 3 | 3,132 | 1,044.000 | $SB/A$ | 20.25[a] | $\sigma_e^2 + \sigma_{SB/A}^2 + an\theta_B^2$ |
| $AB$ | 6 | 1,056 | 176.000 | $SB/A$ | 3.41[a] | $\sigma_e^2 + \sigma_{SB/A}^2 + n\theta_{AB}^2$ |
| $SB/A$ | 45 | 2,320 | 51.556 | | | $\sigma_e^2 + \sigma_{SB/A}^2$ |

[a] $p < .01$.

**TABLE 14.4**  PARAMETERS OF THE MODEL FOR THE MIXED DESIGN OF TABLE 14.1

---

### Population Means[a]

$$\mu_{ijk} = E(Y_{ijk}), \quad \mu_{ij} = \sum_k \frac{\mu_{ijk}}{b}, \quad \mu_{jk} = E(\mu_{ijk}), \quad \mu_j = \sum_k \frac{\mu_{jk}}{b}, \quad \mu_k = \sum_j \frac{\mu_{jk}}{a},$$

$$\mu = \sum_j \frac{\mu_j}{a} = \sum_k \frac{\mu_k}{b}$$

---

### Population Effects and Constraints

$$\varepsilon_{ijk} = Y_{ijk} - \mu_{ijk}, \quad E(\varepsilon_{ijk}) = 0, \quad \eta_{i/j} = \mu_{ij} - \mu_j, \quad E(\eta_{i/j}) = 0,$$

$$\alpha_j = \mu_j - \mu, \quad \sum_j \alpha_j = 0, \quad \beta_k = \mu_k - \mu, \quad \sum_k \beta_k = 0,$$

$$(\alpha\beta)_{jk} = \mu_{jk} - \mu_j - \mu_k + \mu, \quad \sum_j (\alpha\beta)_{jk} = \sum_k (\alpha\beta)_{jk} = 0,$$

$$(\eta\beta)_{ik/j} = \mu_{ijk} - \mu_{ij} - \mu_{jk} + \mu_j, \quad E[(\eta\beta)_{ik/j}] = \sum_k [(\eta\beta)_{ik/j}] = 0$$

---

### Population Variances

$$E(\varepsilon_{ijk}^2) = \sigma_e^2, \quad E(\eta_{i/j}^2) = \sigma_{S/A}^2, \quad E[(\eta\beta)_{ik/j}^2] = \sigma_{SB/A}^2,$$

$$\sum_j \frac{\alpha_j^2}{a-1} = \theta_A^2, \quad \sum_k \frac{\beta_k^2}{b-1} = \theta_B^2, \quad \text{and} \quad \sum_j \sum_k \frac{(\alpha\beta)_{jk}^2}{(a-1)(b-1)} = \theta_{AB}^2$$

---

[a] $E$ stands for the expectation over the population of subjects at $A_j$.

of that model. The following assumptions should be kept in mind when considering that table:

1. $Y_{ijk}$, the observed score for the $i$th subject at the $j$th level of $A$, is made up of a true score component, $\mu_{ijk}$, and a random error component, $\varepsilon_{ijk}$. The $\varepsilon_{ijk}$ are independently and normally distributed with mean zero and variance $\sigma_e^2$.
2. $A$ and $B$ are fixed-effect variables.
3. The $n$ subjects in each of the $a$ groups are randomly sampled from a treatment population consisting of an infinite number of subjects,

Assumptions 2 and 3 justify the definitions and constraints in Table 14.4. For example, we define $\mu_{ij}$ as the arithmetic mean of $b$ values of $\mu_{ijk}$ because the average is taken over the levels of $B$, a fixed-effects variable. In contrast, we define $\mu_j$ as the expectation of the $\mu_{ij}$. This is because $S$ is a random-effects variable; therefore, to obtain the mean of the population of scores at $A_j$, we must average (i.e., take the expectation) over an infinite population of subjects. To consider one other example of the application of Assumptions 2 and 3, note that we have the constraint that $\sum \beta_k = 0$, whereas $E(\eta_{i/j}) = 0$; in one case, fixed effects (the $\beta_k$) are summed and, in the other, we take the expectation of random effects (the $\eta_{i/j}$). The reason for the differences in definitions and constraints as a function of the nature of the effects was discussed in Chapter 13.

Given the definitions and constraints in Table 14.4, we can specify the structural model,

$$Y_{ijk} = \mu + \alpha_j + \eta_{i/j} + \beta_k + (\alpha\beta)_{jk} + (\eta\beta)_{ik/j} + \varepsilon_{ijk} \tag{14.1}$$

The effects in this equation, with the exception of the error component, $\varepsilon_{ijk}$, correspond to sources of variance in Table 14.3. In particular, the nested effects, $\eta_{i/j}$ and $(\eta\beta)_{ik/j}$, correspond to the sources $S/A$ and $SB/A$. There is no source of variance corresponding directly to $\varepsilon_{ijk}$ because there is only one score for each combination of $S$, $A$, and $B$. We saw a similar situation in the repeated-measures designs of Chapter 13.

Equation 14.1, together with the definitions of variances and constraints in Table 14.4, allows us to derive expected mean squares for the design. These were presented in Table 14.3. These expectations can be generated by a set of rules that are general enough to encompass more complex designs as well. Those rules will be presented in Section 14.3 but, before that, again consider the expected mean squares in Table 14.3. The first thing to note is that there are two error terms; the EMS indicate that $MS_{S/A}$ is the appropriate error term against which to test whether the $A$ effect is significant and that $MS_{SB/A}$ is the appropriate error term for $B$ and $AB$. An important difference between the expectations of these two error terms is that $E(MS_{S/A})$ involves the variance of the $\eta_{i/j}$ ($\sigma_{S/A}^2$), whereas $E(MS_{SB/A})$ involves the variance of the $(\eta\beta)_{ik/j}$ ($\sigma_{SB/A}^2$); $\sigma_{S/A}^2$ will typically be greater than $\sigma_{SB/A}^2$. Therefore, within-subjects factors, usually are tested against error terms that are smaller than the error terms used with between-subjects factors, and tests of $B$ and $AB$ effects usually have greater power than test of $A$ effects.

When tests of within-subjects factors are performed, possible violations of the sphericity assumption are a consideration. In Chapter 13, we discussed how violations of sphericity may result in positively biased $F$ tests of within-subjects factors. This is also true for mixed designs. Conservative $F$ tests parallel to those discussed in Chapter 13 can be performed for the current design and are routinely reported by most statistical software. The statistics $MS_B$ and $MS_{AB}$ are distributed on $(b-1)\varepsilon$ and $(a-1)(b-1)\varepsilon$ $df$, respectively, and $MS_{SB/A}$, the error term for both $B$ and $AB$, is distributed on $a(n-1)(b-1)\varepsilon$ $df$. The values that $\varepsilon$ can take on vary between 1 (when there is no violation of the sphericity assumption) and $1/(b-1)$ (when there is maximum violation). The conservative test of the $B$ effect would therefore use 1 and $a(n-1)$ $df$ and that for the $AB$ effect would use $a-1$ and $a(n-1)$ $df$. For the data set of Table 14.1, the degrees of freedom for the conservative $F$ test of $B$ would be 1 and 15 ($3 \times 5$) $df$, and the degrees of freedom for the $AB$ test would be 2 and 15. The conservative test of the $B$ effect would still be significant at the .01 level. However, the conservative test of the $AB$ interaction is not significant at the .05 level; $p = .06$. In this case, the conservative test is very conservative indeed. Using SPSS's repeated-measures program, the Greenhouse-Geisser estimate of $\varepsilon$ ($\hat{\varepsilon}$) was .626, and the $F$ test of the $AB$ interaction, with degrees of freedom adjusted by this value, was significant; $p = .023$. The Huynh-Feldt estimate ($\tilde{\varepsilon}$) was .807; $p = .013$.

## 14.3 RULES FOR GENERATING EXPECTED MEAN SQUARES

There are six components of variance that might potentially contribute to any of the expected mean squares. These are the variances due to subjects ($\sigma_S^2$), the interaction of subjects and $B$ ($\sigma_{SB/A}^2$), and error variance ($\sigma_e^2$), as well as components corresponding to the fixed effects

**TABLE 14.5**  RULES OF THUMB FOR OBTAINING EXPECTED MEAN SQUARES (EMS)

**Rule 1.**  Decide for each independent variable (including subjects) whether it is fixed or random. Assign a letter to designate each variable. Assign another letter to be used as a coefficient that represents the number of levels of each variable. In the example of Table 9.3, the variables are designated $A$, $B$, and $S$; the coefficients are $a$, $b$, and $n$; $A$ and $B$ are fixed-effect variables and $S$ is random.

**Rule 2.**  List $\sigma_e^2$ as part of each EMS

**Rule 3.**  For each EMS, list the null hypothesis component—that is, the component corresponding directly to the SV under consideration. Thus, we add $nb\theta_A^2$ to the EMS for the $A$ line and $b\sigma_{S/A}^2$ to the EMS for the $S/A$ line. Note that a component consists of three parts:

  1. A coefficient representing the number of scores at each level of the effect (e.g.) $nb$ scores at each level of $A$, or $b$ scores for each subject).

  2. A $\sigma^2$ or $\theta^2$, depending on whether the effect is assumed to be random or fixed [$\sigma^2$ is the variance of the population of effects; for example, $\sigma_{S/A}^2 = E(\eta_{i/j}^2)$, $\theta_A^2 = \sum_j \alpha_j^2/(a-1)$].

  3. As subscripts, those letters that designate the effect under consideration.

**Rule 4.**  Now add to each EMS all components whose subscripts contain all the letters designating the $SV$ in question. Since the subscript $SB/A$ contains the letters $S$ and $A$, for example, add $\sigma_{SB/A}^2$ to the EMS for the $S/A$ line (this is later deleted according to Rule 6).

**Rule 5.**  Next, examine the components for each SV. If a slash appears in the subscript, define only the letters to the left of the slash as "essential." If there are several slashes (as in the next chapter), only the letters preceding the leftmost slash are essential. If there is no slash in the subscript, all letters are considered essential.

**Rule 6.**  Among the essential letters, ignore any that are necessary to designate the SV. If the source is $A$, in considering $n\theta_{AB}^2$, for example, ignore the $A$. If the source is $S/A$, in considering the $\sigma_{SB/A}^2$ component, $S$ and $B$ are essential subscripts and $S$ is to be ignored. If any of the remaining essential letters designate fixed variables, delete the entire component from the EMS.

---

in the structural equation, ($\theta_A^2$, $\theta_B^2$, and $\theta_{AB}^2$). Referring to Table 14.3, it is evident that only a few of these terms actually contribute to any expectation, and therefore play a role in the selection of the error term or in the estimation of effect sizes. Our designs are now becoming sufficiently complicated that rules for determining the components of each expected mean square will be useful. Table 14.5 presents such rules. Appendix 14.1 presents a justification for these **"rules of thumb"** by examining the example of $E(MS_A)$.

Consider how the rule of thumb might be used to find $E(MS_B)$. First list $\sigma_e^2$ because it contributes to every EMS. Then, add every additional component of variance that has subscripts containing $B$, multiplying each component by its appropriate coefficient. The result is

$$\sigma_e^2 + na\theta_B^2 + n\theta_{AB}^2 + \sigma_{S/AB}^2$$

Rules 5 and 6 dictate deletion of the $n\theta_{AB}^2$ component, because once $B$ is deleted from its subscripts ($A$ and $B$), we are left with $A$, a subscript that denotes a fixed effect variable. Note that the $\sigma_{S/AB}^2$ component is retained, because when $B$ is deleted from the "essential" subscripts of that component, we are left with $S$, a subscript that denotes a random-effect

**TABLE 14.6** EXPECTED MEAN SQUARES (EMS) WHEN A IS A FIXED-EFFECT VARIABLE AND B IS A RANDOM-EFFECTS VARIABLE

| SV | df | EMS |
|----|-----|-----|
| $A$ | $a - 1$ | $\sigma_e^2 + b\sigma_{S/A}^2 + n\sigma_{AB}^2 + \sigma_{SB/A}^2 + nb\theta_A^2$ |
| $S/A$ | $a(n - 1)$ | $\sigma_e^2 + b\sigma_{S/A}^2 + \sigma_{SB/A}^2$ |
| $B$ | $b - 1$ | $\sigma_e^2 + \sigma_{SB/A}^2 + na\sigma_B^2$ |
| $AB$ | $(a - 1)(b - 1)$ | $\sigma_e^2 + \sigma_{SB/A}^2 + n\sigma_{AB}^2$ |
| $SB/A$ | $a(n - 1)(b - 1)$ | $\sigma_e^2 + \sigma_{SB/A}^2$ |

variable. The final result is

$$E(MS_B) = \sigma_e^2 + \sigma_{S/AB}^2 + na\theta_B^2$$

The reader should apply the rules to the remaining sources of variance and compare the results with those in Table 14.3. The rules also apply to designs with more variables and with additional levels of nesting.

The rules for generating expected mean squares also enable us to construct quasi-$F$ ratios in situations in which no single source of variance provides an appropriate error term. For example, assume $a$ instructional groups of $n$ subjects each. Further assume that the students are tested once on a set of $b$ randomly selected items. The sources of variance, degrees of freedom, and expected mean squares are presented in Table 14.6. Verify that the expected mean squares follow the rules in Table 14.5. Note that the $S/A$ mean square, the usual error term against which to test $A$, is inappropriate under the assumption that $B$ is a random-effects variable. If $A$ is tested against $S/A$, a significant result could be attributed to either effects due to $A$ or $AB$. Assuming a model that includes an $AB$ term—that is, $\sigma_{AB}^2 \neq 0$—we must construct a quasi-$F$ test of the $A$ source or variance. From the developments in Chapter 13,

$$F' = \frac{MS_A + MS_{SB/A}}{MS_{S/A} + MS_{AB}} \tag{14.2}$$

The numerator degrees of freedom are

$$df_{\text{num}} = \frac{(MS_A + MS_{SB/A})^2}{MS_A^2/(a - 1) + MS_{SB/A}^2/a(n - 1)(b - 1)} \tag{14.3}$$

and the denominator degrees of freedom are

$$df_{\text{denom}} = \frac{(MS_{S/A} + MS_{AB})^2}{MS_{S/A}^2/a(n - 1) + MS_{AB}^2/(a - 1)(b - 1)} \tag{14.4}$$

## 14.4 MEASURES OF EFFECT SIZE

Calculations of effect size in the mixed design follow the approach taken in earlier chapters. For convenient reference, Table 14.7 summarizes formulas for the $A$, $B$, and $AB$ effects in the design exemplified by the data set of Table 14.1 and the ANOVA of Table 14.3.

**TABLE 14.7**  EFFECT SIZE MEASURES FOR A DESIGN WITH ONE BETWEEN-SUBJECTS (A) AND ONE WITHIN-SUBJECTS FACTOR

| | Effect | | |
|---|---|---|---|
| | *A* | *B* | *AB* |
| $\eta^2$ | $SS_A/(SS_A + SS_{S/A})$ | $SS_B/(SS_B + SS_{SB/A})$ | $SS_{AB}/(SS_{AB} + SS_{SB/A})$ |
| $\hat{f}$ | $\sqrt{\dfrac{SS_A - (a-1)MS_{S/A}}{abnMS_{S/A}}}$ | $\sqrt{\dfrac{SS_B - (b-1)MS_{SB/A}}{abnMS_{SB/A}}}$ | $\sqrt{\dfrac{SS_{AB} - (a-1)(b-1)MS_{SB/A}}{abnMS_{SB/A}}}$ |
| | $= \sqrt{(a-1)(F_A - 1)/abn}$ | $= \sqrt{(b-1)(F_B - 1)/abn}$ | $= \sqrt{(a-1)(b-1)(F_{AB} - 1)/abn}$ |
| $\omega^2$ | $\hat{f}_A^2/\left(1 + \hat{f}_A^2\right)$ | $\hat{f}_B^2/\left(1 + \hat{f}_B^2\right)$ | $\hat{f}_{AB}^2/\left(1 + \hat{f}_{AB}^2\right)$ |
| | $= \dfrac{(a-1)(F_A - 1)}{(a-1)(F_A - 1) + abn}$ | $= \dfrac{(b-1)(F_B - 1)}{(b-1)(F_B - 1) + abn}$ | $= \dfrac{(a-1)(b-1)(F_{AB} - 1)}{(a-1)(b-1)(F_{AB} - 1) + abn}$ |

## 14.4.1 Partial Eta-Squared ($\eta^2$) Statistics

The general form of the partial $\eta^2$ statistic is

$$\eta^2_{\text{effect}} = SS_{\text{effect}}/(SS_{\text{effect}} + SS_{\text{error}}) \tag{14.5}$$

For example, using the results in Table 14.3, the $\eta^2$ value for $A \times B$ (Instructional Method $\times$ Time of Test) is $1056/(1056 + 2320) = .313$.

## 14.4.2 Cohen's f

As noted in previous discussions of effect sizes, $\eta^2$ is a descriptive statistic whose numerator is inflated by error variance. Cohen's $f$—defined for several designs in Chapters 8, 12, and 13—is a population parameter and is defined as

$$f = \sigma_{\text{effect}}/\sigma_{\text{error}} \tag{14.6}$$

The population standard deviations can be estimated from the expected mean squares in Table 14.3, as in the previous chapters. For example,

$$\hat{\sigma}_A = \sqrt{\frac{(a-1)}{a} \times \frac{(MS_A - MS_{S/A})}{bn}}$$

and

$$\hat{\sigma}_{\text{error(A)}} = \sqrt{MS_{S/A}}.$$

Substituting the estimates, and simplifying, we have the formulas in Table 14.7, where $F_{\text{effect}} = MS_{\text{effect}}/MS_{\text{error}}$. For example, for the interaction effect in Table 14.3, we have $F_{AB} = MS_{AB}/MS_{S/AB}$ and $\hat{f}_{AB} = \sqrt{(6)(2.414)/72} = .45$, a value that would be a large effect according to Cohen's (1988) guidelines.

### 14.4.3 Partial Omega-Squared $\omega^2$

Values of partial $\omega^2$ can be computed as a function of $\hat{f}$,

$$\hat{\omega}^2_{\text{effect}} = \hat{f}^2_{\text{effect}}/(1 + \hat{f}^2_{\text{effect}}), \tag{14.7}$$

or as a function of the $F$ ratio,

$$\hat{\omega}^2_{\text{effect}} = \frac{df_{\text{effect}}(F_{\text{effect}} - 1)}{df_{\text{effect}}(F_{\text{effect}} - 1) + abn} \tag{14.8}$$

Substituting the previously calculated value of $\hat{f}_{AB}$ into Equation 14.7,

$$\hat{\omega}^2_{AB} = .45^2/(1 + .45^2) = .17$$

or, substituting values from Table 14.3 into Equation 14.8,

$$\hat{\omega}^2_{AB} = \frac{(6)(2.41)}{(6)(2.41) + 72} = .17$$

### 14.4.4 Other Measures of Effect Size

The noncentrality parameter of the $F$ distribution, $\lambda$, is needed in some programs for calculating power. It can be calculated simply as a function of $f$:

$$\hat{\lambda}_{\text{effect}} = abn\hat{f}^2_{\text{effect}} \tag{14.9}$$

As stated in earlier chapters, estimates of the index $\phi$ can be used together with charts found in several sources (e.g., Kirk, 1995; Myers & Well, 1995) to compute power, or the $n$ needed to obtain a specified level of power. This index can also be calculated as a function of $f$:

$$\hat{\phi}_{\text{effect}} = \sqrt{\frac{abn\hat{f}^2_{\text{effect}}}{df_{\text{effect}} + 1}} \tag{14.10}$$

## 14.5 POWER CALCULATIONS

Suppose that prior to running the experiment on instructions and time of test, we estimated from pilot work that the effect of instructions ($A$) would be large; that is, $f = .4$. How many subjects should be included in the experiment to have power equal to .8? Assume that $a$ and $b$ are 3 and 4, as in Table 14.1. What should $n$ be? We can use the free program GPOWER, cited at several earlier points in this text, to decide on $n$. Begin by selecting "Other $F$ tests." Then enter .16 for $f^2$, .05 for $\alpha$, and assuming a trial $n$ of 6, 72 for $N$, and 2 and 15 for the numerator and denominator degrees of freedom. The resulting power is .79, almost sufficient to meet our goal. Suppose we also want power equal to .8 to detect a large interaction effect. The numerator and denominator $df = 6$ and 45, and power equals .65.[1] If we increase $n$ to 8, $N$ is now 96 ($3 \times 4 \times 8$), the denominator $df$ are 63, and the power for testing the interaction is .81.

It is important to bear in mind a point discussed in Chapter 13: Power estimates for within-subject variables assume sphericity. If this assumption is not met, the numerator and denominator $df$ for the test of $B$ and $AB$ will be less than those entered into whatever program (or chart) is used, and therefore power will be less that the estimated value. Nevertheless, even an overestimate of power, or an underestimate of $n$, is better than no estimate, particularly if the researcher is aware of the potential nonsphericity effect.

## 14.6 CONTRASTING MEANS IN MIXED DESIGNS

As we noted in previous chapters, many statistical packages can test contrasts among means if the weights involved in the contrasts are provided. If such packages are not used, the tests can still be done in a fairly straightforward way. Procedures developed in Chapters 9 and 12 for between-subjects designs, and in Chapter 13 for within-subjects designs, can be extended to mixed designs.

To have an example in mind, let's take another look at Table 14.1. There were three groups of six subjects, and the groups had either a standard instructional approach ($A_1$), additional problems ($A_2$), or additional problems presented by a computer ($A_3$). Subjects were tested at four points in time ($B_1$ to $B_4$), beginning with a test at the end of the instructional period. In this section, we use the example of Table 14.1 to illustrate tests of four kinds of contrasts. We indicate the first kind by $\psi_{p(A)}$, where $\psi$ indicates a contrast and the subscript $p(A)$ specifies the $p$th contrast among the means of the between-subjects factor, $A$. For example, we might want to test the difference between the means of $A_2$ and $A_3$, the groups receiving additional problems. Or, we might wish to pit the mean of our control, $A_1$, against the average of the combined $A_2$ and $A_3$ groups. In both examples, we are contrasting the marginal means, those obtained by averaging the $bn$ scores at a level of $A$.

We also might wish to test whether the contrast among the $A_j$ differs as a function of the level of $B$. For example, the data of Table 14.1 suggest that the difference between the $A_1$ mean and the average of the $A_2$ and $A_3$ means increases as $B$, the time since training, increases. This suggests a second kind of contrast, $\psi_{p(A) \times B}$, the variation in the $p$th contrast of the $A$ means as a function of the level of $B$.

Still, a third possible contrast is $\psi_{q(B)}$, which would involve the $q$th contrast among the marginal means at the different levels of $B$. For example, it appears from Table 14.1 that there is a trend for the average score to decrease as the delay since instruction increases. Using the weights for polynomial analysis, discussed in Chapter 10, we can test whether this decline (the linear trend component) is a significant contributor to the overall variability due to $B$. We might refer to this contrast as $\psi_{\text{lin}(B)}$.

Finally, note that the decline over time seems more pronounced for the control group ($A_1$) than for either of the groups that received additional problems ($A_2$ and $A_3$). In terms of our discussion of trend analysis in Chapter 11, it appears that there may be a significant $\psi_{A \times \text{lin}(B)}$ source of variance.

In the remainder of this section, the data of Table 14.1 are used to illustrate the calculations involved in testing whether these contrasts are significant. Bear in mind that the discussion in Chapter 9 of familywise error rates applies here as well. For example, if all pairwise comparisons of the $\overline{Y}_{.j.}$ are made, the Tukey or Bonferroni procedure should be used to evaluate whether results are significant.

### 14.6.1 Contrasts of the Levels of the Between-Subjects Factor, A

Suppose we wish to compare the average score at $A_1$ with the average for the combined $A_2$ and $A_3$ conditions. The three group means receive the weights $-1$, $1/2$, and $1/2$ (or

**TABLE 14.8**    A CONTRAST OF THE MEANS AT THE LEVELS OF $A$ IN TABLE 14.1

(a) The totals for the $AB$ combinations ($T_{.jk}$) and the weights for the contrast ($w_j$) are presented; $n = 6$.

|       | $A_1$ | $A_2$ | $A_3$ | $\sum_j w_j T_{.jk}$ |
|-------|-------|-------|-------|----------------------|
| $B_1$ | 384   | 438   | 456   | 63   |
| $B_2$ | 276   | 378   | 408   | 117  |
| $B_3$ | 234   | 372   | 366   | 135  |
| $B_4$ | 210   | 372   | 426   | 189  |
| $T_{.j.}$ | 1,104 | 1,560 | 1,656 | |
| $w_j$ | $-1$  | 1/2   | 1/2   | |

$$\sum_j w_j T_{.j.} = (-1)(1{,}104) + \frac{1}{2}(1{,}560) + \frac{1}{2}(1{,}656)$$

$$= 63 + 117 + 135 + 189 = 504$$

(b) To test $H_0$: $\sum_j w_j \mu_j = 0$,

$$F_{1,a(n-1)} = \frac{SS_{p(A)}}{MS_{S/A}} = \frac{(\sum_j w_j T_{.j.})^2 / nb \sum_j w_j^2}{MS_{S/A}}$$

For the data of Table 14.1,

$$F_{1,15} = \frac{[(-1)(1{,}104) + (1/2)(1{,}560) + (1/2)(1{,}656)]^2 / (6)(4)(3/2)}{480}$$

$$= \frac{254{,}016/36}{480} = \frac{7{,}056}{480} = 14.7$$

(c) To test $H_0$: $\sum_j w_j \mu_{j1} = \sum_j w_j \mu_{j2} = \cdots = \sum_j w_j \mu_{jb}$, first calculate

$$SS_{p(A) \times B} = \frac{\sum_k \left( \sum_j w_j T_{.jk} \right)^2}{n \sum_j w_j^2} - SS_{p(A)}$$

$$= \frac{63^2 + 117^2 + 135^2 + 189^2}{(6)(3/2)} - 7{,}056$$

$$= 900$$

$$MS_{p(A) \times B} = \frac{SS_{p(A) \times B}}{b - 1} = \frac{900}{3} = 300$$

$$F_{b-1,a(n-1)(b-1)} = \frac{MS_{p(A) \times B}}{MS_{SB/A}} = \frac{300}{51.556} = 5.82$$

any multiple of these), respectively. Panel (a) of Table 14.8 presents the cell totals from Table 14.1, together with weighted totals at each level of $B$. For example, the value of 63 in the $B_1$ row is obtained from

$$\sum_J w_j T_{.j1} = (-1)(384) + (1/2)(458) + (1/2)(456) = 63$$

The sum of squares of the A contrast is distributed on 1 *df* and therefore can be tested using either the *t* or its square, the *F*. Throughout this section, we will use *F* ratios to test the hypotheses. From Chapter 9,

$$SS_{p(A)} = \frac{\left(\sum_j w_j \overline{Y}_{.j.}\right)^2}{\sum_j w_j^2/bn} = \frac{\left(\sum_j w_j T_{.j.}\right)^2}{bn\sum_j w_j^2} \tag{14.11}$$

and

$$F_{1,a(n-1)} = SS_{p(A)}/MS_{S/A} \tag{14.12}$$

The denominator is the *S/A* mean square because we are testing a component of the between-groups variability.

In panel (b) of Table 14.8, Equations 14.11 and 14.12 have been applied to the data in panel (a) to test the contrast of the $A_1$ mean with the mean of the combined $A_1$ and $A_2$ data. The value of *F* of 14.7 is significant; the control group ($A_1$) mean differs significantly from the average of the two groups that received extra problems. The reason for this result is apparent in Figure 14.1, in which the control groups curve lies far beneath the other two curves.

Next let's look at the interaction of $p(A)$ and *B*. For our example, we test whether the difference between $\overline{Y}_{.1.}$ and the average of $\overline{Y}_{.2.}$ and $\overline{Y}_{.3.}$ varies significantly as a function of the time of test (*B*). The sum of squares for this comparison of *b* contrasts is

$$SS_{p(A) \times B} = \frac{\sum_k \left(\sum_j w_j T_{.jk}\right)^2}{n\sum_j w_j^2} - SS_{p(A)} \tag{14.13}$$

The *F* test is

$$F_{b-1,a(n-1)(b-1)} = \frac{SS_{p(A) \times B}/(b-1)}{MS_{SB/A}} \tag{14.14}$$

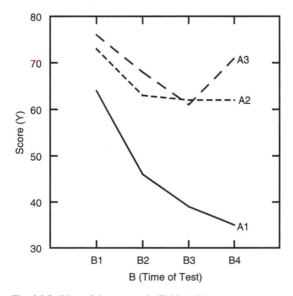

**Fig. 14.1** Plot of the means in Table 14.1.

Note that the numerator sum of squares is distributed on $b - 1$ $df$. The reason is that we are calculating the variance of $b$ contrasts. Also note that the error term is the usual within-subject error term. This is appropriate here because a component of the $AB$ interaction variability is tested.

Equations 14.13 and 14.14 are applied to the data of Table 14.1 in panel (c) of Table 14.8. This result is also significant. Turning to Figure 14.1, it appears that the difference between the $A_1$ curve and the $A_2$ and $A_3$ curves increases as $B$ increases. In terms of our example, the advantage of additional problems ($A_2$ and $A_3$) is greater as the time since instruction ($B$) increases, accounting for the significant $p(A) \times B$ result.

## 14.6.2 Contrasts of the Levels of the Within-Subjects Factor, B

Contrasts of the $b$ means (time of test in the example) can be tested directly by using statistical packages that can provide tests of contrasts of within-subject effects. They can also be tested by transforming the data into contrast scores as we did in Chapter 13.1.[2] For example, suppose we want to test whether the average curve in Fig. 14.1 has a significantly negative slope. This is a test of linear trend, $lin(B)$. From the orthogonal polynomial coefficients of Appendix Table C.6, we obtain weights of 3, 1, $-1$, and $-3$. These weights were applied in Table 14.9 to obtain the 18 contrast scores ($C_{ij}$), one for each subject at each level of $A$. The contrast scores were computed by multiplying each of the four scores for each subject by the corresponding linear coefficient and then summing these products. For example, the four scores for the first subject in group $A_1$ are 82, 48, 41, and 53. Then the contrast score is $(3)(82) + (1)(48) + (-1)(41) + (-3)(53) = 94$. The test for linear trend is a test of whether the average of all $an$ ($3 \times 6$ in our example) contrast scores differs significantly from zero. The test can be performed by submitting the $an$ contrast scores to a program for analyzing data from a one-factor ($A$) design. Table 14.10 presents the output from SPSS's ANOVA of the three groups of contrast scores. The "intercept" term corresponds to the test of linear trend. In general, it tests whether the mean of all the scores differs significantly from zero. The very large $F$ ratio ($p = .000$) indicates that the average of the three curves has a slope different from zero. Again, turning to Figure 14.1, the result of the test of linear trend apparently reflects the average negative slope of the three group curves.

**TABLE 14.9**  CONTRAST SCORES BASED ON THE DATA OF TABLE 14.1

| $A_1$ | $A_2$ | $A_3$ |
|-------|-------|-------|
| 94    | 30    | 26    |
| 90    | 54    | 18    |
| 98    | 34    | 42    |
| 128   | 34    | 26    |
| 64    | 36    | 8     |
| 90    | 16    | 12    |

The weights on the scores at the levels of $B$ are 3, 1, $-1$, and $-3$. These are multiplied by the scores for each subject. For example, the contrast score for Subject 1 in Group $A_1$ is $(3)(82) + (1)(48) + (-1)(41) + (-3)(53) = 94$. In this way, we get 18 contrast scores, one for each subject in each of the three groups.

**TABLE 14.10**   SPSS ANOVA OUTPUT FOR THE CONTRAST SCORES IN TABLE 14.9

**Tests of Between-Subjects Effects**

| Source | Type III Sum of Squares | df | Mean Square | F | Sig. |
|---|---|---|---|---|---|
| Corrected Model | 17856.000[a] | 2 | 8928.000 | 37.283 | .000 |
| Intercept | 45000.000 | 1 | 45000.000 | 187.918 | .000 |
| A | 17856.000 | 2 | 8928.000 | 37.283 | .000 |
| Error | 3592.000 | 15 | 239.467 | | |
| Total | 66448.000 | 18 | | | |
| Corrected Total | 21448.000 | 17 | | | |

Dependent Variable: Y
[a]$R^2 = .833$ (adjusted $R^2 = .810$.)
*Note.* Output is from SPSS.

Another test of interest is that of the interaction of $A$ and $q(B)$. In our example, the significant $AB$ interaction (see the ANOVA of Table 14.3) may be due, at least in part, to differences among the three groups in the rate at which performance drops off over the four test periods. The $A_1$ curve appears to have a more negative slope than those for the other two groups. As with the $q(B)$ term, $A \times q(B)$ can be tested by performing a one-factor ANOVA on the contrast scores. The results are also presented in the SPSS output of Table 14.10 in the line for the $A$ source. Both $q(B)$ (the intercept source) and $A \times q(B)$ (the $A$ source) are very significant sources of variance. We conclude that, averaging over all three levels of $A$, performance in the population declines markedly after the end of the instruction period; however, the rate of decline varies as a function of $A$, presumably because it is greater at $A_1$ than at $A_2$ or $A_3$.

## 14.7 TESTING SIMPLE EFFECTS

In the example of Table 14.1, we might wish to test the effects of type of instruction ($A$) only immediately after instruction; that is, only at $B_1$. Or, we might wish to test the effects of time ($B$) only for the control group ($A_1$). In general, we may wish to test the simple effects of $A$ at $B_k$ ($A/B_k$) or the simple effects of $B$ at $A_j$ ($B/A_j$). Let's consider the appropriate $F$ test for each in turn.

To test the simple main effects of $A$ at $B_k$, we recommend ignoring the data at all other levels of $B$. Then there are $a$ groups of $n$ subjects, each subject having exactly one score, the score at $B_k$. The numerator sum of squares is

$$SS_{A/B_k} = n \sum_j (\overline{Y}_{.jk} - \overline{Y}_{..k})^2 \tag{14.15}$$

and is distributed on $a - 1$ df. The denominator mean square ($MS_{S/A/B_k}$; subjects within $A$ at $B_k$) is just the average of the variances in the $a$ cells at $B_k$ and therefore is distributed on $a(n - 1)$ degrees of freedom.

If the populations of scores corresponding to the $ab$ cells have homogeneous variances, a more powerful test of the simple effects of $A$ at $B_k$ is possible. The numerator of the test statistic is the sum of squares of Equation 14.15, but its denominator is $MS_{W\,cells}$, the average of the $ab$ cell variances. An easy way to calculate this error term is to pool the $S/A$ and $SB/A$ sources of variance in the original analysis of variance of Table 14.3. The reason for the potential power advantage when $MS_{W\,cells}$ is the error term is that $MS_{W\,cells}$ has more degrees of freedom than $MS_{S/A/B_k}$; $ab(n-1)$ $df$ [the sum of $a(n-1)$ and $a(n-1)(b-1)$] is greater than $a(n-1)$ $df$. However, researchers should be cautious about using $MS_{W\,cells}$ as an error term for testing the simple effects of $A$. Averaging variances from cells that are not involved in the numerator of the $F$ ratio may result in an increase in Type 1 or Type 2 errors, depending on whether the additional cell variances are smaller or larger than those at $B_k$. We recommend the more conservative approach of basing the error term only on the cells involved in the contrast.

To test the effects of $B$ at $A_j$, we view the design as a simple subjects $\times B$ design, in which there are $n$ subjects with $b$ scores for each. The error term for testing the simple effect of $B$ is the $S \times B/A_j$ (subjects by $B$ at $A_j$) mean square. This will be on $(n-1)(b-1)$ $df$. As in testing simple effects of $A$, a potentially more powerful alternative exists; the simple effect of $B$ may be tested against $SB/A$, the omnibus error term against which the main effects of $B$ (and the $A \times B$ interaction) are tested. However, we again urge caution in using this error term. Although $SB/A$ is distributed on more degrees of freedom than the error term based only on the $A_j$ data, Type 1 and Type 2 error rates may be severely distorted if the subjects $\times B$ interaction variance changes across the levels of $A$.

## 14.8 PRETEST–POSTTEST DESIGNS

A common mixed design is one in which there is a between-subjects treatment ($A$), and two measures are obtained from each subject: a pretest and a posttest score. Subjects are generally assigned randomly to the levels of $A$ and the pretest scores are obtained before the treatment is applied, so that there are no systematic differences in the pretest scores across levels of $A$. The posttest scores reflect the effects of the treatment, if there are any. Although this design is often analyzed as a mixed design, other analyses are preferable. Because the treatment is applied to the posttest scores but not the pretest scores, the two types of scores are described by different structural models. Assuming that we are interested in whether the variable $A$ effects posttest performance, possible analyses for this design include:

1. *Analysis of covariance.* When its assumptions are met, the most powerful analysis is provided by the **analysis of covariance** (ANCOVA) that will be discussed in Chapter 15. Briefly, this analysis rests on the assumption that the posttest scores are linear functions of the pretest scores and that the slopes of these functions are the same at each level of $A$. The analysis takes advantage of this relationship, reducing error variance in the posttest scores by removing variability accounted for by the pretest scores.

2. *Analysis of gain scores.* Another possible analysis is based on **gain scores**. Each subject's pretest score is subtracted from the posttest score and then a one-factor ($A$) ANOVA is performed on these gain scores. This approach assumes that each treatment adds a constant to the pretest score. Because this model is less likely to be true than that assumed in the analysis of covariance, it will generally provide a less powerful test.

3. *Analysis of posttest scores only.* Because the treatment only affects the posttest scores, one could ignore the pretest scores and simply perform a one-factor ANOVA on the posttest scores. The resulting $F$ would clearly test the effect of $A$ on posttest scores. However, although this approach does not violate any assumptions, it ignores data (the pretest scores), which could help reduce error variance, and therefore this approach will produce less powerful tests than those noted previously.

4. *Using the mixed design analysis.* We raised the issue of testing the effects of $A$ using pretest and posttest scores in this section because such data are frequently analyzed as if generated by a mixed design with $A$ as the between-subjects factor and trials as the within-subjects factor (Huck & McLean, 1975; Jennings, 1988). If this is done, the $F$ test for the $A$ main effect will be very conservative because the pretest scores cannot be affected by the treatment. A better test of $A$ is given by the $F$ for the $A \times$ Trials interaction. This test can be shown to be identical to that obtained by performing a one-factor ANOVA on the gain (posttest–pretest) scores. However, as indicated previously, the analysis of covariance will generally provide a more powerful test. More detailed discussions of these issues are provided by Huck and McLean (1975), Jennings (1988), and Maxwell and Howard (1981).

We emphasize that the discussion in this section has presupposed random assignment of subjects to levels of $A$. Without random assignment, there may be systematic differences in the pretest scores across levels of $A$. If so, interpretation is more difficult, both for analysis of covariance and for analyses of gain scores (see, e.g., Cronbach & Furby, 1970; and Linn & Slinde, 1977). The referenced articles and the material on regression in Chapters 18–21 should be consulted by researchers faced with this problem.

## 14.9 ADDITIONAL MIXED DESIGNS

The approach taken in analyzing data from the design discussed in the preceding sections may be extended to any mixed design. In the present section, two additional designs are presented as illustrations.

### 14.9.1 Two Between-Subjects and One Within-Subjects Factor

Consider a variation of the experimental design that has carried us through the chapter so far. Again assume a between-subjects factor, $A$. This might be the three instructional methods in the example analyzed in previous sections. Furthermore, assume a second between-subjects variable, $B$. For example, there might be an equal number of male and female participants in each instructional condition. In general, as in Chapter 11, there are $ab$ groups of $n$ subjects each. Finally, assume a third, within-subjects, variable, $C$. For example, each of the $abn$ subjects might be tested on each of $c$ occasions. Table 14.11 presents the layout for a group tested under conditions $A_j B_k$. The indices of notation are $i = 1, 2, \ldots, n$; $j = 1, 2, \ldots, a$; $k = 1, 2, \ldots, b$; and $m = 1, 2, \ldots, c$.

The approach taken in developing the ANOVA table for the one between-subjects and one within-subjects design is readily extended to designs in which there are two between-subjects factors. If we ignore the between-subjects factors and write down the sources of

**TABLE 14.11**    THE LAYOUT FOR THE GROUP OF SCORES OBTAINED UNDER CONDITIONS $A_j$ AND $B_k$

| $A$ | $B$ | Subject | $C_1$ | $\ldots$ | $C_m$ | $\ldots$ | $C_c$ |
|---|---|---|---|---|---|---|---|
| | | $S_{1jk}$ | $Y_{1jk1}$ | | $Y_{1jkm}$ | | $Y_{1jkc}$ |
| | | $\ldots$ | | | | | |
| $j$ | $k$ | $S_{ijk}$ | $Y_{ijk1}$ | | $Y_{ijkm}$ | | $Y_{ijkc}$ |
| | | $\ldots$ | | | | | |
| | | $S_{njk}$ | $Y_{njk1}$ | | $Y_{njkm}$ | | $Y_{njkc}$ |

**TABLE 14.12**    ANOVA FOR A DESIGN WITH TWO BETWEEN-SUBJECTS AND ONE WITHIN-SUBJECTS FACTORS

**(a) Appropriate SV and df Terms If Factors A and B Are Ignored**

| SV | df | SS |
|---|---|---|
| Total | $abcn - 1$ | $\sum\sum\sum\sum(Y_{ijkm} - \overline{Y}_{....})^2$ |
| Between-Subjects ($S$) | $abn - 1$ | $c\sum\sum\sum(\overline{Y}_{ijk.} - \overline{Y}_{....})^2$ |
| Within-Subjects ($WSs$) | $abn(c - 1)$ | $\sum\sum\sum\sum(Y_{ijkm} - Y_{ijk.})^2$ |
| $C$ | $c - 1$ | $abn\sum(\overline{Y}_{...m} - \overline{Y}_{....})^2$ |
| $SC$ | $(abn - 1)(c - 1)$ | $SS_{tot} - SS_S - SS_C$ |

**(b) Complete Partitioning of the Variability**

| SV | df | SS |
|---|---|---|
| Total | $abcn - 1$ | $\sum\sum\sum\sum(Y_{ijkm} - \overline{Y}_{....})^2$ |
| Between-Subjects ($S$) | $abn - 1$ | $c\sum\sum\sum(\overline{Y}_{ijk.} - \overline{Y}_{....})^2$ |
| $A$ | $a - 1$ | $bcn\sum(\overline{Y}_{.j..} - \overline{Y}_{....})^2$ |
| $B$ | $b - 1$ | $acn\sum(\overline{Y}_{..k.} - \overline{Y}_{....})^2$ |
| $AB$ | $(a - 1)(b - 1)$ | $cn\sum\sum(\overline{Y}_{.jk.} - \overline{Y}_{....})^2 - SS_A - SS_B$ |
| $S/AB$ | $ab(n - 1)$ | $c\sum\sum\sum(\overline{Y}_{ijk.} - \overline{Y}_{.jk.})^2$ |
| Within-Subjects ($WSs$) | $abn(c - 1)$ | $\sum\sum\sum\sum(Y_{ijkm} - \overline{Y}_{ijk.})^2$ |
| $C$ | $c - 1$ | $abn\sum(\overline{Y}_{...m} - \overline{Y}_{....})^2$ |
| $SC$ | $(abn - 1)(c - 1)$ | $SS_{tot} - SS_S - SS_C$ |
| $AC$ | $(a - 1)(c - 1)$ | $bn\sum\sum(\overline{Y}_{.j.m} - \overline{Y}_{....})^2 - SS_A - SS_C$ |
| $BC$ | $(b - 1)(c - 1)$ | $an\sum\sum(\overline{Y}_{..km} - \overline{Y}_{....})^2 - SS_B - SS_C$ |
| $ABC$ | $(a - 1)(b - 1)(c - 1)$ | $n\sum\sum\sum(\overline{Y}_{.jkm} - \overline{Y}_{....})^2 - SS_A - SS_B - SS_C$ $- SS_{AB} - SS_{AC} - SS_{BC}$ |
| $SC/AB$ | $ab(n - 1)(c - 1)$ | $SS_{SC} - SS_{AC} - SS_{BC} - SS_{ABC}$ |

variance and degrees of freedom for the resulting repeated-measures design, we obtain the result presented in panel (a) of Table 14.12. This preliminary analysis of the data accounts for all $abcn - 1$ $df$; there are $abn - 1$ $df$ for between-subject variability and $abn(c - 1)$ for within-subject variability; that is, $c - 1$ $df$ for each of the $abn$ subjects. The analysis of panel (a) is, however, incomplete because it fails to take account of the between-subjects factors $A$ and $B$. From the analysis of data from completely randomized designs with two factors (Chapter 11), it follows that the between-subjects variability occurs partly because of the main effects of $A$ and $B$, partly because of the joint effect of $A$ and $B$, and partly because subjects tested at a given combination of the levels of $A$ and $B$ differ from one another in ways that affect their scores. The partitioning of the between-subjects variability ($SS_{BSs}$) and degrees of freedom ($df_{BSs}$) can therefore be represented by

$$SS_{BSs} = SS_A + SS_B + SS_{AB} + SS_{S/AB}$$

and

$$abn - 1 = a - 1 + b - 1 + (a - 1)(b - 1) + ab(n - 1)$$

Crossing $C$ with each of the above terms, the $SC$ variability and degrees of freedom of panel (a) can be partitioned as

$$SS_{SC} = SS_{AC} + SS_{BC} + SS_{ABC} + SS_{SC/AB}$$

and

$$(abn - 1)(c - 1) = (a - 1)(c - 1) + (b - 1)(c - 1) + (a - 1)(b - 1)(c - 1)$$
$$+ ab(n - 1)(c - 1)$$

The complete partitioning of the total variability is presented in panel (b) of Table 14.12. Table 14.13 contains the $F$ ratios and expected mean squares. Note that there are two error terms in Table 14.13: one for the between-subjects-terms ($A$, $B$, and $AB$) and another for the within-subjects terms ($C$ and its interactions).

**TABLE 14.13**  EXPECTED MEAN SQUARES AND ERROR TERMS FOR A DESIGN WITH TWO BETWEEN-SUBJECTS AND ONE WITHIN-SUBJECTS VARIABLE

| SV | df | EMS | Error Term |
|----|----|-----|------------|
| $A$ | $a - 1$ | $\sigma_e^2 + c\sigma_{S/AB}^2 + nbc\theta_A^2$ | $S/AB$ |
| $B$ | $b - 1$ | $\sigma_e^2 + c\sigma_{S/AB}^2 + nac\theta_B^2$ | $S/AB$ |
| $AB$ | $(a - 1)(b - 1)$ | $\sigma_e^2 + c\sigma_{S/AB}^2 + nc\theta_{AB}^2$ | $S/AB$ |
| $S/AB$ | $ab(n - 1)$ | $\sigma_e^2 + c\sigma_{S/AB}^2$ | |
| $C$ | $c - 1$ | $\sigma_e^2 + \sigma_{SC/AB}^2 + nab\theta_C^2$ | $SC/AB$ |
| $AC$ | $(a - 1)(c - 1)$ | $\sigma_e^2 + \sigma_{SC/AB}^2 + nb\theta_{AC}^2$ | $SC/AB$ |
| $BC$ | $(b - 1)(c - 1)$ | $\sigma_e^2 + \sigma_{SC/AB}^2 + na\theta_{BC}^2$ | $SC/AB$ |
| $ABC$ | $(a - 1)(b - 1)(c - 1)$ | $\sigma_e^2 + \sigma_{SC/AB}^2 + n\theta_{ABC}^2$ | $SC/AB$ |
| $SC/AB$ | $ab(n - 1)(c - 1)$ | $\sigma_e^2 + \sigma_{SC/AB}^2$ | |

*Note.* $A$, $B$, and $C$ are all assumed to be fixed-effects factors.

## 14.9.2 One Between-Subjects and Two Within-Subjects Factors

Still, another version of the mixed design involves more than one within-subjects factor. For example, in the study by Myers et al. (1983), cited in Chapters 6 and 8, subjects were instructed in probability by one of three methods, then tested on two occasions 48 hours apart. The tests contained story problems and formula problems, which were scored separately. Instructional method ($A$) was a between-subjects factor, and day of test ($B$) and problem type ($C$) were within-subjects factors. The indices of notation for this design are $i = 1, 2, \ldots, n$; $j = 1, 2, \ldots, a$; $k = 1, 2, \ldots, b$; and $m = 1, 2, \ldots, c$, where $Y_{ijkm}$ refers to the score for the $i$th subject at the $j$th level of $A$, tested at $B_k$ and $C_m$.

Once again, we begin partitioning $SS_{tot}$ and $df_{tot}$ by ignoring the variable $A$ and considering an $S \times B \times C$ design in which $an$ subjects are tested under all combinations of $B$ and $C$. We have

$$SS_{tot} = SS_S + SS_B + SS_{SB} + SS_C + SS_{SC} + SS_{BC} + SS_{SBC}$$

The variability among the $an$ subjects is in part due to $A$; therefore, as in the one-factor between-subjects design of Chapter 8, $SS_S = SS_A + SS_{S/A}$. This accounts for the between-subjects variability. Crossing $S$ with $B$, $C$, and $BC$ in turn, we have

$$SS_{SB} = SS_{AB} + SS_{SB/A},$$

$$SS_{SC} = SS_{AC} + SS_{SC/A},$$

**TABLE 14.14**   ANOVA FOR A DESIGN WITH ONE BETWEEN-SUBJECTS AND TWO WITHIN-SUBJECTS FACTORS

| SV | df | SS |
|---|---|---|
| Total | $abcn - 1$ | $\sum\sum\sum\sum(Y_{ijkm} - \overline{Y}_{\ldots})^2$ |
| Between-Subjects ($S$) | $an - 1$ | $bc\sum\sum(\overline{Y}_{ij..} - \overline{Y}_{\ldots})^2$ |
| $A$ | $a - 1$ | $bcn\sum(\overline{Y}_{.j..} - \overline{Y}_{\ldots})^2$ |
| $S/A$ | $a(n - 1)$ | $bc\sum\sum(\overline{Y}_{ij..} - \overline{Y}_{.j..})^2$ |
| Within-Subjects ($WSs$) | $an(bc - 1)$ | $\sum\sum\sum\sum(Y_{ijkm} - \overline{Y}_{ij..})^2$ |
| $B$ | $b - 1$ | $acn\sum(\overline{Y}_{..k.} - \overline{Y}_{\ldots})^2$ |
| $AB$ | $(a - 1)(b - 1)$ | $cn\sum\sum(\overline{Y}_{.jk.} - \overline{Y}_{\ldots})^2 - SS_A - SS_B$ |
| $SB/A$ | $a(n - 1)(b - 1)$ | $c\sum\sum\sum(\overline{Y}_{ijk.} - \overline{Y}_{ij..} - \overline{Y}_{.jk.} + \overline{Y}_{.j..})^2$ |
| $C$ | $c - 1$ | $abn\sum(\overline{Y}_{\ldots m} - \overline{Y}_{\ldots})^2$ |
| $AC$ | $(a - 1)(c - 1)$ | $bn\sum\sum(\overline{Y}_{.j.m} - \overline{Y}_{\ldots})^2 - SS_A - SS_C$ |
| $SC/A$ | $a(n - 1)(c - 1)$ | $b\sum\sum\sum(\overline{Y}_{ij.m} - \overline{Y}_{ij..} - \overline{Y}_{.j.m} + \overline{Y}_{.j..})^2$ |
| $BC$ | $(b - 1)(c - 1)$ | $an\sum\sum(\overline{Y}_{..km} - \overline{Y}_{\ldots})^2 - SS_B - SS_C$ |
| $ABC$ | $(a - 1)(b - 1)(c - 1)$ | $n\sum\sum\sum(\overline{Y}_{.jkm} - \overline{Y}_{\ldots})^2 - SS_A - SS_B$ $-SS_C - SS_{AB} - SS_{AC} - SS_{BC}$ |
| $SBC/A$ | $a(n - 1)(b - 1)(c - 1)$ | $SS_{Wss} - SS_B - SS_{AB} - SS_C - SS_{AC}$ $-SS_{BC} - SS_{ABC} - SS_{SB/A} - SS_{SC/A}$ |

**TABLE 14.15**   EXPECTED MEAN SQUARES AND ERROR TERMS FOR A DESIGN WITH
ONE BETWEEN-SUBJECTS AND TWO WITHIN-SUBJECTS FACTORS

| SV | df | EMS | Error Term |
|---|---|---|---|
| A | $a - 1$ | $\sigma_e^2 + bc\sigma_{S/A}^2 + nbc\theta_A^2$ | S/A |
| S/A | $a(n - 1)$ | $\sigma_e^2 + bc\sigma_{S/A}^2$ | |
| B | $b - 1$ | $\sigma_e^2 + c\sigma_{SB/A}^2 + nac\theta_B^2$ | SB/A |
| AB | $(a - 1)(b - 1)$ | $\sigma_e^2 + c\sigma_{SB/A}^2 + nc\theta_{AB}^2$ | SB/A |
| SB/A | $a(n - 1)(b - 1)$ | $\sigma_e^2 + c\sigma_{SB/A}^2$ | |
| C | $c - 1$ | $\sigma_e^2 + b\sigma_{SC/A}^2 + nab\theta_C^2$ | SC/A |
| AC | $(a - 1)(c - 1)$ | $\sigma_e^2 + b\sigma_{SC/A}^2 + nb\theta_{AC}^2$ | SC/A |
| SC/A | $a(n - 1)(c - 1)$ | $\sigma_e^2 + b\sigma_{SC/A}^2$ | |
| BC | $(b - 1)(c - 1)$ | $\sigma_e^2 + \sigma_{SBC/A}^2 + na\theta_{BC}^2$ | SBC/A |
| ABC | $(a - 1)(b - 1)(c - 1)$ | $\sigma_e^2 + \sigma_{SBC/A}^2 + n\theta_{ABC}^2$ | SBC/A |
| SBC/A | $a(n - 1)(b - 1)(c - 1)$ | $\sigma_e^2 + \sigma_{SBC/A}^2$ | |

*Note.* A, B, and C are all assumed to have fixed effects.

and

$$SS_{SBC} = SS_{ABC} + SS_{SBC/A}.$$

The complete partitioning is presented in Table 14.14 and the expected mean squares and
$F$ tests are presented in Table 14.15. One difference from the previous analyses of this
chapter is that there are four error terms. In descending order, these are $S/A$, $SB/A$, $SC/A$,
and $SBC/A$. Assuming that all three factors have fixed effects, we can use the rules of
Table 14.5 to verify the expected mean squares.

In many experiments, subjects' responses to stimuli ($C$) are obtained under several
conditions ($B$). For example, ratings or times to respond are often recorded. If the investigator wishes to generalize to a population of items represented by the stimuli in the study,
the stimuli are assumed to have random effects. We leave as an exercise the use of the rules
of thumb to derive expected mean squares and $F$ tests of $A$ and $B$ in the design of this
section, with the warning that quasi-$F$s will be involved.

## 14.10 CONCLUDING REMARKS

In mixed designs, the analyses for both between-subjects and within-subjects factors are
essentially the same as in the corresponding pure designs, with the same advantages, assumptions, and costs. Effects of within-subjects factors can potentially be tested for with more
precision because individual differences components are removed from the error terms.
However, as in pure within-subjects designs, the possibility of Subjects × Treatments
interactions is introduced for these factors as well as the possibility of violations of the
sphericity assumption.

For within-subjects factors, if there are large Subjects × Treatments interactions, efficiency will be lowered, and if the sphericity assumption is violated, $F$ tests may be positively biased unless the appropriate degree-of-freedom corrections are used. Conservative $F$ tests that adjust for this bias have been discussed in Chapter 13 and in the current chapter, and are calculated automatically by most statistical software. It should be emphasized that we need not be concerned about the positive bias that arises from violations of the sphericity assumption when testing the effects of between-subjects factors in a mixed design, nor when testing the effects of within-subjects factors that have only two levels, nor when testing single degree-of-freedom contrasts.

## KEY CONCEPTS

| | |
|---|---|
| mixed, or split-plot, designs | crossed factors |
| nested factors | rules of thumb for generating EMS |
| pretest-posttest designs | gain scores |
| analysis of covariance | |

## EXERCISES

**14.1** Consider the following data set:

| | | $B_1$ | $B_2$ | $B_3$ |
|---|---|---|---|---|
| | $S_{11}$ | 23 | 16 | 12 |
| $A_1$ | $S_{21}$ | 27 | 1 | 14 |
| | $S_{31}$ | 22 | 10 | 10 |
| | $S_{12}$ | 25 | 16 | 19 |
| $A_2$ | $S_{22}$ | 17 | 33 | 22 |
| | $S_{32}$ | 9 | 17 | 22 |

(a) Present the complete ANOVA table with all numerical results; assume $A$ and $B$ both have fixed-effects.

(b) Find the mean score for each subject. You now have a one-factor completely randomized design. Perform an ANOVA using the mean scores as the data. (i) How does the $F$ test of $A$ compare with that calculated in part (a)? (ii) How does $MS_A$ in this analysis compare with that obtained in part (a)? Explain the relation.

(c) In this chapter, we stated that $SS_{SB/A}$ was equivalent to the result of calculating the $S \times B$ sum of squares separately at each level of $A$ and then summing the $a$ terms. To demonstrate this, ignore the $A_2$ data and calculate the sum of squares for $S \times B$ at $A_1$ ($SS_{SB/A_1}$). Do the same thing at $A_2$ and check the sum of the two terms against $SS_{SB/A}$ calculated in part (a). Confirm that $MS_{SB/A}$ is the average of the two $S \times B$ mean squares.

**14.2** $A_1$ and $A_2$ in Exercise 14.1 might have been two litters of three animals; in that case, we would assume that $A$ has random effects. Assume $B$ represents trials and is a fixed-effect variable.

(a) State the expected mean squares for the various sources of variance.

(b) Recalculate any $F$ ratios that are not the same as in Exercise 14.1.

**14.3** Suppose $A_1$ and $A_2$ in Exercise 14.1 are two groups of subjects of two different ages and the levels of $B$ correspond to three problems sampled randomly from some very large population of problems. Present the EMS under this model and recalculate $F$ tests where necessary.

**14.4** An investigator is interested in the extent to which children are attentive to violent acts on television. An experiment is run with 120 subjects: half boys and half girls (sex, $X$) at each of three age levels (Age, $A$). Each child views six scenes differing with respect to the level of violence ($V$, 3 levels), and the type of character; half the scenes involve animal cartoon characters and the other involve human characters ($C$, 2 levels). The dependent variable is a measure of attention during presentation of the scene.

(a) State the $SV$, $df$, and error terms for this design.

(b) In an alternative design, each child might view only three scenes involving only one type of character; $C$ would be a between-subjects variable. Present the $SV$, $df$, and EMS for this design. What tests will be affected by this change in design? In what way?

(c) Suppose the children are available for only short periods of time, but the investigator has access to large numbers of subjects. What are the advantages and disadvantages of the original design [part (a)] as opposed to using a design in which each subject is tested only once in some combination of $V$ and $C$?

**14.5** In a study of the development of the concepts of conservation of quantity and weight, two standardized and quantifiable tasks ($T$, 2 levels) are presented to each of 72 children. Mastering the first task requires that a child grasp the notion of conservation of quantity whereas the second task depends on conservation of weight. The score is the number of trials required for the mastery of the task. Both age ($A$, 3 levels: 5, 7, and 9 years) and sex ($X$, 2 levels) are included as major variables in the design.

(a) Present the sources of variance associated with the design of this study as well as the $df$ and EMS (using numbers where possible).

(b) State the error term and its $df$ for tests of the following simple effects: (i) The effect of age for the conservation-of-quantity task ($T_1$); (ii) the effect of age for all male subjects on the $T_1$ task; and (iii) the effects of task on the scores of all male subjects.

**14.6** Thompson, Schellenberg, and Husain (2001) tested the "Mozart effect," the effect on tests of spatial abilities after listening to music by Mozart. Twenty-four participants listened to a tape of music by either Mozart or Albinoni (Group, $g = 2$). They were tested on measures of spatial relations, arousal, mood, and enjoyment after listening to the music and also after a period of silence (Condition, $c = 2$). The order of the two conditions was counterbalanced with half of the subjects receiving the music first and half receiving the silence first (Order, $o = 2$).

(a) The $F$ for Groups on the arousal scores was 6.20. What are the values of $\hat{f}$ and $\hat{\omega}^2$ for this effect? According to Cohen's (1988) guidelines, is the effect small, medium, or large?

(b) Assuming the effect estimated in part (b), what power did the experiment have? Is nonsphericity a potential problem in this calculation? Would it be if we were calculating power for the effect of conditions? Explain.

(c) If we were to redo the experiment, assuming a medium effect on arousal by Cohen's standards, how many subjects would we need to attain power of .8?

**14.7** In the Thompson et al. spatial test data, the means are (approximately)

| Group | Music | Silence |
|---|---|---|
| Mozart | 14.8 | 11.0 |
| Albinoni | 9.8 | 11.4 |

Given the $F$ of 16.89 for Groups $\times$ Conditions, find the .95 confidence interval for $(\mu_{\text{Mozart,Music}} - \mu_{\text{Albioni,Music}}) - (\mu_{\text{Mozart,Silence}} - \mu_{\text{Albioni,Silence}})$.

**14.8** In a small-scale pilot study of the effects of diet on the ability to withstand physical stress, 12 volunteers were divided into three groups of four subjects and each given a different diet. They then underwent a battery of physical tests on each of four successive days. Scores for each day were combined into a single score, with higher scores representing better performance. The data are in the file Ex14_8 on your CD.

(a) Plot the performance curves for each group.

(b) Perform the ANOVA, including a complete trend analysis. Discuss the results in terms of the plot in part (a).

**14.9** (a) For the Ex14_8 data set, calculate the .95 simultaneous confidence intervals on the pairwise differences among diet means (averaging over the 4 days), using Tukey's *HSD* (1953) procedure. Report any significant differences.

(b) After inspecting the data, the researcher notes that diet $C$ yields better performance than $A$ or $B$ on day 4. Calculate a confidence interval for the difference between that mean and the average of the other two means, taking into consideration the fact that the test is post hoc (FWE = .05). Is the difference significant?

**14.10** We have two groups ($A_1$, $A_2$) of four subjects each. Each subject is tested six times with two levels of $B$ and three levels of $C$ crossing to yield six scores for each subject. The data are presented in the Ex14_10 file in the Exercises folder of your CD.

(a) Test the $A$ term, assuming all factors are fixed.

(b) Suppose $C$ represents randomly chosen items. How will your analysis ($F$ tests, EMS) differ from that when all three factors have fixed effects? Again, test the $A$ effect.

(c) Without doing the calculations, set up the $F$ test for $B$ and $AB$, again assuming the effects of $C$ are random.

**14.11** Several different measures are available in the Wiley file in the *Wiley_Voss* folder. Of these, the SVT (sentence verification) and IVT (inference verification) are on the same scale, and differences between the two tap the difference between memory for explicitly stated information and the inferences drawn from the material studied. We might wish to see if these differences are affected by the format and text manipulations.

(a) Plot the cell means and describe the resulting pattern. What effects are suggested?

(b) Perform an ANOVA with format and text as between-subjects variables and test (SVT vs. IVT) as the within-subjects variable. Discuss the results, relating your discussion to the plot of the means.

**14.12** In Exercise 14.11, there is a significant interaction between format and the type of test (SVT vs. IVT). We may better understand this effect if we calculate some additional measures.

(a) Calculate an estimate of $f$ for the effect of format on the difference between test scores.

(b) Calculate a .95 confidence interval for the interaction of format and test.

(c) We wish to have a measure of the effect of instructions on the difference between SVT and IVT scores. Estimate Cohen's $f$ statistic for that difference (i) in the text and (ii) in the web condition.

---

## APPENDIX 14.1

## Justifying the Rules of Thumb for Expected Mean Squares

We begin by noting that $MS_A$ is $bn$ times the variance of the means at the levels of $A$; accordingly, we relate $\overline{Y}_{.j.}$ to the structural equation. Because $\overline{Y}_{.j.} = \sum_k \sum_i Y_{ijk}/nb$, and substituting for $Y_{ijk}$ from Equation 14.1,

$$\overline{Y}_{.j.} = (1/nb) \sum_i \sum_k [\mu + \alpha_j + \eta_{i/j} + \beta_k + (\alpha\beta)_{jk} + (\eta\beta)_{ik/j} + \varepsilon_{ijk}]$$

$$= \mu + \alpha_j + (1/n) \sum_i \eta_{i/j} + (1/b) \sum_k \beta_k + (1/b)(\alpha\beta)_{jk}$$

$$+ (1/bn) \sum_i \sum_k (\eta\beta)_{ik/j} + (1/bn) \sum_i \sum_k \varepsilon_{ijk}$$

As stated in Table 14.4, because $B$ is a fixed-effect variable, $\sum_k \beta_k = 0$, $\sum_k (\alpha\beta)_{jk} = 0$, and $\sum_i \sum_k (\eta\beta)_{ik/j} = 0$. Therefore, the preceding equation simplifies to

$$\overline{Y}_{.j.} = \mu + \alpha_j + \overline{\eta}_{.j.} + \overline{\varepsilon}_{.j.}$$

where $\overline{\eta}_{.j.}$ is the mean subject effect at $A_j$ and equals $(1/n) \sum_i \eta_{i/j}$, and $\overline{\varepsilon}_{.j.}$ is the average error in group $j$ and equals $(1/bn) \sum_i \sum_k \varepsilon_{ijk}$. Because $\mu$ contributes to all $a$ means, it does not contribute to $MS_A$. The group means differ because of the $A$ treatment effect $(\alpha_j)$, individual differences $(\overline{\eta}_{.j.})$, and error of measurement $(\overline{\varepsilon}_{.ij})$. This is reflected in the $E(MS_A)$ of Table 14.3. The other EMS can be justified in a similar manner.

# Chapter 15

## Using Concomitant Variables to Increase Power: Blocking and Analysis of Covariance

## 15.1 INTRODUCTION

In Chapter 8 we introduced an analysis of variance (ANOVA) by discussing a probability-learning study (Myers et al., 1983) in which subjects were randomly assigned to one of three learning conditions—standard text ($S$), low-explanatory text ($LE$), and high-explanatory text ($HE$)—and then tested on 12 probability problems. The dependent variable was the proportion correct on the 12 problems (the data are presented in Table 15.1). When a standard between-subjects ANOVA was performed, we did not have sufficient evidence to reject the omnibus null hypothesis

$$\mu_S = \mu_{LE} = \mu_{HE}$$

That is, the differences among the group means were not sufficiently large, relative to the error variance, to reject the null hypothesis. The present chapter describes ways in which error variance can be reduced, and power consequently increased, through the use of information about a **concomitant variable** or **covariate**, a measure that is correlated with the dependent variable.

One way to reduce the error variance is to use the concomitant variable to generate a **Treatment $\times$ Blocks design** (see Section 12.7). Suppose that before we conducted the probability-learning study, we gave each of the 48 participants a quantitative reasoning test. We could use the scores on this test to assign participants to text conditions. For example, we could rank the scores on the test and form, say, 4 blocks of 12 participants each: The top 12 scorers on the reasoning test would form $B_1$, the next 12 would form $B_2$, the next 12 would form $B_3$, and the 12 lowest scorers would form $B_4$. Then we could randomly distribute the participants in each block among the three treatment conditions, $S$, $LE$, and $HE$, and perform the experiment. We could then conduct a two-factor ANOVA in which the factors are text condition ($A$) and block ($B$) that would have four participants in each of the 12 cells of the design. Instead of having a **completely randomized design** with structural

**TABLE 15.1**   PROPORTION CORRECT IN THE MYERS ET AL. (1983) STUDY ALONG WITH THE
QUANTITATIVE APTITUDE SCORE (*X*) FOR EACH PARTICIPANT

| | S | X | LE | X | HE | X |
|---|---|---|---|---|---|---|
| | .083 | 46 | .083 | 64 | .333 | 61 |
| | .167 | 41 | .167 | 58 | .333 | 61 |
| | .250 | 50 | .250 | 51 | .333 | 67 |
| | .250 | 60 | .250 | 66 | .417 | 52 |
| | .250 | 53 | .250 | 52 | .417 | 29 |
| | .333 | 74 | .333 | 56 | .500 | 38 |
| | .333 | 69 | .333 | 68 | .500 | 58 |
| | .333 | 51 | .417 | 47 | .500 | 60 |
| | .417 | 68 | .417 | 72 | .583 | 74 |
| | .500 | 49 | .417 | 59 | .583 | 59 |
| | .500 | 65 | .417 | 61 | .583 | 72 |
| | .500 | 42 | .500 | 77 | .583 | 48 |
| | .500 | 59 | .583 | 51 | .583 | 66 |
| | .583 | 69 | .583 | 83 | .667 | 75 |
| | .583 | 80 | .667 | 93 | .667 | 81 |
| | .750 | 71 | .833 | 97 | .917 | 90 |
| Mean = | .396 | 59.188 | .406 | 65.938 | .531 | 61.938 |
| | | $\overline{Y}.. = .444$ | | $\overline{X}.. = 62.355$ | | |
| $s^2 =$ | .031 | 146.029 | .038 | 225.929 | .023 | 239.396 |

model

$$Y_{ij} = \mu + \alpha_j + \varepsilon_{ij} \tag{15.1}$$

in which participants are randomly assigned to text conditions without regard to quantitative ability, we would now have a two-factor model Treatments × Blocks design with model

$$Y_{ijk} = \mu + \alpha_j + \beta_k + (\alpha\beta)_{jk} + \varepsilon_{ijk} \tag{15.2}$$

For the completely randomized design, the text main effect would be tested by the ratio $MS_A/MS_{S/A}$, where the error term, $MS_{S/A}$, is an estimate of the variance of $\varepsilon_{ij}$. For the Treatments × Blocks design, the text effect would be tested using the ratio $MS_A/MS_{S/AB}$, where the error term,[1] $MS_{S/AB}$, is an estimate of the variance of $\varepsilon_{ijk}$. If quantitative ability is correlated with performance on the probability problems, we would expect $MS_{S/AB}$ to be smaller than $MS_{S/A}$. Because participants within a cell of the Treatments × Blocks design are less variable with respect to quantitative ability than participants randomly assigned to a treatment condition without regard to their quantitative ability scores, their performance on the probability problems should be also less variable. The resultant reduction in error variance would tend to make the Treatments × Blocks design more powerful, all other things being equal.

However, not all other things are equal; power depends not only on the size of the ratio, but also on the degrees of freedom of the error term. Whenever we increase *b*, the number of blocks, thereby making $MS_{S/AB}$ smaller, we also lose error degrees of freedom, which increases the size of the critical *F*, thereby decreasing power. In the current example with $N = 48$, we would have $df_{error} = N - a = 48 - 3 = 45$ for the completely randomized design; $df_{error} = N - ab = 48 - (3)(4) = 36$ for a Treatments $\times$ Blocks design with 4 blocks; and $df_{error} = 48 - (3)(8) = 24$ if we used 8 blocks. It turns out that, for each combination of $N$, $a$, and the correlation between the dependent and concomitant variables, there is a value of $b$ that maximizes power. Feldt (1958) has discussed these issues and made recommendations for selecting the optimal number of blocks.

We will have more to say about blocking in Section 15.5. However, we now turn to the analysis of covariance (ANCOVA). The ANCOVA can result in even greater gains in power than blocking when there is a high correlation between the concomitant and dependent variables, although at the cost of somewhat increased complexity, and of more and stronger assumptions about the data. In most cases, an ANCOVA is applied to designs in which subjects are assigned to treatments without regard to the covariate. However, as we see later, even greater gains in power may be achieved by an ANCOVA if the covariate is used in forming the treatment groups.

The basic idea of the ANCOVA is similar to that of Treatments $\times$ Blocks in that information about a concomitant variable is used to reduce error variance. However, in the blocking design, this information is used to form a categorical blocking factor to remove the effect of the blocking factor and its interaction with $A$ from the error term. In contrast, in an ANCOVA, we try to remove the error variance predictable from the concomitant variable (which in an ANCOVA is usually called the covariate) by using regression. This may result in a smaller error term and also a reduction in bias of the group means due to the error variance. We can think of the ANCOVA as performing a statistical adjustment to ask what the ANOVA would be like if each participant had the same score on the covariate. The model for a one-factor ANCOVA

$$Y_{ij} = \mu + \alpha_j + \beta(X_{ij} - \overline{X}_{..}) + \varepsilon'_{ij} \qquad (15.3)$$

adds a regression component to the one-factor ANOVA model of Equation 15.1. An increase in power may be achieved, because if $SS_A$ and $SS_{S/A}$ are adjusted by removing the variability accounted for by the regression on $X$ (i.e., variability predictable from $X$), the ratio of the resulting mean squares may be considerably larger than the ratio of the unadjusted mean squares. Comparing the ANOVA and ANCOVA models (Equations 15.1 and 15.3), we see that

$$\varepsilon_{ij} = \beta(X_{ij} - \overline{X}_{..}) + \varepsilon'_{ij} = \varepsilon_{pred} + \varepsilon_{res}$$

That is, the error associated with $i$th participant in the $j$th treatment condition can be considered to be made up of two components: a component predictable from the covariate ($\varepsilon_{pred}$) and the residual component ($\varepsilon_{res}$). In the ANOVA for a completely randomized design, both components contribute to the error variance, so that $\sigma_e^2 = \sigma_{pred}^2 + \sigma_{res}^2$, whereas in the ANCOVA, only the residual component contributes. Graphing the regression of $Y$ on $X$ provides another way of looking at the potential advantage in efficiency of the ANCOVA over the ANOVA. Figure 15.1 schematically indicates how differences between two treatment groups may be easier to observe if the variability in $Y$ predictable from $X$ can be removed. The two ellipses in the central part of the figure represent clouds of data points for two treatment groups. As can be seen from the two distributions plotted on the right vertical axis, the $Y$ scores for the two groups overlap considerably. However, the distributions of the deviations of the data points from the regression lines that are plotted along the left

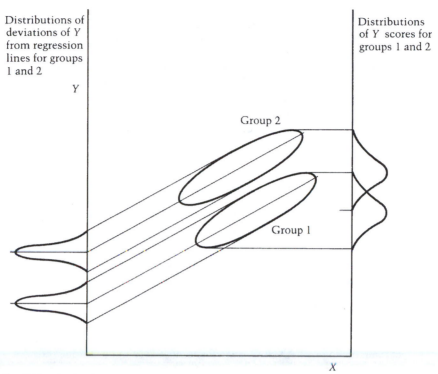

**Fig. 15.1** Distributions of $Y$ scores (right side) and deviations of $Y$ scores from the regression lines (left side) in two groups.

vertical axis show greater separation. We should have more power if we test the equality of the intercepts than if we test the equality of the means.

An ANCOVA may be viewed as a special case of a multiple regression analysis, and we will return to it in that context in Chapter 21. At this point, using the bivariate regression framework developed in Chapter 3, we focus on the basic ideas behind the ANCOVA and on its interpretation—especially on how correct interpretation of the analysis depends on certain assumptions being met. Because we assume that ANCOVAs will be performed using software packages, we will not concern ourselves much with calculations or computational formulas.

## 15.2 EXAMPLE OF AN ANCOVA

### 15.2.1 Introduction

Table 15.1 contains the data for the Myers et al. (1983) probability-learning experiment along with the scores on a quantitative reasoning test, $X$.[2] As mentioned earlier, when we conduct an ANOVA on the dependent variable, $Y$ (proportion of the probability problems solved correctly), we cannot reject the null hypothesis that $\mu_S = \mu_{LE} = \mu_{HE}$, $F(2, 45) = 2.965$,

**TABLE 15.2**    (a) RESULTS OF THE ANOVA OF PROPORTION CORRECT ON THE PROBABILITY PROBLEMS $(Y)$

| SV | df | SS | MS | F | p |
|----|----|----|----|----|----|
| Text [A] | 2 | 0.182 | 0.091 | 2.965 | .062 |
| Error [S/A] | 45 | 1.379 | 0.031 | | |
| Total | 47 | 1.560 | | | |

(b) RESULTS OF THE ANCOVA FOR $Y$ USING $X$ AS A COVARIATE

| SV | df | SS | MS | F | p |
|----|----|----|----|----|----|
| Text [A(adj)] | 2 | 0.205 | 0.102 | 5.081 | .010 |
| X | 1 | 0.492 | 0.492 | 24.383 | .000 |
| Error [S/A(adj)] | 44 | 0.887 | 0.020 | | |
| Total (adj) | 46 | 1.092 | | | |

$p = .062$ [see panel (a) of Table 15.2]. However, we can use $X$ as a covariate and conduct an ANCOVA. When we do so, we find that the null hypothesis can now be rejected, $F(2, 44) = 5.081$, $p = .010$ [see panel (b) of Table 15.2]. In the rest of the section, we explain the logic of ANCOVA and the terms found in the output.

Essentially what we do in an ANCOVA is first to assume that the relation between $Y$ and $X$ is the same in each of the treatment groups, and then estimate what the ANOVA would be like if each subject had the same score on the covariate. Perhaps the best way to think of ANCOVA is in terms of a comparison of two regression models, a **restricted model** $(R)$ in which $Y$ is regressed on $X$ without regard to group membership,

$$Y_{ij} = \mu + \beta_{tot}(X_{ij} - \overline{X}_{..}) + \varepsilon_{ij} \tag{15.4}$$

and a **full model** $(F)$ in which regressions are performed in each group, but it is assumed that they each have the same slope,

$$Y_{ij} = \mu + \alpha_j + \beta_{S/A}(X_{ij} - \overline{X}_{..}) + \varepsilon'_{ij} \tag{15.5}$$

Two points about the preceding equations should be noted. First, the slope parameters in the two models are not the same: $\beta_{tot}$ is estimated by the slope of the overall regression of $Y$ on $X$, whereas $\beta_{S/A}$, the common slope for the within-group regressions, is estimated by an average of the slopes obtained in separate regressions for each of the groups. Therefore, we cannot perform an ANCOVA by simply performing an ANOVA on the residuals of the first regression. The second point is a matter of notation. In ANCOVA, we use $\mu$ to refer to the mean of the $Y$ scores and $\overline{X}$ to refer to the mean of the $X$ scores because, in the usual regression inference model (see Chapter 19), we assume that $X$ is a fixed-effect variable and that $Y$ is random.

The restricted model is represented (for two groups) in panel (a) of Fig. 15.2, and the full model is represented in panel (b). The test of the full against the restricted model asks whether we can account for significantly more variability by performing separate within-groups regressions with a common slope than by performing a single overall regression

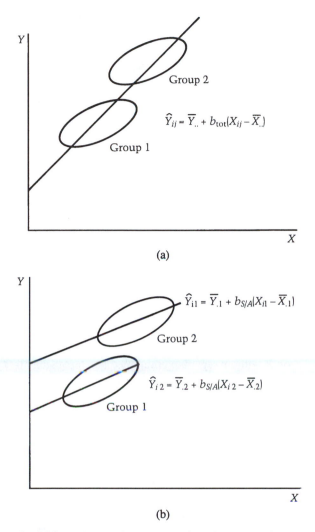

**Fig. 15.2** (a) Schematic representation of the regressions indicated by the model of Equation 15.4. All the data are used to obtain a single regression line. (b) Schematic representation of the regressions indicated by Equation 15.5. Regression lines with equal slopes are obtained for each treatment group.

without regard to group membership. Rejection of the null hypothesis implies that the group intercepts are not all the same.

The appropriate statistic for testing a full model against a restricted one is given by

$$F = \frac{[SS_{\text{error}(R)} - SS_{\text{error}(F)}]/[df_{\text{error}(R)} - df_{\text{error}(F)}]}{SS_{\text{error}(F)}/df_{\text{error}(F)}} \tag{15.6}$$

where $SS_{\text{error}(R)} - SS_{\text{error}(F)}$ represents the reduction in error variability (or equivalently, the additional variability accounted for) when the full model is used instead of the restricted model.

## 15.2.2 Developing Expressions for $SS_{\text{error}(R)}$ and $SS_{\text{error}(F)}$ in an ANCOVA

To perform an ANCOVA, we first need to calculate $SS_{\text{error}(R)}$ and $SS_{\text{error}(F)}$, the error sums of squares associated with the restricted and full models for an ANCOVA. The appropriate equations rest on the development of the error sum of squares for regression in Chapter 3 (see Section 3.7).

$$SS_{\text{error}} = \sum (Y_i - \hat{Y}_i)^2 = (1 - r^2)SS_Y \tag{15.7}$$

where $r$ is the correlation between the dependent variable, $Y$, and the covariate, $X$. Because the equations for an ANCOVA are usually expressed in terms of slopes, we can express $SS_{\text{error}}$ in terms of the slope instead of the correlation. First, we note that from Equation 3.8,

$$b_1 = r\frac{s_Y}{s_X} = r\frac{\sqrt{SS_Y}}{\sqrt{SS_X}} \tag{15.8}$$

where $b_1$ is the slope of the regression of $Y$ on $X$. Substituting $b_1$ for $r$ in Equation 15.7 and rewriting, we obtain

$$SS_{\text{error}} = SS_Y - b_1^2 SS_X \tag{15.9}$$

We can now find the error sums of squares for the restricted and full models. $SS_{\text{error}(R)}$ is the variability in the $Y$ scores not accounted for by the restricted model, that is, not accounted for by a regression of $Y$ on $X$ without regard to group membership, using all $N$ data points. From Equation 15.9,

$$SS_{\text{error}(R)} = SS_Y - b_{\text{tot}}^2 SS_X = SS_{\text{total(adj)}}$$

where

$$b_{\text{tot}} = \frac{\sum_i \sum_j (X_{ij} - \overline{X}_{..})(Y_{ij} - \overline{Y}_{..})}{\sum_i \sum_j (X_{ij} - \overline{X}_{..})^2}$$

is the slope of the overall (or total) regression of $Y$ on $X$. $SS_{\text{error}(R)}$ is sometimes referred to as the **adjusted total sum of squares of $Y$**, or $SS_{\text{total(adj)}}$. For the current example, $SS_Y = 1.560$, $SS_X = 9538.979$, and $b_{\text{tot}} = 0.0070$, so that $SS_{\text{error}(R)} = 1.092$.

$SS_{\text{error}(F)}$ is the variability not accounted for by the full model (Equation 15.5); that is, the variability left unaccounted for by separate regressions in each of the groups in which each slope is assumed to have the same value, $b_{S/A}$. If we label the S, LE, and HE text conditions as Groups 1, 2, and 3, we have

$$
\begin{aligned}
SS_{\text{error}(F)} &= SS_{\text{error(group 1)}} + SS_{\text{error(group 2)}} + SS_{\text{error(group 3)}} \\
&= \left(SS_{Y_1} - b_{S/A}^2 SS_{X_1}\right) + \left(SS_{Y_2} - b_{S/A}^2 SS_{X_2}\right) + \left(SS_{Y_3} - b_{S/A}^2 SS_{X_3}\right) \\
&= \left(SS_{Y_1} + SS_{Y_2} + SS_{Y_3}\right) - b_{S/A}^2 \left(SS_{X_1} + SS_{X_2} + SS_{X_3}\right) \\
&= SS_{S/A} - SS_{\text{regression (within groups)}} = SS_{S/A(\text{adj})}
\end{aligned}
\tag{15.10}
$$

$SS_{\text{error}(F)}$ is sometimes referred to as the adjusted within sum of squares $SS_{S/A(\text{adj})}$. As we will see in Section 15.3.4, the interpretation of an ANCOVA depends on the assumption that, in the population, the slopes of the regression lines are the same for each group. The estimate of this common slope, $b_{S/A}$, is obtained as a weighted average of the slopes found when separate regressions are conducted in each group, where the weights are the sums of squares of $X$ for each group. That is,

$$b_{S/A} = \frac{\sum b_j SS_{X_j}}{\sum SS_{X_j}}$$

In the current example, separate regressions of $Y$ on $X$ for Groups 1, 2, and 3 are 0.00786, 0.00858, and 0.00581, respectively, so that

$$b_{S/A} = \frac{(.00786)(2190.435) + (.00858)(3388.935) + (.00581)(3590.937)}{2190.435 + 3388.935 + 3590.937} = 0.00732$$

Substituting into Equation 15.10, we find $SS_{\text{error}(F)} = 0.887$. The main effect of text can now be tested according to Equation 15.6,

$$F = \frac{[SS_{\text{error}(R)} - SS_{\text{error}(F)}]/[df_{\text{error}(R)} - df_{\text{error}(F)}]}{SS_{\text{error}(F)}/df_{\text{error}(F)}}$$

$$= \frac{SS_{A(\text{adj})}/(a-1)}{SS_{S/A(\text{adj})}/(N-a-1)}$$

Note that there is one fewer degree of freedom for the ANCOVA error term than for the corresponding ANOVA because 1 $df$ is used to estimate $b_{S/A}$. For the current example, $F = [(1.092 - 0.887)/2](0.887/44) = 5.081$ and $p = .010$.

Table 15.2 summarizes the analysis and Table 15.3 describes the terms usually found in the software output. Different software packages present somewhat different outputs, but they all present certain sources of variance. One is the source of variance labeled by the name of the independent variable, which is the $A(\text{adj})$ term listed in Tables 15.2 and 15.3. This has a sum of squares equal to $SS_{\text{error}(R)} - SS_{\text{error}(F)}$. A second source of variance that is usually included is labeled by the name of the covariate; this is $SS_{\text{regression(within groups)}}$. A third source of variance, usually labeled as "error," is the $S/A(\text{adj})$ term that has a sum of squares equal to $SS_{\text{error}(F)}$.

## 15.2.3 Adjusting the Group Means in $Y$ for Differences in $X$

In the previous section, we showed how $SS_A$ and $SS_{S/A}$ could be adjusted for differences in the covariate. Similarly, in certain situations, it is both possible and desirable to adjust the mean of the group $Y$ scores for covariate differences. To do the adjustment, we predict what the group means for $Y$ would be if the value of the covariate was held constant. In our example, the mean of the scores on the covariate is highest for the LE text condition (65.938) and lowest for the S condition (59.188). We define the **adjusted mean** of the scores for Group $j$, $\overline{Y}_{\cdot j(\text{adj})}$, as the score predicted in Group $j$ using the within-group regression equation with common slope $b_{S/A}$ if the value of the covariate is equal to the grand mean of the covariate scores; that is, if $X_{ij} = \overline{X}_{\cdots}$.

Starting with Equation 3.11, a form of the regression equation for predicting $Y$ from $X$,

$$\hat{Y} = \overline{Y} + b_1(X_i - \overline{X})$$

**TABLE 15.3** EXPLANATION OF THE TERMS IN AN ANCOVA

| SV | df | SS | Explanation |
|---|---|---|---|
| A(adj) | $a - 1$ | $SS_{\text{error}(R)} - SS_{\text{error}(F)}$ $= SS_{\text{total(adj)}} - SS_{S/A(\text{adj})}$ | The variability accounted for by the full model (Equation 15.5) over and above that accounted for by the restricted model (Equation 15.4) |
| X | 1 | $SS_{\text{regression (within groups)}}$ $= SS_{\text{regression (group1)}} + \cdots + SS_{\text{regression(group }a)}$ $= b_{S/A}^2 \sum SS_{X_j}$ | The sums of squares accounted for by separate regressions in each group, but with common slope $b_{S/A}$ |
| S/A(adj) | $N - a - 1$ | $SS_{\text{error}(F)} = SS_{S/A} - SS_{\text{regression(within groups)}}$ $= SS_{\text{error(group1)}} + \cdots + SS_{\text{error(group }a)}$ $= \sum \left( SS_{Y_j} - b_{S/A}^2 \, SS_{X_j} \right)$ | The summed residual variability in the groups; that is the variability not accounted for by the within-group regressions using the common slope, $b_{S/A}$ |
| Total (adj) | $N - 2$ | $SS_{\text{error}(R)} = SS_Y - SS_{\text{regression(total)}}$ $= SS_Y - b_{\text{tot}}^2 \, SS_X$ | The residual variability in $Y$ not accounted for by the overall regression on $X$ |

*Note.* If $Y$ is regressed on $X$, $SS_{\text{regression}} = r^2 SS_Y = b^2 SS_X$ and $SS_{\text{error}} = SS_Y - b^2 SS_X$. The common slope, $b_{S/A}$, is obtained as a weighted average of the slopes, $(b_j\text{'s})$, obtained in separate regressions, where the weights are the sums of squares of $X$ for the groups; that is $b_{S/A} = \sum b_j SS_{X_j} / \sum SS_{X_j}$.

the regression equation for scores in Group $j$ is

$$\hat{Y}_{ij} = \overline{Y}_{\cdot j} + b_1(X_{ij} - \overline{X}_{\cdot j})$$

Substituting $b_{S/A}$ for $b_1$ and $\overline{X}_{\cdot\cdot}$ for $X_{ij}$, we have

$$\overline{Y}_{\cdot j(\text{adj})} = \overline{Y}_{\cdot j} + b_{S/A}(\overline{X}_{\cdot\cdot} - \overline{X}_{\cdot j})$$

or

$$\overline{Y}_{\cdot j(\text{adj})} = \overline{Y}_{\cdot j} - b_{S/A}(\overline{X}_{\cdot j} - \overline{X}_{\cdot\cdot}) \tag{15.11}$$

In our example, the adjusted group means for the S, LE, and HE text conditions are

$$\overline{Y}_{\cdot 1(\text{adj})} = .396 - (.00732)(59.188 - 62.355) = .419$$
$$\overline{Y}_{\cdot 2(\text{adj})} = .406 - (.00732)(65.938 - 62.355) = .380$$

and

$$\overline{Y}_{\cdot 3(\text{adj})} = .531 - (.00732)(61.938 - 62.355) = .534$$

## 15.2.4 Testing Contrasts Using the Adjusted Means

If the assumptions for the ANCOVA are met, we can test contrasts based on the adjusted means; these tests are generally more powerful than those using unadjusted means. Suppose we wished to test the null hypothesis

$$H_0: \quad \psi = \mu_{\text{HE}} - \frac{\mu_S + \mu_{\text{LE}}}{2}$$

Using the procedures described in Chapter 9, we would use the test statistic

$$t = \frac{\hat{\psi}}{s_{\hat{\psi}}} = \frac{\overline{Y}_{\text{HE}} - \dfrac{\overline{Y}_S + \overline{Y}_{\text{LE}}}{2}}{\sqrt{MS_{S/A} \sum \dfrac{w_j^2}{n_j}}} = \frac{.531 - \dfrac{.396 + .406}{2}}{\sqrt{(.031)(1.5/16)}} = 2.411 \text{ with 45 } df,$$

so that we could reject the null hypothesis at $p = .019$.

Using procedures described in Huitema (1980), we can form a contrast using the adjusted means. The procedure is essentially the same as that for the unadjusted means, except that the error term contains corrections for the covariate. For a completely randomized design, the recommended test statistic is

$$t = \frac{\hat{\psi}_{(\text{adj})}}{s_{\hat{\psi}(\text{adj})}} = \frac{\overline{Y}_{\text{HE}(\text{adj})} - \dfrac{\overline{Y}_{S(\text{adj})} + \overline{Y}_{\text{LE}(\text{adj})}}{2}}{\sqrt{MS_{S/A(\text{adj})}\left(\sum \dfrac{w_j^2}{n_j}\right)\left(1 + \dfrac{MS_{A(X)}}{SS_{S/A(X)}}\right)}} \tag{15.12}$$

where $MS_{A(X)}$ and $SS_{S/A(X)}$ are the between mean squares and the within sum of squares obtained when an ANOVA is performed on the covariate. Substituting into Equation 15.12, we have

$$t = \frac{\hat{\Psi}_{(adj)}}{s_{\hat{\Psi}(adj)}} = \frac{.534 - \dfrac{.419 + 380}{2}}{\sqrt{(.020)(1.5/16)\left(1 + \dfrac{184.333}{9170.312}\right)}}$$

$$= .135/.044 = 3.089 \text{ with } 44 \ df$$

We can now reject the null hypothesis at $p = .003$. We obtained a larger value of the test statistic using the adjusted means, although we lost one error degree of freedom. In observational studies (i.e., studies in which subjects are not randomly assigned to conditions), the recommended error term is different, and now contains a correction that depends on the specific contrast that is tested,

$$s_{\hat{\Psi}(adj)} = \sqrt{MS_{S/A(adj)}\left(\sum \frac{w_j^2}{n_j} + \frac{\left(\sum w_j \overline{X}_{\cdot j}\right)^2}{SS_{S/A(X)}}\right)}$$

For a good discussion of these issues, see Huitema (1980).

If several contrasts are tested, Type 1 error can be controlled in much the same way as was discussed in Chapter 9. If there are several planned contrasts, we can use the Dunn–Bonferroni method. For post hoc contrasts, if we wish to use the Scheffé test, the $t$ statistics obtained earlier can be referred to the criterion $\sqrt{(a-1)F_{FWE,\,a-1,N-a-1}}$. For the Tukey post hoc test of pairwise differences, the same test statistics can be used with weights $+1$ and $-1$. If the covariate is a fixed-effect variable, the test statistic can be referred to $q_{FWE,a,df_{error}}/\sqrt{2}$, where $q$ is a critical value of the studentized range statistic (Appendix Table C.9) that we used with the Tukey test in Chapter 9. If the covariate is a random variable, as is usually the case, Bryant and Paulson (1976) have shown that $q$ should be replaced by $Q_{FWE,a,c,df_{error}}$, a value of the generalized studentized range statistic in which $c$ is the number of covariates. Tables of the generalized studentized range statistic are available in Huitema (1980) and Kirk (1995).

## 15.3 ASSUMPTIONS AND INTERPRETATION IN AN ANCOVA

### 15.3.1 Introduction

When an ANCOVA is used instead of an ANOVA, increases in power may be achieved at the cost of greater complexity and more assumptions. The standard assumptions for an ANCOVA break down into two groups. As in an ordinary ANOVA, some assumptions are necessary for the ratio of adjusted mean squares to be distributed as $F$. However, unless certain additional assumptions, such as homogeneity of regression and identity of the $X$ populations are met, the ANCOVA $F$ may test a different null hypothesis than an ordinary ANOVA, and the adjusted means may be biased estimates of the population means. In the sections that follow, we will discuss these assumptions and the consequences of violating them.

### 15.3.2 Normality and Homogeneity of Variance

In an ANCOVA, it is assumed that the conditional distributions of $Y$ at different values of $X$ are normal and have equal variances. In general, the consequences of violating these assumptions are similar to those for an ANOVA, with the exception that they depend to some extent on the distribution of the covariate (see Huitema, 1980, for a more detailed discussion of these assumptions). An ANCOVA is unlikely to be severely biased by violations of the normality and homogeneity of variance assumptions, provided there are equal numbers of participants in each group and the covariate itself is approximately normally distributed.

## 15.3.3 Linearity

As we have so far discussed it, an ANCOVA adjusts for differences in the covariate by removing the variability accounted for by a linear regression on $X$. If there is a systematic nonlinear component to the relation between $X$ and $Y$, the use of linear regression will not remove all the variability in $Y$ potentially accounted for by $X$. The effect of moderate nonlinearity is a slight negative bias in the ANCOVA $F$ test. Although it is rare in the behavioral sciences to observe strongly nonlinear relations, they can result in severely biased $F$ tests if a linear ANCOVA is used (Atiqullah, 1964). However, if the nature of the nonlinearities can be specified, transformations of $Y$ or polynomial ANCOVAs (see Section 15.8) may be used. It is recommended that the linearity assumption be checked as a preliminary step in using the ANCOVA. Plotting the group scatter diagrams offers a quick check, and a significance test for nonlinearity is also available (see Chapter 19).

## 15.3.4 Assumption of Homogeneity of Regression Slopes

In an ANCOVA, we adjust for differences in the covariate. However, an ANCOVA makes sense only if the same type of adjustment is appropriate for each treatment group. Therefore, we make the strong assumption that in the population the slopes are equal in each of the groups. This assumption should be tested (see Section 15.4), and the results of an ANCOVA should be reported only if homogeneity cannot be rejected.

In the one-factor ANCOVA design, we estimate the common slope, $\beta_{S/A}$, by using the pooled within-group slope, $b_{S/A}$, essentially an average of the slopes obtained in within-groups regressions. If the slopes in the different groups are not equal, using any kind of "average" adjustment will be inappropriate for at least some of the groups. An analogy can be made between an adjusted $A$ main effect in an ANCOVA in the presence of heterogeneous slopes, and an $A$ main effect in the presence of an interaction between $A$ and a second factor, $B$, in an ANOVA. If there is a large interaction, particularly if the curves cross, the $F$ test of $A$ may not adequately reflect the $A$ effect at any level of $B$. Similarly, if the group regression coefficients vary, the effect of $A$ varies with $X$ and the ANCOVA $F$ test may produce misleading results.

It may help to describe the situation using diagrams. When $Y$ is adjusted for the effects of the covariate, $X$, treatment effects are interpreted in terms of differences in the intercepts of the group regression lines instead of differences in the group means (see Fig. 15.1). Suppose that the lines in each panel of Fig. 15.3 represent regression lines obtained separately for two treatment groups. Parallel lines, illustrated in panel (a), indicate that the

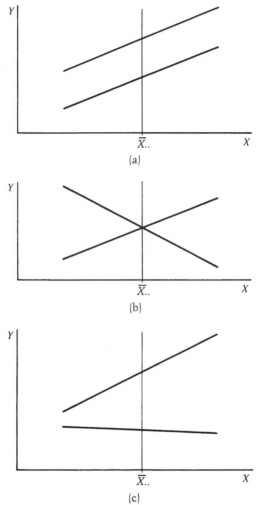

**Fig. 15.3** Regressions with homogeneous and heterogeneous slopes.

treatment effects are the same for each value of the covariate. In this case, we can identify the treatment effects with the vertical distance between the lines. On the other hand, nonparallel lines, illustrated in panels (b) and (c), indicate that the treatment effects are not the same for each value of $X$. In panel (b), the two lines intersect at $X = \overline{X}..$, but differ considerably for high and low values of $X$. In panel (c), there is a separation between the two lines at $X = \overline{X}..$, but the separation is larger for large $X$ and smaller for small $X$. For panels (b) and (c), it is of more interest to ask for what values of $X$, if any, the separations are significant than to consider the separation at any single value of $X$. Johnson and Neyman (1936) have developed a procedure for establishing regions of significance on the covariate. The Johnson–Neyman technique and related procedures are described in several sources; for example, Huitema (1980) and Hunka and Leighton (1997).

## 15.3.5 Assumption That the Treatment and Covariate Are Independent

An ANCOVA should not be used to analyze designs in which the covariate varies systematically with the treatment. If the treatment influences the covariate, or is otherwise systematically related to it, performing an ANCOVA will not simply reduce error variance; it may adjust between-group differences in ways that are difficult to understand and lead to biased tests.

It was appropriate to use an ANCOVA to test the effect of text condition for the Myers et al. experiment because participants were randomly assigned to the text conditions, and there was no way that the treatment could influence the covariate. However, suppose everything else was kept the same, except that participants were given the quantitative reasoning test at the end of the experiment instead of before they saw the text material. In this case, we should not use the quantitative reasoning test as a covariate if material given in the text conditions might affect performance on the test. If test performance was affected and we went ahead and used it as a covariate, the ANCOVA would not only remove some of the error variance, but it would also remove some of the effect of the treatment.

Suppose instead, rather than randomly assigning participants to text conditions, the different text materials were presented to intact groups—say the LE text was given to a class of psychology majors and the S and HE texts were given to classes of English and fine arts majors, thereby confounding text condition with major. We would say that we had a **nonequivalent-groups design**. Some researchers seem to believe that performing an ANCOVA can appropriately adjust the groups for their preexisting differences. However, even though the groups may differ on the covariate, the confounding cannot be magically removed by performing an ANCOVA. The underlying groups may differ on many variables, and many of these differences are not likely to be fully predictable from a covariate. If treatments are applied to intact groups that differ from one another, an ANCOVA presents the same kinds of difficulties that are always associated with interpreting the results of observational studies. Whenever the covariate varies systematically across conditions, it becomes correlated with other variables that differ across groups, including the treatment itself. Performing an ANCOVA tends to adjust the effects of all of these variables, but to different degrees. This will be the case even when the distinctions among the intact groups are more subtle.

Consider another example in which the independent variable and covariate might be correlated. Suppose in an experiment conducted to evaluate three different teaching programs, students are given material to study on their own, and then are tested on it. Suppose the mean test score for Program 1 is larger than the means for Programs 2 and 3, and an ANOVA performed on the test scores is significant, suggesting that the three programs are not all equally effective. However, the experimenter notes that students assigned to Program 1 spend more time actually working with the material than students assigned to the other programs and decides to perform an ANCOVA using "study time" as the covariate. The ANCOVA reveals no significant differences, and so the experimenter concludes that the three programs would be equally effective if study time was held constant. This interpretation is not necessarily correct. Statistically controlling for study time is not the same as experimentally controlling or manipulating it and no causal statements are justified; we simply do not know from these data what would happen if study time was actually held constant. The materials used in Program 1 may be more understandable and interesting to work with than that used in the other programs; these qualities may be the cause of both the superior test performance and the greater study time. Using study time as a covariate will tend to remove the effects of any variables correlated with study time, including the characteristics of the program that are actually responsible for the superior performance. It is therefore entirely possible that Program 1 would produce superior performance even if study time was actually equated.

"Controlling" study time by throwing out data is also not appropriate. Suppose that the mean daily study time is 40 min for the first group and 25 min for the other two groups. What if we analyze only the performance scores for students in the three groups who have comparable study times, say 30–35 min? This is a poor strategy because in selecting students who have comparable study times, we may be selecting students who differ widely on other important characteristics. There is no reason to think that students in the first group whose study times are below that group's average are comparable in ability and motivation to students who have above average study times in the other two groups. If one is interested in the effects of the program and study time, there is simply no substitute for conducting a true experiment in which both variables are manipulated.

The assumption of independence of the treatment and covariate can be tested by performing an ANOVA on the covariate. In nonequivalent groups designs, a significant ANOVA result for a covariate measured before the treatments have been administered indicates that the ANCOVA $F'$s and adjusted means will almost certainly be biased. Unfortunately, a nonsignificant ANOVA cannot be taken as an indication that there will be no bias, although the bias is more likely to be small. In completely randomized designs, there will be no bias for covariates measured before treatments have been administered. However, ANOVAs should be performed on covariates measured during or following treatment.

## 15.3.6 Assumption That the Covariate Is Fixed and Measured Without Error

As we shall see in Chapter 19, the standard model for making statistical inferences about regression assumes that the variable used to predict $Y$ is a fixed-effect variable that is measured without error. In ANCOVA this translates into the assumption that the covariate has these properties. However, the assumption that the covariate is a fixed-effect variable can generally be violated without serious consequences and, indeed, the most common applications of ANCOVA are with random covariates. For randomized designs, measurement error results in reduced power. However, for nonequivalent groups designs, measurement error in the covariate can result in increased bias and, therefore, even greater difficulties in interpretation. In a nonequivalent groups design, if the mean covariate value varies across groups and if the covariate is measured with error, the expected values of the adjusted $Y$s may differ even if the treatment has no effect. Figure 15.4 illustrates the problem for two groups in which the true scores of $X$ and $Y$ are perfectly correlated and there are no treatment effects. In panel (a), $X$ is measured without error and both group equations have the same slope and intercept. Therefore, the adjusted means for these groups must be the same and an ANCOVA would correctly reveal that there are no treatment effects. Panel (b) represents exactly the same situation, except that now $X$ is measured with error. The effect of the measurement error will be to "spread out" the values of $X$ and reduce the slopes for both groups. As can be seen in panel (b), the adjusted $Y$ mean will now be larger for the group that has the larger values of $X$, even though there is no treatment effect. Because groups

**TABLE 15.4** SYSTAT OUTPUT FOR TESTING THE HOMOGENEITY OF GROUP SLOPES

```
Effects coding used for categorical variables in model.
Categorical values encountered during processing are: TEXT (3 levels)
           1,       2,       3

Dep Var: Y   N: 48   Multiple R: 0.66374   Squared multiple R: 0.44055
Analysis of Variance
```

| Source | Sum-of-Squares | df | Mean-Square | F-ratio | P |
|--------|----------------|----|-----|----|----|
| TEXT | 0.048 | 2 | 0.024 | 1.146 | 0.328 |
| X | 0.480 | 1 | 0.480 | 23.114 | 0.000 |
| TEXT*X | 0.014 | 2 | 0.007 | 0.341 | 0.713 |
| Error | 0.873 | 42 | 0.021 | | |

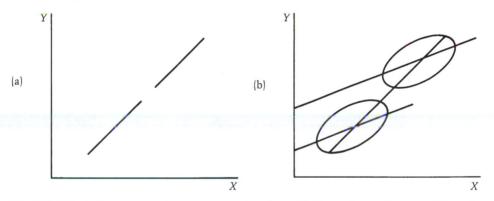

**Fig. 15.4** Effect of measurement error on regression slopes. Both samples are from populations in which the true scores of $Y$ and $X$ are perfectly correlated and no treatment is applied. $X$ is measured (a) without error and (b) with error.

do not differ systematically from one another in randomized designs, measurement error in $X$ will result in reduced power, but will not cause the adjusted means to be biased. However, in nonequivalent groups designs, measurement error in $X$ will introduce bias. Quite apart from the issue of measurement error, Fig. 15.4 provides another illustration that when nonequivalent groups are used, bias is introduced if the dependent variable and covariate are not perfectly correlated.

## 15.4 TESTING HOMOGENEITY OF SLOPES

As we discussed in Section 15.3.4, a necessary assumption for ANCOVA is that the slopes are equal in each of the treatment populations. In practice, the easiest way to test this is to use a software package such as SPSS or SYSTAT to test whether the independent variable interacts with the covariate, a test that is equivalent to testing homogeneity of slopes. Table 15.4 presents the SYSTAT output for this test. The interaction is not significant, $F(2, 42) = 0.341$, $p = .713$. We cannot reject the hypothesis that the slopes are homogeneous and therefore proceed with the ANCOVA. This analysis is equivalent to comparing a restricted model in which regressions with a common slope are performed for the separate groups,

$$Y_{ij} = \mu + \alpha_j + \beta_{S/A}(X_{ij} - \overline{X}_{..}) + \varepsilon'_{ij} \tag{15.5}$$

(note that this is the ANCOVA model), and a full model in which the separate within-group regressions are not constrained to have the same slope

$$Y_{ij} = \mu + \alpha_j + \beta_j(X_{ij} - \overline{X}_{..}) + \varepsilon''_{ij} \tag{15.13}$$

## 15.5 MORE ABOUT ANCOVA VERSUS TREATMENTS × BLOCKS

Both the ANCOVA and the Treatments × Blocks design use information about a concomitant variable, $X$, to increase power. It is therefore of interest to discuss the advantages and disadvantages of both designs. However, in doing so, we must consider how participants are assigned to treatment conditions, as well as what statistical analysis is subsequently used. We distinguish among four cases:

1. *Treatments × Blocks with a priori blocking.* As described in Section 15.1, this design requires that participants be divided into $b$ blocks on the basis of their $X$ scores, where the optimal value of $b$ (Feldt, 1958) depends on $N$, the number of treatment conditions, and the correlation between $X$ and the dependent variable. Within each block, participants are randomly assigned to treatment conditions. Finally, a two-factor Treatments × Blocks ANOVA is performed.
2. *Treatments × Blocks with post hoc blocking.* In this case, participants are assigned to treatment conditions without regard to their $X$ values. Blocks are formed after the $Y$ scores have been collected, and the design is analyzed as a two-factor ANOVA.
3. *ANCOVA with random assignment of participants to treatment conditions.* Participants are assigned to treatment conditions without regard to their $X$ values as in (2); however, an ANCOVA is performed.
4. *ANCOVA with assignment of participants to conditions based on the covariate value.* If the covariate values are available before the experiment is conducted, they can be used in assigning participants to conditions, even if an ANCOVA is to be used. For example, if the independent variable has $a$ levels, the $a$ participants with the highest scores on $X$ can be randomly distributed across the treatment conditions, then the participants with the next $a$ highest scores, and so on. In the case of two treatment groups, several authors (Dalton & Overall, 1977; Maxwell, Delaney, & Dill, 1984) have recommended the alternate ranks design in which the participants are ranked with respect to $X$ and then assigned to conditions $A_1$ and $A_2$ according to an $A_1 A_2 A_2 A_1 A_1 A_2 A_2 \ldots$ sequence. Whether the assignment of each $a$ scores to the levels of $A$ is made randomly or based on the alternative ranks design, the means of $X$ should vary less than in cases 2 and 3.

In a classic paper, Feldt (1958) compared methods 1 and 3. He found that an ANCOVA was more powerful than Treatments × Blocks with the optimal number of blocks when $\rho$, the population correlation between $Y$ and $X$, was greater than .6; that blocking was more powerful for $\rho$ less than .4; and that there was little difference for $.4 < \rho < .6$. Because of these findings and the complexity and stringent assumptions of an ANCOVA, it has often been argued that blocking should be used instead of an ANCOVA, except when $\rho$ is large.

However, in practice, it will not be possible for the experimenter to decide on the optimal number of blocks unless a good estimate of the correlation between $X$ and $Y$ is available before participants are assigned to blocks and the $Y$ scores are obtained. The ANCOVA designs do not require this information in advance. Also, when assignment to groups is considered as well as the method of analysis, there seem to be reasons to favor an ANCOVA over blocking, even for moderate values of $\rho$. Maxwell et al. (1984) used simulation procedures to test the power and precision of nine methods, including the four listed previously. Although in their simulations they used an independent variable with only two levels, it is likely that their findings hold more generally.

When information about $X$ is not used in assigning subjects to treatment conditions, an ANCOVA tends to have strong advantages over post hoc blocking. Maxwell et al. (1984) found method 3 to be more powerful and precise than method 2, even for values of $\rho$ as low as .28. Another disadvantage of post hoc blocking is that it will usually lead to designs with disproportionate cell frequencies. If post hoc blocks are to be formed, they should be based on the $X$ values of all members of the entire sample, without regard to group assignment. If this is done, it is unlikely that there will be equal numbers of scores in each of the $ab$ cells. As discussed in Chapter 12, such designs involve problems of analysis and interpretation. Experimenters should be very careful to avoid forming post hoc blocks within each group. As Myers (1979) has pointed out, this will lead to positively biased $F$ tests.

Maxwell et al. also suggest that advantages in power and precision may be obtained by using the values of $X$ to assign participants to conditions (method 4). They found that when participants were assigned to conditions using an alternative ranks procedure, both the ANCOVA and Treatments × Blocks ANOVA were more powerful than when assignment was made without regard to $X$. Also, both when $X$ was used in assigning participants to treatments and when it was not, the ANCOVA was found to be slightly more powerful than the Treatments × Blocks ANOVA for $\rho = .28$ and had a larger advantage for $\rho = .50$.

In summary, if the concomitant measure is available prior to data collection, greater power may be achieved if it is used in assigning participants to treatment conditions. In addition, if the relation between $Y$ and $X$ is linear and the other assumptions of an ANCOVA are reasonably satisfied, the ANCOVA will generally provide more power than the Treatments × Blocks ANOVA.

Finally, several comments should be made with respect to the ANCOVA assumptions. As we have so far discussed it, the ANCOVA assumes a linear relation between $X$ and $Y$, whereas the Treatments × Blocks analysis does not depend on the nature of the functional relation between $X$ and $Y$. The Treatments × Blocks design will therefore be relatively more powerful to the extent that there are nonlinearities that are not accounted for by the ANCOVA analysis. However, relations in the behavioral sciences are often approximately linear. If there is a nonlinear relation, transformations of $Y$ or generalized ANCOVAs that depend on polynomial regression may be performed.

The fact that the ANCOVA requires the strong assumption of homogeneity of regression slopes is sometimes mentioned as a reason to favor Treatments × Blocks designs. However, heterogeneity of regression slopes is conceptually the same as an interaction in a Treatments × Blocks ANOVA; in both cases, it is not advisable to interpret the treatment main effect. Also, although most researchers are more familiar with simple effects tests, the nature of group differences at different values of the covariate will be revealed in more detail by the Johnson–Neyman technique than by simple effects tests (see, Huitema, 1980, Chapter 13).

## 15.6 ESTIMATING POWER IN AN ANCOVA

We considered how to find the power for a one-factor ANOVA in Chapter 8. We began by estimating the quantity

$$f = \sqrt{\frac{\sigma_A^2}{\sigma_e^2}} \tag{15.14}$$

where, for the current example, $\sigma_A^2$ can be estimated from

$$\left(\frac{a-1}{a}\right)\left(\frac{MS_A - MS_{S/A}}{n}\right) = \left(\frac{2}{3}\right)\left(\frac{.091 - .031}{16}\right) = .0025$$

and $\sigma_e^2$ can be estimated from $MS_{S/A} = .031$. The estimate of $f$ is, therefore,

$$\hat{f} = \sqrt{\frac{.0025}{.031}} \approx .284$$

Using GPOWER (see Table 8.10), we find the post hoc power to be approximately .38. We can also perform a priori power calculations. Again, using GPOWER, we find that given $f = .284$; we need approximately 41 participants per condition to have power = .80.

How can we estimate power for an ANCOVA The major change in an ANCOVA is that the error variance is reduced. It can be shown that the estimated error variance will be

$$\text{estimated } MS_{S/A(\text{adj})} = MS_{S/A}\left(1 - r_{S/A}^2\right)\left(\frac{df_{\text{error(ANOVA)}}}{df_{\text{error(ANCOVA)}}}\right) \tag{15.15}$$

where $r_{S/A}^2$ is the squared within-group correlation between the covariate and the dependent variable. For the current example, this correlation is about .6, so that, substituting into Equation 15.15, the estimated error variance is

$$(.031)(1 - .60^2)\left(\frac{45}{44}\right) = .020,$$

the value actually obtained for $MS_{S/A(\text{adj})}$ when the ANCOVA was performed. Now substituting into the denominator of the expression for $f$ in Equation 15.14, we find

$$\hat{f} = \sqrt{.0025/.020} = \sqrt{.125} = .354.$$

Using GPOWER,[3] we find that the post hoc power for the ANCOVA is .55 and that we would need about 27 participants per condition to achieve a power of .80.

## 15.7 ANCOVA IN HIGHER-ORDER DESIGNS

Sources of variance can be adjusted for a covariate in multifactor designs in much the same way as the one-factor design we have so far considered. Again, the test for each effect can be thought of as a comparison between a full and a restricted model. For example, if we have two between-subjects factors $A$ and $C$, and a covariate $X$, the full model for the ANCOVA is

$$Y_{ijk} = \mu + \alpha_j + \gamma_k + (\alpha\gamma)_{jk} + \beta_{S/AC}(X_{ijk} - \overline{X}...) + \varepsilon_{ijk}$$

where a common slope is assumed in each of the $ac$ groups. The restricted models for the $A$ and $C$ main effects and the $AC$ interaction are, respectively,

$$Y_{ijk} = \mu + \gamma_k + (\alpha\gamma)_{jk} + \beta_{S/AC}(X_{ijk} - \overline{X}...) + \varepsilon_{ijk}$$
$$Y_{ijk} = \mu + \alpha_j + (\alpha\gamma)_{jk} + \beta_{S/AC}(X_{ijk} - \overline{X}...) + \varepsilon_{ijk}$$

and

$$Y_{ijk} = \mu + \alpha_j + \gamma_k + \beta_{S/AC}(X_{ijk} - \overline{X}...) + \varepsilon_{ijk}$$

The adjusted $SS$ for any effect $E$, $SS_{E(\text{adj})}$, is the reduction in $SS_{\text{error}}$ that results when the full model is applied instead of the restricted model in which $E$ is omitted. In each case, the effect is tested using Equation 15.6, which becomes

$$F = \frac{SS_{E(\text{adj})}/df_{E(\text{adj})}}{SS_{\text{error(adj)}}/df_{\text{error(adj)}}}$$

where $SS_{\text{error(adj)}}$ is the error left unaccounted for in the $ac$ cells when the full model is applied. The appropriate $F$ statistics are readily calculated by many software packages.

## 15.8 SOME EXTENSIONS OF THE ANCOVA

In this section, we briefly introduce the ideas of adjustments for more than one covariate and adjustments based on polynomial regression. Because these procedures fit particularly well into a multiple regression framework, we defer more detailed consideration of them until Chapter 21. However, these extensions can easily be accommodated by the standard statistical packages.

### 15.8.1 More Than One Covariate

Suppose that our dependent variable is problem-solving performance ($Y$), but that now we have available two possible covariates: scores on analytic reasoning ($X$) and verbal skills ($W$) tests. We might wish to use either of the covariates in an ANCOVA; however, we may choose to use both of them in the same analysis. This would involve testing a full model that contains a treatment component as well as the covariates

$$Y_{ij} = \mu + \alpha_j + \beta_{YX}(X_{ij} - \overline{X}..) + \beta_{YW}(W_{ij} - \overline{W}..) + \varepsilon_{ij}$$

against a restricted model that contains the covariates, but not the treatment,

$$Y_{ij} = \mu + \beta_{YX}(X_{ij} - \overline{X}..) + \beta_{YW}(W_{ij} - \overline{W}..) + \varepsilon_{ij}$$

If $X$ and $W$ are both correlated with $Y$, but not completely redundant, it is possible that using both covariates will result in a greater gain in power than using either one by itself.

### 15.8.2 Polynomial ANCOVA

Suppose our dependent measure ($Y$) is performance; our possible covariate is a measure of anxiety ($X$), and we know that the relation between $X$ and $Y$ contains both strong linear and quadratic components. It would be inappropriate to use ANCOVA based on the regression of $Y$ on $X$ alone because this will adjust only for the linear component of the relation. However, it is possible to use an ANCOVA model that contains both linear and quadratic components. In this case the full model would be

$$Y_{ij} = \mu + \alpha_j + \beta_1(X_{ij} - \overline{X}..) + \beta_2(X_{ij}^2 - \overline{X..^2}) + \varepsilon_{ijk}$$

and the restricted model would be

$$Y_{ij} = \mu + \beta_1(X_{ij} - \overline{X}..) + \beta_2(X_{ij}^2 - \overline{X..^2}) + \varepsilon_{ijk}$$

(note that $\overline{X..^2}$ is the average of the squared scores, $X_{ij}^2$, not the square of the mean, $\overline{X}..$). The combined linear and quadratic components should together partial out more of the error variability than the linear component alone, and thereby provide a more powerful analysis.

## 15.9 CONCLUDING REMARKS

When used with an understanding of its assumptions and limitations, ANCOVA can be a useful tool. However, ANCOVA is, as Elashoff (1969) has termed it, a "delicate instrument," and there is great potential for its abuse, especially because it is so easy to perform ANCOVAs with the standard statistical packages. The greatest abuses occur when ANCOVA is used to try to equate groups that are basically different from one another. In such cases, Smith (1957) has argued that adjusted means might better be referred to as "fictitious means," and the use of ANCOVA can result in worse inferences than using no adjustment whatsoever. Although it seems trite to repeat it, one must always keep in mind that statistical control is not the same as experimental control, and that correlation and prediction are not the same as causation.

## KEY CONCEPTS

| | |
|---|---|
| error variance | concomitant variable |
| covariate | treatment by blocks design |
| completely randomized design | $SS_{\text{regression (total)}}$ |
| $SS_{\text{regression(within groups)}}$ | $SS_{\text{error}(R)}$ |
| $SS_{\text{error(F)}}$ | $SS_{\text{total(adj)}}$ |
| $SS_{S/A(\text{adj})}$ | $SS_{A(\text{adj})}$ |
| adjusted means | homogeneity of regression slopes |
| Johnson–Neyman procedure | nonequivalent groups |
| a priori blocking | post hoc blocking |
| polynomial regression | |

# EXERCISES

**15.1** Consider an experiment conducted to test the effectiveness of three software packages for teaching problem-solving skills to seventh graders. Thirty-six seventh graders are randomly selected and assigned to the software packages with the restriction that 12 children work with each of the packages. The levels of the independent variable ($P$) are the software packages the children worked with; and the dependent variable ($Y$) is the score obtained on a problem-solving achievement test administered after the children have worked with a package for 6 months. There are also scores ($X$) obtained on a problem-solving pretest administered before the children were assigned to work with the software packages. The data are presented herein:

| $P_1$ | | $P_2$ | | $P_3$ | |
|---|---|---|---|---|---|
| Y | X | Y | X | Y | X |
| 38 | 25 | 47 | 10 | 58 | 19 |
| 61 | 35 | 73 | 28 | 74 | 37 |
| 50 | 23 | 44 | 16 | 65 | 17 |
| 44 | 11 | 85 | 30 | 91 | 40 |
| 69 | 29 | 58 | 21 | 67 | 24 |
| 72 | 36 | 64 | 18 | 45 | 25 |
| 61 | 26 | 67 | 31 | 54 | 23 |
| 41 | 10 | 69 | 34 | 65 | 31 |
| 51 | 23 | 58 | 27 | 59 | 27 |
| 57 | 29 | 81 | 35 | 57 | 14 |
| 46 | 16 | 94 | 41 | 49 | 17 |
| 62 | 27 | 43 | 15 | 74 | 41 |

(a) Perform an ANOVA using $P$ as the independent variable.
(b) Perform an ANCOVA using $P$ as the independent variable and $X$ as the covariate.
(c) Test whether the homogeneity of regression slope assumption is satisfied.

**15.2** Eighteen participants are assigned randomly to three treatment conditions $A_1$, $A_2$, and $A_3$. After the treatment is applied, values of $Y$, the dependent variable, are obtained. However, before the treatment is applied, values of $X$, a variable closely related to $Y$, are recorded. The data are as follows:

| $A_1$ | | $A_2$ | | $A_3$ | |
|---|---|---|---|---|---|
| X | Y | X | Y | X | Y |
| 12 | 26 | 11 | 32 | 6 | 23 |
| 10 | 22 | 12 | 31 | 13 | 35 |
| 7 | 20 | 6 | 20 | 15 | 44 |
| 14 | 34 | 18 | 41 | 15 | 41 |
| 12 | 28 | 10 | 29 | 7 | 28 |
| 11 | 26 | 11 | 31 | 9 | 30 |

(a) Perform an ANOVA on $Y$.

(b) Perform an ANOVA on $X$.

(c) Test for homogeneity of regression in the three groups.

(d) Perform an ANCOVA on $Y$, using $X$ as the covariate.

(e) How do the hypotheses tested by the ANOVA and the ANCOVA differ?

(f) What are the adjusted means for the three treatment groups?

(g) What is the interpretation of the adjusted means?

**15.3** Discuss whether it is appropriate to perform ANCOVAs using $X$ as the covariate in each of the following cases:

(a) Measures of job satisfaction ($Y$) and performance evaluation by supervisors ($X$) are obtained for eight randomly sampled workers in each of the four departments of a company. The researchers desire to test whether job satisfaction is the same in each of the departments. The data are as follows:

| $D_1$ | | $D_2$ | | $D_3$ | | $D_4$ | |
|---|---|---|---|---|---|---|---|
| $X$ | $Y$ | $X$ | $Y$ | $X$ | $Y$ | $X$ | $Y$ |
| 1.4 | 1.0 | 3.2 | 3.0 | 6.2 | 7.3 | 5.8 | 5.6 |
| 2.0 | 2.7 | 6.8 | 5.5 | 3.1 | 4.0 | 6.6 | 7.2 |
| 3.2 | 3.9 | 5.0 | 5.6 | 3.2 | 4.9 | 6.5 | 6.1 |
| 1.4 | 1.0 | 2.5 | 3.2 | 4.0 | 6.9 | 5.9 | 7.1 |
| 2.3 | 4.0 | 6.1 | 4.2 | 4.5 | 2.1 | 5.9 | 5.4 |
| 4.0 | 3.4 | 4.8 | 4.2 | 6.4 | 5.6 | 3.0 | 4.0 |
| 5.0 | 3.7 | 4.6 | 3.7 | 4.4 | 6.0 | 5.9 | 5.6 |
| 4.7 | 2.3 | 4.2 | 3.8 | 4.1 | 4.6 | 5.6 | 5.8 |

(b) Thirty children are each randomly assigned to one of three remedial math skills training programs. Before entering the programs, each child takes a standardized pretest ($X$). At the end of 6 months, a standardized achievement test ($Y$) is given to each of the children. The researchers wish to determine whether the training programs are all equally effective. The data are:

| $A_1$ | | $A_2$ | | $A_3$ | |
|---|---|---|---|---|---|
| $X$ | $Y$ | $X$ | $Y$ | $X$ | $Y$ |
| 29 | 61 | 39 | 79 | 41 | 78 |
| 37 | 73 | 34 | 66 | 36 | 66 |
| 26 | 54 | 35 | 76 | 29 | 56 |
| 32 | 63 | 39 | 84 | 33 | 61 |
| 31 | 62 | 35 | 73 | 42 | 70 |
| 37 | 76 | 27 | 75 | 35 | 65 |
| 33 | 72 | 35 | 66 | 32 | 59 |
| 39 | 80 | 29 | 85 | 42 | 80 |
| 33 | 73 | 34 | 62 | 39 | 65 |
| 36 | 72 | 26 | 79 | 36 | 64 |

**15.4**  If, for the data of Exercise 15.2, all the $Y$ scores are regressed on all of the $X$ scores, the regression equation obtained is

$$\hat{Y} = 9.974 + 1.816X$$

The residuals for this regression are as follows:

| $A_1$ | $A_2$ | $A_3$ |
|---|---|---|
| −5.771 | 2.045 | 2.128 |
| −6.138 | −0.771 | 1.412 |
| −2.689 | −0.872 | 6.780 |
| −1.404 | −1.670 | 3.780 |
| −3.771 | 0.862 | 5.311 |
| −3.955 | 1.045 | 3.678 |

Perform an ANOVA on these residuals. Is the ANOVA on the residuals equivalent to the ANCOVA of part (d) of Exercise 15.2? Why or why not?

**15.5**  Perform an ANCOVA for the following two-factor between-subjects design:

|  | $A_1$ | | $A_2$ | |
|---|---|---|---|---|
|  | X | Y | X | Y |
| | 24.4 | 15.9 | 22.5 | 24.2 |
| | 22.3 | 15.7 | 12.5 | 19.7 |
| | 23.3 | 19.2 | 14.2 | 19.2 |
| $B_1$ | 15.8 | 13.4 | 18.6 | 17.9 |
| | 22.6 | 18.0 | 15.2 | 24.4 |
| | 24.9 | 22.5 | 23.2 | 28.0 |
| | 20.9 | 15.1 | 20.9 | 19.9 |
| | 19.6 | 13.7 | 18.1 | 28.2 |
| | 23.9 | 12.8 | 18.1 | 18.1 |
| $B_2$ | 26.2 | 25.5 | 11.5 | 13.5 |
| | 18.8 | 17.0 | 22.4 | 19.3 |
| | 24.0 | 25.3 | 30.2 | 35.1 |

# Chapter 16
## Hierarchical Designs

## 16.1 INTRODUCTION

This chapter is concerned with two classes of designs that involve the nesting of variables. We refer to these as **hierarchical designs** in reference to the hierarchy of variables that typifies them. The first class of designs is typical of those studies in social, clinical, and educational psychology in which the behavior of individuals is measured following participation in interactive groups. For example, educational researchers have studied the effects of cooperative group learning on academic achievement and attitudes to learning (e.g., Lindauer & Petrie, 1997; Springer, Stanne, & Donovan, 1999), and social psychologists have studied the effects of training within interactive groups on individual problem solving (e.g., Brodbeck & Greitemeyer, 2000). In such designs, subjects are nested within interactive groups (i.e., each subject is in only one group) that often in turn are nested within levels of a factor. For example, groups may differ with respect to gender, number of group participants, or range or level of participant abilities. Or groups may be assigned to different levels of an experimental variable, such as the rule used to decide on the solution to problems (Stasson, Kameda, Parks, Zimmerman, & Davis, 1991).

The reason we treat this **groups-within-treatments design** differently from the completely randomized subjects-within-treatments design of Chapter 8 is the assumption that the scores of individuals within an interactive group will be correlated, whereas it is assumed that the scores of individuals in the completely randomized design are independently distributed. In this view, the interactive group makes a contribution to the total variability beyond that due to the individual. Individuals' scores are not just a function of their personal characteristics and the treatment condition, but also of the particular group of people with whom they interacted during the initial phase of the study. This effect of grouping is also present in other types of research. If several elementary classes are taught reading by one method and several others by another method, the structural model should incorporate an effect of class because scores within a class will not be independently distributed; they are obtained from students taught by the same teacher at the same time of day in the same classroom, and within the context of interaction with the same group of children. Still another example of the design might be taken from the animal laboratory. Different methods of rearing rats might be compared, with each method applied to several litters. Measures obtained from individual rats within a litter may be correlated because of the common genetic heritage.

In summary, the primary new aspect of the groups-within-treatment design is the assumption that social, environmental, and genetic units are a source of variability separate from error variability. Even though the same experimental treatment is applied to two individuals in different social groups (or school classes or litters), their scores will differ, not only because they are different individuals, but also because they are subject to different social interactions (or genetic contributions). Once the possibility of such group effects are recognized, they must be incorporated within the structural model and, therefore, within the data analysis.

We also consider a second class of hierarchical designs in this chapter. These involve **nesting** of items within levels of a within-subjects factor. For example, in Chapter 13, we cited a study by Murray et al. (2000) in which the distortion and orientation of photos of faces were varied, and the photos were then rated as to how bizarre they appeared. In that study, four of eight faces in each condition were female and four were male. We characterize this as nesting of faces within gender levels. Such nesting of one within-subject variable—most often items—within levels of a factor is common in many areas of research. Research in language processing often involves responses to words that differ in various ways, such as English language frequency or grammatical category. Research in education may involve scores on sets of problems differing in complexity. Personality or social psychological research may involve responses to pictures representing different forms of social interaction. In each of these cases, there are several levels of a factor, such as word frequency, problem complexity, or social interaction; there are several different items at each level of the factor; and usually each subject is tested on all items at all levels of the within-subject factor.

Usually items—e.g., words, problems, or pictures—are assumed to have random effects because of the method of selection and because of the wish to generalize beyond the set of items used in the study. Given this assumption, there will be several sources of variance among the means of the conditions within which the stimuli are nested. First, there may be effects of the condition, as when complexity affects the time to solve problems. Second, means of the different conditions may vary because the items are different for different conditions. Third, as in repeated-measurement designs generally, the interaction of subjects with within-subject factors may contribute to the variance of within-subject treatment means. In many instances, it will be necessary to calculate quasi-$F$ ratios to incorporate stimuli-within-treatments and subjects-by-treatments effects into the error term. In this respect, our discussion of the **items-within-treatments design** revisits issues that arose originally in Chapter 13, although in a slightly different context.

## 16.2 GROUPS WITHIN TREATMENTS

### 16.2.1 Partitioning Variability

Consider an experiment in which subjects meet in a first phase in groups to solve a set of five math problems. The groups are assigned to one of two conditions: Their solution to each

**TABLE 16.1**   DATA FOR A GROUPS-WITHIN-TREATMENTS DESIGN

| | $A_1$ (Majority Rule) | | | | $A_2$ (Unanimity Rule) | | |
| | $G_{11}$ | $G_{21}$ | $G_{31}$ | | $G_{12}$ | $G_{22}$ | $G_{32}$ |
|---|---|---|---|---|---|---|---|
| | 19 | 16 | 19 | | 10 | 9 | 12 |
| | 20 | 15 | 15 | | 12 | 8 | 10 |
| | 18 | 15 | 13 | | 15 | 14 | 12 |
| | 15 | 14 | 13 | | 19 | 9 | 14 |
| $\overline{Y}_{.j1} =$ | 18 | 15 | 15 | $\overline{Y}_{.j2} =$ | 14 | 10 | 12 |
| | | $\overline{Y}_{..1} = 16$ | | | | $\overline{Y}_{..2} = 12$ | |

problem is decided either by majority rule or by a unanimous decision of the group members. In a subsequent phase, individual's are tested on a set of five new math problems, and their scores as well as their ratings of satisfaction with the group experience are recorded. For the sake of simplicity, this hypothetical experiment involves three 4-person groups in each of the two conditions.[1] In general, this type of experiment has $a$ levels of the treatment variable, $A$, $g$ groups at each level of $A$, and $n$ participants in each group. In the example, $a = 2$ (decision rules), $g = 3$, and $n = 4$ for a total of $agn = 24$ participants in the experiment.

Table 16.1 presents the satisfaction ratings for the example. An individual score is represented as $Y_{ijk}$, where $i = 1, 2, \ldots, n$; $j = 1, 2, \ldots, g$; and $k = 1, 2, \ldots, a$. The deviation of each score from the grand mean can be partitioned into effects due to the treatment (the decision rule in the example), the group membership, and a residual component attributable to individual differences and error of measurement:

$$Y_{ijk} - \overline{Y}_{...} = (\overline{Y}_{..k} - \overline{Y}_{...}) + (\overline{Y}_{.jk} - \overline{Y}_{..k}) + (Y_{ijk} - \overline{Y}_{.jk})$$
$$\text{treatment} + \text{group} + \text{residual} \qquad (16.1)$$
$$\text{effect} \quad \text{effect}$$

Table 16.2 presents this partitioning of the deviation of the score from the grand mean for the data of Table 16.1. Note that the group effect is the deviation of the group mean from the treatment mean.

The analysis of variance (ANOVA) of Table 16.3 follows directly from Equation 16.1. More precisely, by summing and squaring the values of $Y_{ijk} - \overline{Y}_{...}$, we have the total sum of squares ($SS_{tot}$); similarly, summing and squaring the treatment, group, and residual values in Table 16.1 yields the components of the $SS_{tot}$. In equation form, we have

$$\sum_i \sum_j \sum_k (Y_{ijk} - \overline{Y}_{...}) = ng \sum_k (\overline{Y}_{..k} - \overline{Y}_{...})^2 + n \sum_j \sum (\overline{Y}_{.jk} - \overline{Y}_{..k})^2$$
$$+ \sum_i \sum_j \sum_k (Y_{ijk} - \overline{Y}_{.jk})^2 \qquad (16.2)$$
$$SS_{tot} = SS_A + SS_{G/A} + SS_{S/G/A}$$

The notation, $S/G/A$, is read as "subjects within groups within levels of A," or more briefly, "within groups." Some books and software packages use the notation $S(GA)$. What is critical is the distinction between the variable denoted by the essential subscript(s), and the variables in which they are nested.

**TABLE 16.2** DECOMPOSITION OF THE DATA OF TABLE 16.1

| Score − Grand Mean ($Y_{ijk} - \overline{Y}_{...}$) | | | | | | = | Rule Effect ($\overline{Y}_{..k} - \overline{Y}_{...}$) | | | | | |
|---|---|---|---|---|---|---|---|---|---|---|---|---|
| $A_1$ | | | $A_2$ | | | | $A_1$ | | | $A_2$ | | |
| $G_{11}$ | $G_{21}$ | $G_{31}$ | $G_{12}$ | $G_{22}$ | $G_{32}$ | | $G_{11}$ | $G_{21}$ | $G_{31}$ | $G_{12}$ | $G_{22}$ | $G_{32}$ |
| 5 | 1 | 5 | 1 | −5 | −2 | | 2 | 2 | 2 | −2 | −2 | −2 |
| 6 | 1 | −1 | 5 | −6 | 0 | | 2 | 2 | 2 | −2 | −2 | −2 |
| 4 | 2 | 1 | −4 | 0 | −2 | | 2 | 2 | 2 | −2 | −2 | −2 |
| 1 | 0 | −1 | −2 | −5 | −4 | | 2 | 2 | 2 | −2 | −2 | −2 |

$SS_{tot} = 5^2 + 1^2 + \cdots + (-5)^2 + (-4)^2 = 268$   $SS_A = (12)(2^2) + (12)(-2)^2 = 96$

| + Group Effect ($\overline{Y}_{.jk} - \overline{Y}_{..k}$) | | | | | | | + Residual ($Y_{ijk} - \overline{Y}_{.jk}$) | | | | | |
|---|---|---|---|---|---|---|---|---|---|---|---|---|
| $A_1$ | | | $A_2$ | | | | $A_1$ | | | $A_2$ | | |
| $G_{11}$ | $G_{21}$ | $G_{31}$ | $G_{12}$ | $G_{22}$ | $G_{32}$ | | $G_{11}$ | $G_{21}$ | $G_{31}$ | $G_{12}$ | $G_{22}$ | $G_{32}$ |
| 2 | −1 | −1 | 2 | −2 | 0 | | 1 | 0 | 4 | 1 | −1 | 0 |
| 2 | −1 | −1 | 2 | −2 | 0 | | 2 | 0 | −2 | 5 | −2 | 2 |
| 2 | −1 | −1 | 2 | −2 | 0 | | 0 | 1 | 0 | −4 | 4 | 0 |
| 2 | −1 | −1 | 2 | −2 | 0 | | −3 | −1 | −2 | −2 | −1 | −2 |

$SS_{G/A} = (4)(2^2) + (4)(-1)^2 + \cdots + (4)(0^2) = 56$   $SS_{S/G/A} = 1^2 + 0^2 + \cdots + (-1)^2 + (-2)^2 = 116$

**TABLE 16.3** ANOVA OF THE DATA OF TABLE 16.3

| SV | df | SS | MS | F | EMS | Error Terms |
|---|---|---|---|---|---|---|
| Total | 23 | 268 | | | | |
| Between groups | 5 | 152 | | | | |
| A | 1 | 96 | 96 | 6.86* | $\sigma_e^2 + n\sigma_{G/A}^2 + gn\theta_A^2$ | G/A |
| G/A | 4 | 56 | 14 | 2.17** | $\sigma_e^2 + n\sigma_{G/A}^2$ | S/G/A |
| S/G/A | | | | | | |
| (Within groups) | 18 | 116 | 6.44 | | $\sigma_e^2$ | |

*$p = .06$; **$p = .11$.

The SVs in Table 16.3 are consistent with the partitioning just presented. We have included the lines for the Total and Between Groups sources as an aid in calculating their components. However, only the last three lines are needed, and these would be the only lines listed in the output of statistical software capable of providing an analysis of data from designs involving nested factors (e.g., SPSS, SAS, BMDP). Researchers lacking access to such software, or having only very early versions that may lack the ability to carry out the nesting analysis, can perform the correct analysis in one of two ways. The first approach to calculating the sum of squares for the nested term is based on the fact that the between-group variability is a composite of $A$ and $G/A$. This can be seen in the partitioning of the degrees of freedom:

$$df_{\text{Between Groups}} = df_A + df_{G/A}$$

$$ag - 1 = (a - 1) + a(g - 1)$$

Then,

$$df_{G/A} = df_{\text{Between Groups}} - df_A$$

and, because of the one-to-one correspondence of sums of squares and degrees of freedom,

$$SS_{G/A} = SS_{\text{Between Groups}} - SS_A$$

This suggests carrying out the ANOVA in two passes. In the first, $G$ (with $ag$ levels) is treated as the factor in a one-factor complete randomized design; this pass yields $SS_{\text{Between Groups}}$. In the second pass, the group variable is ignored, and $A$ is treated as the sole factor; this yields $SS_A$. Subtraction provides $SS_{G/A}$.

A second approach can be used with any program that is capable of analyzing a two-factor design, but that has no provision to deal with nesting. This approach is based on viewing groups as if they crossed with $A$. With respect to Table 16.1, we would input the variables as if there were the same three groups at each level of $A$. The result of the analysis would be two main effects and an interaction: $A$, $G$, and $A \times G$. Summing the degrees of freedom for $G$ and $A \times G$,

$$df_G \ + \ df_{AG} \ = \ df_{G/A}$$
$$(g - 1) + (a - 1)(g - 1) = a(g - 1)$$

Summing the corresponding sums of squares yields the nested term:

$$SS_G + SS_{AG} = SS_{G/A}$$

Justification of the expected mean squares requires specification of the underlying structural model that relates each score to population parameters. We do that next, first pausing to note that, given these expected mean squares, the $F$ ratios calculated in Table 16.3 meet the usual requirement of equality of numerator and denominator expectations under $H_0$.

## 16.2.2 The ANOVA Model

In establishing the relation of $Y_{ijk}$ to population parameters, we ignore the variable $A$ and view the design as having one factor, $G$, with $ag$ levels and $n$ subjects at each level. In accord with the one-factor model (Chapter 8), this view suggests

$$Y_{ijk} = \mu + \gamma_{jk} + \varepsilon_{ijk} \tag{16.3}$$

where $\gamma_{jk} = \mu_{jk} - \mu$, the deviation of the population mean for the $j$th group at the $k$th level of $A$ from the grand mean of all the populations, and $\varepsilon_{ijk} = Y_{ijk} - \mu_{jk}$, the residual error component. Equation 16.3 ignores any possible effect of the treatment variable, $A$. However, group means may differ not only because the groups have different compositions, but also because some groups are at one level of $A$, whereas other groups are at a different level of $A$. This line of reasoning suggests that part of the group effect, $\gamma_{jk}$, is due to the treatment effect, $\alpha_k$, the effect due to the particular level of $A$ in which the group is nested. Expressed in terms of the population parameters,

$$\gamma_{jk} = \alpha_k + \gamma_{j/k} \quad \text{or} \quad (\mu_{jk} - \mu) = (\mu_k - \mu) + (\mu_{jk} - \mu_k)$$

Substituting for $\gamma_{jk}$ in Equation 16.3, results in the structural model for the groups-within-treatments design:

$$Y_{ijk} = \mu + \alpha_k + \gamma_{j/k} + \varepsilon_{ijk} \tag{16.4}$$

Each score is contributed to by a treatment effect, a group effect, and a residual component reflecting error of measurement and individual differences. This parallels the development in Table 16.2 in which the deviations of the observed scores from the grand mean were partitioned into estimates of the effects in Equation 16.4.

A common error in analyzing group designs is the failure to incorporate group effects into the model. When this happens, the analysis proceeds as though the design were a completely randomized one-factor design with $gn$ subjects in each of $a$ treatment groups. This failure to separate group variance from the residual error variance may result in positive bias, an increase in the Type 1 error rate beyond the nominal value. The reason for this will be discussed shortly.

To complete the presentation of the theory underlying the ANOVA, and to arrive at the expected mean squares of Table 16.3, we must decide whether the variables have fixed or random effects. Generally, the levels of $A$ have been arbitrarily selected by the researcher and therefore $A$ is a fixed-effect factor. Therefore, the variance component is defined as $\theta_A^2 = \sum_{k=1}^{a} \alpha_k^2/(a-1)$. The nested group effect, $\gamma_{j/k}$, is viewed as a random-effects variable because the groups are assumed to be a random sample from the population of all possible groups of size $n$ that could be composed. Both $\gamma_{j/k}$ and $\varepsilon_{ijk}$ are assumed to be independently and normally distributed with mean zero and variances $\sigma_{G/A}^2$ and $\sigma_e^2$, respectively.

Given these assumptions, the expected mean squares of Table 16.3 can be derived. More simply, we can use the rules of thumb presented in Chapter 14. Considering the $A$ source of variance first, set down $\sigma_e^2$ and the null hypothesis term, $\theta_A^2$. The latter term is multiplied by $ng$, the number of scores at each level of $A$. Because the subscript $G/A$ includes the letter $A$, and the essential letter $G$ represents a random-effects variable, $\sigma_{G/A}^2$ is included in the expectation. Its coefficient is $n$, the number of scores in each group. The remaining two lines should pose no problems. Note, however, that $\sigma_e^2$ combines both variance due to individual difference and variance due to error of measurement. Only when the design involves repeated measures is there a need to distinguish between these two variance components.

## 16.2.3 Pooling Group and Subject Variances

The ANOVA of Table 16.3 failed to yield a significant $A$ effect. However, the test against an error mean square on 4 $df$ is likely to have a very high Type 2 error rate. Admittedly, most experiments are likely to involve more groups, and therefore more error degrees of freedom, than our example. Nevertheless, although exaggerated in our example, the problem of a relatively low value of $df_{G/A}$ is a common one in hierarchical designs. One possible

**TABLE 16.4**   REVISION OF TABLE 16.3 AFTER POOLING

| SV | df | SS | MS | F | EMS | Error Terms |
|----|----|----|----|----|----|----|
| $A$ | 1 | 96 | 96 | 12.28* | $\sigma_e^2 + gn\theta_A^2$ | $S/A$ |
| $S/A$ | 22 | 172 | 7.82 | | $\sigma_e^2$ | |

*$p = .002$.

solution to the problem of low power of the $F$ test is to assume a different structural model. If it is assumed that the group variable does not contribute to the total variability, the effect of $G/A$ is deleted from the model and $\sigma_{G/A}^2$ is deleted from the expected mean squares of Table 16.3. Then, $MS_{G/A}$ and $MS_{S/G/A}$ both estimate $\sigma_e^2$. Assuming this revised model, the two mean squares could be pooled to obtain a single estimate of error variance, $MS_{S/A}$, where

$$MS_{S/A} = \frac{SS_{G/A} + SS_{S/G/A}}{df_{G/A} + df_{S/G/A}} \tag{16.5}$$

If Equation 16.5 is applied to the terms in Table 16.3, the result is Table 16.4. Note that the $F$ test of the $A$ effect is now very significant. There are two reasons for this. First, the error degrees of freedom are now 22, instead of 4. Even if the $F$ ratio had been unchanged from that of Table 16.3, the result would now be significant because an $F$ of 6.86 on 1 and 22 $df$ results in $p = .016$. In the example, there is a second reason for the decreased $p$ value. The pooled mean square, $MS_{S/A}$, is a weighted (by degrees of freedom) average of $MS_{G/A}$ and $MS_{S/G/A}$; that is, Equation 16.5 can be rewritten as

$$MS_{S/A} = \left( \frac{df_{G/A}}{df_{G/A} + df_{S/G/A}} \right) MS_{G/A} + \left( \frac{df_{S/G/A}}{df_{G/A} + df_{S/G/A}} \right) MS_{S/G/A}$$
$$= (W)(MS_{G/A}) + (1 - W)(MS_{S/G/A}) \tag{16.6}$$

Note that $W$ represents a proportion of degrees of freedom. Because, in this example, $MS_{S/G/A}$ is less than $MS_{G/A}$, the average of the two will be less than $MS_{G/A}$. So, the pooled error term has more degrees of freedom than the original error term in Table 16.3, and it is also smaller. However, pooling carries a risk, as we discussed in Chapter 12. If the original structural model is correct, then $\sigma_{G/A}^2 > 0$, and the expectation of the pooled mean square is

$$E(MS_{S/A}) = W \times E(MS_{G/A}) + (1 - W) \times E(MS_{S/G/A})$$
$$= \sigma_e^2 + (W)(n\sigma_{G/A}^2)$$

Therefore, assuming $H_0$ is true, the ratio of expected mean squares involved in the pooled $F$ test of $A$ is

$$\frac{E(MS_A)}{E(MS_{S/A})} = \frac{\sigma_e^2 + n\sigma_{G/A}^2}{\sigma_e^2 + (W)(n\sigma_{G/A}^2)}$$

But because $W$ is a fraction, the above ratio is greater than 1, indicating that we could get a significant result even though the null hypothesis is true.

Bozivich, Bancroft, and Hartlet (1956) and Srivastava and Bozivich (1961) carried out computer simulation studies using exactly the design and model under consideration in this chapter, with $\alpha = .05$. They pooled the $G/A$ and $S/G/A$ terms when a preliminary test of $G/A$ against $S/G/A$ was not significant at the .25 level. Using this procedure, when the null hypothesis was true, the Type 1 error rate for the test of the $A$ source of variance rose to .08 under some conditions. The authors recommended that pooling should be carried out in the hierarchical design only when there are a priori grounds for assuming that the mean squares to be pooled have the same expectation and the $p$ value for the preliminary test, $MS_{G/A}/MS_{S/G/A}$, is greater than .25. Returning to Table 16.3, the .25 criterion is not met ($p = .11$), and a pooled error term should not be used in this example. Generally, groups will differ from each other and pooling will not be proper. Therefore, researchers should have as many groups as is practical, so that the appropriate error term, $MS_{G/A}$, will be distributed on a substantial number of degrees of freedom, and the $F$ test of $A$ will have reasonable power without resorting to pooling.

## 16.3 GROUPS VERSUS INDIVIDUALS

In many studies in which individuals are trained within a group setting, there is also a condition in which in which individuals do not participate in a group. For example, Stasson et al. (1991) had subjects work in groups to solve practice problems and then tested them individually on a new problem set; however, they also included one condition in which other subjects worked on the practice problems individually. Because this group-versus-individual-training design is common, and the data often are improperly analyzed, we consider it here. Assume that there are 15 students assigned to study a topic individually (individual condition, $C_I$) and another 15 students randomly assigned to five discussion groups of three students each (group condition, $C_G$). After the study session, all 30 students are tested individually on the subject matter studied. The data and group means are presented in Table 16.5. Although the subjects in $C_I$ studied individually, we randomly grouped their scores into sets of three. This simplifies the notation, allowing us to denote each score by $Y_{ijk}$: $i = 1, 2, \ldots, n$; $j = 1, 2, \ldots, g$; and $k = 1, 2, \ldots, c$. In the example, $n = 3$, $g = 5$, and $a = 2$ ($I$ or $G$).

The sum of squares for the individual-versus-group condition ($SS_C$) is calculated in Table 16.5, below the data. The denominator against which this is tested has usually been

**TABLE 16.5**   DATA FOR A GROUPS-VERSUS-INDIVIDUALS DESIGN

| Individual Condition ($C_I$) | | | | | | | | | | | | | | | |
|---|---|---|---|---|---|---|---|---|---|---|---|---|---|---|---|
| $Y_{ijI} =$ | 9 | 9 | 11 | 15 | 16 | 12 | 12 | 8 | 15 | 16 | 15 | 16 | 14 | 11 | 13 | |
| $Y_{.jI} =$ | | 9.67 | | | 14.33 | | | 11.67 | | | 15.67 | | | 12.67 | | $\overline{Y}_{..I} = 12.8$ |

| Group Condition ($C_G$) | | | | | | | | | | | | | | | |
|---|---|---|---|---|---|---|---|---|---|---|---|---|---|---|---|
| $Y_{ijG} =$ | 11 | 16 | 15 | 17 | 18 | 19 | 11 | 13 | 15 | 17 | 18 | 19 | 10 | 13 | 13 | |
| $Y_{.jG} =$ | | 14 | | | 18 | | | 13 | | | 18 | | | 12 | | $\overline{Y}_{..G} = 15$ |

$$SS_C = \frac{(15 - 12.8)^2}{2/15} = 36.3$$

**TABLE 16.6**    PSEUDOGROUP ANALYSIS OF THE DATA OF TABLE 16.5

$$SS_{G/C} = n \sum (\overline{Y}_{.jI} - \overline{Y}_{..I})^2 + n \sum (\overline{Y}_{.jG} - \overline{Y}_{..G})^2$$
$$= 3[(9.67 - 12.8)^2 + \cdots + (12.67 - 12.8)^2 + (14 - 15)^2 + \cdots + (12 - 15)^2] = 161$$
$$df_{G/C} = 2(g - 1) = 8$$

Then the pseudogroup $F$ ratio, distributed on 1 and 8 $df$, is

$$F_{PG} = \frac{36.3}{161/8} = 1.80$$

calculated as $MS_{S/C}$. In the data set of Table 16.5, this means calculating the variance of the 15 scores in each condition and averaging the two variances. The result, here distributed on 28 $df$, is 8.37. To the extent that the group factor in Condition $C_G$ contributes to the variance of the 15 scores in that condition, the resulting $F$ test of $C$ will be positively biased. Myers, DiCecco, and Lorch (1981) have shown that this inflation in Type 1 error rate can be quite marked and increases with the number of scores. Using expected mean squares, they justified two methods of analysis that yield unbiased $F$ tests. We present these methods here. The calculations are in Tables 16.6 and 16.7.

### 16.3.1 The Pseudogroup Procedure

This analysis, presented in Table 16.6, is performed as if the randomly constructed post hoc groups (the pseudogroups) in $C_I$ were real groups and $C$ is tested against $G/C$ on 1 and $2(g-1)$ $df$. Assuming $H_0$ is true, the ratio of expected mean squares is 1, so the $F$ ratio is not biased. There is heterogeneity of variance here because the pseudogroup means vary less than the real group means do, but Myers et al. (1981) reported simulation results demonstrating that Type 1 error rates are little affected by this when the number of pseudogroups are equal to the number of experimental groups and are of the same size. This is consistent with our earlier observation (Chapters 6 and 8) that heterogeneity of variance is not a problem except when the numbers of observations vary between conditions.

### 16.3.2 The Quasi-F Procedure

This approach uses the quasi-$F$ statistic. It is identical to the Brown–Forsythe statistic presented in Chapter 8 as a way of testing effects in the presence of heterogeneity of variance. That makes sense here because the error term will be a linear combination of the variance of group means from Condition $C_G$ and the variance of individual scores from Condition $C_I$. The error mean squares ($MS_{QF}$) and degrees of freedom are presented in Table 16.7. The steps in the calculations are:

1.  Find the variance of the $N_I$ scores in $C_I$ (15 in the example); this is $MS_{S/C_I}$.
2.  Find $n$ times the variance of the $g$ group means in $C_G$; this is $MS_{G/C_G}$.
3.  The error term for the quasi-$F$ test is $MS_{QF}$, a weighted average of $MS_{S/C_I}$ and $MS_{G/C_G}$; the weighting is defined in Table 16.7.
4.  As illustrated in Table 16.7, the error degrees of freedom, $df_{QF}$, are calculated and rounded to the nearest integer.

**TABLE 16.7**   QUASI-*F* ANALYSIS OF THE DATA OF TABLE 16.5

The mean square based on the scores in condition $C_I$ is

$$MS_{S/C_I} = \frac{\sum\sum(Y_{ijI} - \overline{Y}_{..I})^2}{gn - 1} = \frac{(9 - 12.8)^2 + \cdots + (13 - 12.8)^2}{14} = 7.6$$

The mean square based on the group means in condition $C_G$ is

$$MS_{G/C_G} = n\sum\frac{(\overline{Y}_{.jG} - \overline{Y}_{..G})^2}{g - 1}$$

$$= \frac{3[(14 - 15)^2 + \cdots + (12 - 15)^2]}{4} = (3)(8.0) = 24$$

Let $N_I$ be the number of scores in $C_I$, $N_G$ be the number of scores in $C_G$, and $N = N_I + N_G$; $N_I = N_G = 15$ in the example. Then the error mean square is

$$MS_{QF} = \frac{N_I}{N}(MS_{S/C_I}) + \frac{N_G}{N}(MS_{G/C_G})$$

$$= \frac{15}{30}(7.6) + \frac{15}{30}(24.0) = 15.8$$

The quasi-*F* statistic is

$$F_{QF} = \frac{MS_C}{MS_{QF}} = \frac{36.3}{15.8} = 2.30$$

The *df* associated with the error term, $MS_{QF}$, are

$$df_{QF} = \frac{MS_{QF}^2}{\left(\frac{N_G}{N}\right)^2\left[\frac{MS_{G/C_G}^2}{g - 1}\right] + \left(\frac{N_I}{N}\right)^2\left[\frac{MS_{S/C_I}^2}{N_I - 1}\right]}$$

$$= \frac{(15.8)^2}{(1/2)^2[(24^2/4 + 7.6^2/14)]} = 6.74$$

that we have rounded to 7 *df*.

### 16.3.3 Which Method?

The pseudogroup and quasi-*F* tests are similar in their power to reject false null hypotheses and both tests have approximately correct Type 1 error rates (Myers et al., 1981). The pseudogroup approach is computationally simpler and should be used when the $N_I$ observations can be partitioned into as many pseudogroups as there are real groups. The quasi-*F* approach is applicable regardless of the value of $N_I$. Also, Myers et al. (1981) have pointed out that the groups-versus-individuals design is a special case of designs in which group size is a variable; the article shows how the quasi-*F* statistic can be used to analyze data from the more general design.

## 16.4 EXTENSIONS OF THE GROUPS-WITHIN-TREATMENTS DESIGN

### 16.4.1 A Within-Groups Variable

The composition of a discussion group or school class might be included as a variable in the study. In the example of Table 16.1, the discussion groups could be composed of

**TABLE 16.8**  THE DATA OF TABLE 16.1 WITH SUBJECT'S GENDER INCLUDED

|  |  | $B_1$ (Males) |  | $\overline{Y}_{..1}$ | $B_2$ (Females) |  | $\overline{Y}_{..2}$ |  |
|---|---|---|---|---|---|---|---|---|
| $A_1$ | $G_{11}$ | 19 | 20 | 19.5 | 18 | 15 | 16.5 | |
|  | $G_{21}$ | 16 | 15 | 15.5 | 15 | 14 | 14.5 | |
|  | $G_{31}$ | 19 | 15 | 17.0 | 13 | 13 | 13.0 | |
|  |  | | $\overline{Y}_{.11} = 17.33$ | | | $\overline{Y}_{.12} = 14.67$ | | $\overline{Y}_{.1.} = 16$ |
| $A_2$ | $G_{12}$ | 10 | 12 | 11.0 | 15 | 19 | 17.0 | |
|  | $G_{22}$ | 9 | 8 | 8.5 | 14 | 9 | 11.5 | |
|  | $G_{31}$ | 12 | 10 | 11.0 | 12 | 14 | 13.0 | |
|  |  | | $\overline{Y}_{.21} = 10.17$ | | | $\overline{Y}_{.22} = 13.83$ | | $\overline{Y}_{.2.} = 12$ |
|  |  | | $\overline{Y}_{..1} = 13.75$ | | | $\overline{Y}_{..2} = 14.25$ | | $\overline{Y}_{....} = 14$ |

two males and two females. In that case, gender is a within-groups variable. The design enables us to ask whether the effect of the group decision rule is different for males than for females. The data of Table 16.1 are presented once more in Table 16.8 with the gender of the subject indicated. Groups are still nested within levels of $A$. However, $A$ and $B$ cross; that is, all possible combinations are present in the design, allowing for a test of the $A \times B$ interaction. Note that groups also cross with $B$; there are both males and females in every group.

In general, there are $g$ groups at each of $a$ levels of $A$ for a total of $ag$ groups. Within each group, there are $b$ levels of $B$, with $n$ subjects at each level. Therefore, there are $bn$ scores in each of $ag$ groups. In the current example, $a = 2$ (decision rule), $g = 3$ (groups within decision rule), $b = 2$ (gender), and $n = 2$ (subjects within each cell formed by $A$, $G$, and $B$), yielding 4 ($b \times n$) scores in each of 6 ($a \times g$) groups for a total of 24 scores. The indices of notation for this design are $i = 1, 2, \ldots, n; j = 1, 2, \ldots, g; k = 1, 2, \ldots, a$; and $m = 1, 2, \ldots, b$.

Whether the data are analyzed using a calculator or statistical software, understanding the structure of the design is critical. It may help to realize that the layout of Table 16.8 is very similar to that of the mixed design of Chapter 14. Rather than partitioning $SS_{tot}$ into between-subjects and within-subjects components, it is divided into between-groups and within-groups components. Table 16.9 illustrates this partitioning; panel (a) presents the general form of the degrees of freedom, sums of squares, and the expected mean squares, and panel (b) presents numerical results for the data of Table 16.8. As we can see in Table 16.9, the between-groups sum of squares can be further divided into $A$ and $G/A$ sources. This reflects the fact that part of the variability among the $ag$ group means may be due to differences in the level of $A$ and part is due to differences among groups within each level of $A$. Similarly, the within-groups sum of squares can be divided further. A potential source of the variability among the $bn$ scores within each group is the factor $B$. This is also reflected in Table 16.8. The $AB$ and $GB/A$ terms fall out naturally as a result of crossing each between-group term with $B$. The last component of the within-group sum of squares, $S/GB/A$, is due to the fact that the $n$ scores vary within each $G \times B$ combination within each level of $A$.

The degrees of freedom follow from the sources of variance. Only two of these represent terms we have not seen before. $GB/A$ represents the interaction of $g$ groups and $b$ levels

**TABLE 16.9** ANOVA FOR THE DESIGN AND DATA OF TABLE 16.8

| (a) Formulas and Expected Mean Squares | | | |
|---|---|---|---|
| SV | df | SS | EMS |
| Between Groups | $ag - 1$ | $nb \sum_{j=1}^{g} \sum_{k=1}^{a} (\overline{Y}_{\cdot jk\cdot} - \overline{Y}_{\cdots})^2$ | |
| A | $a - 1$ | $ngb \sum_{k=1}^{a} (\overline{Y}_{\cdots k\cdot} - \overline{Y}_{\cdots})^2$ | $\sigma_e^2 + bn\sigma_{G/A}^2 + bgn\theta_A^2$ |
| G/A | $a(g-1)$ | $SS_{\text{Between } G} - SS_A$ | $\sigma_e^2 + bn\sigma_{G/A}^2$ |
| Within Groups | $agb(n-1)$ | $\sum_{i=1}^{n} \sum_{j=1}^{g} \sum_{k=1}^{a} \sum_{m=1}^{b} (Y_{ijkm} - \overline{Y}_{\cdots})^2$ $- SS_{\text{Between } G}$ | |
| B | $b - 1$ | $nga \sum_{m=1}^{b} (\overline{Y}_{\cdots m} - \overline{Y}_{\cdots})^2$ | $\sigma_e^2 + n\sigma_{GB/A}^2 + agn\theta_B^2$ |
| AB | $(a-1)(b-1)$ | $ng \sum_{k=1}^{a} \sum_{m=1}^{b} (\overline{Y}_{\cdots km} - \overline{Y}_{\cdots})^2$ $- SS_A - SS_B$ | $\sigma_e^2 + n\sigma_{GB/A}^2 + gn\theta_{AB}^2$ |
| GB/A | $a(g-1)(b-1)$ | $n \sum_{j=1}^{g} \sum_{k=1}^{a} \sum_{m=1}^{b} (\overline{Y}_{jkm} - \overline{Y}_{\cdots})^2$ $- SS_{\text{Between } G} - SS_B - SS_{AB}$ | $\sigma_e^2 + n\sigma_{GB/A}^2$ |
| S/GB/A | $agb(n-1)$ | $SS_{\text{Within } G} - SS_B$ $- SS_{AB} - SS_{GB/A}$ | $\sigma_e^2$ |

| (b) ANOVA of the Data of Table 16.8 | | | | | |
|---|---|---|---|---|---|
| SV | df | SS | MS | F | Error Terms |
| Between Groups | 5 | 152.000 | | | |
| A | 1 | 96.000 | 96.000 | 6.86[a] | G/A |
| G/A | 4 | 56.000 | 14.000 | | |
| Within Groups | 18 | 116.000 | | | |
| B | 1 | 1.500 | 1.500 | .45 | GB/A |
| AB | 1 | 60.167 | 60.167 | 18.05* | GB/A |
| GB/A | 4 | 13.333 | 3.333 | .98 | S/GB/A |
| S/GB/A | 12 | 41.000 | 3.417 | | |

\*$p < .001$.

of $B$, pooled over the $a$ levels of $A$; therefore, $df_{GB/A} = a(g-1)(b-1)$. Similarly, $df_{S/GB/A}$ reflects the variability of $n$ scores in each combination of $G$ and $B$ within each level of $A$, or $gba(n-1)$. Although sums of squares can be computed by hand for a small data set such as this one, the amount of data and the complexity of the design, together with the possibility of doing supplementary analyses, usually will warrant a computer analysis. Several packages expedite the analysis of hierarchical designs. These include SPSS, SAS, and BMDP. The manuals should be consulted for details of the appropriate commands.

The $F$ tests in Table 16.9 follow directly from the expected mean squares presented there. They in turn are derived from the following structural model:

$$Y_{ijkm} = \mu + \alpha_k + \beta_m + \gamma_{j/k} + (\alpha\beta)_{km} + (\gamma\beta)_{jm/k} + \varepsilon_{ijkm} \tag{16.7}$$

Several aspects of the model should be noted. Because subjects do not cross with any of the other variables, there are no interactions involving them. Furthermore, because groups are nested within levels of $A$, the groups $\times$ $B$ interaction effect, $(\gamma\beta)_{jm/k}$, is also nested within levels of $A$. The corresponding source of variance may be viewed as $G/A \times B$, or $GB/A$. The $GB/A$ notation indicates a method of computing the $SS_{GB/A}$. The $G \times B$ sum of squares can be calculated at each level of $A$, and then the $a$ interaction terms are summed.

We assume that $A$ and $B$ are fixed-effects variables; therefore, the corresponding components of the expected mean squares are $\theta_A^2 = \left(\sum_k \alpha_k^2\right)/(a-1)$, $\theta_B^2 = \left(\sum_m \beta_m^2\right)/(b-1)$, and $\theta_{AB}^2 = \left[\sum_k \sum_m (\alpha\beta)_{km}^2\right]/[(a-1)(b-1)]$. The terms $\gamma_{j/k}$, $(\gamma\beta)_{jm/k}$, and $\varepsilon_{ijkm}$ are independently and normally distributed with mean zero and respective variances $\sigma_{G/A}^2$, $\sigma_{GB/A}^2$, and $\sigma_e^2$. These terms are incorporated in the expected mean squares as dictated by the rules stated in Chapter 14.

## 16.4.2 Repeated Measurements in the Groups-Within-Treatments Design

In several articles reporting experiments of the sort considered so far, more than one score has been obtained from each subject. For example, scores might have been obtained on each of $c$ occasions from each of the $abgn$ subjects in a design such as that of Table 16.8. In that case, there are $abcgn - 1$ total degrees of freedom. Of these, $abgn - 1$ are allocated to the between-subjects sources of variance; these are the terms in the SV column of Table 16.9. Then, $abgn(c - 1)$ degrees of freedom remain to be accounted for. These correspond to within-subjects sources of variance that can be obtained by crossing each of the between-subjects terms with the within-subjects variable, $C$. Table 16.10 presents the SV, $df$, EMS, and error terms resulting from partitioning the within-subjects variability. Several software packages are capable of dealing with this and other variations of the groups-within-treatments design provided that the researcher correctly designates nesting and crossing relations among variables. In the current example, $A$ crosses with $B$ and $C$, $B$

**TABLE 16.10**   THE WITHIN-SUBJECT TERMS IN AN EXTENSION OF THE DESIGN OF TABLE 16.8

| SV | df | EMS | Error Term |
|---|---|---|---|
| Within subjects | $abgn\,(c-1)$ | | |
| $C$ | $c-1$ | $\sigma_e^2 + \sigma_{SC/GB/A}^2 + nb\sigma_{GC/A}^2 + nabg\theta_C^2$ | $GC/A$ |
| $AC$ | $(a-1)(c-1)$ | $\sigma_e^2 + \sigma_{SC/GB/A}^2 + nb\sigma_{GC/A}^2 + nbg\theta_{AC}^2$ | $GC/A$ |
| $GC/A$ | $a(g-1)(c-1)$ | $\sigma_e^2 + \sigma_{SC/GB/A}^2 + nb\sigma_{GC/A}^2$ | $SC/GB/A$ |
| $BC$ | $(b-1)(c-1)$ | $\sigma_e^2 + \sigma_{SC/GB/A}^2 + n\sigma_{GBC/A}^2 + nga\theta_{BC}^2$ | $GBC/A$ |
| $ABC$ | $(a-1)(b-1)(c-1)$ | $\sigma_e^2 + \sigma_{SC/GB/A}^2 + n\sigma_{GBC/A}^2 + ng\theta_{ABC}^2$ | $GBC/A$ |
| $GBC/A$ | $a(g-1)(b-1)(c-1)$ | $\sigma_e^2 + \sigma_{SC/GB/A}^2 + n\sigma_{GBC/A}^2$ | $SC/GB/A$ |
| $SC/GB/A$ | $abg(n-1)(c-1)$ | $\sigma_e^2 + \sigma_{SC/GB/A}^2$ | |

crosses with $C$, $G$ is nested in $A$, and $G/A$ crosses with $B$ and with $C$. The $G/A \times C$ and the $G/A \times BC$ are labeled $GC/A$ and $GBC/A$ in Table 16.10.

## 16.5 ITEMS WITHIN TREATMENTS

In many experiments, participants respond to stimuli that are nested within the levels of some variable of interest. For example, in the study by Murray et al. (2000), described in Chapter 13 and cited in the introduction to this chapter, photos of four male and four female faces were presented in different orientations and rated for bizarreness. In this case, faces are nested within levels of gender. Both variables cross with orientation because each face was rated in each physical position. To take another example, researchers have recorded time spent reading words that were either high or low in English-language frequency. In this case, words are nested within levels of frequency. Typically, as in these two examples, the items—faces or words—are most properly viewed as a random sample from a population of items. One approach frequently taken to the analysis is to reduce it to the Subjects $\times$ Treatments design of Chapter 13. For example, the researcher might obtain the means of the ratings of the male and female faces. Then there would be two scores for each subject, the male and female means. The problem with this analysis is that, although the differences between the male and female means is at least in part attributable to the variability of the items, the approach ignores that variability. Ignoring item variability inflates the probability of a Type 1 error because then the error term does not include the variance of the scores on the items, whereas the numerator of the $F$ does. In this section, a small artificial data set is used to illustrate the proper partitioning of the total sums of squares and degrees of freedom, and formulas for quasi-$F$ tests are presented.

### 16.5.1 An Example of the Design

Suppose that a researcher is interested in the effects of problem difficulty on time to solution. Each subject is required to solve 12 problems, 4 of which are easy, 4 of intermediate difficulty, and 4 difficult. In this example, problems are nested within difficulty levels. The study is further complicated by having subjects nested within levels of experience; 5 subjects are novices and 5 are experts. The data from such a study are presented in Table 16.11.

The study just described is a specific example of a general design in which there are $n$ subjects at each of $a$ levels of $A$ for a total of $an$ subjects. Each subject is tested with $b$ different stimuli at each of $c$ levels of $C$; in the above example, $a = 2$ (levels of expertise), $b = 4$ (problems within difficulty levels), and $c = 3$ (difficulty levels). $B$ is nested within levels of $C$ ($B/C$) and is assumed to have random effects; $C$ and $A$ are assumed to have fixed effects. In what follows, we develop an approach to deal with design variations of various degrees of complexity.

### 16.5.2 Partitioning the Sums of Squares and Degrees of Freedom

As in earlier examples involving a between-subjects variable, beginning with Chapter 8, the between-subjects sources are $A$ and $S/A$. The within-subjects sums of squares and degrees of freedom can be partitioned in a similar way. In our problem-solving example, there are

**TABLE 16.11**   DATA FOR A WITHIN-SUBJECTS DESIGN WITH LEVELS OF B NESTED WITHIN LEVELS OF A

| | | $C_1$ | | | | $C_2$ | | | | $C_3$ | | |
| | | $B_{11}$ | $B_{21}$ | $B_{31}$ | $B_{41}$ | $B_{12}$ | $B_{22}$ | $B_{32}$ | $B_{42}$ | $B_{13}$ | $B_{23}$ | $B_{33}$ | $B_{43}$ |
|---|---|---|---|---|---|---|---|---|---|---|---|---|---|
| | $S_{11}$ | 4.4 | 5.2 | 5.8 | 4.5 | 5.5 | 5.7 | 4.2 | 4.8 | 5.4 | 4.2 | 5.6 | 5.6 |
| | $S_{21}$ | 4.4 | 6.0 | 6.1 | 4.3 | 5.7 | 5.3 | 4.0 | 6.4 | 5.5 | 3.7 | 5.2 | 6.7 |
| $A_1$ | $S_{31}$ | 5.0 | 5.9 | 6.3 | 4.8 | 5.3 | 6.8 | 4.6 | 6.2 | 6.3 | 5.1 | 4.9 | 5.3 |
| | $S_{41}$ | 4.4 | 5.0 | 5.5 | 3.4 | 5.2 | 5.2 | 3.5 | 4.9 | 5.8 | 4.6 | 5.4 | 4.5 |
| | $S_{51}$ | 4.8 | 5.5 | 5.3 | 5.4 | 4.9 | 5.1 | 4.0 | 5.2 | 5.1 | 4.5 | 5.2 | 5.1 |
| | $S_{12}$ | 5.0 | 7.8 | 9.8 | 6.0 | 8.4 | 8.7 | 5.9 | 8.4 | 8.9 | 5.1 | 7.9 | 9.5 |
| | $S_{22}$ | 3.9 | 6.6 | 8.6 | 5.2 | 6.1 | 8.3 | 4.9 | 6.1 | 7.6 | 3.9 | 7.7 | 9.0 |
| $A_2$ | $S_{32}$ | 3.9 | 5.6 | 6.5 | 3.6 | 6.5 | 7.2 | 4.1 | 6.2 | 7.6 | 2.8 | 5.6 | 7.1 |
| | $S_{42}$ | 6.1 | 7.1 | 8.3 | 5.7 | 6.9 | 9.1 | 5.2 | 6.5 | 9.5 | 6.4 | 7.5 | 8.9 |
| | $S_{52}$ | 6.0 | 7.8 | 9.1 | 6.6 | 7.9 | 9.9 | 5.9 | 8.0 | 8.8 | 5.4 | 7.0 | 9.2 |

**TABLE 16.12**   ANOVA OF THE DATA OF TABLE 16.11

| SV | df | SS | MS | EMS |
|---|---|---|---|---|
| $A$ | 1 | 94.70 | 94.70 | $\sigma_e^2 + bc\sigma_{S/A}^2 + n\sigma_{AB/C}^2 + nbc\theta_A^2$ |
| $S/A$ | 8 | 41.76 | 5.22 | $\sigma_e^2 + bc\sigma_{S/A}^2$ |
| $C$ | 2 | 4.11 | 2.06 | $\sigma_e^2 + na\sigma_{B/C}^2 + b\sigma_{SC/A}^2 + nba\theta_C^2$ |
| $B/C$ | 9 | 111.47 | 12.39 | $\sigma_e^2 + na\sigma_{B/C}^2$ |
| $AC$ | 2 | 2.80 | 1.40 | $\sigma_e^2 + n\sigma_{AB/C}^2 + b\sigma_{SC/A}^2 + nb\theta_{AC}^2$ |
| $AB/C$ | 9 | 25.27 | 2.81 | $\sigma_e^2 + n\sigma_{AB/C}^2$ |
| $SC/A$ | 16 | 5.00 | .31 | $\sigma_e^2 + b\sigma_{SC/A}^2$ |
| $SB/AC$ | 72 | 18.70 | .26 | $\sigma_e^2$ |

*Note.* We have not included the $\sigma_{SB/AC}^2$ component in the EMS because it contributes to every term.

$c \times b$ or $3 \times 4$, problems. Therefore, there are $bc - 1$, or 11, *df* for problems. Part of the variability among the scores on the $bc$ items is because there are $c$ levels of difficulty. This accounts for $c - 1$, or 2, of the $bc - 1$ *df* for items. The remaining $c(b - 1)$, or 9, *df* account for the $B/C$ term (items within levels of $C$).

To summarize, so far we have listed $A$, $S/A$, $C$, and $B/C$ as sources of variance. The remaining terms follow after deciding about the crossing and nesting of the sources already listed. Because there are scores for all combinations of expertise ($A$) and problem difficulty ($C$), $A$ crosses with $C$ yielding $AC$. Also, because individuals at both expertise levels see all items, $A$ also crosses with $B/C$, yielding $AB/C$. Because all subjects are tested on all items at all difficulty levels, $S/A$ will also cross with $C$ and with $B/C$, yielding $SC/A$ and $SB/AC$. Note that $A$ and $S/A$ do not cross with each other; nor does $C$ cross with $B/C$. If a variable is nested within levels of another variable, the two variables cannot cross. All sources of variance are presented in the SV column of Table 16.12.

As usual, we can check the list of sources by considering the degrees of freedom. The between-subjects degrees of freedom are partitioned into two components:

$$an - 1 = (a - 1) + a(n - 1)$$
$$df_{\text{Between } Ss} = df_A + df_{S/A}$$

The within-subjects sum of squares will be on $an(bc - 1)$ $df$ because the variance of scores for a single subject will be on $bc - 1$ $df$, and there are $an$ subjects. Or, we can subtract $an - 1$ from the total degrees of freedom, $abcn - 1$, again obtaining $an(bc - 1)$ $df$ for the within-subjects sum of squares. This within-subjects term can be partitioned

**TABLE 16.13**   QUASI-$F$ TESTS FOR THE DATA OF TABLE 16.11

These tests follow from the entries in the expected-mean-square column of Table 16.12

$$F_1' = \frac{MS_A}{MS_{S/A} + MS_{AB/C} - MS_{SB/AC}}$$

$$= \frac{94.6963}{5.22 - 2.8073 - .2597}$$

$$= \frac{94.6963}{7.7676} = 12.19$$

$df_A = 1$

$$df_{\text{error}} = \frac{MS_{\text{error}}^2}{MS_{S/A}^2/df_{S/A} + MS_{AB/C}^2/df_{AB/C} + MS_{SB/AC}^2/df_{SB/AC}}$$

$$= \frac{7.7676^2}{5.22^2/8 + 2.8073^2/9 + .2597^2/72}$$

$$= \frac{60.3356}{4.2826} = 14.09 \text{ (or 14)}$$

$$F_2' = \frac{MS_A + MS_{SB/AC}}{MS_{S/A} + MS_{AB/C}}$$

$$= \frac{94.6963 + .2597}{5.22 + 2.8073} = 11.83$$

$$df_A = \frac{(MS_A + MS_{SB/AC})^2}{MS_A^2/df_A + MS_{SB/AC}^2/df_{SB/AC}} = \frac{(94.6963 + .2597)^2}{94.6963^2/1 + .2597^2/72}$$

$$= \frac{9016.6419}{8967.39} = 1.0055 \text{ (or 1)}$$

$$df_{\text{error}} = \frac{(MS_{S/A} + MS_{AB/C})^2}{MS_{S/A}^2/df_{S/A} + MS_{AB/C}^2/df_{AB/C}} = \frac{(5.22 + 2.8073)^2}{5.22^2/8 + 2.8073^2/9}$$

$$= \frac{64.4375}{4.2817} = 15.05 \text{ (or 15)}$$

*Note.* Both quasi-$F$'s are significant at the .01 level. Note that they give very similar results; $F_2'$ is slightly smaller then $F_1'$, but has an error term with one more df.

as follows:

$$an(bc - 1) = (c - 1) + c(b - 1) + (a - 1)(c - 1) + c(a - 1)(b - 1)$$
$$+ a(n - 1)(c - 1) + ac(n - 1)(b - 1)$$
$$df_{\text{Within } Ss} = df_C + df_{B/C} + df_{AC} + df_{AB/C} + df_{SC/A} + df_{SB/AC}$$

The partitioning of sums of squares follows the same pattern. As we noted previously, several software packages provide commands enabling the user to obtain the nested terms. Appendix 16.1 provides an alternative approach that requires only the capability to handle mixed designs such as those in Chapter 14.

The numerical results, together with expected mean squares, are presented in Table 16.12. The lack of a column of $F$ values is not an oversight; the terms in the EMS column indicate the need for quasi-$F$ ratios. We construct these next.

### 16.5.3 Quasi-$F$ Ratios

Turning to the EMS column[2] of Table 16.12, we first note that there is no single source of variance that provides an error term against which to test $A$. If $MS_A$ is divided by $MS_{S/A}$—as was the case in the designs of Chapters 8, 12, and 14—a significant result could be due to $A$ or the nested $AB$ interaction; that is, either $\theta_A^2$ or $\sigma_{AB/C}^2$, or both, could be greater than zero. Table 16.13 illustrates two methods of computing a quasi-$F$ test of $A$. In both cases, the $p$ value is .004. Tests of the $C$ and $AC$ sources of variance can be similarly constructed. We leave this as an exercise for the reader.

## 16.6 CONCLUDING REMARKS

Although there are countless variations of the hierarchical design, all yield to the same principles of analysis that have been applied in the preceding chapters. The first step is to have a sound understanding of the layout of the design. Which variables are nested in which others? Which variables cross each other? Which are between-subjects and which are within-subjects variables? No matter how sophisticated the software used for analysis, these questions must be answered to obtain the correct partitioning of total variability and degrees of freedom. In addition, we must determine which variables are to be viewed as random, which as fixed. This is not always an easy decision; the answer depends on how levels of the variable have been selected and on the range of generalization we intend. Once variables have been classified, application of the rules of thumb will yield the expected mean squares. These provide a check on the error terms and a basis for estimating effect size and for power calculations.

Data analysis is particularly sensitive to the choice of a structural model. If certain variables are assumed to have negligible effects, it is possible to pool terms and consequently have more error degrees of freedom. This results in tests of greater power and the avoidance of quasi-$F$ ratios. Although such consequences of simplifying the model are desirable, we have espoused a more conservative approach to model construction and therefore to data analysis. We prefer to assume a general model, incorporating all possible effects. Ignoring some variance components that make a more than negligible contribution to the variance in the data can lead to Type I errors in testing treatment effects of interest.

The presence of other random-effects variables besides subjects, a characteristic of the designs of this chapter, raises additional considerations in planning the experiment. One important point is that merely running many subjects will not ensure sufficient power to test null hypotheses of interest. In the designs of Sections 16.2–16.4, the value of $g$—the number of social groups, classes, litters, and so on—is the critical determinant of error degrees of freedom and thus of power. It is important to work out the actual analysis of sources of variance and degrees of freedom before collecting data, and to modify the design in whatever ways seem necessary to obtain powerful tests of effects of interest. In the extreme case in which $g = 1$, there is not only a loss of power, but also a confounding of groups and levels of $A$. If one class is taught by one method and another by a second, is a difference in class means due to the different methods or to differences in the interperson interactions within the two classes? To determine the effect of the treatment, we need some measure of variability among classes taught by the same method. Experimenters often don't realize that the failure to replicate groups within levels is not particularly different from running one subject at each level of $A$ in a simple completely randomized one-factor design. Similar comments hold for the designs of Section 16.5. When stimuli are a random sample from some population, the power of the test of treatment effects depends on the number of stimuli.

## KEY CONCEPTS

| | |
|---|---|
| hierarchical designs | crossing |
| nesting | items-within-treatments design |
| pseudogroup procedure | quasi-$F$ procedure |

*Note.* The designs are becoming more complicated. Therefore, in the following problems, indicate which variables are between-subjects variables, which are within-subjects variables, which ones are nested and what they are nested in, and which variables have fixed and which have random effects. Also, a few of these problems will require quasi-$F$ ($F'$) tests of the effects of interest. When this is the case, present the test and the associated degrees of freedom.

## EXERCISES

16.1   A group of personality researchers hypothesized that the self-image children have is related to their socioeconomic background, but that this is less the case for males than for females. To examine this question, they selected three school districts ($D$), each representing a different social stratum, for inclusion in the study. Five sixth-grade classes ($C$) were randomly sampled from each school district, and 10 students of each sex ($X$) from each class were then randomly selected and asked to fill out a self-evaluation form. The researchers performed the following analysis:

| SV | df |
|---|---|
| Total | 299 |
| District ($D$) | 2 |
| Sex ($X$) | 1 |
| $D \times X$ | 2 |
| $S/DX$ | 294 |

(a) Present an alternative ANOVA table (SV, $df$, EMS).

(b) What inferences might be changed by doing the analysis this way? Why?

**16.2** A therapist meets with 12 groups ($G$) for an hour each week. Each group consists of three males and three females (sex, $X$). Six of the groups are engaged in a type of directed therapy and the other six in nondirected therapy ($T$). Self-ratings are collected after a year of therapy and analyzed. Present the SV, $df$, EMS, and $F$ tests.

**16.3** An educational psychologist divides the 240 students in an Introductory Psychology course into 40 six-person discussion groups ($G$). There are four graduate student discussion leaders ($L$), each responsible for 10 groups. Half of the groups for each leader are taught by a didactic method in which the leader lectures and responds to questions from the six group members; the other five groups for each leader are taught by an interactive method in which the leader is strictly a resource person, monitoring the discussion and speaking only when the group can go no further in discussing a problem. Call this variable method ($M$). The dependent variable is the score on the midterm.

Present SV, $df$, EMS, and $F$ tests. Is $L$ a random-effect or fixed-effect variable?

**16.4** Six high schools ($Sc$) are chosen at random for an experiment testing the effectiveness of an educational software package that is to be used at three of the schools, but not at the other three; call this variable $P$ (package). The 120 students in the study come from 12 classes ($C$), two from each school. The measures are the scores on two tests ($T$), a midterm and final given to each subject.

(a) Present the SV, $df$, EMS, and $F$ tests.

(b) Redo your answer assuming the design is changed so that the software package was used in one of the two classes at each of the six schools.

**16.5** A list of 50 stimulus items to be used in a memory task is constructed in the following way: First, 5 large pools of items are selected that differ with respect to meaningfulness ($M$). Then 10 items ($I$) are randomly selected from each pool. The list of 50 items is presented to 20 subjects, so that there is a total of 1000 scores.

Present all SV, $df$, and EMS, and an $F$ test for $M$ (meaningfulness), including its $df$.

**16.6** A researcher wishes to study the effects of viewing televised violence on the behavior of children. She has a large sample of adult viewers rate the level of violence of a large number of episodes randomly selected from typical Saturday morning cartoon presentations. She then chooses 15 episodes; 5 of these are viewed as representative of a population of low-violence episodes; 5 more are medium, and 5 more are high in violence. Thus, there are three levels of violence ($V$), with five different episodes ($E$) at each level. Subjects are 6, 8, and 10 years old. Each of several dependent measures will be subjected to an ANOVA. One way to run the study would be to minimize the number of subjects needed. We might use 10 subjects at each age level. Each child would be tested on each of 15 days with a different episode viewed on each day; the order of episodes would be random.

Present SV, *df*, and EMS, and the *F* test for the *A* effect.

**16.7**   There are many alternative designs for the study in Exercise 16.6. One possibility is to have both age and violence be between-subject variables. There are 9 groups of 10 subjects each, and each child views five episodes, all at the same level of *V*. Again, state SV, *df*, and EMS, and the *F* test for the *A* effect.

**16.8**   The members of each of 10 groups of three monkeys have been raised together. In five of the groups, the group members were separated at 6 months of age; in the other five groups, separation occurred at 1 year. At age 2, all monkeys were tested on four problems in the presence of their original cohorts and on four other problems with no other monkeys present. Thus, we have 2 levels of age (*A*) of separation, 8 different problems (*P*), and 2 test environments (*E*). We also have 30 monkeys who comprise 10 different groups.

Present an *F* test for the *AE* term. Include the *df* and justify with the relevant EMS.

**16.9**   The design in Exercise 16.8 involved 240 observations. We could do the same study using 240 monkeys reared in 80 three-monkey groups. Half of these groups would be separated at 6 months of age and half at 1 year. Of the 40 groups at $A_1$, the members of five would be tested on Problem 1; the members of another five groups would be tested on Problem 2; etc. The same would be done with the 40 groups at $A_2$. Problems 1–4 are those tested in the social environment and Problems 5–8 are those tested in the individual environment.

**(a)** Present an *F* test for the *AE* term. Include the *df* and justify with the relevant EMS.

**(b)** What are the pros and cons of the two designs presented? There are both statistical and practical considerations.

**16.10**   The file Ex16_10 in the Exercise folder of your CD contains problem-solving scores from 60 subjects. The subjects were in one of three conditions: (1) practice in problem solving was conducted in a four-person group with a leader appointed by the experimenter (Leader = appointed); (2) the group practice was led by a leader elected by the group (Leader = elected); and (3) no leader was designated for the group (leader = noleader). In each condition, there were five groups of four members each, two males and two females. Carry out an ANOVA, testing for the effects of leader, gender, and their interaction.

**16.11**   In a follow-up experiment to that in Exercise 16.10, the "noleader" condition was compared with a "nogroup" condition in which subjects practiced individually. The data are in the Ex16_11 file. The 20 individual scores are coded as though they had been in groups (see the discussion of pseudogroups in Section 16.3.1). Test the effect of groups versus individuals using (a) the pseudogroup method and (b) the quasi-*F* method.

**16.12**   In several recent experiments, researchers have presented participants with material to read that was designed to prime their attitudes about subsequently presented descriptions of individuals (e.g., Stapel & Koomen, 2000). For example, on a given trial, a participant might read a sentence designed to prime a positive or negative attitude toward some personality trait. Following that, the participant would read a description of an individual that was ambiguous with respect to the trait and would have to rate the individual on a 1 (very positive) to 7 (very negative) scale. The file Ex16_13 contains a data set we created for a possible study of this sort. One independent variable is Sex $= M$ or $F$. There are four conditions: a sentence primed either a positive ($P$) or negative ($N$) attitude, and was either relevant ($R$) or irrelevant ($I$) to the trait that was rated after reading the subsequent description. There are five items (prime-description pairings) in each condition so that there are 20 ratings for each of 12 male and 12 female participants. Present SV, $df$, SS, and MS. Then test the $V$ and $R \times V$ terms. Discuss the results.

## APPENDIX 16.1

## Calculating Sums of Squares for Nested Terms

In the absence of software capable of calculating nested sums of square for the data in Table 16.11, we can make do with any program that can handle one between-subjects and two within-subjects variables. Enter the data as if the levels of $B$ cross with $C$ in Table 16.11. We now have a variable, $B'$, with the same four levels at each level of $A$. Proceeding with the analysis in this way, the within-subjects sources of variance and degrees of freedom are as follows:

| SV | df |
|----|----|
| $B'$ | $b - 1$ |
| $C$ | $c - 1$ |
| $B'C$ | $(b - 1)(c - 1)$ |
| $AB'$ | $(a - 1)(b - 1)$ |
| $AC$ | $(a - 1)(c - 1)$ |
| $AB'C$ | $(a - 1)(b - 1)(c - 1)$ |
| $SB'/A$ | $a(n - 1)(b - 1)$ |
| $SC/A$ | $a(n - 1)(c - 1)$ |
| $SB'C/A$ | $a(n - 1)(b - 1)(c - 1)$ |

Note that $df_{B'} + df_{B'C} = (b - 1) + (b - 1)(c - 1) = c(b - 1)$, the degrees of freedom for $B/C$, one of the terms in the correct ANOVA of Table 16.12. We take advantage of the one-to-one relation between degrees of freedom and sums of squares to arrive at $SS_{B/C} = SS_{B'} + SS_{B'C}$. Similarly, $SS_{AB/C} = SS_{AB'} + SS_{AB'C}$ and $SS_{SB/AC} = SS_{SB'/A} + SS_{SB'C/A}$. The correct degrees of freedom are arrived at in a parallel manner.

# Chapter 17
## Latin Squares and Related Designs

## 17.1 INTRODUCTION

An important consideration in designing an experiment is the efficiency of the design; all other things being equal, research should be designed to minimize the effects of chance factors. As chance variability decreases, statistical power increases, and with it the probability of detecting effects of the independent variable. One way to increase design efficiency was described in Chapter 12. There we showed that assigning subjects to blocks on the basis of a measure related to the dependent variable could greatly reduce error variance, and thus increase the likelihood of detecting treatment effects if these exist in the population. The repeated-measures design of Chapter 14 is still more efficient. This design permits further reduction in variance due to individual differences; because every subject experiences all conditions, differences among subjects do not contribute to differences among the means for the different conditions. In this chapter, we consider a class of experimental designs that have the potential for still greater reductions in error variance. We begin by considering a research example that should provide a sense of the design, its potential benefits, and some potential problems.

Suppose we wish to compare the relative effects of five different drug dosages on the ability of monkeys to learn a discrimination. Our measure will be the number of correct responses in a block of 20 trials. Monkeys are expensive subjects and so a between-subjects design will not be used. In fact, we will use only five subjects, testing each under a different dosage on a different day. One way to do this is to select a different random order of the five dosages for each subject. Using a random number table, or a computer-generated sequence of random numbers, the resulting five sequences of dosages might be as follows:

| Subject | Days | | | | |
|---------|------|------|------|------|------|
|         | 1    | 2    | 3    | 4    | 5    |
| 1 | $A_3$ | $A_2$ | $A_1$ | $A_4$ | $A_5$ |
| 2 | $A_2$ | $A_1$ | $A_3$ | $A_5$ | $A_4$ |
| 3 | $A_3$ | $A_2$ | $A_1$ | $A_4$ | $A_5$ |
| 4 | $A_4$ | $A_5$ | $A_2$ | $A_3$ | $A_1$ |
| 5 | $A_2$ | $A_3$ | $A_5$ | $A_4$ | $A_1$ |

where $A_j$ is the $j$th dosage. Averaging over the five subjects, some dosages are presented relatively earlier in the sequence than others; $A_2$, for example, never appears later than the third day, whereas only Subject 4 experiences $A_5$ before the third day, This may not have any effect on performance; on the other hand, boredom may slow down, or practice speed up, responses late in the series of days. Because all dosages have an equal chance of presentation on each of the 5 days, no dosage has a systematic advantage over many replications of the experiment; therefore, the statistical test of $A$ is unbiased. Nevertheless, this chance variability due to the day of presentation does reduce the power of the test to detect effects of $A$. In a more efficient design, the variability due to days would be removed from the data much as the variability due to subjects was removed in the repeated-measures design. This could be done by having each dosage appear equally often on each of the 5 days. An example of this would be:

| Subject | Days | | | | |
|---------|------|------|------|------|------|
|         | 1    | 2    | 3    | 4    | 5    |
| 1 | $A_2$ | $A_5$ | $A_1$ | $A_3$ | $A_4$ |
| 2 | $A_1$ | $A_4$ | $A_5$ | $A_2$ | $A_3$ |
| 3 | $A_3$ | $A_1$ | $A_2$ | $A_4$ | $A_5$ |
| 4 | $A_5$ | $A_3$ | $A_4$ | $A_1$ | $A_2$ |
| 5 | $A_4$ | $A_2$ | $A_3$ | $A_5$ | $A_1$ |

This design is called a **Latin square**; it is characterized by the fact that each level of A appears exactly once in each row and column.

Because each subject and each level of A is represented exactly once in each column of the Latin square design, variability due to columns (days in this example) can be extracted from the total sum of squares. The Latin square design allows the removal of variability due to two sources of error, subjects and days in our example. In contrast, in a Subjects × Treatments design, only error variance due to subjects is removed; random variability due to days contributes to $\sigma_e^2$. Because the error variance is potentially smaller in the Latin square than in the Subjects × Treatments design, the Latin square is potentially a more efficient design.

We say "potentially a more efficient design" because there are also some potential problems that do not arise in the Subjects × Treatments design. One problem arises because the Latin square is what is often called an **incomplete block design.** This means that each subject (block) in our example is not tested under the complete set of 25 possible combinations of drug dosage ($A$) and days. Because of this, there are not enough total degrees of freedom to perform independent tests of the $A$, subjects, and days effects, and their interactions. For example, there are $24$ $(25 - 1)$ $df$ available for assessing the variability among the cell means. Twelve $[3 \times (5 - 1)]$ of these are associated with the main effects of subjects, days, and drug dosage. This leaves only 12 $df$ to account for all the possible interactions, any one of which requires at least $16$ $[(5 - 1) \times (5 - 1)]$ $df$. Our inability to calculate interaction sums of squares poses no problem if row, column, and treatment effects are additive; that is, if there are no interactions among these variables in the population. However, if such interactions are present in the population, they may affect our conclusions. We will consider this issue at several points in this chapter.

A second potential problem, as with any repeated-measures design,[1] is **carry-over effects**. Consider the example of tests under different drug dosages on different days. The Latin square controls for any potential effect of practice in the discrimination task by ensuring that each drug dosage is presented once on each of the 5 days. However, it does not control for the sequencing of treatments. If, in our example, $A_1$ has an effect that lasts for more than 1 day, performance under $A_2$ might be affected more than performance under other levels of $A$ because $A_2$ follows $A_1$ twice, whereas other treatments follow $A_1$ zero or one time. One way of minimizing such effects of the sequences of treatments is to increase the time period between treatments. However, using a long enough **recovery period** may not be feasible in some experiments. For example, in research with young children, prolonging a session, or requiring subjects to serve over an extended number of sessions, is often undesirable. An alternative to the recovery period is a variation on the Latin square design in which each treatment is followed equally often by every other treatment. We will consider such variations in this chapter.

A necessary step in using the experimental designs of this chapter is the selection of the Latin square. We begin by demonstrating how this is done. We then proceed to consider the data analysis. Finally, we describe some modifications and extensions of the basic design.

## 17.2 SELECTING A LATIN SQUARE

The expected mean squares we present in this chapter are based on the assumption that the Latin square used in the experiment has been randomly selected from the population of possible squares. In this section, we consider procedures for selecting a square so that the random-selection assumption will be justified. This is straightforward for $2 \times 2$ squares; only two such squares are possible. There are 12 possible $3 \times 3$ squares. We could enumerate these and select a random number from 1 to 12 to choose the one for our experiment. However, it is simpler to obtain a square for an experiment by permuting the rows and columns of a **standard square**; this is a square whose first row and first column is in the standard order: $\langle A_1, A_2, A_3 \rangle$. The only possible $3 \times 3$ standard square is

$$\begin{bmatrix} A_1 & A_2 & A_3 \\ A_2 & A_3 & A_1 \\ A_3 & A_1 & A_2 \end{bmatrix}$$

To construct a random member of the possible set of 12 squares, begin by permuting all rows but the first. To do this, draw the numbers 2 and 3 in random order and reorder the rows accordingly; for example, if the sequence is $\langle 3, 2 \rangle$, the new square is

$$\begin{bmatrix} A_1 & A_2 & A_3 \\ A_3 & A_1 & A_2 \\ A_2 & A_3 & A_1 \end{bmatrix}$$

Now draw the numbers 1, 2, and 3 in random order. This time, permute the columns. Assuming the sequence is $\langle 3, 1, 2 \rangle$, the square is now

$$\begin{bmatrix} A_3 & A_1 & A_2 \\ A_2 & A_3 & A_1 \\ A_1 & A_2 & A_3 \end{bmatrix}$$

Note that the row permutation stage involves two possible orders of rows; this combines with six possible orders of columns to generate the entire population of 12 possible squares. There are four 4 × 4 standard squares:

$$\begin{bmatrix} A_1 & A_2 & A_3 & A_4 \\ A_2 & A_3 & A_4 & A_1 \\ A_3 & A_4 & A_1 & A_2 \\ A_4 & A_1 & A_2 & A_3 \end{bmatrix} \begin{bmatrix} A_1 & A_2 & A_3 & A_4 \\ A_2 & A_4 & A_1 & A_3 \\ A_3 & A_1 & A_4 & A_2 \\ A_4 & A_3 & A_2 & A_1 \end{bmatrix}$$

$$\begin{bmatrix} A_1 & A_2 & A_3 & A_4 \\ A_2 & A_1 & A_4 & A_3 \\ A_3 & A_4 & A_1 & A_2 \\ A_4 & A_3 & A_2 & A_1 \end{bmatrix} \begin{bmatrix} A_1 & A_2 & A_3 & A_4 \\ A_2 & A_1 & A_4 & A_3 \\ A_3 & A_4 & A_2 & A_1 \\ A_4 & A_3 & A_1 & A_2 \end{bmatrix}$$

To obtain a random square from the population of 4 × 4 squares, select a number at random from 1 to 4 and begin with the corresponding standard square. Then permute all rows except the first and all columns as we did in the example of the 3 × 3 square. Note that this procedure generates 3!4! possible squares for each of the four standard squares Therefore, we are selecting one square at random from the population of 576 (4 × 3! × 4!) squares.

The number of standard squares increases rapidly as $a$, the number of treatment levels, increases. Therefore, the procedure used for $a = 4$ is impractical for larger squares. A reasonable approach is to arbitrarily select a standard square, permute all rows, then all columns, and finally all letters. We did this to arrive at the 5 × 5 square presented in Section 17.1. We start with the standard square

$$\begin{bmatrix} A_1 & A_2 & A_3 & A_4 & A_5 \\ A_2 & A_4 & A_5 & A_3 & A_1 \\ A_3 & A_1 & A_2 & A_5 & A_4 \\ A_4 & A_5 & A_1 & A_2 & A_3 \\ A_5 & A_3 & A_4 & A_1 & A_2 \end{bmatrix}$$

A table of random numbers yields the values $\langle 2, 4, 3, 1, 5 \rangle$; the rows are permuted accordingly:

$$\begin{bmatrix} A_2 & A_4 & A_5 & A_3 & A_1 \\ A_4 & A_5 & A_1 & A_2 & A_3 \\ A_3 & A_1 & A_2 & A_5 & A_4 \\ A_1 & A_2 & A_3 & A_4 & A_5 \\ A_5 & A_3 & A_4 & A_1 & A_2 \end{bmatrix}$$

We turn again to the random number table and this time get $\langle 4, 1, 2, 5, 3 \rangle$, resulting in the following column permutation:

$$
\begin{bmatrix}
A_3 & A_2 & A_4 & A_1 & A_5 \\
A_2 & A_4 & A_5 & A_3 & A_1 \\
A_5 & A_3 & A_1 & A_4 & A_2 \\
A_4 & A_1 & A_2 & A_5 & A_3 \\
A_1 & A_5 & A_3 & A_2 & A_4
\end{bmatrix}
$$

Draw one more set of random numbers; this time we have $\langle 4, 2, 5, 1, 3 \rangle$. We will replace the $A_1$s in the above square by the $A_4$s, the $A_2$s will be in the same cells, the $A_3$s will be replaced by the $A_5$s, and so on. Then the final square to be used in the experiment is

$$
\begin{bmatrix}
A_5 & A_2 & A_1 & A_4 & A_3 \\
A_2 & A_1 & A_3 & A_5 & A_4 \\
A_3 & A_5 & A_4 & A_1 & A_2 \\
A_1 & A_4 & A_2 & A_3 & A_5 \\
A_4 & A_3 & A_5 & A_2 & A_1
\end{bmatrix}
$$

This procedure should be used whenever there are five or more treatment levels. Although not all squares have an equal opportunity to be sampled, the approach adequately approximates random sampling from the complete set of squares of size $a \times a$.

## 17.3 THE SINGLE LATIN SQUARE

We begin our discussion of the data analysis using the $5 \times 5$ square selected in Section 17.2 and the example introduced in Section 17.1. Recall that each level of $A$ is a drug dosage, each row is a subject, and the columns are days. This single Latin square is the simplest use of the Latin square principle; possible extensions include running more than one subject through each sequence of treatments, and using more than one $a \times a$ square. When only a single square is used with one subject in each sequence, the square should be at least $5 \times 5$. Anything smaller is likely to have too few degrees of freedom associated with the error mean square to provide adequate power to detect treatment effects.

### 17.3.1 The ANOVA

Table 17.1 presents the data collected using the $5 \times 5$ square obtained in Section 17.2. Most computer packages can analyze these data. Typically, each score is entered with its row, column, and treatment level coded. For the data set of Table 17.1, we would have a data file looking like this:

| S | C | A | Y |
|---|---|---|---|
| 1 | 1 | 1 | 17 |
| 1 | 2 | 2 | 18 |
| 1 | 3 | 4 | 18 |
|   |   |   | . |
|   |   |   | . |
|   |   |   | . |
| 5 | 5 | 3 | 14 |

**TABLE 17.1**   EXAMPLE OF A SINGLE LATIN SQUARE

|        | $C_1$ | $C_2$ | $C_3$ | $C_4$ | $C_5$ | $\overline{Y}_{i..}$ |
|--------|-------|-------|-------|-------|-------|----------------------|
| $S_1$  | $(A_1)17$ | $(A_2)18$ | $(A_4)18$ | $(A_3)19$ | $(A_5)20$ | 18.4 |
| $S_2$  | $(A_3)14$ | $(A_1)16$ | $(A_5)16$ | $(A_2)18$ | $(A_4)17$ | 16.2 |
| $S_3$  | $(A_4)13$ | $(A_3)15$ | $(A_1)18$ | $(A_5)16$ | $(A_2)18$ | 16.0 |
| $S_4$  | $(A_2)14$ | $(A_5)14$ | $(A_3)16$ | $(A_4)17$ | $(A_1)19$ | 16.0 |
| $S_5$  | $(A_5)\ 8$ | $(A_4)10$ | $(A_2)12$ | $(A_1)14$ | $(A_3)14$ | 11.6 |

$$\overline{Y}_{..k} = 13.2 \qquad 14.6 \qquad 16.0 \qquad 16.8 \qquad 17.6 \qquad \overline{Y}_{...} = 15.64$$

The means for the levels of $A$ are

$$\begin{array}{cccccc} & A_1 & A_2 & A_3 & A_4 & A_5 \\ \overline{Y}_{.j.} = & 16.8 & 16.0 & 15.6 & 15.0 & 14.8 \end{array}$$

*Note. $C$ = days; $A$ = drugs.*

where $S$ is the subject number, $C$ is the day, $A$ is the level of $A$, and $Y$ is the score. In SPSS's GLM module, click on the Model option and indicate "Main Effects." The SPSS output is presented in the upper panel of Table 17.2. Other statistical software programs provide other options for analyzing data from Latin square designs.

The lower panel of Table 17.2 presents the expected mean squares that justify the error term for each $F$ test. These expected mean squares, as well as the partitioning of variability into the sources presented, reflect a structural model considered in the next section. The sums of squares for the total, subjects ($S$), drug dosage ($A$), and days ($C$) are calculated exactly as in the preceding chapters. The residual sum of squares (the "error" term in Table 17.2) is exactly that, a residual of the total variability after removal of $SS_S$, $SS_A$, and $SS_C$. All $F$ ratios are constructed by testing the numerator source of variance against the residual term. Note that there is considerable variance due to days ($C$). In a repeated-measures (Subjects $\times A$) design, this variance would have been included in the error variance, and the $F$ test of $A$ might not have had a significant outcome. Also, confidence intervals on trend components or on possible contrasts would have been considerably wider. The success of the design lies in the fact that performance improved over days, and the Latin square design enabled us to remove the variance attributable to days from the error variance. We will have more to say on this point in Section 17.3.3.

## 17.3.2 The Structural Model

We now consider the model that justifies the analysis of Table 17.2. The advantages of the Latin square are clear and the interpretation of the analysis straightforward if the following additive model can reasonably be assumed:

$$Y_{ijk} = \mu + \eta_i + \alpha_j + \gamma_k + \varepsilon_{ijk} \tag{17.1}$$

where $i$ indexes the subjects (rows of the square), $j$ indexes the treatment levels, $k$ indexes the columns, and there are $a$ levels of each of the three variables.

As in Chapter 13, the term "additive" refers to the additivity of main effects; no interactions are assumed to be present in the model. For our example of drug dosages administered over days, we assume that $A$ (treatments) and $C$ (columns) are fixed-effect variables. We

**TABLE 17.2**  SPSS RESULTS OF AN ANOVA OF THE DATA OF TABLE 17.1 AND EXPECTED MEAN SQUARES

## (a) SPSS Results

**Tests of Between-Subjects Effects**

**Dependent Variable: Y**

| Source | | Type III Sum of Squares | df | Mean Square | F | Sig. |
|---|---|---|---|---|---|---|
| Intercept | Hypothesis | 6115.240 | 1 | 6115.240 | 199.584 | .000 |
| | Error | 122.560 | 4 | 30.640[a] | | |
| C | Hypothesis | 61.760 | 4 | 15.440 | 74.710 | .000 |
| | Error | 2.480 | 12 | .207[b] | | |
| A | Hypothesis | 12.960 | 4 | 3.240 | 15.677 | .000 |
| | Error | 2.480 | 12 | .207[b] | | |
| S | Hypothesis | 122.560 | 4 | 30.640 | 148.258 | .000 |
| | Error | 2.480 | 12 | .207[b] | | |

a. MS(S)
b. MS(Error)

*Note.* The Intercept term tests the null hypothesis that the population grand mean is zero.

## (b) Expected Mean Squares

| SV | df | EMS |
|---|---|---|
| S | $a-1$ | $\sigma_e^2 + a\sigma_S^2$ |
| C | $a-1$ | $\sigma_e^2 + a\theta_C^2$ |
| A | $a-1$ | $\sigma_e^2 + a\theta_A^2$ |
| Residual | $(a-1)(a-2)$ | $\sigma_e^2$ |

consider days to be a fixed-effect factor because time periods such as days are usually arbitrarily selected; ordinarily, we do not randomly select the days for testing. Later in this chapter, we will consider cases in which $C$ might be a factor other than time periods and might have random effects. Under the present assumptions, $\sum_j \alpha_j = \sum_k \beta_k = 0$. Also, the $\eta_i$ and $\varepsilon_{ijk}$ are normally distributed random variables with zero means and variances $\sigma_e^2$ and $\sigma_S^2$, respectively. The expected mean squares derived from this model are presented in Table 17.2. If Equation 17.1 adequately describes the population of scores, the Latin square design provides the basis for a very efficient test of effects, because we have removed error variance due to both the row and column variables. It should be emphasized that this efficiency is realized only if the proper analysis is carried out. Frequently, researchers counterbalance treatment levels over positions in time, or with respect to some other variable, and then partition the total $SS$ into only three components: $SS_A$, $SS_S$, and $SS_{SA}$. This partitioning implies a different structural model, one in which the effect of $C$ ($\gamma_k$) is absent:

$$Y_{ijk} = \mu + \eta_i + \alpha_j + \varepsilon_{ijk}$$

If $C$ contributes more than chance variability, this analysis results in a negatively biased $F$ test. The error term in this analysis is a pool of the $C$ and residual mean squares and therefore

$$E(MS_{SA}) = \frac{(a-1)E(MS_C) + (a-1)(a-2)E(MS_{\text{residual}})}{(a-1) + (a-1)(a-2)}$$

$$= \sigma_e^2 + a\theta_C^2/(a-1)$$

Failure to detect an effect of $A$ when tested against this error term might reflect an absence of $A$ effects in the population, or large enough $C$ effects to obscure effects of $A$. To minimize the possibility of a Type 2 error due to the presence of $C$ effects in the denominator of the $F$ test of $A$, the complete analysis of Table 17.2 should always be carried out.

   If the data are properly analyzed, the Latin square should be a more efficient design than the Subjects $\times$ Treatments design of Chapter 13. Let's consider this point next.

### 17.3.3 Relative Efficiency

We argued in the introduction to this chapter that the Latin square design should have less error variance associated with it than the Subjects $\times$ Treatments design, because the former permits us to remove variance due not only to individual differences (or, more generally, rows), but also to columns. This intuitive argument can be supported in a more formal way. Assume a Subjects $\times$ Treatments design with $a$ subjects and $a$ treatment levels, and a Latin square design with the same dimensions. Then it can be shown (Myers & Well, 1995, p. 375) that the relation between the error terms in the two designs is

$$E(MS_{SA}) = E(MS_{\text{residual}}) + E(MS_C - MS_{\text{residual}})/a \tag{17.2}$$

If $MS_C > MS_{\text{residual}}$, $MS_{SA}$ (the Subjects $\times$ Treatments error term) will be larger than $MS_{\text{residual}}$ (the error term in the Latin square design). Therefore, we can expect $F$ tests of treatments to be more powerful with the Latin square design. However, $MS_{\text{residual}}$ has fewer degrees of freedom than $MS_{SA}$, which lessens the advantage of the Latin square error term. To account for this, Fisher (1952) proposed the following measure of relative efficiency of Design 1 to Design 2, originally cited in Chapter 13:

$$RE_{1\text{ to }2} = \left[\frac{df_1 + 1}{df_1 + 3}\right] \cdot \left[\frac{df_2 + 3}{df_2 + 1}\right] \cdot \left[\frac{MS_{\text{error 2}}}{MS_{\text{error 1}}}\right] \tag{17.3}$$

Note the adjustment for error degrees of freedom ($df_1$ and $df_2$).

   In the example of the drug dosage experiment, assume that we have used the Latin square design and want to decide whether it will be more efficient than the Subjects $\times$ Treatments design in future studies. The Latin square degrees of freedom are $df_1 = (a-1)(a-2) = 12$ in our example. The degrees of freedom for the alternative repeated-measures design are $df_2 = (a-1)(n-1) = 16$ (because $n = a$). Applying Equations 17.2 to the mean squares in Table 17.2, the estimate of $MS_{SA}$ is

$$\text{est } MS_{SA} = .207 + (15.440 - .207)/5 = 3.254$$

Replacing $MS_{\text{error 2}}$ in Equation 17.3 by 3.254 and $MS_{\text{error 1}}$ by $MS_{\text{residual}}$ (.207), the efficiency of the Latin square relative to the repeated-measures design is

$$RE_{LS\text{ to }RM} = \left(\frac{13}{15}\right) \cdot \left(\frac{17}{19}\right) \cdot \left(\frac{3.254}{.207}\right) = 12.19$$

To achieve equivalent power with the Subjects × Treatments design would require approximately 12 times more subjects than using (and properly analyzing the data from) the Latin square design. Of course, this conclusion might be quite different if days had not contributed so much variance. However, factors such as practice, fatigue, and boredom can be expected to frequently influence performance, contributing more variability than even the treatment of interest.

### 17.3.4 Estimating Missing Scores

Assuming Equation 17.1, missing scores can be estimated following a derivation similar to that in Chapter 13. Let $X_{ijk}$ be the missing score. Then, its expected value follows from Equation 17.1:

$$E(X_{ijk}) = \mu + \eta_i + \alpha_j + \gamma_k \tag{17.4}$$

Substituting estimates of effects into Equation 17.4, the estimated value of $X$ is

$$\hat{X} = \left[ \frac{T_{...} + \hat{X}}{a^2} \right] + \left[ \frac{T_{i..} + \hat{X}}{a} - \frac{T_{...} + \hat{X}}{a^2} \right] + \left[ \frac{T_{.j.} + \hat{X}}{a} - \frac{T_{...} + \hat{X}}{a^2} \right]$$
$$+ \left[ \frac{T_{..k} + \hat{X}}{a} - \frac{T_{...} + \hat{X}}{a^2} \right]$$

Simplifying and solving,

$$\hat{X} = \frac{a(T_{i..} + T_{.j.} + T_{..k}) - 2T_{...}}{(a-1)(a-2)} \tag{17.5}$$

where $T_{...}$ is the sum of all the scores (except the missing one), $T_{i..}$ is the sum of scores for the $i$th subject, $T_{.j.}$ is the sum of scores for treatment $A_j$, and $T_{..k}$ is the sum of scores in the $k$th column of the square. If several scores are missing, the iterative procedure described in Chapter 13 can be used.

### 17.3.5 Nonadditivity

In the preceding sections, we assumed complete additivity; that is, no interactions among $S$, $C$, and $A$. Because this model is unrealistic in many, perhaps most, situations, it is important to examine the consequences of nonadditivity. A nonadditive model incorporating all possible interactions is

$$Y_{ijk} = \mu + \eta_i + \alpha_j + \gamma_k + (\eta\alpha)_{ij} + (\alpha\gamma)_{jk} + (\eta\gamma)_{ik} + (\eta\alpha\gamma)_{ijk} + \varepsilon_{ijk} \tag{17.6}$$

As in the additive case, $\eta_i$, $\alpha_j$, and $\gamma_k$ reflect $S$, $A$, and $C$ effects.

Wilk and Kempthorne (1957) derived the expected mean squares for the Latin square design based on Equation 17.6. Table 17.3 presents their results for two cases, when $C$ has fixed effects and when $C$ has random effects. In both cases, $S$ represents subjects and is assumed to have random effects, and $A$, the treatment variable, is assumed to have fixed effects. Note that components of variance are present in the expected mean squares that the rules of thumb of Chapter 14 would not suggest. For example, when $C$ has fixed effects, $\theta_{AC}^2$ contributes to the variance of the subject ($S$) means. The reason for this is that the Latin square is an incomplete block design; only a subset of all possible $AC$ interaction effects

**TABLE 17.3** EXPECTED MEAN SQUARE FOR THE SINGLE LATIN SQUARE (NONADDITIVITY ASSUMED)

| | S Random, C and A Fixed |
|---|---|
| SV | EMS |
| $S$ | $\sigma_e^2 + \theta_{AC}^2 + \left(\dfrac{a-1}{a}\right)\sigma_{SCA}^2 + a\sigma_S^2$ |
| $A$ | $\sigma_e^2 + \sigma_{SA}^2 + \sigma_{SC}^2 + \left(\dfrac{a-2}{a}\right)\sigma_{SCA}^2 + a\theta_A^2$ |
| $C$ | $\sigma_e^2 + \sigma_{SA}^2 + \sigma_{SC}^2 \left(\dfrac{a-2}{a}\right)\sigma_{SCA}^2 + a\theta_C^2$ |
| Residual | $\sigma_e^2 + \sigma_{SA}^2 + \sigma_{SC}^2 + \theta_{AC}^2 + \left(\dfrac{a-2}{a}\right)\sigma_{SCA}^2$ |

| | S and C Random A Fixed |
|---|---|
| SV | EMS |
| $S$ | $\sigma_e^2 + \sigma_{SC}^2 + \sigma_{AC}^2 + \left(\dfrac{a-1}{a}\right)\sigma_{SCA}^2 + a\sigma_S^2$ |
| $A$ | $\sigma_e^2 + \sigma_{SA}^2 + \sigma_{AC}^2 + \sigma_{SC}^2 + \left(\dfrac{a-1}{a}\right)\sigma_{SCA}^2 + a\theta_A^2$ |
| $C$ | $\sigma_e^2 + \sigma_{SA}^2 + \sigma_{SC}^2 + \left(\dfrac{a-1}{a}\right)\sigma_{SCA}^2 + a\sigma_C^2$ |
| Residual | $\sigma_e^2 + \sigma_{SA}^2 + \sigma_{AC}^2 + \sigma_{SC}^2 + \left(\dfrac{a-1}{a}\right)\sigma_{SCA}^2$ |

contribute to a subject's data, and the subset differs among subjects, thus contributing to differences among the subjects' mean scores. For a similar reason, $\sigma_{SC}^2$ contributes to $E(MS_A)$ even though the rules previously given for constructing expected mean squares do not require it. In general, whether the effects are fixed or random, $\sigma_{SC}^2$ influences $MS_A$, $\sigma_{SA}^2$ influences $MS_C$, $\theta_{AC}^2$ influences $MS_S$, and the three-way interaction contributes to the mean squares for all three variables. Such **confounding** of effects is typical of incomplete block designs—that is, designs in which all combinations of two variables are not present at each level of a third variable.

Nonadditivity has some undesirable consequences. When the null hypothesis is false, the addition of a component of variance to numerator and denominator tends to reduce the $F$ ratio and therefore tends to reduce power. The presence of some interactions in the population also can cause bias in the $F$ test. If $C$ is a fixed-effect variable, the interaction variance component, $\theta_{AC}^2$, will contribute to $MS_{\text{residual}}$ but not to $MS_A$ or $MS_C$. Thus, if $\theta_{AC}^2 > 0$, the test of $A$ will be negatively biased. If this interaction variance is large relative to variance among the population means for the treatment levels, Type 2 error rates will be high.

Despite such potential bias, the Latin square design often provides a more powerful test than the Subjects × Treatments design. For this to be the case, $\theta_{AC}^2$ should be small, and $\theta_C^2$ should be large. In short, the negative bias should not overwhelm any potential treatment effects, and blocking with respect to columns should have a large payoff in the form of a reduction of error variance. These conditions will often be met.

When $C$ has random effects, the $F$ test of $A$ is unbiased, regardless of which variance components are present in the population. This can be seen in the bottom panel of Table 17.3 in which $\sigma_{AC}^2$ contributes to both the $A$ and residual mean squares. $C$ might be considered a random-effects factor in many experiments. Often, stimuli such as pictures, sentences, or passages are randomly divided into $c$ sets, each of which is assigned to a different level of a treatment variable, $A$. The assignment is counterbalanced so that the design is a Latin square with the levels of $C$ representing sets of items. Assuming that the items represent a random sample from a population of items, the levels of $C$ can be viewed as randomly sampled.

Let's sum up the consequences of nonadditivity in analyzing data from a design using a single Latin square. When $C$ has random effects, or when $\theta_{AC}^2$ is zero, the $F$ test of treatment effects is unbiased. Under other conditions, the bias will be negative because $\theta_{AC}^2$ will contribute to $MS_{\text{residual}}$, but not to $MS_A$. Even if such bias is present, the Latin square usually will provide a more powerful test of $A$ effects than will other designs because row and column main effects will not contribute to the Latin square's error variance. However, estimates of $\theta_A^2$, will be systematically too small in the presence of negative bias.

Provided there are sufficient data, nonadditivity may be detected by plotting residuals. As with the repeated-measures design, we can calculate the values of $Y_{ijk}$ that are expected under the additive model:

$$\hat{Y}_{ijk} = \hat{\mu} + \hat{\eta}_i + \hat{\alpha}_j + \hat{\gamma}_k$$
$$= \overline{Y}_{...} + (\overline{Y}_{i..} - \overline{Y}_{...}) + (\overline{Y}_{.j.} - \overline{Y}_{...}) + (\overline{Y}_{..k} - \overline{Y}_{...}) \tag{17.7}$$

If the data are additive, the residuals, $Y_{ijk} - \hat{Y}_{ijk}$, plotted as a function of the predicted value, $\hat{Y}_{ijk}$, will vary randomly about a line with slope of zero. Figure 17.1 presents such a plot for the data of Table 17.1. Although the points are widely scattered, there is no systematic trend and the slope is clearly not different from zero; the confidence interval for the slope of the best-fitting straight line is bounded by $-.05$ and $.05$. In figures such as Fig. 17.1, one or two deviant points would suggest the possibility of miscalculation of the data point, or a need to replace the subject. A systematic pattern such as a curved function would suggest nonadditivity that may be corrected by a power transformation (i.e., $Y^p$). However, we again emphasize that transformations result in tests of null hypotheses on a scale other than the original data scale. If the original scale has no firm theoretical or practical basis, and the new scale is as readily interpreted, such transformations make sense, but not otherwise.

The residual plot can be supplemented by a test of nonadditivity (Tukey, 1952). The test requires extensive calculations (which are not generally available in computer packages), is not sensitive to all patterns of nonadditivity, and requires a large enough square to ensure power. Our inclination is to rely primarily on plots of residuals to inform us about the presence and nature of nonadditivity in our data. Finally, we note that nonadditivity opens the possibility of nonsphericity. The epsilon ($\epsilon$) adjustment of degrees of freedom, described in Chapter 13 is appropriate for the Latin square as well.

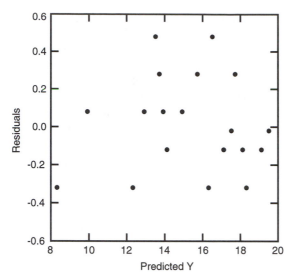

**Fig. 17.1** A plot of residuals for the data of Table 17.1.

## 17.3.6 Incorporating Several Treatment Variables Into a Single Square

Even in a single Latin square, the interaction of two variables, $A$ and $B$, can be analyzed, provided that all possible combinations appear exactly once in each row and column of the square. Consider a study of visual perception in which targets are presented for a brief period of time. The targets are either large or small and are presented for 50 or 100 ms. Each subject experiences a block of 20 trials under each of the four possible treatment combinations, and the dependent variable is the number of correctly identified targets in each block. In this case, the Latin-squared treatments form a $2 \times 2$ design (Size × Duration). An example of the design using one subject in each of four sequences of trial blocks, together with a set of scores, is presented in Table 17.4. Table 17.5 contains the results of the analysis of these data. The calculations are essentially the same as those for a single Latin square. The only difference is that we now calculate $SS_A$, $SS_B$, and $SS_{AB}$ rather than a single treatment sum of squares.

In general, there are $ab$ rows and $ab$ columns; because $a = b = 2$ in Table 17.4, $ab = 4$. The model underlying the sources of variance and the expected mean squares in the ANOVA of Table 17.5 is

$$Y_{ijkm} = \mu + \eta_i + \alpha_j + \beta_k + (\alpha\beta)_{jk} + \gamma_m + \varepsilon_{ijkm} \tag{17.8}$$

where $i$ indexes subjects ($i = 1, 2, \ldots, ab$), $j$ indexes the levels of $A$ (size: $j = 1, 2, \ldots, a$), $k$ indexes the levels of $B$ (duration: $k = 1, 2, \ldots, b$), and $m$ indexes the columns (trial block: $m = 1, 2, \ldots, ab$). In the present example, we assume that the $\alpha_j$, $\beta_k$, $(\alpha\beta)_{jk}$, and $\gamma_m$ are fixed-effect variables, and therefore $\sum_j \alpha_j = \sum_k \beta_k = \sum_m \gamma_m = \sum_j (\alpha\beta)_{jk} = \sum_k (\alpha\beta)_{jk} = 0$. The $\eta_i$ and $\varepsilon_{ijkm}$ are random-effect variables independently and normally distributed with mean zero and variances $\sigma_e^2$ and $\sigma_S^2$, respectively.

**TABLE 17.4**　A LATIN SQUARE DESIGN ALLOWING TESTS OF INTERACTION

| | $C_1$ | $C_2$ | $C_3$ | $C_4$ | $\overline{Y}_{i..}$ |
|---|---|---|---|---|---|
| $S_1$ | 11 $(A_1 B_2)$ | 16 $(A_2 B_1)$ | 20 $(A_1 B_1)$ | 15 $(A_2 B_2)$ | 15.5 |
| $S_2$ | 6 $(A_2 B_1)$ | 13 $(A_2 B_2)$ | 13 $(A_1 B_2)$ | 18 $(A_1 B_1)$ | 12.5 |
| $S_3$ | 2 $(A_2 B_2)$ | 13 $(A_1 B_1)$ | 9 $(A_2 B_1)$ | 10 $(A_1 B_2)$ | 8.5 |
| $S_4$ | 5 $(A_1 B_1)$ | 6 $(A_1 B_2)$ | 4 $(A_2 B_2)$ | 7 $(A_2 B_1)$ | 5.5 |
| $\overline{Y}_{..m} = 6$ | | 12 | 11.5 | 12.5　$\overline{Y}_{...} = 10.5$ | |

Treatment Means $(\overline{Y}_{.jk.})$

| | $B_1$ | $B_2$ | $\overline{Y}_{.j..}$ |
|---|---|---|---|
| $A_1$ | 14 | 10 | 12 |
| $A_2$ | 9.5 | 8.5 | 9 |
| $\overline{Y}_{..k.}$ | 11.75 | 9.25 | 10.5 |

**TABLE 17.5**　THE ANOVA FOR THE DATA OF TABLE 17.4

| SV | df | SS | MS | F | EMS |
|---|---|---|---|---|---|
| $S$ | $ab - 1 = 3$ | 232 | 77.333 | 116.00 | $\sigma_e^2 + ab\sigma_S^2$ |
| $C$ | $ab - 1 = 3$ | 110 | 36.667 | 55.00 | $\sigma_e^2 + ab\theta_C^2$ |
| $A$ | $a - 1 = 1$ | 36 | 36.000 | 54.00 | $\sigma_e^2 + ab^2\theta_A^2$ |
| $B$ | $b - 1 = 1$ | 25 | 25.000 | 37.50 | $\sigma_e^2 + a^2b\theta_B^2$ |
| $AB$ | $(a - 1)(b - 1) = 1$ | 9 | 9.000 | 13.50 | $\sigma_e^2 + ab\theta_{AB}^2$ |
| Residual | $(ab - 1)(ab - 2) = 6$ | 4 | .667 | | $\sigma_e^2$ |
| Total | $(ab)^2 - 1 = 15$ | 416 | | | |

[a] $MS_{residual}$ is the error term for all $F$ tests. All effects are significant at the .01 level.

## 17.4 THE REPLICATED LATIN SQUARE DESIGN

The single Latin square design discussed so far is useful in situations in which it is impractical to collect data from more than a small number of subjects. Perhaps more commonly, the square is replicated $n$ times; that is, $a$ groups of $n$ subjects are assigned to each of the $a$ sequences. Then there are $an$ subjects, each with $a$ scores. In the following sections, we first present the proper partitioning of sums of squares, and then consider the $F$ tests based on two models, one assuming that $C$ is a fixed-effect variable and the other assuming that $C$ has random effects.

### 17.4.1 Partitioning the Sums of Squares

Table 17.6 presents group means from an experiment reported by Cook, Myers, and O'Brien (2000). The column factor, $C$, represents 3 sets of 8 short texts each. The factor, $A$, represents 3 versions of each text, differing with respect to information in the early part of the text

**TABLE 17.6** CELL MEANS FOR A REPLICATED LATIN SQUARE (COOK, MYERS, & O'BRIEN, 2000)

| Group | $C_1$ | $C_2$ | $C_3$ | Mean |
|---|---|---|---|---|
| 1 | $1917.1(A_2)$ | $1726.4(A_1)$ | $1817.8(A_3)$ | 1820.43 |
| 2 | $1753.5(A_3)$ | $1805.4(A_2)$ | $1830.1(A_1)$ | 1796.33 |
| 3 | $1836.1(A_1)$ | $1836.8(A_3)$ | $2018.4(A_2)$ | 1897.10 |

Means at the levels of $C$ are

$$\begin{array}{ccc} C_1 & C_2 & C_3 \\ 1835.57 & 1789.53 & 1888.77 \end{array}$$

Means at the levels of $A$ are

$$\begin{array}{ccc} A_1 & A_2 & A_3 \\ 1797.53 & 1913.63 & 1802.70 \end{array}$$

The grand mean = 1838.96

that was referred to in the last sentence of the text. Note that the design is a Latin square, differing only from the single Latin square in that each value in a cell represents a mean of 10 scores. For example, the 10 subjects in Group 1 read version $A_2$ of the eight texts in set $C_1$; the subjects in Group 2 read version $A_3$ of the $C_1$ texts; and the subjects in Group 3 read version $A_1$ of the $C_1$ texts. The means are based on the time each subject took to read the final sentence of the text; that sentence was the same in all three versions.

We begin the partitioning of degrees of freedom and sum of squares by first considering the variability among the $a^2$ cell means, the $SS_{\text{cells}}$, distributed on $a^2 - 1$ $df$. Subtracting $SS_{\text{groups}}$, $SS_A$, and $SS_C$ from $SS_{\text{cells}}$, we have a **between-cells residual sum of squares ($SS_{\text{BCR}}$)**; that is,

$$SS_{\text{BCR}} = SS_{\text{cells}} - SS_{\text{groups}} - SS_A - SS_C$$

and accordingly,

$$df_{\text{BCR}} = df_{\text{cells}} - df_{\text{groups}} - df_A - df_C = (a - 1)(a - 2)$$

Table 17.7 presents a complete partitioning of sums of squares and degrees of freedom. We will postpone discussion of the $F$ tests until after consideration of expected mean squares. For now, we focus on obtaining the sums of squares. In most software packages, this is done fairly easily. We began by constructing a data file with 30 rows (one for each subject) and 7 columns. The first column contains the group code, in our case a number from 1 to 3, depending on the group. The next three columns contained the scores at each level of $A$. The final three columns contained the same scores, but rearranged so that each column corresponded to a level of $C$. We ran two mixed-design ANOVAs with groups as the between-subjects factor.[2] In the first, $A$ was the within-subjects variable and in the second $C$ was the within-subject variable. The $SS_{\text{groups}}$ and $SS_{S/\text{groups}}$ terms are the same in both analyses. Calculation of $SS_{\text{BCR}}$ follows from its definition:

$$\begin{aligned} SS_{\text{BCR}} &= SS_{\text{cells}} - SS_{\text{groups}} - SS_A - SS_C \\ &= SS_{\text{groups} \times A} - SS_C \end{aligned} \tag{17.9}$$

**TABLE 17.7** PARTITIONING OF THE SUMS OF SQUARES FOR THE DATA OF TABLE 17.6

| SV | df | SS | MS |
|---|---|---|---|
| Between Ss | $an - 1 = 29$ | 12,375,507.81 | |
| *Groups (G)* | $a - 1 = 2$ | 166,125.09 | 83,062.54 |
| *S/G* | $a(n - 1) = 27$ | 12,209,382.72 | 452,199.36 |
| Within Ss | $an(a - 1) = 60$ | 1,473,905.72 | |
| A | $a - 1 = 2$ | 258,121.09 | 129,060.54 |
| C | $a - 1 = 2$ | 147,965.62 | 73,982.81 |
| BCR | $(a - 1)(a - 2) = 2$ | 27,128.14 | 13,564.41 |
| WCR | $a(n - 1)(a - 1) = 54$ | 1,040,690.87 | 19,272.05 |

*Note.* BCR = between-cells residual; WCR = within-cells residual.

The $SS_{\text{Groups} \times A}$ is available in the output of the first analysis. Or we could calculate

$$SS_{\text{BCR}} = SS_{\text{groups} \times C} - SS_A$$

In the example,

$$SS_{\text{groups} \times A} - SS_C = 175,094.04 - 147,965.62 = 27,128.42$$

or

$$SS_{\text{groups} \times C} - SS_A = 285,249.51 - 258,121.09 = 27,128.42$$

The last term in Table 17.7 is the usual mixed-design error term. Because $A$ and $C$ are totally confounded within each group, $SS_{S \times A/\text{groups}}$ must be the same as $SS_{S \times C/\text{groups}}$; in Table 17.7, we chose the more neutral label WCR (within-cells residual) for this term.[3] This completes the partitioning of the total sum of squares. We consider the $F$ tests next.

## 17.4.2 Expected Mean Squares and *F* Tests

In the Cook et al. (2000) experiment, $C$ is most reasonably viewed as having random effects because the sets of passages that constitute the levels of $C$ have been randomly constructed from a pool of passages that may be viewed as a sample from some population of potential items. However, the replicated square design is also used when $C$ is more reasonably considered to have fixed effects; for example, when the levels of $C$ are time periods. Because the designation of $C$ as fixed or random affects the expected mean squares and, consequently, the error term against which the $A$ source of variance is tested, we consider both possibilities.

The structural model for the replicated square design is

$$Y_{ijkm} = \mu + \eta_{i/m} + \alpha_j + \gamma_k + (\alpha\gamma)_{jk} + \varepsilon_{ijkm} \tag{17.10}$$

where $i$ indexes the subject within a row of the Latin square ($i = 1, 2, \ldots, n$), $j$ indexes the level of $A$ ($j = 1, 2, \ldots, a$), $k$ indexes the level of $C$ ($k = 1, 2, \ldots, a$), and $m$ indexes the row within the square (the group; $m = 1, 2, \ldots, a$). The population of subject effects, the $\eta_{i/m}$, is assumed to be independently and normally distributed with mean zero and variance $\sigma^2_{S/G}$. The effects of $a$, the $\alpha_j$, are assumed to be fixed. As indicated, $C$ may have fixed or random effects. If random, then the effects of $C$, the $\gamma_k$, and the $AC$ interaction effects, the $(\alpha\gamma)_{jk}$, are distributed independently and normally with mean zero and respective variances $\sigma_C^2$ and $\sigma_{AC}^2$.

The $AC$ effects require further comment. Although there is no $SS_{AC}$ in the usual sense, the $AC$ interaction effects contribute to the variance of the group means. If there are $AC$ effects in the population, part of their contribution to the data will be reflected in $MS_{\text{groups}}$. This is because the Latin square is an incomplete block design; as a result, each of the three factors (rows, columns, treatments) is potentially confounded with the interaction of the other two factors (see Section 17.4.3). Furthermore, significant residual variability among the $a^2$ cell means (after adjusting for the contribution of the main effects) also reflects part of the variance of $AC$ interaction effects. The $(AC)'$ label in the SV column of Table 17.8 (as well as the expected mean squares) indicates these partial interaction effects.

Turning to Table 17.8, the test of the effects of the treatment variable, $A$, when the effects of $C$ are assumed to be fixed is the same as in the mixed design of Chapter 14. The within-subjects error term is appropriate for testing both $A$ and $C$ main effects, as well as providing a test of the partial interaction $(AC')$ of $A$ and $C$. However, when $C$ is assumed to have random effects, following the rules stated in Chapter 14, $\sigma_{AC}^2$ contributes to $E(MS_A)$ and the appropriate error term is $MS_{\text{BCR}}$. Unless the $A$ effects are large, or the

**TABLE 17.8**  EXPECTED MEAN SQUARES AND F RATIOS FOR THE REPLICATED SQUARE DESIGN (DATA FROM TABLE 17.6)

| SV | EMS | Error Term | F | p |
|---|---|---|---|---|
| **C Has Fixed Effects** | | | | |
| Groups (AC') | $\sigma_e^2 + a\sigma_{S/G}^2 + na\theta_{AC}^2$ | S/G | .18 | .836 |
| S/G | $\sigma_e^2 + a\sigma_{S/G}^2$ | | | |
| A | $\sigma_e^2 + na\theta_A^2$ | WCR | 6.70 | .003 |
| C | $\sigma_e^2 + na\theta_C^2$ | WCR | 3.84 | .028 |
| BCR (AC') | $\sigma_e^2 + n\theta_{AC}^2$ | WCR | .70 | .501 |
| WCR | $\sigma_e^2$ | | | |
| **C Has Random Effects** | | | | |
| Groups (AC') | $\sigma_e^2 + a\sigma_{S/G}^2 + na\sigma_{AC}^2$ | S/G | .18 | .836 |
| S/G | $\sigma_e^2 + a\sigma_{S/G}^2$ | | | |
| A | $\sigma_e^2 + n\sigma_{AC}^2 + na\theta_A^2$ | BCR | 9.51 | .095 |
| C | $\sigma_e^2 + na\sigma_C^2$ | WCR | 3.84 | .028 |
| BCR (AC') | $\sigma_e^2 + n\sigma_{AC}^2$ | WCR | .70 | .501 |
| WCR | $\sigma_e^2$ | | | |

*Note.* Because $\sigma_{AC}^2$ clearly makes no contribution to the residual variance of the cell means, we pooled the *BCR* and *WCR* terms. $SS_{\text{pool}} = 1,067,819.01$ and after dividing by 56, the pooled degrees of freedom, $MS_{\text{pool}} = 19,068.20$. Dividing $MS_A$ by the pooled mean square yields $F = 6.77$, which is significant at the .002 level.

square is, this $F$ test will lack power. In the Cook et al. example, BCR has only 2 $df$ and, as can be seen, what appears to be a rather large $F$ is not significant at the .05 level. A more powerful test of $A$ can be constructed if we have clear evidence that $AC$ interaction effects ($\theta^2_{AC}$) are negligible. In that case, the BCR and WCR mean squares could be pooled and used as an error term against which to test $A$. With this in mind, we tested BCR against WCR. The $p$ value for this preliminary test is considerably greater than .25, the standard suggested by Bozivich et al. (1956), and the test would appear to be reasonably powerful, given the number of error degrees of freedom. Thus, the result offers no evidence of any $AC$ contribution to the $E(MS_{BCR})$. In terms of the Cook et al. experiment, the effects of the text version (their $A$ factor) do not appear to depend on the particular set of texts ($C$) used. In view of this, the BCR and WCR terms have been pooled, and as noted at the bottom of Table 17.8, the $F$ test of $A$ now has a clearly significant result.

What if the preliminary test has a $p$ value less than .25? A transformation may be found that results in a scale on which there is no evidence of $AC$ variance. Failing that, the investigator should consider redoing the experiment with an alternative design that does not involve the confounding associated with the Latin square.

One other issue deserves mention. The means in Table 17.6 are averages not only over subjects, but also over items as well. It may appear that—as we prescribed in Chapter 13—a quasi-$F$ statistic should be calculated to take the variance due to items into account. However, the test against the BCR mean square (or its pool with the WCR mean square) serves that function because variance due to the sets of items, and its interaction with treatments, is included in the expected mean squares (Raaijmakers, Schrijnemakers, & Gremmen, 1999).

## 17.4.3 Including Between-Subjects Variables in the Replicated Square Design

Suppose that, on the basis of a pretest, Cook et al. had divided their subjects into two levels of reading ability; call this factor $B$. Then the design would look like that of Table 17.9 in which the Latin square is a $3 \times 3$, and there are 5 good and 5 poor readers in each row (combinations of $A$ and $C$). In general, the design has $abn$ subjects, divided at random among the $a$ rows of the square and the $b$ levels of $B$. The sources of variance, degrees of freedom, expected mean squares, and error terms are presented in Table 17.10, assuming that $C$ has random effects. As indicated in the SV column and expected mean

**TABLE 17.9**   REPLICATED LATIN SQUARE WITH A BETWEEN-SUBJECTS VARIABLE

| | $B_1$ (Good Readers) | | | | $B_2$ (Poor Readers) | | |
|---|---|---|---|---|---|---|---|
| Row | $C_1$ | $C_2$ | $C_3$ | Row | $C_1$ | $C_2$ | $C_3$ |
| 1 | $A_2$ | $A_1$ | $A_3$ | 1 | $A_2$ | $A_1$ | $A_3$ |
| 2 | $A_3$ | $A_2$ | $A_1$ | 2 | $A_3$ | $A_2$ | $A_1$ |
| 3 | $A_1$ | $A_3$ | $A_2$ | 3 | $A_1$ | $A_3$ | $A_2$ |

*Note.* There are five subjects in each row at each level of $B$. In general, there are $n$ subjects in each of $a$ rows at each of $b$ levels of $B$, for a total of $abn$ subjects with $a$ scores for each subject.

**TABLE 17.10**    ANALYSIS OF THE DESIGN OF TABLE 17.9

| SV | df | EMS[a] | Error Term |
|---|---|---|---|
| Rows (AC′) | $a - 1$ | $\sigma_e^2 + a\sigma_{S/B \times \text{Rows}}^2 + abn\sigma_{AC}^2$ | S/B×Rows |
| B | $b - 1$ | $\sigma_e^2 + a\sigma_{S/B \times \text{Rows}}^2 + a^2 n\theta_B^2$ | S/B × Rows |
| B × Rows (ABC′) | $(a-1)(b-1)$ | $\sigma_e^2 + a\sigma_{S/B \times \text{Rows}}^2 + an\sigma_{ABC}^2$ | S/B × Rows |
| S/B × Rows | $ab(n-1)$ | $\sigma_e^2 + a\sigma_{S/B \times \text{Rows}}^2$ | |
| A | $a - 1$ | $\sigma_e^2 + nb\sigma_{AC}^2 + abn\theta_A^2$ | BCR |
| C | $a - 1$ | $\sigma_e^2 + nb\sigma_{AC}^2 + abn\sigma_C^2$ | BCR |
| AB | $(a-1)(b-1)$ | $\sigma_e^2 + n\sigma_{ABC}^2 + an\theta_{AB}^2$ | B × BCR |
| BC | $(a-1)(b-1)$ | $\sigma_e^2 + n\sigma_{ABC}^2 + an\sigma_{BC}^2$ | B × BCR |
| BCR(AC′) | $(a-1)(a-2)$ | $\sigma_e^2 + nb\sigma_{AC}^2$ | WCR |
| B × BCR (ABC′) | $(a-1)(a-2)(b-1)$ | $\sigma_e^2 + n\sigma_{ABC}^2$ | WCR |
| WCR | $ab(a-1)(n-1)$ | $\sigma_e^2$ | |

[a] The *EMS* are based on the assumption that *C* has random effects. If *C* has fixed effects, the *AC* and *ABC* interaction components are deleted from the *A*, *C*, *AB*, and *BC EMS*, and those effects are accordingly tested against the within-cells residual, *WCR*.

squares of Table 17.10, both the row and between-cells residual (BCR) terms reflect possible *AC* interaction effects. The *B* × Row and *B* × BCR terms reflect possible *ABC* interaction effects. This also is indicated in the SV and *EMS* columns of Table 17.10. These interaction effects are again a function of the confounding inherent in incomplete block designs.

Main and interaction effects are calculated as in all preceding chapters. The only terms whose calculations might pose a problem are the BCR and its interaction with *B*. These can be viewed as differences between terms derived from standard mixed-design ANOVAs. This observation again forms the basis for using computer packages to analyze the data. Any computer program capable of handling two between-subject variables (*B,* Row) and one within-subject variable (*A* or *C* ) can then be used to do two analyses. For example, obtain $SS_A$ from the analysis that treats *A* as the within-subject variable and $SS_{C \times \text{Row}}$ from the analysis that treats *C* as the within-subjects variable. Then $SS_{C \times \text{Row}} - SS_A = SS_{\text{BCR}}$. Similarly, $SS_{B \times C \times \text{Row}} - SS_{AB} = SS_{B \times \text{BCR}}$. The results will be the same if $SS_C$ is subtracted from $SS_{A \times \text{Row}}$, and $SS_{BC}$ is subtracted from $SS_{A \times B \times \text{Row}}$. The entries in the EMS column in Table 17.10 were derived assuming *C* has random effects, the most reasonable assumption when *C* represents sets of items. If *C* is a fixed-effect variable, as when *C* represents time periods, the expected mean squares and error terms are changed as described in the footnote to Table 17.10.

## 17.5 BALANCING CARRY-OVER EFFECTS

When *C* represents time periods, there is a risk that the effects of treatments will be modified by preceding treatments. By the proper choice of squares, carry-over effects from the immediately preceding treatment can be balanced out. This can be done with a single square when there is an even number of treatments, but requires two squares when $a$ is an odd number. Assume $a$ is an even number, say 4. Then the square is constructed in the following steps.

1. Number the treatments from 1 to $a$.
2. Enter numbers in order in every other cell of the first row:

$$
\begin{array}{cccc}
C_1 & C_2 & C_3 & C_4 \\
1 & & 2 &
\end{array}
$$

3. Fill the remaining cells with the remaining numbers in order, starting at the right of the row:

$$
\begin{array}{cccc}
C_1 & C_2 & C_3 & C_4 \\
1 & 4 & 2 & 3
\end{array}
$$

4. Fill each column in order from the first row:

$$
\begin{array}{cccc}
C_1 & C_2 & C_3 & C_4 \\
1 & 4 & 2 & 3 \\
2 & 1 & 3 & 4 \\
3 & 2 & 4 & 1 \\
4 & 3 & 1 & 2
\end{array}
$$

Each number now precedes each other number exactly once. Treatment levels can now be assigned at random to the four numbers. Each row corresponds to a subject or to a group of subjects as in previous versions of the Latin square design.

When $a$ is an odd number, say 3, two squares are needed to balance carry-over effects from the immediately preceding treatment. To construct the squares, follow these steps.

1. Construct a row with $2a$ columns. Then write the numbers from 1 to $a$ in order in every other cell:

$$
\begin{array}{cccccc}
C_1 & C_2 & C_3 & C_1 & C_2 & C_3 \\
1 & & 2 & & 3 &
\end{array}
$$

2. Write the same numbers in order, this time starting at the right of the row:

$$
\begin{array}{cccccc}
C_1 & C_2 & C_3 & C_1 & C_2 & C_3 \\
1 & 3 & 2 & 2 & 3 & 1
\end{array}
$$

3. Fill in each column by proceeding sequentially from the number in the first row:

$$
\begin{array}{cccccc}
C_1 & C_2 & C_3 & C_1 & C_2 & C_3 \\
1 & 3 & 2 & 2 & 3 & 1 \\
2 & 1 & 3 & 3 & 1 & 2 \\
3 & 2 & 1 & 1 & 2 & 3
\end{array}
$$

**4.** Split the columns midway and rearrange with the first $a$ columns placed on top of the remaining $a$ columns:

$$
\begin{array}{ccc}
C_1 & C_2 & C_3 \\
1 & 3 & 2 \\
2 & 1 & 3 \\
3 & 2 & 1 \\
2 & 3 & 1 \\
3 & 1 & 2 \\
1 & 2 & 3 \\
\end{array}
$$

Each of the six rows corresponds to a subject or group of subjects. Each digit, representing a treatment level, precedes each other digit exactly twice.

The data from this **digram-balanced design** is analyzed as in the preceding sections. Because a treatment precedes all other treatments equally often, the carry-over contribution to treatment effects should be equated. However, the design equates only the effect of the immediately preceding treatment and does not deal with effects carried over several time periods. Cochran and Cox (1957, pp. 135–139) describe methods for calculating the sums of squares due to carry-over, and for removing that variability from the sums of squares for treatments. Namboodiri (1972) also describes other related designs.

## 17.6 GRECO-LATIN SQUARES

The designs presented in this chapter are a subset of the many possible variations of the Latin square design. They are an even smaller subset of incomplete block designs. We have limited our presentation to those designs we view as most useful and most often used by researchers. One possible extension occasionally referenced in the experimental literature is the Greco-Latin square. Suppose we have three levels of a variable $A$ and three levels of a variable $B$. To have efficient tests of both, we wish to treat both $A$ and $B$ as within-subject variables. But suppose it is impractical to test each subject under all nine combinations of $A$ and $B$. If the levels of $A$ are represented by the letters $a$, $b$, and $c$ and those of $B$ by $\alpha$, $\beta$, and $\gamma$ (hence "Greco-Latin"), the design might be

$$
\begin{bmatrix}
b\beta & a\alpha & c\gamma \\
c\alpha & b\gamma & a\beta \\
a\gamma & c\beta & b\alpha
\end{bmatrix}
$$

where a subject or group is tested with each sequence (row of the square). Note that the layouts of the Latin letters and the Greek letters each meet the requirements for a Latin square. Furthermore, each combination of levels of $A$ and $B$ appears exactly once in each row and column. The above design has several problems. First, the introduction of another variable reduces the BCR degrees of freedom; for a single square, such as the one above, these degrees of freedom are $(a^2 - 1) - 4(a - 1) = (a - 1)(a - 3)$. This is zero when $a = 3$. To have any chance at rejecting a false null hypothesis, the

Greco-Latin design should involve at least six rows and columns. The second problem is perhaps more serious. The introduction of another factor in this way sets up the possibility of still more interactions that may be confounded with main effects of interest. This may cost us a clean test of such main effects. The third problem is that if $A \times B$ interactions are present, we have no way of assessing them. It is rare that an investigator would want to forego the opportunity to test for an interaction between two experimentally manipulated factors. In short, although there are circumstances in which this design has some appeal, we believe that investigators usually will be better off with some other design.

## 17.7 CONCLUDING REMARKS

Several points about designs that use the Latin square principle deserve emphasis. Such designs are potentially very efficient because they permit blocking with respect to two variables, such as subjects and trials, or subjects and sets of materials. The potential benefits carry with them the risk that the $F$ test may be biased because variability due to interactions cannot be removed from the total pool of variability. Latin squares are incomplete block designs and therefore there are insufficient degrees of freedom to permit independent tests of both main effects and interactions of rows, columns, and treatments. However, even if interaction effects do contribute to various mean squares, the Latin square design will often still be more efficient than the standard repeated-measures design, because of the removal of variance due to the columns factor.

It is often helpful to plot residuals to obtain a sense of the degree, if any, of nonadditivity. Also, the test of the BCR in the replicated squares design is an aid in assessing whether an additive model is appropriate. Given evidence of marked nonadditivity, the researcher might consider transforming the data to a scale on which the additive model is adequate. If such a transformation cannot be found, or if there are reasons to keep the original scale, at least the knowledge of nonadditivity can aid in assessing the implications of the $F$ ratios calculated and perhaps in qualifying the inferences to be drawn. Finally, we again wish to emphasize our sense that the Latin square, particularly the replicated square design, is often used by researchers, but the data are often not properly analyzed (Pollatsek & Well, 1995). Failing to adjust for the variance of group means (i.e., row effects) negatively biases the $F$ test, increasing the probability of a Type 2 error. Also, as we have discussed, the BCR is the proper error term against which to test treatment effects when the columns factor has random effects. Failure to do so can result in an inflated Type 1 error rate.

## KEY CONCEPTS

| | |
|---|---|
| Latin square design | incomplete block design |
| carry-over effects | recovery period |
| standard square | confounding |
| replicated-squares design | between-cells residual sum of squares |
| digram-balanced design | |

## EXERCISES

**17.1**   Consider the following $4 \times 4$ Latin square:

$$
\begin{array}{c}
 & C_1 & C_2 & C_3 & C_4 \\
\begin{array}{c} S_1 \\ S_2 \\ S_3 \\ S_4 \end{array} &
\left[\begin{array}{cccc}
25(A_1) & 16(A_4) & 24(A_2) & 18(A_3) \\
19(A_2) & 19(A_1) & 13(A_3) & 12(A_4) \\
13(A_4) & 18(A_3) & 20(A_1) & 16(A_2) \\
17(A_3) & 19(A_2) & 18(A_4) & 17(A_1)
\end{array}\right]
\end{array}
$$

(a) Calculate the $SS_A$, $SS_C$, $SS_{S.}$, and $SS_{\text{residual}}$.

(b) Calculate the estimates of the 16 $S \times C$ interaction effects $[(\eta\gamma)_{ik}]$. Then subtract each estimate of $(\eta\gamma)_{ik}$ from $Y_{ik}$. Note that

$$
\begin{aligned}
Y_{ik} - \text{est}(\eta\gamma)_{ik} &= Y_{ik} - (Y_{ik} - \overline{Y}_{i\cdot} - \overline{Y}_{\cdot k} + \overline{Y}_{\cdot\cdot}) \\
&= \overline{Y}_{i\cdot} + \overline{Y}_{\cdot k} - \overline{Y}_{\cdot\cdot}
\end{aligned}
$$

Now recalculate the various sums of squares for the adjusted scores. Which sums of squares, if any, change? What potential problem in the use of this design do these results reflect?

**17.2**   Suppose the design in Exercise 17.1 was a repeated-measures design in which the sequence of the $A_j$ had been randomly assigned for each subject.

(a) Estimate $MS_{SA}$ from the data set above.

(b) What is your estimate of the relative efficiency of the two designs?

(c) Suppose every subject had scores 3 points lower at $C_1$ and 3 points higher at $C_2$. Would the efficiency relative to the $S \times A$ design be less than, the same as, or greater than the value you calculated in part (b)? Why?

**17.3**   In a study of decision making, two factors were manipulated. The task either resembled one seen during a practice session or did not (experience, $E$) and the amount of information available was either high or low (information level, $I$). Each subject was tested under all four combinations of $E$ and $I$ with the assignment of $EI$ combinations to four randomly sampled problems ($P$) counterbalanced through the use of a Latin square. Decision times were:

$$
\begin{array}{c}
 & P_1 & P_2 & P_3 & P_4 \\
\begin{array}{c} S_1 \\ S_2 \\ S_3 \\ S_4 \end{array} &
\left[\begin{array}{cccc}
1.4(E_1 I_1) & 2.2\,(E_2 I_2) & 1.5(E_1 I_2) & 1.5(E_2 I_1) \\
2.1(E_1 I_2) & 1.5(E_1 I_1) & 2.0(E_2 I_1) & 2.4(E_2 I_2) \\
2.8(E_2 I_2) & 2.1(E_2 I_1) & 1.4(E_1 I_1) & 1.8(E_1 I_2) \\
2.3(E_2 I_1) & 2.1(E_1 I_2) & 2.7(E_2 I_2) & 1.6(E_1 I_1)
\end{array}\right]
\end{array}
$$

Perform the ANOVA.

**17.4**   A researcher wishes to investigate cognitive performance as a function of drug type ($T$) and dosage ($D$). Thirty-two subjects are randomly assigned to one of two drugs, and each subject is given a different one of four dosages of the same drug on four different occasions ($O$). A Latin square design is used with four sequences of dosages and eight subjects in each sequence. Note that half of the subjects in each sequence receive $D_1$ and half receive $D_2$.

(a) Give the SV, *df*, and error terms.

(b) Another way to run this study would be to create a single $8 \times 8$ Latin square with two subjects in each row (so there are still 128 total scores). The eight treatments would be all possible combinations of the drug ($T$) and dosage ($D$) levels. Write out the SV, *df*, and error terms for this case.

(c) What are the pros and cons of the two designs?

**17.5** A researcher is interested in gambling behavior under variations in initial stake ($I$), payoffs ($P$), and probability of winning ($W$). There are three levels of each of these variables. Eighty-one subjects are available for this experiment. Many possible experimental designs could be used. Suggest several alternative designs and discuss their relative merits.

**17.6** When subjects are tested under different conditions at different points in time, carry-over (residual) effects are a potential problem. The digram-balanced design described in this chapter provides one possible solution.

(a) Construct a digram-balanced design, assuming that there are six levels of the treatment variable.

(b) Construct a digram-balanced design, assuming that there are five levels of the treatment variable.

**17.7** The Ex17_7 file in the *Exercises* folder of your CD contains a data set for a $4 \times 4$ Latin square design. There are 12 subjects with 3 in each row ($R$) of the square. $A$ is the treatment factor and $C$ is the column (or position in time) factor. Assume $C$ has fixed effects. Perform the ANOVA.

**17.8** Presumably, you analyzed the Ex17_7 data set correctly. However, some individuals might treat the data as if they were obtained from a Subjects $\times$ Treatments design. Pool terms from your answer to Exercise 17.7 to arrive at this incorrect ANOVA. How does the $F$ and $p$ value relate to that previously obtained? Explain the reason for the difference in results.

**17.9** The Ex17_9 file contains data (very) loosely modeled after a study by Witvliet, Ludwig, and Vander Laan (2001). Subjects in that experiment were instructed to think of an individual who had mistreated or offended them. They imagined a response to this individual as they read four scripts representing hurting someone ($S_1$), bearing a grudge ($S_2$), empathsizing ($S_3$), and forgiving ($S_4$). Various physiological measures were obtained in each of several segments of time in several counterbalanced blocks. The Ex17_9 file contains heartbeat change scores similar to averages in the Witvliet article. There are 20 cases in the file, 5 in each of the four rows of a Latin square. The within-subject factors are $S$ (the script) and $C$ (the ordinal position in the sequence of presentation). Note that $S_1$ and $S_2$ have negative valences, and $S_3$ and $S_4$ have positive valences; the effect of valence should be considered in the analysis. Perform the analysis and summarize your conclusions.

**17.10** Assume that we had given a scale measuring hostility to 40 subjects, and divided them into two groups of 20 on that basis ($H = 1$ corresponds to the high hostility group and $H = 2$ corresponds to the low hostility group). These subjects then participate in the experiment described in Exercise 17.9. The data are in the Ex17_10 file. Carry out the ANOVA and state your conclusions.

# Chapter 18
## More About Correlation

## 18.1 INTRODUCTION

In Chapter 3 we introduced the Pearson correlation coefficient as a measure of the extent to which two variables are linearly related, and we considered examples in which correlations such as $r = .594$ for multiplication and subtraction accuracy in third graders and $r = .286$ for cholesterol level and age were obtained. Given such correlations, a number of questions immediately arise. How are we to interpret these correlations? Is a correlation of .286 large enough to be meaningful? Is it significantly different from zero? Can we find a confidence interval? What assumptions must we make about the data?

In this chapter, we first extend our discussion of the interpretation of $r$ because although the correlation coefficient is frequently encountered, it often seems to be reported without a great deal of understanding, and without looking at the data. This can lead to serious problems because the correlation coefficient has some important limitations. As we showed in Chapter 3, the correlation coefficient is a measure of the extent to which two variables are *linearly* related; however, two variables may have a systematic nonlinear relation even if their correlation is very small or zero. Also, in general, there is no one-to-one relation between the correlation coefficient and slope of the best-fitting regression line. Although the Pearson correlation coefficient is a measure of the *extent* to which two variables are linearly related, different combinations of the slope, variance of $X$ and $Y$, and error variance can yield the same value of the correlation coefficient. This means that the correlation coefficient is a **sample-specific measure**. That is, the correlation coefficient depends not only on the nature of the linear relation between $X$ and $Y$, but also on the variability of $X$ and $Y$ in the sample.

When we introduced the correlation coefficient in Chapter 3, we discussed a number of important issues. In the present chapter, we discuss some characteristics of the correlation coefficient in more detail and raise a number of additional issues that should be kept in mind when interpreting correlations. We also discuss confidence intervals and significance tests for correlation coefficients, and the power of significance tests for correlation. We also introduce the concept of partial correlation, the correlation between two variables that have been adjusted for the effects of other variables. Finally, we introduce several special cases and alternative measures of correlation.

## 18.2 FURTHER ISSUES IN UNDERSTANDING THE CORRELATION COEFFICIENT

### 18.2.1 The Standard Error of Estimate

Before considering the properties of the correlation coefficient, it is useful to introduce a measure of variability about the regression line. As we shall show, this variability affects the magnitude of $r$. It is measured by $s_e$, the estimated population **standard error of estimate,** the most commonly used measure of variability about the regression line and the one typically given by software packages. It is defined as

$$s_e = \sqrt{\frac{\sum (Y_i - \hat{Y}_i)^2}{N - 2}} = \sqrt{\frac{SS_{\text{residual}}}{N - 2}} = \sqrt{\frac{(1 - r^2)SS_Y}{N - 2}} \tag{18.1}$$

Two things should be noted about Equation 18.1. First, we use $SS_{\text{residual}}$ instead of $SS_{\text{error}}$ to refer to $\sum (Y_i - \hat{Y}_i)^2$, because the term $SS_{\text{error}}$ is often reserved to refer to variability about a mean. Second, in the expression for $s_e$, $SS_{\text{residual}}$ is divided by its $df$, $N - 2$. There are $N - 2$ $df$ because there are $N$ data points and two restrictions; that is, 2 $df$ are used up by estimating the intercept and slope of the regression equation.

### 18.2.2 The Relation Between $r$ and Variability in $X$ and $Y$

In this section, we discuss how the value of $r$ depends on the slope of the regression line, the variability about the regression line, and the variability of $X$ and $Y$. In Chapter 3, we pointed out how the correlation coefficient and the slope of the regression line for predicting $Y$ from $X$ were related:

$$r = b_1 \frac{s_X}{s_Y} = b_1 \sqrt{\frac{SS_X}{SS_Y}} \tag{18.2}$$

where $b_1$ is the slope of the regression line for predicting $Y$ from $X$, $s_X$ and $s_Y$ are the standard deviations of $X$ and $Y$, and $SS_X$ and $SS_Y$ are the sums of squares of $X$ and $Y$. If $s_X$ and $s_Y$ are equal, $r$ is equal to the slope of the regression line. However, when the standard deviations differ, as they usually do, $r$ is not the slope of the regression equation. From Equation 18.2, we see that $r$ depends not only on $b_1$, but also on $s_X$ and $s_Y$. As we shall see, by packaging the information slightly differently, we can show that $r$ depends on $b_1$, $s_X$, and $s_e$, the variability in $Y$ not accounted for by the regression line.

In Chapter 3, we presented several scatterplots (Fig. 3.9) that were each based on the same 20 paired $z$ scores and therefore represented the same correlation ($r = .80$). The scatterplots differ in having different standard deviations for $X$ and $Y$. The correlation coefficient remains the same despite the fact that the slope varies considerably, as does the apparent degree of clustering around the best-fitting straight line. The same value of $r$ can occur for different combinations of $s_X$, $s_Y$, $b_1$, and $s_e$. The fact that the same value of $r$ can occur for these different combinations makes it clear that we must look at the scatterplot and consider not only $r$, but also these other statistics if we wish to understand the relation between $X$ and $Y$. Also, when comparing the nature of the relation between $X$ and $Y$ in two groups, we must think carefully about whether we want to compare $r$s or whether we want to compare regression slopes.

We can write several equations that are useful for understanding how $r$ depends on the regression slope and the different types of variability. Two of these equations are

$$r^2 = \frac{b_1^2 SS_X}{b_1^2 SS_X + SS_{\text{residual}}} = \frac{(N-1)b_1^2 s_X^2}{(N-1)b_1^2 s_X^2 + (N-2)s_e^2} \tag{18.3}$$

and

$$r^2 = 1 - \frac{s_e^2}{s_Y^2}\left[\frac{N-2}{N-1}\right] \tag{18.4}$$

These equations both follow directly from the fact that the total variability in the $Y$ scores can be partitioned into components that correspond to the variability in $Y$ accounted for by the regression ($SS_{\text{regression}}$) and the variability not accounted for by the regression ($SS_{\text{residual}}$); that is,

$$\sum(Y_i - \overline{Y})^2 = \sum(\hat{Y}_i - \overline{Y})^2 + \sum(Y_i - \hat{Y}_i)^2 \tag{18.5}$$
$$SS_Y = \quad SS_{\text{regression}} \quad + SS_{\text{residual}}$$

Equation 18.5 is derived in Appendix 18.1, and Equations 18.3 and 18.4 are derived in Appendix 18.2.

Both Equations 18.3 and 18.4 show that when all the data points fall on the regression line so that $SS_{\text{residual}}$ and $s_e^2$ are zero, then $r^2 = 1$, and $r$ must be $+1$ or $-1$. Equation 18.3 shows that, for a given slope and amount of variability around the regression line, the more variability there is in $X$, the closer $r^2$ is to 1. Also, for given values of $SS_{\text{residual}}$ and $SS_X$, larger values of the slope, $b_1$, lead to increases in $r^2$. Equation 18.4 shows that, for a given amount of variability around the regression line, the more variability there is in $Y$, the closer $r^2$ is to 1. These equations suggest that it is useful to think of the correlation coefficient as a composite measure that combines different features of the linear relation between $X$ and $Y$.

The fact that the correlation coefficient is so strongly influenced by the sample variances of $X$ and $Y$ has some unfortunate consequences. For example, in the Seasons data set, the correlation between total cholesterol level and age for females is .506. If we break the sample into two parts, one subsample consisting of women 50 years of age or over and the other of women under 50, the age variability is less in each of the subsamples (the standard deviations are 6.26 and 6.58 for older and younger women, respectively) than in the combined sample (standard deviation of 11.69). As suggested by Equation 18.3, the correlations between cholesterol level and age are also much smaller in the subsamples: the correlations of .148 and .264 found for the older and younger women represent reductions of 71% and 49% from the correlation of .506 in the whole sample. These results indicate that comparisons of correlations between groups may be ambiguous. A finding that $r$ is larger in one group than in another might occur because the nature of the linear relation between $X$ and $Y$ is different in the two groups. However, we might also find the same result even if the linear relation is the same in both groups, but the variability of $X$ is different.

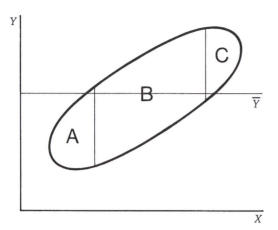

**Fig. 18.1** Scatterplots with different regions marked to illustrate the effect of the variability of $X$ and $Y$ on the correlation coefficient.

If we want to compare the rate at which $Y$ changes with $X$ in the two groups, we should compare their regression coefficients, not their correlations.

Consider what happens when only certain values of $X$ are sampled. Suppose we have a population of data points in which $X$ and $Y$ have an imperfect linear relation with a moderately high correlation, $\rho$, as indicated in Fig. 18.1. Assume further that there is **homoscedasticity**; that is, the variability about the regression line is the same for all values of $X$. Now suppose we select two samples, one from region B and the second from regions A and C. The $r$ for a sample selected from region B will tend to *underestimate* $\rho$, and the $r$ for a sample selected from a region consisting of both A and C will tend to *overestimate* $\rho$. The standard deviation of $Y$ will be smaller in region B (or in any other single region) than it is in the entire population of data points. This is because there are relatively fewer large deviations of $Y$ scores from their mean in a restricted region (see Fig. 18.1). Therefore, $s_Y$ will tend to be smaller for a sample selected from region B than for a sample of the same size selected from the entire population. In contrast, the standard error of estimate, $s_e$, will not systematically differ by very much in the two samples. Therefore, the ratio $s_e/s_Y$ will tend to be larger for the restricted sample than for the sample selected from the entire population, and from Equation 18.4, we can see that $r$ would be expected to be smaller. This type of bias is frequently referred to as the **restriction of range** problem. An oft-cited example of restriction of range is the low correlation between Graduate Record Examination (GRE) scores and success in graduate school as measured by grades or faculty ratings (e.g., Dawes, 1971), which has prompted calls for the abandonment of the GRE scores as predictive measures. Even if GRE scores were an excellent measure of ability, the correlation would be expected to be quite low because only students with relatively high GRE scores get accepted into graduate programs.

Sampling from restricted regions of the distribution can also produce inflated estimates of $\rho$. For example, suppose we select a sample only from regions A and C in Fig. 18.1. The standard deviation of $Y$ in this sample will tend to be larger than the population standard deviation because it is based on the $Y$ values in regions A and C, which tend to deviate considerably from the mean of $Y$, and it fails to include the smaller deviations in area B. Because $s_e$ will not usually differ by much in the two situations, samples from the combined

A and C regions will tend to have smaller $s_e/s_Y$ ratios than samples selected from the entire population, and therefore, as we can see from Equation 18.4, these samples will have larger values of $r$. Investigators interested in the relation between two variables will sometimes drop the middle scores for one or both of them. For example, the gambling behavior of subjects scoring high on the MMPI Psychopathic Deviant Scale may be compared with the gambling behavior of subjects who score low on the scale. Although this procedure is acceptable for determining whether there is a linear component to the relation, the correlation between gambling behavior and MMPI scale scores obtained from the extreme groups should definitely not be considered to be an estimate of the correlation in the whole population. However, as we will show, the correlation for the complete sample may be estimated from that calculated from a subset of scores.

We can also illustrate these points by considering the arithmetic accuracy data for the third graders in the Royer data set. If we consider all the third graders, the correlation between subtraction accuracy and multiplication accuracy is .59. From the preceding discussion, we would expect that the correlation would decrease if we selected scores from only one part of the distribution, so that $s_X$ and $s_Y$ were smaller. This turns out to be true. If we consider only children who scored at least 80% in subtraction, the correlation drops to .34. On the other hand, if we consider only those children who either scored over 90% or under 70% on subtraction, the correlation increases to .72. As expected, selecting from the distribution in ways that increase $s_X$ and $s_Y$ raises the correlation.

When we have a value of $r$ estimated from a sample selected from a particular range of $X$ values, it is possible to estimate what the value would have been if the sample had been based on a different range of $X$ values, if we can assume that the relation between $X$ and $Y$ is linear and that $b_1$ and $s_e$ are exactly the same in both samples. Then, starting with Equation 18.3, it can be shown that if a correlation coefficient of $r'$ is obtained from a sample with standard deviation $s_{X'}$, an estimate of the correlation coefficient in a sample with standard deviation $s_X$ is given by

$$\hat{r} = \frac{r' s_X/s_{X'}}{\sqrt{1 + r'^2 \left[s_X^2/s_{X'}^2 - 1\right]}} \tag{18.6}$$

For example, for those third graders who scored at least 80% on subtraction, the correlation between multiplication and subtraction accuracy was $r' = .34$. The standard deviation of the subtraction scores in this restricted sample was $s_{X'} = 6.04$. If we consider all the third graders, the standard deviation is $s_X = 11.77$. Substituting these values into Equation 18.6, we find the estimated correlation of subtraction and multiplication scores for the third graders to be .58, very close to the actual correlation of .59 in the unrestricted sample.

So far, we have tried to indicate how $r$ depends on the characteristics of the sample by noting what we would expect to happen for samples selected from particular restricted regions of the population. It is important to note that the same kind of bias will occur in samples that are randomly selected from the entire population. All other things being equal, samples that have larger values of $s_X$ because of sampling error will tend to produce higher estimates of $\rho$.

Because the correlation coefficient is sample-specific and generally does not describe the relation between $X$ and $Y$, some writers (e.g., Achen, 1982; Tukey, 1969) have cautioned against its use. Achen (1982) has taken a rather extreme position, arguing

"The fact that a Pearson $r$ (or a gamma, phi, standardized beta, or any other correlational measure) depends in an important way on the variance of the variables involved makes comparisons meaningless in general. Different correlational measures depend on the variance in different ways, but the solution is not to find the one that captures the medieval essence of correlation, but rather to abandon them all." (p. 61)

We agree that if there is a linear relation between $X$ and $Y$, characteristics of the regression equation—such as the intercept, slope, and standard error of estimate—may well describe the nature of the relation more usefully than does $r$. However, we do not believe that the correlation coefficient should be abandoned, only that it should be used with a full understanding of what it does and does not measure.

One possible reason for the popularity of the correlation coefficient is that in the social sciences we frequently work with variables that have arbitrary scales (what does a 1-point difference on a 7-point anxiety scale really mean?). Therefore $r$ may seem attractive because it is based on standardized scores, rather than scores expressed in terms of the actual units of the measuring scales. However, the downside is that when we use $r$ or $r^2$, or any other standardized measure of effect size, we are more likely to ignore the fact that our scales may be inadequate. We may not understand them very well, and they may not be good measures of the underlying variables that are our real concern. When we do have variables with meaningful units, we should consider using measures such as the regression slope, which is expressed in terms of these units. As Tukey (1969) puts it,

"Given two perfectly meaningless variables, one is reminded of their meaninglessness when a regression coefficient is given, since one wonders how to interpret its value. A correlation coefficient is less likely to bring up the unpleasant truth—we think we know what $r = -.7$ means." (p. 89)

### 18.2.3 Measurement Error

If $X$ and $Y$ are measured with error, the obtained correlation coefficient will underestimate the "true" correlation that would be obtained if $X$ and $Y$ could be measured without error. This should not be surprising; if our numbers are contaminated by measurement error, they can hardly be expected to reveal strong systematic relations. To better understand the effect of measurement error on the correlation coefficient, assume that $X$ and $Y$ each consist of a true score and an error component; that is,

$$X = X' + u \quad \text{and} \quad Y = Y' + v$$

where $X'$ and $Y'$ are the true scores, and $u$ and $v$ are error components. Then it can be shown that the correlation that we observe, $r_{XY}$, has the following relation to the correlation of the true, errorless, scores, $r_{X'Y'}$,

$$r_{XY} = r_{X'Y'} \sqrt{r_{XX}} \sqrt{r_{YY}} \tag{18.7}$$

where the quantities $r_{XX}$ and $r_{YY}$ are the **reliability coefficients** for $X$ and $Y$, and estimate the proportion of the variances of $X$ and $Y$ accounted for by the true scores; e.g., $r_{XX}$ estimates

$$\frac{\sigma_{X'}^2}{\sigma_X^2} = 1 - \frac{\sigma_u^2}{\sigma_X^2}$$

From Equation 18.7, if the correlation between the true scores $X'$ and $Y'$ is .6 and the reliability coefficients for both $X$ and $Y$ are .7, then the observed correlation will be only .42. In fact, from Equation 18.7, because the true correlation cannot be larger than $+1$ or less than $-1$, the observed correlation cannot be larger than $\sqrt{r_{XX}}\sqrt{r_{YY}}$ or more negative than $-\sqrt{r_{XX}}\sqrt{r_{YY}}$.

If we know the reliability coefficients for $X$ and $Y$, we can use Equation 18.7 to estimate the correlation of the true scores; that is, we can estimate the correlation that would result if both variables were measured without error. Dividing both sides of Equation 18.7 by $\sqrt{r_{XX}}\sqrt{r_{YY}}$ results in a correlation, $r_c$, that has been "corrected for attenuation,"

$$r_C = r_{XY}\left(\frac{1}{\sqrt{r_{XX}}\sqrt{r_{YY}}}\right)$$

If this is done, it should be kept in mind that $r_c$ is an *estimated* correlation, not a correlation directly obtained from observed scores. We should also note that correcting a correlation for attenuation does not change whether or not it is statistically significant. As pointed out by Hunter and Schmidt (1990), because

$$r_{XY} = \rho_{XY} + e$$

where $e$ is the sampling error, if $r_{XY}$ is multiplied by a factor of $1/\sqrt{r_{XX}}\sqrt{r_{YY}}$, then so is the sampling error. For example, if correcting for attenuation doubles the size of the correlation coefficient, the width of the confidence interval for the correlation coefficient is doubled as well.

## 18.2.4 The Shapes of the *X* and *Y* Distributions

The marginal distributions of $X$ and $Y$ place constraints on the possible values of the correlation between $X$ and $Y$. We noted in Chapter 3 that the correlation is $+1$ if for each data point, $(X, Y)$, $z_X = z_Y$, and the correlation is $-1$ if $z_X = -z_Y$. Therefore, if both $X$ and $Y$ have identical, symmetrical distributions, it is possible that any given value of $z_X$ might be paired with any of the values of $z_Y$, and so it is possible that any value of $r$ from $-1$ to $+1$ might occur, depending on how the values of $X$ and $Y$ are paired. However, if $X$ and $Y$ have distributions that are different from one another, or if they are asymmetric, the full range of correlations from $-1$ to $+1$ cannot occur, no matter how the values of $X$ and $Y$ are paired.

In Figure 18.2, distribution A is positively skewed and distribution B is negatively skewed. If larger scores in A are paired with smaller scores in B, and vice versa, it is possible to obtain a correlation of $-1$; however, it is not possible to obtain a correlation of $+1$. For one thing, there are no scores in B that have positive $z$ scores as large as those in the upper tail of B. For another, if we attempted to pair larger scores in A with those in B, it would soon become apparent that there are not enough large scores in A to match up with those in B. If we did the best we could (i.e., paired off scores that had the same rank order), the scatterplot would show that we had a curvilinear relation with a correlation less than $+1$. Similarly, if we had two variables whose marginal distributions were both positively skewed as in A, or were both negatively skewed as in B, it would be possible to have a correlation of $+1$, but not one of $-1$. Because of these constraints, we should plot the univariate distributions of $X$ and $Y$ as well as the scatterplot when we try to understand the relation between $X$ and $Y$.

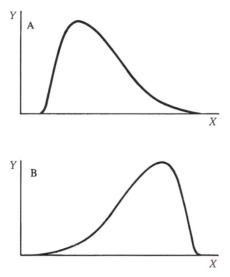

**Fig. 18.2** Two skewed distributions to illustrate how the distributions of $X$ and $Y$ limit the possible values of correlation.

## 18.2.5 Combining Data Across Groups

When the data from different groups are combined, the correlation in the resultant data set may not characterize the relation between $X$ and $Y$ in any of the groups. The problem occurs because the "aggregate" correlation reflects not only the relations between $X$ and $Y$ within the different groups, but also the differences among the group means. In panel (a) of Fig. 18.3, it is apparent that the correlation will be larger if the groups are combined than in either of the separate groups, and in panel (b) it is apparent that the correlation will be lower if the groups are combined.

Suppose, for example, that we were interested in finding the correlation between height and weight. Because men tend to be both taller and heavier than women, we would expect a situation like that depicted in panel (a), in which the correlation would be larger for the combined group than for either men or women. This expectation is confirmed if we consider the Seasons data set. Here, the correlation between height and weight is .29, both for men and for women considered separately. However, if we combine the data for men and women, the correlation is .53. As another example, if we correlated scores on verbal and math skills tests, we would expect positive correlations for both men and women. However, if the data conformed to the stereotypical view that women perform better than men on verbal tests, but worse than men on math tests, we would have a situation like that depicted in panel (b), in which the correlation is lower in the combined group than for either men or women considered separately. In extreme cases, it is conceivable that $X$ and $Y$ could be positively correlated in each of a number of groups but negatively correlated when the groups were combined, as in panel (c), or negatively correlated in each group but positively correlated when combined, as in panel (d).

The message is that one must be very cautious when combining data from meaningful subgroups. The summary statistics for the combined data set may not only fail to accurately

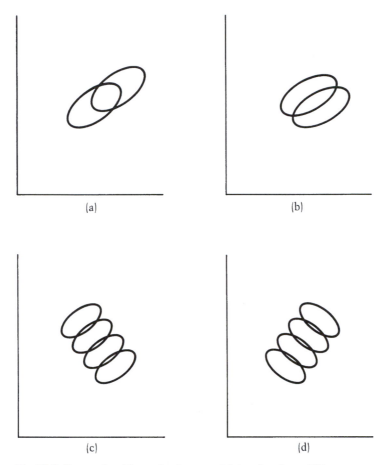

**Fig. 18.3** Scatterplots illustrating how combining data from different groups can affect the correlation coefficient.

describe each of the constituent groups, but also they may fail to describe *any* of the constituent groups appropriately. This is important to keep in mind, not only when considering correlations, but also more complicated analyses that may take correlations as inputs, such as factor analysis. If the correlations do not appropriately characterize the subgroups making up a data set, neither will quantities based on these correlations, such as the factors obtained in a factor analysis. Of course, this caveat does not apply only to the correlation coefficient. For example, the regression slope would be positive for each of the groups represented in panel (c), but would be negative for the combined data set.

## 18.2.6 Ecological Correlations: Correlations Based on Rates or Averages

Similarly, **ecological correlations**, correlations based on the *averages* of groups, may not tell us anything useful about the correlations based on the *individuals* within the groups. For one thing, the group means do not convey information about the within-group variability. For another, factors that cause the variability across the groups may not be the same ones responsible for the within-group variability. For groups such as those represented in panel (c) of Fig. 18.3, we could have strong positive correlations in each of the groups, yet the correlation based on the group means could be strongly negative. In a classic study, Robinson (1950) illustrated the dangers of generalizing from correlations based on means to correlations based on individuals by showing that when measures such as race, national origin, and illiteracy were correlated, the results could differ dramatically depending on the unit of analysis. For measures of race and illiteracy, the correlation was .203 for individuals, .773 for the means of states, and .946 for the means of census tracts (see Pedhazur, 1997, for a more complete discussion). We can also illustrate the problem of generalizing across units of analysis by noting that if we correlate subtraction and multiplication accuracy for third, fourth, fifth, and sixth graders in the Royer data set, we get correlations of .594, −.184, .225, and .431. The correlation based on the means for the four grades is .821, much larger than those for any of the grades.

## 18.3 INFERENCE ABOUT CORRELATION

So far, we have discussed correlation as a descriptive statistic. We have not made any assumptions about the joint distribution of $X$ and $Y$, although we have pointed out that certain characteristics of the distribution can limit the range of values that can be taken on by $r$. Now we turn to the discussion of how to make inferences about correlation; this requires us to state a model for the joint distribution of the population.

### 18.3.1 A Model for Correlation

The model most commonly assumed for inference about correlation asserts that the population of $(X, Y)$ pairs has a **bivariate normal distribution**. Both $X$ and $Y$ are assumed to be random variables and the density function that characterizes their joint distribution is

$$f(X, Y) = \frac{1}{2\pi\sigma_X\sigma_Y\sqrt{1 - \rho_{XY}^2}}e^{-B} \tag{18.8}$$

where

$$B = \frac{1}{2(1 - \rho_{XY}^2)}\left[\frac{(X - \mu_X)^2}{\sigma_X^2} + \frac{(Y - \mu_Y)^2}{\sigma_{YX}^2} - 2\rho_{XY}\frac{(X - \mu_X)(Y - \mu_Y)}{\sigma_X\sigma_Y}\right]$$

Equation 18.8 represents the family of bivariate normal distributions; a member of the family is defined by a combination of the parameters $\mu_X$, $\mu_Y$, $\sigma_X$, $\sigma_Y$, and $\rho$.

We can graphically represent the bivariate normal distribution in several ways. In Fig. 18.4, the plane defined by the $X$ and $Y$ axes contains all possible pairings of $X$ and $Y$. The bivariate normal density function can be thought of as a bell-shaped surface that rises above the $X - Y$ plane. The intersections of this surface with planes perpendicular to the $X - Y$ plane and parallel to either the $X$ or $Y$ axis all define normal distributions. Also, the intersection of the bivariate normal surface with planes parallel to, but above, the $X - Y$ plane define a family of ellipses, as shown in Fig. 18.5. Each point on one of these ellipses will have the same probability density, and hence these ellipses are called **isodensity contours**. Because of the "peaked" shape of the surface, the smaller ellipses in

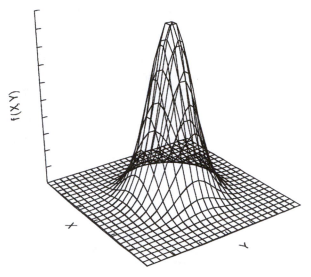

**Fig. 18.4** An example of a bivariate normal distribution.

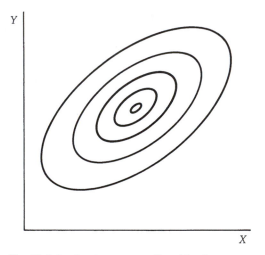

**Fig. 18.5** Isodensity contours for a bivariate
normal distribution.

Fig. 18.5 correspond to larger values of probability density. The more eccentric the ellipses,
the greater the correlation between $X$ and $Y$. A set of concentric circles corresponds to a
correlation of zero.

Some characteristics of a bivariate normal distribution in $X$ and $Y$ are as follows:

1.   The marginal distributions of both $X$ and $Y$ are normal with variances

$$\sigma_X^2 \quad \text{and} \quad \sigma_Y^2.$$

2.   The conditional means of $Y$ fall on the straight line with equation $\mu_{Y \cdot X} = \mu_Y +$
     $\beta_{YX}(X - \mu_X)$, where $\beta_{YX} = \rho \sigma_Y / \sigma_X$ is the slope of the population regression

equation that predicts $Y$ from $X$. The conditional distributions of $Y$ are normal with variance $\sigma_{Y \cdot X}^2 = \sigma_Y^2(1 - \rho^2)$. The conditional means of $X$ fall on the straight line with the equation $\mu_{X \cdot Y} = \mu_X + \beta_{XY}(Y - \mu_Y)$, where $\beta_{XY} = \rho \sigma_X / \sigma_Y$ is the slope for the regression of $X$ on $Y$, and the conditional distributions of $X$ are normal with variance $\sigma_{X \cdot Y}^2 = \sigma_X^2(1 - \rho^2)$. Given bivariate normality, if $X$ and $Y$ have a correlation of zero, then they are independent. That is, given bivariate normality, the only possible systematic relation between $X$ and $Y$ is a linear one.

## 18.3.2 Using the *t* Distribution to Test the Null Hypothesis $H_0$: $\rho = 0$

The null hypothesis $H_0$: $\rho = 0$ may be tested using the test statistic

$$t = r\sqrt{\frac{N - 2}{1 - r^2}} \tag{18.9}$$

with $N - 2$ df. For example, for the 28 third graders in the Royer data set, the correlation between subtraction and multiplication accuracy is .594. The value of the $t$ statistic with 26 df is $(.594)\sqrt{26/(1 - .594^2)} = 3.77$, which yields, from Appendix Table C.3, $p < .001$. Therefore, we can reject the null hypothesis if $\alpha \geq .001$.

Power calculations for the null hypothesis $H_0$: $\rho = 0$ are readily performed. For example, GPOWER calculates both post hoc and a priori power. The post hoc power is .964 for the previous example if a two-tailed test is used. To get this result in GPOWER, simply select "$t$ test (correlations)" from the "Tests" menu, and enter the obtained correlation, $\alpha$, and total sample size, then indicate that a two-tailed test was used, and click on "Calculate." In fact, the post hoc power can be calculated using any noncentral $t$ calculator. An estimate of the noncentrality parameter that is appropriate when using Equation 18.9 is given by

$$\hat{\delta} = \sqrt{\left(\frac{r^2}{1 - r^2}\right) N} \tag{18.10}$$

Substituting $r = .594$ and $N = 28$ yields $\hat{\delta} = 3.907$. The critical $t$ values for a two-tailed test with $\alpha = .05$ and 26 df are $\pm 2.056$. Entering 2.056 as the $X$-value, 26 (for df) and 3.907 (for the noncentrality parameter) in the UCLA noncentral $t$ calculator yields probability = .0360; this indicates that the power in the upper tail is $1 - .0360 = .964$. Entering $-2.056$ yields probability = .000. This indicates that there is no additional power in the lower tail. Therefore, the power of the test is .964.[1]

GPOWER can also calculate the sample size necessary to obtain any desired level of power. Suppose we want the sample size necessary to have a power of .80 for rejecting the null hypothesis $H_0$: $\rho = 0$ using a two-tailed test with $\alpha = .05$ when we expect the correlation to be small[2] ($r = .10$ by Cohen's 1988 guidelines; see Section 3.4). To do this in GPOWER, indicate that an a priori analysis with a two-tailed test is to be performed, then enter $r = .10$, $\alpha = .05$, and power = .80, and click "Calculate." GPOWER indicates that to have power equal to .80, it is necessary to have sample size of $N = 779$. The corresponding $N$s necessary to obtain power equal to .80 for medium ($r = .30$) and large ($r = .50$) correlations are 82 and 26, respectively. It is certainly worth knowing how large the sample size must be before conducting the study, so that a decision can be made about whether it is worth expending the resources necessary to have a reasonable chance of obtaining a significant result. If we simply went ahead with the study, using a sample of size 100 selected from a population in which the $\rho$ was .10, the estimated power for the test of $H_0$: $\rho = 0$ would be only .17.

Although the $t$ test of the null hypothesis that $\rho = 0$ is quite robust with respect to the assumption of normality (see, e.g., Edgell & Noon, 1984), it cannot be used to test other null hypotheses about $\rho$, nor can it be used to develop confidence intervals. This is because the shape and the standard error of the sampling distribution of $r$ depend on $\rho$. When $\rho$ differs from zero, the sampling distribution of $r$ becomes skewed, even for large sample sizes. However, we can test these other hypotheses and find confidence intervals if we use an appropriate transformation.

### 18.3.3 Using the Fisher Z Transform and the Normal Distribution to Find Confidence Intervals and Test Hypotheses About ρ

Fisher showed that if bivariate normality can be assumed, a logarithmic transformation of $r$, henceforth referred to as the **Fisher Z transform**,

$$Z_r = \frac{1}{2}\ln\left[\frac{1+r}{1-r}\right] = \text{arctanh } r \qquad (18.11)$$

(where "ln" is the natural logarithm and "arctanh" is the inverse of the hyperbolic tangent) is approximately normally distributed with mean

$$Z_\rho = \frac{1}{2}\ln\left[\frac{1+\rho}{1-\rho}\right]$$

and standard error

$$\sigma_r = \frac{1}{\sqrt{N-3}}$$

for sample sizes as small as $N = 10$.[3] The effect of the Fisher $Z$ transform is to stretch the tail of the sampling distribution. It has very little effect on small values of $r$ and increasingly large effects as $r$ gets larger. Because the transformed values of $r$ are normally distributed, we can calculate confidence intervals for $\rho$, by first finding the confidence interval for $Z_\rho$ and then transforming back. It also allows us to test null hypotheses of the form $H_0$: $\rho = \rho_{\text{hyp}}$, where $\rho_{\text{hyp}} \neq 0$.

Given an observed correlation $r$, we can find the value of the Fisher transform, $Z_r$, using Appendix Table C.11, or the transformation menu found in most statistical packages, or the inverse hyperbolic tangent function found in many calculators (including the scientific calculator offered as an accessory in the Windows operating system). The $1 - \alpha$ confidence interval for $\rho$ is then given by

$$Z_r \pm z_{\alpha/2}\sigma_r$$

where $z$ is the value that cuts off the upper $\alpha/2$ of the standard normal distribution; for the .95 confidence interval, $z_{.025} = 1.96$. For example, for the 28 third graders in the Royer data set, the correlation between subtraction and multiplication accuracy is .594. The Fisher transform of .594 is approximately .684. The .95 confidence interval for $Z_\rho$ is given by

$$.684 \pm (1.96)/\sqrt{25}$$
$$= .684 \pm .392$$

That is, the confidence interval extends from $Z$ values of .292 to 1.076. Transforming back to $r$ scores using Appendix Table C.11 (or the hyperbolic tangent function of a calculator) yields .95 confidence limits of .284 and .792 for $\rho$. Note that because the Fisher $Z$ transform is a nonlinear function of $r$, the limits are not equally distant from the observed value of $r$.

The confidence interval tells us several important things. For one thing, we can reject the null hypothesis $H_0$: $\rho = \rho_{hyp}$ at $\alpha = .05$ for all values of $\rho_{hyp}$ that do not fall in the confidence interval; that is for all hypothesized values of $\rho$ less than .284 or greater than .792. Note that we can simply test the hypothesis $H_0$: $\rho = \rho_{hyp}$ by using the test statistic

$$z = \frac{Z_r - Z_{\rho_{hyp}}}{\sqrt{\dfrac{1}{N - 3}}} \tag{18.12}$$

Even though we clearly can reject the null hypothesis that $\rho = 0$, we cannot be confident about the exact value of $\rho$ because the .95 confidence interval is quite wide. It is sobering to realize just how large confidence intervals for $\rho$ are, even for moderately large sample sizes. If we had obtained the sample correlation of .594 from a sample of $N = 100$, the .95 confidence interval would extend from approximately .45 to .71; still quite large. We strongly recommend finding confidence intervals for correlation coefficients. These may be calculated as shown previously or alternatively, the approximate .95 confidence intervals may be read off the chart in Fig. 18.6.

Because the Fisher $Z$ transforms are assumed to be normally distributed, we can perform power calculations in a manner analogous to the procedures used in Chapter 5. For example, suppose we wished to test the hypothesis $H_0$: $\rho = .30$ against $H_1$: $\rho \neq .30$ with $\alpha = .05$, and that $r = .594$ was obtained from a sample of $N = 28$. The obtained $z$ using Equation 15.12 is $(.684 - .310)(5) = 1.87$. This is less than the upper critical value of 1.96, so we cannot reject the null hypothesis. The power calculation outlined in Table 18.1 indicates that if $\rho$ really was .594, the power to reject the null hypothesis with a two-tailed test and $N = 28$ would be approximately .46. Also, the calculations in Table 18.2 indicate that if we wanted a power of .80, we would need a sample size of approximately 59. These values are the same as those produced by SYSTAT 10 (see Fig. 18.7, p. 497).

## 18.3.4 What If the Assumption of Bivariate Normality Is Violated?

The model underlying statistical inference in this chapter assumes bivariate normality. Yet, we know that in real data sets, even univariate distributions rarely follow ideal normal distributions (e.g., Micceri, 1989). There have been a number of simulation studies performed to investigate the robustness of significance tests for correlation under violations of the normality assumption (e.g., Edgell & Noon, 1984; Havlicek & Peterson, 1977; Lee & Rodgers, 1998). The results show that tests of the hypothesis $H_0$: $\rho = 0$ are quite robust with respect to Type 1 error. Type 1 error rates are close to their nominal values, even for skewed distributions. The exception occurs when "composite" populations with large correlations are used (e.g., the population might be constructed by selecting data points with $p = .5$ from two populations, one with $\rho = .7$ and the other with $\rho = -.7$). In this case. the Type 1 error rate may actually be two or three times as large as the stated value of $\alpha$.

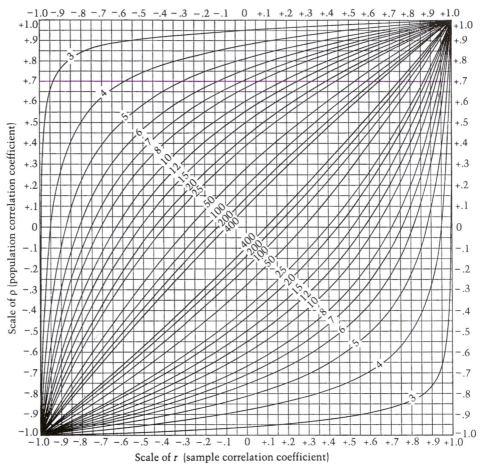

The numbers on the curves indicate sample size. The chart can also be used to determine upper and lower 2.5% significance points for *r*, given ρ.

**Fig. 18.6** Chart giving the .95 confidence intervals for the population correlation coefficient, ρ, given the sample coefficient, *r*.

Other simulation studies have shown that power can be greatly reduced by severe violations of bivariate normality. For example, Lee and Rogers (1998) compared two joint distributions for which ρ was .4. One of them was bivariate normal; for the other, the distribution of one variable was normal, but the distribution of the other variable was highly skewed (an exponential distribution was used). When many samples of sizes 15, 30, and 60 were selected from the normal population, the powers for the test of $H_0$: ρ = 0, using the test statistic in Equation 18.12, were found to be .328, .637, and .892, respectively. When samples were selected from the nonnormal population, the powers were much lower: .203, .301, and .431, respectively. This decline in power suggests that, when we severely violate the normality assumption, we should consider alternatives to the usual tests.

A nonparametric alternative that may be useful when the normality assumption does not seem to be satisfied is **bootstrapping**. Bootstrapping is a general purpose, computationally intensive approach to inference (Efron & Diaconis, 1983), in which the sampling distribution

**TABLE 18.1**  POWER CALCULATIONS USING THE FISHER Z TRANSFORM AND THE NORMAL
DISTRIBUTION

Because the sampling distribution of the $Z_r$'s can be considered to be normally distributed, we can perform all necessary power calculations using the normal distribution. Suppose that $H_0$: $\rho = .30$ and $H_1$: $\rho \neq .30$ with $\alpha = .05$, and that the data from a sample of $N = 28$ indicates that $r = .594$. We showed in the text that this does not provide enough evidence to reject the null hypothesis. The post hoc power (i.e., the power for sample size of 28 if $\rho$ really is .594) can be found by determining what proportion of the sampling distribution centered at $Z_{.594} = .684$ (call this the alternative distribution) lies within the rejection region for the hypothesis test. We can find the power by reasoning as follows:

1.  The upper rejection region for a two-tailed test with $\alpha = .05$ begins at $z_{.025} = 1.96$ standard errors above the mean of the null hypothesis distribution that is centered at $Z_{.30} = .310$.

2.  The mean of the alternative distribution is displaced $(.684 - .310)/\sigma_r = (.684 - .310)(5) = 1.87$ standard errors to the right of the mean of the null hypothesis distribution.

3.  Therefore, the upper rejection region begins $1.96 - 1.87 = .09$ standard errors above the mean of the alternative distribution; therefore, the critical value has a $z$ score of .09, with respect to the alternative distribution.

4.  Therefore, the power in the upper tail is the proportion of the normal distribution above a $z$ score of $.09 = .46$.

Expressing this reasoning in terms of equations, the power in the upper tail is given by the proportion of a normal distribution above a $z$ score of

$$z = z_{\text{crit}} - (Z_r - Z_{\text{phyp}})\sqrt{N - 3}$$

and the power in the lower tail would be given by the proportion of a normal distribution *below* a $z$ score of

$$z = z_{\text{crit}} - (Z_r - Z_{\text{phyp}})\sqrt{N - 3}$$

where for a two-tailed test with $\alpha = .05$, $z_{\text{crit}}$ for the lower tail would be $-1.96$. In the current example, for the lower tail $z = -1.96 - 1.87 = -3.83$. The power in the lower tail is essentially zero, because almost none of the normal distribution lies below a $z$ of $-3.83$. Therefore, the power is approximately .46.

Suppose we had used a one-tailed test with $H_1$: $\rho > .30$. Then, the power would be the proportion of the normal distribution above $z = z_{.05} - (Z_r - Z_{\text{phyp}})\sqrt{N - 3} = 1.645 - 1.87 = -.225$; so the power would be about $1 - .41 = .59$.

of a statistic can be obtained by repeatedly sampling from the observed sample. For example, a .95 confidence interval could be obtained for a correlation coefficient based on a sample of size $N$, using the following steps:

1.  Select 1000 samples (or any other large number of samples) of size $N$ with replacement from the observed sample.
2.  Calculate the correlation coefficient for each sample.
3.  Sort the 1000 correlations, ordering them from smallest to largest.
4.  With 1000 samples, the 25th largest and 976th largest correlation would then form the boundaries of the .95 confidence interval.

**TABLE 18.2**   CALCULATING THE SAMPLE SIZE NECESSARY TO ACHIEVE A DESIRED POWER

Starting with the equations in Table 18.1, we can develop an expression that estimates the sample size necessary to achieve a desired level of power. Suppose we have a positive value of $r$, so that virtually all of the power will be in the upper tail. Then, the power is the area in the normal distribution to the right of a $z$ score of

$$z = z_{\text{crit}} - (Z_r - Z_{\rho\text{hyp}})\sqrt{N - 3}$$

where $z_{\text{crit}}$ is 1.96 if we use a two-tailed test with $\alpha = .05$. If we wish to have a desired power of .80, the desired $z$ score, $z_D$, must be $-.84$. Solving for $N$, we have

$$\sqrt{N - 3} = (z_{\text{crit}} - z_D)/(Z_r - Z_{\rho\text{hyp}})$$

so that

$$N = \frac{(z_{\text{crit}} - z_D)^2}{(Z_r - Z_{\rho\text{hyp}})^2} + 3$$

Therefore, if we wish to test $H_0: \rho = .30$ against $H_1: \rho \neq .30$ with $\alpha = .05$, the sample size necessary to achieve a power of .80 if $\rho$ is really .594 is given by

$$N = [(1.96 + .84)^2/(.684 - .310)^2] + 3 = 59.$$

Note that this is the same as the value provided by the power module of SYSTAT (see Fig. 18.7). When $H_0: \rho = 0$, calculations using the $Z$ transform agree quite well with those performed using the $t$ distribution in Section 18.2.2. For example, to obtain a power of .80 of rejecting $H_0:\rho_{\text{hyp}} = 0$ at $\alpha = .05$ if $\rho$ is really .30, we have

$$N = \frac{(1.96 + .84)^2}{(.310 - 0)^2} + 3$$
$$= 85$$

rounding to the nearest whole number. This compares with the required $N$ of 82 obtained using GPOWER.

---

The preceding steps provide a general approach when there is a concern about the distributional assumptions. However, it has been pointed out (e.g., Rasmussen, 1987) that the confidence intervals produced by the bootstrap tend to be too small, especially for small samples, leading to inflated Type 1 error when they are used to test hypotheses. Strube (1988) used several modifications suggested by Efron (1982) and showed that they performed better than the original bootstrap. Rasmussen (1989) noted that one of these, the "adjusted" bootstrap procedure, in which the width of the usual bootstrap confidence interval is simply increased by a factor of $\sqrt{(N + 2)/(N - 1)}$, controlled Type 1 error better than the standard test using the Fisher $Z$ transforms when composite populations were sampled.

When we used the bootstrapping option in SYSTAT with 1000 samples for the correlation between total cholesterol and age for females in the Seasons study, we found that the .95 confidence interval for the correlation between cholesterol level and age for females extended from .386 to .605. The "adjusted" bootstrap .95 confidence interval extended from .385 to .606. This is close to the interval from .397 to .599 that was found using the Fisher $Z$ transform approach discussed in the previous section.

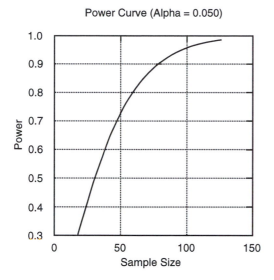

**Power Curve (Alpha = 0.050)**

**Fig. 18.7** Output of SYSTAT power module for a priori power calculation. The goal is to determine the sample size necessary to have power of .80 to reject $H_0$: $\rho = .30$ in favor of $H_1$: $\rho \neq .30$, with $\alpha = .05$, if $\rho$ is really .594. The value produced for $N$ is the same as that obtained by the calculations in Table 8.2.

## 18.3.5 Testing Whether Independent Correlations Are Significantly Different

It is possible to test whether the correlation between $X$ and $Y$ is the same in two different populations; i.e., to test $H_0$: $\rho_1 = \rho_2$, by using the test statistic

$$z = \frac{Z_{r_1} - Z_{r_2}}{\sqrt{\dfrac{1}{N_1 - 3} + \dfrac{1}{N_2 - 3}}} \tag{18.13}$$

We may, for example, want to know whether the correlation between number of years of education and income is the same for African-Americans as it is for Caucasians, or whether math and verbal scores are correlated equally for male and female ninth graders. Of course, if the correlations were different for males and females, we would have to be cautious in interpreting what the difference meant. Even if the slope and standard error of estimate were the same for males and females, the males would have a higher correlation if their scores had greater variability. When comparing two groups, it is always a good idea to display the scatterplots and to find the regression statistics for both groups instead of looking only at the correlations.

As an example, using Equation 18.13 with real data, the correlation between subtraction and multiplication accuracy for the 28 third graders in the Royer data set is .594; for the 25 fifth graders, it is .225. To determine whether these correlations are significantly different

**TABLE 18.3**  POWER AND SAMPLE SIZE CALCULATIONS FOR A TEST OF $H_0$: $\rho_1 - \rho_2$

The logic underlying these calculations is exactly the same as that for the test of $H_0$: $\rho = \rho_{hyp}$; the only difference is that now the standard error reflects the fact that both $\rho_1$ and $\rho_2$ are estimated from the data. In the example discussed in 18.3.5, for a sample of 28 third graders, $r_1 = .594$ and for a sample of 25 fifth graders, $r_2 = .225$. For a two-tailed test of $H_0$: $\rho_1 = \rho_2$ against $H_0$: $\rho_1 \neq \rho_2$ with $\alpha = .05$, the power in the right-hand tail is the area in a standard normal distribution to the right of $z_p$, where

$$z_p = z_{crit} - z_{obtained}$$
$$= z_{crit} - \frac{Z_{r_1} - Z_{r_2}}{\sqrt{[1/(N_1 - 3)] + [1/(N_2 - 3)]}}$$
$$= 1.96 - .455/.292 = .40$$

so the power in the right tail is $p(z > .40) = .34$. The power in the left tail is the area below the $z_p$ given by the same expression, except that now $z_{crit} = -1.96$; this yields $z_p = -1.96 - .455/.292 = -3.52$. The power in the left tail is $p(z < -3.52)$, which is approximately 0. Therefore, the power for the two-tailed test is approximately .34.

To determine the sample size for each group necessary to obtain a desired level of power, we start with the same equation, assuming equal sample size,

$$z_p = z_{crit} - \frac{Z_{r_1} - Z_{r_2}}{\sqrt{2/(N - 3)}}$$

We then substitute for $z_p$ the value necessary for the desired level of power, then solve for $N$. For example, to obtain a power of .80 in the right tail, we substitute the value of $z$ that cuts off the lower .20 of the distribution. From Appendix Table C.2, we see that .20 of the normal distribution lies above $z = .84$; therefore, $z_p$ must be $-.84$. Similarly, if we wish the power to be .90, $z_p$ must be $-1.28$. Solving for $N$, we have

$$N = 2\left[\frac{z_{crit} - z_p}{Z_{r_1} - Z_{r_2}}\right]^2 + 3$$

To find the $N$ necessary to obtain a power of .80 in the current example, we have $N = 2[(1.96 + .84)/.455]^2 + 3 = 79$. Similarly, the $N$ necessary for the power to be .90 is $2[(1.96 + 1.28)/.455]^2 + 3 = 104$.

---

at $\alpha = .05$, we can substitute in Equation 18.13. If so, we obtain

$$z = (.684 - .229)/.292 = 1.56$$

This is less than the upper critical value of $z_{crit} = 1.96$, so we do not have sufficient evidence to reject the null hypothesis that the correlations in the populations of third and fifth graders are equal. The calculations for post hoc power and for the sample size necessary to obtain a desired level of power are analogous to those shown in the previous section and are outlined in Table 18.3. For example, given the current data, the post hoc power for a two-tailed test of $H_0$: $\rho_1 = \rho_2$ at $\alpha = .05$ is .34. Also, assuming that $\rho_1 = .594$ and $\rho_2 = .225$, the sample size for each group that is necessary to achieve a power of .80 is approximately 79.

**TABLE 18.4**   CORRELATIONS BETWEEN SUBTRACTION AND
MULTIPLICATION ACCURACY FOR FOURTH, FIFTH,
AND SIXTH GRADERS IN THE ROYER DATA

| Grade | Correlation | $N$ | .95 CI |
|-------|-------------|-----|--------|
| Fourth | −.194 | 28 | −.528–.194 |
| Fifth | .225 | 23 | −.206–.583 |
| Sixth | .431 | 26 | .052–.701 |

Equation 18.13 provides a basis for obtaining confidence intervals for $Z_{\rho_1} - Z_{\rho_2}$ The .95 confidence interval is given by

$$Z_{r_1} - Z_{r_2} \pm 1.96 \sqrt{\frac{1}{N_1 - 3} + \frac{1}{N_2 - 3}} \tag{18.14}$$

Note that, although Equation 18.14 can be used to find a confidence interval for $Z_{\rho_1} - Z_{\rho_2}$, one cannot transform back to obtain a confidence interval for $\rho_1 - \rho_2$, because $Z_{\rho_1 - \rho_2}$ is not the same as $Z_{\rho_1} - Z_{\rho_2}$. This does not pose a problem for hypothesis testing, because if $Z_{\rho_1} = Z_{\rho_2}$, then $\rho_1$ must be equal to $\rho_2$ .

It is also possible to test for the homogeneity of $J$ independent correlation coefficients. The hypothesis that the set of $J$ $\rho$s are all equal uses the test statistic

$$\chi^2_{J-1} = \sum_j (N_j - 3)Z_j^2 - \frac{\left[\sum_j (N_j - 3)Z_j\right]^2}{\sum_j (N_j - 3)} \tag{18.15}$$

where $Z_j$ is the Fisher $Z$ transform of the $j$th correlation coefficient. For example, Table 18.4 presents the correlations between subtraction accuracy and multiplication accuracy for fourth, fifth, and sixth graders; these are −.194, .225, and .431, respectively. The obtained value of the test statistic is $\chi^2 = 6.899 - (10.283)^2/68 = 5.344$. Because this is less than $\chi^2_{.05,2} = 5.99$, we do not have sufficient evidence to reject the hypothesis that the three population correlations are identical.

## 18.3.6 Testing Hypotheses About Correlation Matrices

When data on a number of variables have been collected from the same set of subjects, the correlations may be displayed as a **correlation matrix**. If the variables are $X_1$, $X_2$, $X_3$, and $X_4$, the correlation matrix is

$$\begin{array}{c} \\ X_1 \\ X_2 \\ X_3 \\ X_4 \end{array} \begin{array}{cccc} X_1 & X_2 & X_3 & X_4 \\ \left[\begin{array}{cccc} 1 & r_{12} & r_{13} & r_{14} \\ r_{21} & 1 & r_{23} & r_{24} \\ r_{31} & r_{32} & 1 & r_{34} \\ r_{41} & r_{42} & r_{43} & 1 \end{array}\right] \end{array}$$

If there are $k$ variables, the correlation matrix consists of $k^2$ elements. The $k$ elements on the major diagonal (the one that goes from the upper left to the lower right) are each equal to 1, because any variable is perfectly correlated with itself. The $k^2 - k = k(k - 1)$ off-diagonal elements can be divided into a set of $k(k - 1)/2$ correlations above the diagonal and a set of equal size below it. The matrix is symmetric because elements on opposite sides of the diagonal are identical; $r_{12} = r_{21}$ and, in general, $r_{ij} = r_{ji}$ for all $i$ and $j$.

When $k$ is large, the number of correlations will be large. For example, if $k = 20$, $k(k-1)/2 = 190$. If we tested each correlation for significance at $\alpha = .05$, the Type 1 error rate for the entire family of correlations would be very high. Although most software packages will dutifully print out the significance level for each correlation coefficient as though it was the only one tested, it is every bit as necessary to control Type 1 error here as when we perform multiple $t$ tests on the differences between means. If we are interested in a limited number of tests based on a priori considerations, we can adjust the significance levels using the Dunn–Bonferroni procedure described in Chapter 9. We can also use the Dunn–Bonferroni adjustment if we have a large number of significance tests, although it will be conservative because the tests are not independent of one another.

To protect against excessive Type 1 error, Steiger (1980) has recommended the routine use of a simple test of the hypothesis that all off-diagonal elements of a correlation matrix are equal to zero. If this hypothesis cannot be rejected, tests on the individual correlations in the matrix are not likely to be meaningful unless motivated by a priori considerations. The hypothesis can be tested using the statistic

$$\chi^2 = (N - 3) \sum\sum_{j > i} Z_{ij}^2 \tag{18.16}$$

with $k(k-1)/2$ $df$, where $Z_{ij}$ is the Fisher $Z$ transform of $r_{ij}$ and the summation is over the $k(k-1)/2$ squared transforms corresponding to the correlations above (or below) the diagonal. For example, if for the Seasons data set, we correlate age, height, total cholesterol (TC), and body mass index (BMI) for the 207 women having scores for all four variables, the correlation matrix is

$$\begin{array}{c} \\ \text{Age} \\ \text{Height} \\ \text{TC} \\ \text{BMI} \end{array} \begin{array}{cccc} \text{Age} & \text{Height} & \text{TC} & \text{BMI} \\ \left[\begin{array}{cccc} 1 & -.129 & .513 & .070 \\ -.129 & 1 & -.198 & -.093 \\ .513 & -.198 & 1 & .152 \\ .070 & -.093 & .152 & 1 \end{array}\right] \end{array}$$

$\sum\sum Z_{ij}^2 = (-.130)^2 + (.567)^2 + (-.201)^2 + (.070)^2 + (-.093)^2 + (.153)^2 = .415$, so, from Equation 18.16, $\chi^2 = (204)(.415) = 84.66$. Because the observed value of $\chi^2$ is much larger than the critical value $\chi^2_{.05,6} = 12.59$, we can reject the hypothesis that all the off-diagonal correlations are zero. Had we failed to reject the overall null hypothesis, and if we had no a priori knowledge about the correlations, we would conduct no further tests on these correlations. In the present example, the null hypothesis was rejected. In any event, we might have tested some of the individual correlations on a priori grounds. For example, the literature suggests that, for women, there is a positive correlation between age and TC. Based on this sample, using the procedures of Section 18.3.3, we find the .95 confidence interval for the correlation between TC and age to be between .41 and .61, and can therefore reject the null hypothesis that this correlation is zero in the population.

We may also choose to determine whether the correlation between TC and age is significantly different than that between TC and BMI. Unfortunately, testing hypotheses about dependent correlations involves expressions that are complicated, nonintuitive, and often tedious to calculate, especially when the correlations to be tested do not have a variable in common. Because these tests have not been incorporated into the standard statistics packages, we must either use specialized software, or calculate the test statistics. Some useful sources that discuss tests of dependent correlations are Meng et al. (1992), Olkin and Finn (1990, 1995), and Steiger (1980). Perhaps the simplest test for two dependent correlations that have a variable in common is given by Meng et al. (1992). Given the null hypothesis $H_0$: $\rho_{YX_1} = \rho_{YX_2}$, we can use the test statistic

$$z = \left(Z_{r_{YX_1}} - Z_{r_{YX_2}}\right)\sqrt{\frac{N-3}{2\left(1 - r_{X_1X_2}\right)h}} \tag{18.17}$$

where

$$h = \frac{1 - f\overline{r^2}}{1 - \overline{r^2}},$$

and

$$f = \frac{1 - r_{X_1X_2}}{2(1 - \overline{r^2})}$$

(where $f$ is not allowed to exceed 1) and $\overline{r^2}$ is the mean of $r_{YX_1}^2$ and $r_{YX_2}^2$. To test whether the correlation between TC and age (.513) is significantly different from the correlation between TC and BMI (.152), we may substitute into Equation 18.17. We have $\overline{r^2} = .143$, $f = .543$, and $h = 1.076$, so that $z = 4.18$. Therefore, we may reject the null hypothesis at $p = .000$. Note that the test statistic given in Equation 18.17 is only appropriate if the two correlations have a common variable. If we wish to test the hypothesis $H_0$:$\rho_{XY} = \rho_{WQ}$, the test statistic is considerably more complicated (see Steiger, 1980) .

One may test many different types of hypotheses about the elements of a correlation matrix by using Steiger's MULTICORR program (Steiger, 1979), which performs tests based on a statistical rationale developed by Dunn and Clark (1969). The program is free, and is available, along with documentation and source code, at http://www.interchg.ubc.ca/steiger/homepage.htm. MULTICORR is a DOS program that requires the preparation of a command file in which certain pieces of information have to be typed in exactly the right columns. However, it can test a variety of hypotheses about whether correlations or groups of correlations are equal to one another, or to specified values, and is much more desirable to use than the corresponding computational formulas. Using MULTICORR to test whether the correlation between TC and age is significantly different from the correlation between TC and BMI yields $\chi_1^2 = 17.819$, which corresponds to $z = 4.22$, a result very similar to the value of 4.18 given by Equation 18.17.

## 18.4 PARTIAL CORRELATIONS

### 18.4.1 The Partial Correlation Coefficient

In Chapter 3, we noted that two variables may be correlated because they are both influenced directly or indirectly by other variables. For example, verbal ability is correlated with shoe size in children, because both verbal ability and shoe size increase with age. However, we may wish to ask whether there would still be a correlation between physical size and verbal ability even if the effects of age could somehow be controlled or "partialed out." For example, we may believe that even at the same ages, students who are more physically mature may tend to be more mentally mature, perhaps because greater physical growth may be an indicator of better health or nutrition, and might therefore be related to mental ability. How can we find a measure of the relation between size and verbal ability that is not contaminated by the effects of chronological age?

If we use the notation $r_{XY} = corr(X, Y)$ to stand for the correlation between two variables $X$ and $Y$, then $r_{XY|W}$, the **partial correlation between $X$ and $Y$ with the effects of $W$ partialed out**, is given by

$$r_{XY|W} = corr(X|W, Y|W)$$

where $X|W = X - \hat{X}$, and $\hat{X}$ is the value of $X$ predicted from the regression of $X$ on $W$; therefore, $X|W$ is the part of $X$ that is not predictable from $W$. Similarly, $Y|W = Y - \hat{Y}$ is the residual that results when $Y$ is regressed on $W$. It is also possible to express $r_{XY|W}$ in terms of the simple correlations between $X$, $Y$, and $W$:

$$r_{XY|W} = \frac{r_{XY} - r_{XW}r_{YW}}{\sqrt{(1 - r_{XW}^2)(1 - r_{YW}^2)}} \tag{18.18}$$

For example, suppose $X$ represents size, $Y$ represents verbal ability, and $W$ represents age. If the correlations of both size and verbal ability with age were .7 ($r_{XW} = r_{YW} = .7$), and the correlation between size and verbal ability was .5 ($r_{XY} = .5$), $r_{size,verbal|age}$ would have a value of $(.5 - .49)/(1 - .49) = .02$. In other words, if we take into account the relation between size and age, and verbal ability and age, the apparent relation between size and verbal ability essentially disappears.

Partial correlations are often calculated on data from observational studies, in an attempt to statistically "control" for the effects of variables that are not of interest. Unfortunately, although partial correlations are easy enough to calculate, the meaning of a partial correlation can usually be properly understood only in terms of a specific theory or causal model of the situation under investigation (see, e.g., Pedhazur, 1997). It should be emphasized that when $r_{XY|W}$ is obtained, what is removed from $X$ and $Y$ are the components that are *predictable* from a linear regression on $W$. Suppose, for example, that $X$ measures parents' education, $Y$ measures their children's performance in school, and $W$ is the number of books in the home. If $r_{XY|W}$ is considerably smaller than $r_{XY}$—that is, if the correlation between school performance and parent's education is much smaller when the number of books in the home is partialed out—this does not necessarily mean that providing the family with lots of books will have much of an effect on performance, or that parental education is unimportant. Partialing books out of the correlation between parental education and school performance removes more than the direct effect of the books; partialing out books removes any components of parental education and children's school performance *predictable* from the number of books in the home. The number of books in the home is correlated with parental education and intelligence, as well as with other potentially important variables, such as socioeconomic level and parental encouragement of achievement. Therefore, when the number of books is partialed out of the relation between $X$ and $Y$, some of the effects of these other variables are removed as well. These types of difficulties in interpretation also arise for other techniques, such as analysis of covariance and multiple regression, in which there are a number of correlated variables and one or more of them are statistically "controlled." We will be in a better position to discuss these issues in more detail after we have introduced multiple regression in Chapter 20.

The ideas in this section can be extended to partialing out the effects of more than one variable. Suppose that we wish to partial out the effects of variables $W$ and $Q$ from the correlation between $X$ and $Y$. The partial correlation $r_{XY|WQ}$ is given by $corr(X|WQ, Y|WQ) = corr(X - \hat{X}, Y - \hat{Y})$, where $\hat{X}$ is the prediction of X based on a linear regression equation that contains both $W$ and $Q$, and $\hat{Y}$ *is the corresponding prediction of Y.* The same logic holds no matter how many variables there are to be partialed out; the partial correlation can always be obtained by correlating the two sets of residuals that result when $X$ and $Y$ are regressed on these variables. Such partial correlations are readily obtained by using statistical packages that either produce the partial correlations directly or provide the appropriate residuals that can then be correlated. If the raw data are not available, but the first-order correlations are, Equation 18.19 indicates how to find the partial correlation between $X$ and $Y$, partialing out $W$ and $Q$. In effect, Equation 18.18 is first used to remove the effects of $Q$ from $r_{XY}$, $r_{XW}$, and $r_{YW}$, then is used again to remove the effects of $W$ from $r_{XY|Q}$.

$$r_{XY|WQ} = \frac{r_{XY|Q} - r_{XW|Q}r_{YW|Q}}{\sqrt{(1 - r_{XW|Q}^2)(1 - r_{YW|Q}^2)}} \tag{18.19}$$

## 18.4.2 Confidence Intervals and Significance Tests for Partial Correlation Coefficients

Confidence intervals and significance tests for partial correlation coefficients are completely analogous to those calculated in Section 18.3. The null hypothesis $H_0{:}\rho_{XY|W} = 0$ can be tested by using

$$t = r_{XY|W}\sqrt{\frac{N - 3}{1 - r_{XY|W}^2}} \quad \text{with} \quad N - 3\, df$$

and the more general null hypothesis $H_0{:}\rho_{XY|W} = \rho_{hyp}$ can be tested using

$$z = (Z_r - Z_{\rho_{hyp}})\sqrt{N - 4}$$

where the $Z$'s are Fisher transforms. The $1 - \alpha$ confidence interval for $\rho$ may be found by finding the limits for $Z_\rho$,

$$Z_r \pm z_{\alpha/2}\sqrt{\frac{1}{N - 4}}$$

and then transforming back to the correlation scale.

In general, if $r$ is the partial correlation with $p$ variables partialed out, the expressions become

$$t = r\sqrt{\frac{N - 2 - p}{1 - r^2}} \quad \text{with} \quad N - 2 - p \text{ df,}$$

and

$$z = (Z_r - Z_{\rho_{hyp}})\sqrt{N - 3 - p},$$

and the confidence limits on $\rho$ can be obtained by transforming

$$Z_r \pm z_{\alpha/2}\sqrt{\frac{1}{N-3-p}}.$$

### 18.4.3 The Semipartial (or Part) Correlation Coefficient

The semipartial correlation coefficient $r_{Y(X|W)}$ is the correlation between $Y$ and $X|W$, where $X|W = X - \hat{X}$, and is the residual when $X$ is regressed on $W$. The coefficient may be obtained by regressing $X$ on $W$, then correlating the resulting residuals with $Y$, or by using Equation 18.20,

$$r_{Y(X|W)} = \frac{r_{XY} - r_{XW}r_{YW}}{\sqrt{1 - r_{XW}^2}} \tag{18.20}$$

Note that the part of $X$ that can be predicted by $W$ has been removed, but no adjustment has been made to $Y$. The part correlation has a useful interpretation in terms of multiple regression and will be discussed further in Chapter 20.

### 18.4.4 Constraints in Sets of Correlation Coefficients

Given three variables—$X$, $Y$, and $W$—there are three correlation coefficients, $r_{XY}$, $r_{XW}$, and $r_{YW}$. The range of possible values that can be taken on by any one of these correlations is constrained by the values taken on by the other two. As the most extreme example, if $W$ has a perfect linear relation with both $X$ and $Y$, then $X$ and $Y$ must have a perfect linear relation. That is, if $|r_{XW}| = |r_{YW}| = 1$, then $|r_{XY}| = 1$. However, what can we say about the possible values of $r_{XY}$ if $r_{XW}$ and $r_{YW}$ are both equal to some other value such as .7?

Because $r_{XY|W}$ is a correlation, it must take on a value between $-1$ and $+1$. If we solve Equation 18.18 for $r_{XY}$, we have

$$r_{XY} = r_{XW}r_{YW} + r_{XY|W}\sqrt{(1 - r_{XW}^2)(1 - r_{YW}^2)}.$$

Therefore, the value of $r_{XY}$ must lie between

$$r_{XY} = r_{XW}r_{YW} - \sqrt{(1 - r_{XW}^2)(1 - r_{YW}^2)}$$

and

$$r_{XY} = r_{XW}r_{YW} + \sqrt{(1 - r_{XW}^2)(1 - r_{YW}^2)}$$

Substituting into these expressions, we see that if $r_{XW} = r_{YW} = .7$, $r_{XY}$ must have a value between $-.02$ and $1.00$. A strong negative correlation between $X$ and $Y$ is not possible if $X$ and $Y$ both have large positive correlations with $W$.

## 18.5 OTHER MEASURES OF CORRELATION

In this section, we introduce several classes of correlation measures other than the usual Pearson product-moment correlation coefficient. We first discuss four measures used when one or both variables are dichotomous (i.e., they have only two possible values). The

**point-biserial** and **phi** ($\phi$) coefficients are simply the Pearson $r$ with one and two dichotomous variables, respectively. The **biserial** and **tetrachoric** coefficients provide estimates of what the Pearson $r$ would be if, instead of dichotomous variables, we actually had normally distributed scores. We then discuss several measures of correlation used with ranked data. The first of these, the **Spearman rho ($\rho$) coefficient**, is simply the usual Pearson $r$ applied to ranks. The **Kendall tau ($\tau$)** and **Goodman–Kruskal gamma ($\gamma$)** coefficients use a different measure of agreement, based on the proportion of pairs of data points in which the rankings of $X$ and $Y$ agree.

## 18.5.1 The Point-Biserial and $\phi$ Correlation Coefficients

We are frequently concerned with dichotomies, such as male/female, pass/fail, and experimental/control. Even though these are each categorical variables and there is nothing inherently quantitative about them, we can express each dichotomy as levels of a quantitative variable that may be correlated with other variables.[4] For example, we can correlate a dichotomous variable with a continuous variable (e.g., passing or failing an individual test item with the overall test score) or correlate two dichotomous variables (e.g., male/female with pass/fail). We can find the correlation by assigning any two different numbers to the categories that make up the dichotomy. Usually the two numbers 0 and 1 are used, but the size of the correlation would be the same for any pair of numbers (e.g., 31 and 57).

When the Pearson $r$ formula is applied to a data set in which one variable is continuous and the other variable takes on the values 0 and 1, the result is called the point-biserial correlation coefficient. There are specialized formulas for the correlation that take advantage of the fact that one of the variables is dichotomous, but they will give the same result as the Pearson $r$ applied to the same variables and therefore will not be presented here. The point-biserial correlation coefficient can be tested for significance using the statistic presented in Equation 18.9.

The $t$ test for the point-biserial correlation is formally identical to the independent-groups $t$ test that we discussed in Chapter 6. Given data from two independent groups, we could test the null hypothesis that their population means are equal using the test statistic given in Chapter 6. If we do this, we get exactly the same observed $t$ as if we formed $N = n_1 + n_2$ data points $(X, Y)$ in which the value of $X$ was determined by group membership, and $Y$ was the value of the dependent variable, then found $r_{XY}$, then tested $H_0$: $\rho = 0$ using Equation 18.9. Solving Equation 18.9 for $r$ yields the relation between $t$ and $r$ in Equation 18.21:

$$r = \sqrt{\frac{t^2}{t^2 + N - 2}} = \sqrt{\frac{t^2}{t^2 + df_{\text{error}}}} \tag{18.21}$$

Because of this relation, some authors recommend that $r$ be used as the primary measure of effect size to accompany $t$ tests and, because $F(1, df_{\text{error}}) = t^2(df_{\text{error}})$, as the measure of effect size for $F$ tests in which $df_1 = 1$ (see, e.g., Rosenthal, 1991).

As an illustration, if we correlate depression score (averaged over seasons) with sex (coded as 0 for males and 1 for females), we find $r = .134$. The positive correlation indicates that depression scores are higher for females. Using the $t$ test statistic of Equation 18.9, we find that the correlation is significant, $t(328) = 2.455$, $p = .015$. If we perform a pooled-variance independent-groups $t$ test on the same data, we find that we can reject $H_0$: $\mu_{\text{females}} = \mu_{\text{males}}$, also with $t(328) = 2.455$ and $p = .015$. The point-biserial correlation coefficient

**TABLE 18.5**  AN EXAMPLE OF THE CALCULATION OF THE PHI COEFFICIENT

$$X$$

|   |   | 1 | 0 |
|---|---|---|---|
|   | 1 | a | b |
| Y |   |   |   |
|   | 0 | c | d |

If there are $a$ cases for which both $X$ and $Y$ are 1, $b$ cases for which $X$ is 0 and $Y$ is 1, $c$ cases for which $X$ is 1 and $Y$ is 0, and $d$ cases for which $X$ and $Y$ are both 0, then $\phi$ may be calculated as

$$\phi = \frac{ad - bc}{\sqrt{(a+b)(c+d)(a+c)(b+d)}}$$

Consider an example in which drug therapy and outcome are correlated. Assume the following contingency table:

|   |   | Outcome | |
|---|---|---|---|
|   |   | Survive | Die |
| Treatment | Drug | 60 | 40 |
|   | No Drug | 40 | 60 |

The $\phi$ coefficient for treatment and outcome is

$$\phi = \frac{(60)(60) - (40)(40)}{\sqrt{(100)(100)(100)(100)}} = .20$$

may be used as a measure of effect size, although the standardized effect size measure that we introduced in Chapter 6, $E_S = (\overline{Y}_{female} - \overline{Y}_{male})/s_{pooled} = (6.217 - 4.720)/5.537 = .270$, seems to have a more direct interpretation.

When the Pearson $r$ formula is applied to two variables that are each coded 0 or 1 to represent dichotomies, the result is called the $\phi$ coefficient. As is the case for the point-biserial coefficient, specialized formulas for $\phi$ exist, but these always give the same result as applying the Pearson $r$ to the dichotomous data. Table 18.5 contains the calculation of the correlation between survival (survive, die) and treatment (drug, no drug), using one of the expressions for $\phi$. The example also demonstrates that, depending on the context, even a small correlation can correspond to an important effect. In the example, the value of the correlation between treatment and survival is .2; only $(.2)(.2) = .04$ or 4% of the variance is accounted for. Yet, this small correlation corresponds to a 20% increase in survival rate when a drug is administered, a difference that no one would deny was important.

The $\phi$ coefficient is closely related to the $\chi^2$ test for independence, and it can be shown that

$$\chi_1^2 = N\phi^2 \tag{18.22}$$

The $\chi^2$ statistic with 1 $df$ can be used to test the hypothesis that $X$ and $Y$ are independent in the population, whereas the $\phi$ coefficient (or $\phi^2$, which can be interpreted as the proportion of variance accounted for) can be used as a measure of the strength of the relation between $X$ and $Y$.

As a final comment, we note that Equation 18.22 provides us with an opportunity to emphasize that with large enough samples, even small effects may be statistically significant. Looking in Appendix Table C.4, we find that we can reject the null hypothesis that $X$ and $Y$ are independent at $\alpha = .05$, as long as $\chi^2 = N\phi^2 > 3.84$ or $\phi^2 > 3.84/N$. It follows that for $N = 1000$, we would be able to reject the null hypothesis of independence even if $\phi^2$ was only .00384. In this case, the "significant" relation would only account for about one third of 1% of the variance.

## 18.5.2 The Biserial and Tetrachoric Correlation Coefficients

The biserial correlation coefficient is analogous to the point-biserial coefficient in that for both measures, one variable is dichotomous and the other is continuous. The difference between them is that whereas the point-biserial coefficient is simply a special case of the Pearson $r$, the biserial correlation coefficient is an *estimate* of what $r$ would be if, instead of having a dichotomous variable, scores on the underlying normally distributed variable were available. The biserial correlation coefficient acts quite differently than the point-biserial one. Unlike the point-biserial, the biserial coefficient is not very sensitive to the proportion of 0s and 1s in the dichotomous variable; moreover, the biserial coefficient can be shown to always be at least 25% larger than the point-biserial coefficient calculated on the same data, and under some circumstances may take on values greater than 1.

The tetrachoric coefficient is also an estimate. Like the $\phi$ coefficient, the tetrachoric coefficient takes as data two dichotomous variables. However, rather than measuring the correlation between the dichotomous variables, the tetrachoric coefficient estimates the $r$ that would result if scores on the two normally distributed underlying variables were available. The idea of representing a dichotomy in terms of an underlying normal variable may make sense in some cases but not in others. For the dichotomy pass/fail, one can imagine passing a test if one has more than a certain amount of a normally distributed ability, and failing the test if one has less than that amount of ability. On the other hand, the idea of a normally distributed underlying variable does not make sense for a variable like sex. Even if there is an underlying continuous variable, the assumption of normality may not be appropriate. For example, the dichotomous data may have been collected in a sample of college students. Even if an underlying ability dimension is normally distributed in the general population, the lowest part of the distribution will not be represented in the population of college students.

The biserial and tetrachoric coefficients depend very strongly on the assumption of normality and should be used only with caution. Because these measures are rarely used, we do not deal with them further, other than to refer the interested reader to sources that provide more detailed discussions, such as Lindeman, Merenda, and Gold (1980).

### 18.5.3 The Spearman Correlation Coefficient for Ranked Data

Sometimes we wish to obtain correlations for data that occur in the form of ranks. We may, for example, have two judges rank a set of stimuli according to some quality and obtain the correlation between the two sets of rankings as a measure of reliability. Even if $X$ and $Y$ are continuous variables, we may wish to convert to ranks, either because we do not believe that equal differences in the $X$ and/or $Y$ scores necessarily correspond to equal differences in the underlying variable that is measured, or because we desire measures that are more resistant to the effects of outliers than the usual Pearson $r$.

The special case of the Pearson $r$ for ranked data is referred to as the Spearman correlation coefficient ($r_s$) or sometimes as the Spearman rho coefficient. Although the value of the Spearman coefficient can always be obtained by applying any of the usual Pearson $r$ formulas to the ranked data, one frequently encounters a fairly simple formula that takes advantage of the characteristics of ranks. If there are no ties, the ranks of $N$ scores are the first $N$ integers. Therefore, the mean of a set of $N$ ranks is $(N + 1)/2$, and the variance can be shown to be $N(N + 1)/12$. Substituting such expressions into the Pearson $r$ formula yields

$$r_s = 1 - \frac{6 \sum_i D_i^2}{N(N^2 - 1)} \tag{18.23}$$

where $D_i$ is the difference between the $X$ and $Y$ ranks for the $i$th case. An example of a calculation using Equation 18.23 is given in Table 18.6. Equation 18.23 should not be used if there are ties, because when there are ties, all the scores in a group of ties are given the mean of the ranks they would have received had there been no ties. For example, if after the nine largest scores have been ranked, we find that four scores are tied for 10th place, each receives the rank of 11.5 (the mean of 10, 11, 12, and 13), and the next largest score receives a rank of 14. The assigning of mean ranks for ties reduces the variance of the ranks so that it is less than the variance of the first $N$ integers. Although there are modifications of Equation 18.23 that can adjust for ties, they are both cumbersome and unnecessary, given that the appropriate value can be obtained by finding the Pearson $r$ for the ranked data, and that most statistical packages will do both the ranking and the calculations.

For $N > 10$, we can test the null hypothesis that the ranks of $X$ and $Y$ have a correlation of zero in the population by using the test statistic given in Equation 18.9 with $N - 2$ $df$. Although this test is not appropriate for small samples, Zar (1972) has developed tables for the critical values of the Spearman coefficient for small $N$; these tables have been reproduced in Siegel and Castellan (1988).

### 18.5.4 The Kendall $\tau$ and Goodman–Kruskal $\gamma$ Coefficients for Ranked Data

Kendall has developed a different approach to the problem of assessing agreement between two sets of ranks. Rather than using a measure of discrepancy that depends on the sum of the squared differences in the ranks of $X$ and $Y$ (i.e., the $\sum D_i^2$ quantity that appears in the formula for the Spearman coefficient), Kendall's approach depends on the number of agreements and disagreements in rank order when pairs of items are considered.

**TABLE 18.6** CALCULATION OF $r_s$ AND $\tau$ FOR A SET OF RANKED DATA

| X | Rank of X | Y | Rank of Y | D | $D^2$ |
|---|---|---|---|---|---|
| 81 | 9 | 20 | 8 | 1 | 1 |
| 59 | 3 | 16 | 5 | −2 | 4 |
| 37 | 1 | 12 | 2 | −1 | 1 |
| 79 | 8 | 21 | 9 | −1 | 1 |
| 63 | 5 | 19 | 7 | −2 | 4 |
| 72 | 7 | 17 | 6 | 1 | 1 |
| 42 | 2 | 9 | 1 | 1 | 1 |
| 61 | 4 | 14 | 3 | 1 | 1 |
| 83 | 10 | 25 | 10 | 0 | 0 |
| 70 | 6 | 15 | 4 | 2 | 4 |

Calculation of $r_s$

$$r_s = 1 - \frac{6\Sigma_i D_i^2}{N(N^2 - 1)}$$

$$= 1 - \frac{(6)(18)}{(10)(99)}$$

$$= .89$$

Calculation of $\tau$

| Ordered ranks of X | 1 | 2 | 3 | 4 | 5 | 6 | 7 | 8 | 9 | 10 |
|---|---|---|---|---|---|---|---|---|---|---|
| Corresponding ranks of Y | 2 | 1 | 5 | 3 | 7 | 4 | 6 | 9 | 8 | 10 |

The number of inversions can most easily be obtained by drawing lines between the same ranks for $X$ and $Y$. The number of times that pairs of lines cross one another is the number of inversions. For the current example, there are six inversions. Therefore,

$$\tau = 1 - \frac{2(\text{number of inversions})}{N(N-1)/2}$$

$$= 1 - \frac{(2)(6)}{(10)(9)/2}$$

$$= .73$$

Suppose we have $N$ objects $O_1, O_2, \ldots, O_N$ that receive two sets of rankings, $X$ and $Y$. If the $X$ and $Y$ rankings are exactly the same, there will be no disagreement, and the Kendall $\tau$ will have a value of 1. We say that an *inversion* occurs if, for any two objects $O_i$ and $O_j$, $O_i$ is ranked higher than $O_j$ in one set of rankings, but lower than $O_j$ in the other set. For $N$ objects, there are $N(N-1)/2$ possible pairings of objects. Therefore, if there are no ties, there are a maximum of $N(N-1)/2$ possible inversions. The Kendall $\tau$

coefficient is defined as

$$r = 1 - \frac{(2)(\text{number of inversions})}{\text{maximum number of inversions}}$$

$$= \frac{\text{number of agreements in order} - \text{number of disagreements in order}}{\text{total number of pairs}}$$

Various procedures exist for obtaining the number of rank inversions, but the simplest is the graphic method illustrated in Table 18.6. The graphic method is appropriate only if there are no tied ranks, and more general procedures when there are ties are outlined in Hays (1988) and Siegel and Castellan (1988). If there are ties, the expression for $\tau$ becomes

$$\tau = \frac{(2)(\text{number of agreements in order} - \text{number of disagreements in order})}{\sqrt{N(N-1) - T_X}\sqrt{N(N-1) - T_Y}}$$

where $T_X = \sum t(t-1)$ and $t$ is the number of tied observations in each group of ties on the $X$ variable; and $T_Y = \sum t(t-1)$, where, $t$ is the number of tied observations in each group of ties on the $Y$ variable. Packages such as SPSS, SYSTAT, and SAS all provide measures that take account of ties. However, the packages differ in whether or not they will perform significance tests; for example, SPSS 10 will provide the results of significance tests[5] for $\rho$ and $\tau$, but SYSTAT 10 will not.

For $N$ greater than 10, the significance of $\tau$ can be tested by using the test statistic $z = \tau/\sigma_\tau$ where $\sigma_\tau = \sqrt{2(2N+5)/9N(N-1)}$, and $z$ is approximately normally distributed under the null hypothesis. We can reject the null hypothesis that $\tau$ is equal to zero in the population at $\alpha = .05$ for the data in Table 18.6, because the obtained value of the test statistic, 2.94, is greater than the critical $z$ of 1.96. Tables that can be used when $N \leq 10$ can be found in Siegel and Castellan (1988).

The Goodman–Kruskal $\gamma$ is closely related to the Kendall $\tau$ and has essentially the same interpretation. The $\gamma$ is simply the ratio of the difference between the number of agreements and disagreements to their sum, after all ties have been thrown out; that is

$$r = \frac{\text{number of agreements in order} - \text{number of disagreements in order}}{\text{number of agreements in order} + \text{number of disagreements in order}}$$

Both $\gamma$ and $\tau$ can be thought of as measures of **monotonicity**, the tendency for the underlying measures to increase or decrease together. The test for significance for $\gamma$ depends on an approximation that requires large samples (e.g., see Siegel & Castellan, 1988), and we shall not consider it here.

On what basis should we decide which measure to use? The Kendall $\tau$ is somewhat more appealing than the Spearman $\rho$ because of its direct interpretation in terms of the proportion of agreements and disagreements in rankings. In contrast, the Spearman $\rho$ is interpretable primarily by analogy to the usual Pearson coefficient. Concerns about power do not help much with the choice. Siegel and Castellan (1988) point out that, although $\tau$ and $\rho$ will generally have different values when calculated for the same data set, when significance tests for $\tau$ and $\rho$ are based on their sampling distributions, they will yield the same $p$ values. However, if a normal approximation is used to perform the significance test, the $\tau$ is a better choice because its sampling distribution approaches normality more rapidly than that of the Spearman $\rho$ as sample size increases.

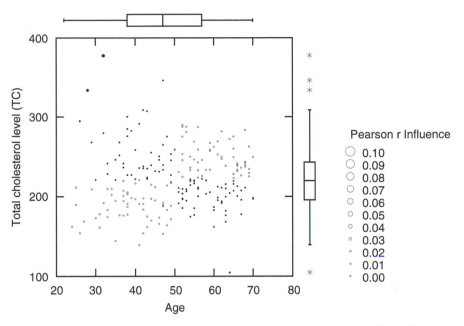

**Fig. 18.8** Influence plot for the correlation between cholesterol level and age for males.

We found the correlation between cholesterol level and age for males, using the Pearson $r$, the $\tau$, and the $\rho$. As stated earlier, $r = .062$ and is not significant, $p = .363$. The Kendall $\tau$ and Spearman $\rho$ values obtained from SPSS are slightly larger than $r$, .093 and .135; and they are both significant, $p = .044$ and .046, respectively. There are several reasons for this discrepancy. One reason is that monotonicity, the tendency for $X$ and $Y$ to increase (or decrease) together, is a weaker condition than linearity, and thus easier to satisfy. Another reason is that, because they are based on ranks, $\tau$ and $\rho$ are more resistant than the Pearson $r$; that is, they are less influenced by outliers. As we can see in Figure 18.8, the influence plot (see Section 3.4.2) of cholesterol level and age for men does have some outliers that reduce the size of the correlation. We conclude that there is a weak tendency for cholesterol level to increase with age for men. We have sufficient evidence to reject the null hypothesis that the relation is nonmonotonic in the population.

## 18.6 CONCLUDING REMARKS

We conclude this chapter by repeating several concerns about correlational measures that should be kept in mind. Although we outlined procedures for testing differences in correlations across groups, the sample-specific nature of the correlation coefficient makes such differences difficult to interpret. Because the correlation depends on the variability within each group, the correlations may be different even if the nature of the linear relation is the same. Also, we must be concerned with the meaningfulness of our variables. Interpreting a regression slope that is expressed in the units of $X$ and $Y$ forces us to consider what changes in $X$ and in $Y$ really mean. We may be less likely to consider our variables carefully if we

**TABLE 18.7** SUMMARY OF SOME OF THE TYPES OF CORRELATIONS DISCUSSED IN CHAPTER 18

| Statistic | Equation or Description |
|---|---|
| Some useful expressions for the Pearson $r$ | $r_{XY} = \dfrac{1}{N-1} \sum z_X z_Y$ <br> $r_{XY} = b_1 \dfrac{s_X}{s_Y}$ <br> $r_{XY} = \sqrt{1 - \dfrac{s_e^2}{s_Y^2}\left[\dfrac{N-2}{N-1}\right]}$ |
| Partial correlation | $r_{XY\|W} = corr(X\|W, Y\|W) = \dfrac{r_{XY} - r_{XW}r_{YW}}{\sqrt{(1 - r_{XW}^2)(1 - r_{YW}^2)}}$ <br> where $X\|W = X - \hat{X}$ is the part of $X$ that is not predictable from $W$ and $Y\|W = Y - \hat{Y}$ is the part of $Y$ that is not predictable from $W$ |
| Semipartial correlation | $r_{Y(X\|W)} = corr(Y, X\|W) = \dfrac{r_{XY} - r_{XW}r_{YW}}{\sqrt{(1 - r_{XW}^2)}}$ |
| Point-biserial $r$ | Pearson $r$, where one variable is continuous and the other is dichotomous |
| $\phi$ coefficient | Pearson $r$, where both variables are dichotomous |
| Spearman $\rho$, $r_s$ | Pearson $r$ for ranked data |
| Kendall $\tau$, if there are no ties | $\dfrac{\text{number of agreements in order} - \text{number of disagreements in order}}{\text{total number of pairs of objects}}$ |
| if there are ties, | $\dfrac{(2)(\text{number of agreements in order} - \text{number of disagreements in order})}{\sqrt{N(N-1) - T_X}\sqrt{N(N-1) - T_Y}}$ |

where $T_X = \sum t(t-1)$, where $t$ is the number of tied observations in each group of ties on the $X$ variable and $T_Y = \sum t(t-1)$ where $t$ is the number of tied observations in each group of ties on the $Y$ variable

use a dimensionless correlational measure. If we are interested in understanding the relation between two variables, it is always a good idea to look at the scatterplot and the regression statistics in addition to the correlation coefficient.

Finally, in Table 18.7, we list some of the major types of correlation discussed in Chapter 18.

# KEY CONCEPTS

| | |
|---|---|
| sample-specific measure | standard error of estimate |
| homoscedasticity | restriction of range |
| reliability coefficient | ecological correlation |
| bivariate normal distribution | Fisher $Z$ transform |
| bootstrapping | correlation matrix |
| partial correlation coefficient | semipartial or part correlation coefficient |
| point-biserial correlation coefficient | $\phi$ coefficient |
| biserial correlation coefficient | tetrachoric correlation coefficient |
| Spearman $\rho$ coefficient | Kendall $\tau$ coefficient |
| Goodman–Kruskal $\gamma$ coefficient | |

# EXERCISES

**18.1**  Given the following data,

| X | Y |
|---|---|
| 1 | 11 |
| 2 | 3 |
| 3 | 7 |
| 4 | 9 |
| 5 | 9 |
| 6 | 21 |

(a) Draw a scatterplot.
(b) What is the correlation between $Y$ and $X$?
(c) What is the proportion of variance in $Y$ accounted for by $X$?
(d) What is the proportion of the variance in $X$ accounted for by $Y$?

**18.2**  For parts (a)–(c) indicate whether the use of the correlation coefficient and/or the conclusion drawn is reasonable. If it is not, indicate why not.

(a) A clinical psychologist reads a description of a study in which a correlation of $-.80$ was obtained between a measure of anxiety and a measure of emotional stability. Deciding to verify the result, he administers the same measures of anxiety and emotional stability to a random sample of patients in a VA hospital. The observed correlation of $-.20$ between measures is not significant. He concludes that he has no evidence of any relation (at least any linear relation) between anxiety and emotional stability.

(b) Martians are tall and skinny and do not weigh very much. Jovians are shorter, but weigh a lot more. Height and weight correlates pretty highly for each group, about $r = .60$. Would you expect the correlation between height and weight for a mixed group consisting of equal numbers of Martians and Jovians to be about the same, bigger, or smaller than .60? Why?

(c) It is reported in the press that getting a degree from a 4-year college is highly correlated with lifetime earnings; i.e., it is worth several hundred thousand dollars a year in lifetime earnings.

**18.3**  Using the *Seasons* data set on the CD, verify that the correlation between total cholesterol (TC) level and age is .506 for women, but only .148 for women 50 years of age or over, and .264 for women under 50 years of age. How do you explain these differences? What are the corresponding results for men?

**18.4**  (a) A psychologist is interested in predicting $Y$ from $X$ in two distinct groups. She finds the following results:

| Group 1 | Group 2 |
|---|---|
| $b_1 = 1$ | $b_1 = 4$ |
| $s_Y = 20$ | $s_Y = 10$ |
| $s_X = 10$ | $s_X = 2$ |

In which situation is the correlation between $X$ and $Y$ higher?

(b) You are given a large number of data points $(X, Y)$, and find that the correlation between $X$ and $Y$ is $r_{XY} = .70$. You now transform $X$ by multiplying each of the $X$ scores by 10 and adding 3 to the each of the products. You also transform $Y$ by multiplying each of the $Y$ scores by 2. What is the correlation coefficient between the transformed variables?

**18.5**  We are concerned with the correlation between two tests. The reliability of the first test is .64; that of the second test is .81.

(a) What is the largest correlation that we could possibly find?

(b) Suppose we actually find that the correlation is .40 in a sample of 40 subjects. What is our best estimate of what the correlation would be if we had perfectly reliable measures?

(c) Is the correlation significantly different from 0?

**18.6**  Using the data for men in the *Seasons* data set, if we consider individual men, the correlation between TC and age is .062. What is this correlation if we consider levels of the variable agegrp; that is, if we find the mean value of TC and age at each level of agegrp, and use these as our data points?

**18.7**  It is found in an introductory statistics course with 19 students that scores on the final examination correlate $-.30$ with the number of hours studied.

(a) Using the $t$ distribution, test the null hypothesis $H_0$: $\rho = 0$, assuming a two-tailed test with $\alpha = .05$?

(b) Test the same hypothesis, using the Fisher $Z$ transform and the normal distribution.

(c) Can we conclude that studying too much interferes with test taking?

(d) Find the .95 confidence interval for the population correlation coefficient, $\rho$. Find the .50 confidence interval.

(e) Using GPOWER, or any other valid procedure or program, what is the post hoc power for the test in (a)?

(f) Calculate the post hoc power for the test in (b). Note that here you cannot use GPOWER.

(g) Assuming that the population correlation really is $-.30$, use GPOWER to find the number of subjects necessary to have a power of .80 for rejecting $H_0$: $\rho = 0$, using a two-tailed test with $\alpha = .05$.

(h) Using the normal distribution, and the test in (b), find the number of subjects that would be necessary to have the power be .80 for the significance test.

**18.8**  Each year, a random sample of $N = 200$ freshmen admitted to the Elite Institute of Technology (EIT) must take a standardized skills test when they first enroll. Two years ago, the correlation between the test and first year GPA (Grade Point Average) was .22. Last year, after the test had been revised, the correlation rose to .35.

(a) If the two entering classes can be considered random samples of EIT freshmen, test whether the two correlations are significantly different at $\alpha = .05$? If the test indicated that the correlations were significantly different, what conclusion(s) could you draw about the standardized skills tests.

(b) What is the post hoc power for the test in (a)?

(c) Assuming that the population correlations for the two versions of the test were actually .22 and .35, how large would $N$ have to be to have a power of .80 to reject the null hypothesis that they were the same? (assume two-tailed test with $\alpha = .05$)

**18.9**   For three independent groups, the data are as follows: (use $\alpha = .05$ for any significance tests)

|     | $G_1$ | $G_2$ | $G_3$ |
| --- | --- | --- | --- |
| $n$ | 103 | 52 | 67 |
| $r$ | .60 | .45 | .20 |

For the following, assume nondirectional alternative hypotheses with $\alpha = .05$.

(a) Test $H_0$: $\rho_2 = 0$.

(b) Test $H_0$: $\rho_1 = \rho_2$.

(c) Test $H_0$: $\rho_2 = \rho_3$.

(d) Find the 95% confidence interval for $\rho_2$.

**18.10**   A random sample of 39 students are given tests of abstract reasoning (A), quantitative reasoning (Q), and verbal skills (V). The resulting correlation matrix is

|     | A | Q | V |
| --- | --- | --- | --- |
| A | 1.00 | | |
| Q | .30 | 1.00 | |
| V | .50 | .20 | 1.00 |

Note that these correlations are not independent, because all the correlations are based on the same students.

(a) Test the hypothesis that all of the off-diagonal elements in the matrix (here the .30, .50, and .20 correlations) are equal to 0 in the population.

(b) Test the hypothesis that, in the population, abstract reasoning correlates equally with verbal ability and quantitative reasoning. That is, test $H_0$: $\rho_{AV} = \rho_{AQ}$ against the alternative hypothesis $H_1$: $\rho_{AV} \neq \rho_{AQ}$.

(c) Find $r_{AV|Q}$, the partial correlation between A and V with Q partialed out. Test whether it is significantly different from zero.

**18.11**   Steiger (1980) used as an example a longitudinal study of sex stereotypes and verbal achievement. Masculinity, femininity, and verbal achievement are measured at Time 1 and Time 2. A random sample of 103 observations are obtained. The resulting correlation matrix is

|     | M1 | F1 | V1 | M2 | F2 | V2 |
| --- | --- | --- | --- | --- | --- | --- |
| M1 | 1.00 | | | | | |
| F1 | .10 | 1.00 | | | | |
| V1 | .40 | .50 | 1.00 | | | |
| M2 | .70 | .05 | .50 | 1.00 | | |
| F2 | .05 | .70 | .50 | .50 | 1.00 | |
| V2 | .45 | .50 | .80 | .50 | .60 | 1.00 |

Note that these correlations are *not independent*, because all the correlations are based on the same students.

**(a)** Test the hypothesis that, in the population, the correlation between masculinity and femininity is the same at Time 1 and Time 2.

**(b)** Test the hypothesis that, in the population, the correlation between V1 and M1 is the same as the correlation between V1 and F1.

**18.12** If we have two binary variables $X$ and $Y$, we can find the correlation between them (called the "$\phi$ coefficient") using the expression in Table 18.5.

**(a)** What is the value of $\phi$ for the following 2 × 2 table?

| | | Item 2 | | |
|---|---|---|---|---|
| | | Pass | Fail | |
| Item 1 | Pass | 20 | 20 | 40 |
| | Fail | 50 | 10 | 60 |
| | | 70 | 30 | 100 |

**(b)** Given the marginal frequencies, what are the minimum and maximum values of $\phi$ that are possible?

**(c)** Given the marginal frequencies, for what cell values would $\phi$ be 0?

**18.13** Sometimes we will find that a correlation has been computed between some variable $X$ and another variable $T$, which is the sum of a number of variables, including $X$ (e.g., $T = X + Y$). Under these circumstances, we can expect a positive correlation between $X$ and $T$, even if $X$ is not related to $Y$ because $X$ is part of $T$. Show that in general

$$r_{X,T-X} = \frac{r_{XT}s_T - s_X}{\sqrt{s_X^2 + s_T^2 - 2r_{XT}s_Xs_T}}$$

where $r_{X,T-X}$ is the correlation between $X$ and the part of $T$ not containing $X$.

**18.14** Note that the previous question has implications for the interpretation of correlations involving change or difference scores. Suppose that $X$ refers to pretest scores and $T$ to posttest scores. Therefore, $T - X$ refers to change scores. If we assume that $s_{\text{pre}} = s_{\text{post}}$, the equation in question 18.13 reduces to

$$r_{X,T-X} = r_{\text{pre,change}} = \frac{r_{\text{pre,post}} - 1}{\sqrt{2(1 - r_{\text{pre,post}})}}$$

We would not expect a perfect correlation between pretest and posttest scores for a lot of reasons, including random error. Suppose $r_{\text{pre,post}} = .70$. What do we expect for $r_{\text{pre,change}}$?

**18.15** A researcher tries to develop a new questionnaire to measure some personality trait. The instrument is made up of a number of items, each of which is scored numerically. The total score, $T$, is supposed to represent the degree to which a person has the trait. The researcher likes the instrument, but thinks it will be too time-consuming to administer all of it, because it contains a large number of items—so she arbitrarily divides the instrument into two parts, each containing half the items. Let's refer to the score on one of the halves as $X$ and the score on the other half as $Y$ (so that $T = X + Y$). She finds that the correlation between $X$ and $T$ is high ($r_{XT} = .7$) and concludes that the correlation between the scores on the two halves of the instrument ($r_{XY}$) must also be pretty high, so that she can get by using only one of the halves to measure the personality trait. If we can assume that the variances of $X$ and $Y$ are equal, what is $r_{XY}$?

## APPENDIX 18.1

## Proof that $\sum (Y_i - \overline{Y})^2 = \sum (Y_i - \hat{Y})^2 + \sum (\hat{Y}_i - \overline{Y})^2$

We start with the identity $Y_i - \overline{Y} = (Y_i - \hat{Y}_i) + (\hat{Y}_i - \overline{Y})$ Squaring both sides and summing, we get

$$\sum (Y_i - \overline{Y})^2 = \sum (Y_i - \hat{Y}_i)^2 + \sum (\hat{Y}_i - \overline{Y})^2 + 2 \sum (Y_i - \hat{Y}_i)(\hat{Y}_i - \overline{Y})$$

We next show that $\sum (Y_i - \hat{Y}_i)(\hat{Y}_i - \overline{Y}) = 0$. We first substitute $\hat{Y}_i = \overline{Y} + b_1(X_i - \overline{X})$ into the left side of the equation. This yields

$$\sum (Y_i - \hat{Y}_i)(\hat{Y}_i - \overline{Y}) = \sum [Y_i - \overline{Y} - b_1(X_i - \overline{X})][b_1(X_i - \overline{X})]$$
$$= \sum [b_1(X_i - \overline{X})(Y_i - \overline{Y}) - b_1^2(X_i - \overline{X})^2] \qquad (18.24)$$
$$= b_1 \sum (X_i - \overline{X})(Y_i - \overline{Y}) - b_1^2 \sum (X_i - \overline{X})^2$$

We then note from the definition of covariance in Chapter 3 that $\sum (X_i - \overline{X})(Y_i - \overline{Y}) = (N-1)s_{XY} = (N-1)b_1 s_X^2$ because $b_1 = s_{XY}/s_X^2$ and that $\sum (X_i - \overline{X})^2 = (N-1)s_X^2$, where $s_X^2$ is the variance of $X$.

Substituting into Equation 18.24, we have

$$\sum (Y_i - \hat{Y}_i)(\hat{Y}_i - \overline{Y}) = (N-1)\left(b_1^2 s_X^2 - b_1^2 s_X^2\right) = 0$$

Therefore, the crossproduct term is 0, and

$$\sum (Y_i - \overline{Y})^2 = \sum (Y_i - \hat{Y}_i)^2 + \sum (\hat{Y}_i - \overline{Y})^2$$
$$SS_Y = \qquad SS_{\text{residual}} \qquad + SS_{\text{regression}}$$

## APPENDIX 18.2

To get Equation 18.3, we start with

$$r^2 = \frac{r^2 SS_Y}{SS_Y} = \frac{SS_{\text{regression}}}{SS_Y} \qquad (18.25)$$

We first note that if we square both sides of Equation 18.3 and multiply both sides of the equation by $SS_Y$, the result is

$$r^2 SS_Y = b_1^2 SS_X = SS_{\text{regression}}$$

Also, from Appendix 18.1, we have $SS_Y = SS_{\text{regression}} + SS_{\text{residual}}$. Substituting into Equation 18.25, we have

$$r^2 = \frac{SS_{\text{regression}}}{SS_{\text{regression}} + SS_{\text{residual}}} = \frac{b_1^2 SS_X}{b_1^2 SS_X + SS_{\text{residual}}}$$

The rest of Equation 18.3 follows if we note that the variance of $X$ is

$$s_X^2 = \frac{SS_X}{N - 1}$$

and that the variance of estimate (the square of the standard error of estimate) is

$$s_e^2 = \frac{SS_{\text{residual}}}{N - 2}.$$

To get Equation 18.4, we note that

$$r^2 = \frac{SS_{\text{regression}}}{SS_Y} = \frac{SS_Y - SS_{\text{residual}}}{SS_Y} = 1 - \frac{SS_{\text{residual}}}{SS_Y}$$

# Chapter 19

## More About Bivariate Regression

## 19.1 INTRODUCTION

In Chapter 3, we indicated how to find linear regression equations that best predict scores on one variable from those on another. For example, we developed linear equations to predict final exam performance from pretest performance in a statistics class and cholesterol level from age in a sample of subjects participating in a medical school study.

In the present chapter, we first consider an important characteristic of regression, the phenomenon of **regression toward the mean**. This term refers to the fact that, whenever prediction is not perfect, the best prediction is always less "extreme" (i.e., is closer to its mean *in standard deviation units*) than the score it is predicted from. This has consequences that are often unappreciated.

We then go on to consider the kinds of inferences we can make about the linear equation that characterizes the relation between two variables in a population on the basis of a random sample selected from the population. Perhaps we wish to form a .95 confidence interval (CI) for the population slope, or determine whether we have sufficient evidence to reject the null hypothesis that the population slope is zero. To form confidence intervals, test hypotheses, or perform power calculations, we must state a model and make certain assumptions about the population. Our strategy will be to begin with the usual regression model that assumes that the predictor, $X$, is a fixed-effect variable and is measured without error, and $Y$ is a random variable that is normally distributed, then discuss what happens when $X$ is also random and when $X$ is measured with error. We also discuss how to check whether the assumptions of the model have been met and whether any of the data points have a particularly strong influence on the regression. We conclude by indicating how to test whether regression coefficients are significantly different from one another and by considering repeated-measures designs.

## 19.2 REGRESSION TOWARD THE MEAN

Whenever there is an imperfect linear relation between $X$ and $Y$, the values of $z_Y$ associated with any given value of $z_X$ will, on the average, be closer to zero than $z_X$ is. This can be seen in Fig. 19.1 in which an elliptical "envelope" has been drawn to represent a large number of standardized data points. In the figure, the envelope is symmetrical about a straight line with a slope of 1 drawn through the origin (i.e., the line with the equation $z_Y = z_X$). Now imagine that the ellipse is divided into a number of narrow vertical strips and that the mean of the data points in each strip is located in the middle of the strip. We can see that the line joining the means of the strip will have a slope that is less than 1. In fact, the line that best fits the points representing the mean values of $z_Y$ in the vertical strips will approximate

$$\hat{z}_Y = r z_X \tag{19.1}$$

the regression equation for predicting $z_Y$ from $z_X$. From Equation 19.1, we see that the predicted $z$ is always closer to zero than the predictor, whenever prediction is not perfect (i.e., whenever $|r| < 1$). We can extend this result to raw scores by rewriting Equation 19.1 as

$$\frac{\hat{Y} - \overline{Y}}{s_Y} = r \frac{X - \overline{X}}{s_X}$$

or, multiplying both sides by $s_Y$, as

$$\hat{Y} - \overline{Y} = r \frac{s_Y}{s_X}(X - \overline{X}) \tag{19.2}$$

In Equation 19.2 we see that the best prediction for $Y$ must be closer to $\overline{Y}$ than the corresponding $X$ is to $\overline{X}$, whenever $s_X = s_Y$ and prediction is not perfect.

Although regression toward the mean must always occur whenever two variables with equal variances are not perfectly linearly related, investigators have often felt compelled to

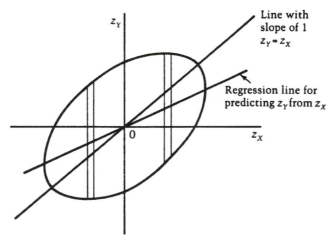

**Fig. 19.1** Regression line for predicting $z_Y$ from $z_X$ when there is an imperfect linear relation between $X$ and $Y$.

explain regression effects in terms of "interesting" variables—ignoring the fact that these effects could have been produced solely by random variability or measurement error or any other factor that results in less-than-perfect correlation. For example, suppose a group of children takes an achievement test, then is given a period of instruction followed by a second test. Children with extremely low scores on the first test will often tend to show some improvement in standing on the second test, and children with extremely high scores on the first test will often tend to show a decline. Although this seems to suggest that the intervening instruction is more effective for the students who scored lower on the first test than for those who scored higher, the changes in performance may merely reflect regression toward the mean. Even if the instruction was equally effective for all children, we would expect regression toward the mean if the two tests did not measure exactly the same thing or if there were random fluctuations in the children's alertness and their success in guessing. Because of such nuisance variables, if we want to assess the effects of instruction, we should include an appropriate control group and conduct an experiment.

Another example of the interpretive problems resulting from regression toward the mean is the so-called "sophomore slump." Individuals who perform particularly well in their first year of academics or athletics will probably perform relatively less well in their second year. It is often thought that this finding requires an explanation in terms of overconfidence and poor work habits that result from early success. However, these explanations may be unnecessary. Even without any interventions or distractions, performance will generally fluctuate so that there are periods of better-than-average performance and periods of worse-than-average performance. Therefore, periods of exceptionally good performance will often be followed by performance that is less good, whether or not there is an intervention. Similar regression effects observed in other everyday situations may elicit unwarranted explanations. Normal fluctuations in children's behavior may cause parents to overestimate the effectiveness of interventions such as punishment. Fluctuations in the intensity of symptoms in sufferers of many chronic diseases may cause patients to overestimate the effectiveness of various remedies and food supplements.

Regression toward the mean may also result in an apparent lack of symmetry that at first glance seems to be counterintuitive. Suppose, for example, that the correlation between the heights of fathers and their adult sons is .5, and that the mean height for males is 69 inches with a standard deviation of 2 inches. From Equation 19.2, the best prediction for the heights of sons whose fathers are 73 inches tall is

$$\hat{Y} = \overline{Y} + r\frac{s_Y}{s_X}(X - \overline{X}) = 69 + (.5)(1)(73 - 69) = 71$$

However, it does not follow from this that the best prediction for the heights of fathers of 71-inch sons is 73 inches. Rather, the best prediction for the heights of fathers of 71-inch-tall sons is 70 inches, again a regression toward the mean.

Regression toward the mean also complicates the study of change. For example, again consider children who take two tests separated by a period of instruction. It might seem desirable to subtract the score on the first test from the score on the second test in the hope of obtaining a "pure" measure of improvement; that is, a measure of change unrelated to initial performance. However, the change scores are *not* free of the influence of the scores on the first test. Whenever there is less than a perfect correlation between the tests, regression effects will occur, and these effects will be larger for more extreme scores. In our example, children who had extremely high scores on the first test will tend to have lower scores on the second one; children with extremely low scores on the first test will tend to score relatively higher on the second. It follows that if the scores have been standardized and if regression toward the mean occurs, change scores will tend to be negatively correlated with the scores on the first test, so that how other variables correlate with the change scores will depend to some extent on how they correlate with initial performance. These considerations, and others, have led to much discussion about whether the best estimate of average treatment effect in a pretest–posttest design is obtained if the pretest score is subtracted or if it is used as a covariate (for a recent discussion, see Maris, 1998).

We conclude this section by emphasizing that regression toward the mean is inevitable only if the variances are equal. As we can see in Equation 19.2, regression effects must occur for raw scores if

$$|r| \frac{s_Y}{s_X} < 1$$

However, if $s_Y > s_Y$, regression toward the mean need not occur for raw scores; in fact, if $|r| s_Y/s_X > 1$, we will have the opposite effect, called "egression from the mean" (see, e.g., Ragosa, 1995). Although there are many situations in which regression effects occur for raw scores, there are others in which these effects occur for standardized, but not for raw, scores.

## 19.3 INFERENCE IN LINEAR REGRESSION

### 19.3.1 The Normal Regression Model

We now go on to develop the theoretical structure necessary to make statistical inferences in regression. We first consider the model for the population that states $Y$ and $X$ are related according to the equation

$$Y_i = \beta_0 + \beta_1 X_i + \varepsilon_i \tag{19.3}$$

where
   $Y_i$ is the value of the dependent variable for the $i$th case
   $\beta_0$ and $\beta_1$ are the $Y$ intercept and slope of the line
   $X_i$ is the value taken on by the predictor variable for the $i$th case
and
   $\varepsilon_i$ is a random error component
We further assume that the error component $\varepsilon$ is independently and normally distributed with mean 0 and variance $\sigma_e^2$; that is,
   $E(\varepsilon_i) = 0$
   $var(\varepsilon_i) = \sigma_e^2$    for all   $i$   (homogeneity of variance or **homoscedasticity**)
   $cov(\varepsilon_i, \varepsilon_i') = 0$    except when $i = i'$   (independence)
These assumptions imply that the conditional population mean of $Y$ corresponding to any given value of $X$, $\mu_{Y.X}$, lies on the straight line $\mu_{Y.X} = \beta_0 + \beta_1 X$, and that the deviation of $Y$ from its conditional population mean is due solely to random error. This is very important; if the systematic relation between $X$ and $Y$ is not linear, our measure of error will include more than chance variability, and the significance tests developed from this model may be biased. In this model, $X$ is assumed to be a fixed-effect variable

that is measured without error. If we replicated the study, exactly the same values of $X$ would be used. If these conditions are satisfied, it can be shown that $b_1$ and $b_0$, the least-squares estimators of $\beta_1$ and $\beta_0$ that we developed in Chapter 3, are both unbiased (e.g., $E(b_1) = \beta_1$) and consistent (i.e., as the sample sizes are made larger, the estimates more closely approximate the parameter values).[1] The estimators are (see Equations 3.8 and 3.9)

$$b_1 = r\frac{s_Y}{s_X}$$

and

$$b_0 = \overline{Y} - b_1\overline{X}$$

As an example, consider the data presented in panel (a) of Table 19.1. In a hypothetical visual search experiment, 20 subjects each look at a screen and are presented with an array of letters. They are asked to respond as quickly as they can whether a specified target letter is present in the array. Groups of five subjects are assigned to array sizes of two, four, six, and eight letters, and the times in (milliseconds) to respond correctly that the target letter is present are recorded. Generally, when the letter arrays are larger, it takes longer to respond to the presence of a target letter, so the data are reasonably well fit by a linear equation. Here, the assumption that $X$ is a fixed-effect variable is satisfied, because the array sizes are chosen by the researcher and can be measured without error. Note that this is not the case for the statistics class example presented in Chapter 3, in which we think of first selecting individuals from the population, then measuring $X$ (pretest score) and $Y$ (final exam score), so that both $X$ and $Y$ are random variables.

In the next few sections, we discuss how to make statistical inferences about the slope and intercept of the regression equation and about the predictions made by the equation. In every case, we can find the $1-\alpha$ confidence interval for $\theta$, the population parameter of interest, by finding

$$\hat{\theta} \pm t_{a/2}\, s_{\hat{\theta}} \tag{19.4}$$

and can test hypotheses about $\theta$ by using the test statistic

$$t = \frac{\hat{\theta} - \theta_{\text{hyp}}}{s_{\hat{\theta}}} \tag{19.5}$$

where $\hat{\theta}$ is the estimate of $\theta$ obtained from the sample and $s_{\hat{\theta}}$ (which, when there are subscripts, will usually be written as $SE(\hat{\theta})$) is the estimated standard error. For example, the .95 confidence interval for $\beta_1$ is given by $b_1 \pm t_{.025} \cdot SE(b_1)$. We have already shown how to find $b_1$ in Chapter 3; all we need to find the confidence interval is $SE(b_1)$, the estimated standard error of $b_1$.

## 19.3.2 Inferences About $\beta_0$ and $\beta_1$

The SYSTAT output for the regression of time on array size is given in panel (b) of Table 19.1. From this output, we see that the bivariate regression equation that best predicts reaction time ($Y$) from array size ($X$) is

$$\hat{Y}_i = 381.90 + 23.92X_i$$

**TABLE 19.1**   DATA AND REGRESSION OUTPUT FOR THE SEARCH EXPERIMENT EXAMPLE

| (a) Data | |
|---|---|
| Size | Time |
| 2 | 418 |
| 2 | 428 |
| 2 | 410 |
| 2 | 445 |
| 2 | 471 |
| 4 | 475 |
| 4 | 455 |
| 4 | 418 |
| 4 | 524 |
| 4 | 516 |
| 6 | 537 |
| 6 | 500 |
| 6 | 480 |
| 6 | 511 |
| 6 | 529 |
| 8 | 550 |
| 8 | 617 |
| 8 | 590 |
| 8 | 608 |
| 8 | 548 |

(b) SYSTAT Regression Output

```
Dep Var: TIME     N: 20     Multiple R: 0.873     Squared multiple R: 0.763
Adjusted squared multiple R: 0.749      Standard error of estimate: 31.452
Effect    Coefficient  Std Error   Std Coef   Tolerance      t     P(2 Tail)
CONSTANT    381.900      17.227      0.000        .        22.169    0.000
SIZE         23.920       3.145      0.873      1.000       7.605    0.000
```

Analysis of Variance

| Source | Sum-of-Squares | df | Mean-Square | F-ratio | P |
|---|---|---|---|---|---|
| Regression | 57216.640 | 1 | 57216.640 | 57.839 | 0.000 |
| Residual | 17806.360 | 18 | 989.242 | | |

*Note.* Output is from SYSTAT.

In the output, the term **multiple R** refers to the **multiple correlation coefficient**, $R_{Y.X} = corr(Y, \hat{Y}) = .873$. This is the correlation between the actual value of $Y$ and $\hat{Y}$, the value of $Y$ predicted from $X$ using the regression equation. Because $\hat{Y}$ is a linear function of $X$, and because the magnitude of a correlation is unchanged by a linear transformation, for bivariate regression the multiple correlation is the absolute value of $r_{XY}$. Note that the multiple correlation coefficient cannot be negative because it is the correlation between $Y$ and a prediction of $Y$ based on a regression equation that has been developed to minimize prediction error. Also, presented in the regression output is the **standard error of**

**TABLE 19.2**   EXPLANATION OF THE ANOVA TABLE IN THE REGRESSION OUTPUT FOR
BIVARIATE REGRESSION

| SV | df | SS | MS | F |
|---|---|---|---|---|
| Regression | 1 | $\sum (\hat{Y}_i - \overline{Y})^2 = r^2 SS_Y = b_1^2 SS_X$ | $SS_{reg}/1$ | $MS_{reg}/MS_{residual}$ |
| Residual | $N - 2$ | $\sum (Y_i - \hat{Y}_i)^2 = (1 - r^2)SS_Y$ | $SS_{residual}/(N - 2)$ | |
| Total | $N - 1$ | $\sum (Y_i - \overline{Y})^2 = SS_Y$ | | |

**estimate,**

$$s_e = \sqrt{\frac{\sum (Y_i - \hat{Y}_i)^2}{N - 2}} = \sqrt{\frac{SS_{residual}}{N - 2}} = 31.452,$$

a measure of the variability around the regression line that we discussed in Chapter 18.

As can be seen in Table 19.2, the ANOVA (analysis of variance) table at the bottom of the output indicates the partitioning of variability (see Appendix 18.1). The total variability in the $Y$ scores, $SS_Y = \sum (Y_i - \overline{Y})^2$, is partitioned into two components, the variability accounted for by the bivariate regression equation,

$$SS_{regression} = \sum (\hat{Y} - \overline{Y})^2 = b_1^2 SS_X = r^2 SS_Y,$$

and the variability not accounted for by the regression,

$$SS_{residual} = \sum (Y - \hat{Y})^2 = (1 - r^2)SS_Y.$$

The $F$ given in the rightmost column of Table 19.2 is the ratio $MS_{regression}/MS_{residual}$. A significant $F$ indicates that both $r$ and $b_1$ are significantly different than zero; that is, that the null hypotheses $H_0: \rho = 0$ and $H_0: \beta_1 = 0$ can both be rejected. The $F$ can be used to test the significance of the correlation coefficient because it can be expressed as the square of the $t$ that was presented in Chapter 18 as the test statistic for the null hypothesis $H_0: \rho = 0$. Also, as we shall soon see, the $F$ can be written as the square of $t = b_1/SE(b_1)$, the test statistic for the null hypothesis $H_0: \beta_1 = 0$.

The regression output also displays $t$ tests for the significance of $b_0$ and $b_1$. Above the ANOVA table in Table 19.1, in the "Effect" column, the terms CONSTANT (i.e., the $Y$ intercept of the regression equation) and SIZE (the predictor variable, $X$) are listed. In the next two columns to the right are the values of the coefficients, $b_0$ and $b_1$, and then their standard errors. The "$t$" column is the ratio of the coefficient to its standard error, which is distributed as $t$ if the assumptions of the model are satisfied and the null hypothesis is true. Note that the square of the $t$ for $b_1$, $(7.605)^2$ is, within rounding error, the same as the value of the $F$ in the ANOVA table. The "Std Coef" column contains information about the regression of $Y$ on $X$ when both variables have been standardized. Because the regression line must pass through the origin when the variables are standardized, the $Y$ intercept must be zero. The standardized slope coefficient, the so-called "$\beta$" coefficient, has the same value as the correlation coefficient in bivariate regression.[2]

We estimate the regression parameters $\beta_0$ and $\beta_1$ using the least-squares estimates $b_0$ and $b_1$ that were presented in Chapter 3. It can be shown (see Appendix 19.2) that $b_0$ and $b_1$ are unbiased estimates of $\beta_0$ and $\beta_1$. The estimated standard errors for $b_0$ and $b_1$ can be expressed as

$$SE(b_0) = s_e \sqrt{\frac{1}{N} + \frac{\overline{X}^2}{SS_X}} \qquad (19.6)$$

and

$$SE(b_1) = \frac{s_e}{\sqrt{SS_X}} \qquad (19.7)$$

where $s_e$ is the standard error of estimate and $SS_X = \sum (X_i - \overline{X})^2$. These equations follow readily from the fact that, under the regression model, $b_0$ and $b_1$ can each be expressed as linear combinations of the $Y$ scores. This discussion is elaborated in Appendix 19.1, and the expressions are derived in Appendix 19.3.

Although the exact forms of the expressions for the standard errors are not completely intuitive, they have characteristics that make sense. For example,

1. We would expect that the greater the variability of the data points around the regression line, the more uncertainty we should have about the location of the regression line. Therefore, the standard errors of $b_0$ and $b_1$ should vary directly with $s_e$.

2. We would expect to get more stable estimates of the regression parameters if the sample contained both large and small $X$ values than if it contained only a narrow range of $X$'s. Therefore, the standard errors of both $b_0$ and $b_1$ should vary *inversely* with some measure of variability in the $X$ scores such as $s_X$ or $SS_X$.

3. Because the least-squares regression line must pass though the point $(\overline{X}, \overline{Y})$, variability in the slope will affect the $Y$ intercept less if $\overline{X}$ is close to the $Y$ axis (i.e., if $\overline{X}$ is close to 0). Therefore, the standard error of $b_0$ increases as $\overline{X}$ increases.

We can use these standard errors to find confidence intervals and test hypotheses about the slope and $Y$ intercept. For the slope of the regression equation, the .95 confidence interval for $\beta_1$ is given by

$$b_1 \pm t_{.025, 18} \cdot SE(b_1)$$
$$= 23.92 \pm (2.101)(3.145) = 17.31, 30.53$$

We can test the null hypothesis $H_0$: $\beta_1 = \beta_{1_{hyp}}$ by using the test statistic

$$t = \frac{b_1 - \beta_{1_{hyp}}}{SE(b_1)} \quad \text{with} \quad N - 2 \; df \qquad (19.8)$$

Note that if we wished to test the null hypothesis $H_0$: $\beta_1 = 0$, a two-tailed $t$ test for the slope is equivalent to the $F$ test in the ANOVA table. This may be seen by squaring the expression for the $t$,

$$t^2 = \frac{b_1^2}{SE(b_1)^2} = \frac{b_1^2}{s_e^2 / SS_X} = \frac{b_1^2 SS_X}{s_e^2} = \frac{MS_{\text{regression}}}{MS_{\text{error}}} = F$$

Suppose we wish to test the hypothesis $H_0$: $\beta_1 = 20$ against the alternative hypothesis

$H_1$: $\beta_1 > 20$. The value of the test statistic is

$$t = \frac{23.92 - 20}{3.145} = 1.246$$

Because this value does not exceed the one-tailed critical value of $t_{.05,18} = 1.734$, we do not have sufficient evidence to reject the null hypothesis.

If we are concerned with the $Y$ intercept, we can find confidence intervals and test hypotheses just as we did for the slope. For example, the .95 confidence interval for $\beta_0$ is

$$b_0 \pm t_{.025,18} \cdot SE(b_0)$$
$$= 381.90 \pm (2.101)(17.227) = 345.71, 418.09$$

We know that the test of $H_0$: $\beta_0 = 350$ against $H_1$: $\beta_0 \neq 350$ at $\alpha = .05$ will not be significant because 350 lies within the .95 confidence interval for $\beta_0$.

### 19.3.3 Power Calculations

Using the noncentral $t$ distribution, we can readily calculate the post hoc power for the tests we just conducted. The noncentrality parameter for the test of the slope coefficient is

$$\delta = \frac{|\beta_1 - \beta_{1_{\text{hyp}}}|}{\sigma_{b_1}} \tag{19.9}$$

If we wish to test $H_0$: $\beta_1 = 20$ against the alternative hypothesis $H_1$: $\beta_1 > 20$ with $\alpha = .05$, as in the previous section, the noncentrality parameter is estimated by the observed value of $t$, here 1.246. Entering the critical value of $t$, 1.734, as the $X$ value, $df = 18$, and the observed value of $t$ as the noncentrality parameter in the UCLA noncentral Student calculator returns probability $= .672$, so the power is $1 - .672 = .328$.

We can also estimate what the power would be if we increased the number of observations. Suppose we had 20 observations at each level of array size instead of 5 and that everything else remained the same. Because $SS_X = \sum(X_i - \overline{X})^2$, increasing the number of observations at each level of $X$ from 5 to 20 would increase $SS_X$ from 100 to 400, a factor of 4. Assuming the slope and standard error of estimate remained the same, we can see from Equation 19.7 that making $SS_X$ four times as large would make the standard error of $b_1$ half as large. Therefore, the test statistic would become twice as large, increasing in value from 1.246 to 2.492. The $df$ would now be $N - 2 = 78$, and the new critical value of $t$ would be $t_{.05,78} = 1.665$. Entering these values into the noncentral $t$ calculator yields a probability of .205, so that the estimated power would be approximately .80 for rejecting $H_0$: $\beta_1 = 20$ in favor of $H_1$: $\beta_1 > 20$.

We can perform power calculations for tests of the $Y$ intercept in exactly the same way. For the test of $H_0$: $\beta_0 = 350$ against $H_1$: $\beta_0 \neq 350$ at $\alpha = .05$, we can use the test statistic $t = (381.90 - 350)/17.227 = 1.852$ as the estimate of the noncentrality parameter. Using this estimate, and the critical value of $t_{.025,18} = 2.101$, yields a post hoc power estimate of .42. If we increased the number of observations at each array size from 5 to 20 and everything else remained the same, the standard error would become

$$SE(b_0) = s_e\sqrt{\frac{1}{N} + \frac{\overline{X}^2}{SS_X}} = (31.452)\sqrt{\frac{1}{80} + \frac{25}{400}} = 8.613$$

and the test statistic would be $(381.90 - 350)/8.613 = 3.703$. Using 3.703 as the estimate of the noncentrality parameter, the critical value $t_{.025,78} = 1.99$, and $df = 78$ yields a power estimate of .96.

GPOWER can also be used to provide power estimates in regression. However, it can only estimate power for tests of the null hypothesis that $\beta_1 = 0$ (or, in the case of multiple regression, for tests of null hypotheses that state that one or more of the set of $\beta$s for different predictors are equal to zero). We illustrate its use in Chapter 20.

### 19.3.4 Inferences About the Population Regression Line

According to the regression model, the expected value of $Y$ for any $X = X_j$ is $\mu_{Y.X_j} = \beta_0 + \beta_1 X_j$. We can think of $\mu_{Y.X_j}$ as the conditional mean of the $Y$ scores that correspond to $X_j$. We can show that $\hat{Y}_j = \hat{\mu}_{Y.X_j} = b_0 + b_1 X_j$ is an unbiased estimator of $\mu_{Y.X_j}$, and that the estimated standard error is given by

$$SE(\hat{\mu}_{Y.X_j}) = s_e \sqrt{h_{jj}} \tag{19.10}$$

where

$$h_{jj} = \frac{1}{N} + \frac{(X_j - \overline{X})^2}{SS_X} \tag{19.11}$$

is the so-called **leverage** of $X_j$ (see Appendix 19.1).

For the search experiment data, the best estimate for the conditional mean of $Y$ at $X = 4$ is given by $\hat{\mu}_{Y.X=4} = 381.90 + (23.92)(4) = 477.58$ and the estimated standard error is

$$SE(\hat{\mu}_{Y.X=4}) = (31.452)\sqrt{\frac{1}{20} + \frac{(4-5)^2}{100}}$$

Therefore, the .95 confidence interval for $\mu_{Y.X=4}$ is

$$477.58 \pm (2.101)(7.70) = 461.39, 493.77$$

As we can see from Equations 19.10 and 19.11, the standard error, and therefore the confidence interval, depends on the value of $X_j$. It is smallest when $X_j = \overline{X}$, and increases as $X_j$ deviates more from $\overline{X}$. This can be clearly seen in Fig. 19.2, which is the scatterplot for the search experiment data, with the regression line and the .95 confidence interval also displayed. Note that hypothesis tests or power calculations may be conducted in the same way as in the previous section.

### 19.3.5 Obtaining a Confidence Interval for $Y_{new j}$, a New Value of $Y$ at $X_j$

In the previous section, we showed how to find a confidence interval for the conditional mean of the $Y$ scores at $X_j$. Here, we show how to find a confidence interval for the $Y$ score of a new individual who has $X = X_j$. That is, we wish to estimate one of the scores from the population of scores with mean $\mu_{Y.X_j}$, where $Y_{new j} = \mu_{Y.X_j} + \varepsilon$. The estimate of the conditional mean, $\hat{\mu}_{Y.X_j} = b_0 + b_1 X_j$, is an unbiased estimate of $Y_{new j}$. However, if we wish to find the confidence interval for $Y_{new j}$, our measure of variability should not only contain the variability associated with $\hat{\mu}_{Y.X_j}$, but should have an additional

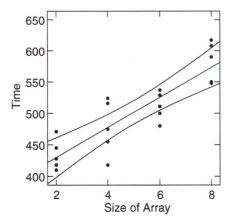

**Fig. 19.2** Scatterplot for the search data of Table 19.1 with the regression line and .95 confidence curves.

component because of the variability of the $Y$ scores around their conditional means. The appropriate standard error is given by $s_e\sqrt{1 + h_{jj}}$, where $h_{jj}$, the leverage, was defined by Equation 19.11.

For the search experiment data, the predicted reaction time for a new subject with an array size of 4 is $381.90 + (23.92)(4) = 477.58$, the same as the predicted conditional mean. However, the estimated standard error is

$$31.452\sqrt{1 + \frac{1}{20} + \frac{(4 - 5)^2}{100}} = 32.38$$

so that the .95 confidence interval for $Y_{\text{new}}$ is $477.58 \pm (2.101)(32.38) = 477.58 \pm 68.03$. Note that this interval is much wider than the .95 confidence interval for the conditional mean that we previously found to be $477.58 \pm 16.19$.

Note that the above result does not allow us to conclude that 95% of the population of $Y$ scores corresponding to $X = 4$ lie within the interval $477.58 \pm 68.03$. As always, the correct interpretation of the confidence interval is based on what would be expected to happen during repeated sampling: Assume that (1) we select many samples of size $N$, using the same values of $X$ in each sample, (2) for each sample, we find the .95 confidence interval for the $Y$ score of a new individual with $X = 4$; and (3) for each sample, we observe whether the $Y$ score actually is contained within the confidence interval. If the assumptions of the model are valid, the .95 confidence intervals will contain the actual scores in 95% of the samples. Table 19.3 lists some of the population parameters that we might wish to estimate, the sample statistics that we use as estimators, and the standard errors that can be used to form confidence intervals.

## 19.3.6 The One-Factor ANOVA with Two Groups: A Special Case of Regression Analysis

It is important to understand that ANOVA is simply a special case of regression analysis. Although we will discuss this in detail after we have introduced multiple regression, we are

**TABLE 19.3**  SUMMARY OF BIVARIATE REGRESSION STATISTICS

| Statistic | Expression | Expected Value | Estimated Standard Error for Finding Confidence Interval |
|---|---|---|---|
| Slope | $b_1 = \sum (X_i - \overline{X})(Y_i - \overline{Y})/SS_X$ <br> $= rs_Y/s_X$ | $\beta_1$ | $s_e/\sqrt{SS_X}$ <br> where $s_e = \sqrt{SS_{\text{residual}}/(N-2)}$ <br> is the standard error of estimate |
| Y intercept | $b_0 = \overline{Y} - b_1\overline{X}$ | $\beta_0$ | $s_e\sqrt{(1/N) + (\overline{X}^2/SS_X)}$ |
| Mean value of $Y$ at $X_j$ | $\hat{\mu}_{Y \cdot X_j} = b_0 + b_1 X_j$ | $\mu_{Y \cdot X_j}$ | $s_e\sqrt{h_{jj}}$, where $h_{jj} = \frac{1}{N} + \frac{(X_j - \overline{X})^2}{SS_X}$ |
| New score at $X_j$ | $\hat{Y}_{\text{new}_j} = \hat{\mu}_{Y \cdot X_j} = b_0 + b_1 X_j$ | $\mu_{Y \cdot X_j}$ | $s_e\sqrt{1 + h_{jj}}$ |
| Residual of the $j$th case | $e_j = Y_j - \hat{Y}_j$ | $0$ | $s_e\sqrt{1 - h_{jj}}$ |

already in a position to demonstrate that a one-factor ANOVA that tests the hypothesis $H_0$: $\mu_1 = \mu_2$ is exactly equivalent to a regression test of the hypothesis $H_0$: $\beta_1 = 0$.

The ANOVA model for a one-factor between-subjects design is

$$Y_{ij} = \mu + \alpha_j + \varepsilon_{ij}$$

with the usual assumption that the $\varepsilon_{ij}$ are independently distributed with mean 0 and variance $\sigma_e^2$ within each population. To consider the two-group design as a problem in regression analysis, we assign the value $X_1$ to all the participants in one group and any different value $X_2$ to all the participants in the second group. The regression model may then be written as

$$Y_{ij} = \beta_0 + \beta_1 X_j + \varepsilon_{ij}$$

The distributional assumptions about $\varepsilon_{ij}$ are the same as for the ANOVA model. Because there are only two populations of $Y$ scores, the two population means must lie on a straight line. The population mean for the first group of $Y$'s is given by $\mu_1 = \beta_0 + \beta_1 X_1$, and the mean of the second group is $\mu_2 = \beta_0 + \beta_1 X_2$. Therefore,

$$\mu_1 - \mu_2 = \beta_1(X_1 - X_2)$$

Because $X_1 \neq X_2, \mu_1 - \mu_2 = 0$ only if $\beta_1 = 0$; therefore, when there are only two groups, testing the null hypothesis that $\beta_1 = 0$ is equivalent to testing the hypothesis $\mu_1 = \mu_2$.

We can also show that, if the factor has only two levels, $SS_{\text{regression}} = SS_A$, and $SS_{\text{residual}} = SS_{S/A}$. Because there are only two groups, the least-squares regression line must pass through the two group means. Therefore, $\hat{Y}_{i1} = \overline{Y}_{\cdot 1}$ and $\hat{Y}_{i2} = \overline{Y}_{\cdot 2}$. Therefore, in the case of one-factor ANOVA with two levels

$$SS_{\text{residual}} = \sum\sum (Y_{ij} - \hat{Y}_{ij})^2 = \sum\sum (Y_{ij} - \overline{Y}_{\cdot j})^2 = SS_{S/A}$$

and

$$SS_{\text{regression}} = \sum\sum (\hat{Y}_{ij} - \overline{Y}_{\cdot \cdot})^2 = \sum\sum (\overline{Y}_{\cdot j} - \overline{Y}_{\cdot \cdot})^2 = SS_A$$

so that $MS_{\text{regression}}/MS_{\text{residual}}$ and $MS_A/MS_{S/A}$ are equivalent if there are only two levels of the factor.

It is important to note that, when there are more than two levels of the factor, $SS_{\text{regression}}$ will in general not be equal to $SS_A$. For the general case in which there are $a$ groups of scores, $SS_{\text{regression}}$ will equal $SS_A$ only if, when $Y$ is plotted against $X$, the $a$ group means all fall on a straight line. However, we will show in Chapter 21 that even complicated ANOVAs can be considered to be special cases of multiple regression.

### 19.3.7 Regression Analysis in Nonexperimental Research

In the regression model introduced in Section 19.3.1, $X$ is assumed to be fixed and measured without error. In other words, the values of $X$ scores are assumed to be known constants. This condition will generally only be fully satisfied when $X$ is an independent variable that is manipulated in an experiment. In an experiment, the researcher selects the levels of the independent variable—array size in the current example. When a statistical inference is made, conclusions are drawn about the populations of $Y$ scores corresponding to these fixed levels of $X$.

However, regression is commonly used with data collected in nonexperimental research in which both $X$ and $Y$ take on values that vary from sample to sample, and are therefore random variables. This will occur in observational studies in which a sample of individuals is selected, and values of $X$ and $Y$ are obtained for each individual. For example, we could perform an observational study in which we selected a sample of patients and measured the body mass index ($X$) and cholesterol ($Y$) for each patient.

Even if $X$ is a random variable, it can be shown that the least-squares estimates are unbiased and consistent, and we can use the *same* calculations for hypothesis tests and confidence intervals as for the fixed-$X$ model we discussed earlier, provided we are willing to make certain assumptions. We must assume that the values of $Y$ are drawn from a normal population with mean $\mu_{Y.X} = \beta_0 + \beta_1 X$ and constant variance $\sigma_e^2$, and that the probability distribution of $X$ does not involve the regression parameters $\beta_0$, $\beta_1$, and $\varepsilon$. In particular, we must assume that $X$ and $\varepsilon$ are not correlated. Note that to ensure that $X$ and $\varepsilon$ are independent, we treat the $X$ scores as though they were fixed by making our statistical inferences "conditional" on them. That is, our inferences are considered to apply to situations having the same distribution of $X$ scores as in the current sample. (For discussions of what happens when both $X$ and $Y$ are random variables, see Fox, 1997, pp. 113–114; Hays, 1994, pp. 637–638; Neter et al., 1996, p. 85; Snedecor & Cochran, 1967, pp. 149–150; and especially Mittelhammer et al.,[3] 2000, pp. 17–24 and 225–235.)

### 19.3.8 Regression When *X* Is Subject to Random Error

So far we have assumed that $X$ is measured without error. As this assumption is often not realistic, we consider what happens when the obtained value of $X$ is made up of two components, $X'$, its true value (i.e., the value it would have if it could be measured without error), and $u$, an error component, so that

$$X = X' + u$$

If we can assume that the measurement is unbiased and that the error component, $u$, is uncorrelated with $X'$, we have $E(u) = 0$ and $\sigma_X^2 = \sigma_{X'}^2 + \sigma_u^2$.

Snedecor and Cochran (1967) point out that, if $\varepsilon$, $u$, and $X'$ are all normally and independently distributed, $Y$ and $X$ will follow a bivariate normal distribution (see Chapter 18) and the regression of $Y$ on $X$ will be linear with a slope of

$$\beta_1 = \frac{\beta_1'}{1 + \lambda} = r_{XX} \beta_1' \tag{19.12}$$

where $\beta_1'$ is the "true" slope (i.e., the slope of the equation that would be obtained by regressing $Y$ on $X'$), $\lambda = \sigma_u^2 / \sigma_{X'}^2$, and $r_{XX} = \sigma_{X'}^2 / \sigma_X^2$ is the **reliability** of $X$. Even if $X'$ is not normally distributed, the result holds for large samples and approximately for small samples when $\lambda$ is small. This means that when $X$ is measured with error, the obtained slope, $b_1$, underestimates the magnitude of the true slope because it estimates $\beta_1$ rather than the true slope, $\beta_1'$. If there is a great deal of measurement error, the reliability will be low, and $\beta_1$ will be much closer to zero than the true slope.

Fortunately, in experimental research, measurement error is usually quite small. Consider a situation in which $\sigma_{X'} = 15$. Even if $\sigma_u = 5$ (this implies that about one third of the measured values of $X$ will be in error by at least 5 units), the reliability will be high. In this case, $r_{XX} = 225/250 = .90$ so that from Equation 19.12, $\beta_1 = .9 \beta_1'$.

However, if instruments that have large amounts of measurement error are used, the magnitudes of the regression coefficients may be seriously underestimated. Also, if the amount of measurement error differs across conditions, this must be kept in mind when comparing slopes obtained in the different conditions. The situation is more complicated if it cannot be assumed that $X'$ is independent of $u$. For further discussion, see Draper and Smith (1998, pp. 89–92).

## 19.4 AN EXAMPLE: REGRESSING CHOLESTEROL LEVEL ON AGE

Suppose we were to explore the extent to which total cholesterol level is related to age. To do this, we consider the scores of the participants in the Seasons study who had their cholesterol measured in every season.[4] The scatterplot of the mean of the four seasonal cholesterol scores against the age of the participant at the first measurement was presented in Figure 3.6 and showed a moderate linear relation. Because the literature suggests that the relation might be different for men and women, we present separate scatterplots for men and women in Fig. 19.3(a) and Fig. 19.3(b).

For the 211 women having cholesterol scores in each season, the scatterplot indicates that there is a positive linear relation between cholesterol and age. Using the inference procedures discussed in Chapter 18, we can determine that the correlation is significantly different from zero, $r = .506$, $p = .000$. The univariate distributions for age and cholesterol are fairly symmetric, and the boxplots indicate only a single outlier on the cholesterol measure. There is considerable scatter around the smoothing curve, especially for several women between the ages of 30–50 who have high cholesterol scores.

Figure 19.4 displays the SYSTAT output for the regression of cholesterol on age for women. From the output, we see that the linear regression equation that best predicts cholesterol ($Y$) from age ($X$) is

$$\hat{Y} = 131.87 + 1.71X$$

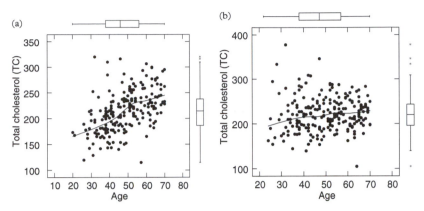

**Fig. 19.3** Scatterplot for total cholesterol and age with LOWESS smoothing for (a) females ($r = .506$) and (b) males ($r = .062$).

For each additional year of age, the predicted cholesterol level increases by 1.71 units. The .95 confidence interval for the slope is

$$1.71 \pm t_{.025, 209}(.202)$$
$$= 1.71 \pm 0.40 = 1.31, 2.11$$

Both the intercept and slope differ significantly from zero, $t(209) = 13.117$, $p = .000$, and $t(209) = 8.476$, $p = .000$, respectively. The output also contains information about the Durbin–Watson statistic (see Section 19.5.5) and the first-order autocorrelation (i.e., the correlation between the residual on trial $i$ and the residual on trial $i - 1$), and warns that case 311 is an outlier, then goes on to plot the residuals (the differences between the actual $Y$ scores and the $Y$ scores predicted by the regression equation) against the estimated $Y$'s. We will discuss these measures in the context of checking the assumptions that underlie our inferences in Section 19.5.

The 220 men with complete data have an age distribution very similar to that for the female sample (the mean age is 48.4 years for women and 50.3 years for men). The mean cholesterol score in the male sample is slightly higher than for the female sample (221.9 as compared with 214.7), but the difference is not sufficient to conclude that they are significantly different (the .95 confidence interval for the difference extends from $-0.19$ to 14.55). There seems to be less change in cholesterol level with age for men than women, and there are also a few more outlying cholesterol scores for men. The correlation between cholesterol and age for men is not significantly different from zero, $r = .062$, $p = .363$. Using the test statistic given in Chapter 18, we find that the correlation between cholesterol and age is significantly larger for women than for men, $z = 5.10$, $p = .000$.

The results of the regression of cholesterol level on age for men are given in Fig. 19.5. The regression equation is

$$\hat{Y} = 211.91 + 0.20X$$

The slope is not significantly different from zero, $t(218) = .912$, $p = .363$; the estimate of the slope is .198, with a .95 confidence interval that extends from $-.23$ to $+.63$. A reasonable question to ask at this point is whether the slope for women is significantly different than

```
Dep Var: TC    N: 211    Multiple R: 0.506    Squared multiple R: 0.256
Adjusted squared multiple R: 0.252    Standard error of estimate: 34.219
Effect    Coefficient  Std Error   Std Coef   Tolerance     t      P(2 Tail)
CONSTANT    131.870     10.053      0.000         .       13.117     0.000
SIZE          1.712      0.202      0.506       1.000      8.476     0.000

                          Analysis of Variance

   Source        Sum-of-Squares       df      Mean-Square    F-ratio       P
Regression         84117.481           1       84117.481     71.838     0.000
Residual          244725.926         209        1170.937

---------------------------------------------------------------------------

***WARNING***
Case     311  is an outlier    (Studentized Residual = 4.068)
Durbin-Watson D Statistic     2.084
First Order Autocorrelation −0.050
```

## Plot of Residuals against Predicted Values

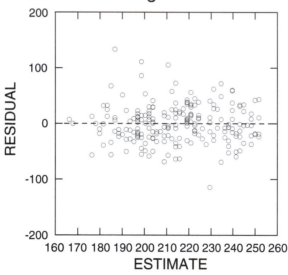

**Fig. 19.4** SYSTAT output for regression of total cholesterol on age for females.

that for men. We shall present this test in Section 19.7. In bivariate regression, if $r$ is significantly different from zero, the slope must also be significantly different from zero. However, because of the characteristics of the correlation coefficient, it does not necessarily follow that, if a correlation is significantly larger in Group 1 than in Group 2, the slope must also be larger in Group 1. In Exercise 19.5 at the end of the chapter, we present an example in which the correlation coefficient is significantly higher for men than for women, but the regression slope is significantly higher for women than for men. We next consider how to check the assumptions underlying our tests.

## 19.5 CHECKING FOR VIOLATIONS OF ASSUMPTIONS

Because our conclusions can be seriously in error if there are severe violations of the assumptions, we next discuss how to check for violations. When we try to understand our

```
Dep Var: TC     N: 220     Multiple R: 0.062     Squared multiple R: 0.004
Adjusted squared multiple R: 0.000        Standard error of estimate: 38.286
Effect     Coefficient  Std Error   Std Coef    Tolerance      t      P(2 Tail)
CONSTANT    211.906       11.249      0.000         .        18.837     0.000
SIZE          0.198        0.218      0.062       1.000       0.912     0.363
```

Analysis of Variance

| Source | Sum-of-Squares | df | Mean-Square | F-ratio | P |
|---|---|---|---|---|---|
| Regression | 1218.673 | 1 | 1218.673 | 0.831 | 0.363 |
| Residual | 319540.841 | 218 | 1465.784 | | |

---

```
***WARNING***
Case     409  is an outlier    (Studentized Residual = 4.362)
Durbin-Watson D Statistic    2.011
First Order Autocorrelation −0.018
```

## Plot of Residuals against Predicted Values

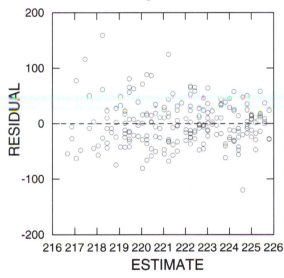

**Fig. 19.5** SYSTAT output for regression of total cholesterol on age for males.

data, we should not rely only on summary statistics such as the correlation coefficient or the slope of the regression line. It is important to plot the data and to use the diagnostics that are usually provided by statistical packages. A dramatic illustration of the dangers of relying exclusively on summary measures has been provided by Anscombe (1973). He developed four very different data sets (see Fig. 19.6; the data are in Table 3.3) that have identical values of $N$, $\overline{X}$, $\overline{Y}$, $b_1$, $b_0$, $SS_X$, $SS_{\text{regression}}$, $SS_{\text{residual}}$, $SE(b_1)$, and $r$. The summary statistics themselves suggest very strongly that the relation between $Y$ and $X$ must be the same for all four data sets. But, if we look at Fig. 19.6, we see that this is not so. In set (a), $Y$ and $X$ have a linear relation with some scatter around the regression line; but, in set (b), there is a curvilinear relation with a strong linear component. In set (c), 10 of the 11 points are well fit by a linear equation, but the remaining point is quite far off the line that fits the other 10. Without knowing more about how the data were generated, we cannot say whether or not it

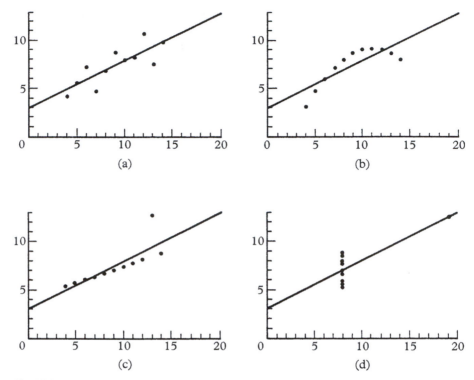

**Fig. 19.6** Scatterplots for four data sets with identical summary statistics (from Anscombe, 1973).

is appropriate to delete the outlying point; however, if we do delete it, the slope changes from .50 to .35. Finally, the regression for set (d) depends very heavily on one case. If this case was deleted, we could not even estimate the slope, and the correlation would be undefined because the variance of $X$ would be zero. We cannot have much confidence in measures of $b_1$ and $r$ that depend so heavily on a single case. These data sets make it clear that summary statistics do not tell the whole story. To understand the relation between $Y$ and $X$, we must look at the scatterplot, check to see whether there are deviations from linearity (whether there are some very influential data points), and check the other assumptions that underlie inference.

### 19.5.1 Checking Assumptions by Using Residuals

Valuable information about whether the assumptions are valid may be obtained by studying residuals, that is, differences between the observed and predicted values of $Y$. The residuals, $e_i = Y_i - \hat{Y} = Y_i - (b_0 + b_1 X_i)$ provide information about the population error components, $\varepsilon_i = Y_i - (\beta_0 - \beta_1 X_i)$. Statistical software packages generally provide residuals and allow them to be plotted in a variety of ways. If the distribution of residuals differs strongly from that assumed for the error components, the assumptions of the model may not be satisfied. Moreover, the nature of the difference can tell us which assumptions have been violated and suggest remedial measures.

Residuals cannot provide information about the assumption $E(\varepsilon_i) = 0$ because when a least-squares regression equation is used, the residuals are constrained to sum to zero. The residuals can, however, provide useful information about whether there are violations of the assumptions of linearity, homogeneity of variance, normality, and independence of error.

If the assumptions of linearity and homoscedasticity (homogeneity of variance) are both valid, when residuals are plotted against either $X$ or $\hat{Y}$, the data points should lie within a horizontal band as indicated in panel (a) of Fig. 19.7. Any other pattern suggests that the assumptions are not valid or that some kind of error has been made. For example, plots such as that in panel (b) indicate that the relation between $Y$ and $X$ is nonlinear, and that the appropriate model should contain additional terms such as $X^2$. Plots such as that in panel (c), in which the residuals are more spread out for some values of $X$ or $Y$ than others, indicate that the variance of estimate is not constant. We plot residuals against $\hat{Y}$ rather than against $Y$ because it can be shown that $e$ is not correlated with $\hat{Y}$ (or, therefore, with $X$), but has a correlation of $\sqrt{1 - r^2}$ with $Y$. It should also be noted that although plots of residuals against $X$ and against $\hat{Y}$ provide equivalent information for bivariate regression (because $Y$ is simply a linear function of $X$), this will not be the case when there is more than one predictor variable. We can determine whether an additional variable, $W$, belongs in the model by plotting the residuals against $W$. If the residual varies systematically with $W$, then $W$ should be included in the model; if it is not included, the error component, $\varepsilon$, will consist of more than chance variability.

## 19.5.2 An *F* Test for Departures From Linearity

The assumption that, in the population, the conditional means of $Y$ are a perfect linear function of $X$ is basic to the inferential procedures that we have discussed in this chapter. Departures from linearity suggested by scatter diagrams or plots of residuals may be tested for significance by using a procedure based on partitioning $SS_{\text{residual}}$ into two components, one based on systematic departures from linearity and the other based on **pure error**—that is, variability around the curve that accounts for all the systematic variability.

If the linear model is appropriate, the conditional means all fall on a straight line. In this case, the variability about the straight line is the same as the variability about the means, so that $SS_{\text{residual}}$ consists only of pure error. If the linear model is not appropriate, $SS_{\text{residual}}$ consists not only of a pure error component that reflects variability about the conditional means, but also a "nonlinearity" component that reflects the extent to which the conditional means are not a perfect linear function of $X$. Assume that $X$ takes on the values $X_1$, $X_2, \ldots, X_j, \ldots, X_a$, and that there are $n_j$ values $Y_{1j}, Y_{2j}, \ldots, Y_{ij}, \ldots, Y_{n_j j}$ of $Y$ at $X_j$. The predicted $Y$ score at $X_j$ is obtained from the linear equation $\hat{Y}_j = b_0 + b_1 X_j$. The identity

$$Y_{ij} - \hat{Y}_j = (Y_{ij} - \overline{Y}._j) + (\overline{Y}._j - \hat{Y}_j)$$
$$\text{residual} = \text{pure error} + \text{nonlinearity}$$

suggests the following partitioning of error variance:

$$\sum\sum (Y_{ij} - \hat{Y}_j)^2 = \sum\sum (Y_{ij} - \overline{Y}._j)^2 + \sum\sum (\overline{Y}._j - \hat{Y})^2 \qquad (19.14)$$
$$SS_{\text{residual}} = \quad SS_{\text{pure error}} \quad + \quad SS_{\text{nonlinearity}}$$

The pure error $SS$ term is associated with $N - a\ df$; there are $n_j - 1\ df$ at each of the $a$ levels of $X$, and $N = \sum n_j$. The corresponding mean square, $\sum\sum (Y_{ij} - \overline{Y}._j)^2/(N - a)$,

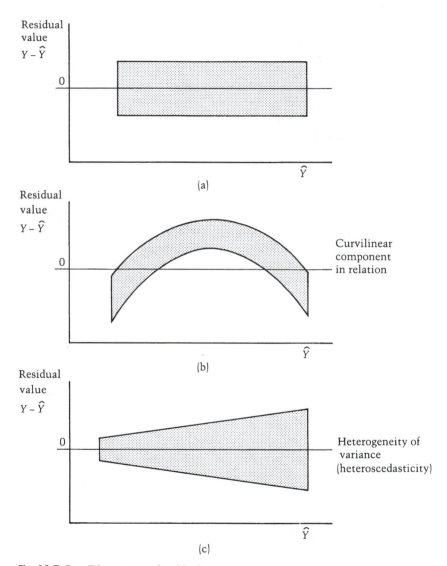

**Fig. 19.7** Possible patterns of residuals.

estimates the variance of the scores around the conditional means of $Y$. The nonlinearity $SS$ term is obtained by subtracting $SS_{\text{pure error}}$ from $SS_{\text{residual}}$. It has $a - 2\ df$ because there are $a$ means and 2 $df$ are used up in estimating the slope and intercept of the linear regression equation; equivalently, $(N - 2) - (N - a) = a - 2$. The corresponding mean square estimates a quantity that is the sum of $\sigma^2_{\text{pure error}}$ and a component that reflects the departure from linearity. Therefore, the linearity assumption may be tested using

$$F = \frac{MS_{\text{nonlinearity}}}{MS_{\text{pure error}}} \tag{19.15}$$

with $a - 2$ and $N - a\ df$.

**TABLE 19.4**    RESULT OF AN ANOVA USING DATA FROM WOMEN IN WHICH THE DEPENDENT VARIABLE IS CHOLESTEROL LEVEL, AND THE INDEPENDENT VARIABLE IS AGE

| Dep Var: TC | N: 211 | | Multiple R: 0.624 | Squared multiple R: 0.389 | |
|---|---|---|---|---|---|
| | | | Analysis of Variance | | |
| Source | Sum-of-Squares | df | Mean-Square | F-ratio | P |
| AGE | 128075.102 | 46 | 2784.241 | 2.274 | 0.000 |
| Error | 200768.305 | 164 | 1224.197 | | |

*Note.*    Output is from SYSTAT.

Suppose we wish to test whether the relation between cholesterol level and age departs significantly from linearity for women. Looking at the regression output in Fig. 19.4, we see that $SS_{residual} = 244,725.926$ with 209 *df*. Now, all we need to complete the analysis is to find $SS_{pure\ error}$. Because the error term in an ANOVA is a measure of pure error (i.e., variability about the group means), the easiest way to do this is to perform an ANOVA in which the dependent variable is cholesterol level and age is treated as a categorical independent variable. We can do this even for predictor variables that we would not normally consider to be categorical (as is the case for age); the test only requires that some of the values of the predictor have more than one value of $Y$ associated with them, so that an estimate of $SS_{pure\ error}$ may be obtained. The results of the ANOVA are displayed in Table 19.4. We see that $SS_{error}$ is 200,768.305 with 164 *df*; this is the $SS_{pure\ error}$ term in Equation 19.14. Subtracting this from $SS_{residual}$, we find $SS_{nonlinearity} = 43,957.621$ with 45 *df*. Substituting into the test statistic of Equation 19.15, we have $F = 976.836/1224.197 = 0.80$; this result does not provide evidence of a significant departure from linearity. We can summarize the steps to test for systematic departures from linearity as follows:

1.  First find $SS_{residual}$:    To do this regress $Y$ on $X$.
2.  Then find $SS_{pure\ error}$:    To do this, perform an ANOVA on $Y$ with $X$ as the factor; the error $SS$ in the ANOVA is $SS_{pure\ error}$.
3.  Find $SS_{nonlinearity} = SS_{residual} - SS_{pure\ error}$ and $df_{nonlinearity} = df_{residual} - df_{pure\ error}$ and substitute into the test statistic given in Equation 19.15.

In Chapter 10, we described tests for specific kinds of deviations from linearity (e.g., quadratic or cubic curvature). The calculations based on the coefficients of orthogonal polynomials found in Appendix Table C.6 were appropriate only when the values of $X$ were equally spaced and the *n*s were equal. We shall consider tests of nonlinear components under more general conditions when we return to trend analysis in Chapter 20.

## 19.5.3 Dealing With Heteroscedasticity

In the current example, when we regress cholesterol level on age for women, the assumption of homoscedasticity is reasonably well satisfied. But what should we do if there are severe violations of the assumption that can result in biased estimates and inflated standard errors? One possibility is to transform the $Y$ variable (see the discussion of variance-stabilizing transformations in Chapter 8). Another possibility, if the variability in the residuals varies systematically with $X$, is to use a procedure called **weighted least-squares (WLS) estimation** instead of the **ordinary least-squares (OLS) estimation** procedures that we have been using. WLS regression is identical to OLS regression, except that residuals based on values of the predictor variable for which there is less error variance are weighted more heavily than residuals based on predictor values that have more error variance. The rationale is that predictor values associated with less error are more useful for making predictions (for more detail about the procedures, see, e.g., Neter et al., 1996). In an appropriate WLS regression, the resulting values of $b_1$ and $b_0$ will have smaller standard errors, and therefore narrower confidence intervals than they would have in the corresponding OLS regression. Some, but not all, of the standard statistical packages can conveniently handle WLS analyses. For example, SPSS 10 offers a WLS option in the Linear Regression dialog box and a Weight Estimation option in the Regression menu to assist in determining which weights to use. On the other hand, although there are ways of performing WLS regression with SYSTAT, they are less convenient.

How do we decide which weights to use in a WLS regression? If the variance in the residuals is proportional to $X^2$, as would be the case if the plot of the residuals against $X$ provided a fan-shaped scatterplot like the one in panel (c) of Fig. 19.7, it would be appropriate to use the weights

$$w_i = \frac{1}{X_i^2}$$

in a program that can perform WLS analyses. The Weight Estimation option in SPSS Regression can help decide which power of $1/X_i$ to use as the weight. When regressing $Y$ on $X$, we indicate that $X$ is to be used as the basis of the weights. Then, SPSS tries out different powers of $1/X$ and indicates for which power the WLS model provides the best fit. For the regression of cholesterol level on age for women, the variability in the residuals does not seem to vary systematically with age. If we nevertheless proceed to use the Weight Estimation option, we find that the most appropriate powers of 1/Age are 0 and $-.5$. The zero power is equivalent to equal weighting, and therefore would result in the usual OLS regression. We tried the alternative weighting, $(1/\text{Age})^{-.5}$ or $\text{Age}^{.5}$, and found a result that was very similar to that for the OLS regression. The regression equation obtained using WLS was $TC_{predicted} = 132.61 + 1.70 \times \text{Age}$; the OLS regression equation was $TC_{predicted} = 131.871 + 1.71 \times \text{Age}$. Had the weight estimation procedure produced a different power, we could have simply used that in the WLS regression.

## 19.5.4 Normality

As indicated earlier, statistical packages are usually capable of constructing histograms and normal probability plots of the residuals. A virtue of the normal probability plot is that if the residuals are normally distributed, the points fall on a straight line, and it is easier to detect departures from a straight line than from a normal histogram. Figure 19.8 displays both a histogram with a normal smoother and a normal probability plot for the residual of the regression of cholesterol on age for females. The distribution of residuals is slightly heavy-tailed and positively skewed. If there were large deviations from normality, we could consider transformations of the $Y$ variable. Violations of the linearity and homogeneity of variance assumptions may cause the residuals to depart from normality, so that generally the linearity and homogeneity of variance assumptions should be checked before looking for violations of the normality assumption.

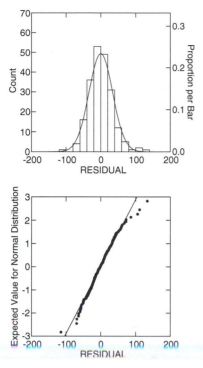

**Fig. 19.8** A histogram with a
superimposed normal curve and a
normal probability plot for the residuals
for the regression of cholesterol on age
for females.

## 19.5.5 Independence

We assume that the error components, the $\varepsilon_i$, are independent of one another. If they are positively correlated, perhaps because of the omission of some important variables from the model, standard errors calculated using the usual OLS procedures may underestimate the true standard deviations of the regression coefficients, and the confidence intervals and hypothesis tests based on these standard errors will not be appropriate. The residuals cannot be strictly independent; there are $N$ residuals and only $N - 2\,df$ (another way to think about this is that the residuals are all based on the same estimates of $b_0$ and $b_1$). Nonetheless, if $N$ is reasonably large, this unavoidable dependency will be very small so that residuals can meaningfully be examined for evidence of lack of independence. Data are usually collected and recorded sequentially. If the error components are independent, the residuals should not vary systematically over time. Systematic variation may reflect changes in subjects, measuring devices, or surroundings. When the residuals are plotted against time or case number, the result should again look like panel (a) of Fig. 19.7.

It is possible for error components to exhibit different kinds of serial correlations: for example, the residual corresponding to case $i$ may tend to be similar (or dissimilar) in size to those corresponding to case $i - 1$ or $i - 2$. Several packages print values of the Durbin-Watson $D$ statistic that forms the basis for a test of serial correlation in adjacent residuals. The statistic

$$D = \frac{\sum_i (e_i - e_{i-1})^2}{\sum_i e_i^2} \qquad (19.16)$$

will be small when sequentially adjacent residuals are positively correlated and large when they are negatively correlated. $D$ is approximately equal to $2(1 - r_{i,i-1})$, where $r_{i,i-1}$ is the correlation between sequentially adjacent residuals. Therefore, $D$ can range from 0 to 4, with larger deviations from a value of 2 providing stronger evidence of serial correlation. A more detailed discussion of the test and appropriate tables for assessing significance may be found in Draper and Smith (1998). Under some conditions, WLS can be used to perform the regression analysis when the data are serially correlated (see Draper & Smith, 1998, Chapter 9). In the current example, as we can see from the output in Fig. 19.4 and 19.5, the $D$ statistic has values close to 2 for both males and females, and the serial correlations are close to zero.

## 19.6 LOCATING OUTLIERS AND INFLUENTIAL DATA POINTS

Because the results of an OLS regression analysis can be markedly affected by a few extreme data points, it is important to identify data points that are unusually influential. If these points can be located, checks can be made to determine whether they reflect different processes than the rest of the data do or occur because of recording or transcription errors. If so, they can be corrected or deleted from the data. If the influential points cannot be attributed to an error or failure of some sort, the appropriate way to deal with them depends on the specific research problem. Given the presence of influential points, we can make the impact of these points clear to the reader by collecting more data and/or by reporting analyses both with the influential cases included and with them deleted. Also, in situations in which predictions are important, the effects of influential points may be partially circumvented by isolating regions where the influence is relatively unimportant. It is also possible to use robust regression procedures that are relatively resistant to the effects of outliers (see Huynh, 1982; Neter et al., 1996; Rousseeuw & Leroy, 1987).

It also may be of interest to locate points that have outlying $X$ and/or $Y$ values, even though such points may not greatly influence the regression equation. These points can be examined for errors or to determine whether there is something "special" about them. Also, depending on the particular research problem, it may be reasonable to treat cases with extreme values of $X$ differently, or to confine discussion to cases that do not have outlying values of $X$.

Table 19.5 contains output for the first 30 cases obtained from the SYSTAT package when we regressed cholesterol on age for females and requested that the residuals be saved. Six quantities are presented. The first two are the predicted value ($\hat{Y}$) and residual ($Y - \hat{Y}$) for each case. Note that estimates are provided for all of the females, including those who did not have complete cholesterol data. However, residuals and related variables can only be obtained for those with complete data. For the others, the missing data are indicated by dots. The last measure, SEPRED, is $SE(\hat{\mu}_{Y.X})$, which, as we have previously noted, takes on different values for different values of $X$. The remaining measures are LEVERAGE (the $h_{jj}$ that we have encountered on several occasions), COOK, and STUDENT. LEVERAGE measures the extent to which the case is an outlier with respect to the distribution of $X$ values, COOK measures the influence exerted by the case on the regression equation, and STUDENT measures the extent to which the case has an outlying residual. In the remainder

**TABLE 19.5**  THE FIRST 30 CASES OF THE SYSTAT RESIDUAL OUTPUT FOR THE REGRESSION OF CHOLESTEROL LEVEL ON AGE FOR WOMEN[a]

| Case | ESTIMATE | RESIDUAL | LEVERAGE | COOK | STUDENT | SEPRED |
|---|---|---|---|---|---|---|
| 1 | 222.583 | . | 0.005 | . | . | 2.532 |
| 2 | 205.467 | . | 0.006 | . | . | 2.596 |
| 3 | 215.736 | −63.486 | 0.005 | 0.008 | −1.871 | 2.359 |
| 4 | 239.698 | −9.198 | 0.012 | 0.000 | −0.270 | 3.774 |
| 5 | 224.294 | 8.456 | 0.006 | 0.000 | 0.247 | 2.613 |
| 6 | 241.410 | −59.535 | 0.013 | 0.021 | −1.760 | 3.934 |
| 7 | 227.717 | . | 0.007 | . | . | 2.812 |
| 8 | 195.198 | −15.823 | 0.009 | 0.001 | −0.464 | 3.294 |
| 9 | 219.159 | 42.716 | 0.005 | 0.004 | 1.253 | 2.414 |
| 10 | 226.006 | . | 0.006 | . | . | 2.707 |
| 11 | 229.429 | . | 0.007 | . | . | 2.927 |
| 12 | 220.871 | 56.004 | 0.005 | 0.007 | 1.648 | 2.465 |
| 13 | 232.852 | . | 0.009 | . | . | 3.183 |
| 14 | 231.140 | 62.110 | 0.008 | 0.013 | 1.833 | 3.051 |
| 15 | 229.429 | . | 0.007 | . | . | 2.927 |
| 16 | 234.563 | 7.187 | 0.009 | 0.000 | 0.211 | 3.322 |
| 17 | 202.044 | −58.669 | 0.007 | 0.010 | −1.728 | 2.790 |
| 18 | 243.121 | −13.246 | 0.014 | 0.001 | −0.389 | 4.097 |
| 19 | 236.275 | −14.025 | 0.010 | 0.001 | −0.411 | 3.468 |
| 20 | 200.332 | . | 0.007 | . | . | 2.903 |
| 21 | 202.044 | −24.419 | 0.007 | 0.002 | −0.715 | 2.790 |
| 22 | 200.332 | 53.293 | 0.007 | 0.009 | 1.568 | 2.903 |
| 23 | 202.044 | 22.456 | 0.007 | 0.001 | 0.658 | 2.790 |
| 24 | 215.736 | . | 0.005 | . | . | 2.359 |
| 25 | 215.736 | −41.361 | 0.005 | 0.004 | −1.213 | 2.359 |
| 26 | 215.736 | 20.889 | 0.005 | 0.001 | 0.611 | 2.359 |
| 27 | 220.871 | −34.871 | 0.005 | 0.003 | −1.022 | 2.465 |
| 28 | 224.294 | 14.706 | 0.006 | 0.001 | 0.430 | 2.613 |
| 29 | 196.909 | 17.341 | 0.009 | 0.001 | 0.508 | 3.156 |
| 30 | 203.755 | −27.005 | 0.006 | 0.002 | −0.791 | 2.687 |

*Note.*  Output is from SYSTAT.
[a] Dots indicate missing data. These come from participants who did not have cholesterol data recorded in each season.

of this section, we attempt to provide an explanation of these, and other related measures, and to indicate why they might be useful.

### 19.6.1 Locating Outliers

There are several types of outliers that may be discussed. We first deal with detecting extreme residuals, then with extreme values of the predictor. Measures for detecting these outliers are listed in Table 19.6.

***Locating Outlying Residuals.***  Whether a given residual is an outlier depends not only on its absolute size, but also on the distribution of the other residuals. Therefore, if one is interested in locating extreme outliers, it makes sense to use some sort of standardized measure in which the raw residual is divided by something like the standard deviation.

**TABLE 19.6**   MEASURES FOR LOCATING OUTLIERS

| Measure | Equation | Criterion |
|---|---|---|
| Measures for detecting extreme residuals | | |
| Internally studentized residual | $t_j = e_j/s_e\sqrt{1 - h_{jj}}$ | |
| Externally studentized residual | $t_j^{(-j)} = e_j/s_e^{(-j)}\sqrt{1 - h_{jj}}$ | $t_{.025/N}$ |
| | where $\quad s_e^{(-j)} = \sqrt{\sum_{i \neq j}\left(Y_i - \hat{Y}_i^{(-j)}\right)^2/(N - 3)}$ | |
| Measures for detecting outlying values of predictors | | |
| Mahalanobis distance | $D_j = \left[(X_j - \overline{X})/s_X\right]^2$ | |
| | $\quad = (N - 1)(X_j - \overline{X})^2/SS_X$ | |
| Leverage | $h_{jj} = \frac{1}{N} + \frac{(X_j - \overline{X})^2}{SS_X}$ | $2(p + 1)/N$ |

Finding that a residual has a $z$ score of 4.50 informs us more directly that it is an outlier than finding that it has an absolute value of 34.58. Although there is nothing very complicated about this basic idea, different statistical packages provide a variety of measures termed standardized or **studentized** residuals. Unfortunately, the packages are not always consistent in the terms they use to refer to these measures.

To discuss the measures, we note (see Appendix 19.3) that the standard error for a given residual $e_j$ is given by

$$SE(e_j) = s_e\sqrt{1 - h_{jj}} \tag{19.17}$$

where $h_{jj}$ is the leverage of $X_j$ (see Equation 19.11).

Dividing a raw residual by its standard error results in an **internally studentized residual** (Velleman & Welsch, 1981),

$$t_j = \frac{e_j}{s_e\sqrt{1 - h_{jj}}} \tag{19.18}$$

Both BMDP and SPSS refer to this as the "studentized residual." However, a somewhat different measure of studentized residual is often considered. If a data point $(X_j, Y_j)$ is far from the other data points, it may have a strong influence on the regression line (see the next section). An influential data point will pull the regression line toward itself, thereby reducing its residual; but, in doing so, increasing the residuals for most of the other data points. Because of this, a better index of the extent to which a data point is an outlier is based on the distance of the data point from the regression line based on the *other N* − 1 data points.

The **deleted prediction** for the $j$th case is defined as

$$\hat{Y}_j^{(-j)} = b_0^{(-j)} + b_1^{(-j)}X_j \tag{19.19}$$

where $\hat{Y}_j^{(-j)}$ is the prediction of $Y$ from $X_j$ using the regression equation in which the $Y$ intercept and slope, $b_0^{(-j)}$ and $b_1^{(-j)}$, are obtained from the $N$ − 1 cases that remain when the data point $(X_j, Y_j)$ is not included.

The **deleted residual** for the $j$th case, $e_j^{(-j)}$, is defined as the difference between $Y_j$ and its deleted prediction,

$$e_j^{(-j)} = Y_j - \hat{Y}_j^{(-j)} = \frac{e_j}{1 - h_{jj}} \tag{19.20}$$

The ratio of the deleted residual to its standard error is called the **externally studentized residual** and can be expressed as

$$t_j^{(-j)} = \frac{e_j^{(-j)}}{SE\left(e_j^{(-j)}\right)} = \frac{e_j}{s_e^{(-j)}\sqrt{1 - h_{jj}}} \tag{19.21}$$

where the deleted standard error of estimate

$$s_e^{(-j)} = \sqrt{\frac{\sum_{i \neq j}\left(Y_i - \hat{Y}_i^{(-j)}\right)^2}{N - 3}} \tag{19.22}$$

is based on the $N - 1$ data points that remain after case $j$ has been deleted. The externally studentized residual is what SYSTAT calls STUDENT in the saved residual output in Table 19.5 and what SPSS calls the "studentized deleted residual."

An advantage of externally studentized residuals is that they can be tested by the $t$ statistic defined in Equation 19.21. However, as usual, when a large number of significance tests are performed, Type 1 error rate should be controlled (see Chapter 9). This can be accomplished conveniently for the family of $N$ residuals by using the Bonferroni inequality, that is, by conducting each test at the $\alpha/N$ level of significance. With $\alpha = .05$ and 211 cases, the critical $t$ is approximately 3.73. The SYSTAT output in Fig. 19.4 automatically alerts us that case 311 is an outlier with an externally studentized residual of 4.068.

### Locating outlying values of the predictor.
Another index of an outlier is the extent to which $X_j$ differs from the center of the distribution of $X$ scores. Statistical packages provide the **Mahalanobis distance**, which for bivariate regression is just a squared $z$ score,

$$D_j = \left[\frac{X_j - \overline{X}}{s_X}\right]^2 = \frac{(N - 1)(X_j - \overline{X})^2}{SS_X} \tag{19.23}$$

Another useful measure of the extent to which $X_j$ is an outlier is the leverage measure provided by SYSTAT when residuals are saved,[5]

$$h_{jj} = \frac{1}{N} + \frac{(X_j - \overline{X})^2}{SS_X}$$

The leverage is closely related to the Mahalanobis distance and can be expressed in terms of it as

$$h_{jj} = \frac{1}{N} + \frac{D_j}{N - 1}$$

It can be shown that the sum of the leverages for a data set is equal to $p + 1$, where $p$ is the number of predictor variables; therefore, for bivariate regression, the $h_{jj}$ must sum to 2 and have a mean value of $2/N$. Hoaglin and Welsch (1978) suggest that values of $h_{jj}$ greater than $2(p + 1)/N$ should be considered large. Belsley, Kuh, and Welsch (1980) caution that this cutoff will identify too many points when there are only a few predictor variables, but recommend it because it is easy to remember and use. SYSTAT uses an $F$ approximation discussed by Belsley et al. (1980) to determine which values should elicit a warning. For the current example, the mean leverage is $2/211 = .0095$, and the largest leverage, .033, comes from the only 20-year-old female with complete cholesterol data. This exceeds the Hoaglin and Welsch criterion, but not that used by SYSTAT.

## 19.6.2 Influential Data Points

We are certainly concerned with cases that have large residuals and should look closely at them. However, we look even more closely at cases that have an unusually large influence on the regression equation and thereby on the predictions made using it. As we shall see, cases that are both outliers and have large residuals will have the greatest influence (see Equation 19.26). There are several measures commonly used to detect influential points. These are listed in Table 19.7.

One way of assessing the influence of the $j$th case on the regression equation is to compare the results of the analysis when the $j$th case is present with the results when it is deleted. Therefore, the difference in the fitted (i.e., predicted) value, $\hat{Y}_j$, when case $j$ is included and when it is excluded from the regression equation doing the prediction,

$$DFFIT_j = \hat{Y}_j - \hat{Y}_j^{(-j)}$$

can be considered an index of the effect of the $j$th case. Both $DFFIT_j$ and its standardized value,

$$DFFITS_j = \frac{\hat{Y}_j - \hat{Y}_j^{(-j)}}{s_e^{(-j)}\sqrt{h_{jj}}} \tag{19.24}$$

**TABLE 19.7**   MEASURES FOR DETECTING INFLUENTIAL DATA POINTS

| Measure | Equation | Criterion |
|---|---|---|
| Measure of the influence of the $j$th data point on the fitted (predicted) value of $Y_j$<br>    *DFFITS* | $DFFITS_j = [\hat{Y}_j - \hat{Y}_j^{(-j)}]/s_e^{(-j)}\sqrt{h_{jj}}$ | $2\sqrt{(p+1)/N}$ |
| Measure of the influence of the $j$th data point on all fitted values<br>    Cook's distance | $CD_j = \sum_i \left(\hat{Y}_i - \hat{Y}_i^{(-j)}\right)^2/(p+1)s_e^2$ | $F_{.50,\,p+1,\,N-p-1}$ |
| Measure of the influence of the $j$th data point on the $k$th regression coefficient<br>    *DFBETAS* | $DFBETAS_{jk} = [b_k - b_k^{(-j)}]/SE^{(-j)}(b_k)$ | $2/\sqrt{N}$ |

where $s_e^{(-j)}$ is as defined in Equation 19.22, can be requested for each data point in both SAS and SPSS. A number of criteria have been suggested for a case to be considered influential. SAS suggests a general cutoff of 2 and a size-adjusted cutoff of $2\sqrt{(p+1)/N}$ for *DFFITS*.

Cook (1977) proposed a measure that takes into consideration the effect of deleting case $j$ on all $N$ residuals. This measure, known as **Cook's distance**, can be expressed as

$$CD_j = \frac{\sum_i \left( \hat{Y}_i - \hat{Y}_i^{(-j)} \right)^2}{(p+1)s_e^2} \tag{19.25}$$

where $p = 1$ for bivariate regression and, in general, $p$ is the number of predictor variables in the regression equation. Cook and Weisberg (1982) suggest that Cook's distance should be referred to an $F$ distribution with $p + 1$ and $N - p - 1$ $df$. A value of Cook's distance is considered large if the $F$ has a $p$ value greater than .5. For regressions with more than 5 or 6 predictor variables, this leads to a criterion value of about 1; however, for bivariate regression with a sample size of about 200, the criterion would be about 0.7. Another useful expression for Cook's distance is

$$CD_j = \left( \frac{t_j^2}{p+1} \right) \left( \frac{h_{jj}}{1 - h_{jj}} \right) \tag{19.26}$$

where $t_j$ is the internally studentized residual of Equation 19.18. This expression makes it clearer that the influence of a data point depends on both its residual and the extent to which it is an outlier.

The final measures we consider here reflect differences in the regression coefficients $b_0$ and $b_1$ that result when case $j$ is excluded from the analysis. The difference

$$DFBETA_{jk} = b_k - b_k^{(-j)} \tag{19.27}$$

where $k = 0$ for the $Y$ intercept and 1 for the slope, indicates the change in the coefficient, and the standardized change,

$$DFBETAS_{jk} = \frac{DFBETA_{jk}}{SE^{(-j)}(b_k)} \tag{19.28}$$

where the denominator is simply the usual standard error for $b_k$, except that $s_e^{(-j)}$ replaces $s_e$. The *DFBETAS* measure is available in both SAS and SPSS and has a suggested size-related cutoff of $2/\sqrt{N}$.

With these measures, we reconsider the regression of cholesterol level on age for females. Case 311 (see Fig. 19.4) deserves special attention. It not only has an externally studentized residual of 4.068 that elicited a warning from SYSTAT, but we calculated a *DFFITS* of .487, which is greater than the criterion of .195. We also found *DFBETAS* values of .452 and −.397 for $b_0$ and $b_1$, respectively, both of which exceed the criterion of 137. The Cook's distance for case 311 was .110. This does not exceed the criterion, but it is more than twice the size of the next largest value. When we examined case 311, we found the data came from a woman who was relatively young (32 years old), but had a high cholesterol level (320), possibly resulting from a very high body mass index (41.1). There does not seem to have been any obvious error in recording the data. Although any one cholesterol reading can be in error, the cholesterol levels for case 311 are over 300 in each season. We cannot drop a data point from our analysis just because we don't like it, but we can assess whether and how much our conclusions would change if the data point was excluded. If we redo the regression analysis excluding case 311, the results are much the same: The slope changes from 1.71 to 1.79, the intercept from 131.87 to 127.49, and the correlation between the observed and predicted values from .51 to .54.

Another possible approach when we are concerned about the presence of influential data points is to use one of the **robust regression** procedures that give less weight to cases with large residuals (see, e.g., Huynh, 1982). Both SPSS and SYSTAT allow us to perform robust regressions in their nonlinear regression modules. SYSTAT offers options that include using **least absolute deviations** estimators (for which the sum of absolute deviations is minimized rather than the sum of squared deviations) and trimming a specified proportion of the cases. Performing a least absolute deviations regression of cholesterol level on age for females yields an intercept of 133.04, a slope of 1.65, and a correlation between observed and predicted values of .51—values not very different from those obtained with the usual OLS regression. The use of robust regression procedures might be particularly useful in situations in which there are groups of data points that collectively, but not individually, have a strong influence on the regression. In the current example, we conclude that the assumptions are reasonably well satisfied and that the regression is not severely distorted by outliers, and would report the results of the OLS regression. In general, the recommendations of Hogg (1979) and Huynh (1982) are reasonable: "Perform the usual OLS regression along with a robust regression procedure. If the resulting estimates are in essential agreement, report the OLS estimates and relevant statistics. If substantial differences occur, however, take a careful look at the observations with large robust residuals and check to determine whether they contain errors of any type or if they represent significant situations under which the postulated regression model is not appropriate." (Huynh, 1982, pp. 511–512)

## 19.7 TESTING INDEPENDENT SLOPES FOR EQUALITY

Suppose we wish to test whether the slopes for men and women differ significantly. This will be particularly easy to do after we have considered multiple regression in the next chapter. However, in Table 19.8, we show that we can test the null hypothesis that two independent slopes are equal ($H_0$: $\beta_{11} - \beta_{12} = 0$) using the test statistic

$$t = \frac{b_{11} - b_{12}}{s_e \sqrt{\dfrac{1}{SS_{X_1}} + \dfrac{1}{SS_{X_2}}}} \quad \text{with} \quad N_1 + N_2 - 4 \ df \tag{19.29}$$

where $s_e$ is the best estimate of the standard error of estimate based on both groups (see Table 19.8). Substituting in the data for the regression of cholesterol and age for men and women, we have

$$t = \frac{1.712 - 0.198}{36.352 \sqrt{\dfrac{1}{28714.56} + \dfrac{1}{30944.92}}} \tag{19.30}$$

$$= 5.08$$

so that the slopes are significantly different with $p = .000$.

DeShon and Alexander (1996) and Overton (2001) have recently emphasized that the assumption of equal within-group error variances is important when testing the homogeneity of regression lines. They point out that violations of this assumption can

**TABLE 19.8** DEVELOPING A TEST FOR THE EQUALITY OF TWO INDEPENDENT SLOPES

Suppose we wish to test the hypothesis that the slopes are identical in populations 1 and 2 (i.e., that $H_0: \beta_{11} - \beta_{12} = 0$). We can estimate the difference in the population slopes by $b_{11} - b_{12}$, and, because under the usual regression assumption, the $b$'s can be expressed as linear combinations of the $Y$'s, the ratio

$$\frac{(b_{11} - b_{12}) - (\beta_{11} - \beta_{12})}{SE(b_{11} - b_{12})}$$

is distributed as $t$ with $df = N_1 + N_2 - 4$ if the null hypothesis is true. From Table 19.4, we know that $\text{var}(b_1) = \sigma_e^2 / SS_X$. Therefore,

$$\text{var}(b_{11} - b_{12}) = \text{var}(b_{11}) + \text{var}(b_{12})$$

because the groups are independent

$$= \sigma_e^2 \left( \frac{1}{SS_{X_1}} + \frac{1}{SS_{X_2}} \right)$$

where $SS_{X_1}$ and $SS_{X_2}$ are the sums of squares of $X$ in Groups 1 and 2, so that

$$SE(b_{11} - b_{12}) = s_e \sqrt{\frac{1}{SS_{X_1}} + \frac{1}{SS_{X_2}}}$$

where the best estimate of $\sigma_e^2$ is given by the weighted average of the estimates from Groups 1 and 2:

$$s_e^2 = \frac{df_1 s_{e_1}^2 + df_2 s_{e_2}^2}{df_1 + df_2} = \frac{SS_{\text{residual}_1} + SS_{\text{residual}_2}}{N_1 + N_2 - 4}$$

Combining this information, the test statistic

$$t = \frac{b_{11} - b_{12}}{s_e \sqrt{\dfrac{1}{SS_{X_1}} + \dfrac{1}{SS_{X_2}}}} \qquad \text{with} \quad N_1 + N_2 - 4\, df$$

can be used to test the null hypothesis $H_0: \beta_{11} = \beta_{12}$.

seriously affect the power of the test, even when the sample sizes are equal, and they consider some possible remedies.

## 19.8 REPEATED-MEASURES DESIGNS

Up to this point, we have considered regressions in which each data point has been contributed by a different subject. However, in many situations, each of the participants provides data points at several levels of $X$. If we ignored the fact that each participant provides a number of data points, and analyzed the data in the usual way, the test of the null hypothesis, $H_0: \beta_1 = 0$, would be biased. When there are repeated measures, it can be shown that

$$E(MS_{\text{regression}}) = \sigma_e^2 + \sigma_{\beta_1}^2 SS_X + N\beta_1^2 SS_X$$

(see Lorch & Myers, 1990). Because the error mean square in the usual analysis (i.e., when all points are viewed as being independent) estimates $\sigma_e^2$, a significant result might indicate only that the slope varies across participants (i.e., that $\sigma_{\beta_1}^2 > 0$). Therefore, repeated-measures designs must be analyzed in ways that take account of the fact that each participant contributes a set of data points.

We would normally run a search experiment of the type discussed in Section 19.3.1 as a repeated-measures design, collecting data from each participant at all four array sizes. Let's say that 20 participants search for particular target letters in arrays of letters and that we obtain 200 detection times from each participant, 50 at each of the four array sizes. The 20 participants provide a total of 4,000 data points.

Regression equations could be obtained using any of the following three procedures:

1. Regress reaction time on array size using the combined data set (4000 data points, 200 from each participant). Values of $b_1$ and $b_0$ could be obtained, as usual, by using Equations 3.8 and 3.9.
2. Regress reaction time on array size using the 80 data points obtained by pairing each array size with the mean detection time for each of the 20 participants at that array size.
3. Regress the mean reaction time on array size separately for each of the 20 participants, basing each equation on four data points. Average the resulting 20 values of $b_1$ and $b_0$ to obtain values that best represent the entire group.

If every participant is tested at exactly the same levels of $X$ and contributes the same number of data points at each level, all three procedures will yield exactly the same values for $b_1$ and $b_0$. However, procedure 3 has the advantage that the values of $b_1$ and $b_0$ obtained for each participant can be treated as scores in subsequent analyses in which we test hypotheses about $\beta_1$ and $\beta_0$ using the procedures that were developed in earlier chapters.[6] In essence, when we test hypotheses about $\beta_1$ or $\beta_0$, we have one score for each participant, either $b_1$ or $b_0$. Suppose we use $b_{1i}$ to represent the slope obtained for the $i$th participant. Then, we could test the null hypothesis that $\beta_1$ is equal to some hypothesized value $\beta_{1hyp}$ by using exactly the same $t$ test that was introduced in Chapter 6 with slope as the dependent variable. The test statistic is

$$t = \frac{\overline{b}_1 - \beta_{1hyp}}{s_{\overline{b}_1}} = \frac{\overline{b}_1 - \beta_{1hyp}}{s_{b_1}/\sqrt{N}} \quad \text{with } N - 1 \, df$$

where $\overline{b}_1$ is the mean slope for the sample of $N$ participants, and $s_{b_1}$ is the estimated standard deviation of the slopes; that is,

$$s_{b_1} = \sqrt{\frac{\sum_i (b_{1i} - \overline{b}_1)^2}{N - 1}}$$

We could find the confidence interval for $\beta_1$ by finding $\overline{b}_1 \pm t_{\alpha/2} s_{\overline{b}_1}$.

Suppose, for example, the values of $b_1$ for the 20 participants are 19, 25, 27, 16, 14, 15, 18, 34, 19, 30, 25, 26, 19, 30, 27, 19, 24, 20, 23, and 25. Then, the mean slope is 22.75, and the estimated population standard deviation $s_{b_1}$ is 5.45, so that $s_{\overline{b}_1} = s_{b_1}/\sqrt{20} = 1.22$. Therefore, the .95 confidence interval around $\beta_1$ is given by $22.75 \pm (2.093)(1.22) = 22.75 \pm 2.55$. The individual values of $b_0$ or $b_1$ could also be used in matched- and independent-groups $t$ tests and in repeated-measures and between-subjects ANOVAs if we wished to test for equality of slopes or intercepts across conditions. We might, for example, want to test whether slopes for arrays consisting of letters and digits are equal.

Note that this so-called "slopes-as-outcomes" approach to repeated-measures regression gives equal weight to the regression coefficients for each participant. This is reasonable in the search example if each participant is tested at the same levels of $X$, and contributes equal amounts of data at each level. But suppose that some participants were tested at only three of the four array sizes, but others at all four, and that some participants contributed more data points than others. Or suppose that some participants saw arrays of sizes 2, 4, and 6, but others saw sizes 2, 4, and 8. We could still perform regressions separately for each participants, but the resulting regression coefficients would have varying standard errors; ideally, those coefficients with larger standard errors should receive less weight because they convey less information. If we did perform some second-order analysis on these coefficients without somehow taking this into account, we would be ignoring an important aspect of the data.

## 19.9 MULTILEVEL MODELING

Repeated-measures studies are only one of the possible types of design with a hierarchically nested structure. As we discussed in Chapter 16, participants may be nested within social groups, schools, or litters. For example, suppose we wanted to assess the effect of the number of hours of assigned homework on a common achievement test for charter and public schools, using data from students in 10 public and 10 charter schools. In a two-level model, we can think of students nested in schools; in a three-level model, we could add class within school. If we simply regressed achievement score on hours of homework for each type of school, we would ignore the variability among schools. On the other hand, if we regressed achievement score on hours of homework separately for each school, and then used only the resulting regression coefficients in subsequent analyses, we would ignore the variability within schools. A number of **multilevel modeling procedures**, given names such as **hierarchical linear modeling** or **random coefficients regression**, have been developed that take both kinds of variability into account (see, e.g., Bryk & Raudenbush,1992; Goldstein 1995; & Kreft & de Leeuw, 1998). Although the basic ideas are not too complicated, a detailed discussion of the estimation procedures is beyond the scope of this book.

## 19.10 CONCLUDING REMARKS

In the present chapter, we discussed statistical inference in bivariate regression and how to check the assumptions on which these inferences are based. In doing so, we presented many new concepts and formulas.

However, in most research situations, we are concerned with more than two variables. If our goal is prediction, we will usually be able to make better predictions of $Y$ if we base these predictions on more information. Using bivariate regression, we showed that age was useful in predicting cholesterol level for females. But, certainly other variables—such as body mass index and various dietary measures such as amount of fat consumed—should also be useful in predicting cholesterol level. A regression equation with several relevant predictors will often make better predictions than an equation with only a single predictor. Similarly, if we are using regression as a tool to develop an explanatory model, we can gain a better understanding of the situation if we study a number of variables simultaneously. We therefore consider multiple regression in Chapter 20.

## KEY CONCEPTS

regression toward the mean

multiple correlation coefficient, $R$

$SS_{regression}$

standard error of $b_1$

reliability

regression assumptions

linearity

homoscedasticity

OLS (ordinary least-squares)
  regression

outliers

Mahalanobis distance

externally studentized residual

influential data points

*DFBETAS*

robust regression

multilevel modeling (hierarchical
  linear modeling)

regression model for inference

standard error of estimate

$SS_{residual}$

standard error of $b_0$

residual

independence

$SS_{pure\ error}$

Durbin–Watson test

WLS (weighted least-squares)
  regression

leverage

studentized residual

internally studentized residual

*DFFITS*

Cook's distance

repeated-measures regression

## EXERCISES

**19.1**    **(a)** After each of two practice landings, pilot trainees discuss their performance
with their instructors. The instructors find that trainees who make poor landings
the first time tend to make better landings the second time, whereas trainees
who make good landings the first time tend to do worse the second time. The
instructors conclude that the criticism that follows poor performance tends to
make pilots do better and that the praise that follows good performance tends
to make them do worse. Therefore, the instructors decide to be critical of all
landings, good or bad. Is this a reasonable strategy?

**(b)** After the first examination in a course, students who scored in the bottom 25%
of the distribution are given special tutoring. On the next examination, all of
these students score above the average for the whole class. Can we conclude
that the tutoring was effective or could the results simply be due to regression
toward the mean?

**(c)** An educational psychologist wants to see if ability to spell has any effect on
ability to read. To this end, he selects two groups of students, a group of poor
spellers and a group of good spellers. However, he is worried that the poor
spellers may not be as intelligent as the good spellers, so he creates a group of
poor spellers and a group of good spellers who are equated on IQ. (To make
this simple, let us assume that his procedure is to use only those students
in both groups who scored 100 on an IQ test that he administered.) He now
administers a reading test to both groups and finds that the good spellers do
better on average than the poor spellers. Does this mean that spelling ability
affects reading ability?

**19.2** Assume that the correlation between the adult heights of fathers and sons is .5, and that the mean and standard deviation of the heights of adult men is 70.0 and 3.0 inches, respectively.

(a) Given the information that a father is 76 inches tall, what is the best linear prediction for the adult height of his son?

(b) Given that the adult height of a son is 73 inches, what is the best linear prediction for the height of his father?

(c) Given the phenomenon of "regression toward the mean," why wouldn't we expect all men to have about the same height in a few more generations?

**19.3** At the end of this exercise are data relating response time ($Y$) to a target on a screen as a function of intensity level ($X$); the intensity levels have been coded from 1 to 5 for convenience. There are 10 participants at each value of $X$.

(a) First, using a statistical package, plot the scatter diagram. Then, test whether there is a linear relationship between $Y$ and $X$. Save the residuals for the regression.

   (i) Write out the best-fitting linear equation, using the numbers from your regression analysis. Use this equation to predict $Y$ for each of the five $X$ values.

   (ii) Is there a significant linear relation? Report the appropriate test statistic and *df*.

(b) Now, plot the residuals against the estimates. That is, produce a plot of residuals as a function of $\hat{Y}$. Include this graph with your answer. Does it suggest any problem with your analysis?

(c) Fill in the following table:

| SV | df | SS | MS | F | p |
|---|---|---|---|---|---|
| Linearity | | | | | |
| Lack of fit (nonlinearity) | | | | | |
| Pure error | | | | | |

Note that if you perform an ANOVA on $Y$ with $X$, treating $X$ as a categorical independent variable, the *SS* accounted for by $X$ is the sum of the linear and nonlinear *SS* (i.e., accounts for all the variability in the group means). The error term of the ANOVA provides an estimate of the "Pure Error" variability (i.e., the residual variability when all the systematic effects are partitioned out).

(d) Now regress $Y$ on both $X$ and $X^2$. That is, $Y$ should be the "dependent" variable and the "independent" (i.e., predictor) variables should be $X$ and $XSQ = X * X$. Again, save the residuals. This estimates the parameters $\beta_0$, $\beta_1$, and $\beta_2$ for the population model

$$Y = \beta_0 + \beta_1 X + \beta_2 X^2 + \varepsilon$$

   (i) Write out the equation for predicting $Y$ with numbers taken from the output. Are $\beta_1$ and $\beta_2$ different from zero? Explain.

   (ii) Does this model provide a better account of the data than the linear model? Explain.

(iii) Plot the residuals for this model against $\hat{Y}$. Do you see any problem now?

| | Data for Exercise 19.3 | | |
|---|---|---|---|
| Intensity Level ($X$) | Response Time ($Y$) | $X$ | $Y$ |
| 1 | 400 | 4 | 501 |
| 1 | 380 | 4 | 497 |
| 1 | 394 | 4 | 495 |
| 1 | 416 | 4 | 494 |
| 1 | 400 | 4 | 504 |
| 1 | 440 | 4 | 469 |
| 1 | 429 | 4 | 430 |
| 1 | 388 | 4 | 434 |
| 1 | 419 | 4 | 470 |
| 1 | 391 | 4 | 474 |
| 2 | 470 | 5 | 431 |
| 2 | 417 | 5 | 407 |
| 2 | 457 | 5 | 430 |
| 2 | 471 | 5 | 387 |
| 2 | 495 | 5 | 418 |
| 2 | 460 | 5 | 422 |
| 2 | 483 | 5 | 433 |
| 2 | 463 | 5 | 419 |
| 2 | 446 | 5 | 455 |
| 2 | 470 | 5 | 415 |
| 3 | 474 | | |
| 3 | 476 | | |
| 3 | 495 | | |
| 3 | 455 | | |
| 3 | 496 | | |
| 3 | 475 | | |
| 3 | 479 | | |
| 3 | 498 | | |
| 3 | 453 | | |
| 3 | 503 | | |

🌑 **19.4** **(a)** Open the *Seasons* data set and select the data for women. Regress cholesterol level on age. Write out the regression equation and indicate the values of the standard error of estimate, $SE(b_1)$, and $SE(b_0)$.

**(b)** Using the regression equation, estimate the means of the populations of cholesterol scores for women of ages (i) 30 and (ii) 50. Find the 95% confidence interval for each of these population means.

**(c)** Which estimate is more likely to be closer to its actual population value, that for 30- or for 50-year-old women? Explain why.

**(d)** What is the 95% confidence interval for the cholesterol score of a randomly chosen 30-year-old woman?

**19.5**  In a large study of income $(Y)$ as a function of years on job $(X)$, the data for 2,000 men and 2,000 women in a certain profession are

|  | Men | | Women | |
|---|---|---|---|---|
|  | Income $(Y)$ | Years $(X)$ | Income | Years |
| $s^2$ | 324 | 100 | 289 | 25 |
| $r_{XY}$ | | .333 | | .235 |

*Note.*   Income is recorded in thousands of dollars.

(a) Test to see whether the correlations for men and women are significantly different. How do you interpret the result?

(b) Find $b_{YX}$ (i.e., $b_{\text{Income, Years}}$), the regression coefficient for the regression of income on years of service for men and for women. What is your best estimate of the amount by which salary increases per year for men and women? Is the rate of increase for men and women significantly different? Is this result consistent with differences in the correlations? Explain.

**19.6**  Given the following data from a between-subjects experiment in which the dependent variable is a performance measure $Y$:

| Drug Dosage $(D)$ | | | |
|---|---|---|---|
| 10 | 20 | 30 | 40 |
| 27 | 38 | 69 | 60 |
| 17 | 32 | 64 | 57 |
| 14 | 10 | 59 | 55 |
| 20 | 26 | 57 | 30 |
| 15 | 29 | 35 | 50 |

(a) Regress $Y$ on $D$. What is the best linear equation? Is the slope of the regression line significantly different from zero?

(b) Perform an ANOVA, using $D$ as the independent variable. Is the $D$ effect significant? How exactly does the null hypothesis in (b) differ from that in (a)?

**19.7**  Use a statistical package to analyze the data in Table 3.2.

(a) Regress FINAL on PRETEST.

(b) Write out the regression equation for this data set. What are the values of the standard errors of estimate for $b_0$ and $b_1$, $SE(b_1)$, and $SE(b_0)$?

(c) Using the regression equation, estimate the mean of the population of FINAL scores with PRETEST scores of (i) 24 and (ii) 37. Find the 95% confidence interval for each of these population means.

(d) On the basis of your answers to (d), which estimate is more likely to be closer to the actual population value? Explain why, in terms of the leverages associated with the two PRETEST values.

(e) Find the 95% confidence interval for the FINAL score of a single student with a PRETEST score of 24.

**19.8** In a search experiment, participants are required to check for the presence of some target character in an array of characters. There are four different array sizes, $X = 2, 4, 6,$ and $8$. Ten participants are assigned to each array size. The time to respond for each of the 40 participants ($Y$) is recorded. The data for the four array sizes are:

| $X_j$ | 2 | 4 | 6 | 8 |
|-------|------|------|------|------|
| $\overline{Y}_{.j}$ | 480 | 520 | 540 | 540 |
| $s_j^2$ | 360 | 315 | 324 | 333 |

Two experimenters, Anne and Reg, have different views about the analysis. Anne uses the ANOVA design model

$$Y_{ij} = \mu + \alpha_j + \varepsilon_{ij}$$

to test the hypothesis $H_0: \mu_1 = \mu_2 = \mu_3 = \mu_4$, and Reg assumes the linear regression model

$$Y_{ij} = \mu_Y + \beta_1(X_j - \overline{X}) + \varepsilon_{ij}$$

and tests the hypothesis $H_0: \beta_1 = 0$.

(a) Are Anne and Reg testing equivalent hypotheses? Briefly, justify your answer. If your answer is "no," are the two null hypotheses related? That is, if Anne's is false, should Reg's be true? Or, if Reg's is false, should Anne's be true?

(b) Use ANOVA to test $H_0: \mu_1 = \mu_2 = \mu_3 = \mu_4$; and use regression to test $H_0: \beta_1 = 0$.

(c) Must $SS_A$ always be larger than $SS_{\text{regression}}$?

(d) Determine whether there is a significant departure from linearity in the data using $\alpha = .05$.

**19.9** Groups of 40 men and 40 women each participate in the kind of search experiment described in the chapter. For each group, $SS_X = 200$. For men, we obtain $b_1 = 30.0$ and $s_e = 15.5$; for women, $b_1 = 20.0$ and $s_e = 12.2$. Test whether the slopes for men and women differ significantly at $\alpha = .05$.

**19.10** (a) The search experiment described in Section 19.3 is rerun as a repeated-measures study. In one condition, letters are used as stimulus material. Each of the 10 men and 10 women in this condition is tested at all four array sizes, and slopes are obtained for each subject by performing separate regressions. The slopes are:

Men      35  25  29  37  20  24  18  31  30  25
Women  17  19  29  19  23  25  20  18  22  25

Find the .95 confidence interval for the difference in population slopes for men and women when letters are used.

(b) In a second condition using different subjects, digits (i.e., the numbers 0 through 9) are used as stimulus material. In this second condition, the slopes are

Men       30  19  28  38  16  26  22  28  33  21
Women   19  21  24  22  20  23  20  15  25  28

Test whether the slopes for men are significantly different from those for women in this condition. What exactly can you conclude from the significance test?

(c) From the results of both conditions, test the following, using slope as the dependent variable:

(i) the interaction between sex and type of stimulus material (letters versus digit)

(ii) the main effect of sex

(iii) the main effect of type of stimulus material

19.11 Using the *Seasons* data set, we established in the chapter that the model assumptions were reasonably well satisfied for the regression of cholesterol level on age for women. We also established that the regression results were not strongly distorted by the presence of outliers and influential data points. Go through the same types of steps for the regression of cholesterol level on age for *men* and write a brief report of what you find out about that regression.

## APPENDIX 19.1

## To Show That $b_1$, $b_0$, and $\hat{Y}$ Are Linear Combinations of the $Y$ Scores

We start by showing that the expression for $b_1$ can be broken into two components, one of which can be shown to be zero, that is,

$$b_1 = \frac{\sum_i (X_i - \overline{X})(Y_i - \overline{Y})}{SS_X} = \frac{\sum_i (X_i - \overline{X})Y_i}{SS_X} - \frac{\sum_i (X_i - \overline{X})\overline{Y}}{SS_X}$$

$$= \frac{\sum_i (X_i - \overline{X})Y_i}{SS_X} \quad \text{because} \quad \overline{Y}\sum_i (X_i - \overline{X}) = 0$$

Therefore, $b_1$ can be expressed as a linear combination of the $Y$s; that is,

$$b_1 = \sum_i f_i Y_i \quad \text{where} \quad f_i = \frac{X_i - \overline{X}}{SS_X}$$

Also,

$$b_0 = \overline{Y} - b_1\overline{X} = \frac{1}{N}\sum_i Y_i - \overline{X}b_1$$

$$= \frac{1}{N}\sum_i Y_i - \overline{X}\sum_i f_i Y_i = \sum_i \left(\frac{1}{N} - \overline{X}f_i\right)Y_i$$

so,

$$b_0 = \sum g_i Y_i \quad \text{where} \quad g_i = \frac{1}{N} - \frac{\overline{X}(X_i - \overline{X})}{SS_X}$$

and

$$\hat{Y}_j = b_0 + b_1 X_j = \sum_i g_i Y_i + X_j \sum_i f_i Y_i$$

$$= \sum_i (g_i + X_j f_i) Y_i = \sum_i \left( \frac{1}{N} - \frac{\overline{X}(X_i - \overline{X})}{SS_X} + \frac{X_j(X_i - \overline{X})}{SS_X} \right) Y_i$$

$$= \sum_i \left( \frac{1}{N} + \frac{(X_j - \overline{X})(X_i - \overline{X})}{SS_X} \right) Y_i$$

so,

$$\hat{Y}_j = \sum_i h_{ij} Y_i, \qquad \text{where } h_{ij} = \frac{1}{N} + \frac{(X_j - \overline{X})(X_i - \overline{X})}{SS_X}$$

$$= h_{jj} Y_j + \sum_{i \neq j} h_{ij} Y_i, \qquad \text{where } h_{jj} = \frac{1}{N} + \frac{(X_j - \overline{X})^2}{SS_X} \text{ is the leverage of case } j.$$

## APPENDIX 19.2

## To Show That $b_1$, $b_0$, and $\hat{Y}_j$ Are Unbiased Estimators of $\beta_1$, $\beta_1$, and $\mu_{Y.X_i}$

To show that $b_1$ is an unbiased estimator of $\beta_1$, we need to show that $E(b_1) = \beta_1$. The regression model states that

$$Y_i = \beta_0 + \beta_1 X_i + \varepsilon_i$$

where $X_i$ is a fixed-effect variable. We can rewrite this equation as

$$Y_i = \mu_Y + \beta_1(X_i - \overline{X}) + \varepsilon_i$$

(Note that we refer to the mean of $X$ as $\overline{X}$ and the mean of $Y$ as $\mu_Y$, because according to the usual regression model, $X$ is a fixed-effect variable and $Y$ is a random variable.)

From Appendix 19.1, we have

$$b_1 = \sum_i f_i Y_i$$

where

$$f_i = \frac{X_i - \overline{X}}{SS_X}$$

Substituting the expression for the model and taking the expectation, we have

$$E(b_1) = E\left(\sum f_i\left[\mu_Y + \beta_1(X_i - \overline{X}) + \varepsilon_i\right]\right)$$
$$= \mu_Y \sum f_i + E\left(\sum f_i\beta_1(X_i - \overline{X})\right) + \sum f_i E(\varepsilon_i)$$

The first and third terms are equal to zero because

$$\sum f_i = \sum (X_i - \overline{X})/SS_X = 0$$

and by assumption, $E(\varepsilon_i) = 0$. The second term is

$$E(b_1) = E\left(\sum \frac{X_i - \overline{X}}{SS_X}\beta_1(X_i - \overline{X})\right)$$
$$= E\left(\sum \frac{\beta_1(X_i - \overline{X})^2}{SS_X}\right)$$
$$= E(\beta_1) \qquad \text{because} \quad \sum (X_i - \overline{X})^2 = SS_X$$
$$= \beta_1$$

To show that $b_0$ is an unbiased estimator of $\beta_0$, we need to demonstrate that $E(b_0) = \beta_0$. We begin by noting that

$$b_0 = \overline{Y} - b_1\overline{X}$$

and that from the model

$$Y_i = \beta_0 + \beta_1 X_i + \varepsilon_i$$

Taking the mean of both sides (and noting that $\beta_0$ and $\beta_1$ are constants), we have

$$\overline{Y} = \frac{1}{N}\sum Y_i = \beta_0 + \beta_1\overline{X} + \overline{\varepsilon}$$

Therefore,

$$E(b_0) = E(\overline{Y} - b_1\overline{X})$$
$$= E(\beta_0 + \beta_1\overline{X} + \overline{\varepsilon} - b_1\overline{X})$$
$$= \beta_0 + \beta_1\overline{X} + 0 - \beta_1\overline{X}$$
$$= \beta_0$$

## APPENDIX 19.3

## Obtaining the Standard Errors of $b_1$, $b_0$, $\hat{Y}_J$, and $e_j$

(Note that we assume here that $X$, the predictor, is a fixed-effect variable that is measured without error—so that if the usual assumptions are satisfied, $\text{var}(Y_i) = \sigma_e^2$.)
(1) From Appendix 19.1, we know that $b_1$ can be expressed as $b_1 = \sum_i f_i Y_i$,

where

$$f_i = \frac{X_i - \overline{X}}{SS_X}$$

Therefore,

$$\text{var}(b_1) = \text{var}\left(\sum_i f_i Y_i\right) = \text{var}(f_1 Y_1 + f_2 Y_2 + \cdots + f_N Y_N)$$

$$= \text{var}(f_1 Y_1) + \text{var}(f_2 Y_2) + \cdots + \text{var}(f_N Y_N), \quad \text{assuming independence}$$

$$= f_1^2 \sigma_1^2 + f_2^2 \sigma_2^2 + \cdots + f_N^2 \sigma_N^2$$

$$= \sigma_e^2 \left(f_1^2 + f_2^2 + \cdots + f_N^2\right), \quad \text{assuming homoscedasticity}$$

$$= \sigma_e^2 \sum_i f_i^2$$

Now, because

$$f_i = \frac{X_i - \overline{X}}{SS_X}$$

$$\text{var}(b_1) = \sigma_e^2 \sum_i f_i^2 = \sigma_e^2 \sum_i \frac{(X_i - \overline{X})^2}{(SS_X)^2}$$

$$= \frac{\sigma_e^2}{SS_X} \quad \text{because} \quad SS_X = \sum_i (X_i - \overline{X})^2$$

so the standard error of $b_1$ is

$$\frac{\sigma_e}{\sqrt{SS_X}}$$

and the estimated standard error is

$$SE(b_1) = \frac{s_e}{\sqrt{SS_X}}$$

(2) To find the standard error of $b_0$, we start with $b_0 = \sum g_i Y_i$. If we can assume independence and homoscedasticity, $\text{var}(b_0) = \sigma_e^2 \sum_i g_i^2$. Substituting

$$g_i = \frac{1}{N} - \frac{\overline{X}(X_i - \overline{X})}{SS_X}$$

and simplifying, we have

$$\text{var}(b_0) = \sigma_e^2 \left(\frac{1}{N} + \frac{\overline{X}^2}{SS_X}\right)$$

so that

$$SE(b_0) = s_e \sqrt{\frac{1}{N} + \frac{\overline{X}^2}{SS_X}}$$

(3) Similarly, we can show that

$$SE(\hat{Y}_j) = s_e \sqrt{h_{jj}}$$

From Appendix 19.1,

$$\hat{Y}_j = \sum_i h_{ij} Y_i \quad \text{where} \quad h_{ij} = \frac{1}{N} + \frac{(X_j - \overline{X})(X_i - \overline{X})}{SS_X}$$

Then

$$\text{var}(\hat{Y}_j) = \text{var}\left[\sum_i h_{ij} Y_i\right] = \sigma_e^2 \sum_i h_{ij}^2$$

But it can be shown that

$$\sum_i h_{ij}^2 = h_{jj}$$

(just expand and simplify to see that this is true). Therefore,

$$\text{var}(\hat{Y}_j) = \sigma_e^2 h_{jj}$$

and so

$$SE(\hat{Y}_j) = s_e \sqrt{h_{jj}}$$

(4) Finally, to show that

$$SE(e_j) = s_e \sqrt{1 - h_{jj}},$$

we begin with

$$e_j = Y_j - \hat{Y}_j = Y_j - \sum_i h_{ij} Y$$

so

$$\text{var}(e_j) = \text{var}(Y_j) + \text{var}\left[\sum_i h_{ij} Y_i\right] - 2\,\text{cov}\left[Y_j, \sum_i h_{ij} Y_i\right]$$

The first term on the right-hand side of the equation is equal to $\sigma_e^2$. The second term is equal to $h_{jj}\sigma_e^2$ from (3). The last term is equal to $-2h_{jj}\sigma_e^2$, because $\text{cov}(Y_j, Y_j) = \sigma_e^2$ and $\text{cov}(Y_j, Y_{j'}) = 0$ for $j \neq j'$. Therefore, $\text{var}(e_j) = \sigma_e^2(1 - h_{jj})$ and

$$SE(e_j) = s_e \sqrt{1 - h_{jj}}$$

# Chapter 20
## Multiple Regression

## 20.1 INTRODUCTION

In Chapters 3 and 19, we considered bivariate regression equations in which a criterion variable was regressed on a single predictor variable. Among the examples we discussed were the regressions of response time on stimulus array size and cholesterol level on age. However, in most research situations, there are many relevant variables and more than one predictor needs to be considered. If our goal is simply to generate accurate predictions, surely predictions should be better if we base them on more information. If, instead, our goal is to use regression as a tool to develop an explanatory model of a research situation—and, as we shall see, this is a much more difficult task—we can usually gain a better understanding of the situation if we study a number of variables simultaneously. For example, if we wish to investigate the influences on cholesterol level, it is worth considering variables such as body mass index and various dietary measures in addition to age. In the statistics class example, we would expect to predict final exam performance better if we considered other measures of ability along with pretest score. In Chapter 20, we develop multiple regression, which is regression based on more than one predictor.

In bivariate regression, our concern was with estimating the parameters of the linear model

$$Y_i = \beta_0 + \beta_1 X_i + \varepsilon_i$$

Estimates of $\beta_0$ and $\beta_1$ were obtained using the least-squares criterion; we found values $b_0$ and $b_1$ that minimized the mean-squared error obtained using the prediction equation

$$\hat{Y}_i = b_0 + b_1 X_i$$

We now extend this discussion to multiple linear regression. We consider models in which the criterion variable, $Y$, is expressed as a linear function of a number of predictor variables, $X_1, X_2, X_3, \ldots, X_p$. Although the additional predictor variables result in some increase in complexity, the basic concepts underlying bivariate and multiple regression are largely the same.

In multiple regression, we can obtain the least-squares estimate of the linear model

$$Y_i = \beta_0 + \beta_1 X_{i1} + \beta_2 X_{i2} + \cdots + \beta_p X_{ip} + \varepsilon_i$$

by finding $b_0, b_1, b_2, \ldots, b_p$ such that the linear regression equation

$$\hat{Y}_i = b_0 + b_1 X_{i1} + b_2 X_{i2} + \cdots + b_p X_{ip}$$

minimizes

$$MSE = \frac{1}{N} \sum_i \left(Y_i - \hat{Y}_i\right)^2$$

for the $N$ data points in our sample.

## 20.2 A REGRESSION EXAMPLE WITH SEVERAL PREDICTOR VARIABLES

In Chapter 19, we found that cholesterol level tends to increase with age in women. However, cholesterol level also changes systematically with other variables. For example, it is commonly thought that heavier people are more likely to have higher cholesterol levels. In the current section, we perform regressions involving total cholesterol level (TC), age, and body mass index (BMI),[1] a measure of weight that takes height into consideration. In doing so, we will use data from women in the Seasons study who were 20–65 years of age when they entered the study.

If we are interested in how TC, BMI, and age are related, the first step is, as always, to look at the data. Figure 20.1 contains the SYSTAT scatterplot matrix for the three variables. The distribution of BMI scores is positively skewed and highly peaked, and from the descriptive statistics in panel (a) of Table 20.1, we find that G1 = 1.684 and G2 = 3.906. The boxplot for BMI scores in Fig. 20.1 indicates that there are outliers, and we can see these points clearly in the scatterplots and in the stem-and-leaf plot in Table 20.2. When we plot TC against BMI in Fig. 20.2 and apply a LOWESS smoother (see Chapter 3), it appears that the BMI outliers tend to have relatively low TC scores and introduce a strong curvilinear component to the relation between TC and BMI. Because we are primarily concerned with describing the relations among the variables for women who do not have extreme scores, we will exclude the data points of the nine women whose BMI scores were greater than 40 (the outliers in Table 20.2) from our initial analyses. As can be seen in panel (b) of Table 20.1, if we exclude the outlying BMI scores, the skewness and kurtosis of the BMI distribution are reduced, so that now G1 = 0.830 and G2 = 0.261.

Information about the correlations among TC, age, and BMI is presented in Table 20.3, which contains SPSS output for the 181 women aged 20–65 years with BMIs of 40 or less who have scores on all three measures. TC is significantly correlated with both age, at $r = .492$, $p = .000$, and with BMI, at $r = .231$, $p = .002$. This suggests that we might be able to predict TC better by using information about both age and BMI than by using information about only one of these measures. Somewhat surprisingly, the correlation between age and BMI is small in this sample, at $r = .116$, $p = .119$.

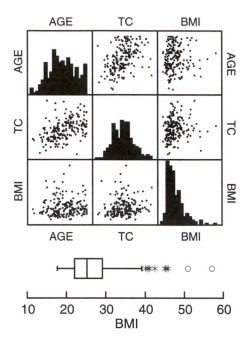

**Fig. 20.1**  Scatterplot matrix for TC, age, and BMI, using data from all women 65 years old or younger and a boxplot for BMI.

Tables 20.4, 20.5, and 20.6 contain the SPSS outputs for the regressions of TC ($Y$) on age ($X_1$), on BMI ($X_2$), and on both age and BMI, respectively. The regressions of TC on age and on BMI yield the equations

$$\hat{Y} = 126.531 + 1.812X_1 \tag{20.1}$$

and

$$\hat{Y} = 161.944 + 1.934X_2 \tag{20.2}$$

In Equation 20.1, the slope of 1.812 indicates that, for each 1-year increase in age, the prediction for TC increases by 1.812 units. Equation 20.2 tells us that predicted TC increases by 1.934 units for each one-unit increase in BMI.

Now let's consider the SPSS output for the regression of TC on both age and BMI. The **B** column in the coefficients table of the output provides the least-squares estimates of the $Y$ intercept ($b_0$) and the **unstandardized partial slope coefficients** or **unstandardized regression coefficients** for $X_1$ and $X_2$ ($b_1$ and $b_2$). The entries tell us that the best regression equation that includes both age and BMI as predictors is

$$\hat{Y} = 92.239 + 1.737X_1 + 1.474X_2 \tag{20.3}$$

This equation corresponds to the regression plane displayed in Fig. 20.3. Equation 20.3 indicates that *if BMI is held constant*, a one-unit (i.e., 1-year) change in age corresponds to a change of 1.737 units in the predicted cholesterol level. Similarly, if age is held constant, a one-unit change in BMI corresponds to a change of 1.474 units in predicted TC. We will use the remainder of this section to introduce some of the other information found in the output. More detailed discussions will be provided in the following sections.

**TABLE 20.1**   DESCRIPTIVE STATISTICS FOR WOMEN AGED 65 YEARS OR LESS

| (a) For all cases with data on all three variables | | | |
| --- | --- | --- | --- |
| | AGE | TC | BMI |
| $N$ of cases | 190 | 190 | 190 |
| Minimum | 20.00000 | 114.87500 | 17.69206 |
| Maximum | 65.00000 | 320.00000 | 57.11127 |
| Median | 47.00000 | 210.50000 | 25.20052 |
| Mean | 46.74211 | 211.61184 | 26.59906 |
| Standard Dev | 10.59359 | 39.60712 | 6.30139 |
| Skewness(G1) | −0.08130 | 0.27696 | 1.68447 |
| SE Skewness | 0.17632 | 0.17632 | 0.17632 |
| Kurtosis(G2) | −0.73470 | −0.00984 | 3.90574 |
| SE Kurtosis | 0.35087 | 0.35087 | 0.35087 |

| (b) For cases with BMI $\leq$ 40 | | | |
| --- | --- | --- | --- |
| | AGE | TC | BMI |
| $N$ of cases | 181 | 181 | 181 |
| Minimum | 20.00000 | 114.87500 | 17.69206 |
| Maximum | 65.00000 | 316.00000 | 39.12482 |
| Median | 48.00000 | 211.12500 | 24.93211 |
| Mean | 46.92818 | 211.58011 | 25.66503 |
| Standard Dev | 10.63016 | 39.17264 | 4.66999 |
| Skewness(G1) | −0.11630 | 0.23947 | 0.83037 |
| SE Skewness | 0.18058 | 0.18058 | 0.18058 |
| Kurtosis(G2) | −0.72168 | −0.16519 | 0.26078 |
| SE Kurtosis | 0.35927 | 0.35927 | 0.35927 |

*Note.*   Output is from SYSTAT.

In the model summary table, we see that the **multiple correlation coefficient**, *R*, is .522. This means that the TC values predicted by Equation 20.3 have a correlation of .522 with the actual TC values in the sample. The squared multiple correlation coefficient, **R Square** is sometimes called the **coefficient of multiple determination**. Here, its value is $.522^2 = .272$, so we may conclude that 27.2% of the variance in TC is accounted for by the regression on age and BMI. This means that the variability not accounted for when the regression equation is used to predict the *Y* scores is $1 - .272 = .728$ of the residual variability that would result if $\overline{Y}$ was used to predict each of the *Y* scores. The **Adjusted R Square** is .264. The sample multiple correlation coefficient is a positively biased estimator of the population coefficient because the regression equation obtained using the sample fits the sample better than it fits the population. The adjusted *R* results from one type of attempt to remove the positive bias. We'll consider the adjusted *R* further in Section 20.4.

The **Standard Error of the Estimate** is 33.603. This provides a measure of how well the regression equation predicts the cholesterol levels. The equation provides a prediction, $\hat{Y}$, for each combination of $X_1$ and $X_2$. The standard error of estimate, $s_e$, is the square root

**TABLE 20.2**   STEM-AND-LEAF PLOT FOR BMI VALUES OF THE
190 FEMALES AGED 65 YEARS OR YOUNGER

Data for the following results were selected according to:
    $(AGE = <65)$ and $(SEX = 1)$ and $(TC <>.)$

Stem-and-leaf plot of variable:    BMI, $N = 190$
   Minimum:                17.69206
   Lower hinge:            22.08871
   Median:                 25.20052
   Upper hinge:            28.97510
   Maximum:                57.11127

```
17   66
18   09
19   334479
20   00112224556777899
21   2223333566677888999
22 H 0012556678999
23   00111122455556677888
24   0002444578899
25 M 01122223345566677789
26   013445579
27   11123489
28 H 00136666688999
29   1266789
30   1235567
31   0344457
32   45
33   013
34
35   257
36   1555
37   29
38   02
39   1
*** Outside Values ***
40   16
41   0
42   4
45   028
50   8
57   1
```

of the sum of the squared deviations of the actual final cholesterol levels from the predicted
levels, divided by the *df*, so that

$$s_e = \sqrt{\frac{\sum (Y_i - \hat{Y}_i)^2}{df}} = \sqrt{\frac{SS_{residual}}{df_{residual}}}$$

**TABLE 20.3**   PEARSON CORRELATIONS FOR TC, AGE, AND BMI FOR WOMEN AGED
20–65 YEARS WITH BMIs ≤ 40

### Correlations

|  |  | TC | AGE | BMI |
|---|---|---|---|---|
| **TC** | **Pearson Correlation**<br>**Sig. (2-tailed)** | 1.000<br>. | .492**<br>.000 | .231**<br>.002 |
| **AGE** | **Pearson Correlation**<br>**Sig. (2-tailed)** | .492**<br>.000 | 1.000<br>. | .116<br>.119 |
| **BMI** | **Pearson Correlation**<br>**Sig. (2-tailed)** | .231**<br>.002 | .116<br>.119 | 1.000<br>. |

*Note.* Output is from SPSS. For correlations, listwise, $N = 181$.
**Correlation is significant at the 0.01 level (two tailed).

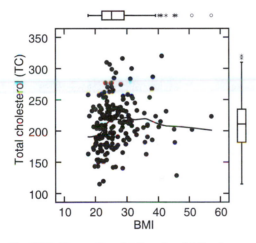

**Fig. 20.2**  Scatterplot of TC against BMI using
LOWESS smoothing for women 65 years old or
younger.

For the general case in which $Y$ is regressed on $p$ predictor variables, the standard error can
be expressed as

$$s_e = \sqrt{\frac{(1 - R^2_{Y \cdot 12 \dots p})SS_Y}{N - 1 - p}} \qquad (20.4)$$

If the underlying model for the population is $Y_i = \beta_0 + \beta_1 X_1 + \beta_2 X_2 + \cdots + \beta_p X_p + \varepsilon_\iota$,
then the standard error of estimate provides an estimate of the standard deviation of $\varepsilon$.

The ANOVA or analysis of variance table tells us that the total sum of squares of
276,209.213 associated with cholesterol scores can be partitioned into two components:
one the sum of squares accounted for by the regression ($SS_{\text{regression}}$) and the other the sum

**TABLE 20.4**   SPSS OUTPUT FOR REGRESSION OF TC ON AGE

**Model Summary**

| Model | R | R Square | Adjusted R Square | Std. Error of the Estimate |
|---|---|---|---|---|
| 1 | .492[a] | .242 | .238 | 34.2029 |

[a] Predictors: (Constant), AGE

**ANOVA[b]**

| Model | | Sum of Squares | df | Mean Square | F | Sig. |
|---|---|---|---|---|---|---|
| 1 | Regression | 66807.777 | 1 | 66807.777 | 57.108 | .000[a] |
|   | Residual | 209401.437 | 179 | 1169.840 | | |
|   | Total | 276209.213 | 180 | | | |

[a]Dependent Variable: TC
[b]Predictors: (Constant), AGE

**Coefficients[a]**

| Model | | Unstandardized Coefficients | | Standardized Coefficients | t | sig. | 95% Confidence Interval for | |
|---|---|---|---|---|---|---|---|---|
| | | B | Std. Error | Beta | | | Lower Bound | Upper Bound |
| 1 | (Constant) | 126.531 | 11.538 | | 10.967 | .000 | 103.763 | 149.299 |
|   | AGE | 1.812 | .240 | .492 | 7.557 | .000 | 1.339 | 2.286 |

[a]Dependent Variable: TC
*Note.* Output is from SPSS.

of squares left unaccounted for, $SS_{residual}$, with

$$SS_{regression} = \sum (\hat{Y}_i - \overline{Y})^2 = R^2 SS_Y = 75,220.300$$

and

$$SS_{residual} = \sum (Y_i - \hat{Y}_i)^2 = (1 - R^2)SS_Y = 200,989.213$$

The $F$ formed by taking the ratio of the regression and residual mean squares, 33.308, is significant, $p = .000$. The null hypothesis that is tested states that the regression coefficients $\beta_1$ and $\beta_2$ are both zero or, equivalently, that the population multiple correlation coefficient is zero. In the **Coefficients table**, we not only have the information about the constant ($b_0$), and the coefficients of $X_1$ and $X_2$ in the regression equation ($b_1$ and $b_2$), but also about their standard errors.

The **Standardized Coefficient (Beta)** column contains the values of the regression coefficients that would result if the regression was performed using $z$ scores. Although standardized regression coefficients offer the advantage of common (standard deviation) units, they are generally not as useful as the unstandardized coefficients. For one thing, if the scales are meaningful, one-unit changes are more understandable than changes of one

**TABLE 20.5**   SPSS OUTPUT FOR REGRESSION OF TC ON BMI

**Model Summary**

| Model | R | R Square | Adjusted R Square | Std. Error of the Estimate |
|---|---|---|---|---|
| 1 | .231[a] | .053 | .048 | 38.2236 |

[a]Predictors: (Constant). BMI

**ANOVA[b]**

| Model | | Sum of Squares | df | Mean Square | F | Sig. |
|---|---|---|---|---|---|---|
| 1 | Regression | 14682.972 | 1 | 14682.972 | 10.050 | .002[a] |
| | Residual | 261526.242 | 179 | 1461.040 | | |
| | Total | 276209.213 | 180 | | | |

[a]Predictors: (Constant), BMI
[b]Dependent Variable: TC

**Coefficients[a]**

| Model | | Unstandardized Coefficients | | Standardized Coefficients | t | sig. | 95% Confidence Interval for | |
|---|---|---|---|---|---|---|---|---|
| | | B | Std. Error | Beta | | | Lower Bound | Upper Bound |
| 1 | (Constant) | 161.944 | 15.913 | | 10.177 | .000 | 130.543 | 193.346 |
| | BMI | 1.934 | .610 | .231 | 3.170 | .002 | .730 | 3.138 |

[a]Dependent Variable: TC
*Note.* Output is from SPSS.

standard deviation. Also, standardized regression coefficients are sample-specific in the same way as correlation coefficients and therefore should not be used to generalize across groups. The magnitudes of the standardized coefficients depend not only on the variances and covariances of the variables included in the model. They also depend on the variances of variables that are not included in the model but contribute to the error term and thereby to the variance of the criterion variable. The unstandardized coefficients, $b_j$, are preferable because they are fairly stable even when variances and covariances vary across samples.

For each coefficient, a $t$ statistic is formed by dividing $b$ by its standard error. This tests the null hypothesis that the corresponding $\beta$ is equal to zero. The $t$ of 7.322 (with $p = .000$) for age indicates that, when BMI is held constant, the rate of change of predicted TC with age is significantly different from zero. The $t$ of 2.730 (with $p = .007$) for BMI indicates that there is a significant rate of change of predicted TC with BMI when age is held constant; that is, there is a significant contribution of BMI to the predictability of TC over and above that provided by age. The significant $t$ for $b_0$ (the constant, or intercept, of the regression equation) indicates that we can reject the null hypothesis that $\beta_0 = 0$ in the population. We requested confidence intervals, and so the table contains the upper and lower bounds of the intervals for each coefficient. Even with a fairly large sample, the confidence

**TABLE 20.6**   SPSS OUTPUT FOR REGRESSION OF TC AGE AND ON BMI

**Model Summary**

| Model | R | R Square | Adjusted R Square | Std. Error of the Estimate |
|---|---|---|---|---|
| 1 | .522[a] | .272 | .264 | 33.6028 |

[a]Predictors: (Constant), BMI, AGE

**ANOVA[b]**

| Model | | Sum of Squares | df | Mean Square | F | Sig. |
|---|---|---|---|---|---|---|
| 1 | Regression | 75220.300 | 2 | 37610.150 | 33.308 | .000[a] |
| | Residual | 200988.913 | 178 | 1129.151 | | |
| | Total | 276209.213 | 180 | | | |

[a]Predictors: (Constant), BMI, AGE
[b]Dependent Variable: TC

**Coefficients[a]**

| Model | | Unstandardized Coefficients | | Standardized Coefficients | t | Sig. | 95% Confidence Interval for B | | Collinearity Statistics | |
|---|---|---|---|---|---|---|---|---|---|---|
| | | B | Std. Error | Beta | | | Lower Bound | Upper Bound | Tolerance | VIF |
| 1 | (Constant) | 92.239 | 16.921 | | 5.451 | .000 | 58.846 | 125.631 | | |
| | AGE | 1.737 | .237 | .471 | 7.322 | .000 | 1.269 | 2.205 | .986 | 1.014 |
| | BMI | 1.474 | .540 | .176 | 2.730 | .007 | .408 | 2.540 | .986 | 1.014 |

[a]Dependent Variable: TC.

**Collinearity Diagnostics[a]**

| Model | Dimension | Eigenvalue | Condition Index | Variance Proportions | | |
|---|---|---|---|---|---|---|
| | | | | (Constant) | AGE | BMI |
| 1 | 1 | 2.949 | 1.000 | .00 | .01 | .00 |
| | 2 | 3.678E-02 | 8.954 | .02 | .79 | .31 |
| | 3 | 1.407E-02 | 14.476 | .98 | .20 | .69 |

[a]Dependent Variable: TC.
*Note.* Output is from SPSS.

intervals are quite wide. For example, the 95% confidence interval for the partial slope of predicted TC with BMI extends from 0.408 to 2.540.

We also requested collinearity statistics, measures that indicate the extent to which the predictor variables are correlated among themselves. As we shall see in Section 20.7, **multicollinearity**, that is, high correlations among the predictors, presents difficulties for multiple regression analysis. The **tolerance** of each predictor variable is a measure of how

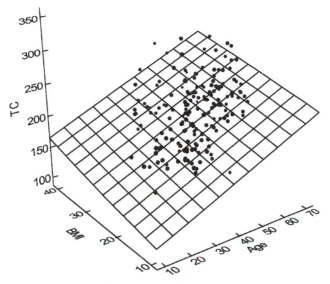

**Fig. 20.3** Regression of total cholesterol (TC) level on age and BMI.

*nonredundant* the predictor is with the other predictor variables in the equation; with only two predictor variables, the tolerance is one minus the square of the correlation between the two predictors. In general, the tolerance of the $j$th predictor variable is $1 - R^2_{j\cdot}$, where $R^2_{j\cdot}$ is the square of the multiple correlation of $X_j$ with all the other predictor variables in the equation. The standard error of the coefficient of the $j$th predictor variable can be shown to be

$$SE(b_j) = \frac{s_e}{\sqrt{SS_j}} \sqrt{\frac{1}{1 - R^2_{j\cdot}}} \tag{20.5}$$

where $s_e$ is the standard error of estimate defined earlier in this section and $SS_j = \sum_i \left( X_{ij} - \overline{X}_{\cdot j} \right)^2$ is the sum of squares of the $j$th predictor. The ratio under the rightmost square root sign, 1 divided by the tolerance of $X_j$, is known as the **variance inflation factor** (**VIF**) for the predictor, which is also presented in the SPSS output. If the predictor $X_j$ has a tolerance of zero (i.e., if $R^2_j = 1$), it can be perfectly expressed as a linear combination of the other predictors in the regression equation. As a consequence, if any of the predictors has a tolerance of zero, we cannot obtain least-squares estimates of the regression coefficients because the set of equations that must be solved to find the $b_j$s does not have a unique solution. From Equation 20.5, we can see that as the tolerance of $X_j$ decreases, the corresponding VIF increases and, consequently, so does the estimated $SE$. This in turn means that a $t$ test of the regression coefficient, $b_j$, will have less power. This makes sense, because if $X_j$ is redundant with the other predictors, we should not expect it to provide a significant increase to the predictability of $Y$. Most packages will allow you to set a minimum tolerance below which a predictor will not be added to the regression equation. In the current analysis, the tolerance for both age and BMI is .986 and the VIF is 1.014, indicating that the correlation between age and BMI is small. The **Collinearity Diagnostics** table contains additional measures that are useful for determining whether the degree of correlation among the predictors is serious enough to present a problem for the regression. We will discuss these measures further in Section 20.7.

## 20.3 THE NATURE OF THE REGRESSION COEFFICIENTS

When a regression equation does a good job predicting the criterion variable, it is tempting to use the equation not only to predict but also as an explanatory model—or at least to think of the regression coefficients in the equation as measures of the "importance" of the corresponding $X$s in influencing $Y$. However, interpretations of regression coefficients as measures of importance should not be made without considerable thought. One reason is that a variable that has no causal importance whatsoever may be a very useful predictor if it happens to be correlated with other variables that are important. For example, the number of books that parents own may be a perfectly good predictor of children's performance in elementary school, even if the children do not read the books. Even though the books themselves do not influence school performance, the number of books is correlated with factors such as parental intelligence and education, that do influence performance.

A second reason for care in interpreting regression coefficients is that the size of a regression coefficient usually depends on the other variables that are included in the equation and how well the equation matches the actual population model. Let's consider this point further.

Suppose we have a population described by the model

$$Y = \beta_0 + \beta_1 X_1 + \varepsilon \tag{20.6}$$

If we ignore the random error component, $Y$ is a linear function of $X_1$ with slope $\beta_1$, where $\beta_1$ is the rate of change of $Y$ with $X_1$. That is, a one-unit change in $X_1$ corresponds to a change of $\beta_1$ units in $Y$. If a sample is drawn from the population described by Equation 20.6, it can be shown that the regression coefficient, $b_1$, is an unbiased estimator of the population parameter, $\beta_1$. Because the population equation has the same predictors as the population model, $b_1$ does not only represent the rate of change of the predicted score, $\hat{Y}$, with changes in $X_1$ in the regression equation based on the sample; it is also an unbiased estimate of the rate at which the actual score, $Y$, changes with changes in $X_1$ in the population.

Now assume that the true population model has an additional predictor:

$$Y = \beta_0 + \beta_1 X_1 + \beta_2 X_2 + \varepsilon \tag{20.7}$$

If we ignore the random error component, $\beta_1$ is the rate of change of $Y$ with $X_1$, *given that $X_2$ is held constant* (i.e., if $X_1$ is changed by one unit and $X_2$ is not changed, then $Y$ will change by $\beta_1$ units). Similarly, $\beta_2$ is the rate of change of $Y$ with $X_2$ given that $X_1$ is held constant. Note that $\beta_1$ in Equation 20.7 does not have the same interpretation as $\beta_1$ in Equation 20.6. To emphasize this distinction, we could write Equation 20.7 as

$$Y = \beta_{0.12} + \beta_{Y1.2} X_1 + \beta_{Y2.1} X_2 + \varepsilon$$

so that the notation for each parameter specifies the other variables in the model; for example, $\beta_{Y1.2}$ indicates the rate of change of $Y$ with $X_1$ when $X_2$ is also in the equation, whereas $\beta_{Y1}$ represents the rate of change of $Y$ with $X_1$ when $X_1$ is the only predictor.

Although the interpretation of the $\beta$s in Equations 20.6 and 20.7 is quite simple, the interpretation of the sample regression coefficients is less straightforward because we usually do not know the underlying model that truly describes the population. If we select a sample from the population described by Equation 20.7 and regress $Y$ only on $X_1$, the sample regression coefficient will be a biased estimator of $\beta_1$ in Equation 20.7—$b_1$ will represent the rate of change of $\hat{Y}$ with $X_1$ in the sample, but it will not necessarily be a good estimator of how $Y$ changes with $X_1$ in the population when $X_2$ is held constant. As we show later, if $X_2$ is left out of the regression equation, $b_1$ will generally reflect the effects of *both* $X_1$ and $X_2$. If $X_2$ is also included in the equation, we obtain a different value of $b_1$, one that now represents the rate of change in $Y$ with $X_2$ held constant.

An example may help. Suppose we want to predict final exam performance in an introductory statistics course on the basis of two predictors: the quantitative SAT score and a pretest. Suppose that (a) the pretest measures algebra skills, (b) the SAT measures abstract mathematical thinking skills, (c) people with better algebra skills also tend to have better abstract thinking skills, and (d) performance on the final exam depends on both types of skills. If we regressed the final exam score only on the pretest score, we would be mistaken if we interpreted the regression coefficient only as a measure of the importance of algebra skills in determining the grade on the final. The change in the predicted final exam score associated with a one-unit difference in the pretest score reflects both the difference in algebra skills and the associated difference in abstract thinking skills. However, if we regressed final exam score on both pretest and SAT score, the coefficient of the pretest variable would no longer reflect the importance of abstract thinking skills. In this case, the pretest score coefficient would represent the rate of change of the predicted score on the final with pretest score, *holding SAT score constant.*

There is one situation in which the inclusion of additional predictors does not affect the other regression coefficients—when the predictors are not correlated. In the example of age, BMI, and cholesterol level, because there is only a small correlation between age and BMI in our sample, the coefficients of age and BMI are similar when both variables are included in the regression equation and when each variable is the only predictor. If age and BMI were completely uncorrelated, the two sets of coefficients would be exactly the same.

## 20.4 THE MULTIPLE CORRELATION COEFFICIENT AND THE PARTITIONING OF VARIABILITY IN MULTIPLE REGRESSION

### 20.4.1 The Multiple Correlation Coefficient

In Chapter 3, we defined the correlation coefficient, $r$, as a measure of the linear relation between $Y$ and $X$ and introduced the coefficient of determination, $r^2$, as the proportion of the variability in one of the variables accounted for by the regression on the other. Both of these concepts have parallels when we investigate the relation between a criterion variable, $Y$, and a collection of predictors, $X_1, X_2, X_3, \ldots, X_p$.

We define the multiple correlation coefficient, $R_{Y \cdot 123 \ldots p}$, as the correlation between $Y$ and $\hat{Y}$, where

$$\hat{Y}_i = b_0 + b_1 X_{i1} + b_2 X_{i2} + \cdots + b_p X_{ip}$$

is the prediction of $Y$ obtained from the multiple regression equation that contains the $p$ predictors. If $Y$ is perfectly predicted by the multiple regression equation, then $R = 1$. If the multiple regression equation predicts no better than the equation $Y = \overline{Y}$, then $R = 0$.

When there is a single predictor variable, $X$, the multiple correlation coefficient reduces to $R_{Y.X} = |r_{XY}|$, the absolute value of the bivariate correlation coefficient. This is because in bivariate regression, $\hat{Y}$ is a linear function of $X$, so that $|r_{YX}| = r_{Y\hat{Y}}$. Note that, although the limits of $r$ are $\pm 1$, $R$ can vary only between 0 and 1.

The proportion of the variability in $Y$ accounted for by the regression on $p$ predictor variables is $r_{Y\hat{Y}}^2 = R_{Y.12...p}^2$. Therefore, we can write

$$R_{Y.12...p}^2 = \frac{SS_{\text{regression}}}{SS_Y}$$

where $SS_{\text{regression}} = \sum_i (\hat{Y} - \overline{Y})^2$ is the amount of variability in $Y$ accounted for by the regression.

## 20.4.2 Partitioning $SS_Y$ into $SS_{\text{regression}}$ and $SS_{\text{residual}}$

As was the case with bivariate regression, the variability of $Y$ can be partitioned into a component accounted for by the regression, $SS_{\text{regression}}$, and a component not accounted for by the regression, $SS_{\text{residual}}$,

$$\sum(Y_i - \overline{Y})^2 = \sum(\hat{Y}_i - \overline{Y})^2 + \sum(Y_i - \hat{Y}_i)^2$$
$$SS_Y = SS_{\text{regression}} + SS_{\text{residual}}$$

where $SS_{\text{regression}} = R^2 SS_Y$ and $SS_{\text{residual}} = (1 - R^2)SS_Y$. It is convenient to express the partitioning of variability in terms of an ANOVA table of the form of Table 20.7. $SS_Y$ is associated with $N - 1$ $df$ because 1 $df$ is used to estimate the population mean. Of these $N - 1$ $df$, $p$ are associated with the regression sum of squares, because coefficients for each of the $p$ predictors must be estimated. The remaining $N - 1 - p$ $df$ are associated with the residual $SS$. Note that, when there is only one predictor, $N - 1 - p = N - 2$, the result presented in Chapter 19.

Under standard assumptions that will be discussed in Section 20.5, if the $p$ population regression coefficients $\beta_1, \beta_2, \ldots, \beta_p$ are all zero, the ratio

$$\frac{MS_{\text{regression}}}{MS_{\text{residual}}} = \frac{R^2 SS_Y/p}{(1 - R^2)SS_Y/(N - 1 - p)} = \frac{R^2/p}{(1 - R^2)/(N - 1 - p)} \tag{20.8}$$

**TABLE 20.7** ANOVA TABLE FOR MULTIPLE REGRESSION

| SV | df | SS | MS | F |
|----|----|----|----|---|
| Regression | $p$ | $\sum(\hat{Y} - \overline{Y})^2$ or $R_{Y1...p}^2 SS_Y$ | $\dfrac{R_{Y1...p}^2 SS_Y}{p}$ | $\dfrac{MS_{\text{reg}}}{MS_{\text{residual}}}$ |
| Residual (or error) | $N - 1 - p$ | $\sum(Y_i - \hat{Y}_i)^2$ or $(1 - R_{Y1...p}^2)SS_Y$ | $\dfrac{(1 - R_{Y1...p}^2)SS_Y}{N - 1 - p}$ | |
| Total | $N - 1$ | $SS_Y = \sum(Y_i - \overline{Y})^2$ | | |

will be distributed as $F$ with $p$ and $N - 1 - p$ df. Therefore, the ratio of mean squares tests the null hypothesis that $\beta_1 = \beta_2 = \cdots = \beta_p = 0$. In the current example, when we regressed TC on both age and BMI score (so that $p = 2$), we found $R = .522$. Substituting the square of this value into Equation 20.8, and replacing $SS_Y$ by the total sum of squares in Table 20.6, we have

$$F = \frac{MS_{\text{regression}}}{MS_{\text{residual}}} = \frac{75,220./2}{200,989./(181 - 1 - 2)} = 33.308$$

Note that the numerator and denominator sums of squares are, within rounding error, the same as the values in the SPSS output of Table 20.6, and the $F$s are accordingly the same. As can be seen in Table 20.6, this large $F$ value clearly provides the basis for rejecting the hypothesis that the population regression coefficients for both age and BMI are zero. $MS_{\text{residual}}$ is the square of the standard error of estimate provided in the SPSS output. If all important systematic sources of variability are included in the regression equation so that the residual variability is due only to random error, $MS_{\text{residual}}$ estimates the random error variance, $\sigma_e^2$. If important sources of variability are omitted from the equation, $MS_{\text{residual}}$ will reflect these sources as well as random error, resulting in a biased $F$ test.

### 20.4.3 Partitioning $SS_{\text{regression}}$

If the $p$ predictor variables in a multiple regression are mutually uncorrelated, $SS_{\text{regression}}$ can be partitioned into nonoverlapping components associated with each of the predictors. Panel (a) of Fig. 20.4 represents this situation. $X_1$ and $X_2$ overlap with $Y$, but not with each other, indicating that the variability in $Y$ collectively accounted for by $X_1$ and $X_2$ is the sum of variabilities accounted for separately by $X_1$ and by $X_2$. In this situation,

$$SS_{\text{regression}} = SS_{Y.1} + SS_{Y.2}$$

where $SS_{Y.j} = r_{Yj}^2 SS_Y$ and $r_{Yj}$ is the correlation between $Y$ and $X_j$. Because $SS_{\text{regression}} = R_{Y.12}^2 SS_Y$ (see Section 20.4), it follows that, when the two predictors are uncorrelated,

$$R_{Y.12}^2 = r_{Y1}^2 + r_{Y2}^2 = \sum_j r_{Yj}^2$$

More generally, if $p$ predictors account for the nonerror variability in $Y$, and are mutually uncorrelated,

$$SS_{\text{regression}} = SS_{Y.1} + SS_{Y.2} + \cdots + SS_{Y.p}$$

and

$$R_{Y.12\ldots p}^2 = r_{Y1}^2 + r_{Y2}^2 + \cdots + r_{Yp}^2 = \sum_j r_{Yj}^2$$

In summary, when the predictors are uncorrelated with one another, the proportion of the variability of $Y$ they collectively account for is the sum of the proportions of variability accounted for by the individual predictors.

However, predictor variables are usually correlated with one another. They usually share variability as in panel (b) of Fig. 20.4, where there is a correlation between $X_1$ and $X_2$ as indicated by the overlap of their circles. Note that if we add the overlap of $Y$ with $X_1$ to the overlap of $Y$ with $X_2$, the $b$ area is added in twice. When any of $p$ predictors

(a)

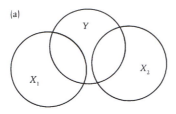

(b)

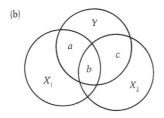

$$R_{Y.1}^2 = a + b$$
$$R_{Y.2}^2 = b + c \qquad r_{Y(2|1)}^2 = c$$
$$R_{Y.12}^2 = a + b + c \qquad r_{Y(1|2)}^2 = a$$

**Fig. 20.4** Representation of variability in the criterion variable accounted for by uncorrelated and correlated predictor variables. (a) Uncorrelated predictors: variabilities accounted for by $X_1$ and $X_2$ do not overlap so that $R_{Y.12}^2 = r_{Y1}^2 + r_{Y2}^2$. (b) Correlated predictors: variabilities accounted for by $X_1$ and $X_2$ overlap so that $R_{Y.12}^2$ is not the sum of the $r_{Yj}^2$s. $R^2$ may be found from $R_{Y.12}^2 = \sum_j b_j r_{Yj} s_j / s_Y$.

are correlated, the proportion of variability in $Y$ they account for is not the sum of the proportions associated with the individual predictors, but must be adjusted for overlapping variability, such as that represented by the $b$ area.

A general expression for $R^2$ that takes the correlations between predictors into account is given by

$$R_{Y.12\dots p}^2 = \frac{\sum r_{Yj} b_j s_j}{s_Y} \tag{20.9}$$

where $b_j$ is the regression coefficient of $X_j$ in the multiple regression equation and $s_j$ and $s_Y$ are the standard deviations of $X_j$ and $Y$, respectively. For example, when TC ($Y$) was regressed on age ($X_1$) and BMI ($X_2$), we obtained the following results:

|       | TC     | Age    | BMI   |
|-------|--------|--------|-------|
| $b_j$ |        | 1.737  | 1.474 |
| $r_{Y_j}$ |    | 0.492  | 0.231 |
| $s_j$ | 39.173 | 10.630 | 4.670 |

so that, substituting in Equation 20.9, we have

$$R^2 = [(0.492)(1.737)(10.630) + (0.231)(1.474)(4.670)]/39.173 = 0.272$$

the same value as that displayed in the SPSS output in 20.6. In the current example, the sum of the $r^2$ values for TC and age and for TC and BMI , 0.295, is not greatly different from the value of 0.272 obtained earlier, because the correlation between age and BMI is small.

The increase in $R^2$ when $X_2$ is added to a regression equation that already contains $X_1$ is $r^2_{Y(2|1)}$, the square of the semipartial correlation coefficient introduced in Chapter 18. As we mentioned there, $r_{Y(2|1)}$ is the correlation of $Y$ with the component of $X_2$ that is not predictable from $X_1$. In terms of the lower panel of Fig. 20.4 we may think of $r^2_{Y(2|1)}$ as the proportion of the $Y$ circle that overlaps $X_2$ but not $X_1$. In general, the squared semipartial correlation coefficient $r^2_{Y(p+1|12...p)}$ is the increase in $R^2$ that follows from adding a $(p + 1)^{\text{st}}$ predictor to a regression equation that already contains $p$ predictors. That is,

$$r^2_{Y(p+1|12...p)} = R^2_{Y\cdot 12...p+1} - R^2_{Y\cdot 12...p} \qquad (20.10)$$

In Equation 20.10, $r_{Y(p+1|12...p)}$ is the correlation between $Y$ and $X_{p+1}|X_1, X_2, \ldots, X_p$, where the latter term represents the residuals of the regression of $X_{p+1}$ on $X_1, X_2, \ldots, X_p$. Applying Equation 20.10 to the TC data, when age is added to a regression equation that already contains BMI as a predictor, the proportion of the variance of TC accounted for is increased by .219. If instead, BMI is added to an equation when age is already included as a predictor, the increase is .030. Note that because age and BMI are somewhat correlated and therefore account for overlapping variability in TC, these increases are smaller than the proportions of variance accounted for by age and BMI when each is the only predictor in the equation. We will soon discuss "partial $F$ tests" that will allow us to test whether the addition of one or more variables significantly increases the variability accounted for by a regression equation.

## 20.4.4 Cross-Validation and the Adjusted (or Shrunken) Multiple Correlation Coefficient

When a multiple regression equation is developed from a sample of data, the multiple correlation coefficient $R$ and its square are commonly used indices of how well the equation fits the data in the sample. These measures are also often used as estimates of how the regression equation fits the population from which the sample was obtained. However, using $R$ or $R^2$ as measures of fit can be misleading, because $R$ is a *positively biased* estimator of the population coefficient. This is a consequence of chance variability that causes the regression equation obtained from the sample to always describe the sample better than the population from which the sample was drawn. Particularly if the sample is small and there are a large number of predictors, a regression equation that predicts well in the sample may predict poorly in the population.

With enough predictors, the regression equation has to fit the sample well no matter how the predictors and the criterion are related in the population. Just as any two data points can be fit by a straight line, any $p + 1$ data points can be fit perfectly by a regression equation with $p$ predictor variables, and the resulting value of the sample $R$ must be 1. With more data points, $R$ in the sample need not be 1, but will tend to be larger than $R$ in the population as long as the $N/p$ ratio (number of cases divided by number of predictor variables) is small because of **capitalization on chance**; that is, because the regression equation takes advantage of chance fluctuations in scores that allow for predictability in the sample, but not in the population. The bias in $R$ can be reduced by working with larger samples. How large should samples be? Although the recommended sample size depends to some extent on the nature of the research problem and the purpose of the analysis, the $N/p$ ratio should be large—perhaps 30 or more—if the size of $R$ is to be taken very seriously.

A common adjustment for this positive bias has been provided by Wherry (1931). The population correlation $\rho$ can be defined as

$$\rho_{XY}^2 = 1 - \frac{\sigma_e^2}{\sigma_Y^2}$$

(compare with Equation 18.4). If we replace the population variances by their unbiased estimates, we have

$$R_{\text{adjusted}}^2 = 1 - \frac{SS_{\text{residual}}/(N - 1 - p)}{SS_Y/(N - 1)}$$

which can be rewritten as

$$R_{\text{adjusted}}^2 = 1 - \left(\frac{SS_{\text{residual}}}{SS_Y}\right)\left(\frac{N - 1}{N - 1 - p}\right)$$

But $SS_{\text{residual}}/SS_Y = 1 - R^2$. Therefore, substituting, we have Wherry's formula,

$$R_{\text{adjusted}}^2 = 1 - (1 - R^2)\left[\frac{N - 1}{N - 1 - p}\right] \tag{20.11}$$

The adjusted (or "shrunken") squared multiple correlation coefficient is provided in the regression output of most statistical packages. For the regression of TC on age and BMI, Equation 20.11 yields an adjusted $R^2$ of $1 - (1 - .272)(180/178) = .264$, the same value, within rounding error, provided by the SPSS output in 20.6. Note that if we set the adjusted $R^2$ equal to zero and solve Equation 20.9 for $R^2$, we get

$$R^2 = \frac{p}{N - 1}$$

This gives the value of $R^2$ for which the adjusted $R^2$ will be zero. Using this equation, we can see that if we have 10 predictors and 50 cases, an $R^2$ value of .204 (or multiple $R$ of .452) would correspond to an adjusted $R$ of zero.

However, if our interest is prediction, the Wherry adjustment may not be appropriate, because we may care less how a regression equation fits the population than in how well the equation fits *another sample* drawn from the same population. Herzberg (1969; see the discussion in Stevens, 1986) gives two adjustment equations that attempt to estimate $R^2$ in a second sample—that is, to estimate $R^2$ if we used the regression equation developed in sample 1 with the data of sample 2. If the predictors are random variables, as is usual in nonexperimental research, the adjustment equation is

$$R^2_{\text{adj}RP} = 1 - \left(\frac{N-1}{N-p-1}\right)\left(\frac{N-2}{N-p-2}\right)\left(\frac{N+1}{N}\right)(1-R^2) \qquad (20.12)$$

If the predictors are fixed, the adjustment equation is

$$R^2_{\text{adj}FP} = 1 - \left(\frac{N-1}{N}\right)\left(\frac{N+p+1}{N-p-1}\right)(1-R^2) \qquad (20.13)$$

The shrinkage is greater if we use the Herzberg equations instead of the Wherry equation. For example, given a sample of size 100 with 10 predictors and an $R^2$ of .50, $R^2_{\text{adjusted}} = .444$, whereas $R^2_{\text{adj}RP} = .374$ and $R^2_{\text{adj}FP} = .383$. In our current example, because of the high $N/p$ ratio, there isn't a great deal of shrinkage: $N = 181$, $p = 2$, and $R^2 = .272$, so that $R^2_{\text{adjusted}} = .264$ and $R^2_{\text{adj}RP} = .252$.

The best way of obtaining a more realistic estimate of the population $R$ is to use a procedure called **cross-validation** that avoids capitalizing on chance by developing the regression equation and testing it in separate samples. One of the samples (the screening sample) is used to develop a regression equation. The regression equation developed in the screening sample is then used to predict $Y$ scores for each case in a second (calibration) sample. The cross-validated $R$ is the correlation between these predicted $Y$ scores and the actual $Y$ scores in the calibration sample. Because the regression weights are obtained from one sample and tested in another, the cross-validated $R$ cannot systematically capitalize on sampling variability. Therefore, a useful estimate of the population $R$ might be obtained by correlating the deleted predictions (see Section 19.6.1) of $Y$ with the actual values of $Y$.

The problem of capitalization on chance is most insidious when the variables in the regression equation are chosen from a larger pool of possible predictors. Variables that are useful for predicting in the sample will be chosen to be in the equation and thus increase the multiple correlation, even if they are not very useful in other samples. If the $N/p$ ratio is small and variables in the regression equation are chosen from a larger set of possible predictors, the shrinkage achieved by cross-validation can be dramatic. We can illustrate this point by using the Seasons data set. We selected the data from the first 40 women aged 65 years or younger with BMI scores $\leq 40$. Then, using TC as the dependent variable and arbitrarily choosing HEIGHT, BMI1, HOST1, ANGER1, IRRIT1, ANXIETY1, DIRWDC1, BECK_D1, BECKD_2, BECK_D3, and BECK_D4 as 11 possible predictors, we found that the best regression equation containing five predictor variables (obtained by using stepwise regression—see Section 20.6) was

$$\hat{\text{TC}} = 78.143 + 2.706 \cdot \text{BMI1} + 16.863 \cdot \text{HOST1}$$
$$- 1.605 \cdot \text{ANGER1} + 16.461 \cdot \text{DIRWDC1} - 1.906 \cdot \text{BECK\_D1}$$

Here, the regression equation is based on the 32 cases in the sample having data on the dependent variable and all five predictors, so the $N/p$ ratio is 6.4. The $R$ obtained for the sample is .504, and the adjusted $R$ is .333. We then cross-validated by first using the equation to predict the TC scores for the remaining 120 women with data on all the variables in the equation, then finding the correlation between the predicted and the actual TC scores for these 120 women. This correlation is very small ($r = .046$, so that the cross-validated $R^2$ is $.046^2 = .002$), indicating that, although the regression equation based on the first 40 cases fits that sample pretty well, it is of no use for predicting outside the sample.

In summary, if the $N/p$ ratio is small, the multiple correlation coefficient for a sample will strongly overestimate the usefulness of the regression equation in the population and in other samples. The situation is much worse when the predictors in the equation are chosen from a larger pool. We strongly recommend the use of cross-validation to counter the effects of capitalization on chance.

## 20.5 INFERENCE IN MULTIPLE REGRESSION

### 20.5.1 Models and Assumptions

As was the case for bivariate regression, the validity of our inferences rests on a model and certain assumptions about the data. Also, we again distinguish between situations in which the predictors are fixed-effect variables and situations in which they are random variables. Fixed predictors generally occur in experimental studies in which the independent variables are manipulated; then $Y$ is a random variable, but the values of the $X$s are selected by the researcher and are therefore considered to be fixed over replications of the experiment. Predictors are considered to be random variables when they, as well as $Y$, are randomly sampled. Fortunately, although somewhat different assumptions are made for fixed and random predictor variables, the procedures for testing hypotheses and forming confidence intervals are the same in both cases when certain assumptions are met. However, the inferences we make are conditional on the joint distribution of the predictors observed in the sample.

Whether $X$ is fixed or random, we assume that the model is

$$Y = \beta_0 + \beta_1 X_1 + \beta_2 X_2 + \cdots + \beta_p X_p + \varepsilon$$
$$= \mu_{Y \cdot X_1 X_2 \ldots X_p} + \varepsilon$$

where $\mu_{Y \cdot X_1 X_2 \ldots X_p}$ is the mean of the population of $Y$ scores corresponding to a particular set of values for the p predictor variables. For the fixed-$X$ situation, we assume:

1.  None of the predictor variables is completely redundant; i.e., no predictor variable, $X_p$, can be perfectly predicted from the other $p - 1$ predictors using a linear equation. If this condition is not satisfied, the set of normal equations that must be solved to obtain the sample regression coefficients will not have a unique solution.
2.  The error components associated with each of the $Y$ scores are normally and independently distributed with mean 0 and variance $\sigma_e^2$.
3.  The values of the predictor variables are fixed and measured without error. This means that the values of the $X$'s will be exactly the same for each replication of the experiment.

If the $X$s are random variables, we assume (1) and (2), and further assume that the distributions of the predictor variables are independent of $\varepsilon$.

In the remainder of Section 20.5, we discuss and illustrate some types of statistical inferences that can be made in multiple regression. We will not derive expressions for standard errors; rather, we state the results and concentrate on the logic and interpretation of the statistical tests.

## 20.5.2 Testing the Hypothesis $\beta_1 = \beta_2 = \cdots = \beta_p$

As we indicated earlier, if the $p$ regression coefficients $\beta_1, \beta_2, \ldots \beta_p$ all have the value 0 in the population, the ratio

$$\frac{MS_{\text{regression}}}{MS_{\text{residual}}} = \frac{R^2 SS_Y/p}{(1 - R^2)SS_Y/(N - 1 - p)} = \frac{R^2/p}{(1 - R^2)/(N - 1 - p)}$$

will be distributed as $F$ with $p$ and $N - 1 - p$ $df$ under standard assumptions. Therefore, $MS_{\text{regression}}/MS_{\text{residual}}$ can serve as the statistic to test the null hypothesis that the $p$ regression coefficients are all zero in the population. This test can be thought of as asking whether we have sufficient evidence to conclude that the model

$$Y = \beta_0 + \beta_1 X_1 + \beta_2 X_2 + \cdots + \beta_p X_p + \varepsilon$$

accounts for $Y$ in the population better than the restricted model

$$Y = \beta_0 + \varepsilon$$
$$= \mu_Y + \varepsilon$$

If the restricted model is appropriate, $\beta_1 = \beta_2 = \cdots = \beta_p = 0$ so that the best predictor for $Y$ is $\beta_0 = \mu_Y$ and the multiple correlation coefficient in the population has the value 0.

In the current example, when we regress TC on age and BMI, we find

$$F = \frac{MS_{\text{regression}}}{MS_{\text{residual}}} = \frac{75,220.300/2}{200,988.913/178} = 33.308$$

and so we can reject the hypothesis that the population regression coefficients are zero for both age and BMI. The test assumes that $MS_{\text{residual}}$ is an estimate of the variance of the random error component. If important variables are left out of the regression equation, $MS_{\text{residual}}$ will reflect their effects as well as random error, and the test will be negatively biased.

## 20.5.3 Testing the Hypothesis $\beta_j = \beta_{\text{hyp}}$ and Finding Confidence Intervals for $\beta_j$

Under standard assumptions, the ratio

$$\frac{b_j - \beta_j}{SE(b_j)}$$

will be distributed as $t$ with $N - 1 - p$ $df$. Therefore, if we can estimate the standard errors (see Equation 20.5), we can test the hypothesis that the population intercept, $\beta_0$, or any of the population regression coefficients, $\beta_j$, are equal to any constant. In practice, the null hypothesis $\beta_j = 0$ is usually tested. Rejection of this hypothesis implies that $X_j$ makes a significant contribution to the predictability of $Y$ when it is added to the other variables in the equation.

Also, once we have obtained the appropriate $SE$s, we can obtain confidence intervals for each parameter using

$$b \pm t_{\alpha/2} SE(b)$$

In the current example, the 95% confidence intervals for the intercept and the coefficients of age and BMI are $92.239 \pm 33.392$, $1.737 \pm 0.468$, and $1.474 \pm 1.066$, respectively.

## 20.5.4 Partial $F$ Tests: Procedures for Testing a Subset of the $\beta_j$s

We can use partial $F$ tests to determine whether adding one or more predictors to a regression equation that already contains $p$ predictors significantly increases the predictability of $Y$. If we consider just one additional predictor, $X_{p+1}$, a test of the model

$$Y = \beta_0 + \beta_1 X_1 + \beta_2 X_2 + \cdots + \beta_p X_p + \beta_{p+1} X_{p+1} + \varepsilon$$

against the restricted model

$$Y = \beta_0 + \beta_1 X_1 + \beta_2 X_2 + \cdots + \beta_p X_p + \varepsilon$$

is equivalent to testing the hypothesis $H_0$: $\beta_{p+1} = 0$.

We can represent the variability in $Y$ accounted for by regression on the variables of the restricted model as

$$SS_{Y \cdot 12 \ldots p} = R^2_{Y \cdot 12 \ldots p} SS_Y$$

and the variability accounted for by the larger model when the predictor $X_{p+1}$ is added as

$$SS_{Y \cdot 12 \ldots p+1} = R^2_{Y \cdot 12 \ldots p+1} SS_Y$$

Therefore, the increment in variability associated with the predictor $X_{p+1}$ is given by

$$SS_{\text{increment}} = SS_{Y \cdot p+1 | 12 \ldots p} = \left( R^2_{Y \cdot 12 \ldots p+1} - R^2_{Y \cdot 12 \ldots p} \right) SS_Y$$

This increment is associated with a single *df* because only one additional regression coefficient must be estimated in the larger model.

Table 20.7 presents these results in the form of an ANOVA table. The hypothesis $H_0$: $\beta_{p+1} = 0$ can be tested using the ratio

$$F = \frac{MS_{\text{increment}}}{MS_{\text{residual}}}$$

where the denominator is the mean square associated with the variability not accounted for by the larger model; that is,

$$MS_{\text{residual}} = \frac{\left( 1 - R^2_{Y \cdot 12 \ldots p+1} \right) SS_Y}{N - p - 2}$$

The numerator of the $F$ is associated with 1 *df* if a single predictor is added and the denominator with $N - p - 2\,df$. The partial $F$ can be expressed as

$$F = \frac{MS_{\text{increment}}}{MS_{\text{residual}}}$$

When a partial $F$ test is used to test whether a single population regression coefficient is zero, the results produced are exactly equivalent to those of the $t$ test discussed in the preceding section. If we use this procedure to test whether BMI adds significantly to the prediction of

**TABLE 20.8** ANOVA TABLE FOR TESTING THE EFFECT OF ADDING k PREDICTOR VARIABLES TO MODEL THAT ALREADY CONTAINS p PREDICTORS

| SV | df | SS | MS |
|---|---|---|---|
| Larger model | $p + k$ | $R^2_{Y1\ldots p+k}SS_Y$ | $\dfrac{R^2_{Y1\ldots p+k}SS_Y}{p + k}$ |
| Smaller model | $p$ | $R^2_{Y1\ldots p}SS_Y$ | $\dfrac{R^2_{Y1\ldots p}SS_Y}{p}$ |
| Increment | $k$ | $SS_{\text{increment}} =$ $\left(R^2_{Y1\ldots p+k} - R^2_{Y1\ldots p}\right)SS_Y$ | $SS_{\text{increment}}/k$ |
| Residual | $N - 1 - p - k$ | $(1 - R^2_{Y1\ldots p+k})SS_Y$ | $\dfrac{\left(1 - R^2_{Y1\ldots p+k}\right)SS_Y}{N - 1 - p - k}$ |

TC over and above age, $SS_{\text{increment}} = 8412.523$, $df_{\text{increment}} = 1$, and $MS_{\text{residual}} = 1129.151$, so that

$$F = \frac{MS_{\text{increment}}}{MS_{\text{residual}}} = \frac{8412.523}{1129.151} = 7.450$$

The $F$ value obtained is the square of the $t$ for the coefficient of BMI in the output for the regression of TC on age and BMI in Table 20.6.

Partial $F$ tests can also be used to test hypotheses that state that some subset of the $\beta_j$s are equal to zero. Suppose, for example, we start with a model containing $p$ predictor variables

$$Y = \beta_0 + \beta_1 X_1 + \beta_2 X_2 + \cdots + \beta_p X_p + \varepsilon$$

and we add $k$ more predictor variables so that the model is now

$$Y = \beta_0 + \beta_1 X_1 + \beta_2 X_2 + \cdots + \beta_p X_p + \beta_{p+1} X_{p+1} + \cdots + \beta_{p+k} X_{p+k} + \varepsilon$$

The appropriate ANOVA table is given in Table 20.8. This general approach can be used to assess the effect of adding any set of predictors to the equation and tests the hypothesis that the regression coefficients for these added predictors are all equal to zero in the population.

### 20.5.5 Inferences About the Predictions of Y

In bivariate regression, the expected value of $Y$ corresponding to a value $X_j$ of $X$ is given by

$$\mu_{Y \cdot X_j} = \beta_0 + \beta_1 X_j$$

that can be estimated by

$$\hat{Y}_j = \hat{\mu}_{Y \cdot X_j} = b_0 + b_1 X_j$$

We showed in Chapter 19 that, for bivariate regression, the estimated standard error associated with the prediction of $Y$ at $X = X_j$ is given by

$$SE(\hat{\mu}_{Y \cdot X_j}) = s_e \sqrt{h_{jj}} \tag{20.14}$$

and that the standard error associated with an individual score is

$$SE(\hat{Y}_j) = s_e\sqrt{1 + h_{jj}} \tag{20.15}$$

where $s_e$ is the standard error of estimate and $h_{jj}$, the leverage of $X_j$, is

$$h_{jj} = \frac{1}{N} + \frac{(X_j - \overline{X})^2}{SS_X}$$

In multiple regression, we can find the estimated standard error for the prediction of $Y$ associated with any combination of values of the $p$ predictor variables in the regression equation. Because there is more than one predictor, the standard errors are most easily presented as matrix expressions. However, if the combination of predictor values is one that occurred for any of the cases in our sample, say case $j$, the estimated standard error for the prediction is again given by Equation 20.14. Although the expression for $h_{jj}$ will now be more complicated because there is more than one predictor, it can be thought of and used in much the same way as in bivariate regression. If we want to find the confidence intervals for the conditional means or individual scores in our data set, we do not have to calculate the leverage; we can simply ask that SPSS add the lower and upper confidence limits to our output, or ask that SYSTAT provide the leverage values that we can then use in Equations 20.14 and 20.15.

However, if we wish to find the standard error for the prediction of $Y$ based on a combination of values for the $p$ predictors, $X_1, X_2, \ldots, X_p$, that did not occur in our sample, the estimated standard errors for $\hat{\mu}$ and $\hat{Y}$ are not directly made available in the computer output and must be calculated. We will not present the relevant matrix expressions or their derivation in the text. They are available, along with a worked-out example, in the brief development of multiple regression using matrix notation in the Supplementary Materials folder on the accompanying CD (Chapter 20A).

## 20.5.6 Outliers and Influential Points in Multiple Regression

In discussing bivariate regression, we introduced measures for identifying cases that had outlying values of $X$ or had inordinate influence in determining the value of the regression coefficient for $X$. The corresponding measures for multiple regression are just generalizations of these measures; and we can think of, and use them, in the same way as in bivariate regression. However, because more than one predictor is involved, the measures are usually expressed in matrix notation. A brief treatment using matrix notation is presented in Chapter 20A on the CD.

In bivariate regression, outliers in $X$ can usually be identified by looking at the distribution of $X$ or at the scatter diagram of $X$ and $Y$. However, in multiple regression, one must depend more heavily on measures such as the leverage, $h_{jj}$, to identify outliers because multivariate outliers can occur in subtle ways. For example, the $j$th case may be an outlier because there are correlated deviations from the mean for several predictors; there need not be an extreme deviation for any predictor. It should be also noted that when leverages are requested, SPSS produces **centered leverages**, $h_{jj} - 1/N$.

As we mentioned in Chapter 19, it can be shown that $\sum h_{jj} = p + 1$ where $p$ is the number of predictor variables; therefore, the mean value of $h_{jj}$ is $(p + 1)/N$. Hoaglin and Welsch (1978) suggest that values of $h_{jj}$ greater than $2(p + 1)/N$ should be considered to be large. Belsley, Kuh, and Welsch (1980) indicate that this cutoff will identify too many data points if $p$ is small, but recommend it because it is easy to remember and use. Other guidelines mentioned by Neter et al. (1996) are that $h_{jj}$ values exceeding .5 indicate very high leverage, whereas those between .2 and .5 indicate moderate leverage. For the regression of TC on age and BMI, for women aged 20–65 years with BMI's $\leq 40$, the largest $h_{jj}$ is .061, a low value according to the Neter et al. guidelines, although above the Hoaglin and Welsh criterion of .033. We can see from the data set that this leverage value comes from case 569, a woman with both predictor values (age $= 64$, BMI $= 39$) near their cutoffs. However, we should emphasize that outlying cases need not exercise inordinate influence on the values of the regression coefficients. We introduced Cook's distance, $CD_j$, in Chapter 19 as a measure of the change that would result in the regression coefficients if the $j$th case was omitted. $CD_j$, can be written as

$$CD_j = \frac{\sum_i \left( \hat{Y}_i^{(-j)} - \hat{Y}_i \right)^2}{(p + 1)s_e^2}$$

where $\hat{Y}_i^{(-j)}$ is the prediction of $Y_i$ obtained from regression coefficients obtained with the $j$th case deleted. A simple guideline given by Cook and Weisberg (1982) is that a Cook's distance of 1 should be considered to be large. However, a guideline that takes sample size and number of predictors into account is that Cook's distance values should be considered large if they exceed the cutoff $F_{.50,p+1,N-p-1}$ (see Section 19.6). Case 569 has a Cook's distance of .029, well below the cutoff of $F_{.50,3,178} = .79$. The largest Cook's distance value for the regression is .084, again well below the cutoff.

Unfortunately, although regression diagnostics that consider the effect of deleting one point at a time work quite well when there is a single influential outlier, it is much more difficult to diagnose outliers when there are several of them. For a useful discussion of developments in the detection of multiple outliers and of robust regression, see Rousseeuw and Leroy (1987).

## 20.5.7 Confidence Intervals for the Squared Multiple Correlation Coefficient

A confidence interval on $\rho^2$, the squared population multiple correlation coefficient, is much more informative than simply stating the sample $R^2$ along with the results of a significance test. Using an example given by Steiger and Fouladi (1997), suppose we obtain an $R^2$ of .40 in a regression using five predictor variables with $N = 45$. The shrunken estimator (i.e., the adjusted $R^2$) is .327 and if a significance test is performed, the $p$ is .0009. However, it is more useful to know that the 95% confidence interval for $\rho^2$ extends from .095 to .562. This interval tells us that the range of possible values is quite wide; the lower limit of the interval for $\rho$ is .31, whereas the upper limit is a relatively high .75.

There are several ways of obtaining these confidence intervals. Olkin and Finn (1995) have pointed out that, for large samples, the variance of $R^2$ is approximately given by

$$\text{var}(R^2) = \frac{4}{N}\rho^2(1 - \rho^2)^2 \left[1 - \frac{(2p + 1)}{N}\right]$$

where $p$ is the number of predictors, and $\rho^2$ is the square of the population multiple correlation coefficient. If $2p + 1$ is small relative to $N$,

$$\text{var}(R^2) \approx \frac{4}{N}\rho^2(1 - \rho^2)^2 \tag{20.16}$$

For example, if we consider the regression of TC on age and BMI for women aged 65 years or younger, using the results in Table 20.5, the variance of $R^2$ can be estimated by

$$\frac{4}{181}(.272)(1 - .272)^2 = .0032$$

Therefore, an estimate of the .95 confidence interval for $\rho^2$ is given by

$$R^2 \pm z_{.025}SE(R^2) = .272 \pm 1.96\sqrt{.0032}$$
$$= .272 \pm .111$$

that is, an interval that extends from approximately .161 to .383.

Steiger and Fouladi (1992) have developed a computer program, R2, that finds confidence intervals and performs significance tests and power calculations for $R^2$. The program is free and may be downloaded from Steiger's web page at http://www.interchg.ubc.ca/steiger/homepage.htm. Using R2 with the current example yields a 95% confidence that extends from .160 to .380, almost exactly the same values we calculated above using the approximation given by Olkin and Finn (1995).

We may also be interested in determining whether a set of predictors is equally useful in separate populations. For example, we may wish to test whether a battery of college placement tests is equally useful for predicting college GPA for city and suburban students, or whether a set of clinical variables is equally useful in predicting cholesterol levels in men and women. For example, when we regressed TC on age and BMI for the 183 men under the age of 65 with BMI $\leq$ 40 who had data on all three variables in the Seasons data set, we found $R^2 = .046$. This seems considerably less than the $R^2$ of .272 that we found for women. Do we have enough evidence to reject the hypothesis that $\rho^2$ is the same for women and men? If $R_1^2$ and $R_2^2$ are obtained from large independent samples with $N_1$ and $N_2$ observations, respectively, the distribution of their difference is approximately normal with a variance that can be estimated by

$$\text{var}\left(R_1^2 - R_2^2\right) = \frac{4}{N_1}R_1^2\left(1 - R_1^2\right)^2 + \frac{4}{N_2}R_2^2\left(1 - R_2^2\right)^2 \tag{20.17}$$

and the confidence interval many be approximated using

$$R_1^2 - R_2^2 \pm z_{\alpha/2} \cdot SE\left(R_1^2 - R_2^2\right) \tag{20.18}$$

For the regression of TC on age and BMI for women and men, the variance is

$$\text{var}(R_1^2 - R_2^2) = \frac{4}{181}(.272)(1 - .272)^2 + \frac{4}{183}(.046)(1 - .046)^2 = .0041$$

(where the subscripts 1 and 2 represent women and men) and the 95% confidence interval for the difference between the population squared multiple correlations for women and men is approximated by

$$R_1^2 - R_2^2 \pm 1.96 SE\left(R_1^2 - R_2^2\right)$$
$$= .272 - .046 \pm 1.96\sqrt{.0041}$$
$$= .226 \pm .126$$

This interval ranges from approximately .10 to .35. Because the interval does not contain zero, we can reject the null hypothesis that the $\rho^2$ values are equal for men and women. Furthermore, we are reasonably certain that the squared correlation is greater for males than for females, but probably not by more than .35.

How big must the samples be to provide a reasonable estimate of the confidence interval using the approximation suggested by Olkin and Finn (1995)? There is no simple answer: Algina and Keselman (1999) performed a simulation study assuming multivariate normality and varying such factors as the sizes of the population multiple correlation coefficients, the number of predictors, and whether or not the sample sizes were equal. They found that the required sample sizes were smaller if the $\rho^2$'s were equal and not extremely close to zero. If $N$s were equal and both were at least 40, both $\rho^2$ values were at least .06, and there were no more than six predictor variables, then the confidence intervals provided reasonable coverage; nominal 95% confidence intervals were somewhere between 92.5% and 97.5% intervals. With more than six predictor variables, the smaller $N$ should be at least 80. The samples must be larger if one or both of the $\rho^2$s is very close to zero. For example, if $\rho_1^2 = .00$, $\rho_2^2 = .02$ and there are 10 predictors, sample sizes should be greater than 900. Algina and Keselman (1999) provide tables that indicate the sample sizes required for various combinations of factors.

It is also possible to use large-sample approximations to find confidence intervals for the difference between dependent $R^2$s (i.e., $R^2$s calculated on the same sample). As was the case with simple correlation coefficients, finding confidence intervals is more complicated when we use dependent measures because we must take account of their covariance. Alf and Graf (1999) discuss how to obtain these confidence intervals and present worked-out examples.

We should point out that the methods discussed in this section will not be accurate unless the assumption of multivariate normality is satisfied and the predictor variables have been specified in advance. In situations in which the predictors have been selected from a larger pool of variables using some sort of stepwise procedure, it is important that cross-validation be used (see Section 20.4).

### 20.5.8 Power Calculations in Multiple Regression

The issue of power calculations in multiple regression is somewhat complicated, largely because there are many hypotheses that might be tested. Consider the model

$$Y = \beta_0 + \beta_1 X_1 + \beta_2 X_2 + \cdots + \beta_j X_j + \cdots + \beta_p X_p + \varepsilon$$

We may wish to test the hypotheses that (a) all $p$ of the partial slope coefficients are equal to zero in the population, (b) a particular coefficient is equal to zero, or (c) all members of a specified subset that contains $k$ of the $p$ coefficients are equal to zero. In calculating power for these cases, it is useful to have in mind a general case from which we can derive power for these three special cases. Specifically, most programs for calculating power will require an estimate of the noncentrality parameter for the $F$ distribution, defined as

$$\hat{\lambda} = N^* \hat{f}^2 \qquad (20.19)$$

When the predictors are fixed-effect variables, $N^*$ is replaced by the sample size, $N$. However, Cohen (1988)[2] recommends that for multiple regression $N^*$ be defined as

$$N^* = df_{\text{numerator}} + df_{\text{denominator}} + 1$$
$$= k + (N - p - 1) + 1 = N - p + k \qquad (20.20)$$

Maxwell comments that Cohen's (1988) formulation appears to provide a small adjustment for the random nature of predictors that are usually encountered in psychological research (Maxwell, 2000, p. 436). Therefore, we will follow Cohen's recommendation for random-effects predictors. In any event, for fairly large values of $N$, the differences in estimated power obtained using $N$, $N - p + k$, and $N - p - 1$ will be small.

The effect size statistic, $\hat{f}^2$, is defined in general as

$$\hat{f}^2 = \frac{\Delta R^2}{1 - R^2} \qquad (20.21)$$

where $\Delta R^2$ is the increment in $R^2$ when $k$ predictors are added to a set of $p - k$ predictors, and $R^2$ is the squared multiple correlation calculated for the full set of $p$ predictors. Then the general form of the noncentrality parameter we will use in most power calculations is, for fixed-effect predictors,

$$\hat{\lambda} = N \left( \frac{\Delta R^2}{1 - R^2} \right) \qquad (20.22a)$$

and, for random-effects predictors,

$$\hat{\lambda} = (N - p - k) \left( \frac{\Delta R^2}{1 - R^2} \right) \qquad (20.22b)$$

We now consider the three cases for which we might require power.

*Case 1—Power for tests that all of the partial slope coefficients are equal to 0 in the population.* The test of the null hypothesis that all partial slope coefficients equal zero is equivalent to the test that $\rho^2 = 0$. Therefore, there are several options that yield similar results. One approach is to use a noncentral $F$ calculator. To obtain an estimate of $\lambda$ as an input for the calculation of power, we need to decide on the values of $N^*$ and $\hat{f}^2$ in Equation 20.19. To do this, we note that we are asking whether adding $p$ predictors to a set with zero predictors increases $R^2$; therefore, we let $k = p$ in Equation 20.20, and accordingly, $N^* = N$. Furthermore, $\Delta R^2 = R^2$ in this case. Therefore, substituting in either Equation 20.22a or 20.22b, we have

$$\hat{\lambda} = N \left( \frac{R^2}{1 - R^2} \right) \qquad (20.23)$$

Suppose, for example, that we plan to regress TC on age and BMI in a sample of 40 women. If we expect $R^2$ to equal .238, substituting into Equation 20.23, we find the estimated value of $\lambda$ to be 12.49. The critical $F$ with 2 and $N - p - 1 = 37$ $df$ is 3.25.

Using the UCLA noncentral $F$ calculator or the NCDF.F function available in SPSS, we find that the estimated power is .87. GPOWER also gives an estimate of .87, whereas the estimate provided by Steiger and Fouladi's R2 program (described in the preceding section) is .84.

GPOWER and R2 can also be used to determine the number of cases necessary to obtain a desired level of power. For example, suppose we have five predictors and wish to determine the number of cases necessary to achieve a power of .80 with $\alpha = .05$ and $f^2 [= R^2/(1 - R^2)] = .02, .15$, and $.35$, the values that, according to Cohens's guidelines, correspond to small, medium, and large effects. Because $R^2 = f^2/(1 + f^2)$, these $f^2$ values correspond to $R^2$ values of .020, .130, and .259. The required values of $N$ produced by the R2 and GPOWER programs are:

| | Effect Size | | |
| --- | --- | --- | --- |
| | Small | Medium | Large |
| R2 | 637 | 95 | 45 |
| GPOWER | 647 | 92 | 43 |

The two programs provide similar results despite the fact that GPOWER assumes the predictors are fixed, whereas R2 assumes they are continuous random variables with a multivariate normal distribution. Gatsonis and Sampson (1989) point out that the approximations would not be expected to be accurate in situations where some variables are continuous random variables with nonnormal distributions and others are dichotomous.

*Case 2—Power calculations for the test that a particular coefficient is zero in the population.* Here, $k = 1$, so that Equation 20.22b becomes

$$\hat{\lambda} = (N - p + 1)\left(\frac{\Delta R^2}{1 - R^2}\right) = (N - p + 1)\hat{f}^2 \qquad (20.24)$$

As an example, suppose we plan to test whether adding BMI to a regression equation that already contains age will significantly improve the predictability of TC. We are considering using $N = 40$, and we have reason to believe that $R^2$ with age as the only predictor will be .203, and that when BMI is added, $R^2$ will be .238, so that $\Delta R^2$ is .035. Substituting in Equation 20.22, we find $\hat{\lambda} = (39)[.035/(1 - .238)] = 1.79$. Using a noncentral $F$ calculator with $F_{\text{crit.05}}(1, 37) = 4.11, df_1 = k = 1, df_2 = N - (p + 1) = 37$, and $\lambda = 1.79$, the estimated power is only .26. If we perform the study, we will need a much larger sample to have a reasonable chance of achieving statistical significance. Trying out different values of $N$, we find that we would need an $N$ of about 175 to obtain an estimated power of .80. Alternatively, we can use GPOWER. If we select the a priori analysis and special hypothesis options of GPOWER, then insert the values $f^2 = 035/(1 - .238) = .046, \alpha = .05$, power $= .80, p = 2$, and numerator $df = 1$, the required $N$ is 173.

If we have a fairly large sample, we can approximate the $N$ required to obtain any desired power. We begin by noting that if $df_{\text{residual}}$ is greater than about 120, the $\lambda$'s required to achieve powers of .80 and .90 are approximately 7.85 and 10.51, respectively. Solving

Equation 20.24 for $N$, we obtain

$$N = \frac{\hat{\lambda}}{\hat{f}^2} + p - 1 \tag{20.25}$$

Assuming we desire power equal to .80, we substitute $\lambda = 7.85$ into Equation 20.23 and, continuing with our example, the $N$ required is $N = (7.85/.0459) + 2 - 1 = 172$, a value consistent with our previous estimates. We can also use Equation 20.25 to estimate the sample sizes required to obtain a specific value of power for small, medium, and large effect sizes (i.e., $f^2$ values of .02, .15, and .35). For power $= .80$, the required $N$'s are $392 + p$, $52 + p$, and $22 + p$, respectively. So, for example, if we expect to obtain a small effect for a specified predictor, and if we have eight predictors in the equation, and wish to have a power of .80, we will need approximately 400 cases.

*Case 3—Power calculations for testing whether all members of a specified subset that contains k of the p coefficients are equal to zero.* Assuming that the predictors are random variables, the noncentrality parameter may be estimated from Equation 20.22b:

$$\hat{\lambda} = (N - p + k)\left(\frac{\Delta R^2}{1 - R^2}\right) = (N - p + k)\hat{f}^2$$

For example, suppose we have a total of five predictors and we wish to test whether a particular subset of three predictors collectively adds significantly to the prediction over and above the contribution of the other two. If we expect that when the subset of three predictors is added to the equation, $R^2$ will increase from .44 to .50, then the $\hat{f}^2$ for the additional three predictors is $.06/.50 = .12$. If we plan to conduct a study with $N = 100$, the estimated noncentrality parameter will be $\hat{\lambda} = (98)(.12) = 11.76$. The critical $F$ for $\alpha = .05$ and $df_1 = k = 3$ and $df_2 = N - (p + 1) = 94$ is 2.70. Using these values with a noncentral $F$ calculator gives an estimated power of .81.

What happens to power when we add more predictor variables to a regression equation? The answer depends on the pattern of correlations among the predictors and the criterion variable, but in general, because predictors tend to be correlated with one another, the unique contribution of any given predictor variable tends to be less when more predictors are added to the equation, even though $R^2$ will increase. Therefore, although there may be a greater probability that *some* test will become significant, the power for the test of *any given* predictor will tend to decline. The consequences of this state of affairs are extremely unfortunate.

Given just enough power to find that *some* predictors are significant, we would expect to find disagreement about *which* predictors are significant. This point is illustrated by a simulation study conducted by Maxwell (2000), who used multivariate normal data for a criterion variable and five predictors. In the population, each predictor had a correlation of .30 with the other predictors and with the criterion variable. When he repeatedly selected samples of $N = 100$, Maxwell found that at least one predictor was significant at the .05 level in .84 of the samples; in other words, power was .84 to reject at least one of the five null hypotheses. However, the probability that any given predictor was significant, alone or in combination with others, was only .26, and the probability that at least four of the five predictors were significant was less than .01. Even though the sample size was sufficiently large to provide a good chance of finding something that was significant, the power for the tests of each of the regression coefficients was very low.

Because researchers, who are usually limited in the number of available subjects, often include many variables to achieve some significant results, power for tests of individual coefficients will often be low. This is a prescription for developing literatures with inconsistent findings. Further discussion of these issues may be found in Maxwell (2000).

## 20.6 SELECTING THE BEST REGRESSION EQUATION FOR PREDICTION

Sometimes we want to predict some criterion of interest by developing a regression equation that contains a subset of the potentially useful predictor variables that are available. In predicting, we are normally concerned both with the accuracy of the predictions and with the costs involved in making them. If our only concern was accuracy, we would be inclined to use as many valid predictors as possible in the regression equation; on the other hand, concerns about costs would motivate us to use fewer predictors. Because in many types of research most of the predictor variables are correlated with one another, including all of them in a regression equation would not only be expensive and cumbersome, but would also introduce a good deal of redundancy. A number of automated procedures that allow a compromise between these concerns have been developed to produce the best possible predictions with regression equations that contain relatively few predictors. These procedures include forward selection, backward elimination, and stepwise regression, and are available in many statistical packages. Using these procedures, it is often possible to select a subset of the potential predictors that accounts for nearly as large a proportion of the variability in $Y$ as does the entire pool of predictors. Before describing them, we should emphasize that these automated procedures have been developed solely to produce the best prediction equations according to certain criteria. These equations need not be best or even very good in any explanatory or theoretical sense. Running an automated regression routine may be useful for predicting, but is a very poor way to develop theory.

### 20.6.1 Forward Selection

In the forward selection procedure, the regression equation is built up one variable at a time. On the first step, the predictor that has the highest correlation (positive or negative) is selected. If it fails to meet the criterion for inclusion, the procedure ends with no predictors in the equation and the final equation is $\hat{Y}_i = \overline{Y}$. If the first predictor meets the criterion and is added to the equation, on the next step a second predictor is selected and tested to determine whether it should be entered into the equation. The predictor selected is the one that would result in the greatest increment in $R^2$ if added to the equation. If the second predictor does not meet the criterion for inclusion, the procedure terminates with only a single predictor in the equation. If it does meet the criterion, on the third step, a third predictor is selected and tested, and so on. At each step, a partial $F$ test (see Section 20.5) is performed on the selected variable, and the criterion for inclusion is stated in terms of the critical value or the significance level of the $F$.

It should be noted that, for procedures like forward selection, the usual significance levels obtained from the $F$ distribution are not appropriate. This is because at each step a number of possible predictors are examined and only one—the one that produces the greatest increment in $R^2$ or, equivalently, the one that has the largest partial $F$—is tested.

If only a single predictor is to be chosen from a pool of $m$ possible predictors, the situation is analogous to choosing the largest member of a family of $m$ contrasts and testing it for significance. As in the case of contrasts, if a single predictor is to be chosen, it is appropriate to use the Bonferroni procedure to control Type 1 error; that is, to use $\alpha^* = \alpha/m$ as the criterion for significance, where $\alpha$ is the probability of at least one Type 1 error (see Chapter 9 for a discussion of the issue of familywise error rates and procedures for controlling them).

If a subset of $k$ predictors is to be chosen, where $1 < k < m$, the distribution of $R^2$ is unknown. Wilkinson (1979) has discussed this problem and has provided tables of the upper 95th and 99th percentage points of the sample $R^2$ distribution in forward selection based on simulations (other tables and discussions of this problem can be found in Hocking, 1983; Rencher & Pun, 1980; Wilkinson & Dallal, 1982). These tables are more conservative than the usual $F$ tables. For example, with $N = 35$, and $\alpha = .05$, if all four members of a set of predictor variables are to be included in the regression equation, it is appropriate to use the standard $F$ test to test $R^2$ for significance. When this is done, it is found that the sample $R^2$ has to exceed .26 to reject the hypothesis that the population multiple correlation coefficient is zero. However, if the four predictors are to be selected from a larger set of 20 predictors using a forward selection procedure, according to Wilkinson's tables, the sample $R^2$ must exceed .51 to reject the null hypothesis. Many researchers do not seem to be aware of this problem; for a sample of 66 published papers that reported significant forward selection analyses according to the usual $F$ tests, Wilkinson found that 19 were not significant when his tables were used.

## 20.6.2 Backward Elimination

Whereas forward selection begins with no predictors in the equation and adds them to the equation one by one, backward elimination begins with all the predictors in the equation and removes them one by one until the final equation is obtained. At each step, the predictor in the equation that produces the smallest increment in $R^2$ is tested to determine whether it should be removed from the equation. Again, the criterion for removal is generally stated in terms of the significance level of a partial $F$ test. If the selected variable is removed, another predictor is selected and tested on the next step. The procedure terminates when a predictor that has been selected for testing is not removed from the equation; it and all the other predictors remaining in the equation are included in the final regression equation.

## 20.6.3 Stepwise Regression

Stepwise regression, the most popular procedure used to obtain the best prediction equation, is a combination of the forward selection and backward elimination procedures. The procedure is essentially the same as forward selection, with the exception that after each new predictor has been added to the regression equation, all the predictors already in the equation are reexamined to determine whether they should be removed. A partial $F$ test is performed on the predictor already in the equation that produces the smallest increment in $R^2$. If the predictor no longer satisfies the criteria for inclusion, it is removed from the equation. Statistical packages allow the user to set the significance levels (or critical $F$ values) for entering or removing a variable.

It is not difficult to see why it is sometimes desirable to remove a predictor that had been entered early in the analysis. For example, suppose that $X_7$ is highly predictable from

$X_4$ and $X_9$, but is more highly correlated with $Y$ than either of them. Even though $X_7$ may enter the equation early because of its high correlation with $Y$, it will become superfluous after $X_4$ and $X_9$ are entered. Even if $X_7$ contributes significantly to the predictability of $Y$ by itself, it may not make a significant contribution over and above that provided by the other two variables.

Again, it is important to emphasize that when predictor variables entered into the equation are selected from a larger pool, the significance levels printed out by stepwise programs are not "real" $p$ values. Because many practitioners seem to be unaware of this fact, stepwise regression outputs are frequently misinterpreted. As Wilkinson states in the SYSTAT manual, stepwise regression programs are probably the most notorious source of "pseudo $p$ values" in the field of automated data analysis. As with forward selection, we recommend that Wilkinson's (1979) tables be used to test $R^2$ for significance.

Finally, we again emphasize that the sole motivation for the automated procedures described in this section is to develop useful prediction equations that include subsets of the available predictors. There is no reason to think that the equations they produce are "best" or even reasonable in any theoretical sense. Variables that are useful predictors need not be important components of a good theory or causal explanation of the situation. The automated procedures may include theoretically uninteresting variables in the regression equations they produce and they may not include the important variables. Consider, for example, a stepwise regression with several predictors that are highly correlated both with the criterion and with each other. The correlation between the criterion and the predictor included on the first step may be only marginally greater than the correlation between the criterion and the other predictors. Nonetheless, including the first predictor may prevent any of the others from being entered into the equation on subsequent steps. Even though the other predictors add significantly to the predictability of $Y$ in the absence of the first variable, they may not do so when the first variable is in the equation.

Because predictor variables are included in the regression equation if they are useful in the sample, stepwise procedures are extremely susceptible to capitalization on chance, especially when the sample is small. Recall that in the discussion of capitalization on chance in Section 20.4, we presented an example in which stepwise regression produced an equation that fit a sample fairly well. Nonetheless, we demonstrated that the equation was of no use for predicting outside of that sample. If stepwise regression is ever to be used, it is critically important to use cross-validation to evaluate the usefulness of the resulting regression equation.

## 20.7 EXPLANATION VERSUS PREDICTION IN REGRESSION

The machinery of regression deals with prediction, not causation. Therefore, regression equations that are useful for prediction may not be useful for explanation or for advancing theory. Nor may regression coefficients be used as measures of causal importance except in the context of a well developed theory. Procedures beyond the scope of this book, such as path analysis and structural modeling (e.g., Bollen, 1989; Joreskog & Sorbom, 1986; Pedhazur, 1997; also see an interesting collection of papers in the Summer 1987 edition of the *Journal of Educational Statistics*), have been seen by some researchers as ways of extracting causal information from correlational data. However, these procedures do not generate causal models; rather, they estimate the strengths of effects within the context of a proposed causal model. The procedures may be able to reject a proposed model if the model can be shown to be inconsistent with the data. However, just because a model is not rejected does not mean that it is correct, or even useful. There may be other, quite different, models that also would not be rejected. Useful causal models are developed by researchers, not by computer programs. However, the programs can be useful in spelling out the consequences of the models and in testing whether they are consistent with the data.

Our goal in Section 20.7 is to extend the discussion, begun in Section 20.3, of reasons why the size of a regression coefficient may not be a good measure of its importance. We have already discussed the fact that a variable that has no causal importance may be a useful predictor if it is correlated with variables that are important. In the next few sections, we discuss the consequences of misspecifying a model and point out that, even in a properly specified causal model, the partial regression coefficient of a predictor variable may not be a good measure of its importance, because the variable may have both direct and indirect effects on the dependent variable, and the partial regression coefficient reflects only the direct effect. Finally, we discuss the consequences of multicollinearity, how to recognize it, and some possible remedies.

## 20.7.1 Specification Errors

If there are **specification errors**, that is, if a regression does not contain the same variables as the true population model, the obtained regression coefficients may be poor estimates of the corresponding population parameters. This is important, because our regression models will rarely match the true population model, either because we do not know the true model, or because we lack information about some of the variables in the true model.

If parameters of the population model

$$Y_i = \beta_0 + \beta_1 X_{i1} + \beta_2 X_{i2} + \cdots + \beta_p X_{ip} + \varepsilon_\iota$$

are estimated by the coefficients of the sample regression equation

$$\hat{Y}_i = b_0 + b_1 X_{i1} + b_2 X_{i2} + \cdots + b_p X_{ip}$$

the $b_j$'s can be shown to be unbiased estimators of the $\beta_j'$s. However, as we pointed out in Section 20.3, if the $b_j$'s are obtained from a regression equation that does not include the same variables as the correct population model, they will generally be biased estimators of the $\beta_j$'s in the population model. Let's consider the consequences of omitting relevant variables from, and including irrelevant variables in our regression equations.

***Omitting Relevant Variables.***    Suppose a variable in the population model is omitted from a regression equation. If it is correlated with one or more of the variables that are included in the equation, the partial regression coefficients may reflect not only the effects of the corresponding predictors, but also the effects of relevant variables that were not included in the regression equation.

Let's be more specific. Suppose that the true model in the population is

$$Y = \beta_{012} + \beta_{Y1\cdot2}X_1 + \beta_{Y2\cdot1} + \varepsilon$$

where we use the notation $\beta_{Y1\cdot2}$ to emphasize that the regression coefficient of $X_1$ comes from a model that includes both $X_1$ and $X_2$. If we attempt to estimate $\beta_{Y1\cdot2}$ and $\beta_{Y2\cdot1}$ from a sample using the regression equation

$$\hat{Y} = b_{012} + b_{Y1\cdot2}X_1 + b_{Y2\cdot1}$$

it can be shown that $E(b_{Y1\cdot2}) = \beta_{Y1\cdot2}$ and $E(b_{Y2\cdot1}) = \beta_{Y2\cdot1}$, so that the sample regression coefficients are unbiased estimators of the model parameters.

If, however, we regress $Y$ only on $X_1$ and thereby misspecify the model, we obtain the sample regression equation

$$\hat{Y} = b_{01} + b_{Y1}X_1$$

Now $b_{Y1}$ will generally be a biased estimator of $\beta_{Y1\cdot2}$. To show this, we first express $b_{Y1}$ as

$$b_{Y1} = \frac{\sum (X_1 - \overline{X}_1)(Y - \overline{Y})}{SS_1}$$

where $SS_1 = \sum (X_1 - \overline{X}_1)^2$ so that

$$E(b_{Y1}) = E\left(\frac{\sum (X_1 - \overline{X}_1)(Y - \overline{Y})}{SS_1}\right)$$

If we assume $X$ is fixed, we can rewrite the preceding equation as

$$E(b_{Y1}) = \frac{\sum (X_1 - \overline{X}_1)E(Y - \overline{Y})}{SS_1}$$

Substituting the population model expressions for $Y$ and $\overline{Y}$ and simplifying, we have

$$E(b_{Y1}) = \frac{\beta_{Y1\cdot2}\sum (X_1 - \overline{X}_1)^2 + E\left[\beta_{Y2\cdot1}\sum (X_1 - \overline{X}_1)(X_2 - \overline{X}_2)\right]}{SS_1}$$

$$= \beta_{Y1\cdot2} + \beta_{Y2\cdot1}E\left(r_{12}\sqrt{\frac{SS_2}{SS_1}}\right)$$

$$= \beta_{Y1\cdot2} + \beta_{Y2\cdot1}E(b_{21})$$

where $r_{12}$ is the correlation between $X_1$ and $X_2$, $SS_1$ and $SS_2$ are the sums of squares of $X_1$ and $X_2$, and $b_{21}$ is the regression coefficient obtained by regressing $X_2$ (the omitted variable) on $X_1$. Therefore, the expected value of $b_{Y1}$ is not $\beta_{Y1\cdot2}$; rather, the expected value also contains a term that depends on $\beta_{Y2\cdot1}$, as well as on the regression of $X_2$ on $X_1$. Note that this biasing term disappears if $X_1$ and $X_2$ are uncorrelated.

Although things get more complicated when there are more predictors, unless all the variables that are in the population model are included in the regression equation, the regression coefficients will be biased estimators of the population parameters—unless all the omitted variables are uncorrelated with those that are included in the regression.

### Including Irrelevant Variables.
Because of the negative consequences of omitting relevant variables, researchers are sometimes inclined to include additional variables in their regression equations, just to make sure that nothing important has been left out. This may result in the addition of irrelevant variables to the equation; that is, variables that are not included in the population model. Adding irrelevant variables does not bias parameter estimates, so the consequences of including irrelevant variables are not as serious as those of omitting relevant ones. Nonetheless, including irrelevant variables will use up degrees

of freedom and will tend to inflate the standard errors of the relevant variables that are in the equation, making parameter estimates less precise.

## 20.7.2 Interpretation of the Regression Coefficients as the Direct Effects of the $X_i$

Even if we include the correct variables in the regression equation and there is a causal relationship between $X_j$ and the criterion, the regression coefficient $b_j$ does not represent the total effect of $X_j$ on $Y$. Rather, the regression coefficient reflects the **direct effect** of $X_j$ on $Y$, that is, the rate of change of $Y$ with $X_j$, *holding all of the other variables in the equation constant*. If we actually changed $X_j$, this would influence other variables in the model, and the resultant changes in these variables will also influence the dependent variable. These are the **indirect effects** of $X_j$. In assessing the causal importance of $X_j$, we must be concerned with both the direct and indirect effects.

Given a valid causal model, path analysis or structural equation modeling can be used to assess the total effect of changing a variable. However, we should note that these estimates may be misleading if important variables are omitted from the model or if the model is otherwise invalid.

## 20.7.3 Multicollinearity

Multicollinearity occurs when predictor variables included in a regression equation can be predicted from the other variables in the equation. If at least one predictor variable can be perfectly predicted from the others, there is perfect multicollinearity. Given perfect multicollinearity, an infinite number of regression equations will fit the data equally well, and the statistical packages will not conduct a regression analysis. Suppose that $Y$ is regressed on $X_1$ and $X_2$. Then, the points $(\hat{Y}, X_1, X_2)$ that satisfy the regression equation $\hat{Y} = b_0 + b_1X_1 + b_2X_2$ will lie along the surface of a plane in the three-dimensional space defined by axes $Y$, $X_1$, and $X_2$. If $X_1$ and $X_2$ are not highly correlated, as in Fig. 20.3, these points constrain the values of $b_0$, $b_1$, and $b_2$ that define the best-fitting regression plane. If the orientation of the plane was changed, resulting in different values for $b_0$, $b_1$, and $b_2$, the predictions would be different. However, if $X_1$ and $X_2$ are perfectly correlated, as in Fig. 20.5, the points $(\hat{Y}, X_1, X_2)$ will lie along a *straight line* in the three-dimensional space, and any of the infinite number of planes that contain the line will fit the data equally well, making it impossible to specify unique values for $b_0$, $b_1$, and $b_2$. It is rare to find perfect multicollinearity unless redundant variables, such as subscale scores and total score, or age and year of birth, are included. However, it is not rare to find situations in which the predictors are highly, but not perfectly, collinear. In such cases, the software packages will perform the regression. However, the values of the regression coefficients, although not totally unconstrained by the data, may be extremely unstable.

High correlations among predictors do not generally result in much difficulty if the only goal is prediction. However, they can present difficulties both for estimating and interpreting regression coefficients. If several highly correlated predictors are included in the regression equation, their combined effect will be split up among them. The nature of the split will depend on the details of the data, and may vary widely from sample to sample, leading to dramatically increased standard errors for the regression coefficients (see Equation 20.5).

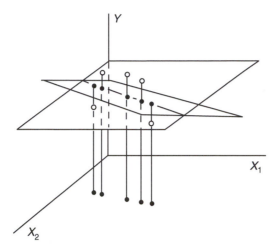

**Fig. 20.5** Illustration of perfect multicollinearity :
The open circles represent data points $(X_1, X_2, Y)$.
The lower group of filled circles represents the $(X_1, X_2)$ coordinates of the data points. If $X_1$ and $X_2$ are
perfectly correlated, these filled circles will fall on a
straight line. The upper set of filled circles represents
the points $(X_1, X_2, \hat{Y})$, where the $\hat{Y}$s are the best
least-squares predictions of $Y$ corresponding to $(X_1, X_2)$. Note that these points fall on a straight line in
the three-dimensional space, and that an infinite
number of planes with different values of $b_0$, $b_1$, and
$b_2$ will contain that straight line. Therefore, it is
impossible to specify a unique regression plane.

The major software packages all contain diagnostic information that can be used to determine if there is a serious multicollinearity problem. In the SPSS output for the regression of TC on age and BMI in Table 20.6, the Coefficients table displays information about the Tolerance $(1 - R_j^2.)$ and VIF $= 1/$Tolerance, measures that we discussed in Section 20.3. Because we asked for collinearity diagnostics, we also have a table containing eigenvalues, condition indices, and variance proportions. Although a complete explanation of these terms is beyond the scope of this book, a rough explanation is as follows: A principal components analysis is first conducted to identify dependencies among the variables; think of this as a data reduction technique in which the first principal component is obtained by finding the linear combination of variables that accounts for the greatest amount of variability, the second principal component is the linear combination that is both uncorrelated with the first component and accounts for the greatest amount of the remaining variability, and so on. The eigenvalues are the amounts of variability accounted for by each of the components. If one or more of the eigenvalues are zero, this indicates that one or more of the variables is completely redundant, so there is perfect multicollinearity. The **condition index** for each component is the square root of the ratio of the largest eigenvalue to the eigenvalue for that component. According to Belsley, Kuh, and Welsh (1980), a condition index greater than 15 suggests a possible multicollinearity problem, and a condition index greater than 30 suggests that there may be a serious multicollinarity problem. The **variance proportions** are the proportions of variance of each regression coefficient estimate associated with each component. There is a serious multicollinearity problem when a component has a large condition index and high variance proportions (say, greater than .50) for two or more regression coefficients. We see in Table 20.6 that none of the condition indices exceed 15 for the regression of TC on age and BMI, so we do not have a multicollinearity problem for this analysis.

A number of remedies have been suggested if we find that there is a multicollinearity problem:

1. One recommendation is to delete some of the predictors that are responsible for the problem. Unfortunately, this might result in specification errors that themselves can have serious consequences, as we discussed in the previous section.

2. Another recommendation is to combine clusters of highly related predictor variables into new variables that represent common underlying factors. Deciding which variables to combine is best done on the basis of theoretical considerations. Other procedures, such as principal components analysis and factor analysis, can provide suggestions about possible underlying processes.

3. Another approach is to use **centering**. This involves replacing each score by the corresponding deviation score; that is, the score minus the mean of the variable. For example, when we regressed TC on age and BMI using data from women aged 20–65 with BMI scores not exceeding 40, the mean of the age scores was 46.928. We would center the age variable by replacing it with a new variable, age − 46.928. Multicollinearity can result in computational errors in the algorithms that are used in standard software packages. Centering can reduce the correlations among predictors and can also reduce the sizes of the numbers used in calculations, thereby reducing rounding error.

4. Finally, a procedure called ridge regression (see, e.g., Draper & Smith, 1998; Rozeboom, 1979) is sometimes used to deal with multicollinearity. This procedure takes advantage of the fact that, under certain conditions, it is possible to obtain biased estimates with small standard errors that are more useful than unbiased estimates with large standard errors.

## 20.8 TESTING FOR CURVILINEARITY IN REGRESSION

### 20.8.1 Testing for Curvilinearity Using Continuous Variables

When we regressed TC on age and BMI, we implicitly assumed that if the variables were related, they were related linearly. However, it is possible that the relation is not strictly linear and that the prediction of TC scores would be better if we included curvilinear components as well. In general, given a dependent variable $Y$ and a predictor $X_1$, we can test for a quadratic component by regressing $Y$ on $X_1^2$ as well as $X_1$, so that the regression equation is of the form

$$\hat{Y} = b_0 + b_1 X_1 + b_2 X_1^2$$

If we find that the quadratic component is significant, we can test for the presence of a cubic component by now regressing $Y$ on $X_1^3$, as well as on $X_1$ and $X_1^2$, and so on. Note that we cannot test for the presence of a quadratic component by regressing only on $X_1^2$, because $X_1^2$ usually will be correlated with $X_1$, so that the regression of $Y$ on $X_1^2$ alone would reflect both linear and quadratic effects. If we wish to test for the presence of a quadratic component, we must include $X_1$ in the equation as well as $X_1^2$, to partial out the linear component. If we regress TC on BMI and BMI$^2$ for women aged 65 or younger who have BMI scores no greater than 40, we find that the coefficient of the BMI$^2$ term is not significant, although it does not miss significance by much; $t(178) = -1.885$, $p = .061$. Because we cannot conclude that the quadratic component differs from zero, we cannot reject the hypothesis that a straight line adequately describes the population.

## 20.8.2 Testing for Curvilinearity Using Quantitative Categorical Variables: Trend Analysis

Multiple regression can readily be used to perform the trend analyses that we discussed in Chapter 10. In fact, using multiple regression to perform trend analysis offers important advantages. When we used orthogonal polynomial contrasts in Chapter 10, the orthogonal

**TABLE 20.9**   AN EXAMPLE OF TREND ANALYSIS

(a) Percent Addition Accuracy as a Function of Grade for Royer Data

| | Grade ($X$) | | | | |
| | 1 | 2 | 3 | 4 | 5 |
|---|---|---|---|---|---|
| $n$ | 19 | 28 | 32 | 30 | 26 |
| $\overline{Y}$ | 71.82 | 84.66 | 91.97 | 92.34 | 91.98 |
| $s$ | 30.23 | 15.26 | 8.24 | 7.30 | 9.20 |

(b) Trend Analysis for the Data in Panel (a)

$$SS_{\text{linear}} = R_{Y \cdot X}^2 SS_Y = 4690.170$$

$$SS_{\text{quadratic}} = \left(R_{Y \cdot X, X^2}^2 - R_{Y \cdot X}^2\right)SS_Y = 6553.310 - 4690.170 = 1863.140$$

$$SS_{\text{cubic}} = \left(R_{Y \cdot X, X^2, X^3}^2 - R_{Y \cdot X, X^2}^2\right)SS_Y = 6617.701 - 6553.310 = 64.391$$

$$SS_{\text{quartic}} = \left(R_{Y \cdot X, X^2, X^3, X^4}^2 - R_{Y \cdot X, X^2, X^3}^2\right)SS_Y = 6626.772 - 6617.701 = 9.071$$

| SV | df | SS | MS | F | p |
|---|---|---|---|---|---|
| Grade | 4 | 6626.772 | 1656.693 | 7.554 | .000 |
| Linear | 1 | 4690.170 | 4690.170 | 21.385 | .000 |
| Quadratic | 1 | 1863.140 | 1863.140 | 8.495 | .004 |
| Cubic | 1 | 64.391 | 64.391 | 0.294 | .589 |
| Quartic | 1 | 9.071 | 9.071 | 0.041 | .840 |
| Error | 130 | 28511.337 | 219.318 | | |

polynomial weights in Appendix Table C.6 assumed equal numbers of subjects at each level of the independent variable and equal spacing between levels of the variable. If either of these equalities are violated, new orthogonal polynomial weights must be calculated. Unequal $n$ and unequal spacing present no difficulties if we perform trend analysis by using hierarchical multiple regression; that is, if we regress $Y$ first on $X$, then on $X$ and $X^2$, then on $X$, $X^2$, and $X^3$, and so on, and test the increments in variability accounted for when higher order components are added to regression equations that already contain the lower order components.

For example, consider the addition accuracy scores for grades 1–5 in the Royer data set that are presented in Table 20.9 and plotted in Fig. 20.6. Accuracy first increases with grade, then levels off. We would expect to find both a linear trend, because the best-fitting straight line would have a positive slope, and a quadratic trend because we have a negatively accelerated curve. If we regress Accuracy ($Y$) on Grade ($X$), $SS_{\text{linear}}$, the variability accounted for by the regression, is $R^2_{Y \cdot X} SS_Y = 4690.170$. If we now regress $Y$ on $X$ and $X^2$, $SS_{\text{quadratic}}$ is the increment in $SS_{\text{regression}}$ that results when $X^2$ is added to a regression equation that already contains $X$. In our example, $SS_{\text{quadratic}}$, $SS_{\text{cubic}}$, and $SS_{\text{quartic}}$, can all be calculated as increments in the regression sum of squares. The contributions are removed in order, linear first, then quadratic, and so on, as illustrated in Table 20.9. As is also indicated in the table, all of these trend components can be tested against the within-groups error term, $MS_{\text{error}} = 219.318$. The ANOVA table in panel (b) of Table 20.9 presents the results of the tests. As expected, we find significant linear and quadratic trends: $F(1, 135) = 21.385$, $p = .000$, and $F(1, 135) = 8.495$, $p = .004$, respectively. We should note that because there are five levels of grade, and therefore 4 $df$, the regression of $Y$ on $X$, $X^2$, $X^3$, and $X^4$ must account for all of the variability in the group means; that is,

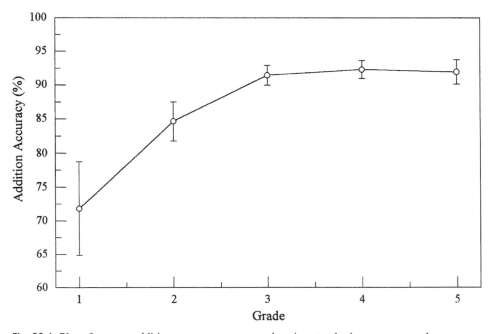

**Fig. 20.6** Plot of percent addition accuracy versus grade using standard errors as error bars.

$R^2_{Y\cdot X, X^2, X^3, X^4} SS_Y = 6626.772 = SS_{\text{Between}}$. Just as any two points can be fit perfectly by a straight line, the points for the five group means can be fit perfectly by a fourth-degree polynomial.

## 20.9 INCLUDING INTERACTION TERMS IN MULTIPLE REGRESSION

### 20.9.1 Introduction

Let's reconsider the population model discussed in Section 20.3,

$$Y = \beta_0 + \beta_1 X_1 + \beta_2 X_2 + \varepsilon$$

If we ignore the random error component, $\beta_1$ is the rate of change of $Y$ with $X_1$, given that $X_2$ is held constant, and $\beta_2$ is the rate of change of $Y$ with $X_2$, given that $X_1$ is held constant. This is an **additive model** because the effect on $Y$ of changing the values of either of the predictors does not depend on the value of the other predictor. This kind of model will be unrealistic whenever the relation between $Y$ and a predictor, $X_1$, is **moderated** by (i.e., it depends on the value taken on by) another variable $X_2$. In this case, we would say we had an **interaction** between $X_1$ and $X_2$.

We dealt with interactions in detail when we discussed ANOVA. In the context of ANOVAs, we would say we had an interaction when the effect of a factor is different for different levels of a second factor. We can translate this thinking directly to multiple regression analyses; however, when we work with multiple regression we can extend the concept, because we can deal not only with categorical factors, but also with a mix of categorical and quantitative continuous variables. Also, it is possible to construct models in which the effect of one factor is a specified function of the levels of a second factor.

### 20.9.2 Testing the Interaction Between Two Quantitative Predictors

In Section 20.2, we regressed TC on age and BMI for women aged 20–65 years and obtained the equation

$$\hat{\text{TC}} = 92.239 + 1.737 \cdot \text{age} + 1.474 \cdot \text{BMI} \tag{20.26}$$

According to this equation, if BMI is held constant, a 1-year increase in age corresponds to a 1.737 unit increase in predicted TC, no matter what value BMI takes on. Also, if age is held constant, a one-unit increase in BMI corresponds to a 1.474 unit increase in predicted TC for subjects at all ages. However, it is possible that Equation 20.26 is unrealistic. Age and BMI may interact; the rate of change of predicted TC with age may differ for different values of BMI, or equivalently, the rate of change of predicted TC with BMI may differ for different ages. We can investigate this possibility by first creating a new variable, Age × BMI, that is the product of age and BMI, and then regressing TC on age, on BMI, and on Age × BMI. As can be seen in the SPSS output in Table 20.10, the resulting regression

**TABLE 20.10**    OUTPUT FOR REGRESSION OF TC ON AGE, BMI, AND AGE × BMI USING DATA
FOR WOMEN AGED 65 YEARS OR YOUNGER WITH BMI ≤ 40

**Model Summary**

| Model | R | R Square | Adjusted R Square | Std. Error of the Estimate |
|---|---|---|---|---|
| 1 | .546[a] | .298 | .286 | 33.0969 |

[a]Predictors: (Constant), AGEXBMI, BMI, AGE.

**ANOVA[b]**

| Model | | Sum of Squares | df | Mean Square | F | Sig. |
|---|---|---|---|---|---|---|
| 1 | Regression | 82322.209 | 3 | 27440.736 | 25.051 | .000[a] |
| | Residual | 193887.004 | 177 | 1095.407 | | |
| | Total | 276209.213 | 180 | | | |

[a]Predictors: (Constant), AGEXBMI, BMI, AGE.
[b]Dependent Variable: TC.

**Coefficients[a]**

| Model | | Unstandardized Coefficients | | Standardized Coefficients | t | sig. |
|---|---|---|---|---|---|---|
| | | B | Std. Error | Beta | | |
| 1 | (Constant) | −70.241 | 65.952 | | −1.065 | .288 |
| | AGE | 5.209 | 1.383 | 1.413 | 3.765 | .000 |
| | BMI | 7.844 | 2.558 | .935 | 3.067 | .003 |
| | AGEXBMI | −.135 | .053 | −1.287 | −2.546 | .012 |

[a]Dependent Variable: TC.
*Note.* Output is from SPSS.

equation is

$$\hat{TC} = -70.241 + 5.209 \cdot \text{Age} + 7.844 \cdot \text{BMI} - 0.135 \cdot \text{Age} \times \text{BMI} \qquad (20.27)$$

The coefficient of the product term is significant, at $t(186) = -2.546$, $p = .012$. It may
help us to understand the interpretation of this coefficient, $-0.135$, by regrouping terms and
rewriting Equation 20.27 as

$$\hat{TC} = -70.241 + 5.209 \cdot \text{Age} + (7.844 - 0.135 \cdot \text{Age}) \text{BMI}$$

or

$$\hat{TC} = -70.241 + (5.209 - 0.135 \cdot \text{BMI}) \text{Age} + 7.844 \cdot \text{BMI}$$

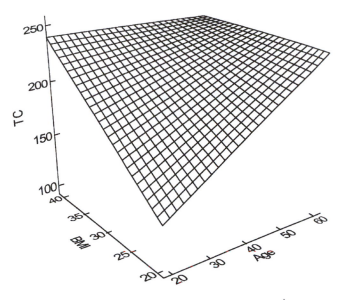

**Fig. 20.7** Plot of the surface generated by the equation $\hat{TC} = -70.241 + 5.209 \cdot \text{Age} + 7.844 \cdot \text{BMI} - 0.135 \cdot \text{Age} \times \text{BMI}$.

We can see from these equations that the rate of change of predicted TC with BMI when age is held constant now depends on the value at which age is held constant. The rate of change of predicted TC with BMI is now a linear function of age, $7.844 - 0.135$ age, and the rate of change of predicted TC with age is a linear function of BMI, $5.209 - 0.135$ BMI. Because of the product term, when we plot Equation 20.27 (see Fig. 20.7), we no longer have a plane, but rather a curved surface on which the partial slopes with one predictor decrease as the value of the other predictor increases.[3] The slope of predicted TC with age decreases by 0.135 for each one-unit increase in BMI, and the slope of TC with BMI decreases by 0.135 for each one-unit increase in age. According to Equation 20.27, the partial slope of predicted TC with age for BMI $= 20$ is $5.209 - (0.135)(20) \approx 2.51$, and for BMI $= 30$ it is approximately 1.16. The partial slope of predicted TC with BMI at age $= 30$ is $7.844 - (.135)(30) \approx 3.79$, and for age $= 55$ it is only approximately 0.42. Therefore, BMI is a less useful predictor of TC for older subjects, and age is a less useful predictor of TC for subjects with large BMIs.

How do we interpret the other regression coefficients in Equation 20.27 and their tests of significance in Table 20.10? The coefficient of age, 5.209, is the partial slope of predicted TC with age for BMI $= 0$. Similarly, the coefficient of BMI, 7.844, is the partial slope of predicted TC with BMI for age $= 0$.

We are not likely to be interested in predictions for age $= 0$ and BMI $= 0$, but we may well be interested in testing whether a partial slope coefficient is significant at a specified value of the other predictor. Suppose we want to test whether the partial slope of TC with BMI is significant at age $= 50$. There are several ways to conduct the test. The easiest way is to transform the variables and redo the regression.

To test the partial slope of TC with BMI at age $= 50$, we can create the variable Agem50 $=$ age $- 50$, then regress TC on Agem50, BMI, and their product, Agem50 $\times$ BMI.

This results in the regression equation

$$\hat{TC} = 190.189 + 5.209 \cdot \text{Agem50} + 1.071 \cdot \text{BMI} - 0.135 \cdot \text{Agem50} \times \text{BMI}$$

In the equation, the coefficient of BMI, 1.071, is the partial slope coefficient of predicted TC with BMI at Agem50 = 0; that is, at age = 50. The coefficient is not significant, $t(177) = 1.93$, $p = 0.055$. We could do similar analyses to test the coefficients of age at different levels of BMI by transforming BMI and redoing the regression.

Finally, we should note that, unless we specify the correct model, we might wind up concluding that we have an interaction when what we actually have is curvilinearity. We do not have space to address this issue here, but we have included a section "Do we actually have an interaction or do we have curvilinearity or do we have both?" in the *Supplementary Materials* folder of the CD.

## 20.9.3 Testing the Interaction Between a Quantitative and a Dichotomous Predictor

In the preceding example, we considered the interaction of two quantitative variables. The approach we took—creating a variable to represent the interaction—can be applied to the common situation in which we have a quantitative variable and a categorical dichotomous (i.e., having only two possible values) variable. For example, consider the regression of TC on age and sex for subjects in the Seasons data set who are of age 65 or younger and have BMI scores no higher than 40. Coding males as 0 and females as 1, we arrive at the output in Table 20.11, which provides the coefficients for the equation

$$\hat{TC} = 178.009 + 0.900 \cdot \text{Age} - 8.645 \cdot \text{Sex} \tag{20.28}$$

A better understanding of the relation of TC to age and sex may be obtained by regressing TC on age separately for males and females; the resulting equations are

$$\hat{TC} = 221.143 - 0.0005 \cdot \text{Age} \tag{20.29}$$

and

$$\hat{TC} = 126.531 + 1.812 \cdot \text{Age} \tag{20.30}$$

These equations are plotted in Figure 20.8; it is apparent that predicted TC changes very little with age for males, but strongly increases for females. We can test this apparent interaction of age and sex by regressing TC on age, sex, and an additional variable, Age × Sex, that is formed by multiplying age and sex. This results in the equation

$$\hat{TC} = 221.143 - 0.0005 \cdot \text{Age} - 94.612 \cdot \text{Sex} + 1.813 \cdot \text{Age} \times \text{Sex} \tag{20.31}$$

As can be seen in the SPSS output in Table 20.12, the coefficient of the product term, 1.813, is significant; $t(363) = 4.909$, $p = .000$. To understand this coefficient, we can regroup the terms in Equation 20.28 and rewrite the equation as either

$$\hat{TC} = 221.143 - 94.612 \cdot \text{Sex} + (-0.0005 + 1.813 \cdot \text{Sex})\text{Age} \tag{20.32}$$

**TABLE 20.11**  OUTPUT FOR REGRESSION OF TC ON AGE AND SEX USING DATA
FOR SUBJECTS AGED 65 YEARS OR YOUNGER WITH BMI ≤ 40

**Model Summary**

| Model | R | R Square | Adjusted R Square | Std. Error of the Estimate |
|-------|------|----------|-------------------|----------------------------|
| 1 | .268[a] | .072 | .067 | 38.5497 |

[a]Predictors: (Constant), SEX, AGE

**ANOVA[b]**

| Model | | Sum of Squares | df | Mean Square | F | Sig. |
|-------|------------|----------------|-----|-------------|--------|---------|
| 1 | Regression | 41436.191 | 2 | 20718.096 | 13.941 | .000[a] |
| | Residual | 536474.480 | 361 | 1486.079 | | |
| | Total | 577910.671 | 363 | | | |

[a]Predictors: (Constant), SEX, AGE
[b]Dependent Variable: TC

**Coefficients[a]**

| Model | | Unstandardized Coefficients B | Std. Error | Standardized Coefficients Beta | t | sig. |
|-------|------------|-------------------------------|------------|-------------------------------|--------|------|
| 1 | (Constant) | 178.009 | 9.562 | | 18.616 | .000 |
| | AGE | .900 | .190 | .240 | 4.723 | .000 |
| | SEX | −8.645 | 4.046 | −.108 | −2.137 | .033 |

[a]Dependent Variable: TC
*Note.* Output is from SPSS.

or as

$$\hat{TC} = 221.143 - 0.0005 \cdot Age + (-94.612 + 1.813 \cdot Age)\,Sex \qquad (20.33)$$

From these equations, we can see that the rate of change of predicted TC with age is a function of sex, namely, $-0.0005 + 1.813$ sex, and the change in predicted TC with sex (i.e., the difference in predicted TC for males and females), is a function of age, $-94.612 + 1.813$ age. For example, at age 60 we would predict the difference in predicted TC for males and females to be $-94.612 + (1.813)(60) = 14.168$, whereas at age 30 we would predict the difference to be $-94.612 + (1.813)(30) = -40.222$. Predicted TC for females is about 40 units lower than for males at age 30, but about14 units higher than for males at age 60.

**TABLE 20.12** OUTPUT FOR REGRESSION OF TC ON AGE, SEX AND AGE × SEX USING DATA FOR WOMEN AGED 65 YEARS OR YOUNGER WITH BMI ≤ 40

**Model Summary**

| Model | R | R Square | Adjusted R Square | Std. Error of the Estimate |
|---|---|---|---|---|
| 1 | .360[a] | .130 | .123 | 37.3727 |

[a]Predictors: (Constant), AGEXSEX

**ANOVA[b]**

| Model | | Sum of Squares | df | Mean Square | F | Sig. |
|---|---|---|---|---|---|---|
| 1 | Regression | 75090.960 | 3 | 25030.320 | 17.921 | .000[a] |
| | Residual | 502819.711 | 360 | 1396.721 | | |
| | Total | 577910.671 | 363 | | | |

[a]Predictors: (Constant), AGEXSEX
[b]Dependent Variable: TC

**Coefficients[a]**

| Model | Unstandardized Coefficients | | Standardized Coefficients | | | Collinearity Statistics | |
|---|---|---|---|---|---|---|---|
| | B | Std. Error | Beta | t | sig. | Tolerance | VIF |
| 1  (Constant) | 221.143 | 12.773 | | 17.313 | .000 | | |
| AGE | 4.57E-04 | .260 | .000 | −.002 | .999 | .502 | 1.990 |
| SEX | −94.612 | 17.947 | −1.187 | −5.272 | .000 | .048 | 20.984 |
| AGEXSEX | 1.813 | .369 | 1.120 | 4.909 | .000 | .046 | 21.554 |

[a]Dependent Variable: TC.

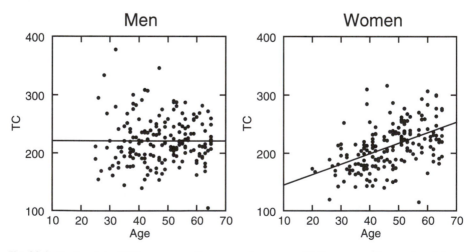

**Fig. 20.8** Scatterplot of TC versus age for men and women with linear smoothers using data from participants aged 65 years or younger with BMI ≤ 40.

## 20.10 MULTIPLE REGRESSION IN REPEATED-MEASURES DESIGNS

When we analyze repeated-measures designs using multiple regression, hypothesis tests can be performed and confidence intervals can be found in the same ways that we indicated in Section 19.8 for bivariate regression. Table 20.13 contains the data for a hypothetical reading experiment described by Lorch and Myers (1990). Each of 10 participants reads a paragraph consisting of seven sentences, and reading times are recorded (in milliseconds) for each sentence. There are three predictor variables for each sentence: the serial position of the sentence in the text (SP), the number of words in the sentence (WORDS), and the number of new arguments in the sentence (NEW). We are interested in whether each of the predictors makes a significant contribution to the prediction of reading time over and above that provided by the other two predictors (i.e., if the rate of change of reading time with the value of the predictor is significant holding the values of the other two predictors constant).

There are several ways of testing hypotheses and forming confidence intervals for the regression coefficients of the predictors. One of them is to regress reading time on the three predictors separately for each participant and then to perform subsequent analyses on the regression coefficients. Table 20.14 contains the regression coefficients for each of the 10 participants along with the mean, standard error, and $t$ (i.e., the ratio of the mean to the standard error) for each coefficient. Because there are 10 participants, there are 9 $df$ associated with each $t$. Because $t_{\text{CRIT}.05,9} = \pm 2.262$, we can reject the hypotheses that $\beta_{\text{SP}} = 0$ and $\beta_{\text{WORDS}} = 0$ at $\alpha = .05$. We cannot reject the hypothesis that $\beta_{\text{NEW}} = 0$.

As we pointed out in Chapter 19, regression analyses of data from repeated-measures designs have frequently been conducted inappropriately. Many researchers would incorrectly analyze the data presented in Table 20.13 by first averaging over participants, and then regressing the mean reading times for each sentence on the predictor variables. If this is done, the resulting significance tests will be positively biased. Even if the expected value of a regression coefficient is zero, the $F$ may be large if the effect of the predictor varies across participants. For a more detailed discussion, see Lorch and Myers (1990).

**TABLE 20.13** VALUES OF THE PREDICTOR VARIABLES FOR THE SEVEN SENTENCES AND THE READING TIMES IN MILLISECONDS FOR EACH OF THE 10 PARTICIPANTS

| SNT | SP | WORDS | NEW | P1 | P2 | P3 | P4 | P5 | P6 | P7 | P8 | P9 | P10 |
|-----|----|-------|-----|------|------|------|------|------|-------|-------|------|------|------|
| 1 | 1 | 13 | 1 | 3429 | 2795 | 4161 | 3071 | 3625 | 3161 | 3232 | 7161 | 1536 | 4063 |
| 2 | 2 | 16 | 3 | 6482 | 5411 | 4491 | 5063 | 9295 | 5643 | 8357 | 4313 | 2946 | 6652 |
| 3 | 3 | 9 | 2 | 1714 | 2339 | 3018 | 2464 | 6045 | 2455 | 4920 | 3366 | 1375 | 2179 |
| 4 | 4 | 9 | 2 | 3679 | 3714 | 2666 | 2732 | 4205 | 6241 | 3723 | 6330 | 1152 | 3661 |
| 5 | 5 | 10 | 3 | 4000 | 2902 | 2991 | 2670 | 3884 | 3223 | 3143 | 6143 | 2759 | 3330 |
| 6 | 6 | 18 | 4 | 6973 | 8018 | 6625 | 7571 | 8795 | 13188 | 11170 | 6071 | 7964 | 7866 |
| 7 | 7 | 6 | 1 | 2634 | 1750 | 2268 | 2884 | 3491 | 3688 | 2054 | 1696 | 1455 | 3705 |

**TABLE 20.14**  REGRESSION COEFFICIENTS FOR THE REGRESSION OF READING TIME ON SP, WORDS, AND NEW FOR EACH OF THE 10 PARTICIPANTS

| Participant | SP | WORDS | NEW |
|---|---|---|---|
| 1 | .23124 | .39103 | .22161 |
| 2 | .30533 | .43415 | .34637 |
| 3 | .20637 | .40360 | −.25294 |
| 4 | .48300 | .50203 | −.27683 |
| 5 | −.06210 | .28778 | .92680 |
| 6 | 1.10982 | .80850 | −.23336 |
| 7 | .25448 | .57498 | .79643 |
| 8 | −.33147 | .11341 | .33124 |
| 9 | .66786 | .50078 | .16320 |
| 10 | .46921 | .56964 | −.50621 |
| Mean | .33337 | .45859 | .15163 |
| SE | .12417 | .05855 | .14982 |
| t | 2.6849 | 7.8329 | 1.0121 |

We also pointed out in Chapter 19 that the approach to repeated-measures regression that we describe above gives equal weight to the regression coefficients for each participant. If the predictors take on different values for different participants or if there are missing data, the multilevel modeling procedures cited in Chapter 19 should be considered.

## 20.11 CONCLUDING REMARKS

In Chapter 20, we extended many of the ideas that we first developed with bivariate regression to the case of two or more predictors. This has allowed us to address important issues within the regression framework, including the ability to detect and describe curvilinearity and interactions. It has also forced us to be more precise about what we can conclude from measures such as the regression coefficients and the coefficient of multiple determination. We have tried to spell out the virtues and limitations of these measures.

In the next and final chapter of this book, we will further extend the regression framework to deal with qualitative categorical variables. To this point, the only qualitative predictors we have used in regression have been those that can take on only two values, such as sex. However, when a qualitative variable has more than two levels, it cannot simply be represented in a regression analysis by a single predictor variable that takes on more than two values. Adequate coding of a $k$-level categorical variable requires $k − 1$ predictors.

When confronted with a mix of continuous and categorical predictors, some researchers have adopted the strategy of transforming the continuous variables into categorical variables—presumably so that they can deal with them by conducting ANOVAs. We strongly argue against arbitrarily categorizing continuous variables, because we believe that this approach is wasteful of data and can be misleading. Once we develop the appropriate coding, we will be able to deal with both quantitative and qualitative variables within the multiple regression framework.

## KEY CONCEPTS

multiple regression

standardized regression coefficient (beta coefficient)

multiple correlation coefficient, $R$

adjusted or shrunken $R^2$

standard error of estimate

$SS_{residual}$

tolerance

capitalization on chance

partial $F$ test

power calculations

backward elimination

specification errors

trend analysis

interaction

influential data point

Cook's distance

unstandardized partial slope coefficient

unstandardized regression coefficient

$R^2$, the coefficient of multiple determination

$R$ as a positively biased statistic

$SS_{regression}$

multicollinearity

variance inflation factor (VIF)

cross validation

conditional mean of $Y$ at $X$

forward selection

stepwise regression

centering

additive model

outlier

leverage

## EXERCISES

**20.1** In a visual "search" experiment, a subject is presented with a display containing an array of letters and makes a response when he or she detects the presence of a specific "target letter" that was specified beforehand. Arrays can differ in the number of letters they contain and (because of differences in brightness and contrast or the presence of visual "noise") how difficult it is to identify the letters. We simulated the results of such an experiment in which number of letters and identification difficulty were varied orthogonally, using the model

$$\text{Time} = 400 + 30 \times \text{Number} + 2 \times \text{Diff} + \varepsilon$$

where Number is the number of letters in the array (2, 4, 6, or 8), Diff stands for identification difficulty (10 or 20 units), and $\varepsilon$ is a number selected randomly from a normal population with mean $= 0$ and standard deviation $= 40$ to generate the 24 cases in the following table:

| Time | 493 | 504 | 483 | 508 | 573 | 515 | 533 | 490 | 614 | 623 | 585 | 542 |
|--------|-----|-----|-----|-----|-----|-----|-----|-----|-----|-----|-----|-----|
| Number | 2 | 2 | 2 | 2 | 2 | 2 | 4 | 4 | 4 | 4 | 4 | 4 |
| Diff | 10 | 10 | 10 | 20 | 20 | 20 | 10 | 10 | 10 | 20 | 20 | 20 |

| Time | 559 | 576 | 618 | 598 | 686 | 656 | 705 | 602 | 570 | 672 | 629 | 709 |
|--------|-----|-----|-----|-----|-----|-----|-----|-----|-----|-----|-----|-----|
| Number | 6 | 6 | 6 | 6 | 6 | 6 | 8 | 8 | 8 | 8 | 8 | 8 |
| Diff | 10 | 10 | 10 | 20 | 20 | 20 | 10 | 10 | 10 | 20 | 20 | 20 |

(a) Find the summary statistics and correlation matrix for these data.

(b) Regress Time on Number and Diff. Are the effects of Number and Diff significant at $\alpha = .05$? Are these significance tests equivalent to the tests of the Number and Diff main effects in a standard ANOVA? Perform an ANOVA on Time using the factors Number and Diff and compare the results with those that follow from the regression.

(c) What are the estimates of the parameters of the model that are obtained from the regression? How do these compare with the actual parameter values ($\beta_0 = 400$, $\beta_1 = 30$, and $\beta_2 = 2$) that were used to generate the data? What are the 95% and 99% confidence intervals for $\beta_0$, $\beta_1$, and $\beta_2$? We should emphasize that, in the real world, we do not know what the parameters of the model are or even the form of the model. We use the sample data to infer something about the underlying model.

**20.2** Given the following data set:

| $Y$ | $X_1$ | $X_2$ |
|-----|-------|-------|
| 4   | 2     | -2    |
| 1   | -1    | -1    |
| 5   | -2    | 0     |
| 7   | -1    | 1     |
| 12  | 2     | 2     |

(a) Verify that $X_1$ and $X_2$ are uncorrelated.

(b) Verify that, in this case ($X_1$ and $X_2$ uncorrelated), $R_{Y.12}^2 = r_{Y1}^2 + r_{Y2}^2$.

(c) For this data set, what is the relation between (i) the regression coefficient for $X_1$ when $Y$ is regressed on $X_1$ alone and (ii) the regression coefficient for $X_1$ when $Y$ is regressed on both $X_1$ and $X_2$? Is this true in general? What is the relation between the standard errors of $b_1$ in (i) and (ii)?

**20.3** For the following 17 cases:

| $X_1$ | $X_2$ | $Y$ |
|-------|-------|-----|
| 2     | 5     | 42, 65 |
| 2     | 6     | 55 |
| 3     | 5     | 68, 55, 65 |
| 3     | 6     | 79, 59, 74, 67 |
| 3     | 7     | 97, 75, 80, 78 |
| 4     | 6     | 83, 72 |
| 4     | 7     | 92 |

(a) Fit the model $Y = \beta_0 + \beta_1 X_1 + \beta_2 X_2 + \varepsilon$.

(b) Test for lack of fit. That is, test for nonlinearity using "pure error" as the error term.

(c) From the data, does it seem that both $X_1$ and $X_2$ should be included in the regression model?

**20.4** Calculate the adjusted $R^2$ given the following information:

(a) $R^2_{Y.1234} = .50,$    $N = 10$

(b) $R^2_{Y.1234} = .50,$    $N = 40$

(c) $R^2_{Y.1234} = .50,$    $N = 200$

(d) $R^2_{Y.12} \phantom{xx} = .30,$    $N = 40$

**20.5** In an experiment designed to determine the effects of drug dosage on performance, the following data are obtained:

| Dosage in milligrams | | | |
|---|---|---|---|
| 10 | 20 | 30 | 40 |
| 6.8 | 10.4 | 10.7 | 8.9 |
| 2.8 | 6.4 | 14.4 | 12.5 |
| 5.2 | 13.1 | 15.9 | 12.7 |
| 4.8 | 8.7 | 10.6 | 7.4 |
| | 12.4 | | 8.5 |
| | 7.2 | | |

(a) Do an ANOVA to test the effect of dosage on performance.

(b) Using multiple regression, perform a trend analysis on the same data.

(c) Find the best-fitting polynomial equations of degrees 2 and 3; that is, of the form

$$\hat{Y} = b_0 + b_1 X + b_2 X^2$$

that expresses performance as a function of dosage.

**20.6** Consider 15 cases selected randomly from the same population:

| | | | | | | | | | | | | | | | |
|---|---|---|---|---|---|---|---|---|---|---|---|---|---|---|---|
| $Y$ | .15 | .09 | −3.36 | −1.34 | −.69 | −1.15 | −.51 | −1.47 | −.38 | .78 | −3.60 | −2.40 | 1.46 | −.71 | 1.42 |
| $X_1$ | .07 | 1.08 | −.40 | −1.25 | −1.31 | 2.16 | 2.26 | 3.69 | −1.44 | −1.80 | −.76 | −2.69 | −1.33 | −.45 | .09 |
| $X_2$ | .27 | .51 | −.78 | −2.92 | −.69 | −.31 | −.83 | −.82 | .34 | .23 | −.60 | 2.33 | .51 | .10 | .72 |
| $X_3$ | .66 | 1.61 | 1.38 | −2.38 | .20 | −.60 | −.16 | −.02 | 2.60 | 2.56 | 2.29 | 4.14 | .20 | −.76 | .07 |

(a) Using only the first four cases, regress $Y$ on $X_1$, $X_2$, and $X_3$. What is the value of $R_{Y.123}$? Comment on why $R_{Y.123}$ must take on the value that it does here.

(b) Use the regression equation obtained in (a) to predict the values of $Y$ for each of the 15 cases.

(c) Find the correlations between the scores predicted in (b) and the actual $Y$ values (i) for the first four cases and (ii) for the remaining 11 cases. Comment on the difference between these correlations.

**20.7** In the following data set, $Y$ is a measure of verbal achievement for students in elementary school, $X_1$ and $X_2$ are measures of school and teacher quality, and $X_3$ and $X_4$ are measures of student and parent background:

| Y | $X_1$ | $X_2$ | $X_3$ | $X_4$ | Y | $X_1$ | $X_2$ | $X_3$ | $X_4$ |
|------|------|------|-------|------|------|------|------|-------|------|
| 7.4 | 7.6 | 5.32 | 17.2 | 2.9 | 4.6 | 4.2 | 4.70 | −2.9 | 1.2 |
| 5.3 | 5.8 | 4.88 | −1.7 | 2.0 | 7.0 | 5.0 | 4.72 | 10.9 | 2.2 |
| 7.3 | 5.9 | 5.14 | 22.3 | 6.9 | 6.9 | 4.4 | 4.90 | 14.8 | 1.4 |
| 8.1 | 5.8 | 5.15 | 24.2 | 6.5 | 6.6 | 5.3 | 5.16 | 9.0 | 3.2 |
| 7.4 | 6.1 | 5.08 | 16.3 | 3.0 | 4.5 | 5.4 | 5.04 | −6.1 | 1.2 |
| 6.7 | 4.1 | 4.32 | 16.2 | 4.5 | 7.9 | 6.3 | 5.01 | 20.6 | 6.8 |
| 8.3 | 5.0 | 4.98 | 22.7 | 7.7 | 6.4 | 7.1 | 5.00 | 12.7 | 4.2 |
| 6.7 | 4.9 | 5.00 | 9.8 | 2.5 | 6.3 | 5.0 | 4.96 | −1.1 | 1.7 |
| 8.2 | 6.2 | 5.32 | 19.9 | 6.5 | 8.6 | 5.4 | 5.11 | 25.1 | 8.6 |
| 7.4 | 4.8 | 5.60 | 10.0 | 1.0 | 8.2 | 4.7 | 5.10 | 22.8 | 7.7 |

(a) Do the school and teacher measures contribute to the predictability of $Y$? Do the student and parent measures? Consider regression equations containing different combinations of predictors in arriving at your answer.

(b) Perform a stepwise regression using one of the standard packages. Do you think that the regression equation identified by the stepwise regression is a reasonable explanatory model of the situation?

(c) Is there a joint effect of the school and teacher measures?

**20.8** In a multiple regression analysis, we wish to reject the hypothesis that all population regression coefficients are equal to zero, using $\alpha = .05$. How many cases do we need to have a power of .80 if we have six predictor variables and expect an $R^2$ of .20?

**20.9** We conduct a multiple regression analysis on data from an observational study with four predictor variables and $N = 40$. We find that adding variable $X_4$ to the other three predictors increases $R^2$ from .21 to .27. Can we reject the null hypothesis that the coefficient of variable $X_4$ has the value 0 in the population? How many cases do we need to have a power of .80 for rejecting the null hypothesis if we use $\alpha = .05$?

**20.10** (a) A researcher is interested in relating measures of mother–child attachment to measures of externalization and criticism obtained from a series of interviews. A regression of the attachment measure on both externalization and criticism yields significant $t$ tests for both the predictor variables. What can be concluded?

(b) The researcher then decides to determine whether the joint effect of externalization and criticism is an important predictor of attachment. She creates a new variable by multiplying the externalization and criticism measures for each case. She then regresses attachment on the externalization and criticism measures as well as on the new variable. The regression now shows that none of the $t$ tests for the three predictors are significant. Is this an appropriate way to assess whether the joint effect of externalization and criticism is an important predictor of attachment? Why or why not? What is the most likely reason that the $t$ tests for the coefficients of externalization and criticism are not significant in the second regression even though they were significant in the first regression, described in part (a)? Considering the results of the two regressions together, what can be concluded?

**20.11** Given the Royer data set, use both ANOVA and multiple regression to perform a trend analysis that will help you understand the functional relation between subtraction accuracy and grade. Determine whether there are significant linear, quadratic, and cubic components and indicate what these suggest. Does there seem to be any additional nonlinearity in the relation?

**20.12** Using the *Seasons* data for men aged 20–65 years who have BMI scores less than or equal to 40:

(a) Determine whether there is a relation between BMI and total cholesterol (TC).

(b) Is there evidence of an interaction between age and BMI in a multiple regression with TC as the dependent variable?

# Chapter 21

## Regression With Categorical and Quantitative Variables: The General Linear Model

### 21.1 INTRODUCTION

In this final chapter, we consider regression with categorical variables that have levels that differ qualitatively from one another. Examples of such variables are sex, with levels female and male; diagnosed mental illness, with levels of schizophrenia, depression, and anxiety disorder; and treatment condition, with levels defined by the different therapies. Our development of regression to this point has focused on quantitative predictor and criterion variables. However, qualitative categorical variables can also be incorporated into regression analyses, providing us with a general and powerful framework within which many of the analyses that we have previously considered, including the analysis of variance (ANOVA) and analysis of covariance (ANCOVA), can be considered as special cases. Learning about this framework can both increase our understanding of how different kinds of analyses are related to one another and allow us to deal with data from designs that cannot be handled easily by the standard ANOVA approach.

In an ANOVA, all factors are treated as though they are qualitative categorical variables that are independent of one another. It is this independence or orthogonality that makes it possible for the ANOVA to partition the variability in factorial designs into distinct, nonoverlapping components associated with main effects and interactions. However, the system breaks down if there is nonorthogonality; when the cell frequencies are unequal, the inequality introduces correlations among the factors, and these correlations cause the variance components associated with the different effects to overlap (see Section 12.4). It is more natural to consider nonorthogonal factorial designs within the multiple regression framework, in which variables are generally correlated with one another. We deal with nonorthogonal ANOVA designs in Section 21.3 and then reconsider within the multiple regression framework several other types of analyses that we discussed previously. However, we first consider how qualitative categorical variables may be coded so that they can be included in regression analyses.

It is important to distinguish between quantitative and qualitative categorical variables in regression. Suppose we have a categorical variable with six levels that refer to qualitatively

different treatment conditions, and use the numbers 1–6 to label these treatments. If we performed a regression analysis that used this variable as a predictor, we would be treating it as a quantitative variable. Such coding implies that the treatment at level 3 is three times "as large" as the treatment at level 1, and the treatment at level 4 is twice "as large" as the one at level 2. However, if the treatments are qualitatively different from one another, we do not want a coding system that imposes relative sizes on the treatments; rather, we want a system that simply specifies that the treatments are *different* from one another. As we shall see, for a factor with six levels, 5 *df* are needed to specify these qualitative differences, and consequently five coding variables will be required to do the job.

In practice, we almost never have to generate these coding variables ourselves. Rather, we let the software packages do it for us in their ANOVA or GLM (general linear model) modules. Our goal here is simply to describe how the coding of categorical variables may be done because this allows greater insight into the analyses.

## 21.2 ONE-FACTOR DESIGNS

### 21.2.1 Coding Categorical Variables

Any qualitative categorical variable can be coded by defining one or more **dummy** or **indicator variables** that take on numerical values. These numbers are not measures of the categories; rather, they are best thought of as labels that together specify category membership. As we discussed in Chapter 19, the coding is particularly simple when a categorical variable has only two levels—as is the case, for example, for the variable sex. If $A$ has only two levels, $X$ could take on any value at one level and any different value at the other level. The overall test of the regression of the dependent variable $Y$ on the dummy variable $X$ is exactly equivalent to the ANOVA $F$ test for the categorical variable.

To be more specific, if we regress $Y$ on $X$, the regression line must pass through the points $(1, \overline{Y}_{.1})$ and $(2, \overline{Y}_{.2})$ as can be seen in Fig. 21.1. This is because the line is defined as the line that minimizes the mean-squared deviations of the $Y$s, and the group means minimize the mean-squared deviations in each of the groups. Because the regression line passes though the two group means, it accounts for all the variability in the group means, so $SS_{\text{regression}}$ must equal the between-group variability, $SS_A$. Also, $SS_{\text{residual}}$, the variability unaccounted for by the regression, must equal $SS_{S/A}$.

However, if the factor $A$ has more than two levels, regression on a single dummy variable will not, in general, account for all of $SS_A$. Consider what happens with three levels: Panel (a) of Table 21.1 presents scores at levels $A_1$, $A_2$, and $A_3$ of the factor $A$. If we code $A$ with a single dummy variable, $X_1$, that takes on the values 1, 2, and 3, as in panel (b) of the table, the points that represent the group means in the space defined by $X_1$ and $Y$ will be $(1, \overline{Y}_{.1})$, $(2, \overline{Y}_{.2})$, and $(3, \overline{Y}_{.3})$—see panel (a) of Fig. 21.2. In general, these three points will not be perfectly fit by a straight line. Therefore, if $Y$ is regressed on $X_1$, the regression will not, in general, account for all the variability in the group means, and $SS_{\text{regression}}$ will be less than $SS_A$. However, we can account for all of $SS_A$ if we define an additional dummy variable, $X_2$, that is not perfectly correlated with $X_1$—for example, the variable that takes on the values given in panel (b) of Table 21.1. Now, if we represent the three group means in the three-dimensional space defined by $Y$, $X_1$, and $X_2$, as in panel (b) of Fig. 21.2, it is apparent that they can be perfectly fit by a regression plane. Therefore, when $Y$ is regressed

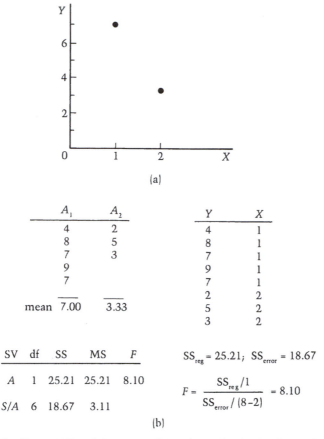

**Fig. 21.1**  (a) Plot of the means of $A$ against $X$ for the data in panel (b). Note that the two points representing group means can be fit perfectly by a straight line. (b) Data and results of ANOVA and multiple regression.

on both dummy variables, all the between-group variability will be accounted for by the regression, so that $SS_{\text{regression}} = SS_A$, and the $F$ test for the overall regression of $Y$ on $X_1$ and $X_2$ is exactly equivalent to the ANOVA $F$ test for the effect of the categorical factor, $A$.

In general, it will take as many independent dummy variables to code a factor as the number of degrees of freedom associated with it, so that a categorical variable with six levels will require five dummy variables. The only requirement on these dummy variables is that they be **linearly independent**—that is, none of them may be obtained as a linear combination of the others. If any dummy variable can be expressed as a linear combination of the other dummy variables, it is redundant and cannot contribute anything to the specification of the categories.

## 21.2.2 Effect and Dummy[1] Coding

In this section, we discuss effect and dummy coding, two of the many possible ways to code categorical variables. Both coding methods allow us to specify group membership

**TABLE 21.1** REGRESSION ON DUMMY VARIABLES FOR A ONE-FACTOR DESIGN

### (a) Data and Results of Standard ANOVA for a One-Factor Design

| | $A_1$ | $A_2$ | $A_3$ |
|---|---|---|---|
| | 4 | 2 | 4 |
| | 8 | 5 | 5 |
| | 7 | 3 | 3 |
| | 9 | | 6 |
| | 7 | | |
| $\overline{Y}_{\cdot j} = $ | 7.00 | 3.33 | 4.50 |

$\overline{Y}_U = (7 + 3.33 + 4.50)/3 = 4.94$

| SV | df | SS | MS | F |
|---|---|---|---|---|
| A | 2 | 28.583 | 14.292 | 5.435 |
| S/A | 9 | 23.667 | 2.630 | |

### (b) Dummy Variable Coding and Some Statistics Obtained From the Regressions of $Y$ on $X_1$ and $X_2$, on $X_{E1}$ and $X_{E2}$, and on $X_{D1}$ and $X_{D2}$

| | Y | $X_1$ | $X_2$ | $X_{E1}$ | $X_{E2}$ | $X_{D1}$ | $X_{D2}$ |
|---|---|---|---|---|---|---|---|
| $A_1$ | 4 | 1 | 0 | 1 | 0 | 1 | 0 |
| | 8 | 1 | 0 | 1 | 0 | 1 | 0 |
| | 7 | 1 | 0 | 1 | 0 | 1 | 0 |
| | 9 | 1 | 0 | 1 | 0 | 1 | 0 |
| | 7 | 1 | 0 | 1 | 0 | 1 | 0 |
| $A_2$ | 2 | 2 | 3 | 0 | 1 | 0 | 1 |
| | 5 | 2 | 3 | 0 | 1 | 0 | 1 |
| | 3 | 2 | 3 | 0 | 1 | 0 | 1 |
| $A_3$ | 4 | 3 | 1 | −1 | −1 | 0 | 0 |
| | 5 | 3 | 1 | −1 | −1 | 0 | 0 |
| | 3 | 3 | 1 | −1 | −1 | 0 | 0 |
| | 6 | 3 | 1 | −1 | −1 | 0 | 0 |

The statistics for the regression of $Y$ on $X_1$ and $X_2$, on $X_{E1}$ and $X_{E2}$, or on $X_{D1}$ and $X_{D2}$ are $R = .740$; $SS_{regression} = 28.583$; $SS_{residual} = 23.667$; $F = MS_{regression}/MS_{residual} = 5.435$. The regression coefficients based on effects coding are:

$$b_{E0} = \overline{Y}_U = 4.94, b_{E1} = \overline{Y}_{\cdot 1} - \overline{Y}_U = 2.06, \quad \text{and} \quad b_{E2} = \overline{Y}_{\cdot 2} - \overline{Y}_U = -1.61$$

and the regression coefficients based on dummy coding are:

$$b_{D0} = \overline{Y}_{\cdot 3} = 4.50, b_{D1} = \overline{Y}_{\cdot 1} - \overline{Y}_{\cdot 3} = 2.50, \quad \text{and} \quad b_{D2} = \overline{Y}_{\cdot 2} - \overline{Y}_{\cdot 3} = -1.17$$

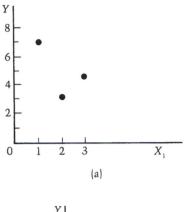

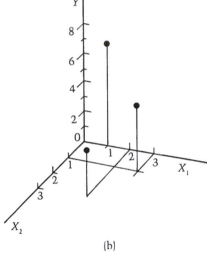

**Fig. 21.2** (a) Plot of the means of $A$ against $X_1$ for the data in Table 21.1. In general, the points representing the three means cannot be fit perfectly by a straight line. (b) Plot of the means of $A$ against $X_1$ and $X_2$. The points representing the three means can always be fit by a plane.

so that a regression of the dependent variable on the dummy variables will produce an analysis identical to the ANOVA. The only difference between them is that the regression coefficients produced by the two coding systems have different interpretations.

***Effect Coding.***    In discussing ANOVA as a special case of multiple regression, we may find it useful to consider the type of dummy variable coding called **effect coding** because, as we show below, it produces regression coefficients that estimate the ANOVA effects $\alpha_1, \alpha_2, \ldots, \alpha_{a-1}$, where $\alpha_j = \mu_j - \mu$. Effect coding represents group membership with dummy variables that contain 1's, 0's, and −1's as illustrated by variables $X_{E1}$ and $X_{E2}$ in panel (b) of Table 21.1. Dummy variables for effect coding are defined as follows:

$$X_{Ej} = 1 \text{ for scores at level } A_j$$
$$= -1 \text{ for scores at some arbitrary level of } A, \text{ here } A_3$$
$$= 0 \text{ otherwise}$$

Because there are three levels of $A$ in Table 21.1, we require two dummy variables to account for all the between-group variability. The coding of $X_{E1}$ and $X_{E2}$ is presented in panel (b) of Table 21.1. As can also be seen there, the regression of $Y$ on $X_{E1}$ and $X_{E2}$ produces a value of $SS_{\text{regression}}$ that is equal to the $SS_A$ obtained from the standard ANOVA, and an overall $F$ statistic for the regression that is equal to the ANOVA $F$.

We can readily find the regression coefficients. As we have just stated, if we use enough dummy variables, regressing on them must account for all the between-group variability. Consequently, the scores predicted by the regression equation for each of the groups must be the group means. Therefore, for $A_1$, we have $\hat{Y} = \overline{Y}_{.1}$, $X_{E1} = 1$ and $X_{E2} = 0$. Substituting into the regression equation that predicts $Y$ from $X_{E1}$ and $X_{E2}$, $\hat{Y} = b_{E0} + b_{E1}X_{E1} + b_{E2}X_{E2}$, we obtain

$$\overline{Y}_{.1} = b_{E0} + b_{E1}(1) + b_{E2}(0) = b_{E0} + b_{E1} \tag{21.1}$$

Similarly, for $A_2$ and $A_3$, respectively, we have

$$\overline{Y}_{.2} = b_{E0} + b_{E1}(0) + b_{E2}(1) = b_{E0} + b_{E2} \tag{21.2}$$

and

$$\overline{Y}_{.3} = b_{E0} + b_{E1}(-1) + b_{E2}(-1) = b_{E0} - b_{E1} - b_{E2} \tag{21.3}$$

Adding Equations 21.1–21.3, we obtain $3b_{E0} = \overline{Y}_{.1} + \overline{Y}_{.2} + \overline{Y}_{.3}$, so that

$$b_{E0} = \frac{\overline{Y}_{.1} + \overline{Y}_{.2} + \overline{Y}_{.3}}{3} = \overline{Y}_U$$

Here, $\overline{Y}_U$ is the unweighted average of the group means. If there are equal numbers of scores in each of the groups, $\overline{Y}_U$ will equal $\overline{Y}_{..}$, the grand mean of all the scores.

We can now write the coefficients of the dummy variables as deviations from the unweighted mean of the group means. Substituting $b_{E0} = \overline{Y}_U$ into Equations 21.1 and 21.2, and solving, we obtain the formulas and numerical results for $b_{E1}$ and $b_{E2}$ that are presented in panel (b) of Table 21.1. Note that for equal-$n$ designs, the regression coefficients correspond exactly to the estimated main effect components of the ANOVA, the $\hat{\alpha}_j$'s. That is, because $\overline{Y}_{.j} = \hat{\mu}_j$ and $\overline{Y}_{..} = \hat{\mu}$,

$$b_{E1} = \overline{Y}_{.1} - \overline{Y}_{..} = \hat{\mu}_1 - \hat{\mu} = \hat{\alpha}_1$$

and

$$b_{E2} = \overline{Y}_{.2} - \overline{Y}_{..} = \hat{\mu}_2 - \hat{\mu} = \hat{\alpha}_2$$

Furthermore, because of the requirement that $\sum \alpha_j = 0$, $\hat{\alpha}_3$ can be found as

$$\hat{\alpha}_3 = -\hat{\alpha}_1 - \hat{\alpha}_2 = -b_{E1} - b_{E2}$$

***Dummy Coding.*** A second way to code categorical variables is to use **dummy coding**, for which the indicator variables only take on the values 0 and 1, as illustrated by $X_{D1}$ and $X_{D2}$ in panel (b) of Table 21.1. For dummy coding, the dummy variables are defined as

$$X_{Dj} = 1 \text{ for scores at level } A_j, \quad \text{and}$$
$$= 0 \text{ otherwise}$$

Note that because we only need $a - 1$ dummy variables to code $a$ groups, one group, referred to as the **reference group**, will receive 0s on all the dummy variables.

Because there are three levels of $A$ in the current example, we require two dummy variables to account for all the between-group variability. Scores at $A_1$ receive a 1 on $X_{D1}$ and a 0 on $X_{D2}$; scores at $A_2$ receive a 0 on $X_{D1}$ and a 1 on $X_{D2}$; and scores at $A_3$ receive values of 0 on both $X_{D1}$ and $X_{D2}$. As we can see in panel (b) of Table 21.1, the regression of $Y$ on $X_{D1}$ and $X_{D2}$ also produces a value of $SS_{\text{regression}}$ equal to the $SS_A$ obtained from the standard ANOVA. Although the variability accounted for by the regression is the same whether we use dummy or effect coding, the regression coefficients are different. If we use dummy coding, the intercept, $b_{D0}$, takes on the value of the mean of the reference group; that is, the group that has 0s on all the indicator variables. The regression coefficients for each of the dummy variables, $b_{D1}$ and $b_{D2}$, take on values equal to the difference between the group coded 1 on the dummy variable and the mean of the reference group. We can see this by noting again that because the regression accounts for all the between-group variability, the prediction for each score will be its group mean. For example, for scores at $A_1$, we have $\hat{Y} = \overline{Y}_{\cdot 1}$. Substituting $\hat{Y} = \overline{Y}_{\cdot 1}$, $X_{D1} = 1$, and $X_{D2} = 0$ into the equation for the regression of $Y$ on $X_{D1}$ and $X_{D2}$, $\hat{Y} = b_{D0} + b_{D1}X_{D1} + b_{D2}X_{D2}$, we obtain

$$\overline{Y}_{\cdot 1} = b_{D0} + b_{D1}(1) + b_{D2}(0) = b_{D0} + b_{D1}$$

Similarly, for scores at $A_2$, we have

$$\overline{Y}_{\cdot 2} = b_{D0} + b_{D1}(0) + b_{D2}(1) = b_{D0} + b_{D2}$$

For the scores at the last level of $A$, each dummy variable has the value 0 so that

$$\overline{Y}_{\cdot 3} = b_{D0} + b_{D1}(0) + b_{D2}(0) = b_{D0}$$

The last equation gives us $b_{D0} = \overline{Y}_{\cdot 3}$, and substitution into the two equations preceding it yields the formulas for the other two coefficients that are found (together with the numerical results) in panel (b) of Table 21.1.

Dummy coding would be particularly useful if the design contained a control group. If so, we could let the control group serve as the reference group, and the regression coefficients would then directly reflect the treatment-control mean differences. There are many other ways to code categorical variables. For example, categorical variables could be coded such that regression coefficients took on the values of contrasts of possible interest. Detailed discussions of these methods may be found in sources such as Cohen and Cohen (1983).

As described previously, although it is important to understand how categorical variables can be represented in regression, we rarely have to code the categorical variables ourselves—we can usually let the standard software packages produce the desired dummy variables for us. For example, once we have specified that we have a categorical factor, the GLM module in SYSTAT 10 allows us to choose whether we wish it to use effect or dummy coding. On the other hand, the GLM module in SPSS 10 does not provide a choice;

it simply uses dummy coding. This does not present any particular problem for us, but we should be aware what the program is doing if we try to interpret the parameter estimates.

## 21.3 REGRESSION ANALYSES AND FACTORIAL DESIGNS

In Section 21.2, we saw how any categorical variable can be coded by a set of dummy variables and that a multiple regression analysis that uses these dummy variables as predictors provides all of the information, and more, that can be obtained from a one-factor ANOVA. In Section 21.3, we extend this discussion to multifactor designs, first considering orthogonal designs and then the issues that arise in analyzing data from nonorthogonal or unbalanced (unequal-$n$) designs.

### 21.3.1 Orthogonal Designs

A regression analysis of a factorial design can be performed if both the factors and their interactions are coded by sets of dummy variables. Panel (a) of Table 21.2 contains data from a $3 \times 3$ design with factors $A$ and $C$ (note that we use $C$ rather than $B$ to refer to the second factor because of the plethora of $b$s already in the chapter), and panel (c) contains the results of an ANOVA on the data. Panel (b) contains the sets of effect dummy variables that code the design. Each set of dummy variables has as many members as the corresponding sources of variance have degrees of freedom. $A$ and $C$ are coded as though each was the only factor in the design, and the set of four dummy variables that code the $AC$ interaction is obtained by multiplying each dummy variable in the $A$ set by each one in the $C$ set. Together, the eight dummy variables code membership in the nine cells of the design.

With effect coding, the dummy variables within any one of the $A$, $C$, and $AC$ sets are correlated. However, if the cell frequencies are all equal, the dummy variables in any set are uncorrelated with all the dummy variables in each of the other sets; therefore, the sums of squares associated with the different sets do not overlap. Let's use the notation $R_{Y.A}$, $R_{Y.AC}$, and $R_{Y.A,AC}$ to represent the multiple correlation coefficients that result when $Y$ is regressed on the sets of dummy variables that code $A$, $AC$, and both $A$ and $AC$, respectively. Then, because the sets of dummy variables corresponding to $A$, $C$, and $AC$ are uncorrelated, we have

$$R_{Y.A,C,AC}^2 = R_{Y.A}^2 + R_{Y.C}^2 + R_{Y.AC}^2$$

Multiplying each of the squared correlations by $SS_Y$, we have

$$SS_{\text{Between cell}} = SS_A + SS_C + SS_{AC}$$

Because we have enough coding variables to account for all the between-subject variability, $SS_{\text{error}} = SS_{\text{residual}} = (1 - R_{Y.A,C,AC}^2)SS_Y$, and tests of the $A$ and $C$ main effects and the $AC$ interaction, respectively, are provided by

$$F = \frac{R_{Y.A}^2/(a-1)}{(1 - R_{Y.A,C,AC}^2)/(N - ac)}$$

$$F = \frac{R_{Y.C}^2/(c-1)}{(1 - R_{Y.A,C,AC}^2)/(N - ac)}$$

**TABLE 21.2**   EFFECT CODING FOR AN ORTHOGONAL 3 × 3 DESIGN

(a) Data

|   | $C_1$ | $C_2$ | $C_3$ |
|---|---|---|---|
| $A_1$ | 53 | 88 | 56 |
|  | 51 | 63 | 42 |
| $A_2$ | 55 | 48 | 79 |
|  | 78 | 42 | 50 |
| $A_3$ | 79 | 80 | 69 |
|  | 99 | 92 | 94 |

(b) Dummy Variables Formed by Using Effect Coding

| | | A | | C | | AC | | | |
|---|---|---|---|---|---|---|---|---|---|
| Effect | Y | $X_1$ | $X_2$ | $X_3$ | $X_4$ | $X_5$ | $X_6$ | $X_7$ | $X_8$ |
| $A_1C_1$ | 53 | 1 | 0 | 1 | 0 | 1 | 0 | 0 | 0 |
|  | 51 | 1 | 0 | 1 | 0 | 1 | 0 | 0 | 0 |
| $A_1C_2$ | 88 | 1 | 0 | 0 | 1 | 0 | 0 | 1 | 0 |
|  | 63 | 1 | 0 | 0 | 1 | 0 | 0 | 1 | 0 |
| $A_1C_3$ | 56 | 1 | 0 | −1 | −1 | −1 | 0 | −1 | 0 |
|  | 42 | 1 | 0 | −1 | −1 | −1 | 0 | −1 | 0 |
| $A_2C_1$ | 55 | 0 | 1 | 1 | 0 | 0 | 1 | 0 | 0 |
|  | 78 | 0 | 1 | 1 | 0 | 0 | 1 | 0 | 0 |
| $A_2C_2$ | 48 | 0 | 1 | 0 | 1 | 0 | 0 | 0 | 1 |
|  | 42 | 0 | 1 | 0 | 1 | 0 | 0 | 0 | 1 |
| $A_2C_3$ | 79 | 0 | 1 | −1 | −1 | 0 | −1 | 0 | −1 |
|  | 50 | 0 | 1 | −1 | −1 | 0 | −1 | 0 | −1 |
| $A_3C_1$ | 79 | −1 | −1 | 1 | 0 | −1 | −1 | 0 | 0 |
|  | 99 | −1 | −1 | 1 | 0 | −1 | −1 | 0 | 0 |
| $A_3C_2$ | 80 | −1 | −1 | 0 | 1 | 0 | 0 | −1 | −1 |
|  | 92 | −1 | −1 | 0 | 1 | 0 | 0 | −1 | −1 |
| $A_3C_3$ | 69 | −1 | −1 | −1 | −1 | 1 | 1 | 1 | 1 |
|  | 94 | −1 | −1 | −1 | −1 | 1 | 1 | 1 | 1 |

| SV | df | SS | MS | F |
|---|---|---|---|---|
| A | 2 | 2862.333 | 1431.167 | 7.577 |
| C | 2 | 64.333 | 32.167 | 0.170 |
| AC | 4 | 1399.333 | 349.833 | 1.852 |
| Error | 9 | 1700.000 | 188.889 | |

and

$$F = \frac{R^2_{Y.AC}/(a-1)(c-1)}{(1 - R^2_{Y.A,C,AC})/(N - ac)}$$

As can be seen in Table 21.2, these test statistics have exactly the same values as the ANOVA $F$s for $A$, $C$, and $AC$.

To carry out the ANOVA, we need only code each factor with a single variable that labels each level with a distinct symbol, such as 1, 2, and 3, then use the ANOVA or GLM module of a standard statistical package to analyze the data. If the variable is specified as a categorical variable or factor, the software creates the dummy variables and performs the analyses as described. The programs differ somewhat in what must be specified in their GLM modules. For example, SPSS 10 GLM assumes that each variable listed as a factor is categorical; continuous variables must be listed as covariates. On the other hand, in SYSTAT 10 GLM, independent variables may be either continuous or categorical; we must specify that a variable is categorical or else it will be treated as though it was continuous.

## 21.3.2 Nonorthogonal Designs

In Chapter 12, we discussed some of the difficulties that stem from the fact that, in nonorthogonal factorial designs, the between-cell variability cannot be neatly partitioned into nonoverlapping components associated with the main effects and interactions. Panel (a) of Table 21.3 contains the data for a nonorthogonal design with factors $A$ and $C$, and panel (b) contains the effect coding for the design. Because of the unequal cell frequencies, the sets of dummy variables that code the $A$, $C$, and $AC$ effects are no longer uncorrelated. Therefore, in general,

$$R^2_{Y.A,C,AC} \neq R^2_{Y.A} + R^2_{Y.C} + R^2_{Y.AC}$$

because the variabilities associated with $A$, $C$, and $AC$ overlap, as represented by Fig. 21.3. Multiple regression analyses allows a variety of possible adjustments for this overlap. For example, in considering the $A$ effect,

1. We may view $SS_A$ as the variability that is uniquely associated with $A$. This is the variability in $A$ that does not overlap with the other effects in the design and is represented by area $t$ in the upper circle of Fig. 21.3. It can be obtained from

$$SS_{A|C,AC} = \left(R^2_{Y.A,C,AC} - R^2_{Y.C,AC}\right)SS_Y$$

   As we discussed in Chapter 12, when we adjust the sum of squares by adjusting for the variability due to all the other main or interaction effects, we obtain what are called **Type III sums of squares**. This is the default for most of the standard statistics packages.

2. We may decide to adjust the $A$ effect only for the other main effect $C$, yielding the variability represented by areas $t$ and $w$ in the upper circle of Fig. 21.3,

$$SS_{A|C} = \left(R^2_{Y.A,C} - R^2_{Y.C}\right)SS_Y$$

   or

3. We may decide not to adjust for the contributions of the other effects at all. This yields

$$SS_A = R^2_{Y.A}SS_Y$$

Summarizing, if we have a nonorthogonal ANOVA with factors $A$ and $C$, we can obtain for the $A$ main effect, $SS_A$, which is the sum of squares for $A$ ignoring overlap with $C$ and $AC$; $SS_{A|C}$, which is the sum of squares for $A$ adjusted for the $C$ main effect; and $SS_{A|C,AC}$, which is the sum of squares for $A$ adjusted for both the $C$ main effect and the $AC$ interaction.

**TABLE 21.3**   EFFECT CODING FOR AN ORTHOGONAL $3 \times 3$ DESIGN

### (a) Data

|        | $C_1$ | $C_2$ | $C_3$ |
|--------|-------|-------|-------|
| $A_1$  | 53    | 88    | 56    |
|        | 51    | 63    | 42    |
|        |       | 50    |       |
|        |       | 71    |       |
| $A_2$  | 55    | 48    | 79    |
|        | 78    | 42    | 50    |
|        | 39    |       | 62    |
| $A_3$  | 79    | 80    | 69    |
|        | 99    | 92    | 94    |
|        |       |       | 80    |
|        |       |       | 77    |

### (b) Dummy Variables Formed by Using Effect Coding

| Effect:   | $Y$ | $X_1$ | $X_2$ | $X_3$ | $X_4$ | $X_5$ | $X_6$ | $X_7$ | $X_8$ |
|-----------|-----|-------|-------|-------|-------|-------|-------|-------|-------|
|           |     | \multicolumn{2}{A} | | \multicolumn{2}{C} | | \multicolumn{4}{AC} | | | |
| $A_1C_1$  | 53  | 1     | 0     | 1     | 0     | 1     | 0     | 0     | 0     |
|           | 51  | 1     | 0     | 1     | 0     | 1     | 0     | 0     | 0     |
| $A_1C_2$  | 88  | 1     | 0     | 0     | 1     | 0     | 0     | 1     | 0     |
|           | 63  | 1     | 0     | 0     | 1     | 0     | 0     | 1     | 0     |
|           | 50  | 1     | 0     | 0     | 1     | 0     | 0     | 1     | 0     |
|           | 71  | 1     | 0     | 0     | 1     | 0     | 0     | 1     | 0     |
| $A_1C_3$  | 56  | 1     | 0     | −1    | −1    | −1    | 0     | −1    | 0     |
|           | 42  | 1     | 0     | −1    | −1    | −1    | 0     | −1    | 0     |
| $A_2C_1$  | 55  | 0     | 1     | 1     | 0     | 0     | 1     | 0     | 0     |
|           | 78  | 0     | 1     | 1     | 0     | 0     | 1     | 0     | 0     |
|           | 39  | 0     | 1     | 1     | 0     | 0     | 1     | 0     | 0     |
| $A_2C_2$  | 48  | 0     | 1     | 0     | 1     | 0     | 0     | 0     | 1     |
|           | 42  | 0     | 1     | 0     | 1     | 0     | 0     | 0     | 1     |
| $A_2C_3$  | 79  | 0     | 1     | −1    | −1    | 0     | −1    | 0     | −1    |
|           | 50  | 0     | 1     | −1    | −1    | 0     | −1    | 0     | −1    |
|           | 62  | 0     | 1     | −1    | −1    | 0     | −1    | 0     | −1    |
| $A_3C_1$  | 79  | −1    | −1    | 1     | 0     | −1    | −1    | 0     | 0     |
|           | 99  | −1    | −1    | 1     | 0     | −1    | −1    | 0     | 0     |
| $A_3C_2$  | 80  | −1    | −1    | 0     | 1     | 0     | 0     | −1    | −1    |
|           | 92  | −1    | −1    | 0     | 1     | 0     | 0     | −1    | −1    |
| $A_3C_3$  | 69  | −1    | −1    | −1    | −1    | 1     | 1     | 1     | 1     |
|           | 94  | −1    | −1    | −1    | −1    | 1     | 1     | 1     | 1     |
|           | 80  | −1    | −1    | −1    | −1    | 1     | 1     | 1     | 1     |
|           | 77  | −1    | −1    | −1    | −1    | 1     | 1     | 1     | 1     |

Column groups: $X_1$–$X_2$ under **A**, $X_3$–$X_4$ under **C**, $X_5$–$X_8$ under **AC**.

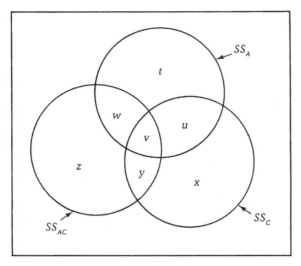

**Fig. 21.3** Partitioning of variability in a nonorthogonal two-factor design.

These sums of squares will all have the same value if the cell frequencies are equal; however, because in nonorthogonal designs the variabilities of the effects may overlap, $SS_A$, $SS_{A|C}$, and $SS_{A|C,AC}$ will generally not be equal. Depending on whether the covariations among the effects are positive or negative, the adjusted sum of squares may be smaller or larger than if there is no adjustment. For the data in Table 21.3, $SS_{A|C,AC} = 4{,}139.42$, $SS_{A|C} = 3{,}609.95$, and $SS_A = 3{,}581.08$.

On what basis are we to decide which, if any, of these sums of squares to use? In Chapter 12, we discussed conditions under which different analyses are appropriate. Here, we review and expand on that discussion. Our view is that the proper analysis depends on the weights that should be given to the levels of the factors in the study. If the variables are manipulated, or if the data in the cells can be viewed as samples from naturally occurring, equal-sized treatment populations, it makes sense to give each cell in the design the same weight, even though chance variations in actual cell frequency may occur. That is, we may plan to have equal cell frequencies, but fail to obtain them because of chance occurrences such as equipment failures or participants failing to show up. In this case, the overall $A$ null hypothesis that is of interest states that the unweighted averages of the $c$ population means at each level of $A$ are equal. That is,

$$\mu_{1.} = \mu_{2.} = \cdots = \mu_{a.}$$

where

$$\mu_{j.} = \frac{1}{c} \sum_k \mu_{jk}$$

is the unweighted mean of the cell means at the $j$th level of $A$.

However, if the cell populations vary systematically in size, we may wish to test hypotheses in which the cell means are weighted according to population size. If we have reliable information about the relative sizes of the cell populations, we can use it to weight the cell means. If we do not have such information, we can use the cell frequencies as weights. In this case, the overall $A$ null hypothesis of interest states that the weighted means of $A$ are equal. That is,

$$\mu_{1*} = \mu_{2*} = \cdots = \mu_{3*}$$

where

$$\mu_{j*} = \frac{1}{n_{j.}} \sum_k n_{jk} \mu_{jk}$$

is the weighted mean of the cell means at the $j$th level of $A$.

It can be shown that adjusting the sums of squares in different ways results in tests of the different hypotheses of interest. Table 21.4 describes three methods of analyzing nonorthogonal factorial designs and indicates the hypotheses tested by each of them. Table 21.5 provides the results of these analyses for the data in Table 21.3. In all three methods, interactions are adjusted for all other effects in the design, resulting in tests of the usual interaction null hypothesis

$$H_0: \mu_{jk} - \mu_{j'k} - \mu_{jk'} + \mu = 0 \quad \text{for all} \quad j, j', k, \text{ and } k'$$

Method 1 adjusts each effect for every other effect in the design. In Method 3, main effect sums of squares are not adjusted for any other effects. In Method 2, adjustments are made only for effects of the same or lower order, so that main effects are adjusted for other main effects, but not for interactions. It can be shown (e.g., Myers & Well, 1995) that Method 1 tests unweighted main effect null hypotheses; therefore, Method 1 is recommended when unequal cell frequencies occur by chance, as is usually the case in experimental designs. Method 3 tests weighted main effect hypotheses and can be useful when cell frequencies are proportional to corresponding population sizes.

The Method 2 approach that is favored by some statisticians (e.g., Cramer & Appelbaum, 1980) corresponds to a hierarchical series of model tests that starts with higher-order effects. On the rationale that main effects are not very meaningful in the presence of an interaction, this approach first tests the interaction by comparing the model

$$Y_{ijk} = \mu + \alpha_j + \gamma_k + (\alpha\gamma)_{jk} + \varepsilon_{ijk}$$

against

$$Y_{ijk} = \mu + \alpha_j + \gamma_k + \varepsilon_{ijk}$$

If there is no interaction, tests of the main effects are then conducted by comparing

$$Y_{ijk} = \mu + \alpha_j + \gamma_k + \varepsilon_{ijk}$$

against

$$Y_{ijk} = \mu + \gamma_k + \varepsilon_{ijk}$$

and

$$Y_{ijk} = \mu + \alpha_j + \gamma_k + \varepsilon_{ijk}$$

against

$$Y_{ijk} = \mu + \alpha_j + \varepsilon_{ijk}$$

**TABLE 21.4**  THREE METHODS FOR ANALYZING NONORTHOGONAL FACTORIAL DESIGNS

| | Method 1: Adjusting for All Main and Interaction Effects | |
|---|---|---|
| SV | df | SS |
| A | $a - 1$ | $SS_{A|C,AC} = \left(R^2_{Y.A,C,AC} - R^2_{Y.C,AC}\right)SS_Y$ |
| C | $c - 1$ | $SS_{C|A,AC} = \left(R^2_{Y.A,C,AC} - R^2_{Y.A,AC}\right)SS_Y$ |
| AC | $(a - 1)(c - 1)$ | $SS_{AC|A,C} = \left(R^2_{Y.A,C,AC} - R^2_{Y.A,C}\right)SS_Y$ |
| Residual | $N - ac$ | $SS_{\text{residual}} = \left(1 - R^2_{Y.A,C,AC}\right)SS_Y$ |

*Hypotheses tested*

$A: \mu_{1.} = \mu_{2.} = \cdots = \mu_{a.}$, where $\mu_{j.} = \frac{1}{c}\sum_k \mu_{jk}$ is the unweighted mean of the population means for the $c$ cells in the $j$th row of $A$

$C: \mu_{.1} = \mu_{.2} = \cdots = \mu_{.c}$, where $\mu_{.k} = \frac{1}{a}\sum_j \mu_{jk}$ is the unweighted mean of the population means for the $a$ cells in the $k$th row of $C$

$AC: \mu_{jk} - \mu_{j'k} - \mu_{jk'} + \mu_{j'k'} = 0$ for all $j, k, j', k'$

*Usage*: This method uses Type III sums of squares to test hypotheses about unweighted column and row means, and will usually be the method of choice when unequal cell frequencies occur by chance. This method is also known as Overall and Spiegel's (1969) Method 1, Yates's (1934) weighted squares of means, and SPSS's classic regression approach.

| | Method 2: Adjusting for the Effects of the Same and Lower Order | |
|---|---|---|
| SV | df | SS |
| A | $a - 1$ | $SS_{A|C} = \left(R^2_{Y.A,C} - R^2_{Y.C}\right)SS_Y$ |
| C | $c - 1$ | $SS_{C|A} = \left(R^2_{Y.A,C} - R^2_{Y.A}\right)SS_Y$ |
| AC | $(a - 1)(c - 1)$ | $SS_{AC|A,C} = \left(R^2_{Y.A,C,AC} - R^2_{Y.A,C}\right)SS_Y$ |
| Residual | $N - ac$ | $SS_{\text{residual}} = \left(1 - R^2_{Y.A,C,AC}\right)SS_Y$ |

*Hypotheses tested*

$A: \sum_k \left[n_{jk} - \frac{n_{jk}^2}{n_{.k}}\right]\mu_{jk} - \sum_{j \neq j'}\sum_k \left[\frac{n_{jk}n_{j'k}}{n_{.k}}\right]\mu_{j'k} = 0 \quad \text{for} \quad j = 1, 2, \ldots, a - 1$

$C: \sum_j \left[n_{jk} - \frac{n_{jk}^2}{n_{j.}}\right]\mu_{jk} - \sum_{k \neq k'}\sum_j \left[\frac{n_{jk}n_{jk'}}{n_{j.}}\right]\mu_{jk'} = 0 \quad \text{for} \quad k = 1, 2, \ldots, c - 1$

$AC: \mu_{jk} - \mu_{j'k} - \mu_{jk'} + \mu_{j'k'} = 0 \quad \text{for all} \quad j, k, j', k'$

*Usage*: If there is *no interaction*, Method 2 tests Method 1's hypotheses with somewhat more power than Method 1 itself. However, if there is the possibility of an interaction, Method 2 should be avoided because it tests data-dependent hypotheses that are not useful (see the hypotheses that are tested above). This method is also known as Overall and Speigel's Method 2, Yates's fitting constants method, and SPSS's classic experimental design approach.

**TABLE 21.4** (continued)

| | Method 3: Main Effects Not Adjusted | |
|---|---|---|
| SV | df | SS |
| $A$ | $a - 1$ | $SS_A = R^2_{Y.A} SS_Y$ |
| $C$ | $c - 1$ | $SS_C = R^2_{Y.C} SS_Y$ |
| $AC$ | $(a - 1)(c - 1)$ | $SS_{AC|A,C} = \left(R^2_{Y.A,C,AC} - R^2_{Y.A,C}\right)SS_Y$ |
| Residual | $N - ac$ | $SS_{\text{residual}} = \left(1 - R^2_{Y.A,C,AC}\right)SS_Y$ |

*Hypotheses tested*

$A$: $\mu_{1*} = \mu_{2*} = \cdots = \mu_{a*}$, where $\mu_{j*} = \frac{1}{n_{j.}} \sum_k n_{jk}\mu_{jk}$ is the weighted mean of the population means for the $c$ cells in the $j$th row of $A$

$C$: $\mu_{*1} = \mu_{*2} = \cdots = \mu_{*c}$, where $\mu_{*k} = \frac{1}{n_{.k}} \sum_k n_{jk}\mu_{jk}$ is the weighted mean of the population means for the $a$ cells in the $k$th row of $C$

$AC$: $\mu_{jk} - \mu_{j'k} - \mu_{jk'} + \mu_{j'k'} = 0$   for all   $j, k, j', k'$

*Usage*: This method tests main-effect hypotheses about the weighted row and column means. These tests may be desirable if the cell frequencies are proportional to the corresponding population sizes. This method is also known as Yates's method for proportional cell sizes.

**TABLE 21.5** RESULTS OBTAINED USING THE THREE METHODS WITH THE DATA OF TABLE 21.3

| | | Method 1 | | |
|---|---|---|---|---|
| SV | df | SS | MS | F |
| $A$ | 2 | $SS_{A|C,AC} = 4139.423$ | 2069.712 | 11.639 |
| $C$ | 2 | $SS_{C|A,AC} = 21.074$ | 10.537 | 0.059 |
| $AC$ | 4 | $SS_{AC|A,C} = 1103.074$ | 275.769 | 1.551 |
| Residual | 15 | $\left(1 - R^2_{Y.A,C,AC}\right)SS_Y = 2667.833$ | 177.882 | |

| | | Method 2 | | |
|---|---|---|---|---|
| SV | df | SS | MS | F |
| $A$ | 2 | $SS_{A|C} = 3609.950$ | 1804.975 | 10.150 |
| $C$ | 2 | $SS_{C|A} = 60.468$ | 30.234 | 0.170 |
| $AC$ | 4 | $SS_{AC|A,C} = 1103.074$ | 275.769 | 1.551 |
| Residual | 15 | $\left(1 - R^2_{Y.A,C,AC}\right)SS_Y = 2667.833$ | 177.882 | |

| | | Method 3 | | |
|---|---|---|---|---|
| SV | df | SS | MS | F |
| $A$ | 2 | $SS_A = 3581.083$ | 1790.542 | 10.089 |
| $C$ | 2 | $SS_C = 31.601$ | 15.800 | 0.089 |
| $AC$ | 4 | $SS_{AC|A,C} = 1103.074$ | 275.769 | 1.551 |
| Residual | 15 | $\left(1 - R^2_{Y.A,C,AC}\right)SS_Y = 2667.833$ | 177.882 | |

The Method 2 tests correspond exactly to these model comparisons. The advantage of this approach is that if there is no interaction, tests of main effects are somewhat more powerful than the comparisons of

$$Y_{ijk} = \mu + \alpha_j + \gamma_k + (\alpha\gamma)_{jk} + \varepsilon_{ijk}$$

against

$$Y_{ijk} = \mu + \gamma_k + (\alpha\gamma)_{jk} + \varepsilon_{ijk}$$

and

$$Y_{ijk} = \mu + \alpha_j + \gamma_k + (\alpha\gamma)_{jk} + \varepsilon_{ijk}$$

against

$$Y_{ijk} = \mu + \alpha_j + (\alpha\gamma)_{jk} + \varepsilon_{ijk}$$

that correspond to the Method 1 main effect tests.

We do not recommend using the Method 2 approach because if an interaction does exist, the hypotheses that it tests are data dependent; that is, they depend on the cell frequencies, and do so in ways that are of little, if any, interest. For example, the null hypothesis for the effect of $A$ can be shown to be

$$\sum_k \left[ n_{jk} - \frac{n_{jk}^2}{n_{\cdot k}} \right] \mu_{jk} - \sum_{j \neq j'} \sum_k \left[ \frac{n_{jk} n_{j'k}}{n_{\cdot k}} \right] \mu_{j'k} = 0 \quad \text{for} \quad j = 1, 2, \dots, a - 1$$

(see Carlson & Timm, 1974). Even interactions that do not approach significance can result in biased tests of the main effects (see, e.g., Overall, Lee, & Hornick, 1981). Therefore, we reaffirm the general rule stated in Chapter 12 that Method 2 should not be used unless there is strong a priori reason to assume no interaction effects, and a clearly nonsignificant interaction effect is observed.

Finally, it is possible that a logical or theoretical analysis of the research problem might dictate the order in which the sets of dummy variables are entered into the regression equation and, therefore, the nature of the adjustments. Suppose, for example, that $A$ and $C$ indicate levels of child and parental educational achievement, respectively. It is reasonable to assume that parental education may influence a child's educational achievement but not the reverse. In this case, it may be desirable to consider the unadjusted effects of parental educational achievement but to adjust the effects of the child's education for that of the parents.

In summary, the ability to use categorical variables in multiple regression analyses enables us to adjust sums of squares in ways that result in tests of the hypotheses of factorial ANOVAs in nonorthogonal designs. We can use the Method 1 approach to test hypotheses about unweighted cell means and the Method 3 approach to test hypotheses about weighted means. Also, if we have logically or theoretically determined orderings of factors, we can perform sequential adjustments.

In most cases, unless otherwise requested, the packages produce Type III sums of squares, and therefore test hypotheses about unweighted means. However, one should check the documentation or perform some test analyses to be sure. SPSS has caused some confusion in its mainframe versions by defaulting to Method 2 for ANOVA commands and Method 1 for MANOVA.

## 21.4 USING CATEGORICAL AND CONTINUOUS VARIABLES IN THE SAME ANALYSIS

### 21.4.1 Testing Homogeneity of Regression Slopes Using Multiple Regression

In Chapters 19 and 20, we discussed tests for equality of slopes when one variable was regressed on another at different levels of a dichotomous (i.e., having only two levels) categorical variable. In Section 20.9, we selected subjects in the *Seasons* data set aged 65 years or younger with BMI (body mass index) scores no larger than 40, and tested whether the rate of change of total cholesterol (TC) level with age was the same for males and females. Although we did not use the term there, the variable sex in the data set is a dummy variable that labels men by 0s and women by 1s. We showed that we could test the hypothesis that the rate of change was the same for men and women by regressing TC on age, sex, and an additional variable Age × Sex that was formed by multiplying age by sex. The resulting regression equation is

$$\hat{T}C = 221.143 - 0.0005 \cdot \text{Age} - 94.612 \cdot \text{Sex} + 1.813 \cdot \text{Age} \times \text{Sex}$$

Because the coefficient of the interaction term Age × Sex is significant, with $t(363) = 4.909$, $p = .000$, we can reject the hypothesis that the slope of TC with age is equal for males and females.

What if the categorical variable has more than two levels? If so, we can still test the hypothesis of homogeneity of regression slopes by determining whether there is a significant interaction. That is, we can test whether the regression of $Y$ on a continuous variable, $X$, is a function of the level of $A$ when $A$ is a categorical variable with more than two levels. However, because now more than one dummy variable is needed to code the categorical variable, the interaction term will have more than 1 *df*, and we will need to use a partial $F$ test (as described in Chapter 20) to determine whether the interaction is significant.

Consider the categorical variable education level, EL. We might be interested not only in its main effect on TC, but also in its interaction with age. Let EL = 1 correspond to individuals with a high school education or less; EL = 2 to education beyond high school, but not including the bachelor's degree, and EL = 3 to at least a bachelor's degree. EL seems to make a difference in TC. Using the same subjects as the previous analysis, to the nearest integer, mean TC is 227, 217, and 210 for EL = 1, 2, and 3, respectively, and an ANOVA with EL as the independent variable is significant; $F(2, 359) = 4.908$, $p = .008$.

Now let's consider whether the effects of EL depend on the age of the subjects. Because EL has three levels, we can code it with two dummy variables—it does not matter whether we use effect, dummy, or any other kind of dummy variable coding. We can then code the interaction of EL with age by using two additional dummy variables, obtained by multiplying the dummy variables used to code EL by age. In general, if we have a continuous predictor variable $X$ and a categorical variable $A$ with $a$ levels, the proportion of the variability in $Y$ accounted for by a regression on $X$ and the $a - 1$ dummy variables coding the categorical variable $A$ is $R^2_{Y.X,A}$. If we now add the $a - 1$ dummy variables that account for the $AX$ interaction to the regression, the proportion of variance accounted for is

$R^2_{Y.X,A,AX}$. The $AX$ interaction can be tested by the partial $F$

$$F = \frac{(R^2_{Y.X,A,AX} - R^2_{Y.X,A})SS_Y/(a-1)}{(1 - R^2_{Y.X,A,AX})SS_Y/(N-2a)}$$

The numerator of the expression corresponds to the increment in the amount of variability accounted for by the interaction and has $df$ equal to the number of dummy variables needed to code the interaction. The denominator is the amount of variability not accounted for by the regression equation that contains the interaction, divided by $df = N - 1-$ the number of predictors in the regression equation $= N - 1 - [1 + 2(a-1)] = N - 2a$. The bracketed quantity, $1 + 2(a-1)$, represents the $a-1$ $df$ for the regression of $Y$ on $A$, the $a-1$ $df$ for the $AX$ interaction, and 1 $df$ for the regression of $Y$ on $X$.

Using the GLM module of a standard statistics package to test the interaction, we would specify that EL is a categorical variable, age is a continuous variable, and that we wanted to include the EL $\times$ Age interaction in the model. The SYSTAT output for the analysis is provided in Table 21.6. The EL $\times$ Age interaction is not significant, $F(2, 356) = 0.641$, $p = .528$. Therefore, we cannot reject the null hypothesis that the effects of EL do not vary with age (or, equivalently, that the rate of change of TC with age is the same at each level of EL).

The procedure can be readily extended to factorial designs. If we had $Y$ and $X$ scores for each cell of a 2 $\times$ 4 design with factors $A$ and $C$, we could test homogeneity of the regression slope in the eight cells of the design by performing analyses that produced partial $F$ tests of the $XA$, $XC$, and $XAC$ interactions.

**TABLE 21.6**  SYSTAT GLM OUTPUT FOR THE TEST OF THE *EL* $\times$ AGE INTERACTION

```
Data for the following results were selected according to:
     (AGE=< 65) AND (BMI=< 40)
```

Effects coding used for categorical variables in model.

Categorical values encountered during processing are:
EL (3 levels)

| | 1, | 2, | 3 |

13 case(s) deleted due to missing data.

Dep Var: TC   N: 362  Multiple R: 0.278  Squared multiple R: 0.077

Analysis of Variance

| Source | Sum-of-Squares | df | Mean-Square | F-ratio | P |
|--------|---------------|-----|-------------|---------|------|
| AGE | 25241.843 | 1 | 25241.843 | 16.971 | 0.000 |
| EL | 2149.938 | 2 | 1074.969 | 0.723 | 0.486 |
| EL*AGE | 1905.416 | 2 | 952.708 | 0.641 | 0.528 |
| Error | 529487.998 | 356 | 1487.326 | | |

*Note.* Output is from SYSTAT.

## 21.4.2 ANCOVA as a Special Case of Multiple Regression

In Chapter 15, we portrayed ANCOVA as a kind of hybrid that incorporated elements of ANOVA to deal with the categorical factors and bivariate regression to adjust for the covariate. Using a multiple regression framework that can deal with both categorical variables and covariates allows a more integrated approach that we believe is easier to understand.

***One-factor ANCOVA.*** Performing an ANCOVA on a design that has a single factor $A$ can now be seen as determining whether $A$ has effects over and above those of the covariate, $X$. First of all, we determine whether there is an $AX$ interaction using the procedures described in the preceding section (see Chapter 15 for a discussion of why the logic of ANCOVA requires homogeneity of regression). If there is no significant interaction, we can go ahead with the ANCOVA by performing a partial $F$ test for the effects of $A$ over and above those of $X$. We find the variability in $Y$ accounted for by $A$ and the covariate, $R^2_{Y.X,A}SS_Y$, and the variability accounted for by the covariate alone, $R^2_{Y.X}SS_Y$, then use the partial $F$ statistic

$$F = \frac{\left(R^2_{Y.X,A} - R^2_{Y.X}\right)SS_Y/df_A}{\left(1 - R^2_{Y.X,A}\right)SS_Y/(N - 2 - df_A)}$$

This partial $F$ test is exactly equivalent to the ANCOVA test for $A$ that was presented in Chapter 15. The adjustments for the covariate that produced $SS_{A(\text{adj})}$ and $SS_{S/A(\text{adj})}$ in Chapter 15 simply involve partialing out the effects of $X$, so that

$$SS_{A(\text{adj})} = \left(R^2_{Y.X,A} - R^2_{Y.X}\right)SS_Y$$

and

$$SS_{S/A(\text{adj})} = \left(1 - R^2_{Y.X,A}\right)SS_Y$$

In practice, we would produce these results by using a standard software package and specifying that $A$ was a categorical variable and $X$ was the covariate. However, recall that if we found a significant $AX$ interaction, we would not proceed with the ANCOVA. Instead, the relation between $X$ and $Y$ can be characterized by obtaining the regression equations for each of the groups and the Johnson–Neyman procedure (see, e.g., Huitema, 1980) can be used to identify regions of the covariate for which the groups differ significantly in $Y$.

***Factorial ANCOVA.*** The multiple regression approach to ANCOVA can be readily extended to factorial designs. For example, if we consider the two-factor design described in the previous section, we can test for homogeneity of regression using Equation 16.4. If homogeneity is not rejected, the ANCOVA tests for $A$, $C$, and $AC$ are provided by

$$F = \frac{\left(R^2_{Y.X,A,C,AC} - R^2_{Y.X,C,AC}\right)SS_Y/df_A}{\left(1 - R^2_{Y.X,A,C,AC}\right)SS_Y/(N - 2 - df_A - df_C - df_{AC})}$$

$$F = \frac{\left(R^2_{Y.X,A,C,AC} - R^2_{Y.X,A,AC}\right)SS_Y/df_C}{\left(1 - R^2_{Y.X,A,C,AC}\right)SS_Y/(N - 2 - df_A - df_C - df_{AC})}$$

and

$$F = \frac{\left(R^2_{Y.X,A,C,AC} - R^2_{Y.X,A,C}\right)SS_Y/df_{AC}}{\left(1 - R^2_{Y.X,A,C,AC}\right)SS_Y/(N - 2 - df_A - df_C - df_{AC})}$$

**Using More Than One Covariate.**  A researcher may wish to adjust for several sources of unwanted variability by using several covariates. For example, suppose we have a one-factor design and information about two covariates $X$ and $W$ that are each linearly related to $Y$. Performing an ANCOVA that uses both covariates tests whether $A$ has significant effects over and above both $X$ and $W$. The appropriate test statistic is the partial $F$:

$$F = \frac{\left(R^2_{Y.X,W,A} - R^2_{Y.X,W}\right)SS_Y/df_A}{\left(1 - R^2_{Y.X,W,A}\right)SS_Y/(N - 3 - df_A)}$$

Note that the denominator of this equation has one less $df$ because of the additional covariate. The adjusted means are the scores predicted by the regression equation for each group if $X = \overline{X}..$ and $W = \overline{W}...$ Homogeneity of regression can be tested by using the partial $F$ for the interactions between $A$ and the covariates,

$$F = \frac{\left(R^2_{Y.X,W,A,AX,AW} - R^2_{Y.X,W,A}\right)SS_Y/2df_A}{\left(1 - R^2_{Y.X,W,A,AX,AW}\right)SS_Y/(N - 3 - 3df_A)}$$

**Nonlinear ANCOVA.**  The relations between the dependent variable and potential covariates are not always linear. For example, according to the Yerkes–Dodson Law, we would expect a quadratic relation between measures of performance and motivation. If we use standard ANCOVA procedures when there is substantial nonlinearity, the ANCOVA $F$ tests may have little power and the adjusted means may be biased estimates of the treatment means. Therefore, it is a good idea to check for severe violations of nonlinearity by plotting scatter diagrams for each group. Also, significance tests for nonlinearity are available.

If the relation between $Y$ and $X$ is nonlinear but monotonic (i.e., $Y$ increases or decreases with $X$ but not in a linear fashion), it may be worth checking to see if there is a simple transformation of $X$, such as $\log X$ or $X$ raised to some power, for which the relation between $Y$ and the transformed $X$ is approximately linear. If such a transformation can be found, the transformed value of $X$ can be used as the covariate in a standard ANCOVA.

If the relation between $Y$ and $X$ is not monotonic, a simple transformation will not achieve linearity. However, in this case, it may be worthwhile to use a polynomial ANCOVA in which the ANCOVA model contains linear and higher-order polynomial components. For a quadratic ANCOVA, it is assumed that the relation between $Y$ and $X$ is of the form

$$Y = b_0 + b_1 X + b_2 X^2$$

for a cubic ANCOVA, the polynomial function contains an $X^3$ term, and so forth. A quadratic ANCOVA is conducted by including both $X$ and $X^2$ as covariates, so that for the one-factor design, the ANCOVA test for $A$ becomes

$$F = \frac{\left(R^2_{Y.X,X^2,A} - R^2_{Y.X,X^2}\right)SS_Y/df_A}{\left(1 - R^2_{Y.X,X^2,A}\right)SS_Y/(N - 3 - df_A)}$$

Higher-order polynomial ANCOVAs can be performed by adding $X^3$, $X^4$, and so on, as covariates. However, it is important to keep in mind that, although more complex models will fit better, using more covariates results in fewer error degrees of freedom. Therefore, one should be careful not to use more complex models or more covariates than are necessary.

Finally, it should be noted that the powers of $X(X, X^2$, etc.) are highly correlated and using them in the same multiple regression will result in multicollinearity (see Chapter 20) that may result in computational difficulties for some software packages. These problems can generally be avoided by centering the covariates, that is, by using deviation scores. For example, $x = (X - \overline{X})$ and $x^2 = (X - \overline{X})^2$ may be used instead of $X$ and $X^2$ in the regression.

## 21.5 CODING DESIGNS WITH WITHIN-SUBJECTS FACTORS

In a repeated-measures design, each subject is tested at every level of at least one independent variable, and subjects are considered to define levels of a factor, $S$, in the design. If there are $n$ subjects, we can code $S$ with $n - 1$ dummy variables in the same way as any other categorical variable.

Table 21.7 contains data for an $S \times A$ design with data from eight subjects at four levels of the repeated-measures factor, $A$. We can code the eight levels of $S$ with the seven dummy variables labeled in Table 21.8 as $S1$–$S7$, the four levels of $A$ with three dummy variables, and the $SA$ interaction with 21 dummy variables ($SA11$–$SA73$) formed by multiplying every dummy variable in the $S$ set by every dummy variable in the $A$ set. The sums of squares can be found from

$$SS_S = R^2_{Y.S}SS_Y$$

$$SS_A = R^2_{Y.A}SS_Y$$

and

$$SS_{SA} = R^2_{Y.SA}SS_Y$$

From Chapter 13, we know that for an $S \times A$ design, the appropriate test for the $A$ main effect is given by $F = MS_A/MS_{SA}$.

The coding procedure can be directly extended to designs in which there are several within-subjects variables, although the number of dummy variables required increases rather dramatically. If we had a $S \times A \times B$ design with eight subjects, four levels of $A$ and two of $B$, coding all the main effects and interactions would require $abn - 1 = 63$ dummy variables, as many dummy variables as $df$ for each source of variance. However, if a multiple regression program was used to analyze such a design, one would really only have to code the $S$, $A$, and $B$ effects. Most software packages have some sort of COMPUTE or TRANSFORM instruction that will create the variables needed to code the interaction effects.

Finally, the coding procedures can be extended to mixed designs that contain both within-subjects and between-subjects factors. Panel (a) of Table 21.8 contains a set of hypothetical data and the ANOVA table for a design that has one between-subjects variable, $A$, and one within-subjects variable, $C$, and panel (b) presents dummy variables that code

**TABLE 21.7** DATA AND DUMMY VARIABLE CODING FOR AN $S \times A$ DESIGN

| Subject | $A_1$ | $A_2$ | $A_3$ | $A_4$ |
|---|---|---|---|---|
| 1 | 1.4 | 3.2 | 3.2 | 3.0 |
| 2 | 2.0 | 2.5 | 3.1 | 5.8 |
| 3 | 1.4 | 4.2 | 4.1 | 5.6 |
| 4 | 2.3 | 4.6 | 4.0 | 5.9 |
| 5 | 4.7 | 4.8 | 4.4 | 5.9 |
| 6 | 3.2 | 5.0 | 6.2 | 5.9 |
| 7 | 4.0 | 6.8 | 4.5 | 6.5 |
| 8 | 5.0 | 6.1 | 6.4 | 6.6 |

| | | | | | $S$ | | | | | $A$ | | | $S \times A$ | | |
|---|---|---|---|---|---|---|---|---|---|---|---|---|---|---|---|
| | $Y$ | $S_1$ | $S_2$ | $S_3$ | $S_4$ | $S_5$ | $S_6$ | $S_7$ | $A_1$ | $A_2$ | $A_3$ | $SA_{11}$ | $SA_{21}$ | ... | $SA_{73}$ |
| $A_1$ | 1.4 | 1 | 0 | 0 | 0 | 0 | 0 | 0 | 1 | 0 | 0 | 1 | 0 | ... | 0 |
| | 2.0 | 0 | 1 | 0 | 0 | 0 | 0 | 0 | 1 | 0 | 1 | 0 | 1 | ... | 0 |
| | 1.4 | 0 | 0 | 1 | 0 | 0 | 0 | 0 | 1 | 0 | 0 | 0 | 0 | ... | 0 |
| | 2.3 | 0 | 0 | 0 | 1 | 0 | 0 | 0 | 1 | 0 | 0 | 0 | 0 | ... | 0 |
| | 4.7 | 0 | 0 | 0 | 0 | 1 | 0 | 0 | 1 | 0 | 0 | 0 | 0 | ... | 0 |
| | 3.2 | 0 | 0 | 0 | 0 | 0 | 1 | 0 | 1 | 0 | 0 | 0 | 0 | ... | 0 |
| | 4.0 | 0 | 0 | 0 | 0 | 0 | 0 | 1 | 1 | 0 | 0 | 0 | 0 | ... | 0 |
| | 5.0 | −1 | −1 | −1 | −1 | −1 | −1 | −1 | 1 | 0 | 0 | −1 | −1 | ... | 0 |
| $A_2$ | 3.2 | 1 | 0 | 0 | 0 | 0 | 0 | 0 | 0 | 1 | 0 | 0 | 0 | ... | 0 |
| | 2.5 | 0 | 1 | 0 | 0 | 0 | 0 | 0 | 0 | 1 | 0 | 0 | 0 | ... | 0 |
| | 4.2 | 0 | 0 | 1 | 0 | 0 | 0 | 0 | 0 | 1 | 0 | 0 | 0 | ... | 0 |
| | 4.6 | 0 | 0 | 0 | 1 | 0 | 0 | 0 | 0 | 1 | 0 | 0 | 0 | ... | 0 |
| | 4.8 | 0 | 0 | 0 | 0 | 1 | 0 | 0 | 0 | 1 | 0 | 0 | 0 | ... | 0 |
| | 5.0 | 0 | 0 | 0 | 0 | 0 | 1 | 0 | 0 | 1 | 0 | 0 | 0 | ... | 0 |
| | 6.8 | 0 | 0 | 0 | 0 | 0 | 0 | 1 | 0 | 1 | 0 | 0 | 0 | ... | 0 |
| | 6.1 | −1 | −1 | −1 | −1 | −1 | −1 | −1 | 0 | 1 | 0 | 0 | 0 | ... | 0 |
| $A_3$ | 3.2 | 1 | 0 | 0 | 0 | 0 | 0 | 0 | 0 | 0 | 1 | 0 | 0 | ... | 0 |
| | 3.1 | 0 | 1 | 0 | 0 | 0 | 0 | 0 | 0 | 0 | 1 | 0 | 0 | ... | 0 |
| | 4.1 | 0 | 0 | 1 | 0 | 0 | 0 | 0 | 0 | 0 | 1 | 0 | 0 | ... | 0 |
| | 4.0 | 0 | 0 | 0 | 1 | 0 | 0 | 0 | 0 | 0 | 1 | 0 | 0 | ... | 0 |
| | 4.4 | 0 | 0 | 0 | 0 | 1 | 0 | 0 | 0 | 0 | 1 | 0 | 0 | ... | 0 |
| | 6.2 | 0 | 0 | 0 | 0 | 0 | 1 | 0 | 0 | 0 | 1 | 0 | 0 | ... | 0 |
| | 4.5 | 0 | 0 | 0 | 0 | 0 | 0 | 1 | 0 | 0 | 1 | 0 | 0 | ... | 1 |
| | 6.4 | −1 | −1 | −1 | −1 | −1 | −1 | −1 | 0 | 0 | 1 | 0 | 0 | ... | −1 |
| $A_4$ | 3.0 | 1 | 0 | 0 | 0 | 0 | 0 | 0 | −1 | −1 | −1 | −1 | 0 | ... | 0 |
| | 5.8 | 0 | 1 | 0 | 0 | 0 | 0 | 0 | −1 | −1 | −1 | 0 | −1 | ... | 0 |
| | 5.6 | 0 | 0 | 1 | 0 | 0 | 0 | 0 | −1 | −1 | −1 | 0 | 0 | ... | 0 |
| | 5.9 | 0 | 0 | 0 | 1 | 0 | 0 | 0 | −1 | −1 | −1 | 0 | 0 | ... | 0 |
| | 5.9 | 0 | 0 | 0 | 0 | 1 | 0 | 0 | −1 | −1 | −1 | 0 | 0 | ... | 0 |
| | 5.9 | 0 | 0 | 0 | 0 | 0 | 1 | 0 | −1 | −1 | −1 | 0 | 0 | ... | 0 |
| | 6.5 | 0 | 0 | 0 | 0 | 0 | 0 | 1 | −1 | −1 | −1 | 0 | 0 | ... | −1 |
| | 6.6 | −1 | −1 | −1 | −1 | −1 | −1 | −1 | −1 | −1 | −1 | 1 | 1 | ... | 1 |

**TABLE 21.8** DUMMY VARIABLE CODING FOR A MIXED DESIGN

### (a) Data and ANOVA Table

|  |  | $C_1$ | $C_2$ | $C_3$ |
|---|---|---|---|---|
| $A_1$ | $S_{11}$ | 7 | 1 | 7 |
|  | $S_{21}$ | 9 | 2 | 10 |
|  | $S_{31}$ | 7 | 3 | 8 |
| $A_2$ | $S_{12}$ | 12 | 7 | 8 |
|  | $S_{22}$ | 16 | 14 | 9 |
|  | $S_{32}$ | 19 | 11 | 12 |

| SV | df | SS | MS | F |
|---|---|---|---|---|
| $A$ | 1 | 162.00 | 162.00 | 13.50 |
| $S/A$ | 4 | 48.00 | 12.00 | |
| $C$ | 2 | 85.33 | 42.67 | 17.66 |
| $AC$ | 2 | 49.33 | 24.67 | 10.21 |
| $SC/A$ | 8 | 19.33 | 2.42 | |

### (b) Dummy Variable Coding for the Design

|  |  | A | S/A | | | | C | | AC | |
|---|---|---|---|---|---|---|---|---|---|---|
|  | Y | $A_1$ | $S/A_{11}$ | $S/A_{12}$ | $S/A_{21}$ | $S/A_{22}$ | $C_1$ | $C_2$ | $AC_{11}$ | $AC_{12}$ |
| $A_1S_1$ | 7 | 1 | 1 | 0 | 0 | 0 | 1 | 0 | 1 | 0 |
|  | 1 | 1 | 1 | 0 | 0 | 0 | 0 | 1 | 0 | 1 |
|  | 7 | 1 | 1 | 0 | 0 | 0 | −1 | −1 | −1 | −1 |
| $A_1S_2$ | 9 | 1 | 0 | 1 | 0 | 0 | 1 | 0 | 1 | 0 |
|  | 2 | 1 | 0 | 1 | 0 | 0 | 0 | 1 | 0 | 1 |
|  | 10 | 1 | 0 | 1 | 0 | 0 | −1 | −1 | −1 | −1 |
| $A_1S_3$ | 7 | 1 | −1 | −1 | 0 | 0 | 1 | 0 | 1 | 0 |
|  | 3 | 1 | −1 | −1 | 0 | 0 | 0 | 1 | 0 | 1 |
|  | 8 | 1 | −1 | −1 | 0 | 0 | −1 | −1 | −1 | −1 |
| $A_2S_1$ | 12 | −1 | 0 | 0 | 1 | 0 | 1 | 0 | −1 | 0 |
|  | 7 | −1 | 0 | 0 | 1 | 0 | 0 | 1 | 0 | −1 |
|  | 8 | −1 | 0 | 0 | 1 | 0 | −1 | −1 | 1 | 1 |
| $A_2S_2$ | 16 | −1 | 0 | 0 | 0 | 1 | 1 | 0 | −1 | 0 |
|  | 14 | −1 | 0 | 0 | 0 | 1 | 0 | 1 | 0 | −1 |
|  | 9 | −1 | 0 | 0 | 0 | 1 | −1 | −1 | 1 | 1 |
| $A_3S_3$ | 19 | −1 | 0 | 0 | −1 | −1 | 1 | 0 | −1 | 0 |
|  | 11 | −1 | 0 | 0 | −1 | −1 | 0 | 1 | 0 | −1 |
|  | 12 | −1 | 0 | 0 | −1 | −1 | −1 | −1 | 1 | 1 |

the design. The $A$, $C$, and $AC$ sources of variance can be coded as in a factorial between-subjects design and $S/A$ can be directly represented by coding subjects separately at each level of $A$ as indicated in Table 21.8. It is not really necessary to code $SC/A$ because $SS_{SC/A}$ can be obtained as a residual

$$SS_{SC/A} = SS_Y \left(1 - R^2_{Y.A,S/A,C,AC}\right)$$

However, $SC/A$ could be coded by the eight dummy variables that would result from multiplying the values of variables in the $C$ and $S/A$ sets.

It should be noted that when there are different numbers of subjects at each level of $A$, the standard ANOVA and GLM modules will produce Type III sums of squares. For example, $SS_C$ will be obtained as $(R^2_{Y.A,C,AC} - R^2_{Y.C,AC})SS_Y$, not as $R^2_{Y.C}SS_Y$.

## 21.6 CONCLUDING REMARKS

The two goals we had in this chapter were to discuss how categorical variables can be coded so that they can be incorporated into multiple regression analysis and to reconsider within the multiple regression framework a number of the analyses we discussed earlier. We did not include this second goal to encourage our readers to perform ANOVAs and ANCOVAs by coding categorical variables in terms of dummy variables and then using multiple regression, although they could do so if the standard ANOVA and ANCOVA programs were not available. Rather, we believe that considering ANOVA and ANCOVA from the multiple regression perspective allows us to gain a deeper understanding of these analyses and their relations to one another.

Also, the generality and flexibility of the multiple regression framework offer some clear advantages. As described previously, the standard ANOVA approach breaks down for disproportionate-$n$ designs. Thinking in terms of multiple regression, a system in which nonorthogonality is the rule, not the exception, facilitates consideration of the kinds of adjustments that might be made. To provide appropriate analyses of nonorthogonal designs, the standard "ANOVA" programs are really multiple regression programs. We hope that this chapter provides some understanding of how these programs might work and what options they allow. Finally, the ability to include categorical and continuous variables in the same analysis not only provides a framework for better understanding ANCOVA, but also makes it clear that it is not necessary to transform inherently continuous variables into categorical ones (by, e.g., using median splits) to analyze the data.

## KEY CONCEPTS

categorical variable

quantitative variable

qualitative variable

dummy (indicator) variable

linearly independent variables

effect coding

dummy coding

orthogonal designs

nonorthogonal designs

Type III sums of squares

Method 1

Method 2

Method 3

## EXERCISES

**21.1**  Test scores are obtained from 8 women and 8 men. Data are as follows:

| Gender | |
|---|---|
| Men | Women |
| 27 | 35 |
| 18 | 33 |
| 16 | 26 |
| 27 | 21 |
| 24 | 38 |
| 30 | 28 |
| 32 | 38 |
| 26 | 32 |

(a) Find the correlation between gender and test score (i.e., the point-biserial correlation coefficient) and test it for significance.

(b) Perform an independent-groups $t$ test to determine whether there is a significant effect of gender.

(c) How many variables are needed to code for gender? Indicate how gender could be coded using (i) effect $(1, -1)$ and (ii) dummy $(1, 0)$ coding.

(d) Regress the dependent variable on the dummy (i.e., indicator) variables for (i) and (ii) above. Compare the significance levels with those found in (a) and (b). What are the interpretations of the regression coefficients for (i) and (ii)?

**21.2**  Create another dummy variable for gender using 33 for males and $-17$ for females. Regress the dependent variable on this "nonsense" variable. What is the interpretation of this analysis?

**21.3**  Given the following data from a between subjects design:

| Condition | | |
|---|---|---|
| $C_1$ | $C_2$ | $C_3$ |
| 17 | 11 | 9 |
| 33 | 18 | 12 |
| 26 | 14 | 10 |
| 27 | 18 | 8 |
| 2 | | 14 |

(a) How many linearly independent dummy (indicator) variables are needed to code the design?

(b) Code the design using (i) dummy coding and (ii) effect coding.

(c) Regress the dependent variable on the indicator variables for (i) and (ii).

(d) What are the interpretations of the regression coefficients in each case?

**21.4** Would the interpretations of the regression coefficients in Exercise 21.3 change if there were equal numbers of scores in each group? If so, how?

**21.5** Given the following data from a $2 \times 3$ nonorthogonal (i.e., unbalanced or unequal $n$) design:

|       | $B_1$ | $B_2$ | $B_3$ |
|-------|-------|-------|-------|
|       | 72    | 49    | 40    |
|       | 63    | 71    | 49    |
| $A_1$ | 57    | 63    | 36    |
|       | 52    | 48    | 50    |
|       | 69    |       | 54    |
|       | 75    |       |       |
|       | 65    | 56    | 41    |
|       | 45    | 55    | 42    |
| $A_2$ | 53    | 49    | 57    |
|       | 52    | 52    | 39    |
|       | 57    | 45    |       |
|       |       | 57    |       |

(a) Perform the ANOVA by using a statistical software package.

(b) Code the design by using effect coding (include variables for the main effects and the interaction).

(c) Are the dummy variables that correspond to the different effects correlated with one another?

(d) Assuming that the unequal $n$s have arisen by chance, and we wish to test hypotheses about the unweighted means, perform the appropriate regression analyses, and do what has to be done to test the $A$, $B$, and $A \times B$ effects. Exactly what hypotheses are tested? Compare your results with the ANOVA performed in (a).

(e) Suppose you regress on just the dummy variable corresponding to the $A$ effect, omitting the dummy variables that code for $B$ and the $A \times B$ interaction. What hypothesis is tested using the $SS_A$ obtained in this analysis?

**21.6** Use the data from Exercise 15.1 to perform an ANCOVA using the ANOVA or GLM module of a software package. Then perform the ANCOVA by coding the variables properly and using regression. Verify that the results are the same.

**21.7** Use multiple regression to test the design in the previous exercise for homogeneity of regression slope.

# Appendix A

## Notation and Summation Operations

We must have a common language to talk about the derivations and computational formulas that relate to psychological experimentation. Such a language exists in the notational system presented here. If you try to master it now, your efforts will be amply repaid. You will find first a few simple rules, which are then applied to some elementary statistical quantities.

## A.1 A SINGLE GROUP OF SCORES

### A.1.1 Some Basic Rules

In a group of scores like $Y_1, Y_2, Y_3, Y_4, \ldots, Y_n$, the subscript has no purpose except to distinguish among the individual scores. The quantity $n$ is the total number of scores in the group. Suppose that $n = 5$ and we want to show that all five scores are to be added together. We could write

$$Y_1 + Y_2 + Y_3 + Y_4 + Y_5$$

or, more briefly,

$$Y_1 + Y_2 + \cdots + Y_5$$

Still more briefly, we write

$$\sum_{i=1}^{5} Y_i$$

This expression is read "sum the values of $Y$ for all $i$ from 1 to 5." In general, $i = 1, 2, \ldots, n$ (that is, $i$ takes on the values of 1 to $n$), and the summation of a group of $n$ scores is indicated by

$$\sum_{i=1}^{n} Y_i$$

The quantity $i$ is the *index*, and 1 and $n$ are the *limits* of summation.[1] When the context of the presentation permits no confusion, the index and limits are often dropped. Thus we may often indicate by $\sum Y$ that a group of scores are to be summed.

Three rules for summation follow.

■ **RULE 1.** The sum of a constant times a variable equals the constant times the sum of the variable; or

$$\sum CY = C \sum Y$$

The term $C$ is a constant in the sense that its value does not change as a function of $i$; the value of $Y$ depends on $i$, and $Y$ is therefore a variable relative to $i$. The rule is easily proved.

$$\sum CY = CY_1 + CY_2 + CY_3 + \cdots + CY_n$$
$$= C(Y_1 + Y_2 + Y_3 + \cdots + Y_n)$$
$$= C \sum Y$$

■ **RULE 2.** The sum of a constant equals $n$ times the constant, where $n$ equals the number of quantities summed; or

$$\sum C = C + C + \cdots + C = nC$$

■ **RULE 3.** The summation sign operates like a multiplier on quantities within parentheses.

■ **EXAMPLE 1.**

$$\sum_{i}^{n}(X_i - Y_i) = \sum_{i}^{n} X_i - \sum_{i}^{n} Y_i$$

*Proof.*

$$\sum(X - Y) = (X_1 - Y_1) + (X_2 - Y_2) + \cdots + (X_n - Y_n)$$
$$= (X_1 + X_2 + \cdots + X_n) - (Y_1 + Y_2 + \cdots + Y_n)$$
$$= \sum X - \sum Y$$

■ **EXAMPLE 2.**

$$\sum(X - Y)^2 = \sum X^2 + \sum Y^2 - 2 \sum XY$$

*Proof.*

$$\sum(X - Y)^2 = (X_1 - Y_1)^2 + \cdots + (X_n - Y_n)^2$$
$$= (X_1^2 + Y_1^2 - 2X_1Y_1) + (X_2^2 + Y_2^2 - 2X_2Y_2) + \cdots + (X_n^2 + Y_n^2 - 2X_nY_n)$$
$$= (X_1^2 + X_2^2 + \cdots + X_n^2) + (Y_1^2 + Y_2^2 + \cdots + Y_n^2)$$
$$\quad -2(X_1Y_1 + X_2Y_2 + \cdots + X_nY_n)$$
$$= \sum X^2 + \sum Y^2 - 2 \sum XY$$

## A.1.2 Applying the Summation Rules

We can apply the rules of summation to prove the properties of means and variances stated in Chapter 2 (Section 2.4). Throughout this section it should be clear that we are summing over $i$ from 1 to $n$ even though the index and limits are not explicitly presented in each expression.

### Properties of the Mean

1. $\sum(Y - \overline{Y}) = 0$; the sum of all deviations of scores about their mean is zero. Applying Rule 3, we get

$$\sum(Y - \overline{Y}) = \sum Y - \sum \overline{Y}$$

However, $\overline{Y}$ is a constant; its value is the same regardless of the value of the index of summation. Therefore, applying Rule 2, we rewrite the last equation as

$$\sum(Y - \overline{Y}) = \sum Y - n\overline{Y}$$

Because $\overline{Y} = \sum Y/n$, we can rewrite this as

$$\sum(Y - \overline{Y}) = \sum Y - n\overline{Y} = \sum Y - n\left(\frac{\sum Y}{n}\right) = \sum Y - \sum Y = 0$$

2. $\sum(Y + k)/n = \overline{Y} + k$; if a constant is added to all scores, the mean is increased by that constant. Applying Rule 3 gives

$$\frac{\sum(Y + k)}{n} = \frac{\sum Y + \sum k}{n} = \frac{\sum Y}{n} + \frac{\sum k}{n}$$

Applying Rule 2 and noting that $\sum Y/n = \overline{Y}$, we have

$$\frac{\sum(Y + k)}{n} = \overline{Y} + \frac{nk}{n} = \overline{Y} + k$$

3. $\sum kY/n = k\overline{Y}$; if all scores are multiplied by a constant, the mean is multiplied by that constant. Applying Rule 1, we have

$$\frac{\sum kY}{n} = \frac{k\sum Y}{n} = k\overline{Y}$$

4. $\sum(Y - \overline{Y})^2$ is a minimum. Assume that there is some value $\overline{Y} + d$ such that the sum of squared deviations of all scores about it is smaller than the sum about any other value. This sum of squared distances is $\sum[Y - (\overline{Y} + d)]^2$. Expanding in accord with Rule 3, we have

$$\sum[Y - (\overline{Y} + d)]^2 = \sum[(Y - \overline{Y}) - d]^2 = \sum(Y - \overline{Y})^2 + \sum d^2 - 2\sum d(Y - \overline{Y})$$

Applying Rule 1, we rewrite the rightmost term as

$$2\sum d(Y - \overline{Y}) = 2d\sum(Y - \overline{Y}) = (2d)(0)$$

because $\Sigma(Y - \overline{Y}) = 0$. Applying Rule 2, we have

$$\sum d^2 = nd^2$$

Therefore,

$$\sum [Y - (\overline{Y} + d)]^2 = \sum (Y - \overline{Y})^2 + nd^2$$

which is as small as possible when $d = 0$, that is, when we sum the squared deviations of scores about their mean.

## Properties of the Variance

1. Adding a constant to all scores leaves the variance unchanged. If a constant $k$ is added to all scores the new variance is

$$s^2_{Y+k} = \frac{\sum [(Y + k) - (\overline{Y + k})]^2}{n - 1} = \frac{\sum (Y - \overline{Y})^2}{n - 1} = s^2_Y$$

2. Multiplying all scores by a constant $k$ is equivalent to multiplying the variance by $k^2$ and the standard deviation by $k$. We have

$$s^2_{ky} = \frac{\sum (kY - \overline{kY})^2}{n - 1} = \frac{\sum k^2(Y - \overline{Y})^2}{n - 1}$$

By Rule 1 this becomes

$$s^2_{kY} = \frac{k^2 \sum (Y - \overline{Y})^2}{n - 1} = k^2 s^2_Y$$

## z Scores

The properties proven allow us to show that the mean of a set of $z$ scores is zero and its variance is 1. Recall that

$$z = \frac{Y - \overline{Y}}{s_Y}$$

To obtain the average of a set of $n$ $z$ scores, we sum them and divide by $n$, keeping in mind that $\sum (Y - \overline{Y}) = 0$. Then

$$\frac{\sum z}{n} = \frac{\sum (Y - \overline{Y})}{n s_Y} = \frac{(0)}{n s_Y} = 0$$

To prove that the variance (and therefore the standard deviation) of the $z$ scores is 1, expand the formula for $z$ as

$$z = \left(\frac{1}{s_Y}\right) Y - \left(\frac{1}{s_Y}\right) \overline{Y}$$

Note that $(1/s_Y)$ is a constant with respect to the index of summation $i$. Because adding (or subtracting) a constant from a variable does not change its variance (see the first property of the variance), the variance of $z$ is the same as the variance of $(1/s_Y)Y$. But, from the second property of a variance, we know that the variance of a constant $(1/s_Y)$ times a variable $(Y)$ is the squared constant times the variance of the variable. That is,

$$s^2_z = \left(\frac{1}{s_Y}\right)^2 s^2_Y = 1$$

### A.1.3 Raw-Score Formulas

The summation rules can be applied to obtain raw-score formulas for quantities such as the variance and covariance. These raw-score or *computational* formulas contain sums of scores, squared scores, and cross products rather than sums of squared differences and cross products of difference scores. This allows them to minimize rounding error and makes them convenient to use with simple hand calculators that do not have variance and correlation keys.

The numerator of the expression for the variance of $Y$ is $SS_Y = \sum(Y_i - \overline{Y})^2$. To get the raw-score formula for $SS_Y$, expand the quantity within the summation sign. Thus

$$\sum(Y - \overline{Y})^2 = \sum(Y^2 + \overline{Y}^2 - 2Y\overline{Y})$$

Applying Rule 3, we have

$$\sum(Y - \overline{Y})^2 = \sum Y^2 + \sum \overline{Y}^2 - \sum 2Y\overline{Y}$$

Noting that $\overline{Y}^2$ is a constant and applying Rule 2, we have

$$\sum(Y - \overline{Y})^2 = \sum Y^2 + n\overline{Y}^2 - \sum 2Y\overline{Y}$$

The quantity $2\overline{Y}$ is a constant and, by Rule 1, can be placed before the summation sign. Thus,

$$\sum(Y - \overline{Y})^2 = \sum Y^2 + n\overline{Y}^2 - 2\overline{Y}\sum Y$$

Now replace $\overline{Y}$ by $\sum Y/n$ to get

$$\sum(Y - \overline{Y})^2 = \sum Y^2 + \frac{n\left(\sum Y\right)^2}{n^2} - 2\left(\frac{\sum Y}{n}\right)\sum Y$$

Simplifying, we have

$$\sum(Y - \overline{Y})^2 = \sum Y^2 - \frac{\left(\sum Y\right)^2}{n} \tag{A.1}$$

Dividing the right-hand side of Equation A.1 by $n - 1$ gives the raw-score formula for $s_Y^2$.

We can find the raw-score formula for the covariance of $X$ and $Y$,

$$s_{XY} = \frac{\sum(X - \overline{X})(Y - \overline{Y})}{n - 1}$$

by noting that Equation A.1 could be rewritten as

$$\sum(Y - \overline{Y})^2 = \sum(Y - \overline{Y})(Y - \overline{Y}) = \sum YY - \frac{\left(\sum Y\right)\left(\sum Y\right)}{n}$$

By analogy, the numerator of $s_{XY}$ has the raw-score formula

$$\sum(X - \overline{X})(Y - \overline{Y}) = \sum XY - \frac{\left(\sum X\right)\left(\sum Y\right)}{n}$$

Dividing by $n - 1$ yields the raw-score formula for $s_{XY}$.

**TABLE A.1** A TWO-DIMENSIONAL MATRIX

| | Groups | | | | | |
|---|---|---|---|---|---|---|
| | $Y_{11}$ | $Y_{12}$ | $\cdots$ | $Y_{1j}$ | $\cdots$ | $Y_{1a}$ |
| | $Y_{21}$ | $Y_{22}$ | $\cdots$ | $Y_{2j}$ | $\cdots$ | $Y_{2a}$ |
| | $\vdots$ | $\vdots$ | | $\vdots$ | | $\vdots$ |
| Subjects | $Y_{i1}$ | $Y_{i2}$ | $\cdots$ | $Y_{ij}$ | $\cdots$ | $Y_{ia}$ |
| | $\vdots$ | $\vdots$ | | $\vdots$ | | $\vdots$ |
| | $Y_{n1}$ | $Y_{n2}$ | $\cdots$ | $Y_{nj}$ | $\cdots$ | $Y_{na}$ |

## A.2 SEVERAL GROUPS OF SCORES

The simplest possible experimental design involves several groups of scores. Thus one might have $a$ groups of $n$ subjects each, which differ in the amount of reward they receive for their performance on some learning task. In setting the data down on paper, there would be a column for each level of amount of reward—that is, for each experimental group. The scores for a group could be written in order within the appropriate column. In referring to a score, we should designate it by its position in the column (or experimental group) and by the position of the column. Table A.1 illustrates this procedure. Note that the first subscript refers to the position in the group (row), the second to the position of the group (column). Thus $Y_{22}$ is the second score in group 2, and in general, $Y_{ij}$ is the $i$th score in the $j$th group.

Suppose we want to refer to the mean of a single column. The term used previously, $\overline{Y}$, is obviously inadequate because it does not designate the row or column that we want. Even $\overline{Y}_1$ is not clear, because it might as easily refer to the mean of the first row as to the mean of the first column.[2] The appropriate designation is $\overline{Y}_{.1} = (1/n) \sum_i^n Y_{i1}$; the dot represents the summation over $i$, the index that ordinarily appears in that position. Similarly, the mean of row $i$ would be designated by $\overline{Y}_{i.} = (1/a) \sum_j^a Y_{ij}$; summation is over the index $j$. The mean of all $an$ scores would be designated by $\overline{Y}_{..} = (1/an) \sum \sum Y_{ij}$, or merely $\overline{Y}$.

Some examples using the double summation ($\sum_i \sum_j$) may be helpful. Suppose we have

$$\sum_{j=1}^{a} \sum_{i=1}^{n} Y_{ij}^2$$

This is an instruction to set $i$ and $j$ initially at 1; the resulting score $Y_{11}$ is then squared. Holding $j$ at 1, we step $i$ from 1 to $n$, squaring each score thus obtained and adding it to those previously squared. When $n$ scores have been squared and summed, we reset the index $i$ at 1 and step $j$ to 2; the squaring and summing is then carried out for all $Y_{i2}$. The process continues until all $an$ scores have been squared and summed. The process just described can be represented by

$$\left( Y_{11}^2 + Y_{21}^2 + \cdots + Y_{na}^2 \right)$$

If we have

$$\sum_{j=1}^{a} \left( \sum_{i=1}^{n} Y_{ij} \right)^2$$

the notation indicates that a sum of $n$ scores is to be squared. We again set $j$ at 1, and after adding together all the $Y_{i1}$, square the total. The index $j$ is then stepped to 2 and $i$ is reset at 1; we get another sum of $n$ scores, which is squared and added to the previous squared sum. We again continue until all $an$ scores have been accounted for. The process can be represented by

$$(Y_{11} + Y_{21} + \cdots + Y_{n1})^2 + \cdots + (Y_{1a} + Y_{2a} + \cdots + Y_{na})^2$$

A third possibility is

$$\left( \sum_{j=1}^{a} \sum_{i=1}^{n} Y_{ij} \right)^2$$

which indicates that the squaring operation is carried out once on the total of $an$ scores; we then have

$$[(Y_{11} + Y_{21} + \cdots + Y_{n1}) + \cdots + (Y_{1a} + Y_{2a} + \cdots + Y_{na})]^2$$

Note that the indices within the parentheses show how many scores are to be summed prior to squaring, and the indices outside the parentheses show how many squared totals are to be summed. When no parentheses appear, as in $\sum \sum Y^2$, we treat the notation as if it were $\sum \sum (Y^2)$. When no indices appear outside the parentheses, it is understood that we are dealing with a single squared term, as in $(\sum \sum Y)^2$. When several indices appear together, whether inside or outside the parentheses, the product of their upper limits tells us the number of terms involved. Thus, $(\sum_{j=1}^{a} \sum_{i=1}^{n} Y)^2$ indicates that $an$ scores are summed before the squaring.

Our three illustrations of the double summation can be further clarified if we use some numbers. Let us use the three groups of four scores each shown in Table A.2. Now,

$$\sum_{j} \sum_{i} Y_{ij}^2 = 30 + 70 + 93 = 193$$

and

$$\sum_{j} \left( \sum_{i} Y_{ij} \right)^2 = (10)^2 + (14)^2 + (19)^2 = 657$$

and

$$\left( \sum_{j} \sum_{i} Y_{ij} \right)^2 = (10 + 14 + 19)^2 = 1849$$

**TABLE A.2**  SOME SAMPLE DATA

|  | Group 1 | Group 2 | Group 3 |
|---|---|---|---|
|  | 4 | 1 | 6 |
|  | 1 | 7 | 4 |
|  | 3 | 2 | 5 |
|  | 2 | 4 | 4 |
| $\sum_i Y_{ij} =$ | 10 | 14 | 19 |
| $\sum_i Y_{ij}^2 =$ | 30 | 70 | 93 |

As another example of how to use double summation, we might derive a raw score formula for the average group variance, often referred to as the *within-group mean square*. This is the sum of the group variances divided by $a$, the number of groups, or

$$\frac{1}{a}\left[\frac{\sum_{i=1}^{n}(Y_{i1}-\overline{Y}_{.1})^2}{n-1}+\cdots+\frac{\sum_{i=1}^{n}(Y_{ia}-\overline{Y}_{.a})^2}{n-1}\right]$$

More briefly, this average is indicated by

$$\frac{1}{a(n-1)}\sum_{j}^{a}\sum_{i}^{n}(Y_{ij}-\overline{Y}_{.j})^2$$

Now, expanding the numerator (or "sums of squares") of this quantity, we get

$$\sum_{j=1}^{a}\sum_{i=1}^{n}(Y_{ij}-\overline{Y}_{.j})^2=\sum_{j=1}^{a}\sum_{i=1}^{n}\left(Y_{ij}^2+\overline{Y}_{.j}^2-2Y_{ij}\overline{Y}_{.j}\right)$$

We "multiply through" by $\sum_i$, noting that $\overline{Y}_{.j}$ varies only with $j$; it is constant when $i$ is the index of summation. Terms are also rearranged so that sums are premultiplied by constants:

$$\sum_{j}\sum_{i}(Y_{ij}-\overline{Y}_{.j})^2=\sum_{j}\left(\sum_{i}Y_{ij}^2+n\overline{Y}_{.j}^2-2\overline{Y}_{.j}\sum_{i}Y_{ij}\right)$$

Note that $\sum_i\overline{Y}_{.j}=n\overline{Y}_{.j}$. Although $\overline{Y}_{.j}$ is a variable relative to the index $j$, it is a constant relative to $i$, the index over which we are currently summing; therefore Rule 2 applies.

Substituting raw-score formulas for the group means gives

$$\sum_{j}\sum_{i}(Y_{ij}-\overline{Y}_{.j})^2=\sum_{j}\left[\sum_{i}Y_{ij}^2+n\frac{(\sum_i Y_{ij})^2}{n^2}-2\left(\frac{\sum_i Y_{ij}}{n}\right)\sum_{i}Y_{ij}\right]$$

Simplifying gives

$$\sum_{j}\sum_{i}(Y_{ij}-\overline{Y}_{.j})^2=\sum_{j}\left[\sum_{i}Y_{ij}^2-\frac{(\sum_i Y_{ij})^2}{n}\right]$$

which can also be written

$$\sum_{j}\sum_{i}Y_{ij}^2-\frac{\sum_j(\sum_i Y_{ij})^2}{n}$$

To simplify notation, we can use $T$ (for "total") to replace $\sum Y$. The sum of scores, for example, for group $j$ is

$$T_{.j}=\sum_{i}Y_{ij}$$

and the raw-score expression just derived can be rewritten as

$$\sum_{j}\sum_{i}Y_{ij}^2-\frac{\sum_j T_{.j}^2}{n}$$

# Appendix B
## Expected Values and Their Applications

The view of a population parameter as the expected value of a statistic is inherent in most inferential procedures. Furthermore, many important results are derived by taking expectations of statistics. The following discussion provides an introduction to these matters. We begin by defining an expected value, and we then present some rules for working with expectations. We then apply these rules to derive some results that were presented earlier in this book.

## B.1 DEFINITIONS AND BASIC RULES

We repeat the earlier definitions of expected values (see Chapter 4) for convenience in dealing with the other material in this appendix. The expected value of a random variable, $Y$, may be viewed as a weighted average of all possible values $Y$ can take. The weights are probabilities, $p(y)$, when $Y$ is discretely distributed and densities, $f(y)$, when $Y$ is continuously distributed. In the discrete case,

$$E(Y) = \sum_y yp(y)$$

and in the continuous case,

$$E(Y) = \int_y yf(y)\,dy$$

$E(Y)$ is read as "the expected value of $Y$" or "the expectation of $Y$." The $y$ under the summation and integral signs is meant to remind us that the sum or integral is over all possible values of $Y$.

The symbol $E$ is often referred to as an *expectation operator*, meaning that it is an instruction to sum or integrate the variable indicated. The expectation operator follows a set of rules similar to those presented in Appendix A for the summation operator. The most important of these rules are presented next.

■ **RULE 1.**    *The expectation of a constant times a variable equals the constant times the sum of the variable:*

$$E(CY) = CE(Y)$$

This may be seen by writing

$$E(CY) = \sum (Cy)p(y) = C \sum yp(y) = CE(Y)$$

■ **RULE 2.**    *The expectation of a constant is the constant:*

$$E(C) = C$$

If several events have the same numerical value $C$, the average value will equal $C$.

■ **RULE 3.**    *E acts like a multiplier.* For example,

$$E(X + Y) = E(X) + E(Y)$$

To prove this, begin with the definition of $E(X + Y)$:

$$E(X + Y) = \sum_x \sum_y (x + y)p(x, y)$$

where the expression on the right indicates that each possible value of $X + Y$ is multiplied by its joint probability, and these products are then summed. Distributing this expression, we obtain

$$E(X + Y) = \sum_x \sum_y xp(x, y) + \sum_x \sum_y yp(x, y)$$

$$= \sum_x x \left[ \sum_y p(x, y) \right] + \sum_y y \left[ \sum_x p(x, y) \right]$$

$$= \sum_x xp(x) + \sum_y yp(y) = E(X) + E(Y)$$

A special case of this expression occurs when one variable is replaced by a constant; then

$$E(Y + C) = E(Y) + E(C) = E(Y) + C$$

This equation provides an immediate basis for asserting that

$$E(Y - \mu) = 0$$

because

$$E(Y - \mu) = E(Y) - \mu = \mu - \mu = 0$$

Another application of Rule 3 is

$$E(X + Y)^2 = E(X)^2 + E(Y)^2 + 2E(XY)$$

This leads to a proof of the statement in Chapter 5 that the variance of $Y$, $E(Y - \mu)^2$, equals $E(Y^2) - \mu^2$:

$$E(Y - \mu)^2 = E(Y^2) + E(\mu)^2 - 2E(Y\mu)$$

$$= E(Y^2) + \mu^2 - 2\mu E(Y), \qquad \text{because } \mu \text{ is a constant}$$

$$= E(Y)^2 + \mu^2 - 2\mu^2, \qquad \text{because } \mu \text{ and } E(Y) \text{ are the same entity}$$
$$= E(Y^2) - \mu^2$$

■ **RULE 4.**    *IF X and Y are independently distributed, then* $E(XY) = E(X)E(Y)$. To prove this, we again begin with the definition of an expectation:

$$E(XY) = \sum_x \sum_y xyp(x, y)$$

$$= \sum_x \sum_y xyp(x)p(y)$$

because the joint probability $p(x, y) = p(x)p(y)$ if $X$ and $Y$ are independently distributed. Rearranging terms gives

$$E(XY) = \left[\sum xp(x)\right]\left[\sum yp(y)\right] = E(X)E(Y)$$

A useful implication of this is that $E(X - \overline{X})(Y - \overline{Y}) = 0$ if $X$ and $Y$ are independent. This follows because $E(X - \overline{X})(Y - \overline{Y})$ then must equal $[E(X - \overline{X})][E(Y - \overline{Y})] = 0 \times 0$. Therefore, if $X$ and $Y$ are independent, their covariance (and consequently $\rho$) must equal zero.

## B.2 APPLICATIONS TO ESTIMATION

We can now show that $\overline{Y}$ is an unbiased estimate of $\mu$; that is, $E(\overline{Y}) = E(Y)$ or $\mu$. We have

$$E(\overline{Y}) = E\left(\frac{\sum Y}{n}\right) = \frac{1}{n}E\left(\sum Y\right) \quad \text{by Rule 1}$$

$$= \frac{1}{n}\sum E(Y)$$

$$= \frac{1}{n}(n)E(Y) = E(Y)$$

We next show that $s^2$ is an unbiased estimator of $\sigma^2$; that is, $E(s^2) = \sigma^2$. Begin by considering the sum of squares, the numerator of $s^2$:

$$E\left[\sum(Y - \overline{Y})^2\right] = E\sum[(Y - \mu) - (\overline{Y} - \mu)]^2$$

$$= E\left[\sum(Y - \mu)^2 + \sum(\overline{Y} - \mu)^2 - 2(\overline{Y} - \mu)\sum(Y - \mu)\right]$$

$$= E\left[\sum(Y - \mu)^2 + n(\overline{Y} - \mu)^2 - 2n(\overline{Y} - \mu)^2\right]$$

$$= E\left[\sum(Y - \mu)^2 - n(\overline{Y} - \mu)^2\right]$$

$$= \sum E(Y - \mu)^2 - nE(\overline{Y} - \mu)^2 \quad \text{by Rule 3}$$

The average squared deviation of a quantity from its average is a variance; that is, $E(Y - \mu)^2 = \sigma^2$ and $E(\overline{Y} - \mu)^2 = \sigma^2/n$. Therefore,

$$E\left[\sum(Y - \overline{Y})^2\right] = n\sigma^2 - \frac{n\sigma^2}{n}$$

$$= (n - 1)\sigma^2$$

Therefore,

$$E\left(\frac{\sum(Y - \overline{Y})^2}{n-1}\right) = E[s^2] = \sigma^2$$

## B.3 THE MEAN AND VARIANCE OF THE BINOMIAL DISTRIBUTION

Consider a series of $n$ Bernoulli trials and let $X = 1$ or $0$, depending upon whether the trial outcome was a success or failure; $p(X = 1) = p$ and $p(X = 0) = q$. The total number of successes in the $n$ trials is $Y = \sum X$. We want to derive expressions for $E(Y)$ and var$(Y)$, the mean and variance of the binomial distribution. We have

$$E(Y) = E\left(\sum X\right) = \sum E(X)$$
$$= \sum \sum x p(x) \quad \text{by definition of an expected value}$$
$$= \sum[(1)(p) + (0)(q)] = \sum p = np$$

We derive the expression for the variance of the binomial distribution in a similar manner:

$$\text{var}(Y) = \text{var}\left(\sum X\right)$$

The variance of a sum of independent variables is the sum of their variances; therefore,

$$\text{var}(Y) = \text{var}\left(\sum X\right) = \sum \text{var}(X)$$

The variance of $X$ is $E[X - E(X)]^2 = E(X^2) - [E(X)]^2$; see the development under Rule 3, immediately preceding Rule 4. We showed above that $E(X) = p$, and

$$E(X^2) = (1^2)(p) + (0^2)(q) \quad \text{by definition of an expected value}$$
$$= p$$

Therefore, var$(X) = E(X^2) - [E(X)]^2 = p - p^2 = p(1 - p) = pq$. Finally, we have

$$\text{var}(Y) = \sum \text{var}(X) = \sum pq = npq$$

# Appendix C
## Statistical Tables

**TABLE C.1**   THE BINOMIAL PROBABILITY: $p(y, n, p)$

| | | | | | $p$ | | | | | |
|---|---|---|---|---|---|---|---|---|---|---|
| y | .05 | .10 | .15 | .20 | .25 | .30 | .35 | .40 | .45 | .50 |
| **n = 4** | | | | | | | | | | |
| 0 | .8145 | .6561 | .5220 | .4096 | .3164 | .2401 | .1785 | .1296 | .0915 | .0625 |
| 1 | .1715 | .2916 | .3685 | .4096 | .4219 | .4116 | .3845 | .3456 | .2995 | .2500 |
| 2 | .0135 | .0486 | .0975 | .1536 | .2109 | .2646 | .3105 | .3456 | .3675 | .3750 |
| 3 | .0005 | .0036 | .0115 | .0256 | .0469 | .0756 | .1115 | .1536 | .2005 | .2500 |
| 4 | .0000 | .0001 | .0005 | .0016 | .0039 | .0081 | .0150 | .0256 | .0410 | .0625 |
| **n = 5** | | | | | | | | | | |
| 0 | .7738 | .5905 | .4437 | .3277 | .2373 | .1681 | .1160 | .0778 | .0503 | .0313 |
| 1 | .2036 | .3281 | .3915 | .4096 | .3955 | .3601 | .3124 | .2592 | .2059 | .1563 |
| 2 | .0214 | .0729 | .1382 | .2048 | .2637 | .3087 | .3364 | .3456 | .3369 | .3125 |
| 3 | .0011 | .0081 | .0244 | .0512 | .0879 | .1323 | .1811 | .2304 | .2757 | .3125 |
| 4 | .0000 | .0005 | .0022 | .0064 | .0146 | .0284 | .0488 | .0768 | .1128 | .1563 |
| 5 | .0000 | .0000 | .0001 | .0003 | .0010 | .0024 | .0053 | .0102 | .0185 | .0313 |
| **n = 6** | | | | | | | | | | |
| 0 | .7351 | .5314 | .3771 | .2621 | .1780 | .1176 | .0754 | .0467 | .0277 | .0156 |
| 1 | .2321 | .3543 | .3993 | .3932 | .3560 | .3025 | .2437 | .1866 | .1359 | .0938 |
| 2 | .0305 | .0984 | .1762 | .2458 | .2966 | .3241 | .3280 | .3110 | .2780 | .2344 |
| 3 | .0021 | .0146 | .0415 | .0819 | .1318 | .1852 | .2355 | .2765 | .3032 | .3125 |
| 4 | .0001 | .0012 | .0055 | .0154 | .0330 | .0595 | .0951 | .1382 | .1861 | .2344 |
| 5 | .0000 | .0001 | .0004 | .0015 | .0044 | .0102 | .0205 | .0369 | .0609 | .0938 |
| 6 | .0000 | .0000 | .0000 | .0001 | .0002 | .0007 | .0018 | .0041 | .0083 | .0156 |
| **n = 7** | | | | | | | | | | |
| 0 | .6983 | .4783 | .3206 | .2097 | .1335 | .0824 | .0490 | .0280 | .0152 | .0078 |
| 1 | .2573 | .3720 | .3960 | .3670 | .3115 | .2471 | .1848 | .1306 | .0872 | .0547 |
| 2 | .0406 | .1240 | .2097 | .2753 | .3115 | .3177 | .2985 | .2613 | .2140 | .1641 |
| 3 | .0036 | .0230 | .0617 | .1147 | .1730 | .2269 | .2679 | .2903 | .2918 | .2734 |
| 4 | .0002 | .0026 | .0109 | .0287 | .0577 | .0972 | .1442 | .1935 | .2388 | .2734 |
| 5 | .0000 | .0002 | .0012 | .0043 | .0115 | .0250 | .0466 | .0774 | .1172 | .1641 |
| 6 | .0000 | .0000 | .0001 | .0004 | .0013 | .0036 | .0084 | .0172 | .0320 | .0547 |
| 7 | .0000 | .0000 | .0000 | .0000 | .0001 | .0002 | .0006 | .0016 | .0037 | .0078 |
| **n = 8** | | | | | | | | | | |
| 0 | .6634 | .4305 | .2725 | .1678 | .1001 | .0576 | .0319 | .0168 | .0084 | .0039 |
| 1 | .2793 | .3826 | .3847 | .3355 | .2670 | .1977 | .1373 | .0896 | .0548 | .0313 |
| 2 | .0515 | .1488 | .2376 | .2936 | .3115 | .2965 | .2587 | .2090 | .1569 | .1094 |
| 3 | .0054 | .0331 | .0839 | .1468 | .2076 | .2541 | .2786 | .2787 | .2568 | .2188 |
| 4 | .0004 | .0046 | .0185 | .0459 | .0865 | .1361 | .1875 | .2322 | .2627 | .2734 |
| 5 | .0000 | .0004 | .0026 | .0092 | .0231 | .0467 | .0808 | .1239 | .1719 | .2188 |
| 6 | .0000 | .0000 | .0002 | .0011 | .0038 | .0100 | .0217 | .0413 | .0703 | .1094 |
| 7 | .0000 | .0000 | .0000 | .0001 | .0004 | .0012 | .0033 | .0079 | .0164 | .0313 |
| 8 | .0000 | .0000 | .0000 | .0000 | .0000 | .0001 | .0002 | .0007 | .0017 | .0039 |
| **n = 9** | | | | | | | | | | |
| 0 | .6302 | .3874 | .2316 | .1342 | .0751 | .0404 | .0207 | .0101 | .0046 | .0020 |
| 1 | .2985 | .3874 | .3679 | .3020 | .2253 | .1556 | .1004 | .0605 | .0339 | .0176 |
| 2 | .0629 | .1722 | .2597 | .3020 | .3003 | .2668 | .2162 | .1612 | .1110 | .0703 |
| 3 | .0077 | .0446 | .1069 | .1762 | .2336 | .2668 | .2716 | .2508 | .2119 | .1641 |
| 4 | .0006 | .0074 | .0283 | .0661 | .1168 | .1715 | .2194 | .2508 | .2600 | .2461 |

**TABLE C.1** (continued)

|  | | | | | | $p$ | | | | |
|---|---|---|---|---|---|---|---|---|---|---|
| $y$ | .05 | .10 | .15 | .20 | .25 | .30 | .35 | .40 | .45 | .50 |
| 5 | .0000 | .0008 | .0050 | .0165 | .0389 | .0735 | .1181 | .1672 | .2128 | .2461 |
| 6 | .0000 | .0001 | .0006 | .0028 | .0087 | .0210 | .0424 | .0743 | .1160 | .1641 |
| 7 | .0000 | .0000 | .0000 | .0003 | .0012 | .0039 | .0098 | .0212 | .0407 | .0703 |
| 8 | .0000 | .0000 | .0000 | .0000 | .0001 | .0004 | .0013 | .0035 | .0083 | .0176 |
| 9 | .0000 | .0000 | .0000 | .0000 | .0000 | .0000 | .0001 | .0003 | .0008 | .0020 |

$n = 10$

| $y$ | .05 | .10 | .15 | .20 | .25 | .30 | .35 | .40 | .45 | .50 |
|---|---|---|---|---|---|---|---|---|---|---|
| 0 | .5987 | .3487 | .1969 | .1074 | .0563 | .0282 | .0135 | .0060 | .0025 | .0010 |
| 1 | .3151 | .3874 | .3474 | .2684 | .1877 | .1211 | .0725 | .0403 | .0207 | .0098 |
| 2 | .0746 | .1937 | .2759 | .3020 | .2816 | .2335 | .1757 | .1209 | .0763 | .0439 |
| 3 | .0105 | .0574 | .1298 | .2013 | .2503 | .2668 | .2522 | .2150 | .1665 | .1172 |
| 4 | .0010 | .0112 | .0401 | .0881 | .1460 | .2001 | .2377 | .2508 | .2384 | .2051 |
| 5 | .0001 | .0015 | .0085 | .0264 | .0584 | .1029 | .1536 | .2007 | .2340 | .2461 |
| 6 | .0000 | .0001 | .0012 | .0055 | .0162 | .0368 | .0689 | .1115 | .1596 | .2051 |
| 7 | .0000 | .0000 | .0001 | .0008 | .0031 | .0090 | .0212 | .0425 | .0746 | .1172 |
| 8 | .0000 | .0000 | .0000 | .0001 | .0004 | .0014 | .0043 | .0106 | .0229 | .0439 |
| 9 | .0000 | .0000 | .0000 | .0000 | .0000 | .0001 | .0005 | .0016 | .0042 | .0098 |
| 10 | .0000 | .0000 | .0000 | .0000 | .0000 | .0000 | .0000 | .0001 | .0003 | .0010 |

$n = 11$

| $y$ | .05 | .10 | .15 | .20 | .25 | .30 | .35 | .40 | .45 | .50 |
|---|---|---|---|---|---|---|---|---|---|---|
| 0 | .5688 | .3138 | .1673 | .0859 | .0422 | .0198 | .0088 | .0036 | .0014 | .0005 |
| 1 | .3293 | .3835 | .3248 | .2362 | .1549 | .0932 | .0518 | .0266 | .0125 | .0054 |
| 2 | .0867 | .2131 | .2866 | .2953 | .2581 | .1998 | .1395 | .0887 | .0513 | .0269 |
| 3 | .0137 | .0710 | .1517 | .2215 | .2581 | .2568 | .2254 | .1774 | .1259 | .0806 |
| 4 | .0014 | .0158 | .0536 | .1107 | .1721 | .2201 | .2428 | .2365 | .2060 | .1611 |
| 5 | .0001 | .0025 | .0132 | .0388 | .0803 | .1321 | .1830 | .2207 | .2360 | .2256 |
| 6 | .0000 | .0003 | .0023 | .0097 | .0268 | .0566 | .0985 | .1471 | .1931 | .2256 |
| 7 | .0000 | .0000 | .0003 | .0017 | .0064 | .0173 | .0379 | .0701 | .1128 | .1611 |
| 8 | .0000 | .0000 | .0000 | .0002 | .0011 | .0037 | .0102 | .0234 | .0462 | .0806 |
| 9 | .0000 | .0000 | .0000 | .0000 | .0001 | .0005 | .0018 | .0052 | .0126 | .0269 |
| 10 | .0000 | .0000 | .0000 | .0000 | .0000 | .0000 | .0002 | .0007 | .0021 | .0054 |
| 11 | .0000 | .0000 | .0000 | .0000 | .0000 | .0000 | .0000 | .0000 | .0002 | .0005 |

$n = 12$

| $y$ | .05 | .10 | .15 | .20 | .25 | .30 | .35 | .40 | .45 | .50 |
|---|---|---|---|---|---|---|---|---|---|---|
| 0 | .5404 | .2824 | .1422 | .0687 | .0317 | .0138 | .0057 | .0022 | .0008 | .0002 |
| 1 | .3413 | .3766 | .3012 | .2062 | .1267 | .0712 | .0368 | .0174 | .0075 | .0029 |
| 2 | .0988 | .2301 | .2924 | .2835 | .2323 | .1678 | .1088 | .0639 | .0339 | .0161 |
| 3 | .0173 | .0852 | .1720 | .2362 | .2581 | .2397 | .1954 | .1419 | .0923 | .0537 |
| 4 | .0021 | .0213 | .0683 | .1329 | .1936 | .2311 | .2367 | .2128 | .1700 | .1208 |
| 5 | .0002 | .0038 | .0193 | .0532 | .1032 | .1585 | .2039 | .2270 | .2225 | .1934 |
| 6 | .0000 | .0005 | .0040 | .0155 | .0401 | .0792 | .1281 | .1766 | .2124 | .2256 |
| 7 | .0000 | .0000 | .0006 | .0033 | .0115 | .0291 | .0591 | .1009 | .1489 | .1934 |
| 8 | .0000 | .0000 | .0001 | .0005 | .0024 | .0078 | .0199 | .0420 | .0762 | .1208 |
| 9 | .0000 | .0000 | .0000 | .0001 | .0004 | .0015 | .0048 | .0125 | .0277 | .0537 |
| 10 | .0000 | .0000 | .0000 | .0000 | .0000 | .0002 | .0008 | .0025 | .0068 | .0161 |
| 11 | .0000 | .0000 | .0000 | .0000 | .0000 | .0000 | .0001 | .0003 | .0010 | .0029 |
| 12 | .0000 | .0000 | .0000 | .0000 | .0000 | .0000 | .0000 | .0000 | .0001 | .0002 |

**TABLE C.1** (continued)

| | | | | | p | | | | | | |
|---|---|---|---|---|---|---|---|---|---|---|---|
| y | .05 | .10 | .15 | .20 | .25 | .30 | .35 | .40 | .45 | .50 |

*n* = 13

| y | .05 | .10 | .15 | .20 | .25 | .30 | .35 | .40 | .45 | .50 |
|---|---|---|---|---|---|---|---|---|---|---|
| 0 | .5133 | .2542 | .1209 | .0550 | .0238 | .0097 | .0037 | .0013 | .0004 | .0001 |
| 1 | .3512 | .3672 | .2774 | .1787 | .1029 | .0540 | .0259 | .0113 | .0045 | .0016 |
| 2 | .1109 | .2448 | .2937 | .2680 | .2059 | .1388 | .0836 | .0453 | .0220 | .0095 |
| 3 | .0214 | .0997 | .1900 | .2457 | .2517 | .2181 | .1651 | .1107 | .0660 | .0349 |
| 4 | .0028 | .0277 | .0838 | .1535 | .2097 | .2337 | .2222 | .1845 | .1350 | .0873 |
| 5 | .0003 | .0055 | .0266 | .0691 | .1258 | .1803 | .2154 | .2214 | .1989 | .1571 |
| 6 | .0000 | .0008 | .0063 | .0230 | .0559 | .1030 | .1546 | .1968 | .2169 | .2095 |
| 7 | .0000 | .0001 | .0011 | .0058 | .0186 | .0442 | .0833 | .1312 | .1775 | .2095 |
| 8 | .0000 | .0000 | .0001 | .0011 | .0047 | .0142 | .0336 | .0656 | .1089 | .1571 |
| 9 | .0000 | .0000 | .0000 | .0001 | .0009 | .0034 | .0101 | .0243 | .0495 | .0873 |
| 10 | .0000 | .0000 | .0000 | .0000 | .0001 | .0006 | .0022 | .0065 | .0162 | .0349 |
| 11 | .0000 | .0000 | .0000 | .0000 | .0000 | .0001 | .0003 | .0012 | .0036 | .0095 |
| 12 | .0000 | .0000 | .0000 | .0000 | .0000 | .0000 | .0000 | .0001 | .0005 | .0016 |
| 13 | .0000 | .0000 | .0000 | .0000 | .0000 | .0000 | .0000 | .0000 | .0000 | .0001 |

*n* = 14

| y | .05 | .10 | .15 | .20 | .25 | .30 | .35 | .40 | .45 | .50 |
|---|---|---|---|---|---|---|---|---|---|---|
| 0 | .4877 | .2288 | .1028 | .0440 | .0178 | .0068 | .0024 | .0008 | .0002 | .0001 |
| 1 | .3593 | .3559 | .2539 | .1539 | .0832 | .0407 | .0181 | .0073 | .0027 | .0009 |
| 2 | .1229 | .2570 | .2912 | .2501 | .1802 | .1134 | .0634 | .0317 | .0141 | .0056 |
| 3 | .0259 | .1142 | .2056 | .2501 | .2402 | .1943 | .1366 | .0845 | .0462 | .0222 |
| 4 | .0037 | .0349 | .0998 | .1720 | .2202 | .2290 | .2022 | .1549 | .1040 | .0611 |
| 5 | .0004 | .0078 | .0352 | .0860 | .1468 | .1963 | .2178 | .2066 | .1701 | .1222 |
| 6 | .0000 | .0013 | .0093 | .0322 | .0734 | .1262 | .1759 | .2066 | .2088 | .1833 |
| 7 | .0000 | .0002 | .0019 | .0092 | .0280 | .0618 | .1082 | .1574 | .1952 | .2095 |
| 8 | .0000 | .0000 | .0003 | .0020 | .0082 | .0232 | .0510 | .0918 | .1398 | .1833 |
| 9 | .0000 | .0000 | .0000 | .0003 | .0018 | .0066 | .0183 | .0408 | .0762 | .1222 |
| 10 | .0000 | .0000 | .0000 | .0000 | .0003 | .0014 | .0049 | .0136 | .0312 | .0611 |
| 11 | .0000 | .0000 | .0000 | .0000 | .0000 | .0002 | .0010 | .0033 | .0093 | .0222 |
| 12 | .0000 | .0000 | .0000 | .0000 | .0000 | .0000 | .0001 | .0005 | .0019 | .0056 |
| 13 | .0000 | .0000 | .0000 | .0000 | .0000 | .0000 | .0000 | .0001 | .0002 | .0009 |
| 14 | .0000 | .0000 | .0000 | .0000 | .0000 | .0000 | .0000 | .0000 | .0000 | .0001 |

*n* = 15

| y | .05 | .10 | .15 | .20 | .25 | .30 | .35 | .40 | .45 | .50 |
|---|---|---|---|---|---|---|---|---|---|---|
| 0 | .4633 | .2059 | .0874 | .0352 | .0134 | .0047 | .0016 | .0005 | .0001 | .0000 |
| 1 | .3658 | .3432 | .2312 | .1319 | .0668 | .0305 | .0126 | .0047 | .0016 | .0005 |
| 2 | .1348 | .2669 | .2856 | .2309 | .1559 | .0916 | .0476 | .0219 | .0090 | .0032 |
| 3 | .0307 | .1285 | .2184 | .2501 | .2252 | .1700 | .1110 | .0634 | .0318 | .0139 |
| 4 | .0049 | .0428 | .1156 | .1876 | .2252 | .2186 | .1792 | .1268 | .0780 | .0417 |
| 5 | .0006 | .0105 | .0449 | .1032 | .1651 | .2061 | .2123 | .1859 | .1404 | .0916 |
| 6 | .0000 | .0019 | .0132 | .0430 | .0917 | .1472 | .1906 | .2066 | .1914 | .1527 |
| 7 | .0000 | .0003 | .0030 | .0138 | .0393 | .0811 | .1319 | .1771 | .2013 | .1964 |
| 8 | .0000 | .0000 | .0005 | .0035 | .0131 | .0348 | .0710 | .1181 | .1647 | .1964 |
| 9 | .0000 | .0000 | .0001 | .0007 | .0034 | .0116 | .0298 | .0612 | .1048 | .1527 |
| 10 | .0000 | .0000 | .0000 | .0001 | .0007 | .0030 | .0096 | .0245 | .0515 | .0916 |
| 11 | .0000 | .0000 | .0000 | .0000 | .0001 | .0006 | .0024 | .0074 | .0191 | .0417 |
| 12 | .0000 | .0000 | .0000 | .0000 | .0000 | .0001 | .0004 | .0016 | .0052 | .0139 |

TABLE C.1 (continued)

| | | | | | $p$ | | | | | |
|---|---|---|---|---|---|---|---|---|---|---|
| y | .05 | .10 | .15 | .20 | .25 | .30 | .35 | .40 | .45 | .50 |
| 13 | .0000 | .0000 | .0000 | .0000 | .0000 | .0000 | .0001 | .0003 | .0010 | .0032 |
| 14 | .0000 | .0000 | .0000 | .0000 | .0000 | .0000 | .0000 | .0000 | .0001 | .0005 |
| 15 | .0000 | .0000 | .0000 | .0000 | .0000 | .0000 | .0000 | .0000 | .0000 | .0000 |

$n = 16$

| y | .05 | .10 | .15 | .20 | .25 | .30 | .35 | .40 | .45 | .50 |
|---|---|---|---|---|---|---|---|---|---|---|
| 0 | .4401 | .1853 | .0743 | .0281 | .0100 | .0033 | .0010 | .0003 | .0001 | .0000 |
| 1 | .3706 | .3294 | .2097 | .1126 | .0535 | .0228 | .0087 | .0030 | .0009 | .0002 |
| 2 | .1463 | .2745 | .2775 | .2111 | .1336 | .0732 | .0353 | .0150 | .0056 | .0018 |
| 3 | .0359 | .1423 | .2285 | .2463 | .2079 | .1465 | .0888 | .0468 | .0215 | .0085 |
| 4 | .0061 | .0514 | .1311 | .2001 | .2252 | .2040 | .1553 | .1014 | .0572 | .0278 |
| 5 | .0008 | .0137 | .0555 | .1201 | .1802 | .2099 | .2008 | .1623 | .1123 | .0667 |
| 6 | .0001 | .0028 | .0180 | .0550 | .1101 | .1649 | .1982 | .1983 | .1684 | .1222 |
| 7 | .0000 | .0004 | .0045 | .0197 | .0524 | .1010 | .1524 | .1889 | .1969 | .1746 |
| 8 | .0000 | .0001 | .0009 | .0055 | .0197 | .0487 | .0923 | .1417 | .1812 | .1964 |
| 9 | .0000 | .0000 | .0001 | .0012 | .0058 | .0185 | .0442 | .0840 | .1318 | .1746 |
| 10 | .0000 | .0000 | .0000 | .0002 | .0014 | .0056 | .0167 | .0392 | .0755 | .1222 |
| 11 | .0000 | .0000 | .0000 | .0000 | .0002 | .0013 | .0049 | .0142 | .0337 | .0667 |
| 12 | .0000 | .0000 | .0000 | .0000 | .0000 | .0002 | .0011 | .0040 | .0115 | .0278 |
| 13 | .0000 | .0000 | .0000 | .0000 | .0000 | .0000 | .0002 | .0008 | .0029 | .0085 |
| 14 | .0000 | .0000 | .0000 | .0000 | .0000 | .0000 | .0000 | .0001 | .0005 | .0018 |
| 15 | .0000 | .0000 | .0000 | .0000 | .0000 | .0000 | .0000 | .0000 | .0001 | .0002 |
| 16 | .0000 | .0000 | .0000 | .0000 | .0000 | .0000 | .0000 | .0000 | .0000 | .0000 |

$n = 17$

| y | .05 | .10 | .15 | .20 | .25 | .30 | .35 | .40 | .45 | .50 |
|---|---|---|---|---|---|---|---|---|---|---|
| 0 | .4181 | .1668 | .0631 | .0225 | .0075 | .0023 | .0007 | .0002 | .0000 | .0000 |
| 1 | .3741 | .3150 | .1893 | .0957 | .0426 | .0169 | .0060 | .0019 | .0005 | .0001 |
| 2 | .1575 | .2800 | .2673 | .1914 | .1136 | .0581 | .0260 | .0102 | .0035 | .0010 |
| 3 | .0415 | .1556 | .2359 | .2393 | .1893 | .1245 | .0701 | .0341 | .0144 | .0052 |
| 4 | .0076 | .0605 | .1457 | .2093 | .2209 | .1868 | .1320 | .0796 | .0411 | .0182 |
| 5 | .0010 | .0175 | .0668 | .1361 | .1914 | .2081 | .1849 | .1379 | .0875 | .0472 |
| 6 | .0001 | .0039 | .0236 | .0680 | .1276 | .1784 | .1991 | .1839 | .1432 | .0944 |
| 7 | .0000 | .0007 | .0065 | .0267 | .0668 | .1201 | .1685 | .1927 | .1841 | .1484 |
| 8 | .0000 | .0001 | .0014 | .0084 | .0279 | .0644 | .1134 | .1606 | .1883 | .1855 |
| 9 | .0000 | .0000 | .0003 | .0021 | .0093 | .0276 | .0611 | .1070 | .1540 | .1855 |
| 10 | .0000 | .0000 | .0000 | .0004 | .0025 | .0095 | .0263 | .0571 | .1008 | .1484 |
| 11 | .0000 | .0000 | .0000 | .0001 | .0005 | .0026 | .0090 | .0242 | .0525 | .0944 |
| 12 | .0000 | .0000 | .0000 | .0000 | .0001 | .0006 | .0024 | .0081 | .0215 | .0472 |
| 13 | .0000 | .0000 | .0000 | .0000 | .0000 | .0001 | .0005 | .0021 | .0068 | .0182 |
| 14 | .0000 | .0000 | .0000 | .0000 | .0000 | .0000 | .0001 | .0004 | .0016 | .0052 |
| 15 | .0000 | .0000 | .0000 | .0000 | .0000 | .0000 | .0000 | .0001 | .0003 | .0010 |
| 16 | .0000 | .0000 | .0000 | .0000 | .0000 | .0000 | .0000 | .0000 | .0000 | .0001 |
| 17 | .0000 | .0000 | .0000 | .0000 | .0000 | .0000 | .0000 | .0000 | .0000 | .0000 |

$n = 18$

| y | .05 | .10 | .15 | .20 | .25 | .30 | .35 | .40 | .45 | .50 |
|---|---|---|---|---|---|---|---|---|---|---|
| 0 | .3972 | .1501 | .0536 | .0180 | .0056 | .0016 | .0004 | .0001 | .0000 | .0000 |
| 1 | .3763 | .3002 | .1704 | .0811 | .0338 | .0126 | .0042 | .0012 | .0003 | .0001 |
| 2 | .1683 | .2835 | .2556 | .1723 | .0958 | .0458 | .0190 | .0069 | .0022 | .0006 |
| 3 | .0473 | .1680 | .2406 | .2297 | .1704 | .1046 | .0547 | .0246 | .0095 | .0031 |

TABLE C.1 (continued)

| | | | | | $p$ | | | | | |
|---|---|---|---|---|---|---|---|---|---|---|
| y | .05 | .10 | .15 | .20 | .25 | .30 | .35 | .40 | .45 | .50 |
| 4 | .0093 | .0700 | .1592 | .2153 | .2130 | .1681 | .1104 | .0614 | .0291 | .0117 |
| 5 | .0014 | .0218 | .0787 | .1507 | .1988 | .2017 | .1664 | .1146 | .0666 | .0327 |
| 6 | .0002 | .0052 | .0301 | .0816 | .1436 | .1873 | .1941 | .1655 | .1181 | .0708 |
| 7 | .0000 | .0010 | .0091 | .0350 | .0820 | .1376 | .1792 | .1892 | .1657 | .1214 |
| 8 | .0000 | .0002 | .0022 | .0120 | .0376 | .0811 | .1327 | .1734 | .1864 | .1669 |
| 9 | .0000 | .0000 | .0004 | .0033 | .0139 | .0386 | .0794 | .1284 | .1694 | .1855 |
| 10 | .0000 | .0000 | .0001 | .0008 | .0042 | .0149 | .0385 | .0771 | .1248 | .1669 |
| 11 | .0000 | .0000 | .0000 | .0001 | .0010 | .0046 | .0151 | .0374 | .0742 | .1214 |
| 12 | .0000 | .0000 | .0000 | .0000 | .0002 | .0012 | .0047 | .0145 | .0354 | .0708 |
| 13 | .0000 | .0000 | .0000 | .0000 | .0000 | .0002 | .0012 | .0045 | .0134 | .0327 |
| 14 | .0000 | .0000 | .0000 | .0000 | .0000 | .0000 | .0002 | .0011 | .0039 | .0117 |
| 15 | .0000 | .0000 | .0000 | .0000 | .0000 | .0000 | .0000 | .0002 | .0009 | .0031 |
| 16 | .0000 | .0000 | .0000 | .0000 | .0000 | .0000 | .0000 | .0000 | .0001 | .0006 |
| 17 | .0000 | .0000 | .0000 | .0000 | .0000 | .0000 | .0000 | .0000 | .0000 | .0001 |
| 18 | .0000 | .0000 | .0000 | .0000 | .0000 | .0000 | .0000 | .0000 | .0000 | .0000 |

$n = 19$

| y | .05 | .10 | .15 | .20 | .25 | .30 | .35 | .40 | .45 | .50 |
|---|---|---|---|---|---|---|---|---|---|---|
| 0 | .3774 | .1351 | .0456 | .0144 | .0042 | .0011 | .0003 | .0001 | .0000 | .0000 |
| 1 | .3774 | .2852 | .1529 | .0685 | .0268 | .0093 | .0029 | .0008 | .0002 | .0000 |
| 2 | .1787 | .2852 | .2428 | .1540 | .0803 | .0358 | .0138 | .0046 | .0013 | .0003 |
| 3 | .0533 | .1796 | .2428 | .2182 | .1517 | .0869 | .0422 | .0175 | .0062 | .0018 |
| 4 | .0112 | .0798 | .1714 | .2182 | .2023 | .1491 | .0909 | .0467 | .0203 | .0074 |
| 5 | .0018 | .0266 | .0907 | .1636 | .2023 | .1916 | .1468 | .0933 | .0497 | .0222 |
| 6 | .0002 | .0069 | .0374 | .0955 | .1574 | .1916 | .1844 | .1451 | .0949 | .0518 |
| 7 | .0000 | .0014 | .0122 | .0443 | .0974 | .1525 | .1844 | .1797 | .1443 | .0961 |
| 8 | .0000 | .0002 | .0032 | .0166 | .0487 | .0981 | .1489 | .1797 | .1771 | .1442 |
| 9 | .0000 | .0000 | .0007 | .0051 | .0198 | .0514 | .0980 | .1464 | .1771 | .1762 |
| 10 | .0000 | .0000 | .0001 | .0013 | .0066 | .0220 | .0528 | .0976 | .1449 | .1762 |
| 11 | .0000 | .0000 | .0000 | .0003 | .0018 | .0077 | .0233 | .0532 | .0970 | .1442 |
| 12 | .0000 | .0000 | .0000 | .0000 | .0004 | .0022 | .0083 | .0237 | .0529 | .0961 |
| 13 | .0000 | .0000 | .0000 | .0000 | .0001 | .0005 | .0024 | .0085 | .0233 | .0518 |
| 14 | .0000 | .0000 | .0000 | .0000 | .0000 | .0001 | .0006 | .0024 | .0082 | .0222 |
| 15 | .0000 | .0000 | .0000 | .0000 | .0000 | .0000 | .0001 | .0005 | .0022 | .0074 |
| 16 | .0000 | .0000 | .0000 | .0000 | .0000 | .0000 | .0000 | .0001 | .0005 | .0018 |
| 17 | .0000 | .0000 | .0000 | .0000 | .0000 | .0000 | .0000 | .0000 | .0001 | .0003 |
| 18 | .0000 | .0000 | .0000 | .0000 | .0000 | .0000 | .0000 | .0000 | .0000 | .0000 |
| 19 | .0000 | .0000 | .0000 | .0000 | .0000 | .0000 | .0000 | .0000 | .0000 | .0000 |

$n = 20$

| y | .05 | .10 | .15 | .20 | .25 | .30 | .35 | .40 | .45 | .50 |
|---|---|---|---|---|---|---|---|---|---|---|
| 0 | .3585 | .1216 | .0388 | .0115 | .0032 | .0008 | .0002 | .0000 | .0000 | .0000 |
| 1 | .3774 | .2702 | .1368 | .0576 | .0211 | .0068 | .0020 | .0005 | .0001 | .0000 |
| 2 | .1887 | .2852 | .2293 | .1369 | .0669 | .0278 | .0100 | .0031 | .0008 | .0002 |
| 3 | .0596 | .1901 | .2428 | .2054 | .1339 | .0716 | .0323 | .0123 | .0040 | .0011 |
| 4 | .0133 | .0898 | .1821 | .2182 | .1897 | .1304 | .0738 | .0350 | .0139 | .0046 |
| 5 | .0022 | .0319 | .1028 | .1746 | .2023 | .1789 | .1272 | .0746 | .0365 | .0148 |
| 6 | .0003 | .0089 | .0454 | .1091 | .1686 | .1916 | .1712 | .1244 | .0746 | .0370 |
| 7 | .0000 | .0020 | .0160 | .0545 | .1124 | .1643 | .1844 | .1659 | .1221 | .0739 |

**TABLE C.1** (continued)

| | | | | | $p$ | | | | | |
|---|---|---|---|---|---|---|---|---|---|---|
| y | .05 | .10 | .15 | .20 | .25 | .30 | .35 | .40 | .45 | .50 |
| 8 | .0000 | .0004 | .0046 | .0222 | .0609 | .1144 | .1614 | .1797 | .1623 | .1201 |
| 9 | .0000 | .0001 | .0011 | .0074 | .0271 | .0654 | .1158 | .1597 | .1771 | .1602 |
| 10 | .0000 | .0000 | .0002 | .0020 | .0099 | .0308 | .0686 | .1171 | .1593 | .1762 |
| 11 | .0000 | .0000 | .0000 | .0005 | .0030 | .0120 | .0336 | .0710 | .1185 | .1602 |
| 12 | .0000 | .0000 | .0000 | .0001 | .0008 | .0039 | .0136 | .0355 | .0727 | .1201 |
| 13 | .0000 | .0000 | .0000 | .0000 | .0002 | .0010 | .0045 | .0146 | .0366 | .0739 |
| 14 | .0000 | .0000 | .0000 | .0000 | .0000 | .0002 | .0012 | .0049 | .0150 | .0370 |
| 15 | .0000 | .0000 | .0000 | .0000 | .0000 | .0000 | .0003 | .0013 | .0049 | .0148 |
| 16 | .0000 | .0000 | .0000 | .0000 | .0000 | .0000 | .0000 | .0003 | .0013 | .0046 |
| 17 | .0000 | .0000 | .0000 | .0000 | .0000 | .0000 | .0000 | .0000 | .0002 | .0011 |
| 18 | .0000 | .0000 | .0000 | .0000 | .0000 | .0000 | .0000 | .0000 | .0000 | .0002 |
| 19 | .0000 | .0000 | .0000 | .0000 | .0000 | .0000 | .0000 | .0000 | .0000 | .0000 |
| 20 | .0000 | .0000 | .0000 | .0000 | .0000 | .0000 | .0000 | .0000 | .0000 | .0000 |

## TABLE C.2 THE STANDARDIZED NORMAL DISTRIBUTION

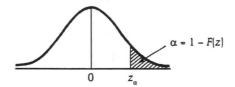

$\alpha = 1 - F(z)$

| z | α | z | α | z | α | z | α | z | α |
|-----|-------|-----|-------|-----|-------|------|-------|------|-------|
| .00 | .5000 | .33 | .3707 | .66 | .2546 | .99  | .1611 | 1.32 | .0934 |
| .01 | .4960 | .34 | .3669 | .67 | .2514 | 1.00 | .1587 | 1.33 | .0918 |
| .02 | .4920 | .35 | .3632 | .68 | .2483 | 1.01 | .1562 | 1.34 | .0901 |
| .03 | .4880 | .36 | .3594 | .69 | .2451 | 1.02 | .1539 | 1.35 | .0885 |
| .04 | .4840 | .37 | .3557 | .70 | .2420 | 1.03 | .1515 | 1.36 | .0869 |
| .05 | .4801 | .38 | .3520 | .71 | .2389 | 1.04 | .1492 | 1.37 | .0853 |
| .06 | .4761 | .39 | .3483 | .72 | .2358 | 1.05 | .1469 | 1.38 | .0838 |
| .07 | .4721 | .40 | .3446 | .73 | .2327 | 1.06 | .1446 | 1.39 | .0823 |
| .08 | .4681 | .41 | .3409 | .74 | .2296 | 1.07 | .1423 | 1.40 | .0808 |
| .09 | .4641 | .42 | .3372 | .75 | .2266 | 1.08 | .1401 | 1.41 | .0793 |
| .10 | .4602 | .43 | .3336 | .76 | .2236 | 1.09 | .1379 | 1.42 | .0778 |
| .11 | .4562 | .44 | .3300 | .77 | .2206 | 1.10 | .1357 | 1.43 | .0764 |
| .12 | .4522 | .45 | .3264 | .78 | .2177 | 1.11 | .1335 | 1.44 | .0749 |
| .13 | .4483 | .46 | .3228 | .79 | .2148 | 1.12 | .1314 | 1.45 | .0735 |
| .14 | .4443 | .47 | .3192 | .80 | .2119 | 1.13 | .1292 | 1.46 | .0721 |
| .15 | .4404 | .48 | .3156 | .81 | .2090 | 1.14 | .1271 | 1.47 | .0708 |
| .16 | .4364 | .49 | .3121 | .82 | .2061 | 1.15 | .1251 | 1.48 | .0694 |
| .17 | .4325 | .50 | .3085 | .83 | .2033 | 1.16 | .1230 | 1.49 | .0681 |
| .18 | .4286 | .51 | .3050 | .84 | .2005 | 1.17 | .1210 | 1.50 | .0668 |
| .19 | .4247 | .52 | .3015 | .85 | .1977 | 1.18 | .1190 | 1.51 | .0655 |
| .20 | .4207 | .53 | .2981 | .86 | .1949 | 1.19 | .1170 | 1.52 | .0643 |
| .21 | .4168 | .54 | .2946 | .87 | .1922 | 1.20 | .1151 | 1.53 | .0630 |
| .22 | .4129 | .55 | .2912 | .88 | .1894 | 1.21 | .1131 | 1.54 | .0618 |
| .23 | .4090 | .56 | .2877 | .89 | .1867 | 1.22 | .1112 | 1.55 | .0606 |
| .24 | .4052 | .57 | .2843 | .90 | .1841 | 1.23 | .1093 | 1.56 | .0594 |
| .25 | .4013 | .58 | .2810 | .91 | .1814 | 1.24 | .1075 | 1.57 | .0582 |
| .26 | .3974 | .59 | .2776 | .92 | .1788 | 1.25 | .1056 | 1.58 | .0571 |
| .27 | .3936 | .60 | .2743 | .93 | .1762 | 1.26 | .1038 | 1.59 | .0559 |
| .28 | .3897 | .61 | .2709 | .94 | .1736 | 1.27 | .1020 | 1.60 | .0548 |
| .29 | .3859 | .62 | .2676 | .95 | .1711 | 1.28 | .1003 | 1.61 | .0537 |
| .30 | .3821 | .63 | .2643 | .96 | .1685 | 1.29 | .0985 | 1.62 | .0526 |
| .31 | .3783 | .64 | .2611 | .97 | .1660 | 1.30 | .0968 | 1.63 | .0516 |
| .32 | .3745 | .65 | .2578 | .98 | .1635 | 1.31 | .0951 | 1.64 | .0505 |

**TABLE C.2**  (continued)

| z | α | z | α | z | α | z | α | z | α |
|---|---|---|---|---|---|---|---|---|---|
| 1.65 | .0495 | 1.98 | .0239 | 2.31 | .0104 | 2.64 | .0041 | 2.97 | .0015 |
| 1.66 | .0485 | 1.99 | .0233 | 2.32 | .0102 | 2.65 | .0040 | 2.98 | .0014 |
| 1.67 | .0475 | 2.00 | .0228 | 2.33 | .0099 | 2.66 | .0039 | 2.99 | .0014 |
| 1.68 | .0465 | 2.01 | .0222 | 2.34 | .0096 | 2.67 | .0038 | 3.00 | .0013 |
| 1.69 | .0455 | 2.02 | .0217 | 2.35 | .0094 | 2.68 | .0037 | 3.01 | .0013 |
| 1.70 | .0446 | 2.03 | .0212 | 2.36 | .0091 | 2.69 | .0036 | 3.02 | .0013 |
| 1.71 | .0436 | 2.04 | .0207 | 2.37 | .0089 | 2.70 | .0035 | 3.03 | .0012 |
| 1.72 | .0427 | 2.05 | .0202 | 2.38 | .0087 | 2.71 | .0034 | 3.04 | .0012 |
| 1.73 | .0418 | 2.06 | .0197 | 2.39 | .0084 | 2.72 | .0033 | 3.05 | .0011 |
| 1.74 | .0409 | 2.07 | .0192 | 2.40 | .0082 | 2.73 | .0032 | 3.06 | .0011 |
| 1.75 | .0401 | 2.08 | .0188 | 2.41 | .0080 | 2.74 | .0031 | 3.07 | .0011 |
| 1.76 | .0392 | 2.09 | .0183 | 2.42 | .0078 | 2.75 | .0030 | 3.08 | .0010 |
| 1.77 | .0384 | 2.10 | .0179 | 2.43 | .0075 | 2.76 | .0029 | 3.09 | .0010 |
| 1.78 | .0375 | 2.11 | .0174 | 2.44 | .0073 | 2.77 | .0028 | 3.10 | .0010 |
| 1.79 | .0367 | 2.12 | .0170 | 2.45 | .0071 | 2.78 | .0027 | 3.11 | .0009 |
| 1.80 | .0359 | 2.13 | .0166 | 2.46 | .0069 | 2.79 | .0026 | 3.12 | .0009 |
| 1.81 | .0351 | 2.14 | .0162 | 2.47 | .0068 | 2.80 | .0026 | 3.13 | .0009 |
| 1.82 | .0344 | 2.15 | .0158 | 2.48 | .0066 | 2.81 | .0025 | 3.14 | .0008 |
| 1.83 | .0336 | 2.16 | .0154 | 2.49 | .0064 | 2.82 | .0024 | 3.15 | .0008 |
| 1.84 | .0329 | 2.17 | .0150 | 2.50 | .0062 | 2.83 | .0023 | 3.16 | .0008 |
| 1.85 | .0322 | 2.18 | .0146 | 2.51 | .0060 | 2.84 | .0023 | 3.17 | .0008 |
| 1.86 | .0314 | 2.19 | .0143 | 2.52 | .0059 | 2.85 | .0022 | 3.18 | .0007 |
| 1.87 | .0307 | 2.20 | .0139 | 2.53 | .0057 | 2.86 | .0021 | 3.19 | .0007 |
| 1.88 | .0301 | 2.21 | .0136 | 2.54 | .0055 | 2.87 | .0021 | 3.20 | .0007 |
| 1.89 | .0294 | 2.22 | .0132 | 2.55 | .0054 | 2.88 | .0020 | 3.21 | .0007 |
| 1.90 | .0287 | 2.23 | .0129 | 2.56 | .0052 | 2.89 | .0019 | 3.22 | .0006 |
| 1.91 | .0281 | 2.24 | .0125 | 2.57 | .0051 | 2.90 | .0019 | 3.23 | .0006 |
| 1.92 | .0274 | 2.25 | .0122 | 2.58 | .0049 | 2.91 | .0018 | 3.24 | .0006 |
| 1.93 | .0268 | 2.26 | .0119 | 2.59 | .0048 | 2.92 | .0018 | 3.25 | .0006 |
| 1.94 | .0262 | 2.27 | .0116 | 2.60 | .0047 | 2.93 | .0017 | | |
| 1.95 | .0256 | 2.28 | .0113 | 2.61 | .0045 | 2.94 | .0016 | | |
| 1.96 | .0250 | 2.29 | .0110 | 2.62 | .0044 | 2.95 | .0016 | | |
| 1.97 | .0244 | 2.30 | .0107 | 2.63 | .0043 | 2.96 | .0015 | | |

*Source*: Adapted from Table 1 in Pearson, E. S. and Hartley, H. O. (1958). *Biometrika Tables for Statisticians*, Vol. 1, 2nd ed. Cambridge University Press: Cambridge, with the kind permission of the trustees of *Biometrika*.

**TABLE C.3** PERCENTAGE POINTS OF THE $t$ DISTRIBUTION

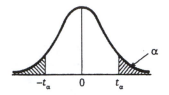

| | Level of Significance for a One-Tailed Test | | | | | | | | | |
|---|---|---|---|---|---|---|---|---|---|---|
| | 0.4 | 0.25 | 0.1 | 0.05 | 0.025 | 0.01 | 0.005 | 0.0025 | 0.001 | 0.0005 |

| | Level of Significance for a Two-Tailed Test | | | | | | | | | |
|---|---|---|---|---|---|---|---|---|---|---|
| df | 0.8 | 0.5 | 0.2 | 0.1 | 0.05 | 0.02 | 0.01 | 0.005 | 0.002 | 0.001 |
| 1 | 0.325 | 1.000 | 3.078 | 6.314 | 12.706 | 31.821 | 63.657 | 127.32 | 318.31 | 636.62 |
| 2 | .289 | 0.816 | 1.886 | 2.920 | 4.303 | 6.965 | 9.925 | 14.089 | 22.326 | 31.598 |
| 3 | .277 | .765 | 1.638 | 2.353 | 3.182 | 4.541 | 5.841 | 7.453 | 10.213 | 12.924 |
| 4 | .271 | .741 | 1.533 | 2.132 | 2.776 | 3.747 | 4.604 | 5.598 | 7.173 | 8.610 |
| 5 | 0.267 | 0.727 | 1.476 | 2.015 | 2.571 | 3.365 | 4.032 | 4.773 | 5.893 | 6.869 |
| 6 | .265 | .718 | 1.440 | 1.943 | 2.447 | 3.143 | 3.707 | 4.317 | 5.208 | 5.959 |
| 7 | .263 | .711 | 1.415 | 1.895 | 2.365 | 2.998 | 3.499 | 4.029 | 4.785 | 5.408 |
| 8 | .262 | .706 | 1.397 | 1.860 | 2.306 | 2.896 | 3.355 | 3.833 | 4.501 | 5.041 |
| 9 | .261 | .703 | 1.383 | 1.833 | 2.262 | 2.821 | 3.250 | 3.690 | 4.297 | 4.781 |
| 10 | 0.260 | 0.700 | 1.372 | 1.812 | 2.228 | 2.764 | 3.169 | 3.581 | 4.144 | 4.587 |
| 11 | .260 | .697 | 1.363 | 1.796 | 2.201 | 2.718 | 3.106 | 3.497 | 4.025 | 4.437 |
| 12 | .259 | .695 | 1.356 | 1.782 | 2.179 | 2.681 | 3.055 | 3.428 | 3.930 | 4.318 |
| 13 | .259 | .694 | 1.350 | 1.771 | 2.160 | 2.650 | 3.012 | 3.372 | 3.852 | 4.221 |
| 14 | .258 | .692 | 1.345 | 1.761 | 2.145 | 2.624 | 2.977 | 3.326 | 3.787 | 4.140 |
| 15 | 0.258 | 0.691 | 1.341 | 1.753 | 2.131 | 2.602 | 2.947 | 3.286 | 3.733 | 4.073 |
| 16 | .258 | .690 | 1.337 | 1.746 | 2.120 | 2.583 | 2.921 | 3.252 | 3.686 | 4.015 |
| 17 | .257 | .689 | 1.333 | 1.740 | 2.110 | 2.567 | 2.898 | 3.222 | 3.646 | 3.965 |
| 18 | .257 | .688 | 1.330 | 1.734 | 2.101 | 2.552 | 2.878 | 3.197 | 3.610 | 3.922 |
| 19 | .257 | .688 | 1.328 | 1.729 | 2.093 | 2.539 | 2.861 | 3.174 | 3.579 | 3.883 |
| 20 | 0.257 | 0.687 | 1.325 | 1.725 | 2.086 | 2.528 | 2.845 | 3.153 | 3.552 | 3.850 |
| 21 | .257 | .686 | 1.323 | 1.721 | 2.080 | 2.518 | 2.831 | 3.135 | 3.527 | 3.819 |
| 22 | .256 | .686 | 1.321 | 1.717 | 2.074 | 2.508 | 2.819 | 3.119 | 3.505 | 3.792 |
| 23 | .256 | .685 | 1.319 | 1.714 | 2.069 | 2.500 | 2.807 | 3.104 | 3.485 | 3.767 |
| 24 | .256 | .685 | 1.318 | 1.711 | 2.064 | 2.492 | 2.797 | 3.091 | 3.467 | 3.745 |
| 25 | 0.256 | 0.684 | 1.316 | 1.708 | 2.060 | 2.485 | 2.787 | 3.078 | 3.450 | 3.725 |
| 26 | .256 | .684 | 1.315 | 1.706 | 2.056 | 2.479 | 2.779 | 3.067 | 3.435 | 3.707 |
| 27 | .256 | .684 | 1.314 | 1.703 | 2.052 | 2.473 | 2.771 | 3.057 | 3.421 | 3.690 |
| 28 | .256 | .683 | 1.313 | 1.701 | 2.048 | 2.467 | 2.763 | 3.047 | 3.408 | 3.674 |
| 29 | .256 | .683 | 1.311 | 1.699 | 2.045 | 2.462 | 2.756 | 3.038 | 3.396 | 3.659 |
| 30 | 0.256 | 0.683 | 1.310 | 1.697 | 2.042 | 2.457 | 2.750 | 3.030 | 3.385 | 3.646 |
| 40 | .255 | .681 | 1.303 | 1.684 | 2.021 | 2.423 | 2.704 | 2.971 | 3.307 | 3.551 |
| 60 | .254 | .679 | 1.296 | 1.671 | 2.000 | 2.390 | 2.660 | 2.915 | 3.232 | 3.460 |
| 120 | .254 | .677 | 1.289 | 1.658 | 1.980 | 2.358 | 2.617 | 2.860 | 3.160 | 3.373 |
| $\infty$ | .253 | .674 | 1.282 | 1.645 | 1.960 | 2.326 | 2.576 | 2.807 | 3.090 | 3.291 |

*Source*: Adapted from Table 12 in Pearson, E. S. and Hartley. H. O. (1958). *Biometrika Tables for Statisticians,* Vol. 1, 2nd ed. Cambridge University Press: Cambridge, with the kind permission of the trustees of *Biometrika*.

**TABLE C.4** PERCENTAGE POINTS OF THE CHI-SQUARE DISTRIBUTION

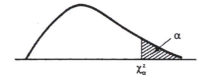

| df \ α | 0.995 | 0.990 | 0.975 | 0.950 | 0.900 | 0.750 | 0.500 |
|---|---|---|---|---|---|---|---|
| 1 | $392704.10^{-10}$ | $157088.10^{-9}$ | $982069.10^{-9}$ | $393214.10^{-8}$ | 0.0157908 | 0.1015308 | 0.454937 |
| 2 | 0.0100251 | 0.0201007 | 0.0506356 | 0.102587 | 0.210720 | 0.575364 | 1.38629 |
| 3 | 0.0717212 | 0.114832 | 0.215795 | 0.351846 | 0.584375 | 1.212534 | 2.36597 |
| 4 | 0.206990 | 0.297110 | 0.484419 | 0.710721 | 1.063623 | 1.92255 | 3.35670 |
| 5 | 0.411740 | 0.554300 | 0.831211 | 1.145476 | 1.61031 | 2.67460 | 4.35146 |
| 6 | 0.675727 | 0.872085 | 1.237347 | 1.63539 | 2.20413 | 3.45460 | 5.34812 |
| 7 | 0.989265 | 1.239043 | 1.68987 | 2.16735 | 2.83311 | 4.25485 | 6.34581 |
| 8 | 1.344419 | 1.646482 | 2.17973 | 2.73264 | 3.48954 | 5.07064 | 7.34412 |
| 9 | 1.734926 | 2.087912 | 2.70039 | 3.32511 | 4.16816 | 5.89883 | 8.34283 |
| 10 | 2.15585 | 2.55821 | 3.24697 | 3.94030 | 4.86518 | 6.73720 | 9.34182 |
| 11 | 2.60321 | 3.05347 | 3.81575 | 4.57481 | 5.57779 | 7.58412 | 10.3410 |
| 12 | 3.07382 | 3.57056 | 4.40379 | 5.22603 | 6.30380 | 8.43842 | 11.3403 |
| 13 | 3.56503 | 4.10691 | 5.00874 | 5.89186 | 7.04150 | 9.29906 | 12.3398 |
| 14 | 4.07468 | 4.66043 | 5.62872 | 6.57063 | 7.78953 | 10.1653 | 13.3393 |
| 15 | 4.60094 | 5.22935 | 6.26214 | 7.26094 | 8.54675 | 11.0365 | 14.3389 |
| 16 | 5.14224 | 5.81221 | 6.90766 | 7.96164 | 9.31223 | 11.9122 | 15.3385 |
| 17 | 5.69724 | 6.40776 | 7.56418 | 8.67176 | 10.0852 | 12.7919 | 16.3381 |
| 18 | 6.26481 | 7.01491 | 8.23075 | 9.39046 | 10.8649 | 13.6753 | 17.3379 |
| 19 | 6.84398 | 7.63273 | 8.90655 | 10.1170 | 11.6509 | 14.5620 | 18.3376 |
| 20 | 7.43386 | 8.26040 | 9.59083 | 10.8508 | 12.4426 | 15.4518 | 19.3374 |
| 21 | 8.03366 | 8.89720 | 10.28293 | 11.5913 | 13.2396 | 16.3444 | 20.3372 |
| 22 | 8.64272 | 9.54249 | 10.9823 | 12.3380 | 14.0415 | 17.2396 | 21.3370 |
| 23 | 9.26042 | 10.19567 | 11.6885 | 13.0905 | 14.8479 | 18.1373 | 22.3369 |
| 24 | 9.88623 | 10.8564 | 12.4011 | 13.8484 | 15.6587 | 19.0372 | 23.3367 |
| 25 | 10.5197 | 11.5240 | 13.1197 | 14.6114 | 16.4734 | 19.9393 | 24.3366 |
| 26 | 11.1603 | 12.1981 | 13.8439 | 15.3791 | 17.2919 | 20.8434 | 25.3364 |
| 27 | 11.8076 | 12.8786 | 14.5733 | 16.1513 | 18.1138 | 21.7494 | 26.3363 |
| 28 | 12.4613 | 13.5648 | 15.3079 | 16.9279 | 18.9392 | 22.6572 | 27.3363 |
| 29 | 13.1211 | 14.2565 | 16.0471 | 17.7083 | 19.7677 | 23.5666 | 28.3362 |
| 30 | 13.7867 | 14.9535 | 16.7908 | 18.4926 | 20.5992 | 24.4776 | 29.3360 |
| 40 | 20.7065 | 22.1643 | 24.4331 | 26.5093 | 29.0505 | 33.6603 | 39.3354 |
| 50 | 27.9907 | 29.7067 | 32.3574 | 34.7642 | 37.6886 | 42.9421 | 49.3349 |
| 60 | 35.5346 | 37.4848 | 40.4817 | 43.1879 | 46.4589 | 52.2938 | 59.3347 |
| 70 | 43.2752 | 45.4418 | 48.7576 | 51.7393 | 55.3290 | 61.6983 | 69.3344 |
| 80 | 51.1720 | 53.5400 | 57.1532 | 60.3915 | 64.2778 | 71.1445 | 79.3343 |
| 90 | 59.1963 | 61.7541 | 65.6466 | 69.1260 | 73.2912 | 80.6247 | 89.3342 |
| 100 | 67.3276 | 70.0648 | 74.2219 | 77.9295 | 82.3581 | 90.1332 | 99.3341 |
| z | −2.5758 | −2.3263 | −1.9600 | −1.6449 | −1.2816 | −0.6745 | 0.0000 |

**TABLE C.4** (continued)

| df \ α | 0.250 | 0.100 | 0.050 | 0.025 | 0.010 | 0.005 | 0.001 |
|---|---|---|---|---|---|---|---|
| 1 | 1.32330 | 2.70554 | 3.84146 | 5.02389 | 6.63490 | 7.87944 | 10.828 |
| 2 | 2.77259 | 4.60517 | 5.99147 | 7.37776 | 9.21034 | 10.5966 | 13.816 |
| 3 | 4.10835 | 6.25139 | 7.81473 | 9.34840 | 11.3449 | 12.8381 | 16.266 |
| 4 | 5.38527 | 7.77944 | 9.48773 | 11.1433 | 13.2767 | 14.8602 | 18.467 |
| 5 | 6.62568 | 9.23635 | 11.0705 | 12.8325 | 15.0863 | 16.7496 | 20.515 |
| 6 | 7.84080 | 10.6446 | 12.5916 | 14.4494 | 16.8119 | 18.5476 | 22.458 |
| 7 | 9.03715 | 12.0170 | 14.0671 | 16.0128 | 18.4753 | 20.2777 | 24.322 |
| 8 | 10.2188 | 13.3616 | 15.5073 | 17.5346 | 20.0902 | 21.9550 | 26.125 |
| 9 | 11.3887 | 14.6837 | 16.9190 | 19.0228 | 21.6660 | 23.5893 | 27.877 |
| 10 | 12.5489 | 15.9871 | 18.3070 | 20.4831 | 23.2093 | 25.1882 | 29.588 |
| 11 | 13.7007 | 17.2750 | 19.6751 | 21.9200 | 24.7250 | 26.7569 | 31.264 |
| 12 | 14.8454 | 18.5494 | 21.0261 | 23.3367 | 26.2170 | 28.2995 | 32.909 |
| 13 | 15.9839 | 19.8119 | 22.3621 | 24.7356 | 27.6883 | 29.8194 | 34.528 |
| 14 | 17.1170 | 21.0642 | 23.6848 | 26.1190 | 29.1413 | 31.3193 | 36.123 |
| 15 | 18.2451 | 22.3072 | 24.9958 | 27.4884 | 30.5779 | 32.8013 | 37.697 |
| 16 | 19.3688 | 23.5418 | 26.2962 | 28.8454 | 31.9999 | 34.2672 | 39.252 |
| 17 | 20.4887 | 24.7690 | 27.5871 | 30.1910 | 33.4087 | 35.7185 | 40.790 |
| 18 | 21.6049 | 25.9894 | 28.8693 | 31.5264 | 34.8053 | 37.1564 | 42.312 |
| 19 | 22.7178 | 27.2036 | 30.1435 | 32.8523 | 36.1908 | 38.5822 | 43.820 |
| 20 | 23.8277 | 28.4120 | 31.4104 | 34.1696 | 37.5662 | 39.9968 | 45.315 |
| 21 | 24.9348 | 29.6151 | 32.6705 | 35.4789 | 38.9321 | 41.4010 | 46.797 |
| 22 | 26.0393 | 30.8133 | 33.9244 | 36.7807 | 40.2894 | 42.7956 | 48.268 |
| 23 | 27.1413 | 32.0069 | 35.1725 | 38.0757 | 41.6384 | 44.1813 | 49.728 |
| 24 | 28.2412 | 33.1963 | 36.4151 | 39.3641 | 42.9798 | 45.5585 | 51.179 |
| 25 | 29.3389 | 34.3816 | 37.6525 | 40.6465 | 44.3141 | 46.9278 | 52.620 |
| 26 | 30.4345 | 35.5631 | 38.8852 | 41.9232 | 45.6417 | 48.2899 | 54.052 |
| 27 | 31.5284 | 36.7412 | 40.1133 | 43.1944 | 46.9630 | 49.6449 | 55.476 |
| 28 | 32.6205 | 37.9159 | 41.3372 | 44.4607 | 48.2782 | 50.9933 | 56.892 |
| 29 | 33.7109 | 39.0875 | 42.5569 | 45.7222 | 49.5879 | 52.3356 | 58.302 |
| 30 | 34.7998 | 40.2560 | 43.7729 | 46.9792 | 50.8922 | 53.6720 | 59.703 |
| 40 | 45.6160 | 51.8050 | 55.7585 | 59.3417 | 63.6907 | 66.7659 | 73.402 |
| 50 | 56.3336 | 63.1671 | 67.5048 | 71.4202 | 76.1539 | 79.4900 | 86.661 |
| 60 | 66.9814 | 74.3970 | 79.0819 | 83.2976 | 88.3794 | 91.9517 | 99.607 |
| 70 | 77.5766 | 85.5271 | 90.5312 | 95.0231 | 100.425 | 104.215 | 112.317 |
| 80 | 88.1303 | 96.5782 | 101.879 | 106.629 | 112.329 | 116.321 | 124.839 |
| 90 | 98.6499 | 107.565 | 113.145 | 118.136 | 124.116 | 128.299 | 137.208 |
| 100 | 109.141 | 118.498 | 124.342 | 129.561 | 135.807 | 140.169 | 149.449 |
| z | +0.6745 | +1.2816 | +1.6449 | +1.9600 | +2.3263 | +2.5758 | +3.0902 |

For df > 100 take

$$\chi^2 = df\left(1 - \frac{2}{9\,df} + z\sqrt{\frac{2}{9\,df}}\right)^3 \quad \text{or} \quad \chi^2 = \frac{1}{2}(z + \sqrt{2df - 1})^2$$

according to the degree of accuracy required. $z$ is the standardized normal deviate corresponding to α and is shown in the bottom line of the table.

*Source*: Adapted from Table 8 in Pearson, E. S. and Hartley, H. O. (1958). *Biometrika Tables for Statisticians*, Vol. 1, 2nd ed. Cambridge University Press: Cambridge, with the kind permission of the trustees of *Biometrika*.

**TABLE C.5** UPPER PERCENTAGE POINTS OF THE *F* DISTRIBUTION

| $df_2$ | $\alpha$ | 1 | 2 | 3 | 4 | 5 | 6 | 8 | 12 | 24 | $\infty$ |
|---|---|---|---|---|---|---|---|---|---|---|---|
| 1 | .001 | 405284 | 500000 | 540379 | 562500 | 576405 | 585937 | 598144 | 610667 | 623497 | 636619 |
|   | .005 | 16211 | 20000 | 21615 | 22500 | 23056 | 23437 | 23925 | 24426 | 24940 | 25465 |
|   | .01 | 4052 | 4999 | 5403 | 5625 | 5764 | 5859 | 5981 | 6106 | 6234 | 6366 |
|   | .025 | 647.79 | 799.50 | 864.16 | 899.58 | 921.85 | 937.11 | 956.66 | 976.71 | 997.25 | 1018.30 |
|   | .05 | 161.45 | 199.50 | 215.71 | 224.58 | 230.16 | 233.99 | 238.88 | 243.91 | 249.05 | 254.32 |
|   | .10 | 39.86 | 49.50 | 53.59 | 55.83 | 57.24 | 58.20 | 59.44 | 60.70 | 62.00 | 63.33 |
|   | .25 | 5.83 | 7.50 | 8.20 | 8.58 | 8.82 | 8.98 | 9.19 | 9.41 | 9.63 | 9.85 |
| 2 | .001 | 998.5 | 999.0 | 999.2 | 999.2 | 999.3 | 999.3 | 999.4 | 999.4 | 999.5 | 999.5 |
|   | .005 | 198.50 | 199.00 | 199.17 | 199.25 | 199.30 | 199.33 | 199.37 | 199.42 | 199.46 | 199.51 |
|   | .01 | 98.49 | 99.00 | 99.17 | 99.25 | 99.30 | 99.33 | 99.36 | 99.42 | 99.46 | 99.50 |
|   | .025 | 38.51 | 39.00 | 39.17 | 39.25 | 39.30 | 39.33 | 39.37 | 39.42 | 39.46 | 39.50 |
|   | .05 | 18.51 | 19.00 | 19.16 | 19.25 | 19.30 | 19.33 | 19.37 | 19.41 | 19.45 | 19.50 |
|   | .10 | 8.53 | 9.00 | 9.16 | 9.24 | 9.29 | 9.33 | 9.37 | 9.41 | 9.45 | 9.49 |
|   | .25 | 2.56 | 3.00 | 3.15 | 3.23 | 3.28 | 3.31 | 3.35 | 3.39 | 3.44 | 3.48 |
| 3 | .001 | 167.5 | 148.5 | 141.1 | 137.1 | 134.6 | 132.8 | 130.6 | 128.3 | 125.9 | 123.5 |
|   | .005 | 55.55 | 49.80 | 47.47 | 46.20 | 45.39 | 44.84 | 44.13 | 43.39 | 42.62 | 41.83 |
|   | .01 | 34.12 | 30.81 | 29.46 | 28.71 | 28.24 | 27.91 | 27.49 | 27.05 | 26.60 | 26.12 |
|   | .025 | 17.44 | 16.04 | 15.44 | 15.10 | 14.89 | 14.74 | 14.54 | 14.34 | 14.12 | 13.90 |
|   | .05 | 10.13 | 9.55 | 9.28 | 9.12 | 9.01 | 8.94 | 8.84 | 8.74 | 8.64 | 8.53 |
|   | .10 | 5.54 | 5.46 | 5.39 | 5.34 | 5.31 | 5.28 | 5.25 | 5.22 | 5.18 | 5.13 |
|   | .25 | 2.02 | 2.28 | 2.36 | 2.39 | 2.41 | 2.42 | 2.44 | 2.45 | 2.46 | 2.47 |
| 4 | .001 | 74.14 | 61.25 | 56.18 | 53.44 | 51.71 | 50.53 | 49.00 | 47.41 | 45.77 | 44.05 |
|   | .005 | 31.33 | 26.28 | 24.26 | 23.16 | 22.46 | 21.98 | 21.35 | 20.71 | 20.03 | 19.33 |
|   | .01 | 21.20 | 18.00 | 16.69 | 15.98 | 15.52 | 15.21 | 14.80 | 14.37 | 13.93 | 13.46 |
|   | .025 | 12.22 | 10.65 | 9.98 | 9.60 | 9.36 | 9.20 | 8.98 | 8.75 | 8.51 | 8.26 |
|   | .05 | 7.71 | 6.94 | 6.59 | 6.39 | 6.26 | 6.16 | 6.04 | 5.91 | 5.77 | 5.63 |
|   | .10 | 4.54 | 4.32 | 4.19 | 4.11 | 4.05 | 4.01 | 3.95 | 3.90 | 3.83 | 3.76 |
|   | .25 | 1.81 | 2.00 | 2.05 | 2.06 | 2.07 | 2.08 | 2.08 | 2.08 | 2.08 | 2.08 |
| 5 | .001 | 47.04 | 36.61 | 33.20 | 31.09 | 29.75 | 28.84 | 27.64 | 26.42 | 25.14 | 23.78 |
|   | .005 | 22.79 | 18.31 | 16.53 | 15.56 | 14.94 | 14.51 | 13.96 | 13.38 | 12.78 | 12.14 |
|   | .01 | 16.26 | 13.27 | 12.06 | 11.39 | 10.97 | 10.67 | 10.29 | 9.89 | 9.47 | 9.02 |
|   | .025 | 10.01 | 8.43 | 7.76 | 7.39 | 7.15 | 6.98 | 6.76 | 6.52 | 6.28 | 6.02 |
|   | .05 | 6.61 | 5.79 | 5.41 | 5.19 | 5.05 | 4.95 | 4.82 | 4.68 | 4.53 | 4.36 |
|   | .10 | 4.06 | 3.78 | 3.62 | 3.52 | 3.45 | 3.40 | 3.34 | 3.27 | 3.19 | 3.10 |
|   | .25 | 1.70 | 1.85 | 1.89 | 1.89 | 1.89 | 1.89 | 1.89 | 1.89 | 1.88 | 1.87 |

**TABLE C.5** (continued)

| $df_2$ | $\alpha$ | 1 | 2 | 3 | 4 | 5 | 6 | 8 | 12 | 24 | $\infty$ |
|---|---|---|---|---|---|---|---|---|---|---|---|
| 6 | .001 | 35.51 | 27.00 | 23.70 | 21.90 | 20.81 | 20.03 | 19.03 | 17.99 | 16.89 | 15.75 |
| | .005 | 18.64 | 14.54 | 12.92 | 12.03 | 11.46 | 11.07 | 10.57 | 10.03 | 9.47 | 8.88 |
| | .01 | 13.74 | 10.92 | 9.78 | 9.15 | 8.75 | 8.47 | 8.10 | 7.72 | 7.31 | 6.88 |
| | .025 | 8.81 | 7.26 | 6.60 | 6.23 | 5.99 | 5.82 | 5.60 | 5.37 | 5.12 | 4.85 |
| | .05 | 5.99 | 5.14 | 4.76 | 4.53 | 4.39 | 4.28 | 4.15 | 4.00 | 3.84 | 3.67 |
| | .10 | 3.78 | 3.46 | 3.29 | 3.18 | 3.11 | 3.05 | 2.98 | 2.90 | 2.82 | 2.72 |
| | .25 | 1.62 | 1.76 | 1.78 | 1.79 | 1.79 | 1.78 | 1.78 | 1.77 | 1.75 | 1.74 |
| 7 | .001 | 29.22 | 21.69 | 18.77 | 17.19 | 16.21 | 15.52 | 14.63 | 13.71 | 12.73 | 11.69 |
| | .005 | 16.24 | 12.40 | 10.88 | 10.05 | 9.52 | 9.16 | 8.68 | 8.18 | 7.65 | 7.08 |
| | .01 | 12.25 | 9.55 | 8.45 | 7.85 | 7.46 | 7.19 | 6.84 | 6.47 | 6.07 | 5.65 |
| | .025 | 8.07 | 6.54 | 5.89 | 5.52 | 5.29 | 5.12 | 4.90 | 4.67 | 4.42 | 4.14 |
| | .05 | 5.59 | 4.74 | 4.35 | 4.12 | 3.97 | 3.87 | 3.73 | 3.57 | 3.41 | 3.23 |
| | .10 | 3.59 | 3.26 | 3.07 | 2.96 | 2.88 | 2.83 | 2.75 | 2.67 | 2.58 | 2.47 |
| | .25 | 1.57 | 1.70 | 1.72 | 1.72 | 1.71 | 1.71 | 1.70 | 1.68 | 1.67 | 1.65 |
| 8 | .001 | 25.42 | 18.49 | 15.83 | 14.39 | 13.49 | 12.86 | 12.04 | 11.19 | 10.30 | 9.34 |
| | .005 | 14.69 | 11.04 | 9.60 | 8.81 | 8.30 | 7.95 | 7.50 | 7.01 | 6.50 | 5.95 |
| | .01 | 11.26 | 8.65 | 7.59 | 7.01 | 6.63 | 6.37 | 6.03 | 5.67 | 5.28 | 4.86 |
| | .025 | 7.57 | 6.06 | 5.42 | 5.05 | 4.82 | 4.65 | 4.43 | 4.20 | 3.95 | 3.67 |
| | .05 | 5.32 | 4.46 | 4.07 | 3.84 | 3.69 | 3.58 | 3.44 | 3.28 | 3.12 | 2.93 |
| | .10 | 3.46 | 3.11 | 2.92 | 2.81 | 2.73 | 2.67 | 2.59 | 2.50 | 2.40 | 2.29 |
| | .25 | 1.54 | 1.66 | 1.67 | 1.66 | 1.66 | 1.65 | 1.64 | 1.62 | 1.60 | 1.58 |
| 9 | .001 | 22.86 | 16.39 | 13.90 | 12.56 | 11.71 | 11.13 | 10.37 | 9.57 | 8.72 | 7.81 |
| | .005 | 13.61 | 10.11 | 8.72 | 7.96 | 7.47 | 7.13 | 6.69 | 6.23 | 5.73 | 5.19 |
| | .01 | 10.56 | 8.02 | 6.99 | 6.42 | 6.06 | 5.80 | 5.47 | 5.11 | 4.73 | 4.31 |
| | .025 | 7.21 | 5.71 | 5.08 | 4.72 | 4.48 | 4.32 | 4.10 | 3.87 | 3.61 | 3.33 |
| | .05 | 5.12 | 4.26 | 3.86 | 3.63 | 3.48 | 3.37 | 3.23 | 3.07 | 2.90 | 2.71 |
| | .10 | 3.36 | 3.01 | 2.81 | 2.69 | 2.61 | 2.55 | 2.47 | 2.38 | 2.28 | 2.16 |
| | .25 | 1.51 | 1.62 | 1.63 | 1.63 | 1.62 | 1.61 | 1.60 | 1.58 | 1.56 | 1.53 |
| 10 | .001 | 21.04 | 14.91 | 12.55 | 11.28 | 10.48 | 9.92 | 9.20 | 8.45 | 7.64 | 6.76 |
| | .005 | 12.83 | 9.43 | 8.08 | 7.34 | 6.87 | 6.54 | 6.12 | 5.66 | 5.17 | 4.64 |
| | .01 | 10.04 | 7.56 | 6.55 | 5.99 | 5.64 | 5.39 | 5.06 | 4.71 | 4.33 | 3.91 |
| | .025 | 6.94 | 5.46 | 4.83 | 4.47 | 4.24 | 4.07 | 3.85 | 3.62 | 3.37 | 3.08 |
| | .05 | 4.96 | 4.10 | 3.71 | 3.48 | 3.33 | 3.22 | 3.07 | 2.91 | 2.74 | 2.54 |
| | .10 | 3.28 | 2.92 | 2.73 | 2.61 | 2.52 | 2.46 | 2.38 | 2.28 | 2.18 | 2.06 |
| | .25 | 1.49 | 1.60 | 1.60 | 1.60 | 1.59 | 1.58 | 1.56 | 1.54 | 1.52 | 1.48 |

$df_1$

| | α | | | | | | | | | | |
|---|---|---|---|---|---|---|---|---|---|---|---|
| 11 | .001 | 19.69 | 13.81 | 11.56 | 10.35 | 9.58 | 9.05 | 8.35 | 7.63 | 6.85 | 6.00 |
| | .005 | 12.23 | 8.91 | 7.60 | 6.88 | 6.42 | 6.10 | 5.68 | 5.24 | 4.76 | 4.23 |
| | .01 | 9.65 | 7.20 | 6.22 | 5.67 | 5.32 | 5.07 | 4.74 | 4.40 | 4.02 | 3.60 |
| | .025 | 6.72 | 5.26 | 4.63 | 4.28 | 4.04 | 3.88 | 3.66 | 3.43 | 3.17 | 2.88 |
| | .05 | 4.84 | 3.98 | 3.59 | 3.36 | 3.20 | 3.09 | 2.95 | 2.79 | 2.61 | 2.40 |
| | .10 | 3.23 | 2.86 | 2.66 | 2.54 | 2.45 | 2.39 | 2.30 | 2.21 | 2.10 | 1.97 |
| | .25 | 1.46 | 1.58 | 1.58 | 1.58 | 1.56 | 1.55 | 1.54 | 1.51 | 1.49 | 1.45 |
| 12 | .001 | 18.64 | 12.97 | 10.80 | 9.63 | 8.89 | 8.38 | 7.71 | 7.00 | 6.25 | 5.42 |
| | .005 | 11.75 | 8.51 | 7.23 | 6.52 | 6.07 | 5.76 | 5.35 | 4.91 | 4.43 | 3.90 |
| | .01 | 9.33 | 6.93 | 5.95 | 5.41 | 5.06 | 4.82 | 4.50 | 4.16 | 3.78 | 3.36 |
| | .025 | 6.55 | 5.10 | 4.47 | 4.12 | 3.89 | 3.73 | 3.51 | 3.28 | 3.02 | 2.72 |
| | .05 | 4.75 | 3.88 | 3.49 | 3.26 | 3.11 | 3.00 | 2.85 | 2.69 | 2.50 | 2.30 |
| | .10 | 3.18 | 2.81 | 2.61 | 2.48 | 2.39 | 2.33 | 2.24 | 2.15 | 2.04 | 1.90 |
| | .25 | 1.46 | 1.56 | 1.56 | 1.55 | 1.54 | 1.53 | 1.51 | 1.49 | 1.46 | 1.42 |
| 13 | .001 | 17.81 | 12.31 | 10.21 | 9.07 | 8.35 | 7.86 | 7.21 | 6.52 | 5.78 | 4.97 |
| | .005 | 11.37 | 8.19 | 6.93 | 6.23 | 5.79 | 5.48 | 5.08 | 4.64 | 4.17 | 3.65 |
| | .01 | 9.07 | 6.70 | 5.74 | 5.20 | 4.86 | 4.62 | 4.30 | 3.96 | 3.59 | 3.16 |
| | .025 | 6.41 | 4.97 | 4.35 | 4.00 | 3.77 | 3.60 | 3.39 | 3.15 | 2.89 | 2.60 |
| | .05 | 4.67 | 3.80 | 3.41 | 3.18 | 3.02 | 2.92 | 2.77 | 2.60 | 2.42 | 2.21 |
| | .10 | 3.14 | 2.76 | 2.56 | 2.43 | 2.35 | 2.28 | 2.20 | 2.10 | 1.98 | 1.85 |
| | .25 | 1.45 | 1.55 | 1.55 | 1.53 | 1.52 | 1.51 | 1.49 | 1.47 | 1.44 | 1.40 |
| 14 | .001 | 17.14 | 11.78 | 9.73 | 8.62 | 7.92 | 7.43 | 6.80 | 6.13 | 5.41 | 4.60 |
| | .005 | 11.06 | 7.92 | 6.68 | 6.00 | 5.56 | 5.26 | 4.86 | 4.43 | 3.96 | 3.44 |
| | .01 | 8.86 | 6.51 | 5.56 | 5.03 | 4.69 | 4.46 | 4.14 | 3.80 | 3.43 | 3.00 |
| | .025 | 6.30 | 4.86 | 4.24 | 3.89 | 3.66 | 3.50 | 3.29 | 3.05 | 2.79 | 2.49 |
| | .05 | 4.60 | 3.74 | 3.34 | 3.11 | 2.96 | 2.85 | 2.70 | 2.53 | 2.35 | 2.13 |
| | .10 | 3.10 | 2.73 | 2.52 | 2.39 | 2.31 | 2.24 | 2.15 | 2.05 | 1.94 | 1.80 |
| | .25 | 1.44 | 1.53 | 1.53 | 1.52 | 1.51 | 1.50 | 1.48 | 1.45 | 1.42 | 1.38 |
| 15 | .001 | 16.59 | 11.34 | 9.34 | 8.25 | 7.57 | 7.09 | 6.47 | 5.81 | 5.10 | 4.31 |
| | .005 | 10.80 | 7.70 | 6.48 | 5.80 | 5.37 | 5.07 | 4.67 | 4.25 | 3.79 | 3.26 |
| | .01 | 8.68 | 6.36 | 5.42 | 4.89 | 4.56 | 4.32 | 4.00 | 3.67 | 3.29 | 2.87 |
| | .025 | 6.20 | 4.77 | 4.15 | 3.80 | 3.58 | 3.41 | 3.20 | 2.96 | 2.70 | 2.40 |
| | .05 | 4.54 | 3.68 | 3.29 | 3.06 | 2.90 | 2.79 | 2.64 | 2.48 | 2.29 | 2.07 |
| | .10 | 3.07 | 2.70 | 2.49 | 2.36 | 2.27 | 2.21 | 2.12 | 2.02 | 1.90 | 1.76 |
| | .25 | 1.43 | 1.52 | 1.52 | 1.51 | 1.49 | 1.48 | 1.46 | 1.44 | 1.41 | 1.36 |

**TABLE C.5** (continued)

| $df_2$ | $\alpha$ | $df_1$ = 1 | 2 | 3 | 4 | 5 | 6 | 8 | 12 | 24 | $\infty$ |
|---|---|---|---|---|---|---|---|---|---|---|---|
| 16 | .001 | 16.12 | 10.97 | 9.00 | 7.94 | 7.27 | 6.81 | 6.19 | 5.55 | 4.85 | 4.06 |
|  | .005 | 10.58 | 7.51 | 6.30 | 5.64 | 5.21 | 4.91 | 4.52 | 4.10 | 3.64 | 3.11 |
|  | .01 | 8.53 | 6.23 | 5.29 | 4.77 | 4.44 | 4.20 | 3.89 | 3.55 | 3.18 | 2.75 |
|  | .025 | 6.12 | 4.69 | 4.08 | 3.73 | 3.50 | 3.34 | 3.12 | 2.89 | 2.63 | 2.32 |
|  | .05 | 4.49 | 3.63 | 3.24 | 3.01 | 2.85 | 2.74 | 2.59 | 2.42 | 2.24 | 2.01 |
|  | .10 | 3.05 | 2.67 | 2.46 | 2.33 | 2.24 | 2.18 | 2.09 | 1.99 | 1.87 | 1.72 |
|  | .25 | 1.42 | 1.51 | 1.51 | 1.50 | 1.48 | 1.47 | 1.45 | 1.43 | 1.39 | 1.34 |
| 17 | .001 | 15.72 | 10.66 | 8.73 | 7.68 | 7.02 | 6.56 | 5.96 | 5.32 | 4.63 | 3.85 |
|  | .005 | 10.38 | 7.35 | 6.16 | 5.50 | 5.07 | 4.78 | 4.39 | 3.97 | 3.51 | 2.98 |
|  | .01 | 8.40 | 6.11 | 5.18 | 4.67 | 4.34 | 4.10 | 3.79 | 3.45 | 3.08 | 2.65 |
|  | .025 | 6.04 | 4.62 | 4.01 | 3.66 | 3.44 | 3.28 | 3.06 | 2.82 | 2.56 | 2.25 |
|  | .05 | 4.45 | 3.59 | 3.20 | 2.96 | 2.81 | 2.70 | 2.55 | 2.38 | 2.19 | 1.96 |
|  | .10 | 3.03 | 2.64 | 2.44 | 2.31 | 2.22 | 2.15 | 2.06 | 1.96 | 1.84 | 1.69 |
|  | .25 | 1.42 | 1.51 | 1.51 | 1.49 | 1.47 | 1.46 | 1.44 | 1.41 | 1.38 | 1.33 |
| 18 | .001 | 15.38 | 10.39 | 8.49 | 7.46 | 6.81 | 6.35 | 5.76 | 5.13 | 4.45 | 3.67 |
|  | .005 | 10.22 | 7.21 | 6.03 | 5.37 | 4.96 | 4.66 | 4.28 | 3.86 | 3.40 | 2.87 |
|  | .01 | 8.28 | 6.01 | 5.09 | 4.58 | 4.25 | 4.01 | 3.71 | 3.37 | 3.00 | 2.57 |
|  | .025 | 5.98 | 4.56 | 3.95 | 3.61 | 3.38 | 3.22 | 3.01 | 2.77 | 2.50 | 2.19 |
|  | .05 | 4.41 | 3.55 | 3.16 | 2.93 | 2.77 | 2.66 | 2.51 | 2.34 | 2.15 | 1.92 |
|  | .10 | 3.01 | 2.62 | 2.42 | 2.29 | 2.20 | 2.13 | 2.04 | 1.93 | 1.81 | 1.66 |
|  | .25 | 1.41 | 1.50 | 1.49 | 1.48 | 1.46 | 1.45 | 1.43 | 1.40 | 1.37 | 1.32 |
| 19 | .001 | 15.08 | 10.16 | 8.28 | 7.26 | 6.61 | 6.18 | 5.59 | 4.97 | 4.29 | 3.52 |
|  | .005 | 10.07 | 7.09 | 5.92 | 5.27 | 4.85 | 4.56 | 4.18 | 3.76 | 3.31 | 2.78 |
|  | .01 | 8.18 | 5.93 | 5.01 | 4.50 | 4.17 | 3.94 | 3.63 | 3.30 | 2.92 | 2.49 |
|  | .025 | 5.92 | 4.51 | 3.90 | 3.56 | 3.33 | 3.17 | 2.96 | 2.72 | 2.45 | 2.13 |
|  | .05 | 4.38 | 3.52 | 3.13 | 2.90 | 2.74 | 2.63 | 2.48 | 2.31 | 2.11 | 1.88 |
|  | .10 | 2.99 | 2.61 | 2.40 | 2.27 | 2.18 | 2.11 | 2.02 | 1.91 | 1.79 | 1.63 |
|  | .25 | 1.41 | 1.50 | 1.49 | 1.48 | 1.46 | 1.44 | 1.42 | 1.40 | 1.36 | 1.31 |
| 20 | .001 | 14.82 | 9.95 | 8.10 | 7.10 | 6.46 | 6.02 | 5.44 | 4.82 | 4.15 | 3.38 |
|  | .005 | 9.94 | 6.99 | 5.82 | 5.17 | 4.76 | 4.47 | 4.09 | 3.68 | 3.22 | 2.69 |
|  | .01 | 8.10 | 5.85 | 4.94 | 4.43 | 4.10 | 3.87 | 3.56 | 3.23 | 2.86 | 2.42 |
|  | .025 | 5.87 | 4.46 | 3.86 | 3.51 | 3.29 | 3.13 | 2.91 | 2.68 | 2.41 | 2.09 |
|  | .05 | 4.35 | 3.49 | 3.10 | 2.87 | 2.71 | 2.60 | 2.45 | 2.28 | 2.08 | 1.84 |
|  | .10 | 2.97 | 2.59 | 2.38 | 2.25 | 2.16 | 2.09 | 2.00 | 1.89 | 1.77 | 1.61 |
|  | .25 | 1.40 | 1.49 | 1.48 | 1.47 | 1.45 | 1.44 | 1.42 | 1.39 | 1.35 | 1.29 |

| | α | | | | | | | | | | |
|---|---|---|---|---|---|---|---|---|---|---|---|
| 21 | .001 | 14.59 | 9.77 | 7.94 | 6.95 | 6.32 | 5.88 | 5.31 | 4.70 | 4.03 | 3.26 |
| | .005 | 9.83 | 6.89 | 5.73 | 5.09 | 4.68 | 4.39 | 4.01 | 3.60 | 3.15 | 2.61 |
| | .01 | 8.02 | 5.78 | 4.87 | 4.37 | 4.04 | 3.81 | 3.51 | 3.17 | 2.80 | 2.36 |
| | .025 | 5.83 | 4.42 | 3.82 | 3.48 | 3.25 | 3.09 | 2.87 | 2.64 | 2.37 | 2.04 |
| | .05 | 4.32 | 3.47 | 3.07 | 2.84 | 2.68 | 2.57 | 2.42 | 2.25 | 2.05 | 1.81 |
| | .10 | 2.96 | 2.57 | 2.36 | 2.23 | 2.14 | 2.08 | 1.98 | 1.88 | 1.75 | 1.59 |
| | .25 | 1.40 | 1.49 | 1.48 | 1.46 | 1.44 | 1.43 | 1.41 | 1.37 | 1.34 | 1.29 |
| 22 | .001 | 14.38 | 9.61 | 7.80 | 6.81 | 6.19 | 5.76 | 5.19 | 4.58 | 3.92 | 3.15 |
| | .005 | 9.73 | 6.81 | 5.65 | 5.02 | 4.61 | 4.32 | 3.94 | 3.54 | 3.08 | 2.55 |
| | .01 | 7.94 | 5.72 | 4.82 | 4.31 | 3.99 | 3.76 | 3.45 | 3.12 | 2.75 | 2.31 |
| | .025 | 5.79 | 4.38 | 3.78 | 3.44 | 3.22 | 3.05 | 2.84 | 2.60 | 2.33 | 2.00 |
| | .05 | 4.30 | 3.44 | 3.05 | 2.82 | 2.66 | 2.55 | 2.40 | 2.23 | 2.03 | 1.78 |
| | .10 | 2.95 | 2.56 | 2.35 | 2.22 | 2.13 | 2.06 | 1.97 | 1.86 | 1.73 | 1.57 |
| | .25 | 1.40 | 1.48 | 1.47 | 1.46 | 1.44 | 1.42 | 1.40 | 1.37 | 1.33 | 1.28 |
| 23 | .001 | 14.19 | 9.47 | 7.67 | 6.69 | 6.08 | 5.65 | 5.09 | 4.48 | 3.82 | 3.05 |
| | .005 | 9.63 | 6.73 | 5.58 | 4.95 | 4.54 | 4.26 | 3.88 | 3.47 | 3.02 | 2.48 |
| | .01 | 7.88 | 5.66 | 4.76 | 4.26 | 3.94 | 3.71 | 3.41 | 3.07 | 2.70 | 2.26 |
| | .025 | 5.75 | 4.35 | 3.75 | 3.41 | 3.18 | 3.02 | 2.81 | 2.57 | 2.30 | 1.97 |
| | .05 | 4.28 | 3.42 | 3.03 | 2.80 | 2.64 | 2.53 | 2.38 | 2.20 | 2.00 | 1.76 |
| | .10 | 2.94 | 2.55 | 2.34 | 2.21 | 2.11 | 2.05 | 1.95 | 1.84 | 1.72 | 1.55 |
| | .25 | 1.39 | 1.47 | 1.47 | 1.45 | 1.43 | 1.41 | 1.40 | 1.37 | 1.33 | 1.27 |
| 24 | .001 | 14.03 | 9.34 | 7.55 | 6.59 | 5.98 | 5.55 | 4.99 | 4.39 | 3.74 | 2.97 |
| | .005 | 9.55 | 6.66 | 5.52 | 4.89 | 4.49 | 4.20 | 3.83 | 3.42 | 2.97 | 2.43 |
| | .01 | 7.82 | 5.61 | 4.72 | 4.22 | 3.90 | 3.67 | 3.36 | 3.03 | 2.66 | 2.21 |
| | .025 | 5.72 | 4.32 | 3.72 | 3.38 | 3.15 | 2.99 | 2.78 | 2.54 | 2.27 | 1.94 |
| | .05 | 4.26 | 3.40 | 3.01 | 2.78 | 2.62 | 2.51 | 2.36 | 2.18 | 1.98 | 1.73 |
| | .10 | 2.93 | 2.54 | 2.33 | 2.19 | 2.10 | 2.04 | 1.94 | 1.83 | 1.70 | 1.53 |
| | .25 | 1.39 | 1.47 | 1.46 | 1.44 | 1.43 | 1.41 | 1.39 | 1.36 | 1.32 | 1.26 |
| 25 | .001 | 13.88 | 9.22 | 7.45 | 6.49 | 5.88 | 5.46 | 4.91 | 4.31 | 3.66 | 2.89 |
| | .005 | 9.48 | 6.60 | 5.46 | 4.84 | 4.43 | 4.15 | 3.78 | 3.37 | 2.92 | 2.38 |
| | .01 | 7.77 | 5.57 | 4.68 | 4.18 | 3.86 | 3.63 | 3.32 | 2.99 | 2.62 | 2.17 |
| | .025 | 5.69 | 4.29 | 3.69 | 3.35 | 3.13 | 2.97 | 2.75 | 2.51 | 2.24 | 2.91 |
| | .05 | 4.24 | 3.38 | 2.99 | 2.76 | 2.60 | 2.49 | 2.34 | 2.16 | 1.96 | 1.71 |
| | .10 | 2.92 | 2.53 | 2.32 | 2.18 | 2.09 | 2.02 | 1.93 | 1.82 | 1.69 | 1.52 |
| | .25 | 1.39 | 1.47 | 1.46 | 1.44 | 1.42 | 1.41 | 1.39 | 1.36 | 1.32 | 1.25 |

**TABLE C.5** (continued)

| $df_2$ | $\alpha$ | 1 | 2 | 3 | 4 | 5 | 6 | 8 | 12 | 24 | $\infty$ |
|---|---|---|---|---|---|---|---|---|---|---|---|
| 26 | .001 | 13.74 | 9.12 | 7.36 | 6.41 | 5.80 | 5.38 | 4.83 | 4.24 | 3.59 | 2.82 |
|  | .005 | 9.41 | 6.54 | 5.41 | 4.79 | 4.38 | 4.10 | 3.73 | 3.33 | 2.87 | 2.33 |
|  | .01 | 7.72 | 5.53 | 4.64 | 4.14 | 3.82 | 3.59 | 3.29 | 2.96 | 2.58 | 2.13 |
|  | .025 | 5.66 | 4.27 | 3.67 | 3.33 | 3.10 | 2.94 | 2.73 | 2.49 | 2.22 | 1.88 |
|  | .05 | 4.22 | 3.37 | 2.98 | 2.74 | 2.59 | 2.47 | 2.32 | 2.15 | 1.95 | 1.69 |
|  | .10 | 2.91 | 2.52 | 2.31 | 2.17 | 2.08 | 2.01 | 1.92 | 1.81 | 1.68 | 1.50 |
|  | .25 | 1.38 | 1.46 | 1.45 | 1.44 | 1.42 | 1.41 | 1.38 | 1.35 | 1.31 | 1.25 |
| 27 | .001 | 13.61 | 9.02 | 7.27 | 6.33 | 5.73 | 5.31 | 4.76 | 4.17 | 3.52 | 2.75 |
|  | .005 | 9.34 | 6.49 | 5.36 | 4.74 | 4.34 | 4.06 | 3.69 | 3.28 | 2.83 | 2.29 |
|  | .01 | 7.68 | 5.49 | 4.60 | 4.11 | 3.78 | 3.56 | 3.26 | 2.93 | 2.55 | 2.10 |
|  | .025 | 5.63 | 4.24 | 3.65 | 3.31 | 3.08 | 2.92 | 2.71 | 2.47 | 2.19 | 1.85 |
|  | .05 | 4.21 | 3.35 | 2.96 | 2.73 | 2.57 | 2.46 | 2.30 | 2.13 | 1.93 | 1.67 |
|  | .10 | 2.90 | 2.51 | 2.30 | 2.17 | 2.07 | 2.00 | 1.91 | 1.80 | 1.67 | 1.49 |
|  | .25 | 1.38 | 1.46 | 1.45 | 1.43 | 1.42 | 1.40 | 1.38 | 1.35 | 1.31 | 1.24 |
| 28 | .001 | 13.50 | 8.93 | 7.19 | 6.25 | 5.66 | 5.24 | 4.69 | 4.11 | 3.46 | 2.70 |
|  | .005 | 9.28 | 6.44 | 5.32 | 4.70 | 4.30 | 4.02 | 3.65 | 3.25 | 2.79 | 2.25 |
|  | .01 | 7.64 | 5.45 | 4.57 | 4.07 | 3.75 | 3.53 | 3.23 | 2.90 | 2.52 | 2.06 |
|  | .025 | 5.61 | 4.22 | 3.63 | 3.29 | 3.06 | 2.90 | 2.69 | 2.45 | 2.17 | 1.83 |
|  | .05 | 4.20 | 3.34 | 2.95 | 2.71 | 2.56 | 2.44 | 2.29 | 2.12 | 1.91 | 1.65 |
|  | .10 | 2.89 | 2.50 | 2.29 | 2.16 | 2.06 | 2.00 | 1.90 | 1.79 | 1.66 | 1.48 |
|  | .25 | 1.38 | 1.46 | 1.45 | 1.43 | 1.41 | 1.40 | 1.38 | 1.34 | 1.30 | 1.24 |
| 29 | .001 | 13.39 | 8.85 | 7.12 | 6.49 | 5.59 | 5.18 | 4.64 | 4.05 | 3.41 | 2.64 |
|  | .005 | 9.23 | 6.40 | 5.28 | 4.66 | 4.26 | 3.98 | 3.61 | 3.21 | 2.76 | 2.21 |
|  | .01 | 7.60 | 5.42 | 4.54 | 4.04 | 3.73 | 3.50 | 3.20 | 2.87 | 2.49 | 2.03 |
|  | .025 | 5.59 | 4.20 | 3.61 | 3.27 | 3.04 | 2.88 | 2.67 | 2.43 | 2.15 | 1.81 |
|  | .05 | 4.18 | 3.33 | 2.93 | 2.70 | 2.54 | 2.43 | 2.28 | 2.10 | 1.90 | 1.64 |
|  | .10 | 2.89 | 2.50 | 2.28 | 2.15 | 2.06 | 1.99 | 1.89 | 1.78 | 1.65 | 1.47 |
|  | .25 | 1.38 | 1.45 | 1.45 | 1.43 | 1.41 | 1.40 | 1.37 | 1.34 | 1.30 | 1.23 |
| 30 | .001 | 13.29 | 8.77 | 7.05 | 6.12 | 5.53 | 5.12 | 4.58 | 4.00 | 3.36 | 2.59 |
|  | .005 | 9.18 | 6.35 | 5.24 | 4.62 | 4.23 | 3.95 | 3.58 | 3.18 | 2.73 | 2.18 |
|  | .01 | 7.56 | 5.39 | 4.51 | 4.02 | 3.70 | 3.47 | 3.17 | 2.84 | 2.47 | 2.01 |
|  | .025 | 5.57 | 4.18 | 3.59 | 3.25 | 3.03 | 2.87 | 2.65 | 2.41 | 2.14 | 1.79 |
|  | .05 | 4.17 | 3.32 | 2.92 | 2.69 | 2.53 | 2.42 | 2.27 | 2.09 | 1.89 | 1.62 |
|  | .10 | 2.88 | 2.49 | 2.28 | 2.14 | 2.05 | 1.98 | 1.88 | 1.77 | 1.64 | 1.46 |
|  | .25 | 1.38 | 1.45 | 1.44 | 1.42 | 1.41 | 1.39 | 1.37 | 1.34 | 1.29 | 1.23 |

$df_1$

| | | | | | | | | | | | |
|---|---|---|---|---|---|---|---|---|---|---|---|
| 40 | .001 | 12.61 | 8.25 | 6.60 | 5.70 | 5.13 | 4.73 | 4.21 | 3.64 | 3.01 | 2.23 |
| | .005 | 8.83 | 6.07 | 4.98 | 4.37 | 3.99 | 3.71 | 3.35 | 2.95 | 2.50 | 1.93 |
| | .01 | 7.31 | 5.18 | 4.31 | 3.83 | 3.51 | 3.29 | 2.99 | 2.66 | 2.29 | 1.80 |
| | .025 | 5.42 | 4.05 | 3.46 | 3.13 | 2.90 | 2.74 | 2.53 | 2.29 | 2.01 | 1.64 |
| | .05 | 4.08 | 3.23 | 2.84 | 2.61 | 2.45 | 2.34 | 2.18 | 2.00 | 1.79 | 1.51 |
| | .10 | 2.84 | 2.44 | 2.23 | 2.09 | 2.00 | 1.93 | 1.83 | 1.71 | 1.57 | 1.38 |
| | .25 | 1.36 | 1.44 | 1.42 | 1.41 | 1.39 | 1.37 | 1.35 | 1.31 | 1.27 | 1.19 |
| 60 | .001 | 11.97 | 7.76 | 6.17 | 5.31 | 4.76 | 4.37 | 3.87 | 3.31 | 2.69 | 1.90 |
| | .005 | 8.49 | 5.80 | 4.73 | 4.14 | 3.76 | 3.49 | 3.13 | 2.74 | 2.29 | 1.69 |
| | .01 | 7.08 | 4.98 | 4.13 | 3.65 | 3.34 | 3.12 | 2.82 | 2.50 | 2.12 | 1.60 |
| | .025 | 5.29 | 3.93 | 3.34 | 3.01 | 2.79 | 2.63 | 2.41 | 2.17 | 1.88 | 1.48 |
| | .05 | 4.00 | 3.15 | 2.76 | 2.52 | 2.37 | 2.25 | 2.10 | 1.92 | 1.70 | 1.39 |
| | .10 | 2.79 | 2.39 | 2.18 | 2.04 | 1.95 | 1.87 | 1.77 | 1.66 | 1.51 | 1.29 |
| | .25 | 1.35 | 1.42 | 1.41 | 1.39 | 1.37 | 1.35 | 1.32 | 1.29 | 1.24 | 1.15 |
| 120 | .001 | 11.38 | 7.31 | 5.79 | 4.95 | 4.42 | 4.04 | 3.55 | 3.02 | 2.40 | 1.56 |
| | .005 | 8.18 | 5.54 | 4.50 | 3.92 | 3.55 | 3.28 | 2.93 | 2.54 | 2.09 | 1.43 |
| | .01 | 6.85 | 4.79 | 3.95 | 3.48 | 3.17 | 2.96 | 2.66 | 2.34 | 1.95 | 1.38 |
| | .025 | 5.15 | 3.80 | 3.23 | 2.89 | 2.67 | 2.52 | 2.30 | 2.05 | 1.76 | 1.31 |
| | .05 | 3.92 | 3.07 | 2.68 | 2.45 | 2.29 | 2.17 | 2.02 | 1.83 | 1.61 | 1.25 |
| | .10 | 2.75 | 2.35 | 2.13 | 1.99 | 1.90 | 1.82 | 1.72 | 1.60 | 1.45 | 1.19 |
| | .25 | 1.34 | 1.40 | 1.39 | 1.37 | 1.35 | 1.33 | 1.30 | 1.26 | 1.21 | 1.10 |
| ∞ | .001 | 10.83 | 6.91 | 5.42 | 4.62 | 4.10 | 3.74 | 3.27 | 2.74 | 2.13 | 1.00 |
| | .005 | 7.88 | 5.30 | 4.28 | 3.72 | 3.35 | 3.09 | 2.74 | 2.36 | 1.90 | 1.00 |
| | .01 | 6.64 | 4.60 | 3.78 | 3.32 | 3.02 | 2.80 | 2.51 | 2.18 | 1.79 | 1.00 |
| | .025 | 5.02 | 3.69 | 3.12 | 2.79 | 2.57 | 2.41 | 2.19 | 1.94 | 1.64 | 1.00 |
| | .05 | 3.84 | 2.99 | 2.60 | 2.37 | 2.21 | 2.09 | 1.94 | 1.75 | 1.52 | 1.00 |
| | .10 | 2.71 | 2.30 | 2.08 | 1.94 | 1.85 | 1.77 | 1.67 | 1.55 | 1.38 | 1.00 |
| | .25 | 1.32 | 1.39 | 1.37 | 1.35 | 1.33 | 1.31 | 1.28 | 1.24 | 1.18 | 1.00 |

*Source:* Adapted from Table 18 in Pearson, E. S. and Hartley, H. O. (1958). *Biometrika Tables for Statisticians*, Vol. 1, 2nd ed. Cambridge University Press: Cambridge, with the kind permission of the trustees of *Biometrika*.

**TABLE C.6** COEFFICIENTS OF ORTHOGONAL POLYNOMIALS

| $k$ | Polynomial | $X=1$ | 2 | 3 | 4 | 5 | 6 | 7 | 8 | 9 | 10 | $\Sigma \xi'^2$ | $\lambda$ |
|---|---|---|---|---|---|---|---|---|---|---|---|---|---|
| 3 | Linear | −1 | 0 | 1 | | | | | | | | 2 | 1 |
| | Quadratic | 1 | −2 | 1 | | | | | | | | 6 | 3 |
| 4 | Linear | −3 | −1 | 1 | 3 | | | | | | | 20 | 2 |
| | Quadratic | 1 | −1 | −1 | 1 | | | | | | | 4 | 1 |
| | Cubic | −1 | 3 | −3 | 1 | | | | | | | 20 | 10/3 |
| 5 | Linear | −2 | −1 | 0 | 1 | 2 | | | | | | 10 | 1 |
| | Quadratic | 2 | −1 | −2 | −1 | 2 | | | | | | 14 | 1 |
| | Cubic | −1 | 2 | 0 | −2 | 1 | | | | | | 10 | 5/6 |
| | Quartic | 1 | −4 | 6 | −4 | 1 | | | | | | 70 | 35/12 |
| 6 | Linear | −5 | −3 | −1 | 1 | 3 | 5 | | | | | 70 | 2 |
| | Quadratic | 5 | −1 | −4 | −4 | −1 | 5 | | | | | 84 | 3/2 |
| | Cubic | −5 | 7 | 4 | −4 | −7 | 5 | | | | | 180 | 5/3 |
| | Quartic | 1 | −3 | 2 | 2 | −3 | 1 | | | | | 28 | 7/12 |
| 7 | Linear | −3 | −2 | −1 | 0 | 1 | 2 | 3 | | | | 28 | 1 |
| | Quadratic | 5 | 0 | −3 | −4 | −3 | 0 | 5 | | | | 84 | 1 |
| | Cubic | −1 | 1 | 1 | 0 | −1 | −1 | 1 | | | | 6 | 1/6 |
| | Quartic | 3 | −7 | 1 | 6 | −3 | −7 | 3 | | | | 154 | 7/12 |
| 8 | Linear | −7 | −5 | −3 | −1 | 1 | 3 | 5 | 7 | | | 168 | 2 |
| | Quadratic | 7 | 1 | −3 | −5 | −5 | −3 | 1 | 7 | | | 168 | 1 |
| | Cubic | −7 | 5 | 7 | 3 | −3 | −7 | −5 | 7 | | | 264 | 2/3 |
| | Quartic | 7 | −13 | −3 | 9 | 9 | −3 | −13 | 7 | | | 616 | 7/12 |
| | Quintic | −7 | 23 | −17 | −15 | 15 | 17 | −23 | 7 | | | 2184 | 7/10 |
| 9 | Linear | −4 | −3 | −2 | −1 | 0 | 1 | 2 | 3 | 4 | | 60 | 1 |
| | Quadratic | 28 | 7 | −8 | −17 | −20 | −17 | −8 | 7 | 28 | | 2772 | 3 |
| | Cubic | −14 | 7 | 13 | 9 | 0 | −9 | −13 | −7 | 14 | | 990 | 5/6 |
| | Quartic | 14 | −21 | −11 | 9 | 18 | 9 | −11 | −21 | 14 | | 2002 | 7/12 |
| | Quintic | −4 | 11 | −4 | −9 | 0 | 9 | 4 | −11 | 4 | | 468 | 3/20 |
| 10 | Linear | −9 | −7 | −5 | −3 | −1 | 1 | 3 | 5 | 7 | 9 | 330 | 2 |
| | Quadratic | 6 | 2 | −1 | −3 | −4 | −4 | −3 | −1 | 2 | 6 | 132 | 1/2 |
| | Cubic | −42 | 14 | 35 | 31 | 12 | −12 | −31 | −35 | −14 | 42 | 8580 | 5/3 |
| | Quartic | 18 | −22 | −17 | 3 | 18 | 18 | 3 | −17 | −22 | 18 | 2860 | 5/12 |
| | Quintic | −6 | 14 | −1 | −11 | −6 | 6 | 11 | 1 | −14 | 6 | 780 | 1/10 |

*Source:* Adapted from Table 47 in Pearson, E. S. and Hartley. H. O. (1958). *Biometrika Tables for Statisticians*, Vol. 1, 2nd ed. Cambridge University Press: Cambridge, with the kind permission of the trustees of *Biometrika*.

**TABLE C.7**  CRITICAL VALUES OF THE BONFERRONI *t* STATISTIC (note that the tabled values are two-tailed)

| df | FWE | 2 | 3 | 4 | 5 | 6 | 7 | 8 | 9 | 10 | 15 |
|---|---|---|---|---|---|---|---|---|---|---|---|
| | | | | | | Number of contrasts (*K*) | | | | | |
| | .01 | 7.453 | 8.575 | 9.465 | 10.215 | 10.869 | 11.453 | 11.984 | 12.471 | 12.924 | 14.819 |
| 3 | .05 | 4.177 | 4.857 | 5.392 | 5.841 | 6.232 | 6.580 | 6.895 | 7.185 | 7.453 | 8.575 |
| | .10 | 3.182 | 3.740 | 4.177 | 4.541 | 4.857 | 5.138 | 5.392 | 5.625 | 5.841 | 6.741 |
| | .01 | 5.598 | 6.254 | 6.758 | 7.173 | 7.529 | 7.841 | 8.122 | 8.376 | 8.610 | 9.568 |
| 4 | .05 | 3.495 | 3.961 | 4.315 | 4.604 | 4.851 | 5.068 | 5.261 | 5.437 | 5.598 | 6.254 |
| | .10 | 2.776 | 3.186 | 3.495 | 3.747 | 3.961 | 4.148 | 4.315 | 4.466 | 4.604 | 5.167 |
| | .01 | 4.773 | 5.247 | 5.604 | 5.893 | 6.138 | 6.352 | 6.541 | 6.713 | 6.869 | 7.499 |
| 5 | .05 | 3.163 | 3.534 | 3.810 | 4.032 | 4.219 | 4.382 | 4.526 | 4.655 | 4.773 | 5.247 |
| | .10 | 2.571 | 2.912 | 3.163 | 3.365 | 3.534 | 3.681 | 3.810 | 3.926 | 4.032 | 4.456 |
| | .01 | 4.317 | 4.698 | 4.981 | 5.208 | 5.398 | 5.563 | 5.709 | 5.840 | 5.959 | 6.434 |
| 6 | .05 | 2.969 | 3.287 | 3.521 | 3.707 | 3.863 | 3.997 | 4.115 | 4.221 | 4.317 | 4.698 |
| | .10 | 2.447 | 2.749 | 2.969 | 3.143 | 3.287 | 3.412 | 3.521 | 3.619 | 3.707 | 4.058 |
| | .01 | 4.029 | 4.355 | 4.595 | 4.785 | 4.944 | 5.082 | 5.202 | 5.310 | 5.408 | 5.795 |
| 7 | .05 | 2.841 | 3.128 | 3.335 | 3.499 | 3.636 | 3.753 | 3.855 | 3.947 | 4.029 | 4.355 |
| | .10 | 2.365 | 2.642 | 2.841 | 2.998 | 3.128 | 3.238 | 3.335 | 3.422 | 3.499 | 3.806 |
| | .01 | 3.833 | 4.122 | 4.334 | 4.501 | 4.640 | 4.759 | 4.864 | 4.957 | 5.041 | 5.374 |
| 8 | .05 | 2.732 | 3.016 | 3.206 | 3.355 | 3.479 | 3.584 | 3.677 | 3.759 | 3.833 | 4.122 |
| | .10 | 2.306 | 2.566 | 2.752 | 2.896 | 3.016 | 3.117 | 3.206 | 3.285 | 3.355 | 3.632 |
| | .01 | 3.690 | 3.954 | 4.146 | 4.297 | 4.422 | 4.529 | 4.622 | 4.706 | 4.781 | 5.076 |
| 9 | .05 | 2.685 | 2.933 | 3.111 | 3.250 | 3.364 | 3.462 | 3.547 | 3.622 | 3.690 | 3.954 |
| | .10 | 2.262 | 2.510 | 2.685 | 2.821 | 2.933 | 3.028 | 3.111 | 3.184 | 3.250 | 3.505 |
| | .01 | 3.581 | 3.827 | 4.005 | 4.144 | 4.259 | 4.357 | 4.442 | 4.518 | 4.587 | 4.855 |
| 10 | .05 | 2.634 | 2.870 | 3.038 | 3.169 | 3.277 | 3.368 | 3.448 | 3.518 | 3.581 | 3.827 |
| | .10 | 2.228 | 2.466 | 2.634 | 2.764 | 2.870 | 2.960 | 3.038 | 3.107 | 3.169 | 3.409 |
| | .01 | 3.497 | 3.728 | 3.895 | 4.025 | 4.132 | 4.223 | 4.303 | 4.373 | 4.437 | 4.685 |
| 11 | .05 | 2.593 | 2.820 | 2.981 | 3.106 | 3.208 | 3.295 | 3.370 | 3.437 | 3.497 | 3.728 |
| | .10 | 2.201 | 2.431 | 2.593 | 2.718 | 2.820 | 2.906 | 2.981 | 3.047 | 3.106 | 3.334 |
| | .01 | 3.428 | 3.649 | 3.807 | 3.930 | 4.031 | 4.117 | 4.192 | 4.258 | 4.318 | 4.550 |
| 12 | .05 | 2.560 | 2.779 | 2.934 | 3.055 | 3.153 | 3.236 | 3.308 | 3.371 | 3.428 | 3.649 |
| | .10 | 2.179 | 2.403 | 2.560 | 2.681 | 2.779 | 2.863 | 2.934 | 2.998 | 3.055 | 3.273 |
| | .01 | 3.372 | 3.584 | 3.735 | 3.852 | 3.948 | 4.030 | 4.101 | 4.164 | 4.221 | 4.440 |
| 13 | .05 | 2.533 | 2.746 | 2.896 | 3.012 | 3.107 | 3.187 | 3.256 | 3.318 | 3.372 | 3.584 |
| | .10 | 2.160 | 2.380 | 2.533 | 2.650 | 2.746 | 2.827 | 2.896 | 2.957 | 3.012 | 3.223 |
| | .01 | 3.326 | 3.530 | 3.675 | 3.787 | 3.880 | 3.958 | 4.026 | 4.086 | 4.140 | 4.349 |
| 14 | .05 | 2.510 | 2.718 | 2.864 | 2.977 | 3.069 | 3.146 | 3.214 | 3.273 | 3.326 | 3.530 |
| | .10 | 2.145 | 2.360 | 2.510 | 2.624 | 2.718 | 2.796 | 2.864 | 2.924 | 2.977 | 3.181 |
| | .01 | 3.286 | 3.484 | 3.624 | 3.733 | 3.822 | 3.897 | 3.963 | 4.021 | 4.073 | 4.273 |
| 15 | .05 | 2.490 | 2.694 | 2.837 | 2.947 | 3.036 | 3.112 | 3.177 | 3.235 | 3.286 | 3.484 |
| | .10 | 2.131 | 2.343 | 2.490 | 2.602 | 2.694 | 2.770 | 2.837 | 2.895 | 2.947 | 3.146 |
| | .01 | 3.252 | 3.444 | 3.581 | 3.686 | 3.773 | 3.846 | 3.909 | 3.965 | 4.015 | 4.208 |
| 16 | .05 | 2.473 | 2.673 | 2.813 | 2.921 | 3.008 | 3.082 | 3.146 | 3.202 | 3.252 | 3.444 |
| | .10 | 2.120 | 2.328 | 2.473 | 2.583 | 2.673 | 2.748 | 2.813 | 2.870 | 2.921 | 3.115 |

**TABLE C.7**  (continued)

| df | FWE | Number of contrasts ($K$) | | | | | | | | | |
|----|-----|-------|-------|-------|-------|-------|-------|-------|-------|-------|-------|
| | | 2 | 3 | 4 | 5 | 6 | 7 | 8 | 9 | 10 | 15 |
| 17 | .01 | 3.222 | 3.410 | 3.543 | 3.646 | 3.730 | 3.801 | 3.862 | 3.917 | 3.965 | 4.152 |
| | .05 | 2.458 | 2.655 | 2.793 | 2.898 | 2.984 | 3.056 | 3.119 | 3.173 | 3.222 | 3.410 |
| | .10 | 2.110 | 2.316 | 2.458 | 2.567 | 2.655 | 2.729 | 2.793 | 2.848 | 2.898 | 3.089 |
| 18 | .01 | 3.197 | 3.380 | 3.510 | 3.610 | 3.692 | 3.762 | 3.822 | 3.874 | 3.922 | 4.104 |
| | .05 | 2.445 | 2.639 | 2.775 | 2.878 | 2.963 | 3.034 | 3.095 | 3.149 | 3.197 | 3.380 |
| | .10 | 2.101 | 2.304 | 2.445 | 2.552 | 2.639 | 2.712 | 2.775 | 2.829 | 2.878 | 3.065 |
| 19 | .01 | 3.174 | 3.354 | 3.481 | 3.579 | 3.660 | 3.727 | 3.786 | 3.837 | 3.883 | 4.061 |
| | .05 | 2.433 | 2.625 | 2.759 | 2.861 | 2.944 | 3.014 | 3.074 | 3.127 | 3.174 | 3.354 |
| | .10 | 2.093 | 2.294 | 2.433 | 2.539 | 2.625 | 2.697 | 2.759 | 2.813 | 2.861 | 3.045 |
| 20 | .01 | 3.153 | 3.331 | 3.455 | 3.552 | 3.630 | 3.697 | 3.754 | 3.804 | 3.850 | 4.023 |
| | .05 | 2.423 | 2.613 | 2.744 | 2.845 | 2.927 | 2.996 | 3.055 | 3.107 | 3.153 | 3.331 |
| | .10 | 2.086 | 2.285 | 2.423 | 2.528 | 2.613 | 2.683 | 2.744 | 2.798 | 2.845 | 3.026 |
| 25 | .01 | 3.078 | 3.244 | 3.361 | 3.450 | 3.523 | 3.584 | 3.637 | 3.684 | 3.725 | 3.884 |
| | .05 | 2.385 | 2.566 | 2.692 | 2.787 | 2.865 | 2.930 | 2.986 | 3.035 | 3.078 | 3.244 |
| | .10 | 2.060 | 2.252 | 2.385 | 2.485 | 2.566 | 2.634 | 2.692 | 2.742 | 2.787 | 2.959 |
| 30 | .01 | 3.030 | 3.189 | 3.300 | 3.385 | 3.454 | 3.513 | 3.563 | 3.607 | 3.646 | 3.796 |
| | .05 | 2.360 | 2.536 | 2.657 | 2.750 | 2.825 | 2.887 | 2.941 | 2.988 | 3.030 | 3.189 |
| | .10 | 2.042 | 2.231 | 2.360 | 2.457 | 2.536 | 2.601 | 2.657 | 2.706 | 2.750 | 2.915 |
| 35 | .01 | 2.996 | 3.150 | 3.258 | 3.340 | 3.407 | 3.463 | 3.511 | 3.553 | 3.591 | 3.735 |
| | .05 | 2.342 | 2.515 | 2.633 | 2.724 | 2.797 | 2.857 | 2.910 | 2.955 | 2.996 | 3.150 |
| | .10 | 2.030 | 2.215 | 2.342 | 2.438 | 2.515 | 2.579 | 2.633 | 2.681 | 2.724 | 2.885 |
| 40 | .01 | 2.971 | 3.122 | 3.227 | 3.307 | 3.372 | 3.426 | 3.473 | 3.514 | 3.551 | 3.691 |
| | .05 | 2.329 | 2.499 | 2.616 | 2.704 | 2.776 | 2.836 | 2.887 | 2.931 | 2.971 | 3.122 |
| | .10 | 2.021 | 2.204 | 2.329 | 2.423 | 2.499 | 2.562 | 2.616 | 2.663 | 2.704 | 2.862 |
| 60 | .01 | 2.915 | 3.057 | 3.156 | 3.232 | 3.293 | 3.344 | 3.388 | 3.426 | 3.460 | 3.590 |
| | .05 | 2.299 | 2.463 | 2.575 | 2.660 | 2.729 | 2.785 | 2.834 | 2.877 | 2.915 | 3.057 |
| | .10 | 2.000 | 2.178 | 2.299 | 2.390 | 2.463 | 2.524 | 2.575 | 2.620 | 2.660 | 2.811 |
| 120 | .01 | 2.860 | 2.995 | 3.088 | 3.160 | 3.217 | 3.265 | 3.306 | 3.342 | 3.373 | 3.494 |
| | .05 | 2.270 | 2.428 | 2.536 | 2.617 | 2.683 | 2.737 | 2.783 | 2.824 | 2.860 | 2.995 |
| | .10 | 1.980 | 2.153 | 2.270 | 2.358 | 2.428 | 2.486 | 2.536 | 2.579 | 2.617 | 2.761 |

**TABLE C.8**  DISTRIBUTION OF DUNNETT'S *d* STATISTIC FOR COMPARING TREATMENT MEANS WITH A CONTROL (note that the tabled values are two-tailed)

| df for MS$_{error}$ | FWE | \multicolumn{9}{c}{Number of means (including control)} |
|---|---|---|---|---|---|---|---|---|---|---|
| | | 2 | 3 | 4 | 5 | 6 | 7 | 8 | 9 | 10 |
| 6 | .10 | 1.94 | 2.34 | 2.56 | 2.71 | 2.83 | 2.92 | 3.00 | 3.07 | 3.12 |
| | .05 | 2.45 | 2.86 | 3.18 | 3.41 | 3.60 | 3.75 | 3.88 | 4.00 | 4.11 |
| | .02 | 3.14 | 3.61 | 3.88 | 4.07 | 4.21 | 4.33 | 4.43 | 4.51 | 4.59 |
| | .01 | 3.71 | 4.22 | 4.60 | 4.88 | 5.11 | 5.30 | 5.47 | 5.61 | 5.74 |
| 7 | .10 | 1.89 | 2.27 | 2.48 | 2.62 | 2.73 | 2.82 | 2.89 | 2.95 | 3.01 |
| | .05 | 2.36 | 2.75 | 3.04 | 3.24 | 3.41 | 3.54 | 3.66 | 3.76 | 3.86 |
| | .02 | 3.00 | 3.42 | 3.66 | 3.83 | 3.96 | 4.07 | 4.15 | 4.23 | 4.30 |
| | .01 | 3.50 | 3.95 | 4.28 | 4.52 | 4.17 | 4.87 | 5.01 | 5.13 | 5.24 |
| 8 | .10 | 1.86 | 2.22 | 2.42 | 2.55 | 2.66 | 2.74 | 2.81 | 2.87 | 2.92 |
| | .05 | 2.31 | 2.67 | 2.94 | 3.13 | 3.28 | 3.40 | 3.51 | 3.60 | 3.68 |
| | .02 | 2.90 | 3.29 | 3.51 | 3.67 | 3.79 | 3.88 | 3.96 | 4.03 | 4.09 |
| | .01 | 3.36 | 3.77 | 4.06 | 4.27 | 4.44 | 4.58 | 4.70 | 4.81 | 4.90 |
| 9 | .10 | 1.83 | 2.18 | 2.37 | 2.50 | 2.60 | 2.68 | 2.75 | 2.81 | 2.86 |
| | .05 | 2.26 | 2.61 | 2.86 | 3.04 | 3.18 | 3.29 | 3.39 | 3.48 | 3.55 |
| | .02 | 2.82 | 3.19 | 3.40 | 3.55 | 3.66 | 3.75 | 3.82 | 3.89 | 3.94 |
| | .01 | 3.25 | 3.63 | 3.90 | 4.09 | 4.24 | 4.37 | 4.48 | 4.57 | 4.65 |
| 10 | .10 | 1.81 | 2.15 | 2.34 | 2.47 | 2.56 | 2.64 | 2.70 | 2.76 | 2.81 |
| | .05 | 2.23 | 2.57 | 2.81 | 2.97 | 3.11 | 3.21 | 3.31 | 3.39 | 3.46 |
| | .02 | 2.76 | 3.11 | 3.31 | 3.45 | 3.56 | 3.64 | 3.71 | 3.78 | 3.83 |
| | .01 | 3.17 | 3.53 | 3.78 | 3.95 | 4.10 | 4.21 | 4.31 | 4.40 | 4.47 |
| 11 | .10 | 1.80 | 2.13 | 2.31 | 2.44 | 2.53 | 2.60 | 2.67 | 2.72 | 2.77 |
| | .05 | 2.20 | 2.53 | 2.76 | 2.92 | 3.05 | 3.15 | 3.24 | 3.31 | 3.38 |
| | .02 | 2.72 | 3.06 | 3.25 | 3.38 | 3.48 | 3.56 | 3.63 | 3.69 | 3.74 |
| | .01 | 3.11 | 3.45 | 3.68 | 3.85 | 3.98 | 4.09 | 4.18 | 4.26 | 4.33 |
| 12 | .10 | 1.78 | 2.11 | 2.29 | 2.41 | 2.50 | 2.58 | 2.64 | 2.69 | 2.74 |
| | .05 | 2.18 | 2.50 | 2.72 | 2.88 | 3.00 | 3.10 | 3.18 | 3.25 | 3.32 |
| | .02 | 2.68 | 3.01 | 3.19 | 3.32 | 3.42 | 3.50 | 3.56 | 3.62 | 3.67 |
| | .01 | 3.05 | 3.39 | 3.61 | 3.76 | 3.89 | 3.99 | 4.08 | 4.15 | 4.22 |
| 13 | .10 | 1.77 | 2.09 | 2.27 | 2.39 | 2.48 | 2.55 | 2.61 | 2.66 | 2.71 |
| | .05 | 2.16 | 2.48 | 2.69 | 2.84 | 2.96 | 3.06 | 3.14 | 3.21 | 3.27 |
| | .02 | 2.65 | 2.97 | 3.15 | 3.27 | 3.37 | 3.44 | 3.51 | 3.56 | 3.61 |
| | .01 | 3.01 | 3.33 | 3.54 | 3.69 | 3.81 | 3.91 | 3.99 | 4.06 | 4.13 |
| 14 | .10 | 1.76 | 2.08 | 2.25 | 2.37 | 2.46 | 2.53 | 2.59 | 2.64 | 2.69 |
| | .05 | 2.14 | 2.46 | 2.67 | 2.81 | 2.93 | 3.02 | 3.10 | 3.17 | 3.23 |
| | .02 | 2.62 | 2.94 | 3.11 | 3.23 | 3.32 | 3.40 | 3.46 | 3.51 | 3.56 |
| | .01 | 2.98 | 3.29 | 3.49 | 3.64 | 3.75 | 3.84 | 3.92 | 3.99 | 4.05 |
| 16 | .10 | 1.75 | 2.06 | 2.23 | 2.34 | 2.43 | 2.50 | 2.56 | 2.61 | 2.65 |
| | .05 | 2.12 | 2.42 | 2.63 | 2.77 | 2.88 | 2.96 | 3.04 | 3.10 | 3.16 |
| | .02 | 2.58 | 2.88 | 3.05 | 3.17 | 3.26 | 3.33 | 3.39 | 3.44 | 3.48 |
| | .01 | 2.92 | 3.22 | 3.41 | 3.55 | 3.65 | 3.74 | 3.82 | 3.88 | 3.93 |

**TABLE C.8** (continued)

| df for MS$_{error}$ | FWE | 2 | 3 | 4 | 5 | 6 | 7 | 8 | 9 | 10 |
|---|---|---|---|---|---|---|---|---|---|---|
| | | | | | Number of means (including control) | | | | | |
| 18 | .10 | 1.73 | 2.04 | 2.21 | 2.32 | 2.41 | 2.48 | 2.53 | 2.58 | 2.62 |
| | .05 | 2.10 | 2.40 | 2.59 | 2.73 | 2.84 | 2.92 | 2.99 | 3.05 | 3.11 |
| | .02 | 2.55 | 2.84 | 3.01 | 3.12 | 3.21 | 3.27 | 3.33 | 3.38 | 3.42 |
| | .01 | 2.88 | 3.17 | 3.35 | 3.48 | 3.58 | 3.67 | 3.74 | 3.80 | 3.85 |
| 20 | .10 | 1.72 | 2.03 | 2.19 | 2.30 | 2.39 | 2.46 | 2.51 | 2.56 | 2.60 |
| | .05 | 2.09 | 2.38 | 2.57 | 2.70 | 2.81 | 2.89 | 2.96 | 3.02 | 3.07 |
| | .02 | 2.53 | 2.81 | 2.97 | 3.08 | 3.17 | 3.23 | 3.29 | 3.34 | 3.38 |
| | .01 | 2.85 | 3.13 | 3.31 | 3.43 | 3.53 | 3.61 | 3.67 | 3.73 | 3.78 |
| 24 | .10 | 1.71 | 2.01 | 2.17 | 2.28 | 2.36 | 2.43 | 2.48 | 2.53 | 2.57 |
| | .05 | 2.06 | 2.35 | 2.53 | 2.66 | 2.76 | 2.84 | 2.91 | 2.96 | 3.01 |
| | .02 | 2.49 | 2.77 | 2.92 | 3.03 | 3.11 | 3.17 | 3.22 | 3.27 | 3.31 |
| | .01 | 2.80 | 3.07 | 3.24 | 3.36 | 3.45 | 3.52 | 3.58 | 3.64 | 3.69 |
| 30 | .10 | 1.70 | 1.99 | 2.15 | 2.25 | 2.33 | 2.40 | 2.45 | 2.50 | 2.54 |
| | .05 | 2.04 | 2.32 | 2.50 | 2.62 | 2.72 | 2.79 | 2.86 | 2.91 | 2.96 |
| | .02 | 2.46 | 2.72 | 2.87 | 2.97 | 3.05 | 3.11 | 3.16 | 3.21 | 3.24 |
| | .01 | 2.75 | 3.01 | 3.17 | 3.28 | 3.37 | 3.44 | 3.50 | 3.55 | 3.59 |
| 40 | .10 | 1.68 | 1.97 | 2.13 | 2.23 | 2.31 | 2.37 | 2.42 | 2.47 | 2.51 |
| | .05 | 2.02 | 2.29 | 2.47 | 2.58 | 2.67 | 2.75 | 2.81 | 2.86 | 2.90 |
| | .02 | 2.42 | 2.68 | 2.82 | 2.92 | 2.99 | 3.05 | 3.10 | 3.14 | 3.18 |
| | .01 | 2.70 | 2.95 | 3.10 | 3.21 | 3.29 | 3.36 | 3.41 | 3.46 | 3.50 |
| 60 | .10 | 1.67 | 1.95 | 2.10 | 2.21 | 2.28 | 2.35 | 2.39 | 2.44 | 2.48 |
| | .05 | 2.00 | 2.27 | 2.43 | 2.55 | 2.63 | 2.70 | 2.76 | 2.81 | 2.85 |
| | .02 | 2.39 | 2.64 | 2.78 | 2.87 | 2.94 | 3.00 | 3.04 | 3.08 | 3.12 |
| | .01 | 2.66 | 2.90 | 3.04 | 3.14 | 3.22 | 3.28 | 3.33 | 3.38 | 3.42 |
| 120 | .10 | 1.66 | 1.93 | 2.08 | 2.18 | 2.26 | 2.32 | 2.37 | 2.41 | 2.45 |
| | .05 | 1.98 | 2.24 | 2.40 | 2.51 | 2.59 | 2.66 | 2.71 | 2.76 | 2.80 |
| | .02 | 2.36 | 2.60 | 2.73 | 2.82 | 2.89 | 2.94 | 2.99 | 3.03 | 3.06 |
| | .01 | 2.62 | 2.84 | 2.98 | 3.08 | 3.15 | 3.21 | 3.25 | 3.30 | 3.33 |
| ∞ | .10 | 1.64 | 1.92 | 2.06 | 2.16 | 2.23 | 2.29 | 2.34 | 2.38 | 2.42 |
| | .05 | 1.96 | 2.21 | 2.37 | 2.47 | 2.55 | 2.62 | 2.67 | 2.71 | 2.75 |
| | .02 | 2.33 | 2.56 | 2.68 | 2.77 | 2.84 | 2.89 | 2.93 | 2.97 | 3.00 |
| | .01 | 2.58 | 2.79 | 2.92 | 3.01 | 3.08 | 3.14 | 3.18 | 3.22 | 3.25 |

*Source*: Adapted from tables in Dunnett, C. W. (1955). A multiple comparison procedure for comparing several treatments with a control. *Journal of the American Statistical Association, 50*, 1096–1121, and from Dunnett, C. W. (1964). New tables for multiple comparisons with a control. *Biometrics, 20*, 482–491, with permission of the author and the editors.

**TABLE C.9** CRITICAL VALUES OF THE STUDENTIZED RANGE DISTRIBUTION

| Error df | FWE | Number of Ordered Means | | | | | | |
|---|---|---|---|---|---|---|---|---|
| | | 2 | 3 | 4 | 5 | 6 | 7 | 8 |
| 2 | .01 | 14.04 | 19.02 | 22.29 | 24.72 | 26.63 | 28.20 | 29.53 |
| | .05 | 6.09 | 8.33 | 9.80 | 10.88 | 11.74 | 12.44 | 13.03 |
| | .10 | 4.13 | 5.73 | 6.77 | 7.54 | 8.14 | 8.63 | 9.05 |
| 3 | .01 | 8.26 | 10.62 | 12.17 | 13.33 | 14.24 | 15.00 | 15.64 |
| | .05 | 4.50 | 5.91 | 6.83 | 7.50 | 8.04 | 8.48 | 8.85 |
| | .10 | 3.33 | 4.47 | 5.20 | 5.74 | 6.16 | 6.51 | 6.81 |
| 4 | .01 | 6.51 | 8.12 | 9.17 | 9.96 | 10.58 | 11.10 | 11.55 |
| | .05 | 3.93 | 5.04 | 5.76 | 6.29 | 6.71 | 7.05 | 7.35 |
| | .10 | 3.02 | 3.98 | 4.59 | 5.04 | 5.39 | 5.68 | 5.93 |
| 5 | .01 | 5.70 | 6.98 | 7.80 | 8.42 | 8.91 | 9.32 | 9.67 |
| | .05 | 3.64 | 4.60 | 5.22 | 5.67 | 6.03 | 6.33 | 6.58 |
| | .10 | 2.85 | 3.72 | 4.26 | 4.66 | 4.98 | 5.24 | 5.46 |
| 6 | .01 | 5.24 | 6.33 | 7.03 | 7.56 | 7.97 | 8.32 | 8.61 |
| | .05 | 3.46 | 4.34 | 4.90 | 5.31 | 5.63 | 5.90 | 6.12 |
| | .10 | 2.75 | 3.56 | 4.07 | 4.44 | 4.73 | 4.97 | 5.17 |
| 7 | .01 | 4.95 | 5.92 | 6.54 | 7.01 | 7.37 | 7.68 | 7.94 |
| | .05 | 3.34 | 4.17 | 4.68 | 5.06 | 5.36 | 5.61 | 5.82 |
| | .10 | 2.68 | 3.45 | 3.93 | 4.28 | 4.56 | 4.78 | 4.97 |
| 8 | .01 | 4.75 | 5.64 | 6.20 | 6.63 | 6.96 | 7.24 | 7.47 |
| | .05 | 3.26 | 4.04 | 4.53 | 4.89 | 5.17 | 5.40 | 5.60 |
| | .10 | 2.63 | 3.37 | 3.83 | 4.17 | 4.43 | 4.65 | 4.83 |
| 9 | .01 | 4.60 | 5.43 | 5.96 | 6.35 | 6.66 | 6.92 | 7.13 |
| | .05 | 3.20 | 3.95 | 4.42 | 4.76 | 5.02 | 5.24 | 5.43 |
| | .10 | 2.59 | 3.32 | 3.76 | 4.08 | 4.34 | 4.55 | 4.72 |
| 10 | .01 | 4.48 | 5.27 | 5.77 | 6.14 | 6.43 | 6.67 | 6.88 |
| | .05 | 3.15 | 3.88 | 4.33 | 4.65 | 4.91 | 5.12 | 5.31 |
| | .10 | 2.56 | 3.27 | 3.70 | 4.02 | 4.26 | 4.47 | 4.64 |
| 11 | .01 | 4.39 | 5.15 | 5.62 | 5.97 | 6.25 | 6.48 | 6.67 |
| | .05 | 3.11 | 3.82 | 4.26 | 4.57 | 4.82 | 5.03 | 5.20 |
| | .10 | 2.54 | 3.23 | 3.66 | 3.97 | 4.21 | 4.40 | 4.57 |
| 12 | .01 | 4.32 | 5.05 | 5.50 | 5.84 | 6.10 | 6.32 | 6.51 |
| | .05 | 3.08 | 3.77 | 4.20 | 4.51 | 4.75 | 4.95 | 5.12 |
| | .10 | 2.52 | 3.20 | 3.62 | 3.92 | 4.16 | 4.35 | 4.51 |
| 13 | .01 | 4.26 | 4.96 | 5.40 | 5.73 | 5.98 | 6.19 | 6.37 |
| | .05 | 3.06 | 3.74 | 4.15 | 4.45 | 4.69 | 4.89 | 5.05 |
| | .10 | 2.51 | 3.18 | 3.59 | 3.89 | 4.12 | 4.31 | 4.46 |
| 14 | .01 | 4.21 | 4.90 | 5.32 | 5.63 | 5.88 | 6.09 | 6.26 |
| | .05 | 3.03 | 3.70 | 4.11 | 4.41 | 4.64 | 4.83 | 4.99 |
| | .10 | 2.49 | 3.16 | 3.56 | 3.85 | 4.06 | 4.27 | 4.42 |
| 15 | .01 | 4.17 | 4.84 | 5.25 | 5.56 | 5.80 | 5.99 | 6.16 |
| | .05 | 3.01 | 3.67 | 4.08 | 4.37 | 4.60 | 4.78 | 4.94 |
| | .10 | 2.48 | 3.14 | 3.54 | 3.83 | 4.05 | 4.24 | 4.39 |
| 16 | .01 | 4.13 | 4.79 | 5.19 | 5.49 | 5.72 | 5.92 | 6.08 |
| | .05 | 3.00 | 3.65 | 4.05 | 4.33 | 4.56 | 4.74 | 4.90 |
| | .10 | 2.47 | 3.12 | 3.52 | 3.80 | 4.03 | 4.21 | 4.36 |

**TABLE C.9**  CRITICAL VALUES OF THE STUDENTIZED RANGE DISTRIBUTION

| Error df | FWE | Number of Ordered Means | | | | | | |
|---|---|---|---|---|---|---|---|---|
| | | 2 | 3 | 4 | 5 | 6 | 7 | 8 |
| 17 | .01 | 4.10 | 4.74 | 5.14 | 5.43 | 5.66 | 5.85 | 6.01 |
| | .05 | 2.98 | 3.63 | 4.02 | 4.30 | 4.52 | 4.71 | 4.86 |
| | .10 | 2.46 | 3.11 | 3.50 | 3.78 | 4.00 | 4.18 | 4.33 |
| 18 | .01 | 4.07 | 4.70 | 5.09 | 5.38 | 5.60 | 5.79 | 5.94 |
| | .05 | 2.97 | 3.61 | 4.00 | 4.28 | 4.50 | 4.67 | 4.82 |
| | .10 | 2.45 | 3.10 | 3.49 | 3.77 | 3.98 | 4.16 | 4.31 |
| 19 | .01 | 4.05 | 4.67 | 5.05 | 5.33 | 5.55 | 5.74 | 5.89 |
| | .05 | 2.96 | 3.59 | 3.98 | 4.25 | 4.47 | 4.65 | 4.79 |
| | .10 | 2.45 | 3.09 | 3.47 | 3.75 | 3.97 | 4.14 | 4.29 |
| 20 | .01 | 4.02 | 4.64 | 5.02 | 5.29 | 5.51 | 5.69 | 5.84 |
| | .05 | 2.95 | 3.58 | 3.96 | 4.23 | 4.45 | 4.62 | 4.77 |
| | .10 | 2.44 | 3.08 | 3.46 | 3.74 | 3.95 | 4.12 | 4.27 |
| 24 | .01 | 3.96 | 4.55 | 4.91 | 5.17 | 5.37 | 5.54 | 5.69 |
| | .05 | 2.92 | 3.53 | 3.90 | 4.17 | 4.37 | 4.54 | 4.68 |
| | .10 | 2.42 | 3.05 | 3.42 | 3.69 | 3.90 | 4.07 | 4.21 |
| 30 | .01 | 3.89 | 4.46 | 4.80 | 5.05 | 5.24 | 5.40 | 5.54 |
| | .05 | 2.89 | 3.49 | 3.85 | 4.10 | 4.30 | 4.46 | 4.60 |
| | .10 | 2.40 | 3.02 | 3.39 | 3.65 | 3.85 | 4.02 | 4.16 |
| 40 | .01 | 3.83 | 4.37 | 4.70 | 4.93 | 5.11 | 5.27 | 5.39 |
| | .05 | 2.86 | 3.44 | 3.79 | 4.04 | 4.23 | 4.39 | 4.52 |
| | .10 | 2.38 | 2.99 | 3.35 | 3.61 | 3.80 | 3.96 | 4.10 |
| 60 | .01 | 3.76 | 4.28 | 4.60 | 4.82 | 4.99 | 5.13 | 5.25 |
| | .05 | 2.83 | 3.40 | 3.74 | 3.98 | 4.16 | 4.31 | 4.44 |
| | .10 | 2.36 | 2.96 | 3.31 | 3.56 | 3.76 | 3.91 | 4.04 |
| 120 | .01 | 3.70 | 4.20 | 4.50 | 4.71 | 4.87 | 5.01 | 5.12 |
| | .05 | 2.80 | 3.36 | 3.69 | 3.92 | 4.10 | 4.24 | 4.36 |
| | .10 | 2.34 | 2.93 | 3.28 | 3.52 | 3.71 | 3.86 | 3.99 |
| $\infty$ | .01 | 3.64 | 4.12 | 4.40 | 4.60 | 4.76 | 4.88 | 4.99 |
| | .05 | 2.77 | 3.31 | 3.63 | 3.86 | 4.03 | 4.17 | 4.29 |
| | .10 | 2.33 | 2.90 | 3.24 | 3.48 | 3.66 | 3.81 | 3.93 |

| Error df | FWE | Number of Ordered Means | | | | | | |
|---|---|---|---|---|---|---|---|---|
| | | 9 | 10 | 11 | 12 | 13 | 14 | 15 |
| 2 | .01 | 30.68 | 31.69 | 32.59 | 33.40 | 34.13 | 34.81 | 35.43 |
| | .05 | 13.54 | 13.99 | 14.39 | 14.75 | 15.08 | 15.38 | 15.65 |
| | .10 | 9.41 | 9.73 | 10.01 | 10.26 | 10.49 | 10.70 | 10.89 |
| 3 | .01 | 16.20 | 16.69 | 17.13 | 17.53 | 17.89 | 18.22 | 18.52 |
| | .05 | 9.18 | 9.46 | 9.72 | 9.95 | 10.15 | 10.35 | 10.53 |
| | .10 | 7.06 | 7.29 | 7.49 | 7.67 | 7.83 | 7.98 | 8.12 |
| 4 | .01 | 11.93 | 12.27 | 12.57 | 12.84 | 13.09 | 13.32 | 13.53 |
| | .05 | 7.60 | 7.83 | 8.03 | 8.21 | 8.37 | 8.53 | 8.66 |
| | .10 | 6.14 | 6.33 | 6.50 | 6.65 | 6.78 | 6.91 | 7.03 |

TABLE C.9   (continued)

| Error df | FWE | Number of Ordered Means | | | | | | |
|---|---|---|---|---|---|---|---|---|
| | | 9 | 10 | 11 | 12 | 13 | 14 | 15 |
| 5 | .01 | 9.97 | 10.24 | 10.48 | 10.70 | 10.89 | 11.08 | 11.24 |
| | .05 | 6.80 | 7.00 | 7.17 | 7.32 | 7.47 | 7.60 | 7.72 |
| | .10 | 5.65 | 5.82 | 5.97 | 6.10 | 6.22 | 6.34 | 6.44 |
| 6 | .01 | 8.87 | 9.10 | 9.30 | 9.48 | 9.65 | 9.81 | 9.95 |
| | .05 | 6.32 | 6.49 | 6.65 | 6.79 | 6.92 | 7.03 | 7.14 |
| | .10 | 5.34 | 5.50 | 5.64 | 5.76 | 5.88 | 5.98 | 6.08 |
| 7 | .01 | 8.17 | 8.37 | 8.55 | 8.71 | 8.86 | 9.00 | 9.12 |
| | .05 | 6.00 | 6.16 | 6.30 | 6.43 | 6.55 | 6.66 | 6.76 |
| | .10 | 5.14 | 5.28 | 5.41 | 5.53 | 5.64 | 5.74 | 5.83 |
| 8 | .01 | 7.68 | 7.86 | 8.03 | 8.18 | 8.31 | 8.44 | 8.55 |
| | .05 | 5.77 | 5.92 | 6.05 | 6.18 | 6.29 | 6.39 | 6.48 |
| | .10 | 4.99 | 5.13 | 5.25 | 5.36 | 5.46 | 5.56 | 5.64 |
| 9 | .01 | 7.33 | 7.50 | 7.65 | 7.78 | 7.91 | 8.03 | 8.13 |
| | .05 | 5.60 | 5.74 | 5.87 | 5.98 | 6.09 | 6.19 | 6.28 |
| | .10 | 4.87 | 5.01 | 5.13 | 5.23 | 5.33 | 5.42 | 5.51 |
| 10 | .01 | 7.06 | 7.21 | 7.36 | 7.49 | 7.60 | 7.71 | 7.81 |
| | .05 | 5.46 | 5.60 | 5.72 | 5.83 | 5.94 | 6.03 | 6.11 |
| | .10 | 4.78 | 4.91 | 5.03 | 5.13 | 5.23 | 5.32 | 5.40 |
| 11 | .01 | 6.84 | 6.99 | 7.13 | 7.25 | 7.36 | 7.47 | 7.56 |
| | .05 | 5.35 | 5.49 | 5.61 | 5.71 | 5.81 | 5.90 | 5.98 |
| | .10 | 4.71 | 4.84 | 4.95 | 5.05 | 5.15 | 5.23 | 5.31 |
| 12 | .01 | 6.67 | 6.81 | 6.94 | 7.06 | 7.17 | 7.27 | 7.36 |
| | .05 | 5.27 | 5.40 | 5.51 | 5.62 | 5.71 | 5.80 | 5.88 |
| | .10 | 4.65 | 4.78 | 4.89 | 4.99 | 5.08 | 5.16 | 5.24 |
| 13 | .01 | 6.53 | 6.67 | 6.79 | 6.90 | 7.01 | 7.10 | 7.19 |
| | .05 | 5.19 | 5.32 | 5.43 | 5.53 | 5.63 | 5.71 | 5.79 |
| | .10 | 4.60 | 4.72 | 4.83 | 4.93 | 5.02 | 5.10 | 5.18 |
| 14 | .01 | 6.41 | 6.54 | 6.66 | 6.77 | 6.87 | 6.96 | 7.05 |
| | .05 | 5.13 | 5.25 | 5.36 | 5.46 | 5.55 | 5.64 | 5.71 |
| | .10 | 4.56 | 4.68 | 4.79 | 4.88 | 4.97 | 5.05 | 5.12 |
| 15 | .01 | 6.31 | 6.44 | 6.56 | 6.66 | 6.76 | 6.85 | 6.93 |
| | .05 | 5.08 | 5.20 | 5.31 | 5.40 | 5.49 | 5.57 | 5.65 |
| | .10 | 4.52 | 4.64 | 4.75 | 4.84 | 4.93 | 5.01 | 5.08 |
| 16 | .01 | 6.22 | 6.35 | 6.46 | 6.56 | 6.66 | 6.74 | 6.82 |
| | .05 | 5.03 | 5.15 | 5.26 | 5.35 | 5.44 | 5.52 | 5.59 |
| | .10 | 4.49 | 4.61 | 4.71 | 4.81 | 4.89 | 4.97 | 5.04 |
| 17 | .01 | 6.15 | 6.27 | 6.38 | 6.48 | 6.57 | 6.66 | 6.73 |
| | .05 | 4.99 | 5.11 | 5.21 | 5.31 | 5.39 | 5.47 | 5.54 |
| | .10 | 4.46 | 4.58 | 4.68 | 4.77 | 4.86 | 4.94 | 5.01 |
| 18 | .01 | 6.08 | 6.20 | 6.31 | 6.41 | 6.50 | 6.58 | 6.66 |
| | .05 | 4.96 | 5.07 | 5.17 | 5.27 | 5.35 | 5.43 | 5.50 |
| | .10 | 4.44 | 4.55 | 4.66 | 4.75 | 4.83 | 4.91 | 4.98 |
| 19 | .01 | 6.02 | 6.14 | 6.25 | 6.34 | 6.43 | 6.51 | 6.59 |
| | .05 | 4.92 | 5.04 | 5.14 | 5.23 | 5.32 | 5.39 | 5.46 |
| | .10 | 4.42 | 4.53 | 4.63 | 4.72 | 4.80 | 4.88 | 4.95 |

**TABLE C.9** (continued)

| Error df | FWE | \multicolumn{7}{c}{Number of Ordered Means} |
|---|---|---|---|---|---|---|---|---|
| | | 9 | 10 | 11 | 12 | 13 | 14 | 15 |
| 20 | .01 | 5.97 | 6.09 | 6.19 | 6.29 | 6.37 | 6.45 | 6.52 |
| | .05 | 4.90 | 5.01 | 5.11 | 5.20 | 5.28 | 5.36 | 5.43 |
| | .10 | 4.40 | 4.51 | 4.61 | 4.70 | 4.78 | 4.86 | 4.92 |
| 24 | .01 | 5.81 | 5.92 | 6.02 | 6.11 | 6.19 | 6.26 | 6.33 |
| | .05 | 4.81 | 4.92 | 5.01 | 5.10 | 5.18 | 5.25 | 5.32 |
| | .10 | 4.34 | 4.45 | 4.54 | 4.62 | 4.71 | 4.78 | 4.85 |
| 30 | .01 | 5.65 | 5.76 | 5.85 | 5.93 | 6.01 | 6.08 | 6.14 |
| | .05 | 4.72 | 4.82 | 4.92 | 5.00 | 5.08 | 5.15 | 5.21 |
| | .10 | 4.28 | 4.38 | 4.47 | 4.56 | 4.64 | 4.71 | 4.77 |
| 40 | .01 | 5.50 | 5.60 | 5.69 | 5.76 | 5.84 | 5.90 | 5.96 |
| | .05 | 4.64 | 4.74 | 4.82 | 4.90 | 4.98 | 5.04 | 5.11 |
| | .10 | 4.22 | 4.32 | 4.41 | 4.49 | 4.56 | 4.63 | 4.70 |
| 60 | .01 | 5.36 | 5.45 | 5.53 | 5.60 | 5.67 | 5.73 | 5.79 |
| | .05 | 4.55 | 4.65 | 4.73 | 4.81 | 4.88 | 4.94 | 5.00 |
| | .10 | 4.16 | 4.25 | 4.34 | 4.42 | 4.49 | 4.56 | 4.62 |
| 120 | .01 | 5.21 | 5.30 | 5.38 | 5.44 | 5.51 | 5.56 | 5.61 |
| | .05 | 4.47 | 4.56 | 4.64 | 4.71 | 4.78 | 4.84 | 4.90 |
| | .10 | 4.10 | 4.19 | 4.28 | 4.35 | 4.42 | 4.49 | 4.54 |
| $\infty$ | .01 | 5.08 | 5.16 | 5.23 | 5.29 | 5.35 | 5.40 | 5.45 |
| | .05 | 4.39 | 4.47 | 4.55 | 4.62 | 4.69 | 4.74 | 4.80 |
| | .10 | 4.04 | 4.13 | 4.21 | 4.29 | 4.35 | 4.41 | 4.47 |

| Error df | FWE | \multicolumn{7}{c}{Number of Ordered Means} |
|---|---|---|---|---|---|---|---|---|
| | | 16 | 17 | 18 | 19 | 20 | 30 | 40 |
| 2 | .01 | 36.00 | 36.53 | 37.03 | 37.50 | 37.95 | 41.32 | 43.61 |
| | .05 | 15.91 | 16.14 | 16.37 | 16.57 | 16.77 | 18.27 | 19.28 |
| | .10 | 11.07 | 11.24 | 11.39 | 11.54 | 11.68 | 12.73 | 13.44 |
| 3 | .01 | 18.81 | 19.07 | 19.32 | 19.55 | 19.77 | 21.44 | 22.59 |
| | .05 | 10.69 | 10.84 | 10.98 | 11.11 | 11.24 | 12.21 | 12.87 |
| | .10 | 8.25 | 8.37 | 8.48 | 8.58 | 8.68 | 9.44 | 9.95 |
| 4 | .01 | 13.73 | 13.91 | 14.08 | 14.24 | 14.40 | 15.57 | 16.37 |
| | .05 | 8.79 | 8.91 | 9.03 | 9.13 | 9.23 | 10.00 | 10.53 |
| | .10 | 7.13 | 7.23 | 7.33 | 7.41 | 7.50 | 8.14 | 8.57 |
| 5 | .01 | 11.40 | 11.55 | 11.68 | 11.81 | 11.93 | 12.87 | 13.52 |
| | .05 | 7.83 | 7.93 | 8.03 | 8.12 | 8.21 | 8.88 | 9.33 |
| | .10 | 6.54 | 6.63 | 6.71 | 6.79 | 6.86 | 7.44 | 7.83 |
| 6 | .01 | 10.08 | 10.21 | 10.32 | 10.43 | 10.54 | 11.34 | 11.90 |
| | .05 | 7.24 | 7.34 | 7.43 | 7.51 | 7.59 | 8.19 | 8.60 |
| | .10 | 6.16 | 6.25 | 6.33 | 6.40 | 6.47 | 7.00 | 7.36 |
| 7 | .01 | 9.24 | 9.35 | 9.46 | 9.55 | 9.65 | 10.36 | 10.85 |
| | .05 | 6.85 | 6.94 | 7.02 | 7.10 | 7.17 | 7.73 | 8.11 |
| | .10 | 5.91 | 5.99 | 6.06 | 6.13 | 6.20 | 6.70 | 7.04 |

**TABLE C.9** (continued)

| Error df | FWE | Number of Ordered Means | | | | | | |
|---|---|---|---|---|---|---|---|---|
| | | 16 | 17 | 18 | 19 | 20 | 30 | 40 |
| 8 | .01 | 8.66 | 8.76 | 8.85 | 8.94 | 9.03 | 9.68 | 10.13 |
| | .05 | 6.57 | 6.65 | 6.73 | 6.80 | 6.87 | 7.40 | 7.76 |
| | .10 | 5.72 | 5.80 | 5.87 | 5.94 | 6.00 | 6.48 | 6.80 |
| 9 | .01 | 8.23 | 8.33 | 8.41 | 8.49 | 8.57 | 9.18 | 9.59 |
| | .05 | 6.36 | 6.44 | 6.51 | 6.58 | 6.64 | 7.15 | 7.49 |
| | .10 | 5.58 | 5.66 | 5.72 | 5.79 | 5.85 | 6.31 | 6.62 |
| 10 | .01 | 7.91 | 7.99 | 8.08 | 8.15 | 8.23 | 8.79 | 9.19 |
| | .05 | 6.19 | 6.27 | 6.34 | 6.41 | 6.47 | 6.95 | 7.28 |
| | .10 | 5.47 | 5.54 | 5.61 | 5.67 | 5.73 | 6.17 | 6.48 |
| 11 | .01 | 7.65 | 7.73 | 7.81 | 7.88 | 7.95 | 8.49 | 8.86 |
| | .05 | 6.06 | 6.13 | 6.20 | 6.27 | 6.33 | 6.79 | 7.11 |
| | .10 | 5.38 | 5.45 | 5.51 | 5.57 | 5.63 | 6.07 | 6.36 |
| 12 | .01 | 7.44 | 7.52 | 7.59 | 7.67 | 7.73 | 8.25 | 8.60 |
| | .05 | 5.95 | 6.02 | 6.09 | 6.15 | 6.21 | 6.66 | 6.97 |
| | .10 | 5.31 | 5.37 | 5.44 | 5.50 | 5.55 | 5.98 | 6.27 |
| 13 | .01 | 7.27 | 7.35 | 7.42 | 7.49 | 7.55 | 8.04 | 8.39 |
| | .05 | 5.86 | 5.93 | 6.00 | 6.06 | 6.11 | 6.55 | 6.85 |
| | .10 | 5.25 | 5.31 | 5.37 | 5.43 | 5.48 | 5.90 | 6.19 |
| 14 | .01 | 7.13 | 7.20 | 7.27 | 7.33 | 7.40 | 7.87 | 8.20 |
| | .05 | 5.79 | 5.85 | 5.92 | 5.97 | 6.03 | 6.46 | 6.75 |
| | .10 | 5.19 | 5.26 | 5.32 | 5.37 | 5.43 | 5.84 | 6.12 |
| 15 | .01 | 7.00 | 7.07 | 7.14 | 7.20 | 7.26 | 7.73 | 8.05 |
| | .05 | 5.72 | 5.79 | 5.85 | 5.90 | 5.96 | 6.38 | 6.67 |
| | .10 | 5.15 | 5.21 | 5.27 | 5.32 | 5.38 | 5.78 | 6.06 |
| 16 | .01 | 6.90 | 6.97 | 7.03 | 7.09 | 7.15 | 7.60 | 7.92 |
| | .05 | 5.66 | 5.73 | 5.79 | 5.84 | 5.90 | 6.31 | 6.59 |
| | .10 | 5.11 | 5.17 | 5.23 | 5.28 | 5.33 | 5.73 | 6.00 |
| 17 | .01 | 6.81 | 6.87 | 6.94 | 7.00 | 7.05 | 7.49 | 7.80 |
| | .05 | 5.61 | 5.68 | 5.73 | 5.79 | 5.84 | 6.25 | 6.53 |
| | .10 | 5.07 | 5.13 | 5.19 | 5.24 | 5.30 | 5.69 | 5.96 |
| 18 | .01 | 6.73 | 6.79 | 6.85 | 6.91 | 6.97 | 7.40 | 7.70 |
| | .05 | 5.57 | 5.63 | 5.69 | 5.74 | 5.79 | 6.20 | 6.47 |
| | .10 | 5.04 | 5.10 | 5.16 | 5.21 | 5.26 | 5.65 | 5.92 |
| 19 | .01 | 6.65 | 6.72 | 6.78 | 6.84 | 6.89 | 7.31 | 7.61 |
| | .05 | 5.53 | 5.59 | 5.65 | 5.70 | 5.75 | 6.15 | 6.42 |
| | .10 | 5.01 | 5.07 | 5.13 | 5.18 | 5.23 | 5.62 | 5.88 |
| 20 | .01 | 6.59 | 6.65 | 6.71 | 6.77 | 6.82 | 7.24 | 7.52 |
| | .05 | 5.49 | 5.55 | 5.61 | 5.66 | 5.71 | 6.10 | 6.37 |
| | .10 | 4.99 | 5.05 | 5.10 | 5.16 | 5.21 | 5.59 | 5.85 |
| 24 | .01 | 6.39 | 6.45 | 6.51 | 6.56 | 6.61 | 7.00 | 7.27 |
| | .05 | 5.38 | 5.44 | 5.49 | 5.55 | 5.59 | 5.97 | 6.23 |
| | .10 | 4.91 | 4.97 | 5.02 | 5.07 | 5.12 | 5.49 | 5.74 |
| 30 | .01 | 6.20 | 6.26 | 6.31 | 6.36 | 6.41 | 6.77 | 7.02 |
| | .05 | 5.27 | 5.33 | 5.38 | 5.43 | 5.48 | 5.83 | 6.08 |
| | .10 | 4.83 | 4.89 | 4.94 | 4.99 | 5.03 | 5.39 | 5.64 |

**TABLE C.9**  (continued)

| Error df | FWE | Number of Ordered Means | | | | | | |
|---|---|---|---|---|---|---|---|---|
| | | 16 | 17 | 18 | 19 | 20 | 30 | 40 |
| 40 | .01 | 6.02 | 6.07 | 6.12 | 6.17 | 6.21 | 6.55 | 6.78 |
| | .05 | 5.16 | 5.22 | 5.27 | 5.31 | 5.36 | 5.70 | 5.93 |
| | .10 | 4.75 | 4.81 | 4.86 | 4.91 | 4.95 | 5.29 | 5.53 |
| 60 | .01 | 5.84 | 5.89 | 5.93 | 5.97 | 6.02 | 6.33 | 6.55 |
| | .05 | 5.06 | 5.11 | 5.15 | 5.20 | 5.24 | 5.57 | 5.79 |
| | .10 | 4.68 | 4.73 | 4.78 | 4.82 | 4.86 | 5.20 | 5.42 |
| 120 | .01 | 5.66 | 5.71 | 5.75 | 5.79 | 5.83 | 6.12 | 6.32 |
| | .05 | 4.95 | 5.00 | 5.04 | 5.09 | 5.13 | 5.43 | 5.64 |
| | .10 | 4.60 | 4.65 | 4.69 | 4.74 | 4.78 | 5.10 | 5.31 |
| $\infty$ | .01 | 5.49 | 5.54 | 5.57 | 5.61 | 5.65 | 5.91 | 6.09 |
| | .05 | 4.85 | 4.89 | 4.93 | 4.97 | 5.01 | 5.30 | 5.50 |
| | .10 | 4.52 | 4.57 | 4.61 | 4.65 | 4.69 | 5.00 | 5.20 |

*Source*: Adapted from Table II.2 in *The Probability Integrals of the Range and of the Studentized Range*. prepared by H. L. Harter. D. S. Clemm, and E. H. Guthrie. The original tables are published in WADC Tech. Rep. 58–484, Vol. 2, 1959, Wright Air Development Center, and are reproduced with the permission of the authors.

**TABLE C.10** CRITICAL VALUES FOR THE WILCOXON SIGNED-RANK TEST

| One-tailed | Two-tailed | Number of Pairs | | | | | | | | | |
|---|---|---|---|---|---|---|---|---|---|---|---|
| | | 5 | 6 | 7 | 8 | 9 | 10 | 11 | 12 | 13 | 14 |
| .05 | .10 | 0 | 2 | 3 | 5 | 8 | 10 | 13 | 17 | 21 | 25 |
| .025 | .05 | | 0 | 2 | 3 | 5 | 8 | 10 | 13 | 17 | 21 |
| .01 | .02 | | | 0 | 1 | 3 | 5 | 7 | 9 | 12 | 15 |
| .005 | .01 | | | | 0 | 1 | 3 | 5 | 7 | 9 | 12 |
| | | 15 | 16 | 17 | 18 | 19 | 20 | 21 | 22 | 23 | 24 |
| .05 | .10 | 30 | 35 | 41 | 47 | 53 | 60 | 67 | 75 | 83 | 91 |
| .025 | .05 | 25 | 29 | 34 | 40 | 46 | 52 | 58 | 65 | 73 | 81 |
| .01 | .02 | 19 | 23 | 27 | 32 | 37 | 43 | 49 | 55 | 62 | 69 |
| .005 | .01 | 15 | 19 | 23 | 27 | 32 | 37 | 42 | 48 | 54 | 61 |
| | | 25 | 26 | 27 | 28 | 29 | 30 | 31 | 32 | 33 | 34 |
| .05 | .10 | 100 | 110 | 119 | 130 | 140 | 151 | 163 | 175 | 187 | 200 |
| .025 | .05 | 89 | 98 | 107 | 116 | 126 | 137 | 147 | 159 | 170 | 182 |
| .01 | .02 | 76 | 84 | 92 | 101 | 110 | 120 | 130 | 140 | 151 | 162 |
| .005 | .01 | 68 | 75 | 83 | 91 | 100 | 109 | 118 | 128 | 138 | 148 |
| | | 35 | 36 | 37 | 38 | 39 | 40 | 41 | 42 | 43 | 44 |
| .05 | .10 | 213 | 227 | 241 | 256 | 271 | 286 | 302 | 319 | 336 | 353 |
| .025 | .05 | 195 | 208 | 221 | 235 | 249 | 264 | 279 | 294 | 310 | 327 |
| .01 | .02 | 173 | 185 | 198 | 211 | 224 | 238 | 252 | 266 | 281 | 296 |
| .005 | .01 | 159 | 171 | 182 | 194 | 207 | 220 | 233 | 247 | 261 | 276 |
| | | 45 | 46 | 47 | 48 | 49 | 50 | | | | |
| .05 | .10 | 371 | 389 | 407 | 426 | 446 | 466 | | | | |
| .025 | .05 | 343 | 361 | 378 | 396 | 415 | 434 | | | | |
| .01 | .02 | 312 | 328 | 345 | 362 | 379 | 397 | | | | |
| .005 | .01 | 291 | 307 | 322 | 339 | 355 | 373 | | | | |

**TABLE C.11** TRANSFORMATION OF r TO Z

| r | Z | r | Z | r | Z | r | Z | r | Z |
|---|---|---|---|---|---|---|---|---|---|
| 0.000 | 0.000 | 0.200 | 0.203 | 0.400 | 0.424 | 0.600 | 0.693 | 0.800 | 1.099 |
| 0.005 | 0.005 | 0.205 | 0.208 | 0.405 | 0.430 | 0.605 | 0.701 | 0.805 | 1.113 |
| 0.010 | 0.010 | 0.210 | 0.213 | 0.410 | 0.436 | 0.610 | 0.709 | 0.810 | 1.127 |
| 0.015 | 0.015 | 0.215 | 0.218 | 0.415 | 0.442 | 0.615 | 0.717 | 0.815 | 1.142 |
| 0.020 | 0.020 | 0.220 | 0.224 | 0.420 | 0.448 | 0.620 | 0.725 | 0.820 | 1.157 |
| 0.025 | 0.025 | 0.225 | 0.229 | 0.425 | 0.454 | 0.625 | 0.733 | 0.825 | 1.172 |
| 0.030 | 0.030 | 0.230 | 0.234 | 0.430 | 0.460 | 0.630 | 0.741 | 0.830 | 1.188 |
| 0.035 | 0.035 | 0.235 | 0.239 | 0.435 | 0.466 | 0.635 | 0.750 | 0.835 | 1.204 |
| 0.040 | 0.040 | 0.240 | 0.245 | 0.440 | 0.472 | 0.640 | 0.758 | 0.840 | 1.221 |
| 0.045 | 0.045 | 0.245 | 0.250 | 0.445 | 0.478 | 0.645 | 0.767 | 0.845 | 1.238 |
| 0.050 | 0.050 | 0.250 | 0.255 | 0.450 | 0.485 | 0.650 | 0.775 | 0.850 | 1.256 |
| 0.055 | 0.055 | 0.255 | 0.261 | 0.455 | 0.491 | 0.655 | 0.784 | 0.855 | 1.274 |
| 0.060 | 0.060 | 0.260 | 0.266 | 0.460 | 0.497 | 0.660 | 0.793 | 0.860 | 1.293 |
| 0.065 | 0.065 | 0.265 | 0.271 | 0.465 | 0.504 | 0.665 | 0.802 | 0.865 | 1.313 |
| 0.070 | 0.070 | 0.270 | 0.277 | 0.470 | 0.510 | 0.670 | 0.811 | 0.870 | 1.333 |
| 0.075 | 0.075 | 0.275 | 0.282 | 0.475 | 0.517 | 0.675 | 0.820 | 0.875 | 1.354 |
| 0.080 | 0.080 | 0.280 | 0.288 | 0.480 | 0.523 | 0.680 | 0.829 | 0.880 | 1.376 |
| 0.085 | 0.085 | 0.285 | 0.293 | 0.485 | 0.530 | 0.685 | 0.838 | 0.885 | 1.398 |
| 0.090 | 0.090 | 0.290 | 0.299 | 0.490 | 0.536 | 0.690 | 0.848 | 0.890 | 1.422 |
| 0.095 | 0.095 | 0.295 | 0.304 | 0.495 | 0.543 | 0.695 | 0.858 | 0.895 | 1.447 |
| 0.100 | 0.100 | 0.300 | 0.310 | 0.500 | 0.549 | 0.700 | 0.867 | 0.900 | 1.472 |
| 0.105 | 0.105 | 0.305 | 0.315 | 0.505 | 0.556 | 0.705 | 0.877 | 0.905 | 1.499 |
| 0.110 | 0.110 | 0.310 | 0.321 | 0.510 | 0.563 | 0.710 | 0.887 | 0.910 | 1.528 |
| 0.115 | 0.116 | 0.315 | 0.326 | 0.515 | 0.570 | 0.715 | 0.897 | 0.915 | 1.557 |
| 0.120 | 0.121 | 0.320 | 0.332 | 0.520 | 0.576 | 0.720 | 0.908 | 0.920 | 1.589 |
| 0.125 | 0.126 | 0.325 | 0.337 | 0.525 | 0.583 | 0.725 | 0.918 | 0.925 | 1.623 |
| 0.130 | 0.131 | 0.330 | 0.343 | 0.530 | 0.590 | 0.730 | 0.929 | 0.930 | 1.658 |
| 0.135 | 0.136 | 0.335 | 0.348 | 0.535 | 0.597 | 0.735 | 0.940 | 0.935 | 1.697 |
| 0.140 | 0.141 | 0.340 | 0.354 | 0.540 | 0.604 | 0.740 | 0.950 | 0.940 | 1.738 |
| 0.145 | 0.146 | 0.345 | 0.360 | 0.545 | 0.611 | 0.745 | 0.962 | 0.945 | 1.783 |
| 0.150 | 0.151 | 0.350 | 0.365 | 0.550 | 0.618 | 0.750 | 0.973 | 0.950 | 1.832 |
| 0.155 | 0.156 | 0.355 | 0.371 | 0.555 | 0.626 | 0.755 | 0.984 | 0.955 | 1.886 |
| 0.160 | 0.161 | 0.360 | 0.377 | 0.560 | 0.633 | 0.760 | 0.996 | 0.960 | 1.946 |
| 0.165 | 0.167 | 0.365 | 0.383 | 0.565 | 0.640 | 0.765 | 1.008 | 0.965 | 2.014 |
| 0.170 | 0.172 | 0.370 | 0.388 | 0.570 | 0.648 | 0.770 | 1.020 | 0.970 | 2.092 |
| 0.175 | 0.177 | 0.375 | 0.394 | 0.575 | 0.655 | 0.775 | 1.033 | 0.975 | 2.185 |
| 0.180 | 0.182 | 0.380 | 0.400 | 0.580 | 0.662 | 0.780 | 1.045 | 0.980 | 2.298 |
| 0.185 | 0.187 | 0.385 | 0.406 | 0.585 | 0.670 | 0.785 | 1.058 | 0.985 | 2.443 |
| 0.190 | 0.192 | 0.390 | 0.412 | 0.590 | 0.678 | 0.790 | 1.071 | 0.990 | 2.647 |
| 0.195 | 0.198 | 0.395 | 0.418 | 0.595 | 0.685 | 0.795 | 1.085 | 0.995 | 2.994 |

# Answers to Selected Exercises

**2.1** (a) $\bar{Y} = 30.562$, (b) $\tilde{Y}$ (median) $= 33.5$; (c) $(\sum Y)^2 - 239{,}121$; (d) $\sum Y^2 = 16{,}311$; (e) $9.543$;
(f) $H_L = 23.5$, $H_U = 37.5$.

**2.3** Outliers in box or stem-and-leaf plots and the shape of a normal probability plot suggest a heavy-tailed distribution in data set (a) Both a stem-and-leaf (or a histogram) and a normal probability plot indicate that data set (c) is skewed to the right. Data set (b) appears to be normally distributed.

**2.5** (a) $Y_6 = 57$. (b) Adding a score equal to the mean will yield the smallest variance.

**2.7** (a) $\bar{Y}_{.1} = 22$; (b) $\bar{Y}_{2.} = 19.333$; (c) $\bar{Y}.. = 21.067$; (d) $\sum_{i=1}^{5} \sum_{j=1}^{3} Y_{ij}^2 = 9{,}422$; and
(e) $\sum_{j=1}^{3} \bar{Y}_{.j}^2 = 1{,}532.72$.

**2.9** Standardizing each of the three sets of scores equates their means (at 0) and standard deviations (at 1). The ranges and medians are not necessarily ordered as they were for the original three distributions. However, the shapes are the same; the skewness and kurtosis values, and their standard errors, as well as the normal probability plot are unchanged.

**2.11** (a) The line graph is preferable in that it more clearly reveals differences among age groups in trends over seasons.

(b) Two aspects of the graph are notable. First, the younger age groups (Agegrp $= 1$ and 2) have higher mean Beck anxiety scores than the older groups. Second, this is particularly pronounced in the winter season; although three of the four groups are most anxious then, this is markedly so for the youngest group.

(c) Median trends over seasons within each age group show a trend similar to that for the means, though the differences among age groups are not quite as large when the median is viewed instead of the mean.

**2.13** (a) $z_1 = (41 - 38.6)/4.616 = .520$; $z_2 = (51 - 46.84)/9.496 = .438$. Performance has declined in standard deviation units.

(b) A score of 52 is the lowest integer value that transforms the Test 2 score into a $z$ score exceeding .52.

(c) The distributions appear to be symmetric as suggested by near equality of means and medians, symmetric box plots, and normal probability plots indicating that the points lie fairly close to a straight line.

# CHAPTER 3

**3.1** (b) $r = .620$; (c) $\hat{Y} = 3 + 2X$; (d) $r^2 = .385$; (e) $\hat{X} = 1.577 + 0.192Y$; (f) $r^2 = .385$.

**3.3** (a) $r = -.487$. (c) If the most influential point (case 64) is removed, $r = -.743$.

**3.5** (a) The reasoning of the committee member is that because there is a high correlation between the pretest and posttest scores, no change in IQ has occurred. This reasoning is silly; the correlation is sensitive to the relative standing on the two tests but not the absolute scores. The correlation says nothing about the means. For example, if all the students had their scores increase by about 20 points, the correlation would be very high.

(b) Of course, the longer you live the more time you have to smoke cigarettes. If we are concerned about the infuence of smoking on longevity, we should look at the rate of cigarette smoking (cigarettes/day), not the total number.

(c) The data do not allow us to make a causal statement. It could be that less able or motivated students spent less time on schoolwork and therefore had more time to watch TV. We cannot conclude that the TV watching caused the poor performance.

**3.7** The overall correlation between height and weight is .529; however, it is only .288 for both men and women considered separately. As we discuss in more detail in Chapter 18, statistics of combined distributions may not describe any of the constituent distributions. Here, because men tend to be both taller and heavier than women, the variance of both height and weight is greater for the combined male and female distributions than for men and women considered separately:

|  | Men | Women | Overall |
|---|---|---|---|
| Mean height (cm) | 176.24 | 161.43 | 169.08 |
| *SD* height | 6.81 | 6.73 | 10.03 |
| Mean weight (kg) | 86.21 | 69.55 | 75.12 |
| *SD* weight | 13.81 | 16.36 | 17.24 |

**3.9** Given that $r_{XY} = .6$, we find the following: (a) The correlation between $Y$ and $\hat{Y}$ must also be .6 because $\hat{Y}$ is just a linear transformation of $X$; (b) the correlation between $Y$ and $\hat{Y}$ is $\text{corr}(Y, Y - \hat{Y}) = .8$; (c) $\text{corr}(\hat{Y}, Y - \hat{Y}) = 0$.

# CHAPTER 4

**4.1** (a) .2; (b) $.2^3 = .008$; (c) $(.8)(.2)(.8) = .128$; (d) $(3)(.128) = .384$; (e) $1 - p(\text{none correct}) = 1 - .8^3 = 1 - .512 = .488$; (f) $(3)(.2^2)(.8) = .096$; (g) $(.8^4)(.2) = .08192$.

**4.3** (a)

| Test Results | HIV | No HIV | Total |
|---|---|---|---|
| Positive | 997 | 1,485 | 2,482 |
| Negative | 3 | 97,515 | 97,518 |
| Total | 1,000 | 99,000 | 100,000 |

(b) $997/2,482 = .402$; (c) $97,515/97,518 = .99997$.

**4.5**   (a) $p(\text{reject}|\text{true}) = \alpha = .05$; (b) $p(\text{don't reject}|\text{false}) = \beta = 1 - \text{power} = .2$; (c) $p(\text{true}|$ nonreject$) = .67$; (d) $p(\text{reject}) = .575$.

**4.7**   (a) $H_0: p = .25$; $H_1: p > .25$; (b) $H_0: p = .20$; $H_1: p > .20$, although those espousing ESP often also take below-chance performance as evidence for their cause—in this case, $H_1: p \neq .20$; (c) $H_0: p = .60$; $H_1: p > .60$.

**4.9**   (a) No; $p = p(\text{data at least as extreme as that obtained}|H_0 \text{ true})$, not $p(H_0 \text{ true}|\text{data})$; (b) no, for the same reason as in part (a).

**4.11**  (a) Reject if $r < 7$; $p(\text{reject}) = .058$; (b) power $= .42$; (c) reject if $r > 14$ or $r < 6$; (d) power now equals .25.

**4.13**  (a) $H_0: p = .5$, $H_1: p \neq .5$; $p$ is the probability that the imagery is better than the rote procedure. Let $n = 12$ and $\alpha = .05$. Then the decision rule is: reject if $r > 9$ or $r < 3$ where $r$ is the number of participants who performed better by using the imagery method. The null hypothesis cannot be rejected.
   (b) Power $= .89$.

**4.15**  (a) $E(Y) = 5$; (b) the completed sampling distribution is

$$\overline{Y} = \begin{matrix} 2 & 3 & 4 & 5 & 6 & 7 & 8 \end{matrix}$$
$$p(\overline{Y}) = \begin{matrix} .0625 & .125 & .1875 & .250 & .1875 & .125 & .0625 \end{matrix}$$

   (c) $E(\overline{Y}) = 5 = E(Y)$; $\text{var}(\overline{Y}) = 2.5 = \text{var}(Y)/2$; in general, the variance of the sample mean equals the sample variance divided by the sample size.

**4.17**  (a) The best estimate of the mean of the other four students is still 100; (b) the best estimate of the sample mean is $550/5 = 110$; (c) only the answer to (b) is changed; the estimate is 105.

# CHAPTER 5

**5.1**   (a) (i) $p(Y > 30) = .023$; (ii) $p(85 < Y < 145) = .840$; (iii) $p(Y > 70) = .977$; (iv) $p(70 < Y < 80) = .069$. (b) $Y_{\text{upper}} = 119.2$ and $Y_{\text{lower}} = 80.8$. (c) $Y_{.75} = 110.125$. (d) $p = .159$. (e) The area is essentially zero.

**5.3**   (a) (i) $p = .401$; (ii) $p = .067$; (iii) $p = .464$; (b) $p = .69$; (c) $p = .72$; (d) $p = .69$.

**5.5**   (a) $H_0: \pi = .4$; $H_1: \pi < .4$.
   (b) Then $z = -2.12$. The decision rule is as follows: Reject $H_0$ if $z < -1.645$. Therefore, reject the null hypothesis. We conclude that the new drug has reduced the probability of recurrence of symptoms.
   (c) (i) We assumed that the sampling distribution of $p$ was normal. (ii) Because $p$ is an average of 48 ones (failures) and zeros (successes), the central limit theorem provides the rationale for using the normal distribution. (iii) Because the distribution of $p$ approaches normality as $n$ increases, the normal approximation will not be as good when $n = 10$ than when $n = 48$.

**5.7**   (a) (i) $E(X) = .2$; $\text{var}(X) = \pi(1 - \pi) = .16$. (ii) $\text{var}(\overline{X}) = .16/3 = .053$.
   (b)

| $Y$ | $p(Y)$ | $\overline{X}$ | $S_X^2$ | $S_{\overline{X}}^2$ | $s_{\overline{X}}^2$ |
|---|---|---|---|---|---|
| 0 | $.8^3 = .512$ | 0 | 0 | 0 | 0 |
| 1 | $(3)(.8^2)(.2) = .384$ | 1/3 | 2/9 | 2/27 | 1/9 |
| 2 | $(3)(.8)(.2^2) = .096$ | 2/3 | 2/9 | 2/27 | 1/9 |
| 3 | $.2^3 \qquad = .008$ | 0 | 0 | 0 | 0 |

(c) (i) $E(Y) = .6$; (ii) $E(\overline{X}) = .2$; (iii) $E(S_{\overline{X}}^2) = .036$; (iv) $E(s_{\overline{X}}^2) = .053$.

(d) $E(Y) = N \times E(X)$ and $E(\overline{X}) = E(X)$.

(e) $S_{\overline{X}}^2 = [(N-1)/N] \times var(\overline{X})$; $s_{\overline{X}}^2 = var(\overline{X})$.

**5.9** (a) $E(T - C) = \mu_T - \mu_C = .5\sigma$; $var(T - C) = \sigma_T^2 + \sigma_C^2 = 2\sigma^2$; (b) $p = .64$; (c) (i) $p = .86$; (ii) $p = .66$.

**5.11** (a) Let $\overline{d} = \overline{Y}_1 - \overline{Y}_2$. Then $s_{\overline{d}} = \sqrt{(1/N)(s_1^2 + s_2^2 - 2rs_1s_2)} = 1.469$.

(b) CI $= 2.36, 8.12$

(c) $t = \overline{d}/s_{\overline{d}} = 5.241/1.469 = 3.57$. TC levels are significantly higher in the winter than in the spring season.

(d) SPSS yields confidence bounds of 2.347 and 8.135, and a value of $t$ of 3.569; all of these values are close to those obtained by using the $z$ test.

**5.13** (a) CI $= 3.217, 23.735$; (b) power $= .84$.

**5.15** (a) The medians and means for women are higher than those for men. Female depression scores are also more variable. Skewness and kurtosis measures are high for both sexes. Graphs of histograms, box plots, normal probability curves, and stem-and-leaf plots indicate that the data are markedly skewed to the right in both groups with many outliers (roughly, a little more than 7%).

(b) CI $= .333, 2.735$. The interval does not include zero, so the null hypothesis of no difference can be rejected. Although the populations of scores are not normal, the sampling distributions of the means are likely to be, given the size of the samples, and therefore the significance test is likely to be valid.

(c) From stem-and-leaf plots, we find that male scores greater than 13.250 and female scores greater than 16.659 are outliers.

(d) When outliers, as defined in part (c), are deleted from the data set, there is still considerable skew but less than previously. Some scores that previously were not outliers are so now, but there are fewer outliers than before. Also, the mean and median are closer together in both groups than in the original full data set. The removal of outliers greatly reduces the variances. Consequently, the new CI bounds, .430 and 2.076, are closer than those obtained in part (b). Therefore, the population difference in means is more precisely estimated, and power to test the null hypothesis is greater.

# CHAPTER 6

**6.1** (a) CI $= 4.5 \pm (2.201)(1.555) = 1.077, 7.923$.

(b) $H_0$: $\mu_d = 0$; $H_1$: $\mu_d \neq 0$;  reject if  $|t| > 2.201$. $t = \overline{d}/s_{\overline{d}} = 4.5/1.555 = 2.895$. Reject $H_0$.

(c) CI $= -6.559, 15.584$ and $t = 4.5/5.332 = .844$, clearly less than the critical value on 22 $df$ of 2.074. The independent-groups analysis is considerably less efficient as evidenced by the fact that the CI is more than three times wider than in the repeated-measures design. The independent-groups design has twice as many degrees of freedom, but this is more than compensated for by the much smaller $SE$ for the repeated-measures data. However, one potential problem is that performance exposure to one condition may affect performance under the other condition, and sometimes it is impossible to test the same subjects in two conditions.

**6.3** (a) $t = 2/(5.6/4) = 1.43$. The null hypothesis cannot be rejected. (b) $E_S = .36$; (c) power $= .39$ when $N = 16$; (d) when $N = 36$, power $= .68$; (e) $N = 50$; (f) the power values for various $N$s and the two distributions are as follows:

|   | Distributions | |
| --- | --- | --- |
| $N$ | $t$ | $z$ |
| 16 | .39 | .41 |
| 36 | .68 | .69 |
| 49 | .80 | .81 |

The normal distribution ($z$) provides a reasonable approximation to the power of the $t$ test, even when $N$ is relatively small. Also, because the $t$ distribution approaches the normal with increasing degrees of freedom, the approximation improves as $N$ increases.

**6.5** (a) On 30 $df$, with $\alpha = .05$ (two tailed), the critical $t = 2.042$. $t = 2.20$. Therefore, reject $H_0$.

(b) Applying Equation 6.19, we have $t' = 3.2/1.763 = 1.82$. From Equation 6.20, $df' = 13$. The null hypothesis cannot be rejected against a two-tailed alternative.

(c) The pooled-variance test gives heavy weight to the smaller variance, producing a positive bias (i.e., too many Type 1 errors) in the $t$ test. The separate-variance test corrects this bias.

**6.7** (a) $H_0: \mu_H - \mu_L = 0$; $H_1: \mu_H - \mu_L \neq 0$; for $\alpha = .05$ and $df = 34$, reject if $|t| > 2.034$. $t = .621$, which is not significant.

(b) $H_0: \mu_M - (.5)(\mu_H + \mu_L) = 0$; $H_1: \mu_M - (.5)(\mu_H + \mu_L)_L > 0$; $df = N - 3 = 51$ and for $\alpha = .05$, reject $H_0$ if $t > 1.676$. $\hat{\psi} = 3.921$. Assuming homogeneous variances, we have $s_{\hat{\psi}} = 1.776$ and $t = \hat{\psi}/s_{\hat{\psi}} = 3.931/1.776 = 2.21$. The null hypothesis can be rejected.

(c) For the contrast in part (a), $\hat{\psi}_g = .21$. For part (b), $\hat{\psi}_s = .64$.

**6.9** (a) When Sayhlth $= 2$, then $E_S = .22$, a small standardized effect; when Sayhlth $= 4$, then $E_S = 11.087/19.375 = .57$, a medium standardized effect.

(b) Sayhlth $= 2, t_{181, .05} = 1.973$; CI $= 1.59, 7.53$; $t = 4.56/1.506 = 3.030$; $p = .003$. Sayhlth $= 4, t_{22, .05} = 2.074$; CI $= 11.087 \pm (2.074)(4.040) = 2.71, 19.47$; $t = 11.087/4.04 = 2.744$; $p = .012$.

(c) The statistics in part (b) might suggest that the increase in TC scores in the winter relative to the spring is more pronounced in the Sayhlth $= 2$ group. However, this probably reflects the fact that there are many more participants in the study who rated themselves in very good health (Sayhlth $= 2$) than who rated themselves in fair health (Sayhlth $= 4$). The comparison of effect sizes serves to remind us of this because the standardized effect size is considerably larger in the Sayhlth $= 4$ group. Because of the small $n$ in that group, we can reach no firm conclusion about the relative effects in the two groups. We need a considerably larger sample of people who rate themselves in only fair health.

**6.11** Response time data are—like the accuracy data—quite similar for boys and girls. Again, effect sizes are very small, all less than .01, and all $t$ statistics are less than one. All distributions are skewed to the right, with the bulk of scores falling between 1 and 3 seconds. Perhaps the one notable difference between boys and girls is that the variances of the male scores are higher for all four measures. However, the ratios are less than 2 and tests of significance will have to await developments in Chapter 7.

# CHAPTER 7

**7.1** (a) (i), $p(\chi_5^2 < 9.236) = .90$; (ii) $p(1.145 < \chi_5^2 < 6.626) = .70$.

(b) $\chi^2 = (N - 1)s^2/\sigma^2 = 5s^2/10 = s^2/2$. If $s^2 < 8.703$, then $\chi^2 < 8.703/2$, or 4.351. Therefore, $p = .50$.

**7.3** (a) $H_0: \sigma^2 = 12.64$; $H_1: \sigma^2 < 12.64$. $\chi^2 = (9)(3.51)/12.64 = 2.499$. $p(\chi_9^2 < 2.499) = .019$. Therefore, reject $H_0$; the variance has decreased.

(b) The ratio, $(N - 1)s^2/\sigma^2$, is distributed as $\chi^2$ under the assumption that the distribution of scores in the population is normal. As sample size increases, the sample distribution is more likely to approach the (nonnormal) distribution so that increasing the sample size will not remedy the situation.

**7.5** (a) Appendix Table C.5 is entered with $df_1 = 4$ and $df_2 = 10$ because the boys' variance is in the numerator. The required probabilities are (i) .10 and (ii) .975.

(b) We assume the samples were drawn from two independently and normally distributed populations with the same variances.

**7.7** $F = 3.75$. Reject if $F > F_{10,20,.025}$ or $F < F_{10,20,.975}$; $F_{10,20,.025} = 2.77$ and $F_{10,20,.975.} = 1/F_{20,10,.025} = .29$. The variances differ significantly.

**7.9** (a) The CI limits are 1.70 and 16.58.

(b) The decision rule is: reject $H_0$ if $F > F_{12,14,.025}$ or $F < F_{12,14,.975}$. $F_{12,14,.975} = 3.05$ and therefore $H_0$ is rejected; the variance of the girls' multiplication accuracy scores is significantly greater than that for the boys.

(c) A stem-and-leaf plot reveals two outliers in the boys' data: 37.5 and 41.429. When these are deleted, the variance shrinks to 22.791, less than one tenth of the original variance. The effect of outliers in small data sets can be very large.

(d) The data are clearly not normally distributed.

**7.11** (a) Plots of the means as a function of grade show a steep decline from third to sixth grade, and then a leveling off at approximately 1.8 seconds. The standard deviations also decrease from the third to the sixth grade, with the sharpest drop occurring between Grades 5 and 6. Surprisingly, variability increases from the sixth to the eighth grade. This could be investigated by plotting the distributions. Outlying scores may be responsible. It is also possible that the upturn is not statistically significant.

(b) $H_0: \sigma_1^2 = \sigma_2^2$; $H_1: \sigma_1^2 \neq \sigma_2^2$. $F = 2.028$. The critical $F$ value is 2.44; therefore, we cannot reject $H_0$.

# CHAPTER 8

**8.1** (a) The variances will be multiplied by $100^2$.

(b) The $F$ ratio will not change because both numerator and denominator increase by the same factor.

(c) The variance is increased by the square of the constant.

(d) Adding a constant to all scores will not change the mean squares or the $F$ ratios.

(e) Because the spread of the group means is changed, the $MS_A$ changes. However, adding the same constant to all scores in a group will not change the within-group variance and therefore $MS_{S/A}$ is unaffected.

**8.3** (a) $F = 44.1/53.0 = .832$. We cannot reject $H_0$. (b) $t = .912$. Squaring $t$, we have $.912^2 = .832 = F$.

**8.5** The treatment effects are $\hat{\alpha}_j = \overline{Y}_{.j} - \overline{Y}_{..} = -9.333, -1.400,$ and 10.733. The mean is zero as it should be. The residuals are $\hat{\varepsilon}_{ij} = Y_{ij} - \overline{Y}_{.j}$; these also have a mean of zero.

(b) $15 \sum_j \hat{\alpha}_j^2 = 3064.133 = SS_A$ and $\sum_j \sum_i \hat{\varepsilon}_{ij}^2 = 20547.067 = SS_{S/A}$.

**8.7** (a) $p = .057$. The effects of $A$ are not significant. (b) Cohen's $f = .383$. (c) Power = .41. (d) $N = 159$, or 53 in each group.

**8.9** (a) The test of the means of the absolute deviations from the median yields $F = .472$, $p = .627$.

(b) Normal probability plots for each text indicate that deviations from normality are small, mostly for the highest scores. Also, neither the Kolmogorov–Smirnov or Shapiro–Wilk test (available in SPSS's Explore module) yield a significant result for any of the three groups.

(c) The rank sums for the three groups are 333, 341, and 502, and $H = 5.922$, which is distributed approximately as $\chi^2$ on 2 $df$ and has $p = .052$. Although slightly less than the $p$ value from the $F$ test, the result is again not significant.

**8.11** (a) For men (sex = 0), $F_{3,156} = 268.793/16.523 = 16.268$; $p = .000$. For women (sex = 1), $F_{3,163} = 242.595/32.009 = 7.579$; $p = 000$.

(b) $\hat{f} = \sqrt{\hat{\sigma}_A^2/\hat{\sigma}_e^2} = \sqrt{4.730/16.523} = .54$. Similar calculations for the female data yield $\hat{f} = \sqrt{\hat{\sigma}_A^2/\hat{\sigma}_e^2} = \sqrt{3.783/32.009} = .34$. According to the guidelines suggested by Cohen, the effect for men is large, and that for women nearly so.

# CHAPTER 9

**9.1** (a) $H_0$: $(1/2)(\mu_{F1} + \mu_{F2}) - \mu_C \leq 0$; $H_1$: $(1/2)(\mu_{F1} + \mu_{F2}) - \mu_C > 0$.

$$t_{95} = \frac{\hat{\psi}}{\sqrt{MS_{S/A}\sum_j w_j^2/n}} = \frac{(1/2)(14.6 + 14.9) - 13.8}{\sqrt{(4)(.5^2 + .5^2 + 1^2)/20}} = 1.73$$

The $p$ value is .043. Reject $H_0$.

(b) $H_0$: $\mu_C - (1/2)(\mu_{I1} + \mu_{I2}) = 0$; $H_1$: $(1/2)(\mu_{I1} + \mu_{I2}) - \mu_C \neq 0$. Proceeding as in part (a), $t = 3.74$, which is clearly significant.

(c) $H_0$: $(1/2)(\mu_{F1} + \mu_{F2}) - (1/2)(\mu_{I1} + \mu_{I2}) = 0$; $H_1$: $(1/2)(\mu_{F1} + \mu_{F2}) - (1/2)(\mu_{I1} + \mu_{I2}) \neq 0$. $t = 6.71$. The null hypothesis can be rejected.

**9.3** (a) $SS_A = 560$. (b) (i) $SS_{\hat{\psi}_1} = 320$; (ii) $SS_{\hat{\psi}_2} = (20 - 14)^2/(1.5/10) = 240$; (iii) $SS_{\hat{\psi}_3} = (24 - 14)^2/(2/10) = 500$. Because the contrasts are orthogonal, $SS_{\hat{\psi}_2} + SS_{\hat{\psi}_1} = SS_A$.

(c) $SS_{\hat{\psi}_2}$ is unchanged because the contrast is orthogonal to the first contrast. However, $SS_{\hat{\psi}_3}$ is changed because it is not orthogonal to the first contrast.

**9.5** (a) $\hat{\psi}_S = .2$. (b) $\hat{\psi}_S = .185$.

**9.7** (a) (i) Let $\psi = \mu_B - (1/2)(\mu_A + \mu_C)$; then $H_0$: $\psi \leq 0$; $H_1$: $\psi > 0$; (ii) $s_{\hat{\psi}}^2 = MS_{error}\sum_j w_j^2/n_j. = 10.5$; (iii) $t = \hat{\psi}/s_{\hat{\psi}} = 6.5/3.24 = 2.01$.

(b) (i) The standard $t$ test, on 27 $df$, is appropriate if this test is the only one and has been planned. For $\alpha = .05$ and a one-tailed alternative, reject $H_0$ if $t > 1.703$; therefore reject $H_0$.

(ii) The Scheffé method is appropriate here; $t$ is compared with $S = \sqrt{df_1 \cdot F_{.05, df_1, df_2}}$, where $df_1$ and $df_2$ refer to the numerator and denominator degrees of freedom. Substituting values, we have $S = \sqrt{(2)(3.35)} = 2.59$. We cannot reject $H_0$.

**9.9** (a) The critical distance is 6.26, and all comparisons, except $A_4$ versus $A_5$, are significant.

(b) The null hypothesis is $H_0$: $(\mu_1 - \mu_2) - (\mu_3 - \mu_4) = 0$. Therefore, $\hat{\psi} = 13$, $s_{\hat{\psi}} = 3.381$, and $t = 3.85$, which leads us to reject $H_0$.

(c) Reject $H_0$ if $|t| > 2.90$, or if the absolute difference between two means is greater than 6.93.

**9.11** (a) $F = 86.679/28.895 = 3.00$; with 2 and 323 $df$, $p = .051$.

(b) There are 323 $df_e$. In part (b), the Tukey–Kramer test is appropriate and for three groups, $q_{.05, 323} \approx 3.31$; therefore, $t_{crit} = 3.31/\sqrt{2} = 2.34$. In part (c), the Dunn–Bonferroni method is appropriate; therefore, $\alpha = .017$ (two tailed), and with 323 $df$, $t_{crit} = 2.408$. Let $\overline{D} = \overline{Y}._j - \overline{Y}._{j'}$ and $SE = s_{\overline{D}}$. Then, we have the following:

| Employ. Cat. | $\overline{D}$ | SE | CI Part (b) | CI Part (c) |
|---|---|---|---|---|
| 1,2 | 1.274 | 0.872 | −0.77, 3.31 | −0.83, 3.37 |
| 1,3 | 1.730 | 0.783 | −0.10, 3.56 | −0.16, 3.62 |
| 2,3 | 0.456 | 1.053 | −2.01, 2.92 | −2.08, 2.99 |

The confidence limits are $\overline{D} \pm t_{\text{crit}}\ SE$ and $SE = \sqrt{MS_{\text{error}}\,(1/n_j + 1/n_{j'})}$. The Dunn–Bonferroni intervals are slightly wider than the Tukey–Kramer ones.

# CHAPTER 10

**10.1**  (a) $b_1 = -.864$. (b) $\overline{Y}_{\text{pre},j} = 6.136, 5.272, 4.408$, and $3.544$. (c) (i) $SS_{\text{lin}} = 29.860$; (ii) $SS_{\text{lin}} = 29.860$; $F_{1,28} = 29.860/1.42 = 21.028$; (iii) The best-fitting straight line has a slope significantly different from zero.

**10.3**  Only lin($A$) is significant; $F_{1,16} = 7.33$, $p = .016$. The results support Smith's hypothesis of an increasing trend with increased group size.

**10.5**  (a) According to the theoretical model, the function relating $d'$ and time should increase with time and should be S shaped. This suggests linear and cubic polynomial components.

(b) As predicted, only the linear ($F_{1,35} = 78.81$, $p = .000$) and cubic ($F_{1,35} = 738.50$, $p = .000$) components of *Time* are significant.

**10.7**  (a) The means increase from $A_1$ to $A_3$ and then decrease at $A_4$, suggesting linear and quadratic components.

(b) All three components of $A$ are significant. lin($A$): $F_{1,36} = 5.72$, $p = .022$; quad($A$): $F_{1,36} = 20.39$, $p = .000$; cubic($A$): $F_{1,36} = 14.84$, $p = .000$.

(c) The means at the $A_1$, $A_2$, and $A_3$ levels are increasing, contributing to the significant linear component. The downturn at $A_4$ is apparently responsible for the quadratic component. The inflection point at $A_2$ is the most likely reason for the cubic contribution.

# CHAPTER 11

**11.1**  (a) The cell and marginal means are as follows:

| | $A_1$ | $A_2$ | $A_3$ | $A_4$ | $\overline{Y}_{..k}$ |
|---|---|---|---|---|---|
| $B_1$ | 17.333 | 26.667 | 35.667 | 19.333 | 24.750 |
| $B_2$ | 28.000 | 27.000 | 20.000 | 38.333 | 28.333 |
| $\overline{Y}_{.j.}$ | 22.667 | 26.834 | 23.824 | 28.833 | 26.542 |

In a plot of the cell means, the only clear pattern is one of interaction. The $B_1$ means increase as $A$ does until $A_3$, whereas the $B_2$ means exhibit the opposite pattern, falling until $A_3$ and then rising.

(b) The estimates for the $A$ and $B$ main effects are as follows:

| $A_1$ | $A_2$ | $A_3$ | $A_4$ | | $B_1$ | $B_2$ |
|-------|-------|-------|-------|---|-------|-------|
| $-3.875$ | $0.292$ | $1.292$ | $2.291$ | | $-1.792$ | $1.792$ |

The interaction effects are $(\overline{Y}_{\cdot jk} - \overline{Y}...) - \hat{\alpha}_j - \hat{\beta}_k$:

| | $A_1$ | $A_2$ | $A_3$ | $A_4$ |
|-------|---------|---------|---------|---------|
| $B_1$ | $-3.542$ | $1.625$ | $9.625$ | $-7.708$ |
| $B_2$ | $3.542$ | $-1.625$ | $-9.625$ | $7.708$ |

(c) $SS_A = 440.423$; $SS_B = 256.794$; $SS_{AB} = 3344.960$.

**11.3** (a) Calculate the $A$, $B$, and $AB$ mean squares from the cell means. We also know that $MS_{AB}/MS_{S/AB} = 8.0$ so that we can solve for $MS_{S/AB}$. The result is as follows:

| SV | df | SS | MS | F | p |
|------|-----|-----|-----|-----|------|
| $A$ | 1 | 4 | 4 | 0.5 | .485 |
| $B$ | 2 | 32 | 16 | 2.0 | .153 |
| $AB$ | 2 | 128 | 64 | 8.0 | .002 |
| $S/AB$ | 30 | 240 | 8 | | |

(b) $MS_{B/A_2} = 56$; $F_{2,30} = 7.00$; $p = .003$. We assume that the six population variances are equal because we are using the error mean square from the omnibus $F$ tests.

**11.5** $SS_A = 399.361$; $SS_B = 121.522$; $SS_{AB} = 43.389$.

**11.7** (a) The effects of $A$ ($F_{2,81} = 82.56$, $p = .000$) and $B$ ($F_{2,81} = 7.68, p = .001$) are significant, but not $AB$ ($F_{4,81} = 1.38$, $p = .248$).

(b) $\hat{\psi} = 7.667$; $s_{\hat{\psi}} = 1.978$; $CI = 3.73, 11.60$. The contrast differs significantly from zero.

(c) $\hat{\psi} = 7$ and $s_{\hat{\psi}} = 4.844$; $t_{81} = 1.45$; this is not significant.

**11.9** (a) The means at the four ages are (in order from age 5 to 8) 14.20, 7.25, 6.60, and 6.80. The only significant sources are age ($F_{3,32} = 15.38$, $p = .000$), linear(age) ($F_{1,32} = 29.84$, $p = .000$), and quad(age) ($F_{1,32} = 14.61$, $p = .001$). The slope of the best-fitting straight line differs significantly from zero, and there is significant (quadratic) curvature.

(b) There are no significant differences between the sexes with respect to any of the three polynomial components; for lin(Age) $\times$ Sex, ($F_{1,32} = 1.18$, $p = .285$), for quad(Age) $\times$ Sex, ($F_{1,32} = 2.32$, $p = .138$); and for cubic(Age) $\times$ Sex, ($F_{1,32} = .10$, $p = .754$).

**11.11** (a) A plot of the means for the three groups suggests both a linear and a quadratic component of the time source of variance. The ANOVA confirms the linear trend and the quadratic is almost significant.

| SV | df | SS | MS | F | p |
|---|---|---|---|---|---|
| Time | 3 | 35.00 | 11.67 | 6.38 | .001 |
| Linear | 1 | 27.00 | 27.00 | 14.75 | .000 |
| Quadratic | 1 | 6.67 | 6.67 | 3.64 | .062 |
| Cubic | 1 | 1.33 | 1.33 | 0.73 | .398 |
| Method | 2 | 8.13 | 4.07 | 2.22 | .119 |
| $T \times M$ | 6 | 16.40 | 2.73 | 1.49 | .201 |
| $S/TM$ | 48 | 87.84 | 1.83 | | |

(b) (i) $H_0$: $(1/2)(\beta_{11} + \beta_{12}) - \beta_{13} = 0$

(ii) $F_{1,48} = 10.14/1.83 = 5.54$; $p = .023$ and we reject the null hypothesis; the slope is significantly flatter in the $M_3$ condition.

**11.13** (a) In both format conditions, instructions influence mean performance, with means highest in the argument ($A$) condition, and tending to be lowest in the narrative ($N$) and summary ($S$) conditions. Means are consistently higher in the web than in the text condition. There may be an interaction with the largest format effects present in the $N$ and $A$ conditions. There appears to be considerable heterogeneity of variance, with variances highly correlated with the means. Levene's $F_{7,56} = 2.437$, $p = .03$. Finally, normal probability plots, the Kolmogorov–Smirnov test, and skewness and kurtosis statistics all make clear that the data are not normally distributed. In particular, the text/$N$ and text/$S$ distributions are skewed to the right with a pileup of scores near the median.

(b) The format effects are significant ($F_{1,56} = 4.71$, $p = .034$), as are the instruction effects ($F_{3,56} = 6.37$, $p = .034$); the interaction is not ($F_{3,56} = .30$, $p = .824$).

(c) The pattern of means is similiar to that on the original scale, although there is a more marked trend toward interaction; the effect of format decreases as we move from the narrative to the explanation condition. The most evident change is that the differences among the variances are much reduced; in fact, the Levene test of homogeneity, which previously yielded a $p$ value of .03, now yields $F_{7,56} = .384$, $p = .91$. Although $p$ values are somewhat less than on the original data scale, conclusions are essentially the same. For format, $F_{1,56} = 7.86$, $p = .007$; for instructions, $F_{3,56} = 8.41$, $p = .000$; for the interaction, $F_{3,56} = 1.45$, $p = .239$, and $SS_{ABC} = 45$.

# CHAPTER 12

**12.1** (a) For $A$, $H_0$: $(\mu_{111} + \mu_{112} + \mu_{121} + \mu_{122}) - (\mu_{211} + \mu_{212} + \mu_{221} + \mu_{222}) = 0$. For $BC$, $H_0$: $(\mu_{111} + \mu_{211} + \mu_{122} + \mu_{222}) - (\mu_{112} + \mu_{212} + \mu_{121} + \mu_{221}) = 0$. For $ABC$, $H_0$: $(\mu_{111} + \mu_{122} + \mu_{212} + \mu_{221}) - (\mu_{211} + \mu_{222} + \mu_{112} + \mu_{121}) = 0$.

(b) $SS_A = 145$, $SS_{BC} = 180$, and $SS_{ABC} = 45$.

**12.3** (a) Let $A$, $I$, and $X$ represent age, irrelevant information, and sex, respectively. Then the SV, $df$, and EMS are:

| SV | df | EMS |
|------|------|------|
| $A^*$ | 2 | $\sigma_e^2 + 60\theta_A^2$ |
| $I^*$ | 2 | $\sigma_e^2 + 60\theta_I^2$ |
| $X$ | 1 | $\sigma_e^2 + 90\theta_X^2$ |
| $AI^*$ | 4 | $\sigma_e^2 + 20\theta_{AI}^2$ |
| $AX$ | 2 | $\sigma_e^2 + 30\theta_{AX}^2$ |
| $IX$ | 2 | $\sigma_e^2 + 30\theta_{IX}^2$ |
| $AIX^*$ | 4 | $\sigma_e^2 + 10\theta_{AIX}^2$ |
| $S/AIX$ | 162 | $\sigma_e^2$ |

    (b) Sources followed by an asterisk are hypothesized to be significant.

**12.5** (a) $SS_{\text{cells}} = 240$.

    (b) $SS_A = 240$; $SS_B = 52.267$. Because $A$ and $B$ effects are correlated, the variability due to $A$ and $B$ is greater then the variability among the four cell means, an impossible result. Subtracting from $SS_{\text{cells}}$, the $SS_{AB}$ is negative, a meaningless result.

    (c) $\hat{\alpha}_1 = 5$; $\hat{\alpha}_2 = -3$.

    (d) Adjusting for the effects of $A$, the cell means are now all 5. The $SS_B$ and $SS_{AB}$ are now both zero. This peculiar state of affairs exists because the $A$, $B$, and $AB$ effects are perfectly correlated in this "data set."

**12.7** (a) $\hat{f}_B = .21$; $\hat{\omega}_B^2 = .04$. The effect is roughly medium in size by Cohen's guidelines.

    (b) The power to detect $f = .25$ with 2 and 81 $df$ is .54.

**12.9** (a) The means (and *SEM*s) for the Wiley–Voss SVT data are:

| Format | Narrative | Summary | Explanation | Argument | Means |
|------|------|------|------|------|------|
| Text | 80.00 (3.27) | 80.00 (3.78) | 70.00 (5.35) | 71.25 (4.80) | 75.31 |
| Web | 71.88 (4.32) | 69.38 (3.59) | 62.50 (2.67) | 75.62 (2.74) | 69.84 |
| Means | 75.94 | 74.69 | 66.25 | 73.44 | 72.58 |

    (b) The ANOVA table is:

| SV | df | SS | MS | F | p |
|------|------|------|------|------|------|
| Format | 1 | 478.52 | 478.52 | 3.90 | .053 |
| Instructions | 3 | 904.30 | 301.43 | 2.45 | .073 |
| $F \times I$ | 3 | 538.67 | 179.56 | 1.46 | .235 |
| Error | 56 | 6878.13 | 122.82 | | |

    (c) $\hat{f} = \hat{\sigma}_{\text{effect}}/\hat{\sigma}_e$ and, for example, in a two-factor design,

$$\hat{\sigma}_A = \sqrt{[df_A/df_A + 1)](MS_A - MS_{\text{error}})/nb}.$$

| Source | $\hat{\sigma}_{effect}$ | $\hat{f}$ |
|---|---|---|
| Format | $\sqrt{(1/2)(478.52 - 122.82)/32} = 2.358$ | .21 |
| Instructions | $\sqrt{(3/4)(301.43 - 122.82/16} = 2.894$ | .26 |
| $F \times I$ | $\sqrt{(3/4)(179.56 - 122.82/8} = 2.306$ | .21 |

    (d) Although the Format $F$ is larger, and its $p$ value smaller, than that for Instructions, the estimated effect of Instructions is larger. $E(MS_{Format}) = \sigma_e^2 + 32\theta_{Format}^2$, whereas $E(MS_{Instructions}) = \sigma_e^2 + 16\theta_{Instructions}^2$. The larger coefficient of the $\theta^2$ term in the Format $F$ test contributes to its larger $F$. However, the estimated ratio of population standard deviations is not affected by the coefficients.

    (e) We require $N = 128$ to detect $f = .25$ with power $= .80$ for the format effects, but $N = 176$ for the instructional effects. It may seem surprising that a much larger $N$ is needed to have the same power. However, note that, for fixed $N$, each of the four instructional means is based on fewer scores than each of the two format means and therefore has a larger standard error. To compensate for this, a larger sample size is needed to test Instructions.

**12.11**  Dunnett's method should be used. Because the control group variance ($s^2 = 4.5^2$) is quite similar to the $MS_{error}$, we pooled them, obtaining the standard error, $s_{diff} = 2.064$. The critical value of Dunnett's $d$, with $\alpha = .10$ and 81 $df$, is approximately 2.43. The means of experimental conditions differed significantly from the mean of the control only when subjects were sad and focused on the content of a strongly worded message, or when subjects were happy and focused on the language of a weakly worded message.

# CHAPTER 13

**13.1**(a, b)

| SV | df | MS | F | EMS |
|---|---|---|---|---|
| Subjects | 3 | 23.556 | | $\sigma_e^2 + 3\sigma_S^2$ |
| A | 2 | 16.583 | 14.559 | $\sigma_e^2 + 4\theta_A^2$ |
| $S \times A$ | 6 | 1.139 | | $\sigma_e^2$ |

    (c) partial $\hat{\omega}_A^2 = .69$. (d) est $MS_{S/A} = 7.253$.

    (e) For the repeated-measures design, assuming sphericity, $\hat{f} = 1.50$ or $\hat{\lambda} = 27$. Then, power $\approx .95$. For the between-subjects design, $\hat{f} = .596$ and $\hat{\lambda} = 4.259$. Then, power $= .28$.

**13.3**  The matrix does not exhibit compound symmetry because the variances are not equal, nor are the covariances. However, it does meet the sphericity definition because $\text{var}(d_{12}) = \text{var}(d_{13}) = \text{var}(d_{23}) = 3$.

**13.5**  Following is SPSS's output for a trend analysis:

| | **Tests of Within-Subjects Contrasts** | | | | | |
|---|---|---|---|---|---|---|
| **Source   A** | **Type III Sum of Squares** | **df** | **Mean Squares** | **F** | **Significance** |
| **A**     **Linear** | 2.809 | 1 | 2.809 | 10.566 | .014 |
| **Quadratic** | .911 | 1 | .911 | 3.777 | .093 |
| **Cubic** | 4.225E-02 | 1 | 4.225E-02 | .495 | .505 |
| **Error (A)  Linear** | 1.861 | 7 | .266 | | |
| **Quadratic** | 1.689 | 7 | .241 | | |
| **Cubic** | .598 | 7 | 8.539E-02 | | |

Measure: MEASURE_1.

**13.7**  (a)

$$\hat{X}_{ij} = (nT_{i.} + aT_{.j} - T_{..})/[(n-1)(a-1)]$$
$$= [(4)(61) + (3)(78) - 331]/[(3)(2)] = 24.5$$

(b)  Our results are:

| | Cycles | | | |
|---|---|---|---|---|
| | 1 | 2 | 3 | 4 |
| $\hat{X}_{12}$ | 30.5000 | 24.6806 | 24.5189 | 24.5144 |
| $\hat{X}_{43}$ | 37.9167 | 38.8866 | 38.9135 | 38.9143 |

**13.9**  (a)

| SV | df | EMS |
|---|---|---|
| Subjects (S) | $n - 1$ | $\sigma_e^2 + ot\sigma_S^2$ |
| Occasions (O) | $o - 1$ | $\sigma_e^2 + nt\sigma_O^2$ |
| Tasks (T) | $t - 1$ | $\sigma_e^2 + no\sigma_T^2$ |
| Residual | $not - (n + o + t - 2)$ | $\sigma_e^2$ |

(b)  $\hat{\sigma}_S^2 = (MS_S - MS_{\text{residual}})/ot$; $\hat{\sigma}_O^2 = MS_O - MS_{\text{residual}}/nt$; $\hat{\sigma}_T^2 = (MS_T - MS_{\text{residual}})/no$.

(c)

| SV | df | EMS |
|----|----|-----|
| Subjects ($S$) | $n - 1$ | $\sigma_e^2 + o\sigma_{ST}^2 + ot\sigma_S^2$ |
| Occasions ($O$) | $o - 1$ | $\sigma_e^2 + nt\sigma_O^2$ |
| Tasks ($T$) | $t - 1$ | $\sigma_e^2 + o\sigma_{ST}^2 + noo_T^2$ |
| $ST$ | $(n - 1)(t - 1)$ | $\sigma_e^2 + o\sigma_{ST}^2$ |
| Residual | $(nt - 1)(o - 1)$ | $\sigma_e^2$ |

$$\hat{\sigma}_S^2 = (MS_S - MS_{ST})/ot; \hat{\sigma}_O^2 = (MS_O - MS_{\text{residual}})/nt$$
$$\hat{\sigma}_T^2 = (MS_T - MS_{ST})/no$$

**13.11**    (a)

| SV | df | SS | MS | Error | F |
|----|----|----|----|-------|---|
| $S$ | 4 | 34.467 | 8.617 | | |
| $A$ | 1 | 112.133 | 112.133 | $SA$ | 30.170 |
| $B$ | 2 | 9.800 | 4.900 | $SB$ | 15.474 |
| $AB$ | 2 | 4.067 | 2.033 | $SAB$ | .859 |
| $SA$ | 4 | 14.867 | 3.717 | | |
| $SB$ | 8 | 2.533 | .317 | | |
| $SAB$ | 8 | 18.933 | 2.367 | | |

(b)

| SV | df | SS | MS | F |
|----|----|----|----|---|
| $S$ | 4 | 11.489 | 2.872 | |
| $A$ | 1 | 37.378 | 37.378 | 30.170 |
| $SA$ | 4 | 4.956 | 1.239 | |

*Note.* The *MS* and *SS* are one-third of their original values because the "scores" in part (b) are an average of three scores in part (a). The *F* ratio for *A* is unchanged. Therefore, as long as *B* has fixed effects, averaging over its levels will not change the test of the effects of interest.

(c) The EMS are presented in the table. The terms in parentheses do not contribute to the variability in the data when *B* has fixed effects.

| SV | EMS |
|----|-----|
| $S$ | $\sigma_e^2 + (a\sigma_{SB}^2) + ab\sigma_S^2$ |
| $A$ | $\sigma_e^2 + b\sigma_{SA}^2 + (n\sigma_{AB}^2) + (\sigma_{SAB}^2) + nb\theta_A^2$ |
| $B$ | $\sigma_e^2 + a\sigma_{SB}^2 + na\sigma_B^2$ |
| $SA$ | $\sigma_e^2 + \sigma_{SAB}^2 + b\sigma_{SA}^2$ |
| $SB$ | $\sigma_e^2 + a\sigma_{SB}^2$ |
| $AB$ | $\sigma_e^2 + \sigma_{SAB}^2 + n\sigma_{AB}^2$ |
| $SAB$ | $\sigma_e^2 + \sigma_{SAB}^2$ |

(d) Using Equation 13.19, $F_2' = 19.91$. From Equations 20.20 and 20.21, the $df = 1.042$ and 5.98. Therefore, $p = .004$. When $B$ is viewed as fixed [part (a)], $p = .0006$.

(e) Averaging over the levels of $B$ and analyzing the data as if there were only $a$ scores for each subject ignores the $A \times B$ and $S \times A \times B$ variability that contributes to the $A$ mean square if $B$ has random effects. Therefore, in such circumstances, that procedure will generally lead to an inflated Type 1 error rate.

**13.13** (a) The sum of the negative ranks is 6. For $\alpha = .05$ (two tailed) and $n = 8$, to reject $H_0$, $T_- \leq 3$ (see Appendix Table C.10). Therefore, we cannot reject $H_0$.

(b) For each subject, multiply the scores from $A_1$ to $A_4$ by $-3$, $-1$, 1, and 3, respectively, and sum the cross products to obtain an index of linearity. Only the contrast for $S_7$ is negative. It has the smallest absolute value of the eight contrasts and therefore has a rank of 1. Because $T_- \leq 3$, we can reject the null hypothesis.

**13.15** (a) The results of the ANOVA are:

| SV | SS | df | MS | F | p |
|---|---|---|---|---|---|
| Seasons | 57.989 | 3 | 19.330 | 12.924 | .000 |
| Error | 215.372 | 144 | 1.496 | | |

(b) The partial $\omega^2 = .154$, a large value.

(c) The results of the trend analysis are:

**Tests of Within-Subjects Contrasts**

| Source | SEASONS | Type III Sum of Squares | df | Mean Squares | F | Significance |
|---|---|---|---|---|---|---|
| SEASONS | Linear | 3.629 | 1 | 3.629 | 5.043 | .029 |
| | Quadratic | 48.133 | 1 | 48.133 | 31.725 | .000 |
| | Cubic | 6.227 | 1 | 6.227 | 2.767 | .103 |
| Error (SEASONS) | Linear | 34.539 | 48 | .720 | | |
| | Quadratic | 72.824 | 48 | 1.517 | | |
| | Cubic | 108.009 | 48 | 2.250 | | |

Measure: MEASURE_1.

# CHAPTER 14

**14.1** (a) The results of the ANOVA are:

| SV | df | SS | MS | F | p |
|---|---|---|---|---|---|
| Between $Ss$ | 5 | 226.5 | | | |
| $A$ | 1 | 112.5 | 112.50 | 3.947 | .118 |
| $S/A$ | 4 | 114.0 | 28.50 | | |
| Within $Ss$ | 12 | 758.0 | | | |
| $B$ | 2 | 84.0 | 42.00 | .994 | .412 |
| $AB$ | 2 | 336.0 | 168.00 | 3.976 | .063 |
| $S \times B/A$ | 8 | 338.0 | 42.25 | | |

(b) The ANOVA based on the mean scores for the subjects is:

| SV | df | SS | MS | F | p |
|---|---|---|---|---|---|
| Total | 5 | 75.5 | | | |
| A | 1 | 37.5 | 37.5 | 3.947 | .118 |
| S/A | 4 | 38.0 | 9.5 | | |

(i) The $F$s in parts (a) and (b) are identical. (ii) The $SS$ and $MS$ in part (b) are one third of their counterparts in part (a). The reason for this is that, in part (a), $SS_A = bn \sum_j (\overline{Y}._j. - \overline{Y}...)^2$, whereas in part (b), $SS_A = n \sum_j (\overline{Y}._j. - \overline{Y}...)^2$.

(c) $SS_{SB/A_1} = 118$ and $SS_{SB/A_2} = 220$; the sum is 338, the result in part (a). Also, $MS_{SB/A_1} = 29.5$ and $MS_{SB/A_2} = 55$; the average is 42.25, the result in part (a).

**14.3**

| SV | df | EMS |
|---|---|---|
| A | 1 | $\sigma_e^2 + \sigma_{SB/A}^2 + 3\sigma_{S/A}^2 + 3\sigma_{AB}^2 + 9\theta_A^2$ |
| S/A | 4 | $\sigma_e^2 + \sigma_{SB/A}^2 + 3\sigma_{S/A}^2$ |
| B | 2 | $\sigma_e^2 + \sigma_{SB/A}^2 + 6\theta_B^2$ |
| AB | 2 | $\sigma_e^2 + \sigma_{SB/A}^2 + 3\sigma_{AB}^2$ |
| SB/A | 8 | $\sigma_e^2 + \sigma_{SB/A}^2$ |

To test the $A$ effect, $F' = (MS_A + MS_{SB/A})/(MS_{S/A} + MS_{AB}) = (112.5 + 42.25)/(28.5 + 168) = .79$. The result is clearly not significant.

**14.5** (a) The ANOVA table is:

| SV | df | EMS |
|---|---|---|
| Between Ss | 71 | |
| X | 1 | $\sigma_e^2 + 2\sigma_{S/XA}^2 + 72\theta_X^2$ |
| A | 2 | $\sigma_e^2 + 2\sigma_{S/XA}^2 + 48\theta_A^2$ |
| X × A | 2 | $\sigma_e^2 + 2\sigma_{S/XA}^2 + 24\theta_{XA}^2$ |
| S/XA | 66 | $\sigma_e^2 + 2\sigma_{S/XA}^2$ |
| Within Ss | 72 | |
| T | 1 | $\sigma_e^2 + \sigma_{ST/XA}^2 + 72\theta_T^2$ |
| XT | 1 | $\sigma_e^2 + \sigma_{ST/XA}^2 + 36\theta_{XT}^2$ |
| AT | 2 | $\sigma_e^2 + \sigma_{ST/XA}^2 + 24\theta_{AT}^2$ |
| XAT | 2 | $\sigma_e^2 + \sigma_{ST/XA}^2 + 12\theta_{XAT}^2$ |
| ST/XA | 66 | $\sigma_e^2 + \sigma_{ST/XA}^2$ |

$S/XA$ is the error term for the between-subjects terms, and $ST/XA$ is the error term for the within-subjects terms.

(b) We base the error term only on those scores involved in these tests of simple effects; that is the default in most statistical packages. For part (i), we find the variance of $T_1$

scores within each Age × Sex combination and average these. We might notate this as $MS_{S/A \times X/T_1}$ (subjects within Age × Sex combinations for the $T_1$ task). The $df = ax(n-1) = (3)(2)(11) = 66$.

(ii) The error term is $MS_{S/A/\text{Male}/T_1}$. The $df = a(n-1) = (3)(11) = 33$.

(iii) The error term is $MS_{ST/A/\text{Male}}$. The $df = a(n-1)(t-1) = (3)(11)(1) = 33$.

**14.7** The confidence interval is CI $= 5.4 \pm (1.314)(2.086) = 2.66, 8.14$.

**14.9** (a) Using Appendix Table C.10, the $B{-}A$ interval $= -1.03, 4.28$; the $C{-}A$ interval $= 2.22, 7.53$; and the $C{-}B$ interval is $= .60, 5.90$. Diet $C$ differs significantly from both Diets $A$ and $B$; Diets $A$ and $B$ do not differ significantly from each other.

(b) Scheffé's method is appropriate here. The confidence interval $= 2.07, 9.68$. Because the interval does not contain zero, we conclude that the mean for Diet $C$ does differ from the average of the other two means on Day 4.

**14.11** (a) Mean SVT scores are higher than IVT scores in the text format, though the advantage diminishes as we move from $N$ (narrative) to $A$ (argument) instructions. In the web format, IVT scores are higher than SVT scores and the advantage is greatest with $A$ instructions. This suggests a Test × Format interaction, and Test × Instruction interaction.

(b)

| SV | df | SS | MS | F | p |
|---|---|---|---|---|---|
| Format ($F$) | 1 | 9.570 | 9.570 | .05 | .818 |
| Instructions ($I$) | 3 | 1430.273 | 476.758 | 2.67 | .056 |
| $F \times I$ | 3 | 1064.648 | 354.883 | 1.99 | .126 |
| $S/FI$ | 36 | 9993.312 | 170.400 | | |
| | | | | | |
| Test ($T$) | 1 | 164.258 | 164.258 | 1.67 | .202 |
| $T \times F$ | 1 | 1158.008 | 1158.008 | 11.75 | .001 |
| $T \times I$ | 3 | 616.211 | 205.404 | 2.08 | .113 |
| $T \times F \times I$ | 3 | 3.711 | 1.237 | .01 | .998 |
| $S \times T/FI$ | 56 | 5520.312 | 98.577 | | |

The one source that is significant at the .05 level is the Test × Format interaction; $F_{1,56} = 11.75$, $p = .001$. This interaction reflects the fact that the sentence memory (SVT) mean is higher when participants have studied the material from a textbook chapter but that the inferences (IVT) mean is higher when participants have been required to integrate information from the Web site.

# CHAPTER 15

**15.1** (a) The effect of $P$ is not significant when an ANOVA is performed.

```
Dep Var: Y  N: 36  Multiple R: 0.344  Squared multiple R: 0.119
Analysis of Variance
```

| Source | Sum of Squares | df | Mean Squares | F Ratio | P |
|---|---|---|---|---|---|
| P | 806.167 | 2 | 403.083 | 2.221 | 0.124 |
| Error | 5988.583 | 33 | 181.472 | | |

(b) Using an ANCOVA, the effect of $P$ is significant.

```
Dep Var: Y  N: 36  Multiple R: 0.830  Squared multiple R: 0.688
Analysis of Variance
```

| Source | Sum of Squares | df | Mean Squares | F Ratio | P |
|---|---|---|---|---|---|
| X | 3869.741 | 1 | 3869.741 | 58.443 | 0.000 |
| P [P (adj)] | 539.495 | 2 | 269.748 | 4.074 | 0.027 |
| Error [S/P (adj)] | 2118.843 | 32 | 66.214 | | |

(c) We use the GLM module in one of the software packages to add a $P^*X$ term to the model. The interaction term is not significant, so we do not reject the hypothesis of homogeneity of slopes.

```
Dep Var: Y  N: 36  Multiple R: 0.844  Squared multiple R: 0.712
Analysis of Variance
```

| Source | Sum of Squares | df | Mean Squares | F Ratio | P |
|---|---|---|---|---|---|
| X | 3725.614 | 1 | 3725.614 | 57.130 | 0.000 |
| P | 75.463 | 2 | 37.731 | 0.579 | 0.567 |
| $P^*X$ | 162.458 | 2 | 81.229 | 1.246 | 0.302 |
| Error | 1956.385 | 30 | 65.213 | | |

**15.3** (a) No, it is not appropriate to use ANCOVA here. We have a nonequivalent-groups design because the workers for whom we have satisfaction scores have not been randomly assigned to the four departments. Moreover, an ANOVA with $X$ as the dependent variable yields a significant effect of department, $F(3, 28) = 5.602, p = .004$.

(b) No, it is not appropriate to use ANCOVA here. The data violate the assumption of homogeneity of the slopes. The test of heterogeneity of slope indicates that there is a significant interaction between the covariate $X$ and the factor $A$, $F(2, 24) = 7.137, p = .004$.

**15.5** The ANOVA on $Y$ does not indicate any significant effects; however, the ANCOVA on $Y$ using $X$ as a covariate reveals a significant $A$ effect, $F(1, 19) = 17.376, p = .001$. There are no significant effects when an ANOVA is performed using $X$ as the dependent variable; also, there is no suggestion that the homogeneity of regression slopes has been violated.

Dep Var: Y   N: 24   Multiple $R$: 0.409   Squared multiple $R$: 0.168
Analysis of Variance

| Source | Sum of Squares | df | Mean Squares | F Ratio | P |
|---|---|---|---|---|---|
| A | 118.815 | 1 | 118.815 | 3.963 | 0.060 |
| B | 1.215 | 1 | 1.215 | 0.041 | 0.842 |
| A*B | 0.667 | 1 | 0.667 | 0.022 | 0.883 |
| Error | 599.577 | 20 | 29.979 | | |

Dep Var: Y   N: 24   Multiple $R$: 0.762   Squared multiple $R$: 0.581
Analysis of Variance

| Source | Sum of Squares | df | Mean Squares | F Ratio | P |
|---|---|---|---|---|---|
| A | 276.023 | 1 | 276.023 | 17.376 | 0.001 |
| B | 2.513 | 1 | 2.513 | 0.158 | 0.695 |
| A*B | 11.878 | 1 | 11.878 | 0.748 | 0.398 |
| X | 297.762 | 1 | 297.762 | 18.745 | 0.000 |
| Error | 301.814 | 19 | 15.885 | | |

Dep Var: X   N: 24   Multiple $R$: 0.421   Squared multiple $R$: 0.177
Analysis of Variance

| Source | Sum of Squares | df | Mean Squares | F Ratio | P |
|---|---|---|---|---|---|
| A | 64.354 | 1 | 64.354 | 3.334 | 0.083 |
| B | 9.500 | 1 | 9.500 | 0.492 | 0.491 |
| A*B | 9.250 | 1 | 9.250 | 0.479 | 0.497 |
| Error | 386.082 | 20 | 19.304 | | |

# CHAPTER 16

**16.1**   (a)

| SV | df | EMS |
|---|---|---|
| D | 2 | $\sigma_e^2 + 20\sigma_{C/D}^2 + 100\theta_D^2$ |
| C/D | 12 | $\sigma_e^2 + 20\sigma_{C/D}^2$ |
| X | 1 | $\sigma_e^2 + 10\sigma_{CX/D}^2 + 150\theta_X^2$ |
| DX | 2 | $\sigma_e^2 + 10\sigma_{CX/D}^2 + 50\theta_{DX}^2$ |
| CX/D | 12 | $\sigma_e^2 + 10\sigma_{CX/D}^2$ |
| S/CX/D | 270 | $\sigma_e^2$ |

(b) $MS_{S/DX}$ is the pool of the $C/D$, $CX/D$, and $S/CX/D$ mean squares; $E(MS_{S/DX}) = \sigma_e^2 + (12/294)(20\sigma_{C/D}^2) + (12/294)(10\sigma_{CX/D}^2)$. If the variance due to $C/D > 0$, the test of $X$ will be negatively biased; if the variance due to $CX/D > 0$, the test of $D$ will be negatively biased.

**16.3** Presumably, we wish to generalize beyond the four leaders used in the study. Therefore, $L$ is viewed as a random-effects variable. The ANOVA is:

| SV | df | EMS | Error Term |
|----|----|-----|------------|
| $L$ | 3 | $\sigma_e^2 + 6\sigma_{G/LM}^2 + 600\theta_L^2$ | $G/LM$ |
| $M$ | 1 | $\sigma_e^2 + 6\sigma_{G/LM}^2 + 30\sigma_{LM}^2 + 120\theta_M^2$ | $LM$ |
| $L \times M$ | 3 | $\sigma_e^2 + 6\sigma_{G/LM}^2 + 30\sigma_{LM}^2$ | $G/LM$ |
| $G/LM$ | 32 | $\sigma_e^2 + 6\sigma_{G/LM}^2$ | $S/G/LM$ |
| $S/G/LM$ | 200 | $\sigma_e^2$ | |

If each leader has been selected for a particular quality, we may view $L$ as fixed, in which case $M$ is tested against $G/LM$.

**16.5**

| SV | df | EMS |
|----|----|-----|
| $S$ | 19 | $\sigma_e^2 + 50\sigma_S^2$ |
| $M$ | 4 | $\sigma_e^2 + 20\sigma_{I/M}^2 + 10\sigma_{SM}^2 + 200\theta_M^2$ |
| $I/M$ | 45 | $\sigma_e^2 + 20\sigma_{I/M}^2$ |
| $S \times M$ | 76 | $\sigma_e^2 + 10\sigma_{SM}^2$ |
| $S \times I/M$ | 855 | $\sigma_e^2$ |

To test $M$, a quasi-$F$ is needed; $F' = (MS_M + MS_{SI/M})/(MS_{I/M} + MS_{SM})$. The numerator $df = (MS_M + MS_{SI/M})^2/(MS_M^2/4 + MS_{SI/M}^2/855)$; the denominator $df = (MS_{I/M} + MS_{SM})^2/(MS_{I/M}^2/45 + MS_{SM}^2/76)$.

**16.7**

| SV | df | EMS |
|----|----|-----|
| $A$ | 2 | $\sigma_e^2 + 5\sigma_{S/AV}^2 + 10\sigma_{AE/V}^2 + 150\theta_A^2$ |
| $V$ | 2 | $\sigma_e^2 + 5\sigma_{S/AV}^2 + 30\sigma_{E/V}^2 + 150\theta_V^2$ |
| $AV$ | 4 | $\sigma_e^2 + 5\sigma_{S/AV}^2 + 10\sigma_{AE/V}^2 + 50\theta_{AV}^2$ |
| $S/AV$ | 81 | $\sigma_e^2 + 5\sigma_{S/AV}^2$ |
| $E/V$ | 12 | $\sigma_e^2 + 30\sigma_{E/V}^2$ |
| $AE/V$ | 24 | $\sigma_e^2 + 10\sigma_{AE/V}^2$ |
| $SE/AV$ | 324 | $\sigma_e^2$ |

To test the $A$ source of variance, $F' = (MS_A + MS_{SE/AV})/(MS_{S/AV} + MS_{AE/V})$. The numerator $df = (MS_A + MS_{SE/AV})^2/(MS_A^2/2 + MS_{SE/AV}^2/324)$ and the denominator $df = (MS_{S/AV} + MS_{AE/V})^2/(MS_{S/AV}^2/81 + MS_{AE/V}^2/24)$.

**16.9** (a)

| SV | df | EMS | Error Term |
|---|---|---|---|
| $A$ | 1 | $\sigma_e^2 + 3\sigma_{G/AP/E}^2 + 15\sigma_{AP/E}^2 + 120\theta_A^2$ | $AP/E$ |
| $E$ | 1 | $\sigma_e^2 + 3\sigma_{G/AP/E}^2 + 30\sigma_{P/E}^2 + 120\theta_E^2$ | $P/E$ |
| $AE$ | 1 | $\sigma_e^2 + 3\sigma_{G/AP/E}^2 + 15\sigma_{AP/E}^2 + 60\theta_{AE}^2$ | $AP/E$ |
| $P/E$ | 6 | $\sigma_e^2 + 3\sigma_{G/AP/E}^2 + 30\sigma_{P/E}^2$ | $G/AP/E$ |
| $AP/E$ | 6 | $\sigma_e^2 + 3\sigma_{G/AP/E}^2 + 15\sigma_{AP/E}^2$ | $G/AP/E$ |
| $G/AP/E$ | 64 | $\sigma_e^2 + 3\sigma_{G/AP/E}^2$ | $S/G/AP/E$ |
| $S/G/AP/E$ | 160 | $\sigma_e^2$ | |

(b) This analysis is likely to involve less error variance and provide more powerful, and certainly simpler, tests of $A$, $E$, and $AE$. However, monkeys are expensive to purchase and maintain, and the design Exercise 16.8 involves far fewer subjects.

**16.11** (a) $F_{1,30} = 6.646$, $p = .03$.

(b) Let $NL$ be the "noleader" group condition and $I$ be the individual (no group) condition. Then, $F' = MS_L/[(^1/_2)(MS_{G/NL} + MS_{S/I})] = 26.150/(1/2)(8.825 + 5.937) = 3.543$. The error $df \approx 10$; $p = .09$.

# CHAPTER 17

**17.1** (a) $SS_A = 79.5$, $SS_C = 22.5$, $SS_S = 56$, and $SS_{\text{residual}} = 29$.

(b) The estimates of the $S \times C$ effects and the scores after adjustment are:

| | est$(\gamma\gamma)_{ij}$ | | | | $Y_{ijk} - $est$(\gamma\gamma)_{ij}$ | | | |
|---|---|---|---|---|---|---|---|---|
| | $C_1$ | $C_2$ | $C_3$ | $C_4$ | $C_1$ | $C_2$ | $C_3$ | $C_4$ |
| $S_1$ | 3.500 | −5.000 | 2.250 | −0.750 | 21.500 | 21.000 | 21.750 | 18.750 |
| $S_2$ | 2.500 | 3.000 | −3.750 | −1.750 | 16.500 | 16.000 | 16.750 | 13.750 |
| $S_3$ | −4.500 | 1.000 | 2.250 | 1.250 | 17.500 | 17.000 | 17.750 | 14.750 |
| $S_4$ | −1.500 | 1.000 | −0.750 | 1.250 | 18.500 | 18.000 | 18.750 | 15.750 |

$SS_S$ and $SS_C$ are unchanged; however, $SS_A$ and $SS_{\text{residual}}$ now both equal zero. If there is an interaction of two variables in the population, effects attributed to the third variable may be due to the interaction.

**17.3**

| SV | df | SS | MS | F | p |
|----|----|----|----|----|----|
| S | 3 | .593 | .198 | 47.4 | .000 |
| P | 3 | .232 | .077 | 18.6 | .002 |
| E | 1 | 1.323 | 1.323 | 197.6 | .000 |
| I | 1 | .903 | .903 | 144.4 | .000 |
| E × I | 1 | .023 | .023 | 3.6 | .107 |
| Residual | 6 | .025 | .004 | | |

**17.5**  The simplest design is a $3 \times 3 \times 3$ completely randomized design with three subjects in each of the 27 cells. This requires the least time from each subject, involves the fewest assumptions, runs no risk of carry-over effects, and has 54 error $df$. However, it is also the least efficient design because the error term includes variance due to individual differences. A second possibility would be to create a $3 \times 3$ Latin square with one variable, perhaps ($W$) varied in a counterbalanced order. Twenty-seven subjects would be run in each row of the square (sequence of levels of $w$). These 27 individuals would be divided among the nine combinations of the remaining two factors. The advantage of this design is that whichever factor is the within-subject factor, and its interactions, can be tested more efficiently than in the first, completely randomized design. The disadvantage is the possibility of carry-over effects, and the added assumptions (e.g., sphericity) involved in any within-subject design. A third possibility is a variation on the second, in which two factors are within subjects, so that the basic design is a replicated Latin square. The advantage is that now two variables are efficiently tested. The possible disadvantages are those cited for the second design, and the added time for each participant. There are other possibilities, including Latin-Greco squares. The main disadvantage of this design is that it rests on the assumption of no interaction between the two within-subject variables.

**17.7**  $A$ and $C$ are tested against the within-cell residual (WCR). These are the only significant sources. For $A$, $F_{3,24} = 10.24$, $p = .000$; for $C$, $F_{3,24} = 18.68$, $p = .000$.

**17.9**  The key to the analysis is to recognize that scripts ($S$) are nested within valences ($V$). The script means and the ANOVA table are:

| $S_1$ | $S_2$ | $S_3$ | $S_4$ |
|----|----|----|----|
| 2.321 | 1.909 | .766 | .617 |

| SV | df | SS | MS | F | p |
|----|----|----|----|----|----|
| R | 3 | 10.375 | 3.458 | 1.80 | .188 |
| Ss/R | 16 | 30.825 | 1.927 | | |
| Script (S) | 3 | 42.462 | 14.154 | 53.82 | .000 |
| V | 1 | 40.527 | 40.527 | 154.95 | .000 |
| S/V | 2 | 1.895 | .948 | 3.60 | .035 |
| C | 3 | 5.953 | 1.984 | 7.54 | .000 |
| BCR | 6 | 1.783 | .297 | 1.13 | .359 |
| WCR | 48 | 12.606 | .263 | | |

Heartbeat change scores are affected by the script, and this variance is primarily due to the difference between the negative and positive scripts; the change is greater for the two scripts with negative valence. All terms are tested against the within-cells residual (WCR) except $R$, which is tested against $S/R$.

# CHAPTER 18

**18.1**   (b) $r = .620$; (b) $r^2 = .385$; (c) $r^2 = .385$.

**18.3**   The reduction in the correlation between age and TC for older and younger women occurs because of the reduction in the variability of age (see the discussion in Section 18.2.2). The corresponding figures for men are $r = .062$ for the overall correlation of age and TC in the sample; $r = .008$ for men under 50 and $r = -.035$ for men 50 and over.

**18.5**   (a) Because $r_{XY} = r_{X'Y'}\sqrt{r_{XX}}\sqrt{r_{YY}}$ (Equation 18.7), the largest correlation that we could find would be $r_{XY} = \sqrt{r_{XX}}\sqrt{r_{YY}} = \sqrt{.64}\sqrt{.81} = .72$.

   (b) The estimated correlation if we "correct for attenuation" due to low reliability is $.40/\sqrt{r_{XX}}\sqrt{r_{YY}} = .40/\sqrt{.64}\sqrt{.81} = .40/.72 = .56$.

   (c) To test the correlation, we use the "uncorrected" correlation of .40. The test statistic is $t = r/\sqrt{(1 - r^2)/(N - 2)} = 2.690$, $p < .05$. The correlation is significant.

**18.7**   (a) Using Equation 18.9, $t(17) = -1.30$, so we cannot reject $H_0$.

   (b) $z = (Z_r - Z_{hyp})/\sqrt{1/(N - 3)} = -1.24$, so again we cannot reject $H_0$.

   (c) No, even if the correlation had been significant, we could not conclude that studying interferes with test performance. More likely, students having difficulty may study more, but still perform more poorly.

   (d) The .95 CI for $Z_\rho$ is given by $Z_r \pm z_{.025}\sqrt{1/(N - 3)} = -.310 \pm (1.96)(1/4) = -.80, .18$. Translating back to correlations, the .95 CI for $\rho$ extends from $-.66$ to $+.18$. The .50 CI for $Z_\rho$ is $-.310 \pm (.675)(1/4) = -.48$ to $-.14$. Translating back to correlations, the interval extends from $-.44$ to $-.14$.

   (e) Using GPOWER, the post hoc power is approximately .25.

   (f) To calculate directly as in Table 18.1, recall from part (b) that the test statistic was $z = -1.24$. The lower critical value therefore has a $z$ score of $-1.96 - (-1.24) = -.72$ with respect to the sampling distribution given $\rho = .30$, so that the power is $p(z < -.72) = .24$, about the same value given by GPOWER.

   (g) From GPOWER, we need $N = 82$ to get power of .80.

   (h) Using the procedure illustrated in Table 18.2, we get $N = 85$.

**18.9**   (a) $z = (Z_{.45} - 0)/\sqrt{1/49} = 3.395$, so we can reject $H_0$.

   (b) $z = (Z_{.60} - Z_{.45})/\sqrt{[1/49] + [1/64]} = 1.193$, we cannot reject $H_0$.

   (c) $z = (Z_{.45} - Z_{.20})/\sqrt{[1/49] + [1/64]} = 1.486$; the correlations do not differ significantly.

   (d) The .95 CI for $Z_\rho$ is $.485 \pm (1.96)(1/7) = .205, .765$; the interval for $\rho$ is .202, .644.

**18.11**   (a) Using Steiger's MULTICORR program, we find $\chi_1^2 = 34.007$, $p = .000$. The correlation between masculinity and femininity is significantly different at times 1 and 2.

   (b) Again using the program, we find $\chi_1^2 = 0.798$, $p = .375$. We cannot reject the hypothesis that the correlation between V1 and M1 is the same as the correlation between V1 and F1.

**18.13**

$$r_{X,XT} = \frac{1}{N - 1}\sum z_X z_{T-X} = \frac{1}{N - 1}\sum\left(\frac{X - \overline{X}}{s_X}\right)\left(\frac{T - X - \overline{T - X}}{s_{T-X}}\right)$$

$$= \frac{1}{N-1} \sum \frac{(X - \overline{X})\left[(T - \overline{T}) - (X - \overline{X})\right]}{s_X \sqrt{\frac{1}{N-1} \sum \left[(T - \overline{T}) - (X - \overline{X})\right]^2}} = \frac{r_{XT} s_X s_T - s_X^2}{s_X \sqrt{s_T^2 + s_X^2 - 2r_{XT} s_X s_T}}$$

$$= \frac{r_{XT} s_T - s_X}{\sqrt{s_X^2 + s_T^2 - 2r_{XT} s_X s_T}}$$

**18.15** There are several ways of doing the problem. We could start by expressing $r_{XT} = r_{X(X+Y)}$ in terms of $r_{XY}$:

$$r_{X(X+Y)} = \frac{1}{N-1} \sum z_X z_{X+Y} = \frac{1}{N-1} \sum \left(\frac{X - \overline{X}}{s_X}\right)\left(\frac{X + Y - \overline{X+Y}}{s_{X+Y}}\right)$$

$$= \frac{1}{N-1} \sum \left(\frac{X - \overline{X}}{s_X}\right)\left(\frac{(X - \overline{X}) + (Y - \overline{Y})}{\sqrt{s_X^2 + s_Y^2 + 2r_{XY} s_X s_Y}}\right) = \frac{s_X^2 + r_{XY} s_X s_Y}{s_X \sqrt{s_X^2 + s_Y^2 2r_{XY} s_X s_Y}}$$

$$= \frac{s_X + r_{XY} s_Y}{\sqrt{s_X^2 + s_Y^2 + 2r_{XY} s_X s_Y}}$$

Now, if $s_X = s_Y = s$, then

$$r_{X(X+Y)} = \frac{s^2 + r_{XY} s^2}{s \sqrt{s^2 + s^2 + 2r_{XY} s^2}} = \sqrt{\frac{1 + r_{XY}}{2}} = r_{XT} = .70$$

Squaring both sides, $(1 + r_{XY})/(2) = .49$, so that $r_{XY} = -.02$. Here, the two parts of the test are not correlated. The reason $r_{XT}$ is high is because $X$ is part of $T$.

# CHAPTER 19

**19.1** (a) The strategy is not a good one. Given inconsistent behavior, very bad performance is likely to followed by better performance, and exceptionally good performance may well be followed by performance that is not as good, whether or not feedback is given.

(b) The improvement cannot be explained as regression toward the mean. Regression toward the mean by itself would not account for above average performance by the group that received tutoring.

(c) Not necessarily. Regression toward the mean complicates matching. Suppose that good spellers on the average have much higher IQs than poor spellers. If we were to form a mixed group of good and poor spellers matched for IQ on the basis of a single test, then the mixed group might largely consist of more intelligent good spellers who just happened to perform poorly on the IQ test and less intelligent poor spellers who performed well on the test. If they were to be given a second IQ test, the two groups might regress to separate means.

**19.3** (a) The scatterplot indicates that there is a strong curvilinear relation between the two variables. The results of the regression of $Y$ on $X$ are:

| Dep Var: Y   N: 50   Multiple $R$: 0.178   Squared multiple $R$ : 0.032 |
| Adjusted squared multiple $R$: 0.012   Standard error of estimate: 36.309 |

| Effect | Coefficient | Std Error | Std Coef | Tolerance | $t$ | $p$(2-tail) |
|---|---|---|---|---|---|---|
| CONSTANT | 435.880 | 12.042 | 0.000 | . | 36.196 | 0.000 |
| $X$ | 4.560 | 3.631 | 0.178 | 1.000 | 1.256 | 0.215 |

Analysis of Variance

| Source | Sum of Squares | df | Mean Square | F Ratio | p |
|---|---|---|---|---|---|
| Regression | 2079.360 | 1 | 2079.360 | 1.577 | 0.215 |
| Residual | 63280.960 | 48 | 1318.353 | | |

Durbin-Watson $D$ Statistic   0.677
First-Order Autocorrelation 0.633

and the results of an ANOVA with $X$ as the factor are as follows:

Analysis of Variance

| Source | Sum of Squares | df | Mean Square | F Ratio | p |
|---|---|---|---|---|---|
| X | 45790.520 | 4 | 11447.630 | 26.323 | 0.000 |
| Error | 19569.800 | 45 | 434.884 | | |

To test whether there is also a significant linear effect, we note that from the regression, $SS_{linear} = MS_{linear} = 2079.360$. To test for linearity, form the ratio $F = MS_{linear}/MS_{error}$, where $MS_{error}$ is obtained from the ANOVA; $F(1, 45) = 2079.360/434.884 = 4.781$; there is a significant linear effect, $p < .05$. The best-fitting regression equation is $\hat{Y} = 435.88 + 4.56X$; this predicts values of 440.44, 445.00, 449.56, 454.12, and 458.68 for $X = 1–5$, respectively.

(b) The plot of residuals ($Y$ against $\hat{Y}$) is curvilinear, indicating that a curvilinear component in the relation between $Y$ and $X$ has not been accounted for by the regression.

(c) We can now fill in the table:

| SV | df | SS | MS | F | p |
|---|---|---|---|---|---|
| Between | 4 | 45790.52 | 11447.63 | 26.32 | .000 |
| Linearity | 1 | 2079.36 | 2079.36 | 4.78 | <.05 |
| Lack of fit (nonlinearity) | 3 | 43711.16 | 14570.39 | 33.50 | <.001 |
| Pure error | 45 | 19569.80 | 434.88 | | |

(d) We can create a new variable $XSQ = X*X$ and regress $Y$ on $X$ and $XSQ$. This yields the following output:

Dep Var: Y   N: 50   Multiple R: 0.833   Squared multiple R: 0.693
Adjusted squared multiple R: 0.680 Standard error of estimate: 20.657

| Effect | Coefficient | Std Error | Std Coef | Tolerance | t | p (2-tail) |
|---|---|---|---|---|---|---|
| CONSTANT | 312.880 | 14.010 | 0.000 | . | 22.332 | 0.000 |
| X | 109.989 | 10.677 | 4.302 | 0.037 | 10.302 | 0.000 |
| XSQ | −17.571 | 1.746 | −4.203 | 0.037 | −10.065 | 0.000 |

Analysis of Variance

| Source | Sum of Squares | df | Mean Square | F Ratio | p |
|---|---|---|---|---|---|
| Regression | 45305.074 | 2 | 22652.537 | 53.087 | 0.000 |
| Residual | 20055.246 | 47 | 426.707 | | |

Durbin-Watson $D$ statistic  1.793
First-Order Autocorrelation 0.101

The regression equation is $\hat{Y} = 312.88 + 109.99X + 17.571X^2$. The quadratic component is highly significant. $R^2$ is now .69 as opposed to .03 in the original regression. The residual plot no longer suggests any obvious nonlinearity.

**19.5** (a) Using Equation 18.13, $z = 3.38$, so there is a higher correlation between salary and years of service for males and females; that is, there is a stronger linear relation for men than for women.

(b) Using $b_1 = rs_Y/s_X$, we find there is a slope of .599 for men and .799 for women. Each additional year of service corresponds to about an additional $600 (.599 × $1000) for males and about $800 for females. We can test whether the slope difference is significant using the test statistic (see Table 19.8)

$$t = \frac{b_M - b_F}{SE(b_M - b_F)} = \frac{b_M - b_F}{s_e\sqrt{(1/SS_{X_M}) + (1/SS_{X_F})}}$$

where

$$s_e^2 = \frac{SS_{\text{residual}}}{N_M + N_F - 4} = \frac{(1 - r_M^2)SS_{Y_M} + (1 - r_F^2)SS_{YF}}{3996}$$
$$= \frac{575855.86 + 545806.95}{3996} = 280.70.$$

so that $s_e = 16.75$, substituting we find $t(3996) = -2.38$, $p < .02$. The salary increment per year for women is significantly greater than that for men. So here we have a situation in which the correlation is significantly larger for men than women, but the slope is significantly higher for women than men. The reason for this apparent paradox is that the men have greater variability in their years of service.

**19.7** (a) Regressing FINAL on PRETEST produces the following output:

Dep Var: FINAL  N: 18   Multiple R: 0.725   Squared multiple R:  0.526
Adjusted squared multiple R: 0.496   Standard error of estimate: 10.638

| Effect | Coefficient | Std Error | Std Coef | Tolerance | t | p (2-tail) |
|---|---|---|---|---|---|---|
| CONSTANT | −36.083 | 27.295 | 0.000 | . | −1.322 | 0.205 |
| PRETEST | 3.546 | 0.842 | 0.725 | 1.000 | 4.212 | 0.001 |

Analysis of Variance

| Source | Sum of Squares | df | Mean Square | F Ratio | p |
|---|---|---|---|---|---|
| Regression | 2007.497 | 1 | 2007.497 | 17.738 | 0.001 |
| Residual | 1810.780 | 16 | 113.174 | | |

(b) The regression equation is $\widehat{FINAL} = -36.08 + 3.55$ PRETEST. The standard error of estimate is 10.64, and the standard errors of $b_0$ and $b_1$ are 27.295 and 0.842, respectively.

(c) Using the regression equation, estimates of the conditional means of the population of FINAL scores for PRETEST $= 24$ and $37$ are 49.02 and 95.12, respectively. To find the confidence intervals for the conditional means, we need the standard errors for the predicted final scores, $SE(\widehat{FINAL}) = s_e\sqrt{h_{jj}} = s_e\sqrt{1/N + (X - \overline{X})^2/SS_X}$. For PRETEST $= 24$, $N = 18$; $(X - \overline{X})^2 = (24 - 32.278)^2$; $SS_X = (N - 1)s_X^2 = 159.60$. So, $SE(\widehat{FINAL}) = (10.638)\sqrt{1/18 + (24 - 32.278)^2/159.60} = 7.408$. Similarly, the $SE$ for PRETEST $= 37$ is 4.708. The .95 CI for the conditional mean of FINAL scores at PRETEST $= 24$ is given by $49.02 \pm t_{16,.025}\,SE = 49.02 \pm (2.12)(7.408) = 49.02 \pm 15.71$. Similarly, the .95 CI at PRETEST $= 37$ is given by $95.12 \pm 9.98$.

(d) The estimate at PRETEST $= 37$ is likely to be more accurate. Because it is closer to the mean of the PRETEST scores, it has a smaller leverage and therefore a smaller standard error.

(e) To find the .95 CI for the FINAL score of a single student with PRETEST score $= 24$, we need the appropriate standard error given by

$$s_e\sqrt{1 + \frac{1}{N} + \frac{(X - \overline{X})^2}{SS_X}} = 10.638\sqrt{1 + \frac{1}{18} + \frac{(24 - 32.378)^2}{159.60}} = 12.96$$

so the confidence interval is $49.02 \pm 27.48$.

**19.9** The null hypothesis that the population slopes are equal can be tested using the test statistic $t = (b_{1_M} - b_{1_F})/(SE(b_{1_M} - b_{1_F}))$, where $SE(b_{1_M} - b_{1_F})$ can be estimated by $s_e\sqrt{1/SS_{X_M} + 1/SS_{X_F}}$ (see Table 19.8). In general, $s_e^2$ is the weighted average of $s_{e_M}^2$ and $s_{e_F}^2$, here 194.55, so $s_e = 13.95$. Therefore, we test the null hypothesis using $t = (30.0 - 20.0)/(13.95\sqrt{1/200 + 1/200}) = 7.17$ with $N_M - 2 + N_F - 2 = 76$ df. We can reject the null hypothesis.

**19.11** If we regress TC on age for males, we get the following results:

Dep Var: TC  N: 220   Multiple $R$: 0.062   Squared multiple  $R$:  0.004
Adjusted squared multiple $R$: 0.000   Standard error of estimate: 38.286

| Effect | Coefficient | Std Error | Std Coef | Tolerance | t | p (2-tail) |
|---|---|---|---|---|---|---|
| CONSTANT | 211.906 | 11.249 | 0.000 | . | 18.837 | 0.000 |
| AGE | 0.198 | 0.218 | 0.062 | 1.000 | 0.912 | 0.363 |

```
Analysis of Variance
```

| Source | Sum of Squares | df | Mean Square | F Ratio | p |
|---|---|---|---|---|---|
| Regression | 1218.673 | 1 | 1218.673 | 0.831 | 0.363 |
| Residual | 319540.841 | 218 | 1465.784 | | |

```
*** WARNING ***
Case            409 is an outlier        (Studentized Residual =      4.362)
Durbin—Watson D Statistic      2.011
First-order Autocorrelation   −0.018
```

The slope is not significant; $t(218) = 0.912$, $p = .363$. To check assumptions, we begin by noting that the residual plot does not show any obvious nonlinearity, although there is perhaps a tendency for the lower estimates to have larger residuals, indicating a possible problem with homogeneity of variance. If we use a weighted least-squares regression, as described in Section 19.5.3, we get the results that are not greatly different from those obtained in the original analysis.

| Effect | Coefficient | Std Error | t | p (2-tail) |
|---|---|---|---|---|
| CONSTANT | 212.89 | 12.27 | 17.36 | 0.000 |
| AGE | 0.180 | 0.22 | 0.81 | 0.42 |

We can check for nonlinearity by first conducting an ANOVA in which age is the independent variable. We obtain the following output:

```
Dep Var: TC    N: 220    Multiple R: 0.461    Squared multiple R: 0.212
Analysis of Variance
```

| Source | Sum of Squares | df | Mean Square | F Ratio | p |
|---|---|---|---|---|---|
| AGE | 68150.767 | 46 | 1481.538 | 1.015 | 0.457 |
| Error | 252608.747 | 173 | 1460.166 | | |

$SS_{\text{nonlinearity}} = SS_{\text{residual}} - SS_{\text{error}} = 319{,}540.841 - 252{,}608.094 = 66{,}932.094$ with 45 $df$. So we test the null hypothesis of no nonlinearity using $F(45, 173) = MS_{\text{nonlinearity}}/MS_{\text{error}} = (66932.094/45)/1460.166 = 1.019$, so there is no significant nonlinearity.

The Durbin–Watson test does not show any evidence of serial correlation; $D$ is close to 2 and $r$ is only $-.018$. SYSTAT identifies the case with ID = 686 as an outlier, having an externally Studentized residual of 4.362. This score comes from a 32-year-old male with very high cholesterol readings (all seasonal TC levels at least 358). But even this case is not extremely influential. Cook's distance is .137—much less than $F_{.50}(2{,}218) = .695$. Redoing the regression omitting this case results in a slope of 0.294, which is higher than but not greatly different from the original value.

There is some modest nonnormality. Plots of the residual indicate somewhat heavy tails and a slight positive skew. The kurtosis = 1.485 and skewness = .616. Finally, when we tried out several types of robust regression, the obtained results were not very different from those in the original regression. We therefore conclude that the assumption for the original least-squares regression were reasonably well satisfied.

# CHAPTER 20

**20.1** (a)

| Pearson correlation matrix | | | |
|---|---|---|---|
| | TIME | NUMBER | DIFF |
| TIME | 1.000 | | |
| NUMBER | 0.756 | 1.000 | |
| DIFF | 0.339 | 0.000 | 1.000 |

| NUMBER | 2 | 2 | 4 | 4 | 6 | 6 | 8 | 8 |
|---|---|---|---|---|---|---|---|---|
| DIFF | 10 | 20 | 10 | 20 | 10 | 20 | 10 | 20 |
| Mean | 493.33 | 532.00 | 545.67 | 583.33 | 584.33 | 646.67 | 625.67 | 670.00 |
| SD | 10.50 | 35.68 | 62.96 | 40.53 | 30.37 | 44.74 | 70.54 | 40.04 |

(b) In the regression, the effects of both Number and Diff are significant, $t(21) = 6.192$, $p = .000$ and $t(21) = 2.775$, $p = .011$, respectively. If an ANOVA is conducted, we find significant main effects for both Number and Diff, $F(3, 16) = 10.216$, $p = .001$ and $F(1, 16) = 6.091$, $p = .025$, respectively. The results of the regression are not equivalent to that of an ANOVA. The regression treats the predictors as quantitative variables and tests whether the rate of change of time with one of the variables is different from zero in the population, holding the other variable constant. In the ANOVA, the test of the number main effect addresses the question of whether the population means for the different levels of number are all the same.

(c) The regression yields estimates of 402.375, 22.825, and 4.575 for $\beta_0$, $\beta_1$, and $\beta_2$. The 95% confidence intervals are 335.99 − 468.76, 15.16 − 30.49, and 1.157 − 8.00. The 99% confidence intervals are 312.01 − 492.75, 12.39 − 33.27, and − 0.09 − 9.25.

**20.3** (a) Regressing $Y$ on $X_1$ and $X_2$ yields the regression equation $\hat{Y} = -16.294 + 9.196X_1 + 9.941X_2$.

(b) The ANOVA table for the regression indicates that $SS_{residual} = 1030.745$ with 14 $df$. Next, to obtain $SS_{pure\ error}$, we perform an ANOVA, using $X_1$ and $X_2$ as factors. The error term of the ANOVA is $SS_{pure\ error} = 937.417$ with 10 $df$. Therefore, $SS_{nonlinearity} = 1030.745 - 937.417 = 93.328$ with 4 $df$. $F = MS_{nonlinearity}/MS_{pure\ error} = .249$, so there is no significant departure from linearity.

(c) In the initial regression, the coefficients of $X_1$ and $X_2$ both differ significantly from zero, $t(14) = 2.420$, $p = .030$ and $t(14) = 3.378$, $p = .005$, respectively. Therefore, both variables should be included.

**20.5** (a) For the data set, a standard ANOVA yields:

| SV | df | SS | MS | F | p |
|---|---|---|---|---|---|
| Dosage (D) | 3 | 132.306 | 44.102 | 7.290 | .003 |
| Error (S/D) | 15 | 90.740 | 6.049 | | |

(b) A trend analysis yields:

| SV | df | SS | MS | F | p |
|---|---|---|---|---|---|
| Dosage (D) | 3 | 132.306 | 44.102 | 7.290 | .003 |
| Linear | 1 | 62.110 | 62.110 | 10.268 | <.01 |
| Quadratic | 1 | 65.375 | 65.375 | 10.808 | <.01 |
| Cubic | 1 | 4.821 | 4.821 | 0.797 | ns |
| Error (S/D) | 15 | 90.740 | 6.049 | | |

(c) The best-fitting quadratic equation is $\hat{Y} = -4.714 + 1.122X - 0.019X^2$.

**20.7** (a) When individual bivariate regressions are performed, student background and parent background are both significant. However, the background measures are highly correlated, and if both measures are included as predictors, the student background measure remains significant, but the parental background measure does not. Also, although the teacher quality does not predict significantly by itself, it adds significantly to predictability if either student or parental background is included.

(b) Here, the stepwise regression enters student background on the first step and teacher quality on the second. Although these seem like useful predictors, the predictor variables that are first selected in a stepwise regression need not be the ones that are important in an explanatory model.

(c) There are no significant interactions between either of the background measures and either of the quality measures.

**20.9** If including $X_4$ in the regression equation results in $R^2$ increasing from .21 to .27, then $\Delta R^2 = .06$ and $f^2 = .06/(1 - .27) = .082$. To test whether the increment in predictability afforded by the addition of $X_4$ is significant, we form the partial $F$ ratio

$$F = \frac{\left(R^2_{Y.1234} - R^2_{Y.123}\right)/1}{\left(1 - R^2_{Y.1234}\right)/(N - p - 1)} = \frac{.06}{(1 - .27)/35} = 2.877$$

The obtained $F$ is less than the critical $F_{.05, \, 1, \, 35}$ of 4.121. To determine the $N$ necessary to have a power of .80 for the test of $X_4$, we try out several values for $N$, finding the noncentrality parameter and critical $F$ value for each, then use a noncentral $F$ calculator to determine the power. For $N = 101$, $N^* = 98$, the noncentrality parameter $\lambda$ is 8.036, and the critical value of $F$ (with 1 and 96 $df$) is 3.940. This yields estimated power of .801, approximately the desired value.

**20.11**   The ANOVA table is as follows:

| SV | df | SS | MS | F | p |
|---|---|---|---|---|---|
| Grade | 7 | 10,040.060 | 1434.294 | 17.491 | .000 |
| Linear | 1 | 5,668.646 | 5,668.646 | 69.128 | .000 |
| Quadratic | 1 | 2,170.851 | 2,170.851 | 26.473 | .000 |
| Cubic | 1 | 684.947 | 684.947 | 8.351 | .002 |
| Other nonlinear | 4 | 1,515.516 | 378.879 | 4.620 | .003 |
| Error | 185 | 15,170.367 | 82.002 | | |

There are highly significant linear, quadratic, and cubic components. There is a significant linear component—the best-fitting straight line has a slope other than zero. There are also significant tendencies to level off and possibly decrease as grade increases, then to increase again. Some of the other bumps in the curve are probably due to other than chance variation, because the remaining nonlinearity is significant.

# CHAPTER 21

**21.1**   (a)  We can create a gender variable with levels, say, 1 for men and 0 for women. If we correlate gender with the dependent variable, we find $r(14) = -.509$, $p = .044$.

   (b)  We find that there is a significant effect of gender; $t(14) = 2.210$, $p = .044$. As we noted in Section 18.5.1, the test of the point-biserial correlation is equivalent to an independent-groups $t$ test.

   (c)  Because it has only two levels, we only need a single dummy variable to code for gender. If men and women were assigned values of 1 and $-1$, we would have effect coding; if the values were 1 and 0, we would have dummy coding.

   (d)  For effect coding, we find the output:

Dep Var: Y   N: 16  Multiple R: 0.509  Squared multiple R: 0.259
Adjusted squared multiple R: 0.206    Standard error of estimate: 5.769

| Effect | Coefficient | Std Error | Std Coef | Tolerance | t | p (2-tail) |
|---|---|---|---|---|---|---|
| CONSTANT | 28.187 | 1.442 | 0.000 | . | 19.545 | 0.000 |
| EFFECT | −3.188 | 1.442 | −0.509 | 1.000 | −2.210 | 0.044 |

Analysis of Variance

| Source | Sum of Squares | df | Mean Square | F Ratio | p |
|---|---|---|---|---|---|
| Regression | 162.563 | 1 | 162.563 | 4.885 | 0.044 |
| Residual | 465.875 | 14 | 33.277 | | |

and for dummy coding, we obtain:

---

Dep Var: Y   N: 16   Multiple $R$: 0.509   Squared multiple $R$: 0.259
Adjusted squared multiple $R$: 0.206     Standard error of estimate: 5.769

| Effect | Coefficient | Std Error | Std Coef | Tolerance | t | p (2-tail) |
|--------|-------------|-----------|----------|-----------|---|------------|
| CONSTANT | 31.375 | 2.040 | 0.000 | . | 15.384 | 0.000 |
| DUMMY | −6.375 | 2.884 | −0.509 | 1.000 | −2.210 | 0.044 |

Analysis of Variance

| Source | Sum of Squares | df | Mean Square | F Ratio | p |
|--------|----------------|-----|-------------|---------|---|
| Regression | 162.563 | 1 | 162.563 | 4.885 | 0.044 |
| Residual | 465.875 | 14 | 33.277 | | |

---

Note that the ANOVA tables are the same for both analyses; in both cases the gender variable accounts for all the variability in the means. However, the slope coefficients are not the same. The coefficient of EFFECT in the first analysis, −3.188, indicates that the mean for men is 3.188 units less than the average of the male and female means, whereas the coefficient of DUMMY in the second analysis, −6.375, indicates that the mean of the male scores is 6.375 units less than the mean of the female scores.

**21.3**   (a) With three levels of the factor, we would need two dummy variables.
(b) The coding is as follows:

| | Effect Coding | | Dummy Coding | |
|---|---|---|---|---|
| Y | E1 | E2 | D1 | D2 |
| 17 | 1 | 0 | 1 | 0 |
| 33 | 1 | 0 | 1 | 0 |
| 26 | 1 | 0 | 1 | 0 |
| 27 | 1 | 0 | 1 | 0 |
| 21 | 1 | 0 | 1 | 0 |
| 11 | 0 | 1 | 0 | 1 |
| 18 | 0 | 1 | 0 | 1 |
| 14 | 0 | 1 | 0 | 1 |
| 18 | 0 | 1 | 0 | 1 |
| 9 | −1 | −1 | 0 | 0 |
| 12 | −1 | −1 | 0 | 0 |
| 10 | −1 | −1 | 0 | 0 |
| 8 | −1 | −1 | 0 | 0 |
| 14 | −1 | −1 | 0 | 0 |

(c) (i) For effect coding, the regression output is:

```
Dep Var: Y   N: 14  Multiple R: 0.846    Squared multiple    R: 0.716
Adjusted squared multiple R: 0.664    Standard error of estimate: 4.335
```

| Effect | Coefficient | Std Error | Std Coef | Tolerance | t | p (2-tail) |
|---|---|---|---|---|---|---|
| CONSTANT | 16.883 | 1.165 | 0.000 | . | 14.491 | 0.000 |
| E1 | 7.917 | 1.616 | 0.928 | 0.720 | 4.900 | 0.000 |
| E2 | −1.633 | 1.710 | −0.181 | 0.720 | −0.955 | 0.360 |

Analysis of Variance

| Source | Sum of Squares | df | Mean Square | F Ratio | p |
|---|---|---|---|---|---|
| Regression | 521.250 | 2 | 260.625 | 13.866 | 0.001 |
| Residual | 206.750 | 11 | 18.795 | | |

(ii) For dummy coding, the regression output is:

```
Dep Var: Y   N: 14  Multiple R: 0.846  Squared multiple R: 0.716
Adjusted squared multiple R: 0.664    Standard error of estimate: 4.335
```

| Effect | Coefficient | Std Error | Std Coef | Tolerance | t | p (2-tail) |
|---|---|---|---|---|---|---|
| CONSTANT | 10.600 | 1.939 | 0.000 | . | 5.467 | 0.000 |
| D1 | 14.200 | 2.742 | 0.944 | 0.778 | 5.179 | 0.000 |
| D2 | 4.650 | 2.908 | 0.291 | 0.778 | 1.599 | 0.138 |

Analysis of Variance

| Source | Sum of Squares | df | Mean Square | F Ratio | p |
|---|---|---|---|---|---|
| Regression | 521.250 | 2 | 260.625 | 13.866 | 0.001 |
| Residual | 206.750 | 11 | 18.795 | | |

Note that the ANOVA tables are exactly the same for the two regressions.

(d) The interpretation of the coefficients for the regression on the effect coding variables are $b_0 = (\overline{Y}_{\cdot 1} + \overline{Y}_{\cdot 2} + \overline{Y}_{\cdot 3})/(3)$; $b_1 = \overline{Y}_{\cdot 1} - b_0$; and $b_2 = \overline{Y}_{\cdot 2} - b_0$. For the regression on the dummy coding variables, if the reference group, i.e., the group coded by 0's by both variables is Group 3, the coefficients are:

$$b_0 = \overline{Y}_{\cdot 3}; b_1 = \overline{Y}_{\cdot 1} - \overline{Y}_{\cdot 3}; \quad \text{and} \quad b_2 = \overline{Y}_{\cdot 2} - \overline{Y}_{\cdot 3}.$$

**21.5** (a) The ANOVA output (using SYSTAT) is:

```
Dep Var: Y   N: 30  Multiple R: 0.696  Squared multiple R: 0.484
Analysis of Variance
```

| Source | Sum of Squares | df | Mean Square | F Ratio | p |
|--------|----------------|-----|-------------|---------|-----|
| A      | 227.031        | 1   | 227.031     | 3.566   | 0.071 |
| B      | 1019.342       | 2   | 509.671     | 8.004   | 0.002 |
| A*B    | 104.836        | 2   | 52.418      | 0.823   | 0.451 |
| Error  | 1528.167       | 24  | 63.674      |         |     |

(b) We would need five dummy variables to code the design: one for $A$, two for $B$, and two for the $A \times B$ interaction. The effect coding is presented here:

| Y | A $X_1$ | B $X_2$ | $X_3$ | A × B $X_4$ | $X_5$ |
|----|----|----|----|----|----|
| 72 | 1 | 1 | 0 | 1 | 0 |
| 63 | 1 | 1 | 0 | 1 | 0 |
| 57 | 1 | 1 | 0 | 1 | 0 |
| 52 | 1 | 1 | 0 | 1 | 0 |
| 69 | 1 | 1 | 0 | 1 | 0 |
| 75 | 1 | 1 | 0 | 1 | 0 |
| 49 | 1 | 0 | 1 | 0 | 1 |
| 71 | 1 | 0 | 1 | 0 | 1 |
| 63 | 1 | 0 | 1 | 0 | 1 |
| 48 | 1 | 0 | 1 | 0 | 1 |
| 40 | 1 | −1 | −1 | −1 | −1 |
| 49 | 1 | −1 | −1 | −1 | −1 |
| 36 | 1 | −1 | −1 | −1 | −1 |
| 50 | 1 | −1 | −1 | −1 | −1 |
| 54 | 1 | −1 | −1 | −1 | −1 |
| 65 | −1 | 1 | 0 | −1 | 0 |
| 45 | −1 | 1 | 0 | −1 | 0 |
| 52 | −1 | 1 | 0 | −1 | 0 |
| 53 | −1 | 1 | 0 | −1 | 0 |
| 57 | −1 | 1 | 0 | −1 | 0 |
| 56 | −1 | 0 | 1 | 0 | −1 |
| 55 | −1 | 0 | 1 | 0 | −1 |
| 49 | −1 | 0 | 1 | 0 | −1 |
| 52 | −1 | 0 | 1 | 0 | −1 |
| 45 | −1 | 0 | 1 | 0 | −1 |
| 57 | −1 | 0 | 1 | 0 | −1 |
| 41 | −1 | −1 | −1 | 1 | 1 |
| 42 | −1 | −1 | −1 | 1 | 1 |
| 57 | −1 | −1 | −1 | 1 | 1 |
| 39 | −1 | −1 | −1 | 1 | 1 |

(c) The correlation matrix for the dummy variables is:

| | Pearson Correlation Matrix | | | | |
|---|---|---|---|---|---|
| | $X_1$ | $X_2$ | $X_3$ | $X_4$ | $X_5$ |
| $X_1$ | 1.000 | | | | |
| $X_2$ | 0.000 | 1.000 | | | |
| $X_3$ | −0.126 | 0.460 | 1.000 | | |
| $X_4$ | 0.082 | 0.100 | 0.051 | 1.000 | |
| $X_5$ | 0.042 | 0.062 | −0.048 | 0.465 | 1.000 |

Yes, the dummy variables are correlated with one another. However, the variables belonging to different effects would not be correlated if the design was orthogonal (had an equal number of scores in each cell).

(d) In this case, we would want to test hypotheses about unweighted means, i.e.,

$$H_{0_A}: \mu_1. = \mu_2.$$

where

$$\mu_1. = \frac{\mu_{11} + \mu_{12} + \mu_{13}}{3}$$

$$H_{0_B}: \mu._1 = \mu._2 = \mu._3$$

where

$$\mu._1 = \frac{\mu_{11} + \mu_{21}}{2}$$

and $H_{0_{AB}}: \mu_{jk} - \mu_j. - \mu._k - \mu.. = 0$ for all $j, k$. We could test the first of these hypotheses by finding $SS_{A|B,AB} = (R^2_{Y \cdot A,B,AB} - R^2_{Y \cdot B,AB})SS_Y$, then use

$$F = \frac{(R^2_{Y \cdot A,B,AB} - R^2_{Y \cdot B,AB})SS_Y / df_A}{(1 - R^2_{Y \cdot A,B,AB})SS_Y / df_{\text{error}}}.$$

Here, this is

$$F_A = \frac{(1433.20 - 1206.17)/1}{1528.17/24} = 3.56, \quad p = .071$$

$$F_B = \frac{(1433.20 - 413.86)/2}{1528.17/24} = 8.00, \quad p = .002$$

and

$$F_{AB} = \frac{52.42}{63.67} = 0.82, \quad p = .451.$$

The results are identical to those of the standard ANOVA using Type III $SS$.

(e) If we regress only on $X_1$, we get $F = MS_A / MS_{\text{error}} = (229.63)/(2731.73/28) = 2.354$, $p = .136$. This a test of the hypothesis $\mu_{1*} = \mu_{2*}$ where

$$\mu_{1*} = \frac{n_{11}\mu_{11} + n_{12}\mu_{12} + n_{13}\mu_{13}}{n_{11} + n_{12} + n_{13}} \quad \text{and} \quad \mu_{2*} = \frac{n_{21}\mu_{21} + n_{22}\mu_{22} + n_{23}\mu_{23}}{n_{21} + n_{22} + n_{23}}$$

are weighted means. The same result may be obtained by performing an ANOVA, but only including $X_1$ as a factor.

**21.7**  To test for homogeneity of slope, find:

$$F = \frac{(R^2_{Y \cdot X, X_1, X_2, X_3, X_4, X_5} - R^2_{Y \cdot X, X_1, X_2, X_3})/2}{(1 - R^2_{Y \cdot X, X_1, X_2, X_3, X_4, X_5})/30} = \frac{(.7121 - .6882)/2}{(1 - .7121)/30} = 1.246$$

We cannot reject the hypothesis that the population regression slopes are the same.

# Endnotes

## FOOTNOTES TO CHAPTER 2

1. The normal distribution is referred to as the *Gaussian* distribution in many articles and books. This name refers to the mathematician and statistician, K. F. Gauss, and reflects the fact that normal distributions are not very normal; that is, they are not commonly observed with real data.
2. Percent correct and response time scores for students in Grades 1–8 in the Royer study are available on the CD accompanying this book. Students are classified by gender and grade, and scores are available for several skills, including addition, subtraction, and multiplication. Table 2.1 contains values that have been rounded to the nearest integer value, and the statistics and graphs we present for the second-grade addition accuracy are based on these integer values.
3. These data are available on the accompanying CD in the *Seasons* folder.
4. The means are averages of the four seasonal depression scores and were calculated only for those participants who had been tested in all four sessions. The absence of a bar for participants in category 4 indicates not that there were no women in that category but only that there were no women for whom four scores were available.

## FOOTNOTES TO CHAPTER 3

1. The mean of the absolute errors, $\sum |Y_i - \hat{Y}_i|/N$, also has the value 0 only if prediction is perfect, and it has the additional virtue of being more resistant to outliers than the mean of the squared errors. However, it is not as easy to work with mathematically.
2. Note that whenever the prediction of $Y$ from $X$ is not perfect, the predicted $Y$ will always be fewer standard deviations away from the mean of the $Y$ scores than $X$ is from the mean of the $X$ scores. We have more to say about this phenomenon of "regression toward the mean" in Chapter 19. Here we merely note that the prediction equations discussed in this chapter are referred to as "regression" equations in recognition of these regression effects.
3. Because $r$ is symmetric in $X$ and $Y$, $r^2$ is also the proportion of the variability in $X$ accounted for by $Y$.

## FOOTNOTES TO CHAPTER 4

1. The actual experiment was a bit more complicated than described here. Chen and Myers included a control group and the teenagers were tested on more than one trial. The results suggest that the teenagers retained some memory for the objects they had seen more than a decade earlier. They chose previously presented objects significantly more often than would be expected by chance, and significantly more often than a control group that had not been in the earlier experiment.

## FOOTNOTES TO CHAPTER 5

1. The central limit theorem states that the sampling distribution of a variable of the general form $L = w_1 Y_1 + w_2 Y_2 + \cdots + w_N Y_N$ will approach normality as $N$ increases. The $Y_i$ are random variables, but each of the $w_i$ is constant across samples. If the $w_i$ all equal 1, $L$ is the sum of scores in the sample, and if the $w_i$ all equal $1/n$, $L$ is the mean of the sample. In general, we refer to variables of the form of $L$ as **linear combinations**. Appendix 5.1 contains more information about linear combinations, including expressions for their means and variances.
2. Technically, $\hat{\theta}$ is a consistent estimate of $\theta$ if the probability that $|\theta - \hat{\theta}|$ is less than an arbitrarily chosen small value approaches 1 as $N$ increases.
3. As noted earlier, because $N$ is large, the results based on the normal distribution are quite similar to those based on the $t$ distribution; the confidence limits using the $t$ distribution are 218.64 and 230.14. Generally, we base inferences about population means on the $t$ distribution because we usually do not know the value of $\sigma$.
4. As we show in Appendix 5.1, the variance of the difference of two dependent means equals the sum of the variances of the two means minus twice their covariance (see Chapter 3 for a definition of covariance). If we treat the means as independent when they are not, we fail to subtract the covariance from our measure of variability, and therefore have too large an estimate of the $SE$ of the difference of the means.
5. We do not wish to suggest that the true population distribution looks exactly like the sample distribution; samples are not miniature replicas of populations. However, in this instance, the sample provided a convenient way of conceptualizing a nonnormal distribution that is similar to data distributions that have been examined in several studies.
6. Because of sampling error inherent in drawing a finite number of samples, we do not expect a perfect match to the theoretical value of .95.

## FOOTNOTES TO CHAPTER 6

1. There have been a number of expressions for effect size, and various notations have been used (e.g., Cohen, 1988; Glass, 1976; Hedges, 1981). The $E_s$ of Equation 6.4 is an estimate of Cohen's $d$, essentially $\hat{d}$.
2. A listing of available software packages that compute power may be found at http://sustain.forestry.ubc.ca/cacb/power. A review of the packages (as of 1997) may be found at http://sustain.forestry.ubc.ca/cacb/review/powrev.html.
3. When "Other $t$ Tests" is selected in GPOWER, the label for effect size is "$f$" and the listed sample size conventions are those for $f$. However, we should ignore this. When calculating power for matched-group or single-group $t$ tests, insert the value of $E_s$ (Cohen's $d$) for effect size and use the effect size conventions for $d$. The index $f$ is another of Cohen's effect size measures, defined as $\sigma_m / \sigma$ where $\sigma_m$ is the standard deviation of the group means and $\sigma$ is the within-group standard deviation. When there are two groups, $d = 2f$.

# FOOTNOTES TO CHAPTER 8

1. The researchers found that the relative performances of the three groups depended significantly on the type of problem, with the HE group performing better than the other two groups on story problems but worse on formula problems. We refer to this as a significant interaction and discuss this concept in Chapter 11.

2. The studentized residual is the deviation of the score from its group mean divided by a measure of error variability from which the score has been deleted. Note that the outliers found by this procedure are not the same ones found in the box plot. Those are based on a different definition of outliers (see Chapter 2).

3. Gatti and Harwell (1998) provide a detailed comparison of the results of charts and computer program calculations, and they illustrate the use of SAS in calculating power. SAS takes the same inputs as the UCLA calculator, whose use is illustrated in Table 8.10.

4. We must be cautious because some of the options provided by the programs overestimate power. We will get overestimates if we select the observed (i.e., post hoc) power option in the SPSS General Linear Model Univariate module, or if we provide observed sample means and an estimate of the within-group standard deviation to GPOWER or the power module of SYSTAT instead of providing $f$ or $f^2$ ourselves. The reason for this is that the programs treat all the variation in sample means as though it was due to variation in the population means. The estimate of the component of variation in the group means that occurs because of random variability is not subtracted. This results in the noncentrality parameter being estimated as $\hat{\lambda} = (a - 1)MS_A/MS_{S/A} = (a - 1)F$ instead of as $\hat{\lambda} = (a - 1)(MS_A - MS_{S/A})/MS_{S/A} = (a - 1)(F - 1)$, the estimate we provide in Table 8.9.

5. Vargha and Delaney (1998) note that if the distributions of the ranks have equal variance (a weaker condition than homogeneity of variance of the original scores), $H$ and $F_R$ test the null hypothesis that the expected values of the ranks are the same for the $a$ treatments. This hypothesis is equivalent to one in which for every pair of treatments, the probability is .5 that a randomly chosen score under one treatment exceeds a randomly chosen score under the other treatment.

# FOOTNOTES TO CHAPTER 9

1. A review of the sections of Chapter 6 that deal with contrasts may be helpful. It includes material on CIs and standardized effect sizes.

2. We could conduct only two tests, a $t$ test contrasting the fifth graders against the average of the other three grades, and an $F$ test of the equality of the remaining three group means. However, if the $F$ was significant, we might still wish to carry out pairwise comparisons within the set of three means to determine the possible source of the significant $F$.

3. A possible sequential test alternative in the face of unequal variances would be to use the Welch test or the Brown–Forsythe test of the omnibus null hypothesis in the first stage (Brown & Forsythe, 1974b; Welch, 1951). If that proves significant, pairwise contrasts could be tested by the Games–Howell or the Dunnett T3 method, using a critical value based on $a - 1$, rather than $a$, means. Because of a lack of information of the properties of this method, it cannot be recommended. However, investigation of its FWE and power might prove fruitful.

# FOOTNOTES TO CHAPTER 11

1. The $E$/web plot contains no median line or "whiskers" because all scores are either 60 or 80, and the median is at 80, the value of the upper hinge and the highest score.

2. Because the two independent variables are qualitative, a bar graph is appropriate. However, we have used a line graph here so that the parallelism of the text and web means is more clearly displayed.

3. If there were more than two formats, we could test for equality of the contrast of the four types of instructions across the three formats. However, the calculations are somewhat different from those we present here, and the associated degree of freedom would be $a - 1$, where $a$ is the number of formats, because we are calculating the variance of $a$ contrasts. We believe that tests of simple differences between two contrasts are most useful, and therefore we focus on these. Readers interested in the general analysis may consult Myers (1959, 1979).

4. Several individuals (e.g., Marascuilo & Levin, 1970; Rosnow & Rosenthal, 1989, 1991, 1995) have argued that when the interaction is significant, tests should be performed not on the simple effects of each factor but on interaction effects; for example, those in the four cells defined by the crossing of the $A$ and $N$ instructions with the web and format conditions. In contrast, Tukey (1991) gave equal "first class" status to comparisons of simple effects and "cross comparisons" of interaction effects (p. 112). We have taken this approach.

## FOOTNOTES TO CHAPTER 13

1. We will never observe perfect sphericity in a real data set, but, to make some points more clearly, we have eliminated error from these "data."

2. The design actually involved four within-subject variables. The original photos were of 4 men and 4 women. Therefore, gender was a third within-subject variable, and photos-within-gender (or items) was a fourth variable.

3. Some programs (e.g., SYSTAT 10) do not correct for ties. This will lead to an underestimate of the $\chi^2$.

4. The actual comparisons in the cited articles involved $F_F$, a function of $\chi_F^2$, which is somewhat more powerful and has the $F$ distribution under the null hypothesis. However, because statistical software packages report values of $\chi_F^2$, and it will have similar properties to $F_F$, we continue to refer to the chi-square statistic.

## FOOTNOTES TO CHAPTER 14

1. It may be counterintuitive that, with increased degrees of freedom and the same effect size, power for the test of the interaction is less than that for the $A$ main effect. Comparing the equations for $\hat{f}$ in Table 14.7, note that because here $b > 2$, $(a - 1)(b - 1) > a - 1$, so that $F_{AB}$ must be less than $F_A$ to maintain the same value of $f$. The distance between the noncentral and central $F$ distributions is smaller, and therefore power is less, for the $AB$ source. Another way to view the problem is to note that, in Equation 14.10, if $f$ is held constant, then $\phi$ decreases as the degrees of freedom increase.

2. Most statistical packages have the option of providing these results as part of the output of an analysis of the original data, avoiding the necessity of obtaining contrast scores. Although that is the procedure we recommend, we present the trend analysis in terms of an analysis of contrast scores to emphasize that what is being done is essentially a between-subjects analysis in which the "scores" for each subject reflect the polynomial component of the subject's curve.

## FOOTNOTES TO CHAPTER 15

1. Whether blocks selected in the manner described should be viewed as a fixed- or random-effects variable is open to debate. We have chosen to treat them as fixed in their effects. This has two

implications: first, generalizations should be restricted to levels of ability defined by the blocks in the experiment. Second, the error term is the within-cells mean square, whereas, if blocks are viewed as having random effects, the appropriate error term is the Blocks × Treatment interaction mean square.

2. We made up the scores on the quantitative reasoning variable by first generating scores that correlated approximately .6 with the dependent variable in each of the text conditions, and then scaling them so that the overall mean of the quantitative reasoning scores was approximately 63 and the standard deviation was approximately 15 in each of the groups.

3. To use GPOWER to calculate the post hoc power for an ANCOVA, we select $F$ Test (ANOVA) and specify that we have a "Special" hypothesis (this simply tells GPOWER that the $df_e$ is not $N - a$, and will have to be calculated on the basis of other information). We insert a value for $f$ (here .354), Alpha (here .05), total sample size (48), and numerator degrees of freedom (here 2). In order to have the correct $df_e$, we insert for groups the number of cells in the design plus the number of covariates (here $3 + 1 = 4$). When we click on "Calculate," we get post hoc power $= .55$. If we request a priori power and specify Power $= .80$, we get $N = 80$; we need about 27 subjects per condition to achieve the desired power.

## FOOTNOTES TO CHAPTER 16

1. Although this example is patterned after the experiment by Stasson et al. (1991), it simplifies their design considerably. They had several hundred subjects, included a no-concensus and an individual condition, and a first phase in which they obtained a baseline (or pretest) score from individuals prior to group training. The satisfaction means in their study were 14.02 for the majority condition and 13.03 for the unanimity condition.

2. We have not included the $\sigma^2_{SB/AC}$ component in the EMS because it contributes to every term.

## FOOTNOTES TO CHAPTER 17

1. The Latin square design can be used with different subjects in each cell; this application of the Latin square is discussed in several sources (e.g., Kirk, 1995; Myers, 1979; Myers & Well, 1995). However, in our experience, the great majority of examples of application of the Latin square principle involve repeated measures, and we have chosen to focus exclusively on such examples in this edition.

2. Note that all we really need from the second analysis is $SS_C$ (or $SS_A$ if $C$ was the within-subjects factor in the first analysis). Therefore, there is no need to do a complete second analysis, although if a file is set up and a statistical package is used for analysis, this will be the easiest procedure.

3. The within-cell sum of squares is distributed on $a^2(n - 1)$ $df$. Subtracting $a(n - 1)$ $df$ for the $S/G$ sum of squares leaves a within-cell residual distributed on $a(n - 1)(a - 1)$ $df$. Equivalently, this may be thought of as the within-subjects residual.

## FOOTNOTES TO CHAPTER 18

1. Different power programs may produce slightly different answers. For example, for power calculations for tests of the hypothesis $H_0$: $\rho = 0$, the SYSTAT power module (newly introduced with version 10) uses tests based on the Fisher $Z$ transform (see Subsection 18.3.3) instead of the $t$ and produces a power estimate of .928, instead of the value of .964 obtained by using the $t$.

2. We should emphasize that, depending on the context, even small correlations may be important. See the example in Subsection 18.5.1.
3. Strictly speaking, the $Z$ transformation is biased by an amount $r/2(N-1)$; see Pearson and Hartley (1954, p. 29). This bias will generally be negligible unless $N$ is small and $\rho$ is large, and we ignore it here.
4. As we see in Chapter 21, this general idea can be extended to categorical variables that have more than two levels; in that case, more than a single quantitative variable is required to accomplish the coding. In general, a categorical variable with $a$ levels can be coded in terms of $a - 1$ numerical "indicator" or "dummy" variables.
5. Details of the tests are available at ftp://ftp.spss.com/pub/spss/statistics/spss/algorithms/, as is information about all the algorithms used by SPSS. Look for npcorr.pdf.

## FOOTNOTES TO CHAPTER 19

1. If the assumptions of linearity, homoscedasticity, and independence are satisfied, the Gauss–Markov theorem shows that the least-squares estimators are the most efficient (i.e., have the smallest sampling variance); that is, they are the best linear unbiased estimators (often given the acronym BLUE). If one adds the assumption of normality, it can be shown that the least-squares estimators are the most efficient of all unbiased estimators. In some applications, such as ridge regression (see, eg., Draper & Smith, 1998), it is desirable to choose estimators that have some bias but are more efficient than any of the unbiased estimators.
2. Unfortunately, both the standardized coefficients and the population parameters of the unstandardized coefficients are commonly referred to as "betas." We will be mostly concerned with unstandardized coefficients and will usually reserve the use of $\beta$ notation to refer to the population parameters.
3. Mittelhammer et al. (2000) offer a detailed discussion of the consequences of having random predictor variables. They also provide simulation programs in the GAUSS language that allow exploration of the properties of estimators, significance tests, and power functions with random predictors.
4. In drawing inferences from these data, keep in mind that the eligibility requirements of the study excluded people with extremely high cholesterol scores (Merriam et al., 1999). Specifically, the subjects were members of a large HMO who were between the ages of 20 and 70 years and were not receiving medication to lower lipids, were not on a lipid-lowering or weight-control diet, and did not have a secondary cause of hyperlipidemia or a history of cancer during the previous 5 years.
5. Note that if you request that leverages be saved in SPSS, you get "centered leverages," $h_{jj} - 1/N$.
6. Because $b_1$ and $b_0$ are both linear combinations of the $Y$ scores, we can think of their repeated-measures significance tests as analogous to those for repeated-measures contrasts. Any repeated-measures contrast can be tested by first obtaining a contrast score for each subject and then using the contrast score as the dependent variable in a subsequent analysis.

## FOOTNOTES TO CHAPTER 20

1. A BMI (i.e., weight in kilograms divided by the square of height in meters) of 40 corresponds to a weight of about 300 lb (135.9 kg) for an individual who is 6 ft (1.82m) tall.
2. Cohen's (1988) recommendation that $N^* = N - p + k$ represents a change from the 1977 edition of his power analysis book in which he used $N^* = df_{\text{residual}} = N - p - 1$. This latter value is consistent with the post hoc power analyses available in SPSS. However, GPOWER uses $N^* = N$.

3. If the coefficient of the product was positive, the partial slope of predicted $Y$ with one predictor would become larger as the value of the other predictor increased.

## FOOTNOTE TO CHAPTER 21

1. The term "dummy variables" refers to the variables that code a categorical variable by using any of the coding procedures. "Dummy coding" refers to a particular kind of coding procedure in which each dummy variable takes on the values 1 and 0 as described in the text.

## FOOTNOTES TO APPENDIX A

1. To conserve space, when we wish to indicate an index of summation in a line of text or a fraction, we will often write it as a subscript. The expression $\Sigma_i Y_i$, should be considered equivalent to

$$\sum_i Y_i.$$

2. In the design we used for an example, the mean of the first row would not be a quantity of interest, since we stipulated that the order within each column was arbitrary. There are designs, however, giving rise to tables like Table A.1 for which it is as interesting to obtain row means as it is to obtain column means.

# References

Achen, C. H. (1982). *Interpreting and using regression*. Beverly Hills, CA: Sage.

Alexander, R. A., & Govern, D. M. (1994). A new and simpler approach to ANOVA under variance heterogeneity. *Journal of Educational Statistics, 19*, 91–101.

Alf, E. F., & Graf, R. G. (1999). Asymptotic confidence limits for the difference between two squared multiple correlations: A simplified approach. *Psychological Methods, 4*, 70–75.

Algina, J., & Keselman, H. J. (1997). Detecting repeated measures effects with univariate and multivariate statistics. *Psychological Methods, 2*, 208–218.

Algina, J., & Keselman, H. J. (1999). Comparing squared multiple correlation coefficients: Examination of an interval and a test of significance. *Psychological Methods, 4*, 76–83.

American Psychological Association. (1994). *Publication manual of the American Psychological Association* (4th ed.). Washington, DC: Author.

Anderson, L. R., & Ager, J. W. (1978). Analysis of variance in small group research. *Personality & Social Psychology Bulletin, 4*, 341–345.

Anscombe, F. J. (1973). Graphs in statistical analysis. *American Statistician, 27*, 17–21.

Anscombe, F. J., & Tukey, J. W. (1963). The examination and analysis of residuals. *Technometrics, 5*, 141–160.

Appelbaum, M. I., & Cramer, E. M. (1974). Some problems in the nonorthogonal analysis of variance. *Psychological Bulletin, 81*, 335–343.

Atiqullah, M. (1964). The robustness of the covariance analysis of a one-way classification. *Biometrika, 51*, 365–373.

Balanda, K. P., & MacGillivray, H. L. (1988). Kurtosis: A critical review. *American Statistician, 42*, 111–119.

Bartlett, M. S. (1937). Properties of sufficiency and statistical tests. *Proceedings of the Royal Society, A, 160*, 268–282.

Belsley, D. A., Kuh, E., & Welsch, R. E. (1980). *Regression diagnostics*. New York: Wiley.

Bevan, M. F., Denton, J. Q., & Myers, J. L. (1974). The robustness of the $F$ test to violations of continuity and form of treatment populations. *British Journal of Mathematical and Statistical Psychology, 27*, 199–204.

Bishop, Y. M. M., Fienberg, S. E., & Holland, P. W. (1975). *Discrete multivariate analysis: Theory and practice*. Cambridge, MA: MIT Press.

Blair, R. C., & Higgins, J. J. (1980). A comparison of the power of Wilcoxon's rank-sum statistic to that of Student's *t* statistic under various non-normal distributions. *Journal of Educational Statistics, 5*, 309–335.

Blair, R. C., & Higgins, J. J. (1985). A comparison of the paired samples *t* test to that of Wilcoxon's signed-rank test under various population shapes. *Psychological Bulletin, 97*, 119–128.

Bless, H., Bohner, G., Schwarz, N., & Strack, F. (1990). Mood and persuasion: A cognitive response analysis. *Personality and Social Psychology Bulletin, 16*, 331–345.

Boik, R. J. (1981). A priori tests in repeated measures designs: Effects of nonsphericity. *Psychometrika, 46*, 241–255.

Bollen, K. A (1989). *Structural equations with latent variables*. New York: Wiley.

Bower, G. H. (1961). Application of a model to paired-associate learning. *Psychometrika, 26*, 255–280.

Box, G. E. P. (1954). Some theorems on quadratic forms in the study of analysis of variance problems: Effect of inequality of variance in the one-way classification. *Annals of Mathematical Statistics, 25*, 290–302.

Bozivich, H., Bancroft, T. A., & Hartley, H. O. (1956). Power of analysis of variance test procedures for certain incompletely specified models. *Annals of Mathematical Statistics, 27*, 1017–1043.

Brodbeck, F. C., & Greitemeyer, T. (2000). Effects of individual versus mixed individual and group experience in rule induction on group member learning and group performance. *Journal of Experimental Social Psychology, 36*, 621–648.

Brown, M. B., & Forsythe, A. B. (1974a). Robust tests for the equality of variances. *Journal of the American Statistical Association, 69*, 364–367.

Brown. M. B., & Forsythe, A. B. (1974b). The ANOVA and multiple comparisons for data with heterogeneous variances. *Biometrics, 30*, 719–724.

Bryk, A. S., & Raudenbush, S. W. (1992). *Hierarchical linear models: Applications and data analysis methods*. Newbury Park, CA: Sage.

Carlson, J. E., & Timm, N. H. (1974). Analysis of nonorthogonal fixed-effect designs. *Psychological Bulletin, 81*, 563–570.

Church, J. D., & Wike, E. L. (1976). The robustness of homogeneity of variance tests for asymmetric distributions: A Monte Carlo study. *Bulletin of the Psychonomic Society, 7*, 417–420.

Clark, H. H. (1973). The language-as-fixed-effect fallacy: A critique of language statistics in psychological research. *Journal of Verbal Learning and Verbal Behavior, 12*, 335–359.

Cleveland, W. (1979). Robust locally weighted regression and smoothing scatterplots. *Journal of the American Statistical Association, 78*, 158–161.

Clinch, J. J., & Keselman, H. J. (1982). Parametric alternatives to the analysis of variance. *Journal of Educational Statistics, 7*, 207–214.

Cochran, W. G. (1941). The distribution of the largest of a set of estimated variances as a fraction of their total. *Eugenics, 11*, 47–52.

Cochran, W. G. (1950). The comparison of percentages in matched samples. *Biometrika, 37*, 256–266.

Cochran, W. G., & Cox, G. M. (1957). *Experimental designs* (2nd ed.). New York: Wiley.

Cohen, J. (1977). *Statistical power analysis for the behavioral sciences* (rev. ed.). New York: Academic Press.

Cohen, J. (1988). *Statistical power analysis for the behavioral sciences* (2nd ed.). New York: Academic Press.

Cohen, J., & Cohen, P. (1983). *Applied multiple regression/correlation analysis for the behavioral sciences* (2nd ed.). Hillsdale, NJ: Lawrence Erlbaum Associates.

Conover, W. J., & Iman, R. L. (1981). Rank transformations as a bridge between parametric and nonparametric statistics. *The American Statistician, 35*, 124–129.

Cook, A. E., Myers, J. L., & O'Brien, E. J. (2000, November). *Processing an anaphor when there is no antecedent*. Poster presented at the meeting of the Psychonomic Society, New Orleans, LA.

Cook, R. D. (1977). Detection of influential observations in linear regression. *Technometrics, 19*, 15–18.

Cook, R. D., & Weisberg, S. (1982). *Residuals and influence in regression*. New York: Chapman and Hall.

Cook, R. D., & Weisberg, S. (1999). *Applied regression including computing and graphics*. New York: Wiley.

Coombs, W. T., Algina, J., & Oltman, D. O. (1996). Univariate and multivariate omnibus hypothesis tests selected to control type I error rates when population variances are not necessarily equal. *Review of Educational Research, 66*, 137–179.

Corbett, A. T., & Wicklegren, W. A. (1978). Semantic memory retrieval: Analysis by speed-accuracy tradeoff functions. *Quarterly Journal of Experimental Psychology, 30*, 1–15.

Cramer, E. M., & Appelbaum, M. I. (1980). Nonorthogonal analysis of variance—once again. *Psychological Bulletin, 87*, 51–57.

Cronbach, L. J., & Furby, L. (1970). How should we measure "change"—or should we? *Psychological Bulletin, 74*, 68–80.

Cumming, G., & Finch, S. (2001). A primer on the understanding, use, and calculation of confidence intervals that are based on central and noncentral distributions. *Educational and Psychological Measurement, 61*, 532–574.

D'Agostino, R. B., Belanger, A., & D'Agostino, R. B., Jr. (1990). A suggestion for using powerful and informative tests of normality. *The American Statistician, 44*, 316–321.

Dalton, S., & Overall, J. C. (1977). Nonrandom assignment in ANCOVA: The alternative ranks design. *The Journal of Experimental Education, 46*, 58–62.

Davenport, J. M., & Webster, J. T. (1973). A comparison of some approximate *F* tests. *Technometrics, 15*, 779–789.

Dawes, R. M. (1971). A case study of graduate admissions: Application of three principles of human decision making. *American Psychologist, 26*, 180–188.

DeCarlo, L. T. (1997). On the meaning and uses of kurtosis. *Psychological Methods, 2*, 292–307.

DeShon, R. P., & Alexander, R. A. (1996). Alternative procedures for testing regression slope homogeneity when group error variances are unequal. *Psychological Methods, 1*, 261–277.

Donaldson, T. S. (1968). Robustness of the *F* test to errors of both kinds and the correlation between the numerator and denominator of the *F* ratio. *Journal of the American Statistical Association, 63*, 660–676.

Draper, N. R., & Smith, H. (1998). *Applied regression analysis* (3rd ed). New York: Wiley.

Duncan, D. B. (1955). Multiple range and multiple *F* tests. *Biometrics, 11*, 1–42.

Dunn, O. J. (1961). Multiple comparisons among means. *Journal of the American Statistical Association, 56*, 52–64.

Dunn, O. J., & Clark, V. A. (1969). Correlation coefficients measured on the same individuals. *Journal of the American Statistical Association, 64,* 366–377.

Dunnett, C. W. (1955). A multiple comparison procedure for combining several treatments with a control. *Journal of the American Statistical Association, 50,* 1096–1121.

Dunnett, C. W. (1964). New tables for multiple comparisons with a control. *Biometrics, 20,* 482–491.

Dunnett, C. W. (1980). Pairwise multiple comparisons in the unequal variance case. *Journal of the American Statistical Association, 75,* 796–800.

Edgell, S. E., & Noon, S. N. (1984). Effect of the violation of normality on the *t* test of the correlation coefficient. *Psychological Bulletin, 95,* 576–583.

Efron, B. (1982). *The jackknife, the bootstrap, and other resampling plans.* Philadelphia: Society for Industrial and Applied Mathematics.

Efron, B., & Gong, G. (1983). A leisurely look at the bootstrap, the jackknife, and cross-validation. *The American Statistician, 37,* 36–48.

Efron, B. E. (1988). Bootstrap confidence intervals: Good or bad? *Psychological Bulletin, 104,* 293–296.

Efron, B. E., & Diaconis, B. (1983). Computer-intensive methods in statistics. *Scientific American, 248,* 115–130.

Elashoff, J. D. (1969). Analysis of covariance: A delicate instrument. *American Educational Research Journal, 6,* 383–401.

Elashoff, J. D., & Elashoff, R. M. (1978). Effects of errors in statistical assumptions. In W. H. Kruskal & J. M. Tanur (Eds.), *International encyclopedia of statistics* (pp. 229–250). New York: Free Press.

Emerson, J. D., & Stoto, M. A. (1983). Transforming data. In D. C. Hoaglin, F. Mosteller, & J. F. Tukey (Eds.), *Understanding robust and exploratory data analysis* (pp. 97–128). New York: Wiley.

Erdfelder, E., Faul, F., & Buchner, A. (1996). GPOWER: A general power analysis program. *Behavior Research Methods, Instrumentation, & Computers, 28,* 1–11.

Falk, R., & Well, A. D. (1996). Correlation as probability of common descent. *Multivariate Behavioral Research, 31,* 219–238.

Falk, R., & Well, A. D. (1998). The many faces of the correlation coefficient. *Journal of Statistical Education, 5*(3), 1–18.

Feldt, L. S. (1958). A comparison of the precision of three experimental designs employing a concomitant variable. *Psychometrika, 23,* 335–353.

Fenz, W., & Epstein, S. (1967). Gradients of physiological arousal of experienced and novice parachutists as a function of an approaching jump. *Psychosomatic Medicine, 29,* 33–51.

Fienberg, S. E. (1977). *The analysis of cross-classified data.* Cambridge, MA: MIT Press.

Fisher, R. A. (1935). *The design of experiments.* Edinburgh, Scotland: Oliver and Boyd.

Fisher, R. A. (1952). *Statistical methods for research workers* (12th ed.). London: Oliver and Boyd.

Fliess, J. L. (1973). *Statistical methods for rates and proportions.* New York: Wiley.

Forster, K. I., & Dickinson, R. G. (1976). More on the language-as-fixed-effect fallacy: Monte Carlo estimates of error rates for $F_1$, $F_2$, $F'$, and *min F*. *Journal of Verbal Learning and Verbal Behavior, 15,* 135–142.

Fox, J. (1997). *Applied regression analysis, linear models, and related methods.* Thousand Oaks, CA: Sage.

Friedman M. (1937). The use of ranks to avoid the assumption of normality implication the analysis of variance. *Journal of the American Statistical Association, 32,* 675–701.

Games, P. A., & Howell, J. F. (1976). Pairwise multiple comparison procedures with unequal $n$'s and/or variances: A Monte Carlo study. *Journal of Educational Statistics, 1*, 113–125.

Games, P. A., Keselman, H. J., & Clinch, J. J. (1979). Tests for homogeneity of variance in factorial designs. *Psychological Bulletin, 86*, 978–984.

Games, P. A., Keselman, H. J., & Rogan, J.C. (1981). Simultaneous pairwise multiple comparison procedures when sample sizes are unequal. *Psychological Bulletin, 90*, 594–598.

Gary, H. E., Jr. (1981). *The effects of departures from circularity on type 1 error rates and power for randomized block factorial experimental designs.* Unpublished doctoral dissertation, Baylor University, Waco, TX.

Gatsonis, C., & Sampson, A. R. (1989). Multiple correlation: Exact power and sample size calculations. *Psychological Bulletin, 106*, 516–524.

Gatti, G. G., & Harwell, M. R. (1998). Advantages of computer programs over power charts for the estimation of power. *Journal of Statistical Education, Volume 6, number 3.*

Glass, G. V. (1976). Primary, secondary, and meta-analysis of research. *Educational Researcher, 5*, 3–8.

Goldstein, H. (1995). Multilevel statistical models. London: Edward Arnold.

Goodman, L. A., & Kruskal, W. H. (1954). Measures of association for cross-classifications. *Journal of the American Statistical Association, 49*, 732–764.

Greenhouse, S. W., & Geisser, S. (1959). On methods in the analysis of profile data. *Psychometrika, 55*, 431–433.

Grissom, R. J. (2000). Heterogeneity of variance in clinical data. *Journal of Consulting and Clinical Psychology, 68*, 155–165.

Grissom, R. J., & Kim, J. J. (2001). Review of assumptions and problems in the appropriate conceptualization of effect size. *Psychological Methods, 6*, 135–146.

Harlow, L. L. (1997). Significance testing introduction and overview. In L. L. Harlow, S. A. Mulaik, & J. H. Steiger (Eds.), *What if there were no significance tests?* (pp. 1–17). Mahwah, NJ: Lawrence Erlbaum Associates.

Harris, R. J. (1985). *A primer of multivariate statistics* (2nd ed.). New York: Academic Press.

Harter, H. L., Clemm, D. S., & Guthrie, E. H. (1959). *The probability integrals of the range and of the studentized range* (WADC Tech. Rep. 58–484). Wright-Patterson Air Force Base, OH: Wright Air Development Center.

Hartley, H. O. (1950). The maximum $F$-ratio as a short-cut test for heterogeneity of variance. *Biometrika, 37*, 308–312.

Havlicek, L. L., & Peterson, N. L. (1977). Effect of the violations of assumptions upon significance levels for the Pearson $r$. *Psychological Bulletin, 84*, 373–377.

Hays, W. L. (1988). *Statistics* (4th ed.). New York: Holt, Rinehart, and Winston.

Hays, W. L. (1994). *Statistics* (5th ed.). New York: Holt, Rinehart, & Winston.

Hayter, A. J. (1986). The maximum familywise error rate of Fisher's least significant difference test. *Journal of the American Statistical Association, 81*, 1000–1004.

Hedges, L. V. (1981). Distributional theory for Glass's estimator of effect size and related estimators. *Journal of Educational Statistics, 6*, 107–128.

Hedges, L. V., & Olkin, I. (1985). *Statistical methods for meta-analysis.* New York: Academic Press.

Herzberg, P. A. (1969). The parameters of cross validation. *Psychometrika* (Monograph supplement, No. 16), *34* (2, pt. 2).

Hill, M., & Dixon, W. J. (1982). Robustness in real life: A study of clinical laboratory data. *Biometrics, 38*, 377–396.

Hoaglin, D. C. (1983). Letter values: A set of ordered statistics. In D. C, Hoaglin, F. Mosteller, & J. F. Tukey (Eds.), *Understanding robust and exploratory data analysis* (pp. 33–57). New York: Wiley.

Hoaglin, D. C., Mosteller, F., & Tukey, J. F. (1983). *Understanding robust and exploratory data analysis*. New York: Wiley.

Hoaglin, D. C., Mosteller, F., & Tukey, J. F. (1985). *Exploring data tables, trends and shapes*. New York: Wiley.

Hoaglin, D. C., Mosteller, F., & Tukey, J. F. (1991). *Fundamentals of exploratory analysis of variance*. New York: Wiley.

Hoaglin, D. C., & Welsch, R. (1978). The hat matrix in regression and ANOVA. *American Statistician, 32*, 17–22.

Hochberg, Y. (1988). A sharper Bonferroni procedure for multiple tests of significance. *Biometrika, 75*, 800–803.

Hocking, R. R. (1983). Developments in linear regression methodology: 1959–1982. *Technometrics, 25*, 219–245.

Hogg, R. V. (1974). Adaptive robust procedures: A partial review and some suggestions for future applications and theory. *Journal of the American Statistical Association, 69*, 909–927.

Hogg, R. V. (1979). Statistical robustness: One view of its use in application today. *American Statistician, 33*, 108–115.

Hogg, R. V., Fisher, D. M., & Randles, R. K. (1975). A two-sample adaptive distribution-free test. *Journal of the American Statistical Association, 70*, 656–667.

Holm, S. (1979). A simple sequentially rejective multiple test procedure. *Scandinavian Journal of Statistics, 6*, 65–70.

Hommel, G. (1988). A stepwise rejective multiple test procedure based on a modified Bonferroni test. *Biometrika, 75*, 383–386.

Hora, S. C., & Iman, R. L. (1988). Asymptotic relative efficiencies of the rank-transformation procedure in randomized complete-block designs. *Journal of the American Statistical Association, 83*, 462–470.

Horst, P., & Edwards, A. L. (1982). Analysis of nonorthogonal designs: The $2^k$ factorial experiment. *Psychological Bulletin, 91*, 190–192.

Hotelling, H. (1931). The generalization of Student's ratio. *Annals of Mathematical Statistics, 2*, 360–378.

Hsu, T. C., & Feldt, L. S. (1969). The effect of limitations on the number of criterion score values on the significance of the $F$ test. *American Educational Research Journal, 6*, 515–527.

Huck, S. W., & McLean, R. A. (1975). Using a repeated measures ANOVA to analyze the data from a pretest-posttest design: A potentially confusing task. *Psychological Bulletin, 82*, 511–518.

Hudson, J. D., & Krutchkoff, R. C. (1968). A Monte Carlo investigation of the size and power of tests employing Satterthwaite's synthetic mean squares. *Biometrika, 55*, 431–433.

Huitema, B. E. (1980). *The analysis of covariance and alternatives*. New York: Wiley.

Hunka, S., & Leighton, J. (1997). Defining Johnson-Neyman regions of significance in the three-covariate ANCOVA using Mathematica. *Journal of Educational and Behavioral Statistics, 22*, 361–387.

Hunter, J. E., & Schmidt, F. L. (1990). *Methods of meta-analysis: Correcting error and bias in research studies*. Newbury Park, CA: Sage.

Huynh, H. (1982). A comparison of four approaches to robust regression. *Psychological Bulletin, 92*, 505–512.

Huynh, H., & Feldt, L. S. (1976). Estimation of the Box correction for degrees of freedom from sample data in randomized block and split-plot designs. *Journal of Educational Statistics, 1*, 69–82.

Iman, R. L., Hora, S. C., & Conover, W. J. (1984). Comparison of asymptotically distribution-free procedures for the analysis of complete blocks. *Journal of the American Statistical Association, 79*, 674–685.

James, G. S. (1951). The comparison of several groups of observations when the ratios of the population variances are unknown. *Biometrika, 38*, 324–329.

James, G. S. (1954). Tests of linear hypotheses in univariate and multivariate analysis when the ratios of the population variances are unknown. *Biometrika, 41*, 19–43.

Jennings, E. (1988). Models for pretest-posttest data: Repeated measures ANOVA revisited. *Journal of Educational Statistics, 13*, 273–280.

Johnson, P. O., & Neyman, J. (1936). Tests of certain linear hypotheses and their application to some educational problems. *Statistical Research Memoirs, 1*, 57–93.

Joreskog, K. G., & Sorbom, D. (1986). LISREL: Analysis of linear structural relationships by the method of maximum likelihood (Version VI). Mooresville, IN: Scientific Software, Inc.

Kepner, J. L., & Robinson, D. H. (1988). Nonparametric methods for detecting treatment effects in repeated-measures designs. *Journal of the American Statistical Association, 83*, 456–461.

Keuls, M. (1952). The use of the studentized range in connection with an analysis of variance. *Euphytica, 1*, 112–122.

Kirk, R. E. (1995). *Experimental design: Procedures for the behavioral sciences* (3rd ed.). Belmont, CA: Brooks/Cole.

Koele, P. (1982). Calculating power in analysis of variance. *Psychological Bulletin, 92*, 513–516.

Kraemer, H. C., & Thiemann, S. (1987). *How many subjects? Statistical power analysis in research*. Beverly Hills, CA:Sage.

Kramer, C. Y. (1956). Extension of multiple range tests to group means with unequal numbers of replications. *Biometrics, 12*, 307–310.

Kreft, I., & de Leeuw, J. (1998). *Introducing multilevel modeling*. London: Sage.

Kruskal, W. H., & Wallis, W. A. (1952). Use of ranks in one-criterion variance analysis. *Journal of the American Statistical Association, 47*, 583–621.

Lee, W.-C., & Rodgers, J. L. (1998). Bootstrapping correlation coefficients using univariate and bivariate sampling. *Psychological Methods, 3*, 91–103.

Lee, Y. S. (1972). Tables of the upper percentage points of the multiple correlation coefficient. *Biometrika, 59*, 175–189.

Lehmann, E. L. (1975). *Nonparametrics*. San Francisco: Holden-Day.

Levene, H. (1960). Robust tests for equality of variances. In I. Olkin (Ed.), *Contributions to probability and statistics*. Stanford: Stanford University Press.

Levine, D. W., & Dunlap, W. P. (1982). Power of the *F* test with skewed data: Should one transform or not? *Psychological Bulletin, 92*, 272–280.

Lindauer, P., & Petrie, G. (1997). A review of cooperative learning: An alternative to everyday instructional strategies. *Journal of Instructional Psychology, 24*, 183–187.

Lindeman, R. H., Merenda, P. F., & Gold, R. Z. (1980). *Introduction to bivariate and multivariate analysis*. Glenview, IL: Scott Foresman.

Lindquist, E. F. (1953). *Design and analysis of experiments in education and psychology*. Boston: Houghton-Mifflin.

Linn, R. L., & Slinde, J. A. (1977). The determination of the significance of change between pre- and posttesting periods. *Review of Educational Research, 47*, 121–150.

Lix, L. M., & Keselman, H. J. (1998). To trim or not to trim: Tests of location equality under heteroscedasticity and nonnormality. *Educational and Psychological Measurement, 58*, 409–429.

Lix, L. M., Keselman, J. C., & Keselman, H. J. (1996). Consequences of assumption violations revisited: A quantitative review of alternatives to the one-way analysis of variance *F* test. *Review of Educational Research, 66*, 579–620.

Lorch, R. F., & Myers, J. L. (1990). Regression analyses of repeated measures data: A comparison of three different methods. *Journal of Experimental Psychology: Learning, Memory, and Cognition, 16*, 149–157.

Lunney, G. H. (1970). Using analysis of variance with a dichotomous variable: An empirical study. *Journal of Educational Measurement, 7*, 263–269.

Marascuilo, L. A., & Levin, J. R. (1970). Appropriate post hoc comparisons for interaction and nested hypotheses in analysis of variance designs: The elimination of type IV errors. *American Educational Research Journal, 7*, 397–421.

Marascuilo, L. A., & Serlin, R. C. (1988). *Statisical methods for the behavioral and social sciences*. New York: Freeman.

Maris. E. (1998). Covariance adjustment versus gain scores—revisited. *Psychological Methods, 3*, 309–327.

Mauchly, J. W. (1940). Significance test for sphericity of a normal *n*-variate distribution. *Annals of Mathematical Statistics, 11*, 204–209.

Maxwell, S. E. (1980). Pairwise multiple comparisons in repeated measures designs. *Journal of Educational Statistics, 5*, 269–287.

Maxwell, S. E. (2000). Sample size and multiple regression analysis. *Psychological Methods, 5*, 434–458.

Maxwell, S. E., & Bray, J. H. (1986). Robustness of the quasi *F* statistic to violations of sphericity. *Psychological Bulletin, 99*, 416–421.

Maxwell, S. E., Camp, C. J., & Arvey, R. D. (1981). Measures of strength of association. *Journal of Applied Psychology, 66*, 525–534.

Maxwell, S. E., Delaney, H. D., & Dill, C. A. (1984). Another look at ANCOVA versus blocking. *Psychological Bulletin, 95*, 136–147.

Maxwell, S. E., & Howard, G. S. (1981). Change scores—necessarily anathema? *Educational and Psychological Measurement, 41*, 747–756.

Mead, R., Bancroft, T. A., & Han, C. (1975). Power of analysis of variance test procedures for incompletely specified fixed models. *Annals of Statistics, 3*, 797–808.

Meng, X.-L., Rosenthal, R., & Rubin, D. B. (1992). Comparing correlated correlation coefficients. *Psychological Bulletin, 111*, 172–175.

Merriam, P. A., Ockene, I. S., Hebert, J. R., Rosal, M. C., & Matthews, C. E. (1999). Seasonal variation of blood cholesterol levels. *Journal of Biological Rhythms, 14*, 330–330.

Micceri, T. (1989). The unicorn, the normal curve, and other improbable creatures. *Psychological Bulletin, 105*, 156–166.

Miller, R. G. (1974). The jackknife—a review. *Biometrika, 61*, 1–17.

Miller, R. G., Jr. (1981). *Simultaneous statistical inference* (2nd ed.). New York: Springer-Verlag.

Mittlehammer, R. C., Judge, G. C., & Miller, D. J. (2000). *Econometric foundations*. Cambridge: Cambridge University Press.

Morrison, D. F. (1990). Multivariate statistical methods (3rd ed.). New York: McGraw-Hill.

Morrow, L. M., & Young, J. (1997). A family literacy program connecting school and home: Effects on attitude, motivation, and literacy achievement. *Journal of Educational Psychology, 89*, 736–742.

Mosteller, F., & Tukey, J. W. (1977). *Data analysis and regression: A second course in statistics*. Reading, MA: Addison-Wesley.

Muller, K. E., & Barton, C. N. (1989). approximate power for repeated-measures ANOVA lacking sphericity. *Journal of the American Statistical Association, 84*, 549–555.

Muller, K. E., & Barton, C. N. (1991). Correction to "approximate power for repeated-measures ANOVA lacking sphericity." *Journal of the American Statistical Association, 86*, 255–256.

Muller, K. E., LaVange, L. M., Ramey, S. L., & Ramey, C. T. (1992). Power calculations for general linear multivariate models including repeated measures applications. *Journal of the American Statistical Association, 87*, 1209–1226.

Murray, J. E, Yong, E., & Rhodes, G. (2000). Revisiting the perception of upside-down faces. *Psychological Science, 11*, 492–496.

Myers, J. L. (1959). On the interaction of two scaled variables. *Psychological Bulletin, 56*, 385–391.

Myers, J. L. (1979). *Fundamentals of experimental design* (3rd ed.). Boston: Allyn and Bacon.

Myers, J. L., DiCecco, J. V., & Lorch, R. F. (1981). Group dynamics and individual performances: Pseudogroup and quasi-$F$ analyses. *Journal of Personality and Social Psychology, 40*, 86–98.

Myers, J. L., DiCecco, J. V., White, J. B., & Borden, V. M. (1982). Repeated measurements on dichotomous variables: $Q$ and $F$ tests. *Psychological Bulletin, 92*, 517–525.

Myers, J. L., Hansen, R. S., Robson, R. R., & McCann, J. (1983). The role of explanation in learning elementary probability. *Journal of Educational Psychology, 75*, 374–381.

Myers, J. L., & Well, A. D. (1995). *Research design and statistical analysis*. Hillsdale, NJ: Lawrence Erlbaum Associates.

Myers, N. A., & Chen, Z. (1996). A decade beyond: Recognizing objects from an early childhood event. Unpublished manuscript.

Namboodiri, N. K. (1972). Experimental designs in which each subject is used repeatedly. *Psychological Bulletin, 77*, 54–64.

Neter, J., Kutner, M. H., Nachtscheim, C. J., & Wasserman, W. (1996). *Applied linear statistical models* (4th ed.). Boston: WCB McGraw-Hill.

Newman, D. (1939). The distribution of range in samples from a normal population, expressed in terms of independent estimate of a standard deviation. *Biometrika, 31*, 20–30.

Odeh, R. E. (1977). Extended tables of the distribution of Friedman's S-statistic in the two-way layout. *Communications in Statistics, Part B. Simulation and Computation, 6*, 29–48.

Olkin, I., & Finn, J. (1990). Testing correlated correlations. *Psychological Bulletin, 108*, 330–333.

Olkin, I., & Finn, J. (1995). Correlations redux. *Psychological Bulletin, 118*, 155–164.

Oshima, T. C., & Algina, J. (1992). Type I error rates for James' second order test and Wilcox's $H_m$ test under heteroscedasticity and non-normality. *British Journal of Mathematical and Statistical Psychology, 45*, 225–263.

Overall, J. E., Lee, D. M., & Hornick, C.W. (1981). Comparison of two strategies for analysis of variance in nonorthogonal designs. *Psychological Bulletin, 90*, 367–375.

Overall, J. E., & Spiegel, D. K. (1969). Concerning least squares analysis of experimental data. *Psychological Bulletin, 72*, 311–322.

Overton, R. C. (2001). Moderated multiple regression for interactions involving categorical variables: A statistical control for heterogeneous variance across two groups. *Psychological Methods, 6*, 218–233.

Pearson, E. S., & Hartley, H. (1954). *Biometrika tables for statisticians*. London: Cambridge University Press.

Pedhazur, E. J. (1997). *Multiple regression in behavioral research: Explanation and prediction*. Fort Worth, TX: Harcourt Brace.

Pedhazur, E. J., & Schmelkin, L. (1991). *Measurement, design, and analysis: An integrated approach*. Hillsdale, NJ: Lawrence Erlbaum Associates.

Peritz, E. (1970). A note on multiple comparisons. Unpublished manuscript, Hebrew University, Jerusalem, Israel.

Perlmutter, J., & Myers, J. L. (1973). A comparison of two procedures for testing multiple contrasts. *Psychological Bulletin, 79*, 181–184.

Pollatsek, A., & Well, A. D. (1995). On the use of counterbalanced designs in cognitive research: A suggestion for a better and more powerful analysis. *Journal of Experimental Psychology: Learning, Memory, and Cognition, 21*, 783–794.

Raaijmakers, J. G. W, Schrijnemakers, J. M. C., & Gremmen, F. (1999). How to deal with "the language-as-fixed-effect fallacy": Common misconceptions and alternative solutions. *Journal of Memory & Language, 41*, 416–426.

Ragosa, D. (1995). Myths and methods: "Myths about longitudinal research" plus supplemental questions. In M. Gottman (Ed.), *The analysis of change*. Mahwah, NJ: Lawrence Erlbaum Associates.

Räkkönen, K., Matthews, K. A., Flory, J. D., Owens, J. F., & Gump. B. B. (1999). Effects of optimism, pessimism, and trait anxiety on ambulatory blood pressure and mood during everyday life. *Journal of Personality and Social Psychology, 76*, 104–113.

Ramsey, P. H. (1978). Power differences between pairwise multiple comparisons. *Journal of the American Statistical Association, 73*, 479–485.

Ramsey, P. H. (1981). Power of univariate pairwise multiple comparison procedures. *Psychological Bulletin, 90*, 352–366.

Rasmussen, J. L. (1987). Estimating correlation coefficients: Bootstrap and parametric approaches. *Psychological Bulletin, 101*, 136–139.

Rasmussen, J. L. (1988). "Bootstrap confidence intervals: Good or bad": Comments on Efron (1988) and Strube (1988) and further evaluation. *Psychological Bulletin, 104*, 297–299.

Rasmussen, J. L. (1989). Computer-intensive correlational analysis: Bootstrap and approximate randomization techniques. *British Journal of Mathematical and Statistical Psychology, 42*, 103–111.

Ratcliff, R. (1993). Methods for dealing with reaction time outliers. *Psychological Bulletin, 114*, 510–532.

Rencher, A. C., & Pun, F. C. (1982). Inflation of *R*-squared in best subset regression. *Technometrics, 22*, 49–54.

Robinson, W. S. (1950). Ecological correlations and the behavior of individuals. *American Sociological Review, 15*, 351–357.

Rodgers, J. L., & Nicewander, W. A. (1988). Thirteen ways to look at the correlation coefficient. *American Statistician, 42*, 59–66.

Roediger, H. L., III, Meade, M. L., & Bergman, E. T. (2001). Social contagion of memory. *Psychonomic Bulletin & Review, 8*, 365–371.

Rogan, J. C., Keselman, H. J., & Mendoza, J. L. (1979). Analysis of repeated measurements. *British Journal of Mathematical and Statistical Psychology, 32*, 269–286.

Rom, D. M. (1990). A sequentially rejective test procedure based on a modified Bonferroni inequality. *Biometrika, 77*, 663–665.

Rosenberger, J. L., & Gasko, M. (1983). Comparing location estimators: Trimmed means, medians, and trimeans. In D. C. Hoaglin, F. Mosteller, & J. F. Tukey (Eds.), *Understanding robust and exploratory data analysis* (pp. 297–328). New York: Wiley.

Rosenthal, R. (1991). *Meta-analytic procedures for social research* (rev. ed.). Newbury Park, CA: Sage.

Rosenthal, R. R., & Rubin, D. B. (1983). Ensemble-adjusted *p* values. *Psychological Bulletin, 94*, 540–541.

Rosnow, R. L., & Rosenthal, R. (1989). Definition and interpretation of interaction effects. *Psychological Bulletin, 105*, 143–146.

Rosnow, R. L., & Rosenthal, R. (1991). If you're looking at the cell means, you're not looking at only the interaction (unless all main effects are zero). *Psychological Bulletin, 110*, 574–576.

Rosnow, R. L., & Rosenthal, R. (1995). "Some things you learn aren't so": Cohen's paradox, Asch's paradigm, and the interpretation of interaction. *Psychological Science, 6*, 3–9.

Rouanet, H., & Lepine, D. (1970). Comparisons between treatments in a repeated-measurement design: ANOVA and multivariate methods. *British Journal of Mathematical and Statistical Psychology, 23*, 147–163.

Rousseeuw, J. R., & Leroy, A. M. (1987). *Robust regression and outlier detection*. New York: Wiley.

Rovine, M. J., & Von Eye, A. (1997). A 14th way to look at a correlation coefficient: Correlation as the proportion of matches. *American Statistician, 51*, 42–46.

Royer, J. M., Tronsky, L. M., & Chan, Y. (1999). Math-fact retrieval as the cognitive mechanism underlying gender differences in math test performance. *Contemporary Educational Psychology, 24*, 181–266.

Rozeboom, W. W. (1979). Ridge regression: Bonanza or beguilement? *Psychological Bulletin, 86*, 242–249.

Satterthwaite, F. E. (1946). An approximate distribution of variance components. *Biometrics Bulletin, 2*, 110–114.

Sawilosky, S. S., & Blair, R. C. (1992). A more realistic look at the robustness and type II error properties of the *t* test to departures from population normality. *Psychological Bulletin, 111*, 352–360.

Scheffé, H. (1959). *The analysis of variance*. New York: Wiley.

Seaman, M. A., Levin, J. R., & Serlin, R. C. (1991). New developments in pairwise multiple comparisons: Some powerful and practicable procedures. *Psychological Bulletin, 110*, 577–586.

Shaffer, J. P. (1979). Comparison of means: An *F* test followed by a modified multiple range procedure. *Journal of Educational Statistics, 4*, 14–23.

Shaffer, J. P. (1986). Modified sequentially rejective multiple test procedures. *Journal of the American Statistical Association, 81*, 826–831.

Shaffer, J. P. (1995). Multiple hypothesis testing. *Annual Review of Psychology, 46*, 561–584.

Shapiro, S. S., & Wilk, M. B. (1965). An analysis of variance test for normality (complete samples). *Biometrika, 52*, 591–611.

Sidak, Z. (1967). Rectangular confidence regions for the means of multivariate normal distributions. *Journal of the American Statistical Association, 62*, 626–633.

Siegel, S., & Castellan, N. J. (1988). *Nonparametric statistics for the behavioral sciences* (2nd ed.). New York: McGraw-Hill.

Smith, H. F. (1957). Interpretation of adjusted treatment means and regressions in analysis of covariance. *Biometrics, 13*, 282–308.

Smith, J. F. K. (1976). Data transformations in analysis of variance. *Journal of Verbal Learning and Verbal Behavior, 15*, 339–346.

Snedecor, G. W., & Cochran, W. G. (1967). *Statistical methods* (6th ed.). Ames, IA: Iowa University Press.

Springer, L., Stanne, M. E., & Donovan, S. S. (1999). Effects of small-group learning on undergraduates in science, mathematics, engineering, and technology: A meta-analysis. *Review of Educational Research, 69*, 21–51.

Srivastava, S. R., & Bozivich, H. (1961). Power of certain analyses of variance test procedures involving preliminary tests. *Bulletin de l'Institut International Statistique*, 33rd Session.

Stapel, D. A., & Koomen, W. (2000). The impact of opposites: Implications of trait inferences and their antonyms for personal judgment. *Journal of Experimental Social Psychology, 36*, 439–464.

Stasson, M. F., Kameda, T., Parks, C. D., Zimmerman, S. K., & Davis, J. (1991). Effects of assigned group consensus requirement on group problem solving and group members' learning. *Social Psychology Quarterly, 54*, 25–35.

Steiger, J. H. (1979). Multicorr: A computer program for fast, accurate, small-sample tests of correlational pattern hypotheses. *Educational and Psychological Measurement, 39*, 677–680.

Steiger, J. H. (1980). Tests for comparing elements of a correlation matrix. *Psychological Bulletin, 87*, 245–251.

Steiger, J. H., & Fouladi, R. T. (1992). R2: A computer program for interval estimation, power calculation, and hypothesis testing for the squared multiple correlation. *Behavior Research Methods, Instruments, and Computers, 4*, 581–582.

Steiger, J. H., & Fouladi, R. T. (1997). Noncentrality interval estimation and the evaluation of statistical models. In L. L. Harlow, S. A. Mulaik, & J. H. Steiger (Eds.), *What if there were no significance tests?* (pp. 221–257). Mahwah, NJ: LEA.

Stevens, J. (1986). *Applied multivariate statistics for the social sciences*. Hillsdale, NJ: Lawrence Erlbaum Associates.

Stolberg, S. G. (2001, April 22). Science, studies, and motherhood. *The New York Times,* p. WK3.

Strube, M. J. (1988). Bootstrap type 1 error rates for the correlation coefficient: An examination of alternative procedures. *Psychological Bulletin, 104*, 290–292.

Thompson, W. F., Schellenberg, E. G., & Husain, G. (2001). Arousal, mood, and the Mozart effect. *Psychological Science, 12*, 248–251.

Tomarken, A. J., & Serlin, R. C. (1986). Comparison of ANOVA alternatives under variance heterogeneity and specific noncentrality structures. *Psychological Bulletin, 99*, 90–99.

Toothaker, L. E. (1993). *Multiple comparison procedures*. Newbury Park, CA: Sage.

Tukey, J. W. (1949). One degree of freedom for nonadditivity. *Biometrics, 5*, 232–242.

Tukey, J. W. (1952). A test for nonadditivity in the Latin square. *Biometrics, 11*, 111–113.

Tukey, J. W. (1953). The problem of multiple comparisons. Unpublished manuscript, Princeton University.

Tukey, J. W. (1969). Analyzing data: Sanctification or detective work? *American Psychologist, 24*, 83–91.

Tukey, J. W. (1991). The philosophy of multiple comparisons. *Statistical Science, 6*, 100–116.

Vargha, A., & Delaney, H. D. (1998). The Kruskal-Wallis test and stochastic homogeneity. *Journal of Educational and Behavioral Statistics, 23*, 170–192.

Velleman, P., & Welsch, R. (1981). Efficient computing of regression diagnostics. *American Statistician, 35*, 234–242.

Welch, B. L. (1938). The significance of the difference between two means when the population variances are unequal. *Biometrika, 25*, 350–362.

Welch, B. L. (1947). The generalization of Student's problem when several different population variances are involved. *Biometrika, 34*, 28–35.

Welch, B. L. (1951). On the comparison of several mean values: An alternative approach. *Biometrika, 38*, 330–336.

Welsch, R. E. (1977). Stepwise multiple comparison procedures. *Journal of the American Statistical Association, 72*, 566–575.

Wherry, R. J. (1931). A new formula for predicting the shrinkage of the coefficient of multiple correlation. *Annals of Mathematical Statistics, 2*, 440–457.

Wilcox, R. R. (1987). New designs in analysis of variance. *Annual Review of Psychology, 38*, 29–60.

Wilcox, R. R. (1997). *Introduction to robust estimation and hypothesis testing*. San Diego, CA: Academic Press.

Wiley, J., & Voss, J. F. (1999). Constructing arguments from multiple sources: Tasks that promote understanding and not just memory for texts. *Journal of Educational Psychology, 91*, 301–311.

Wilk, M. B., & Kempthorne, O. (1957). Nonadditivities in a Latin square. *Journal of the American Statistical Association, 52*, 218–236.

Wilkinson, L. (1979). Tests of significance in stepwise regression. *Psychological Bulletin, 86*, 168–174.

Wilkinson, L., & Dallal, G. E. (1982). Tests of significance in forward selection regression with an *F*-to-enter stopping rule. *Technometrics, 24*, 25–28.

Wilkinson, L., & the Task Force on Statistical Inference. (1999). Statistical methods in psychology journals: Guidelines and explanations. *American Psychologist, 54*, 594–904.

Witvliet, C. V., Ludwig, T. E., & Vander Laan, K. L. (2001). Granting forgiveness or harboring grudges: Implications for emotion, physiology, and health. *Psychological Science, 12*, 117–123.

Yates, F. (1934). The analysis of multiple classifications with unequal numbers in the different classes. *Journal of the American Statistical Association, 29*, 57–66.

Zar, J. H. (1972). Significance testing of the Spearman rank correlation coefficient. *Journal of the American Statistical Association, 67*, 578–580.

Zimmerman, D. W., & Zumbo, B. D. (1993). The relative power of parametric and nonparametric statistical methods. In G. Keren & C. Lewis (Eds.), *A handbook for data analysis in the behavioral sciences: Methodological issues* (pp. 481–517). Hillsdale, NJ: LEA.

Zwick, R. (1993). Pairwise multiple comparison procedures for one-way analysis of variance designs. In G. Keren & C. Lewis (Eds.), *A handbook for data analysis in the behavioral sciences: Statistical issues* (pp. 43–71). Hillsdale, NJ: LEA.

# Author Index

# Subject Index